HUMAN RESOURCE MANAGEMENT

Visit the *Human Resource Management*, sixth edition Companion Website at **www.pearsoned.co.uk/torrington** to find valuable student learning material including:

- Learning objectives for each chapter
- Over 250 multiple choice questions to help test your learning
- FT articles with exercises and activities
- Three extra chapters on organisational processes and structures
- Links to relevant sites on the web
- A glossary of key concepts

PEARSON
Education

sixth edition

HUMAN RESOURCE MANAGEMENT

Derek Torrington

Laura Hall

Stephen Taylor

An imprint of Pearson Education

Harlow, England • London • New York • Boston • San Francisco • Toronto
Sydney • Tokyo • Singapore • Hong Kong • Seoul • Taipei • New Delhi
Cape Town • Madrid • Mexico City • Amsterdam • Munich • Paris • Milan

Pearson Education Limited
Edinburgh Gate
Harlow
Essex CM20 2JE
England

and Associated Companies throughout the world

Visit us on the World Wide Web at:
www.pearsoned.co.uk

First published in Great Britain under the Prentice Hall Europe imprint in 1987
Second edition published 1991
Third edition published 1995
Fourth edition published 1998
Fifth edition published 2002
Sixth edition published 2005

ISBN: 0 273 68713 1

British Library Cataloguing-in-Publication Data
A catalogue record for this book is available from the British Library

Library of Congress Cataloging-in-Publication Data
A catalog record for this book is available from the Library of Congress

10 9 8 7 6 5 4 3 2 1
08 07 06 05

Typeset in 10/12.5pt Sabon by 35
Printed and Bound by Mateu Cromo Artes Graficas, Spain

The publisher's policy is to use paper manufactured from sustainable forests.

Brief contents

Contents

Preface

This book and its antecedent have been through many editions in the quarter of a century since first publication in 1979 as Torrington, D.P. and Chapman, J.B., *Personnel Management*, Prentice Hall International: London. Over that period it has steadily evolved in line with the development of the personnel/HR function and the changing mix of students studying the subject. In 1979 Personnel Management or Manpower Administration was given little respect in academia. It was rarely taught on undergraduate courses and the UK did not have a single professor of personnel management, although there was a reasonable number of professors of industrial relations. Teaching was mainly focused on professional courses leading to a qualification from the then Institute of Personnel Management (IPM). Twenty-five years later human resource management is found in virtually all undergraduate teaching of business and management, as well as in MBAs and specialist masters' programmes. The number of professors of industrial relations is declining and professors of HRM are everywhere.

We have been very glad to see the number of people buying the book increase year by year, despite the great growth in the number of available texts, and the steady growth of translations into foreign languages, with Georgian and Serbian being the latest versions. It is also gratifying to see that the use of the text is equally strong at all academic levels from specialist master's, through MBA to all undergraduate and professional courses, and that it is being used by many practitioners.

For this latest edition we have comprehensively updated and revised the material to encompass legislative changes, emerging issues of professional and academic debate, findings and commentary from our own recent research into contemporary business practices, and other recent data and survey findings. Despite adding much new material we have maintained the same general structure that has been appreciated in the past, taking each of the main functional areas of HRM in turn. We have also been careful to retain all of the material that regularly receives special commendation and requests for permission to copy.

For the first time we have dropped the part of the text on organisation, as several of the people who were kind enough to review our previous edition for us felt that this material was now more appropriately located in a text on general management. Also following reviewers' comments we have a new Part VII dealing with developing issues that affect all the functional areas of human resource management.

There is a range of assessment material and illustrations, as well as several design features to assist readers further in using and learning from the text; these include:

- Integrated Window on practice boxes provide a range of illustrative material throughout the text, including examples of real company practice, survey results, anecdotes and quotes, and court cases.
- Integrated Activity boxes encourage readers to review and critically apply their understanding at regular intervals throughout the text, either by responding to a question or by undertaking a small practical assignment, individually or as part of a group. In recognition that this text is used on both professional and academic courses, most of the exercises reflect the fact that many students will have little or no business experience. Others may appear to exclude students who are not in employment by asking readers to consider an aspect in their own organisation; however, the organisation could be a college or university, the students' union, a political body or sports team.
- Discussion topics: at the end of each chapter there are two or three short questions intended for general discussion in a tutorial or study group.
- Case study problems: at the end of each part we have included one short case study with several questions to enable readers to review, link and apply their understanding of the previous chapters to a business scenario.
- Examination questions: at the end of each part of the text we have included eight sample questions from past examinations at various levels: undergraduate, MBA, master's and professional.
- Web links are given as appropriate at various points in the text. These are either to the text's companion website, where there is a great deal of further material, or to other websites containing useful information relating to the topics covered.
- Further reading lists for each chapter suggest further relevant readings, with guidance on their value.
- Each part of the text includes a brief introduction to its scope and purpose.
- Chapter objectives to open and Summary propositions to conclude each chapter set readers' expectations and review their understanding progressively.
- There are full References at the end of each chapter to aid further exploration of the chapter material, as required.
- In previous editions there have always been a number of chapters dealing with the face-to-face situations that make up a large part of the HR manager's day. This time they are re-styled as 'Focus on skills' at the end of each part; they have a twofold purpose. Not only do they introduce a basic aspect of human resource management activity, they also act as a means of focusing one's understanding of the myriad other activities discussed in the part of the text which they conclude.
- For the first time we include a Glossary. This is not a comprehensive repetition of all the terms used throughout the text. Rather, it provides further notes on a selection of words and phrases that benefit from more background than is already provided. Words that appear in the glossary are emboldened the first time they appear in the text.

- **Website**: the companion website **www.pearsoned.co.uk/torrington** has more material, including further case studies or exercises for each chapter and support for both tutor and student. The HRP Exercise is directly referred to in Chapter 3, as this is an integral part of the chapter. This exercise is a case study giving worked examples of how the techniques referred to in the chapter have been used.

Supporting resources

Visit **www.pearsoned.co.uk/torrington** to find valuable online resources

Companion Website for students

- Learning objectives for each chapter
- Over 250 multiple choice questions to help test your learning
- FT articles with exercises and activities
- Three extra chapters on organisational processes and structures
- A glossary of key concepts
- Links to relevant sites on the web

For instructors

- Complete, downloadable Instructor's Manual
- PowerPoint slides that can be downloaded and used as OHTs

Also: The Companion Website provides the following features:

- Search tool to help locate specific items of content
- E-mail results and profile tools to send results of quizzes to instructors
- Online help and support to assist with website usage and troubleshooting

For more information please contact your local Pearson Education sales representative or visit **www.pearsoned.co.uk/torrington**

OneKey: All you and your students need to succeed

OneKey is an exclusive new resource for instructors and students, giving you access to the best online teaching and learning tools 24 hours a day, 7 days a week.

OneKey means all your resources are in one place for maximum convenience, simplicity and success.

A OneKey product is available for *Human Resource Management, sixth edition* for use with Blackboard™, WebCT and CourseCompass. It contains:

- Online Study Guide
- Additional FT articles with exercises and activities
- Flashcards to test knowledge of key terms

For more information about the OneKey product please contact your local Pearson Education sales representative or visit **www.pearsoned.co.uk/onekey**

Acknowledgements

We are grateful to the following for permission to reproduce copyright material:

Table 2.1 from *Academy of Management Executive* by Schuler and Jackson, copyright 1987 by Academy of Management, reproduced with permission of Academy of Management in the format textbook via Copyright Clearance Center; Table 8.2 from Labour Market Trends (2001) 'length of time continuously employed by occupation and industry,' *Labour Market Trends*, February, and Table 20.1 adapted from Labour Market Trends (2003c) 'Labour disputes in 2002,' *Labour Market Trends*, June, Crown copyright material is reproduced with the permission of the Controller of HMSO and the Queen's Printer for Scotland; Table 14.2 adapted from *Managerial Organizational Behavior: Utilizing Human Resources*, 5th edition, © copyrighted material, adapted/reprinted with permission of Center for Leadership Studies, Escondido, CA 92025, all rights reserved (Hersey, P. and Blanchard, K. H. 1988); Table 14.3 adapted from 'Leadership that gets results' by D. Goleman, Mar/Apr 2000, Table 19.2 from 'Toward a career-resilient workforce' by R. H. Waterman, J. A. Waterman and B. A. Collard, July/Aug 1994, Figure 3.1 from 'The fall and rise of strategic planning' by H. Mintzberg, Jan/Feb 1994, reprinted by permission of *Harvard Business Review*, copyright © 2000, 1994, 1994 by the Harvard Business School Publishing Corporation; all rights reserved; Table 14.4 From 'Take it from the top,' *People Management*, Vol. 23, October, pp. 26 and 28, originally published in *People Management* 1997 and reproduced with permission of Dr Amin Rajan (Rajan, A. and van Eupen, P. 1997); Table 16.1 from 'A strategic look at management development,' *Personnel Management*, August 1991, p. 47, © Paul Miller, Managing Director of Trends Business Research, reproduced with permission of Personnel Publications Ltd and the author (Miller, P. 1991); Tables 17.2 and 17.3 from *The Competent Manager*, New York, Wiley (Boyatzis, R. 1982), Figures 2.3 and 2.4 from *Strategic Human Resource Management*, New York, Wiley, p. 35 (Fombrun, C. *et al.* 1984), Figure 4.2 from 'Strategic determinants of managerial labour markets,' *Human Resource Management*, Vol. 27, No. 4, New York, Wiley (Sonnefield, J. A. *et al.* 1992), Figure 24.1 from 'Baxter Healthcare organization' by F. LaFasto in 'Diversity,' *Human Resource Management*, Vol. 31, No. 1/2, p. 28 (Jackson, B. W. *et al.* 1992), copyright © 1982, 1984, 1992, 1992, respectively, John Wiley & Sons, reprinted with permission of John Wiley & Sons, Inc.; Table 18.1 adapted from 'Planned and emergent learning: a framework and a method,' *Executive Development*, Vol. 7, No. 6, pp. 29–32, reproduced with permission of Emerald Group Publishing Limited (Megginson, D. 1994); Table 20.2 from 'Strategies and practice in the management of industrial relations,' in G. S. Bain (ed.) *Industrial Relations in Britain*, Oxford, Blackwell (Purcell, J. and Sisson, K. 1983);

Table 24.1 based on data from 'Employers move on equal pay,' *IDS Report 897*, January, London, Incomes Data Services (IDS, 2004); Figure 2.2 from *Managing Human Assets*, New York, The Free Press, reproduced with permission (Beer, M. *et al.* 1984); Figure 2.5 from 'Human resources and sustained competitive advantage: a resource-based perspective,' *International Journal of Human Resource Management*, Vol. 5, No. 2, p. 318, reproduced with permission of Taylor & Francis Ltd, http://www.tandf.co.uk/journals (Wrights, P. *et al.* 1994); Figure 4.1 from 'Manpower strategies for flexible organizations,' *Personnel Management*, August, pp. 28–31, reproduced with permission of People Management (Aktinson, J. 1984); Figure 8.1 is taken from *Personnel and Profit: The Pay-off from People* by H. Fair (1984) and Figure 17.1 is taken from *The Competencies Handbook by* S. Whiddett and S. Hollyforde (1999), with the permission of the publisher, the Chartered Institute of Personnel and Development, London; Figure 10.1 from 'Human resource management: employee well-being and organisational performance,' figure 1, paper presented at *CIPD Professional Standards Conference*, 11 July 2000, reproduced with the permission of the author (Guest, D. E. 2000); Figure 11.1 from *The Learning Company*, Maidenhead, McGraw-Hill, copyright 1991, reproduced with the kind permission of the McGraw-Hill Publishing Company (Pedlar, M. *et al.* 1991); Figure 11.2 adapted from *Becoming a Learning Organisation*, Wokingham, Addision Wesley, reproduced with permission of Professor A. F. M. Wierdsma (Swieringa, J. and Wierdsma, A. 1992); Figure 13.2 from *Partners not Competitors*, p. 76, copyright 1992 Idea Group Publishing, reprinted with permission (Oliva, L. M. 1992); Figure 33.2 adapted from Figure 3.7, page 65, *The Human Value of the Enterprise* by Andrew Mayo 2001 (published by Nicholas Brealey Publishing), reproduced with permission of Nicholas Brealey Publishing and of the author.

AstraZeneca plc for the extract from *Management of Team and Individual Performance* (2000), copyright AstraZeneca plc; 'The Preying Mantis' from *The Bottom Line* by Bertie Ramsbottom, published by Hutchinson, used by permission of The Random House Group Limited; extract p. 217, abridged from *Finding and Keeping the Right People*, London, Pearson Education Limited, pp. 225–6, copyright Pearson Education (Billsberry, J. 2000).

Photographs: p. 1, 3, 27 and 48 Herb Watson/Corbis; p. 68 Stockbyte/Royalty Free; pp. 81, 83, 99, 120, 140, 163, 180 Peter Bowater/Alamy; p. 201 Corbis/Royalty Free; pp. 221, 223, 239, 258, 278, 299, 317 Action Plus/Chris Barry; p. 335 Dorling Kindersley; pp. 353, 355, 368, 384, 406 Alamy/Frank Chmura; pp. 428, 449, 451, 470, 480, 506, 528, 553, 573, 668 Alamy/Royalty Free; p. 769 Getty/Photodisc Green.

In some instances we have been unable to trace the owners of the copyright material, and we would appreciate any information that would enable us to do so.

Guided tour

Windows on Practice
Provides a range of interesting and topical illustrations of HRM in practice

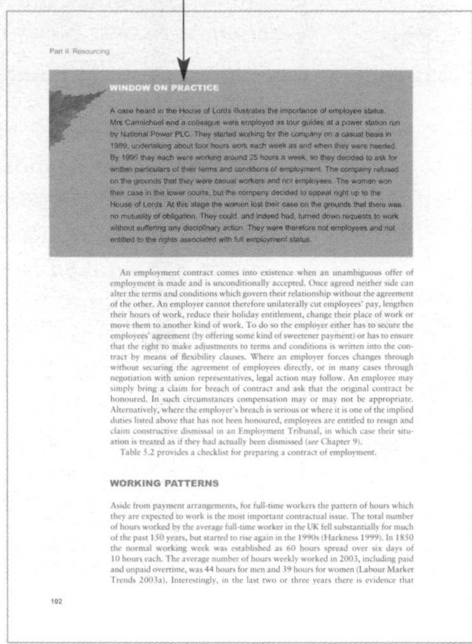

Part opening page
Provides a visual guide to the part contents

Activity boxes
Allow you to review and apply your understanding at regular intervals throughout the text

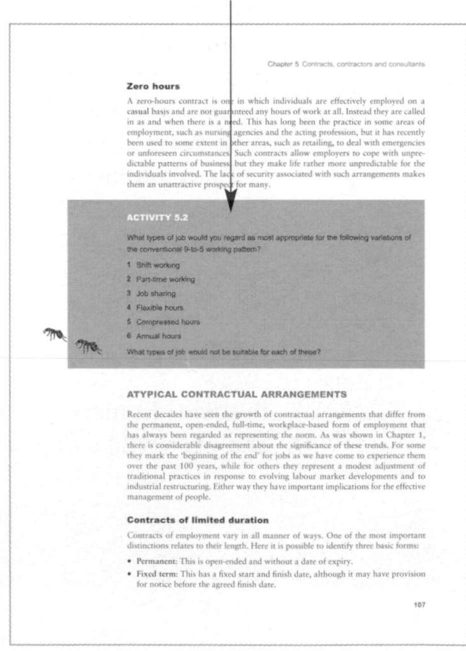

Chapter opening page
Learning objectives help you focus on what you should have learned by the end of the chapter

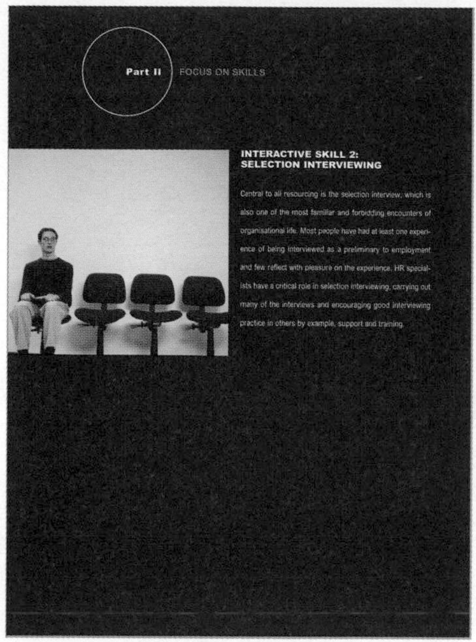
Part II FOCUS ON SKILLS

INTERACTIVE SKILL 2: SELECTION INTERVIEWING

Central to all resourcing is the selection interview, which is also one of the most familiar and forbidding encounters of organisational life. Most people have had at least one experience of being interviewed as a preliminary to employment and few reflect with pleasure on the experience. HR specialists have a critical role in selection interviewing, carrying out many of the interviews and encouraging good interviewing practice in others by example, support and training.

Focus on skills

Appear at the end of each part, offering clear guidance and a range of exercises to help you to develop the skills required of a Human Resource Manager

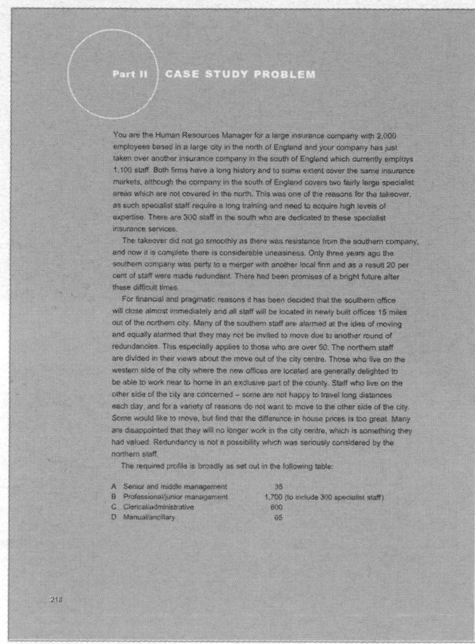
Part II CASE STUDY PROBLEM

You are the Human Resources Manager for a large insurance company with 2,000 employees based in a large city in the north of England and your company has just taken over another insurance company in the south of England which currently employs 1,100 staff. Both firms have a long history and to some extent cover the same insurance markets, although the company in the south of England covers two fairly large specialist areas which are not covered in the north. This was one of the reasons for the takeover, as such specialist staff require a long training and need to acquire high levels of expertise. There are 300 staff in the south who are dedicated to these specialist insurance services.

The takeover did not go smoothly as there was resistance from the southern company, and now it is complete there is considerable uneasiness. Only three years ago the southern company was party to a merger with another local firm and as a result 20 per cent of staff were made redundant. There had been promises of a bright future after these difficult times.

For financial and pragmatic reasons it has been decided that the southern office will close almost immediately and all staff will be located in newly built offices 15 miles out of the northern city. Many of the southern staff are alarmed at the idea of moving and equally alarmed that they may not be invited to move due to another round of redundancies. This especially applies to those who are over 50. The northern staff are divided in their views about the move out of the city centre. Those who live on the western side of the city where the new offices are located are generally delighted to be able to work near to home in an exclusive part of the county. Staff who live on the other side of the city are concerned – some are not happy to travel long distances each day, and for a variety of reasons do not want to move to the other side of the city. Some would like to move, but find that the difference in house prices is too great. Many are disappointed that they will no longer work in the city centre, which is something they had valued. Redundancy is not a possibility which was seriously considered by the northern staff.

The required profile is broadly as set out in the following table:

A	Senior and middle management	35
B	Professional/junior management	1,700 (to include 300 specialist staff)
C	Clerical/administrative	600
D	Manual/ancillary	65

218

Case study problems

Offer a variety of business scenarios, encouraging you to apply your understanding of the issues covered in the text

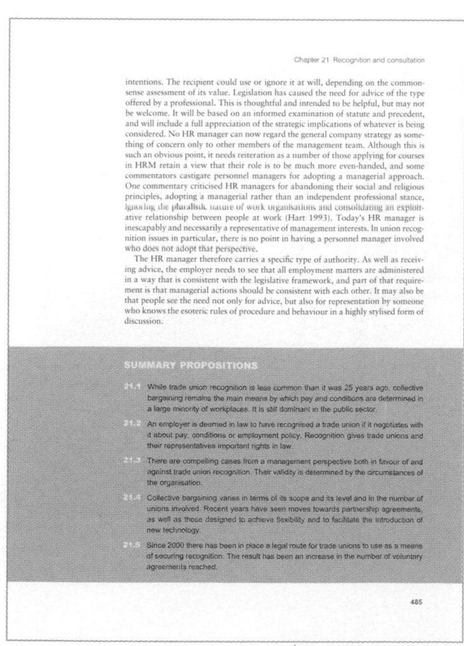
Chapter 21 Recognition and consultation

intentions. The recipient could use or ignore it at will, depending on the commonsense assessment of its value. Legislation has caused the need for advice of the type offered by a professional. This is thoughtful and intended to be helpful, but may not be welcome. It will be based on an informed examination of statute and precedent, and will include a full appreciation of the strategic implications of whatever is being considered. No HR manager can now regard the general company strategy as something of concern only to other members of the management team. Although this is such an obvious point, it needs reiteration as a number of those applying for courses in HRM retain a view that their role is to be much more even-handed, and some commentators castigate personnel managers for adopting a managerial approach. One commentary criticised HR managers for abandoning their social and religious principles, adopting a managerial rather than an independent professional stance, ignoring the pluralistic nature of work organisations and consolidating an exploitative relationship between people at work (Hart 1993). Today's HR manager is inescapably and necessarily a representative of management interests. In union recognition issues in particular, there is no point in having a personnel manager involved who does not adopt that perspective.

The HR manager therefore carries a specific type of authority. As well as receiving advice, the employer needs to see that all employment matters are administered in a way that is consistent with the legislative framework, and part of that requirement is that managerial actions should be consistent with each other. It may also be that people see the need not only for advice, but also for representation by someone who knows the esoteric rules of procedure and behaviour in a highly stylised form of discussion.

SUMMARY PROPOSITIONS

21.1 While trade union recognition is less common than it was 25 years ago, collective bargaining remains the main means by which pay and conditions are determined in a large minority of workplaces. It is still dominant in the public sector.

21.2 An employer is deemed in law to have recognised a trade union if it negotiates with it about pay, conditions or employment policy. Recognition gives trade unions and their representatives important rights in law.

21.3 There are compelling cases from a management perspective both in favour of and against trade union recognition. Their validity is determined by the circumstances of the organisation.

21.4 Collective bargaining varies in terms of its scope and its level and in the number of unions involved. Recent years have seen moves towards partnership agreements, as well as those designed to achieve flexibility and to facilitate the introduction of new technology.

21.5 Since 2000 there has been in place a legal route for trade unions to use as a means of securing recognition. The result has been an increase in the number of voluntary agreements reached.

485

Summary propositions

Help you to check your understanding of chapter content and provide a useful revision tool

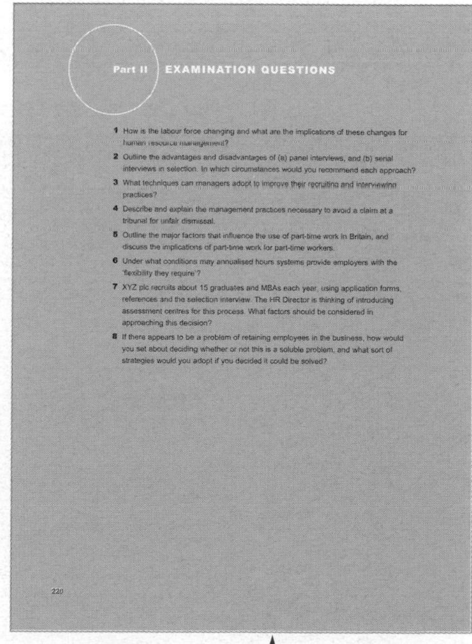
Part II EXAMINATION QUESTIONS

1 How is the labour force changing and what are the implications of these changes for human resource management?
2 Outline the advantages and disadvantages of (a) panel interviews, and (b) serial interviews in selection. In which circumstances would you recommend each approach?
3 What techniques can managers adopt to improve their recruiting and interviewing practices?
4 Describe and explain the management practices necessary to avoid a claim at a tribunal for unfair dismissal.
5 Outline the major factors that influence the use of part-time work in Britain, and discuss the implications of part-time work for part-time workers.
6 Under what conditions may annualised hours systems provide employers with the 'flexibility they require'?
7 XYZ plc recruits about 15 graduates and MBAs each year, using application forms, references and the selection interview. The HR Director is thinking of introducing assessment centres for this process. What factors should be considered in approaching this decision?
8 If there appears to be a problem of retaining employees in the business, how would you set about deciding whether or not this is a soluble problem, and what sort of strategies would you adopt if you decided it could be solved?

220

Exam questions

Each part concludes with sample questions from past examinations at various levels

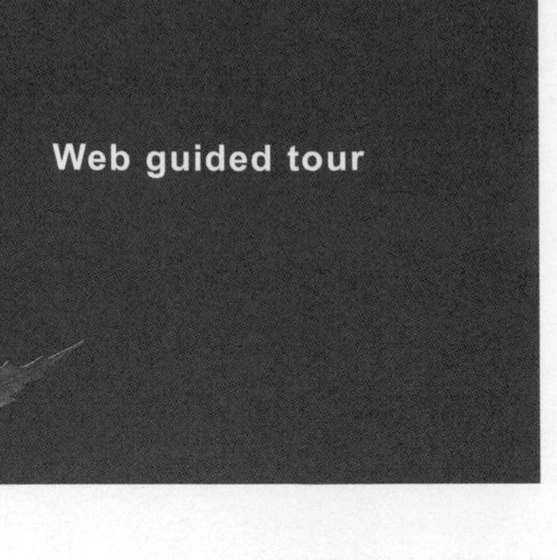

Web guided tour

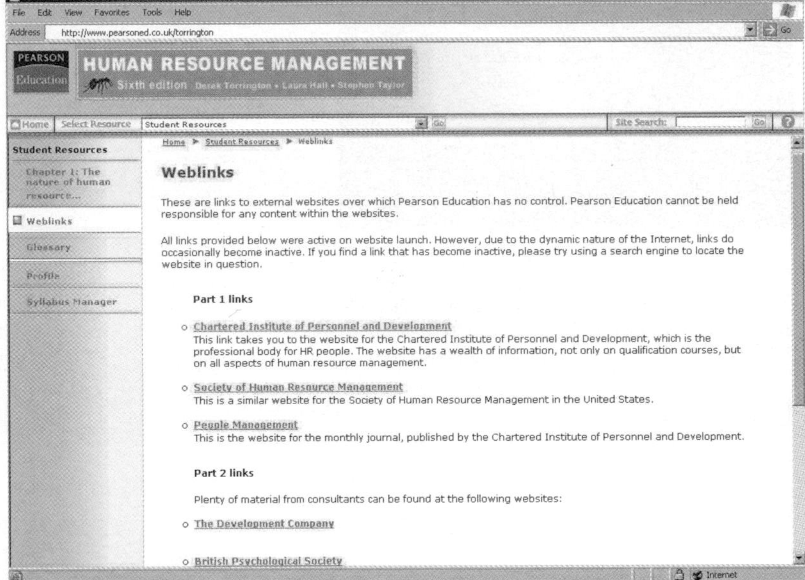

Links to relevant sites on the web

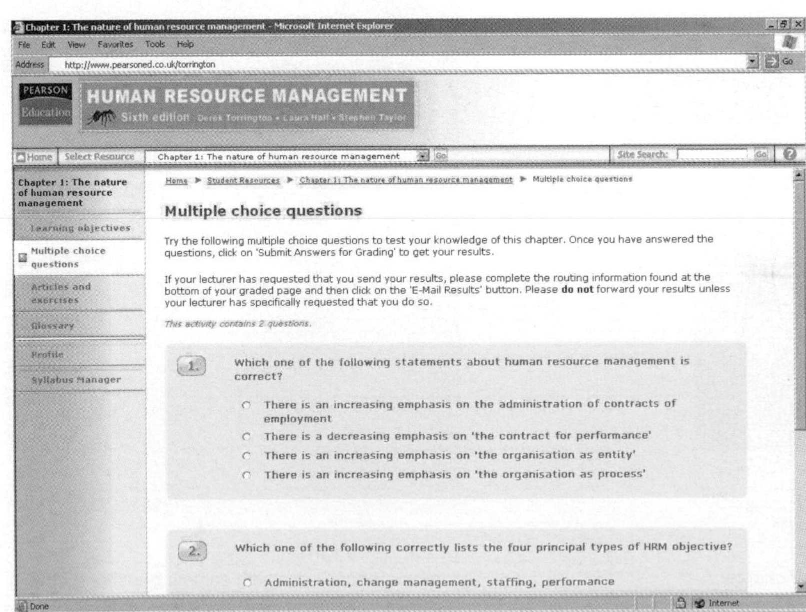

Over 250 **Multiple Choice Questions** to test your learning

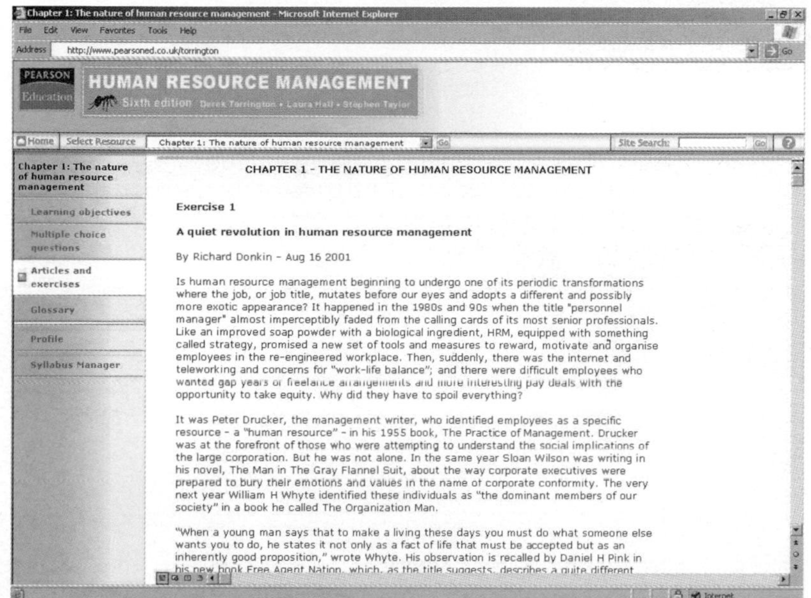

FT articles with exercises and activities

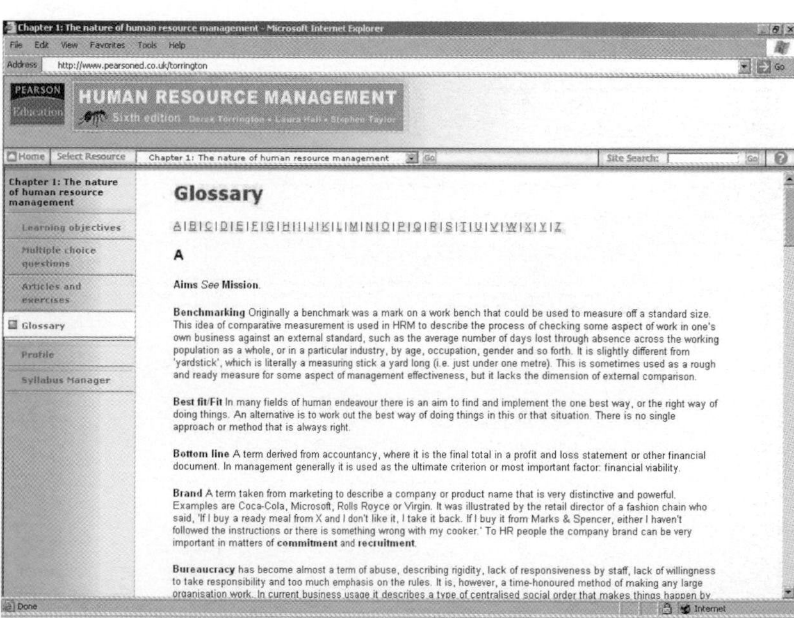

Searchable **Glossary** of Key Concepts

PART 1

INTRODUCTION

The first part of the book has three chapters and a Focus on skills to introduce various dimensions of what human resource management involves. Chapter 1 sets the scene by describing the way in which human resource management works today and then explains how it has evolved to its present form over the hundred years of its existence as a separate function of management. It shows that present-day practice is not only a response to contemporary business demands and social expectations, but also an amalgam of different features which built up throughout the twentieth century and continue in the twenty-first. Later there is a philosophy for human resource management. This is followed by summaries of major debates in the field.

Chapter 2 concentrates on strategy in personnel and human resource management. We see the way in which HR specialists make their strategic contribution, drawing a distinction between a human resource strategy and strategic human resource.

Chapter 3 is different from all the others in having a strong focus on the analytical techniques and processes involved in planning relating to jobs and people.

The Part I Focus on skills begins a series of treatments of the way in which being effective in different face-to-face situations is a fundamental feature of life for all in human resource management.

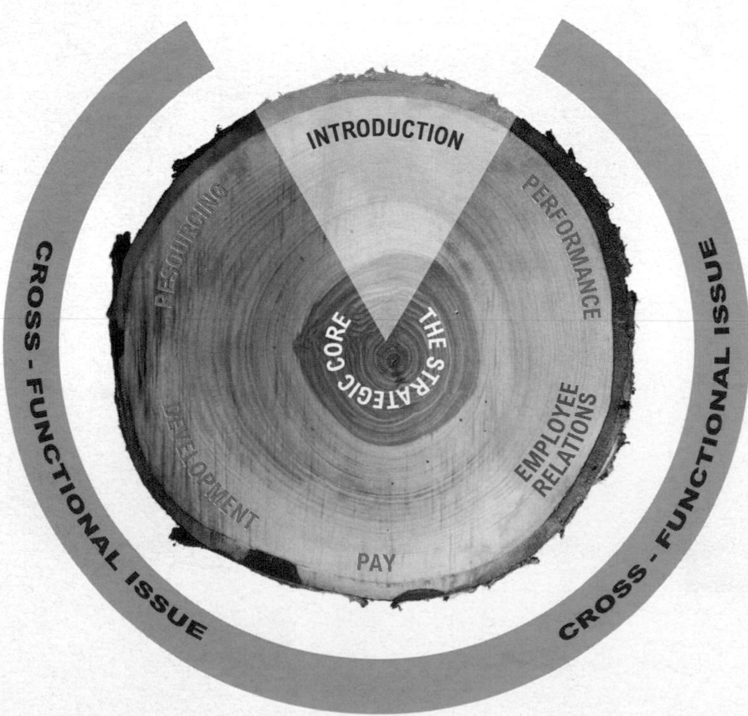

CHAPTER 1

THE NATURE OF HUMAN RESOURCE MANAGEMENT

THE OBJECTIVES OF THIS CHAPTER ARE TO:

1 REVIEW KEY CURRENT DEVELOPMENTS IN HUMAN RESOURCE MANAGEMENT

2 EXPLAIN THE DIFFERENT WAYS IN WHICH THE TERM 'HUMAN RESOURCE MANAGEMENT' IS USED

3 SET OUT THE MAIN OBJECTIVES OF THE HUMAN RESOURCE FUNCTION

4 REVIEW THE HISTORICAL EVOLUTION OF THE MODERN HR FUNCTION

5 EXPLAIN THE PHILOSOPHY OF HRM THAT IS ADOPTED IN THIS BOOK

6 INTRODUCE MAJOR CURRENT DEBATES IN THE FIELD OF HRM

Human resource management (HRM) is the basis of all management activity, but it is not the basis of all business activity. A business may depend fundamentally on having a unique product, like the Dyson vacuum cleaner, or on obtaining the necessary funding, like the London bid to stage the Olympic Games, or on identifying a previously unnoticed market niche, like Saga Services. The basis of management is always the same: getting the people of the business to make things happen in a productive way, so that the business prospers and the people thrive.

HUMAN RESOURCE MANAGEMENT FOR THE TWENTY-FIRST CENTURY

Businesses are diverse. Prisons, restaurants, oil companies, corner shops, fire brigades, churches, hotel chains, hospitals, schools, newspapers, charities, doctors' and dentists' surgeries, professional sports teams, airlines, barristers' chambers and universities are all businesses in the sense that they have overall corporate missions to deliver and these have to be achieved within financial constraints. They all need to have their human resources managed, no matter how much some of the resourceful humans may resent aspects of the management process which limit their individual freedom of action.

Managing resourceful humans requires a constant balancing between meeting the human aspirations of the people and meeting the strategic and financial needs of the business. At times the balance can shift too far in one direction. Through the 1960s and 1970s the human aspirations of senior people in companies and public sector operations tended to produce large staffs, with heavyweight **bureaucracies** and stagnant businesses. One consultancy in the 1970s produced monthly comparative data measuring company success in terms of profitability and the number of employees – the more the better. At the same time the aspirations of employees lower down in the bureaucracy tended to maintain the status quo and a concentration on employee benefits that had scant relevance to business effectiveness. By the end of the twentieth century financial imperatives had generated huge reactions to this in the general direction of '**downsizing**' or reducing the number of people employed to create businesses that were lean, fit and flexible. **Hierarchies** were '**delayered**' to reduce numbers of staff and many functions were '**outsourced**', so as to simplify the operation of the business, concentrating on core expertise at the expense of peripheral activities, which were then bought in as needed from consultants or specialist suppliers. Reducing headcount became a fashionable criterion for success.

By the beginning of the twenty-first century the problems of the scales being tipped so considerably towards rationalisation were beginning to show. Businesses became more than slim; some became anorexic. Cost cutting achieved impressive short-tem results, but it cannot be repeated year after year without impairing the basic viability of the business. Steadily the number of problem cases mounted. In Britain there was great public discussion about problems with the national rail network and the shortage of skilled staff to carry out maintenance and repairs or lack of trained guards.

WINDOW ON PRACTICE

In February 2003 the *Columbia* space shuttle disintegrated over Texas during re-entry to the earth's atmosphere. All seven crew died. In August an official inquiry was severe and unequivocal in its condemnation of cost cutting that took no account of safety requirements. NASA staff had been reduced from 32,000 to 19,000 and its budget had been cut by 40 per cent. Much of the responsibility for safety had been subcontracted to Boeing, and NASA's safety culture had become 'reactive, complacent and dominated by unjustified optimism, displaying no interest in understanding a problem and its implications'.

HR managers need to be particularly aware of the risks associated with cost cutting, as they may be the greatest culprits. The British National Health Service has long been criticised for inefficient use of resources, so large numbers of managers and administrators have been recruited to make things more efficient. Many of these new recruits are HR people who may be perceived by health professionals as creating inefficient and costly controls at the expense of employing more health professionals. We are not suggesting that these criticisms are necessarily justified, but there are undoubtedly situations in which the criticisms *are* justified.

There is now a move towards redressing that balance in search for an equilibrium between the needs for financial viability and success in the **marketplace** on the one hand and the need to maximise **human capital** on the other.

BUSINESSES, ORGANISATIONS AND HUMAN RESOURCE MANAGEMENT

Most books on management and the academic study of management use the term 'organisation' as the classifier: organisational behaviour, organisational psychology, organisational sociology and organisation theory are standard terms because they focus on the interaction between the organisation as an entity and its people or with the surrounding society. So far we have used the word 'business'. We will not stick to this throughout the book, but we have used it to underline the fact that HR people are concerned with the management of resourceful humans *not* employed within the organisation as well as those who are. The above criticism of NASA's complacency was because they had lost the sense of ownership and responsibility for a human capital input simply because the people were employed by a different organisation. HR people have to be involved in the effective management of all the people of the business, not only those who are directly employed within the organisation itself. We need to remember that organisation is a process as well as an entity.

ACTIVITY 1.1

We use the word 'organisation' to describe an entity when we are describing the place where we work ('my organisation'), a particular business enterprise ('Shell is an international organisation') or as a general term to describe undertakings ('over 200 organisations were represented at the conference'). Organisation as a process describes how something is done ('the organisation of the conference was very efficient'; 'the project failed due to poor organisation'). Think of examples of HR work which are organisation as a process.

Human resource managers administer the **contract of employment**, which is the legal basis of the employment relationship, but within that framework they also administer a psychological contract for **performance**. To have a viable business the employer obviously requires those who do its work to produce an appropriate and effective performance and the performance may come from employees, but is just as likely to come from non-employees. A business which seeks to be as lean and flexible as it can needs to reduce long-term cost commitments and focus its efforts on the activities which are the basis of its **competitive advantage**. It may be wise to buy in standard business services, as well as expertise, from specialist providers. Performance standards can be unambiguously agreed and monitored (although they rarely are), while the contract can be ended a great deal more easily than is the case with a department full of employees.

We refer to a **contract** for performance because both parties have an interest in performance. The employer needs it from the employee, but an employee also has a psychological need to perform, to do well and to fulfil personal needs that for many can best be met in the employment context. Schoolteachers cannot satisfy their desire to teach without a school to provide premises, equipment and pupils. A research chemist can do little without a well-equipped laboratory and qualified colleagues; very few coach drivers can earn their living unless someone else provides the coach.

DEFINING HUMAN RESOURCE MANAGEMENT

The term 'human resource management' is not easy to define. This is because it is commonly used in two different ways. On the one hand it is used generically to describe the body of management activities covered in books such as this. Used in this way HRM is really no more than a more modern and supposedly imposing name for what has long been labelled 'personnel management'. On the other hand, the term is equally widely used to denote a particular approach to the management of people which is clearly distinct from 'personnel management'. Used in this way 'HRM' signifies more than an updating of the label; it also suggests a distinctive philosophy towards carrying out people-oriented organisational activities: one which is held to serve the modern business more effectively than 'traditional' personnel management. We explore the substance of these two meanings of human resource management in the following paragraphs, referring to the first as 'HRM mark 1' and the second as 'HRM mark 2'.

HRM mark 1: the generic term

The role of the human resource functions is explained by identifying the key **objectives** to be achieved. Four objectives form the foundation of all HR activity.

Staffing objectives

Human resource managers are first concerned with ensuring that the business is appropriately staffed and thus able to draw on the human resources it needs. This involves designing organisation structures, identifying under what type of contract different groups of employees (or subcontractors) will work, before recruiting, selecting and developing the people required to fill the roles: the right people, with the right skills to provide their services when needed. There is a need to compete effectively in the employment market by recruiting and retaining the best, affordable workforce that is available. This involves developing employment packages that are sufficiently attractive to maintain the required employee skills levels and, where necessary, disposing of those judged no longer to have a role to play in the organisation.

Performance objectives

Once the required workforce is in place, human resource managers seek to ensure that people are well motivated and committed so as to maximise their performance in their different roles. Training and development has a role to play, as do reward systems to maximise effort and focus attention on performance targets. In many organisations, particularly where trade unions play a significant role, human resource managers negotiate improved performance with the workforce. The achievement of performance objectives also requires HR specialists to assist in disciplining employees effectively and equitably where individual conduct and/or performance standards are unsatisfactory. Welfare functions can also assist performance by providing constructive assistance to people whose performance has fallen short of their potential because of illness or difficult personal circumstances. Last but not least, there is the range of employee involvement initiatives to raise levels of commitment and to engage employees in developing new ideas.

Change-management objectives

A third set of core objectives in nearly every business relates to the role played by the HR function in effectively managing change. Frequently change does not come along in readily defined episodes precipitated by some external factor. Instead it is endemic and well-nigh continuous, generated as much by a continual need to innovate as from definable environmental pressures. Change comes in different forms. Sometimes it is merely structural, requiring reorganisation of activities or the introduction of new people into particular roles. At other times cultural change is sought in order to alter attitudes, philosophies or long-present organisational norms. In any of these scenarios the HR function can play a central role. Key activities include the recruitment and/or development of people with the necessary leadership skills to drive the change process, the employment of change agents to encourage acceptance of change and the construction of reward systems which underpin the change process. Timely and effective employee involvement is also crucial because 'people support what they help to create'.

Administration objectives

The fourth type of objective is less directly related to achieving competitive advantage, but is focused on underpinning the achievement of the other forms of objective. In part it is simply carried out in order to facilitate an organisation's smooth running. Hence there is a need to maintain accurate and comprehensive data on individual employees, a record of their achievement in terms of performance, their attendance and training records, their terms and conditions of employment and their personal details. However, there is also a legal aspect to much administrative activity, meaning that it is done because the business is required by law to comply. Of particular significance is the requirement that payment is administered professionally and lawfully, with itemised monthly pay statements being provided for all employees. There is also the need to make arrangements for the deduction of taxation and national insurance, for the payment of pension fund contributions and to be on top of the complexities associated with Statutory Sick Pay and Statutory Maternity Pay, as well as maternity and paternity leave. Additional legal requirements relate to the monitoring of health and safety systems and the issuing of contracts to new employees. Accurate record keeping is central to ensuring compliance with a variety of newer legal obligations such as the National Minimum Wage and the Working Time Regulations.

ACTIVITY 1.2

Each of the four types of HR objective is important and necessary for organisations in different ways. However, at certain times one or more can assume greater importance than the others. Can you identify types of situation in which each could become the most significant or urgent?

Delivering HRM objectives

The larger the organisation, the more scope there is to employ people to specialise in particular areas of HRM. Some, for example, employ employee relations specialists to look after the **collective relationship between management and employees**. Where there is a strong tradition of collective bargaining, the role is focused on the achievement of satisfactory outcomes from ongoing negotiations. Increasingly, however, employee relations specialists are required to provide advice about legal developments, to manage consultation arrangements and to preside over employee involvement initiatives.

Another common area of specialisation is in the field of training and development. Although much of this is now undertaken by external providers, there is still a role

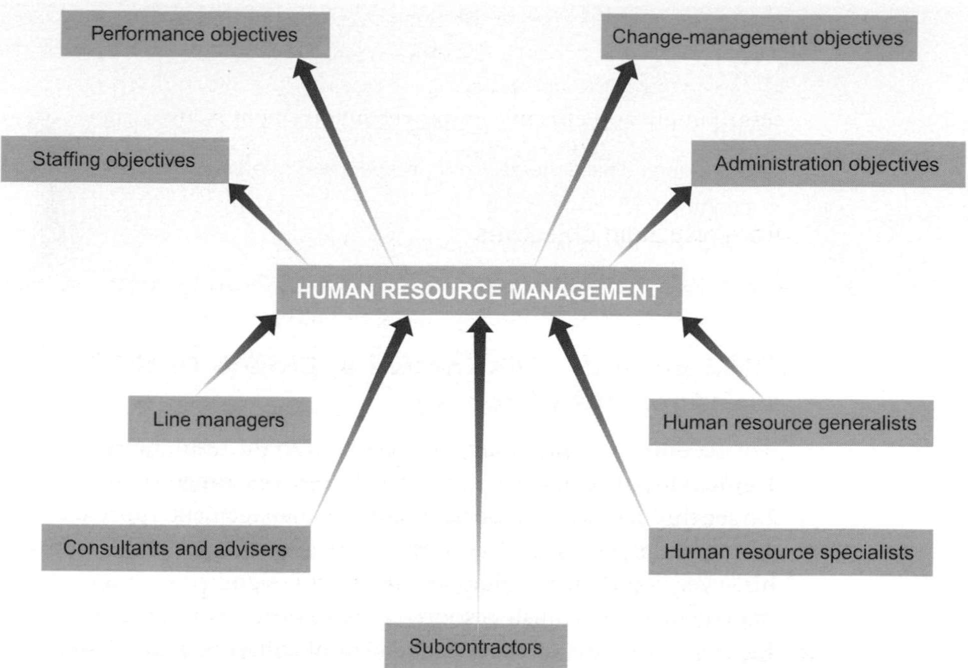

Figure 1.1 HRM roles and objectives

for in-house trainers, particularly in management development. Increasingly the term 'consultant' is used instead of 'officer' or 'manager' to describe the training specialist's role, indicating a shift towards a situation in which line managers determine the training *they* want rather than the training section providing a standardised **portfolio** of courses. The other major specialist roles are in the fields of **recruitment and selection**, health, safety and welfare, compensation and benefits and human resource planning.

In addition to the people who have specialist roles there are many other people who are employed as human resources or personnel generalists. Working alone or in small teams, they carry out the range of HR activities and seek to achieve all the objectives outlined above. In larger businesses generalists either look after all personnel matters in a particular division or are employed at a senior level to develop policy and take responsibility for HR issues across the organisation as a whole. In more junior roles, human resource administrators and assistants undertake many of the administrative tasks mentioned earlier. Figure 1.1 summarises the roles and objectives of HRM.

Most HR practitioners working at a senior level are now professionally qualified, having secured membership of the Chartered Institute of Personnel and Development (CIPD). The wide range of elective subjects which can now be chosen by those seeking qualification through the Institute's examinations has made it as relevant to those seeking a specialist career as to those who prefer to remain in generalist roles. However, many smaller businesses do not need, or cannot afford, HR managers at all. They may use consultants or the advisory services of university departments. They may use their bank's computer to process the payroll, but there is still a human resource dimension to their managers' activities.

ACTIVITY 1.3

Which of the various HR roles described above would you be most interested in undertaking? The generalist role, a specialist role or perhaps that of a consultant or subcontractor?

What are the main reasons for your choice?

HRM mark 2: a distinctive approach to the management of people

The second meaning commonly accorded to the term 'human resource management' denotes a particular way of carrying out the range of activities discussed above. Under this definition, a 'human resource management approach' is something qualitatively different from a 'personnel management approach'. Commentators disagree, however, about how fundamental a shift is signified by a movement from personnel management to human resource management. For some, particularly those whose focus of interest is on the management of collective relationships at work, the rise of HRM in the last two decades of the twentieth century represents something new and very different from the dominant personnel management approach in earlier years. A particular theme in their work is the contention that personnel management is essentially *workforce centred*, while HRM is *resource centred*. Personnel specialists direct their efforts mainly at the organisation's employees; finding and training them, arranging for them to be paid, explaining management's expectations, justifying management's actions, satisfying employees' work-related needs, dealing with their problems and seeking to modify management action that could produce an unwelcome employee response. The people who work in the organisation are the starting point, and they are a resource that is relatively inflexible in comparison with other resources, like cash and materials.

Although indisputably a management function, personnel management is not totally identified with management interests. Just as sales representatives have to understand and articulate the aspirations of the customers, personnel managers seek to understand and articulate the aspirations and views of the workforce. There is always some degree of being in between management and the employees, mediating the needs of each to the other.

HRM, by contrast, is directed mainly at management needs for human resources (not necessarily employees) to be provided and deployed. Demand rather than supply is the focus of the activity. There is greater emphasis on planning, monitoring and control, rather than mediation. Problem solving is undertaken with other members of management on human resource issues rather than directly with employees or their representatives. It is totally identified with management interests, being a general management activity, and is relatively distant from the workforce as a whole. David Guest (1987) emphasises the differences between the two approaches in his model illustrating 'stereotypes of personnel management and human resource management' (see Figure 1.2).

An alternative point of view, while recognising the differences, downplays the significance of a break between personnel and human resources management. Such

	Personnel management	Human resource management
Time and planning perspective	Short term, reactive, ad hoc, marginal	Long term, proactive, strategic, integrated
Psychological contract	Compliance	Commitment
Control systems	External controls	Self-control
Employee relations perspective	Pluralist, collective, low trust	Unitarist, individual, high trust
Preferred structures/ systems	Bureaucratic/mechanistic, centralised, formal defined roles	Organic, devolved, flexible roles
Roles	Specialist/professional	Largely integrated into line management
Evaluation criteria	Cost minimisation	Maximum utilisation (human asset accounting)

Figure 1.2 Personnel versus HRM

a conclusion is readily reached when the focus of analysis is on what HR/personnel managers actually do, rather than on the more profound developments in the specific field of collective employee relations. Legge (1989 and 1995) concludes that there is very little difference in fact between the two, but that there are some differences that are important; first, that human resource management concentrates more on what is done to managers than on what is done by managers to other employees; second, that there is a more proactive role for line managers; and, third, that there is a top management responsibility for managing culture – all factors to which we return later in the book. From this perspective, human resource management can simply be seen as the most recent mutation in a long line of developments that have characterised personnel management practice as it evolved during the last century. HRM is therefore the latest new dimension to be added to a role which has developed in different directions at different stages in its history. Below we identify four distinct stages in the historical development of the personnel management function. HRM, as described above, is a fifth. On the companion website there is a journalist's view of contemporary HRM to which we have added some discussion questions.

THE EVOLUTION OF PERSONNEL AND HR MANAGEMENT

Theme 1: social justice

The origins of personnel management lie in the nineteenth century, deriving from the work of social reformers such as Lord Shaftesbury and Robert Owen. Their criticisms of the free enterprise system and the hardship created by the exploitation of workers by factory owners enabled the first personnel managers to be appointed and provided the first frame of reference in which they worked: to ameliorate the lot of the workers. Such concerns are not obsolete. There are still regular reports of employees being exploited by employers flouting the law, and the problem of organisational distance between decision makers and those putting decisions into practice remains a source of alienation from work.

In the late nineteenth and early twentieth centuries some of the larger employers with a paternalist outlook began to appoint welfare officers to manage a series of new initiatives designed to make life less harsh for their employees. Prominent examples were the progressive schemes of unemployment benefit, sick pay and subsidised housing provided by the Quaker family firms of Cadbury and Rowntree, and the Lever Brothers' soap business. While the motives were ostensibly charitable, there was and remains a business as well as an ethical case for paying serious attention to the welfare of employees. This is based on the contention that it improves **commitment** on the part of staff and leads potential employees to compare the organisation favourably *vis-à-vis* competitors. The result is higher productivity, a longer-serving workforce and a bigger pool of applicants for each job. It has also been argued that a commitment to welfare reduces the scope for the development of adversarial industrial relations. The more conspicuous welfare initiatives promoted by employers today include employee assistance schemes, childcare facilities and health-screening programmes.

Theme 2: humane bureaucracy

The second phase marked the beginnings of a move away from a sole focus on welfare towards the meeting of various other organisational objectives. Personnel managers began to gain responsibilities in the areas of staffing, training and organisation design. Influenced by social scientists such as F.W. Taylor (1856–1915) and Henri Fayol (1841–1925) personnel specialists started to look at management and administrative processes analytically, working out how organisational structures could be designed and labour deployed so as to maximise efficiency. The humane bureaucracy stage in the development of personnel thinking was also influenced by the **Human Relations School**, which sought to ameliorate the potential for industrial conflict and dehumanisation present in too rigid an application of these **scientific management** approaches. Following the ideas of thinkers such as Elton Mayo (1880–1949), the fostering of social relationships in the workplace and employee morale thus became equally important objectives for personnel professionals seeking to raise productivity levels.

Theme 3: negotiated consent

Personnel managers next added expertise in bargaining to their repertoire of skills. In the period of full employment following the Second World War labour became a scarce resource. This led to a growth in trade union membership and to what Allan Flanders, the leading industrial relations analyst of the 1960s, called 'the challenge from below'. Personnel specialists managed the new collective institutions such as joint consultation committees, joint production committees and suggestion schemes set up in order to accommodate the new realities. In the industries that were nationalised in the 1940s, employers were placed under a statutory duty to negotiate with unions representing employees. To help achieve this, the government encouraged the appointment of personnel officers and set up the first specialist courses for them in the universities. A personnel management advisory service was also set up at the Ministry of Labour, which still survives as the first A in ACAS (the Advisory, Conciliation and Arbitration Service).

Theme 4: organisation

The late 1960s saw a switch in focus among personnel specialists, away from dealing principally with the rank-and-file employee on behalf of management, towards dealing with management itself and the integration of managerial activity. This phase was characterised by the development of career paths and of opportunities within organisations for personal growth. This too remains a concern of personnel specialists today, with a significant portion of time and resources being devoted to the recruitment, development and retention of an elite core of people with specialist expertise on whom the business depends for its future. Personnel specialists developed techniques of manpower or workforce planning. This is basically a quantitative activity, boosted by the advent of information technology, which involves forecasting the likely need for employees with different skills in the future.

Theme 5: human resource management

This has already been explained in the previous pages.

ACTIVITY 1.4

Think of an HR management role with which you are familiar. To what extent can you identify in it the presence of activities inherited from each of the five stages in the development of modern HRM?

A PHILOSOPHY OF HUMAN RESOURCE MANAGEMENT

The philosophy of human resource management that is the basis of this book has been only slightly modified since it was first put forward in 1979 (Torrington and Chapman 1979, p. 4). Despite all the changes in the labour market and in the government approach to the economy, this seems to be the most realistic and constructive approach, based on the earlier ideas of Enid Mumford (1972) and McCarthy and Ellis (1973). The original was:

> Personnel management is most realistically seen as a series of activities enabling working man and his employing organisation to reach agreement about the nature and objectives of the employment relationship between them, and then to fulfil those agreements. (Torrington and Chapman 1979, p. 4)

Our definition for the fifth edition in 2002 was:

> Human resource management is a series of activities which: first enables working people and the organisation which uses their skills to agree about the objectives and nature of their working relationship and, secondly, ensures that the agreement is fulfilled.
> (Torrington, Hall and Taylor 2002, p. 13)

This remains our philosophy. Only by satisfying the needs of the individual contributor will the business obtain the commitment to organisational objectives that is needed for organisational success, and only by contributing to organisational success will individuals be able to satisfy their personal employment needs. It is when employer and employee – or business and supplier of skills – accept that mutuality and reciprocal dependence that human resource management is exciting, centre stage and productive of business success. Where the employer is concerned with employees only as factors of production, personnel management is boring and a cost that will always be trimmed. Where employees have no trust in their employer and adopt an entirely instrumental orientation to their work, they will be fed up and will make ineffectual the work of any HR function.

Figure 1.3 represents the contents of this book in the six main parts. After the three-chapter introduction in Part I come the six parts, which each have the same format: strategic aspects, operational features and a concluding Focus on skills which highlights an interaction that is central to that set of operations. This is the HRM process, a strategic core with operational specialist expertise and a strong focus on dealing with people face to face.

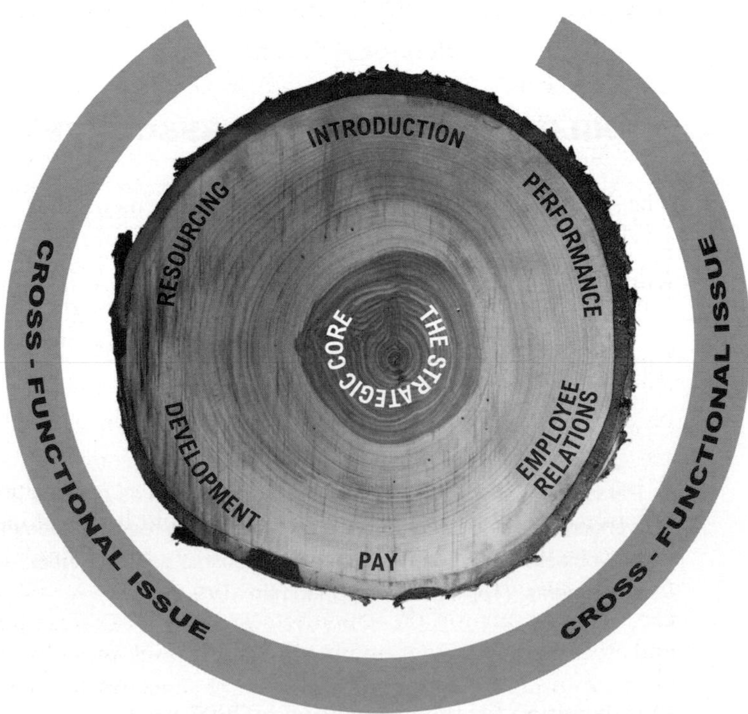

Figure 1.3 The personnel/HR process

Human resource managers are like managers in every other part of the organisation. They have to make things happen rather than wait for things to happen, and to make things happen not only do they need to have the right approach; they also have to know their stuff. Read on!

DEBATES IN HRM

The world in which human resource managers exist and with which they interact is continually changing, generating new issues and conundrums to consider. While in most cases managers have a fair degree of choice about how to deal with new ideas and new sets of circumstances, the choices themselves are often difficult. Our final task in this opening chapter is to introduce readers to a number of these issues in general terms. All raise themes to which we will return at various stages later in the book.

In one way or another all the major debates that occupy HR professionals, analysts and commentators concern the appropriate response to the major trends which are evolving in our business environment. But people differ in their analysis of the extent and nature of these developments and this colours their ideas about whether or not radical **change** in the way that people are managed is or is not appropriate. Here we can usefully distinguish between three separate fields of debate.

The first is concerned with understanding and conceptualising the nature of current responses. How are organisations dealing with the issues that they face in terms of the management of their people? Are they developing new approaches that differ fundamentally from those that have been established for some time or are we witnessing a more steady, considered evolution of practice?

The second field of debate concerns what HR managers *should* be doing. Are new or radical changes in policy and practice necessary? Or is the correct response to environmental developments the further refinement of more familiar approaches? Further debate concerns the extent to which the answer to these questions is broadly the same for all employing organisations or whether it differs quite profoundly from industry to industry or firm to firm.

A third debate is oriented towards longer-term future developments. Many believe and have argued persuasively that we are currently witnessing changes in our business environment which are as fundamental and significant as those which accompanied the industrial revolution two hundred years ago. They further argue that the world of work which will emerge in future decades will be wholly different in major respects from that we currently inhabit. It follows that those organisations which 'see the future' most clearly and change accordingly stand to gain most. But are these predictions really accurate? Could the analysis on which they are built be faulty in key respects?

Of course it is also possible to ask rather different kinds of questions about the HR practices that are being, will be or should be developed, which in turn lead us to engage in various types of debate. Some, for example, focus exclusively on the requirements of the organisation and the search for competitive advantage. What can the HR function do which will maximise organisational growth, effectiveness and efficiency? However, many also like to think more broadly and to concern themselves with the impact of employment practice on the workforce and on society in more general terms. Hence we also engage in debates that are essentially ethical in nature or which have a prominent ethical dimension.

Key environmental developments

The major trends in our contemporary **business environment** are well understood, well documented and uncontroversial. People differ, though, in their understanding of the speed of change and of the extent to which all organisations are or will be affected. As far as product markets are concerned the big trend is towards ever more intense competitive pressures, leading some to argue that we are now entering the era of hyper-competition (Sparrow 2003, p. 371). This is being driven by two major developments, the significance of which has increased considerably in recent years.

First, we are witnessing moves towards the globalisation of economic activity on a scale that has not been experienced before in human history. More and more the markets for the goods and products we sell are international, which means of course that competition for those markets as well as our established ones is also increasingly becoming international. Large organisations that were able to dominate national markets a decade or two ago (many owned and operated by governments) are now mainly privately owned and faced with vastly more competition from similar organisations based all over the world. This has led to consolidation through the construction of global corporations and strategic alliances whose focus in terms of people management is also international.

The second major antecedent of hyper-competition is technology, which moves forward at an ever-accelerating pace year by year. Developments in information technology, energy production, chemical engineering, laser technology, transportation and biotechnology are in the process of revolutionising the way that many industries operate. It is partly the sheer pace of change and the need for organisations to stay ahead of this very fast-moving game which drives increased competition. Being the first to develop and make efficient use of new technologies is the means by which many organisations maintain their competitive position and can thus grow and prosper.

But IT, and in particular the growth of e-business, is significant too because it has the potential vastly to increase the number of competitors that any one organisation faces. This is because it makes it much easier for customers and potential customers to compare what your organisation can offer in terms of price and quality with what others can offer.

What does this mean in practical terms from the point of view of the HR manager? First, it means that practices continually have to be developed which have the effect of enhancing an organisation's competitive position. Ways need to be found of improving quality and of bringing to market attractive new products and services, while at the same time ensuring that the organisation remains competitive in terms of its cost base. Second, it means that a good deal of volatility is the norm and that change, often of a profound nature, is something that people working in organisations must expect and be ready for. So a capacity for organisational flexibility has become central to the achievement and maintenance of competitive advantage. Third, there are direct practical outcomes. For example, HR managers have to learn how to manage an international workforce effectively and how best to attract, retain and develop and motivate people with those relatively scarce skills that are essential if an organisation is effectively to harness and deploy evolving technologies.

For the HR manager, however, unlike colleagues in other areas of management, responding to product market developments is only part of what is needed. Other major environmental trends are equally important and must also be understood and built into decision making. There are two areas which are particularly important:

- labour market trends
- the evolution of employment regulation

Developments in the labour market are significant partly in terms of the numbers of people and skills available, and partly in terms of attitudes towards work and the workplace. Major developments appear to be occurring in both these areas. Many industries, for example, have found themselves facing skills shortages in recent years. The impact varies from country to country depending on relative economic prosperity, but most organisations in the UK have seen a tightening of their key labour markets in recent years. Unemployment levels have remained low, while demographic trends have created a situation in which more older people are retiring than younger people are entering the job market. There are all kinds of implications. For a start, employers are having to make themselves more attractive to employees than has been necessary in recent years. No longer can they simply assume that people will seek work with them or seek to remain employed with them. In a tight labour market individuals have more choice about where and when they work, and do not need to put up with a working environment in which they are unhappy. If they do not like their jobs there are more opportunities for them to look elsewhere. So organisations are increasingly required to compete with one another in labour markets as well as in product markets. This has implications for policy in all areas of HRM, but particularly in the areas of reward, employee development and recruitment.

Labour market conditions along with other social trends serve to shape the attitudes of people towards their work. In order to mobilise and motivate a workforce, HR managers must be aware of how these are changing and to respond effectively. One of the most significant trends in recent years, for example, has been a reduced interest on the part of employees in joining trade unions and taking part in their activities. A more individualistic attitude now prevails in the majority of workplaces, people focusing on themselves and their own career development rather than standing in solidarity with fellow workers. Another well-documented trend is the increased desire for employees to achieve a better balance between their home and work lives and their increased willingness to seek out employers who can provide this.

The growth in the extent and complexity of employment regulation is a third area which HR managers are obliged to grasp and the elements of which they must implement in their organisations. Prior to 1970, with one or two exceptions, there was no **statutory regulation** of the employment relationship in the UK. An individual's terms and conditions of employment were those that were stated in the contract of employment and in any collective agreements. The law did not intervene beyond providing some basic health and safety protection, the right to modest redundancy payments and a general requirement on employers and employees to honour the contractual terms agreed when the employment began. Since 1970 this situation has wholly changed. The individual contract of employment remains significant and can be enforced in court if necessary, but there has been added to this a whole range of statutory rights which employers are obliged to honour. The most significant are in the fields of health and safety, equal pay, unlawful discrimination and unfair dismissal. Much recent new law such as that on working time, family-friendly rights, consultation and discrimination on grounds of sexual orientation and belief has a European origin, and a great deal more can be expected in the years ahead.

Debates about how HR managers are and should be responding to these various trends form the focus of much of what follows in this book and you will find a much more detailed treatment of some in other chapters. The international dimension, for example, is discussed in Chapter 30 and ethical matters in Chapter 31. We focus on the work-life balance in Chapter 32, on labour market trends in Part 2 and on regulatory matters in Part 5. Below we briefly set out the main contours of three specific debates that have a general relevance to many of the topic areas we discuss later.

The psychological contract

According to many, one consequence of these evolving environmental pressures is a significant and fundamental change in what has become known as 'the psychological contract'. This refers to the expectations that employees have about the role that they play and to what the employer is prepared to give them in return. Whereas a legal contract of employment sets out terms and conditions of employment, remuneration arrangements and the basic rules which are to govern the employment relationship, the psychological contract concerns broad expectations about what each party thinks it will gain from the relationship. By its nature the psychological contract is not a written document. Rather, it exists entirely within people's heads. But this has not prevented researchers from seeking to pin it down and to track the extent to which we are witnessing ongoing change in established psychological contracts.

While people disagree about the extent to which this change has in fact occurred, there is general agreement about the phenomenon itself and the notion that an 'old' psychological contract to which generations of employees have become accustomed is being superseded to some extent by a 'new' psychological contract which reflects the needs of the present business environment. From the employee perspective we can sum up the old psychological contract as follows:

> I will work hard for and act with loyalty towards my employer. In return I expect to be retained as an employee provided I do not act against the interests of the organisation. I also expect to be given opportunities for development and promotion should circumstances make this possible.

By contrast, the new psychological contract takes the following form:

> I will bring to my work effort and creativity. In return I expect a salary that is appropriate to my contribution and market worth. While our relationship may be short term, I will remain for as long as I receive the developmental opportunities I need to build my career.

A switch from the 'old' approach to the 'new' involves employers giving less job security and receiving less loyalty from employees in return. Instead, employees are given developmental opportunities and are expected to give the employer flexibility. The whole perception of the employment relationship on both sides is thus radically different. Moreover, moving from old psychological contracts towards new ones is a problematic process that involves managers 'breaching' the established deal. This is likely to lead to dissatisfaction on the part of employees who are affected and to some form of collective industrial action in unionised settings.

The big question is how far has a change of this nature actually occurred? Are we really witnessing a slow decline in the old psychological contract and its replacement by the new one, or have reports of its death been exaggerated?

On this issue there is a great deal of disagreement. Many researchers claim to have found evidence of substantial change in many industries, particularly as regards reduced employee loyalty (e.g. Coyle-Shapiro and Kessler 2000, Maguire 2002). Yet others, notably Guest and Conway in their many studies conducted on behalf of the Chartered Institute of Personnel and Development (CIPD), have found relatively little evidence of any change in the state of the psychological contract. Their findings (e.g. Guest and Conway 2000 and 2001) suggest that while some change has occurred in the public sector, perceptions closer to the 'old' psychological contract remain a great deal more common than those associated with the 'new' approach.

It is difficult to reach firm conclusions about why these very marked differences of opinion exist. It is possible that the old psychological contract remains intact for most people, but that a significant minority, particularly managers and some public sector workers, have had to adjust to profound change. It is also possible that organisations have tried to move away from the old approach towards the new one, but have found it difficult to take their employees with them and have thus sought other methods of increasing their competitiveness. A third possibility, suggested by Atkinson (2003), is that the differences in the conclusions people reach about this issue derive from the methodologies they adopt when studying it. She argues that large-scale studies which involve sending questionnaires to employees have tended to report little change in the state of the psychological contract, while smaller-scale studies based on interviews with managers and trade union officials tend to report the opposite.

ACTIVITY 1.5

How would you characterise your current psychological contract at work? To what extent and in what ways does it differ from psychological contracts you have experienced in previous jobs or from those of your friends and family?

Best practice v. best fit

The debate between **best practice** and **best fit** is an interesting one of general significance which has consequences across the field of HRM. As well as being a managerial issue it concerns one of the most significant academic controversies in the HR field at present. At root it is about whether or not there is an identifiable 'best way' of carrying out HR activities which is universally applicable. It is best understood as a debate between two schools of thought, although in practice it is quite possible to take a central position which sees validity in both the basic positions.

Adherents of a best practice perspective argue that there are certain HR practices and approaches to their operation which will invariably help an organisation in achieving competitive advantage. There is therefore a clear link between HR activity and business performance, but the effect will only be maximised if the 'right' HR policies are pursued. A great deal of evidence has been published in recent years, using various methodologies, which appears to back up the best practice case (e.g. Pfeffer 1994; Huselid 1995; Wood and Albanese 1995; Delery and Doty 1996; Fernie and Metcalf 1996; Patterson *et al.* 1998; Guest and Conway 2000). While there are differences of opinion on questions of detail, all strongly suggest that the same basic bundle of human resource practices or general human resource management orientation tends to enhance business performance in all organisations irrespective of the particular product market strategy being pursued. According to David Guest this occurs through a variety of mechanisms:

> human resource practices exercise their positive impact by (i) ensuring and enhancing the competence of employees, (ii) by tapping their motivation and commitment, and (iii) by designing work to encourage the fullest contribution from employees. Borrowing from elements of expectancy theory (Vroom 1964, Lawler 1971), the model implies that all three elements should be present to ensure the best outcome. Positive employee behaviour should in turn impact upon establishment level outcomes such as low absence, quit rates and wastage, as well as high quality and productivity. (Guest 2000, p. 2)

The main elements of the 'best practice bundle' that these and other writers identify are those which have long been considered as examples of good practice in the HRM field. They include the use of the more advanced selection methods, a serious commitment to employee involvement, substantial investment in training and development, the use of individualised reward systems and harmonised terms and conditions of employment as between different groups of employees.

The alternative 'best fit' school also identifies a link between human resource management practice and the achievement of competitive advantage. Here, however, there is no belief in the existence of universal solutions. Instead, all is **contingent** on the particular circumstances of each organisation. What is needed is HR policies and practices which 'fit' and are thus appropriate to the situation of individual employers. What is appropriate (or 'best') for one will not necessarily be right for another. Key variables include the size of the establishment, the dominant product market strategy being pursued and the nature of the labour markets in which the organisation competes. It is thus argued that a small organisation which principally achieves competitive advantage through innovation and which competes in very tight labour markets should have in place rather different HR policies than those of a large firm which produces low-cost goods and faces no difficulty in attracting staff. In order to maximise competitive advantage, the first requires informality combined with sophisticated human resource practices, while the latter needs more bureaucratic systems combined with a 'low cost – no frills' set of HR practices.

The best fit or contingency perspective originated in the work of Joan Woodward and her colleagues at Imperial College in the 1950s. In recent years it has been developed and applied to contemporary conditions by academics such as Randall Schuler and Susan Jackson, John Purcell and Ed Lawler. In addition, a number of influential models have been produced which seek to categorise organisational contingencies and suggest what mix of HR practices is appropriate in each case. Examples are those of Miles and Snow (1978), Fombrun *et al.* (1984) and Sisson and Storey (2000) – a number of which we look at in more detail in Chapter 2.

To a great extent the jury is still out on these questions. Proponents of both the 'best practice' and 'best fit' perspectives can draw on bodies of empirical evidence to back up their respective positions and so the debate continues.

The future of work

Debates about what will happen in the future are inevitably speculative and impossible to prove one way or the other, but a great deal of attention and government research funding is currently being devoted to this issue. It matters a great deal from a public policy point of view because judgements about employers' human resource needs in the future must determine decisions about education and training now. Government actions in the fields of economic policy, employment legislation and immigration are also affected.

A good starting point is the work of influential writers such as Charles Handy (1994 and 2001), William Bridges (1995) and Jeremy Rifkin (1995). In different ways they have argued that the product market forces identified above will lead in future decades to the emergence of a world of work which is very different in many respects from that which most in western industrialised countries currently experience. Both the type of work we do and the nature of our contractual arrangements will, it is argued, change profoundly as we complete our journey out of the industrial era and into a new post-industrial age.

The first consequence will be a marked shift towards what is described as knowledge work. In the future, it is claimed, most people will be employed, in one way or another, to carry out tasks which involve the generation, interpretation, processing or application of knowledge. Automation and the availability of cheaper labour in developing countries will see further declines in much manufacturing activity, requiring the western economies to create wealth from the exploitation of scientific and technological advances. It follows that many more people will be employed for their specialist knowledge and that far fewer routine jobs will exist than is currently the case. Demand for professional and technical people will increase, while demand for manual and lower-skilled workers will decrease. It also means that competitive advantage from an employer's perspective will derive from the capacity to create and deploy knowledge more effectively than others can.

The second major claim that is made is that the 'job' as we have come to know it will become rarer and rarer. In the future many fewer people will occupy defined jobs in organisations. Instead we will tend increasingly to work on a self-employed basis carrying out specific, time-limited projects for organisations. This is inevitable, so the argument goes, in a highly volatile business climate. Organisations simply will not be able to offer long-term guarantees of work and so will be forced to stop offering contracts of employment in the way that they currently do. The future is therefore bleak for people who want job security, but bright for those who are happy working for many employers and periodically re-educating themselves for a new type of career.

In many respects these arguments are persuasive. They are based on a rational analysis of likely developments in the business environment as globalisation and technological advances further evolve. They remain, however, highly controversial and are increasingly subject to challenge by researchers who argue that change on this kind of scale is not currently happening and will not happen in the near future.

A prominent critic of the views expressed by the predictors of radical change is Peter Nolan (*see* Nolan 2001 and Nolan and Wood 2003), who argues that the case is often overstated to a considerable degree:

> Change is evident, to be sure, but the shifts in the patterns and rhythms of work are not linear, pre-determined by technology or, as some writers have uncritically assumed, driven by universal trends in market globalisation. (Nolan and Wood 2003, p. 165)

Instead, according to Nolan and his colleagues, we are witnessing the resolute continuation of established approaches and some reversal of trends that began to develop in the 1980s and 1990s but which have since petered out. Job tenure in the UK, for example, has risen significantly in recent years while the proportion of people employed on fixed-term contracts and a self-employed basis has fallen. While we are seeing a slow growth in the proportion of people employed in professional and scientific roles (from 34 per cent to 37 per cent in the 1990s), there is no fall occurring in the number of manual jobs. At the same time the proportion of people employed in relatively low-skilled jobs in the service sector is growing quickly. Critics of Handy and the other futurologists have thus identified a gap between a rhetoric which emphasises fundamental change and a reality which gives little support to the view that we are in the process of shaping a 'new world of work'.

These different conceptions of the future may well derive from a preference for a focus on different types of environmental development. A reading of the major contemporary product market trends can easily lead to predictions of radical change. The twin forces of technological advance and globalisation do indeed point to a transformation of many aspects of our lives. But trends in employment are equally determined by developments in the labour market and regulatory environments. These suggest a strong preference on the part of both employees and law makers for a continuation of traditional approaches towards employment.

WINDOW ON PRACTICE

Flexicurity in Denmark

Government intervention is commonly seen as a barrier blocking the creation of **flexible labour markets** such as those that it is argued are necessary if the Western economies are to thrive in an increasingly volatile and knowledge-driven business environment. Labour market regulation serves to slow down progress towards a world of work in which most people are self-employed or employed on a series of short-term contracts for different organisations. In fact, as Madsen (2003) shows, the Danish experience appears to show that the opposite is the case.

Denmark has the highest level of employee turnover in Europe (30 per cent on average in recent years). It is also has a very high level of job turnover, between

10 per cent and 15 per cent of its jobs disappearing each year and being replaced with new ones. Around a quarter of the Danish workforce finds itself unemployed for some portion of every year, while as many as 10 per cent of the country's people are employed on fixed-term contracts. The proportion of small and medium-sized enterprises is also the highest in Europe. Economically, Denmark is a success story. Inflation has been low for a decade, overall unemployment rates are well below those of other major EU economies and growth has been stronger. In short, Denmark appears to be a good deal further down the road to the kind of 'future world of work' envisaged by Charles Handy than the other EU countries.

The major reason for this appears to be the Danish social security system, which is very generous in comparison with those of other countries. It is relatively easy to dismiss people (although less easy than in the UK), but people who do find themselves out of work suffer a great deal less in financial terms than equivalents elsewhere. They are, however, obliged as a condition of receiving benefit to take part in government-sponsored retraining and educational programmes. It is this highly sophisticated and expensive unemployment benefit system that seems to have allowed Denmark to develop highly flexible labour markets. It means that people are more willing to take on insecure roles and that employers are less concerned than they are elsewhere to avoid redundancies at all costs.

SUMMARY PROPOSITIONS

1.1 Human resource management is fundamental to all management activity.

1.2 It is possible to identify two distinct definitions of the term 'human resource management'. The first describes a body of management activities, while the second signifies a particular approach to carrying out those activities.

1.3 Human resource managers are concerned with meeting four distinct sets of organisational objectives: staffing, performance, change management and administration.

1.4 HRM activities are carried out in various ways through various forms of organisational structure. In some larger organisations HR generalists work alongside specialists in particular HR disciplines.

1.5 Human resource management can be characterised as the latest in a series of incarnations that personnel practitioners have developed since the origins of the profession over 100 years ago.

1.6 The philosophy of human resource management in this book is that it is a series of activities which: first, enables working people and the business which uses their skills to agree about the nature and objectives of their working relationship; and, second, ensures that the agreement is fulfilled.

1.7 Most current debates about human resource management in general focus on the extent and nature of the responses needed in the face of developments in the business environment.

1.8 Three of the most prominent current debates focus on the nature of the psychological contract, the relative wisdom of the 'best fit' and 'best practice' approaches and predictions about the future of work.

GENERAL DISCUSSION TOPICS

1. How do you understand the suggestion that the contract of employment is gradually changing to a contract for performance?
2. The philosophy of HRM set out at the end of this chapter makes no reference to the customer. David Ulrich, a professor at Michigan Business School, believes that it is important to refocus HR activities away from the firm towards the customer so that suppliers, employees and customers are woven together into a value-chain team. What difference do you think that would make?
3. How far do you think it is possible to agree with both the 'best fit' and 'best practice' perspectives on HRM? In what ways are they compatible with each other?

FURTHER READING

British Journal of Industrial Relations (Vol. 41, No. 2)
The special edition, published in June 2003 was devoted to research on and debates about the future of work. Many leading writers in the field contributed articles which set out the first findings from a major national research project that has involved 22 universities.

Legge, K. (1995) *Human Resource Management: Rhetorics and Realities*. London: Macmillan
This provides a rigorous discussion of the differences between personnel management and HRM, as well as introducing and considering a series of other debates about the nature of HRM and its purpose for organisations. Other useful discussions include Guest (1999 and 2001), Tyson (1995) and Maund (2001).

Sparrow, P. and Cooper, C. (2003) *The Employment Relationship: Key Challenges for HR*. London: Butterworth-Heinemann
An excellent introduction to the major issues facing HR managers in the current business environment. The psychological contract and the evolution of new organisational structures are particularly well covered.

REFERENCES

Atkinson, C. (2003) 'Exploring the state of the psychological contract: the impact of research strategies on outcomes'. Paper presented to the CIPD Professional Standards Conference, Keele University, 2003.

Bridges, W. (1995) *Jobshift: How to prosper in a workplace without jobs*. London: Nicholas Brealey.

Coyle-Shapiro, J. and Kessler, I. (2000) 'Consequences of the psychological contract for the employment relationship: a large scale survey', *Journal of Management Studies*, Vol. 37, No. 7.

Delery, J. and Doty, D.H. (1996) 'Modes of Theorising in Strategic Human Resource Management: Tests of Universalistic, Contingency and Configurational Performance Predictions', *Academy of Management Journal*, Vol. 39, No. 4.

Fernie, S. and Metcalf, D. (1996) 'Participation, Contingent Pay, Representation and Workplace Performance: Evidence from Great Britain', *Discussion Paper 232*, Centre for Economic Performance, London School of Economics.

Fombrun, C., Tichy, N.M. and Devanna, M.A. (1984) *Strategic Human Resource Management*. New York: Wiley.

Guest, D.E. (1987) 'Human resource management and industrial relations', *Journal of Management Studies*, Vol. 24, No. 5.

Guest, D.E. (1999) 'Human resource management: the workers' verdict', *Human Resource Journal*, Vol. 9, No. 3, pp. 5–25.

Guest, D.E. (2000) 'Human resource management, employee well-being and organisational performance', Paper given at the CIPD Professional Standards Conference, University of Warwick.

Guest, D.E. (2001) 'Human resource management: when research confronts theory', *International Journal of Human Resource Management*, Vol. 12, No. 7, pp. 1092–1106.

Guest, D.E. and Conway, N. (2000) *The Psychological Contract in the Public Sector*. London: CIPD.

Guest, D.E. and Conway, N. (2001) *Public and Private Sector Perceptions on the Psychological Contract*. London: CIPD.

Handy, C. (1994) *The Empty Raincoat: Making Sense of the Future*. London: Hutchinson.

Handy, C. (2001) *The Elephant and the Flea: Looking Backwards to the Future*. London: Hutchinson.

Huselid, M. (1995) 'The impact of Human Resource Management practices on Turnover, Productivity and Corporate Financial Performance', *Academy of Management Journal*, Vol. 38, No. 3.

Lawler, E.E. (1971) *Pay and Organizational Effectiveness. A Psychological View*. New York: McGraw-Hill.

Legge, K. (1989) 'Human resource management: a critical analysis', in J. Storey (ed.), *New Perspectives on Human Resource Management*. London: Routledge.

Legge, K. (1995) *Human Resource Management: Rhetorics and Realities*. London: Macmillan.

Madsen, P.K. (2003) 'Flexicurity through labour market policies and institutions in Denmark', in P. Auer and S. Cazes (eds) *Employment stability in an age of flexibility: Evidence from industrialised countries*. Geneva: ILO.

Maguire, H. (2002) 'Psychological contracts: are they still relevant?' *Career Development International*, Vol. 7, No. 3 pp. 167–80.

Maund, L. (2001) *An Introduction to Human Resource Management: Theory and Practice*. Basingstoke: Palgrave.

McCarthy, W.E.J. and Ellis, N.D. (1973) *Management by Agreement*. London: Hutchinson.

Miles, R.E. and Snow, C.C. (1978) *Organisational Strategy, Strategy and Process*. New York: McGraw-Hill.

Mumford, E. (1972) 'Job satisfaction: a method of analysis', *Personnel Review*, Vol. 1, No. 3.

Nolan, P. (2001) 'Shaping things to come', *People Management*, 27 December.

Nolan, P. and Wood, S. (2003) 'Mapping the Future of Work', *British Journal of Industrial Relations*, Vol. 41, No. 2, pp. 165–74.

Patterson, M.G., West, M.A., Lawthom, R. and Nickell, S. (1998) *Impact of People Management Practices on Business Performance*. Issues in People Management No. 22. London: IPD.

Pfeffer, J. (1994) *Competitive Advantage Through People*. Boston: Harvard Business School Press.

Rifkin, J. (1995) *The End of Work: The decline of the global labour force and the dawn of the post market era*. New York: Putnam.

Sisson, K. and Storey, J. (2000) *The Realities of Human Resource Management: Managing the Employment Relationship*. Buckingham: Open University Press.

Sparrow, P.L. (2003) 'The Future of Work?' in D. Holman, T. Wall, C. Clegg, P. Sparrow and A. Howard (eds) *The New Workplace: a guide to the human impact of modern working practices*. Chichester: Wiley.

Sparrow, P.L. and Cooper, C.L. (2003) *The Employment Relationship: Key Challenges for HR*. London: Butterworth-Heinemann.

Torrington, D.P. and Chapman, J.B. (1979) *Personnel Management*. Hemel Hempstead: Prentice Hall.

Torrington, D.P., Hall, L.A. and Taylor, S. (2002) *Human Resource Management* (5th edition). Harlow: Pearson Education.

Tyson, S. (1995) *Human Resource Strategy: Towards a General Theory of Human Resource Management*. London: Pitman.

Vroom, V.H. (1964) *Work and Motivation*. New York: Wiley.

Wood, S. and Albanese, M. (1995) 'Can We Speak of High Commitment Management on the Shop Floor?' *Journal of Management Studies*, Vol. 32, No. 2.

An extensive range of additional materials, including multiple choice questions, answers to questions and links to useful websites can be found on the Human Resource Management Companion Website at www.pearsoned.co.uk/torrington.

CHAPTER 2

STRATEGIC HUMAN RESOURCE MANAGEMENT

THE OBJECTIVES OF THIS CHAPTER ARE TO:

1. CLARIFY THE USE OF THE TERMS STRATEGIC HUMAN RESOURCE MANAGEMENT AND HUMAN RESOURCE STRATEGY, AND ARRIVE AT WORKABLE DEFINITIONS OF EACH
2. EXPLAIN THE FEASIBILITY AND NATURE OF THE LINK BETWEEN BUSINESS STRATEGY AND HR STRATEGY
3. EVALUATE THREE THEORETICAL PERSPECTIVES ON THE NATURE OF HR STRATEGY AND SHOW HOW EACH EXPRESSES A DIFFERENT VIEW ON HOW THE CONTRIBUTION OF PEOPLE TO THE ORGANISATION MIGHT BE UNDERSTOOD AND ENHANCED
4. EXPLORE THE EXTENT TO WHICH THE HR FUNCTION OPERATES STRATEGICALLY

There is a strong lobby propounding the view that human resources are *the* source of competitive advantage for the business, rather than, say, access to capital or use of technology. It is therefore logical to suggest that attention needs to be paid to the nature of this resource and its management as this will impact on human resource behaviour and performance and consequently the performance of the organisation. Indeed Boxall and Steeneveld (1999) argue that there is no need to prove the relationship between firm performance and labour management as it is self-evident that the quality of human resource management is a critical influence on the performance of the firm. It is not, therefore, surprising that the rhetoric of strategic human resource management has been readily adopted, especially as a strategic approach is considered to be one of the characteristics of HRM as opposed to personnel management, which is seen as operational. If, as Boxall and Purcell (2003) suggest, HR is strategic to business success, then HR needs to be a strategic player and the role of business strategist will be a key role for HR specialists in the future (Cleland *et al.* 2000).

STRATEGIC HUMAN RESOURCE MANAGEMENT AND HUMAN RESOURCE STRATEGY

Our understanding of HR strategy has changed considerably since strategy first became the subject of great attention. We have moved from viewing strategy as a physical document to seeing it as an incremental process, affected by political influences and generating learning. Tyson's (1995) definition of human resource strategy is a useful starting point, although somewhat limited, as will be seen from our later discussion:

> the intentions of the corporation both explicit and covert, toward the management of its employees, expressed through philosophies, policies and practices. (Tyson 1995)

This definition is helpful because research on human resource strategy in the early 1980s tended to focus on seeking an HR strategy document in order to determine whether there was a strategic approach to HR and what that approach was. This was rather like searching for the Holy Grail. Not surprisingly few complete HR strategies were found and HR specialists berated themselves for having failed in this critical area. Gradually the thinking changed to encompass a view that HR strategy need not be written on a piece of paper or need not, indeed, be explicit, as the Tyson quotation illustrates. Further developments in thinking began to accept the idea that strategies are neither finished, nor complete, but rather incremental and piecemeal. There is compelling evidence to suggest that strategic HR tends to be issue based rather than the formulation of a complete and integrated strategy (for example, Grundy 1998; Hall and Torrington 1998). Strategic thinking, strategic decision making and a strategic orientation (for example, Hunt and Boxall 1998) were gradually understood as much more realistic expectations.

In parallel with this thinking there were developments in the general strategy literature which viewed strategy as a process which was not necessarily rational and top down, but a political and evolutionary process (*see*, for example, Mintzberg 1994). Mintzberg argues that strategy is 'formed' rather than 'formulated' and that any intended strategy is changed by events, opportunities, the actions of employees and so on – so that the realised strategy is different from the initial vision. Strategy, Mintzberg argues, can only be identified in retrospect and, as Boxall and Purcell suggest, is best seen in the ultimate behaviour of the organisation. Wrapped up in this view is also the idea that strategy is not necessarily determined by top management alone but can be influenced 'bottom up', as ideas are tried and tested in one part of the organisation and gradually adopted in a wholesale manner if they are seen to be applicable and successful. This is not to say that producing a strategy is an unhelpful act, and indeed research carried out by PriceWaterhouseCoopers indicated that those organisations with a written HR strategy generated 35 per cent greater revenues per employee than those without (Higginbottom 2002).

This leads on to the concept of strategy as learning both in content and in process (*see*, for example, Senge 1990; Pedler *et al.* 1991), which is supported by the notion of strategy as a process of change (*see*, for example, Hendry and Pettigrew 1992). Literature draws out the need to sense changes in the environment, develop a resultant strategy and turn this strategy into action. While the HR function has often found itself excluded from the strategy formation process, HR strategy has more often been seen in terms of the implementation of organisational strategies. However, implementation of HR strategy has been weak, at best. Among the qualities of the most successful organisations is the ability to turn strategy into action quickly (Ulrich 1998), in other words to implement the chosen strategy (Grensing-Pophel 1999), and Guest (1987) maintained that the capability to implement strategic plans is an important feature of successful HRM. However, a lack of attention to the implementation of HR strategy has been identified (Beaumont 1992; Lundy and Cowling 1996; Skinner and Mabey 1997), and the information that does exist suggests that this is a problematic area. Legge (1995) maintained that the evidence of implementation of HR strategies was patchy and sometimes contradictory, and Skinner and Mabey (1997) found that responsibility for implementation was unclear, with only 54 per cent of respondents, in organisations with an HR director, perceiving that the HR function played a major part in implementation. In their research Kane and Palmer (1995) found that the existence of an HR strategy was only a minor influence on the HR policies and procedures that were used. Frameworks such as the HR scorecard (Becker *et al.* 2001) are aimed, at least in part, at facilitating the management and implementation of HR architecture ('the sum of the HR function, the broader HR system, and the resulting employee behaviors' p. 1) as a strategic asset.

THE LINK BETWEEN BUSINESS AND HR STRATEGY

The nature, desirability and feasibility of the link between business strategy and HR strategy is a consistent theme which runs through the strategy literature, although, as we shall discuss later, some theories suggest that implementing 'best practice' in HRM is even more important than this. Figure 2.1 is a simple model that is useful in visualising different ways in which this relationship may be played out and has relevance for the newer conceptions of strategy based on the resource-based view of the firm, as well as earlier conceptions.

In the *separation model* (A) there is no relationship at all, if indeed organisational and human resource strategy *does* exist in an explicit form in the organisation. This

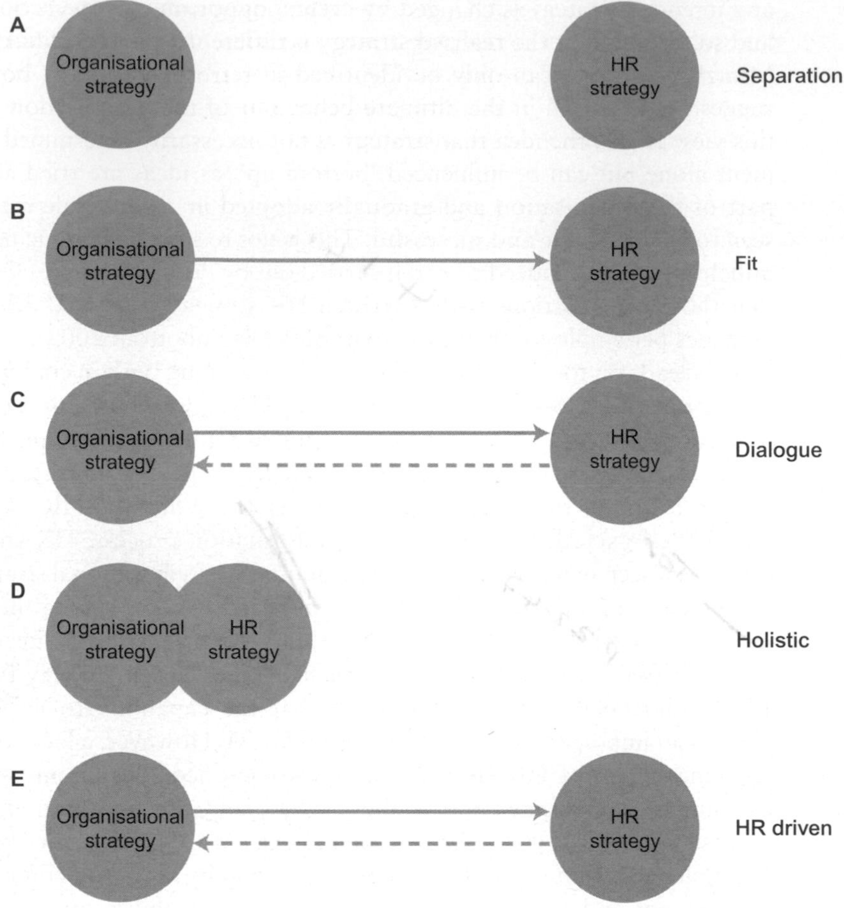

Figure 2.1 Potential relationships between organisational strategy and HR strategy

is a typical picture of twenty years ago, but it still exists today, particularly in smaller organisations.

The *fit model* (B) represents a growing recognition of the importance of people in the achievement of organisational strategy. Employees are seen as key in the implementation of the declared organisational strategy, and human resource strategy is designed to fit with this. Some of the early formal models of human resource strategy, particularly that proposed by Fombrun *et al.* (1984), concentrate on how the human resource strategy can be designed to ensure a close fit, and the same approach is used in the Schuler and Jackson example in Table 2.1.

This whole approach depends on a view of strategy formulation as a logical rational process, which remains a widely held view. The relationship in the fit model is exemplified by organisations which cascade their business objectives down from the senior management team through functions, through departments, through teams and so on. Functions, for example, have to propose a functional strategy which enables the organisational strategy to be achieved. Departments have to propose a strategy which enables the functional strategy to be achieved, and so on. In this way the HR function (as with any other) is required to respond to organisational strategy by defining a strategy which meets organisational demands.

The *dialogue model* (C) takes the relationship one step further, as it recognises the need for two-way communication and some debate. What is demanded in the organisation's strategy may not be viewed as feasible and alternative possibilities need to be reviewed. The debate, however, is often limited, as shown in the example in the Window on practice which follows.

WINDOW ON PRACTICE

In one large multinational organisation an objectives-setting cascade was put in place. This cascade allowed for a dialogue between the planned organisation strategy and the response of each function. In the organisation strategy there was some emphasis on people growth and development and job fulfilment. The HR Department's response included among other things an emphasis on line management involvement in these areas, which would be supported by consultancy help from the HR Department.

The top management team replied to this by asking the HR Department to add a strategic objective about employee welfare and support. The HR Department strongly argued that this was a line management responsibility, along with coaching, development and so on. The HR Function saw its customers as the managers of the organisation, not the employees. The result of the debate was that the HR function added the strategic objective about employee welfare.

Although the approach in this case appeared two-way, the stronger of the parties was the management team, and they were determined that their vision was the one that would be implemented!

The holistic model and the HR-driven model (D and E) show a much closer involvement between organisational and human resource strategy.

The *holistic model* (D) represents the people of the organisation being recognised as the key to competitive advantage rather than just the way of implementing organisational strategy. In other words HR strategy is not just the means for achieving business strategy (the ends), but an end in itself. Human resource strategy therefore becomes critical and, as Baird *et al.* (1983) argued, there can be no strategy without human resource strategy. Boxall (1996) develops this idea in relation to the resource-based firm, and argues convincingly that business strategy can usefully be interpreted as more broad than a competitive strategy (or positioning in the marketplace). In this case business strategy can encompass a variety of other strategies including HRM, and he describes these strategies as the pieces of a jigsaw. This suggests mutual development and some form of integration, rather than a slavish response to a predetermined business strategy.

The *HR-driven model* (E) offers a more extreme form, which places human resource strategy in prime position. The argument here is that if people are the key to competitive advantage, then we need to build on our people strengths. Logically, then, as the potential of our employees will undoubtedly affect the achievement of any planned strategy, it would be sensible to take account of this in developing our strategic direction. Butler (1988/89) identifies this model as a shift from human resources as the implementors of strategy to human resources as a driving force in the formulation of the strategy. Again this model is a reflection of a resource-based strategic HRM perspective, and sits well with the increasing attention being given to the notion of 'human capital' where it is the collective nature and quality of the people in the organisation which provide the potential for future competitive advantage (*see*, for example, Lengnick-Hall and Lengnick-Hall 2003).

ACTIVITY 2.1

- Which of these approaches to human resource strategy most closely fits your organisation? (If you are a full-time student read one or two relevant cases in *People Management* and interpret these as 'your organisation'.)
- Why did you come to this conclusion?
- What are the advantages and disadvantages of the approach used?

THEORETICAL PERSPECTIVES OF STRATEGIC HUMAN RESOURCE MANAGEMENT

Three theoretical approaches to strategic HRM can be identified. The first is founded on the concept that there is 'one best way' of managing human resources in order to improve business performance. The second focuses on the need to align employment policies and practice with the requirements of business strategy in order that the latter will be achieved and the business will be successful. This second approach is based on the assumption that different types of HR strategies will be suitable for different types of business strategies. Thirdly, a more recent approach to strategic HRM is derived from the resource-based view of the firm, and the perceived value of human capital. This view focuses on the quality of the human resources available to the organisation and their ability to learn and adapt more quickly than their competitors. Supporters of this perspective challenge the need to secure a mechanistic fit with business strategy and focus instead on long-term sustainability and survival of the organisation via the pool of human capital.

Universalist approach

The perspective of the universalist approach is derived from the conception of human resource management as 'best practice', as we discussed in Chapter 1. In other words it is based on the premise that one model of labour management – a high-commitment model – is related to high organisational performance in all contexts, irrespective of the particular competitive strategy of the organisation. An expression of this approach can be seen in Guest's theory of HRM, which is a prescriptive model based on four HR policy goals: strategic integration, commitment, flexibility and quality. These policy goals are related to HRM policies which are expected to produce desirable organisational outcomes.

Guest (1989) describes the four policy goals as follows:

- **Strategic integration** – ensuring that HRM is fully integrated into strategic planning, that HRM policies are coherent, that line managers use HRM practices as part of their everyday work.
- **Commitment** – ensuring that employees feel bound to the organisation and are committed to high performance via their behaviour.
- **Flexibility** – ensuring an adaptable organisation structure, and functional flexibility based on multiskilling.
- **Quality** – ensuring a high quality of goods and services through high-quality, flexible employees.

Guest sees these goals as a package – all need to be achieved to create the desired organisational outcomes which are high job performance, problem solving, change, innovation and cost effectiveness; and low employee turnover, absence and grievances.

Clarity of goals gives a certain attractiveness to this model – but this is where the problems also lie. Whipp (1992) questions the extent to which such a shift is possible, and Purcell (1991) sees the goals as unattainable. The goals are also an expression of human resource management, as opposed to personnel management, and as such bring us back to the debate about what human resource management really is and the inherent contradictions in the approach (Legge 1991, 1995). Ogbonna and Whipp (1999) argue that internal consistency within such a model is extremely difficult to achieve because of such contradictions (for example the tension between flexibility and commitment). Because the prescriptive approach brings with it a set of values, it suggests that there is only one best way and this is it. Although Guest (1987) has argued that there is no best practice, he also encourages the use of the above approach as the route to survival of UK businesses.

Pfeffer (1994) and Becker and Gerhart (1996) are well-known exponents of this view. While there is some support for this perspective, there remains some debate as to which particular human resource practices will stimulate high commitment. We consider this perspective in more depth in Chapter 10 on Strategic aspects of performance. The following Window on practice gives an example of one interpretation of a high-commitment, high-performance approach to human resource management strategy.

WINDOW ON PRACTICE

High performance teams at Digital, Ayr

In an extremely competitive market the Ayr plant had to demonstrate that they could manufacture specified computer systems at a 'landed cost' competitive with other Digital plants, especially those in the Far East. To do this management had to rapidly introduce a package of changes. They had a strategic focus and a clear vision of the changes (both technical and organisational) required to promote success and they 'sold' this to the employees and corporate management. The high-performance team concept they sold had two great advantages – inbuilt quality and flexibility.

Supportive policies were put in place – such as a new skills-based pay system.

Employment policies in terms of career planning, training and development and other reward policies were also designed to be consistent with and reinforce the initiative. Management introduced unsupervised autonomous groups called 'high performance teams' with around a dozen members with full 'back to front' responsibility for product assembly, testing, fault finding, and problem solving, as well as some equipment maintenance. They used flexitime without time clocks and organised their own team discipline. Individuals were encouraged to develop a range of skills and help others in developing their capability. The ten key characteristics of the teams were as follows:

- self-managing, self-organising, self-regulating;
- front-to-back responsibility for core process;
- negotiated production targets;
- multiskilling – no job titles;
- share skills, knowledge, experience and problems;
- skills-based payment system;
- peer selection, peer review;
- open layout, open communications;
- support staff on the spot;
- commitment to high standards and performance.

Management had to learn to stand back and let the groups reach their own decisions – an approach that eventually released considerable management time. A great deal of attention was given to how the transition was managed and this was seen as critical to the success of the approach. Time was taken to ensure maximum formal and informal communication and consultation, and there was a critical mass of key individuals prepared to devote themselves to ensure success. Employees were involved to the fullest extent so they eventually felt they owned the concepts and techniques that they used. Training covered job skills, problem-solving techniques and 'attitude training' in the concepts of high-performance organisational design.

Source: Adapted from D.A. Buchanan (1992) 'High performance: new boundaries of acceptability in worker control', in G. Salaman *et al.* (eds), *Human Resource Strategies*. California: Sage.

Falling somewhere between the universalist approach and the fit approach is the Harvard model of HRM. This model, produced by Beer *et al.* (1984), is analytical rather than prescriptive. The model, shown in Figure 2.2, recognises the different stakeholder interests that impact on employee behaviour and performance, and also gives greater emphasis to factors in the environment that will help to shape human resource strategic choices – identified in the **Situational factors** box. Poole (1990) also notes that the model has potential for international or other comparative analysis, as it takes into account different sets of philosophies and assumptions which may be operating.

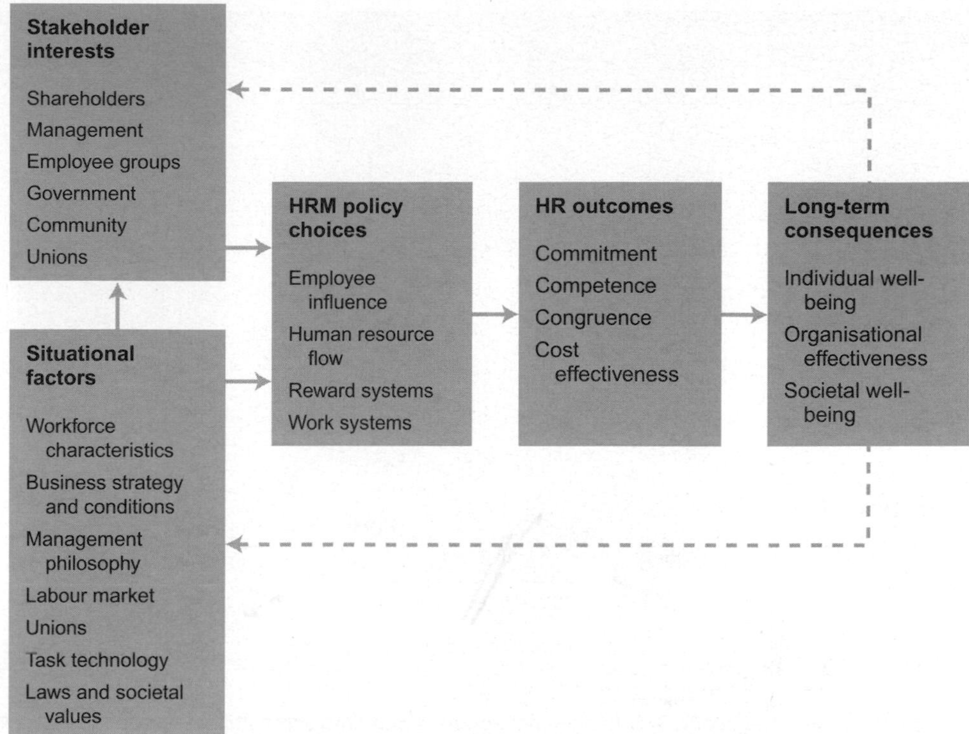

Figure 2.2 The Harvard framework for human resource management (Source: Adapted with permission of The Free Press, a Division of Simon & Schuster, Inc., from *Managing Human Assets* by Michael Beer, Bert Spector, Paul R. Lawrence, D. Quinn Mills, Richard E. Walton. New York: The Free Press. Copyright © 1984 by The Free Press.)

Although Beer *et al.*'s model is primarily analytical, there are prescriptive elements leading to some potential confusion. The prescription in Beer *et al.*'s model is found in the **HR outcomes** box, where specific outcomes are identified as universally desirable.

Fit or contingency approach

The fit or contingency approach is based on two critical forms of fit. The first is external fit (sometimes referred to as vertical integration) – that HR strategy fits with the demands of business strategy; the second is internal fit (sometimes referred to as horizontal integration) – that all HR policies and activities fit together so that they make a coherent whole, are mutually reinforcing and are applied consistently. One of the foundations of this approach is found in Fombrun *et al.* (1984), who proposed a basic framework for strategic human resource management, shown in Figures 2.3 and 2.4. Figure 2.3 represents the location of human resource management in relation to organisational strategy, and you should be able to note how the Fit model (B) is used (*see* Figure 2.1). Figure 2.4 shows how activities within human resource management can be unified and designed in order to support the organisation's strategy.

The strength of this model is that it provides a simple framework to show how selection, appraisal, development and reward can be mutually geared to produce the required type of employee performance. For example, if an organisation required

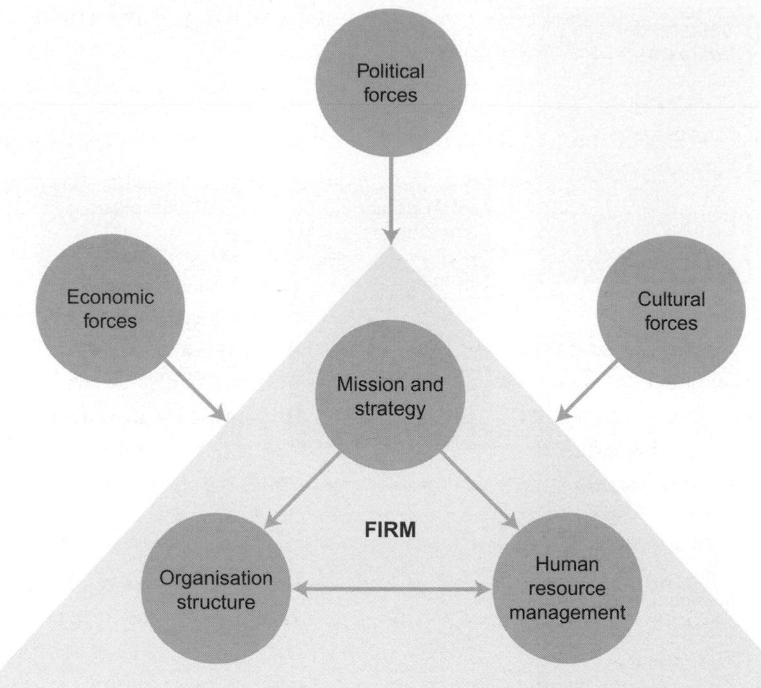

Figure 2.3 Strategic management and environmental pressures (Source: C. Fombrun, N.M. Tichy and M.A. Devanna (1984) *Strategic Human Resource Management*, p. 35. New York: John Wiley and Sons, Inc. © John Wiley and Sons Inc., 1984. Reprinted by permission of John Wiley and Sons, Inc.)

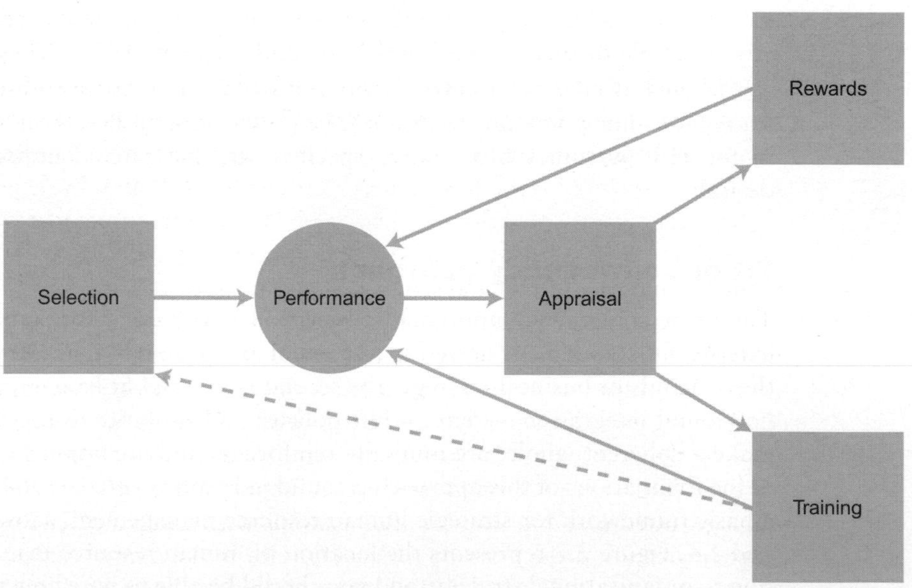

Figure 2.4 The human resource cycle (Source: C. Fombrun, N.M. Tichy and M.A. Devanna (1984) *Strategic Human Resource Management*, p. 41. New York: John Wiley and Sons, Inc. © John Wiley and Sons Inc., 1984. Reprinted by permission of John Wiley and Sons, Inc.)

cooperative team behaviour with mutual sharing of information and support, the broad implications would be:

- **Selection**: successful experience of teamwork and sociable, cooperative personality; rather than an independent thinker who likes working alone.
- **Appraisal**: based on contribution to the team, and support of others; rather than individual outstanding performance.
- **Reward**: based on team performance and contribution; rather than individual performance and individual effort.

There is little doubt that this type of internal fit is valuable. However, questions have been raised over the model's simplistic response to organisation strategy. The question 'what if it is not possible to produce a human resource response that enables the required employee behaviour and performance?' is never addressed. So, for example, the distance between now and future performance requirements, the strengths, weaknesses and potential of the workforce, the motivation of the workforce and employee relations issues are not considered.

This model has been criticised because of its dependence on a rational strategy formulation rather than on an emergent strategy formation approach; and because of the nature of the one-way relationship with organisational strategy. It has also been criticised owing to its unitarist assumptions, as no recognition is made for employee interests and their choice of whether or not to change their behaviour.

Taking this model and the notion of fit one step further, human resource strategy has been conceived in terms of generating specific employee behaviours. In the ideal form of this there would be analysis of the types of employee behaviour required to fulfil a predetermined business strategy, and then an identification of human resource policies and practices which would bring about and reinforce this behaviour. A very good example of this is found in Schuler and Jackson (1987). They used the three generic business strategies defined by Porter (1980) and for each identified employee role behaviour and HRM policies required. Their conclusions are shown in Table 2.1.

Similar analyses can be found for other approaches to business strategy, for example in relation to the **Boston matrix** (Purcell 1992) and the developmental stage of the organisation (Kochan and Barocci 1985). Some human resource strategies describe the behaviour of all employees, but others have concentrated on the behaviour of Chief Executives and senior managers; Miles and Snow (1984), for example, align appropriate managerial characteristics to three generic strategies of prospector, defender and analyser. The rationale behind this matching process is that if managerial attributes and skills are aligned to the organisational strategy, then a higher level of organisational performance will result. There is little empirical evidence to validate this link, but work by Thomas and Ramaswamy (1996) does provide some support. They used statistical analysis to investigate if there was a match between manager attributes and skills in organisations with either a defender or a prospector strategy in 269 of the Fortune 500 companies in the United States. They found an overall statistical relationship between manager attributes and strategy. Taking the analysis a step further they then compared 30 organisations which were misaligned with 30 which were aligned and found that performance in the aligned companies (whether prospector or defender) was statistically superior. While this work can be criticised, it does provide an indication of further research which can be developed to aid our understanding of the issues. Sanz-Valle *et al.* (1999) found some partial

Strategy	Employee role behaviour	HRM policies
1 Innovation	A high degree of creative behaviour	Jobs that require close interaction and coordination among groups of individuals
	Longer-term focus	Performance appraisals that are more likely to reflect longer-term and group-based achievements
	A relatively high level of co-operative, interdependent behaviour	Jobs that allow employees to develop skills that can be used in other positions in the firm
		Compensation systems that emphasise internal equity rather than external or market-based equity
	A moderate degree of concern for quality	Pay rates that tend to be low, but that allow employees to be stockholders and have more freedom to choose the mix of components that make up their pay package
	A moderate concern for quantity; an equal degree of concern for process and results	Broad career paths to reinforce the development of a broad range of skills
	A greater degree of risk taking; a higher tolerance of ambiguity and unpredictability	
2 Quality enhancement	Relatively repetitive and predictable behaviours	Relatively fixed and explicit job descriptions
	A more long-term or intermediate focus	High levels of employee participation in decisions relevant to immediate work conditions and the job itself
	A moderate amount of co-operative, interdependent behaviour	A mix of individual and group criteria for performance appraisal that is mostly short term and results orientated
	A high concern for quality	A relatively egalitarian treatment of employees and some guarantees of employment security
	A modest concern for quantity of output	Extensive and continuous training and development of employees
	High concern for process: low risk-taking activity; commitment to the goals of the organisation	
3 Cost reduction	Relatively repetitive and predictable behaviour	Relatively fixed and explicit job descriptions that allow little room for ambiguity
	A rather short-term focus	Narrowly designed jobs and narrowly defined career paths that encourage specialisation, expertise and efficiency
	Primarily autonomous or individual activity	Short-term results-orientated performance appraisals
	Moderate concern for quality	Close monitoring of market pay levels for use in making compensation decisions
	High concern for quantity of output	Minimal levels of employee training and development
	Primary concern for results; low risk-taking activity; relatively high degree of comfort with stability	

Table 2.1 Business strategies, and associated employee role behaviour and HRM policies

Source: R.S. Schuler and S.E. Jackson (1987) 'Linking competitive strategies with human resource management practices', *Academy of Management Executive*, No. 3, August. Reproduced with permission of the Academy of Management.

support for the Schuler and Jackson model in terms of the link between business strategy and HR practices, but they did not investigate the implications of this link for organisational performance. The types of strategies described above are generic, and there is more concentration in some organisations on tailoring the approach to the particular needs of the specific organisation.

Many human resource strategies aim not just to target behaviour, but through behaviour change to effect a movement in the culture of the organisation. The target is, therefore, to change the common view of 'the way we do things around here' and to attempt to manipulate the beliefs and values of employees. There is much debate as to whether this is achievable.

We have previously recounted some of the concerns expressed about Fombrun *et al.*'s specific model; however, there is further criticism of the fit or matching perspective as a whole. Grundy (1998) claims that the idea of fit seems naive and simplistic. Ogbonna and Whipp (1999) argue that much literature assumes that fit can be targeted, observed and measured and there is an underlying assumption of stability. Given that most companies may have to change radically in response to the environment, any degree of fit previously achieved will be disturbed. Thus, they contend that fit is a theoretical ideal which can rarely be achieved in practice. Boxall (1996) criticises: the typologies of competitive advantage that are used, arguing that there is evidence that high-performing firms are good 'all rounders'; the fact that strategy is a given and no account is made of how it is formed or by whom; the assumption that employees will behave as requested; and the aim for consistency, as it has been shown that firms use different strategies for different sections of their workforce.

However, in spite of the criticisms of this perspective, it is still employed in both the academic and practitioner literature – see, for example, Holbeche's (1999) book entitled *Aligning Human Resources and Business Strategy*.

Resource-based approach

The resource-based view of the firm (Barney 1991) has stimulated attempts to create a resource-based model of strategic HRM (Boxall 1996). The resource-based view of the firm is concerned with the relationships between internal resources (of which human resources are one), strategy and firm performance. It focuses on the promotion of sustained competitive advantage through the development of human capital rather than merely aligning human resources to current strategic goals. Human resources can provide competitive advantage for the business, as long as they are unique and cannot be copied or substituted for by competing organisations. The focus is not just on the behaviour of the human resources (as with the fit approach), but on the skills, knowledge, attitudes and competencies which underpin this, and which have a more sustained impact on long-term survival than current behaviour (although this is still regarded as important). Briggs and Keogh (1999) maintain that business excellence is not just about 'best practice' or 'leapfrogging the competition', but about the intellectual capital and business intelligence to anticipate the future, today.

Barney states that in order for a resource to result in sustained competitive advantage it must meet four criteria, and Wright *et al.* (1994) demonstrate how human resources meet these. First, the resource must be *valuable*. Wright and his colleagues argue that this is the case where demand for labour is heterogeneous, and where the supply of labour is also heterogeneous – in other words where different firms require different competencies from each other and for different roles in the organisation, and where the supply of potential labour comprises individuals with different competencies. On this basis value is created by matching an individual's competencies with the requirements of the firm and/or the job, as individuals will make a variable contribution, and one cannot be substituted easily for another.

The second criterion, *rarity*, is related to the first. An assumption is made that the most important competence for employees is cognitive ability due to future needs for adaptability and flexibility. On the basis that cognitive ability is normally distributed in the population, those with high levels of this ability will be rare. The talent pool is not unlimited and many employers are currently experiencing difficulties in finding the talent that they require.

Third, resources need to be *inimitable*. Wright *et al.* argue that this quality applies to the human resource as competitors will find it difficult to identify the exact source of competitive advantage from within the firm's human resource pool. Also competitors will not be able to duplicate exactly the resource in question, as they will be unable to copy the unique historical conditions of the first firm. This history is important as it will affect the behaviour of the human resource pool via the development of unique norms and cultures. Thus even if a competing firm recruited a group of individuals from a competitor they would still not be able to produce the same outcomes in the new firm as the context would be different. Two factors make this unique history difficult to copy. The first is causal ambiguity – in other words it is impossible to separate out the exact causes of performance, as the sum is always more than the parts; and, second, social complexity – that the complex of relationships and networks developed over time which have an impact on performance is difficult to dissect.

Finally resources need to be *non-substitutable*. Wright and his co-authors argue that although in the short term it may be possible to substitute human resources with others, for example technological ones, in the long term the human resource is different as it does not become obsolete (like technology) and can be transferred across other products, markets and technologies.

Wright *et al.* noted that attention has often been devoted to leaders and top management in the context of a resource-based approach, and indeed Boxall (1996) contends that this approach provides the theoretical base on which to concentrate in the renewal and development of the critical resource of leaders in the organisation. However, Wright and his co-authors view all human resources in the organisation as the pool of capital. This sits well with the view of strategy as evolutionary and strategy being influenced from the bottom up as well as from the top down. Also it is likely that top managers are more easily identified for their contribution to the organisation and hence are more likely to be mobile, therefore, than other employees who may not be so easily identified. However, different segments of the human resource are viewed differently by organisations in terms of their contribution to competitive advantage, so for some organisations the relevant pool of human capital may not be the total pool of employees.

Whereas fit models focus on the means of competitive advantage (HR practices) the resource-based view focuses on the source (the human capital). Wright *et al.* argue that while the practices are important they are not the source of competitive advantage as they can be replicated elsewhere, and they will produce different results in different places because of the differential human capital in different places. The

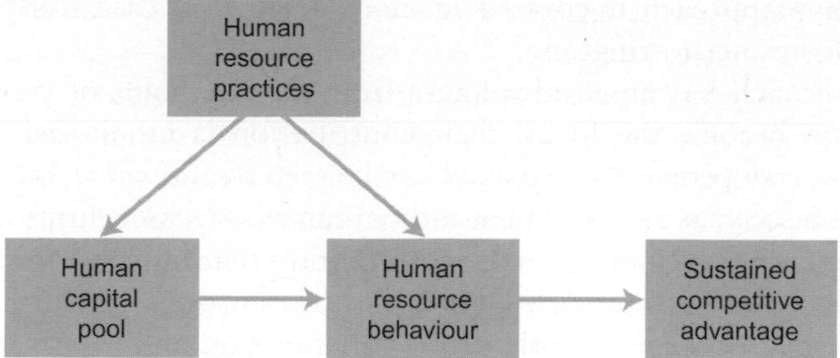

Figure 2.5 A model of human resources as a source of sustained competitive advantage
Source: P. Wright, G. McMahon and A. McWilliams (1994) 'Human resources and sustained competitive advantage: a resource-based perspective', *International Journal of Human Resource Management*, Vol. 5, No. 2, p. 318. Reproduced with the permission of Taylor and Francis Ltd. *See* www.tandf.co.uk/journals.

relationship between human capital, human resource practices and competitive advantage is shown in Figure 2.5.

Boxall (1996) argues that this theoretical perspective provides a conceptual base for asserting that human resources are a source of competitive advantage, and as such valued as generating strategic capability. Thus there is a case for viewing HR strategy as something more than a reactive matching process. Indeed Wright *et al.* argue that it provides the case for HR to be involved in the formulation of strategy rather than just its implementation. They suggest that it provides a grounding for asserting that not every strategy is universally implementable, and that alternatives may have to be sought or the human capital pool developed further, via human resource practices, where this is possible.

The importance of this perspective is underlined by the current emphasis on a firm's intangible assets. Numerous studies have shown that a firm's market value (the sum of the value of the shares) is not fully explained by its current financial results (*see*, for example, Ulrich and Smallwood 2002) or its tangible assets and the focus has moved to a firm's intangible assets such as intellectual capital and customer relationships – all of which are derived from human capital (*see*, for example, Schmidt and Lines 2002). This emphasis has resulted in a great deal of attention being paid to the evaluation of human capital through measuring, reporting and managing it. Human capital can be reported both internally and externally (as in the annual financial report, or similar), and Angela Baron from the CIPD has been reported as commenting that 'investors are demanding information on human capital' (Roberts 2002).

But human capital is loaned: 'human capital is not owned by the organization, but secured through the employment relationship' (Scarborough 2003a, p. 2) and because this is so, the strategy for the management of people is also critical. The government's White Paper, *Modernising Company Law*, suggests that the largest 1,000 companies should publish an annual operating review. Experts believe this will need to include a review about the ways that employees are managed (*People Management* 2002). In addition the Accounting Standards Board recommend that people management measures should be included in annual reports (Brown 2002).

The perceived importance of people as an intangible asset is demonstrated in the action of Barclays Group who on their Investor's Day were keen to demonstrate not only their financial results but people strategies and improvements in staff satisfaction which they believe have contributed to the results (Arkin and Allen 2002).

The Barclays approach is covered in more detail in a case study on the website **www.booksites.net/torrington**.

This approach has great advantages from an HR point of view. People in the organisation become the focus, their contribution is monitored and made more explicit, the way people are managed can be seen to add value and money spent on people can be seen as an investment rather than a cost. Some firms are using the balanced scorecard to demonstrate the contribution that human capital makes to firm performance, such as Norwich Union, and Scarborough (2003b) argues that this builds a bridge between the role of the HR function and the strategy of the firm. However, there are in-built barriers in the language of the resource-based view. One is the reference to people as 'human capital' which some consider to be unnecessarily instrumental. Another is the focus on 'firms' and 'competitive advantage' which makes it harder to see the relevance of this perspective for organisations in the public sector. There is also the issue of what is being measured and who decides this. The risk is that too much time is spent measuring and that not everything that is measured is of critical value to the organisation. So far, such measures appear very varied, although different firms will, of course, need to measure different things. Measures often appear to be taken without a coherent framework, as appears to be the case in the results documented by Scarborough and Elias (2002) for their 10 case study organisations. The balanced scorecard and the HR scorecard, however, appear to be a useful mechanism in this respect. The evaluation of human capital is considered in greater depth in Chapter 33.

Why does the theory matter?

It is tempting to think of these theories of strategic HRM as competing with each other. In other words one is right and the others are wrong. If this were the case HR managers/directors and board members would need only to work out which is the 'right' theory and apply that. This is, of course, a gross oversimplification, as each theory can be interpreted and applied in different ways, and each has advantages and disadvantages. It could be argued that different theories apply in different sectors or competitive contexts. For example Guest (2001) suggests that there is the possibility that a 'high performance/high commitment' approach might always be most appropriate in manufacturing, whereas strategic choice (which could be interpreted as choice to fit with business strategy) might be more realistic in the services sector. This could be taken one step further to suggest that different theories apply to different groups in the workforce.

Consequently, these three theories do not necessarily represent simple alternatives. It is also likely that some board directors and even HR managers are not familiar with any of these theories (*see*, for example, Guest and King 2001). In spite of that, organisations, through their culture, and individuals within organisations operate on the basis of a set of assumptions, and these assumptions are often implicit. Assumptions about the nature and role of human resource strategy, whether explicit or implicit, will have an influence on what organisations actually do. Assumptions will limit what are seen as legitimate choices.

Understanding these theories enables HR managers, board members, consultants and the like to interpret the current position of HR strategy in the organisation, confront current assumptions and challenge current thinking and potentially open up a new range of possibilities.

THE ROLE OF THE HR FUNCTION IN STRATEGY

The extent to which the HR function is involved in both organisational and human resource strategy development is dependent on a range of factors, the most often quoted being whether the most senior HR person is a member of the board of directors. Sparkes (2001) identifies a key role for the HR director as promoting the connection between organisational strategy, culture and people strategy. He maintains that being an HR director means that 'we can almost guarantee that a human element is built into everything strategic from the start' (p. 45).

There is evidence to suggest that over the past 20 years HR board membership has increased and surveys suggest that around three-fifths of larger organisations have an HR director (*see*, for example, Hall and Torrington 1998), although some surveys indicate lower percentages. However, we found, as did Kelly and Gennard (1996), that board membership, while generally identified as desirable, does not guarantee the involvement of specialists in strategy, and it was not necessarily seen as essential to strategic involvement, and this is perhaps why currently very little attention is given to assessing the percentage of organisations with an HR director:

> Thus whilst board membership is often treated as a proxy for strategic involvement, the reality of the situation is far more complex. Even looking at the most favourable evidence from the research, a picture emerges of limited involvement in strategic matters. The good news is that the IPM's survey found that representation on the top management team was predicted to increase, although there is contradictory evidence. (Tyson 1995)

While a seat on the board is undoubtably an advantage and, as Sparkes suggests, improves HR's understanding of the business context in which HR strategies need to be developed and implemented, this is not essential. Other factors influencing the role of the HR function in strategic concerns include the overall philosophy of the organisation towards the value of its people, the mindset of the Chief Executive, and the working relationship between the Chief Executive and the most senior HR person.

These influences are not particularly easy to manipulate, but what the HR function *can* do is look for opportunities in these areas, and *use* them. Building a good working relationship with the Chief Executive is critical, and doubly so, as Stiles (2001) confirms the power of the Chief Executive in selecting who should be appointed to the board. There is evidence that HR managers have to prove themselves before being given a seat on the board (*see*, for example, Hall and Torrington 1998) so building key competencies is essential. Barney and Wright (1998) suggest that one of the real reasons why HR are not involved in strategic planning is that they are not displaying the required competencies. In 2001 IRS (2001) found that only 72 per cent of HR managers in their survey reported the HR function as having a strategic/business focus. The website case study, 'People issues are central to the success of any organisation', focuses on these issues.

It is suggested that HR managers need to use business and financial language; describe the rationale for HR activities in terms of added value; act as a business manager first and an HR manager second; appoint line managers into the HR function; concentrate on priorities as defined by the business; understand the business they work in, and offer well-developed change-management skills that can be used immediately. Guest and King (2001) argue that, as senior managers and board members appear to have limited knowledge of research linking people management and performance, there is an opportunity for enthusiastic HR managers/directors to feed new ideas to Chief Executives. Increasingly, HR managers need to become closer to their accounting colleagues. In addition, the function needs to prepare itself by thinking strategically, identifying a functional mission and strategy and involving line management in the development and implementation of human resource strategy.

SUMMARY PROPOSITIONS

2.1 It is more helpful to focus on the concept of strategic HRM than on HRM strategy as the former directs us to consider strategic thinking and a strategic orientation, rather than a 'strategy' which is written down and exists as a physical entity.

2.2 The nature of the link between business strategy and HR strategy is critical and can be played out in a variety of ways.

2.3 Three theoretical perspectives on strategic HR management can be identified: universalist/best practice; contingency/fit; and the resource-based/human capital view.

2.4 The extent to which HR specialists are involved in HR strategy is influenced by the environment of the business, its culture, the perspective of the Chief Executive, HR board membership and the qualities, characteristics and working relationships of the most senior HR specialist.

GENERAL DISCUSSION TOPICS

1. Is it feasible to link business strategy with the management of people in organisations?
2. Does it really matter whether the most senior HR person is on the board of directors, or are personal work relationships, political alliances and personal track records more important?
3. Human resource strategies can be stimulating to produce and satisfying to display, but how can we make sure that they are implemented?

FURTHER READING

Khatri, N. and Budhwar, P. (2001) 'A study of strategic HR issues in an Asian context', *Personnel Review*, Vol. 31, No. 2, pp. 166–87

This article investigates strategic HR issues which are often neglected. Rather than focusing on strategic content issues, the research reported here concentrates on the structure of the HR function and its strategic relationships; HR competencies; the nature of HR strategy (for example formal or informal); and HR outsourcing. Although the study is located in a very specific context – the electronics and components sector and the machinery and equipment sector in Singapore – the literature review and results are both very useful and informative and straightforward reading.

Mayo, A. (2001) *The Human Value of the Enterprise*. London: Nicholas Brealey
Mayo provides one approach to the measurement of human capital – the human capital monitor, which is based on people as assets, people's motivation and commitment and people's contribution to added value. There is advice on maximising human capital, motivation and commitment, innovation and learning and the challenges of mergers, acquisitions and alliances.

REFERENCES

Arkin, A. and Allen, R. (2002) 'Satisfaction guaranteed', *People Management*, Vol. 8, No. 21, October, pp. 40–2.

Baird, L., Meshoulam, I. and DeGive, G. (1983) 'Meshing human resources planning with strategic business planning: a model approach', *Personnel*, Vol. 60, Part 5 (Sept./Oct.), pp. 14–25.

Barney, J. (1991) 'Firm resources and sustained competitive advantage', *Journal of Management*, Vol. 17, No. 1, pp. 99–120.

Barney, J. and Wright, P. (1998) 'On becoming a strategic partner: the role of human resources in gaining competitive advantage', *Human Resource Management*, Vol. 37, No. 1, pp. 31–46.

Beaumont, P. (1992) 'The US human resource management literature: a review', in G. Salaman (ed.) *Human Resource Strategies*. London: Sage in association with OUP.

Becker, B. and Gerhart, B. (1996) 'The impact of Human Resource Management on Organisational Performance: Progress and Prospects', *Academy of Management Journal*, Vol. 39, pp. 779–801.

Becker, B., Huselid, M. and Ulrich, D. (2001) *The HR Scorecard: Linking People, Strategy and Performance*. Boston: Harvard Business School Press.

Beer, M., Spector, B., Lawrence, P.R., Quinn Mills, D. and Walton, R.E. (1984) *Managing Human Assets*. New York: Free Press.

Boxall, P.F. (1992) 'Strategic human resource management: beginnings of a new theoretical sophistication?' *Human Resource Management Journal*, Vol. 2, No. 3.

Boxall, P.F. (1996) 'The strategic HRM debate and the resource-based view of the firm', *Human Resource Management Journal*, Vol. 6, No. 3, pp. 59–75.

Boxall, P. and Purcell J. (2003) *Strategy and Human Resource Management*. Basingstoke: Palgrave, Macmillan.

Boxall, P. and Steeneveld, M. (1999) 'Human Resource Strategy and competitive advantage: A longitudinal study of engineering consultancies', *Journal of Management Studies*, Vol. 36, No. 4, pp. 443–63.

Briggs, S. and Keogh, W. (1999) 'Integrating human resource strategy and strategic planning to achieve business excellence', *Total Quality Management*, July, p. 447.

Brown, D. (2002) 'Top-down and bottom-up', *People Management*, Vol. 8, No. 17, 29 August, p. 18.

Buchanan, D.A. (1992) 'High performance: new boundaries of acceptability in worker control', in G. Salaman *et al.* (eds) *Human Resource Strategies*. California: Sage Publications.

Butler, J. (1988/89) 'Human resource management as a driving force in business strategy', *Journal of General Management*, Vol. 13, No. 4.

Cleland, J., Pajo, K. and Toulson, P. (2000) 'Move it or lose it: an examination of the evolving role of the human resources professional in New Zealand', *International Journal of Human Resource Management*, Vol. 11, No. 1, pp. 143–60.

Fombrun, C., Tichy, N.M. and Devanna, M.A. (1984) *Strategic Human Resource Management*. New York: John Wiley and Sons.

Grensing-Pophel, L. (1999) 'Taking your "seat at the table" (the role of Human Resource Managers in companies)', *HRMagazine*, March, Vol. 44, No. 3, pp. 90–4.

Grundy, T. (1998) 'How are corporate strategy and human resources strategy linked?' *Journal of General Management*, Vol. 23, No. 3, Spring, pp. 49–72.

Guest, D. (1987) 'Human resource management and industrial relations' *Journal of Management Studies*, Vol. 24, No. 5.

Guest, D. (1989) 'Personnel and HRM: Can you tell the difference?' *Personnel Management* (January).

Guest, D. (2001) 'Human resource management: when research confronts theory', *International Journal of Human Resource Management*, Vol. 12, No. 7, pp. 1092–1106.

Guest, D. and King, Z. (2001) 'Personnel's Paradox', *People Management*, Vol. 17, No. 19, 27 September, pp. 24–9.

Hall, L. and Torrington, D. (1998) *The Human Resource Function: The Dynamics of change and development*. London: Financial Times Pitman Publishing.

Hendry, C. and Pettigrew, A. (1992) 'Patterns of strategic change in the development of Human Resource Management', *British Journal of Management*, Vol. 3, No. 3, pp. 137–56.

Higginbottom, K. (2002) 'Profits rise with a written HR strategy', *People Management*, Vol. 8, No. 25, 26 December, p. 9.

Holbeche, L. (1999) *Aligning Human Resources and Business Strategy*. Oxford: Butterworth-Heinemann. © Roffey Park Management Institute.

Hunt, J. and Boxall, P. (1998) 'Are top Human Resource Specialists strategic partners? Self-perceptions of a corporate elite', *International Journal of Human Resource Management*, Vol. 9, pp. 767–81.

IRS (2001) 'HR in 2001: the HR audit', *IRS Employment Trends*, No. 728, May, pp. 4–10.

Kane, B. and Palmer, I. (1995) 'Strategic HRM or managing the employment relationship?' *International Journal of Manpower*, Vol. 15, No. 5, pp. 6–16.

Kelly, J. and Gennard, J. (1996) 'The role of personnel directors in the Board of Directors', *Personnel Review*, Vol. 25, No. 1, pp. 7–24.

Kochan, T.A. and Barocci, T.A. (1985) *Human Resource Management and Industrial Relations: Text, Readings and Cases*. Boston: Little Brown.

Legge, K. (1991) 'Human resource management: a critical analysis', in J. Storey (ed.) *New Perspectives on Human Resource Management*. London: Routledge.

Legge, K. (1995) *Human Resource Management: Rhetorics and realities*. Basingstoke: Macmillan.

Lengnick-Hall, M. and Lengnick-Hall, C. (2003) *Human Resource Management in the Knowledge Economy*. San Francisco: Berrett-Koehler Inc.

Lundy, O. and Cowling, A. (1996) *Strategic Human Resource Management*. London: Routledge.

Miles, R.E. and Snow, C.C. (1984) 'Organisation strategy, structure and process', *Academy of Management Review*, Vol. 2, pp. 546–62.

Mintzberg, H. (1994) 'The fall and rise of strategic planning', *Harvard Business Review* (February).

Ogbonna, E. and Whipp, R. (1999) 'Strategy, culture and HRM: evidence from the UK food retailing sector', *Human Resource Management Journal*, Vol. 9, No. 4, pp. 75–90.

Pedler, M., Burgoyne, J. and Boydell, T. (1991) *The Learning Company*. Maidenhead: McGraw-Hill.

People Management (2002) 'Human Capital Review', *People Management*, Vol. 8, No. 15, 25 July, p. 9.

Pfeffer, J. (1994) *Competitive Advantage through People*. Boston: Harvard Business School Press.

Poole, M. (1990) 'Editorial: HRM in an international perspective', *International Journal of Human Resource Management*, Vol. 1, No. 1.

Porter, M. (1980) *Competitive Strategy*. New York: Free Press.

Purcell, J. (1991) 'The impact of corporate strategy on human resource management', in J. Storey (ed.) *New Perspectives on Personnel Management*. London: Routledge.

Purcell, J. (1992) 'The impact of corporate strategy on human resource management', in G. Salaman *et al.* (eds) *Human Resource Strategies*. London: Sage Publications.

Roberts, Z. (2002) 'CIPD task force to create new framework for external reporting of human capital' *People Management*, Vol. 8, No. 23, 21 November, p. 7.

Sanz-Valle, R., Sabater-Sánchez, R. and Aragón-Sánchez, A. (1999) 'Human Resource management and business strategy links: an empirical study', *International Journal of Human Resource Management*, Vol. 10, No. 4, pp. 655–71.

Scarborough, H. (2003a) *Human Capital – External Reporting Framework*. London: CIPD.

Scarborough, H. (2003b) 'Recipe for success', *People Management*, Vol. 9, No. 2, 23 January, pp. 32–5.

Scarborough, H. and Elias, J. (2002) *Evaluating Human Capital – Research Report*. London: CIPD.

Schmidt, J. and Lines, S. (2002) 'A measure of success', *People Management*, Vol. 8, No. 9, May, pp. 32–4.

Schuler, R.S. and Jackson, S.E. (1987) 'Linking competitive strategies with human resource management practices', *Academy of Management Executive*, No. 3 (August).

Senge, P. (1990) *The Fifth Discipline: The Art and Practice of the Learning Organization*. London: Century Business, Random House.

Skinner, D. and Mabey, C. (1997) 'Managers' perceptions of strategic HR change', *Personnel Review*, Vol. 26, No. 6, pp. 467–84.

Sparkes, J. (2001) 'Job's a good un', *People Management*, Vol. 7, No. 20, 11 October, pp. 44–7.

Stiles, P. (2001) 'The impact of the board on strategy: an empirical examination', *Journal of Management Studies*, Vol. 38, No. 5, pp. 627–650.

Thomas, A. and Ramaswamy, K. (1996) 'Matching managers to strategy: further tests of the Miles and Snow typology', *British Journal of Management*, Vol. 7, pp. 247–61.

Tyson, S. (1995) *Human Resource Strategy*. London: Pitman.

Ulrich, D. (1998) 'A new mandate for human resources', *Harvard Business Review*, Jan.–Feb., pp. 125–34.

Ulrich, D. and Smallwood, N. (2002) 'Seven Up', *People Management*, Vol. 8, No. 10, May, pp. 42–4.

Whipp, R. (1992) 'Human resource management, competition and strategy: some productive tensions', in P. Blyton and P. Turnbull (eds) *Reassessing Human Resource Management*. California: Sage Publications.

Wright, P., McMahon, G. and McWilliams, A. (1994) 'Human Resources and sustained competitive advantage: a resource-based perspective', *International Journal of Human Resource Management*, Vol. 5, No. 2, May, pp. 301–26.

An extensive range of additional materials, including multiple choice questions, answers to questions and links to useful websites can be found on the Human Resource Management Companion Website at **www.pearsoned.co.uk/torrington.**

CHAPTER 3

PLANNING: JOBS AND PEOPLE

THE OBJECTIVES OF THIS CHAPTER ARE TO:

1 DISCUSS THE CONTRIBUTION AND FEASIBILITY OF HR PLANNING

2 EXPLORE THE SCOPE OF HR PLANNING

3 EXPLAIN AN INTEGRATED HR PLANNING FRAMEWORK

Planning for human resources has experienced a chequered history. In the 1960s and 1970s it was heralded as a critical tool for business success, as planning to get the right people in the right place at the right time was seen to be essential to achieving rapid growth. In the 1980s and 1990s planning was viewed as a suitable tool for managing downsizing and redundancies. On the other hand it has been argued that planning is no longer meaningful in an era of rapid and discontinuous change where it been recognised that strategies emerge rather than being precisely planned in advance. However, good planning still has an important contribution in supporting strategic HRM in this context (*see*, for example, Boxall and Purcell 2003; Stiles 2001).

THE CONTRIBUTION AND FEASIBILITY OF HR PLANNING

A useful starting point is to consider the different contributions that strategy and planning make to the organisation. A common view has been that they are virtually one and the same – hence the term 'strategic planning'. Henry Mintzberg (1994, p. 108) distinguished between *strategic thinking*, which is about synthesis, intuition and creativity to produce a not too precisely articulated vision of direction, and *strategic planning*, which is about collecting the relevant information to stimulate the visioning process and also programming the vision into what needs to be done to get there. It is helpful to look at human resource planning in the same way, and this is demonstrated in Figure 3.1. In more detail he suggests:

- **Planning as strategic programming** – planning cannot generate strategies, but it can make them operational by clarifying them; working out the consequences of them; and identifying what must be done to achieve each strategy.
- **Planning as tools to communicate and control** – planning can ensure coordination and encourage everyone to pull in the same direction; planners can assist in finding successful experimental strategies which may be operating in just a small part of the organisation.
- **Planners as analysts** – planners need to analyse hard data, both external and internal, which managers can then use in the strategy development process.
- **Planners as catalysts** – raising difficult questions and challenging the conventional wisdom which may stimulate managers into thinking in more creative ways.

Organisational and human resource planners make an essential contribution to strategic visioning. Sisson and Storey (2000) identify HR planning as 'one of the basic building blocks of a more strategic approach'. Starting with some ideas of Lam and Schaubroeck (1998) we identify four specific ways in which HR planning is critical to strategy, as it can identify:

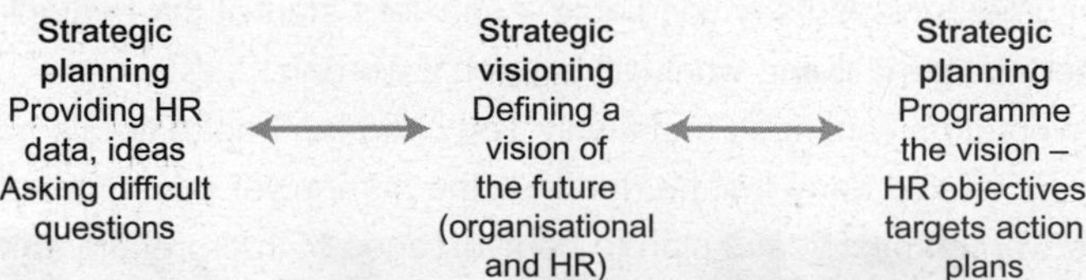

Figure 3.1 Human resource strategic visioning and strategic planning (Source: After Mintzberg 1994.)

- *gaps in capabilities* – lack of sufficient skills, people or knowledge in the business which will prevent the strategy being implemented successfully;
- *surpluses in capabilities* – providing scope for efficiencies and new ventures to capitalise on the skills, people and knowledge that are currently underused in order to influence or shape the strategy;
- *poor utilisation of people* – suggesting inappropriate human resource practices that need to be altered;
- *developing a talent pool.*

If you turn back to Chapter 2 and look again at the resource-based view of the firm you will see how these four aspects are crucial to sustaining competitive advantage through making the most of human resources.

Our environment of rapid and discontinuous change makes any planning difficult, and HR planning is especially difficult as people have free will, unlike other resources, such as finance or technology. The contribution and implementation of HR planning is likely to be enhanced if:

- plans are viewed as flexible and reviewed regularly, rather than being seen as an end point in the process;
- stakeholders, including all levels of manager and employee, are involved in the process. Surveys and focus groups are possible mechanisms, in addition to line manager representatives on the HR planning team;
- planning is owned and driven by senior managers rather than HR specialists, who need to facilitate the process;
- plans are linked to business and HR strategy;
- plans are user-friendly and not overly complex;
- it is recognised that while a comprehensive plan may be ideal, sometimes it may only be feasible to plan on an issue-by-issue basis.

WINDOW ON PRACTICE

Tony, the Personnel Manager, shouted at Ian, the Chief Executive: 'What do you mean, it wasn't agreed?'

'I mean it's the first I've heard that you need £22k for a new apprentice scheme.'

'Well, it was in the plan.'

'What plan?'

'The manpower plan, what other f*****g plan would I mean!'

'You didn't ask me for the money.'

'I asked you in the plan, and you didn't come back and say we couldn't have it.'

'I didn't come back and say you could – now let's start at the beginning – tell me why we need to spend it and what will happen if we don't.'

The conversation continued and finally Tony and Ian began to talk about the real issues. Ian never told Tony that he had filed the manpower plan unread, but he did tell him that he wanted next year's plan to be five pages of interpretation and recommendations and not 85 pages of figures.

THE SCOPE OF HUMAN RESOURCE PLANNING

Traditionally human resource planning, generally termed manpower planning, was concerned with the numbers of employees and the levels and types of skill in the organisation. A typical model of traditional manpower planning is shown in Figure 3.2. In this model the emphasis is on balancing the projected demand for and supply of labour, in order to have the right number of the right employees in the right place at the right time. The demand for manpower is influenced by corporate strategies and objectives, the environment and the way that staff are utilised within the business. The supply of manpower is projected from current employees (via calculations about expected leavers, retirements, promotions, etc.) and from the availability of the required skills in the labour market. Anticipated demand and supply are then reconciled by considering a range of options, and plans to achieve a feasible balance are designed.

As the world has moved on this model has been viewed as too narrow, being heavily reliant on calculations of employee numbers or potential employee numbers. It has also been criticised for giving insufficient attention to skills (Hendry 1994; Taylor 1998). In addition there has been an increasing recognition of the need to plan, not just for hard numbers, but for the softer issues of employee behaviour, organisation culture and systems; these issues have been identified as having a key impact on business success in the current environment.

Increasingly there is a need for organisations to integrate the process of planning for numbers and skills of employees; employee behaviour and organisational culture; organisation design and the make-up of individual jobs; and formal and informal systems. These aspects are all critical in terms of programming and achieving the vision. Each of these aspects interrelates with the others. However, reality has always

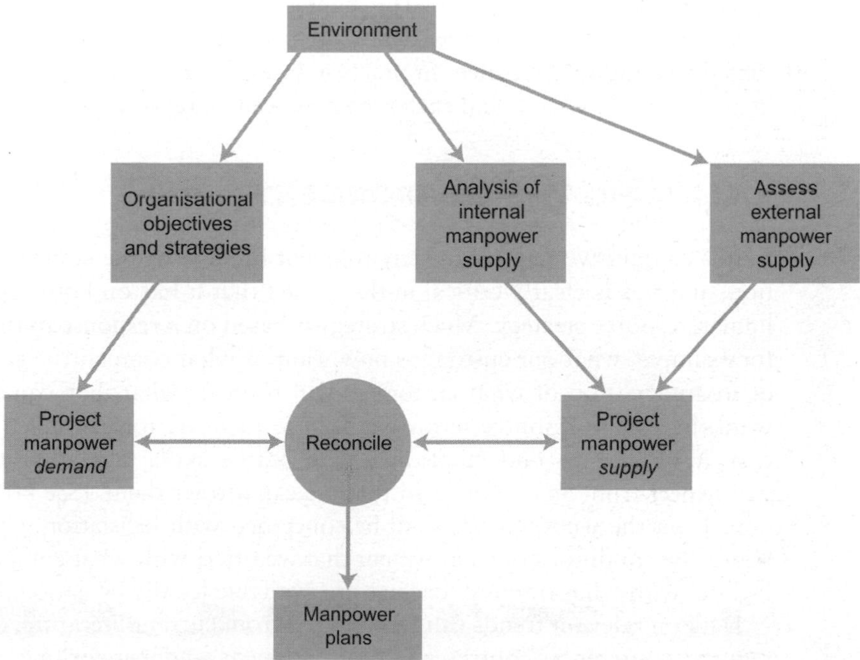

Figure 3.2 A model of traditional manpower planning

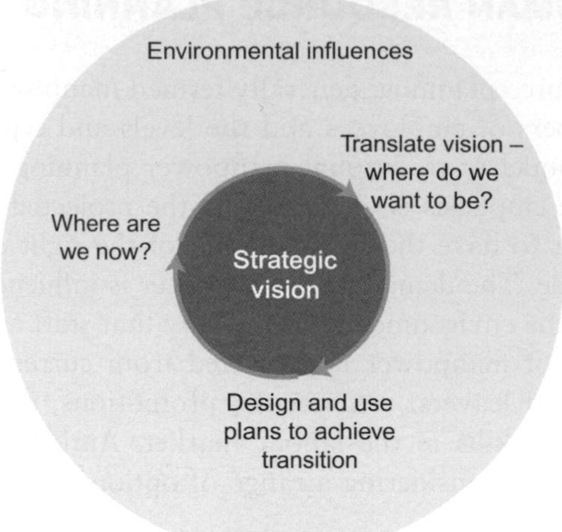

Figure 3.3 Integrated human resource planning framework

been recognised as being a long way from identified best practice. Undoubtedly different organisations will place different emphases on each of these factors, and may well plan each separately or plan some and not others.

The framework we shall use in this chapter attempts to bring *all* aspects of HR planning together, incorporating the more traditional approach to 'manpower planning', but going beyond this to include behaviour, culture, systems and so on. Our framework identifies 'where we want to be', translated from responses to the strategic vision; 'where we are now'; and 'what we need to do to make the transition' – all operating within the organisation's environment. The framework is shown in diagrammatic form in Figure 3.3. An alternative framework to use may be the HR scorecard (*see* Becker *et al.* 2001). Chapter 33 provides more details.

We shall now look in more depth at each of these four areas. The steps are presented in a logical sequence. In practice, however, they may run in parallel, and/or in an informal fashion, and each area may well be revisited a number of times.

ANALYSING THE ENVIRONMENT

In this chapter we refer to the environment broadly as the context of the organisation, and this is clearly critical in the impact that it has on both organisational and human resource strategy. Much strategy is based on a response to the environment – for example, what our customers now want or what competitors are now offering – or in anticipation of what customers will want or what they can be persuaded to want. In human resource terms we need to identify, for example, how difficult or easy it will be to find employees with scarce skills and what these employees will expect from an employer so that we can attract them. (*See* HRP Exercise, 3.1, note 1, on the website.) We shall be concerned with legislation which will limit or widen the conditions of employment that we offer, with what competitors are offering and with what training schemes are available locally or nationally.

Data on relevant trends can be collected from current literature, company annual reports, conferences/courses and from contacts and networking. Table 3.1 gives examples of the many possible sources for each major area.

Table 3.1 Sources of information on environment trends

Trend area	Possible sources
Social	Census information CIPD journals News media *Social Trends* *General Household Survey* *Employment Gazette* Local papers
Demographics	*Labour Market Quarterly* Census information *Employment Gazette* Local Council, Learning and Skills Councils
Political and legislative	News media *Proceedings of European Parliament* *Proceedings of British Parliament* *Hansard* *Industrial Relations Review and Report* *Industrial Law Journal* *IDS Brief*
Industrial and technological	*Employment Digest* Journals specifically for the industry *Financial Times* Employers' association Trade association
Competitors	Annual reports Talk to them!

WINDOW ON PRACTICE

The impact of demographics

The number of younger people in the population is reducing in proportion to the number of older people, as birth rates are lower than previously and people are living longer. This has an impact on many organisations. For example skills loss and shortages will require organisational planners to devise novel solutions. One of these is to delay retirement age, so that vital skills are retained for longer. Alternatively a flexible retirement age could be applied by companies rather than a mandatory age (typically 65 for men and 60 for women in the UK). This is a markedly different perspective than that taken in the 1990s, when early retirement was viewed as a favourable means to downsize the organisation. There is a further pressure from a legal perspective – mandatory retirement ages may constitute age discrimination, and different retirement ages for men and women may constitute sex discrimination. This is not just a UK phenomenon, and Gomez *et al.* (2002) explore this in the Canadian context, making the point that a flexible retirement age will make HR planning much more difficult for companies particularly in respect of succession planning and planning for disability, medical and pension costs.

Once one has acquired and constantly updated data on the environment, a common method of analysis is to produce a map of the environment, represented as a wheel. The map represents a time in the future, say three years away. In the centre of the wheel can be written the core purpose of the organisation as it relates to people, or potential future strategies or goals. Each spoke of the wheel can then be filled in to represent a factor of the external environment, for example, potential employees, a specific local competitor, competitors generally, regulatory bodies, customers, government. From all the spokes the six or seven regarded as most important need to be selected.

These can then be worked on further by asking what demands each will make of the organisation, and how the organisation will need to respond in order to achieve its goals. From these responses can be derived the implications for human resource activities. For example, the demands of potential employees may be predicted as:

- We need a career not just a job.
- We need flexibility to help with childrearing.
- We want to be treated as people and not as machines.
- We need a picture of what the organisation has in store for us.
- We want to be better trained.

And so on.

Managers then consider what the organisation would need to offer to meet these needs in order to meet a declared organisational goal or strategy. It is a good way of identifying human resource issues which need to be addressed. The analysis can also be fed back into identifying and clarifying the future vision or goals in human resource terms. Figure 3.4 gives an outline for the whole process. (For a worked example *see* HRP Exercise, 3.1, note 2, on the website.)

ACTIVITY 3.1

Draw a map of the external environment, for any organisation in which you are involved, for three to five years ahead. Individually, or as a group, brainstorm all the spokes in the wheel and select the six most important ones. Draw up a demands and responses list for each. Write a summary (one side of A4) of what you think your organisation's priorities should be in the people area over the next 3–5 years.

FORECASTING FUTURE HUMAN RESOURCE NEEDS

Organisation, behaviour and culture

There is little specific literature on the methods used to translate the strategic objectives of the organisation and environmental influences into qualitative or soft human resource goals. In general terms, they can be summed up as the use of managerial judgement. Brainstorming, combined with the use of structured checklists or matrices, can encourage a more thorough analysis. Organisation-change literature

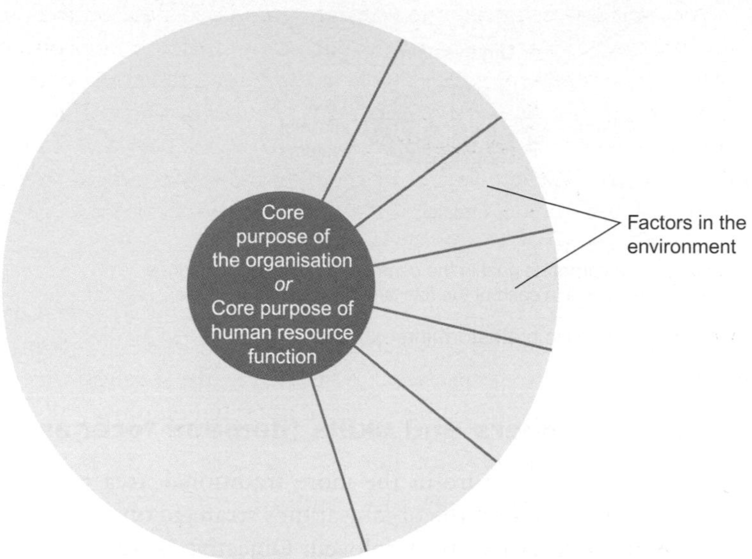

Individual factors in the environment

Demands from the factor	*Responses from the organisation*

Figure 3.4 Mapping the environment

and corporate planning literature are helpful as sources of ideas in this area. Three simple techniques are a human resource implications checklist (*see* Figure 3.5), a strategic brainstorming exercise (Figure 3.6) and a behavioural expectation chart (HRP Exercise, 3.1, note 3, on the website). The HR scorecard may be a useful tool for this aspect of planning, and the use of **scenarios** may also be helpful (*see*, for example, Boxall and Purcell 2003; Turner 2002). Scenarios can be used to provide a picture of alternative organisational futures and alternative HR responses to these.

Corporate goal	Human resource implications in respect of:	Methods of achieving this
	New tasks? For whom? What competencies needed? Relative importance of team/individual behaviour Deleted tasks? How will managers need to manage?	

Figure 3.5 The beginnings of a human resource implications checklist

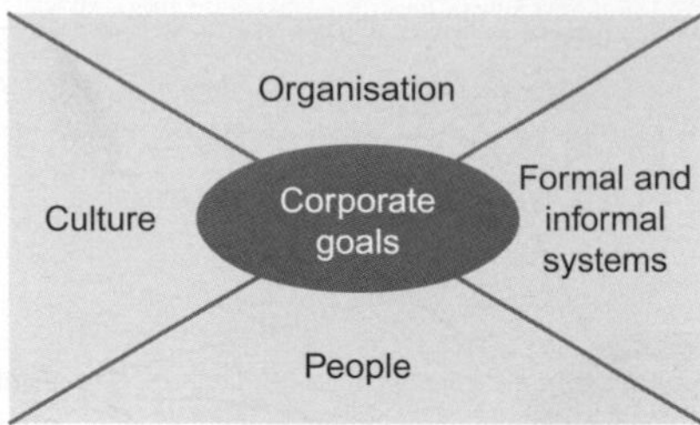

Managers write a corporate goal in the centre and brainstorm changes that need to take place in each of the four areas, one area at a time

Figure 3.6 Strategic brainstorming exercise

Employee numbers and skills (demand forecasting)

There is far more literature in the more traditional area of forecasting employee number demand based on the organisation's strategic objectives. Both objective and subjective approaches can be employed. Objective methods include statistical and work study approaches.

Statistical models generally relate employee number demand to specific organisational circumstances and activities. Models can take account of determining factors, such as production, sales, passenger miles, level of service. A simple model might relate people demand to production, using a constant relationship, without making any assumptions about economies of scale. In this model if output is to be doubled, then employees would also need to be doubled. (*See* HRP Exercise, 3.1, note 4, on the website.)

More complicated equations can be formulated which describe the way that a combination of independent factors is expected to affect the dependent employee demand. By inserting new values for the independent factors, such as new projected sales figures, we can work out the demand for employees from the equation. The equations can also be represented as graphs, making the relationships clear to see. These models can be adapted to take account of projected changes in utilisation, owing to factors such as the introduction of new technology, or alternative organisational forms, such as high-performance teams.

The work-study method is based on a thorough analysis of the tasks to be done, and the time each takes. From this the person-hours needed per unit of output can be calculated, and standards are developed for the numbers and levels of employees required. These are most useful when one is studying production work. They need to be checked regularly to make sure they are still appropriate. Work study is usually classified as an objective measure; however, it is often accepted that since the development of standards and the grouping of tasks is partly dependent on human judgement, it could be considered as a subjective method.

The most common subjective method of demand forecasting is managerial judgement (sometimes referred to as managerial opinion or the inductive method), and this can also include the judgements of other operational and technical staff, as well as all levels of managers. This method relies on managers' estimates of human resource demand based on past experience and on corporate plans. Managerial judgements can be collected from the 'bottom up' with lower-level managers providing estimates to go up the hierarchy for discussion and redrafting. Alternatively, a 'top-down' approach can be used with estimates made by the highest level of

Table 3.2 A Range of methods to change employee utilisation

- Introducing new materials or equipment, particularly new technology
- Introducing changes in work organisation, such as:
  - quality circles
  - job rotation
  - job enlargement
  - job enrichment
  - autonomous work groups
  - high-performance teams
  - participation
- Organisation development
- Introducing changes in organisation structure, such as:
  - centralisation/decentralisation
  - new departmental boundaries
  - relocation of parts of the organisation
  - flexible project structures
- Introducing productivity schemes, bonus schemes or other incentive schemes
- Encouraging greater staff flexibility and work interchangeability
- Altering times and periods of work
- Training and appraisal of staff
- Developing managers and use of performance management

management to go down the hierarchy for discussion and redrafting. When this method is used it is difficult to cope with changes that are very different from past experiences. It is also less precise than statistical methods, but it is more comprehensive. Managerial judgement is a simple method, which can be applied fairly quickly and is not restricted by lack of data, particularly historical data, as are statistical techniques. However, managerial judgement is important even when statistical techniques are used. (*See* HRP Exercise, 3.1, note 5, on the website.)

A specialised procedure for the collection of managerial opinions is based on the idea of the oracle at Delphi. A group of managers anonymously and independently answer questions about anticipated human resource demand. A compilation of the answers is fed back to each individual, and the process is repeated until all the answers converge.

The way that human resources are utilised will change the number of employees required and the necessary skills needed. There are many ways to change how employees are used, and these are shown in Table 3.2. Some methods are interrelated or overlap and would therefore be used in combination. (*See* HRP Exercise, 3.1, note 6, on the website.) Interconnections between most of these areas and soft human resources planning are also apparent.

ANALYSING THE CURRENT SITUATION AND PROJECTING FORWARD

Organisation, behaviour and culture

It is in this area that more choice of techniques is available, and the possibilities include the use of questionnaires to staff (HRP Exercise, 3.1, note 7, on the website), interviews with staff and managerial judgement. Focus groups are an increasingly popular technique where, preferably, the Chief Executive meets with, say, 20 representative

staff from each department to discuss their views of the strengths and weaknesses of the organisation, and what can be done to improve. These approaches can be used to provide information on, for example:

- Motivation of employees.
- Job satisfaction.
- Organisational culture.
- The way that people are managed.
- Attitude to minority groups and equality of opportunity.
- Commitment to the organisation and reasons for this.
- Clarity of business objectives.
- Goal-focused and other behaviour.
- Organisational issues and problems.
- What can be done to improve.
- Organisational strengths to build on.

WINDOW ON PRACTICE

Jennifer Hadley is the Chief Executive of Dynamo Castings, a long-established organisation which had experienced rapid growth and healthy profits until the past three years. Around 800 staff were employed mostly in production, but significant numbers were also employed in marketing/sales and research/development. Poor performance over the last three years was largely the result of the competition who were able to deliver a quality product quicker and at a competitive price. Dynamo retained the edge in developing new designs, but this consumed a high level of resources and was a lengthy process from research to eventual production. Most employees had been with the company for a large part of their working lives and the culture was still appropriate to the times of high profit where life had been fairly easy and laid back. Messages about difficult times, belt tightening and higher productivity with fewer people had been filtered down to employees, who did not change their behaviour but did feel threatened.

It was with some trepidation that Jennifer decided to meet personally with a cross-section of each department to talk through company and departmental issues. The first meeting was with research/development. As expected, the meeting began with a flood of concerns about job security. No promises could be given. However, the mid-point of the meeting was quite fruitful, and the following points, among others, became clear:

- that development time could be reduced to one year from two if some production staff were involved in the development process from the very beginning;

- that many development staff felt their career prospects were very limited and a number expressed the wish to be able to move into marketing. They felt this would also be an advantage when new products were marketed;
- that staff felt fairly paid and would be prepared to forgo salary rises for a year or two if this would mean job security; they liked working for Dynamo and didn't want to move;
- that staff were aware of the difficult position the company was in but they really didn't know what to do to make it any better;
- development staff wanted to know why Dynamo didn't collaborate with Castem Ltd on areas of mutual interest (Jennifer didn't know the answer to this one).

The meeting gave Jennifer not only a better understanding of what employees felt, but also some good ideas to explore. Departmental staff knew their problems had not been wiped away, but did feel that Jennifer had at least taken the trouble to listen to them.

Turnover figures, performance data, recruitment and promotion trends and characteristics of employees may also shed some light on these issues.

Data relating to current formal and informal systems, together with data on the structure of the organisation, also need to be collected, and the effectiveness, efficiency and other implications of these need to be carefully considered. Most data will be collected from within the organisation, but data may also be collected from significant others, such as customers, who may be part of the environment.

Current and projected employee numbers and skills (employee supply)

Current employee supply can be analysed in both individual and overall statistical terms. To gain an overview of current supply the following factors may be analysed either singly or in combination: number of employees classified by function, department, occupation job title, skills, qualifications, training, age, length of service, performance appraisal results. (*See* HRP Exercise, 3.1, note 8, on the website.)

Forecasting employee supply is concerned with predicting how the current supply of employees will change, primarily how many will leave, be internally promoted or transferred. These changes are forecast by analysing what has happened in the past, in terms of staff retention and/or movement, and projecting this into the future to see what would happen if the same trends continued. The impact of changing circumstances would also need to be taken into account when projecting analyses forward. Bell (1989) provides an extremely thorough coverage of possible analyses, on which this section is based. Behavioural aspects are also important, such as investigating the reasons why staff leave, the criteria that affect promotions and transfers and changes in working conditions and in HR policy. Analyses fall broadly into two categories: analyses of staff leaving, and analyses of internal movements. The following calculations are the most popular forms of analysing staff leaving the organisation.

Annual labour turnover index

The annual labour turnover index is sometimes called the percentage wastage rate, or the conventional turnover index. This is the simplest formula for wastage and looks at the number of staff leaving during the year as a percentage of the total number employed who could have left.

$$\frac{\text{Leavers in year}}{\text{Average number of staff in post during year}} \times 100 = \text{percentage wastage rate}$$

(*See* HRP Exercise, 3.1, note 9, on the website.)

This measure has been criticised because it gives only a limited amount of information. If, for example, there were 25 leavers over the year, it would not be possible to determine whether 25 different jobs had been left by 25 different people, or whether 25 different people had tried and left the same job. Length of service is not taken into account with this measure, yet length of service has been shown to have a considerable influence on leaving patterns, such as the high number of leavers at the time of induction.

Stability index

The stability index is based on the number of staff who could have stayed throughout the period. Usually, staff with a full year's service are expressed as a percentage of staff in post one year ago.

$$\frac{\text{Number of staff with one year's service at date}}{\text{Number of staff employed exactly one year before}} \times 100 = \text{percent stability}$$

(*See* HRP Exercise, 3.1, note 10, on the website.)

This index, however, ignores joiners throughout the year and takes little account of length of service.

Cohort analysis

A cohort is defined as a homogeneous group of people. Cohort analysis tracks what happens as some people leave a group of people with very similar characteristics who all joined the organisation at the same time. Graduates are an appropriate group for this type of analysis. A graph showing what happens to the group can be in the form of a survival curve or a log-normal wastage curve, which can be plotted as a straight line and can be used to make predictions. The disadvantage of this method of analysis is that it cannot be used for groups other than the specific group for which it was originally prepared. The information has also to be collected over a long time-period, which produces problems of availability and reliability of data.

Half-life

The half-life is a figure expressing the time taken for half the cohort to leave the organisation. The figure does not give as much information as a survival curve, but it is useful as a summary and as a method of comparing different groups.

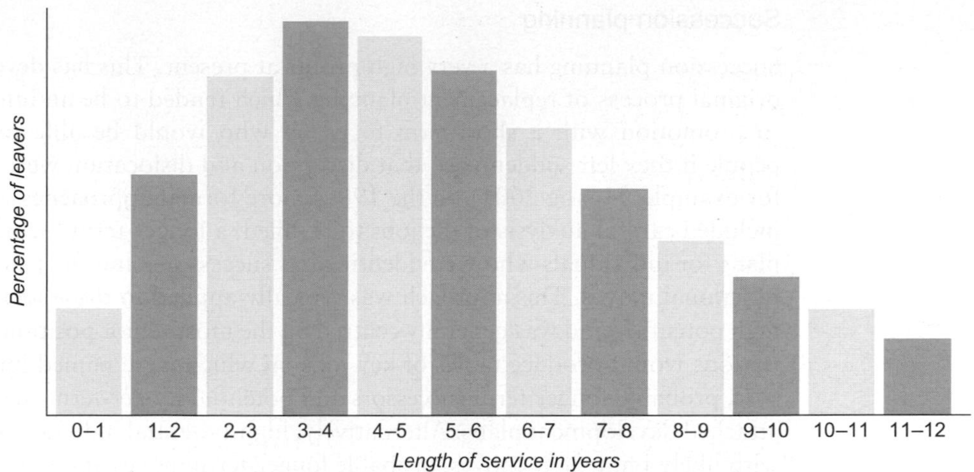

Figure 3.7 Census analysis: percentage of leavers with differing lengths of service

Census method

The census method is an analysis of leavers over a reasonably short period of time – often over a year. The length of completed service of leavers is summarised by using a histogram, as shown in Figure 3.7. (*See* HRP Exercise, 3.1, note 11, on the website.)

Retention profile

Staff retained, that is those who remain with the organisation, are allocated to groups depending on the year they joined. The number in each year group is translated into a percentage of the total number of individuals who joined during that year.

We move now to methods of analysing internal movements. These focus on either overall analyses of movement patterns in the organisation or succession planning, which has a more individual emphasis.

Analyses of internal movements

And now we turn to employee movements. Age and length of service distributions can be helpful to indicate an overall pattern of problems that may arise in the future, such as promotion blocks. They need to be used in conjunction with an analysis of previous promotion patterns in the organisation. (*See* HRP Exercise, 3.1, note 12, on the website.) An alternative is a stocks and flows analysis of the whole organisation or a part of it, such as a department. The model is constructed to show the hierarchy of positions and the numbers employed in each. Numbers moving between positions, and in and out of the organisation over any time-period, can be displayed. The model displays visually promotion and lateral move channels in operation, and shows what happens in reality to enable comparison to be made with the espoused approach, but users need to recognise, and work within, the limitation that the structure of jobs will change more rapidly than in the past.

Succession planning

Succession planning has a very high profile at present. This has developed from the original process of replacement planning which tended to be an informal approach to promotion with a short-term focus on who would be able to replace senior people if they left suddenly, so that disruption and dislocation were minimised (*see*, for example, Huang 2001). In the 1980s more formal approaches were used which included careful analysis of the jobs to be filled, a longer-term focus, developmental plans for individuals who were identified as successors, and the possibility of cross-functional moves. This approach was typically applied to those identified as having high potential, and was generally centred on the most senior positions. Larger organisations would produce tables of key jobs on which were named immediate successors, probable longer-term successors and potential longer-term successors, all with attached development plans. Alternatively, high-potential individuals were identified with likely immediate moves, probable longer-term moves and possible longer-term moves. However, as Hirsh (2000) points out, this model is appropriate to a stable environment and career structure, and the emphasis in current succession planning has changed yet again.

The focus now is on the need to build and develop a pool of talent, without such a clear view of how the talent will be used in the future. This is a more dynamic approach and fits well with the resource-based view of the firm. While the link to business strategy is emphasised, there is more recognition of individual aspirations and a greater opportunity for people to put themselves forward to be considered for the talent pool. Developing talent at different leadership levels in the organisation is considered important. Much greater openness in succession planning is encouraged, and more consideration is given to the required balance between internal talent development and external talent. Simms (2003) provides an interesting debate on these issues, which is provided as case study 3.2, on the website.

WINDOW ON PRACTICE

Succession planning at Astra Zeneca

Astra Zeneca have designed a new succession planning programme which replaces an older more complex Zeneca one, and an Astra one which reflected the competition rather than collaboration between local sites. The new programme was designed to bring the best out of both systems.

The business drivers for the new system were to:

- develop leadership capability to move a larger global business forward
- integrate the business culturally (Zeneca was UK based and demerged from ICI; Astra was Swedish)
- ensure a diverse, cross-functional base of talent
- develop the ability to lead cross-functional and cross-national teams

In the new system there is greater integration with business and strategic planning, and the focus is on identifying an international key talent pool rather than identifying successors to current jobs which may not exist in the future. Individuals in the pool are provided with challenging opportunities to foster their development. They are also made aware that they are valued and supported, and are involved in an open dialogue. While it is also necessary for future leaders to be identified and developed, they must be broadly based, come from diverse backgrounds and possess strategic capability.

Source: Summarised from: Industrial Relations Services (2002) 'The changing face of succession planning', *IRS Employment Review*, No. 756, July, pp. 37–42.

ACTIVITY 3.2

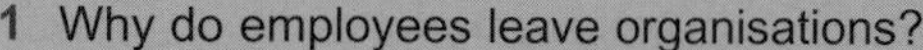

1 Why do employees leave organisations?

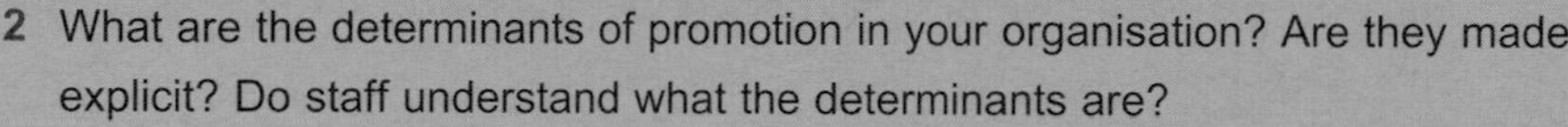

2 What are the determinants of promotion in your organisation? Are they made explicit? Do staff understand what the determinants are?

3 What would be your criteria for promotion in your organisation?

RECONCILIATION, DECISIONS AND PLANS

We have already said that, in reality, there is a process of continuous feedback between the different stages of human resource planning activities, as they are all interdependent. On the soft side (organisation, behaviour and culture) there is a dynamic relationship between the future vision, environmental trends and the current position. Key factors to take into account during reconciliation and deciding on action plans are the acceptability of the plans to both senior managers and other employees, the priority of each plan, key players who will need to be influenced and the factors that will encourage or be a barrier to successful implementation.

On the hard side, feasibility may centre on the situation where the supply forecast is less than the demand forecast. Here, the possibilities are to:

- Alter the demand forecast by considering changes in the utilisation of employees (such as training and productivity deals, or high-performance teams): by using different employees with higher skills; employing staff with insufficient skills and training them immediately; or outsourcing the work.
- Alter the supply forecast by, say, reducing staff turnover or delaying retirement.
- Change the company objectives, as lack of human resource will prevent them from being achieved in any case. Realistic objectives need to be based on the resource that is, and is forecast to be, available either internally or externally.

When the demand forecast is less than the internal supply forecast in some areas, the possibilities are to:

- Consider and calculate the costs of overemployment over various timespans.
- Consider the methods and cost of losing staff.
- Consider changes in utilisation: work out the feasibility and costs of retraining, redeployment and so on.
- Consider whether it is possible for the company objectives to be changed. Could the company diversify, move into new markets, etc.?

We have also noted the interrelationship between the soft and the hard aspects of planning. For example, the creation of high-performance teams may have implications for different staffing numbers, a different distribution of skills, alternative approaches to reward and a different management style. The relocation of supplier's staff on to premises of the company that they supply, in order to get really close to this customer, could have implications for relocation, recruitment, skills required and culture encouraged. The development of a learning organisation may have implications for turnover and absence levels, training and development provision, culture encouraged and approach to reward.

Once all alternatives have been considered and feasible solutions decided, specific action plans can be designed covering all appropriate areas of HRM activity. For example:

1 **Human resource supply plans.** Plans may need to be made concerning the timing and approach to recruitment or downsizing. For example, it may have been decided that in order to recruit sufficient staff, a public relations campaign is needed to promote a particular company image. Promotion, succession, transfer and redeployment and redundancy and retirement plans would also be relevant here. Increasingly there is the need to focus on plans for the development and retention of the talent pool.

2 **Organisation and structure plans.** These plans may concern departmental existence, remit and structure and the relationships between departments. They may also be concerned with the layers of hierarchy within departments and the level at which tasks are done, and the organisational groups within which they are done. Changes to organisation and structure will usually result in changes in employee utilisation.

3 **Employee utilisation plans.** Any changes in utilisation that affect human resource demand will need to be planned. Some changes will result in a sudden difference in the tasks that employees do and the numbers needed; others will result in a gradual movement over time. Other plans may involve the distribution of hours worked, for example the use of annual hours contracts; or the use of functional flexibility where employees develop and use a wider range of skills. There are implications for communications plans as the employees involved will need to be consulted about the changes and be prepared and trained for what will happen. There will be interconnections with supply plans here: for example, if fewer employees will be needed, what criteria will be used to determine who should be made redundant and who should be redeployed and retrained, and in which areas?

4 **Learning and development plans.** There will be development implications from both the human resource supply and utilisation plans. The timing of development can be a critical aspect. For example, training for specific new technology skills loses most of its impact if it is done six months before the equipment arrives. If the

organisation wishes to increase recruitment by promoting the excellent development that it provides for employees, then clear programmes of what will be offered need to be finalised and resourced so that these can then be used to entice candidates into the organisation. If the organisation is stressing customer service or total quality, then appropriate development will need to be developed to enable employees to achieve this.

5 **Performance management and motivation plans.** These plans may include the development or renewal of a performance management system; ensuring that employees are assessed on objectives or criteria that are key to organisational success, and which may then be linked to reward. They may also include setting performance and quality standards; culture change programmes aimed at encouraging specified behaviour and performance; or empowerment or career support to improve motivation.

6 **Reward plans.** It is often said that what gets rewarded gets done, and it is key that rewards reflect what the organisation sees as important. For example, if quantity of output is most important for production workers, bonuses may relate to number of items produced. If quality is most important, then bonuses may reflect reject rate, or customer complaint rate. If managers are only rewarded for meeting their individual objectives there may be problems if the organisation is heavily dependent on teamwork.

7 **Employee relations plans.** These plans may involve unions, employee representatives or all employees. They would include any matters which need to be negotiated or areas where there is the opportunity for employee involvement and participation.

8 **Communications plans.** The way that planned changes are communicated to employees is critical. Plans need to include not only methods for informing employees about what managers expect of them, but also methods to enable employees to express their concerns and needs for successful implementation. Communications plans will also be important if, for example, managers wish to generate greater employee commitment by keeping employees better informed about the progress of the organisation.

Once the plans have been made and put into action, the planning process still continues. It is important that the plans be monitored to see if they are being achieved and if they are producing the expected results. Plans will also need to be reconsidered on a continuing basis in order to cope with changing circumstances.

SUMMARY PROPOSITIONS

3.1 Even in a context of rapid and discontinuous change HR planning still has a valuable contribution to make, but as human resource planning deals with people, planners need to plan for what is acceptable as well as what is feasible.

3.2 The scope of human resource planning covers not only numbers of people and skills, but also structure, culture, systems and behaviour.

3.3 An integrated framework which attempts to cover all aspects of HR planning involves:

- analysing the external environment and business strategy;
- analysing where do we want to be? (forecasting HR requirements);
- analysing where are we now? (defining the current HR position and projecting this forward);
- comparing the two and forming plans to bridge the gap.

3.4 Human resource planning is a continuous process rather than a one-off activity.

GENERAL DISCUSSION TOPICS

1 Discuss the proposition that traditional (numbers) human resource planning is only of interest to organisations in periods of growth when unemployment levels are low.

2 'It is worthwhile planning even if you have no strategy.' For what reasons might you agree or disagree with this statement?

FURTHER READING

McNeilly, M. (2002) 'Gathering information for strategic decisions', *Strategy and Leadership*, Vol. 30, No. 5, pp. 29–34
Focuses on information gathering, making strategic decisions and taking action, and provides some useful tools for each of these three stages. Some interesting suggestions for making strategic decisions include scenario planning and acting out scenarios in advance.

Turner, P. (2002) *Strategic Human Resource Forecasting*. London: CIPD
An excellent and detailed text which covers issues involved in forecasting, strategy and planning and the HR role in this. Turner includes a wide range of aspects of HR from employee numbers to employee relations and organisation design.

Walker, G. and MacDonald J. (2001) 'Designing and Implementing an HR scorecard', *Human Resource Management*, Vol. 40, No. 4, pp. 365–77
This is a useful introduction to the concept of an HR scorecard developed from Kaplan and Norton's balanced scorecard model. The article is practical rather than academic and demonstrates how companies have constructed and applied the card.

REFERENCES

Becker, B., Huselid, M. and Ulrich, D. (2001) *The HR Scorecard: Linking People, Strategy and Performance*. Boston: Harvard Business School Press.

Bell, D.J. (1989) *Planning Corporate Manpower*. London: Longman.

Boxall, P. and Purcell, J. (2003) *Strategy and Human Resource Management*. Basingstoke: Palgrave, Macmillan.

Gomez, R., Gunderson, M. and Luchak, A. (2002) 'Mandatory retirement: a constraint in transitions to retirement?' *Employee Relations*, Vol. 24, No. 4, pp. 403–22.

Hendry, C. (1994) *Human Resource Strategies for International Growth*. London: Routledge.

Hirsh, W. (2000) *Succession planning demystified*. Brighton: Institute for Employment Studies.

Huang, T.-C. (2001) 'Succession Management Systems and human resource outcomes', *International Journal of Manpower*, Vol. 22, No. 8, pp. 736–47.

Industrial Relations Services (2002) 'The changing face of succession planning', *IRS Employment Review*, No. 756, July, pp. 37–42.

Lam, S.S. and Schaubroeck, J. (1998) 'Integrating HR planning and organizational strategy', *Human Resource Management Journal*, Vol. 8, No. 3, pp. 5–19.

Mintzberg, H. (1994) 'The fall and rise of strategic planning', *Harvard Business Review* (Jan./Feb.).

Simms, J. (2003) 'The generation game', *People Management*, Vol. 9, No. 9, 1 May, pp. 26–31.

Sisson, K. and Storey, J. (2000) *The Realities of Human Resource Management*. Buckingham: Open University Press.

Stiles, P. (2001) 'The impact of the board on strategy: an empirical examination', *Journal of Management Studies*, Vol. 38, No. 5, pp. 627–50.

Taylor, S. (1998) *Employee Resourcing*. London: IPD.

Turner, P. (2002) 'How to do HR forecasting and planning', *People Management*, Vol. 8, No. 6, March, pp. 48–9.

An extensive range of additional materials, including multiple choice questions, answers to questions and links to useful websites can be found on the Human Resource Management Companion Website at **www.pearsoned.co.uk/torrington**.

Part I FOCUS ON SKILLS

INTERACTIVE SKILL 1 – FACE-TO-FACE SKILLS

Managers of all types spend most of their time talking with people; information is the stock in which they trade. HR specialists have skilfulness in interaction as their core expertise. We have already seen how interactive skill is essential to enable HR people to have an impact on strategy formulation. Throughout this book we shall see how effective handling of face-to-face situations is essential throughout human resource management. As well as being articulate and receptive in any face-to-face situation, HR specialists need to develop their skills in various different types of encounter.

The recruiter has to be effective in the highly specialised interaction of the selection interview, where the task is to find out a great deal of relevant information about an applicant on which to base a judgement as to whether or not that person would match the skills, experience and attitudes required in the job to be filled. The skilled recruiter knows that such information will only come from an applicant who has confidence in the interviewer's integrity and who volunteers the information, responding willingly and helpfully to the questions that are posed.

The industrial relations manager, in contrast, needs to be an effective negotiator, explaining a position that those on the other side of the table may not appreciate and who have themselves a position which the industrial relations manager may not appreciate. Common ground has to be established, differences clarified and possibilities for reconciling those differences explored.

Both interactions have things in common, but they require different skills. Each Part of this book is rounded up by focusing on an interaction central to the theme of the Part. Understanding that interaction helps with understanding the other activities that have been reviewed.

Our objectives in this introductory Focus on skills are to:

1. Explain what makes for effectiveness in interaction
2. Explain the different types of interaction
3. Review the fundamental skills of (a) setting the tone, (b) listening, (c) questioning and (d) feedback

There is also a brief case study, typical examination questions and some suggested web links.

Effectiveness in interaction

In the remainder of this focus on skills we concentrate on methods, but we also must remember the need to understand non-verbal behaviour. We all reveal our feelings by what we do as well as in what we say. Someone blushing is obviously embarrassed and someone crying is clearly distressed, but there are a host of other signs or *tells* that indicate what a person is feeling. The person who is able to read these signals has a great advantage in interactions. The term '**tell**' comes from the study of poker players, who are as anxious to conceal their own hand as they are to guess what is in someone else's (Caro 1994).

Effective face-to-face people are likely to have some basic qualities. *Poise* enables a person to be at ease in a wide variety of social situations, often enjoying them, and able to talk with different types of people in a relaxed and self-confident way. This self-confidence derives partly from the feedback of willing responses constantly provided by other people.

Another element of poise is knowing what you are talking about, so we demonstrate our poise much more in situations with which we are familiar than we do in strange circumstances. There is less fear of what the other may say and less apprehension about appearing naive. Questions, and even criticism, are easier to deal with and are often wanted, so stimulating the interchange.

Poise is often associated with maturity, due to a person having succeeded in developing a rounded view of themselves without feeling too much anxiety about the possible adverse opinions of others. The process of acquiring poise can be accelerated by experience which involves meeting a variety of people from differing backgrounds.

A necessary adjunct to poise is the quality of being *responsive* to the needs, feelings and level of understanding in other people. This prevents poise from becoming too egocentric. The teacher, for instance, will be looking for signs of misunderstanding in the student so that the message can be restated or clarified, and the market research interviewer will be looking for signals that the question has been accurately construed, or that it needs elaboration. Responsiveness can also include offering rewards, like friendliness, warmth, sympathy and helpfulness as features of general style or as part of a relationship with other participants. These not only sustain and strengthen the relationship, but may also be held back as a means of trying to get one's own way.

There are certain general problems that impair effectiveness. They mostly concern ways in which people tend to hear what they expect to hear rather than what they are being told.

The frame of reference is the standpoint from which a person views an issue, and understanding of the issue will be shaped by that perspective rather than any abstract 'reality'. It is a set of basic assumptions or standards that frame our behaviour. These are developed through childhood conditioning, through social background, education and affiliations. Differences in the frames of reference held by participants in interactions present inescapable problems. Can Israelis and Arabs ever really understand each other? How can those who manage and direct ever appreciate the point of view of those who are managed and directed?

The frame of reference on any particular matter is largely determined by opinions developed within a group with which we identify, as few of us alter our opinions alone. We both follow and participate in the formulation of opinion in our group, and most of us are in a number of such reference groups. Because this is so, complexities arise: some people can be vociferously anti-union as citizens and voters in general elections, yet support a union of which they are members at their workplace.

The *stereotype* is the standardised expectation we have of those who have certain dominant characteristics: typical stereotypes are that all Scots are mean, all shop stewards are disruptive, women are more caring than men and that men are more aggressive than women. The behaviour of some people in a category makes us expect all in that category to behave in the same way. This is obviously invalid, but is a tendency to which we are prone. We must always listen to what people are actually saying to us rather than hearing what we think a person of that type *would say*.

At first making use of stereotypes is necessary in working relationships; it is not feasible to deal with every individual we meet as being a void until we have collected enough information to know how to treat them, so we always try to find a pigeon-hole in which to put someone. We begin conversations with a working stereotype, so that, for example, we stop someone in the street to ask directions only after we have selected a person who looks intelligent and sympathetic. If we are giving directions to a stranger we begin our explanation having made an assessment of their ability to understand quickly, or their need for a more detailed, painstaking explanation. The stereotype becomes a handicap only when we remain insensitive to new information enabling us to develop a fuller and more rational appraisal of the individual with whom we are interacting.

Being aware of the dangers of stereotyping others, and trying to exercise self-discipline, can reduce the degree to which you misunderstand other people, but you still have the problem that your respondents will put you into a stereotype and hear what you say in accordance with whatever their predetermined notion may be.

Cognitive dissonance is the difficulty we all have in coping with behaviour that is not consistent with our beliefs. Such behaviour will make us uncomfortable and we will try to cope with the dissonance in various ways in order to reduce the discomfort. Either we persuade ourselves that we believe in what we are doing, or we avoid the necessary behaviour. When we are given new information that is not consistent with what we already believe, we are likely to massage it to fit our existing pattern of behaviour rather than discard the beliefs of a lifetime.

Different types of interaction

Meetings are needed to make decisions, to overcome misunderstanding and to develop ideas. Interviews are used for selection, discipline, appraisal, counselling, problem solving and grievance handling. Managers 'put things across' in selling, persuasion, presentation and negotiation.

It is helpful to group interactions into four broad types: enquiry, exposition, joint problem solving and conflict resolution, as indicated in Figure I.1.

Enquiry is that group of situations where the HR specialist needs to find things out from someone else, with the selection interview being the classic example. What needs to be found out may be factual information, attitudes, feelings, levels of understanding or misunderstanding. The main skill is in types of questioning.

Exposition is almost the direct opposite. Instead of finding things out, the HR person is trying to convey information, to develop in the other person a level of knowledge and understanding, acceptance of an argument or agreement with a proposition. Although some questioning is often an integral part of exposition, the main skill is in clear articulation, fluency, good organisation of material and effective illustration.

Joint problem solving is a different type of activity as it involves developing an exchange in which both parties work together to unravel a problem or understand a situation which neither fully understands beforehand. It is not one person transferring an 'answer' to another, but both trying to understand together something which they can only partly understand alone. The skills involve some questioning and explanation, but also careful listening and feedback.

Joint problem solving assumes that both parties trust each other and see a common interest in helping the other. *Conflict resolution* begins without that mutual confidence, as the parties have interests that inevitably conflict and they are not likely fully to trust each other. The skills here are first those of presentation and then listening, questioning and feedback.

A very specialised skill is that of *chairing*, which is dealt with at the end of the book.

Enquiry Selection Attitude survey Health screening	**Exposition** Presentation Lecture Briefing
Joint problem solving Appraisal Counselling Discipline	**Conflict resolution** Negotiation Arbitration

Figure I.1 Four categories of interaction

Fundamental skills in setting the tone

Any interaction begins by someone setting the tone of what is to follow. A shop assistant who says, 'Can I help you', or the peculiarly common, 'Are you all right *there*?' is trying to set a tone of knowledgeable helpfulness to a customer that might eventually result in a sale. It is the inclusion of the apparently superfluous 'there' that is puzzling. Of course you are there; where else would you be? Presumably the reason is to make the question less blunt, avoiding the implication that you are not all right. The HR specialist will set the tone of a selection interview, for instance, by explaining what is to happen and providing other contextual information that will enable the candidate to engage in the process constructively. There will also be a process of conveying more subtle messages to say, 'I'm in charge; I know what I'm doing; you can trust me.' In other interactions the way of setting the tone is different, but some features are common:

- Speak first.
- Smile, looking confident and relaxed (much easier said than done).
- Have brief, harmless exchanges that enable the parties to speak to each other without the answers mattering (weather, travel problems, etc.), but always react appropriately to answers.
- Explain your understanding of what is to happen.
- Check that that is understood and accepted.

Fundamental skills in listening

Tone of voice

Different feelings express themselves in different voice characteristics. Possible meanings for various characteristics are tabulated below:

Characteristic	Probable meaning
Monotone voice	Boredom
Slow speed, low pitch	Depression
High voice, emphasis	Enthusiasm
Ascending tone	Astonishment
Abrupt speech	Defensiveness
Terse speed, loud tone	Anger
High pitch, drawn-out speech	Disbelief

Giving attention

Inclining the body towards the other person is a signal of attentiveness, so our posture should be inclined forward and facing the other squarely with an open posture: folded arms can be inhibiting.

Eye contact is crucial to good listening, but is a subtle art:

> Effective eye contact expresses interest and a desire to listen. It involves focusing one's eyes softly on the speaker and occasionally shifting the gaze from his face to other parts of the body, to a gesturing hand, for example, and then back to the face and then to eye contact once again. Poor eye contact occurs when a listener repeatedly looks away from the speaker, stares at him constantly or blankly, or looks away as soon as the speaker looks at the listener. (Bolton 1987, p. 36)

The distinction between 'focusing one's eyes softly' and staring is vital, though difficult to describe, and competence in eye contact is never easy to establish. It is one of the most intimate ways of relating to a person and many managers fear that the relationship may become too close.

We also show *physical responses* in our attentiveness. First we have to avoid distracting the other person by physical behaviour that is unrelated to what is being said; fiddling with a pen, playing with car keys, scrutinising our fingernails, wringing our hands, brushing specks of dust off our sleeves are a few typical behaviours that indicate inattention. Skilled listeners not only suppress these, they also develop minor gestures and posture variants that are directly responsive to what the other is saying.

Being silent helps you to listen by providing space for incoming messages, but it also provides opportunities to observe the other person and to think about what is being said. Most people are uncomfortable with silence and try to fill it with inconsequential chat, but this interferes with listening. Silence still has to be attentive and the longer the silence, the harder it is to be attentive: think of the last lecture you attended and how hard it was to maintain attentiveness.

Fundamental skills in questioning

Closed questions seek precise, terse information and are useful when you want clear, straightforward data. Most encounters feature closed questioning at some point.

Open-ended questions avoid terse replies by inviting respondents to develop their opinions without the interviewer prescribing what the answer should be. The question does little more than introduce a topic to talk about. Their main purpose is to obtain the type of deeper information that the closed question misses, as the shape of the answer is not predetermined by the questioner. You are informed not simply by the content of the answers, but by what is selected and emphasised.

Indirect questions take an oblique approach on a difficult matter. A blunt 'Did you like that job?' almost suggests you didn't, or at least raises the suspicion that the interviewer thinks you didn't; it is a bit like the shop assistant avoiding being too blunt. Put indirectly as 'What gave you the most satisfaction in that job?' it has the merit of concentrating on the work rather than the person.

The *probe* is a form of questioning to obtain information that the respondent is trying to conceal. When the questioner becomes aware that the respondent is doing so he or she has to make an important, and perhaps difficult, decision: whether to respect the candidate's unwillingness and let the matter rest, or to persist with the enquiry. Reluctance is quite common in selection interviews where a candidate may wish to gloss over an aspect of the recent employment history. The most common sequence for the probe takes the following form: (a) direct questions, replacing the more comfortable open-ended approach ('What were you doing in the first six months of 2001?'). Careful phrasing may avoid a defensive reply, but those skilled at avoiding unwelcome enquiries may still deflect the question, leading to (b) supplementaries, which reiterate the first question with different phrasing ('Yes, I understand about that period. It's the first part of 2001 that I'm trying to get clear: after you came back from Belgium and before you started with Amalgamated Widgets'). Eventually this should produce the information the questioner needs. (c) Closing. If the information has been wrenched out like a bad tooth and the interviewer looks horrified or sits in stunned silence, then the candidate will feel put down beyond redemption. The interviewer needs to make the divulged secret less awful than the candidate had feared, so that the interview can proceed with reasonable confidence ('Yes, well you must be glad to have that behind you'). It may be that the interviewer will feel able to develop the probe by developing the answer by a further question such as 'And how did that make you feel?' or 'And how did you react to that? It must have been a terrible blow.' It is only reasonable to do this if the resultant exchange adds something useful to the questioner's understanding of the client: simple nosiness is not appropriate.

WINDOW ON (MAL)PRACTICE

One rather dubious version of the probe is to offer an exaggerated explanation for something being avoided. In the imaginary situation described above the selector might do this:

> *Selector*: Yes, I understand about that period. It's the first part of 2001 that I'm trying to get clear: after you came back from Belgium and before you started with Amalgamated Widgets. You weren't in prison or anything, were you?
> *Candidate*: Oh no. I had a nervous breakdown

The explanation offered by the selector is so appalling that the candidate rushes to offer a less appalling explanation. This is not recommended, but it is interesting to know about. It might happen to you one day.

Some common lines of questioning should be avoided because they can produce an effect that is different from what is intended.

Leading questions ('Would you agree with me that . . . ?') will not necessarily produce an answer that is informative, but an answer in line with the lead that has been given.

Multiple questions give the candidate too many inputs at one time ('Could you tell me something of what you did at university, not just the degree, but the social and sporting side as well, and why you chose to backpack your way round the world? You didn't travel on your own, did you?'). This sort of questioning is sometimes adopted by interviewers who are trying very hard to efface themselves and let the respondent get on with the talking. However helpful the interviewer intends to be, the effect is that the candidate will usually forget the later parts of the question, feel disconcerted and ask, 'What was the last part of the question?' By this time the interviewer has also forgotten, so they are both embarrassed.

Taboo questions are those that infringe the reasonable personal privacy of the candidate. There is a proper place for the probe, but some questions have to be avoided, especially in selection interviews, as they could be interpreted as discriminatory. It is at least potentially discriminatory, for instance, to ask women how many children they have and what their husbands do for a living. Questions about religion or place of birth are also to be avoided. Some questions may do no more than satisfy the idle curiosity of the questioner. If there is no point in asking them, they should not be put.

Fundamental skills in feedback

As well as listening, it is necessary to provide feedback to demonstrate that you have received and understood what you are being told.

In *reflection*, the listener picks up and re-states the content of what has just been said. In a difficult situation the listener picks out the emotional overtones of a statement and 'reflects' them back to the respondent without any attempt to evaluate them. The interviewer expresses neither approval nor disapproval, neither sympathy nor condemnation.

At a more prosaic level, there is *summary and re-run* to show you are listening and providing the opportunity for any misunderstanding to be pointed out. In appraisal, for instance, the respondent will produce lots of information in an interview and you will be selecting that which is to be retained and understood. From time to time you interject a summary sentence or two with an interrogative inflection. This shows that you are listening, gives the respondent the chance to correct any false impressions and reinforces the key points that are being retained. It is also a useful way of making progress, as the interjection is easily followed by another open-ended question – 'Now perhaps we can turn to . . . ?'

The standard method in both reflection and summary is *paraphrasing*, by which the listener states the essence of what has been said. This is done concisely, giving the speaker a chance to review what has been said and, perhaps, to correct it.

We all respond positively when a listener shows *interest* in what is being said. If it is possible also to agree with what is being said, the reinforcement of the respondent will be greater.

The most common form of *affirmation* in feedback is the head nod, and many public speakers look for head nods (not to be confused with nodding off) as a way of judging the supportive mood of the audience. Other ways of affirming involve the use of the eyes. These are too subtle and individual to describe, but we each have a repertoire of signals to indicate such reactions as encouragement, surprise and understanding. When the eyes are part of a smile, there will be stronger reward to the talker. There are also words and phrases: 'Really?' 'Go on . . .', 'Yes . . .', 'Of course . . .', 'My word . . .', 'You were saying . . .'

Interaction contains a variety of noises that are ways of feeding back to the other party. They are impossible to reproduce in words but are usually variations of a theme of 'Mmm . . .' and they form a part of the exchanges that is inarticulate yet meaningful, keeping things going without interrupting.

SUMMARY PROPOSITIONS

I.1 Interactive skills are a fundamentally important aspect of all managerial work.

I.2 Effectiveness in interaction is aided by poise and being responsive to others, as well as by understanding the effects of the frame of reference, stereotyping and cognitive dissonance.

I.3 The basic types of interaction can be categorised as enquiry, exposition, joint problem solving and conflict resolution. A specialised skill is chairing.

I.4 Listening skills include tone of voice, giving attention, eye contact, physical responses and being silent.

I.5 The main types of question are closed, open ended, indirect and the probe. Inappropriate questions are leading, multiple and taboo.

I.6 Methods of feedback include reflection, summary and re-run, paraphrasing, showing interest, affirmation and using appropriate noises.

GENERAL DISCUSSION TOPICS

1 What are the advantages of face-to-face conversation compared with a combination of e-mail, fax, text messages and telephone calls?

2 If a central part of HRM is getting things done by other people, what is the difference between telling them what to do and asking them to do things? In what sort of situations would each approach be appropriate?

FURTHER READING

Argyle, M. (1994) *The Psychology of Interpersonal Behaviour*. Harmondsworth, Middlesex: Penguin Books
This is a classic that was first published in 1967 and remains the ideal introduction to understanding the dynamics of interpersonal skills.

Collett, P. (2003) *The Book of Tells*. London: Doubleday
This book provides a comprehensive explanation of non-verbal behaviours that reveal a person's true feelings. The author is a social psychologist who combines research at the Oxford University Department of Experimental Psychology with acting as resident psychologist for the television programme *Big Brother*.

Glass, L. (1992) *He Says, She Says*. London: Piatkus
This shows the differences in communication behaviour between men and women, which lead to such extensive misunderstanding of motives. The author explains differences in body language, voice tone, speech patterns and even choice of words.

WEB LINKS

www.cipd.co.uk takes you to the Chartered Institute of Personnel and Development, which is the professional body for HR people. The site has a wealth of information, not only on qualification courses, but on all aspects of human resource management.

www.shrm.org is a similar site for the Society of Human Resource Management in the United States.

www.peoplemanagement.co.uk is the website for the monthly journal, published by CIPD.

The book's companion website contains more practical advice on interaction techniques.

REFERENCES

Bolton, R. (1987) *People Skills*. Brookvale, New South Wales: Simon & Schuster.

Caro, M. (1994) *The Body Language of Poker*. Secaucus, New Jersey: Carol Publishing Group.

REVIEW OF PART I

The early chapters of this book indicated that many controversial incidents in human life have what might be called an HR dimension. If someone fails in a job, was the right person chosen in the first place? Was the 'right' person unfairly rejected? If a train crashes with serious loss of life, was the driver properly trained and supervised? Are employees effectively disciplined when they make mistakes, or does the manager concerned avoid the issue for fear of jeopardising a working relationship? And so they go on, issues of fitting people to jobs and jobs to people, issues of training, appraisal, motivation, payment and many more. All go to the core of human resource management, yet the role of the human resource manager is not directly to manage these situations, but to ensure they are managed and to enable other people to manage them well.

The challenge for HRM people is thus, somehow or other, to get the job done by other people, not all of whom will welcome assistance and guidance because they are quite sure of their own ability to deal with the matters. Furthermore, they may well outrank the HR people and disparage HR expertise, although the latter problem seems to be getting less common.

The human resource manager needs to understand the range and potential of human resource management, its traditions, its problems and its expertise, so as to adopt a perspective on any situation (as in the case study that follows) that is realistic and fit for the purpose.

Advice from HR will always be strengthened when based on sound analysis, so expertise in planning methods and the ability to use this quickly and appropriately is a necessary part of the HR manager's toolkit.

Because human resource management deals with such a variety of situations and people, a skill that is even more important is that of being effective in face-to-face interaction. This is where advice works or is disregarded, where the 'right' person is spotted and selected or lost to a competitor, where the disgruntled employee is brought back on board or the union agreement is sealed, and so on. Because human resource management is one of the great tasks of getting things done through other people, it is appropriate to conclude this short review with a quotation from an obscure English poet of the eighteenth century, James Thomson. In a eulogy to the recently deceased Lord Talbot, he wrote:

> How the heart listened while he pleading spoke!
> While on the enlightened mind, with winning art,
> His gentle reason so persuasive stole
> That the charmed hearer thought it was his own.

Clearly a man deserving immediate Chartered Personnel Practitioner status!

Part I CASE STUDY PROBLEM

You have just been appointed to replace the personnel manager in an organisation where members of the Board felt that HR practice had become over-preoccupied with fashionable ideas and was not meeting the needs of the business and the people who worked there. They have asked you to:

1. Review the ways in which human resource management is being conducted across the entire business, within the line as well as by the HR specialists.
2. Identify aspects of best practice that are currently being employed by leading-edge HR practitioners in other organisations and which would be relevant to your situation.
3. Draft proposals for a programme of strategic initiatives to enhance human resource management throughout the business.

On investigation you find:

1. A scheme of employee involvement in management decision making has foundered because of resistance from two unions with members in the organisation, whose representatives were excluded from discussions about the proposals; and by reservations held by a number of senior managers, who felt that the scheme had not been properly thought through and that it was too radical a development.
2. The concept of performance management has been introduced at the same time as moves to empower line managers. Many line managers feel that empowerment means no more than taking the blame for things that go wrong, and many of their subordinates feel that they are now cut off from the centralised, expert services of the HR function.
3. A case for the Investors in People award was turned down because what actually happened in practice did not match what the policy statement claimed.
4. Members of the HR function say that they have lost credibility and job satisfaction by a series of grandiose schemes that were not fully developed and which could not be fully implemented in a short time.

Required

Produce outline proposals for the Board to consider, setting out what you would do in the first six months and in the following 12 months to deal with this situation and what you expect to achieve in that time.

Locate the organisation in a real context, either in a company or other organisation with which you are familiar or in a particular industry that interests you.

Part I EXAMINATION QUESTIONS

1 Summarise the stages in development of personnel management and human resource management.

2 Examine some likely future trends in human resource management. Which developments do you expect to be prevalent, and why?

3 Explain the problems of integrating HR strategy with corporate strategy. How can these problems be addressed?

4 'The employment relationship is not just an economic transaction; it also has social and moral connotations.' Discuss the arguments for and against this view and the implications for HRM practice.

5 Analyse the links between business strategy and HRM, using examples to support your answer.

6 'HRM is a second-order function with the task of managing the administrative side of the employment relationship. It should not aspire to more than that.' Do you agree or disagree?

7 In May 1993 *Fortune* magazine set out 'six trends that will re-shape the workplace':

- The average organisation will become smaller, employing fewer people.
- The traditional hierarchical organisation will give way to a variety of forms, foremost being the network of specialists.
- Technicians will replace manufacturing operatives as the worker elite.
- The vertical division of labour will be replaced by a horizontal division.
- The paradigm of doing business will shift from making a product to providing a service.
- Work will be redefined towards constant learning, more higher-order thinking, less nine to five.

How far do you see these trends exemplified in (a) the economy generally and (b) your own organisation?

8 In what ways have the methods and objectives of human resource planning changed as the workforce has become more diverse?

RESOURCING

The first major activity of the human resource specialist is to find and bring in the people that the business needs for its success. The people may not be employees; they may be consultants or subcontractors. They may be temporary, full time, part time or occasional, and the working relationship between the business and its people is the contract, which sums up the features of that relationship so that both parties know where they stand. Nearly always there is a face-to-face meeting between the parties to agree terms before the relationship begins. The process of 'coming to terms' is one of mutual assessment. Many prospective employees reject a prospective employer by deciding not to apply for a post, or by discontinuing their application. Employers usually choose between many, and often feel there are too few applicants. Once recruited, people have to be retained within the business by a series of strategies that sustain their interest and motivation as well as keeping the focus of their activities within a changing organisational and business context. Contracts end as well as begin, and we have to be sure that the arrangements to end the contract are as sound as those for it to start.

The whole resourcing process is symbolised by the mutual assessment of the selection interview: 'Is this person right for us?' and 'Is this job and situation right for me?' The answers to both those questions have major implications for both parties. The uncertainty about whether or not the right answers are found at the interview is why we have to examine resourcing so closely.

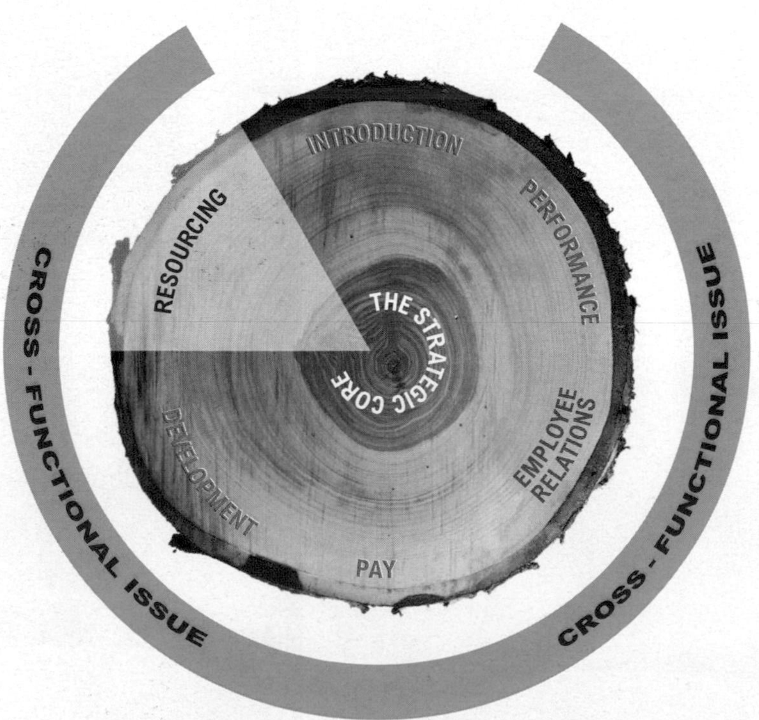

STRATEGIC ASPECTS OF RESOURCING

THE OBJECTIVES OF THIS CHAPTER ARE TO:

1 REVIEW KEY CONTEMPORARY LABOUR MARKET TRENDS

2 DESCRIBE DIFFERENT WAYS IN WHICH LABOUR MARKETS CAN BE USEFULLY ANALYSED

3 EXPLAIN DIFFERENT TYPES OF FLEXIBLE WORKING

4 DEBATE THE MERITS OF MOVING TOWARDS A HIGHER DEGREE OF ORGANISATIONAL FLEXIBILITY

5 ASSESS DIFFERENT STRATEGIES TO USE IN ORDER TO MOBILISE A WORKFORCE

'Angela's leaving – quick, we must make sure to get the ad in this month's journal.'

'It's hopeless – they all leave just as soon as we've trained them. What's the point?'

'It's not my fault – we just can't get the staff. No wonder quality is so poor.'

'That's it. The results are so bad we'll have to let some of them go. Tony, draw up a shortlist of possibles and we'll try and get it sorted this week.'

All too often employee resourcing is a reactive activity, without any link to organisational strategy and without internal coherence. To bridge this gap we suggest a range of aspects which together can form the framework for a resourcing strategy to facilitate the future direction of the business. Each of these aspects offers choices for managers.

RESPONDING TO LABOUR MARKET TRENDS

The starting point for all strategic activity in HRM is to understand the environment in which an organisation operates. It is only possible to formulate the most appropriate policies and practices once its key features have been identified and their importance grasped. In the field of employee resourcing the environment with which we are concerned is the labour market, the pool of available talent in which employers compete to recruit and subsequently retain staff. Later we look at different types of labour market and their implications for employers. Here we focus on three major trends in the UK labour market as a whole and look at how they are affecting decision making in organisations.

Demographic developments

In 2003 the UK's population numbered 59.25 million, of whom just under half (27.9 million) were in work. Both figures are projected to rise marginally during the coming decade. The overall population is increasing, despite falling birth rates, because of lengthening life expectancy. The number of people who are economically active is increasing largely because of women spending a greater proportion of their lives in paid work than has been the case historically. Over the longer term, however, the proportion of the population that is of working age will shrink in comparison with the total population as more and more people live longer after reaching retirement age. This process has already begun in countries such as Japan and Germany with significant implications for the provision of care and pensions for the growing number of elderly people. In the UK there are currently 21 people over the age of 65 for every 100 people of working age. After 2010 this number will start to rise significantly. By 2030 more than a quarter of the population will be over 65. The coming years will therefore see a substantial change in the age profile of the workforce, as the population as a whole gets older and a greater proportion of young people remain in full-time education for longer.

There are two major implications for employers. First, because their numbers will fall, it will be progressively harder to recruit and retain the more talented younger workers. Organisations that have sought to resource their organisations by recruiting and training new graduates or school leavers will either have to work a good deal harder at competing for them or have to bring in older people in their place. Second, there are implications for the capacity of the state to provide a reasonable level of pension for so many retired people. Increasingly, therefore, people are likely to look at the nature of occupational pension being provided by employers when deciding on their career options. Organisations offering good, well-communicated pension benefits will be better placed than others to attract and retain the employees they need.

WINDOW ON PRACTICE

Global demographic trends vary considerably from region to region. According to United Nations statistics, many major European countries can expect to see an overall fall in their populations over the next fifty years. The biggest projected falls are in Eastern Europe. Russia, for example, can anticipate a fall in its population of 30 per cent before 2050, while the highest figure of all (a 52 per cent population fall) is projected in Estonia. Substantial population falls are also predicted for Italy (22 per cent), Switzerland (19 per cent) and Poland (15 per cent). These figures partly reflect low birth rates, but also the likelihood that more people will emigrate from than immigrate into these economies.

Where birth rates are high and where the likelihood of net immigration is also relatively high, population rates are projected to increase. One such country is the United States of America, where fertility rates (i.e. number of children born per couple) are currently running at 2.11 and around two million immigrants settle each year (many illegally). As a result, the US population will overtake that of the EU in the 2030s, passing 400 million by 2050.

Diversity

According to the most recent government figures 84 per cent of men and 73 per cent of women are either in work or actively seeking work in the UK (Hibbett and Meager 2003). Increased female participation in the workforce has been one of the most significant social trends over recent decades. In 1980 the employment rate for women of working age was 59 per cent, since when the figure has risen steadily, while that for men has declined somewhat. This has happened as more women with young children have opted to work while more men have taken early retirement. As a result there has been some decline in the number of workplaces where women are heavily outnumbered by men and an increase in the number where men are outnumbered by women. Although the vast majority of management posts are still held by men, we have also seen a substantial increase in the number of women occupying such positions – another trend that is going to continue in the years ahead. Despite these developments there remain many areas of work which are dominated by either men or women and a continued substantial **gender gap** in overall pay levels (women's average salary is 82 per cent of that for men). A trend which has been identified in many surveys is the growth in the number of part-time workers in the UK. They now account for over a quarter of the total workforce and over 80 per cent of them are women. Representation of ethnic minorities has also increased over recent years. In the early 1980s around 4.5 per cent of employees came from ethnic minorities. Twenty years on the figure is 6.5 per cent. Whereas in 1980 two-thirds of workplaces employed no one from an ethnic minority, over half now do (Millward *et al.* 2000, p. 43). Increases in representation have occurred across the industrial sectors.

Taken together, these various trends mean that the workforce is steadily becoming more diverse in its make-up. While there remains a strong degree of segregation in terms of the types of work performed, the trend is towards heterogeneity at all organisational levels. There are a number of important implications for human resource managers:

- In order to attract and retain the best employees it is necessary to take account of the needs of dual-career families. The law now requires employers to offer a measure of support with recent measures on parental leave, the right to time off for family emergencies, and the right to request flexible working, but there is a great deal more that can be done. Career-break entitlements, crèches and job-share schemes are the most common initiatives. (See Chapter 32 for more on work-life balance issues.)
- There is a heightened need for awareness of the possibility of discrimination against any group which is underrepresented in the workplace. The perception of inequity, however justifiable in practice, is all that is needed for staff turnover rates to increase and for an employer to gain a poor reputation in its labour markets.
- Employers are required to pay more serious attention to the issue of sexual and racial harassment in a workplace characterised by diversity than in one which is less heterogeneous. It is advisable to have written policies covering such matters and to ensure that line managers are fully aware of the developing law on harassment.

Skills and qualifications

The third major development in the labour market is the changing occupational structure, leading to a greater demand for skilled staff. In recent decades the chief job growth areas have been in the managerial and professional occupations, and in service industries such as retailing, security and catering. By contrast there has been an ongoing decline in demand for people to work in the manufacturing and agricultural sectors (Office for National Statistics 2003). While technical skills are not required for all the new jobs, social skills are necessary, as is the ability to work effectively without close supervision.

The past two decades have also seen a strong increase in demand for graduates. Over 400,000 now graduate from universities in the UK every year, including 260,000 with first degrees. Unemployment among this group is considerably lower than for the rest of the population whatever the economic conditions, indicating a capacity on the part of employers to absorb the growing numbers into their labour forces. However, despite the increasing numbers of people gaining formal qualifications at all levels, there remain skills shortages. When the economy is performing well these can be significant. The annual CIPD Labour Turnover Survey for 2003 reported that 70 per cent of employers had had problems filling vacancies (CIPD 2003), while surveys of graduate recruiters found that 53 per cent of public sector organisations and 44 per cent of private sector companies have problems filling their vacancies (Graduate Market Trends 2003). There are still too few people with high-level IT and scientific qualifications entering the labour market and far too many people lacking basic numeracy and literacy skills. It is estimated that 20 per cent of adults in the UK are innumerate and unable to read beyond the most basic level (Department for Education and Employment 2000).

Policy initiatives are in place to improve skills levels at both ends of the scale, but it will take a number of years before the effects are apparent in the labour market. Until then employers have to devise strategies to deal with skills shortages in key areas. One approach is simply to work harder at recruiting and retaining employees. Another is to find ways of reducing reliance on the hard-to-recruit groups by reorganising work and dividing tasks up differently so that people with particular skills spend 100 per cent of their time undertaking the duties for which only they are qualified. A third response is to look overseas for recruits interested in working in the UK. Where skills shortages are particularly acute there is also the possibility of re-locating one or more organisational functions abroad. Finally, of course, it is possible to recruit people without the required skills and to provide the necessary training and development opportunities.

ANALYSING LABOUR MARKETS

While the general trends outlined above have significant implications for employers, more important for individual organisations are developments in the particular labour markets which have relevance to them. An understanding of what is going on in these can then form the basis of decision making across the employee resourcing field. There are several different ways in which labour markets vary.

Geographical differences

For most jobs in most organisations the relevant labour market is local. Pay rates and career opportunities are not so great as to attract people from outside the district in which the job is based. The market consists of people living in the 'travel to work area', meaning those who are able to commute within a reasonable period of time. In determining rates of pay and designing recruitment campaigns there is a need to compare activities with those of competitors in the local labour market and to respond accordingly. Skills shortages may be relieved by increases in the local population or as a result of rival firms contracting. New roads and improved public transport can increase the population in the travel to work area, with implications for recruitment budgets and the extent to which retention initiatives are necessary. For other jobs, usually but not always those which are better paid, the relevant labour market is national or even international. Here different approaches to recruitment are necessary and there is a need to keep a close eye on what a far larger number of rival employers are doing to compete for staff.

Tight v. loose

A tight labour market is one in which it is hard to recruit and retain staff. Where the labour market is loose, there are few problems finding people of the required calibre.

Labour market conditions of this type clearly vary over time. The higher the rate of unemployment in an area, the looser the labour market will be. However, some labour markets always remain tight whatever the economic conditions simply because there are insufficient numbers of people willing or able to apply for the jobs concerned. In recent years, even at the depths of the recessions of the 1980s and 1990s, it has been difficult to find good IT staff and effective sales people.

A number of researchers have looked at the responses of employers faced with either loose or tight labour markets. Windolf (1986) identified four types of approach used in the UK and Germany which varied depending not only on the tightness of the market, but also on the capacity of the organisation to respond intelligently to the situation. He found that many organisations with high market power (that is, faced with a relatively loose labour market) made little effort at all in the employee resourcing field. They simply took the opportunity to spend as little as possible on recruitment and selection and waited for people to come to them. When there was a vacancy it tended to be filled by a similar person to the one who had left, thus maintaining the status quo. According to Windolf, the more intelligent organisations took the opportunity afforded by favourable labour market conditions to seek out people with the capacity to innovate and who would develop their roles proactively. All available recruitment channels were used, leading to the development of a richly diverse and creative workforce. A similar dichotomy was identified in the case of tight labour markets. Here many organisations simply 'muddled through', finding people where they could, giving them training and hoping that they would stay long enough to give a decent return on the investment. By contrast, the more intelligent organisations were looking at restructuring their operations, introducing flexible working patterns and devising ways of reducing their reliance on people who were difficult to recruit.

Occupational structure

Labour markets also differ according to established behavioural norms among different occupational groups. The attitudes of people to their organisations and to their work vary considerably from profession to profession, with important implications for their employers. A useful model developed by Mahoney (1989) illustrates these differences. He identifies three distinct types of occupational structure: craft, organisation career and unstructured. In craft-oriented labour markets, people are more committed over the long term to their profession or occupation than they are to the organisation for which they work. In order to develop a career they perceive that it is necessary for them to move from employer to employer, building up a portfolio of experience on which to draw. Remaining in one organisation for too long is believed to damage or at least to slow down career prospects. Examples include teaching, where there is often a stronger loyalty to the profession as a whole than towards the employing institution. By contrast, an organisation-career occupation is one in which progress is primarily made by climbing a promotion ladder within an organisation. People still move from employer to employer, but less frequently, and will tend to stay in one organisation for as long as their careers are advancing. Mahoney's third category, the unstructured market, consists of lower-skilled jobs for which little training is necessary. Opportunities for professional advancement are few, leading to a situation where people move in and out of jobs for reasons which are not primarily career related.

To an extent employers can seek to influence the culture prevailing among members of each type of occupational group. There is much to be gained in terms of employee retention, for example, by developing career structures which encourage craft-oriented workers to remain for longer than they otherwise would. However, a single employer can have limited influence of this kind. It is therefore necessary to acknowledge the constraints associated with each labour market and to manage within them. Different areas of HR activity have to be prioritised in each case. It is necessary to work harder at retaining people in craft-oriented labour markets than in those which are organisation oriented, because people will be more inclined to stay with one employer in the latter than in the former. Recruitment and selection will be different too. Where career advancement is generally achieved within organisations, as in banking or the civil service, there is a good case for giving a great deal of attention to graduate recruitment. It is worth spending large sums to ensure that a good cohort is employed and subsequently developed because there is likely to be a long period in which to recoup the investment. The case is a good deal weaker in craft-oriented labour markets where there is less likelihood of a long association with individual employees.

Generational differences

Employee resourcing practices should also be adapted to take account of variations in the age profile of those whom the organisation is seeking to employ. While it is clearly wrong to assert that everyone of a certain age shares the same attitudes and characteristics, broad differences between the generations can be identified. Sparrow and Cooper (2003), in their review of recent research in this area, argue that there are good reasons for believing that the workforce of the future (i.e. made up of young people currently in full-time education) will have decidedly different 'work values' from those of the current workforce. This is because the shared experiences which shape the attitudes and expectations of each generation are different. Evidence suggests that future employees will be less trusting of organisations, more inclined to switch jobs, and more prepared to relocate, and indeed emigrate, than is the case today.

Research on generational differences from a management perspective remains underdeveloped, but a number of writers have put forward interesting ideas. Zemke *et al.* (2000), for example, identify four groups defined by their dates of birth. They go on to argue that each must be treated rather differently if they are to be successfully managed. The four categories are Veterans (born before and during the Second World War), Baby Boomers (late 1940s and 1950s), Generation X (1960s and 1970s) and a group labelled 'Nexters' (born after 1980). Some of the points made about each are as follows:

- Veterans are attracted to workplaces which offer stability and which value experience.
- Boomers place a high value on effective employee participation.
- Xers enjoy ambiguity and are at ease with insecurity.
- Nexters are wholly intolerant of all unfair discrimination.
- Boomers do not object to working long hours.
- Xers require a proper 'work-life balance'.

- Veterans are loyal to their employers and are less likely to look elsewhere for employment opportunities than younger colleagues.
- Xers are strongly resistant to tight control systems and set procedures.
- Nexters, being serious minded and principled, prefer to work for ethical employers.
- Xers and Nexters work more easily with new technology than veterans and boomers.

Where a workforce is dominated by a particular age group, it makes sense to manage the workers in a way with which they feel comfortable. Organisational performance as well as turnover rates improve as a result. Similarly, where a recruitment drive is aimed at a particular age group, it is important to give out appropriate messages about what the organisation is able to offer.

ACTIVITY 4.1

Zemke and his colleagues developed their theories of intergenerational difference in the context of labour markets in the USA. Their analysis is based on the idea that successive generations of Americans have been shaped by shared formative influences.

In what ways has the historical experience of these generational groups differed in the UK or in other EU countries?

What implications might such differences have from an employer's perspective?

FLEXIBLE RESOURCING CHOICES

Understanding the dynamics of the organisational environment is only one part of taking a strategic approach to employee resourcing. Having gained an understanding one must decide how the organisation can best interact with its environment to maximise its performance. One set of key choices concerns the extent to which the organisation can aspire to flexibility and in what ways this can be achieved. Three types of flexibility are often identified in the literature: numerical flexibility, temporal flexibility and functional flexibility. A fourth type, financial flexibility, is discussed in Chapter 28.

Numerical flexibility

Numerical flexibility allows the organisation to respond quickly to the environment in terms of the numbers of people employed. This is achieved by using alternatives to traditional full-time, permanent employees. The use, for example, of short-term contract staff, staff with rolling contracts, staff on short-term, government-supported training schemes, outworkers, and so on, enable the organisation to reduce or expand the workforce quickly and cheaply.

Atkinson is one of a number of commentators who has described the way in which firms may develop flexibility in their approach to employment, as shown in

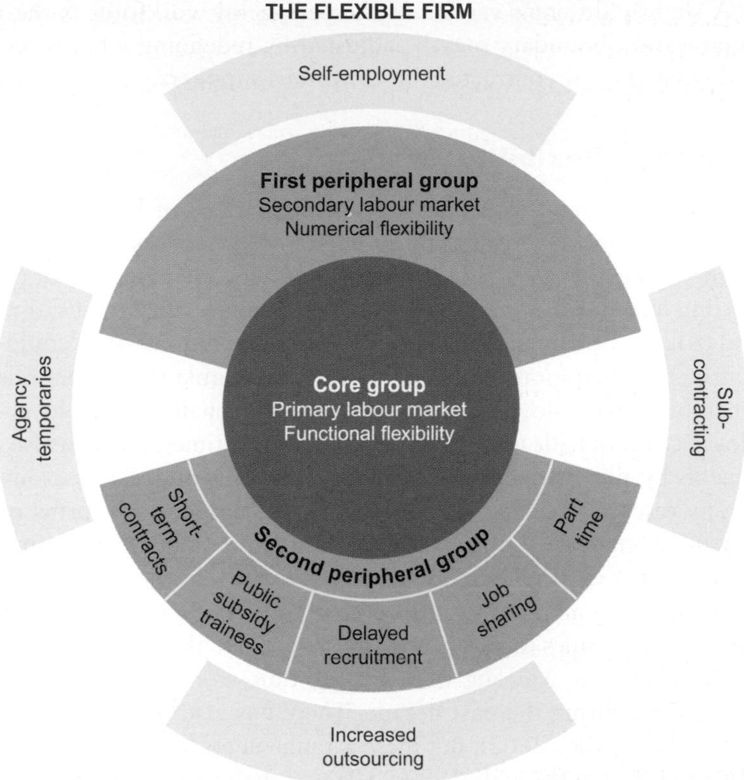

Figure 4.1 Atkinson's model of the flexible firm (Source: J. Atkinson (1984) 'Manpower strategies for flexible organisations', *Personnel Management*, August. Used with the permission of the author.)

Figure 4.1. The flexible firm in this analysis has a variety of ways of meeting the need for human resources. First are core employees, who form the primary labour market. They are highly regarded by the employer, well paid and involved in those activities that are unique to the firm or give it a distinctive character. These employees have improved career prospects and offer the type of flexibility to the employer that is so prized in the skilled craftworker who does not adhere rigidly to customary protective working practices.

There are then two peripheral groups: first, those who have skills that are needed but not specific to the particular firm, like typing and word processing. The strategy for these posts is to rely on the external labour market to a much greater extent, to specify a narrow range of tasks without career prospects, so that the employee has a job but not a career. Some employees may be able to transfer to core posts, but generally limited scope is likely to maintain a fairly high turnover, so that adjustments to the vagaries of the product market are eased.

The second peripheral group is made up of those enjoying even less security, as they have contracts of employment that are limited, either to a short-term or to a part-time attachment. There may also be a few job sharers and many participants on government training schemes find themselves in this category. An alternative or additional means towards this flexibility is to contract out the work that has to be done, either by employing temporary personnel from agencies or by subcontracting the entire operation.

A slightly different version of the peripheral workforce is the way in which the organisation boundary may be adjusted by redefining what is to be done in-house and what is to be contracted out to various suppliers.

Temporal flexibility

Temporal flexibility concerns varying the pattern of hours worked in order to respond to business demands and employee needs. Moves away from the 9–5, 38-hour week include the use of annual hours contracts, increased use of part-time work, job sharing and flexible working hours. For example, an organisation subject to peaks and troughs of demand (such as an ice cream manufacturer) could use annual hours contracts so that more employee hours are available at peak periods and less are used when business is slow. Flexitime systems can benefit the employer by providing employee cover outside the 9–5 day and over lunchtimes, and can also provide employee benefits by allowing personal demands to be fitted more easily around work demands.

The research evidence suggests increased usage of all forms of temporal flexibility in recent years. Longer opening hours in retailing and the growth of the leisure sector means that many more people now work in the evening (17 per cent) and at night (6 per cent) than used to be the case. The proportion of jobs that are part time also continues to rise, albeit at a slower rate than in the 1970s and 1980s, while the length of the working week for full-time workers has increased by three hours on average during the past decade. There has also been some growth in the use of annual hours (IRS 2002), but these arrangements have not become as widespread as was predicted in the early 1990s. The vast majority of employers have not chosen to adopt this approach.

Functional flexibility

The term 'functional flexibility' refers to a process in which employees gain the capacity to undertake a variety of tasks rather than specialising in just one area. Advocates of such approaches have been influenced by studies of Japanese employment practices as well as by criticisms of monotonous assembly-line work. Horizontal flexibility involves each individual employee becoming multiskilled so that they can be deployed as and where required at any time. It is often associated with shop-floor manufacturing work, but can be applied equally in other workplace settings. Vertical flexibility entails gaining the capacity to undertake work previously carried out by colleagues higher up or lower down the organisational hierarchy.

The primary purpose of functional flexibility initiatives is to deploy human resources more efficiently. It should mean that employees are kept busy throughout their working day and that absence is more easily covered than in a workplace with rigidly defined demarcation between jobs. Another source of efficiency gains arises because employees are more stretched, fulfilled and thus productive than is the case in a workplace with narrowly defined jobs. Despite its potential advantages research suggests that employers in the UK have been less successful than competitors elsewhere in Europe at developing functional flexibility. According to Blyton (1998, p. 748), this is primarily because of a reluctance to invest in the training necessary to support these new forms of working. By contrast, Reilly (2001, p. 132) points to employee resistance and the increased likelihood of errors occurring when functional flexibility programmes are introduced.

Debates about flexibility

The growth in flexible working arrangements combined with their promotion by governments since the 1990s has led to the development of robust debates about their desirability and usage in practice. As much controversy has centred on the Atkinson model of the flexible firm as on the rather different elements that go to make it up. There has been a continuing debate, for example, about whether the model of core and periphery is a description of trends or a prescription for the future. Two streams of research have flowed from these interpretations. The first concerns the extent to which the model has been adopted in practice, the second focuses on the advantages and disadvantages of the model as a blueprint for the future organisation of work.

Evidence on the first of these questions is patchy. There is no question that rhetoric about flexibility and the language of flexibility is increasingly used. The flexible firm model appears to be something that managers aspire to adopt, but the extent to which they have actually adopted it is questionable. In many organisations the drive for economies of scale means that far from becoming more flexible, organisations are just as likely to introduce bureaucratic systems and standardised practices in response to competitive pressures. And yet we also have seen for a long period now increased use of part-time workers, consultants, subcontractors, agency workers and of moves towards multiskilling. Karen Legge's (1995) conclusion that flexibility is used in a pragmatic and opportunistic way rather than as a strategic HRM initiative thus seems to hold true today.

On the question of the desirability of flexibility a number of views have been expressed. The theoretical advantages for organisations arise from productivity gains. In different ways each type of flexibility aims to deploy employee time and effort more efficiently so that staff are only at work when they need to be and are wholly focused on achieving organisational objectives throughout that time. However, the extent to which this is achieved in practice is not clear. Many writers equate the term 'flexibility' with 'insecurity' and argue that the consequences for organisations in terms of staff commitment and willingness to work beyond contract are damaging. Staff turnover is likely to increase in response to the introduction of flexible working practices, while recruitment of talented people will be harder too. In short it is plausibly argued that the flexible firm model, at least as far as the 'peripheral' workforce is concerned, is incompatible with best practice approaches to HRM which seek to increase employees' commitment. Sisson and Storey (2000, p. 83) make the further observation that too much 'hollowing out' can impair organisational learning and lead to the loss of expertise, a loss from which it is difficult to recover. These unintended consequences, it is argued, can worsen rather than improve an organisation's competitive position. Others (*see* Heery and Salmon 2000 and Burchell *et al.* 2002) see too much flexibility as having damaging longer-term economic consequences. For example, it can lead to a reduced willingness on the part of employers to invest in training, the absence of which creates skills shortages that hold back economic development. It can also lead to a situation in which managers exploit the vulnerability of peripheral workers by intensifying their work to an unacceptable degree. Finally, it can be argued that in dividing people into 'core' and 'peripheral' groups, flexible firms perpetuate inequality in society more generally and that this leads to poverty, crime, family breakdown and political alienation.

WINDOW ON PRACTICE

Tuselmann (1996) argues that a high degree of interdependence exists between the different forms of flexibility, that there are costs and benefits of each, and that organisations choose an optimal mix dependent on their market conditions and the country in which they operate. He suggests that a high degree of functional flexibility may be generally inconsistent with a high degree of numerical or financial flexibility. It has been argued that while Britain pursues numerical flexibility, in an unregulated and decentralised labour market, there is a greater emphasis in other parts of Europe on functional flexibility. In particular Germany has successfully followed this route within a highly regulatory framework with a high degree of centralisation and industrial relations consensus. Tuselmann notes that this framework also constrains organisations' pursuit of numerical, temporal and financial flexibility, and that as Germany experiences increasing competitive pressures, their model of labour flexibility is at a crossroads.

There are other balances in resourcing strategy that can be addressed, for example the balance between numbers of permanent staff employed and the hours that each employee works. In November 1993 Volkswagen in Germany announced that in their current poor financial situation they were employing too many people. In order to avoid redundancies they agreed with the workforce that hours would be reduced by 20 per cent so that they worked a four-day week, and that wages would be reduced by 10 per cent. There is a good deal of emphasis in Europe on reducing the working week to help reduce redundancies, unemployment and absence levels, and to improve family life.

ACTIVITY 4.2

What evidence can you find in your organisation to support a more flexible approach to resourcing? What were the driving forces behind these changes?

How have employees responded and why?

READY MADE OR HOME GROWN?

Organisations have a choice whether to depend extensively on the talent available in the external labour market or to invest heavily in training and development and career systems to exploit the potential in the internal labour market. Some organisations thrive despite having high levels of staff turnover, while others thrive on the development of employees who remain with the organisation in the long term. The emphasis on either approach, or a balance between the two, can be chosen to support organisational strategy.

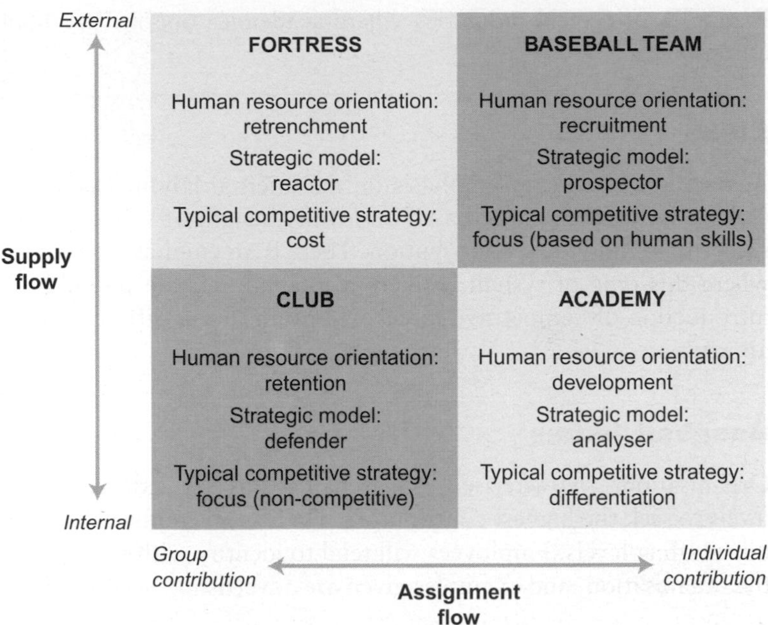

Figure 4.2 A typology of career systems (Source: J.A. Sonnenfield *et al.* (1992) 'Strategic determinants of managerial labour markets', *Human Resource Management*, Vol. 27, No. 4. Copyright © 1992 John Wiley and Sons, Inc. Reproduced with permission of John Wiley and Sons, Inc.)

Sonnenfield *et al.* (1992) propose a model which relates entry and exit of staff with promotion and development of staff in the organisation. One axis of the model is supply flow. They argue that, strategically, organisations that focus on internal supply tend to see people as assets with a long-term development value rather than costs in terms of annual expenditure. The other axis is labelled the assignment flow, which describes the basis on which individuals are assigned new tasks in the organisation. The criteria for allocation may be in terms of individual contribution to organisational performance, or on group contribution – which Sonnenfield *et al.* identify as factors such as loyalty, length of service and support of others. They argue that, strategically, organisations that emphasise individual contribution expect individuals to provide value on a continuous basis, whereas those that emphasise group contribution see employees as having intrinsic value.

The model proposed describes the combination of these two aspects of resourcing and results in four typical 'career systems' as shown in Figure 4.2. In each box alongside the career system label (academy, club, baseball team and fortress) Sonnenfield *et al.* identify the strategic organisation model and the competitive strategy which are most likely to drive each career system. They also identify the likely orientation of the human resource function. In this chapter we are concerned with the characteristics of the career systems, which are discussed below.

Academies

In academies there is a heavy emphasis on individual contribution, in terms of reward and promotion. They are characterised by stability and low turnover of staff, with many employees remaining until retirement. There is an emphasis on development and often competitions for promotion and barriers to leaving the organisation.

Examples of typical industries where academies operate are pharmaceuticals and automobiles.

Clubs

Again there is a heavy emphasis on the internal labour market, but promotion in clubs is more likely to be based on loyalty, length of service, seniority and equality rather than individual contribution. There is an emphasis on staff retention. Sectors where this type of system is likely to operate include public bodies, although the introduction of competitive forces will mean that a different career system may be appropriate.

Baseball teams

Organisations characterised as baseball teams use external labour sources at all levels to seek the highest contributors. There is an emphasis on recruitment to maintain staffing levels. Employees will tend to identify with their profession rather than the organisation, and examples given are advertising, accountancy and legal firms.

Fortresses

Fortress organisations are concerned with survival and cannot afford to be concerned with individuals, in terms of either reward or promotion. They are more likely to depend on external recruitment, often for generalists who meet the needs of a retrenchment or turnaround situation. Examples given are publishing, retailing and the hotel sector.

ACTIVITY 4.3

Which of the four career systems in the Sonnenfield *et al.* model typifies your organisation? What characteristics lead you to this conclusion?

How does this career systems strategy fit with your organisational strategy and organisational mission (either explicitly stated or implicit)?

SUMMARY PROPOSITIONS

4.1 A strategic approach to resourcing requires that account is taken of the changes taking place in the labour market.

4.2 Individual labour markets vary in key respects. These too need to be taken into account when formulating resourcing policy.

4.3 Models incorporating numerical, temporal and functional flexibility have been influential determinants of HRM thinking in recent years, leading to their adoption in many organisations.

4.4 The extent to which increased flexibility is evidence of a strategic approach to employee resourcing is a matter of debate. The extent to which such approaches are desirable in the long term is also open to question.

4.5 Organisations have strategic choices concerning the use they make of their internal and external labour market.

GENERAL DISCUSSION TOPICS

1 In times of high unemployment, many employers still continue to experience skills shortages. What steps can employers take to alleviate this situation? What steps might the government take?

2 Discuss the claim that flexible resourcing strategies should be welcomed by the individual as they provide new areas of opportunity rather than a threat.

FURTHER READING

Brown, P., Green, A. and Lauder, H. (2001) *High Skills: globalization, competitiveness and skill formation*. Oxford: Oxford University Press
The authors draw on the results of a large international study to compare and contrast the different approaches being used around the globe to promote skills acquisition and to create a high-skill labour force. Their analysis focuses in particular on the impact of economic globalisation on skills development.

IRS (2002) 'Internal applicants – handle with care', *IRS Employment Review*, 25 March
This article focuses on the practical implications that arise when organisations opt to recruit and promote staff internally rather than sourcing new people from the external labour market. The article draws on a recent study by researchers at the Institute of Employment Studies to set out best practice guidelines.

Pollert, A. (1988) 'The flexible firm: fixation or fact?' *Work, Employment and Society*, Vol. 2, No. 3, pp. 281–316
Although published some years ago, this article is the best and most coherent critique of Atkinson's model of the flexible firm and the management trends it has influenced for two decades.

REFERENCES

Atkinson, J. (1984) 'Manpower strategies for flexible organisations', *Personnel Management*, August.

Blyton, P. (1998) 'Flexibility', in M. Poole and M. Warner (eds) *The IEBM Handbook of Human Resource Management*. London: Thomson.

Burchell, B., Ladipo, D. and Wilkinson, F. (2002) *Job Insecurity and Work Intensification*. London: Routledge.

Chartered Institute of Personnel and Development (2003) *CIPD Labour Turnover 2003: A Survey of Ireland and the UK*. London: CIPD.

Department for Education and Employment (2000) *Labour Market and Skill Trends*. London: HMSO.

Graduate Market Trends (2003) 'The Lure of the Public Sector', *Graduate Market Trends*, Autumn, pp. 9–12.

Heery, E. and Salamon, J. (eds) (2000) *The Insecure Workforce*. London: Routledge.

Hibbett, A. and Meager, N. (2003) 'Key indicators of women's position in Britain', *Labour Market Trends*, October.

IRS (2002) 'Internal applicants – handle with care', *IRS Employment Review*, 25 March.

Legge, K. (1995) *Human Resource Management: Rhetorics and realities*. Basingstoke: Macmillan.

Mahoney, T.A. (1989) 'Employment Compensation Planning and Strategy', in L. Gomez-Mejia (ed.) *Compensation and Benefits*. Washington, DC: BNA.

Millward, N., Bryson, A. and Forth, J. (2000) *All Change at Work? British employment relations 1980–1998, as portrayed by the Workplace Industrial Relations Survey series*. London: Routledge.

Office for National Statistics (2003) *Workforce Jobs by Industry 1959–2003*, www.statistics.gov.uk.

Reilly, P. (2001) *Flexibility at Work: Balancing the interests of employer and employee*. Aldershot: Gower.

Sisson, K. and Storey, J. (2000) *The Realities of Human Resource Management: Managing the Employment Relationship*. Buckingham: Open University Press.

Sonnenfield, J.A. *et al.* (1992) 'Strategic determinants of managerial labour markets', in G. Salaman *et al.* (eds) *Human Resource Strategies*. London: Sage.

Sparrow, P. and Cooper, C. (2003) *The Employment Relationship: Key Challenges for HR*. London: Butterworth-Heinemann.

Tuselmann, H.-J. (1996) 'The path towards greater labour flexibility in Germany: hampered by past success?' *Employee Relations*, Vol. 18, No. 6, pp. 26–47.

Windolf, P. (1986) 'Recruitment, Selection and Internal Labour Markets in Britain and Germany', *Organizational Studies*, Vol. 7, No. 3, pp. 235–54.

Zemke, R., Raines, C. and Filipczak, B. (2000) *Generations at Work*. New York: AMACOM.

An extensive range of additional materials, including multiple choice questions, answers to questions and links to useful websites can be found on the Human Resource Management Companion Website at **www.pearsoned.co.uk/torrington**.

CHAPTER 5

CONTRACTS, CONTRACTORS AND CONSULTANTS

THE OBJECTIVES OF THIS CHAPTER ARE TO:

1. REVIEW THE MAJOR DUTIES AND RIGHTS WHICH DERIVE FROM THE CONTRACT OF EMPLOYMENT
2. DESCRIBE THE RANGE OF HOURS AND SHIFT PATTERNS SPECIFIED IN CONTRACTS
3. EVALUATE THE ADVANTAGES AND DISADVANTAGES ASSOCIATED WITH DIFFERENT APPROACHES TO TEMPORAL FLEXIBILITY
4. EXAMINE THE REASONS FOR GROWTH IN ATYPICAL CONTRACTUAL ARRANGEMENTS AND OF REGULATION IN THIS AREA
5. DEBATE THE ADVANTAGES AND DISADVANTAGES OF EMPLOYING CONSULTANTS
6. ASSESS THE RECENT TREND TOWARDS MORE OUTSOURCING OF ACTIVITIES TRADITIONALLY CARRIED OUT IN-HOUSE

WINDOW ON PRACTICE

A case heard in the House of Lords illustrates the importance of employee status. Mrs Carmichael and a colleague were employed as tour guides at a power station run by National Power PLC. They started working for the company on a casual basis in 1989, undertaking about four hours work each week as and when they were needed. By 1995 they each were working around 25 hours a week, so they decided to ask for written particulars of their terms and conditions of employment. The company refused on the grounds that they were casual workers and not employees. The women won their case in the lower courts, but the company decided to appeal right up to the House of Lords. At this stage the women lost their case on the grounds that there was no mutuality of obligation. They could, and indeed had, turned down requests to work without suffering any disciplinary action. They were therefore not employees and not entitled to the rights associated with full employment status.

An employment contract comes into existence when an unambiguous offer of employment is made and is unconditionally accepted. Once agreed neither side can alter the terms and conditions which govern their relationship without the agreement of the other. An employer cannot therefore unilaterally cut employees' pay, lengthen their hours of work, reduce their holiday entitlement, change their place of work or move them to another kind of work. To do so the employer either has to secure the employees' agreement (by offering some kind of sweetener payment) or has to ensure that the right to make adjustments to terms and conditions is written into the contract by means of flexibility clauses. Where an employer forces changes through without securing the agreement of employees directly, or in many cases through negotiation with union representatives, legal action may follow. An employee may simply bring a claim for breach of contract and ask that the original contract be honoured. In such circumstances compensation may or may not be appropriate. Alternatively, where the employer's breach is serious or where it is one of the implied duties listed above that has not been honoured, employees are entitled to resign and claim constructive dismissal in an Employment Tribunal, in which case their situation is treated as if they had actually been dismissed (*see* Chapter 9).

Table 5.2 provides a checklist for preparing a contract of employment.

WORKING PATTERNS

Aside from payment arrangements, for full-time workers the pattern of hours which they are expected to work is the most important contractual issue. The total number of hours worked by the average full-time worker in the UK fell substantially for much of the past 150 years, but started to rise again in the 1990s (Harkness 1999). In 1850 the normal working week was established as 60 hours spread over six days of 10 hours each. The average number of hours weekly worked in 2003, including paid and unpaid overtime, was 44 hours for men and 39 hours for women (Labour Market Trends 2003a). Interestingly, in the last two or three years there is evidence that

Table 5.2 Checklist for preparing a contract of employment

1. Name of employer; name of employee.
2. Date on which employment began.
3. Job title.
4. Rate of pay, period and method of payment.
5. Normal hours of work and related conditions, such as meal-breaks.
6. Arrangements for holidays and holiday pay, including means whereby both can be calculated precisely.
7. Terms and conditions relating to sickness, injury and sick pay.
8. Terms and conditions of pension arrangements.
9. Length of notice due to and from employee.
10. Disciplinary rules and procedure.
11. Arrangements for handling employee grievances.
12. (Where applicable) Conditions of employment relating to trade union membership.

people have started working rather fewer hours again, the number working in excess of 45 hours a week falling by nearly 10 per cent (Office for National Statistics 2003).

A return to the downward trend in terms of hours worked may be a direct response to new regulation in this area. The European Union's Working Time Directive was introduced into UK law in 1998 as a health and safety initiative (*see* Chapter 22). Among other measures, it seeks to ensure that no one is required to work more than an average of 48 hours a week against their will. In some countries legislation limiting working hours is primarily seen as a tool for reducing unemployment. In France, for example, the 'loi Aubry' was introduced limiting people to an average working week of only 35 hours (EIRR 1998).

ACTIVITY 5.1

Would you like to see legislation passed in the UK limiting to 35 the number of hours in a week that each person can work?

What would be the main arguments for and against the introduction of such legislation?

The past two decades have also seen some increase in the proportion of the working population engaged in shiftworking. This is nothing new in the manufacturing sector where the presence of three eight-hour shifts has permitted plants to work round the clock for many years. Recently, however, there has been a substantial rise in the number of service-sector workers who are employed to work shifts. They, unlike most factory-based staff, are not generally paid additional shift payments to reward them for working unsocial hours. According to IDS (2000), the change has come about because of moves towards 'a 24-hour society' which have followed on from globalisation, the emergence of e-commerce and consumer demand. Each year more and more people are reported to be watching TV and making phone calls in the early hours of the morning, while late-night shopping has become the norm for a third of adults in the UK. Banks, shops, airports and public houses are now round-the-clock operations. The result is a steadily increasing demand for employees to work outside the standard hours of 9–5, Monday to Friday, a trend long established in the USA where fewer than a third of people work the standard weekday/daytime shift (IDS 2000, p. 1).

While some people remain attached to the 'normal' working week and would avoid working 'unsocial hours' wherever possible, others like the flexibility it gives them, especially where they are rewarded with shift premia for doing so. Shift-working particularly appeals to people with family responsibilities as it permits at least one parent to be present at home throughout the day. Several types of distinct shift pattern can be identified, each of which brings with it a slightly different set of problems and opportunities.

Part-timer shifts require employees to come to work for a few hours each day. The most common groups are catering and retail workers employed to help cover the busiest periods of the day (such as a restaurant at lunchtime) and office cleaners employed to work early in the morning or after hours in the evening. This form of working is convenient for many and clearly meets a need for employers seeking people to come in for short spells of work.

Permanent night shifts create a special category of employee set apart from everyone else. They work full time, but often have little contact with other staff who leave before they arrive and return after they have left. Apart from those working in 24-hour operations, the major categories are security staff and maintenance specialists employed to carry out work when machinery is idle or when roads are quiet. There are particular problems from an HR perspective as they are out of touch with company activities and may be harder to motivate and keep committed as a result. Some people enjoy night work and maintain this rhythm throughout their working lives, but for most such work will be undertaken either reluctantly or for relatively short periods. Night working is now heavily regulated under the Working Time Regulations 1998.

Double day shifts involve half the workforce coming in from early in the morning until early afternoon (an early shift), while the other half work from early afternoon until 10.00 or 11.00 at night (a late shift). A handover period occurs between the two shifts when everyone is present, enabling the organisation to operate smoothly for 16–18 hours a day. Such approaches are common in organisations such as hospitals and hotels which are busy throughout the day and evening but which require relatively few people to work overnight. Rotation between early and late shifts permits employees to take a 24-hour break every other day.

Three-shift working is a well-established approach in manufacturing industry and in service-sector organisations which operate around the clock. Common patterns are 6–2, 2–10 and 10–6 or 8–4, 4–12 and 12–8. A further distinction can be made between discontinuous three-shift working, where the plant stops operating for the weekend, and continuous three-shift working, where work never stops. Typically the workforce rotates between the three shifts on a weekly basis, but in doing so workers suffer the consequences of a 'dead fortnight' when normal evening social activities are not possible. This is avoided by accelerating the rotation with a 'continental' shift pattern, whereby a team spends no more than three consecutive days on the same shift.

Split shifts involve employees coming into work for two short periods twice in a day. They thus work on a full-time basis, but are employed on part-timer shifts to cover busy periods. They are most commonly used in the catering industry so that chefs and waiting staff are present during meal times and not during the mornings and afternoons when there is little for them to do. Drawbacks include the need to commute back and forth from home to work twice and relatively short rest-periods in between shifts in which staff can wind down. For these reasons split shifts are unpopular and are best used in workplaces which provide live-in accommodation for staff.

Compressed hours shifts are a method of reducing the working week by extending the working day, so that people work the same number of hours but on fewer days. An alternative method is to make the working day more concentrated by reducing the length of the midday meal-break. The now commonplace four-night week on the night shift in engineering was introduced in Coventry as a result of absenteeism on the fifth night being so high that it was uneconomic to operate.

WINDOW ON PRACTICE

The banking group Lloyds TSB has recently introduced a 'work options scheme' to help it recruit and retain effective performers. It aims to help employees to find ways of meeting both their work and home obligations without having to compromise one or the other. According to the group's website, the major options offered are:

- reduced hours – working less than a full-time schedule
- job sharing – two individuals sharing the duties of a full-time position
- variable hours – varying the start and finish time of a standard day
- compressed workweek – working a full working week in fewer than five days a week
- tele-working – working at home or off-site for up to three days a week.

Source: www.lloydstsbjobs.com/pages/what_we_offer.html.

FLEXIBLE WORKING HOURS

Another way of dealing with longer operating hours and unpredictable workloads is to abandon regular, fixed hours of working altogether. This allows an organisation to move towards the 'temporal flexibility' we discussed in Chapter 4. The aim is to ensure that employees are present only when they are needed and are not paid for being there during slack periods. However, there are also advantages for employees. Three types of arrangement are reasonably common in the UK: flexitime, annual hours and zero-hours contracts.

Flexitime

A flexitime system allows employees to start and finish the working day at different times. Most systems identify core hours when everyone has to be present (for example 10–12 and 2–4) but permit flexibility outside those times. Staff can then decide for themselves when they start and finish each day and for how long they are absent at lunchtime. Some systems require a set number of hours to be worked every day, while others allow people to work varying lengths of time on different days provided they complete the quota appropriate for the week or month or whatever other settlement period is agreed. This means that someone can take a half-day or full day off from time to time when they have built up a sufficient bank of hours.

There are great advantages for employees working under flexitime. Aside from the need formally to record time worked or to **clock in**, the system allows them considerable control over their own hours of work. They can avoid peak travel times, maximise the amount of time they spend with their families and take days off from time to time without using up holiday entitlement. From an employer's perspective flexitime should reduce the amount of time wasted at work. In particular, it tends to eliminate the frozen 20-minute periods at the beginning and end of the day when nothing much happens. If the process of individual start-up and slowdown is spread over a longer period, the organisation is operational for longer. Moreover, provided choice is limited to a degree, the system encourages staff to work longer hours at busy times in exchange for free time during slack periods.

Annual hours

Annual hours schemes involve an extension of the flexitime principle to cover a whole year. They offer organisations the opportunity to reduce costs and improve performance by providing a better match between working hours and a business's operating profile. Unlike flexitime, however, annual hours systems tend to afford less choice for employees.

Central to each annual hours agreement is that the period of time within which full-time employees must work their contractual hours is defined over a whole year. All normal working hours contracts can be converted to annual hours; for example, an average 38-hour week becomes 1,732 annual hours, assuming five weeks' holiday entitlement. The principal advantage of annual hours in manufacturing sectors, which need to maximise the utilisation of expensive assets, comes from the ability to separate employee working time from the operating hours of the plant and equipment. Thus we have seen the growth of five-crew systems, in particular in the continuous process industries. Such systems are capable of delivering 168 hours of production a week by rotating five crews. In 365 days there are 8,760 hours to be covered, requiring 1,752 annual hours from each shift crew, averaging just over 38 hours for 46 weeks. All holidays can be rostered into 'off' weeks, and 50 or more weeks of production can be planned in any one year without resorting to overtime. Further variations can be incorporated to deal with fluctuating levels of seasonal demand.

The move to annual hours is an important step for a company to take and should not be undertaken without careful consideration and planning. Managers need to be aware of all the consequences. The tangible savings include all those things that are not only measurable but capable of being measured before the scheme is put in. Some savings, such as reduced absenteeism, are quantifiable only after the scheme has been running and therefore cannot be counted as part of the cost justification. A less tangible issue for both parties is the distance that is introduced between employer and employee, who becomes less a part of the business and more like a subcontractor. Another problem can be the carrying forward of assumptions from the previous working regime to the new. One agreement is being superseded by another and, as every industrial relations practitioner knows, anything that happened before, which is not specifically excluded from a new agreement, then becomes a precedent.

Zero hours

A zero-hours contract is one in which individuals are effectively employed on a **casual** basis and are not guaranteed any hours of work at all. Instead they are called in as and when there is a need. This has long been the practice in some areas of employment, such as nursing agencies and the acting profession, but it has recently been used to some extent in other areas, such as retailing, to deal with emergencies or unforeseen circumstances. Such contracts allow employers to cope with unpredictable patterns of business, but they make life rather more unpredictable for the individuals involved. The lack of security associated with such arrangements makes them an unattractive prospect for many.

ACTIVITY 5.2

What types of job would you regard as most appropriate for the following variations of the conventional 9-to-5 working pattern?

1 Shift working
2 Part-time working
3 Job sharing
4 Flexible hours
5 Compressed hours
6 Annual hours

What types of job would not be suitable for each of these?

ATYPICAL CONTRACTUAL ARRANGEMENTS

Recent decades have seen the growth of contractual arrangements that differ from the permanent, open-ended, full-time, workplace-based form of employment that has always been regarded as representing the norm. As was shown in Chapter 1, there is considerable disagreement about the significance of these trends. For some they mark the 'beginning of the end' for jobs as we have come to experience them over the past 100 years, while for others they represent a modest adjustment of traditional practices in response to evolving labour market developments and to industrial restructuring. Either way they have important implications for the effective management of people.

Contracts of limited duration

Contracts of employment vary in all manner of ways. One of the most important distinctions relates to their length. Here it is possible to identify three basic forms:

- **Permanent:** This is open-ended and without a date of expiry.
- **Fixed term:** This has a fixed start and finish date, although it may have provision for notice before the agreed finish date.

- **Temporary:** Temporary contracts are for people employed explicitly for a limited period, but with the expiry date not precisely specified. A common situation is where a job ends when a defined source of funding comes to an end. Another is where someone is employed to carry out a specified task, so that the expiry date is when the task is complete. The employer is obliged to give temporary workers an indication in writing at the start of their employment of the expected duration of the job.

Around half of all employers in the UK, including a good majority of public sector bodies, employ some people on a fixed-term basis or make use of agency temps. In 2003 a total of 1.5 million people worked under some form of non-permanent contract, which is 6.4 per cent of all employees (Labour Market Trends 2003b). This is appreciably more than the 5 per cent who were employed on such a basis in the 1980s, but represents a substantial fall over the past few years; in 1998 the figure was close to 1.8 million. As unemployment has fallen and the economy has grown employers have found that they have to offer permanent positions if they are to attract effective employees. Although only around a quarter of temporary staff now claim that they would prefer a permanent job, in the mid-1990s this figure was close to half.

Some of the reasons for employing people on a temporary or fixed-term basis are obvious. Retail stores need more staff immediately before Christmas than in February and ice cream manufacturers need more people in July than November, so both types of business have seasonal fluctuations. Nowadays, however, there is the additional factor of flexibility in the face of uncertainty. Will the new line sell? Will there be sustained business after we have completed this particular contract? In the public sector fixed-term employment has grown with the provision of funds to carry out one-off projects, while the signing of time-limited service provision agreements with external private-sector companies has also become a great deal more common.

Often temporary staff are needed to cover duties normally carried out by a permanent employee. This can be due to sickness absence or maternity leave, or it may occur when there is a gap between one person resigning and another taking up the post. Another common approach is to employ new starters on a probationary basis, confirming their appointments as permanent when the employer is satisfied that they will perform their jobs successfully.

Some argue (e.g. Geary 1992) that managers have a preference for temporary staff because the use of such people gives them a greater degree of control over labour. This control derives from the fact that many temporary staff would dearly love to secure greater job security in order to gain access to mortgages and to allow them to plan their future lives with greater certainty. As a result temporary workers are often keenest to impress and will work beyond their contract in a bid to gain permanent jobs. Their absence levels also tend to be low. Because they work under the constant, unspoken threat of dismissal, they feel the need to behave with total compliance to avoid this. Managers sometimes take advantage of such a situation and push people into working harder than is good for them.

The law on the employment of fixed-term workers has changed in recent years and this may well in part account for the reduction in their numbers. Until October 1999 it was possible to employ staff on fixed-term contracts which contained clauses waiving the right to claim unfair dismissal. This meant that the employer could terminate the relationship by failing to renew the contract whether or not there was a good reason for doing so. It was thus possible substantially to avoid liability for claims of unfair dismissal by employing people on a succession of short contracts. For fixed-term contracts entered into after October 1999 waiver clauses no longer apply. Henceforth employers who do not renew a fixed-term contract have had to be able justify their decision just as they do with any other dismissal, if they want to avoid court action. Temporary and fixed-term workers also gained a number of further rights via the Employment Act 2002 which implemented the EU's Fixed-term Work Directive. This seeks to ensure that temporary employees enjoy the same terms and conditions as permanent employees undertaking equivalent roles, that employers inform them of permanent vacancies and allow them access to training opportunities. The new law also seeks to limit the number of times that an employer can renew a fixed-term contract without making it permanent without good reason. After October 2006 people who have been employed on a temporary basis for four years or more will be entitled to permanent contracts unless the employer can objectively justify less favourable treatment. People entering temporary contracts after October 2002 are also now entitled to redundancy payments if they are laid off.

A special type of contract is that for apprenticeship. Although this is not to be seen as a contract of employment for the purpose of accumulating employment rights, it is a form of legally binding working relationship that pre-dates all current legislative rights in employment, and the apprentice therefore has additional rights at common law relating to training. An employer cannot lawfully terminate an apprentice's contract before the agreed period of training is complete, unless there is closure or a fundamental change of activity in the business to justify redundancy.

Part-time contracts

At one time part-time working was relatively unusual and was scarcely economic for the employer as the national insurance costs of the part-time employee were disproportionate to those of the full-timer. The part-time contract was regarded as an indulgence for the employee and only a second-best alternative to the employment of someone full time. This view was endorsed by lower rates of pay, little or no security of employment and exclusion from such benefits as sick pay, holiday pay and pension entitlement. The situation has now wholly changed.

Since the 1960s the proportion of the employed workforce on part-time contracts has increased dramatically. Over a quarter of us (seven million) now work on a part time basis, compared to just 9 per cent in 1961. Table 5.3 shows that this proportion

Table 5.3 Proportion of the total workforce working part time in EU countries (2002)

Country	Per cent	Country	Per cent
Greece	4.5	Austria	18.9
Spain	8.0	Belgium	19.4
Italy	8.6	Denmark	20.6
Portugal	11.3	Germany	20.8
Luxembourg	11.7	Sweden	21.4
Finland	12.4	UK	25.0
France	16.2	Netherlands	43.8
Ireland	16.5	EU Average	18.2

Source: Table compiled from data in Eurostat, *Labour Force Survey*, 2003.

is greater than that in most other EU countries, although there is some difficulty of definition. What is part time? At the moment the British method of calculation classifies anything less than the normal weekly hours at the place of work to be part time, so a part-timer could be working six hours a week or 35. Whatever the definition used, it is clear that the number of part-timers across the EU is steadily growing.

Women account for four-fifths of all part-time workers in the UK, 44 per cent of all female workers being employed on a part-time basis and only 10 per cent of men. Male part-timers are overwhelmingly in the 16–19 and over 65 age groups, suggesting that full-time work is the preference for most men between leaving school and retiring. In the case of women the age pattern is markedly different. Around a quarter of women work on a part-time basis in their twenties, but this figure rises to 40 per cent for women aged 30–34 and to 50 per cent for those aged 35–39. After that the proportion declines somewhat until close to retirement. Among women, therefore, part-time work appears very frequently to be undertaken during the time that their children are at school and that it is the preference for many. Among women with dependent children who work part time, government statistics report that 94 per cent do not want a full-time job (Labour Market Trends 2003c).

Many part-timers work short shifts and sometimes two will share a full working day. Others will be in positions for which only a few hours within the normal day are required or a few hours at particular times of the week. Retailing is an occupation that has considerable scope for the part-timer, as there is obviously a greater need for counter personnel on Saturday mornings than on Monday mornings. Also many shops are now open for longer periods than would be normal hours for a full-time employee, so that the part-timer helps to fill the gaps and provide the extra staffing at peak periods. Catering is another example, as is market research interviewing, office cleaning, clerical work and some posts in education.

Unjustified discrimination against part-time workers has effectively been outlawed in the UK since 1994 when it was held by the courts potentially to amount to indirect discrimination on grounds of sex. Since 2000, however, statute has required that all part-timers and full-timers are treated equally. The Part-time Workers (Prevention of Less Favourable Treatment) Regulations provide that part-time workers are to be given the same pay per hour and the same terms and conditions of employment as full-time colleagues undertaking the same or similar work. All benefits must also be provided to part-timers on a pro-rata basis. Moreover, the regulations state that employers cannot subject workers to a detriment of any kind simply because they work part time. This means, for example, that both part-time and full-time workers must be given equal access to training. It also means that the fact that an employee works part time should not be taken into account when deciding who is to be made redundant. Unlike other forms of direct discrimination, however, in the case of part-timers employers can seek to justify their actions on objective grounds.

Distance working

In the quest for greater flexibility many employers are beginning to explore new ways of getting work done which do not involve individuals working full time on their premises. Working overseas, selling in the field and home-working are the most obvious types of distance working, but advances in information technology have led to increased interest in the concepts of teleworking and tele-cottaging. The term *tele* is the Greek for distant, which is familiar to us in words such as telegram and television.

However, despite the possibilities for such arrangements deriving from new technologies, as few as one in every 50 UK employees are mainly based at home, only a further 2 per cent or so being categorised as 'occasional teleworkers' (IDS 2002c, p. 2).

The main advantage, for both the employer and the employee, is the flexibility that teleworking can provide, but the employer also benefits from reduced office accommodation costs and potential increases in productivity. Employees avoid the increasingly time-consuming activity of commuting to work and can manage their own workload around their home responsibilities and leisure interests. But there is a downside too. Many find working from home all the time to be a rather isolating experience and miss the social life and sense of belonging to a community of colleagues that comes with traditional employment.

The main problem for employers, aside from fostering staff morale, commitment and a sense of corporate identity, is the need to maintain a reasonable degree of management control when the workforce is so geographically diffused. Drawing up an appropriate job specification is thus particularly important in the case of teleworking jobs. It is important to set out clearly defined parameters of action, criteria for decisions and issues which need reference back. Person specifications are also crucial since in much distance working there is less scope for employees to be trained or socialised on the job. In addition, 'small business' skills are likely to be needed by teleworkers, networkers, consultants and subcontractors.

Attention also needs to be given to the initial stages of settling in distance workers. Those off-site need to know the pattern of regular links and contacts to be followed. Those newly recruited to the company need the same induction information as regular employees. In fact, those working independently with less supervision may need additional material, particularly on health and safety. Heightened team-building skills will also be needed to encompass staff who are working on a variety of different contracts and at different locations.

The final key aspect of employing distance workers is the need for a close link between pay and performance. Managers must be able to specify job targets and requirements accurately and to clarify and agree these with the employees concerned. Where a fee rather than a salary is paid, the onus is on the manager to ensure the work has been completed satisfactorily.

Self-employment

In the UK just over three million people are self-employed, which is around 11 per cent of the total workforce. The proportion is somewhat higher in London and the south-east than elsewhere in the country because that is where the industries which employ most self-employed people are most common. Weir (2003) shows that demand for the services of self-employed people is lowest in manufacturing and in the public services. By contrast there are many more opportunities for self-employment in the construction, retailing, property, business services and personal services industries. Three-quarters of self-employed people work for themselves or in partnership with one other person and they are heavily concentrated in skilled trades and professional services occupations. They also tend to be a good deal older than average workers, as many as 31 per cent of older workers employing themselves.

The 1980s saw a substantial growth in the number of self-employed people, but the growth slowed down in the 1990s and has now apparently come to an end. Why this should be is not clear, but it may simply reflect a preference among most people for employment if they are able to secure a job which they enjoy. The growth in self-employment in previous decades, like the growth in temporary working, may therefore simply be a reaction to conditions of relatively high unemployment and low job security. What is clear is that most employed people earn considerably more than most self-employed people (Weir 2003, p. 449). While around 17 per cent of self-employed people earn well in excess of the national average, the big majority earn substantially less. Some running fledgling businesses struggle to earn anything at all. Some of these earnings figures may be subject to some under-reporting for tax avoidance reasons, but they firmly dispel the myth that self-employment is a route to affluence and an easy life. Many more self-employed people work longer hours for less reward than those employed by organisations.

Increasing the proportion of the workforce that is hired on a self-employed basis has both attractions and drawbacks for employers. While self-employed people typically cost more per hour to employ, they only need to be paid for the time they actually spend completing a job or can simply be paid a set fee for the completion of a project irrespective of how long it takes. The fact that they can be asked to tender for work in competition with others tends to further reduce costs, as does the fact that a self-employed person manages their own taxation and pension arrangements. So overall there are often major savings to be made in replacing certain jobs in an organisation with self-employed people. Moreover, as was shown at the start of this chapter, huge swathes of employment rights such as unfair dismissal and paid maternity leave apply only to employees and not to those employed on a subcontracted basis. The negative implications derive from the inevitable fact that a self-employed person is not obliged to work exclusively for one employer or even to work uniquely in the interests of any one organisation. The relationship is thus more distant and conditional on external influences for its continuance. This can mean that only the minimum acceptable levels of quality are achieved in practice and that the contribution made by the worker to longer-term business development is severely limited. An employer can buy a self-employed person's expertise, but cannot draw on the full range of their energies and commitment as is possible in the case of well-managed employees to whom a longer-term commitment has been made and with whom a closer personal relationship has been forged.

CONSULTANTS

Some management consultants are self-employed people who have gained considerable experience over some years and are in a position to sell their expertise to organisations for a fee. Many more are employed by larger firms which also provide a range of other business services. These tend to be younger people who have substantial, specialist, technical knowledge of particular areas of business activity. Consultants offer advice about issues faced by organisations, but they are also in a position to carry out research, to design new policies and procedures, and to brief or train staff in their effective use. Nowadays a lot of their work involves selling already developed IT products to clients and assisting them to put these into operation. In the HR field this is true of consultancies that specialise in job evaluation and in the provision of personnel information systems.

In many ways consultants thus provide a service analogous to that of an accountant, a lawyer or a financial adviser. However the service is packaged, organisations are being invited to buy their professional expertise and to apply it (or not) as they see fit. Substantial demand for such services over recent years has meant that consultancy has grown into a major multi-billion pound international industry employing hundreds of thousands of highly qualified people, many of whom are in a position to charge their clients upwards of £3,000 per day. Yet, despite their having been a fixture on the management scene for decades, there remains considerable cynicism about consultancy as a trade (*see* the poem below entitled 'The Preying Mantis'). The following quotation from the leading industrialist Lord Weinstock is born of disappointing experiences:

> Consultants are invariably a waste of money. There has been the occasional instance where a useful idea has come up, but the input we have received has usually been banal and unoriginal, wrapped up in impressive sounding but irrelevant rhetoric.
> (Caulkin 1997)

WINDOW ON PRACTICE

The Preying Mantis

Of all the businesses, by far,
Consultancy's the most bizarre.
For, to the penetrating eye,
There's no apparent reason why,
With no more assets than a pen,
This group of personable men
Can sell to clients more than twice
The same ridiculous advice,
Or find, in such a rich profusion,
Problems to fit their own solution.
The strategy that they pursue –
To give advice instead of do –
Keeps their fingers on the pulses
Without recourse to stomach ulcers,
And brings them monetary gain,
Without a modicum of pain.
The wretched object of their quest,
Reduced to cardiac arrest,
Is left alone to implement
The asinine report they've sent.
Meanwhile the analysts have gone
Back to client number one,
Who desperately needs their aid
To tidy up the mess they made.
And on and on – ad infinitum –

The masochistic clients invite 'em.
Until the merciful reliever
Invokes the company receiver.
No one really seems to know
The rate at which consultants grow.
By some amoeba-like division?
Or chemobiologic fission?
They clone themselves without an end
Along their exponential trend.
The paradox is each adviser,
If he makes his client wiser,
Inadvertently destroys
The basis of his future joys.
So does anybody know
Where latter-day consultants go? ('Bertie Ramsbottom')

Source: Ralph Windle (1985) *The Bottom Line*. London: Century Hutchinson. Reprinted by permission of the Random House Group Ltd.

The use of consultants is thus a matter about which managers are very divided. In some companies, and increasingly in public-sector organisations, they are employed regularly and found to offer a useful if expensive service. Elsewhere it appears almost to be a matter of policy to resist their blandishments and to tap into alternative sources of advice. The best approach, as with all major purchasing decisions, is to employ them only in situations where there is a good business case for doing so and where they are likely to add value. The most likely scenario is where the organisation needs specialist advice and cannot gain access to it through its internal resources. In the HR field an example would be the need to develop a competitive employment package for an individual who is being sent on long-term expatriate assignment to a country with which people within the organisation are largely unfamiliar. It makes sense in such a situation to take advice from someone who has technical knowledge of the tax systems, pay rates and living standards in that country. Another common situation in which consultants are employed in the HR field is to administer psychometric selection tests to candidates applying for jobs and then to interpret and provide feedback on the results. However, there can also be other reasons for their employment, as Duncan Wood (1985) found in his interviews with well-established HR consultants:

1 To provide specialist expertise and wider knowledge not available within the client organisation.
2 To provide an independent view.
3 To act as a catalyst.
4 To provide extra resources to meet temporary requirements.
5 To help develop a consensus when there are divided views about proposed changes.
6 To demonstrate to employees the impartiality/objectivity of personnel changes or decisions.
7 To justify potentially unpleasant decisions.

ACTIVITY 5.3

What personnel problems currently facing your organisation do you think might best be approached by using outside consultants? Why? How would you specify the requirements?

What personnel problems currently facing your organisation would you not remit to outside consultants? Why not?

The likelihood of securing a positive outcome when employing consultants depends on two conditions being present. First, it is essential that the consultant is given very clear instructions both about the nature of the issue or problem that they are being asked to advise about, and about what the client expects of them. Second, they should only be employed once it has first been established that they are likely to be able to provide knowledge and ideas that cannot be sourced in-house, and that the costs associated with their employment are justified.

WINDOW ON PRACTICE

Typical views about using outside consultants

A Favourable views

1 The HR manager knows what to do, but proposals are more likely to be implemented if endorsed by outside experts.
2 The outsider can often clarify the HR manager's understanding of an issue.
3 Specialist expertise is sometimes needed.
4 The HR manager has insufficient time to deal with a particular matter on which a consultant could work full time.
5 The consultant is independent.
6 Using consultants can be cheaper than employing your own full-time, permanent specialists.

B Less favourable views

1 The HR function should contain all the necessary expertise.
2 In-house HR specialists know what is best for the company.
3 Other members of the organisation are prejudiced against the use of outside advisers.
4 Using consultants can jeopardise the position of the HR specialists and reduce their influence.

OUTSOURCING

Consultants are mainly employed to give advice or to carry out a defined project. In employing them an organisation is effectively subcontracting part of its management process. But organisations can and do subcontract out to specialist service providers a great deal more. The outsourcing of functions which either could be or were previously carried out in-house has become more common in recent years. It is a trend that creates its own momentum because the more outsourcing that occurs, the bigger and better the providers become, making it an increasingly viable proposition for more organisations. Of particular interest to readers of this book is the strong trend that can now be discerned towards the outsourcing (either in whole or in part) of activities that have traditionally been carried out by the HR function in organisations.

According to Colling (2000) the organisational functions which are most commonly outsourced by UK organisations are ancillary services such as cleaning, catering, security, transportation and buildings maintenance. There is nothing new about organisations subcontracting such functions to external providers, but there is clearly an increased trend in that direction. Twenty years ago most larger corporations and the entire public sector managed these ancillary services themselves, employing their own people to carry them out. This is less and less true. Increasingly managers are keen to focus all their energies on their 'core business activities', by which they mean those activities which are the source of competitive advantage and which determine the success or failure of their organisations. There is thus a desire to minimise the amount of management time and effort which is spent carrying out more marginal activities. The decision to outsource is made easier by the fact that specialist security, cleaning and catering companies are often in a position to provide a higher-quality standard of service at a lower cost than can be achieved by in-house operations. This is because for them the provision of ancillary services is the core business and they have the expertise, up-to-date equipment, and staff to run highly efficient operations. Moreover, their size means that they can benefit from economies of scale that are not available to the far smaller locally run operations.

The nature and standard of services that the external company provides are determined by the service level agreement that is signed. This will usually follow on from a competitive tendering exercise in which providers of outsourced services compete with one another to secure a three- or five-year contract. If the standards of service fall short of those set out in the agreement, the purchasing organisation is then able to look elsewhere, and can in any case sign a new agreement with a different provider at the end of the contract. This should ensure that high standards are maintained, but the evidence suggests that outsourcing frequently disappoints in practice. Reilly (2001, p. 135) lists all manner of problems that occur due to poor communication, differences of opinion about the service levels being achieved and different interpretations of terms in the contract. These occur because it will always be in the interests of the providing company to keep its costs low and in the interests of the purchasing company to demand higher standards of service and value for money.

In practice the theoretical advantages of outsourcing thus often fail to materialise. Serious cost savings are often difficult to achieve, largely because the Transfer of Undertakings laws require existing staff to be retained by the new service provider on their existing terms and conditions, yet standards of service may actually decline. Loss of day-to-day control means that problems take longer to rectify because complaints have to be funnelled through to managers of the providing company and cannot simply be addressed on the spot. It is also hard in practice to replace one contractor with another, as well as being costly, because there are a limited number of companies that are both viable over the long term and interested in putting in a bid. So great care has to be taken when adopting this course of action. Expectations need to be managed and deals should only be signed with providers who can demonstrate a record of satisfactory service achieved in comparable organisations.

These potential obstacles have not stopped a number of large corporations from outsourcing large portions of their HR functions in recent years. The service level agreements that are signed typically involve a specialist provider taking over responsibility for the more routine administrative tasks that are traditionally carried out by in-house HR teams. These include payroll administration, the maintenance of personnel databases, the provision of intranet services which set out HR policies, recruitment administration and routine training activities. Such arrangements enable the organisation to dispense with the services of junior HR staff and to retain small teams of more senior people to deal with policy issues, sensitive or confidential matters and union negotiations.

ACTIVITY 5.4

Make a list of all the major activities carried out by your organisation's HR function. Which of these could realistically be outsourced and which could not and why?

SUMMARY PROPOSITIONS

5.1 The law distinguishes between 'employees' and 'workers', the former enjoying a wider range of statutory and contractual rights than the latter.

5.2 Once a contract is established its terms cannot be broken by either party without the consent of the other.

5.3 Patterns of work vary considerably. The traditional Monday to Friday, 9–5 pattern is increasingly giving way to new shift patterns and contractual arrangements.

5.4 In recent years we have seen a growth in the number of 'atypical contracts' such as those which provide work on a temporary or fixed-term basis.

5.5 New technologies allow a greater proportion of people to work from home. This development brings all manner of new challenges for HR managers.

5.6 The use of outside consultants to undertake HR activities is rising.

5.7 Larger organisations and public-sector bodies are increasingly outsourcing functions that are not considered to be 'core' to their operations. This includes some HR activities.

GENERAL DISCUSSION TOPICS

1 What are the advantages and disadvantages of part-time working for the employer and for the employee? In what ways do the age and domestic situation of the employee alter the answer?

2 The chapter indicates some of the problems in employing consultants and specialist outsourcing companies. How can these be overcome?

3 What is the future for teleworking?

FURTHER READING

Beynon, H., Grimshaw, D., Rubery, J. and Ward, K. (2002) *Managing Employment Change: The New Realities of Work*. Oxford: Oxford University Press
This provides a critical perspective on many of the trends introduced in this chapter. The authors draw on seven case studies of UK organisations to explore why employment restructuring is occurring and its consequences.

Colling, T. (2000) 'Personnel management in the extended organisation', in S. Bach and K. Sisson (eds) *Personnel Management: A Comprehensive Guide to Theory and Practice in Britain*. Oxford: Blackwell
This article gives an excellent summary of research into the increased use of outsourcing in the UK and the implications of the trend for HR practice. The author explores all the problematic issues and presents useful case study evidence.

Incomes Data Services (IDS) publications
Incomes Data Services regularly publish studies focusing on different types of contractual arrangement which draw on the experiences of larger UK employers. Recent publications have covered *Annual Hours*, IDS Study 721 (January 2002), *Flexitime Schemes*, IDS Study 725 (March 2002), *Teleworking*, IDS Study 729 (May 2002) and *Outsourcing HR Administration*, IDS Study 746 (Spring 2003).

REFERENCES

Caulkin, S. (1997) 'The great consultancy cop-out', *Management Today*, February, pp. 32–8.

Colling, T. (2000) 'Personnel management in the extended organisation', in S. Bach and K. Sisson (eds) *Personnel Management: A Comprehensive Guide to Theory and Practice in Britain*. Oxford: Blackwell.

European Industrial Relations Review (EIRR) (1998) 'Making way for the 35-hour working week', *EIRR 294*. London: Eclipse Group Ltd.

Eurostat (2003) *Labour Force Survey*. Brussels: European Communities.

Geary, J.F. (1992) 'Employment flexibility and human resource management: the case of three electronics plants', *Work, Employment and Society*, Vol. 4, No. 2, pp. 157–88.

Harkness, S. (1999) 'Working 9–5?' in P. Gregg and J. Wadsworth (eds) *The State of Working Britain*. Manchester: Manchester University Press.

IDS (2000) *24-hour society*, IDS Focus 93. London: Incomes Data Services Ltd.

IDS (2002a) *Annual Hours*, IDS Study 721. London: Incomes Data Services Ltd.

IDS (2002b) *Flexitime Schemes*, IDS Study 725. London: Incomes Data Services Ltd.

IDS (2002c) *Teleworking*, IDS Study 729. London: Incomes Data Services Ltd.

IDS (2003) *Outsourcing HR Administration*, IDS Study 746. London: Incomes Data Services Ltd.

Labour Market Trends (2003a) 'Labour Market Spotlight', *Labour Market Trends*, January, p. 15.

Labour Market Trends (2003b) 'Employment: full-time, part-time and temporary workers', *Labour Market Trends*, November, p. S26.

Labour Market Trends (2003c) 'Part-time Working Patterns', *Labour Market Trends*, March, p. 116.

Lloyds TSB (2003) www.lloydstsbjobs.com.

Office for National Statistics (2003) www.statistics.gov.uk.

Reilly, P. (2001) *Flexibility at Work*. Aldershot: Gower.

Weir, G. (2003) 'Self-employment in the UK labour market', *Labour Market Trends*, September, pp. 441–51.

Windle, R. (1985) *The Bottom Line*. London: Century-Hutchinson.

Wood, D. (1985) 'The uses and abuses of personnel consultants', *Personnel Management*, October, pp. 40–7.

An extensive range of additional materials, including multiple choice questions, answers to questions and links to useful websites can be found on the Human Resource Management Companion Website at www.pearsoned.co.uk/torrington.

CHAPTER 6

RECRUITMENT

THE OBJECTIVES OF THIS CHAPTER ARE TO:

1 IDENTIFY ALTERNATIVE COURSES OF ACTION TO TAKE WHEN AN EMPLOYEE LEAVES AN ORGANISATION

2 EXPLAIN THE ROLE PLAYED BY JOB DESCRIPTIONS AND PERSON SPECIFICATIONS IN THE RECRUITMENT PROCESS

3 COMPARE AND CONTRAST THE MAJOR ALTERNATIVE RECRUITMENT METHODS

4 ASSESS DEVELOPMENTS IN RECRUITMENT ADVERTISING AND INTERNET RECRUITMENT

5 INTRODUCE THE CONCEPT OF EMPLOYER BRANDING

6 CLARIFY THE NEED FOR CONTROL AND EVALUATION PROCEDURES IN RECRUITMENT

7 ASSESS DIFFERENT APPROACHES TO SHORTLISTING

There is always a need for replacement employees and those with unfamiliar skills that business growth makes necessary. Recruitment is also an area in which there are important social and legal implications, but perhaps most important is the significant part played in the lives of individual men and women by their personal experience of recruitment and the failure to be recruited. Virtually everyone reading these pages will know how significant those experiences have been in their own lives.

WINDOW ON PRACTICE

On graduating from university, Howard was employed as a management trainee by a large bank and was soon assigned to taking part in interviews of prospective graduate recruits, which he found interesting and a boost to his ego. After two years in the bank a programme of reorganisation led to Howard being out of a job. It was seven months before he was employed again and he had undergone many disappointments and frustrations. His new post was again in recruitment and he wrote himself a short homily on a postcard which he kept propped up on his desk. It said:

- When you turn someone down, remember:
  - First, what the experience of rejection can do to a person.
  - Second, that the rejected person may be a customer.
  - Third, you may want to recruit that person later.

Over three million people are recruited by employers in the UK each year. It can be a costly and difficult process when skills are in short supply and labour markets are tight. In such circumstances the employer needs to 'sell' its jobs to potential employees so as to ensure that it can generate an adequate pool of applicants. According to Barber (1998) it is important that employers do not consider the recruitment process to be finished at this point. It continues during the shortlisting and interviewing stages and is only complete when an offer is made and accepted. Until that time there is an ongoing need to ensure that a favourable impression of the organisation as an employer is maintained in the minds of those whose services it wishes to secure.

DETERMINING THE VACANCY

Is there a vacancy? Is it to be filled by a newly recruited employee? These are the first questions to be answered in recruitment. Potential vacancies occur either through someone leaving or as a result of expansion. When a person leaves, there is no more than a prima facie case for filling the vacancy thus caused. There may be other ways of filling the gap. Vacancies caused by expansion may be real or imagined. The desperately pressing need of an executive for an assistant may be a plea more for recognition than for assistance. The creation of a new post to deal with a specialist activity may be more appropriately handled by contracting that activity out to a supplier. Recruiting a new employee may be the most obvious tactic when a vacancy occurs, but it is not necessarily the most appropriate. Listed below are some of the options, several of which we discussed in Chapters 4 and 5:

- Reorganise the work
- Use overtime
- Mechanise the work
- Stagger the hours
- Make the job part time
- Subcontract the work
- Use an agency

ACTIVITY 6.1

Can you think of further ways of avoiding filling a vacancy by recruiting a new employee? What are the advantages and disadvantages of the methods you have thought of? For what types of job with which you are familiar would each of your methods, and those listed above, be most appropriate?

If your decision is that you are going to recruit, there are four questions to determine the vacancy:

1. What does the job consist of?
2. In what way is it to be different from the job done by the previous incumbent?
3. What are the aspects of the job that specify the type of candidate?
4. What are the key aspects of the job that the ideal candidate wants to know before deciding to apply?

The conventional HR approach to these questions is to produce job descriptions and personnel specifications. Methods of doing this are well established. Good accounts are provided by Pearn and Kandola (1988), Brannick and Levine (2002) and IRS (2003a). The approach involves breaking the job down into its component parts, working out what its chief objectives will be and then recording this on paper. A person specification listing the key attributes required to undertake the role can then be derived from the job description and used in recruiting the new person. An example of a job description is given in Figure 6.1.

An alternative approach which allows for more flexibility is to dispense with the job description and to draw up a person specification using other criteria. One way of achieving this is to focus on the characteristics or competences of current job holders who are judged to be excellent performers. Instead of asking 'What attributes are necessary to undertake this role?' this second method involves asking 'What attributes are shared by the people who have performed best in the role?' According to some (for example Whiddett and Kandola 2000), the disadvantage of the latter

Job title: SENIOR SALES ASSISTANT

Context
The job is in one of the thirteen high-technology shops owned by 'Computext'
Location: Leeds
Supervised by, and reports directly to, the Shop Manager
Responsible for one direct subordinate: Sales Assistant

Job summary
To assist and advise customers in the selection of computer hardware and software, and to arrange delivery and finance where appropriate.
Objective is to sell as much as possible, and for customers and potential customers to see 'Computext' staff as helpful and efficient.

Job content

Most frequent duties in order of importance

1 Advise customers about hardware and software.
2 Demonstrate the equipment and software.
3 Organise delivery of equipment by liaising with distribution department.
4 Answer all after-sales queries from customers.
5 Contact each customer two weeks after delivery to see if they need help.
6 Advise customers about the variety of payment methods.
7 Develop and keep up to date a computerised stock control system.

Occasional duties in order of importance

1 Arrange for faulty equipment to be replaced.
2 Monitor performance of junior sales assistant as defined in job description.
3 Advise and guide, train and assess junior sales assistant where necessary.

Working conditions
Pleasant, 'business-like' environment in new purpose-built shop premises in the city centre. There are two other members of staff and regular contact is also required with the Delivery Department and Head Office. Salary is £18,000 p.a. plus a twice-yearly bonus, depending on sales. Five weeks' holiday per year plus statutory holidays. A six-day week is worked.

Other information
There is the eventual possibility of promotion to shop manager in another location depending on performance and opportunities.

Performance standards
There are two critically important areas:

1 Sales volume. Minimum sales to the value of £700,000 over each six-month accounting period.
2 Relations with customers:
   - Customers' queries answered immediately.
   - Customers always given a demonstration when they request one.
   - Delivery times arranged to meet both customer's and delivery department's needs.
   - Complaints investigated immediately.
   - Customers assured that problem will be resolved as soon as possible.
   - Customers never blamed.
   - Problems that cannot be dealt with referred immediately to Manager.

Figure 6.1 Job description for a senior sales assistant

approach is that it tends to produce employees who are very similar to one another and who address problems with the same basic mindset (corporate clones). Where innovation and creativity are wanted it helps to recruit people with more diverse characteristics.

INTERNAL RECRUITMENT

Vacancies, of course, are often filled internally. Sometimes organisations advertise all vacancies publicly as a matter of course and consider internal candidates along with anyone from outside the organisation who applies. This approach is generally considered to constitute good practice and is widely used in the UK's public sector. However, many organisations prefer to invite applications from internal candidates *before* they look to their external labour markets for new staff (Newell and Shackleton 2000, pp. 116–17; CIPD 2003, p. 11). There are considerable advantages from the employer's perspective. First it is a great deal less expensive to recruit internally, there being no need to spend money on job advertisements or recruitment agencies. Instead a message can simply be placed in a company newsletter or posted on its intranet or staff noticeboards. Further cost savings and efficiency gains can be made because internal recruits are typically able to take up new posts much more quickly than people being brought in from outside. Even if they have to work some notice in their current positions, they are often able to take on some of their new responsibilities or undergo relevant training at the same time. The other advantage stems from the fact that internal candidates, as a rule, are more knowledgeable than new starters coming in from other organisations about what exactly the job involves. They are also more familiar with the organisation's culture, rules and geography, and so take less time to settle into their new jobs and to begin working at full capacity.

Giving preference to internal recruits, particularly as far as promotions are concerned, has the great advantage of providing existing employees with an incentive to work hard, demonstrate their commitment and stay with the organisation when they might otherwise consider looking for alternative employment. The practice provides a powerful signal from management to show that existing employees are valued and that attractive career development opportunities are available to them. Failing to recruit internally may thus serve to put off good candidates with potential from applying for the more junior positions in an organisation.

The main disadvantage of only advertising posts internally stems from the limited field of candidates that it permits an organisation to consider. While it may mean that someone who 'fits in well' is recruited, it may also very well mean that the best available candidate is not even considered. Over the long term the organisation can thus end up being less well served than it would have been had internal candidates been required to compete with outside people for their posts. For this reason internal recruitment sits uneasily with a commitment to equal opportunities and to the creation of a diverse workforce. Talented candidates from under-represented groups are not appointed because they never get to know about the vacancies that the organisation has.

It is also important to note that the management of internal recruitment practices is difficult to carry out effectively in practice. Research carried out by the Institute of Employment Studies (2002) shows that serious problems often occur when internal candidates fail to be selected. This is because they tend to enter the selection process with higher expectations of being offered the position than is the case with external candidates. Bitterness, antipathy and low morale are thus likely to follow. Moreover, failed internal candidates are considerably more likely to pursue claims of unfair discrimination following a selection process than external candidates. For these reasons it is essential that great care is taken when managing internal recruitment to ensure that the approach taken is both fair and seen to be fair. Giving honest, full, accurate and constructive feedback to failed candidates is an essential part of the process.

METHODS OF RECRUITMENT

Once an employer has decided that external recruitment is necessary, a cost-effective and appropriate method of recruitment must be selected. There are a number of distinct approaches to choose from, each of which is more or less appropriate in different circumstances. As a result most employers use a wide variety of different recruitment methods at different times. In many situations there is also a good case for using different methods in combination when looking to fill the same vacancy. Table 6.1 sets out the usage of different methods reported in a recent CIPD survey of 557 UK employers (CIPD 2003).

It is interesting to compare the figures in Table 6.1 with those reported in surveys of how people actually find their jobs in practice. These repeatedly show that informal methods (such as word of mouth and making unsolicited applications) are as common as, if not more common than, formal methods such as recruitment advertising. In 2002, the Labour Force Survey asked over a million people how they had obtained their current job. The results are shown in Table 6.2.

Table 6.1 Usage of various methods of recruitment by 557 organisations in 2003

Advertisements in local press	84%	Recruiting temporary employees	43%
Specialist journals and trade press	73%	Executive recruitment consultants	41%
Corporate website	72%	Promotional events/careers fairs	37%
Recruitment agencies	71%	Apprentices/work placements	34%
National newspaper advertisements	64%	Speculative applications	34%
Internal intranet	61%	Secondments	32%
Word of mouth	58%	Commercial job-board internet sites	15%
Job Centres/Employment Service	46%	Radio/TV	14%
Education liaison	45%	Posters/billboards	13%

Source: Table compiled from data in CIPD (2003) *Recruitment and Selection Survey*. London: CIPD.

Table 6.2 Methods of obtaining a job

	Men	Women
Hearing from someone who worked there	30%	25%
Reply to an advertisement	25%	31%
Direct application	14%	17%
Private employment agency	10%	10%
Job centre	9%	8%
Other	12%	9%

Source: Labour Market Trends (2002), 'Labour market spotlight', *Labour Market Trends*, August.

THE RECRUITMENT METHODS COMPARED

All the various methods of recruitment have benefits and drawbacks, and the choice of a method has to be made in relation to the particular vacancy and the type of labour market in which the job falls. A general review of advantages and drawbacks is given in Table 6.3.

Table 6.3 Advantages and drawbacks of different methods of recruitment

Job centres		
Advantages:	(a)	Applicants can be selected from nationwide sources with convenient, local availability of computer-based data.
	(b)	Socially responsible and secure.
	(c)	Can produce applicants very quickly.
	(d)	Free service for employers.
Drawbacks:	(a)	Registers are mainly of the unemployed rather than of the employed seeking a change.
	(b)	Produces people for interview who are not genuinely interested in undertaking the job.
Commercial employment agencies and recruitment consultancies		
Advantages:	(a)	Established as the normal method for filling certain vacancies, e.g. secretaries in London.
	(b)	Little administrative chore for the employer.
Drawbacks:	(a)	Can produce staff who are likely to stay only a short time.
	(b)	Widely distrusted by employers.
	(c)	Can be very expensive.
Management selection consultants		
Advantages:	(a)	Opportunity to elicit applicants anonymously.
	(b)	Opportunity to use expertise of consultant in an area where employer will not be regularly in the market.
Drawbacks:	(a)	Internal applicants may feel, or be, excluded.
	(b)	Cost.
Executive search consultants ('headhunters')		
Advantages:	(a)	Known individuals can be approached directly.
	(b)	Useful if employer has no previous experience in specialist field.
	(c)	Recruiting from, or for, an overseas location.
Drawbacks:	(a)	Cost.
	(b)	Potential candidates outside the headhunter's network are excluded.
	(c)	Recruits remain on the consultant's list and can be hunted again.
Visiting universities		
Advantages:	(a)	The main source of new graduates from universities.
	(b)	Rated by students as the most popular method.
Drawbacks:	(a)	Need to differentiate presentations from those of other employers.
	(b)	Time taken to visit a number of universities (i.e. labour intensive).
Schools and the Careers Service		
Advantages:	(a)	Can produce a regular annual flow of interested enquirers.
	(b)	Very appropriate for the recruitment of school-leavers, who seldom look further than the immediate locality for their first employment.
Drawbacks:	(a)	Schools and the advisers are more interested in occupations than organisations.
	(b)	Taps into a limited potential applicant pool.

ACTIVITY 6.2

We have seen the significance of informal methods of recruitment whereby new employees come as a result of hearing about a vacancy from friends, or putting their names down for consideration when a vacancy occurs. Employees starting employment in this way present the employer with certain advantages as they come knowing that they were not wooed by the employer: the initiative was theirs. Also they will probably have some contacts in the company already that will help them to settle and cope with the induction crisis.

What are the drawbacks of this type of arrangement?

RECRUITMENT ADVERTISING

In order to assist them in drafting advertisements and placing them in suitable media, many employers deal with a recruitment advertising agency. Such agencies provide expert advice on where to place advertisements and how they should be worded and will design them attractively to achieve maximum impact. Large organisations often subcontract all their advertising work to an agency with whom a mutually acceptable service-level agreement has been signed.

Recruitment advertising companies (as opposed to headhunters and recruitment consultants) are often inexpensive because the agency derives much of its income from the commission paid by the journals on the value of the advertising space sold, the bigger agencies being able to negotiate substantial discounts because of the amount of business they place with the newspapers and trade journals. A portion of this saving is then passed on to the employer so that it can easily be cheaper *and* a great deal more effective to work with an agent providing this kind of service. The HR manager placing, say, £50,000 of business annually with an agency will appreciate that the agency's income from that will be between £5,000 and £7,500, and will expect a good standard of service. The important questions relate to the experience of the agency in dealing with recruitment, as compared with other types of advertising, the quality of the advice they can offer about media choice and the quality of response that their advertisements produce.

In choosing where to place a recruitment advertisement the aim is to attract as many people as possible with the required skills and qualifications. You also want to reach people who are either actively looking for a new job or thinking about doing so. The need is therefore to place the advertisement where job seekers who are qualified to take on the role are most likely to look. Except in very tight labour markets, where large numbers of staff are required at the same time, there is no point in placing a recruitment advertisement outside a newspaper or journal's recruitment pages. In some situations newspaper readership figures are helpful when deciding where to advertise. An example would be where there are two or more established trade journals or local newspapers competing with one another, both of which carry extensive numbers of recruitment advertisements. Otherwise readership figures are unimportant because people tend to buy different newspapers when job searching than they do the rest of the time. It is often more helpful to look at the share of different recruitment advertising markets achieved by the various publications, as this gives an indication of where particular types of job are mostly advertised. In the UK in recent years the *Guardian* newspaper has gained and sustained a 40 per cent market share of national recruitment advertising. For many jobs in the media, education and the public sector it is now established as the first port of call for job seekers. This has been achieved by cutting rates to less than half those charged by other national newspapers. For the more senior private sector jobs, however, the established market leaders are the *Daily Telegraph*, the *Sunday Times* and the *Financial Times*. While recruitment advertising agents are well placed to advise on these issues, it is straightforward to get hold of information about rates charged by different publications and their respective market shares. Good starting points are the websites of British Rate and Data (www.brad.co.uk), which carries up-to-date information about thousands of publications, and the National Readership Survey (www.nrs.co.uk) which provides details of readership levels among different population groups. Table 6.4 reviews the advantages and drawbacks of various methods of job advertising.

Drafting the advertisement

The decision on what to include in a recruitment advertisement is important because of the high cost of space and the need to attract attention; both factors will encourage the use of the fewest number of words. Where agencies are used they will be able to advise on this, as they will on the way the advertisement should be worded, but the following is a short checklist of items that must be included.

- Name and brief details of employing organisation
- Job role and duties
- Training to be provided
- Key points of the personnel specification or competency profile
- Salary
- Instructions about how to apply

Many employers are coy about declaring the salary that will accompany the advertised post. Sometimes this is reasonable as the salary scales are well known and inflexible, as in much public sector employment. Elsewhere the coyness is due either to the fact that the employer has a general secrecy policy about salaries and does not want to publicise the salary of a position to be filled for fear of dissatisfying holders of other posts, or does not know what to offer and is waiting to see 'what the mail brings'. All research evidence, however, suggests that a good indication of the salary is essential if the employer is to attract a useful number of appropriate replies (*see* Barber 1998, pp. 42–3).

Table 6.4 The advantages and drawbacks of various methods of job advertising

Internal advertisement		
Advantages:	(a)	Maximum information to all employees, who might then act as recruiters.
	(b)	Opportunity for all internal candidates to apply.
	(c)	If an internal candidate is appointed, there is a shorter induction period.
	(d)	Speed.
	(e)	Cost.
Drawbacks:	(a)	Limit to number of applicants.
	(b)	Internal candidates not matched against those from outside.
	(c)	May be unlawful if indirect discrimination. (*See* Chapter 23.)
Vacancy lists outside premises		
Advantage:	(a)	Economical way of advertising, particularly if premises are near a busy thoroughfare.
Drawbacks:	(a)	Vacancy list likely to be seen by few people.
	(b)	Usually possible to put only barest information, like the job title, or even just 'Vacancies'.
Advertising in the national press		
Advantages:	(a)	Advertisement reaches large numbers.
	(b)	Some national newspapers are the accepted medium for search by those seeking particular posts.
Drawbacks:	(a)	Cost.
	(b)	Much of the cost 'wasted' in reaching inappropriate people.
Advertising in the local press		
Advantages:	(a)	Recruitment advertisements more likely to be read by those seeking local employment.
	(b)	Little 'wasted' circulation.
Drawback:	(a)	Local newspapers appear not to be used by professional and technical people seeking vacancies.
Advertising in the technical press		
Advantage:	(a)	Reaches a specific population with minimum waste.
Drawbacks:	(a)	Relatively infrequent publication may require advertising copy six weeks before appearance of advertisement.
	(b)	Inappropriate when a non-specialist is needed, or where the specialism has a choice of professional publications.
Internet		
Advantages:	(a)	Information about a vacancy reaches many people.
	(b)	Inexpensive once a website has been constructed.
	(c)	Speed with which applications are sent in.
	(d)	Facilitates online shortlisting.
Drawbacks:	(a)	Can produce thousands of unsuitable applications.
	(b)	Worries about confidentiality may deter good applications.

ACTIVITY 6.3

Table 6.5 contains phrases about the value in pay terms of 12 different jobs. Try putting them in rank order of actual cash value to the recipient. Then ask a friend to do the same thing and compare your lists.

Table 6.5 Phrases from a quality newspaper about salary

1	*c.*£60,000 + bonus + car + benefits
2	from *c.*£35k
3	£30,000–£40,000 + substantial bonus + car
4	You will already be on a basic annual salary of not less than £40,000
5	Six-figure remuneration + profit share + benefits
6	*c.*£60,000 package
7	Attractive package
8	Substantial package
9	£50,000 OTE, plus car and substantial benefits
10	£ excellent + benefits
11	£ Neg.
12	*c.*£60k package + banking benefits

E-RECRUITMENT

The use of the internet for recruitment purposes is undoubtedly the most striking recent development in the field, but its practical significance remains a question of debate. When the internet first became widely used a decade ago it was often predicted that it would revolutionise the recruitment industry. In the future, it was argued, most of us would find out about jobs through web searches. It now appears that these predictions greatly overstated the influence that the internet would have. Incomes Data Services (2003) came to the following conclusion having carried out an extensive survey of approaches used by UK organisations:

> While advertising on the Internet is fairly common – many organisations now place vacancies on their own websites and make use of third party job boards – among the employers featured in this study this is clearly seen as complementary to, rather than replacing traditional advertising media. Placing advertisements in local and national newspapers and in the trade press continues to be the most important way for many companies to reach potential applicants. IDS (2003, p. 1)

Internet recruitment takes two basic forms. The first is centred on the employer's own website, jobs being advertised alongside information about the products and services offered by the organisation. The second approach makes use of the growing number of cyber-agencies which combine the roles traditionally played by both newspapers and employment agents. They advertise the job and undertake shortlisting before sending on a selection of suitable CVs to the employer.

For employers the principal attraction is the way that the internet allows jobs to be advertised inexpensively to a potential audience of millions. According to Frankland (2000) the cost of setting up a good website is roughly equivalent to that associated with advertising a single high-profile job in a national newspaper. Huge savings can also be made by dispensing with the need to print glossy recruitment brochures and other documents to send to potential candidates. The other big advantage is speed. People can respond within seconds of reading about an opportunity by emailing their CV to the employer. Shortlisting can also be undertaken quickly with the use of CV-matching software or online application forms.

In principle e-recruitment thus has a great deal to offer. In practice, however, there are major problems which may take many years to iron out. A key drawback is the way that employers advertising jobs tend to get bombarded with hundreds of applications. This occurs because of the large number of people who read the advertisement and because it takes so little effort to email a copy of a pre-prepared CV to the employer concerned. In order to prevent 'spamming' of this kind it is necessary to make use of online shortlisting software which is able to screen out unsuitable applications. Such technologies, however, are not wholly satisfactory. Those which work by looking for key words in CVs inevitably have a 'hit and miss' character and can be criticised for being inherently unfair. The possibility that good candidates may not be considered simply because they have not chosen a particular word or phrase is strong. The alternative is to require candidates to apply online by completing an application form or pschyometric test. This approach has the advantage of deterring candidates who are not prepared to invest the time and effort required to complete the forms, but is unreliable in important respects – there is no guarantee that the test is in fact being completed by the candidate, nor is it completed within a standard, pre-determined time limit. Other problems concern fears about security and confidentiality which serve to deter people from submitting personal details over the web:

> Everybody should be familiar with the fear of using a credit card on-line even though good e-commerce sites have secure servers that enable these transactions to take place safely. The job-seeker's equivalent of this is 'how safe is it to put my CV on-line?' Although the figures prove that plenty of people have overcome this fear (there are an estimated 4.5 million CVs on-line), horror stories of candidates' CVs ending up on their employer's desktop aren't entirely without foundation. (Weekes 2000, p. 35)

Criticisms have also been made about poor standards of ethicality on the part of cyber-agencies. As with conventional employment agents there are a number who employ sharp practices such as posting fictional vacancies and falsely inflating advertised pay rates in order to build up a bank of CVs which can be circulated to employers on an unsolicited basis. Some cyber-agencies also copy CVs from competitors' sites and send them on to employers without authorisation. Over time, as the industry grows, professional standards will be established and a regulatory regime established, but for the time being such problems remain.

The fact that there are so many drawbacks alongside the advantages explains why so many employers appear to use the internet for recruitment while rating it relatively poorly. When asked to rank recruitment methods in terms of their effectiveness very few employers place the internet at the top of the list (7 per cent according to the 2003 CIPD survey). Established approaches such as newspaper advertising and education liaison are much more highly rated and are thus unlikely to be replaced by e-recruitment in the near future. However, over the longer term, technological developments and increased web usage may improve the effectiveness of e-recruitment considerably. This will occur when one or two very well-funded job sites emerge from the current mass and are able command substantial shares of the market. We will then have a situation in which anyone seeking a new job in a particular field will make a familiar website rather than the newspaper or journal their first port of call.

WINDOW ON PRACTICE

In 2000 an unemployed 53-year-old electronics manager called David Hall took part in a project commissioned by Wynnwith, an established recruitment company. He spent three months unsuccessfully looking for a job using the services of twelve well-known cyber-agencies. He registered with each, giving full details of his background and skills. At the end of the period he concluded that 'these sites appear to offer little more than pretty coloured graphics and empty promises about job opportunities'. He was offered one interview during the twelve weeks, for a role that was unsuitable given his experience. Of the hundreds of job opportunities emailed to him, he reckoned that only 5 per cent matched his capabilities. Among his criticisms were the following:

- the same jobs were advertised week after week
- very little information was provided about most vacancies
- salary levels were inflated to make jobs more appealing
- he received no feedback on applications that failed
- he was concerned that his CV was being circulated without his consent
- his emails were often not acknowledged

Source: 'Online Recruitment Study' at www.wynnwith.com.

EMPLOYER BRANDING

In recent years considerable interest has developed in the idea that employers have much to gain when competing for staff by borrowing techniques long used in marketing goods and services to potential customers. In particular, many organisations have sought to position themselves as 'employers of choice' in their labour markets with a view to attracting stronger applications from potential employees. Those who have succeeded have often found that their recruitment costs fall as a result because they get so many more unsolicited applications (*see* Taylor 2002, p. 449).

Central to these approaches is the development over time of a positive **'brand image'** of the organisation as an employer, so that potential employees come to regard working there as highly desirable. Developing a good brand image is an easier task for larger companies with household names than for those which are smaller or highly specialised, but the possibility of developing and sustaining a reputation as a good employer is something from which all organisations stand to benefit.

The key, as when branding consumer products, is to build on any aspect of the working experience that is distinct from that offered by other organisations competing in the same broad applicant pool. It may be relatively high pay or a generous benefits package, it may be flexible working, or a friendly and informal atmosphere, strong career development potential or job security. This is then developed as a 'unique selling proposition' and forms the basis of the employer branding exercise.

The best way of finding out what is distinct and positive about working in your organisation is to carry out some form of staff attitude survey. Employer branding exercises simply amount to a waste of time and money when they are not rooted in the actual lived experience of employees because people are attracted to the organisation on false premises. As with claims made for products that do not live up to their billing, the employees gained are not subsequently retained, and resources are wasted recruiting people who resign quickly after starting.

Once the unique selling propositions have been identified they can be used to inform all forms of communication that the organisation engages in with potential and actual applicants. The aim must be to repeat the message again and again in advertisements, in recruitment literature, on internet sites and at careers fairs. It is also important that existing employees are made awarc of their employer's brand proposition too as so much recruitment is carried out informally through word of mouth. Provided the message is accurate and provided it is communicated effectively over time, the result will be a 'leveraging of the brand' as more and more people in the labour market begin to associate the message with the employer.

WINDOW ON PRACTICE

Like many fast food chains, Burger King has found it hard to recruit mangers to run its restaurants. Such workplaces have a poor image in the labour market and lose out as a result in the recruitment of graduates and junior managerial staff, many of whom would prefer to work pretty well anywhere else. Burger King reversed its fortunes to a great extent during 2002 and 2003 by running a shrewd recruitment advertising campaign rooted in an employer branding exercise. The advertisements were strikingly designed and printed in colour to attract attention. A small corporate logo was featured in one corner, but this was dwarfed by slogans which set out what made working as a Burger King manager distinct. The focus was on the following:

- The fact that the job was never dull
- The career development opportunities that were available to ambitious people
- The relatively attractive salary package on offer

In the week after the first advertisement was placed in a local paper two hundred people phoned for further details leading to the appointment of eight new managers. The company's equivalent old-style advertisement had only yielded twenty applicants, none of whom were considered appointable.

Source: IRS (2003b).

CONTROL AND EVALUATION

The HR manager needs to monitor the effectiveness of advertising and all other methods of recruitment, first, to ensure value for money and, second, to ensure that the pool of applicants produced by the various methods is suitable.

Wright and Storey (1994, p. 209) suggest that information on the following should be collected:

1 Number of initial enquiries received which resulted in completed application forms.
2 Number of candidates at various stages in the recruitment and selection process, especially those shortlisted.
3 Number of candidates recruited.
4 Number of candidates retained in organisation after six months.

There is also a good case for monitoring the numbers of men and women who are successful at each stage of the process and the numbers of people from different ethnic minorities. Where an imbalance becomes apparent the organisation can then take remedial action.

There needs, however, to be more information than this in order to get to the more intangible questions, such as 'Did the best candidate not even apply?' The most important source of information about the quality of the recruitment process is the people involved in it. Do telephonists and receptionists know how to handle the tentative employment enquiry? What did they hear from applicants in the original enquiries that showed the nature of their reaction to the advertisement? Is it made simple for enquirers to check key points by telephone or personal visit? Is there an unnecessary emphasis on written applications before anything at all can be done? Useful information can also be obtained from both successful and unsuccessful applicants. Those who have been successful will obviously believe that recruitment was well done, while the unsuccessful may have good reason to believe that it was flawed. However, those who are unsuccessful sometimes ask for feedback on the reasons. If a recruiter is able to give this, it is also a simple development to ask the applicant for comment on the recruitment process.

CORRESPONDENCE

If an organisation is to maximise its chances of recruiting the best people to the jobs it advertises it must ensure that all subsequent communication with those who express an interest is carried out professionally. The same is true of casual enquirers and those who find out about possible vacancies informally through word of mouth. Failing to make a positive impression may well result in good candidates losing interest or developing a preference for a rival organisation which takes greater care to project itself effectively in its labour markets. Providing information to would-be candidates who express an interest is the first step. This is often seen as unnecessary and costly, but it should be seen as the organisation's opportunity to sell itself as an employer to its potential applicant pool. The following are commonly provided:

- a copy of the relevant job description and personnel specification;
- a copy of the advertisement for reference purposes;
- a copy of any general recruitment brochure produced by the organisation;
- the staff handbook or details of a collective agreement;
- details of any occupational pension arrangements;
- general information about the organisation (e.g. a mission statement, annual report or publicity brochures).

It is also essential to have some method of tracking recruitment, either manually or by computer, so that an immediate and helpful response can be given to applicants enquiring about the stage their application has reached. Moreover, it is necessary to ensure that all applicants are informed about the outcome of their application. This will reduce the number of enquiries that have to be handled, but it is also an important aspect of public relations, as the organisation dealing with job applicants may also be dealing with prospective customers. Many people have the experience of applying for a post and then not hearing anything at all. Particularly when the application is unsolicited, HR managers may feel that there is no obligation to reply, but this could be bad business as well as disconcerting for the applicant. Standard letters ('I regret to inform you that there were many applications and yours was not successful . . .') are better than nothing, but letters containing actual information ('out of the seventy-two applications, we included yours in our first shortlist of fifteen, but not in our final shortlist of eight') are better. Best of all are the letters that make practical suggestions, such as applying again in six months' time, asking if the applicant would like to be considered for another post elsewhere in the organisation, or pointing out the difficulty of applying for a post that calls for greater experience or qualifications than the applicant at that stage is able to present.

ACTIVITY 6.4

Recruiters are interested in the job to be done, so that they concentrate on how the vacancy fits into the overall structure of the organisation and on the type of person to be sought. Applicants are interested in the work to be done, as they want to know what they will be doing and what the work will offer to them. Think of your own job and list both types of feature.

The job to be done

1 ....

2 ....

3 ....

4 ....

5 ....

The work that is offered

1 ....

2 ....

3 ....

4 ....

5 ....

How does your listing of features in the second list alter the wording of advertisements and other employment documentation?

SHORTLISTING

Shortlisting of candidates can be difficult in some instances because of small numbers of applicants and in other instances because of extremely large numbers of applicants. Such difficulties can arise unintentionally when there is inadequate specification of the criteria required or intentionally in large-scale recruitment exercises such as those associated with an annual intake of graduates.

In such circumstances it is tempting for the HR department to use some form of arbitrary method to reduce the numbers to a more manageable level. Examples include screening people out because of their age, because of their handwriting style or because their work history is perceived as being unconventional in some way. No doubt there are other whimsical criteria adopted by managers appalled at making sense of 100 or so application forms and assorted curricula vitae. Apart from those that are unlawful, these criteria are grossly unfair to applicants if not mentioned in the advertisement, and are a thoroughly unsatisfactory way of recruiting the most appropriate person.

It is far more satisfactory to have in place a fair and objective system for shortlisting candidates which produces the best group of alternative candidates to move forward to the interview stage. This can be achieved in one of three basic ways – which can be used separately or in combination. The first involves using a panel of managers to undertake shortlisting, reducing the likelihood that individual prejudices will influence the process. A number of distinct stages can be identified:

- **Stage 1:** Panel members agree essential criteria for those to be placed on the shortlist.
- **Stage 2:** Using those criteria, selectors individually produce personal lists of, say, ten candidates. An operating principle throughout is to concentrate on who can be included rather than who can be excluded, so that the process is positive, looking for strengths rather than shortcomings.
- **Stage 3:** Selectors reveal their lists and find their consensus. If stages 1 and 2 have been done properly the degree of consensus should be quite high and probably sufficient to constitute a shortlist for interview. If it is still not clear, they continue to:
- **Stage 4:** Discuss those candidates preferred by some but not all in order to clarify and reduce the areas of disagreement. A possible tactic is to classify candidates as 'strong', 'possible' or 'maverick'.
- **Stage 5:** Selectors produce a final shortlist by discussion, guarding against including compromise candidates: not strong, but offensive to no one.

The second approach involves employing a scoring system as advocated by Roberts (1997) and Wood and Payne (1998). As with the panel method, the key shortlisting criteria are defined at the start of the process (e.g. three years' management experience, a degree in a certain discipline, current salary in the range of £20,000–£30,000, evidence of an ability to drive change, etc.). The shortlister then scores each CV or application form received against these criteria awarding an A grade (or high mark) where clear evidence is provided that the candidate matches the criteria, a B grade where there is some evidence or where the candidate partially meets the criteria and a C grade where no convincing evidence is provided. Where a structured application form has been completed by the candidates, this process can be undertaken quickly (two or three minutes per application) because a candidate can be screened out whenever, for example, more than one C grade has been awarded.

The third approach involves making use of the software systems on the market which shortlist candidates electronically. The different types of system and some of the drawbacks were described above in the section on e-recruitment. Despite the problems, such systems can be useful where the criteria are very clearly and tightly defined, and where an online application form is completed which makes use of multiple-choice answers. Such forms can be scored speedily and objectively, the candidate being given feedback on whether or not they have been successful. Only those who make the 'right' choices when completing the online questionnaire are then invited to participate in the next stage of the recruitment process.

SUMMARY PROPOSITIONS

6.1 Alternatives to filling a vacancy include reorganising the work; using overtime; mechanising the work; staggering the hours; making the job part time; subcontracting the work; using an employment agency.

6.2 Recent trends indicate a greater use by employers of recruitment agencies and executive consultants, open days, recruitment fairs, etc. Relocation constraints have also prompted a move towards the use of regional as opposed to national recruitment advertising.

6.3 Advertising agencies and specialist publications provide a wealth of information to ensure that advertisements reach the appropriate readership.

6.4 E-recruitment provides great potential advantages for employers but is not seen as being especially effective at present.

6.5 Employer branding involves actively selling the experience of working for an organisation by focusing on what makes the experience both positive and distinct.

6.6 Increasing the amount of information provided to potential applicants reduces the number of inappropriate applications.

6.7 Care with shortlisting increases the chances of being fair to all applicants and lessens the likelihood of calling inappropriate people for interview.

GENERAL DISCUSSION TOPICS

1 What are the advantages and disadvantages of graduate recruitment fairs from an employer's point of view?

2 Why is it that the national newspapers which sell the fewest copies (broadsheets) dominate the market for recruitment advertising in the UK, while the more popular tabloids carry virtually none at all?

3 Can you improve on the suggestions for shortlisting that the chapter contains?

FURTHER READING

Barber, A.E. (1998) *Recruiting Employees: Individual and Organizational Perspectives*. Thousand Oaks, Calif.: Sage

Taylor, S. and Collins, C. (2000) 'Organizational Recruitment: Enhancing the Intersection of Research and Practice', in C. Cooper and E. Locke (eds) *Industrial and Organizational Psychology*. Oxford: Blackwell
Academic research on recruitment as opposed to selection processes is relatively undeveloped and there remain many central issues that have not been rigorously studied. In the USA the gap has been filled to some extent in recent years. The best summary and critique of this work is provided by Barber (1998). Taylor and Collins (2000) provide a shorter treatment with an additional practical focus.

Chartered Institute of Personnel and Development
CIPD commissions a large survey each year on recruitment and selection issues which tracks all the major trends and provides authoritative evidence about employer practices. The institute's journal, *People Management*, also publishes a very useful supplement each July reviewing developments in the recruitment industry.

Incomes Data Services, IDS Study No. 751 (June 2003)

Industrial Relations Service (2003d) 'The effective recruitment of managers', *IRS Employment Review*, No. 759, September

Industrial Relations Service (2003e) 'The effective recruitment of computer staff', *IRS Employment Review*, No. 760, October

Industrial Relations Service (2003f) 'The effective recruitment of sales staff', *IRS Employment Review*, No. 761, October
The IDS and IRS publications regularly feature articles and surveys about recruitment practices in UK organisations. The case studies they write are especially useful.

REFERENCES

Barber, A.E. (1998) *Recruiting Employees: Individual and Organizational Perspectives*. Thousand Oaks, Cal.: Sage.

Brannick, M.T. and Levine, E.L. (2002) *Job Analysis: Methods, research and applications for human resource management in the new millennium*. Thousand Oaks, Cal.: Sage.

CIPD (2003) *Recruitment and Retention 2003: survey report*. London: CIPD.

Frankland, G. (2000) 'If you build it, they will come', *People Management*, 16 March, p. 45.

IDS (2003) *Recruitment Practices*, IDS Study No. 751, June. London: Incomes Data Services.

Institute of Employment Studies (2002) *Free, fair and efficient? Open internal job advertising* (W. Hirsh, E. Pollard and P. Tamkin). Brighton: IES.

IRS (2003a) 'Job descriptions and person specifications', *IRS Employment Review*, No. 776, 23 May.

IRS (2003b) 'Better recruitment processes', *IRS Employment Review*, No. 780, 18 July.

Labour Market Trends (2002) 'Labour market spotlight', *Labour Market Trends*, August.

Newell, S. and Shackleton, V. (2000) 'Recruitment and selection', in S. Bach and K. Sisson (eds), *Personnel Management: A Comprehensive Guide to theory and practice*. Oxford, Blackwell.

Pearn, M. and Kandola, R. (1988) *Job Analysis: A practical guide for managers*. London: IPM.

Roberts, G. (1997) *Recruitment and Selection*. London: IPD.

Taylor, S. (2002) *People Resourcing*. London, CIPD.

Weekes, S. (2000) 'Hire on the wire', *Personnel Today*, 2 May, pp. 31–5.
Whiddett, S. and Kandola, B. (2000) 'Fit for the job?' *People Management*, 25 May, pp. 30–4.
Wood, R. and Payne, T. (1998) *Competency Based Recruitment and Selection: A Practical Guide*. Chichester: Wiley.
Wright, M. and Storey, J. (1994) 'Recruitment', in I. Beardwell and L. Holden (eds) *Human Resource Management*. London: Pitman.

An extensive range of additional materials, including multiple choice questions, answers to questions and links to useful websites can be found on the Human Resource Management Companion Website at **www.pearsoned.co.uk/torrington.**

CHAPTER 7

SELECTION METHODS AND DECISIONS

THE OBJECTIVES OF THIS CHAPTER ARE TO:

1. EXPLAIN THE IMPORTANCE OF VIEWING SELECTION AS A TWO-WAY PROCESS
2. EXAMINE THE DEVELOPMENT AND USE OF SELECTION CRITERIA
3. EVALUATE THE RANGE OF SELECTION METHODS THAT ARE AVAILABLE (INTERVIEWING WILL BE DEALT WITH IN DETAIL IN THE INTERACTIVE SKILLS SECTION OF THE FOCUS ON SKILLS AT THE END OF PART II) AND CONSIDER THE CRITERIA FOR CHOOSING DIFFERENT METHODS
4. REVIEW APPROACHES TO SELECTION DECISION MAKING
5. EXPLAIN HOW SELECTION PROCEDURES CAN BE VALIDATED

While the search for the perfect method of selection continues, in its absence HR and line managers continue to use a variety of imperfect methods to aid the task of predicting which applicant will be most successful in meeting the demands of the job, and/or be the best fit with the work group and culture of the organisation. Selection is increasingly important as more attention is paid to the costs of poor selection, in a very competitive market for talent. This context has promoted greater attention to the applicant's perspective and increasing use of technology in selection. In addition equal opportunities legislation has underlined the importance of using well-validated selection procedures, so that the selection process discriminates fairly, and not unfairly, between applicants. Chapters 23 and 24 deal with equal opportunity issues.

SELECTION AS A TWO-WAY PROCESS

The various stages of the selection process provide information for decisions by both the employer and the potential employee. While employment decisions have long been regarded as a management prerogative there is considerable evidence that the two-way nature of the process is now being widely acknowledged, and Lievens *et al.* (2002) suggest that labour market shortages have promoted a concern for the organisation's image and the treatment of applicants during the recruitment and selection process. We must also be concerned not only with the job to be done, but also with the work and the organisational context that is offered.

Throughout the selection process applicants choose between organisations by evaluating the developing relationship between themselves and the prospect. This takes place in the correspondence from potential employers; in their experience of the selection methods used by the employer; and in the information they gain on interview. Applicants will decide not to pursue some applications. Either they will have accepted another offer, or they will find something in their dealings with the organisation that discourages them and they withdraw. When large numbers of candidates withdraw it may be because the information provided by the organisation was sufficiently detailed, accurate and realistic that they were able to make a wise decision that they were not suited to the organisation and that time would be wasted by continuing. On the other hand, it might be that potentially admirable recruits were lost because of the way in which information was presented, lack of information, or the interpretation that was put on the 'flavour' of the correspondence.

The frame of reference for the applicant is so different from that of the manager in the organisation that the difference is frequently forgotten. It would not be unrealistic to suggest that the majority of applicants have a mental picture of their application being received by the company and immediately being closely scrutinised and discussed by powerful figures. The fact that the application is one element in a varied routine for the recipient is incomprehensible to some and unacceptable to many. The thought that one person's dream is another's routine is something the applicant cannot cope with.

If they have posted or emailed an application with high enthusiasm about the fresh prospects that the new job would bring, they are in no mood for delay and they may quickly start convincing themselves that they are not interested, because their initial euphoria has not been sustained. If candidates get as far as interview they will also be influenced by recruiter behaviour in deciding whether to accept a job offer, if one is made. Papadopoulou *et al.* (1996), for example, demonstrated that candidates were influenced by the recruiter's ability to supply adequate and accurate information, as this is what they had expected from the interview. In addition they were influenced by the way the recruiter managed the interaction, as well as the content, so the recruiter's control of the interaction, their listening ability and in particular their ability/willingness to allow the candidate to present themselves effectively are all important.

Some of the points that seem to be useful about interacting with the candidate are:

1 Reply, meaningfully, fast. The printed postcard of acknowledgement is not a reply, neither is the personal letter or email which says nothing more than that the application has been received. Web-based selection can speed things up considerably (for a useful discussion *see* IRS 2001).
2 Conduct correspondence in terms of what the applicants want to know. How long will they have to wait for an answer? If you ask them in for interview, how long will it take, what will it involve, do you defray expenses, can they park their car, how do they find you, etc.?
3 Interviewers should be trained to ensure that they have not only full knowledge of the relevant information, but also the skills to manage the interaction effectively.

SELECTION CRITERIA AND THE PERSON SPECIFICATION

Unless the criteria against which applicants will be measured are made explicit, it is impossible to make credible selection decisions. It will be difficult to select the most appropriate selection procedure and approach, and it will be difficult to validate the selection process. Selection criteria are typically presented in the form of a person specification representing the ideal candidate, and cover such areas as skills, experience, qualifications, education, personal attributes, special attributes, interests and motivation (IRS 2003a). Although the IRS found that person specifications were used by three-quarters of the organisations in their study, Lievens *et al.* (2002) challenge the use of traditional person specifications as jobs become less defined and constantly change. Three perspectives can be used to determine selection criteria – organisational fit, team/functional fit and job fit.

Fit with the organisation

The organisational criteria are those attributes that an organisation considers valuable in its employees and that affect judgements about a candidate's potential to be successful within an organisation. For example, the organisation may be expanding and innovating and require employees who are particularly flexible and adaptable. Previously, these organisational criteria were rarely made explicit and they were often used at an intuitive level. However, Townley (1991) argues that organisations are increasingly likely to focus on more general attitudes and values than narrow task-based criteria. Barclay (1999) explains how fit with the organisation is often expressed in terms of personality, attitudes, flexibility, commitment and goals, rather than the ability to do the specific job for which the person is being recruited. Such organisational criteria are important where jobs are ill defined and constantly changing. There are also some groups who are recruited into the organisation rather than into specific jobs or even a specific function – new/recent graduates, for example, and, here again, organisation criteria are important.

Functional and team fit

Between the generality of the organisational criteria and the preciseness of job criteria there are functional criteria, such as the definition of appropriate interpersonal skills for all members of the HR department. Criteria may also be important when the new appointee will have to fit into a pre-existing work team. For a useful discussion of person/group fit *see* Werbel and Johnson 2001.

Individual job criteria

Individual job criteria contained in job descriptions and person specifications are derived from the process of job analysis. Although it is reasonably easy to specify the factors that should influence the personnel specification, the process by which the specification is formed is more difficult to describe. Van Zwanenberg and Wilkinson (1993) offer a dual perspective. They describe 'job first – person later' and 'person first – job later' approaches. The first starts with analysing the task to be done, presenting this in the form of a job description and from this deriving the personal qualities and attributes or competencies that are necessary to do the task. The difficulty here is in the translation process and the constant change of job demands and tasks. The alternative approach suggested by van Zwanenberg and Wilkinson starts with identifying which individuals are successful in a certain job and then describing their characteristics. There is also a trend towards making the person specification appropriate for a broad band of jobs rather than one particular job.

In addition to, or sometimes instead of, a person specification, many organisations are developing a competency profile as a means of setting the criteria against which to select. Competencies have been defined as underlying characteristics of a person which result in effective or superior performance; they include personal skills, knowledge, motives, traits, self-image and social role (*see* Boyatzis 1982). The advantage of competencies is that they can be used in an integrated way for selection, development, appraisal and reward activities; and also that from them behavioural indicators can be derived against which assessment can take place. For a fuller discussion of the nature and role of competencies, *see* Chapter 17. Woodruffe (2000) and Whiddett and Hollyforde (1999) are useful practical sources of information on how to use competencies in the selection process. It should be noted, however, that using competencies as the only selection criteria is considered to be limiting and unhelpful (*see*, for example, Brittain and Ryder (1999) and Whiddett and Kandola (2000)).

ACTIVITY 7.1

Write a brief job description and a person specification for the anti-rape detective job as described in case 7.1 on the website.

CHOOSING SELECTION METHODS

It is unusual for one selection method to be used alone. A combination of two or more methods is generally used, and the choice of these is dependent upon a number of factors:

1 **Selection criteria for the post to be filled.** For example, group selection methods and assessment centre activities would be most useful for certain types of job, such as managerial, professional, supervisory and those who will be part of self-managing teams.

2 **Acceptability and appropriateness of the methods.** For the candidates involved, or likely to be involved, in the selection. The use, for example, of intelligence tests may be seen as insulting to applicants already occupying senior posts.

3 **Abilities of the staff involved in the selection process.** This applies particularly in the use of tests and assessment centres. Only those staff who are appropriately qualified by academic qualification and/or attendance on a recognised course may administer psychological tests.

4 **Administrative ease.** For administrative purposes it may be much simpler, say, to arrange one or two individual interviews for a prospective candidate than to organise a panel consisting of four members, all needing to make themselves available at the same time. Web-based testing may save much administrative time, particularly when there are large numbers of candidates.

5 **Time factors.** Sometimes a position needs to be filled very quickly, and time may be saved by using telephone or video-based interviews, or organising individual interviews rather than group selection methods, which would mean waiting for a day when all candidates are available.

6 **Accuracy.** Accuracy in selection generally increases in relation to the number of appropriate selection methods used (*see*, for example, IRS 2002a).

7 **Cost.** Tests may cost a lot to set up but once the initial outlay has been made they are reasonably cheap to administer. Assessment centres would involve an even greater outlay and continue to be fairly expensive to administer. Interviews, on the other hand, cost only a moderate amount to set up in terms of interviewer training and are fairly cheap to administer. For the costlier methods great care needs to be taken in deciding whether the improvement in selection decision making would justify such costs.

SELECTION METHODS

Application forms

Growing use is being made of the application form as a basis for employment decisions, and the CIPD (2003) found that they were used in 80 per cent of the organisations they surveyed. For a long time the application form was not suitable for use in that way; it was a personal details form, which was intended to form the nucleus of the personnel record for the individual when they began work. As reservations grew about the validity of interviews for employment purposes, the more productive use of the application form was one of the avenues explored for improving the quality of decisions.

Forms were considered to act as a useful preliminary to employment interviews and decisions, either to present more information that was relevant to such deliberations, or to arrange such information in a standard way. This made sorting of applications and shortlisting easier and enabled interviewers to use the form as the basis for the interview itself, with each piece of information on the form being taken and developed in the interview. While there is heavy use of CVs for managerial and professional posts, many organisations, especially in the public sector, require both – off-putting to the applicant but helpful to the organisation in eliciting comparable data from all applicants.

The application form has been extended by some organisations to take a more significant part in the employment process. One form of extension is to ask for very much more, and more detailed, information from the candidate.

Another extension of application form usage has been in weighting, or biodata. Biodata have been defined by Anderson and Shackleton (1990) as 'historical and verifiable pieces of information about an individual in a selection context usually reported on application forms'. Biodata are perhaps of most use for large organisations filling fairly large numbers of posts for which they receive extremely high numbers of applications. This method is an attempt to relate the characteristics of applicants to characteristics of a large sample of successful job holders. The obvious drawbacks of this procedure are, first, the time that is involved and the size of sample needed, so that it is only feasible where there are many job holders in a particular type of position. Second, it smacks of witchcraft to the applicants who might find it difficult to believe that success in a position correlates with being, *inter alia*, the first born in one's family. Such methods are not currently well used and Taylor (1998) notes the controversial nature and high development costs. In addition the 1998 Data Protection Act prohibits the use of an automated selection process (which biodata invariably are) as the *only* process used at any stage in the procedure.

Generally, application forms are used as a straightforward way of giving a standardised synopsis of the applicant's history. This helps applicants present their case by providing them with a predetermined structure, it speeds the sorting and shortlisting of applications and it guides the interviewers as well as providing the starting point for personnel records. There remain concerns about the reliability of applications forms and CVs and this issue is dealt with in case study 7.2 on the website. Application forms are increasingly available electronically; this not only speeds up the process but also enables 'key word' searches of the data on the forms (for alternative ways in which this may be carried out *see* Mohamed *et al.* (2001)), but there are questions about the legality of this method when used alone.

WINDOW ON PRACTICE

Using application forms electronically at KPMG

KPMG introduced e-selection for graduates in 2000. The driving forces were company image and quicker and smarter recruitment. They first attempted to use the existing application form in electronic format, and then printed out completed forms. They found this unsatisfactory and developed some more radical ideas. The existing application was stripped down to collect only essential information to the selection decision, and so that it takes one hour to complete. It is possible for applicants to fill in the form in one sitting or do it over several sessions, as there are facilities to save separate sections of the form on the web. In addition to the application form candidates complete a self-assessment profile which KPMG match against a standard profile which was developed as a benchmark by an occupational psychology company. Once the candidate has sent the completed application form and self-assessment profile to KPMG via the website KPMG aim to email a decision back to the candidate by the following day, as to whether they will progress to the next stage of the selection procedure.

As a result of these procedures KPMG made cost savings – they have reduced headcount in the central recruitment department by 20 per cent, even though in addition to the electronic procedures they also scrutinise each application form individually. They comment that such systems cannot be introduced quickly and should not just replicate the old paper-based system.

Source: Summarised from IRS (2002b) 'Press to select', *Employment Review*, No. 755, 8 July, pp. 37–42.

Self-assessment and peer assessment

There is increasing interest in providing more information to applicants concerning the job. This may involve a video, an informal discussion with job holders or further information sent with the application form. This is often termed giving the prospective candidate a 'realistic job preview' (Wanous 1992), enabling them to assess their own suitability to a much greater extent. However, the CIPD survey (2003) found that only 2 per cent of organisations have taken the opportunity to provide a self-selection questionnaire on the company website. Another way of achieving this is by asking the candidates to do some form of pre-work. This may also involve asking them questions regarding their previous work experiences which would relate to the job for which they are applying.

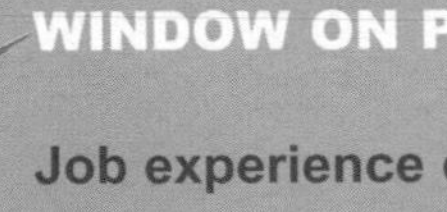

WINDOW ON PRACTICE

Job experience day at Pret à Manger

Pret à Manger have reduced staff turnover from 130 per cent (not high for the industry) to 98 per cent. They put this down to the use of a job experience day, which candidates have to do after an initial interview, but before they are granted a further competency-based interview.

Applicants do a day's work for which they are paid and they receive guidance and mentoring from an existing team member who is assigned to them for the day. But the aim is to enable applicants to work across a wide range of tasks with a wide range of team members. During the day the candidate also has an interview with the shop manager.

Team members who would be the applicant's future colleagues assess the applicant on competencies relevant to the job and then vote at the end of the day as to whether they would employ the applicant. The manager does not get a vote but can lobby for or against any candidate.

The success rate for the day is around 50 per cent. Pret à Manger have found this a good way of sifting large numbers of applicants and at the same time developing team commitment to new recruits.

Source: Summarised from L. Carrington (2002) 'At the cutting edge', *People Management*, Vol. 8, No. 10, 16 May, pp. 30–1.

Telephone interviewing

Telephone interviews can be used if speed is particularly important, and if geographical distance is an issue, as interviews with appropriate candidates can be arranged immediately. CIPD (2003) report that 28 per cent of organisations use this method of selection. There is evidence that telephone interviews are best used as a part of a structured selection procedure, rather than alone – generally in terms of pre-selection for a face-to-face interview. However, they may also have in important role when selecting for jobs in which telephone manner is critical such as call centre and contact centre staff. IRS (2002c) report problems such as lack of non-verbal information and difficulties getting hold of the applicant. However, positive aspects have been reported, such as concentration on content rather than the person. From an applicant perspective IDS found that face-to-face interviews are preferred.

WINDOW ON PRACTICE

One large employer requests CVs from applicants, and, on the basis of these, invites a selected number to take part in a telephone interview. A date and time are given and an idea of the questions that will be asked so that the candidate can prepare. The interview takes about 15–20 minutes, and time is allowed for the candidate to ask questions of the interviewer as well. Candidates are also told in advance of the telephone interview that if they are successful at this stage they will be invited to a one-day assessment centre on a specified date. After the telephone interview candidates are notified in writing whether or not they will move on to the assessment centre stage of the selection procedure.

ACTIVITY 7.2

What are the advantages of using telephone interviews of the type described in the box? For what types of job would you use this approach to selection?

Testing

The use of tests in employment procedures is surrounded by strong feelings for and against. Those in favour of testing in general point to the unreliability of the interview as a predictor of performance and the greater potential accuracy and objectivity of test data. Tests can be seen as giving credibility to selection decisions. Those against them either dislike the objectivity that testing implies or have difficulty in incorporating test evidence into the rest of the evidence that is collected. Questions have been raised as to the relevance of the tests to the job applied for and the possibility of unfair discrimination and bias. Also, some candidates feel that they can improve their prospects by a good interview performance and that the degree to which they are in control of their own destiny is being reduced by a dispassionate routine.

Tests remain heavily used, and the key issue debated currently is the extent to which tests should be administered over the web (*see*, for example, IRS 2002a). IRS reported (in 2003b) that 80 per cent of organisations studied used ability tests and 85 per cent used personality tests, although the CIPD (2003) with a larger sample found much lower figures (around 45 per cent for both). IRS found that testing is more likely to be used for management, professional and graduate jobs (2003b) – although as testing on the web becomes more common it is likely to be used for a wider range of jobs.

Tests are chosen on the basis that test scores relate to, or correlate with, subsequent job performance, so that a high test score would predict high job performance and a low test score would predict low job performance.

WINDOW ON PRACTICE

Online testing at B&Q

B&Q have been using online psychological testing for managers, and this is being extended to all managerial and shop floor appointments. The system cost £12,000 to install and it is expected that costs will be recouped by the end of the first year of full use. B&Q have introduced this in a context of a growing company in a competitive recruitment market, and the tests are open to anyone who can access the website (www.diy.com). Tests are assessed as they are completed and feedback is immediately given to candidates to tell them if they can progress to the next stage of the selection procedure. B&Q argue that this approach avoids bias which may be present when initially assessing CVs. If candidates do not have online access a telephone test is available as an alternative.

E. Davidson (2003) 'You can do it', *People Management*, Vol. 9, No. 4, 20 February, pp. 42–3.

Critical features of test use

Validity

Different types of validity can be applied to psychological tests. Personnel managers are most concerned with predictive validity, which is the extent to which the test can predict subsequent job performance. Predictive validity is measured by relating the test scores to measures of future performance, such as error rate, production rate, appraisal scores, absence rate or whatever criteria are important to the organisation. Sometimes performance is defined as the level of the organisation to which the individual has been promoted – so the criteria here are organisational rather than job specific. If test scores relate highly to future performance, however defined, then the test is a good predictor.

Reliability

The reliability of a test is the degree to which the test measures consistently whatever it does measure. If a test is highly reliable, then it is possible to put greater weight on the scores that individuals receive on the test. However, a highly reliable test is of no value in the employment situation unless it also has high validity.

Use and interpretation

Tests need to be used and interpreted by trained or qualified testers. Test results, especially personality tests, require very careful interpretation as some aspects of personality will be measured that are irrelevant to the job. The British Psychological Society (BPS) can provide a certificate of competence for occupational testing at levels A and B. Both the BPS and CIPD have produced codes of practice for occupational test use. It is recommended that tests are not used in a judgemental, final way, but to stimulate discussion with the candidate based on the test results and that feedback is given to candidates.

In addition it is recommended in the CIPD code that test data alone should not be used to make a selection decision (which could contravene the 1998 Data Protection Act), but should always be used as part of a wider process where inferences from test results can be backed up by other sources. Norm tables and the edition date of a test are also important features to check. For example Ceci and Williams (2000) warn that intelligence is a relative concept and that the norm tables change over time – so using an old test with old norm tables may be misleading.

Problems with using tests

A number of problems can be incurred when using tests.

1 In the last section we commented that a test score that was highly related to performance criteria has good validity. The relationship between test scores and performance criteria is usually expressed as a correlation coefficient (r). If $r = 1$ then test scores and performance would be perfectly related; if $r = 0$ there is no relationship whatsoever. A correlation coefficient of $r = 0.4$ is comparatively good in the testing world and this level of relationship between test scores and performance is generally seen as acceptable. Tests are, therefore, not outstanding predictors of future performance.

2 Validation procedures are very time consuming, but are essential to the effective use of tests. There are concerns that with the growth of web testing, new types of tests, such as emotional intelligence tests, are being developed without sufficient validation (Tulip 2002).

3 The criteria that are used to define good job performance in developing the test are often inadequate. They are subjective and may account to some extent for the mediocre correlations between test results and job performance.

4 Tests are often job specific. If the job for which the test is used changes, then the test can no longer be assumed to relate to job performance in the same way. Also, personality tests only measure how individuals see themselves at a certain time and cannot therefore be reliably reused at a later time.

5 Tests may not be fair as there may be a social, sexual or racial bias in the questions and scoring system. People from some cultures may, for example, be unused to 'working against the clock'.

6 Increasingly organisations are using competencies as a tool to identify and develop the characteristics of high performance. However, as Fletcher (1996) has pointed out, it is difficult to relate these readily to psychological tests. Rogers (1999) reports research which suggests the two approaches are compatible – but there is little evidence to support this so far.

WINDOW ON PRACTICE

Ensuring tests are 'fair and reasonable' and free from ethnic or sexual bias

Indirect discrimination would result when a test unfairly and unjustifiably disadvantages one race or sex compared with another, and test results need to be monitored to show that is not happening. Organisations need to be able to demonstrate that the test has been developed or tailored and assessed in relation to the job content and person specification. Alternative means of taking the test also need to be developed when the use of tests would disadvantage a disabled person.

Source: Summarised from M. Palmer (2002) 'Very testing testing', *People Management*, Vol. 8, No. 1, 10 January, pp. 18–19.

ACTIVITY 7.3

In what ways could you measure job performance for the following?

- A data input clerk
- A mobile plumber
- A call centre operator
- A supervisor

Types of test for occupational use

Aptitude tests

People differ in their performance of tasks, and tests of aptitude (or ability) measure an individual's potential to develop in either specific or general terms. This is in contrast to attainment tests, which measure the skills an individual has already acquired. When considering the results from aptitude tests it is important to remember that a simple relationship does not exist between a high level of aptitude and a high level of job performance, as other factors, such as motivation, also contribute to job performance.

Aptitude tests can be grouped into two categories: those measuring general mental ability or general intelligence, and those measuring specific abilities or aptitudes.

General intelligence tests

Intelligence tests, sometimes called mental ability tests, are designed to give an indication of overall mental capacity. A variety of questions are included in such tests, including vocabulary, analogies, similarities, opposites, arithmetic, number extension and general information. Ability to score highly on such tests correlates with the capacity to retain new knowledge, to pass examinations and to succeed at work. However, the intelligence test used would still need to be carefully validated in terms of the job for which the candidate was applying. And Ceci and Williams (2000) note that intelligence is to some extent determined by the context – so an individual's test score may not reflect capacity to act intelligently. Indeed practical intelligence, associated with success in organisations, may be different from the nature of intelligence as measured by tests (Williams and Sternberg 2001). Examples of general intelligence tests are found in IDS (2000).

Special aptitude tests

There are special tests that measure specific abilities or aptitudes, such as spatial abilities, perceptual abilities, verbal ability, numerical ability, motor ability (manual dexterity) and so on. An example of a special abilities test is the Critical Reasoning Test developed by Smith and Whetton (*see* IDS 2000).

Trainability tests

Trainability tests are used to measure a potential employee's ability to be trained, usually for craft-type work. The test consists of the applicants doing a practical task that they have not done before, after having been shown or 'trained' how to do it. The test measures how well they respond to the 'training' and how their performance on the task improves. Because it is performance at a task that is being measured, these tests are sometimes confused with attainment tests; however, they are more concerned with potential ability to do the task and response to training.

Attainment tests

Whereas aptitude tests measure an individual's potential, attainment or achievement tests measure skills that have already been acquired. There is much less resistance to such tests of skills. Few candidates for a secretarial/administrative post would refuse to take a typing speed test, or a test on 'Word', 'PowerPoint' or 'Excel' software before interview. The candidates are sufficiently confident of their skills to welcome the opportunity to display them and be approved. Furthermore, they know what they are doing and will know whether they have done well or badly. They are in control, while they feel that the tester is in control of intelligence and personality tests as the candidates do not understand the evaluation rationale. Attainment tests are often devised by the employer.

Personality tests

The debate still rages as to the importance of personality for success in some jobs and organisations. The need for personality assessment may be high but there is even more resistance to tests of personality than to tests of aptitude, partly because of the reluctance to see personality as in any way measurable. There is much evidence to suggest that personality is also context dependent, and Iles and Salaman (1995) also argue that personality changes over time. Both of these factors further complicate the issue. Personality tests are mainly used for management, professional and graduate jobs, although there is evidence of their use when high-performance teams are developed.

Theories of human personality vary as much as theories of human intelligence. Jung, Eysenck and Cattell, among others, have all proposed different sets of factors/traits which can be assessed to describe personality. Based on research to date Robertson (2001) argues that it is now possible to state that there are five basic building blocks of personality: extroversion/introversion; emotional stability; agreeableness; conscientiousness and openness to new experiences.

It is dangerous to assume that there is a standard profile of 'the ideal employee' (although this may fit nicely with theories of culture change) or the ideal personality for a particular job, as the same objectives may be satisfactorily achieved in different ways by different people. Another problem with the use of personality tests is that they rely on an individual's willingness to be honest, as the socially acceptable answer or the one best in terms of the job are seemingly easy to pick out, although 'lie detector' questions are usually built in. Ipsative* tests may seek to avoid the social desirability problem by using a different test structure – but other problems arise from this approach. Dalen *et al.* (2001) did show that tests are manipulable but not sufficiently for the candidate to match an ideal profile, and that such manipulation would be exposed by detection measures within the test. There is a further problem that some traits measured by the test will not be relevant in terms of performance on the job. Myers–Briggs is a well used personality test; for details *see* McHenry (2002). There is at the time of writing an interest in emotional intelligence – tests measure self-awareness, self-motivation, emotional control, empathy and the ability to understand and inspire others.

---

* Ipsative tests require the candidate to make a *choice*, usually between two statements or adjectives, rather than allowing the candidate to answer, for example, 'true' or 'false' against every statement.

WINDOW ON PRACTICE

Online testing: the case for and against

While online tests are not widely used at present, there is much interest in developing this area. Tests can be used in one of three different ways:

- uncontrolled – anyone can register to use them on the open internet;
- controlled – the candidate needs first to be registered by the organisation using the test, and their identity must be checked;
- supervised – as above, and a qualified tester from the organisation also logs on and ensures that time limits and other requirements are met.

For:

- Cheaper in the long run
- Immediate analysis
- Immediate feedback to candidate
- Can be used for wider range of (lower-paid) jobs
- Speeds processes and helps to retain potential candidates
- Good for company image
- Can use a wider range of different tests – e.g. video scenarios, followed by 'what would you do next?'
- Can be convenient for applicants

Against:

- Worries over confidentiality and security of personal data
- Appears cold and impersonal
- Open to misuse – who is actually completing the test?
- Can encourage the rapid development of new tests which are not properly validated

Group selection methods and assessment centres

Group methods

The use of group tasks to select candidates is not new – the method dates back to the Second World War – but such measures have gained greater attention through their use in assessment centres. Plumbley (1985) describes the purpose of group selection methods as being to provide evidence about the candidate's ability to:

- get on with others;
- influence others and the way they do this;
- express themselves verbally;
- think clearly and logically;

- argue from past experience and apply themselves to a new problem;
- identify the type of role they play in group situations.

These features are difficult on the whole to identify using other selection methods and one of the particular advantages of group selection methods is that they provide the selector with examples of behaviour on which to select. When future job performance is being considered it is behaviour in the job that is critical, and so selection using group methods can provide direct information on which to select rather than indirect verbal information or test results. The increasing use of competencies and behavioural indicators, as a way to specifiy selection criteria, ties in well with the use of group methods.

Plumbley (1985) identifies three main types of group task that can be used, each of which would be observed by the selectors:

1 **Leaderless groups:** A group of about 6–8 individuals are given a topic of general interest to discuss.
2 **Command or executive exercises:** The members of the group are allocated roles in an extensive brief based on a real-life situation. Each member outlines his or her solution on the basis of their role and defends it to the rest of the group.
3 **Group problem solving:** The group is leaderless and has to organise itself in order to solve, within time limits, a problem that is relevant to the job to be filled. Such tasks may be developed into business games and case studies.

Group selection methods are most suitable for management, graduate and sometimes supervisory posts. One of the difficulties with group selection methods is that it can be difficult to assess an individual's contribution, and some people may be unwilling to take part.

ACTIVITY 7.4

To what extent does a person's behaviour on these group selection tasks accurately reflect behaviour on the job? Why?

Assessment centres

Assessment centres incorporate multiple selection techniques, and group selection methods outlined above form a major element, together with other work simulation exercises such as in-basket tasks, psychological tests, a variety of interviews and presentations. Assessment centres are used to assess, in depth, a group of broadly similar applicants, using a set of competencies required for the post on offer and a series of behavioural statements which indicate how these competencies are played out in practice. Even assuming that the competencies for the job in question have already been identified, assessment centres require a lengthy design process to select the appropriate activities so that every competency will be measured via more than one task. IRS (2002d) note that assessment centres have been proven to be one of the most effective ways of selecting candidates – this is probably due to the use of multiple measures.

Day One Times	Activity	Who is involved
9.30–10.00	Introduction to centre	All
10.00–10.45	General discussion – given topics	All
10.45–11.15	Coffee	
11.15–12.00	General intelligence test	All
12.00–12.30	One-to-one interviews (30 mins each)	Candidates A, B, C
12.30–1.30	Lunch	
1.30–2.00	One-to-one interviews (30 mins each)	Candidates B, E, C
2.00–2.45	Spatial reasoning test	All
2.45–3.15	Coffee	
3.15–4.00	Personality test	All
4.00–4.30	One-to-one interviews (30 mins each)	Candidates C, F, D

Day Two Times	Activity	Who is involved
9.30–10.15	Verbal reasoning test	All
10.15–10.45	One-to-one interviews (30 mins each)	Candidates D, A, F
10.45–11.15	Coffee	
11.15–12.00	Critical thinking test	All
12.00–12.30	One-to-one interviews (30 mins each)	Candidates E, B, A
12.30–1.30	Lunch	
1.30–3.00	In-tray exercise	All
3.00–3.30	Coffee	
3.30–4.00	One-to-one interviews (30 mins each)	Candidates F, D, E

Note: Based on six candidates (A, B, C, D, E, F) and three assessors.

Figure 7.1 An example of the scheduling of events – based on an assessment centre for a professional post (central government)

A matrix is usually developed to show how the required competencies and the activities link up together. In terms of running the centre sufficient well-trained assessors will be needed, usually based on the ratio of one assessor for two candidates to ensure that the assessor can observe each candidate sufficiently carefully. Lists of competencies and associated behaviours will need to be drawn up as checklists and a careful plan will need to be made of how each candidate will move around the different activities – an example of which is found in Figure 7.1. Clearly candidates will need to be very well briefed both before and at the start of the centre.

At the end of the procedure the assessors have to come to agreement on a cumulative rating for each individual, related to job requirements, taking into account all the selection activities. The procedure as a whole can then be validated against job performance rather than each separate activity. The predictive validities from such procedures are not very consistent, but there is a high 'face validity' – a feeling that this is a fairer way of selecting people. Reliability can also be improved by the quality of assessor training, careful briefing of assessors and a predetermined structured approach to marking. The chief disadvantages of these selection methods are that they are a costly and time-consuming procedure, for both the organisation and the candidates. The time commitment is extended by the need to give some feedback to candidates who have been through such a long procedure which involves psychological assessment – although feedback is still not always available for candidates. There is evidence of increasing use of assessment centres and CIPD (2003) reports that 47.5 per cent of organistaions in its survey used such centres for selection. Some organisations have been improving their centres (*see* IRS 2002d) by making the activities more connected or by using longer simulations or scenarios which are a reflection of real-life experience on the job, and are carrying out testing separately from the centre. Some are assessing candidates against the values of the company rather than a specific job, in view of the rapid change in the nature of jobs, and others, such as Britvic, are running a series of assessment centres which candidates must attend, rather than only one. A helpful text relating competency profiles and assessment centre activities is Woodruffe (2000) and IDS (2002) provides examples of different company experiences.

Work sampling/portfolios

Work sampling of potential candidates for permanent jobs can take place by assessing candidates' work in temporary posts or on government training schemes in the same organisation. For some jobs, such as photographers and artists, a sample of work in the form of a portfolio is expected to be presented at the time of interview. Kanter (1989) suggests that managers and professionals should also be developing portfolios of their work experiences and achievements as one way of enhancing their employability.

References

One way of informing the judgement of managers who have to make employment offers to selected individuals is the use of references. Candidates provide the names of previous employers or others with appropriate credentials and then prospective employers request them to provide information. Reference checking is increasing as organisations react to scandals in the media and aim to protect themselves from rogue applicants (IRS 2002e). There are two types: the factual check and the character reference.

The factual check

The factual check is fairly straightforward as it is no more than a confirmation of facts that the candidate has presented. It will normally follow the employment interview and decision to offer a post. It simply confirms that the facts are accurate. The knowledge that such a check will be made – or may be made – will help focus the mind of candidates so that they resist the temptation to embroider their story.

The character reference

The character reference is a very different matter. Here the prospective employer asks for an opinion about the candidate before the interview so that the information gained can be used in the decision-making phases. The logic of this strategy is impeccable: who knows the working performance of the candidate better than the previous employer? The wisdom of the strategy is less sound, as it depends on the writers of references being excellent judges of working performance, faultless communicators and – most difficult of all – disinterested. The potential inaccuracies of decisions influenced by character references begin when the candidate decides who to cite. They will have some freedom of choice and will clearly choose someone from whom they expect favourable comment, perhaps massaging the critical faculties with such comments as: 'I think references are going to be very important for this job' or 'You will do your best for me, won't you?'

Other methods

A number of other less conventional methods such as physiognomy, phrenology, body language, palmistry, graphology and astrology have been suggested as possible selection methods. While these are fascinating to read about there is little evidence to suggest that they could be used effectively. Thatcher (1997) suggests that the use of graphology is around 10 per cent in Holland and Germany and that it is regularly used in France; in the UK he found nine per cent of small firms (with fewer than 100 employees), one per cent of medium-sized firms (100–499 employees) and five per cent of larger firms used graphology as a selection method. In 1990 Fowler suggested that the extent of use of graphology is much higher in the UK than reported figures indicate, as there is some reluctance on the part of organisations to admit that they are using graphology for selection purposes. There are also concerns about the quality of graphologists – who can indeed set themselves up with no training whatsoever. The two main bodies in this field in the UK are the British Institute of Graphology and the International Graphology Association and both these organisations require members to gain qualifications before they can practise.

WINDOW ON PRACTICE

It is interesting to contrast different approaches to selection in different countries. Bulois and Shackleton (1996) note that interviews are the cornerstone of selection activity in both Britain and France, but that they are consciously used in different ways. In Britain they argue that interviews are increasingly structured and criterion referenced, whereas in France the approach tends to be deliberately unstructured and informal. They note that in France the premise is that 'the more at ease the candidates are, the higher the quality of their answer', whereas in Britain they characterise the premise as 'the more information you get about an individual, the better you know him/her and the more valid and reliable your judgement is' (p. 129). Tixier (1996), in a survey covering the EU (but excluding France), Switzerland, Sweden and Austria, found that structured interviews were favoured in the UK, Scandinavia, Germany and Austria. This contrasted with Italy, Portugal, Luxembourg and Switzerland where unstructured styles were preferred.

Bulois and Shackleton identify selectors in Britain as more aware of the limitations of interviews and as attempting to reduce the subjectivity by also carrying out assessment centres and psychological tests; whereas in France these methods were identified as unnatural, tedious and frustrating. Interviews are much more likely to be supplemented by handwriting analysis in France – both methods being identified as valuable, flexible and cheap sources of information. Shackleton and Newell (1991) report that handwriting analysis was used in 77 per cent of the organisations that they surveyed in France compared with 2.6 per cent of the organisations they surveyed in the UK.

Both culture and employment legislation clearly have an influence on the selection methods adopted in any country and the way in which they are used.

ACTIVITY 7.5

Design an assessment centre for the anti-rape detective job as described in case 7.1 on the website.

FINAL SELECTION DECISION MAKING

The selection decision involves measuring each candidate against the selection criteria defined in the person specification, and not against each other. A useful tool to achieve this is the matrix in Figure 7.2. This is a good method of ensuring that every candidate is assessed against each selection criterion and in each box in the matrix the key details can be completed. The box can be used whether a single selection method was used or multiple methods. If multiple methods were used and contradictory information is found against any criterion, this can be noted in the decision-making process.

When more than one selector is involved there is some debate about how to gather and use the information and judgement of each selector. One way is for each selector to assess the information collected separately, and then for all selectors to meet to discuss assessments. When this approach is used, there may be some very different assessments, especially if the interview was the only selection method used. Much heated and time-consuming debate can be generated, but the most useful aspect of this process is sharing the information in everyone's matrix to understand how judgements have been formed. This approach is also helpful in training interviewers.

An alternative approach is to fill in only one matrix, with all selectors contributing. This may be quicker, but the drawback is that the quietest member may be the one who has all the critical pieces of information. There is a risk that all the information may not be contributed to the debate in progress. Iles (1992), referring to assessment centre decisions, suggests that the debate itself may not add to the quality of the decision, and that taking the results from each selector and combining them is just as effective.

Selection criteria	**Candidate 1**	**Candidate 2**	**Candidate 3**	**Candidate 4**
Criterion a				
Criterion b				
Criterion c				
Criterion d				
Criterion e				
General comments				

Figure 7.2 A selection decision-making matrix

VALIDATION OF SELECTION PROCEDURES

We have already mentioned how test scores may be validated against eventual job performance for each individual in order to discover whether the test score is a good predictor of success in the job. In this way we can decide whether the test should be used as part of the selection procedure. The same idea can be applied to the use of other individual or combined selection methods.

The critical information that is important for determining validity is the selection criteria used, the selection processes used, an evaluation of the individual at the time of selection and current performance of the individual.

Unfortunately we are never in a position to witness the performance of rejected candidates and compare this with those we have employed. However, if a group of individuals are selected at the same time, for example, graduate trainees, it will be unlikely that they were all rated equally highly in spite of the fact that they were all considered employable. It is useful for validation purposes if a record is made of the scores that each achieved in each part of the selection process. Test results are easy to quantify, and for interview results a simple grading system can be devised.

Current performance includes measures derived from the job description, together with additional performance measures:

1 **Measures from the job description:** quantitative measures such as volume of sales, accuracy, number of complaints and so on may be used, or qualitative measures such as relations with customers and quality of reports produced.
2 **Other measures:** these may include appraisal results, problems identified, absence data and, of course, termination.

Current performance is often assessed in an intuitive, subjective way, and while this may sometimes be useful it is no substitute for objective assessment.

Selection ratings for each individual can be compared with eventual performance over a variety of time periods. Large discrepancies between selection and performance ratings point to further investigation of the selection criteria and methods used. The comparison of selection rating and performance rating can also be used to compare the appropriateness of different selection criteria, and the usefulness of different selection methods.

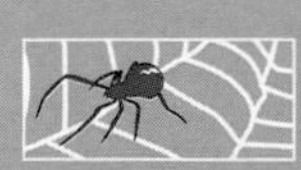

ACTIVITY 7.6

How would you validate the selection process for the anti-rape detective job as described in case 7.1 on the website?

SUMMARY PROPOSITIONS

7.1 Selection is a two-way process. The potential employer and the potential employee both make selection decisions.

7.2 A combination of selection methods is usually chosen, based upon the job, appropriateness, acceptability, time, administrative ease, cost, accuracy and the abilities of the selection staff. Different countries often have a different view on which methods are most appropriate.

7.3 The most well-used selection methods are application forms, interviews (including those conducted by video and telephone), tests, group selection procedures, assessment centres and references.

7.4 A procedure for selection decision making needs to be agreed which can integrate all the selection information available.

7.5 Selection methods should be validated. A simple system is better than no system at all.

GENERAL DISCUSSION TOPICS

1 It could be argued that the selection process identifies candidates who are competent in the selection process rather than candidates who are most competent to perform the job on offer. Discuss this in relation to all forms of selection.

2 'It is unethical and bad for business to make candidates undergo a selection assessment centre without providing detailed feedback and support.' Discuss.

FURTHER READING

International Journal of Selection and Assessment, Vol. 11, No. 2/3, June/September 2003
This is a special edition of the journal and it is devoted to the role of technology in shaping the future of staffing and assessment. Contains some highly relevant articles, including, for example, using technology in the recruiting, screening and selection process; applicant and recruiter reactions to technology; internet-based personality testing and privacy in internet-based selection systems.

IRS (2002) 'Of good character: supplying references and providing access', *Employment Review*, No. 754, 24 June, pp. 34–6
Second of a two-part series on references – this one concentrating on providing references and employee access to references about them. Useful to read this in conjunction with No. 752, 27 May, entitled 'The check's in the post' which focuses on the legal position and on the content and nature of references.

Strudwick, L. (2002) *Training for Assessment Centres*. Aldershot: Gower
A good resource pack, although expensive. Includes the development of exercises, roles of assessors, competencies, the nature of evidence, observation and recording techniques, planning and organising the centre.

REFERENCES

Anderson, N. and Shackleton, V. (1990) 'Staff selection decision making into the 1990s', *Management Decision*, Vol. 28, No. 1.

Barclay, J. (1999) 'Employee Selection: a question of structure', *Personnel Review*, Vol. 28, No. 1/2, pp. 134–51.

Boyatzis, R. (1982) *The Competent Manager*. Chichester: John Wiley.

Brittain, S. and Ryder, P. (1999) 'Get complex', *People Management*, 25 November, pp. 48–51.

Bulois, N. and Shackleton, V. (1996) 'A qualitative study of recruitment and selection in France and Britain: the attitudes of recruiters in multinationals', in I. Beardwell (chair), *Contemporary Developments in Human Resource Management*. Paris: Editions ESKA, pp. 125–35.

Carrington L. (2002) 'At the cutting edge', *People Management*, Vol. 8, No. 10, pp. 30–1.

Ceci, S. and Williams, W. (2000) 'Smart Bomb', *People Management*, 24 August, pp. 32–6.

CIPD (2003) *Recruitment and Retention 2003*. London: CIPD.

Dalen, L., Stanton, N. and Roberts, A. (2001) 'Faking personality questionnaires in selection', *Journal of Management Development*, Vol. 20, No. 8, pp. 729–41.

Davidson, E. (2003) 'You can do it', *People Management*, Vol. 9, No. 4, 20 February, pp. 42–3.

Fletcher, C. (1996) 'Mix and match fails to work on competencies', *People Management*, September.

Fowler, A. (1990) 'The writing on the wall', *Local Government Chronicle*, 26 January, pp. 20–8.

Iles, P. (1992) 'Centres of excellence? Assessment and development centres, managerial competence and human resource strategies', *British Journal of Management*, Vol. 3, pp. 79–90.

Iles, P. and Salaman, G. (1995) 'Recruitment, selection and assessment', in J. Storey (ed.) *Human Resource Management: A critical text*. London: Routledge.

Incomes Data Services (2000) *IDS Study Plus: Psychological Tests*, Spring. London: IDS.

Incomes Data Services (2002) *Assessment Centres*, IDS Study No. 735, 25 September. London: IDS.

IRS (2001) 'Screen Test', *Employee Development Bulletin*, No. 140, pp. 7–10.

IRS (2002a) 'Psychometrics: the next generation', *Employment Review*, No. 744, 28 January, pp. 36–40.

IRS (2002b) 'Press to select', *Employment Review*, No. 755, 8 July, pp. 37–42.

IRS (2002c) 'I've got your number: telephone interviewing', *Employment Review*, No. 756, 22 July, pp. 34–6.

IRS (2002d) 'Focus of attention', *Employment Review*, No. 749, 15 April, pp. 36–41.

IRS (2002e) 'The check's in the post', *Employment Review*, No. 752, 27 May, pp. 34–42.

IRS (2003a) 'Setting the tone: job descriptions and person specifications', *Employment Review*, No. 776, 23 May, pp. 42–8.

IRS (2003b) 'Testing times for selectors', *Employment Review*, No. 769, 7 February, pp. 32–8.

Kanter, R.M. (1989) *When Giants Learn to Dance*. New York: Simon and Schuster.

Lievens F., van Dam, K. and Anderson N. (2002) 'Recent trends and challenges in personnel selection', *Personnel Review*, Vol. 31, No. 5, pp. 580–601.

McHenry, R. (2002) 'The Myers–Briggs Response', *People Management*, Vol. 8, No. 24, 5 December, p. 34.

Mohamed, A., Orife, J. and Wibowo, K. (2001) 'The legality of a key word search as a personnel selection tool', *Personnel Review*, Vol. 24, No. 5, pp. 516–22.

Palmer, M. (2002) 'Very testing testing', *People Management*, Vol. 8, No. 1, 10 January, pp. 18–19.

Papadopoulou, A., Ineson, E. and Williams, D. (1996) 'The graduate management trainee pre-selection interview', *Personnel Review*, Vol. 25, No. 4, pp. 21–37.

Plumbley, P.R. (1985) *Recruitment and Selection*, 4th edn. London: Institute of Personnel Management.

Robertson, I. (2001) 'Undue diligence', *People Management*, Vol. 7, No. 23, 22 November, pp. 42–3.

Rogers, G. (1999) 'All round vision', *People Management*, 2 July.

Shackleton, V. and Newell, S. (1991) 'Management selection: a comparative survey of methods used in top British and French companies', *Journal of Occupational Psychology*, Vol. 64, pp. 23–36.

Sigman, A. (2002) 'Body of evidence' *People Management*, Vol. 8, No. 5, 7 March, pp. 48–9.

Taylor, S. (1998) *Employee Resourcing*. London: IPD.

Thatcher, M. (1997) 'A test of character', *People Management*, 15 May.

Tixier, M. (1996) 'Employers' recruitment tools across Europe', *Employee Relations*, Vol. 18, No. 6, pp. 67–78.

Townley, B. (1991) 'Selection and appraisal: reconstituting social relations?' in J. Storey (ed.) *New Perspectives in Human Resource Management*. London: Routledge.

Tulip, S. (2002) Personality trait secrets', *People Management*, Vol. 8, No. 17, pp. 34–8.

van Zwanenberg, N. and Wilkinson, L.J. (1993) 'The person specification – a problem masquerading as a solution?' *Personnel Review*, Vol. 22, No. 7, pp. 54–65.

Wanous, J.P. (1992) *Organisational Entry: Recruitment, Selection, Orientation and Socialisation of Newcomers*. Reading, Mass.: Addison-Wesley.

Werbel, J. and Johnson, D. (2001) 'The use of person-group fit for employment selection: a missing link in person-environment fit' *Human Resource Management*, Vol. 40, No. 3, pp. 227–40, Fall.

Whiddett, S. and Hollyforde, S. (1999) *The competencies handbook*. London: IPD.

Whiddett, S. and Kandola, B. (2000) 'Fit for the job?' *People Management*, 25 May.

Wilkinson, L.J. and van Zwanenberg, N. (1994) 'Development of a person specification system for managerial jobs', *Personnel Review*, Vol. 23, No. 1, pp. 25–36.

Williams, W. and Sternberg, R. (2001) *Success for Managers*. London: Lawrence Erlbaum Associates.

Woodruffe, C. (2000) *Development and Assessment Centres: Identifying and assessing competence*, 3rd edn. London: IPD.

An extensive range of additional materials, including multiple choice questions, answers to questions and links to useful websites can be found on the Human Resource Management Companion Website at **www.pearsoned.co.uk/torrington.**

CHAPTER 8

STAFF RETENTION

THE OBJECTIVES OF THIS CHAPTER ARE TO:

1. EXAMINE RECENT TRENDS IN JOB TENURE AND TURNOVER IN THE UK
2. ASSESS THE ARGUMENTS FOR AND AGAINST INVESTING RESOURCES IN STAFF TURNOVER REDUCTION PROGRAMMES
3. OUTLINE THE MAIN REASONS FOR VOLUNTARY RESIGNATIONS
4. SET OUT HOW STAFF TURNOVER CAN BE COSTED
5. EXPLORE SOME APPROACHES WHICH IMPROVE STAFF RETENTION RATES

The last three chapters focused on the processes used to mobilise a workforce: activities which are often expensive and time consuming. It is estimated that the costs associated with recruiting and training a new employee average between half and one and a half times the annual salary for the post in question, depending on the approaches used (Thompson 2000). In this chapter we consider the most important way in which human resource managers seek to reduce the time and money spent on these activities, namely by trying to ensure that people choose not to leave an organisation voluntarily in the first place.

The extent of interest in employee retention issues varies over time as labour markets become successively tighter and looser depending on economic conditions. In recent years, as unemployment has fallen, making it harder to recruit staff with the necessary skills and attitudes, the subject has again moved up the HRM agenda. This has led to the publication of several new books and articles exploring how organisations can ensure that they have the best chance of retaining the people they employ. The authors tend to take one of two distinct perspectives on the subject. The first focuses on the organisation as a whole, tracking staff turnover rates over time, benchmarking the figures against industry or regional averages and developing organisational policy aimed at improving retention generally. The second, illustrated in recent work by Hiltrop (1999), Woodruffe (1999), Williams (2000) and Cappelli (2000), concentrates primarily on retaining high-performing key players. Each of these authors uses the expression 'the war for talent' to illustrate the significance and difficulty faced by those competing for the services of individuals who have the capacity to make a real difference to an organisation's competitive position. While the methods put forward to reduce turnover are similar in each case, the second group advocate more sophisticated retention practices aimed specifically at those whose talents are the most scarce.

ACTIVITY 8.1

Employee retention becomes an important item on the HRM agenda when organisations are faced with skills shortages. When labour is in reasonably good supply leavers can easily be replaced by new starters.

Aside from working harder at retaining staff, what alternative approaches could be adopted to help staff an organisation when the skills it requires are in short supply?

TURNOVER RATES AND TRENDS

In recent years there has been a mismatch between the rhetoric about job tenure and the reality. Much mileage continues to be made by some consultants, academics and management gurus out of the claim that 'there are no longer any jobs for life', suggesting that the length of time we spend working for organisations has fallen substantially in recent years. In fact this is a misleading claim. Detailed analyses of data from the *New Earnings Survey*, the *General Household Survey* and the *British Labour Force Survey* show that relatively little actually changed in terms of employee retention during recent decades (*see* Gregg and Wadsworth 1999). Turnover always

Table 8.1
Job tenure in the UK since 1975

Year	Male job tenure	Female job tenure	Average tenure
1975	6 years, 6 months	3 years, 7 months	4 years, 9 months
1985	7 years, 2 months	3 years, 10 months	5 years, 6 months
1990	6 years	3 years, 9 months	4 years, 4 months
1995	6 years, 10 months	4 years, 6 months	5 years, 7 months
1998	5 years, 9 months	4 years, 4 months	4 years, 10 months

Source: Table compiled from data in P. Gregg and J. Wadsworth (1999) 'Job tenure, 1975–98', in P. Gregg and J. Wadsworth (eds) *The State of Working Britain*. Manchester: Manchester University Press, p. 115.

rises when the economy is strong and jobs are plentiful because there are more opportunities available for people to change employers. Conversely, during recessions staff turnover falls because relatively few attractive permanent positions are advertised. These trends are reflected in Table 8.1 which shows how job tenure rates fluctuated for men and women between 1975 and 1998 while the overall tenure rate for the UK as a whole remained stable. What happened over this period is that male tenure rates fell as men in their fifties and early sixties took early retirement or accepted redundancy packages, while job tenure among women rose. Gregg and Wadsworth (1999, p. 116) show that the biggest increase has been among women with children. In 1975, on average, they remained in a job for 20 months; the figure in 1998 was 46 months. This reflects the greater propensity of women during this period to return to work following maternity leave and the improved career opportunities available to them.

These trends continue today. Table 8.2 shows that long periods of job tenure remain the norm for a substantial portion of the working population. People tend to move from employer to employer early on in their careers, often staying in one employment for just a few months. But once they find a job (or an employer) that they like, the tendency is to remain for several years. 'Jobs for life' have, in truth, always been a relative rarity, but the evidence suggests that they remain a reality for many employees, despite the predictions of the management gurus. Nearly a third of workers have been in their current jobs for over ten years.

The overall figures mask substantial differences between tenure and turnover rates in different industries. Studies undertaken annually by the Chartered Institute of

Table 8.2
Job tenure in the UK

Length of service	% of the workforce
0–3 months:	6%
3–6 months:	6%
6–12 months:	10%
1–2 years:	12%
2–5 years:	21%
5–10 years:	15%
10–20 years:	19%
Over 20 years:	10%

Source: *Labour Market Trends* (2001), 'Length of time continuously employed by occupation and industry', *Labour Market Trends*, February.

Personnel and Development persistently show retailing and catering to be the sectors with the highest turnover levels, with rates averaging over 40 per cent in recent years. By contrast the most stable workforces are to be found in the public services, where reported annual turnover rates are only 10 or 11 per cent (CIPD 2003, p. 9). Rates also vary from region to region and over time, being highest when and where average pay levels are highest and unemployment is low, and between different professions. As a rule, the more highly paid a person is, the less likely they are to switch jobs, but there remain some highly paid professions such as sales where turnover is always high. It is also interesting to observe how much more inclined younger workers are to switch jobs than their older colleagues. Macaulay (2003) recently calculated what proportion of employees had completed more than a year's service with their employer. For the over-fifties the figure was 86 per cent, for the 18–24 age group it was only 51 per cent.

ACTIVITY 8.2

Why do you think staff turnover rates are so much higher in some industries than others? Make a list of the different factors you consider may account for variations.

THE IMPACT OF STAFF TURNOVER

There is some debate about the level which staff turnover rates have to reach in order to inflict measurable damage on an employer. The answer varies from organisation to organisation. In some industries it is possible to sustain highly successful businesses with turnover rates that would make it impossible to function in other sectors. Some chains of fast food restaurants, for example, are widely reported as managing with turnover rates in excess of 300 per cent. This means that the average tenure for each employee is only four months (Ritzer 1996, p. 130; Cappelli 2000, p. 106), yet the companies concerned are some of the most successful in the world. By contrast, in a professional services organisation, where the personal relationships established between employees and clients are central to ongoing success, a turnover rate in excess of 10 per cent is likely to cause damage to the business.

There are sound arguments that can be made in favour of a certain amount of staff turnover. First, it is fair to say that organisations need to be rejuvenated with 'fresh blood' from time to time if they are to avoid becoming stale and stunted. This is particularly true at senior levels, where new leadership is often required periodically to drive change forward. More generally, however, new faces bring new ideas and experiences which help make organisations more dynamic. Second, it is possible to argue that a degree of turnover helps managers to keep firmer control over labour costs than would otherwise be the case. This is particularly true of organisations which are subject to regular and unpredictable changes in business levels. When income falls it is possible to hold back from replacing leavers until such time as it begins to pick up again. In this way organisations are able to minimise staffing budgets while maintaining profit levels during leaner periods. Redundancy bills are also lower in organisations with relatively high staff turnover because they are able to use natural wastage as the main means of reducing their workforce before compulsory lay-offs are needed. Third, it can be plausibly argued that some employee turnover is 'functional' rather than 'dysfunctional' because it results in the loss of poor performers and their replacement with more effective employees.

The arguments against staff turnover are equally persuasive. First are the sheer costs associated with replacing people who have left, ranging from the cost of placing a recruitment advertisement, through the time spent administering and conducting the selection process, to expenses required in inducting and training new employees. On top of these there are less easily measurable losses sustained as a result of poorer performance on the part of less experienced employees. For larger organisations employing specialist recruiters these costs can add up to millions of pounds a year, with substantial dividends to be claimed from a reduction in staff turnover levels by a few percentage points. The second major argument in favour of improving staff retention results from a straightforward recognition that people who leave represent a lost resource in whom the organisation has invested time and money. The damage is all the greater when good people, trained and developed at the organisation's expense, subsequently choose to work for competitors. Finally, it is argued that high turnover rates are symptomatic of a poorly managed organisation. They suggest that people are dissatisfied with their jobs or with their employer and would prefer to work elsewhere. It thus sends a negative message to customers and helps create a poor image in the labour market, making it progressively harder to recruit good performers in the future.

We may thus conclude that the case for seeking to reduce staff turnover varies from organisation to organisation. Where replacement employees are in plentiful supply, where new starters can be trained quickly and where business levels are subject to regular fluctuation it is possible to manage effectively with a relatively high level of turnover. Indeed, it may make good business sense to do so if the expenditure required to increase employee retention is greater than the savings that would be gained as a result. In other situations the case for taking action on turnover rates is persuasive, particularly where substantial investment in training is required before new starters are able to operate at maximum effectiveness. Companies which achieve turnover rates below their industry average are thus likely to enjoy greater competitive advantage than those whose rates are relatively high.

TURNOVER ANALYSIS AND COSTING

There is little that an organisation can do to manage turnover unless there is an understanding of the reasons for it. Information about these reasons is notoriously difficult to collect. Most commentators recommend exit interviews (that is, interviews with leavers about their reasons for resigning), but the problem here is whether the individual will feel able to tell the truth, and this will depend on the culture of the organisation, the specific reasons for leaving and support that the individual will need from the organisation in the future in the form of references. Despite their disadvantages, exit interviews may be helpful if handled sensitively and confidentially – perhaps by the HR department rather than the line manager. In addition, analyses of turnover rates between different departments and different job groups may well shed some light on causes of turnover. Attitude surveys can also provide relevant information.

WINDOW ON PRACTICE

It is very easy for an organisation to get itself into a vicious circle of turnover if it does not act to stem a retention problem. Modest turnover rates can rapidly increase as the pressures on remaining staff become greater, leading to serious operational difficulties. As soon as more than one or two people leave an established team, more is demanded of those left to carry the burden. First, there may be a sizeable time gap between leavers resigning and new starters coming into post. Then there is the period when the new people are learning their jobs, taking more time to accomplish tasks and needing assistance from more established employees. The problem can be compounded with additional pressure being placed on managers and HR specialists faced with the need to recruit people quickly, leading to the selection of people who are not wholly suited to the jobs in question. The result is greater turnover as people respond by looking for less pressured job opportunities elsewhere.

Problems of this kind were faced by the Japanese engineering company, Makita. It addressed the issue by increasing its induction programme from half a day to four weeks and by taking a good deal more care over its recruitment and selection processes. The result was a reduction in turnover levels from 97 per cent in 1997 to 38 per cent in 1999.

Source: IDS (2000) *Improving Staff Retention*, IDS Study 692, July, pp. 14–17.

People leave jobs for a variety of different reasons, many of which are wholly outside the power of the organisation to influence. One very common reason for leaving, for example, is retirement. It can be brought forward or pushed back for a few years, but ultimately it affects everyone. In many cases people leave for a mixture of reasons, certain factors weighing more highly in their minds than others. The following is one approach to categorising the main reasons people have for voluntarily leaving a job, each requiring a different kind of response from the organisation.

Outside factors

Outside factors relate to situations in which someone leaves for reasons that are largely unrelated to their work. The most common instances involve people moving away when a spouse or partner is relocated. Others include the wish to fulfil a long-term ambition to travel, pressures associated with juggling the needs of work and family and illness. To an extent such turnover is unavoidable, although it is possible to reduce it somewhat through the provision of career breaks, forms of flexible working and/or childcare facilities.

Functional turnover

The functional turnover category includes all resignations which are welcomed by both employer and employee alike. The major examples are those which stem from an individual's poor work performance or failure to fit in comfortably with an organisational or departmental culture. While such resignations are less damaging than others from an organisation's point of view they should still be regarded as lost opportunities and as an unnecessary cost. The main solution to the reduction of functional turnover lies in improving recruitment and selection procedures so that fewer people in the category are appointed in the first place. However, some poorly engineered change management schemes are also sometimes to blame, especially where they result in new work pressures or workplace ethics.

Push factors

With push factors the problem is dissatisfaction with work or the organisation, leading to unwanted turnover. A wide range of issues can be cited to explain such resignations. Insufficient development opportunities, boredom, ineffective supervision, poor levels of employee involvement and straightforward personality clashes are the most common precipitating factors. Organisations can readily address all of these issues. The main reason that so many fail to do so is the absence of mechanisms for picking up signs of dissatisfaction. If there is no opportunity to voice concerns, employees who are unhappy will inevitably start looking elsewhere.

Pull factors

The opposite side of the coin is the attraction of rival employers. Salary levels are often a factor here, employees leaving in order to improve their living standards. In addition there are broader notions of career development, the wish to move into new areas of work for which there are better opportunities elsewhere, the chance to work with particular people, and more practical questions such as commuting time. For the employer losing people as a result of such factors there are two main lines of attack. First, there is a need to be aware of what other employers are offering and to ensure that as far as possible this is matched – or at least that a broadly comparable package of pay and opportunities is offered. The second requirement involves trying to ensure that employees appreciate what they are currently being given. The emphasis here is on effective communication of any 'unique selling points' and of the extent to which opportunities comparable to those offered elsewhere are given.

What are the most common reasons?

Taylor and his colleagues (2002) interviewed 200 people who had recently changed employers about why they left their last jobs. They found a mix of factors at work in most cases but concluded that push factors were a great deal more prevalent than pull factors as causes of voluntary resignations. Very few people appear to leave jobs in which they are broadly happy in search of something even better. Instead the picture is overwhelmingly one in which dissatisfied employees seek alternatives because they no longer enjoy working for their current employer.

Interestingly this study found relatively few examples of people leaving for financial reasons. Indeed more of the interviewees took pay cuts in order to move from one job to another than said that a pay rise was their principal reason for switching employers. Other factors played a much bigger role:

1 Dissatisfaction with the conditions of work, especially hours
2 A perception that they were not being given sufficient career development opportunities
3 A bad relationship with their immediate supervisor

This third factor was by far the most commonly mentioned in the interviews, lending support to the often stated point that people leave their managers and not their organisations.

ACTIVITY 8.3

Think about jobs that you or members of your family have left in recent years. What were the key factors that led to the decision to leave? Was there one major factor or did several act together in combination?

Costing

When deciding what kind of measures to put in place in order to improve staff retention generally or the retention of particular individuals, organisations need to balance the costs involved against those that are incurred as a direct result of voluntary resignations. Although it is difficult to cost turnover accurately, it is possible to reach a fair estimate by taking into account the range of expenses involved in replacing one individual with another. Once a figure has been calculated for a job, it is relatively straightforward to compute the savings to be gained from a given percentage reduction in annual turnover rates. Figure 8.1 shows the approach to turnover costing recommended by Hugo Fair (1992).

STAFF RETENTION STRATEGIES

The straightforward answer to the question of how best to retain staff is to provide them with a better deal, in the broadest sense, than they perceive they could get by working for alternative employers. Terms and conditions play a significant role, but other factors are often more important. For example, there is a need to provide jobs which are satisfying, along with career development opportunities, as much autonomy as is practicable and, above all, competent line management. Indeed, at one level, most of the practices of effective human resource management described in this book can play a part in reducing turnover. Organisations which make use of them will enjoy lower rates than competitors who do not. Below we look at six measures that have been shown to have a positive effect on employee retention, focusing particularly on those practices which are not covered in any great depth elsewhere in the book.

Figure 8.1 A sample form for costing labour turnover

Enter number of employees		______ (a),
Enter average weekly wage	£	______ (b),
Multiply (a) × (b)	£	______ (c),
Multiply (c) × 52	£	______ (d) = *Total paybill*
Enter current turnover rate		______% (e),
Multiply (e) × (a)		______ (f) = *Staff loss p.a.*
Enter average number of days to replace		______ (g),
Multiplier rate for overtime/temps.		______ (h),
Multiply (b) × (h)	£	______ (i),
Multiply (f) × (g) × [(i)/5]	£	______ (j) = Immediate cover costs
Preparation and interview time per applicant (days)		______ (k),
Shortlisted applicants per position		______ (l),
Enter average manager weekly wage	£	______ (m),
Multiply (f) × (k) × (l) × [(m)/5]	£	______ (n) = Interview time costs
Enter average recruitment fees		______% (o),
Multiply (d) × (e) × (o)	£	______ (p) = Recruitment fee costs
Length of induction training (days)		______ (q),
Frequency of this training (p.a.)		______ (r),
Multiply [(b)/5] × (q) × [(f) + (r)]	£	______ (s) = Induction training cost
Duration of learning curve (months)		______ (t),
Enter non-productive element		______% (u),
Multiply (d) × (e) × [(t)/12] × (u)	£	______ (v) = Non-productive costs
Multiply (t) × (u) (months)	£	______ (w),
Multiply (d) × (e) × (h) × [(w)/12]	£	______ (x) = Continuing cover costs
Multiply (g) × [(b)/5] × (f)	£	______ (y) = Salary savings
Add (j) + (n) + (p) + (s) + (v) + (x) − (y)	£	______ (z) = *Turnover cost p.a.*
Potential cost saving		
Enter expected turnover reduction		______% (1),
Multiply (z) × [(1)/(e)]	£	______ (2) = Labour turnover savings
Enter reduction in replacement time		______% (3),
Multiply (j) × (3)	£	______ (4) = Added cover savings
Add (2) + (4)	£	______ (5) = *Total savings p.a.*

Source: H. Fair (1992) *Personnel and Profit: The pay-off from people*, p. 41. London: IPM. Used with permission of CIPD Publications.

Pay

There is some debate in the retention literature about the extent to which raising pay levels reduces staff turnover. On the one hand there is evidence to show that, on average, employers who offer the most attractive reward packages have lower attrition rates than those who pay poorly (Gomez-Mejia and Balkin 1992, pp. 292–4), an assumption which leads many organisations to use pay rates as their prime weapon in retaining staff (Cappelli 2000, pp. 105–6; IRS 2000a, p. 10; IRS 2000b, p. 9). On the other, there is questionnaire-based evidence which suggests that pay is a good deal less important than other factors in a decision to quit one's job (Bevan *et al.* 1997, p. 25; Hiltrop 1999, p. 424). The consensus among researchers specialising in retention issues is that pay has a role to play as a satisfier, but that it will not usually have an effect when other factors are pushing an individual towards quitting. Raising pay levels may thus result in greater job satisfaction where people are already happy with their work, but it will not deter unhappy employees from leaving. Sturges and Guest (1999), in their study of leaving decisions in the field of graduate employment, summed up their findings as follows:

> As far as they are concerned, while challenging work will compensate for pay, pay will never compensate for having to do boring, unstimulating work. (Sturges and Guest 1999, p. 19)

Recent research findings thus appear to confirm the views expressed by Herzberg (1966) that pay is a 'hygiene factor' rather than a motivator. This means that it can be a cause of dissatisfaction at work, but not of positive job satisfaction. People may be motivated to leave an employer who is perceived as paying badly, but once they are satisfied with their pay additional increases have little effect.

The other problem with the use of pay increases to retain staff is that it is an approach that is very easily matched by competitors. This is particularly true of 'golden handcuff' arrangements which seek to tie senior staff to an organisation for a number of years by paying substantial bonuses at a defined future date. As Cappelli (2000, p. 106) argues, in a buoyant job market, recruiters simply 'unlock the handcuffs' by offering equivalent signing-on bonuses to people they wish to employ.

It is important that employees do not perceive their employers to be treating them inequitably. Provided pay levels are not considerably lower than those paid by an organisation's labour market competitors, other factors will usually be more important contributors towards high turnover levels. Where the salaries that are paid are already broadly competitive, little purpose is served by increasing them further. The organisation may well make itself more attractive in recruitment terms, but the effect on staff retention will be limited. Moreover, of course, wage costs will increase.

There is potentially more to be gained from enhancing benefits packages, because these are less easily imitated or matched by competitors. Where particular benefits, such as staff discounts, holiday entitlements or private healthcare schemes, are appreciated by staff, they are more likely to have a positive effect on staff turnover than simply paying higher base wages. Potentially the same is true of pension schemes, which are associated with relatively high levels of staff retention. However, the research evidence suggests that except for older employees who have completed many years of service, most pension schemes are not sufficiently valued by staff to cause them to stay in a job with which they are dissatisfied (Taylor 2000). Arguably, the best way of using benefits to keep a lid on staff turnover is to move towards flexible schemes such as those discussed in Chapter 29. An employer which allows individual employees to choose how they make up their own remuneration package will generally be more attractive than one which only offers a 'one size fits all' set of benefits.

ACTIVITY 8.4

The case for arguing that pay rates have a relatively minor role to play in explaining individual resignations rests partly on the assumption that other elements of the employment relationship are more important. It is argued that people will 'trade in' high pay in order to secure other perceived benefits and that consequently low-paying employers can retain staff effectively.

What other factors do you think employees consider to be more important than pay? What role can the HRM function play in helping to develop these?

Managing expectations

For some years research evidence has strongly suggested that employers benefit from ensuring that potential employees gain a 'realistic job preview' before they take up a job offer. The purpose is to make sure that new staff enter an organisation with their eyes wide open and do not find that the job fails to meet their expectations. A major cause of job dissatisfaction, and hence of high staff turnover, is the experience of having one's high hopes of new employment dashed by the realisation that it is not going to be as enjoyable or stimulating as anticipated.

Several researchers have drawn attention to the importance of these processes in reducing high turnover during the early months of employment (e.g. Wanous 1992, pp. 53–87; Hom and Griffeth 1995, pp. 193–203). The need is to strike a balance at the recruitment stage between sending out messages which are entirely positive and sending out those which are realistic. In other words, it is important not to mislead candidates about the nature of the work that they will be doing.

Realistic job previews are most important when candidates, for whatever reason, cannot know a great deal about the job for which they are applying. This may be because of limited past experience or it may because the job is relatively unusual and not based in a type of workplace with which job applicants are familiar. An example quoted by Carroll *et al.* (1999, p. 246) concerns work in nursing homes, which seems to attract people looking to undertake a caring role but who are unfamiliar with the less attractive hours, working conditions and job duties associated with the care assistant's role. The realistic job preview is highly appropriate in such a situation as a means of avoiding recruiting people who subsequently leave within a few weeks.

The importance of unmet expectations as an explanation for staff turnover is also stressed by Sturges and Guest (1999, pp. 16 and 31) in their work on the retention of newly recruited graduates. Here the problem is one of employers overselling graduate careers when competing with others to secure the services of the brightest young people:

> False impressions are given and a positive spin put on answers to questions so as to deter able applicants from taking up alternative offers. As a result, graduates start work confident in the belief that their days will be filled with interesting work, that they will be treated fairly and objectively in terms of performance assessment, that their career development will be fostered judiciously, and that their working lives will in some way be 'fun' and 'exciting'. That is fine if it really can be guaranteed. Unfortunately such is often not the case, and unsurprisingly it leads to early dissatisfaction and higher turnover rates than are desirable. (Jenner and Taylor 2000, p. 155)

A solution, aside from the introduction of more honest recruitment literature, is to provide periods of work experience for students before they graduate. A summer spent working somewhere is the best possible way of finding out exactly what a particular job or workplace is really like. The same argument can be deployed in support of work experience for young people who are about to leave school in order to enter the job market.

Induction

Another process often credited with the reduction of turnover early in the employment relationship is the presence of effective and timely induction. It is very easy to overlook in the rush to get people into key posts quickly and it is often carried out badly, but it is essential if avoidable early turnover is to be kept to a minimum. Gregg and Wadsworth (1999, p. 111) show in their analysis of 870,000 workers starting new jobs in 1992 that as many as 17 per cent had left within three months and 42 per cent within 12 months. No doubt a good number of these departures were due either to poorly managed expectations or to ineffective inductions.

Induction has a number of distinct purposes, all of which are concerned with preparing new employees to work as effectively as possible and as soon as is possible in their new jobs. First, it plays an important part in helping new starters to adjust emotionally to the new workplace. It gives an opportunity to ensure that they understand where things are, who to ask when unsure about what to do and how their role fits into the organisation generally. Second, induction provides a forum in which basic information about the organisation can be transmitted. This may include material about the organisation's purpose, its mission statement and the key issues it faces. More generally a corporate induction provides a suitable occasion to talk about health and safety regulations, fire evacuation procedures and organisational policies concerning matters like the use of telephones for private purposes. Third, induction processes can be used to convey to new starters important cultural messages about what the organisation expects and what employees can expect in return. It thus potentially forms an important stage in the establishment of the psychological contract, leaving new employees clear about what they need to do to advance their own prospects in the organisation. All these matters will be picked up by new starters anyway in their first months of employment, but incorporating them into a formal induction programme ensures that they are brought up to speed a good deal quicker, and that they are less likely to leave at an early date.

There is no 'right' length for an induction programme. In some jobs it can be accomplished effectively in a few days, for others there is a need for some form of input over a number of weeks. What is important is that individuals are properly introduced both to the organisation and to their particular role within it. These introductons are usually best handled by different people. Organisational induction, because it is given to all new starters, is normally handled centrally by the HR department and takes place in a single place over one or two days. Job-based induction takes longer, will be overseen by the individual's own line manager and will usually involve shadowing colleagues. The former largely takes the form of a presentation, while the latter involves the use of a wider variety of training methods. IRS (2000c, pp. 10–12) draws attention to the recent development of web-based training packages which allow new employees to learn about their organisations and their jobs at their own pace, when they get the opportunity.

Family-friendly HR practices

Labour Force Survey statistics show that between 5 per cent and 10 per cent of employees leave their jobs for 'family or personal reasons' (IRS 1999, p. 6), while Hom and Griffeth (1995, p. 252) quote American research indicating that 33 per cent of women quit jobs to devote more time to their families – a response given by

WINDOW ON PRACTICE

IRS (2000c, p. 11) describes an original approach taken to the induction of staff at a large Novotel Hotel in London. Unusually for the hotel industry the induction programme here lasts for three weeks. It includes some job shadowing of experienced staff, but also consists of several days spent in a training room learning about the hotel's main services and learning how to deal with difficult customers. A variety of training techniques are used including quizzes, games, discussion forums and role play exercises. The management saw their retention rates increase by 12 per cent after the introduction of the new programme.

only one per cent of men. To these figures can be added those quoted by Gregg and Wadsworth (1999, p. 116) which show average job tenure among women with children in the UK to be over a year shorter than that of women without children and almost two years shorter than that of men. These statistics suggest that one of the more significant reasons for voluntary resignations from jobs is the inability to juggle the demands of a job with those of the family. They indicate that there is a good business case, particularly where staff retention is high on the agenda, for considering ways in which employment can be made more family friendly.

As a result of legislation under the Working Time Regulations 1998, the Employment Relations Act 1999 and the Employment Act 2002, UK employers are now obliged by law to provide the following as a minimum floor of rights:

- 26 weeks' maternity leave for all employees with more than six months' service paid according to a formula set out in the Act;
- an additional 26 weeks' unpaid maternity leave for employees with over a year's service;
- reasonable paid time off for pregnant employees to attend ante-natal clinics;
- specific health and safety measures for workers who are pregnant or have recently given birth;
- four weeks' paid holiday each year;
- a total of three months' unpaid parental leave for mothers and fathers on the birth or adoption of a child;
- reasonable unpaid time off for employees to deal with family emergencies such as the sickness of a child or dependent relative;
- consideration of reasonable requests by parents of young children to work flexibly;
- two weeks' paid paternity leave for new fathers.

Many employers, however, have decided to go a good deal further down this road than is required by law. The most common example is the provision of more paid maternity leave and the right, where possible, for mothers to return to work on a part-time or job-share basis if they so wish. Crèche provision is common in larger workplaces, while others offer childcare vouchers instead. Career breaks are offered by many public sector employers, allowing people to take a few months off without pay and subsequently to return to a similar job with the same organisation. Flexitime systems such as those described in Chapter 4 are also useful to people with families and may thus serve as a retention tool in some cases. In the USA the literature indicates growing interest in 'elder care' arrangements (Lambert 2000) aimed specifically at providing assistance to those seeking to combine work with responsibility for the care of elderly relatives. An example in the UK is the 'granny crèche' established by Peugeot for employees at its plant in Coventry. You can read much more about these and other work-life-balance initiatives in Chapter 32.

Training and development

There are two widely expressed, but wholly opposed, perspectives on the link between training interventions and employee turnover. On the one hand is the argument that training opportunities enhance commitment to an employer on the part of individual employees, making them less likely to leave voluntarily than they would if no training were offered. The alternative view holds that training makes people more employable and hence more likely to leave in order to develop their careers elsewhere. The view is thus put that money spent on training is money wasted because it ultimately benefits other employers.

Green *et al.* (2000, pp. 267–72) report research on perceptions of 1,539 employees on different kinds of training. They found that the overall effect is neutral, 19 per cent of employees saying that training was 'more likely to make them actively look for another job' and 18 per cent saying it was less likely to do so. However, they also found the type of training and the source of sponsorship to be a significant variable. Training which is paid for by the employer is a good deal less likely to raise job mobility than that paid for by the employee or the government. Firm-specific training is also shown in the study to be associated with lower turnover than training which leads to the acquisition of transferable skills. The point is made, however, that whatever the form of training an employer can develop a workforce which is both 'capable and committed' by combining training interventions with other forms of retention initiative.

The most expensive types of training intervention involve long-term courses of study such as an MBA, CIPD or accountancy qualification. In financing such courses, employers are sending a very clear signal to the employees concerned that their contribution is valued and that they can look forward to substantial career advancement if they opt to stay. The fact that leaving will also mean an end to the funding for the course provides a more direct incentive to remain with the sponsoring employer.

Improving the quality of line management

If it is the case that many, if not most, voluntary resignations are explained by dissatisfaction on the part of employees with their supervisors, it follows that the most effective means of reducing staff turnover in organisations is to improve the performance of line managers. Too often, it appears, people are promoted into supervisory positions without adequate experience or training. Organisations seem to assume that their managers are capable supervisors, without recognising that the role is difficult and does not usually come naturally to people. Hence it is common to find managers who are 'quick to critise but slow to praise', who are too tied up in their own work to show an interest in their subordinates and who prefer to impose their own solutions without first taking account of their staff's views. The solution is to take action on various fronts to improve the effectiveness of supervisors:

- select people for line management roles following an assessment of their supervisory capabilities;
- ensure that all newly appointed line managers are trained in the art of effective supervision;
- regularly appraise line managers on their supervisory skills.

This really amounts to little more than common sense, but such approaches are the exception to the rule in most UK organisations.

WINDOW ON PRACTICE

An interesting approach to improving retention is reported by Cappelli (2000, p. 108) as being used at a computer company in the USA. It is believed to have played a major role in keeping turnover rates among software engineers to seven per cent – unusually low for computer workers.

The aim has been to work hard at creating a sense of community among employees so that 'leaving the company means leaving your social network of company-sponsored activities'. Strong social ties are fostered by organising all manner of out-of-work activities including sports teams and investment clubs. In addition to this, the company tries to place employees in closely knit teams when they are at work. Because team members rely so much on one another, it makes people think twice about resigning and abandoning their team-mates.

SUMMARY PROPOSITIONS

8.1 Staff turnover tends to decrease in recessions and increase during economic booms.

8.2 Contrary to much popular perception, average job tenure has not reduced substantially over the past thirty years.

8.3 Retention rates vary very considerably between industries and between different regions.

8.4 While there are arguments that can be deployed in favour of modest staff turnover, it is generally agreed that too great a rate is damaging for an organisation.

8.5 In planning retention initiatives it is important both to analyse the causes of turnover and to calculate the current costs associated with each voluntary resignation.

8.6 Specific programmes which lead to improved retention include flexible benefits, better induction, the effective management of expectations, family-friendly initiatives, training opportunities and the improvement of line management in organisations.

GENERAL DISCUSSION TOPICS

1 What are the main reasons for the trends in job tenure illustrated in Table 8.1?

2 Staff turnover is generally low during recessions, but it increases substantially in firms which get into financial difficulty. What factors account for this phenomenon?

3 Think about your own experiences at work or those of close friends and family. What were the key factors that affected decisions to leave a particular job? What, if anything, could the employer have done to ensure that no resignation took place?

FURTHER READING

Chartered Institute of Personnel and Development (annual) *Labour Turnover Survey*. London: CIPD

Confederation of British Industry (annual) *Absence and Labour Turnover Survey*. London: CBI
Each year the CIPD and the CBI carry out major surveys looking at staff turnover across the UK. They report the labour turnover rates among different groups as well as estimates of turnover costs. Many smaller surveys covering specific employee groups (like graduates) or particular industries are also published annually. *IRS Employment Review* always carries a number of 'benchmarking turnover' articles towards the end of the year which report the key findings from all these surveys.

Hom, P. and Griffeth, R. (1995) *Employee Turnover*. Cincinnati, Ohio: South Western College Publishing
This is by far the best source of information about academic research on turnover and staff retention issues. It is now out of print, but the same authors' more recent book, Griffeth, R. and Hom P. (2001) *Retaining Valued Employees*, Thousand Oaks, Cal.: Sage, is widely available.

Taylor S. (2002) *The Employee Retention Handbook*. London: CIPD
This is a useful source of information about UK research on the topic. It contains chapters focusing on measuring and costing turnover, identifying the causes of turnover and several looking at different strategies for improving retention rates.

REFERENCES

Bevan, S., Barber, L. and Robinson, D. (1997) *Keeping the Best: a practical guide to retaining key employees*. Brighton: Institute for Employment Research.

Cappelli, P. (2000) 'A market-driven approach to retaining talent', *Harvard Business Review*, January/February, pp. 103–11.

Carroll, M., Marchington, M., Earnshaw, J. and Taylor, S. (1999) 'Recruitment in small firms: processes, methods and problems', *Employee Relations*, Vol. 21, No. 3, pp. 236–50.

Chartered Institute of Personnel and Development (2003) *Labour Turnover 2003: A survey of Ireland and the UK*. London: CIPD.

Fair, H. (1992) *Personnel and Profit: The pay-off from people*. London: IPM.

Gomez-Mejia, L. and Balkin, D. (1992) *Compensation, Organizational Strategy and Firm Performance*. Cincinnati, Ohio: South Western College Publishing.

Green, F., Felstead, A., Mayhew, K. and Pick, A. (2000) 'The impact of training on labour mobility: individual and firm-level evidence from Britain', *British Journal of Industrial Relations*, Vol. 38, No. 2.

Gregg, P. and Wadsworth, J. (1999) 'Job tenure, 1975–98', in P. Gregg and J. Wadsworth (eds) *The State of Working Britain*. Manchester: Manchester University Press.

Griffeth, R. and Hom, P. (2001) *Retaining Valued Employees*. Thousand Oaks, Cal.: Sage.

Herzberg, F. (1966) *Work and the Nature of Man*. Cleveland, Ohio: World Publishing.

Hiltrop, J.-M. (1999) 'The quest for the best: human resource practices to attract and retain talent', *European Management Journal*, Vol. 17, No. 4, pp. 423–31.

Hom, P. and Griffeth, R. (1995) *Employee Turnover*. Cincinnati, Ohio: South Western College Publishing.

IDS (2000) *Improving Staff Retention*, IDS Study No. 692, July.

IRS (1999) 'Benchmarking labour turnover: annual guide 1999/2000', *Employee Development Bulletin*, No. 118, October.

IRS (2000a) 'Employee Retention 1 – the tools and techniques', *Employee Development Bulletin*, No. 128, pp. 6–10, August.

IRS (2000b) 'Retention 2 – effective methods', *Employee Development Bulletin*, No. 129, pp. 6–16, September.

IRS (2000c) 'Improving retention and performance through induction', *Employee Development Bulletin*, No. 130, pp. 10–16, October.

Jenner, S. and Taylor, S. (2000) *Recruiting, Developing and Retaining Graduate Talent*. London: Financial Times/Prentice Hall.

Labour Market Trends (2001) 'Length of time continuously employed by occupation and industry', *Labour Market Trends*, February.

Lambert, S. (2000) 'Added benefits: The link between work-life benefits and organizational citizen behavior', *Academy of Management Journal*, Vol. 43, No. 5, pp. 801–15.

Macaulay, C. (2003) 'Job mobility and job tenure in the UK', *Labour Market Trends*, November.

Ritzer, G. (1996) *The Macdonaldisation of Society: an investigation into the changing character of contemporary social life*, revised edn. Thousand Oaks, Cal.: Pine Forge.

Sturges, J. and Guest, D. (1999) *Shall I Stay or Should I go?* Warwick: Association of Graduate Recruiters.

Taylor, S. (2000) 'Occupational pensions and employee retention: debate and evidence', *Employee Relations*, Vol. 22, No. 3, pp. 246–59.

Taylor, S. (2002) *The Employee Retention Handbook*. London: CIPD.

Thompson, H. (2000) 'If you leave me now . . .' *Daily Telegraph*, 2 November 2000.

Wanous, J.P. (1992) *Recruitment, Selection, Orientation and Socialization of Newcomers*. Reading, Mass.: Addison Wesley.

Williams, M. (2000) *The War for Talent*. London: CIPD.

Woodruffe, C. (1999) *Winning the Talent War*. Chichester: Wiley.

An extensive range of additional materials, including multiple choice questions, answers to questions and links to useful websites can be found on the Human Resource Management Companion Website at www.pearsoned.co.uk/torrington.

CHAPTER 9

ENDING THE CONTRACT

THE OBJECTIVES OF THIS CHAPTER ARE TO:

1 OUTLINE THE FRAMEWORK IN WHICH THE LAW OF UNFAIR DISMMISSAL OPERATES

2 SET OUT THE MAJOR REASONS FOR WHICH AN EMPLOYER CAN AND CANNOT LAWFULLY DISMISS EMPLOYEES

3 EXPLAIN THE CONCEPT OF 'REASONABLENESS' IN UNFAIR DISMISSAL CASES AND ITS SIGNIFICANCE

4 REVIEW THE LAW ON DISMISSALS ON GROUNDS OF CAPABILITY, MISCONDUCT AND REDUNDANCY

5 DESCRIBE THE OPERATION OF THE LAW OF CONSTRUCTIVE DISMISSAL AND THE LAW OF WRONGFUL DISMISSAL

6 REVIEW SOME CURRENT TRENDS IN RETIREMENT PRACTICE

In the last chapter we looked at situations in which employees decide to end their contracts of employment by giving their employers notice. Here we focus on circumstances when the contract is brought to an end by the employer through a dismissal of one kind or another, something that over a million employees experience in the UK each year (DTI 1999). In some cases employees are happy to leave (or at least not unhappy) such as when they are retiring or when they are due to receive a large redundancy payment. More common, however, are situations where the person dismissed is distinctly unhappy about the contract being brought to an end. When someone feels that they have been treated unfairly in terms of the reason for, or the manner of, their dismissal they can take their case to an employment tribunal. In practice, between five per cent and ten per cent of all dismissed workers who qualify do bring such claims (DTI 1999). If someone wins their case they may ask to be reinstated, but will usually settle for a compensation payment. The size of such awards is not generally substantial (around £3,000 on average), but occasionally people are awarded larger sums. Whatever the final outcome there are often additional legal costs for the employer to bear, not to mention the loss of a great deal of management time. An organisation's reputation as a good employer can also be damaged by adverse publicity arising from such cases. Employers generally take careful account of the requirements of the law when dismissing employees. The alternative is to run the risk of being summoned to an employment tribunal and possibly losing the case. To a great extent the law therefore effectively determines practice in the field of dismissal.

In the UK there are three forms of dismissal claim that can be brought to a **tribunal**. Rights associated with the law of **wrongful dismissal** are the longest established. A person who claims wrongful dismissal complains that the way that they were dismissed breached the terms of their contract of employment. **Constructive dismissal** occurs when someone feels forced to resign as a direct result of their employer's actions. In this area the law aims to deter employers from seeking to avoid dismissing people by pushing them into resignation. The third category, **unfair dismissal**, is by far the most common. It is best defined as a dismissal which falls short of the expectations of the law as laid down in the Employment Rights Act 1996.

UNFAIR DISMISSAL

The law of unfair dismissal dates from 1971, since when it has been amended a number of times. Although new additions and the outcomes of leading cases have made it more complex than it was originally, the basic principles have stood the test of time and remain in place. The latest major changes were contained in the Statutory Dispute Resolution Regulations which came into effect in 2004. Their aim was to reduce the number of claims being brought before employment tribunals by providing strong incentives for employers and employees to exhaust internal disciplinary and grievance procedures first. These regulations also adjusted the position of the law in respect of dismissals that are for justified reasons but which are carried out using an incomplete or deficient procedure.

In most circumstances the right to bring a claim of unfair dismissal applies to employees who have completed a year's continuous service with their employer on the date their contract was terminated. This allows the employer a period of 12 months to assess whether or not an individual employee is suitable before the freedom to dismiss is restricted. For a number of years until 1999 the time limit was two years. In reducing the period, the government brought an additional 2.8 million more people within the scope of unfair dismissal law (DTI 1999).

At the time of writing (2004) the right not to be unfairly dismissed was not available for people who were over the age of 65 or 'the normal retiring age' in a particular employment. However, it is very likely that such provisions will be removed from the statutes or extended by some years to 70 or 75 as a result of new measures on age discrimination that are due to come into effect from October 2006.

Restrictions on qualification apply except where the reason for the dismissal is one of those listed below which are classed as 'automatically unfair' or 'inadmissible'. A further requirement is that the claim form is lodged at the tribunal office before three months have elapsed from the date of dismissal. Unless there are circumstances justifying the failure to submit a claim before the deadline, applications received after three months are ruled out of time.

Before a case comes to tribunal, officers of the Advisory, Conciliation and Arbitration Service (ACAS) will often try to help the parties reach a settlement. The papers of all cases lodged with the employment tribunals' offices are sent to ACAS with a view to conciliation taking place ahead of a tribunal hearing. As a result the majority of cases either get settled or are withdrawn without the need for the parties to attend a full hearing.

When faced with a claim of unfair dismissal, and where it is not disputed that a dismissal took place, an employment tribunal asks two separate questions:

1 Was the reason for the dismissal one which is classed by the law as legitimate?
2 Did the employer act reasonably in carrying out the dismissal?

Where the answer to the first question is 'no', there is no need to ask the second because the dismissed employee will already have won his or her case. Interestingly the burden of proof shifts as the tribunal moves from considering the first to the second question. It is for the employer to satisfy the tribunal that it dismissed the employee for a legitimate reason. The burden of proof then becomes neutral when the question of reasonableness is addressed.

ACTIVITY 9.1

Consider the working activities of some of your colleagues (and perhaps your own working activities). What examples are there of behaviour that you feel justify dismissal? Make a list of your ideas and check them when you have finished this chapter and see how many might be classified by a tribunal as unfair dismissals.

Automatically unfair reasons

Certain reasons for dismissal are declared in law to be inadmissable or automatically unfair. Where the tribunal finds that one of these was the principal reason for the dismissal, they find in favour of the claimant (i.e. the ex-employee) whatever the circumstances of the case. In practice, therefore, there is no defence that an employer can make to explain its actions that will be acceptable to the tribunal. Some of these relate to other areas of employment law such as non-discrimination, working time and the minimum wage, which are discussed in more detail elsewhere in this book. The list of automatically unfair reasons for dismissal has grown steadily in recent years as new employment rights have come on to the statute book; in 2004 it was as follows:

- on grounds of sex, marital status or gender reassignment;
- on racial grounds;
- on grounds of disability (unless objectively justified);
- on grounds of sexual orientation;
- on grounds of religion or belief;
- on grounds of having committed a criminal offence where the conviction is spent;
- on grounds of pregnancy or maternity;
- on grounds of being a part-time worker;
- for exercising the right to parental leave or time off for dependants;
- for carrying out duties as a safety representative;
- for carrying out duties as a pension fund trustee;
- for refusing to work on a Sunday (retail workers only);
- for taking part, or proposing to take part, in lawful trade union activity;
- for joining or refusing to join a trade union;
- for taking part in official industrial action (i.e. organised and approved by a trade union executive) during the first eight weeks that the action takes place;
- for refusing to work in unsafe conditions;
- for asserting a statutory right.

This last provision relates to the various other employment protection rights set out in statute. It is designed to ensure that no one is victimised by being dismissed (unfairly or constructively) simply because they sought to exercise their rights under employment law.

The following are the principal Acts covered:

- Trade Union and Labour Relations (Consolidation) Act 1992
- Employment Rights Act 1996
- Working Time Regulations 1998
- Public Interest Disclosure Act 1998 (often known as the 'Whistleblowers' Act')
- National Minimum Wage Act 1998
- Tax Credits Act 1999
- Employment Relations Act 1999
- Employment Act 2002

A further situation which is classed as automatically unfair is a dismissal which occurs directly as a result of a business changing hands (known as a transfer of undertakings case). Dismissals for this reason will be judged as unfair by employment tribunals unless it can be shown that the dismissals were for economic, technical or organisational reasons. Unlike the other automatically unfair dismissals, transfer of undertakings cases can only be brought by ex-employees who have completed a year's continuous service and are under the 'normal' age of retirement at the time of their dismissal.

Under the Dispute Resolution Regulations 2004 the government added to the list a further situation in which a dismissal could be found automatically unfair after the completion of a year's service. This is where someone is dismissed *without* the employer first having initiated the following basic three-step procedure:

- **Step 1:** The employer sends the employee a letter setting out the nature of the circumstances that may lead to the employee's dismissal.
- **Step 2:** The employer invites the employee to a meeting to discuss the issue at which both parties put their views across. After the meeting the employer informs the employee about the outcome. If it is to dismiss, then the right of appeal is confirmed.
- **Step 3:** The employee exercises their right to appeal and a further meeting is held for this purpose.

In exceptional cases of gross misconduct employers are permitted to omit stage 2 of this procedure. This does not, however, make the dismissal fair, it just means that it is not automatically unfair. A failure to investigate properly or hold a hearing would mean that such a dismissal would usually be found to have been carried out unreasonably.

Potentially fair reasons

From an employer's perspective it is important to be able to satisfy the tribunal that the true reason for the dismissal was one of those reasons classed as potentially fair in unfair dismissal law. Only once this has been achieved can the second question (the issue of reasonableness) be addressed. The potentially fair grounds for dismissal are as follows:

- **Lack of capability or qualifications:** if an employee lacks the skill, aptitude or physical health to carry out the job, then there is a potentially fair ground for dismissal.
- **Misconduct:** this category covers the range of behaviours that we examine in considering the grievance and discipline processes: disobedience, absence, insubordination and criminal acts. It can also include taking industrial action.
- **Redundancy:** where an employee's job ceases to exist, it is potentially fair to dismiss the employee for redundancy.
- **Statutory bar:** when employees cannot continue to discharge their duties without breaking the law, they can be fairly dismissed. Most cases of this kind follow disqualification of drivers following convictions for speeding, drunk or dangerous driving. Other common cases involve foreign nationals whose work permits have been terminated.
- **Some other substantial reason:** this most intangible category is introduced in order to cater for genuinely fair dismissals for reasons so diverse that they could not realistically be listed. Examples have been security of commercial information (where an employee's husband set up a rival company) or employee refusal to accept altered working conditions.
- **Dismissals arising from official industrial action after eight weeks have passed.**

Determining reasonableness

Having decided that potentially fair grounds for the dismissal exist, the tribunal then proceeds to consider whether the dismissal is fair in the circumstances. There are two questions: was the decision reasonable in the circumstances, and was the dismissal carried out in line with the procedure? When considering the first, tribunal members pay particular attention to consistency of treatment, seeking to satisfy themselves that the dismissed employee has not been treated more severely than others have been in similar circumstances. They are also required to have regard to the size and resources of the employer concerned. Higher standards are thus expected of a large PLC with a well-staffed HR department than of a small owner-managed business employing a handful of people. The former, for example, might be expected to give two or three warnings and additional training before dismissing someone on grounds of incapability. One simple warning might suffice in a small business which relied heavily on an acceptable level of performance from the individual concerned.

The significance attached to procedure has varied over the years. Until 1987 employers were able to argue successfully that although the procedure used was deficient in some respects, the outcome was not affected. This changed following the judgment of the House of Lords in the leading case of *Polkey* v. *AE Dayton Services* (1987). This particular case concerned the fairness of a redundancy when the employer had failed to consult the employee and had also failed to give proper notice. In giving judgment Lord Mackay ruled that the fact that consultation would have made no difference to the final outcome did not render the dismissal fair. Henceforth, tribunals were obliged to find dismissals unfair where the employer had not completed a proper procedure before making the final decision to dismiss. Typical procedural defects were identified as follows by Earnshaw (1997):

- no chance given to the applicants to give an explanation;
- dismissal without any prior disciplinary hearing;
- no procedure in cases involving senior staff;
- the procedure used did not comply with the respondent's own rules;
- unwillingness to have a procedure because of disliking formality; and
- no chance for the applicant to rectify their shortcomings.

The Dispute Resolution Regulations 2004 go some way to overturning the House of Lords judgment in the *Polkey* case, but the extent to which common practice changes will only become clear as tribunals consider cases over time and set new precedents. In its guide to the 2004 provisions the government explained its measure as follows:

> To alter the way unfair dismissals are judged so that, provided the minimum standards are met and the dismissal is otherwise fair, procedural shortcomings can be disregarded. (Employers will always have to follow the basic procedures but will no longer be penalised for irrelevant mistakes beyond that – provided the dismissal would otherwise be fair). (Department of Trade and Industry (2003))

The standard used by the tribunal in reaching decisions about the fairness of a dismissal is that of the reasonable employer. Tribunal members are not required to judge cases on the basis of what they would have done in the circumstances or what the best employers would have done. Instead they have to ask themselves whether what the employer did in the circumstances of the time fell within a possible band of reasonable responses. In practice this means that the employer wins the case if it can show that the decision to dismiss was one that a reasonable employer *might* conceivably have taken.

In this book we have separated the consideration of discipline from the consideration of dismissal in order to concentrate on the practical aspects of discipline (putting things right) rather than the negative aspects (getting rid of the problem). The two cannot, however, be separated in practice and the question of dismissal needs to be reviewed in the light of the material in Chapter 25.

WINDOW ON PRACTICE

In 1999 the Employment Appeal Tribunal made a landmark decision in the case of *Haddon* v. *Van den Bergh Foods* only to be overturned a few months later in another case. Mr Haddon was dismissed in extraordinary circumstances when he failed to return to work after having attended a ceremony at which he had been presented with a long service award. Rather than completing the last few hours of his shift, he decided to take the time off. This was contrary to the workplace rules; so he was fired. When the case came to an employment tribunal Mr Haddon lost on the grounds that the employer's decision, though harsh, fell within the band of reasonable responses open to an employer in the circumstances. He appealed to the EAT, who took the opportunity not only to overturn the original decision, but also to hold that the long-established 'band of reasonable responses' test was unhelpful. Instead, they suggested that tribunals should simply make a general judgment about whether or not an employer had acted reasonably, taking into account their own opinion about what is appropriate.

For a few months the new ruling stood and tribunals began to use it in order to find in favour of ex-employees in many more cases than had been their practice previously. In March 2000, the EAT (with a new chairman) overturned its own decision in Haddon's case, putting back the band of reasonable responses test in the case of *Midland Bank* v. *Madden* (IRS 2000a). It argued that only a higher court, such as the Court of Appeal or the House of Lords, could discard the test, so it must remain until this occurs.

Lack of capability or qualifications

The first aspect of capability relates to skill or aptitude. Although employers have the right and opportunity to test an applicant's suitability for a particular post before that individual is engaged, or before promotion, the law recognises that mistakes may be made so that dismissal can be an appropriate remedy for the error, if the unsuitability is gross and beyond redemption. In order for such a dismissal to be fair and reasonable at least one warning has to be given and a reasonable opportunity to improve before the dismissal is implemented.

Where an employee is going through a period of probation at the time of termination, the following are appropriate check questions:

1 Has the employer shown that reasonable steps were taken to maintain the appraisal of the probationer through the period of probation?
2 Was there guidance by advice or warning when it would have been useful or fair to provide it?
3 Did an appropriate person make an honest effort to determine whether the probationer came up to the required standard, after reviewing the appraisals made by supervisors and other facts recorded about the probationer?

The employer will always need to demonstrate the employee's unsuitability to the satisfaction of the tribunal by producing evidence of that unsuitability. This evidence must not be undermined by, for instance, giving the employee a glowing testimonial at the time of dismissal or by the presence of positive appraisal reports on the individual's personal file. Lack of skill or aptitude is a fair ground when the lack can be demonstrated and where the employer has not contributed to it by, for instance, ignoring it for a long period. Normally there must be the chance to state a case and/or improve before the dismissal will be procedurally fair. Redeployment to a more suitable job is also an option employers are expected to consider before taking the decision to dismiss.

The second aspect of capability is qualifications: the degree, diploma or other paper qualification needed to qualify the individual to do the work for which they are employed. The simple cases are those of misrepresentation, where an employee claims qualifications he or she does not have. More difficult are the situations where the employee cannot acquire the necessary qualifications.

WINDOW ON PRACTICE

Dr Al-Tikriti was a senior registrar employed by the South Western Regional Health Authority. The practice of the authority was to allow registrars three attempts at passing the examination of the Royal College of Pathologists. Dr Al-Tikriti failed on the third attempt and was subsequently dismissed. He claimed that the dismissal was unfair on the grounds that he had had insufficient training to pass the exams. The tribunal, having heard evidence from the Royal College, decided that the training had been adequate and found the dismissal to have been fair (*Al-Tikriti* v. *South Western RHA* (1986)).

The third aspect of employee capability is health. It is potentially fair to dismiss someone on the grounds of ill health which renders the employee incapable of discharging the contract of employment. Even the most distressing dismissal can be legally admissible, provided that it is not too hasty and that there is consideration of alternative employment. Employers are expected, however, to take account of any medical advice available to them before dismissing someone on the grounds of ill health. Companies with occupational health services are well placed to obtain detailed medical reports to help in such judgements but the decision to terminate someone's employment is ultimately for the manager to take and, if necessary, to justify at a tribunal. Medical evidence will be sought and has to be carefully considered but dismissal remains an employer's decision, not a medical decision.

Normally, absences through sickness have to be frequent or prolonged in order for dismissal on the grounds of such absence to be judged fair, although absence which seriously interferes with the running of a business may be judged fair even if it is neither frequent nor prolonged. In all cases the employee must be consulted before being dismissed.

In the leading case of *Egg Stores* v. *Leibovici* (1977) the EAT set out nine questions that have to be asked to determine the potential fairness of dismissing someone after long-term sickness:

> (a) how long has the employment lasted; (b) how long had it been expected the employment would continue; (c) what is the nature of the job; (d) what was the nature, effect and length of the illness; (e) what is the need of the employer for the work to be done, and to engage a replacement to do it; (f) if the employer takes no action, will he incur obligations in respect of redundancy payments or compensation for unfair dismissal; (g) are wages continuing to be paid; (h) why has the employer dismissed (or failed to do so); and (i) in all the circumstances, could a reasonable employer have been expected to wait any longer?

This case was of frustration of contract, and there is always an emphasis in all tribunal hearings that the decision should be based on the facts of the particular situation of the dismissal that is being considered, rather than on specific precedents. For this reason the nine questions are no more than useful guidelines for managers to consider: they do not constitute 'the law' on the matter.

A different situation is where an employee is frequently absent for short spells. Here too it is potentially reasonable to dismiss, but only after proper consideration of the illnesses and after warning the employee of the consequences if their attendance record does not improve. As is made clear by Duggan (1999, pp. 140–1) each case has to be decided on its own merits. Medical evidence must be sought and a judgement reached about how likely it is that high levels of absence will continue in the future. The fact that an employee is wholly fit at the time of his or her dismissal does not mean that it is necessarily unfair. What matters is the overall attendance record and its impact on the organisation.

In another leading case, that of *International Sports Ltd* v. *Thomson* (1980), the employer dismissed an employee who had been frequently absent with a series of minor ailments ranging from althrugia of one knee, anxiety and nerves to bronchitis, cystitis, dizzy spells, dyspepsia and flatulence. All of these were covered by medical notes. (While pondering the medical note for flatulence, you will be interested to know that althrugia is water on the knee.) The employer issued a series of warnings and the company dismissed the employee after consulting its medical adviser, who saw no reason to examine the employee as the illnesses had no connecting medical theme and were not chronic. The Employment Appeals Tribunal held that this dismissal was fair because proper warning had been given and because the attendance record was deemed so poor as not to be acceptable to a reasonable employer. This position was confirmed by the Court of Appeal in *Wilson* v. *The Post*

Office (2000) where it was held to be quite acceptable, in principle, for an employer to dismiss someone simply because of a poor absence record.

The law on ill-health dismissals was affected in important ways by the passing of the Disability Discrimination Act 1995. In Chapter 23 we look at this important piece of legislation in detail. Here it is simply necessary to state that dismissing someone who is disabled according to the definition given in the Act, without first considering whether adjustments to working practices or the working environment would allow them to continue working, is unlawful. Reasonable adjustments might well include tolerance of a relatively high level of absence, especially where the employer is large enough to be able to cope perfectly well in the circumstances. Employers are well advised to pay particular attention to disability discrimination issues when dismissing people on the grounds of ill health because the level of compensation that can be awarded by tribunals in such cases is considerably higher than it is for unfair dismissal.

WINDOW ON PRACTICE

In 1998 Mr Kirker, a man with a visual impairment, was selected for redundancy by managers at British Sugar PLC. The selection criteria included assessments of competence and potential, on both of which measures he scored poorly because of his disability. He took his case to an employment tribunal and won. It was ruled that in dismissing him, the employer had unlawfully discriminated on grounds of disability. Had it not been for the visual impairment, he would have been retained.

There are no limits on the amount of compensation that can be awarded in disability discrimination cases, so the tribunal can make an award based on their estimate of the true level of financial loss suffered by the individual concerned. In Mr Kirker's case the figure was £103,146. British Sugar subsequently lost their appeal to the Employment Appeal Tribunal.

Source: *British Sugar* v. *Kirker* [1998] IRLR 624.

Misconduct

The law expects employers to make a distinction between two classes of misconduct when dismissing employees or considering doing so.

1 **Gross misconduct.** This occurs when an employee commits an offence which is sufficiently serious to justify summary dismissal. To qualify, the employee must have acted in such a way as to have breached either an express term of their contract or one of the common law duties owed by an employee to an employer (*see* Chapter 4).

2 **Ordinary misconduct.** This involves lesser transgressions, such as minor breaches of rules and relatively insignificant acts of disobedience, insubordination, lateness, forgetfulness or rudeness. In such cases the employer is deemed by the courts to be acting unreasonably if it dismisses as a result of a first offence. The dismissal would only be fair if, having been formally warned at least once, the employee failed to improve his/her conduct.

Employers have a wide degree of discretion when it comes to deciding what exactly does and does not constitute gross misconduct, and this will vary from workplace to workplace. For example, a distinction can be made between smoking in an office where there is a no-smoking policy (ordinary misconduct) and smoking on the factory floor near to combustible materials (gross misconduct). While much depends on the circumstances, the tribunals also look carefully at an employer's established policies on matters of conduct:

> Where the disciplinary rules spell out clearly the type of conduct that will warrant dismissal then a dismissal for this reason may be fair. Conversely, if the rules are silent or ambiguous as to whether particular conduct warrants dismissal, a dismissal for a first offence may be unfair. (Duggan 1999, p. 178)

It is important, therefore, for employers to set out in writing what standards of conduct they expect, to make clear what will be regarded as 'sackable misconduct', and to ensure that everyone is aware of these rules.

The second key principle in misconduct cases concerns procedure. Whether the individual is dismissed summarily for gross misconduct or after a number of warnings for ordinary misconduct, the tribunals look to see if a reasonable procedure has been used. This basic requirement is unaffected by the Dispute Resolution Regulations (2004) which clearly state that employers are required to adhere to basic procedures. However, these regulations do permit employers to dispense with the need for a disciplinary hearing in 'extreme' cases of gross misconduct. We look in more detail at disciplinary procedures in Chapter 25. Here it is necessary to note the main questions that an employment tribunal asks when faced with such cases:

1. Was the accusation thoroughly, promptly and properly investigated by managers before the decision was made to dismiss or issue a formal warning?
2. Was a formal hearing held at which the accused employee was given the opportunity to state their case and challenge evidence brought forward by managers?
3. Was the employee concerned permitted to be accompanied at the hearing by a colleague or trade union representative?
4. Was the employee treated consistently when compared with other employees who had committed similar acts of misconduct in the past?

Only if the answers to all these questions is 'yes' will a tribunal find a dismissal fair. They do not, however, expect employers to adhere to very high standards of evidence gathering such as those employed by the police in criminal investigations. Here, as throughout employment law, the requirement is for the employer to act reasonably in all the circumstances, conforming to the principles of natural justice and doing what it thought to be right at the time, given the available facts.

Conversely, if an employee is found guilty by court proceedings, this does not automatically justify fair dismissal; it must still be procedurally fair and reasonable. A theft committed off duty and away from the workforce is not necessarily grounds for dismissal; it all depends on the nature of the work carried out by the employee concerned. For example, it might well be reasonable to dismiss members of staff with responsibility for cash if they commit an offence of dishonesty while off duty.

On the other hand, evidence that would not be sufficient to bring a prosecution may be sufficient to sustain a fair dismissal. Clocking-in offences will normally merit dismissal. Convictions for other offences like drug handling or indecency will only justify dismissal if the nature of the offence will have some bearing on the work done by the employee. For someone like an instructor of apprentices it might justify summary dismissal, but in other types of employment it would be unfair, just as it would be unfair to dismiss an employee for a driving offence when there was no need for driving in the course of normal duties and there were other means of transport for getting to work.

WINDOW ON PRACTICE

In the past few years employment tribunals have had to come to grips with a new type of dismissal case, situations in which people are dismissed for downloading and storing pornographic images from the internet. Tribunals have had to consider whether or not such actions constitute gross misconduct (leading to summary dismissal without notice), or whether they should be considered as ordinary misconduct, in which case summary dismissal for a first offence would be regarded as being unfair.

Cases have been decided in different ways depending on the clarity of established rules and procedural matters. In *Parr* v. *Derwentside District Council* (1998), Mr Parr was summarily dismissed having been caught by his employers accessing pornography from his computer while at work. He claimed that he had visited the site concerned by accident, had got himself stuck in it and had subsequently 'revisited it only because he was disturbed by the prospect that entry could easily be made by children'. His claim for unfair dismissal failed because the employers had used a fair procedure and because they were able to show that Mr Parr had broken established codes of conduct.

By contrast, in *Dunn* v. *IBM UK Ltd* (1998), a summary dismissal occurring in similar circumstances was found to fall outside the 'band of reasonable responses'. In this case the employers were found not to have investigated the matter properly and not to have convened a fair disciplinary hearing, the whole matter having been handled far too hastily. Moreover, there was no company policy on internet usage for Mr Dunn to have broken and he was unaware that he had done anything that would be construed as gross misconduct. He won his case, but had his compensation reduced by 50 per cent on the grounds that he was partly responsible for his own dismissal.

In a third case, *Humphries* v. *VH Barnett & Co* (1998), a tribunal stated that in normal circumstances the act of accessing pornography from the internet while at work should not be construed as gross misconduct unless such a policy was made clear to employees and established as a workplace rule. However, in this case, the tribunal decided that the pictures downloaded were so obscene that Mr Humphries could be legitimately treated as having commited an act of gross misconduct.

Source: IDS (1999), 'Downloading pornography', *IDS Brief 637*, May.

Redundancy

Dismissal for redundancy is protected by compensation for unfair redundancy, compensation for genuine redundancy and the right to consultation before the redundancy takes place:

> An employee who is dismissed shall be taken to be dismissed by reason of redundancy if the dismissal is attributable wholly or mainly to:
> (a) the fact that his employer has ceased, or intends to cease, to carry on the business for the purposes of which the employee was employed by him, or has ceased, or intends to cease, to carry on that business in the place where the employee was so employed, or
> (b) the fact that the requirements of that business for employees to carry out work of a particular kind, or for employees to carry out work of a particular kind in the place where he was so employed, have ceased or are expected to cease or diminish.
> (Employment Rights Act 1996, s. 139(1))

Apart from certain specialised groups of employees, anyone who has been continuously employed for two years or more is guaranteed a compensation payment from an employer, if dismissed for redundancy. The compensation is currently assessed on a sliding scale relating to length of service, age and rate of pay per week. If the employer wishes to escape the obligation to compensate, then it is necessary to show that the reason for dismissal was something other than redundancy. The inclusion of age in the criteria for calculating redundancy payments is likely to end with the introduction of age discrimination law in 2006.

Although the legal rights relating to redundancy have not altered for 35 years, there have been persistent problems of interpretation, different courts reaching different decisions when faced with similar sets of circumstances (*see* IRS 2000b). In 1999 the House of Lords provided some long-needed clarification of key issues in the cases of *Murray et al.* v. *Foyle Meats Ltd*, where it was decided that tribunals should look at the actual facts of someone's working situation rather than at their written contractual terms when deciding whether or not their jobs were redundant. In so doing it confirmed that the practice of 'bumping', where the employer dismisses a person whose job is remaining to retain the services of another employee whose job is disappearing, is acceptable under the statutory definition. The questions laid out by the Employment Appeals Tribunal (EAT) in *Safeway* v. *Burrell* (1997) are thus now confirmed as those that tribunals should ask when considering these cases:

1 Has the employee been dismissed?
2 Has there been an actual or prospective cessation or diminution in the requirements for employees to carry out work of a particular kind?
3 Is the dismissal wholly or mainly attributable to the state of affairs?

The employer has to consult with the individual employee before dismissal takes place, but there is also a separate legal obligation to consult with recognised trade unions or some other body of employee representatives where no union is recognised. If 20 or more employees are to be made redundant, then the employer must give written notice of intention to any recognised unions concerned and the Department of Trade and Industry (DTI) at least 30 days before the first dismissal. If it is proposed to make more than 100 employees redundant within a three-month period, then 90 days' advance notice must be given. Having done this, the employer has a legal duty to consult on the redundancies. There is no obligation to negotiate with employees, merely to explain, listen to comments and reply with reasons. Employees also have the right to reasonable time off with pay during their redundancy notice so that they can seek other work.

One of the most difficult aspects of redundancy for the employer is the selection of who should go. The traditional approach provides that people should leave on a last-in-first-out basis, or LIFO, as this provides a rough-and-ready justice with which it is difficult to argue. In recent years, however, an increasing number of employers are using a mix of other criteria, including skill, competence and attendance record. A third approach involves drawing up a new post-redundancy organisation structure and inviting everyone to apply for the jobs that will remain. In principle all are acceptable as far as the law is concerned provided they are carried out objectively and consistently.

Increasingly, employers are trying to avoid enforced redundancy by a range of strategies, such as not replacing people who leave, early retirement and voluntary redundancy. The large scale of redundancies in recent years has produced a variety of managerial initiatives to mitigate the effects. One of the most constructive has been a redundancy counselling or outplacement service. Sometimes this is administered by the HR department, but many organisations use external services. Contrary to some popular perception there is no legal requirement to offer such services or to ask for volunteers before carrying through a programme of compulsory redundancies.

Some other substantial reason

As the law of unfair dismissal has evolved since 1971 the most controversial area has been the category of potentially fair dismissals known as 'some other substantial reason'. Many commentators see this as a catch-all or dustbin category which enables employers to dismiss virtually anyone provided a satisfactory business case can be made. All manner of cases have been successfully defended under this heading including the following: dismissals resulting from personality clashes, pressure to dismiss from subordinates or customers, disclosure of damaging information, the dismissal of a man whose wife worked for a rival firm, and the dismissal of a landlord's wife following her husband's dismissal on grounds of capability.

The majority of cases brought under this heading, however, result from business reorganisations where there is no redundancy. These often occur when the employer seeks to alter terms and conditions of employment and cannot secure the employee's agreement. Such circumstances can result in the dismissal of the employee together with an offer of re-employment on new contractual terms. Such dismissals are judged fair provided a sound business reason exists to justify the changes envisaged. It will usually be necessary to consult prior to the reorganisation but the tribunal will not base its judgment on whether the employee acted reasonably in refusing new terms and conditions. The test laid down in *Hollister* v. *The National Farmers' Union* (1979) by the Court of Appeal merely requires the employer to demonstrate that the change would bring clear organisational advantage.

WRITTEN STATEMENT OF REASONS

The Employment Rights Act 1996 (s. 92) gives employees the right to obtain from their employer a written statement of the reasons for their dismissal, if they are dismissed after completing a year's continuous service. If asked, the employer must provide the statement within 14 days. If it is not provided, the employee can complain to an employment tribunal that the statement has been refused and the tribunal will award the employee two weeks' pay if they find the complaint justified. The same right applies where a fixed-term contract is not renewed after having expired. The employee can also complain, and receive the same award, if the employer's reasons are untrue or inadequate, provided that the tribunal agrees.

Such an award is in addition to anything the tribunal may decide about the unfairness of the dismissal, if the employee complains about that. The main purpose of this provision is to enable the employee to test whether there is a reasonable case for an unfair dismissal complaint or not. Although the statement is admissible as evidence in tribunal proceedings, the tribunal will not necessarily be bound by what the statement contains. If the tribunal members were to decide that the reasons for dismissal were other than stated, then the management case would be jeopardised.

CONSTRUCTIVE DISMISSAL

When the behaviour of the management causes the employee to resign, the ex-employee may still be able to claim dismissal on the grounds that the behaviour of the employer constituted a repudiation of the contract, leaving the employee with no alternative but to resign. The employee may then be able to claim that the dismissal was unfair. It is not sufficient for the employer simply to be awkward or whimsical; the employer's conduct must amount to a significant breach, going to the root of the contract, such as physical assault, demotion, reduction in pay, change in location of work or significant change in duties. The breach must, however, be significant, so that a slight lateness in paying wages would not involve a breach, neither would a temporary change in place of work.

Some of the more interesting constructive dismissal cases concern claims that implied terms of contract have been breached, such as the employer's duty to maintain safe systems of working or mutual trust and confidence.

WINDOW ON PRACTICE

In 1994 a former manager of an off-licence called Mrs Gullyes won a case of constructive dismissal. She argued successfully that her employer had breached an implied term of her contract and that this had led directly to her resignation.

At the time of her resignation, Mrs Gullyes had been employed as a branch manager for four years – a job she carried out with conspicuous success. As a result she had been promoted into a manager's role in a larger branch with severe staffing problems. She accepted the new post with some reluctance after agreeing with the company that she could transfer again if things did not work out.

She found the new job hard from the start, finding herself working 76 hours a week and gaining insufficient help from other members of staff. After a few months she went away on holiday, returning to find that two of her staff had been transferred to other branches in her absence. At this point she requested a transfer herself and was refused. She resigned and brought a claim of constructive dismissal.

Mrs Gullyes won her case by arguing that the company had breached its common law duty to provide adequate support to her in the new job. The case was appealed to the EAT, where she won again.

Sources: L. Macdonald (1998) 'Termination of Employment: Breach of contract, constructive dismissal and wrongful dismissal', *Personnel Manager's Fact Finder*. London: Gee Publishing. *Whitbread PLC/Thresher* v. *Gullyes* (1994).

Constructive dismissal, like unfair dismissal, dates from 1971. It too only applies to employees who have completed a year's continuous service. The cases are harder for employees to win and easier for employers to defend because of the need to establish that a dismissal has taken place, before issues of reasonableness in the circumstances are addressed. The burden of proof is on the employee to show that they were forced into resigning as a result of a repudiatory breach on the part of the employer.

COMPENSATION FOR DISMISSAL

Having found in favour of the applicant in cases of unfair or constructive dismissal, the tribunal can make two types of decision: either they can order that the ex-employee be re-employed or they can award some financial compensation from the ex-employer for the loss that the employee has suffered. Originally it was intended that re-employment should be the main remedy, although this was not previously available under earlier legislation. In practice, however, the vast majority of ex-employees (over 95 per cent) want compensation.

Tribunals will not order re-employment unless the dismissed employee wants it, and tribunals can choose between reinstatement or re-engagement. In reinstatement the old job is given back to the employee under the same terms and conditions, plus any increments, etc., to which the individual would have become entitled had the dismissal not occurred, plus any arrears of payment that would have been received. The situation is just as it would have been, including all rights deriving from length of service, if the dismissal had not taken place. The alternative of re-engagement will be that the employee is employed afresh in a job comparable to the last one (usually in a different department), but without continuity of employment. The decision as to which of the two to order will depend on assessment of the practicability of the alternatives, the wishes of the unfairly dismissed employee and the natural justice of the award taking account of the ex-employee's behaviour.

Tribunals currently calculate the level of compensation under a series of headings. First is the **basic award** which is based on the employee's age and length of service. It is calculated in the same way as statutory redundancy payments, and like them will have to be reviewed to ensure that it complies with age discrimination law when it is introduced in 2006:

- half a week's pay for every year of service below the age of 22;
- one week's pay for every year of service between the ages of 22 and 41;
- one and a half weeks' pay for every year of service over the age of 41.

The basic award is limited, however, because tribunals can only take into account a maximum of 20 years' service when calculating the figure to be awarded. A maximum weekly salary figure is also imposed by the Treasury. This was £270 in 2004. The maximum basic award that can be ordered is therefore £8,100. In many cases, of course, where the employee has only a few years' service the figure will be far lower. In addition a tribunal can also order compensation under the following headings:

- **Compensatory awards** take account of loss of earnings, pension rights, future earnings loss, etc. The maximum level in 2004 was £55,000.
- **Additional awards** are used in cases of sex and race discrimination and also when an employer fails to comply with an order of reinstatement or re-engagement. In the former case the maximum award is 52 weeks' pay, in the latter 26 weeks' pay.
- **Special awards** are made when unfair dismissal relates to trade union activity or membership. They can also be used when the dismissal was for health and safety reasons.

A tribunal can reduce the total level of compensation if it judges the individual concerned to have contributed to his or her own dismissal. For example, a dismissal on grounds of poor work performance may be found unfair because no procedure was followed and consequently no warnings given. This does not automatically entitle the ex-employee concerned to compensation based on the above formulae. If the tribunal judges them to have been 60 per cent responsible for their own dismissal the compensation will be reduced by 60 per cent. Reductions are also made if an ex-employee is judged not to have taken reasonable steps to mitigate his or her loss.

ACTIVITY 9.2

In what circumstances do you think a dismissed employee might welcome reinstatement or re-engagement, and in what circumstances might the employer welcome it?

WRONGFUL DISMISSAL

In addition to the body of legislation defining unfair and constructive dismissal there is a long-standing common law right to damages for an employee who has been dismissed wrongfully.

Cases of wrongful dismissal are taken to employment tribunals where the claim is for less than £25,000; otherwise they are taken to the the county court. These cases are concerned solely with alleged breaches of contract. Employees can thus only bring cases of wrongful dismissal against their employers when they believe their dismissal to have been unlawful according to the terms of their contract of employment.

Wrongful dismissal can, therefore, be used when the employer has not given proper notice or if the dismissal is in breach of any clause or agreement incorporated into the contract. This remains a form of remedy that very few people use, but it could be useful to employees who do not have sufficient length of service to claim unfair dismissal and whose contracts include the right to a full disciplinary procedure. There may also be cases where a very highly paid employee might get higher damages in an ordinary court than the maximum that the tribunal can award.

WINDOW ON PRACTICE

In order to bring a claim of unfair dismissal ex-employees must have been employed continuously for at least 12 months by the organisation concerned when they are dismissed. As a result it is common for employers to dismiss people after 11 months' service in the belief that they will never have to justify their actions in court. However, such approaches can backfire, as was shown in the case of *Raspin* v. *United News* (1999). Here the applicant brought a case of wrongful dismissal, basing the claim on the presence in the contract of employment of a disciplinary procedure. The Employment Appeals Tribunal decided that had the employer fulfilled its contractual duties and dismissed the employee using the procedure, the date of the dismissal would have occurred after 12 months' service had been completed. In assessing compensation the matter was thus treated as if it was an unfair dismissal claim.

RETIREMENT

The final mode of contract termination is retirement, and this has the advantage for the employer that there is usually plenty of notice, so that succession arrangements can be planned smoothly. It is now rare for people to retire abruptly after working at high pressure to the very end. Some sort of phased withdrawal is much preferred, so that the retiree adjusts gradually to the new state of being out of regular employment and with a lower level of income, while the employing organisation is able to prepare a successor to take office.

Another advantage of this arrangement is that there may be 'a life after death', with the retiree continuing to work part time after retirement, or coming back to help out at peak periods or at holiday times. Many organisations go to great lengths to keep in touch with their retired personnel, often arranging Christmas parties, excursions and other events, with people returning year after year.

Early retirement has become a widespread method of slimming payrolls and making opportunities both for some people to retire early and for others to take their place. The nature of the pension arrangements are critical to early retirement strategies, as early retirements are ideally voluntary and the majority of people will accept, or volunteer for, early retirement if the financial terms are acceptable. It is not, of course, possible to draw state retirement pension until the official retirement ages of 65 for men and 60 for women (born before 1 April 1950), but many people will accept an occupational pension and a lump sum in their 50s if they see the possibility of a new lease of life to pursue other interests or to start their own business. According to Disney (1999, p. 64) another reason is a substantial increase in the numbers who are able to claim incapacity benefit on a long-term basis. Between a fifth and a quarter of men in these age groups now claim the benefit. As a result, since the mid-1970s the proportion of men aged between 55 and 59 in the labour force has fallen from 90 per cent to 75 per cent. For those aged 60–65 participation rates have fallen from 80 per cent to under 50 per cent. By contrast, the proportion of women in these age groups undertaking paid work has risen during the same period (Disney 1999, p. 59). As a result of this trend, and a demographic context in which the population is ageing and living much longer, the government is considering proposals to push the date at which people can claim a state pension back to 70.

NOTICE

An employee qualifies for notice of dismissal on completion of four weeks of employment with an employer. At that time the employee is entitled to receive one week's notice. This remains constant until the employee has completed two years' service, after which it increases to two weeks' notice, thereafter increasing on the basis of one week's notice per additional year of service up to a maximum of 12 weeks for 12 years' unbroken service with that employer. These are minimum statutory periods. If the employer includes longer periods of notice in the contract, which is quite common with senior employees, then they are bound by the longer period.

The employee is required to give one week's notice after completing four weeks' service and this period does not increase as a statutory obligation. If an employee accepts a contract in which the period of notice to be given is longer, then that is binding, but the employer may have problems of enforcement if an employee is not willing to continue in employment for the longer period.

Neither party can withdraw notice unilaterally. The withdrawal will be effective only if the other party agrees. Therefore, if an employer gives notice to an employee and wishes later to withdraw it, this can be done only if the employee agrees to the contract of employment remaining in existence. Equally, employees cannot change their minds about resigning unless the employer agrees.

Notice exists when a date has been specified. The statement 'We're going to wind up the business, so you will have to find another job' is not notice: it is a warning of intention.

SUMMARY PROPOSITIONS

9.1 Of the many dismissals that take place in a year, a minority are reported to tribunals and a small minority are found in favour of the ex-employee.

9.2 The main grounds on which an employee can be dismissed without the likelihood of an unfair dismissal claim are lack of capability, misconduct, redundancy, statutory bar or some other substantial reason.

9.3 If an employee is dismissed on one of the above grounds, the dismissal must still be procedurally acceptable and fair in the circumstances.

9.4 An employee who resigns as a result of unreasonable behaviour by the employer can claim constructive dismissal and, if successful, have their case treated as if they had in fact been dismissed.

9.5 When employees retire from an organisation, a phased withdrawal rather than abrupt termination is likely to be a better arrangement for both employer and employee.

GENERAL DISCUSSION TOPICS

1 If you were dismissed in circumstances that you regarded as legally unfair, would you prefer to seek satisfaction through ACAS conciliation or through a tribunal hearing? Why?

2 In some countries a dismissal cannot be made until *after* a tribunal hearing, so that its 'fairness' is decided before it takes effect. What do you see as the benefits and drawbacks of that system?

3 What changes would you make in the criteria for dismissal on the grounds of misconduct?

FURTHER READING

Collins, H. (1992) *Justice in Dismissal: The Law of Termination of Employment.* Oxford: Oxford University Press

Dickens, L., Jones, M., Weekes, B. and Hant, M. (1985) *Dismissed: A Study of Unfair Dismissal and the Industrial Tribunal System.* Oxford: Blackwell
Many of the best scholarly critiques of unfair dismissal law were published some years ago, but they remain the best source of arguments about how the law might be reformed. These two works make major contributions to the literature.

Hepple, B. and Morris, G. (2002) 'The Employment Act 2002 and the crisis of individual employment rights', *Industrial Law Journal*, Vol. 33, No. 3
The Dispute Resolution Regulations 2004 (derived from principles set out in the Employment Act 2002) have proved highly controversial and have generated a great deal of critical comment. Much of this focuses on the likely impact the regulations will have on the operation of unfair dismissal law. A strongly argued critique is provided by the leading academic labour lawyers Bob Hepple and Gillian Morris (2002).

Rojot, J. (2001) 'Security of employment and employability', in R. Blanpain and C. Engels (eds) *Comparative Labour Law and Industrial Relations in Industrialized Market Economies.* The Hague: Kluwer
There is a huge variety of different laws regulating dismissal in different countries. In the USA most states retain the doctrine of 'employment at will', placing no general statutory restrictions on the right of an employer to dismiss. In the Netherlands, by contrast, employers cannot generally dismiss without first getting the approval of a government officer. A good account of the various systems in use around the globe is provided by Rojot (2001).

REFERENCES

Disney, R. (1999) 'Why have older men stopped working?' in P. Gregg and J. Wadsworth (eds) *The State of Working Britain*. Manchester: Manchester University Press.

DTI (1999) *The Unfair Dismissal and Statement of Reasons for Dismissal (variation of qualifying period) Order 1999 – regulatory impact assessment*. London: Department of Trade and Industry.

DTI (2003) *Statutory Dispute Resolution Procedures*. London: Department of Trade and Industry.

Duggan, M. (1999) *Unfair Dismissal: Law, practice & guidance*. Welwyn Garden City: CLT Professional Publishing.

Earnshaw, J.M. (1997) 'Tribunals and tribulations', *People Management*, May, pp. 34–6.

IDS (1999) 'Downloading pornography', *IDS Brief 637*, May.

IRS (2000a) 'Range of reasonable responses test is not wrong', *Industrial Relations Law Bulletin*, No. 638, April.

IRS (2000b) 'The (re)definition of redundancy', *Industrial Relations Law Bulletin*, No. 633, January.

Macdonald, L. (1998) 'Termination of Employment: Breach of contract, constructive dismissal and wrongful dismissal', *Personnel Manager's Fact Finder*. London: Gee Publishing.

LEGAL CASES

Al-Tikriti v. *South Western RHA* (1986).

British Sugar v. *Kirker* [1998] IRLR 624.

Dunn v. *IBM UK Ltd* (1998) IDS Brief 637, May 1999.

Egg Stores v. *Leibovici* [1977] ICR 260.

Haddon v. *Van den Bergh Foods* [1999] IRLR 672, EAT.

Hollister v. *The National Farmers' Union* [1979] ICR 542.

Humphries v. *VH Barnett & Co* (1998) IDS Brief 637, May 1999.

International Sports Ltd v. *Thomson* [1980] IRLR 340.

Midland Bank v. *Madden* [2000] IRLR 288.

Murray et al. v. *Foyle Meats Ltd* [1999] IRLR 562.

Parr v. *Derwentside District Council* (1998) IDS Brief 637, May 1999.

Polkey v. *AE Dayton Services* [1987] ICR 142.

Raspin v. *United News* [1999] IRLR 9.

Safeway v. *Burrell* [1997] IRLR 200.

Whitbread PLC/Thresher v. *Gullyes* [1994] EAT 478/92.

Wilson v. *The Post Office* [2000] IRLR 834.

An extensive range of additional materials, including multiple choice questions, answers to questions and links to useful websites can be found on the Human Resource Management Companion Website at www.pearsoned.co.uk/torrington.

Part II FOCUS ON SKILLS

INTERACTIVE SKILL 2: SELECTION INTERVIEWING

Central to all resourcing is the selection interview, which is also one of the most familiar and forbidding encounters of organisational life. Most people have had at least one experience of being interviewed as a preliminary to employment and few reflect with pleasure on the experience. HR specialists have a critical role in selection interviewing, carrying out many of the interviews and encouraging good interviewing practice in others by example, support and training.

In this Focus on skills our objectives are to:

1 Review the varieties of selection interview and its purpose

2 Explain interview strategy and to consider the number of interviews and interviewers

3 Explain interview structure and the five key aspects of method

Varieties of interview

There are various practices in selection interviewing. At one extreme we read of men seeking work in the docks of Victorian London and generally being treated as if they were in a cattle market. They had to queue up in a series of gangways, similar to those used today to corral cattle at market, and had to vie with each other for the attention of the foreman hiring labourers for the day. Some of the older men apparently used to dye their hair in a pathetic attempt to appear younger and fitter than they really were and thereby catch the foreman's eye. At the opposite extreme we hear of people being telephoned by complete strangers and being offered handsome contracts to work in Hollywood studios.

There is a neat spectrum of employee participation in the employment process which correlates with social class and type of work. While the London docks situation of the 1890s is not found today, there are working situations where the degree of discussion between the parties is limited to perfunctory exchanges about trade union membership, hours of work and rates of pay: labourers on building sites and extras on film sets being two examples. As interviews move up the organisational hierarchy there is growing equilibrium, with the interviewer becoming more courteous and responsive to questions from the applicant, who will probably be described as a 'candidate' or someone who 'might be interested in the position'. For the most senior positions it is less likely that people will be invited to respond to vacancies advertised in the press. Individuals will be approached, either directly or through consultants, and there will be an elaborate pavane in which each party seeks to persuade the other to declare an interest first.

Another indication of the variety of employment practice is in the titles used. The humblest of applicants seek 'jobs' or 'vacancies', while the more ambitious are looking for 'places', 'posts', 'positions', 'openings' or 'opportunities'. The really high-flyers seem to need somewhere to sit down, as they are offered 'seats on the board', 'professorial chairs' or 'places on the front bench'.

The purpose of the selection interview

The interview is a controlled conversation with a purpose. There are more exchanges in a shorter period related to a specific purpose than in an ordinary conversation. In the selection interview the purposes are:

- to collect information in order to predict how well the applicants would perform in the job for which they have applied, by measuring them against predetermined criteria;
- to provide candidates with full details of the job and organisation to facilitate their decision making;
- to conduct the interview in such a way that candidates feel that they have been given a fair hearing.

The selection interview has been extensively criticised as being unreliable, invalid and subjective, although such criticism is directed towards the decisions made and ignores the importance of the interview as a **ritual** in the employment process. Recent comprehensive analysis of selection interview effectiveness, however, concludes that their validity is now much greater than previously believed (McDaniel *et al.* 1994 and Judge 2000), provided that the interview is structured.

Handling this most crucial of encounters is a key skill for personnel and other managers as the interview provides a number of important advantages which cannot be provided by any other means.

The selection interview cannot be bettered as a means of exchanging information and meeting the human and ritual aspects of the employment process.

Exchanging information

The interview is a flexible and speedy means of exchanging information, over a broad range of topics. The employer has the opportunity to sell the company and explain job details in depth. Applicants have the chance to ask questions about the job and the company in order to collect the information they require for their own selection decision. The interview is also the logical culmination of the employment process, as information from a variety of sources, such as application forms, tests and references, can be discussed together.

Human and ritual aspects

In an interview some assessment can be made of matters that cannot be approached any other way, such as the potential compatibility of two people who will have to work together. Both parties need to meet before the contract begins, to 'tune in' to each other and begin the process of induction. The interview is valuable in that way to both potential employee and potential employer. It gives interviewees the feeling that they matter, as another person is devoting time to them and they are not being considered by a computer. Also, giving applicants a chance to ask questions underlines their decision-making role, making them feel less helpless in the hands of the all-powerful interviewer. Selection interviewing has powerful ritual elements, as the applicant is seeking either to enter, or to rise within, a social system. This requires the display of deferential behaviours:

> upward mobility involves the presentation of proper performances and . . . efforts to move upward . . . are expressed in terms of sacrifices made for the maintenance of front. (Goffman 1974, p. 45)

At the same time those who are already inside and above display their superiority and security, even unconsciously, in contrast with the behaviour of someone so obviously anxious to share the same privileged position. Reason tells us that this is inappropriate at the beginning of the twenty-first century as it produces an unreasonable degree of dependency in the applicant; and the books are full of advice to interviewers not to brandish their social superiority, but to put applicants at their ease and to reduce the status differentials. This, however, still acknowledges their superiority as they are the ones who take the initiative; applicants are not expected to help the interviewer relax and feel less apprehensive. Also the reality of the situation is usually that of applicant anxious to get in and selector choosing among several. Status differentials cannot simply be set aside. The selection interview is at least partly an initiation rite, not as elaborate as entry to commissioned rank in the armed forces, nor as whimsical as finding one's way into the Brownie ring, but still a process of going through hoops and being found worthy in a process where other people make all the rules.

ACTIVITY II.1

For a selection interview in which you recently participated, either as selector or as applicant, consider the following:

1 What were the ritual features?

2 Were any useful ritual features missing?

3 Could ritual have been, in any way, *helpfully* reduced?

No matter what other means of making employment decisions there may be, the interview is crucial, and when worries are expressed about its reliability, this is not a reason for doing away with it: it is a reason for conducting it properly.

Interview strategy

The approach to selection interviewing varies considerably from the amiable chat in a bar to the highly organised, multi-person panel.

Frank and friendly strategy

By far the most common is the approach which has been described as frank and friendly. Here the interviewer is concerned to establish and maintain rapport. This is done in the belief that if interviewees do not feel threatened, and are relaxed, they will be more forthcoming in the information that they offer. It is straightforward for both interviewer and interviewee and has the potential advantage that the interviewees will leave with a favourable impression of the business.

Problem-solving strategy

A variation of the frank and friendly strategy is the problem-solving approach. It is the method of presenting the candidate with a hypothetical problem and evaluating his or her answer, like the king in the fairy tale who offered the hand of the princess in marriage to the first suitor who could answer three riddles.

These are sometimes called situational interviews. The questions asked are derived from the job description and candidates are required to imagine themselves as the job holder and describe what they would do in a variety of hypothetical situations. This method is most applicable to testing elementary knowledge, such as the colour coding of wires in electric cables or maximum dosages of specified drugs. It is less effective to test understanding and ability.

There is no guarantee that the candidate would actually behave in the way suggested. The quick thinker will score at the expense of the person who can take action more effectively than they can answer riddles. A useful analysis and commentary on situational interviews is in Latham *et al.* (1980).

Biographical strategy

Similar to the problem-solving strategy is the biographical method. The focus is on the candidate's past behaviour and performance, which is a more reliable way of predicting future performance than asking interviewees what they would do in a certain situation. Candidates are requested to describe the background to a situation and explain what they did and why; what their options were; how they decided what to do; and the anticipated and real results of their action. The success of this method depends on in-depth job analysis, and preferably competency analysis, in order to frame the best questions. Bearing in mind the importance of structure in selection interviewing, the biographical approach is an excellent method.

Stress strategy

In the stress approach the interviewer becomes aggressive, disparages the candidates, puts them on the defensive or disconcerts them by strange behaviour. The advantage of the method is that it may demonstrate a necessary strength or a disqualifying weakness that would not be apparent through other methods. The disadvantages are that evaluating the behaviour under stress is problematic, and those who are not selected will think badly of the employer. The likely value of stress interviewing is so limited that it is hardly worth mentioning, except that it has spurious appeal to many managers, who are attracted by the idea of injecting at least some stress into the interview 'to see what they are made of', or 'to put them on their mettle'. Most candidates feel that the procedures are stressful enough, without adding to them.

Number of interviews and interviewers

There are two broad traditions governing the number of interviewers. One says that effective, frank discussion can only take place on a one-to-one basis, so candidates meet one interviewer, or several interviewers, one at a time. The other tradition is that fair play must be demonstrated and nepotism prevented so the interview must be carried out, and the decision made, by a panel of interviewers. Within this dichotomy there are various options.

The individual interview

The individual interview gives the greatest chance of establishing rapport, developing mutual trust and is the most efficient deployment of time in the face-to-face encounter, as each participant has to compete with only one other speaker. It is usually also the most satisfactory method for the candidate, who has to tune in to only one other person instead of needing constantly to adjust to different interlocutors.

The candidate can more readily ask questions, as it is difficult to ask a panel of six people to explain the workings of the pension scheme, and it is the least formal type of interview. The disadvantages lie in the reliance the organisation places on the judgement of one of its representatives, although this can be mitigated by a series of individual interviews, and the ritual element is largely missing. Candidates may not feel they have been 'done' properly. A sole interview with the line manager is very popular in the selection of blue-collar staff, being used in over one-third of cases. It is less popular for white-collar and management staff.

Sequential interviews

Sequential interviews are a series of individual interviews. The series most often consists of just two interviews for blue- and white-collar staff, but more than two for managerial staff. The most frequent combination is an interview with the line manager and one with a representative of the HR department. For managerial posts this will be extended to interviews with other departmental managers, top managers and significant prospective colleagues. Sequential interviews can give the employer a broader picture of the candidate and they also allow the applicant to have contact with a greater number of potential colleagues. However, for the advantages of sequential interviews to be realised there is a need for effective organisation and for all interviews to be held on the same day. It is important that all interviewers meet beforehand to agree on the requirements of the post and to decide how each will contribute to the overall theme. Immediately following the interviews a further meeting needs to take place so that the candidates can be jointly evaluated. One disadvantage of the method is the organisation and time that it takes from both the employer's and the candidate's point of view. It requires considerable commitment from the candidate who may have to keep repeating similar information and whose performance may deteriorate throughout the course of the interviews due to fatigue.

Panel interviews

The panel interview method has the specious appeal of sharing judgement and may appear to be a way of saving time in interviewing as all panel members are operating at once. It is also possible to legitimise a quick decision, always popular with candidates, and there can be no doubt about the ritual requirements being satisfied. Panel interviews reduce the likelihood of personal bias in interviewing, particularly in guarding against possible infringements of legal requirements. They can also ensure the candidate is acceptable to the whole organisation, and allow the candidate to get a good feel for the business and its organisation. The drawbacks lie in the tribunal nature of the panel. They are not having a conversation with the candidates; they are sitting in judgement upon them and assessing the evidence they are able to present in response to the panel's requests. There is little prospect of building rapport and developing discussion, and there is likely to be as much interplay between members of the panel as there is between the panel and the candidate.

Panel interviews tend towards over-rigidity and give ironic point to the phrase, 'it is only a formality'. They are ritualistically superb, but dubious as a useful preliminary to employment. However, the benefits of the panel interview can be increased, and the disadvantages reduced, if the interviewers are properly trained and the interview well organised, thoroughly planned and made part of a structured selection process.

ACTIVITY II.2

In your organisation how many interviews and interviewers are used? How effective is this approach and why? In what ways could the approach be improved?

The selection interview sequence

Preparation

We assume that the preliminaries of job analysis, recruitment and shortlisting are complete and the interview is now to take place. The first step in preparation is for the interviewers to brief themselves. They will collect and study a job description or similar details of the post to be filled, a candidate specification or statement of required competencies and the application forms or curricula vitae of the candidates.

If there are several people to be interviewed the interview timetable needs greater planning than it usually receives. The time required for each interview can be determined beforehand only approximately. A rigid timetable will weigh heavily on both parties, who will feel frustrated if the interview is closed arbitrarily at a predetermined time and uncomfortable if an interview that has 'finished' is drawn out to complete its allotted timespan. However, the disadvantages of keeping people waiting are considerable and underrated.

The experience of Barbara Trevithick reflects the thinking of some selectors that candidates are supplicants waiting on interviewers' pleasure, they have no competing calls on their time and a short period of waiting demonstrates who is in charge. There are flaws in this reasoning. Most candidates will have competing calls on their time, as they will have taken time off to attend and have earmarked the anticipated interview time to fit in a busy schedule. Some may have other interviews to go to. An open-ended waiting period can be worrying, enervating and a poor preliminary to an interview. If the dentist keeps you waiting you may get distressed, but when the waiting is over you are simply a passive participant and the dentist does not have the success of the operation jeopardised. The interview candidate has, in a real sense, to perform when the period of waiting is over and the success of the interaction could well be jeopardised.

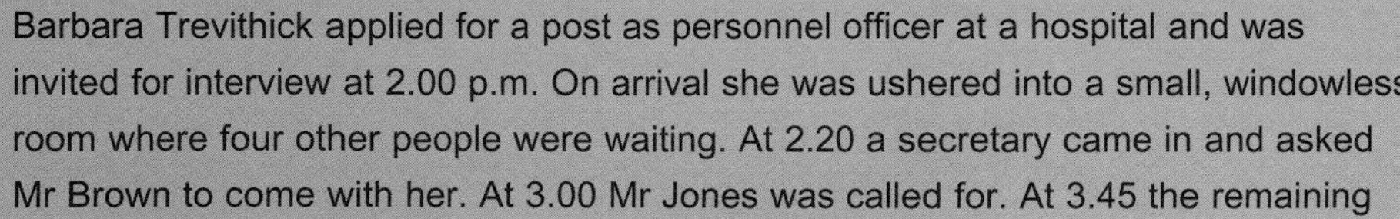

WINDOW ON PRACTICE

Barbara Trevithick applied for a post as personnel officer at a hospital and was invited for interview at 2.00 p.m. On arrival she was ushered into a small, windowless room where four other people were waiting. At 2.20 a secretary came in and asked Mr Brown to come with her. At 3.00 Mr Jones was called for. At 3.45 the remaining three candidates went out in search of the secretary to ask what the remaining timetable for the day was to be. The secretary replied that she did not know but the panel members had just gone to the canteen for a cup of coffee. By now Barbara had figured out that her surname was the last in alphabetical order. Miss Mellhuish was called for interview at 4.10 and Miss Roberts left because her last train home to Scotland was due in 20 minutes. Barbara Trevithick went in for interview at 4.45 to find that two members of the panel 'had had to leave', so she was interviewed by the two surviving members: a personnel officer and a nursing officer. At the close of the interview she asked when the decision would be made and was told that the two interviewers would have to consult with their two absent colleagues in the morning. Three weeks later Barbara rang to ask the outcome, as she had not received a letter, to be told that Mr Brown had been appointed and 'I'm surprised they didn't tell you, as it was offered to him that afternoon, after the coffee break'.

The most satisfactory timetable is the one that guarantees a break after all but the most voluble candidates. If candidates are asked to attend at hourly intervals, for example, this would be consistent with interviews lasting between 40 and 60 minutes. This would mean that each interview began at the scheduled time and that the interviewers had the opportunity to review and update their notes in the intervals.

Reception

Candidates arrive on the premises of their prospective employer on the lookout for every scrap of evidence they can obtain about the business, what it looks like, what the people look like and what people say. A candidate is likely to meet at least one and possibly two people before meeting the interviewer. First will be the commissionaire or receptionist. There is frequently also an emissary from the HR department to shepherd them from the gate to the waiting-room. Both are valuable sources of information, and interviewers may wish to prime such people so that they can see their role in the employment process and can be cheerful, informative and helpful.

The candidate will most want to meet the interviewer, the unknown but powerful figure on whom so much depends. Interviewers easily forget that they know much more about the candidates than the candidates know about them, because the candidates have provided a personal profile in the application form.

Interviewers do not reciprocate. To bridge this gap it can be very useful for interviewers to introduce themselves to the candidate in the waiting-room, so that contact is made quickly, unexpectedly and on neutral territory. This makes the opening of the interview itself rather easier.

Candidates wait to be interviewed. Although there are snags about extended, open-ended waiting periods, some time is inevitable and necessary to enable candidates to compose themselves. It is a useful time to deal with travelling expenses and provide some relevant background reading about the employing organisation.

Setting

The appropriate setting for an interview has to be right for the ritual and right from the point of view of enabling a full and frank exchange of information. It is difficult to combine the two. Many of the interview horror stories relate to the setting in which it took place. A candidate for a post as Deputy Clerk of Works was interviewed on a stage while the panel of 17 sat in the front row of the stalls, and a candidate for a Headteacher post came in to meet the interview panel and actually moved the chair on which he was to sit. He only moved it two or three inches because the sun was in his eyes, but there was an audible frisson and sharp intake of breath from the members of the panel.

Remaining with our model of the individual interviewer, here are some simple suggestions about the setting:

- The room should be suitable for a private conversation.
- If the interview takes place across a desk, as is common, the interviewer may wish to reduce the extent to which the desk acts as a barrier, inhibiting free flow of communication.
- All visitors and telephone calls should be avoided, as they do not simply interrupt: they intrude and impede the likelihood of frankness.
- It should be clear to the candidates where they are to sit.

Interview structure

There are several important reasons why the employment interview should be structured, making use of the application or CV:

- The candidate expects the proceedings to be decided and controlled by the interviewer and will anticipate a structure within which to operate.
- It helps the interviewer to make sure that they cover all relevant areas and avoid irrelevancies.
- It looks professional.
- Structure can be used to guide the interview and ensure that it makes sense.
- It assists the interviewer in using the time available in the most effective way.
- The application form can be used as a memory aid by the interviewer when making notes directly after the interview.
- It makes it easier to compare candidates.

The interview

There are several different ways to structure the interview. We recommend the form set out in Table II.1. This divides activities and objectives into three interview stages: opening, middle and closing. While there are few, if any, alternative satisfactory ways for conducting the beginning and the end of the interview, the middle can be approached from a number of different angles, depending on the circumstances.

The interviewer needs to work systematically through the structure that has been planned but the structure does not have to be adhered to rigidly. Interviewers should abandon their own route whenever the candidate chooses one that seems more promising.

Table II.1 Interview structure: a recommended pattern

Stage	Objectives	Activities
Opening	To put the candidate at ease, develop rapport and set the scene	Greet candidate by name Introduce yourself Explain interview purpose Outline how purpose will be achieved Obtain candidate's assent to outline
Middle	To collect and provide information	Asking questions within a structure that makes sense to the candidate, such as biographical, areas of the application form, or competencies identified for the job Listening Answering questions
Closing	To close the interview and confirm future action	Summarise interview Check candidate has no more questions Indicate what happens next and when

The opening of the interview is the time for mutual preliminary assessment and tuning in to each other. A useful feature of this phase is for the interviewer to sketch out the plan or procedure for the interview and how it fits in with the total employment decision process. It is also likely that the application form will provide an easy, non-controversial topic for these opening behaviours.

One objective is for the two parties to exchange words so that they can adjust their receiving mechanism to be mutually intelligible. It also provides an opportunity for both to feel comfortable in the presence of the other. Interviewers able to achieve these two objectives may then succeed in developing a relationship in which candidates trust the interviewer's ability and motives so that they will speak openly and fully. This is known as 'rapport', which was dealt with in the Part I Focus on skills. The interviewer's effectiveness will greatly depend on their being skilled at this process.

We are working on the assumption that candidates will behave in a reasonably genuine way, provided the interviewer can convince them that the process is fair. Some candidates do not and such people have been labelled as 'white collar psychopaths', although it has to be said that they are rare. They are very good at presenting themselves as being exactly what the interviewer is looking for. Not only are they manufacturing the truth about their experience, the trait (or psychopathic tendency) that drives them causes them to wreak havoc once they are appointed. A New York psychologist cites the example of 'Ron' who was appointed to a sales post in a pharmaceuticals company:

> Ron fiddled his sales figures, charged call girls to the company and nearly succeeded in using his charm to get his new boss fired when he was questioned about his behaviour. Psychopaths are motivated by three things: thrill-seeking, game-playing and hurting people. Once inside the organization they build networks of influence that make it very difficult to get rid of them and can help them join the management fast track. (Paul Babiak, quoted in *Financial Times*, 12 January 2004)

For the middle of the interview the biographical approach is the most straightforward. It works on the basis that candidates at the time of the interview are the product of everything in their lives that has gone before. To understand the candidate the interviewer must understand the past and will talk to the candidate about the episodes of his or her earlier life, education, previous employment, etc.

The advantage of this is that the objectives are clear to both interviewer and interviewee, there is no deviousness or 'magic'. Furthermore, the development can be logical and so aid the candidate's recall of events. Candidates who reply to enquiries about their choice of A level subjects will be subconsciously triggering their recollection of contemporaneous events, such as the university course they took, which are likely to come next in the interview. The biographical approach is the simplest for the inexperienced interviewer to use as discussion can develop from the information provided by the candidate on the application form. Some version of sequential categories, such as employment, education and training, seems the most generally useful, but it will need the addition of at least two other categories: the work offered and the organisational context in which it is to be done. The middle of the interview can be structured by systematically working through items of the job description or the person specification. Increasingly, where competencies have been identified for the job, these are used as the basis of the structure.

In the preparatory stage of briefing, the interviewer will also prepare notes on two elements to incorporate in their plan: key issues and checkpoints.

Key issues will be the two or three main issues that stand out from the application form for clarification or elaboration. This might be the nature of the responsibilities carried in a particular earlier post, the content of a training course, the reaction to a period of employment in a significant industry or whatever else strikes the interviewer as being productive of useful additional evidence.

Checkpoints are matters of detail that require further information: grades in an examination, dates of an appointment, rates of pay, and so forth.

At the close of the interview the explanation of the next step needs especial attention. The result of the interview is of great importance to the candidates and they will await the outcome with anxiety. Even if they do not want the position they will probably hope to have it offered. This may strengthen their hand in dealings with another prospective employer, or with their present employer, and will certainly be a boost to their morale. The great merit of convention in the public sector is that the chosen candidate is told before the contenders disperse: the great demerit is that they are asked to say yes or no to the offer at once.

In the private sector it is unusual for an employment offer to be made at the time of the interview, so there is a delay during which the candidates will chafe. Their frustration will be greater if the delay is longer than expected and they may start to tell themselves that they are not going to receive an offer, in which case they will also start convincing themselves that they did not want the job either! It is important for the interviewer to say as precisely as possible when the offer will be made, but ensuring that the candidates hear earlier rather than later than they expect, if there is to be any deviation.

The interviewer will need to call into play at least five key aspects of method.

1 Some data can be collected by simple observation of the candidate. Notes can be made about dress, appearance, voice, height and weight, if these are going to be relevant, and the interviewer can also gauge the candidate's mood and the

appropriate response to it by the non-verbal cues that are provided. The study of body language has achieved great popularity in the last twenty years, largely because of its alleged potential for interpreting the thoughts and intentions of members of the opposite sex in social situations. Although the available books are designed for a popular market, they are usually sound and contain useful advice for the selection interviewer.

2 The remainder of the evidence will come from listening to what is said, so the interviewer has to be very attentive throughout; not only listening to the answers to questions, but also listening for changes in inflection and pace, nuances and overtones that provide clues on what to pursue further. The amount of time that the two spend talking is important, as an imbalance in one direction or the other will mean that either the candidate or the interviewer is not having enough opportunity to hear information.

Being silent and deliberately leaving verbal lulls in face-to-face situations provide the opportunity for the other person to say more, perhaps more than was initially intended. Silence still has to be attentive and the longer the silence, the harder it is to be attentive.

3 In order to have something to hear, the interviewer will have to direct the candidate. This, of course, is done by questioning, encouraging and enabling the candidate to talk, so that the interviewer can learn. The art of doing this depends on the personality and style of the interviewer who will develop a personal technique through a sensitive awareness of what is taking place in the interviews.

The selection interviewer needs to distinguish between different types of question. In the Part I Focus on skills we explained the difference in nature and usage of various questioning methods.

4 The best place for the interviewer to make notes is on the application form or CV. In this way they can be joined to information that the candidate has already provided and the peculiar shorthand that interviewers use when making notes during interviews can be deciphered by reference to the form and the data that the note is embellishing. It also means that the review of evidence after the interview has as much information as possible available on one piece of paper. An alternative is to record notes on the interview plan where the structure is based on job specification, person specification or competencies. Interviewers are strangely inhibited about note taking, feeling that it in some way impairs the smoothness of the interaction. This apprehension seems ill founded as candidates are looking for a serious, businesslike discussion, no matter how informal, and note taking offers no barrier, provided that it is done carefully in the form of jottings during the discussion, rather than pointedly writing down particular comments by the candidate which make the interviewer seem like a police officer taking a statement.

5 Data exchange marks a change of gear in the interview. Rapport is necessarily rather rambling and aimless, but data exchange is purposeful and the interviewer needs to control both the direction and the pace of the exchanges. Candidates will be responsive throughout to the interviewer's control, and the better the rapport the more responsive they will be. Skilled interviewers close out areas of discussion and open fresh ones. They head off irrelevant reminiscences and probe where matters have been glossed over. They can never abandon control. Even when the time has come for the candidates to raise all their queries, they will do this at the behest of the interviewer and will look to him or her constantly for a renewal of the mandate to enquire by using conversational prefixes such as, 'Can I ask you another question?' 'If it's not taking up your time, perhaps I could ask . . . . ?' 'I seem to be asking a lot of questions, but there was just one thing . . . .'

6 Closing the interview can be as skilful as opening it. Most of the suggestions so far have been to encourage a response, but it is easy to nod and smile your way into a situation of such cosy relaxation that the respondent talks on and on . . . . and on. A surprising number of interviewers have great difficulty closing.

Braking slows the rate of talking by the candidate by working through a series of steps. You will seldom need to go beyond the first two or three, but five are described in case of you having to deal with a really tough case. (a) One or two closed questions to clarify specific points may stem the tide. (b) The facial expression changes with the brow furrowed to indicate mild disagreement, lack of understanding or professional anxiety. The reassuring nods stop and the generally encouraging, supportive behaviours of reward are withdrawn. (c) Abstraction is when the eyes glaze over, showing that they belong to a person whose attention has now shifted away from the respondent and towards lunch. (d) To look at one's watch during a conversation is a very strong signal indeed, as it clearly indicates that time is running out. Other, milder ways of looking away are: looking for your glasses, looking at your notes or looking at the aircraft making a noise outside the window. A rather brutal variant is to allow your attention to be caught by something the respondent is wearing, a lapel badge, a tie, a ring or piece of jewellery, maybe. Putting on your glasses to see it more clearly is really going too far! (e) If all else fails, you simply have to interrupt.

Closing requires the interview to end smoothly. Future action is either clarified or confirmed. Also, candidates take a collection of attitudes away with them, and these can be influenced by the way the interview is closed. There is a simple procedure. (a) First signal, verbal plus papers. The interviewer uses a phrase to indicate that the interview is nearing its end ('Well now, I think we have covered the ground, don't you? There isn't anything more I need to ask you. Is there anything further you want from me?'). In this way you signal the impending close at the same time as obtaining the candidate's confirmation. There is additional emphasis provided by some paper play. A small collection of notes can be gathered together and stacked neatly, or a notebook can be closed. (b) Second signal, the interviewer confirms what will happen next ('There are still one or two people to see, but we will write to you no later than the end of the week'). (c) The final signal is to stand up: the decisive act to make the close. By standing up the interviewer forces the candidate to stand as well and there remain only the odds and ends of handshakes and parting smiles.

PRACTICAL EXERCISE IN SELECTION INTERVIEWING

For this exercise you need a cooperative, interested relative, or a very close friend, who would welcome interview practice.

1 Follow the sequence suggested in Table II.1 to give your partner practice in being interviewed for a job, and giving yourself practice in interviewing and note taking.

2 After the interview, discuss your mutual feelings about the process around questions such as:

Selector Did you ever feel you were being misled? When? Why?
Did you feel the interview got out of your control? When? Why?
How could you have avoided the problem?
How was your note taking?
What, if anything, made you bored or cross?
What did you find most difficult?
How comprehensive are the data you have collected?

Candidate Were you put at your ease?
Were you at any time inhibited by the selector?
Did you ever mislead the selector? When? How?
Did the selector ever fail to follow up important points? When? Which?
Were you in any way disconcerted by the note taking?
Has the selector got a comprehensive set of data about you, so that you could feel any decision made about you would be soundly based?
What did you think of the interview experience?

3 Now swap roles.

SUMMARY PROPOSITIONS

II.1 Despite criticisms and shortcomings, the selection interview remains a central feature of the recruitment and selection process.

II.2 Typical interview strategies are frank and friendly, problem solving, behavioural event and stress.

II.3 Aspects of interview preparation are timetabling, reception and deciding the right setting.

II.4 Features of the interview itself are the opening for preliminary mutual assessment; data gathering, involving a logical sequence, key issues and checkpoints; and the closure, which prepares candidates for the next step in the process.

II.5 The main types of questions are closed, open ended, probes and reflection. Questions to avoid are leading, multiples or taboo questions.

GENERAL DISCUSSION TOPICS

1 Our examination of the selection interview assumes that the candidate is seeking to become an employee. How would the interview be different if the candidate was being interviewed with a view to becoming a freelance consultant doing work for the organisation rather than being an employee in it?

2 'HR are constantly wanting to "involve me" in their recruitment and selection of staff. I'm too busy to spend time doing that. I want HR to do their job properly and send the people through to me when everything is sorted out and a new recruit is ready to start.' How do you react to that comment from an operations manager in an airline?

FURTHER READING

Anderson, N. and Shackleton, V. (1993) *Successful Selection Interviewing*. Oxford: Blackwell

Newell, S. and Shackleton, V. (2000) 'Recruitment and Selection', in S. Bach and K. Sisson (eds) *Personnel Management: A Comprehensive Guide to Theory and Practice*. Oxford: Blackwell

Both of these books provide full treatment of the selection interview in all its forms.

Brewster, C. and Tyson, S. (eds) (1991) *International Comparisons in Human Resource Management*. London: Pitman

Lawler, J.J., Zaidi, M.A. and Atriyanandana, V. (1989) 'Human Resources Strategies in South East Asia: the Case of Thailand', in A. Nedd, G.R. Ferris and K.M. Rowland (eds) *Research in Personnel and Human Resources Management* Supplement 1, Greenwich, Conn.: JAI Press, pp. 201–23

Tan, K.H. (1995) *Planning, Recruiting and Selecting Human Resources*. Shah Alam, Malaysia: Federal Publications

Each of these works provides research findings on interview validity.

McDaniel, M.A., Whetzel, D.A., Schmidt, F.L. and Maurer, S.D. (1994) 'The validity of the employment interviews', *Journal of Applied Psychology*, Vol. 79, No. 19, pp. 599–616

Smith, M. (2002) 'Personnel Selection Research', *International Journal of Organizational and Occupational Psychology*

Williamson, L.G. *et al.* (1996) 'Employment Interview on Trial', *Journal of Applied Psychology*, Vol. 82, No. 6

Selection interviewing varies considerably across different cultures. This Focus on skills and most of the available literature is rooted in Anglo-American practice. Some insights into practice in other situations can be found in the three works given above.

WEB LINKS

Apart from material on the companion website for this book, plenty of material from consultants can be reached.

www.thedevco.com (the Development Company).
www.bps.org.uk (British Psychological Society).
www.opp.co.uk (Oxford Psychologists Press).
www.shlgroup.com/uk (Saville and Holdsworth, test developer/supplier).
www.psl.net (test developer).

REFERENCES

Babiak, P. (2004) quoted in Butcher, S., 'When the ideal applicant is too good to be true', *Financial Times*, 12 January 2004, p. 12.

Billsberry, T. (2000) *Finding and Keeping the Right People*, London: Pearson Education.

Goffman, E. (1974) *The Presentation of Self in Everyday Life*. London: Penguin Books.

Judge, T. (2000) 'The Employment Interview: A Review of Recent Research', *Human Resource Management*, Vol. 10, No. 4.

Latham, G., Saari, L.M., Pursell, E.D. and Campion, M.A. (1980) 'The Situational Interview', *Journal of Applied Psychology*, Vol. 65, No. 4, pp. 422–7.

McDaniel, M.A., Whetzel, D.A., Schmidt, F.L. and Maurer, S.D. (1994) 'The validity of the employment interview', *Journal of Applied Psychology*, Vol. 79, No. 19, pp. 599–616.

REVIEW OF PART II

'Angela's leaving – quick, we must make sure to get the ad in this month's journal.'
'It's hopeless – they all leave just as soon as we've trained them. What's the point?'
'It's not my fault – we just can't get the staff. No wonder quality is so poor.'
'That's it. The results are so bad we'll have to let some of them go. Tony, draw up a shortlist of possibles and we'll try and get it sorted this week.'

We opened Part II with that hypothetical conversation in a business that clearly had not even the most basic grasp of HR realities and the last six chapters have been taken up with how best to avoid that sort of unsatisfactory situation. With any staffing situation there is potentially the basic question, should we recruit an employee to do this work, should we reorganise things to cover the duties with existing personnel, or should we contract the work out to a supplier, a subcontractor or a consultant? Answers to that question come from the facts of the particular situation in the context of the resourcing strategy and the plans that have been developed along the lines outlined in Chapter 3.

Whenever a new employee is to be recruited a further set of actions is triggered to decide the method of approach to the labour market, including an assessment of which labour market you are working in, the approach that is best to use, specifying the vacancy for the benefit of the potential applicants as well as to guide the selectors, and working up a shortlist of people from among whom you hope to select.

Various methods of selection can be used to get as close as possible to the ideal match between the work that is being offered and the person best suited to do the job in its particular context. Central to that is the face-to-face situation of the selection interview, where the two-way discussion needs to ensure that the selected person is the most suitably equipped for the job and for the organisational position and the culture in which it is set, as well as making sure that that same person will derive from the appointment the satisfactions and rewards of the psychological contract that the post provides.

After being appointed employees need to be retained as long as they are doing what is required of them, so work has to be done to ensure that their expectations of the employment contract continue to be met. Eventually employees leave and HR people need to understand the various ways in which the contract can be terminated with as little difficulty as possible. It would be unrealistic to suggest that every termination leaves the ex-employee content, but the level of any discontent can always be reduced by treating matters thoroughly, fairly, with consideration and, of course, within the law.

We close this review with a metaphor or parable slightly abridged from the original by Jon Billsberry:

A gardener wakes up one morning to find that, overnight, thieves have stolen the ornamental pot containing a number of plants that formed the centrepiece in a prize-winning border. The BBC programme *Gardener's World* is due to visit in a few months to film the garden in full bloom, so he has to do something about it. He needs to find a replacement.

Looking at the border, he realises that he has several options. His initial reaction is to rush to the garden centre to purchase another ornamental pot, replant it in a similar fashion and thereby re-create what had existed. But he pauses; he has a 'development opportunity'. Could he make things even better? Have the thieves done him a favour? That pot had always been a bit of a problem, it had come with the garden and had always seemed such a formidable, if impressive, thing. Now the pot's gone, the other plants in the border seem much more prominent and much more attractive. Perhaps, rather than finding another centrepiece, he could replace the pot with something that helps the others stand out even more. Eventually he chooses this option and decides to buy some smaller shrubs that will enhance the other plants in the border. His choice is limited by the nature of the soil and the sunlight, so he carries out a lot of analysis to identify suitable plants.

Where to buy the plants? He has several options, but as time is tight, he decides to get in the car and go straight to his local garden centre which he knows has the sort of shrubs he is looking for. At the garden centre his choice of plants is easy as he knows exactly what he is looking for. He also buys the right fertiliser and compost to ensure that the new plants bed in properly.

Before planting the shrubs he spends a lot of time preparing the border and getting the conditions just right. When the new plants are in he waters them daily and keeps predatory birds away. He continues to tend the new plantings carefully to make sure they develop in the way he wants to complement the other plants in the border.

When the *Gardener's World* team come to film the producer says that the border is much different from when he saw it before, but just as good; perhaps even better.
(Based on Billsberry (2000), pp. 225–6)

Part II CASE STUDY PROBLEM

You are the Human Resources Manager for a large insurance company with 2,000 employees based in a large city in the north of England and your company has just taken over another insurance company in the south of England which currently employs 1,100 staff. Both firms have a long history and to some extent cover the same insurance markets, although the company in the south of England covers two fairly large specialist areas which are not covered in the north. This was one of the reasons for the takeover, as such specialist staff require a long training and need to acquire high levels of expertise. There are 300 staff in the south who are dedicated to these specialist insurance services.

The takeover did not go smoothly as there was resistance from the southern company, and now it is complete there is considerable uneasiness. Only three years ago the southern company was party to a merger with another local firm and as a result 20 per cent of staff were made redundant. There had been promises of a bright future after these difficult times.

For financial and pragmatic reasons it has been decided that the southern office will close almost immediately and all staff will be located in newly built offices 15 miles out of the northern city. Many of the southern staff are alarmed at the idea of moving and equally alarmed that they may not be invited to move due to another round of redundancies. This especially applies to those who are over 50. The northern staff are divided in their views about the move out of the city centre. Those who live on the western side of the city where the new offices are located are generally delighted to be able to work near to home in an exclusive part of the county. Staff who live on the other side of the city are concerned – some are not happy to travel long distances each day, and for a variety of reasons do not want to move to the other side of the city. Some would like to move, but find that the difference in house prices is too great. Many are disappointed that they will no longer work in the city centre, which is something they had valued. Redundancy is not a possibility which was seriously considered by the northern staff.

The required profile is broadly as set out in the following table:

A	Senior and middle management	35
B	Professional/junior management	1,700 (to include 300 specialist staff)
C	Clerical/administrative	600
D	Manual/ancillary	65

Current staffing

	Northern	Southern	Total
A	30	20	50
B	1,400	700	2,100
(there are no specialist professional staff in the north and 300 in the south)			
C	540	370	910
D	30	10	40

In terms of staffing demand it has been estimated that a total staffing of 2,400 is required for the next three-year period with hopes of some increase after this period, based on growth.

The reduction in the number of professional/junior management staff required reflects a general reduction of all types of professional staff due to the economies of scale and more sophisticated IT use. The only professional staff group to increase in size is the IT group.

The reduction in clerical/administrative staff is due largely to the use of more sophisticated IT systems.

The increase in the number of manual/ancillary staff is due to the move to a much larger site with substantial grounds, including a range of on-site facilities due to a non-city centre location.

You are informed that staffing levels and the move should be complete in six months' time and that, as HR Manager, you are to have a high-profile role. You have initially been asked for a recommended strategy and plan to achieve the target resourcing figures with the least possible disruption and damage to morale.

Required

1 What information would you gather before putting your proposal together?

2 What issues would you address in the proposal?

3 What options are there for achieving the target, what impact might each have, and which would you recommend and why?

Part II EXAMINATION QUESTIONS

1. How is the labour force changing and what are the implications of these changes for human resource management?
2. Outline the advantages and disadvantages of (a) panel interviews, and (b) serial interviews in selection. In which circumstances would you recommend each approach?
3. What techniques can managers adopt to improve their recruiting and interviewing practices?
4. Describe and explain the management practices necessary to avoid a claim at a tribunal for unfair dismissal.
5. Outline the major factors that influence the use of part-time work in Britain, and discuss the implications of part-time work for part-time workers.
6. Under what conditions may annualised hours systems provide employers with the 'flexibility they require'?
7. XYZ plc recruits about 15 graduates and MBAs each year, using application forms, references and the selection interview. The HR Director is thinking of introducing assessment centres for this process. What factors should be considered in approaching this decision?
8. If there appears to be a problem of retaining employees in the business, how would you set about deciding whether or not this is a soluble problem, and what sort of strategies would you adopt if you decided it could be solved?

PART 3

PERFORMANCE

10 Strategic aspects of performance

11 Organisational performance: knowledge and learning

12 Individual performance management

13 Team performance

14 Leadership and motivation

15 Managing absence and attendance

Part III Focus on skills
Interactive skill 3: Appraisal interviewing

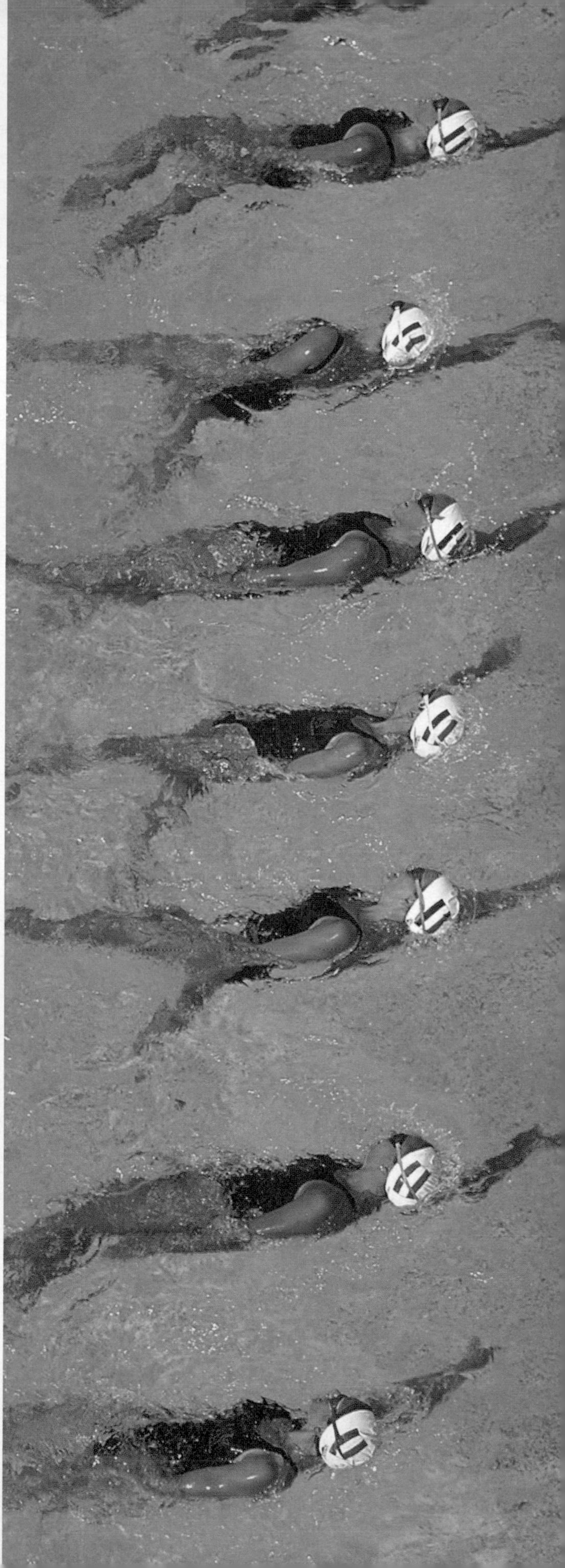

It is no good having all the right people all in the right place, but not delivering the goods. It was suggested in the opening chapter of this book that there is a general move away from the contract of employment towards a contract for performance. We all have to perform effectively. A large part of achieving effective performance is getting the organisational processes right, but within the organisational framework there are the teams, groups and individuals who do the work. Also within that framework we have to understand what it is that motivates people to perform and deploy leadership skills that match those motivations.

Performance management is an idea that has been developed to coordinate several features, especially targets, training, appraisal and payment, in order to deliver effectiveness. Within that sequence is the hardest type of meeting most managers ever have to handle: the appraisal interview. Also included here is the management of absence or of attendance. Are you managing processes which encourage people to attend or are you dealing with the problem of people being absent? It is not simply an alternative way of wording the question.

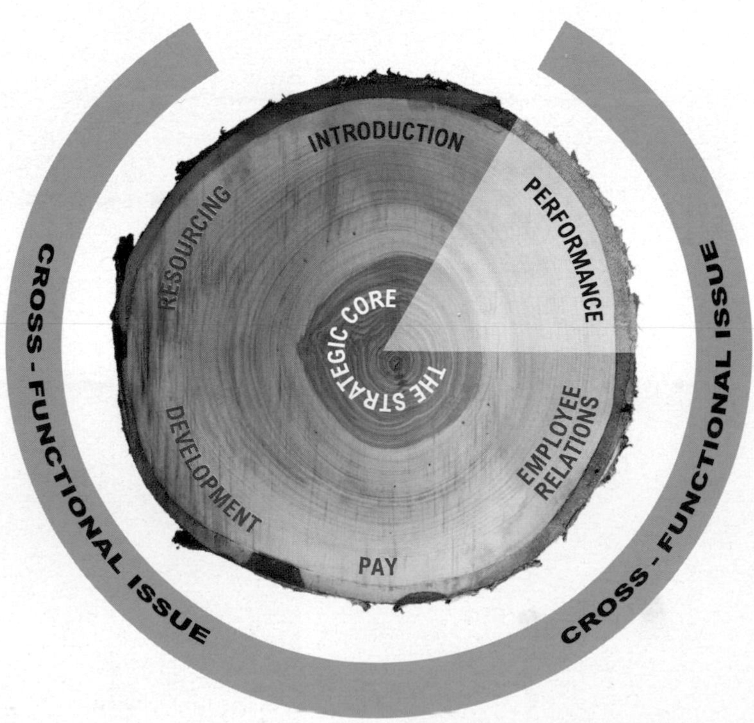

CHAPTER 10

STRATEGIC ASPECTS OF PERFORMANCE

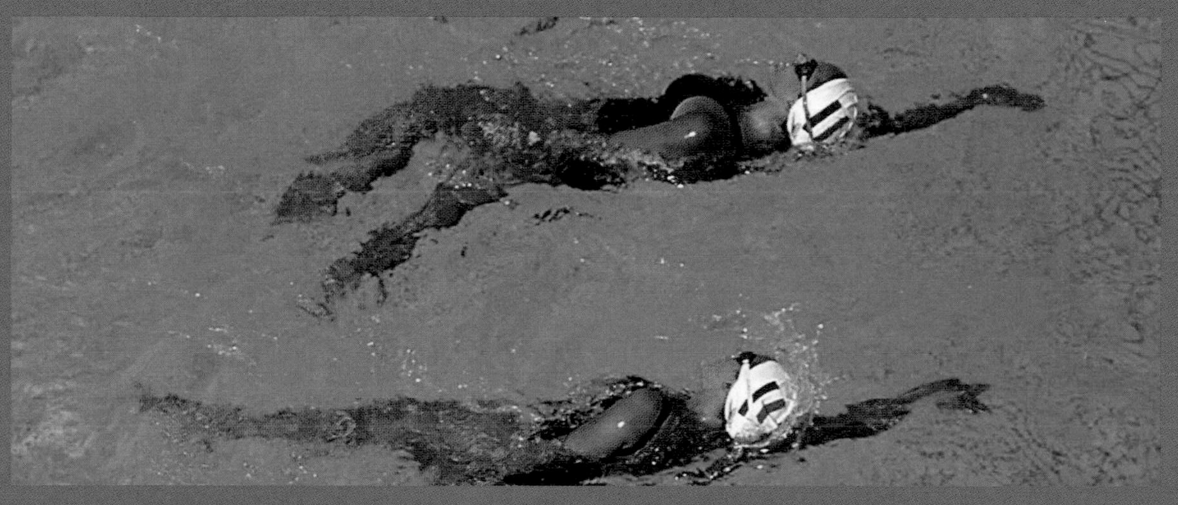

THE OBJECTIVES OF THIS CHAPTER ARE TO:

1. IDENTIFY A CHANGING PERSPECTIVE ON PERFORMANCE
2. REVIEW SOME MAJOR INFLUENCES ON OUR CURRENT THINKING ABOUT PERFORMANCE
3. EXAMINE THE RESEARCH WHICH LINKS HUMAN RESOURCE POLICIES AND PRACTICES WITH INTERNAL AND EXTERNAL MEASURES OF COMPANY PERFORMANCE
4. EXPLORE THE MECHANISMS WHICH LINK HR POLICIES AND PRACTICES AND PERFORMANCE
5. REVIEW, BRIEFLY, A RANGE OF PERFORMANCE INITIATIVES
6. IDENTIFY SOME OF THE PROBLEMS WITH PERFORMANCE INITIATIVES

In our opening chapters we described the shift in emphasis away from the contract of employment towards the contract for performance. Even before the development of Taylor's scientific management methods a century ago, getting the most out of the workforce has always been a predominant management preoccupation, and the management literature is full of studies on the topic. Psychologists have studied motivation and leadership, ergonomists have dismantled and reconstructed every aspect of the physical environment in which people work, industrial relations specialists have pondered power relationships and reward, while sociologists discussed the design of organisations and their social structure, and operations experts have looked for ways to engineer process improvements. In 2001, Caulkin asserts:

> more than 30 studies in the US and UK leave no room for doubt; how organizations manage and develop people has a powerful – perhaps the most powerful – effect on overall performance, including the **bottom line**. (Caulkin 2001, p. 32)

A CHANGE IN PERSPECTIVE: FROM EMPLOYMENT TO PERFORMANCE

The traditional HRM approach to enhancing individual performance has centred on the assessment of past performance and the allocation of reward – rewards were provided in exchange for performance. This has been powerfully influenced by the industrial relations history, as trade unions have developed the process of collective bargaining and negotiation.

The prime purpose of trade unions has always been to improve the terms and working conditions of their members; the union has only one thing to offer in exchange for improvements in terms and conditions, that is, some opportunity for improvement in productivity or performance. With the steadily increasing influence of unions in most industrial countries through most of the twentieth century, it was inevitable that performance improvement was something of direct interest only to management. Performance therefore became stereotyped as something of no intrinsic interest to the person doing the work.

The influence of trade unions has altered and collective bargaining does not dominate the management agenda as much as it used to. This is the most significant feature in the general change in attitudes about what we go to work for. Managements are gradually waking up to this fact and realising that there is now scope for integration in a way that was previously unrealistic. Not only is it possible to say, 'Performance is rewarded', one can now begin to say, 'Performance *is* a reward.' The long-standing motivational ideas of job enlargement, job enrichment, and so forth, become more cogent when those at work are able to look for the satisfaction of their needs not only in the job, but also in their performance at the job.

Although it may seem like playing with words, this subtle shift of emphasis is fundamental to understanding the strategic approach to performance.

WINDOW ON PRACTICE

Mavis has worked in a retail store for 18 years and has recently attended a training course in customer care. She says:

> I always regarded the customer as some sort of enemy; we all did. In our coffee breaks we chatted away about the customer from hell, who was never satisfied, or who always put you down. Also I used to feel that I had to grin and bear it in trying to be nice to these enemies in order to earn commission.
>
> Since the course I feel much more in control and have more self-respect. I really feel that most customers will respond positively if I approach them in the right way. It is my performance that largely affects how they behave. I actually enjoy what I am doing most of the time (and I never thought I'd say that!), because I can see myself doing a bit of good as well as selling more than I used to.

INFLUENCES ON OUR UNDERSTANDING OF PERFORMANCE

The Japanese influence

In the 1980s the success of Japanese companies and the decline of Western organisations encouraged an exploration and adoption of Japanese management ideas and practices in order to improve performance. Thurley (1982) described the objectives of personnel policies in Japan as performance, motivation, flexibility and mobility. Delbridge and Turnbull (1992) described type 'J' organisations (based on Japanese thinking) as characterised by commitment, effort and company loyalty. A key theme in Japanese thinking appears to be people development and continuous improvement, or 'kaizen'.

Much of this thinking and the specific management techniques used in Japan, such as JIT (just in time), have been adopted into UK organisations, often in an uncritical way and without due regard for the cultural differences between the two nations. It is only where the initiatives are developed *and modified* for their location that they appear to succeed.

The American literature

Key writers from the American 'excellence' school, Peters and Waterman (1982), identified eight characteristics that they found to be associated with excellent companies – all American. These companies were chosen as excellent on the basis of their innovativeness and on a set of financial indicators, compared on an industry-wide basis. The characteristics they identified were:

- a bias for action – rather than an emphasis on bureaucracy or analysis;
- close to the customer – concern for customer wishes;
- autonomy and entrepreneurship – the company is split into small operational units where innovation and initiative are encouraged;

- productivity through people – employees are seen as the key resource, and the value of the employees' contribution is reinforced;
- hands on, value driven – strong corporate culture promoted from the top;
- stick to the knitting – pursuing the core business rather than becoming conglomerates;
- simple form, lean staff – simple organisation structure and small HQ staffing;
- simultaneous loose and tight properties – company values strongly emphasised, but within these considerable freedom and errors tolerated.

Peters and Waterman identified a shift from the importance of strategy and structural factors to style, systems, staff and skills (from the hard 's's to the soft 's's). In a follow-on book Peters and Austin (1985) identify four key factors related to excellence as concern for customers, innovation, attention to people and leadership.

However, there are problems with the research methodology used; for example, no comparison was made with companies not considered to be excellent. We do not, therefore, know whether these principles were applied to a greater extent in excellent organisations. In addition, a number of the companies quoted have experienced severe problems since the research was carried out, and there remains the problem of the extent to which we can apply the results to UK organisations.

Whatever the reservations, the influence of this work on strategic thinking about performance remains profound. Even the use of the term 'excellence' means that there is a change of emphasis away from deadpan, objective terms such as profitability, effectiveness, value added and competitive advantage towards an idea that may trigger a feeling of enthusiasm and achievement. 'Try your best' becomes 'Go for it'.

More recently there has been considerable quantitative research in the USA that aims to identify HR practices which lead to high organisational performance, for example Huselid (1995) and Pfeffer (1998). The HR practices identified are termed 'high performance work practices' and have encouraged similar investigations in the UK to determine 'high commitment work practices'.

HRM and the strategy literature

The HRM strategy literature provides different ways to understand the contribution of HR policies and practices to organisational performance. We noted in Chapter 2 that three distinct approaches to HR strategy can be identified. The universalist or best practice approach presupposes that certain HR policies and practices will always result in high performance, and the question is to identify exactly what these are. The contingency or fit approach suggests that different HR policies and practices will be needed to produce high performance in different firms depending on their business strategy and environment. Finally the resource-based view of the firm suggests that neither of these approaches is sufficient, but that every organisation and its employees should be considered as unique and that the set of HR policies and practices that will result in high performance will also be unique to that firm. From this perspective no formula can be applied, and the way that people processes contribute to organisational performance can only be understood within the context of the particular firm. These three perspectives have resulted in different investigational approaches to understanding the impact of people management on organisational performance, as will become clear in the following section.

DO PEOPLE-MANAGEMENT PROCESSES CONTRIBUTE TO HIGH PERFORMANCE?

The investigations to date have had a dual purpose, the first being to seek to establish a link between people-management practices and organisational performance. In other words, does the way that people are managed affect the bottom line? The second one follows logically from this, and is: If the answer to the first question is yes, then which particular policies and practices result in high performance? Both these questions are usually investigated in parallel. A variety of different definitions of performance have been used in these studies. These range from bottom line financial performance (profitability), through productivity measures, to measurement of outcomes such as wastage, quality and labour turnover (which are sometimes referred to as internal performance outcomes). Sometimes the respondent's view of performance is used, on the basis that bottom line figures can be influenced by management accounting procedures. The studies have generally used large datasets and complex statistical analysis to determine relationships.

Some researchers argue that the performance effects of HR policies and practices are multiplicative rather than additive, and this is often termed the 'bundles' approach (*see*, for example, MacDuffie 1995), and this highlights an emphasis on internal rather than external fit. In other words, a particular set of mutually reinforcing practices is likely to have more impact on performance than applying one or just some of these in isolation. Pfeffer (1998), for example, identifies seven critical people-management policies: emphasising employment security; recruiting the 'right' people; extensive use of self-managed teams and decentralisation; high wages solidly linked to organisational performance; high spending on training; reducing status differentials; and sharing information; and he suggests that these policies will benefit *every* organisation. In the UK the Sheffield Enterprise Programme (Patterson *et al.* 1997) has studied 100 manufacturing organisations over 10 years (1991–2001) and used statistical techniques to identify which factors affect profitability and productivity. It has been reported that aspects of culture, supervisory support, concern for employee welfare, employee responsibility, and training were all important variables in relation to organisational performance. Also in the UK, Wood and de Menezes (1998) identify a bundle of HR practices which they term high-commitment management, and these comprise recruitment and selection processes geared to selecting flexible and highly committed individuals; processes which reward commitment and training by promotion and job security; and the use of direct communication and teamwork.

This avenue of work has a very optimistic flavour, suggesting that not only are people-management practices related to high organisational performance, but that we can identify the innovative and sophisticated practices that will work best in combination. On a practical level there are problems because different researchers identify different practices or 'bundles' associated with high performance (*see*, for example, Becker and Gerhard 1996).

There have been many criticisms of this approach, partly based on the methods used – which involve, for example, the view of a single respondent as to which practices are in place, with no account taken of how the practices are implemented. A further confusion is that some studies are at establishment level, some at corporate level, some are sector based and some are cross-sector. Each of these approaches has inbuilt problems and creates extreme difficulties for any meta-analysis of the studies so far. A further problem is causality. It could be that profitable firms use best practice people-management methods, because they can afford to since they are profitable, rather than that such methods lead to profitability. A further issue concerns the conflict between different aspects of the bundle. Such contradictions are, for example, between individualism and teamwork and between a strong culture and adaptability. Lastly, this approach ignores the business strategy of the organisation.

The work we have described so far comes from a universalist/best practice perspective and an alternative way forward is to use the contingency or fit point of view (*see*, for example, the work of Wright and Snell 1998), asking the question, 'Which people-management policies create high performance in which different organisational circumstances?' This approach does bring the integration with business strategy to the fore, and draws attention to sectoral differences; for example Guest (2001) has suggested that 'high performance work practices' may be effective in producing high performance in manufacturing rather than services. However, it fails to provide a more useful way forward. Attempting to model all the different factors that influence the appropriate set of HR policies and practices that lead to high performance is an extremely complex, if not impossible, task. In addition to this Purcell *et al.* (2000) argue that the speed of change poses a real problem for the fit approach.

In summary, the extent to which all the statistical work that has been done proves the relationship between people-management practices and organisational performance continues to be hotly contested. Reviewing the academic literature Richardson and Thompson (1999) come to the conclusion that the evidence indicates a positive relationship between innovative and sophisticated people-management practices and better business performance. Guest *et al.* (2003), however, recognise that although the statistical work so far provides some associations between people management and organisational performance there is a lack of convincing evidence. Guest (2000), Hall (2002) and particularly Purcell (1999) all provide detailed expositions of the problems with the above approaches.

Purcell (1999) suggests that a more useful approach is to focus on the resource-based view of the firm, which is the third perspective on HR strategy that we considered in Chapter 2. From this perspective each organisation is a unique and complex whole, so we need to look beyond lists of HR policies and practices to explain organisational performance. We also need to consider long-term performance capability and not just short-term performance improvements. From this perspective Paauwe and Richardson (2001) argue that the move to longitudinal studies and case study work is useful, and suggest that organisational context and institutional arrangements need greater attention; Becker and Gerhart (1996) suggest that it is more likely to be the architecture of the system, not just a group of HR practices, that results in high performance, and Purcell suggests that it is how practices are implemented and change is managed that makes the difference. Hutchinson *et al.* (2000) term this 'idiosyncratic fit'. The work of Purcell and his colleagues from Bath University, which forms part of the CIPD's research in this area, attempts to address some of the deficits in large sample statistical work. They have investigated 12 case study organisations on a longitudinal basis, collecting the employees' view and concentrating on the line manager's role in implementation.

They collected data on 11 HR policy/practice areas identified from previous research as being linked to high organisational performance. In testing the link between people management and performance this study differs from others in that the measures taken were ones that were the most meaningful to each organisation.

Also the organisations were each visited twice over a two-and-a-half-year period so comparisons could be made over time. Their results are not clear-cut, but a major conclusion is that it is the way policies are implemented and the role of line mangers which are critical. They also acknowledge that it is difficult to disentangle the performance impact of HR policies from the performance impact of changing environmental circumstances and other changes such as technology. They do argue, however, that those organisations with a 'big idea', which expresses what the organisation stands for and what it is trying to achieve, were more able to sustain their performance over the longer term. For example the big idea in Jaguar is quality and in Nationwide it is mutuality. They also found that such big ideas have five characteristics in high-performing organisations:

- **Embedded** – in policies and practices
- **Connected** – connects relationships with customers, values, culture and the way people are managed
- **Enduring** – stable, longlasting values which survive even in difficult times
- **Collective** – acts as corporate glue
- **Measured and managed** – often through the use of balanced scorecard type approaches

HOW DO HR POLICIES AND PRACTICES AFFECT PERFORMANCE?

We have sufficient evidence to claim that HR policies and practices do affect company performance, although some studies (for example Lahteenmaki and Storey 1998) do not support this. We then need to understand better the processes which link these HR practices to business performance. As Purcell *et al.* (2000) point out, 'what remains unclear is what is actually happening in successful organisations to make this connection' (p. 30). Currently the focus is on commitment in mediating the impact of HR policies and practices on business performance, and we shall consider this in more detail.

Commitment

Commitment has been described as:

- **Attitudinal commitment** – that is, loyalty and support for the organisation, strength of identification with the organisation (Porter 1985), a belief in its values and goals and a readiness to put in effort for the organisation.
- **Behavioural commitment** – actually remaining with the company and continuing to pursue its objectives.

Walton (1985) notes that commitment is *thought* to result in better quality, lower turnover, a greater capacity for innovation and more flexible employees. In turn these are seen to enhance the ability of the organisation to achieve competitive advantage. Iles, Mabey and Robertson (1990) add that some of the outcomes of commitment have been identified as the industrial relations climate, absence levels, turnover levels and individual performance. Pfeffer (1998) and Wood and Albanese

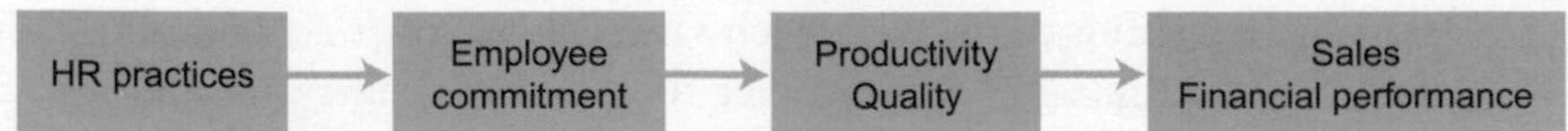

Figure 10.1 A simple model of HRM and performance (Source: D. Guest (2000) 'Human resource management, employee well-being and organizational performance'. Paper presented to the CIPD Professional Standards Conference, 11 July. Reproduced with the permission of the author.)

(1995) argue that commitment is a core variable, and Guest (1998, p. 42) suggests that:

> The concept of organizational commitment lies at the heart of any analysis of HRM. Indeed the whole rationale for introducing HRM policies is to increase levels of commitment so that other positive outcomes can ensue.

Hence we see the adoption of the terms 'high commitment work practices' and 'high commitment management' and their linkage with high performance. Meyer and Allen (1997) argue that there is not a great deal of *evidence* to link high commitment and high levels of organisational performance. Guest (2000) reports analyses of the Workplace Employment Relations Survey (WERS) data and the Future of Work Survey data to show some support for the model that HR practices have an impact on employee attitudes and satisfaction, which in turn have an impact on internal performance outcomes. He is, however, cautious about identifying causal links. In this context Guest uses commitment as shorthand for employee attitudes and values, as shown in his model in Figure 10.1.

Some authors, however, have argued that high commitment could indeed reduce organisational performance. Cooper and Hartley (1991) suggest that commitment might decrease flexibility and inhibit creative problem solving. If commitment reduces staff turnover, this may result in fewer new ideas coming into the organisation. Staff who would like to leave the organisation but who are committed to it in other ways, for example through high pay and benefits, may stay, but may not produce high levels of performance.

As well as the debate on the value of commitment to organisational performance, there is also the debate on the extent to which commitment can be managed, and how it can be managed. Guest (1992) suggests that commitment is affected by: personal characteristics; experiences in job role; work experiences; structural factors; and personnel policies.

WINDOW ON PRACTICE

Rebecca Johnson (1999) reports on performance initiatives at the Holiday Inn, Mayfair. Through a 'back to the floor' experience senior managers realised that front line staff did not have sufficient authority and autonomy to solve routine customer problems and that this was having an adverse impact on customer perceptions. A range of initiatives were thus implemented:

- training to equip front line staff to take greater responsibility in solving customer problems;
- new recruitment and selection strategies to help identify potential employees who are 'focused on going the extra mile', rather than those who have technical skills, which can be learned on appointment. Processes include 'auditions' to identify favourable attitudes;
- demonstrating a genuine commitment to employees. Initiatives included attitude surveys, continued IIP recognition, a training resource centre and a network of mentors and 'buddies';
- encouraging a sense of fun and openness;
- a performance appraisal system which is also geared towards career development, and internal promotions where possible;
- measuring customer feedback through a 'guest tracking system'.

Johnson reports that all these policies are paying off as profits have been increasing steadily for the last five years. She also reports the views of a recently appointed corporate sales executive who claims to have joined the organisation partly because of the training programme, and who noted that 'the commitment is very strong'.

Source: Adapted from a case study by R. Johnson (1999) 'Case 2: Holiday Inn Mayfair', in A. Baron and R. Collard 'Realising our assets', *People Management*, 14 October.

Lastly, it is important to consider whether using commitment as a shorthand for attitudes and satisfaction is sufficient, and whether there are other important dimensions which may be lost, by focusing on commitment alone. Patterson *et al.* (1997) found that in addition to commitment, employee satisfaction was related to organisational performance. Purcell and his colleagues (2003) give equal prominence to job satisfaction and motivation. In their model HR policies and practices are seen to impact on employee ability/skills, motivation and incentive (in that people can be motivated to use their ability productively via intrinsic and extrinsic rewards) and opportunity. In turn these three factors have an impact on commitment, individual motivation and job satisfaction, all of which have an impact on employee discretionary behaviour which in turn impacts on performance. In relation to HR practices they found that:

- job influence, career opportunities, job challenge, involvement in management decisions, training and line manager respect all influence employee motivation;
- job influence, career opportunities, job challenge and teamworking all influence job satisfaction;
- training, career opportunities, job challenge, management leadership, performance appraisal, work-life balance and communication on organisational performance all influence commitment.

MAJOR PERFORMANCE INITIATIVES

We have previously considered some HR policies and practices that have been identified as related to high performance, and have noted the idea of using practices in bundles. Many of the popular performance initiatives that companies have adopted represent similar (but not the same) bundles of HR policies and practices, and we now turn to these. There are many small initiatives every day that help to improve performance, but we are concentrating here on major strategic initiatives although the labels may, of course, mean different things in practice in different organisations. Interestingly, Guest and King (2001) found that many senior managers were not aware of the research on performance, and it is therefore unclear what is informing senior managers' choice of performance initiatives.

This brings us to the concern that too many initiatives in the same organisation will give conflicting messages to employees, particularly when they are introduced by different parts of the business. There may, for example, be contradictions between the messages of total quality management ('right first time') and those of the learning organisation type of approach ('it's OK to make mistakes as long as you learn from them').

The performance research to date focuses very much on the individual, but we agree with Caulkin (2001) who suggests that organisations also need to develop the capability of the organisation as a whole, and to this end we include in Table 10.1 three levels of initiative depending on the primary focus: organisational, team or individual. Some of them partly cover the same ground, and it would be surprising to find them in the same business at the same time.

Table 10.1 Some major performance initiatives

Organisational focus	Learning organisation
	Knowledge management
	Organisational development
	Investors in people
	Total quality management (TQM)
	Performance culture
	Lean production
	Business process re-engineering
	Just in time (JIT)
	Standards: e.g. ISO9000
	Customer care/orientation
Individual focus	Performance management
	Performance-related pay
	Self-development/continuous development
	Empowerment
Team focus	High-performance teams
	Cross-functional teams
	Self-regulating teams

ACTIVITY 10.1

1 Identify the main performance initiatives in your organisation.
2 What/who is the source of each initiative?
3 In what ways do they mutually support each other, and in what ways do they conflict?

THINGS THAT GO WRONG

The level of satisfaction with performance initiatives is typically low (Antonioni 1994), so we close this chapter with a summary of the problems most often reported.

The process/people balance

Schemes rarely strike the right balance between a people emphasis and a process emphasis. Concentrating on being brilliant at talking to the people, getting them going and talking them down gently if they don't quite make it will not suffice if there is not a clear, disciplined process that brings in the essential features of consistency and defining sensible goals. Getting the goals and measures right is a waste of time if there is not the necessary input to changing attitudes, developing skills and winning consent.

Getting the measures right

On the basis of what gets measured gets done, it is critical that the organisation selects the most useful measure of performance for the organisaton as a whole and for the individuals within it. Single measures are unlikely to be sufficiently robust. Kaplan and Norton (1992) argue convincingly that the mix of measures which an organisation should use to assess its performance should be based around four different perspectives:

- **Financial measures** – such as sales growth, profits, cash flow and increased market share.
- **Customer measures** – that is, the customer perspective, which looks at, for example, delivery time, service quality, product quality.
- **Internal business measures** – cycle time, productivity, employee skills, labour turnover.
- **Innovation and learning perspective** – including such elements as ability to innovate and improve.

The focus must be on what is achieved: results are what count. At an individual level a focus on behaviour rather than results achieved can be unhelpful, leading to personality clashes, and misleading. Doing things in the right way is no substitute for doing the right things. For a further exploration of the difficulties with performance measures see case 10.1 on the website.

Management losing interest

A constant axiom with any initiative is the need for endorsement from senior management. With a performance initiative there is the need to go a great deal further. First, senior managers have to accept that the initiative is something in which they have to participate continuously and thoroughly. They cannot introduce it, say how important it is and then go off to find other games to play:

> studies have shown that in organisations that utilise performance management, 90 per cent of senior managers have not received performance reviews in the last two years. Clearly the problem here is that PM is not used, modelled and visibly supported at the top of the organisation. Sooner or later people at lower levels catch on and no longer feel compelled to take the time to make PM work. (Sparrow and Hiltrop 1994, p. 565)

The second aspect is indicated in that quotation. Performance initiatives will not work unless people at all levels either believe in them or are prepared to give them a try with the hope that they will be convinced by the practice.

The team/individual balance

Individuals can rarely perform entirely on their own merits; they are part of a department or team of people whose activities interact in innumerable ways. Trevor Macdonald may read the television news with a clarity and sureness that is outstanding, but it would be of little value if the lights did not work or the script contained errors. Most working people, no matter how eminent, are not solo performers to that extent. Somehow the performance initiative has to stimulate both individual and team performance, working together within the envelope of organisational objectives.

ACTIVITY 10.2

Think of situations in your own experience outside working life, where there has been a potential clash between individual performance and team performance. Examples might be:

(a) the opening batsman more concerned with his batting average than with the team winning the match;

(b) the person playing the lead in the amateur operatic society's production of *The Merry Widow* who ignores the chorus; or

(c) the local councillor more concerned with doing what is needed to earn an MBE than with supporting the collective view of the council.

How was the potential clash avoided, or not? How could it have been managed more effectively to harmonise individual and team performance?

Leaving out the development part

A key feature of managing performance is developing people so that they *can* perform. This is the feature that is most often not delivered. It is often the lack of follow-up on development needs that is the least satisfactory aspect of performance management systems.

Implementing and managing the change

If, as Purcell (1999) identifies, 'our concern should be less about the precise policy mix in the "bundle" and more about how and when organisations manage the HR side of change', then the way that large and small performance initiatives are implemented and managed is critical. While this is well-trodden ground, there is considerable evidence of attempted changes which have failed for a wide range of reasons including: trust is low; change is seen as a management fad which will go away; change has been poorly communicated and understood; change is just a way to get us to work harder for the same money. Changing employee behaviour is also influenced by the culture of the organisation, and for a further exploration of the link between culture and performance initiatives see case 10.2 on the website.

GETTING IT RIGHT

Here are four suggestions for running a successful performance initiative:

1. Develop and promulgate a clear vision for the business as a framework for individual/team goals and targets.
2. In consultation, develop and agree individual goals and targets with three characteristics: (a) what to do to achieve the target; (b) how to satisfy the customer rather than pleasing the boss; (c) targets that are precise, difficult and challenging, but attainable, *with feedback*.
3. Do not begin until you are sure of: (a) unwavering commitment from the top; (b) an approach that is driven by the line and bought into and owned by middle and first-line managers; (c) a system that is run, monitored and updated by HR specialists; (d) an agreement that every development commitment or pay commitment is honoured, or a swift, full explanation is given of why not.
4. Train all participants.

SUMMARY PROPOSITIONS

10.1 Central to understanding management interest in performance is understanding the subtle change in attitudes: not only is performance rewarded, performance is also a reward.

10.2 In the UK our views of performance improvement have been influenced by the US literature, the Japanese experience and the HRM strategy literature.

10.3 There has been considerable research effort devoted to investigating the link between a bundle of people-management practices and organisational performance, and some would argue that the link has been successfully demonstrated.

10.4 Much less clear are the processes by which the link is made, for example how, why and in what context? Commitment as the moderating variable between HR practices and organisational performance is insufficient.

10.5 Things that typically go wrong with performance initiatives are getting the people/process balance wrong, not selecting the right performance measures, management losing interest and getting the team/individual balance wrong.

10.6 Factors likely to produce success relate to a clear, understood vision, effective target setting, full management commitment, training and honouring commitments.

GENERAL DISCUSSION TOPICS

1 To what extent can the American excellence literature be applied in a UK setting?

2 Can commitment, empowerment and job flexibility be pursued together? If yes, how can this be achieved? If no, why not – what are the alternatives?

FURTHER READING

Purcell J., Kinnie, N. and Hutchinson, S. (2003) 'Open minded', *People Management*, Vol. 9, No. 10, 15 May, pp. 30–3
A useful summary of the Bath research to date, if you can't afford or haven't time to read the full report – provided in the reference list below (Purcell *et al.* 2003). Displays the whole people and performance model and discuses the importance of implementation of policies. Provides some detail on the importance of the 'big picture' and the five key attributes of this.

Truss, C. (2003) 'Complexities and controversies in linking HRM with organizational outcomes', *Journal of Management Studies*, Vol. 38, No. 8, pp. 1121–48
An excellent critique of the quantitative approach to establishing the link between people policies and organisational performance. Useful case study of Hewlett-Packard which demonstrates that even high-performing companies do not necessarily follow best practice in all areas of people management. The approach taken in this research is different in that it tracks back from high performance and looks at the people management processes which contribute to this.

REFERENCES

Antonioni, D. (1994) 'Improve the performance management process before discontinuing performance appraisals', *Compensation and Benefits Review*, Vol. 26, No. 2, pp. 29–37.

Becker, B. and Gerhard, B. (1996) 'The impact of human resource management on organizational progress and prospects', *Academy of Management Journal*, Vol. 39, No. 4, pp. 779–801.

Caulkin, S. (2001) 'The time is now', *People Management*, Vol. 7, No. 17, 30 August, pp. 32–4.

Cooper, J. and Hartley, J. (1991) 'Reconsidering the case for organisational commitment', *Human Resource Management Journal*, Vol. 3, Spring, pp. 18–32.

Delbridge, R. and Turnbull, P. (1992) 'Human resource maximisation: The management of labour under just-in-time manufacturing systems', in P. Blyton and P. Turnbull (eds) *Reassessing Human Resource Management*. Beverly Hills: Sage.

Guest, D. (1992) 'Right enough to be dangerously wrong; an analysis of the "In search of excellence" phenomenon', in G. Salaman *et al.* (eds) *Human Resource Strategies*. London: Sage.

Guest, D. (1998) 'Beyond HRM: Commitment and the contract culture', in P. Sparrow and M. Marchington (eds) *Human Resource Management: The New Agenda*. London: Financial Times Pitman Publishing.

Guest, D. (2000) 'Human Resource Management, employee well-being and organizational performance'. Paper presented at the CIPD Professional Standards Conference, 11 July.

Guest, D. (2001) 'Human resource management: when research confronts theory', *International Journal of Human Resource Management*, Vol. 12, No. 7, pp. 1092–1106.

Guest, D. and King, Z. (2001) 'Personnel's Paradox', *People Management*, Vol. 17, No. 19, 27 September, pp. 24–9.

Guest, D., Michie, J, Conway, N. and Sheehan, M. (2003) 'Human Resource management and corporate performance in the UK', *British Journal of Industrial Relations*, Vol. 41, No. 2, pp. 291–314.

Hall, L. (2002) 'HRM practices and employee and organisational performance: a critique of the research and Guest's model'. Paper presented to Manchester Metropolitan University Business School *Performance and Reward* conference, 11 April 2002.

Huselid, M. (1995) 'The impact of human resource management practices on turnover, productivity and corporate financial performance', *Academy of Management Journal*, Vol. 38, No. 3, pp. 635–73.

Hutchinson, S., Purcell, J. and Kinnie, N. (2000) 'Evolving high commitment management and the experience of the RAC call center', *Human Resource Management Journal*, Vol. 10, No. 1, pp. 63–78.

Iles, P., Mabey, C. and Robertson, I. (1990) 'Human resource management practices and employee commitment. Possibilities, pitfalls and paradoxes', *British Journal of Management*, Vol. 1, pp. 147–57.

Johnson, R. (1999) 'Case 2: Holiday Inn Mayfair', in A. Baron and R. Collard, 'Realising our assets', *People Management*, 14 October.

Kaplan, R. and Norton, D. (1992) 'The balanced scorecard – measures that drive performance', *Harvard Business Review*, Jan.–Feb., pp. 71–9.

Lahteenmaki, S. and Storey, J. (1998) 'HRM and company performance: the use of measurement and the influence of economic cycles', *Human Resource Management Journal*, Vol. 8, No. 2, pp. 51–65.

MacDuffie, J. (1995) 'Human resource bundles and manufacturing performance: organizational logic and flexible production systems in the world auto industry', *Industrial and Labor Relations Review*, Vol. 48, No. 2, pp. 197–221.

Meyer, J. and Allen, N. (1997) *Commitment in the workplace: theory, research and application*. London: Sage.

Paauwe, J. and Richardson, R. (2001) 'Editorial introduction: HRM and performance: confronting theory and reality', *International Journal of Human Resource Management*, Vol. 12, No. 7, pp. 1085–91.

Patterson, J., West, M., Lawthom, R. and Nickell, S. (1997) *The Impact of People Management Practices on Business Performance*. London: IPD.

Peters, T. and Austin, N. (1985) *A Passion for Excellence*. New York: Harper and Row.

Peters, T. and Waterman, R. (1982) *In Search of Excellence*. New York: Harper and Row.

Pfeffer, J. (1998) *The Human Equation*. Boston: Harvard Business School Press.

Porter, M. (1985) *Competitive Advantage*. New York: Free Press.

Purcell, J. (1999) 'Best practice and best fit: chimera or cul-de-sac?' *Human Resource Management Journal*, Vol. 9, No. 3, pp. 26–41.

Purcell, J., Kinnie, N., Hutchinson, S. and Rayton, B. (2000) 'Inside the box', *People Management*, 26 October.

Purcell, J., Kinnie, N., Hutchinson, S., Rayton, B. and Swart, J. (2003) *Understanding the People Performance Link: Unlocking the black box*, Research report. London: CIPD.

Richardson, R. and Thompson, M. (1999) *The Impact of People Management Practices – A Review of the Literature*. London: IPD.

Sparrow, P. and Hiltrop, J.-M. (1994) *European Human Resource Management in Transition*. London: Prentice Hall.

Thurley, K. (1982) 'The Japanese model: practical reservations and surprising opportunities', *Personnel Management*, February.

Walton, R.E. (1985) 'From control to commitment in the workplace', *Harvard Business Review*, March–April, pp. 77–84.

Wood, S. and Albanese, M. (1995) 'Can we speak of high commitment management on the shop floor?' *Journal of Management Studies*, Vol. 32, No. 2, pp. 215–47.

Wood, S. and de Menezes, L. (1998) 'High commitment management in the UK: evidence from the Workplace Industrial Relations Survey and employers' manpower and skills practices survey', *Human Relations*, Vol. 51, No. 4, pp. 485–515.

Wright, P. and Snell, S. (1998) 'Towards a unifying framework for exploring fit and flexibility in strategic human resource management', *Academy of Management Review*, Vol. 23, No. 4, pp. 756–72.

An extensive range of additional materials, including multiple choice questions, answers to questions and links to useful websites can be found on the Human Resource Management Companion Website at **www.pearsoned.co.uk/torrington**.

ORGANISATIONAL PERFORMANCE: KNOWLEDGE AND LEARNING

THE OBJECTIVES OF THIS CHAPTER ARE TO:

1 REVIEW THE NATURE OF ORGANISATIONAL INITIATIVES AND PROCESSES WHICH FOCUS ON ORGANISATIONAL PERFORMANCE

2 EXPLORE THE CONCEPTS OF LEARNING ORGANISATIONS AND ORGANISATIONAL LEARNING

3 EXPLAIN THE CONCEPT AND PRACTICE OF KNOWLEDGE MANAGEMENT

it. In particular, he describes the idea of becoming a learning organisation as one grand project, as 'utopian and unrealistic', and he recognises the value of a more incremental approach.

Easterby-Smith and Araujo (1999) note that a number of different disciplines have made a contribution to the debate on organisational learning and learning organisations, producing a plurality of perspectives. Part of the confusion, though, lies in the practices adopted by organisations under the banner of a learning organisation, rather than in the fundamental ideas. Academics and theorists may place different emphases on different aspects, but these are mutually supportive rather than conflicting. There is a common thread of a holistic approach and that organisational learning is greater than the sum of individual learning in the organisation. Different organisations appear to have been inspired by some aspects of this approach and, having adopted these, they see themselves as learning organisations. In essence they have taken some steps towards their goal, and have certainly improved the level of learning going on in the organisation, but have taken a partial rather than a holistic approach. A further confusion lies in the difference between the nature of organisational learning and the learning organisation, which we consider in the following section.

Organisational learning and the learning organisation

The study of *organisational learning* is based on the detached observation of individual and collective learning processes in the organisation. The approach is critical and academic, and the focus is the nature and processes of learning, whereas Easterby-Smith and Araujo (1999) suggest that the study of *learning organisations* is focused on 'normative models for creating change in the direction of improved learning processes'. Much of the research on learning organisations has been produced by consultants and organisations that are involved in the process. In other words the data come from an action learning perspective and are produced by interested parties, giving, inevitably, a positive spin to what is produced. This is not to say that the learning organisation perspective is devoid of theory. The study of learning organisations often focuses on organisational learning mechanisms, and these can be seen as a way of making the concept of organisational learning more concrete, and thus linking the two perspectives. Popper and Lipshitz (1998) describe organisational learning mechanisms as the structural and procedural arrangements that allow organisations to learn, in other words:

> that is to collect, analyse, store, disseminate and use systematically information that is relevant to their and their members' performance.

These issues are well reflected in Pedler *et al.*'s (1991) model of the learning organisation, which we will describe shortly. Easterby-Smith and Araujo (1999) argue that the literature on the learning organisation draws heavily on the concepts of organisational learning, from a utilitarian perspective, and there is some commonality in the literature, as Argyris and Schon (1996) suggest. It is generally agreed that there is a lack of critical research from both perspectives.

Organisational and individual learning

Although some pragmatic definitions of learning organisations centre on more and more individual learning, learning support and self-development, organisational learning is more than just the sum of individual learning in the organisation. It is only when an individual's learning has an impact on and interrelates with others that organisation members learn together and gradually begin to change the way things are done.

WINDOW ON PRACTICE

The difference between individual and organisational learning

Brian learns from the last research project team he ran that it would be much more effective if a member of the marketing department were fully involved at an early stage. Therefore he includes a marketing specialist from the outset on the next project team and finds that this reduces the time needed for the project team and results in less hassle towards the end of the project. Brian and the organisation have gained from this learning, but if *only* Brian learns this lesson the learning will be lost when he leaves the organisation. If, however, Brian discusses the idea with colleagues, or if there is heated debate at the beginning of the project team due to resistance to marketing specialists being included, and/or if there is some appraisal at the end of the project, there is some chance that others may learn from being involved in this experience. Others may feel that marketing specialists should be involved from the outset, may request that this happens, may apply it to other teams, and the new practice may become the way that the organisation operates. In this second scenario, if Brian leaves the organisation, he may take his learning with him, but the organisation also retains the learning as it has become embedded in the way that the organisation operates.

In this way mutual behaviour change is achieved which increases the collective competence, rather than just individual competence. Argyris and Schon (1978) see such learning as a change in the 'theory in use' (that is, the understanding, whether conscious or unconscious, that determines what we actually *do*) rather than merely a change in the 'espoused' theory (what we *say* we do). In other words the often unspoken rules of the organisation have changed. The question of how individual learning feeds into organisational learning and transformation, and how this is greater than the sum of individual learning, is only beginning to be addressed. Viewing the organisation as a process rather than an entity may offer some help here. Another perspective is that of viewing the organisation as a living organism. Pedler *et al.* (1991) make a useful start with their company energy flow model, shown in Figure 11.1.

Argyris and Schon (1978) describe different levels, or loops, of organisational learning, which others have developed. These levels are:

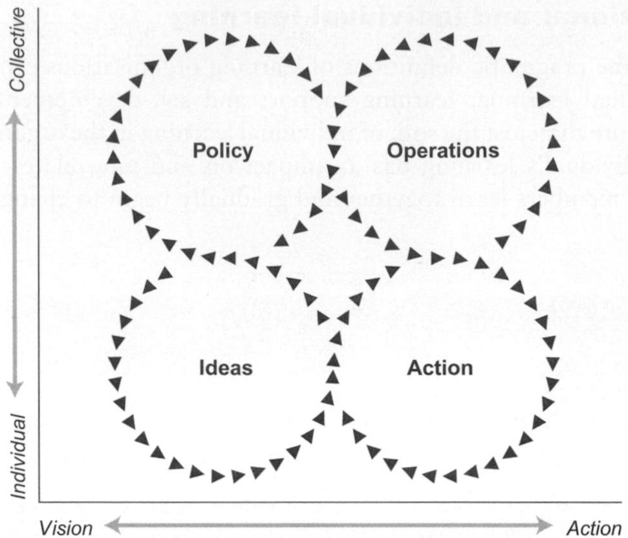

Figure 11.1 The energy flow model (Source: M. Pedler, J. Burgoyne and T. Boydell (1991) *The Learning Company*. Maidenhead: McGraw-Hill. Copyright © 1991 McGraw-Hill Europe. Reproduced with the permission of McGraw-Hill Book Company, Europe.)

- **Level 1: Single loop learning:** Learning about *how* we can do better, thus improving what we are currently doing. This is seen as learning at the operational level, or at the level of rules.
- **Level 2: Double loop learning:** A more fundamental level, which is concerned with '*why*' questions in relation to what we are doing rather than with doing the same things better, that is, questioning whether we should be *doing different things*. This level is described as developing knowledge and understanding due to insights, and can result in strategic changes and renewal.
- **Level 3: Triple loop learning:** This level of learning is the hardest of all to achieve as it is focused on the purpose or principles of the organisation, challenging whether these are appropriate, and is sometimes described as learning at the level of will or being.

All these levels of organisational learning are connected, as shown in Figure 11.2.

What are the characteristics of learning organisations?

There are many different approaches to describing the characteristics of a learning organisation, and we shall briefly consider three of these. First, we look at the approach of Pedler *et al.* (1991), who identify 11 characteristics of a learning organisation, grouped into five general themes.

Strategy

Two characteristics within this theme are suggested, first that a *learning approach to strategy* should be taken. Strategy formation, implementation, evaluation and improvement are deliberately structured as learning experiences by using feedback loops. Second, *participative policy making* infers that this is shared with all in the

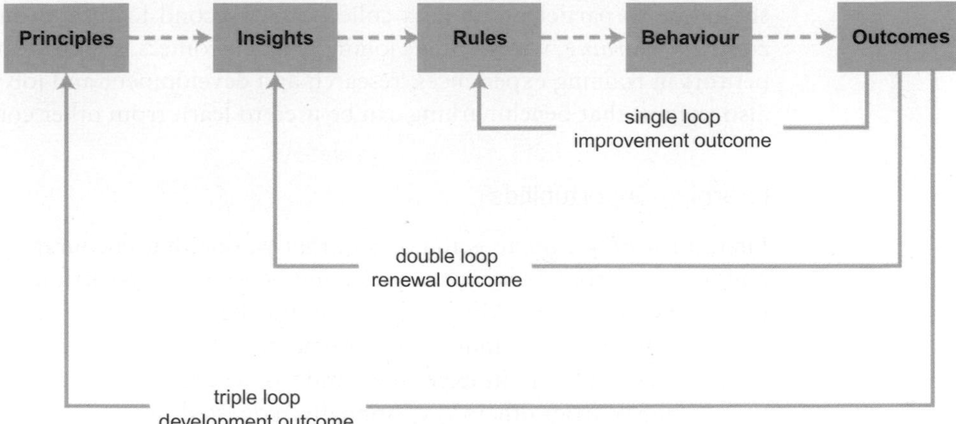

Figure 11.2 Three levels of organisational learning (Source: Adapted from J. Swieringa and A. Wierdsma (1992) *Becoming a Learning Organisation*. Wokingham: Addison-Wesley.)

organisation, and even further, that suppliers, customers and the total community have some involvement. The aim of the policy is to 'delight customers', and the differences of opinion and values that are revealed in the participative process are seen as productive tensions.

Looking in

Four characteristics are suggested within this theme – the first being *informating* which involves using technology to empower and inform employees, and is made widely available. They note that such information should be used to understand what is going on in the company, and so stimulate learning, rather than used to reward, punish or control. Second, there is *formative accounting and control* which involves designing accounting, budgeting and reporting systems to assist learning. Third, there is *internal exchange* which involves all internal units seeing themselves as customers and suppliers of each other. Fourth, they identify *reward flexibility*, which implies that the question of why some receive more money than others is a debate to be brought out into the open. They recommend that alternatives are discussed and tried out, but recognise that this is the most difficult of the 11 characteristics to put into practice.

Structures

Enabling structures suggest that roles are loosely structured in line with the needs of internal customers and suppliers, and in a way that allows for personal growth and experimentation. Internal boundaries can be flexible. For example, project groups and transient structures help to break down barriers between units, provide mechanisms for spreading new ideas and encourage the idea of change.

Looking out

Boundary workers as environmental scanners implies that part of the role of all workers in contact with suppliers, customers and neighbours of the organisation should be to participate in data collection. A second feature in this theme is *inter-company learning*, which entails joining with customers, suppliers and possibly competitors in training experiences, research and development and job exchanges. They also suggest that benchmarking can be used to learn from other companies.

Learning opportunities

First, a *learning climate* is important, that is, one that encourages experimentation and learning from experience, questioning current ideas, attitudes and actions and trying out new ideas. Mistakes are allowed because not all new ideas will work. There is a focus on continuous improvement, and the involvement of customers, suppliers and neighbours in experimentation is suggested. A learning climate suggests that feedback from others is continually requested, is made available and is acted upon. Second, *self-development opportunities for all* requires resources and facilities for self-development for employees at all levels in the organisation, and coaching, mentoring, peer support, counselling, feedback and so on must be available to support individuals in their learning.

ACTIVITY 11.1

Which of the 11 dimensions identified by Pedler *et al.* (1991) are currently being pursued in your organisation, or any organisation with which you are familiar? How is this being done?

Apart from 'reward flexibility' which of the 11 would be the most difficult for this organisation to pursue? What are the barriers, and how might they be overcome?

Peter Senge (1990) takes a slightly different perspective. In his book about the art and practice of a learning organisation he identified five vital dimensions in building organisations which can learn, which he refers to as disciplines:

1 **Systems thinking.** This is an understanding of the interrelatedness between things, seeing the whole rather than just a part and concentrating on processes. In terms of organisational actions it suggests that connections need to be constantly made and that there must be consideration of the implications that every action has elsewhere in the organisation.
2 **Personal mastery.** This underlines the need for continuous development and individual self-development.
3 **Mental models.** This is about the need to expose the 'theories in use' in the organisation. These can block change and the adoption of new ideas, and can only be confronted, challenged and changed if they are brought to the surface rather than remaining unconscious.
4 **Shared visions.** This is expressing the need for a common purpose or vision which can inspire members of the organisation and break down barriers and mistrust. Senge argues that such a vision plus an accurate view of the present state results in a creative tension which is helpful for learning and change.

5 **Team learning.** Teams are seen as important in that they are microcosms of the organisation, and the place where different views and perspectives come together, which Senge sees as a productive process.

Senge acknowledges that he presents a very positive vision of what organisations can do, and recognises that without the appropriate leadership this will not happen. He goes on to identify three critical leadership roles: designer, teacher and steward. As designer the leader needs to engage employees at all levels in designing the vision, core purpose and values of the organisation: design processes for strategic thinking and effective learning processes. As teacher the leader needs to help all organisation members gain more insight into the organisational reality, to coach, guide and facilitate, and help others bring their theories into use. As steward the leader needs to demonstrate a sense of personal commitment to the organisation's mission and take responsibility for the impact of leadership on others.

Bob Garratt (1990) concentrates on the role that the directors of an organisation have in encouraging a learning organisation and in overcoming learning blocks. He suggests:

- the top team concentrate on strategy and policy and hold back from day-to-day operational issues;
- thinking time is needed for the top team to relate changes in the external environment to the internal working of the organisation;
- the creation of a top team, involving the development and deployment of the strengths of each member;
- the delegation of problem solving to staff close to the operation;
- acceptance that learning occurs at all levels of the organisation, and that directors need to create a climate where this learning flows freely.

Clearly, a learning organisation is not something that can be developed overnight and has to be viewed as a long-term strategy.

Easterby-Smith (1990) makes some key points about encouraging experimentation in organisations in relation to flexible structures, information, people and reward. We have discussed flexibility and information in some detail. In respect of people he argues that organisations will seek to select those who are similar to current organisation members. The problem here is that such a strategy, in reinforcing homogeneity and reducing diversity, restrains the production of innovative and creative ideas. He sees diversity as a positive stimulant and concludes that organisations should therefore select some employees who would not normally fit their criteria, and especially those who would be likely to experiment and be able to tolerate ambiguity. In relation to the reward system he notes the need to reinforce rather than punish risk taking and innovation.

Critique

The initial idealism of the learning organisation concept has been tempered by experiences, and more pragmatic material is gradually being developed. Popper and Lipshitz (2000) have identified four conditions under which organisational learning is likely to be productive. These are in situations where there is:

1 **Valid information** – that is, complete, undistorted and verifiable information.

2 **Transparency** – where individuals are prepared to hold themselves open to inspection in order to receive valid feedback. This reduces self-deception, and helps to resist pressures to distort information.

3 **Issues orientation rather than a personal orientation** – that is, where information is judged on its merits and relevance to the issue at hand, rather than on the status or attributes of the individual who provides the information.

4 **Accountability** – that is, 'holding oneself responsible for one's own actions and their consequences and for learning from these consequences'.

In a different approach Burgoyne (1999) provides a list of nine things that need to happen for continuous learning to become a reality.

There remains a wide range of concerns regarding the concept of the learning organisation. Hawkins (1994) notes the evangelistic fervour with which learning organisations and total quality management (TQM) are recommended to the uninitiated and fears that the commercialisation of these ideas means that they become superficial. He argues that an assumption may be made that all learning is good whatever is being learned, whereas the value of learning is where it is taking us and, as Stewart (2001) points out, learning is neither objective nor neutral. Learning should be seen as the means rather than the end in itself. Learning to be more efficient at what is being done does not necessarily make one more effective; it depends on the appropriateness of the activity itself. It is not surprising therefore that there is a lack of evidence linking learning organisation strategies with financial performance (*see*, for example, Sonsino 2002).

Nor does the literature cover adequately the barriers to becoming a learning organisation – for example, the role of politics within the organisation. If learning requires sharing of information, and information is power, then how can individuals be encouraged to let go of the power they have? There has also been a lack of attention to emotion, ethics and human irrationality. Harris (2002), for example, demonstrates how the potential for learning in her retail bank case studies was constrained by the overwhelming desire to maintain continuity in the organisation.

In particular, both Senge (1990) and Garratt (1990) have high expectations of the leaders of organisations. To what extent are these expectations realistic, and how might they be achieved? The literature of learning organisations has a clear unitarist perspective – the question of whether employees desire to be involved in or united by a vision of the organisation needs to be addressed. The question of willing participation was also raised by Harris when she found that contractors were unwilling to share their learning when leaving the organisation, even though this expectation was built into their contracts. For a useful critique of the assumptions behind learning organisations, see Coopey (1995). In addition, the full complexity of the ideas implicit in the words 'learning organisation' requires more explanation.

The problems in implementing learning organisation prescriptions has led Sun and Scott (2003) to suggest that attention needs to refocus on organisational learning in order really to understand how individual learning can be transformed into collective learning, and they suggest some useful ways forward. An alternative development is that of the 'living company' which extends the learning organisation concept, and this is the subject of case 11.1 on the website. Another focus has been the

more recent attention to knowledge management which is generally presented in a more practical/applicable manner, and yet as we have previously suggested has some similar foundations to the learning organisation.

KNOWLEDGE MANAGEMENT

Knowledge and its perceived value

Knowledge is increasingly viewed as a critical organisational resource which provides competitive advantage. As the speed of change gets faster organisations increasingly need innovations, new ideas and new ways of doing things to keep ahead of the competition, and they constantly need to know what their competitors and customers are doing. Increasing organisational knowledge is seen to underpin this. In addition knowledge-based organisations, such as consultancies and finance companies, are growing. The growth of knowledge work and the increasing number of knowledge workers has been well reported. Examples of knowledge workers would be research and development staff, legal, IT, accounting and other professionals. But, although the prevalence of knowledge work still accounts for only a minority of workers in the UK (Nolan 2001), it would be a mistake to see knowledge as relevant just to such a narrow range of staff (*see*, for example, Evans 2003). We take the view in this chapter that knowledge is important for everyone in the organisation.

Providing a definition of knowledge is surprisingly difficult, and there are many different perspectives in the literature. For an academic debate about the nature of knowledge *see* Tsoukas and Vladimirou (2001). At a simple level we can say that data are raw facts, that analysis and contextualisation of raw data so that they become something meaningful produce information, and that knowledge is more than information in that it has been reflected on and processed to the extent that it can be applied and is with the person who needs to apply it. Explicit knowledge, sometimes referred to as operational knowledge, or 'know what' type knowledge, can be codified and stored for others to access. Examples here might be competitors' price changes, new competitor products, customer buying patterns and changes in employment legislation.

However, most knowledge is more complex than this, it is something which resides in a person's head and we are often unaware of what we know until we come to use it. This is usually referred to as tacit knowledge, or 'know how' type knowledge. This is made up of our accumulated experiences about how things are done, how problems can be solved, what works, what doesn't and in what contexts and under what conditions. An example of this might be a fireman who during a fire would be able to work out when a backdraught would be likely to occur and could then make sure the immediate area is clear of people. Working this out involves a series of decision processes about the current conditions of the fire and comparing this with previous experiences when backdraughts have occurred. This is usually done intuitively. For anyone else to use this knowledge it needs to be made explicit, which is recognised by many as difficult, and by some as unachievable. Knowledge management initiatives may cover either or both types of knowledge.

WINDOW ON PRACTICE

We have just cited changing employment legislation as an example of explicit knowledge which could easily be written down and shared. But an experienced lawyer would bring deeper and more detailed tacit knowledge to enhance this. For example, from past experiences and case law they may have some feel for the way new regulations will be interpreted, or the stance that different judges may take on such regulations.

Knowledge in itself is not enough as it has to be accessed, applied appropriately and used to enhance the organisation's ability to achieve its objectives. Thus for knowledge to be of value it needs to be turned into action. Given this, it is not surprising that attention has been focused on how to generate knowledge, how to share knowledge and how to reuse it – in other words knowledge management.

ACTIVITY 11.2

Think of an activity in which you are skilled, where you will have a high level of tacit knowledge. You could even think of riding a bike or crossing a busy road.

Try to write down all the comparisons and decisions that you make when applying your knowledge to the task in hand.

MANAGING KNOWLEDGE

Knowledge management has been variously defined and the term is ambiguous. In this chapter we will use a definition suggested by Scarbrough and Swan (2001):

> defined broadly and inclusively to cover a loosely connected set of ideas, tools and practices centring on the communication and exploitation of knowledge in organisations. (p. 3)

Our understanding of what knowledge is will have implications for the way we try to manage it. Early approaches to knowledge management focused on IT systems as a means of codifying an individual's knowledge, storing it and making it available to others in the organisation. This somewhat simplistic approach was based on the concept that knowledge is an abstract objective truth which can be easily recorded and manipulated, separately from the person who created the knowledge. The resultant activity led to a proliferation of organisational databases, search programmes, yellow pages type directories, intranets and extranets. An example of an extranet is provided by Hunter *et al.* (2002) in the context of a legal firm which offered professional knowledge in this format to valued clients as part of the service that they paid for. While this may be useful for the explicit knowledge referred to above, and is the focus of much research work in the area, it has very limited value.

WINDOW ON PRACTICE

Kermally (2002) provides a case study of 'ResearchNet' demonstrating a simple knowledge-sharing mechanism which demonstrates how explicit knowledge can be effectively shared without IT.

The marketing department of this company wanted to collect external information relevant to its operations. To do this all marketing staff were asked to put Post-it ® notes on the departmental notice board of any information they came across which they felt was relevant. Every week a coordinator would collate the information and produce a short report for discussion. This process then spread to other departments. Kermally suggests this was a useful approach as it involved all staff, used resources effectively, was a meaningful activity, and hence motivational, and was evolutionary.

Source: Summarised from S. Kermally (2002) *Effective Knowledge management*. Chichester: John Wiley.

The alternative perspective is that knowledge is personal and socially constructed. In other words, knowledge is an ongoing interpretation of the external world, as suggested by Blackler (2000):

> knowledge to be . . . pragmatic, partial, tentative and always open to revision – it is no more, and no less, than a collective interpretation. (p. 61)

This perspective suggests that codifying knowledge and using IT systems to store and share it is inadequate. Instead attention needs to be focused on 'communities of interest' – in other words the way in which individuals with a common interest network to share knowledge and spark off new ideas. A second focus is on the way that knowledge becomes embedded into systems, processes and culture within the organisation. This perspective requires that individuals need to be willing to share their knowledge, and since knowledge is power, there can be no assumptions that individuals will comply. To this end encouraging and perhaps facilitating various types of networking would be more appropriate. Trust in the organisation is critical here as sharing knowledge may involve admitting to failures and what has been learned from them and giving bad news. Project write-ups and reports may also be used in trying to make tacit knowledge explicit, especially when individuals holding the knowledge may leave the organisation. An example of this is a Department Head in a university who was aware that a valued member of staff teaching a very specialist area was about to retire and instigated a project to document their teaching content and methods so that their particular knowledge would not be lost to the university.

Kermally identifies a range of knowledge management initiatives, based on Nonaka and Takeuchi's (1995) model of how organisational knowledge can be created. Kermally suggests that to develop knowledge through *socialisation* activities such as brainstorming, informal meetings, conversations, coaching, mentoring, interacting with customers, on-the-job training and observation may be helpful; to develop knowledge through *externalisation*, databases, exchange of best practices, building models, after-action reviews and master classes would be helpful; for a *combined approach*, conferences, publications and electronic libraries are suggested; and for knowledge *internalisation*, feedback from customers, facilitation skills and development counselling would be helpful.

WINDOW ON PRACTICE

Knowledge management at Thames Water

Lank and Windle (2003) report an interview with Peter Hemmings, Director of Knowledge Management at Thames Water, on the progress that the company is making. Hemmings explains that Thames Water's strategy for knowledge management rests on four key building blocks:

- Making knowledge visible
- Increasing knowledge intensity
- Creating a knowledge infrastructure
- Developing a knowledge culture

He suggests that cross-boundary knowledge-sharing communities are critical in achieving this strategy. These communities focus on groups of professionals who share knowledge on common interests, say bidding, negotiations and contracts or the avoidance of water diversion and loss. Each community is initiated with a facilitator and they start by designing the remit of the group including a mission statement, terms of membership, and how the group will use the organisation's electronic 'tea rooms'. Thereafter the communities manage themselves and decide which issues they need to concentrate on. In addition Thames Water has developed an internal electronic directory to help people find needed expertise and people with shared business interests. Knowledge sharing is explicitly encouraged in the company value statements and reinforced through training.

Source: Summarised from E. Lank and I. Windle (2003) 'Catch me if you can', *People Management*, Vol. 9, No. 2, 6 February, pp. 40–2.

The barriers to knowledge management have been variously identified as the culture of the organisation, the risk of admitting to failure, lack of incentive to change, resistance to ideas and learning from other contexts, internal competition and individual reward practices. Factors identified as encouraging knowledge management are an organisation which engenders trust and openness, a knowledge-centric culture, defined roles and responsibilities in knowledge management, support through the performance management system (such as targets about sharing knowledge and team/organisational rewards), building on informal practices which already exist.

WINDOW ON PRACTICE

Knowledge sharing across organisational boundaries

Reporting on a two-year study of six knowledge-intensive firms Swart and Kinnie (2003) found that it was as important for these firms to share knowledge with other firms as to share knowledge within their own organisation. Some of these companies work closely with fellow suppliers of a client to form a network in order to provide an integrated service or product. This demands a lot of trust as it requires commercially sensitive information to be shared with other companies which, at other times, may be their competitor. Such hybrid teams will often involve the client. This poses a dilemma as such teams can develop a strong identity, and result in members becoming isolated from their employer. This may inhibit the sharing of knowledge within the employing company.

Source: Summarised from J. Swart and N. Kinnie (2003) 'Free Transfer', *People Management*, Vol. 9, No. 4, 20 February, pp. 38–40.

It has been suggested that organisations need to make all their knowledge management activities explicit in order to justify the investment made and demonstrate the organisation's commitment to knowledge. Strategies for making knowledge management explicit are the subject of case 11.2 on the website.

Roles in knowledge management

Evans (2003) notes that there is still much confusion about the responsibility for and accountabilities in knowledge management, and Lank (2002) suggests three new organisational roles intended to promote knowledge management:

- **The knowledge architects:** Lank suggests that these are senior, strategic roles such as Chief Knowledge Officer and involve, among other things, working out which knowledge is critical and how it will be shared, how technology could be used, how people will be trained, how they will be rewarded for collaborative working.
- **The knowledge facilitators:** These are the people who run processes to help knowledge flow, for example company journalists who write up customer case studies and project reviews; librarians who develop indexes for storage and retrieval of information; information service providers who provide an internal consultancy service to find and deliver information to staff – including external and internal information; webmasters who develop the company intranet; and learning facilitators who can facilitate post-event reviews to elicit lessons learned.
- **The knowledge aware:** These include all employees, who have a responsibility to share their own expertise and knowledge, who will participate in post-event reviews, and who act to reinforce the value of collaboration.

There are two critical roles missing here – the line manager and the HR specialist. MacNeil (2003) makes a convincing case for the importance of the line manager in knowledge management which she suggests has been overlooked to date. She identifies the line manager's contribution as creating a positive learning climate, encouraging open exchange, reinforcing that making mistakes is acceptable and that it is helpful to share errors. Although she does note that there are questions about the extent to which line managers have the skills to facilitate knowledge management.

Given a broader understanding of knowledge as above, then knowledge management is inevitably bound up with human resource management in overcoming barriers and in proactively supporting knowledge management. HR professionals may, for example, utilise facilitation skills in supporting knowledge management, or they align human resource activities with knowledge management needs.

Knowledge management and human resource management

MacNeil (2003) goes on to suggest that there has been a lack of research on the links between HRM and knowledge management, yet Lengnick-Hall and Lengnick-Hall (2003) suggest that knowledge facilitator is a key HR role. They suggest that HR has a key role in:

> developing the motivation, competencies, value orientation, and knowledge of the firm's strategic intent to use knowledge to enhance organisational capabilities. (p. 90)

In more detail they recommend that HR managers need to design organisational structures and processes that promote knowledge diffusion, contribute to designing user-friendly systems for accessing knowledge and training people in their use, develop a knowledge-centric culture, provide mechanisms for people to share knowledge – for example allowing teams to work together long enough to develop knowledge together and then move people around the organisation to cross-fertilise.

Scarbrough and Carter (2000) asked their sample of researchers in the knowledge management area what implications their work had for HRM, and found that:

- 27 per cent claimed there were implications for recruitment and selection policy;
- 63 per cent claimed there were implications for training and development in the workplace;
- 27 per cent claimed there were implications for rewards and appraisal;
- 77 per cent claimed there were implications for organisational and cultural change policy and practice.

At a strategic level Scarbrough and Carter identify five different perspectives in the work on knowledge management and draw out the implications that each has for HRM:

- **Best practice perspective**: Encouraging employees to share knowledge and co-operate with knowledge management initiatives. If commitment is required in order that individuals are prepared to share their knowledge and remain with the organisation then 'best practice' HRM will be important to generate that commitment. (*See* Chapter 2 for a reminder of this approach.)

- **Knowledge work perspective:** Managing knowledge work and knowledge workers. Such workers may have distinctive needs in terms of motivation, job challenge, autonomy, careers and so on. These will need to be addressed by HR policies. For further depth on this issue *see* Beaumont and Hunter (2002).
- **Congruence perspective:** Increasing performance by aligning HRM and knowledge management practices. For a reminder of this *see* the fit model of HR strategy in Chapter 2.
- **Human and social capital perspective:** This involves the development of human and social resources in the organisation. This both underpins the success of knowledge management initiatives and mobilises longer-term capabilities. This perspective is based on the resource-based view of the firm that we explored in Chapter 2.
- **Learning perspective:** This perspective incorporates two different approaches. First is the notion of communities of learning, discussed above, which draws attention to the way tacit knowledge is developed and shared in practitioner groups. Second, there is organisational learning which focuses on how learning can be embedded in organisational routines and processes to improve organisational performance.

SUMMARY PROPOSITIONS

11.1 There is an increasing emphasis on organisational performance and the factors that affect it. Systems, structures, processes, resources and culture will all have an impact on organisational performance.

11.2 The concentration on the learning organisation has not fulfilled its potential and it is suggested that further investigation into the process of organisational learning would be helpful.

11.3 Knowledge management is an alternative way forward which is packaged in a more user-friendly way, but is not without significant problems.

GENERAL DISCUSSION TOPICS

1. 'Knowledge management is nothing other than learning organisation strategies presented in a more user-friendly way.' To what extent would you support this statement, and why?
2. 'Learning organisations are dreams which can never come true.' Discuss why you agree or disagree with this statement.

FURTHER READING

Alvesson, M. and Karreman, D. (2001) 'Odd couple: making sense of the curious concept of knowledge management', *Journal of Management Studies*, Vol. 38, No. 7, pp. 995–1018

In complete contrast to the following suggestion, this is theoretical and conceptual analysis of the subject of knowledge management. It is, however, quite accessible and thought provoking.

Alvesson and Karreman, among other issues, identify the contradiction of putting knowledge and management together; suggest the possibility that trying to manage knowledge may reduce its value; identify the potential that knowledge management has for control; and question the assumption that knowledge is always a good thing.

Funes, M. and Johnson, N. (1998) *Honing your knowledge skills*. Oxford: Butterworth Heinemann
A useful collection of skills aimed at enabling the individual to be a better knowledge manager. There is some background on the role of knowledge management and then sections which explain practical skills, tools and techniques which can be applied. For example there are sections on gathering data, creating knowledge frameworks, developing intuition and the use of IT. User-friendly style and format, although some of the tools themselves can be complex.

REFERENCES

Argyris, C. and Schon, D.A. (1978) *Organisational Learning*. Reading, Mass.: Addison-Wesley.

Argyris and Schon (1996) *Organisation Learning II: Theory, Method and Practice*, Reading, Mass.: Addison-Wesley.

Beaumont, P. and Hunter, L. (2002) *Managing Knowledge Workers: Research Report*, London: CIPD.

Blackler, F. (2000) 'Collective wisdom', *People Management*, Vol. 6, No. 13, 22 June, p. 61.

Burgoyne, J. (1999) 'Design of the times', *People Management*, 3 June, pp. 38–44.

Coopey, J. (1995) 'The learning organisation, power, politics and ideology', *Management Learning*, Vol. 26, No. 2, pp. 193–213.

Easterby-Smith, M. (1990) 'Creating a learning organisation', *Personnel Review*, Vol. 19, No. 5, pp. 24–8.

Easterby-Smith, M. and Araujo, L. (1999) 'Organisational Learning: Current debates and opportunities', in M. Easterby-Smith, J. Burgoyne and L. Araujo (eds), *Organisational Learning and the Learning Organisation*. London: Sage.

Edmonson, A. and Moingeon, B. (1998) 'From organizational learning to the Learning Organisation', *Management Learning*, Vol. 29, pp. 5–20.

Evans C. (2003) *Managing for Knowledge: HR's strategic role*, Oxford: Butterworth Heinemann.

Garratt, B. (1990) *Creating a Learning Organisation*. Hemel Hempstead: Director Books.

Harris, L. (2002) 'The learning organization – myth or reality? Examples from the UK retail banking industry', *The Learning Organisation*, Vol. 9, No. 2, pp. 78–88.

Hawkins, P. (1994) 'Organisational learning; Taking stock and facing the challenge', *Management Learning*, Vol. 25, No. 1.

Hunter, L., Beaumont, P. and Lee, M. (2002) 'Knowledge management practice in Scottish law firms', *Human Resource Management Journal*, Vol. 12, No. 2, pp. 4–21.

Jones, M. (2001) 'Sustainable organizational capacity building: is organizational learning the key?' *International Journal of Human Resource Management*, Vol. 12, No. 1, pp. 91–8.

Kermally, S. (2002) *Effective Knowledge management*. Chichester: John Wiley.

Lank, E. (2002) 'Head to head', *People Management*, Vol. 8, No. 4, pp. 46–9.

Lank, E. and Windle, I. (2003) 'Catch me if you can', *People Management*, Vol. 9, No. 2, 6 February, pp. 40–2.

Lengnick-Hall, M. and Lengnick-Hall, C. (2003) *Human Resource Management in the Knowledge Economy*. San Fransisco: Berrett-Koehler Inc.

MacNeil, C. (2003) 'Line managers: facilitators of knowledge sharing in teams', *Employee Relations*, Vol. 25, No. 3, pp. 294–307.

Nolan, P. (2001) 'Shaping things to come', *People Management*, Vol. 7, No. 25, 27 December, pp. 30–1.

Nonaka, I. and Takeuchi, H. (1995) *The Knowledge-Creating Company: How Japanese companies create the dynamics of innovation*. Oxford: Oxford University Press.

Ortenblad, A. (2001) 'On differences between organizational learning and learning organisation', *The Learning Organisation*, Vol. 8, No. 3, pp. 125–33.

Pedler, M., Boydell, T. and Burgoyne, J. (1989) 'Towards the learning company', *Management Education and Development*, Vol. 20, Pt 1.

Pedler, M., Burgoyne, J. and Boydell, T. (1991) *The Learning Company*. Maidenhead: McGraw-Hill.

Popper, M. and Lipshitz, R. (1998) 'Organisational learning mechanisms: A cultural and structural approach to organizational learning', *Journal of Applied Behavioural Science*, Vol. 34, pp. 161–78.

Popper, M. and Lipshitz, R. (2000) 'Organisational Learning', *Management Learning*, Vol. 31, No. 2, pp. 181–96.

Scarbrough, H. and Carter, C. (2000) *Investigating Knowledge Management: Research Report*. London: CIPD.

Scarbrough, H. and Swan, J. (2001) 'Explaining the diffusion of knowledge management: the role of fashion', *British Journal of Management*, Vol. 12, pp. 3–12.

Senge, P. (1990) *The Fifth Discipline: The art and practice of the learning organisation*. London: Century Business, Random House.

Sloman, M. (1999) 'Seize the Day', *People Management*, Vol. 5, No. 10, 20 May, p. 31.

Sonsino, S. (2002) 'How convincing is the evidence that learning organizations generate better financial returns?' *People Management*, Vol. 8, No. 12, p. 65.

Stewart, D. (2001) 'Reinterpreting the learning organisation', *The Learning Organisation*, Vol. 8, No. 4, pp. 141–52.

Sun, Y. and Scott, J. (2003) 'Explore the divide – organisational learning and learning organisation', *The Learning Organisation*, Vol. 10, No. 4, pp. 202–15.

Swart, J. and Kinnie, N. (2003) 'Free Transfer', *People Management*, Vol. 9, No. 4, 20 February, pp. 38–40.

Swieringa, J. and Wierdsma, A. (1992) *Becoming a Learning Organisation*. Wokingham: Addison-Wesley.

Tsoukas, H. and Vladimirou, E. (2001) 'What is organisational knowledge?' *Journal of Management Studies*, Vol. 38, No. 7, pp. 973–93.

Vince, R., Sutcliffe, K. and Olivera, F. (2002) 'Organisational Learning: New Directions', *British Journal of Management*, Vol. 13, special edition, pp. S1–S6.

Wang, C. and Ahmed, P. (2003) 'Organisational Learning: a critical review', *The Learning Organisation*, Vol. 10, No. 1, pp. 8–17.

An extensive range of additional materials, including multiple choice questions, answers to questions and links to useful websites can be found on the Human Resource Management Companion Website at **www.pearsoned.co.uk/torrington.**

CHAPTER 12

INDIVIDUAL PERFORMANCE MANAGEMENT

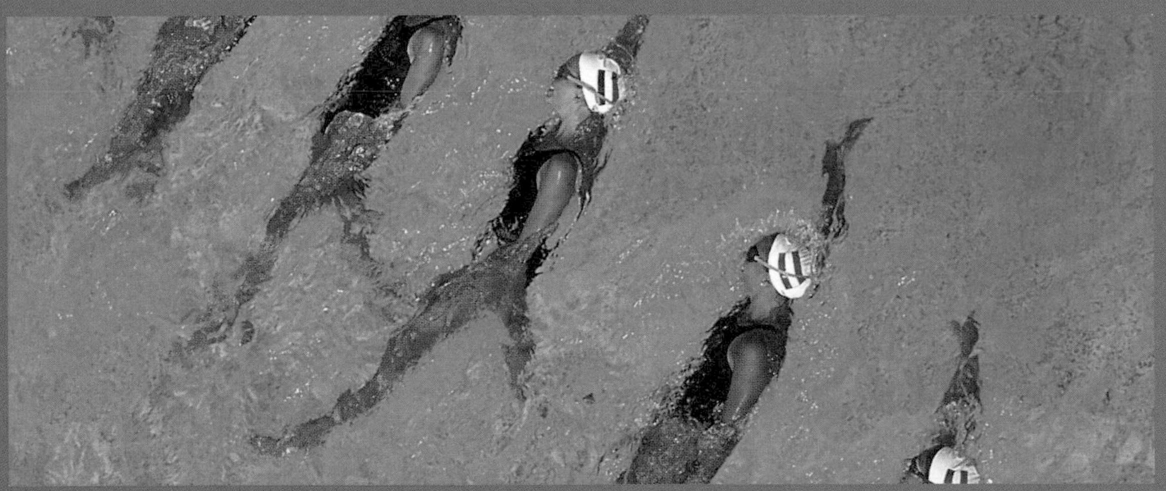

THE OBJECTIVES OF THIS CHAPTER ARE TO:

1 CLARIFY THE NATURE AND PURPOSE OF PERFORMANCE MANAGEMENT AND PERFORMANCE APPRAISAL

2 EXAMINE THE STAGES OF A TYPICAL PERFORMANCE MANAGEMENT SYSTEM

3 REVIEW THE IMPLEMENTATION OF PERFORMANCE MANAGEMENT SYSTEMS

4 EXPLORE THE CONTRIBUTION OF 360-DEGREE/ MULTI-RATER FEEDBACK

The treatment of individual performance in organisations has traditionally centred on the assessment of performance and the allocation of reward. Performance was typically seen as the result of the interaction between individual ability and motivation.

Increasingly, organisations recognise that planning and enabling performance have a critical effect on individual performance. So, for example, clarity of performance goals and standards, appropriate resources, guidance and support from the individual's manager all become central.

PERFORMANCE MANAGEMENT AND PERFORMANCE APPRAISAL

Appraisal systems

Traditionally performance appraisal systems have provided a formalised process to review the performance of employees. They are typically designed on a central basis, usually by the HR function, and require each line manager to appraise the performance of their staff, usually on an annual basis. This normally requires the manager and employee to take part in a performance review meeting. Elaborate forms are often completed as a record of the process, but these are not living documents, they are generally stored in the archives of the HR department, and the issue of performance is often neglected until the next round of performance review meetings.

The nature of what is being appraised varies between organisations and might cover personality, behaviour or job performance. These areas might be measured either quantitively or qualitatively. Qualitative appraisal often involves the writing of an unstructured narrative on the general performance of the appraisee. Alternatively, some guidance might be given as to the areas on which the appraiser should comment. The problem with qualitative appraisals is that they may leave important areas unappraised, and that they are not suitable for comparison purposes.

Coates (1994) argues that what is actually measured in performance appraisal is the extent to which the individual conforms to the organisation. Some traditional appraisal was based on measures of personality traits that were felt to be important to the job. These included traits such as resourcefulness, enthusiasm, drive, application and other traits such as intelligence. One difficulty with these is that everyone defines them differently. Raters, therefore, are often unsure of what they are rating, leaving more scope for bias and prejudice. Another problem is that since the same scales are often used for many different jobs, traits that are irrelevant to an appraisee's job may still be measured.

Other approaches concentrate on linking ratings to behaviour and performance on the job. So performance may be reviewed against key aspects of the job or major headings on the job description. Specific methods of linking ratings with behaviour at work have been developed such as behaviourally anchored rating scales (BARS) and behavioural observation scales (BOS) although evidence suggests that these are not widely used (Williams 2002).

Another method of making appraisal more objective is to use the process to set job objectives over the coming year and, a year later, to measure the extent to which these objectives have been met. The extent to which the appraisee is involved in setting these objectives varies considerably. When a competency profile has been identified for a particular job, it is then possible to use this in the appraisal of

private sector. Similarly, Armstrong and Baron (1998a) report from their survey that no such correlation was found. They do report, however, that 77 per cent of organisations surveyed regarded their systems as effective to some degree and Houldsworth (2003), using the Henley and Hay Group survey of top FTSE companies and public sector respondents, reports that 68 per cent of organisations rated their performance management effectiveness as excellent. So performance management, such as HR systems and processes, still remains an act of faith.

As with appraisal systems, some performance management systems are development driven and some are reward driven. Whereas in the 1992 IPD survey 85 per cent of organisations claimed to link performance management to pay (Bevan and Thompson 1992), Armstrong and Baron found that only 43 per cent of survey respondents reported such a link. However, 82 per cent of the organisations visited had some form of performance-related pay (PRP) or competency-based pay, so the picture is a little confusing. They suggest that a view is emerging of performance management which centres on 'dialogue', 'shared understanding', 'agreement' and 'mutual commitment', rather than rating for pay purposes. While they may feature in more sophisticated systems, Houldsworth (2003) reports a figure of 77 per cent link with pay, and it appears that many organisations are trying to achieve both development and reward outcomes. She also contrasts systems driven by either performance development or performance measurement, finding that the real experience of developmental performance management is that it is motivational, encourages time spent with the line manager, encourages two-way communication and is an opportunity to align roles and training with business needs. Alternatively, where there is a measurement focus, performance management is seen as judgemental, a chance to assess and get rid of employees, emphasises control and getting more out of staff, raises false expectations and is a way to manage the salaries bill.

ACTIVITY 12.1

Think of the performance appraisal or performance management system at your place of work.

- To what extent does it focus on development and to what extent does it focus on reward?
- How, and how well, are each of these purposes achieved? Explain why this is.
- What would you do to improve the system, and what impacts would these actions have?

There are many different definitions of performance management and some have identified it as 'management by objectives' under another name. There are, however, some key differences. Management by objectives was primarily an off-the-peg system which was bought in and generally involved objectives being imposed on managers from above. Performance management tends to be tailor-made and produced in-house (which is why there are so many different versions), with an emphasis on mutual objective setting and on ongoing performance support and review. The term,

Table 12.1 Characteristics of performance management systems

- Top-down link between business objectives and individual objectives (compared with performance appraisal where there may be no objectives, or objectives not explicitly linked to business objectives)
- Line manager driven and owned (rather than being owned by the HR function, as typically with performance appraisal)
- A living document where performance plans, support and ongoing review are documented as work progresses, and prior to annual review (rather than an archived document retrieved at appraisal time to compare achievement with intentions)
- Performance is rewarded and reinforced

therefore, remains beyond precise definition, and rightly so, as it is critical that the system adopted fits with the culture and context of the organisation (*see*, for example, Audit Commission 2000; Hendry *et al.* 2000). As well as the right sort of culture, the right sort of leadership is needed together with a focus on the right priorities. Interestingly, though, Williams (2002) notes that performance management can be used as a tool of culture change. (*See* Table 12.1.)

STAGES IN A PERFORMANCE MANAGEMENT SYSTEM

Figure 12.1 shows a typical system, including both development and reward aspects, the main stages of which are discussed below.

Business mission, values, objectives and competencies

There is an assumption that before it is able to plan and manage individual performance the organisation will have made significant steps in identifying the performance required of the organisation as a whole. In most cases this will involve a mission statement so that performance is seen within the context of an overriding theme. Bevan and Thompson (1992) found that performance management organisations were more likely than others to have an organisational mission statement and to communicate this to employees. In addition many organisations will identify the strategic business objectives that are required within the current business context to be competitive and that align with the organisation's mission statement.

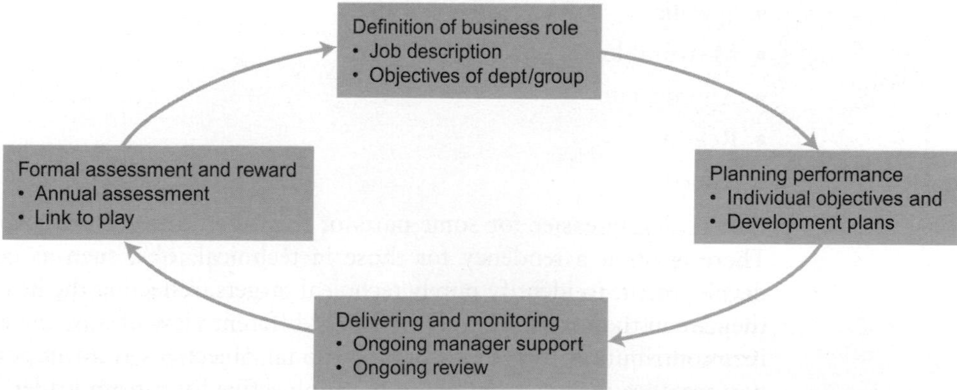

Figure 12.1 Stages of a typical performance management system

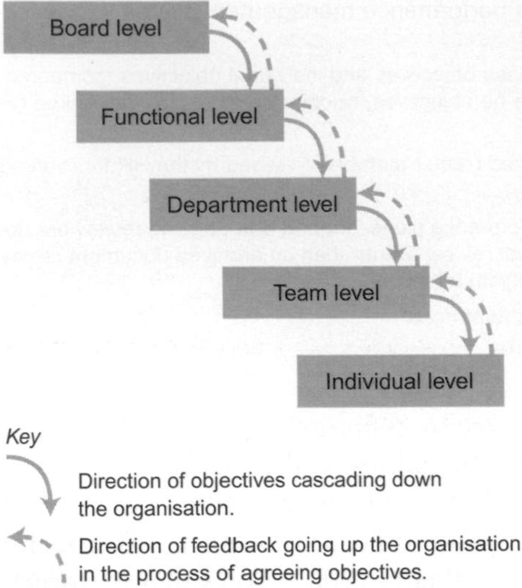

Figure 12.2 An objective-setting cascade

Many organisations will also identify core values of the business and the key competencies required. Each of these has a potential role in managing individual performance. Organisational objectives are particularly important, as it is common for such objectives to be cascaded down the organisation in order to ensure that individual objectives contribute to their achievement (for an example of an objective-setting cascade, *see* Figure 12.2).

Planning performance: a shared view of expected performance

Individual objectives derived from team objectives and an agreed job description can be jointly devised by manager and employee. These objectives are outcome/results oriented rather than task oriented, are tightly defined and include measures to be assessed. The objectives are designed to stretch the individual, and offer potential development as well as meeting business needs. It is helpful to both the organisation and the individual if objectives are prioritised. Many organisations use the 'SMART' acronym for describing individual objectives or targets:

- Specific
- Measurable
- Appropriate
- Relevant
- Timed

It is clearly easier for some parts of the organisation than others to set targets. There is often a tendency for those in technical jobs, such as computer systems development, to identify purely technical targets, reflecting the heavy task emphasis they see in their jobs. Moving staff to a different view of how their personal objectives contribute to team and organisational objectives is an important part of the performance management process. An objective for a team leader in systems development could be:

To complete development interviews with all team members by end July 2005. (written March 2005)

Clearly, the timescale for each objective will need to reflect the content of the objective and not timescales set into the performance management system. As objectives are met, managers and their staff need to have a brief review meeting to look at progress in all objectives and decide what other objectives should be added, changed or deleted. Five or six ongoing objectives are generally sufficient for one individual to work on at any time.

The critical point about a *shared* view of performance suggests that handing out a job description or list of objectives to the employee is not adequate. Performance expectations need to be understood and, where possible, to involve a contribution from the employee. For example, although key accountabilities may be fixed by the manager, they will need to be discussed. Specific objectives allow for and benefit from a greater degree of employee input as employees will have a valid view of barriers to overcome, the effort involved and feasibility. Expressing objectives as a 'what' statement rather than a 'how' statement gives employees the power to decide the appropriate approach once they begin to work on the issue. Incorporating employee input and using 'what' statements are likely to generate a higher degree of employee ownership and commitment. However, difficulties have been experienced with purely 'what' objectives as there may be appropriate and inappropriate ways of achieving an objective. For example, a manager with an objective to ensure that another department agrees to a plan of action could achieve this in different ways. The manager may pressure susceptible members of the other department and force agreement through without listening to the other department's perspective. This may alienate the other department and damage future good relations. Alternatively the manager could adopt a collaborative approach so that the needs of both departments are met, providing a sound basis for future cooperation between the departments. More sophisticated systems now incorporate the 'how' as well (*see* IDS 2003).

Planning the support, development and resources necessary for employees to achieve their objectives is imperative. Without this support it is unlikely that even the most determined employees will achieve the performance required.

Concerns have been expressed over restricting the objectives to those which specify output targets, and there is now evidence of increasing use of input targets, such as developing a critical competency which is valued by the organisation and relevant to the achievement of objectives. Williams (2000) argues that as individuals cannot always control their results it is important to have behavioural targets as well as output targets. It is also recommended that there is a personal development plan which would again underpin the achievement of objectives.

Delivering and monitoring performance

While the employee is working to achieve the performance agreed, the manager retains a key enabling role. Organising the resources and off-job training is clearly essential. So too is being accessible. There may well be unforeseen barriers to the agreed performance which the manager needs to deal with, and sometimes the situation will demand that the expected performance needs to be revised. The employee may want to sound out possible courses of action with the manager before proceeding, or may require further information. Sharing 'inside' information that will affect the employee's performance is often a key need, although it is also something that managers find difficult, especially with sensitive information. Managers can identify information sources and other people who may be helpful.

Ongoing **coaching** during the task is especially important. Managers can guide employees through discussion and by giving constructive feedback. They are in a position to provide practical job experiences to develop the critical skills and competencies that the employee needs, and can provide job-related opportunities for practice. Managers can identify potential role models to employees, and help to explain how high achievers perform so well.

Although it is the employee's responsibility to achieve the performance agreed, the manager has a continuous role in providing support and guidance, and in oiling the organisational wheels.

ACTIVITY 12.2

Do managers actively support employee performance in your organisation? If they do, by what means do they do this and how effective is it? If they do not, why not, and what is the impact of this?

or

Think of any organisation in which you have had some involvement:

- How has individual performance been supported?
- How effective was/is this?
- How would you improve the way in which performance was/is supported?

Ongoing review is an important activity for employees to carry out in order to plan their work and priorities and also to highlight to the manager well in advance if the agreed performance will not be delivered by the agreed dates. Joint employee/manager review is essential so that information is shared. For example, a manager needs to be kept up to date on employee progress, while the employee needs to be kept up to date on organisational changes that have an impact on the agreed objectives. Both need to share perceptions of how the other is doing in their role, and what they could do that would be more helpful.

These reviews are normally informal, although a few notes may be taken of progress made and actions agreed. They need not be part of any formal system and therefore can take place when the job or the individuals involved demand, and not according to a pre-set schedule. The purpose of the review is to facilitate future employee performance, and provide an opportunity for the manager to confirm that the employee is 'on the right track', or redirect him or her if necessary. They thus provide a forum for employee reward in terms of recognition of progress. A 'well done' or an objective signed off as completed can enhance the motivation to perform well in the future. During this period evidence collection is also important. In the Scottish Prison Service (IDS 2003) line managers maintain a performance monitoring log of their team members' positive and negative behaviours in order to provide regular feedback and to embed the practice on ingoing assessment. Employees are expected to build up a portfolio of evidence of their performance over the period to increase the objectivity of reviews and to provide an audit trail to back up any assessment ratings. It is also during this part of the cycle that employees in many organisations can collect 360-degree feedback to be used developmentally and as part of an evidence base.

Formal performance review/assessment

Regular formal reviews are needed to concentrate on developmental issues and to motivate the employee. Also, an annual review and assessment is needed, of the extent to which objectives have been met which may well affect pay received. In many organisations employees are now invited to prepare an initial draft of achievement against objectives, for example Microsoft and AstraZeneca (IDS 2003). Some organisations continue to have overall assessment ratings which have to conform to a forced distribution. So if there were a five-point rating scale percentages would be set requiring each team/department to have, say, 10 per cent of employees on the top point, 20 per cent on the next point, and so on. AstraZeneca does not encourage its managers to give an overall rating to staff as its research suggested that this was demotivating (IDS 2003). Research by the Institute for Employment Studies (IRS 2001) found that review was only seen as fair if the targets set were seen as reasonable, managers were seen to be objective and judgements were consistent across the organisation.

Some organisations encourage employees to give upward feedback to their managers at this point in the cycle. For further details of this stage in the process *see* the Focus on skills at the end of Part III.

Reward

Many systems still include a link with pay, but Fletcher and Williams (1992) point to some difficulties experienced. Some public and private organisations found that the merit element of pay was too small to motivate staff, and sometimes seen as insulting. Although performance management organisations were more likely than others to have merit or performance-related pay (Bevan and Thompson 1992), some organisations have regretted its inclusion. Armstrong and Baron (1998a) report that staff almost universally disliked the link with pay, and a manager in one of their case study companies reported that 'the whole process is an absolute nightmare' (p. 172). Mabey and Salaman (1995) provide a good discussion of the problems with the pay link and we include a detailed discussion of performance related pay in Chapter 28.

There are other forms of reward than monetary and the Institute of Employment Studies (IRS 2001) found that there was more satisfaction with the system where promotion and development, rather than money, was used as a reward for good performance.

WINDOW ON PRACTICE

AstraZeneca performance management principles

AstraZeneca had in place several different approaches to performance management from the time that Astra and Zeneca merged in 1999, and from that time these approaches have been developed on an ongoing basis. The company is now working to define a globally consistent approach which will apply to its 60,000+ employees.

Performance management is defined as the process by which objectives are agreed, progress towards objectives is reviewed, individuals are supported and developed through the year, *and performance (which includes 'what' and 'how') is reviewed at the year end.*

There are four principles that will govern the structures, processes and systems and behaviours for performance management, and the following is a selective summary of these:

1 **Aligned Objectives** – individual, department/function and team objectives are cascaded and aligned with current business objectives so that everyone is working towards the same overall objectives in the most effective manner.

This enables everyone in AstraZeneca to know what is expected of them and how this helps to deliver overall business objectives. Individual, departmental/functional and team objectives are regularly reviewed and updated as business need or individual circumstances change. Managers are accountable for ensuring that individual and team objectives are clear, relevant, measurable, and documented. The way in which delivery against objectives will be reviewed throughout the year will also be agreed. Managers will encourage and support managed risk-taking, creativity, innovation and challenge when agreeing an individual's objectives.

2 **Joint Responsibility** – individuals, managers, and project leaders are jointly responsible for the effectiveness of the performance management process.

Managers are accountable for creating a challenging and supportive environment in which all individuals are able to give *of their best performance, and for ensuring a reasonable total workload for individuals.* Individuals, managers and project leaders must have an equal commitment to the objectives set, including agreeing the means by which to achieve them. In addition to meeting their own objectives, individuals are expected to support others in delivering outstanding team performance.

3 **Constructive Conversations** – there is open and honest dialogue between individuals, managers and project leaders.

Individuals, managers and project leaders need to have frequent, clear, open and fair conversations with each other about the level of performance they are achieving and also how they work together. There should be clear, open and honest conversations about learning and development needs, and about aspirations and opportunities for growth and development, and plans agreed to meet these needs. Where an individual's performance and/or behaviour are not to the required standards, the manager will discuss this promptly with the individual and will work with him/her to address this.

4 **Reviewing and Rewarding Performance** – everyone in AstraZeneca is given the opportunity to understand the link between their performance and their reward and recognition.

Managers will communicate openly Performance Management and Global Remuneration principles. Managers and project leaders will demonstrate capability to carry out their performance management and reward responsibilities. There will be a demonstrable link between an individual's performance and the level of reward and recognition they achieve. AstraZeneca will deliver higher rewards to higher-performing *individuals, and also reward contribution to team performance.*

Source: Summarised from AstraZeneca (2004) *AstraZeneca Performance Management Principles*, AstraZeneca.

Implementation and critique of performance management

Performance management needs to be line driven rather than HR driven, and therefore mechanisms need to be found to make this happen. The incorporation of line managers alongside HR managers in a working party to develop the system is clearly important as it not only takes account of the needs of the line in the system design, it also demonstrates that the system is line led. Training in the introduction and use of the system is also ideally line led, and Fletcher and Williams (1992) give us an excellent example of an organisation where line managers were trained as 'performance management coaches' who were involved in departmental training and support for the new system. However, some researchers have found that line managers are the weak link in the system (*see*, for example, Hendry *et al.* 1997). The Department of Trade and Industry (DTI) (*see* IRS 2001) notes that any system is only as good as the people who operationalise it. See case 12.1 on the website which deals with the introduction of a performance management system.

WINDOW ON PRACTICE

Fletcher and Williams (1992) report on a scheme that was introduced by training a series of nominated line manager coaches from each department of an organisation. They had then to take the message back to their colleagues and train them, tailoring the material to their department (Personnel/Training providing the back-up documentation). These were serving line managers who had to give up their time to do the job. Many of them were high-flyers, and they have been important opinion leaders and influencers – though they themselves had to be convinced first. Their bosses could refuse to nominate high-quality staff for this role if they wished, but they would subsequently be answerable to the Chief Executive. This approach was taken because it fits with the philosophy of performance management (i.e. high line-management participation), and because it was probably the only way to train all the departmental managers in the timescale envisaged.

Source: Summarised from C. Fletcher and R. Williams (1992b) *Performance Management in the UK: Organisational Experience*. London: IPM, p. 133.

Bevan and Thompson (1992) found incomplete take-up of performance management, with some aspects being adopted and not others. They noted that there was a general lack of integration of activities. This is rather unfortunate as one of the key advantages of performance management is the capacity for integration of activities concerned with the management of individual performance. This problem is still apparent. Hendry *et al.* (1997) reported the comments of Phil Wills from GrandMet, that there is still little understanding of what an integrated approach to performance management means. While alignment is critical, some organisations do not understand whether their HR processes are aligned or pulling in different directions. Williams (2002) suggests that there is still confusion over the nature of performance management.

Performance management seems to suffer from the same problems as traditional appraisal systems. Armstrong and Baron (1998a) report, for example, that over half the respondents to their survey feel that managers give their best ratings to people that they like (p. 202), and over half the managers surveyed felt that they had not received sufficient training in performance management processes (p. 203). They also report (1998b) that the use of ratings was consistently derided by staff and seen as subjective and inconsistent. Performance ratings can be seen as demotivating, and forced distributions are felt to be particularly unfair. Yet Houldsworth (2003) found 44 per cent of the Henley and Hay Group survey sample did this.

In terms of individual objective setting linked to organisational performance objectives, there are problems when strategy is unclear and when it evolves. Rose (2000) also reports a range of problems, particularly the fact that SMART targets can be problematic if they are not constantly reviewed and updated, although this is a time-consuming process. Pre-set objectives can be a constraining factor in such a rapidly changing business context, and they remind us of the trap of setting measurable targets, precisely because they are measurable and satisfy the system, rather than because they are most important to the organisation. He argues that a broader approach which assesses the employee's accomplishments as a whole and their contribution to the organisation is more helpful than concentrating on pre-set objectives. Williams (2002) also notes that there is more to performance than task performance, such as volunteering and helping others. He refers to this as contextual performance; it is sometimes referred to as collegiate behaviour.

A further concern with SMART targets is that they inevitably have a short-term focus, yet what is most important to the organisation is developments which are complex and longer term, which are very difficult to pin down to short-term targets (*see*, for example, Hendry *et al.* 1997). In this context systems which also focus on the development of competencies will add greater value in the longer term. Armstrong and Baron (1998b) do note that a more rounded view of performance is gradually being adopted, which involves the 'how' as well as the 'what', and inputs such as the development of competencies. There is, however, a long way to go adequately to describe performance and define what is really required for organisational success.

For an in-depth example of performance management in the Scottish Prison Service *see* case 12.2 on the website.

360-DEGREE FEEDBACK

360-degree feedback, which is a very specific term used to refer to multi-rater feedback, is increasingly being used within performance management systems and as a separate development activity.

The nature of 360-degree feedback

This approach to feedback refers to the use of the whole range of sources from which feedback can be collected about any individual. Thus feedback is collected from every angle on the way that the individual carries out their job: from immediate line manager; peers; subordinates; more senior managers; internal customers; external customers; and from individuals themselves. It is argued that this breadth of feedback provides superior feedback to feedback from the line manager's perspective only, since the latter will only be able to observe the individual in a limited range of situations, and Atwater and his colleagues (2002) suggest that 360-degree feedback provides a better way to capture the complexities of performance. Hogetts *et al.* (1999) report that more than 70 per cent of United Parcels Service employees found that feedback from multiple sources was more useful in developing self-insight than feedback from a single source. Individuals, it is argued, will find feedback from peers and subordinates compelling and more valid (*see*, for example, Borman 1998 and Atwater *et al.* 2001), and Edwards and Ewen (1996, p. 4) maintain that:

> No organizational action has more power for motivating employee behaviour change than feedback from credible work associates.

Such all-round feedback enables the individual to understand how they may be seen differently (or similarly) by different organisational groups, and how this may contrast with their own views of their strengths and weaknesses. This provides powerful information for the development of self-awareness. While 360-degree feedback may be collected using informal methods, as shown in the Window on practice box on Humberside Tec, the term itself is a registered trade mark, and refers to a very specific method of feedback collection and analysis which was devised in the United States (*see* Edwards and Ewen 1996, p. 19), and they suggest that 'simplistic, informal approaches to multi-source assessment are likely to multiply rather than reduce error'. However, informal approaches to 360-degree feedback are sometimes used quite successfully as an alternative to a survey questionnaire and statistical analysis.

team, as Hurley (1998) suggests. Thus raters may feel uncomfortable about being open and honest. The dangers of collusion and bias need to be eliminated, and it is suggested that the appropriate software systems can achieve this, but they are of course expensive, as are well-validated off-the-peg systems. Follow-up is critical and if the experience of 360-degree feedback is not built on via the construction of development goals and the support and resources to fulfil these, the process may be viewed negatively and may be demotivating.

London *et al.* (1997) report concerns about the way systems are implemented, and that nearly one-third of respondents they surveyed experienced negative effects. Atwater and his colleagues (2002) found some negative reactions such as reduced effort, dissatisfaction with peers who provided the feedback and a lower commitment to colleagues. Fletcher and Baldry (2001) note that there are contradictions in the results from 360-degree feedback so far, and they suggest that further research is needed on how feedback affects self-esteem, motivation, satisfaction and commitment. The DTI (2001) suggests that sufficient resources need to be devoted to planning a system and that it should be piloted before general use. Clearly, 360-degree feedback needs to be handled carefully and sensitively and in the context of an appropriate organisational climate so that it is not experienced as a threat. The DTI (2001) suggests that there needs to be a climate of openness and trust for 360-degree feedback to work. Atwater *et al.* (2002) suggest that to counteract any negative effects it is important to prepare people for making their own ratings and on how they can provide honest and constructive feedback to others, ensure confidentiality and anonymity of raters, make sure the feedback is used developmentally and owned by the person being rated (for example they may be the only person to receive the report), provide post-feedback coaching and encouragement and encourage people to follow up the feedback they have received.

WINDOW ON PRACTICE

Johnson (2001) reports on the merger between two pharmaceuticals companies – UniChem from the UK and Alliance Sante from France to form Alliance UniChem. In an attempt to focus managers from diverse cultures on a single vision the HR department concentrated on all aspects of performance management, in particular 360-degree feedback which was felt to be a pragmatic and practical tool. Four key values were identified, excellence, service, innovation and partnership, and competencies were drawn up to reflect these. The process had to be introduced very sensitively as 360-degree feedback was virtually unheard of in three countries covered by the company – Italy, Spain and Portugal, and in France it was seen very much as an American tool and regarded with considerable suspicion.

The most senior managers went through the process first, and it was then piloted in different countries. The tool was developed to be used in five different languages, and the customised package adopted came with development activities for each competency, and coaching sessions to ensure that feedback was not interpreted without analysis and support. The whole process formed part of a self-development programme.

Source: Summarised from R. Johnson (2001) 'Doubled entente', *People Management*, Vo. 7, No. 9, 3 May, pp. 38–9.

SUMMARY PROPOSITIONS

12.1 Performance management systems incorporate appraisal activity, but include other aspects such as a link to organisational objectives, an emphasis on ongoing review, motivation, coaching and support, and reinforcement/reward for performance achieved.

12.2 There is a conflict in many appraisal and performance management systems as managers frequently have a dual role as assessor and developer.

12.3 Current trends in sophisticated appraisal systems include greater employee ownership, emphasis on the how as well as the what, emphasis on evidence collection from both manager and employee, upward feedback to the line manager as well as downward feedback to the employee.

12.4 360-degree feedback is increasingly being used to provide individuals with a basis for changing behaviour and improving performance. It is important to use this process developmentally rather than linking it directly to pay awards.

GENERAL DISCUSSION TOPICS

1. In what ways is the concept of performance management different from the way in which management has been traditionally practised? What are the advantages and disadvantages for employees and employers?
2. 360-degree feedback may have many advantages, but there is the argument that it can never really work because of the built-in biases, such as marking a boss well because you're due for a pay rise; marking yourself low so that you can be happily surprised by others' evaluations; marking peers down to make oneself look better. Discuss as many built-in biases as you can think of, and suggest how they might be tackled and whether substantive improvements could be made.

FURTHER READING

Neary, D. (2002) 'Creating a company-wide on-line performance management system: A case study at TRW Inc', *Human Resource Management*, Vol. 41, No. 4, Winter, pp. 491–8
An interesting example of an IT-based system across 100,000 employees based in 36 countries. Explains the design and implementation of the system.

Swinburne, P. (2001) 'How to use feedback to improve performance', *People Management*, Vol. 7, No. 11, 31 May, pp. 46–7
Short but extremely helpful and full of practical detail. Excellent guidelines on the dos and don'ts of giving feedback and some very useful tips for receiving feedback.

REFERENCES

Armstrong, M. and Baron, A. (1998a) *Performance Management – The New Realities*. London: IPD.

Armstrong, M. and Baron, A. (1998b) 'Out of the Tick Box', *People Management*, 23 July, pp. 38–41.

AstraZeneca (2000) *Management of Team and Individual Performance*. London: AstraZeneca plc.

Atwater, L., Waldman, D. and Brett, J. (2002) 'Understanding and optimising multi-source feedback', *Human Resource Management*, Vol. 41, No. 2, summer, pp. 193–208.

Audit Commission (2002) *Performance Breakthrough: improving performance in public sector organizations*. London: The Audit Commission.

Barlow, G. (1989) 'Deficiencies and the perpetuation of power: latent functions in management appraisal', *Journal of Management Studies*, Vol. 26, No. 5, pp. 499–518.

Bevan, S. and Thompson, M. (1992) 'An overview of policy and practice', in *Personnel Management in the UK: an anaylsis of the issues*. London: IPM.

Borman, W. (1998) '360 ratings: an analysis of assumptions and a research agenda for evaluating their validity', *Human Resource Management Review*, Vol. 7, pp. 299–315.

Coates, G. (1994) 'Performance appraisal as icon: Oscar winning performance or dressing to impress?' *International Journal of Human Resource Management*, No. 1, February.

Cook, S. and Macauley, S. (1997) 'How colleagues and customers can help improve team performance', *Team Performance Management*, Vol. 3, No. 1.

DTI (2001) *360 degree feedback: Best practice guidelines* (Prof C. Farrell). dti.gov.uk/mbp/360feedback.

Edwards, M.R. and Ewen, A.J. (1996) *360 Degree Feedback*. New York: Amacom, American Management Association.

Egan, G. (1995) 'A clear path of peak performance', *People Management*, 18 May, pp. 34–7.

Fletcher, C. and Baldry, C. (2001) 'Multi-source feedback systems: a research perspective', in I. Robertson and C. Cooper (eds) *Personnel Psychology and HRM*. Chichester: John Wiley and Sons Ltd.

Fletcher, C. and Williams, R. (1992) *Performance Management in the UK: Organisational experience*. London: IPM.

Goodge, P. and Watts, P. (2000) 'How to manage 360° feedback', *People Management*, 17 February, pp. 50–2.

Grint, K. (1993) 'What's wrong with performance appraisals? – a critique and a suggestion', *Human Resource Management Journal*, Vol. 3, No. 3, pp. 61–77.

Hendry, C., Bradley, P. and Perkins, S. (1997) 'Missed a motivator?' *People Management*, 15 May, pp. 20–5.

Hendry, C., Woodward, S., Bradley, P. and Perkins, S. (2000) 'Performance and rewards: cleaning out the stables', *Human Resource Management Journal*, Vol. 10, No. 3, pp. 46–62.

Hogetts, R., Luthans, F. and Slocum, J. (1999) 'Strategy and HRM initiatives for the '00s: environment redefining roles and boundaries, linking competencies and resources', *Organizational Dynamics*, Autumn, p. 7.

Houldsworth, E. (2003) 'Managing Individual performance', paper presented to the CIPD National Conference, Harrogate 22–24 November 2003.

Hurley, S. (1998) 'Application of team-based 360° feedback systems', *Team Performance Management*, Vol. 4, No. 5.

IDS (2003) *IDS Studies: Performance Management*, No. 748, April, London: IDS.

IRS (2001) 'Performance appraisal must try harder', *IRS Employment Trends*, No. 724, March, pp. 2–3.

IRS (2003) 'Time to talk – how and why employers conduct appraisals', *IRS Employment Trends*, No. 769, 7 February, pp. 7–14.

Johnson, R. (2001) 'Doubled entente', *People Management*, Vol. 7, No. 9, 3 May, pp. 38–9.

Locke, E. and Latham, G. (1990) *A Theory of Goal Setting and Task Performance*. Englewood Cliffs, NJ: Prentice-Hall.

Locke, E. (1968) 'Towards a theory of task performance and incentives', *Organisational Behaviour and Human Performance*, Vol. 3, No. 2, pp. 157–89.

London, M., Smither, J. and Adsit, D. (1997) 'Accountability: the achilles heel of multi-source feedback', *Group and Organizational Dynamics*, Vol. 22, No. 2, pp. 162–84.

Longenecker, C. (1997) 'Why managerial performance appraisals are ineffective: causes and lessons', *Career Development International*, Vol. 2, No. 5.

Mabey, C. and Salaman, G. (1995) *Strategic Human Resource Management*. Oxford: Blackwell.

Newton, T. and Findlay, P. (1996) 'Playing God? – the performance of appraisal', *Human Resource Management Journal*, Vol. 6, No. 3, pp. 42–58.

Rose, M. (2000) 'Target Practice', *People Management*, 23 November, pp. 44–5.

Sewell, G. and Wilkinson, B. (1992) 'Someone to watch over me: surveillance, discipline and the just-in-time process', *Sociology*, Vol. 26, pp. 271–89.

Storr, F. (2000) 'This is not a circular', *People Management*, 11 May, pp. 38–40.

Townley, B. (1989) 'Selection and appraisal: reconstituting social relations', in J. Storey (ed.) *New Perspectives on Human Resource Management*. London: Routledge.

Townley, B. (1993) 'Performance appraisal and the emergence of management', *Journal of Management Studies*, Vol. 30, No. 2, pp. 27–44.

Ward, P. (1995) 'A 360 degree turn for the better', *People Management*, 9 February.

Williams, R. (2002) *Managing Employee Performance*. London: Thompson Learning.

An extensive range of additional materials, including multiple choice questions, answers to questions and links to useful websites can be found on the Human Resource Management Companion Website at **www.pearsoned.co.uk/torrington.**

CHAPTER 13

TEAM PERFORMANCE

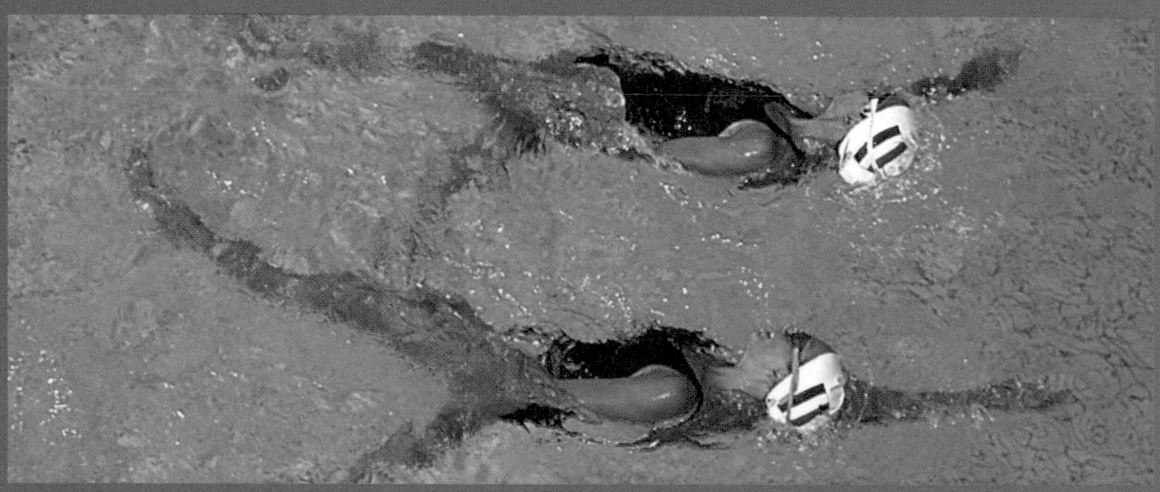

THE OBJECTIVES OF THIS CHAPTER ARE TO:

1 IDENTIFY THE PURPOSE, NATURE AND IMPACT OF TEAMWORK

2 REVIEW A RANGE OF BROAD TYPES OF TEAM

3 EXPLORE THE NOTION OF TEAM EFFECTIVENESS

The appointments pages of *Personnel Management, People Management* and other periodicals have since the early 1990s been littered with advertisements from organisations that are seeking 'proactive', 'natural', 'enthusiastic', 'genuine' and 'effective' team players, who 'enjoy' or 'have a preference for' working in a team environment, and who are 'committed' to team working. The report of the 1998 Workplace Employee Relations survey (Cully *et al.* 1999) acknowledged that teamworking is central to new forms of work organisation, Geary and Dobbins (2001) suggest that teams are repeatedly identified as an aspect of post-industrial society and we could say that 'the team is now the norm at work' (Blau 2002). Yet again, however, a gap between rhetoric and reality has been identified due to unevenness of current practices (Griffith 2002).

PURPOSE, NATURE AND IMPACT OF TEAMWORK

While it is generally accepted that teamworking has increased, there are continued debates about the prevalence of teamwork, its definition and the advantages and disadvantages of this way of working.

Determining the prevalence of teamwork is extremely difficult because of differences in the definition used and the criteria applied. Teamwork is frequently seen as an aspect of high-performance work systems (*see*, for example, Bacon and Blyton 2003), in which case the focus is on lean production teams/semi-autonomous teams, usually in the production sector. However, teams are used in a much wider context than this, as we shall explore later. Even in this narrower context there is much debate about what might constitute a team. In teamworking surveys lists of team characteristics are typically used and only if the organisation being surveyed ticks off a sufficient percentage of these is it considered that teamworking exists. In addition, for an organisation to be identified as being based on teamworking, there has to be a specified percentage of employees, or employees in the largest employee group organised by team. Benders and others (2002) provide an excellent discussion of the definitions used in teamworking surveys across a range of European countries.

In spite of a more critical perspective being taken of late, teamwork is still used and introduced as a way of empowering employees and facilitating the development of their full potential in order to enhance organisational performance. A heavy emphasis on teamwork usually corresponds with 'flatter' organisations, which have diminished status differentials, and reduced staffing. Teamwork, of course, is not a recent idea, and the autonomous working groups of the 1960s and 1970s are its clear forerunners. The similarities are increasing responsibility, authority and a sense of achievement among group members. The protagonists of autonomous working groups were also intent on improving the quality of working life of employees by providing a wider range of tasks to work on (job enrichment) and a social environment in which to carry them out. The emphasis currently is quite different. While it is argued that team members will gain intrinsic rewards from autonomy, job satisfaction, identification with work and greater skills development, performance is the unvarying aim. Higher performance is expected due to increased flexibility and communication within teams, increased ownership of the task and commitment to team goals. Some of the most famous autonomous working groups at Volvo in Sweden have now been disbanded because their production levels were too low compared with other forms of production. Current teams are designed to outperform other production methods, and Natale *et al.* (1998), for example, argue that they are fundamental to continuous corporate improvement. They are also seen as critical in the development of a learning organisation (*see*, for example, Senge 1990).

There remain many strong supporters of teamwork and many organisations committed to this approach, although it is also criticised as management control by another means and has often failed to improve performance. Van den Beukel and Molleman (2002) found a range of unintended consequences of teamwork, and others have reported loss of skills, work intensification and peer pressure as problems. Butcher and Bailey (2000), for example, note that teamwork has not always achieved the desired result, and Attaran and Nguyen (2000) found that flexible structures, such as teamwork, have sometimes been abandoned in favour of returning to more traditional approaches. Not only have organisations begun to consider whether teamwork will produce the expected productivity gains, employees who have experienced teamwork have sometimes viewed it as unsuccessful and feel less optimistic about it than previously (Proehl 1997). Part of the problem may also be unrealistic expectations. Very often performance dips when teamwork is introduced, and the performance improvements only come later on. Teamwork is not a 'quick fix', as has been noted by many of those who have been involved (*see*, for example, Scott and Harrison 1997; Arkin 1999). Part of the problem may also be that, as Church (1998) notes, there has been a tendency to think that teamwork is a solution for all our problems. Thus teamwork has undoubtedly been used in some situations where it was inappropriate, or where there was insufficient support to make it effective.

WINDOW ON PRACTICE

Sharpe (2002) analyses the way that teamwork was enacted by an assembly team with 22 associates and a team leader on a greenfield manufacturing site of a UK subsidiary of a Japanese-owned firm. Team meetings were held at the beginning of every day and these were a central element of management control in which individual performance was discussed and those associates making faults were recognised. The supervisor aimed to reduce faults through developing a positive attitude and encouraging a sense of responsibility amongst the team to ensure improved performance. Break times were taken together, and away from other teams, in a hot corner where production charts were displayed, and this was systematically used to develop a sense of team and commitment to shared objectives. This team exhibited high co-operation, dependency and communication which provided a suitable context for the development of team spirit and unitary goals, and a sense of not letting the team down. As jobs were interdependent there was increased pressure on the team associates not to stop the manufacturing line, there being little slack in deadlines. However, each member had a quality control role in checking the work of the person before them in the line, and was required to press 'red' to stop the line and report quality problems when they occurred. In practice this system was also used to express antagonism against another worker who was in a different clique. Alternatively, in order to protect friends, associates would not press red when a fault was passed to them, and they would help friends out further down the line so as not to have to press red. Pressing the red light was also used as a form of protest when the whole team felt that the work they were being given was too difficult.

Sharpe concludes that while this team was a clear example of a system of managerial control that encouraged worker compliance, the workers still engaged in a form of resistance, albeit in a form less overt and direct than in traditional manufacturing settings.

Source: Adapted from D. Sharpe (2002) 'Teamworking and managerial control within a Japanese manufacturing subsidiary in the UK', *Personnel Review*, Vol. 31, No. 3, pp. 267–82.

So, what is a team? How does it differ from all the other groups in organisations? A team can be described as more than the sum of the individual members. In other words, a team demands collaborative, not competitive, effort, where each member takes responsibility for the performance of the team rather than just their own individual performance. The team comes first, the individual comes second, and everything the individual member does is geared to the fulfilment of the team's goals rather than their individual agenda. If you think of a football team, a surgical team or an orchestra, it is easier to see how each member is assigned a specific role depending on their skills and how individuals use their skills for the benefit of the team performance rather than selectively using them for personal achievement. In a football game, for example, a player making a run towards the goal would pass to another player in a better position to score rather than risk trying to score themselves for the sake of personal glory.

Moxon (1993) defines a team as having a common purpose; agreed norms and values which regulate behaviour; members with interdependent functions and a recognition of team identity. Katzenbach and Smith (1993) and Katzenbach (1997) have also described the differences that they see between teams and work-groups, and identify teams as comprising individuals with complementary skills, shared leadership roles, mutual accountability and a specific team purpose, among other attributes. In organisations this dedication only happens when individuals are fully committed to the team's goals. This commitment derives from an involvement in defining how the goals will be met and having the power to make decisions within teams rather than being dependent on the agreement of external management. These are particularly characteristics of self-managing teams.

Organisational teams differ, though, in terms of their temporary or permanent nature, the interchangeability of individual members and tasks and the breadth of tasks or functions held within the team:

- **Timespan.** Some teams are set up to solve a specific problem, and when this has been solved the team disbands. Other teams may be longer term and project based, and may disband when the project is complete. Some teams will be relatively permanent fixtures, such as production teams, where the task is ongoing.
- **Leadership.** Some teams are based on shared responsibility, although a leader may emerge, and this leader may change depending on the task. Other teams will have a hierarchically appointed leader.
- **Interchangeability.** Teams differ in the range of specific skills that are required and as to whether there is an expectation that all members will learn all skills. In some production teams interchangeability of skills is key, and all members will have the potential and will be expected to learn all skills eventually. In other types of team, for example cross-functional teams (surgical teams, product development teams),

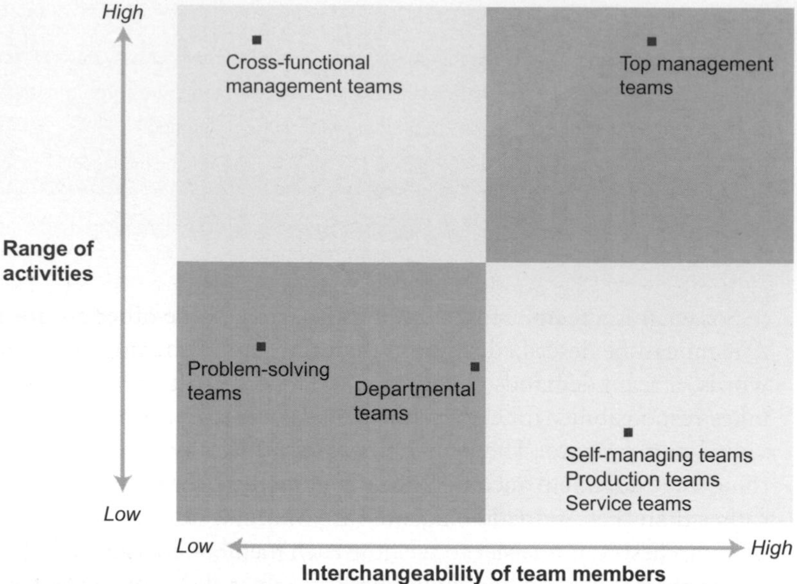

Figure 13.1 Different types of team (*Note*: High range of activities indicates activities over a broad range of functions; low range of activities indicates activities within a function and within a single task.)

each member is expected to bring their specialist skills to use for the benefit of the team, and they are not expected to be able to learn all the skills of each other member.

- **Task and functional range.** Many production teams will often be designed to cover a whole task and within this there will be a wide range of activities. This clearly differs from the traditional line form of production where the tasks are broken down and segmented. Other teams will span a range of functions – for example cross-functional teams involving, say, research, development, marketing and production staff.

Figure 13.1 shows how different types of teams can be represented on a framework representing interchangeability and task/functional spread.

In this chapter we shall go on to look at the characteristics of four broad types of team: production or service teams; cross-functional management teams; problem-solving teams; and departmental teams. We then look at what factors affect teams' performance and what can be done to improve team effectiveness, as these matters are currently of critical concern.

ACTIVITY 13.1

Think of the different types of teams in your organisation, or any organisation in which you have been involved (such as school, university, sports clubs, etc.) and plot them on the framework given in Figure 13.1.

What does this tell you about:

(a) your organisation's approach to teamwork?
(b) the different purposes of the different types of team?

BROAD TEAM TYPES

Production and service teams

It is producton and service teams that are often referred to as **self-managing teams, self-managing work teams** or **self-directed teams**. They are typically given the authority to submit a team budget, order resources as necessary within budget, organise training required, select new team members, plan production to meet predefined goals, schedule holidays and absence cover and deploy staff within the team. There is a clear emphasis on taking on managerial tasks that would previously have been done by a member of the managerial hierarchy. These managerial tasks are delegated to the lowest possible organisational level in the belief that these tasks will be carried out in a responsible manner for the benefit of the team and the organisation. The payoff from this self-management has been shown in Monsanto, for example, to be a 47 per cent increase in productivity and quality over four years (Attaran and Nguyen 2000). These teams are often used in such areas as car production and the production of electrical and electronic equipment. Teams will be based around a complete task so that they perform a whole chunk of the production process and in this way have something clear to manage. For example, the team will normally include people with maintenance skills, specific technical skills and different types of assembly skills so that they are self-sufficient and not dependent on waiting for support from other parts of the organisation. The ultimate aim is usually for all members to have all the skills needed within the team, in other words to be multiskilled. Examples of well-known companies using teams are Coca-Cola, Motorola, Procter & Gamble and Federal Express (Piczak and Hause 1996). Although used initially in the manufacturing sector such teams have increasingly been used in the service sector too.

WINDOW ON PRACTICE

Vesuvius

Arkin (1999) reports how Vesuvius, an isolated Scottish outpost of a large international conglomerate, used self-managed teams throughout the production process, and how this, together with an emphasis on employee development, has driven rapid company growth. Vesuvius introduced self-managed teams in a careful manner and built upon a period of gradual change in working practices, negotiated (with the union) where the job and wage structure was changed, and where production workers were given training so that they could do all jobs within the new teams. There were suspicions to begin with and some resistance, and the new teams were slow to start operating effectively. Inevitable concerns were about job losses, but management tried to develop trust by taking out the time clocks so there was no more checking in and out. Teams became responsible 'for the tasks they carried out, the materials they used and the problems they encountered'. Foremen were extensively developed in their new role as facilitators to the teams, and began to focus on safety, quality and training. In addition every employee had a personal development plan. Opinion surveys show that the workforce is more enthusiastic, the number of customer complaints has decreased and the company has made cost savings of £500,000 a year. While it is not possible to attribute these satisfactory outcomes purely to the introduction of self-managed teams, it is reasonable to conclude that these have contributed.

Source: Summarised from A. Arkin (1999) 'Peak practice', *People Management*, 11 November.

Nationwide

In a very different setting the Nationwide Building Society decided to introduce self-managed teamworking into the administrative centre at Northampton as an approach which would further develop multiskilling in a flatter structure (Scott and Harrison 1997). Teams were introduced into the mortgage and insurance customer service department, based on previous work-groups, and were accompanied by increased training and support for decision making, conflict management and team-building skills. Each team has between 9 and 18 members, and the leader's role is defined as a coaching rather than a directing role. The team allocates work as it comes in, depending on skills and workloads. Gradually teams took on the responsibility of liaising with branches to improve mutual understanding and develop better ways to work together. The results of each team are charted in a variety of league tables and there is a conscious competitive element between teams. This spurred teams to manage absence levels, among other performance criteria. At first there were concerns that self-managed teams were a way to get greater work out of the employees with no more pay, and some team leaders feared a loss of control. There was a temporary dip in performance after the teams were initially set up, but eventually performance improved and absence declined. The approach is now being spread to other locations, although the presence of other initiatives means that it is difficult to tie improvements to the introduction of self-managed teams.

Source: Summarised from W. Scott and H. Harrison (1997). 'Full team ahead', *People Management*, 9 October.

The are, however, two major variations of such teams. In some teams there is a hierarchically distinct team leader, and these are sometimes referred to as lean teams, compared with teams where everyone is on an equal level (*see*, for example, Kerrin and Oliver 2002). Doorewaard *et al.* (2002) distinguish between 'hierarchical teams' and 'shared responsibility teams', making the point that in the hierarchical teams, team autonomy does not mean team member autonomy. They go on to say that a lot of so-called autonomous teams are lean teams and there is not much autonomy for team members as responsibility is in the hands of the team leader. In shared-responsibility teams a leader may emerge, or the leadership may vary according to the nature of task, resting with whoever has the most appropriate skills to offer. Leaders, in both forms of team, will need to take on managerial tasks such as planning, organising, supporting individuals, presenting information and representing the team to the rest of the organisation. The way that the leader carries out these activities and involves others in them will clearly have an impact on the effectiveness of the team. Where leadership is static the leader's role is often defined in terms of a coaching rather than a directing role.

WINDOW ON PRACTICE

The British company Whitbread has established a small, upmarket chain of restaurants called 'Thank God it's Friday', which is abbreviated to 'Friday's' or 'TGIF'. The marketing is directed towards the relatively young and affluent and a part of this strategy has been to avoid the traditional hierarchy of the good-food restaurant – maître d'hôtel, *chef de rang*, commis waiter and so forth – by empowering the person with whom the customer deals directly: the waiter. This person can take decisions on such matters as complimentary drinks without reference to anyone else. There is no manager, but each restaurant has a team leader known as the Coach.

The nature of self-management also has an impact on the role of managers outside the team. Traditionally these managers would carry out the tasks described above and would monitor and control the performance of the team. If these tasks are no longer appropriate, what is the role of the manager – is there a role at all? It will come as no surprise that the formation of self-managed teams is seen as a threat to some managers. However, Casey (1993) comments that 'self-managed teams do not deny the role of manager, they redefine it'. He also notes that the management of the team is a balance between responsibility within the team and management without, rather than an all-or-nothing situation. He suggests a move towards 90 per cent within the team in a self-management situation rather than nearer 30 per cent in a traditional management situation.

Where there are self-managed teams the role of the traditional manager outside the team changes to adviser and coach, as they have now delegated most of their responsibilities for directly managing the team. These managers become a resource to be called on when needed in order to enable the team to solve their own problems.

Oliva (1992) draws a helpful framework for understanding the respective managerial roles of traditional managers and teams in a team environment, shown in Figure 13.2.

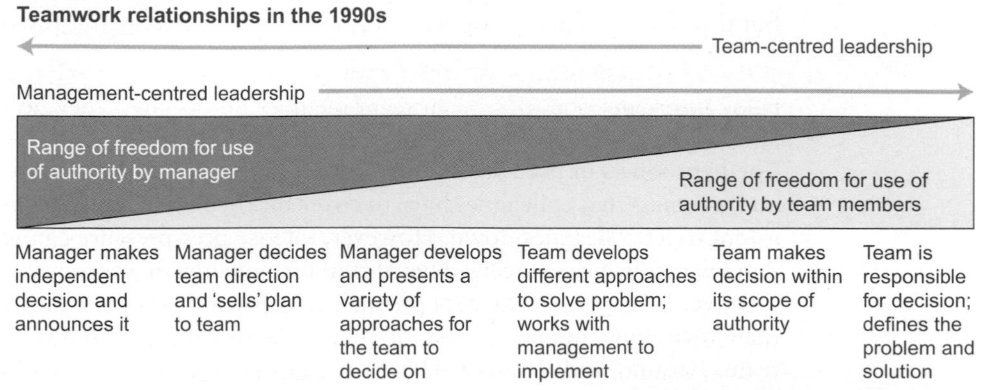

Figure 13.2 Teamwork relationships (Source: L.M. Oliva (1992) *Partners not Competitors*, p. 76. London: Idea Group Publishing. Reproduced with the permission of Idea Group Publishing.)

The self-managing team concept has much to offer in terms of increasing employee ownership and control and thereby releasing their commitment, creativity and potential. There are, of course, potential problems with this approach too. These include the difficulty of returning to traditional systems once employees have experienced greater autonomy; resistance from other parts of the organisation; and peer pressure and its consequences. We would also add resistance from team members too. Let us look at some of these in more detail.

Resistance from other parts of the organisation

As self-managing teams have clear knock-on effects for other parts of the organisation these other parts will react. If traditional managers do not give direction and control over to the team an immediate conflict is set up as to 'who makes the decisions around here'; if they fail to support and coach, the team may feel abandoned and insecure. In general, the climate of the organisation needs to be supportive in terms of the value placed on individual autonomy and learning. Marchington (2000) points out that it is unrealistic to assess teamworking in isolation from management's perceived commitment to employees and their approach to the employment relationship as a whole. There are situations also where the rhetoric of the organisation is about delegating responsibility to the team, but where management fail to give up ownership of the task.

Resistance within the team

Individuals who have spent many years being told what to do may need some time to take this responsibility for themselves. It is clear that operating self-managed teams will be easier on a greenfield site. However, for locations which want to make the transition, the importance of team selection of newcomers and of selecting skills relevant to a team environment as well as essential technical skills will be key. Salem, Lazarus and Cullen (1992) note that the most often cited individual characteristics for a team environment are 'interpersonal skills, self-motivation, ability to cope with peer pressure, level of technical/administrative experience, communication skills and the ability to cope with stress'. Other characteristics that have been noted elsewhere include the ability to deal with ambiguous situations and cope with conflict in a constructive way. Team members may feel resistant due to fear of loss of valued skills, but this seldom actually happens (*see*, for example, Bacon and Blyton 2003).

Peer pressure

The byproducts of peer pressure have been identified as lower absence levels, due to an awareness that colleagues have to cover for them; and a higher production rate so as not to let colleagues down. However, intense peer pressure can lead to stress and destroy many of the perceived benefits of team involvement from the employees' perspective. It is argued that peer pressure makes team members active participants in their own work intensification, as they develop rules to monitor behaviour in the team. Ezzamel and Willmott (1998) found that social loafing within the team (i.e. not pulling your weight) provoked other team members to act as supervisors, when team performance was related to rewards, adding yet more pressure.

WINDOW ON PRACTICE

Bacon and Blyton investigated the impact of teamworking in a range of different teams at British Steel's (now Corus) Shotton Mill. They compared evidence from an attitude survey a numbers of years prior to teamworking and a similar survey after teamworking had been introduced. Follow-up interviews were also carried out. They found that team participants, overall, reported that there was greater development of skills, greater variety and job satisfaction, although work had been intensified. However, they also identified a differential effect depending on previous occupation and job grade. Previous craft workers reported increased training, freedom to choose own method of working and involvement in decisions to a (statistically) significantly greater extent than previous production workers. Those on a lower job grade were least likely to report increased job satisfaction due to teamworking with aspects such as job variety, freedom to choose own working methods, amount of training and opportunity to use abilities.

Source: Adapted from N. Bacon and P. Blyton (2003) 'The impact of teamwork on skills: employee perceptions of who gains and who loses', *Human Resource Management Journal*, Vol. 13, No. 2, pp. 13–29.

Cross-functional management teams

Cross-functional management teams are very different from the teams described above, and members are more likely to retain other roles in the organisation. Typically they will see themselves as members of their function, whether it be marketing, research, sales, development and members of a specific project team as well. In fact the term 'project' (for example as in 'projects for change') rather than 'team' is being used increasingly to minimise any negative connotations of the word 'team' (*see*, for example, Proehl 1997; Butcher and Bailey 2000). Very often the project team will manage the development of a particular product, such as a computer package, a drug, a piece of electrical equipment from creation to sales. Members may be allocated to the team by their home function for all or part of their time. In fact many cross-functional teams are virtual teams, and although they may work closely together, they are rarely physically together. Henry and Hartzler (1998) define virtual teams as 'groups of people who work closely together even though they are geographically separated and may reside in different time zones in different parts of the world'. It is in this context that technology comes into its own – video conferencing, for example. However, Bal and Grundy (1999) argue that all too often the emphasis is the technology, rather than the all-important human processes.

The thinking behind a cross-functional team is that each member brings with them the expertise in their own function and the dedication to the team task around a certain product or project. By bringing individuals together as a team the project gains through the commitment of team members to a task that they feel that they own. Bringing these individuals together enables the development of a common language and the overcoming of departmental boundaries. Such teams are a key feature of a matrix organisation where individuals may be, simultaneously, members of a functional department and a product-based team, frequently with two direct line managers.

Meyer (1994) expresses the importance of measures of performance for cross-functional teams, and sees process measures as key rather than just measures of achievements. His argument is that process measures help the team to gauge their progress, and identify and rectify problems. It follows from this that the performance measures used need to be designed by the team and not imposed on them from senior management, as the team will know best what measures will help them to do their job. Inevitably these measures will need to be designed against a strategic context set by higher management. Meyer describes a good example of the problems that can result if managers try to control the performance measurement process rather than empowering team members.

The process of agreeing their own performance measures will also enable the team to identify different assumptions and perceptions that each team member holds, and generate discussion on the exact goals of the team. All this is helpful in bringing the team together, generating a common language and ensuring that everyone is pulling in the same direction.

One special form of cross-functional management team is the top management team of the organisation. Clearly, this team is different in that it is permanent and not project based, but its members still need to work as a team rather than a collection of individuals. Katzenbach and Smith (1993) note that it is more difficult to get this group to work together as a team as they are more likely to be individualist than are team members elsewhere in the organisation. Directors often still see themselves as representatives of their function rather than members of a team, and thus will be more likely to defend their position and attempt to influence each other than to pull together. Katzenbach (1997) suggests that strong executive leadership and true teamwork require different, but equally important disciplines, which need to be integrated rather than being seen as alternatives. Garratt (1990) asks three key questions of top teams to assess whether they are truly direction-giving teams. He asks about regular processes, outside formal meetings, to discuss what is going on in the organisation and what possibilities exist; to what extent the team involve themselves in unstructured visioning before grappling with the practical matters of plans and budgets; and to what extent they assess individual contributions and the skills and resources owned within the team. He finds little evidence of any of these activities taking place. Case 13.1 on the website focuses on senior management teams, and their development needs.

Functional teams

Functional teams, as the name implies, are made up of individuals within a function. For example, the training section of the HR department may well be referred to as the training team – different groups of nurses on a specific ward are sometimes divided into, say, the 'red' team and the 'blue' team. Sales staff for a particular product or region may refer to themselves as the 'games software sales team' or the 'north west sales team'. Some of the rationale behind this is to give the customer, internal or external, an identified set of individuals to liaise with. Given that these will be a smaller set than those in the whole department, they will be able to gain a much closer knowledge of particular customers and a better understanding of customer needs. The extent to which these are really teams as opposed to groups of individuals will vary enormously.

ACTIVITY 13.2

Think of some functional teams that you either belong to or have belonged to, or have had some contact with.

To what extent, and why, is each truly a team, or just a group of individuals with the title 'team'?

Use the ideas presented in this chapter and Figure 13.1 to to help you with this assessment.

Problem-solving teams

Problem-solving teams may be within a function or cross-functional. Within-function teams may typically be in the form of quality circles where employees voluntarily come together to tackle production and quality issues affecting their work. Unfortunately, many of these teams have had little impact and it has not been possible to implement recommended changes and improvements, owing to the retention of management control. Other within-function problem-solving teams may consist of specially selected individuals who will be involved in the implementation of a major development within the function or department. For example, the implementation of performance management may be supported by specific coaches in each department who carry out related training, offer counselling and advice and who tailor organisation policy so that it meets department needs. These coaches may become the departmental performance management team.

Cross-functional problem-solving teams may be brought together to solve an identified and specific organisational problem, and will remain together for a short period until that problem has been solved. They differ from cross-functional management teams as their role is not to manage anything, but rather to collect and analyse data and perspectives and develop an understanding of the nature of the problem. From this they will make recommendations on how to solve the problem which are then passed on to higher management. Usually their remit ends here, and they have little or no involvement in implementation. Team members will retain their normal work role at the same time as being a team member.

ACTIVITY 13.3

If you have belonged to, or observed, a problem-solving team:

(a) What were the barriers to team formation?

(b) In what ways did team members support the team?

(c) In what ways did team members concentrate on themselves as individuals?

TEAM EFFECTIVENESS

For a team to be effective its members need a clear and agreed vision, objectives and set of rules by which they will work together. Proehl (1997), for example, identifies the need for a clear project purpose, which members agree is worthy. In addition, he found that clear project boundaries, deadlines and specific follow-up activities by a designated co-ordinator were all important to team effectiveness.

Team members will need to feel able to be open and honest with each other and be prepared to confront difficulties and differences. It is also important for members to be able to tolerate conflict and be able to use this in a collaborative way in the achievement of the team's objectives. Some researchers have commented upon the size of the team and suggest it should be small enough, say no more than 20, for communications to be feasible. Others have suggested that proximity is important in maintaining communications and team spirit.

We have previously mentioned support from management as being critical to team success. Edwards and Wright (1998) note from their case study the problems caused by managers who interfere with team autonomy. Next we explore the key issues of selection, training and development, assessment and reward in relation to team effectiveness.

Selecting team members

The effectiveness of a team largely depends on the appropriateness of the team members. For self-managing teams there is a strong lobby for newcomers to be appointed by the team themselves, and indeed some would argue that unless this happens the team is not truly self-managing. Other case studies suggest that team members, whether selected by the team or by others, are chosen very carefully in the likeness of the team and with the 'right attitudes'. For all teamwork Katzenbach and Smith (1993) identify three critical selection criteria: technical or functional expertise, problem-solving and decision-making skills and interpersonal skills, and it also seems that successful teams have team members with high levels of emotional intelligence.

Another approach to selection of team members is to gain an understanding of the team roles that they are best able to play, so that the team is endowed with a full range of the roles that it will need to be effective. Meredith Belbin (1993), through extensive research and the evolution of his original ideas, has identified nine team roles which are important to a team and which individuals may have as strengths or weaknesses. The absence of some or many of these roles can cause problems in team effectiveness. Too many individuals playing the same type of role can cause undue friction in the team and again damage effectiveness. The key is achieving a balance. These team roles are as follows:

1 **Coordinator.** This person will have a clear view of the team objectives and will be skilled at inviting the contribution of team members in achieving these, rather than just pushing his or her own view. The coordinator (or chairperson) is self-disciplined and applies this discipline to the team. They are confident and mature, and will summarise the view of the group and will be prepared to take a decision on the basis of this.

2 **Shaper.** The shaper is full of drive to make things happen and get things going. In doing this they are quite happy to push their own views forward, do not mind being challenged and are always ready to challenge others. The shaper looks for the pattern in discussions and tries to pull things together into something feasible which the team can then get to work on.

3 **Plant.** This member is the one who is most likely to come out with original ideas and challenge the traditional way of thinking about things. Sometimes they become so imaginative and creative that the team cannot see the relevance of what they are saying. However, without the plant to scatter the seeds of new ideas the team will often find it difficult to make any headway. The plant's strength is in providing major new insights and ideas for changes in direction and not in contributing to the detail of what needs to be done.

4 **Resource investigator.** The resource investigator is the group member with the strongest contacts and networks, and is excellent at bringing in information and support from the outside. This member can be very enthusiastic in pursuit of the team's goals, but cannot always sustain this enthusiasm.

5 **Implementer.** The individual who is a company worker is well organised and effective at turning big ideas into manageable tasks and plans that can be achieved. Such individuals are both logical and disciplined in their approach. They are hardworking and methodical but may have some difficulty in being flexible.

6 **Team worker.** The team worker is the one who is most aware of the others in the team, their needs and their concerns. They are sensitive and supportive of other people's efforts, and try to promote harmony and reduce conflict. Team workers are particularly important when the team is experiencing a stressful or difficult period.

7 **Completer.** As the title suggests, the completer is the one who drives the deadlines and makes sure they are achieved. The completer usually communicates a sense of urgency which galvanises other team members into action. They are conscientious and effective at checking the details, which is a vital contribution, but sometimes get 'bogged down' in them.

8 **Monitor evaluator.** The monitor evaluator is good at seeing all the options. They have a strategic perspective and can judge situations accurately. The monitor evaluator can be overcritical and is not usually good at inspiring and encouraging others.

9 **Specialist.** This person provides specialist skills and knowledge and has a dedicated and single-minded approach. They can adopt a very narrow perspective and sometimes fail to see the whole picture.

ACTIVITY 13.4

Think of a team situation in which you have been involved, in either a work or a social/family setting:

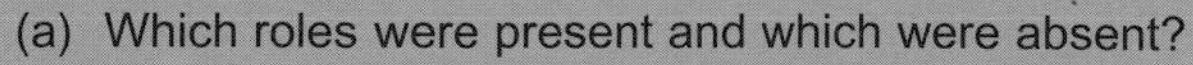
(a) Which roles were present and which were absent?

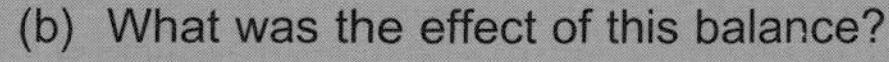
(b) What was the effect of this balance?

An individual's potential team roles can be interpreted from some of the psychometric tests used in the normal selection procedure (for example, Cattell's 16PF). They can also be assessed in a different way. Belbin designed a specific questionnaire to identify the individual's perceived current team role strengths (that is, the roles they have developed and are actually playing). This is particularly helpful for development within the current team, but may be less useful for selection purposes. Although helpful, current team role strengths may not be automatically transferred into another team situation.

The psychometric properties of the Belbin Team Roles Self-perception Inventory (BTRSPI) have been assessed by Furnham *et al.* (1993), whose work has cast doubt on the ability of the BTRSPI to be a reliable measure of team role preference. Fisher *et al.* (1996) raise similar doubts but conclude that despite questions over its reliability, the model has intuitive appeal and some empirical support and it would be a pity to disregard it. Further research by Fisher *et al.* (2001) provides more support for Belbin's model. Using the 16PF, Fisher *et al.* (2000) found in a study of almost 1,800 managers that some roles were more scarce than others. Although coordinators and resource investigators were plentiful, there were few completers, monitor evaluators, plants and shapers. They suggest that selection preferences may be causing this pattern and recommend that managers consider wider selection criteria if they wish to broaden their base of employees adequately to represent all team roles.

Team leader and manager training

Both team leaders and senior managers begin to play new roles in team situations. Team leaders suddenly find themselves with a host of new responsibilities for the support of team members and the planning and organising of team activities, responsibilities for which they have little experience and often no training. Similarly managers will need some training support in moving from a directive, controlling role to a coaching and counselling role. Training needs to encompass not only new skills but an opportunity to discuss the changing philosophy of the organisation and to encourage attitude change. Support in understanding the nature of involvement, empowerment and participation will also be relevant.

Team member training

Whether or not the team has an appointed leader all team members will need some training support in working in a different environment with different rules about what they should and should not be doing. Being more involved and taking on more responsibility, and sometimes leading activities, will require some initial training support. Attaran and Nguyen (2000) suggest that training in problem solving, communications and time management is important. Applebaum *et al.* (1999) recommend training in conflict management. Further training in new technical skills can often be handled within the team once at least one member has the required knowledge and has gained some training skills themselves.

Team development

Blau (2002) suggests that the current interest in team building is due to the fact that many teams are not working effectively. Teams can be developed in many different ways, and perhaps one of the most critical is early development through the task itself. For example, teams can develop by jointly describing the core purpose of the team, visualising the future position that they are aiming to achieve, developing the rules and procedures they will use, performance measures and so on. If the team are given some support to do this, perhaps a facilitator from the HR function or externally, they can not only develop vital guidelines but also gain an understanding of a way of working things out together, a process which they can use by themselves in the future.

Teams can also develop by looking at the way they have been working since they came together. One way of doing this is by completing a team roles questionnaire to identify the strengths and weaknesses of each member. This will help to promote a better understanding of why things happen as they do, and also pave the way for some changes. On this basis some individuals can develop their potential in team roles that they are not presently using, but for which they have some preference, and in this way a better balance may be struck, making the team more effective. Another process is to review what the team as a whole are good at and bad at, what different individuals can do to enable others to carry out their tasks more effectively, and what improvements can be made in the way that the team organises itself. Simple suggestions can be surprisingly effective, such as: 'It would really help me if you gave me a list of telephone numbers where I can leave a message for you when I need to get hold of you urgently' (cross-functional team); and 'I don't understand why we need to lay the figures out in this way and it really gets my back up – will someone take some time out to explain it to me?' Rubin, Plovnick and Fry (1975) identified four major problem areas in relation to group effectiveness – goals, roles, processes and relationships – and these four can be used to provide a framework for team development activities.

WINDOW ON PRACTICE

What is the most effective approach to team building?

Blau reports on a range of teambuilding activities which focus on forcing people into new situations. She found safaris in South Africa, interactive murder mysteries, 'bomb disposal' events, Harry Potter style potion making, working in a kitchen and dog sledding in Finland, among others. Suppliers of such courses say that while they may create a fun environment it is still possible to work on serious issues which can be applied back at work. For example Tim Sheply from 'Thyme management' says that working in a kitchen brings with it the same stresses and time pressures as at work, and Celia Francis at Leith's School of Food and Wine suggests it is important that participants come away with new knowledge – in this case gourmet cooking. Such offerings are now big business. While getting to know fellow workers better may be helpful, Michael West from Aston University argues that developing transferable skills in a team setting is much more valuable, and argues against team activities which centre around fun. Instead he suggests that the focus needs to be on specific skills relevant to the work context. Briner from Birkbeck College, London, suggests that there should be more emphasis on how people operate doing a real job task.

Source: Adapted from R. Blau (2002) 'Playing the game', *People Management*, Vol. 9, No. 11, 30 May, pp. 38–9.

Other less direct methods of development involve working through simulated exercises as a team, such as building a tower out of pieces of paper, and learning from this how the team operate and what they could do to operate better. Outdoor training is also used to good effect in team situations, where the team tackle new, and perhaps dangerous, activities in the outdoors. Typically, some activities involve learning to trust and to depend on each other in a real and risky situation, and the learning from this, and the trust developed, can then be transferred back into the work situation.

The approach taken to team building needs to be appropriate to the stage of development of the team. Tuckman (1965) identified four stages of team development – forming, storming, norming and performing. Forming centres on team members working out what they are supposed to be doing, and trying to feel part of it. At this stage they are quite likely to be wary of each other and hide their feelings. Storming is the stage where members are prepared to express strongly held views, where there is conflict and competition and where some push for power while others withdraw. The norming stage is characterised by a desire to begin to organise themselves. Members actually begin to listen to each other, become more open and see problems as belonging to the whole group. Performing is where a sense of group loyalty has developed and where all contribute in an atmosphere of openness and trust. Proehl (1997) identifies the importance of mutual respect, and Ingram and Descombe (1999) found in their research that camaraderie was very important in getting the work done.

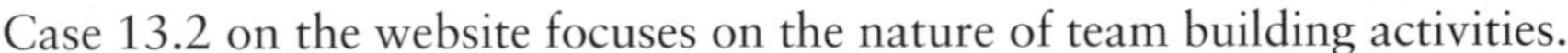

Case 13.2 on the website focuses on the nature of team building activities.

Recognition and reward

Like individuals, teams need some form of recognition and reward for their efforts. Recognition may be in the form of articles in company newsletters or local papers about team successes, inscribing the team name on the product or monetary rewards. A sense of team identity is often encouraged by the use of team T-shirts, coffee mugs and other usable items. It is most important that other reward systems in the organisation, say based on individual contribution, do not cut across the reinforcement for team performance. Kerrin and Oliver (2002), for example, found contradictions between the team structure of work and an individual focus in terms of reward. For example, workers did not put improvement ideas directly to the team, but submitted them to the company suggestion scheme instead as they could gain monetary awards from this. Also when new processes were suggested they did not voice their concerns about the problems they foresaw – instead they waited until the process was implemented and then put suggestions into the suggestion scheme. John Stevens, CIPD Director of Professional Policy (Glover 2002), argues that if we want to identify what teams contribute, team assessment needs to be fitted into the performance management framework of the organisation. The AstraZeneca Window on practice in Chapter 12 on individual performance management demonstrates one way of doing this. For teams where the longer-term objective is for all members to acquire the whole range of skills, a payment system which pays for skills gained rather than job done will be important.

Are teams always the right answer?

Team-based work seems set to increase – on the premise that it will improve organisational commitment and performance. The three difficult issues that will need to be tackled are that not all employees will feel comfortable or perform their best in a team-based situation; that teamwork is not always the best approach; and that not all teams are effective teams. Critics of a team environment suggest that it can have a downward levelling effect, that it stunts creativity and is generally limiting (Stott and Walker 1995). Generating the essential openness, trust and commitment is also a potential difficulty, and decision making can become a lengthy process. Where teams have been introduced inappropriately the result has been lower productivity, poorer decisions and increased dissatisfaction, as noted by Applebaum *et al.* (1999), and this finding conflicts with all the case examples of performance improvement due to the use of teams. These contradictory reports may be explained, as Edwards and Wright (1998) suggested, by the many different types of teams that are set up, and by the impact of different organisational environments.

ACTIVITY 13.5

Using the information in this chapter and other organisational experiences (your own, published case studies, or the experiences of people you know), identify the implications for the HR function of an organisation moving to a heavy emphasis on teamwork.

SUMMARY PROPOSITIONS

13.1 Team-based working has been increasing, due to a belief that this empowers employees, encourages them to use their full potential and results in better performance, although these aspirations are not always achieved in practice, or take some time to be achieved.

13.2 Three key variables in different types of team are timespan of the team, interchangeability of team members and range of activities and functions involved.

13.3 There are four broad team types – production/service teams; cross-functional management teams; departmental teams; and problem-solving teams.

13.4 Team effectiveness is dependent on the team having agreed goals and methods of working, and a climate where team members can be open and honest and use conflict in a constructive way.

13.5 Selection of team members is key and it is important to have a well-balanced team in terms of the team roles described by Belbin.

GENERAL DISCUSSION TOPICS

1 In an organisation which is moving into teamwork the supervisor's role will change from direct supervision to team facilitation and development. What problems are these supervisors likely to experience in their change of role, and what forms of training and development would help them?

2 The need to work as a team depends on the kinds of work that are carried out. Discuss.

FURTHER READING

Bateman, B., Wilson, F. and Bingham, D. (2002) 'Team Effectiveness – development of an audit questionnaire', *Journal of Management Development*, Vol. 21, No. 3, pp. 215–26
Aims to link organisational effectiveness and team building in a coherent way. An audit has been produced to assess six measures of team effectiveness: team synergy, clear objectives, required skills, effective use of resources, innovation/constant improvement and the identification and measurement of quality standards. The article provides an example of how this tool is used on a team development day to elicit the different perspectives of each team member.

Sheard, A. and Kakabadse, A. (2002) 'From loose groups to effective teams', *Journal of Management Development*, Vol. 21, No. 2, pp. 133–51
A framework is developed which reflects how loose groups can transform themselves into effective teams. The framework is based on the combination of Tuckman's four stages of team development and the Kubler Ross acceptance of change curve to form a matrix. (The Kubler Ross curve was developed in the context of research on reactions to bereavement and has been adopted in the management arena as representing the stages in the acceptance of change. Change of course involves both taking on the new and letting go of the old.) Also provided are nine key factors essential to the effectiveness of teams.

REFERENCES

Applebaum, S., Abdallah, C. and Shapiro, B. (1999) 'The self-directed team: A conflict resolution analysis', *Team Performance Management*, Vol. 5, No. 2.

Arkin, A. (1999) 'Peak Practice', *People Management*, 11 November.

Attaran, M. and Nguyen, T. (2000) 'Creating the right structural fit for self-directed teams', *Team Performance Management*, Vol. 6, No. 1/2.

Bacon, N. and Blyton, P. (2003) 'The impact of teamwork on skills: employee perceptions of who gains and who loses', *Human Resource Management Journal*, Vol. 13, No. 2, pp. 13–29.

Bal, J. and Grundy, J. (1999) 'Virtual Teaming in the automotive supply chain', *Team Performance Management*, Vol. 5, No. 6.

Belbin, M. (1993) *Team Roles at Work*. London: Butterworth Heinemann.

Benders, J., Huijen, F. and Pekruhl, U. (2002) 'What do we know about the incidence of groupwork (if anything)?' *Personnel Review*, Vol. 31, No. 3, pp. 371–85.

Blau, R. (2002) 'Playing the game', *People Management*, Vol. 9, No. 11, 30 May, pp. 38–9.

Butcher, D. and Bailey, C. (2000) 'Crewed awakenings', *People Management*, 3 August.

Casey, D. (1993) *Managing Learning in Organisations*. Milton Keynes: Open University Press, p. 60.

Church, A. (1998) 'From both sides now: the power of teamwork – fact or fiction?' *Team Performance Management*, Vol. 4, No. 2.

Cully, M., Woodland, S., O'Reilly, A. and Dix, G. (1999) *Britain at Work: As depicted by the 1998 WERS*. London: Routledge.

Dooreward, H., van Hootegem, G. and Huys, R. (2002) 'Team responsibility structure and team performance', *Personnel Review*, Vol. 31, No. 3, pp. 356–70.

Edwards, P. and Wright, M. (1998) 'HRM and commitment: a case study of teamworking', in P. Sparrow and M. Marchington (eds) *Human Resource Management: The New Agenda*. London: Financial Times Pitman Publishing.

Ezzamel, M. and Willmott, H. (1998) 'Accounting for teamwork: a critical study of group-based systems of organizational control', *Administrative Science Quarterly*, Vol. 43, pp. 358–96.

Fisher, S., Hunter, T. and Macrosson, W.D.K. (2000) 'The distribution of Belbin team roles among UK managers', *Team Performance Management*, Vol. 29, No. 2.

Fisher, S.G., Macrosson, W.D.K. and Sharp, G. (1996) 'Further evidence concerning the Belbin team role self-perception inventory', *Personnel Review*, Vol. 25, No. 2, pp. 61–7.

Fisher, S.G., Macrosson, W.D.K. and Semple, J. (2001) 'Control and Belbin's team roles', *Personnel Review*, Vol. 30, No. 5, pp. 578–88.

Furnham, A., Steele, H. and Pendleton, D. (1993) 'A psychometric assessment of the Belbin team role self-perception inventory', *Journal of Occupational and Organisational Psychology*, pp. 245–57.

Garratt, B. (1990) *Creating a Learning Organisation*. Hemel Hempstead: Director Books.

Geary, J. and Dobbins, A. (2001) 'Teamworking: a new dynamic in the pursuit of management control', *Human Resource Management Journal*, Vol. 11, No. 1, pp. 3–23.

Glover, C. (2002) 'Variations on a team', *People Management*, Vol. 8, No. 3, pp. 36–40.

Griffith, W. (2002) 'Performance Testing', *People Management*, Vol. 8, No. 8, p. 65.

Henry, J. and Hartzler, M. (1998) *Tools for Virtual Teams – A Team Fitness Companion*. Milwaukee, WI: ASQ Quality Press.

Ingram, H. and Descombe, T. (1999) 'Teamwork: comparing academic and practitioners' perceptions', *Team Performance Management*, Vol. 5, No. 1.

Katzenbach, J. (1997) 'The myth of the Top Management Team', *Harvard Business Review*, November–December.

Katzenbach, J.R. and Smith, D.K. (1993) 'The discipline of teams', *Harvard Business Review*, March–April.

Kerrin, M. and Oliver, N. (2002) 'Collective and individual improvement activities: the role of reward systems', *Personnel Review*, Vol. 31, No. 3, pp. 320–37.

Marchington, M. (2000) 'Teamworking and employee involvement: terminology, evaluation and context' in S. Procter and F. Mueller (eds) *Teamworking*. Basingstoke: MacMillan.

Meyer, C. (1994) 'How the right measures help teams excel', *Harvard Business Review*, May–June, pp. 95–103.

Moxon, P. (1993) *Building a Better Team*. Aldershot: Gower in association with ITD.

Natale, S., Libertella, A. and Edwards, B. (1998) 'Team management: Developing concerns', *Team Performance Management*, Vol. 4, No. 8.

Oliva, L.M. (1992) *Partners not Competitors*. London: Idea Group Publishing.

Piczak, M. and Hause, R. (1996) 'SDWTs: a guide to implementation', *Quality Progress*, May.

Proehl, R. (1997) 'Enhancing the effectiveness of cross-functional teams', *Team Performance Management*, Vol. 3, No. 3.

Rubin, I.M., Plovnick, M.S. and Fry, R.E. (1975) *Improving the coordination of care: a program for health team development*. Cambridge, Mass.: Ballinger.

Salem, M., Lazarus, H. and Cullen, J. (1992) 'Developing self-managing teams: structure and performance', *Journal of Management Development*, Vol. 11, No. 3, pp. 24–32.

Scott, W. and Harrison, H. (1997) 'Full team ahead', *People Management*, 9 October.

Senge, P. (1990) *The Fifth Discipline: The art and practice of the learning organisation*. London: Century Business, Random House.

Sharpe, D. (2002) 'Teamworking and managerial control within a Japanese manufacturing subsidiary in the UK', *Personnel Review*, Vol. 31, No. 3, pp. 267–82.

Stott, K. and Walker, A. (1995) *Teams, Teamwork and Teambuilding*. Hemel Hempstead: Prentice Hall.

Tuckman, B.W. (1965) 'Development Sequences in Small Groups', *Psychological Bulletin*, Vol. 63, pp. 384–99.

Van den Beukel, A. and Mollerman, E. (2002) 'Too little, too much: Downsides of multi-functionality in team-based work', *Personnel Review*, Vol. 31, No. 4, pp. 482–94.

An extensive range of additional materials, including multiple choice questions, answers to questions and links to useful websites can be found on the Human Resource Management Companion Website at www.pearsoned.co.uk/torrington.

CHAPTER 14

LEADERSHIP AND MOTIVATION

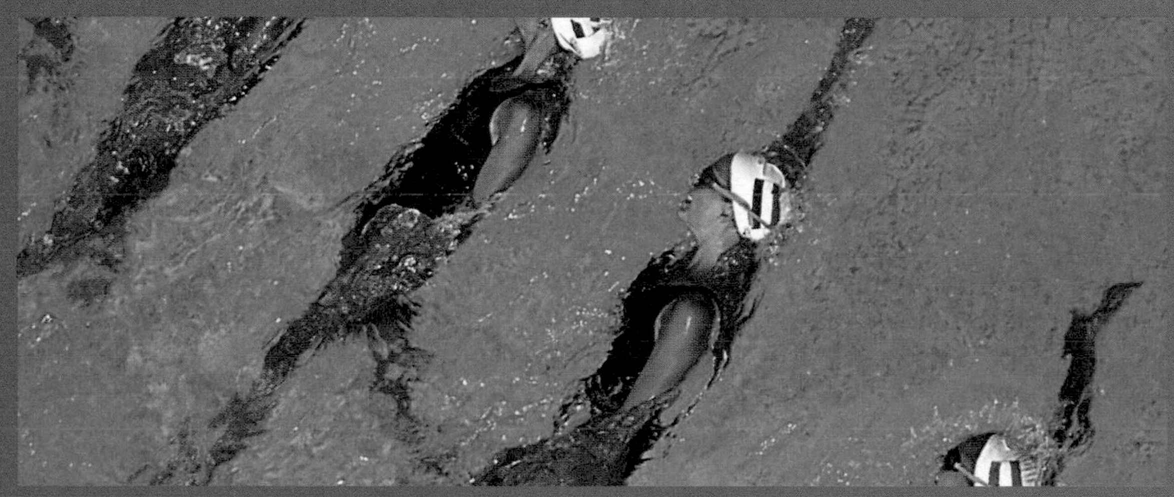

THE OBJECTIVES OF THIS CHAPTER ARE TO:

1 INTRODUCE A WORKING DEFINITION WHICH REFLECTS THE GENERAL NATURE OF LEADERSHIP

2 EXAMINE THE TRAIT APPROACH TO LEADERSHIP

3 EXAMINE THE STYLE (BEHAVIOURAL) AND CONTINGENCY APPROACH TO LEADERSHIP

4 EXPLORE THE NATURE OF HEROIC AND POST-HEROIC LEADERSHIP

5 INVESTIGATE THE LINK BETWEEN LEADERSHIP AND MOTIVATION

Leadership and motivation are two of the most loaded and misunderstood words in management. Individual managers are often seduced by concepts of leadership that show them to be knights in shining armour with superhuman qualities and (this is the really dangerous bit) adoring followers. The followers rarely have that view of their managers. Motivation is often constructed in the same way, 'How can I motivate the members of my team?', although this ignores the mainsprings of motivation, which are in the performer rather than in the manager of the performer.

We must not, however, underestimate the importance of leadership, motivation *and the link between the two*. There are indeed sometimes needs for individual leaders who have outstanding personal qualities and who achieve extraordinary change in their business, sometimes more subtle leadership qualities are more important, and there are infinitely more roles which call on different and more modest leadership skills, which can be learned and which are equally important, even if they do not merit shining armour and a white charger.

Understanding of both leadership and motivation was well developed in the second half of the twentieth century and it is this work which is the basis of our understanding and analysis today. The one major addition of recent years has been an appreciation of the impact of changing circumstances of contemporary business and the role of women. All of the twentieth-century studies and theories were based on two complementary assumptions; first, the business norm was of large, stable organisations steadily getting bigger; second, management was almost exclusively a male activity, with male norms. This led to explanations and suggestions based on those two givens. We now see a weakening of both these assumptions. Effective businesses are not necessarily large, growing organisations and there are many more women in the workforce and in management positions within it. Although charismatic leaders (a predominantly male concept) are still needed in some situations, empowering leaders are increasingly required. We reach this at the close of the chapter, but we can only get there by starting further back.

LEADERSHIP AND MANAGEMENT

Northouse (1997) suggests that there are four components that characterise leadership: that leadership is a process; it involves influence; it occurs within a group context; and it involves goal attainment. This corresponds with Shackleton's (1995) definition, which we shall use as a working definition for the remainder of the chapter:

> Leadership is the process in which an individual influences other group members towards the attainment of group or organizational goals. (Shackleton 1995, p. 2)

This definition is useful as it leaves open the question of whether leadership is exercised in a commanding or a facilitative manner. It does suggest, however, that the leader in some way motivates others to act in such a way as to achieve group goals.

The definition also makes no assumptions about who is the leader; it may or may not be the nominal head of the group. Managers, therefore, may or may not be leaders, and leaders may or may not be managers. Some authors distinguish very clearly between the nature of management and the nature of leadership but this draws on a particular perspective, that of the transformational leader, and we will consider this in the section on whether the organisation needs heroes. This is a school of thought that concentrates on the one leader at the top of the organisation, which is very different from organisations and individuals who use the terms manager and leader interchangeably with nothing more than a vague notion that managers should be leaders. Indeed, any individual may act as a manager one day and a leader the next, depending on the situation.

The flow of articles on leadership continues unabated, but it would be a mistake to think that there is an ultimate truth to be discovered; rather, there is a range of perspectives from which we can try to make sense of leadership and motivation. Grint (1997) puts it well when he comments that

> What counts as leadership appears to change quite radically across time and space. (p. 3)

In the following three sections we will look at three questions which underlie virtually all the work on leadership. First, what are the traits of a leader, or an effective leader? Second, what is the 'best' leadership style or behaviour? Third, if different styles are appropriate at different times, what factors influence the desired style?

WHAT ARE THE TRAITS OF LEADERS AND EFFECTIVE LEADERS?

Trait approaches, which were the earliest to be employed, seek to identify the traits of leaders – in other words what characterises leaders as opposed to those who are not leaders. These approaches rest on the assumption that some people were born to lead due to their personal qualities, while others are not. It suggests that leadership is only available to the chosen few and not accessible to all. These approaches have been discredited for this very reason and because there has been little consistency in the lists of traits that research has uncovered. However, this perspective is frequently resurrected.

Kilpatrick and Locke (1991), in a **meta-analysis**, did seem to find some consistency around the following traits: drive to achieve; the motivation to lead; honesty and integrity; self-confidence, including the ability to withstand setbacks, standing firm and being emotionally resilient; cognitive ability; and knowledge of the business. They also note the importance of managing the perceptions of others in relation to these characteristics. Northouse (1997) provides a useful historical comparison of the lists of traits uncovered in other studies. Perhaps the most well-known expression of the trait approach is the work relating to charismatic leadership. House (1976), for example, describes charismatic leaders as being dominant, having a strong desire to influence, being self-confident and having a strong sense of their own moral values. We will pick up on this concept of leadership in the later section on heroes.

In a slightly different vein Goleman (1998) carried out a meta-analysis of leadership competency frameworks in 188 different companies. These frameworks represented the competencies related to outstanding leadership performance. Goleman analysed the competencies into three groups: technical, cognitive and emotional, and found that, in terms of the ratios between each group, emotional competencies 'proved to be twice as important as the others'. Goleman goes on to describe five components of emotional intelligence:

- **Self-awareness:** this he defines as a deep understanding of one's strengths, weaknesses, needs, values and goals. Self-aware managers are aware of their own limitations.
- **Self-regulation:** the control of feelings, the ability to channel them in constructive ways. The ability to feel comfortable with ambiguity and not panic.
- **Motivation:** the desire to achieve beyond expectations, being driven by internal rather than external factors, and to be involved in a continuous striving for improvement.
- **Empathy:** considering employees' feelings alongside other factors when decision making.
- **Social skill:** friendliness with a purpose, being good at finding common ground and building rapport. Individuals with this competency are good persuaders, collaborative managers and natural networkers.

Goleman's research is slightly different from previous work on the trait approach, as here we are considering what makes an effective leader rather than what makes a leader (irrespective of whether they are effective or not). It is also different in that Goleman refers to competencies rather than traits. There is a thorough discussion of competencies in Chapter 17; it is sufficient for now to say that competencies include a combination of traits and abilities, among other things. There is some debate over whether competencies can be developed in people. The general feeling is that some can and some cannot. Goleman maintains that the five aspects of emotional intelligence can be learned and provides an example in his article of one such individual. In spite of his argument we feel that it is still a matter for debate, and as many of the terms used by Goleman are similar to those of the previous trait models of leadership, we have categorised his model as an extension of the trait perspective. To some extent his work sits between the trait approach and the style approach which follows. It is interesting that a number of researchers and writers are recognising that there is some value in considering a mix of personality characteristics and behaviours, and in particular Higgs (2003) links this approach to emotional intelligence.

Rajan and van Eupen (1997) also consider that leaders are strong on emotional intelligence, and that this involves the traits of self-awareness, zeal, resilience and the ability to read emotions in others. They argue that these traits are particularly important in the development and deployment of people skills. Heifetz and Laurie (1997) similarly identify that in order for leaders to regulate emotional distress in the organisation, which is inevitable in change situations, the leader has to have 'the emotional capacity to tolerate uncertainty, frustration and pain' (p. 128). Along the same lines Goffe (2002) identifies that inspirational leaders need to understand and admit their own weaknesses (within reason); sense the needs of situations; have empathy and self-awareness.

ACTIVITY 14.1

Think of different leaders you have encountered – in particular those that were especially effective or ineffective:

1 What differences can you identify in terms of their traits (personal characteristics)?
2 What differences can you identify in terms of their behaviour?
3 Are the trait and behaviour lists connected in any way? If so how?
4 Which of these two approaches – trait or behaviour – do you find more helpful in helping you to understand the nature of effective leadership?

WHAT IS THE 'BEST WAY TO LEAD'? LEADERSHIP STYLES AND BEHAVIOURS

Dissatisfaction with research on leadership that saw leadership as a set of permanent personal characteristics that describe the leader led to further studies that emphasised the nature of the leadership process – the interaction between leader and follower – aiming to understand how the leaders *behave* rather than what they *are*. The first such studies sought to find the 'best' leadership style; from this perspective leadership comprises an ideal set of behaviours that can be learned. Fulop *et al.* (1999) suggest that Douglas McGregor's (1960) work, *The Human Side of Enterprise*, can be understood from this perspective. McGregor argued that American corporations managed their employees as if they were work-shy, and needed constant direction, monitoring and control (theory 'x'), rather than as if they were responsible individuals who were willing and able to take on responsibility and organise their own work (theory 'y'). McGregor argued that the underlying assumptions of the manager determined the way they managed their employees and this in turn determined how the employees would react. Thus if employees were managed as if they operated on theory 'x' then they would act in a theory 'x' manner; conversely if employees were managed as if they operated on theory 'y' then they would respond as theory 'y' employees would respond. The message was that management style should reinforce theory 'y' and thus employees would take on responsibility, be motivated by what they were doing and work hard. Although the original book was written over forty years ago, this approach is being revisited (*see*, for example, Heil *et al.* 2000) and it fits well with the empowering or post-heroic approach to leadership that we discuss later in the chapter. Another piece of research from the style approach is that by Blake and Mouton (1964), who developed the famous 'Managerial Grid'. The grid is based on two aspects of leadership behaviour. One is concern for production,

Table 14.1 Blake and Mouton's four leadership styles

High concern for people Low concern for production **Country Club management**	High concern for people High concern for production **Team management**
Low concern for people Low concern for production **Impoverished management**	Low concern for people High concern for production **Authority-compliance management**

Source: Adapted from R.R. Blake and J.S. Mouton (1964) *The Managerial Grid*. Houston, Texas: Gulf Publishing.

that is, task-oriented behaviours such as clarifying roles, scheduling work, measuring outputs; the second is concern for people, that is, people-centred behaviour such as building trust, camaraderie, a friendly atmosphere. These two dimensions are at the heart of many models of leadership. Blake and Mouton proposed that individual leaders could be measured on a nine-point scale in each of these two aspects, and by combining them in grid form they identified the four leadership styles presented in Table 14.1.

Such studies, which are well substantiated by evidence, suggest that leadership is accessible for all people and that it is more a matter of learning leadership behaviour than of personality characteristics. Many leadership development courses have therefore been based around this model. However, as Northouse (1997) argues, there is an assumption in the model that the team management style (high concern for people and high concern for production; sometimes termed 9,9 management) is the ideal style; and yet this claim is not substantiated by the research. This approach also fails to take account of the characteristics of the situation and the nature of the followers.

WINDOW ON PRACTICE

A large organisation adopted the Managerial Grid as the framework for its leadership development programme. The programme was generally well accepted and successful application of the team management style was seen to be connected to future promotions. Most managers, on leaving the programme, set out to display 9,9 leadership behaviours. However, this had unexpected and undesirable consequences. Not only were team members daunted by their managers suddenly displaying a different style, but sometimes the 9,9 style was not appropriate in the circumstances in which it was used. The organisation eventually discontinued the programme due to the damage that it was causing.

Much of the recent work on the notion of transformational/heroic leadership, and empowering/post-heroic leadership, similarly assumes that what is being discussed is the one best way for a leader to lead, and we return to this leadership debate later on.

DO LEADERS NEED DIFFERENT STYLES FOR DIFFERENT SITUATIONS?

WINDOW ON PRACTICE

Mintzberg (1998) spent some time observing the conductor of an orchestra, Bramwell Tovey, to see whether this could help managers understand a different perspective on leadership. He found what he called covert as opposed to overt leadership, and proposed that this leadership approach was more appropriate than a traditional approach for professionals and knowledge workers. He argued that such employees respond better to inspiration than supervision, as they do not need to be told what to do, but rather to have their expertise coordinated. Mintzberg also makes the important point that such professionals need the support and protection of their leader in respect of dealings at the boundary of the organisation (in this case the orchestra).

A variety of models, sometimes termed contingency models, have been developed to address the importance of context in terms of the leadership process, and as a consequence these models become more complex. Many, however, retain the concepts of production-centred and people-centred behaviour as ways of describing leadership behaviour, but use them in a different way. Hersey and Blanchard (1988) developed a model which identified that the appropriate leadership style in a situation should be dependent on their diagnosis of the 'readiness', that is, developmental level or maturity, of their followers. The model is sometimes referred to as 'situational leadership', and works on the premise that leaders can 'adapt their leadership style to meet the demands of their environment' (Hersey and Blanchard 1988, p. 169). Readiness of followers is defined in terms of ability and willingness. Level of ability includes the experience, knowledge and skills that an individual possesses in relation to the particular task at hand; and level of willingness encompasses the extent to which the individual has the motivation and commitment, or the self-confidence, to carry out the task. Having diagnosed the developmental level of the followers, Hersey and Blanchard suggest that the leader then adapts their behaviour to fit. They identify two dimensions of leader behaviour: task behaviour, which is sometimes termed 'directive'; and relationship behaviour, which is sometimes termed 'supportive'. Task behaviour refers to the extent to which leaders spell out what has to be done. This includes 'telling people what to do, how to do it, when to do it, where to do it, and who is to do it' (Hersey 1985, p. 19). On the other hand, relationship behaviour is defined as 'the extent to which the leader engages in two-way or multiway communication. The behaviours include listening, facilitating and supporting behaviours' (ibid.). The extent to which the leader emphasises each of these two types of behaviour results in the usual two-by-two matrix. The four resulting styles are identified, as shown in Table 14.2.

There is an assumption that the development path for any individual and required behaviour for the leader is to work through boxes 1, 2, 3 and then 4 in the matrix. Hersey and Blanchard produced questionnaires to help managers diagnose the readiness of their followers.

Table 14.2 Hersey and Blanchard's four styles of leadership

High relationship behaviour Low task behaviour Followers are able, but unwilling or insecure **Supportive (participating) style (3)**	High relationship behaviour High task behaviour Followers are unable, but willing or confident **Coaching (selling) style (2)**
Low relationship behaviour Low task behaviour Followers are both able and willing or confident **Delegation style (4)**	Low relationship behaviour High task behaviour Followers are unable and unwilling or insecure **Directing (telling) style (1)**

Source: Adapted from P. Hersey and K.H. Blanchard (1988) *Management of Organizational Behavior: Utilizing Human Resources*, 5th edn. Englewood Cliffs, NJ: Prentice-Hall International. © Copyright material, adapted and reprinted with the permission of Center for Leadership Studies, Escondido, CA92025.

Other well-known contingency models include Fielder's (1967) contingency model where leadership behaviour is matched to three factors in the situation: the nature of the relationship between the leader and members, the extent to which tasks are highly structured and the position power of the leader. The appropriate leader behaviour (that is, whether it should be task oriented or relationship oriented) depends on the combination of these three aspects in any situation. Fielder's model is considered to be well supported by the evidence. The research was based on the relationship between style and performance in existing organisations in different contexts. For a very useful comparison of contingency models *see* Fulop *et al.* (1999).

WINDOW ON PRACTICE

Hilary Walmsley (1999) reports some of her work as a consultant with BUPA. One of the aims of the exercise she was involved in was to:

> raise individuals' awareness of their own management styles and encourage them to stop and think about which approach to adopt rather than automatically respond to every challenge in a similar way. (p. 48)

She recounts the experiences of Brian Atkins, General Manager of BUPA's Gatwick Park and Redwood Hospitals, as an illustration of this learning process. On joining the hospital group, which was undergoing a critical phase of change, in 1990, Atkins consciously used an authoritative leadership style, at the directive and controlling end of the spectrum. Once the hospital was soundly on course for recovery he began to use a more empowering and facilitative style. Atkins describes modern managers as 'style travellers', and suggests that they need to be skilled at using different styles, even though they may naturally prefer one approach. Walmsley notes that managers are tempted to use the same styles out of habit, and are often unaware of alternative styles they could use.

Table 14.3 Six leadership styles reported by Goleman

Coercive style	Leader demands immediate compliance
Authoritative style	Leader mobilises people towards a vision
Affiliative style	Leader creates emotional bonds and harmony
Democratic style	Leaders use participation to build consensus
Pacesetting style	Leader expects excellence and self-direction from followers
Coaching style	Leader develops people for the future

Source: Reprinted by permission of *Harvard Business Review*. Adapted from 'Leadership that gets results', by D. Goleman, March–April, pp. 80 and 82–3.

Goleman (2000) reports the results of some research carried out by Hay/McBer who sampled almost 20 per cent of a database of 20,000 executives. The results were analysed to identify six different leadership styles, which are shown in Table 14.3, but most importantly Goleman reports that 'leaders with the best results do not rely on only one leadership style' (p. 78).

Goleman goes on to consider the appropriate context and impact of each style, and argues that the more styles the leader uses the better. We have already reported Goleman's work on emotional intelligence, and he links this with the six styles by suggesting that leaders need to understand how the styles relate back to the different competencies of emotional intelligence so that they can identify where they need to focus their leadership development.

ACTIVITY 14.2

For each of Goleman's six styles think of a leader you have worked with, or know of. For each of these individuals write a list of the *behaviours* that they use. Then consider the impact that these behaviours have on followers.

Do the behaviours have the same impact on all followers? If not, why not?

One of the differences between the contingency models we have just discussed and the 'best' style models is the implications for development. The Blake and Mouton model suggests leaders can be developed to lead in the one best way. The Hersey and Blanchard model, and most other contingency models, stress the flexibility of the leader – to learn to lead differently with different employees depending on their needs; hence the leader should learn many styles and learn to diagnose the needs of their employees. Fielder's model, however, emphasises matching the leader to the context (a selection decision), rather than developing leaders in the context.

WINDOW ON PRACTICE

International perspectives on leadership style

Kakabadse *et al.* (1997) carried out a 600-respondent survey of top management styles in Europe (the Cranfield study). The analysis produced four distinct styles:

Leading from the front – where charisma, dominance and self-motivation were valued, with a reliance on an individual's leadership ability and a view that rules and procedures were a hindrance.

Consensus – where team spirit, effective communication and an open dialogue were valued, with attention to organisational detail and consensual decision making.

Managing from a distance – where strategic and conceptual thinking was valued, with a tendency to pursue personal agendas coupled with ineffective communication, lack of discipline and ambiguity.

Towards a common goal – where functional-based expertise, clear roles, systems and controls and discipline are valued, with authority-based leadership.

The researchers found that leading from the front was most common in the UK, Ireland and Spain; consensus was most common in Sweden and Finland; managing from a distance, most common in France; and towards a common goal most common in Germany and Austria.

Source: Summarised from A. Kakabadse, A. Myers, T. McMahon and G. Spony (1997) in K. Grint (ed.) *Leadership*. Oxford: Oxford University Press.

DO WE REALLY NEED HEROES?

A different approach to understanding leadership is transformational leadership, which focuses on the leader's role at a strategic level, so there is a concentration on the one leader at the top of the organisaton. There is a wide range of literature in this vein, most of it written in the 1980s. Since that time the academic literature may have moved on but the image of the transformational leader still remains widely attractive. While this is a different approach it links back to our original three questions about leadership. Transformational leadership shows elements of the trait approach, as leaders are seen to 'have' charisma, which sets them apart as extraordinary and exceptional, and they are also seen to use a set of 'ideal' behaviours, with the assumption in many writings that this is the 'best' approach.

The leader is usually characterised as a hero, although Steyrer (1998) proposes that there are other charismatic types such as the father figure, the saviour and the king. Such leaders appear to know exactly what they are doing and how to 'save' the organisation from its present predicament (and consequently such leadership is found more often when organisations are in trouble). Leaders involve followers by generating a high level of commitment, partly due to such leaders focusing on the needs of followers and expressing their vision in such a way that it satisfies these needs. They communicate high expectations to followers and also the firm belief that followers will be able to achieve these goals. In this way the leader promotes self-confidence in the followers and they are motivated to achieve more than they ordinarily expect to achieve. In terms of behaviours, perhaps the most important is the vision of the future that the leader offers and that they communicate this and dramatise this to the followers. Such leaders are able to help the followers make sense of what is going on and why as well as what needs to be done in the future. It is from this perspective that the distinction between management and leadership is often made. Bennis and Nanus (1985), for example, suggest leadership is path finding while management is path following; and that leadership is about doing the right thing whereas management is about doing things right. Kotter (1990) identified leaders as establishing a direction (whereas managers plan and budget); leaders align people with the vision (whereas managers organise things); leaders motivate and inspire (whereas managers control and solve problems); and leaders encourage change (whereas managers encourage order and predictability). Other writers analysing leadership from this perspective include Tichy and Devanna (1986) and Bass (1985), and there is a wide research base to support the findings. The approach does have a great strength in taking followers' needs into account and seeking to promote their self-confidence and potential, and the idea of the knight in shining armour is very attractive and potentially exciting – Tichy and Devanna, for example, present the process of such leadership as a three-act drama. However, in spite of the emphasis on process there is also an emphasis on leadership characteristics which harks back to the trait approach to leadership, which has been characterised as elitist. There is also the ethical concern of one person wielding such power over others.

Maybe we should ask whether organisations really require such leaders. A very different conception of leadership is now offered as an alternative, partly a reaction to the previous approach, and partly a response to a changing environment. This is termed empowering or post-heroic leadership, and could be described as the currently favoured ideal way to lead.

WINDOW ON PRACTICE

Arkin (1997) reports on the leadership experiences of Percy Barnevik who was Chief Executive of the engineering company ABB. Arkin explains how this charismatic leader transformed ABB into a 'competitive fighting force across the globe' (p. 27). Ten years later, on leaving the role of Chief Executive, Barnevik is reported to have said, 'Ten years after our big merger, we have come a long way from the large dependence on one man at the top' (p. 28).

Source: Summarised from A. Arkin (1997) 'The secret of his success', *People Management*, 23 October, pp. 27–8.

Fulop *et al.* (1999) identify factors in a rapidly changing turbulent environment which by the 1990s dilute the appropriateness of concentrating on the one leader at the top of the organisation. These factors include: globalisation making centralisation more difficult; technology enabling better sharing of information; and change being seen as a responsibility of all levels of the organisation – not just the top. They also note a dissatisfaction with corporate failures, identify few transformational leaders as positive role models, suggest that such a model of male authoritarian leadership is less relevant, and in particular that the macho leader with all the answers does not necessarily fit well with the encouragement of creativity and innovation. In addition they suggest that increasing teamwork and an increasing emphasis on knowledge workers mean that employees will be less responsive now to a transformational leader. The emphasis has therefore moved away from understanding the traits and style of the one leader at the top of the organisation who knows how to solve all the organisation's problems, to how empowering or post-heroic leaders can facilitate many members of the organisation in taking on leadership roles. In this context Applebaum *et al.* (2003) comment that female leadership styles are more effective in today's team-based consensually driven organisations. Many commentators speak of leaders with integrity and humility, the ability to select good people and to remove barriers so they can fulfil their potential and perform (*see*, for example, Collins 2003; Alimo-Metcalfe and Alban-Metcalfe 2002).

The leader becomes a developer who can help others identify problems as opportunities for learning, and who can harness the collective intelligence of the organisation, and Fulop *et al.* (1999) note that this means in practice that they encourage the development of a learning organisation. Senge (1990), who is a protagonist of the learning organisation (*see* Chapter 11 for further details), sees the leader's new roles in encouraging a learning organisation as designer, teacher and steward, rather than a traditional charismatic decision maker. He suggests that leaders should *design* the organisation in terms of vision, purpose, core values and the structures by which these ideas can be translated into business decisions. However, he also suggests that the leader should involve people at all levels in this design task. It is the role of the leader not to identify the right strategy, but to encourage strategic thinking in the organisation, and to design effective learning processes to make this happen. The leader's role as a *teacher* is not to teach people the correct view of reality, but to help employees gain more insight into the current reality. The leader therefore coaches, guides and facilitates. As a *steward* the leader acts as a servant in taking responsibility for the impact of their leadership on others, and in the sense that they override their own self-interest by personal commitment to the organisation's larger mission. To play this role effectively Senge suggests that the leader will need many new skills, in particular vision-making skills – a never-ending sharing of ideas and asking for feedback. Skills that will encourage employees to express and test their views of the world are also key. These involve actively seeking others' views, experimenting, encouraging enquiry and distinguishing 'the way things are done' from 'the way we think things are done'.

WINDOW ON PRACTICE

The role that leaders play in the organisation in the twenty-first century is seen by some as very different from the hero roles of the past, and leaders are no longer expected always to know the solutions to problems.

Williams (2000), who talks about enabling and empowering leadership, suggests that 'twenty first century leaders are not expected to be all-knowing gurus and peddlers of panaceas' (p. 113). However, they are expected to know the right questions to ask, as Heifetz and Laurie (1997) suggest: 'leaders do not need to know all the answers. They do need to know the right questions' (p. 124).

Building on this a speaker from Henley Management College (Radio 4, 25 February 2001) argued that leaders need to be able to admit that they do not know all the answers, and that there was a paradox in leadership, as leaders need to display both boldness and humility.

Taking this one step further Anne Atkinson (Radio 4, 29 November 2000), speaking in relation to the tussle over who won the American presidential election, described the leader as a servant, arguing that the best leaders are unwilling leaders and do not seek power, but instead have a desire to benefit the people they lead.

These ideas take us some way from the charismatic and transformational view of the leader.

This changing perspective on leadership is well demonstrated by a survey on leadership skills reported by Rajan and van Eupen (1997). The research is based on interviews with 49 top business leaders, 50 HR directors and a postal questionnaire of 375 companies in the service sector. They asked what were the most important leadership skills during the period 1995–7 and compared the results with those of a similar survey conducted in the late 1980s. The change in skills base shown in Table 14.4 reflects very well the change in the idealised leadership role and the increasing importance of facilitative people-related skills. They also note the prediction that the future will require an equal balance of traditionally masculine and feminine personality traits.

Higgs (2003) argues that leaders need a combination of skills and personality: envisioning, engaging, enabling, enquiring and developing skills are needed, together with authenticity, integrity, will, self-belief and self-awareness.

Table 14.4 Leadership skills compared

	Top five skills in order of importance
1995–7	1 Ability to inspire trust and motivation
	2 Visioning
	3 Ability, willingness and self-discipline to listen
	4 Strategic thinking
	5 Interpersonal communication skills
Late 1980s	1 Strategic thinking
	2 Entrepreneurial skills
	3 Originality
	4 Flair
	5 Problem-solving skills

Source: Adapted from A. Rajan and P. van Eupen (1997) 'Take it from the top', *People Management*, 23 October, pp. 26 and 28.

From a slightly different perspective Heifetz and Laurie (1997) propose six guiding principles of post-heroic leadership, and they conclude that leadership is about learning and that the idea of having a vision and aligning people to this is bankrupt. The idea of one leader at the top creating major changes in order to solve a one-off challenge is no longer appropriate, as organisations now face a constant stream of adaptive challenges, and leadership is required of many in the organisation, not just one person at the top. They argue that employees should be allowed to identify and solve problems themselves and learn to take responsibility. The role of the leader is to develop collective self-confidence. As Grint (1997) puts it, 'the apparent devolvement (or desertion – depending on your perspective) of responsibility has become the new standard in contemporary models of leadership' (p. 13). For further discussion on the devolution of responsibility *see* case 14.1 on the website.

These visions of leadership are very attractive but they do require a dramatic change in thinking for both leaders and followers. For leaders there is the risk of giving away power, learning to trust employees, developing new skills, developing a different perspective of their role and overriding self-interest. For followers there is the challenge of taking responsibility – which some may welcome, but others shun. Yet, if sustained competitive advantage is based on human capital and collective intelligence, it is difficult to relegate this perspective to 'just an ideal'.

While empowering leaders have been shown to fit with the current climate we may sometimes need heroic leaders. Kets de Vries (2003) makes the point that heroic leadership will never die as change makes people anxious and we need heroic leaders to calm them down, but since no one can live up to the expectations of heroic leaders, they will eventually become a disappointment. We conclude with the thought that there is no one best way – different leaders and different leader behaviours are needed at different times. For an example of a mixed approach to leadership *see* case 14.2 on the website about Tim Smit of the Eden Project.

LEADERSHIP AND MOTIVATION

All leadership models are based on the assumption that one person can motivate another to act, and we have looked at different explanations of how leaders may do this – based on their traits, their employment of the one best leadership style or their use of a style which matches (in some ways) the needs of their followers, and is responsive (in some ways) to the context. We have also explained how the leader may be reconceptualised as heroic (transformational leader) and as empowering or post-heroic.

Some interconnections can be made between these theories and motivation theories. It is not our purpose here to recount any motivation theories in detail (for this *see* texts such as Buchanan and Huczynski 1997; Mullins 1999; Fulop and Linstead 1999; or Hollyforde and Whiddett 2002). Below we identify some of the key concepts addressed in motivation theories and suggest which leadership perspectives tap into these concepts:

- **Expectancy has an impact on motivation.** We have already mentioned McGregor's (1960) model and his argument that if you treat people as responsible and self-motivated then they will act in a responsible and motivated manner. In addition Vroom's (1964) expectancy theory of motivation recognises that in the process of motivation the extent to which the individual feels they can realistically achieve the target will have an influence on whether they are motivated even to try. In respect of transformational leadership it is argued that followers can be inspired to achieve beyond the normal, partly because the leader has high expectations of the followers and in addition the leader expresses the belief that the followers are capable of achieving these great things. From a different perspective the post-heroic leader concept is based on trusting organisation members to play their part, trusting them with information and expecting them to use this wisely for the good of the organisation.

- **Social needs are important.** Maslow (1943), Mayo (1953) and McClelland (1971), among others, highlight the need for affiliation as a motivational factor. Some leadership models specifically respond to this, for example Blake and Mouton (1964) ('one best style' theory), Hersey and Blanchard (1988) and Fielder (1967) (contingency theory) all use 'concern for people' in some form as one of the key aspects of their leadership models. The concept of post-heroic leadership concerns involving those who may previously have been excluded, and concerns the impact of their leadership on individuals. In addition this perspective concentrates on the importance of learning and acting collectively.
- **Importance of the work itself.** Maslow (1943), Herzberg (1968), and Hackman and Oldham (1976), for example, all underline the way in which individuals are motivated to seek and may achieve satisfaction through their jobs. Herzberg, for example, identifies how opportunities for achievement, recognition, responsibility, autonomy, challenging tasks and opportunities for development may all be motivational. In some ways, Hersey and Blanchard's (1988) model addresses these needs in their 'delegation' style. In the post-heroic model many people in the organisation need to be involved in meeting adaptive challenges, in working out solutions and in contributing to vision building and many need to take on the responsibility of leadership. This is very different from the transformational leadership model in which the leader at the top of the organisation is seen to have all the responsibility.
- **Recognising different people are motivated by different things.** Expectancy theory, previously mentioned, also identifies that different individuals value different things and hence have different motivational needs. In the process of motivation, only those things that the individual values will spur them to act. Contingency models of leadership take this on board to some extent. From a different perspective the transformational leader develops an interpretation of the world, or narrative, that plays to the followers' needs. However, while post-heroic leadership identifies that different people may play a different part, there is an assumption that all will be prepared to be involved, to share information and to develop themselves in line with the needs of the organisation.
- **Social influences on motivation.** Recent work in the area of motivation suggests that motivations are socially or culturally determined, and to a limited extent the transformational leader ties into this as they reinterpret the world for their followers.

In spite of the links between leadership and motivation theories, there are many aspects of motivation that the leadership theories ignore. For example, some people have less internal energy and drive than others and less need for growth. Also, individuals with high levels of energy and drive may satisfy these outside the work environment. While we may try to motivate people externally the greatest power for motivation comes from within and is therefore under the control of the individual rather than another. The best we can say is that leaders can enhance followers' motivation by the way they treat them, and at worst leaders may neutralise the motivational energy in their followers. There will always be some factors on which leaders have no impact whatsoever.

SUMMARY PROPOSITIONS

14.1 Leadership is a process where one person influences a group of others to achieve group or organisational goals – leadership is thus about motivation.

14.2 The trait model of leadership, although often discredited, continues to play a part in our understanding of leadership.

14.3 Behavioural models are more helpful than earlier models as they concentrate on what leaders do rather than on what they are.

14.4 Some behavioural models offer a 'one best way' of leadership, but more sophisticated models take account of contingency factors such as maturity of followers and the nature of the task.

14.5 Models of transformational leadership treat the leader as a hero who can (single-handedly) turn the organisation around and deliver it from a crisis.

14.6 Empowering and post-heroic leadership models conceptualise the leader as teacher and facilitator, who involves many in the leadership task.

14.7 While there are many ways in which leadership theories tap into concepts of motivation, at best leaders may enhance the motivation of their followers and at worst they may neutralise it.

GENERAL DISCUSSION TOPICS

1 Do we need leaders at all? Discuss what alternatives there might be.

2 Consider the four types of charismatic leader identified by Steyrer (1998): hero, father figure, missionary and saviour. Discuss the ways in which the types of leader are similar or different.

FURTHER READING

IDS (2003) *IDS Studies: Leadership Development*, No. 753. London: Incomes Data Services

A useful book outlining the work of five case study organisations, in terms of their conception of leadership, what prompted their leadership development programmes and an outline of the programmes themselves. The case organisations are the Dixons group, the Inland Revenue, Novartis Pharmaceuticals, Portsmouth City Council and Skipton Building Society.

Nicholson, N. (2003) 'How to motivate your problem people', *Harvard Business Review*, January, pp. 57–65
Despite the title this article is focused on the perspective of the employee rather than the leader. Nicholson takes the view that leaders need to decentre, in other words put aside their views and look at the world in terms of how the employee sees it – the employee not being a problem to be solved but a person to be understood.

REFERENCES

Alimo-Metcalfe, B. and Alban-Metcalfe, J. (2002) 'The great and the good', *People Management*, Vol. 8, No. 1, 10 January, pp. 32–4.

Applebaum, S., Audet, L. and Miller, J. (2003) 'Gender and leadership? Leadership and gender? A journey through the landscape of theories', *Leadership and Organisation*, Vol. 24, No. 1, pp. 43–51.

Arkin, A. (1997) 'The secret of his success', *People Management*, 23 October, pp. 27–8.

Bass, B.M. (1985) 'Leadership: Good, Better, Best', *Organisational Dynamics*, Winter, pp. 26–40.

Bennis, W.G. and Nanus, B. (1985) *Leaders: the strategies for taking charge*. New York: Harper and Row.

Blake, R.R. and Mouton, J.S. (1964) *The Managerial Grid*. Houston, Texas: Gulf Publishing.

Buchanan, D. and Huczynski, A. (1997) *Organisational Behaviour*. London: Prentice Hall.

Collins, J. (2003) 'From good to great', presentation to the CIPD National Conference, Harrogate, 22–24 November 2003.

Fielder, F.E. (1967) *A Theory of Leadership Effectiveness*. New York: McGraw-Hill.

Fulop, L. and Linstead, S. (1999) *Management. A Critical Text*. South Yarra: Macmillan Business.

Fulop, L., Linstead, S. and Dunford, R. (1999) 'Leading and managing', in L. Fulop and S. Linstead, *Management. A Critical Text*. South Yarra: Macmillan Business.

Goffe, R. (2002) 'Send out the right signals', *People Management*, Vol. 8, No. 21, 24 October, pp. 32–8.

Goleman, D. (1998) 'What makes . . . a leader?' *Harvard Business Review*, Nov.–Dec., pp. 93–102.

Goleman, D. (2000) 'Leadership that gets results', *Harvard Business Review*, March–April, pp. 78–90.

Grint, K. (1997) 'Introduction' in K. Grint (ed.) *Leadership*. Oxford: Oxford University Press.

Hackman, J. and Oldham, G. (1976) 'Motivation through the design of work; test of a theory', *Organisational Behaviour and Human Performance*, Vol. 16, pp. 250–79.

Heifetz, R. and Laurie, D. (1997) 'The work of leadership', *Harvard Business Review*, Jan.–Feb., pp. 124–34.

Heil, G., Bennis, W. and Stephens, D.C. (2000) *Douglas McGregor, revisited: managing the human side of the enterprise*. New York: Wiley.

Hersey, P. (1985) *Situational Selling*. Escondido, Calif.: Centre for Leadership Studies.

Hersey, P. and Blanchard, K.H. (1988) *Management of Organizational Behavior: Utilizing Human Resources*, 5th edn. Englewood Cliffs, NJ: Prentice-Hall International.

Herzberg, F. (1968) 'One more time. How do you motivate employees?' *Harvard Business Review*, Vol. 46, pp. 53–62.

Higgs, M. (2003) 'How can we make sense of leadership in the 21st century?' *Leadership and Organisation Development Journal*, Vol. 24, No. 5, pp. 273–84.

Hollyforde, S. and Whiddett, S. (2002) *The Motivation Handbook*. London: CIPD.

House, R. (1976) 'A 1976 theory of charismatic leadership', in J. Hunt and L. Larson (eds) *Leadership: the Cutting Edge*. Carbondale, Ill.: Southern Illinois University Press.

Kakabadse, A., Myers, A., McMahon, T. and Spony, G. (1997) in K. Grint (ed.) *Leadership*. Oxford: Oxford University Press.

Kets de Vries, M. (2003) 'The dark side of leadership', *Business Strategy Review*, Vol. 14, No. 3, pp. 25–8.

Kilpatrick, S. and Locke, E. (1991) 'Leadership: Do Traits Matter?' *Academy of Management Executive*, Vol. 5, No. 2, pp. 48–60.

Kotter, J. (1990) *A Force for change: How leadership differs from management*. New York: Free Press.

McClelland, D.C. (1971) *Motivational Trends in Society*. Morristown, NJ: General Learning Press.

McGregor, D. (1960) *The Human Side of Enterprise*. New York: McGraw-Hill.

Maslow, A. (1943) 'A theory of human motivation', *Psychological Review*, Vol. 50, pp. 370–96.

Mayo, E. (1953) *The problems with an industrialized civilization*. New York: Macmillan.

Mintzberg, H. (1998) 'Covert leadership: Notes on managing professionals', *Harvard Business Review*, Nov.–Dec., pp. 140–7.

Mullins, L. (1999) *Management and Organisational Behaviour*, 5th edn. Harlow: Financial Times Pitman Publishing.

Northouse, P. (1997) *Leadership – Theory and Practice*. California: Sage.

Rajan, A. and van Eupen, P. (1997) 'Take it from the top', *People Management*, 23 October, pp. 26–9.

Senge, P. (1990) *The Fifth Discipline: The art and practice of the learning organisation*. London: Century Business, Random House.

Shackleton, V. (1995) *Business Leadership*. London: Routledge.

Steyrer, J. (1998) 'Charisma and the Archetypes of leadership', *Organisation Studies*, Vol. 19, No. 5, pp. 807–28.

Tichy, N. and Devanna, M. (1986) *The Transformational Leader*. New York: Wiley.

Vroom, V. (1964) *Work and Motivation*. Chichester: John Wiley.

Walmsley, H. (1999) 'A suitable ploy', *People Management*, 8 April, pp. 48–50.

Williams, M. (2000) *The war for talent: Getting the best from the best*. London: CIPD.

An extensive range of additional materials, including multiple choice questions, answers to questions and links to useful websites can be found on the Human Resource Management Companion Website at www.pearsoned.co.uk/torrington.

CHAPTER 15

MANAGING ABSENCE AND ATTENDANCE

THE OBJECTIVES OF THIS CHAPTER ARE TO:

1 REVIEW THE NATIONAL CONTEXT ON EMPLOYEE ABSENCE

2 IDENTIFY THE IMPACT OF ABSENCE ON THE ORGANISATION

3 EXPLORE THE PROCESS OF ABSENCE FROM WORK AND ABSENCE CAUSATION

4 DISCUSS METHODS BY WHICH LONG- AND SHORT-TERM ABSENCE CAN BE MINIMISED

For organisations to achieve their optimum performance the extent to which employees are absent from their place of work clearly needs to be minimised. Absence has always been a matter of concern to all employers, and methods for reducing it have frequently focused on disciplinary or punitive measures. More recently absence has been framed in a more positive discourse, and the focus is now on what organisations can do to promote attendance and rehabilitation of employees with long-term absence. In an IRS survey (IRS 2001) absence was second among the top ten priorities of HR managers.

THE NATIONAL CONTEXT

The CIPD (2003) found a level of 3.9 per cent sickness absence (defined as the percentage of working time missed, and often referred to as the headline rate) from a survey they carried out in early 2003 with responses from 1,330 public sector and private sector organisations. This represents nine days' absence per employee per year. CIPD commented that this is a reduction on the figure of 4.4 per cent reported by a similar survey in the previous year. Other surveys produce fairly similar figures, for example the CBI survey in 2003 reports a rate of 2.9 per cent (equating to 6.8 days lost per person per year). However, for two reasons it is difficult to argue yet that there is a downward trend in absence rates. First, the rate in the CIPD 2001 survey was 3.8 per cent, and in 2000 was 4.1 per cent. Second, while the methodology of the survey remains constant the actual organisations responding each year are not necessarily the same, within either the CIPD or CBI survey.

In terms of the patterns of absence most surveys report that absence is higher in larger than in smaller organisations, which is likely to be why the CBI figures are generally lower than the ones from the CIPD, as their sample includes a higher proportion of smaller organisations. Public sector absence is usually found to be higher than that in the private sector: for example in 2003 the CIPD found the public sector absence rate to be 4.6 per cent. Reviewing the Labour Force Survey, the General Household Survey and employer surveys, Barham and Leonard (2002) found that absence does tend to be concentrated in some groups of people rather than others: in addition to higher rates in the public sector they found higher rates for women, full-time workers and those aged under 30. They also found differences by occupational group, with managers, professionals and administrative professionals having lower levels than other groups. The CBI found that sickness absence was higher among manual workers, and this to some extent must reflect the nature of job demands. The CIPD (2003) found that absence levels were greatest in the food, drink and tobacco sector and lowest in consultancy, IT services, legal, property services, media and publishing.

The CBI reports that absence costs the UK economy around £11 billion per year. At a national level the government has an interest in reducing absence and loss of employment due to sickness. Roberts (2003) reports that while there are 1.46 million people claiming unemployment pay, there are 2.7 million people out of work claiming long-term sickness and disability benefits. Roberts goes on to explain how this situation has stimulated a focus on how society manages long-term sickness and rehabilitation. The government has an interest in reducing NHS costs and the Department for Work and Pensions has arranged a two-year series of job rehabilitation pilot studies. The pilots will test three different approaches, healthcare interventions, workplace interventions and combined interventions, and the aim is to learn which approaches are most successful.

WINDOW ON PRACTICE

International approaches to long-term absence

James and his colleagues (2002) explain how different countries have enacted legislation in respect of sickness absence. For example, in Sweden employers must ensure that they have assessed rehabilitation needs at an early stage, and are then obliged to put any relevant rehabilitation measures in place. In the Netherlands employers must submit a report on any employee who is unable to work within 13 weeks of the start of the absence. They are required to submit this to a social security agency and must produce a 'work resumption plan'. In New South Wales, Australia, where workers have been absent for 12 weeks, employers must establish a work rehabilitation programme, and if there are more than 20 people employed, they must appoint a rehabilitation coordinator and prepare plans for return to work.

Source: Summarised from P. James, I. Cunningham and P. Dibben (2002) 'Absence management and the issues of job retention and return to work', *Human Resource Management Journal*, Vol. 12, No. 2, pp. 82–94.

THE ORGANISATIONAL CONTEXT

Barham and Leonard (2002) question the accuracy of data in absence surveys. They argue that given the low response rates to such surveys, there is no evidence to suggest that the survey findings are representative of the whole population. In addition the CIPD found that much management absence is not recorded. It is likely that respondents are those with better absence information. On this basis they argue that absence costs to the organisation are underestimated.

The CIPD found that over 90 per cent of organisations in their survey considered absence to be a significant cost to the organisation, but less that half monitored this cost. The average cost was reported to be £567 per year per employee. Barham and Leonard (2002) suggest that estimating the costs of absence is complicated, and that the estimate needs to include not only the direct costs (i.e., paying salary and benefits for a worker who is not there), but also indirect costs such as organising replacement staff, overall reductions in productivity and administrative costs. Bevan (2002), reporting research from the Employment Studies Institute, suggests that there is virtually no robust data on direct and indirect costs of absence and that most employers underestimate the true costs of sickness absence, particularly in respect of long-term sickness. Costing currently does not distinguish between short-term and long-term sickness. Using case study research Bevan reports that long-term sickness costs account for between 30 per cent and 70 per cent of absence costs. He goes on to argue, on the basis of this research, that even the most sophisticated companies are not well equipped to calculate such costs.

Statutory Sick Pay (SSP) changes in 1994 have given absence costs a higher profile as the burden has been passed to the employer, although there were compensatory mechanisms in place, direct costs to the employer are increased and are more prominent.

Traditionally employers have concentrated on short-term absence, and while long-term absence accounts for only around 20 per cent of absence incidents it can represent more than 40 per cent of total working time lost, according to the CBI, although figures do vary. CIPD (2003) found that long-term absence was most significant in the public sector where it accounts for 27 per cent of absence, compared with 18 per cent in manufacturing and 11 per cent in private services. Reducing such absence is increasingly seen as having the potential to create significant costs savings. Cost is not the only factor in influencing organisations to attend to long-term absence, and we have already mentioned government interest in this. In addition, the Disability Discrimination Act 1995 requires employers to provide reasonable adjustments to enable disabled workers to continue in employment, and the term 'disabled' extends to those suffering from long-term ill health. It has been argued that employers have a more explicit duty of care to their employees due to UK and EU legislation, and there is a growing concern for the well-being of employees, partly due to fear of litigation.

PROCESS AND CAUSES OF ABSENCE

The CIPD (2003) found that 81 per cent of organisations collected data on the causes of absence, with the public sector being more likely to do this. The most frequent stated causes of absence are minor illness for short-term absence and back pain (for manual workers) and stress (for non-manual workers) for long-term absence. The increase in stress as a cause may well be partly due to the fact that this is now a more legitimate reason for non-attendance than previously. Case 15.1 on the website focuses on stress as a reason for absence. It is important to bear in mind that recorded causes of absence in organisations will be those causes which employees perceive the organisation to view as legitimate.

The causes of absence are complex and interrelated and a process approach is generally agreed to be the most useful way of understanding absence behaviour, although there are criticisms that such models are not supported by the evidence. One of the most widely quoted models is from Rhodes and Steers (1990) and in our view this is the most useful of the process models. For an alternative model *see* Nicholson (1977).

The Rhodes and Steers model (*see* Figure 15.1) not only includes content information on the causes of absence but also incorporates a range of interdependent processes. In essence the model focuses on attendance motivation and the ability to attend in terms of resulting attendance behaviour.

Rhodes and Steers suggest that *attendance motivation* is directly affected by two factors: *satisfaction with the job* and *pressure to attend*. Pressure to attend may result from such factors as market conditions. Examples include the likelihood that there will be redundancies at their workplace and how easy it would be to get another job; incentives to attend, such as attendance bonuses; work-group norms on what is acceptable in the work-group and the effects of absence on other group members; personal work ethic producing internal pressure to attend based on beliefs about what is right; and commitment to the organisation through an identification with the beliefs and values of the organisation and an intention to remain with the organisation. On this basis threat of redundancies, attendance bonuses, team structures

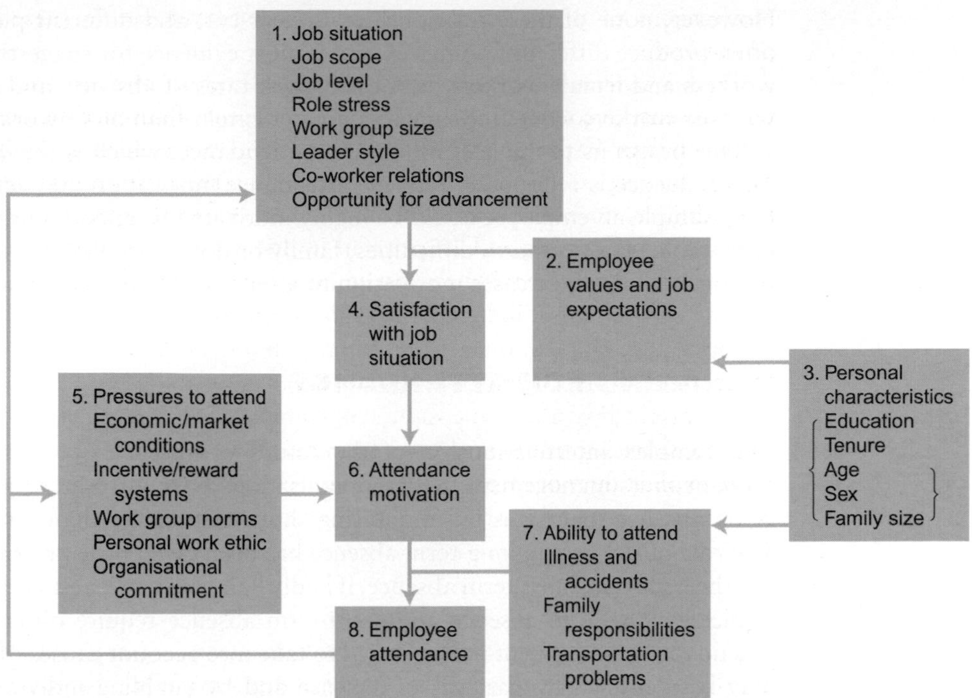

Figure 15.1 The Rhodes and Steers process model of attendance (Source: S. Rhodes and R. Steers (1990) *Managing Employee Absenteeism*, Reading, Mass.: Addison Wesley.)

where team members have to cover the workload of an absent member, a personal ethic about the need to attend work wherever possible, and feelings of loyalty to the organisation should all promote the motivation to attend.

Rhodes and Steers suggest that satisfaction with the job is determined by the *job situation* and moderated by *employee values and job expectations*. Factors in the job situation are identified as job scope and level of responsibility and decision making; role stress such as work overload, underload, difficult working conditions or hours; work-group size; leadership style of their immediate manager, particularly the openness of the relationship and how easy it is to discuss and solve problems jointly; strength of relationships with co-workers; and the opportunity for promotion. On this basis higher levels of responsibility and the opportunity to make decisions in relation to job demands, balanced workload and good working conditions, small work group size, an open relationship with immediate manager, good relationships with colleagues and the opportunity for promotion should all improve attendance motivation.

However job satisfaction is moderated by the values and expectations of the employee. Such values and expectations are shaped by both personality and personal characteristics and life experiences, but can also change during the course of one's life. The extent to which the job matches up with expectations and values will have a bearing on job satisfaction; a close match is more likely to lead to satisfaction than a mismatch.

Personality and personal characteristics influence expectations and values and job satisfaction. We have previously referred to the influence of age and sex on absence rates. Length of service has also been identified as having an influence.

However, none of these relationships is clear-cut, and different pieces of research often produce different findings. There is most evidence for suggesting that younger workers and female workers have the highest rates of absence, and it is argued that younger workers value free time to a greater extent than older workers.

This brings us to the last influence on attendance, which is the *ability to attend*. This influence is interposed between attendance motivation and actual attendance. For example an employee could be highly motivated to attend, but may have insurmountable transportation difficulties, family or domestic responsibilities, or may be genuinely ill. In these cases motivation to attend does not result in attendance.

MANAGING FOR ATTENDANCE

The complex interrelationship of the causes of absence needs to be taken into account in its management. Many organisations have introduced policies for managing absence that focus on minimising short-term rather than long-term absence. The role of sickness in long-term absence has been given little priority in the past, as has the issue that short-term absence, if badly handled, can lead to long-term absence. Typically long-term absence and short-term absence require different approaches. Attendance management policies need to take into account causes of absence, which may be identified by patterns of absence and by enabling individuals to be open about why they are not at work. Measures range from proactive methods intended to reduce the risk of ill health; measures intended to reduce spells of absence and those intended to reduce the length of absence. Typically there is a mix of processes both to discourage absence and positively to encourage attendance, but these work differently with those on long- and short-term sickness absence.

Whatever approach is chosen, there is a great need for consistency in the construction and implementation of absence management policies and procedures, not only in terms of ensuring fairness and as a support for any disciplinary action taken, but also in terms of providing employees with clear expectations about how absence will be tackled, and promoting an attendance culture. While different approaches work in different sectors and with different types of staff, there is a strong argument that the policies themselves need to be consistent in any organisation, to encourage employee acceptance and line manger support. For example Dunn and Wilkinson (2002) report the difficulties that a line manager in a production company experienced due to the fact that manufacturing staff were subject to more stringent absence procedures than other staff in the company.

Lack of consistency in implementation also weakens any policy and procedures. The role of the line manager is key and there is much emphasis on giving the line manager ownership of absence and attendance issues, with support from HR. Whatever policies and procedures are set up it is critical that the line manger feels ownership of these and applies them in practice. James and his colleagues (2002) found that two-thirds of their interviewees in a long-term absence management study noted that there were problems in the way that line managers carried out their responsibilities. Managers frequently did not follow the guidelines in matters such as ongoing contact with absent employees, and consequently HR did not know what was going on and often had to step in and manage cases. James and his colleagues found that managers' behaviour resulted from time pressures, lack of awareness of what the procedure was and lack of training.

WINDOW ON PRACTICE

Managing absence at HBOS

Mary McFadzean (2003) reports on a pilot project at HBOS which encouraged HR to look at absence from a different perspective. The project was intended to test two theories: first, that much absence had non-medical causes and therefore could be tackled by HR and, second, that absence could be reduced without buying in any extra resources.

To introduce the project workshops were held with HR members and best practice guidelines were made available, HR advisers were then encouraged to go out and talk to managers about absence. The best practice model included an emphasis on finding the underlying cause of absence in terms of social or work-related issues, based on the belief that this is the root cause of much absence, and if issues are not dealt with they will gradually produce medical symptoms. The skill was therefore in getting beyond the symptoms on the medical note to understand the underlying cause of absence. Once the underlying cause was understood then temporary or permanent changes could be made to help, such as reducing targets, hours and responsibilities or changing work patterns.

HBOS promoted an absence champion network in its first-tier approach which would adopt the best practice principles provided by HR, and would receive up-to-date information on absence and target cases for intervention (over 20 days' absence for long-term absence and four periods in a year for short-term absence). HR received consistent management information, and progress was monitored in all cases. A health provider network was also set up, as a second-tier approach (for long-term absence), to target high-risk areas and the two top causes of absence. Individuals were referred after 10 days' absence in these cases, and the health provider network included a psychologist and a physiotherapist. Treatment was considered justified if there was deemed to be an 80 per cent chance of return to work. HBOS feel that rehabilitation back into work needs to become part of the business culture.

The project was only carried out in some areas and performance was measured against control groups. HBOS saved 21,000 days over the six-month period (6,000 headcount) and £880,000. Short-term absence was reduced by 35 per cent, but there was no impact on long-term absence, which continues to creep up.

Source: Summarised from M. McFazdean (2003) 'Managing Absence' paper presented at the CIPD National Conference, Harrogate, 22–24 October 2003.

It has been found that some measures to manage absence actually increase absence, so monitoring any new policies and procedures is critical. In terms of implementing a new absence strategy, the advice given by Huczynski and Fitzpatrick (1989) still holds good. The ALIEDIM process they suggest comprises the following stages:

Assess the absence problem
Locate the absence problem
Identify and prioritise absence causes
Evaluate the current absence control methods
Design the absence control programme
Implement the absence control programme
Monitor the effectiveness of the absence control programme

The mix of policies and methods chosen will be specific to the needs of the individual organisation, and case 15.2 on the website explains the mix chosen by Newry and Mourne Police Unit in Ireland. Below are some of the most frequently used approaches to managing absence. Some are most appropriate for short-term absence, and some better suited to long-term absence, others meet the needs of both.

Accurate records

Managing absence is almost impossible without an accurate picture of current absence levels and patterns in terms of the identification of areas of high absence and the most common reasons for absence in the organisation. The CIPD (2003) found that aggregate information about sickness absence rates was collected by 84 per cent of survey respondents, but such data collection was carried out more often in the public sector and manufacturing industry than in the rest of the private sector. Prior to its review of absence Carlsberg-Tetley (IDS 2001) did not have an accurate picture of sickness absence. Although some records were kept, absence was inconsistently measured and recorded, so there was no reliable information about level of absence and patterns. This was their first task in tackling absence. They decided to adopt the 'Bradford factor' method for scoring absence where both frequency of absence spells and absence duration are used but with the weight being given to the former. The Bradford factor formula, devised by Bradford University, is shown in Figure 15.2.

Absence reports are frequently produced by HR and sent to line managers – and such reports will often include details of employees where trigger points have been hit and where intervention is required by the line manager. However, Dunn and Wilkinson (2002) found that the attention line managers gave to these reports varied, and some managers never even looked at the reports, because they did not agree that this was the best way to manage staff. As one manager commented, 'I know my staff well enough not to need these reports . . . at the end of the day it all comes down to good management and knowing your staff'. Some managers argued that the reports were of little use because the employees they managed often worked long hours (beyond contract) and came in at weekends. It was felt that to punish such employees, who were clearly committed to the company, because they had reached certain absence levels was unreasonable, and would be counter-productive.

Absence score = (spells of absence × spells of absence) × duration of absence

Figure 15.2 The Bradford factor formula for scoring absence (Note: The score is usually calculated over a year.)

Absence review and trigger points

In order to focus attention on those with less satisfactory absence records many organisations identify trigger points in terms of absence spells or length, or Bradford factor scores which indicate that action is needed when an individual's absence record hits the trigger. Such policies for reviewing absence appear to be critical in absence reduction, and the CIPD (2003) reports that 77 per cent of organisations reporting a decrease in absence levels put this down to tightened policies for reviewing absence. The HBOS Window on practice above describes the trigger points that they use. However, such trigger points may be well known to employees, and Connex (IDS 2001) found that some employees were able to manipulate the system and regularly have absence levels just below the trigger point. To overcome this some organisations have a rolling year, rather than, say, a calendar year or a financial year, against which absence levels are assessed – on the grounds that it will be much more difficult for employees to keep track of their absence levels and manipulate the system. In fact Dunn and Wilkinson (2002) found organisations where the trigger system was avoided because it was felt that it would encourage employees to take off time until they were just under the trigger limit.

Some organisations have absence review groups, such as the absence champion network at HBOS, and the safety, health and absence unit at HM Customs and Excise (IDS 2001). While the role of these groups varies, they are frequently used to review all absences and identify those who have hit trigger points which will then require intervention, such as an absence review meeting with the employee.

Absence targets and benchmarking

Many organisations have absence targets phrased in terms of a reduction on current absence levels or a lower absence level to attain. However, the CIPD (2003) found that although 90 per cent of the organisations they surveyed believed that absence levels could be reduced, only around half of these had set targets for this, and only around 50 per cent benchmarked their absence levels against other organisations. An alternative approach, used by some organisations, is to give managers absence targets for their group, and tie this into their performance review and performance payments. This is the approach used in Connex (IDS 2001). Such overall and local targets need to be carefully used, however, so as not to give the impression to employees that absence is not allowed.

ACTIVITY 15.1

We have noted that some organisations link improvements in absence levels in their departments to managers' performance assessments and performance-related pay.

What are the potential advantages of this approach?
What are the potential problems?
How else might managers be encouraged to treat absence levels as a key priority?

Training and support for line managers

Most organisations recognise that line managers play a key role in making absence procedures work and in reducing absence levels, and training is usually available when a new absence system is introduced. Connex (IDS 2001) has introduced a creative form of training. The company takes managers to an employment tribunal to view an absence-related case so that managers will understand the consequences of not dealing fairly and consistently with employees when they have to deal with similar situations at work. HM Customs and Excise (IDS 2001) uses training videos showing role plays of return to work interviews (*see* below). These demonstrate that such a meeting is not about accusation or recrimination. The idea is that managers watch the video with their team of supervisory staff and then discuss the issues that arise.

However, there is evidence that further training is needed. Both James *et al.* (2002) and Dunn and Wilkinson (2002) found managers who could not understand how 'sickness' could be managed, were scared of dealing with the situation and were embarrassed about asking personal questions about an employee's state of health.

Absence notification procedures

Many organisations specify that when employees phone in as absent they must phone themselves, rather than asking another person to phone on their behalf. Many also specify that the employee must speak to their direct line manager or nominated representative. This means that such a telephone conversation can be the first stage of the absence management process. The conversation is welfare based and the intention is that the manager is able to ask about the nature of the problem and the anticipated date of return to work. Some organisations, such as First Direct (IDS 2001), make every effort to offer alternative work. For example, a telephone operator who cannot do telephone work with a sore throat may be able to do other work, and managers are asked to bear this in mind when employees phone in sick and to try to encourage the employees to come in, where appropriate, to carry out other tasks. This telephone conversation is also seen as an important tool in reducing the length of the absence.

Better understanding of the causes of absence

Analysis of absence data can show the primary causes of absence in any particular organisation and this may help employers develop absence management methods relevant to the most frequent causes. However, as we have said, the reasons employees give for absence will be those that the organisation considers legitimate, and further investigation may be necessary.

Organisations can encourage individuals to be open about the real cause for their absence, for example a minor illness may be used as an excuse to cover for caring responsibilities, a stressful working environment or alcohol or drug problems. However, this is easier said than done. The London Borough of Brent (IRS 2002b) has decided that the next stage in its efforts to tackle long-term absence is to try to unpick the causes of such absence. The employer has a feeling that the explanation may be partly related to issues of stress and the nature and organisation of the work. Helping employees to feel they can trust the employer sufficiently to admit the real cause of absence means that absence can then effectively be tackled by providing the appropriate form of support. Another key tool is risk assessment, so, for example, some organisations will assess the risk of back pain or stress and then training can be provided to meet identified needs.

WINDOW ON PRACTICE

Risk assessments for stress

Stress accounts for a large proportion of sickness absence in the NHS, and researchers from the Institute of Work, Health and Organisations at Nottingham University studied five groups of hospital staff working under pressure: nurses, healthcare assistants, technical and professional staff, catering staff and clerical/reception staff. The aim was to measure and tackle stress at work. The intervention began with risk assessment, and a well-being questionnaire was used to gather employee feelings about tiredness and exhaustion. Employees were asked to identify not only causes of stress but also changes to management practice which would provide a solution. One of the examples provided is the catering team who identified causes as peak-time high workloads, poorly maintained equipment and inadequate training. Resultant interventions included regular equipment maintenance, additional peak-time staff and regular team briefings.

Source: Summarised from HSE (2002b) *Interventions to control stress at work in hospital staff*, HSE Contract Research Paper no. 435.

Ongoing contact during absence

Maintaining contact during absence is considered by many organisations as a method of reducing length of absence, demonstrating to the employee that the organisation is interested in them, and maintaining employee motivation. In some organisations it is the line manager who will keep in touch, and in others, such as Walter Holland and Son (IDS 2001), there are liaison officers who fulfil this role. Contact may be by telephone, and with longer periods of absence may involve home visits. The Employers Organisation for Local Government (EO) (HSE 2002a) suggests that more effort should be made to keep in touch with employees after operations, partly to keep them up to date, but also to see if it is possible for them to come back to work on light duties or on a part-time basis. In working out its policy of visits, Bracknell Forest Council (IRS 2002a) pays due attention to the requirements of the Human Rights Act 1998. The council recommends one visit per month in working hours and considers this is reasonable in terms of the need to demonstrate 'respect for private and family life', and the wish to avoid putting pressure on employees to return to work too early.

Return to work interviews and formal absence reviews

Return to work interviews are increasingly used as a key part of attendance procedures, and CIPD (2003) reports that these were used by 77 per cent of organisations in 2003 compared with 57 per cent in 2000. CIPD also reports that these interviews are regarded as the most effective way of managing short-term absence. For some organisations these interviews are mandatory, even following a single day's absence, but there is frequently some flexibility about the nature of the interview depending on the circumstances. In general the purposes of such interviews are identified as to: welcome the employee back and update them on recent events; check that the employee is well enough to resume normal duties and whether any further organisational support is needed; reinforce the fact that the employee has been missed and that attendance is a high priority in the organisation; and review the employee's absence record. Dunn and Wilkinson (2002) found managers in their research who said that there was not time to concentrate on return to work interviews, as the practicalities of getting the job done were more critical. They also found a view among line managers that they were just so glad to get the employee back that they did not want to 'rock the boat'. Where formal absence reviews are held these need to be handled with sensitivity and tact, and care needs to be taken so that the interview does not become recriminatory or accusatory.

Use of disciplinary procedures

If someone is genuinely ill and unable to work as a result, disciplinary action whether threatened or real is unlikely to bring about a return to work. It would not be desirable from the point of view of the employee or the employing organisation were this to be the case. There are, however, situations in which people who are too ill to work have to be dismissed. This is never a pleasant task, but it often falls to the HR manager to carry it out. The key is to make sure that the dismissal is carried out in a legally sound manner. This issue is covered in greater detail in Chapters 9 and 23, so it is only necessary here to summarise the main points:

1. Dismissing someone who is unable to work because of ill health is potentially fair under unfair dismissal law.
2. It is necessary to warn the individual concerned that they may be dismissed if they do not return to work and to consult with them ahead of time to establish whether a return in the foreseeable future is feasible.
3. It is necessary to act on whatever medical advice is available.
4. In larger organisations, except where a person's job is very specialised or senior, it is normally considered reasonable to refrain from dismissing a sick employee for at least six months.
5. In any case no dismissal should occur if the employee falls under the definition of 'disabled' as set out in the Disability Discrimination Act 1995. In these cases an employee should only be dismissed once the employer is wholly satisfied that no reasonable adjustments could be made to accommodate the needs of the sick employee so as to allow them to return to work.

Where someone is persistently absent for short periods of time, the course of action taken will depend on whether or not there is a genuine underlying medical condition which explains most of the absences. If so, the matter should be handled in the same way as cases of long-term absence due to ill health outlined above. If not, then it is feasible for the employer to take a tougher line and to threaten disciplinary action at an earlier stage. It is quite acceptable in law to dismiss someone whose absence record is unacceptably high, provided they have been warned ahead of time and given a fair opportunity to improve their attendance. It is also necessary to treat different employees in a consistent fashion. Taking disciplinary action in the form of issuing a formal warning is therefore credible and likely to be successful.

Absence levels and performance assessments

Some organisations have communicated to employees the message that attendance levels are a measure of their performance so they are included in annual assessments. Dunn and Wilkinson (2002) found that in the three retail companies in their case sample, employees were assessed via a separate rating category on their absence levels. In addition employees with unacceptable absence levels would not be put forward for transfers or promotion. The Metropolitan Police service considers absence records as an indication of reliability, although it does not wish to give the message that absence is not permitted (IDS 2001).

Attendance bonus and rewards

Some organisations pay bonuses direct to employees on the basis of their attendance records. For example Connex (IDS 2001) will pay a quarterly attendance bonus of £155 at the end of each 13-week period for full attendance and an additional lump sum of £515 if an employee has had no sickness absence during a full calendar year. In addition Connex sends out letters commending employees for improving their absence record. The company considers that its absence scheme is a success as 80 per cent of eligible employees now qualify for payments. However, some managers do not support attendance bonuses as they feel that employees are already paid to turn up, and they are effectively being paid twice. Connex also found managers who felt that attendance bonuses were a signal to employees that managers cannot control the work environment themselves and that they have relinquished all responsibility for managing absence. On the other hand, Dunn and Wilkinson (2002) found that managers felt attendance bonuses were unfair as they penalised those employees who were genuinely ill.

ACTIVITY 15.2

In terms of your own organisation consider the approaches by which sickness absence is minimised in terms of proactive ill-health prevention methods, discouragement of sickness absence, and encouragement of attendance:

Where is the emphasis in terms of approach?
Why do you think this is so?
Is this the most appropriate approach? Why?

To what extent are different employee groups treated differently?
Why do you think this is so?
Is this the most appropriate approach? Why?

Occupational health support and health promotion

A number of organisations carry out pre-employment screening to identify any potential health problems at this stage. Others screen employees for general fitness and for potential job hazards, such as working with radiation, or VDUs. General screening may involve heart checks, blood tests, eye tests, well-woman/man clinics, ergonomics and physiotherapy, and discussions about weight and lifestyle, such as smoking, drinking and fitness levels. The value of such screening is that problems can be identified at an early stage so that the impact on sickness absence will be minimised. In some organisations positive encouragement will be given to employees to follow healthy lifestyles, such as healthy eating, giving up smoking, taking up exercise routines.

For long-term absence the CIPD (2003) reported that the involvement of occupational health professionals was seen to be the most effective management tool, although HSE (2002c) shows that only one in seven workers has the benefit of comprehensive occupational health support. However, such support does not have to be in-house and can be purchased: this is the course followed by the London Borough of Brent (IRS 2002b).

Physiotherapists, counsellors and psychologists are often employed, and the occupational health role may include remedial fitness training and exercise therapy for those recovering from an illness. Stress counselling is increasingly being provided and if this is offered as part of an employee assistance programme can reduce the liability in stress-related personal injury cases. Also training in stress management may be offered.

James and his colleagues (2002) found that the role of occupational health was ambiguous and problematic. Their respondents suggested that while occupational health worked on behalf of the employer, they tended to see themselves as representing employee interests. They also found that employees were very sceptical about visiting occupational health workers as they saw it as the first step in the termination of their employment.

Changes to work and work organisation

Many employers appear to offer flexible working hours, part-time work and working from home. Employers also sometimes consider offering light duties or redeployment. However, James and his colleagues (2002) found that operational factors often limited what was possible. In the three manufacturing organisations they visited it was not always feasible to offer light duties or make adjustments to the workplace. They also found that other departments were reluctant to accept someone who was being redeployed after sickness, partly because they felt the employee might have lost the work habit, and also because there might be problems with pay if the levels of the old and new job differed. They also noted that might be no budget to pay for adaptations to equipment or purchase further equipment.

WINDOW ON PRACTICE

Flexible working cuts sickness absence

People Management reports that the London Borough of Merton has halved its sickness absence rate and improved productivity by introducing flexible working as part of a work-life balance pilot project. The flexible patterns of work involved a compressed working week, working from home, career breaks, job sharing and special leave including compassionate leave. Keith Davis, the Assistant Chief Executive, explained that the management style had to change from managing attendance to managing output, and significant training was required. The Council plans to roll out the scheme over the entire Council.

Source: Summarised from *People Management* (2002): 'Flexible working cuts sickness absence', *People Management*, Vol. 8, No. 1, 10 January, p. 1.

Practical support

There are many ways in which the employer can provide practical support to minimise sickness absence. Many organisations have experienced frustrations while employees are on waiting lists for diagnostic procedures and operations. In order to speed up medical treatment that employees need some organisations are prepared to pay the medical costs for employees where there is a financial case to do this. Training in areas such as stress management and time management may help employees minimise feelings of stress, and childcare support may simplify childcare arrangements.

SUMMARY PROPOSITIONS

15.1 Employee absence continues to be a major problem for both the country and business in terms of direct costs and lost performance.

15.2 The most often reported cause of short-term absence is minor illness; however, back pain for manual workers and stress for non-manual workers are the leading causes of long-term absence.

15.3 It is important to understand the true nature of the causation of absence, as remedies can only be developed with this knowledge. The causation of absence can result from a complex interrelationship of factors.

15.4 Typical attendance management policies include absence monitoring and reporting, absence review and trigger points, training and support for line managers, absence notification procedures, better understanding of the causes of absence, risk assessments, ongoing contact during absence, return to work interviews and absence review interview, use of disciplinary procedure, absence-influenced performance assessments, absence bonus and rewards, occupational health support, changes to work and work organisation, and practical support. The mix of policies and processes used needs to be tailored to the needs of the organisation.

GENERAL DISCUSSION TOPICS

1 'If we gave employees longer holidays and more flexibility in the hours that they worked it would reduce the conflict between personal responsibilities/interests and work responsibilities. This reduction in conflict would reduce unplanned absence from work.' To what extent do you agree with this statement and why?

2 To what extent do you consider that absence statistics underestimate the extent of absence in the UK, and why?

3 It could be argued that encouraging employees to engage in exercise and keep fit will improve their work motivation and sense of well-being, and that this would reduce absence. To what extent do you agree with this notion?

FURTHER READING

Evans, A. and Walters, M. (2002) *From Absence to Attendance*. London: CIPD
A thorough text which covers absence measuring and monitoring; understanding the causes of absence; absence management policies; the disciplinary and legal framework of absence management; and developing and implementing absence management strategies.

Johns, G. (2001) 'Contemporary research on absence from work: correlates, causes and consequences', in I. Robertson and C. Cooper, *Personnel Psychology and HRM*. Chichester: John Wiley and Sons Ltd
A useful chapter which provides a wide range of perspectives on understanding the nature of absence from work. Johns considers process and decision models, the withdrawal model, demographic models, the medical model, the stress model, social and cultural models, the conflict model, the deviance model and the economic model. An awareness of such a range of perspectives is useful as it provides a context against which to understand any one approach to absence.

REFERENCES

Bevan, S. (2002) 'Counting the cost of absence', *IRS Employment Review*, No. 739, pp. 46–7.

Barham, C. and Leonard, J. (2002) 'Trends and sources of data on sickness absence', *Labour Market Trends*, April, pp. 177–85.

CBI (2003) *Absence and Labour Turnover 2003. The lost billions: addressing the cost of absence*. London: Confederation of British Industry.

CIPD (2003) *Employee Absence 2003*. London: CIPD.

Dunn, C. and Wilkinson, A. (2002) 'Wish you were here: managing absence', *Personnel Review*, Vol. 31, No. 2, pp. 228–46.

HSE (2002a) *Initiative Evaluation Report: Back in Work,* HSE Research Report No. 441.

HSE (2002b) *Interventions to control stress at work in hospital staff*, HSE Contract Research Paper No. 435.

HSE (2002c) *Survey of the use of occupational health support*, HSE Research Report No. 445.

Huczynski, A.A. and Fitzpatrick, M.J. (1989) *Managing Employee Absence for a Competitive Edge*. London: Pitman.

IDS (2001) *Absence Management*, No. 702, January. London: IDS.

IRS (2002a) 'Tackling long-term absence in local government (1): Bracknell Forest Borough Council', *Employment Review*, No. 762, 21 October, pp. 42–6.

IRS (2002b) 'Tackling long-term absence (2): London Borough of Brent', *IRS Employment Review*, No. 763, 11 November, pp. 44–6.

James, P., Cunningham, I. and Dibben, P. (2002) 'Absence management and the issues of job retention and return to work', *Human Resource Management Journal*, Vol. 12, No. 2, pp. 82–94.

McFadzean, M. (2003) 'Managing Absence', paper presented at the CIPD National Conference, Hanogate, 22–24 October 2003.

Nicholson, N. (1977) 'Absence behaviour and attendance motivation: a conceptual synthesis', *Journal of Management Studies*, Vol. 14, pp. 231–52.

People Management (2002) 'Flexible working cuts sickness absence', *People Management*, Vol. 8, No. 1, 10 January, p. 13.

Roberts, Z. (2003) 'Get well sooner', *People Management*, Vol. 9, No. 7, 3 April, pp. 10–11.

Rhodes, S. and Steers, R. (1990) *Managing Employee Absenteeism*. Reading, Mass.: Addison Wesley.

An extensive range of additional materials, including multiple choice questions, answers to questions and links to useful websites can be found on the Human Resource Management Companion Website at www.pearsoned.co.uk/torrington.

INTERACTIVE SKILL 3: APPRAISAL INTERVIEWING

We open with an examination of the performance appraisal process, with particular reference to the appraisal interview. We have seen how effective performance may be that of the organisation as a complete entity, of a team within that framework or of an individual person. We have also seen the place of leadership and motivation in producing a situation where effective performance is likely. Face-to-face appraisal is crucial within the whole complex process of achieving an effective focused performance. In conversations with our colleagues, our bosses and perhaps our customers or clients, we move forward in our understanding of how we are doing. Usually it is an erratic sequence of a word here, an observation there, a complaint, an argument, an explanation of why something failed or was brilliantly successful. As we build up our understanding of who we are, where we want to be, what we want to do and how we can make progress towards whatever our goals may be, we call up and fit together the products of dozens of such inputs. There are occasional landmark conversations, which crystallise our thinking. These are most likely to be appraisal interviews, and they are landmarks because of their relative formality, their official nature and because they are dedicated solely to bringing our personal performance up to an even higher level than it is already.

The objectives of this Focus on skills are:

1 To explain the purpose and nature of the appraisal interview

2 To suggest a model sequence for conducting appraisal interviews

THE APPRAISAL INTERVIEW

The novelist, the textbook writer, the popular vocalist, the newspaper editor, the sculptor or painter, the athlete or the owner of a corner shop all have in common the fact that their performance is measurable in an absolute way by numbers. When Madonna releases an album or writes a book for children, she can see the effectiveness of her performance in the irrefutable logic of the numbers sold. When Paula Radcliffe runs a race the effectiveness of that performance is measured in the time taken. The measure of both performances can then be compared with that of competitors. There are no mitigating circumstances. The writer may feel that the publisher should have done a better job or that the reviewers were incompetent, but that has no weight compared with the inescapable fact of the numbers. The shop owner may grumble about local authority planners or about unfair competition from the local hypermarket, but that explanation will not stop customers from drifting away.

Most working people do not have that same absolute measure for their own personal performance, which is all part of a more general, corporate endeavour. Individual effectiveness is not measurable by an indicator of customer appreciation, as so many other members of the corporate body contribute to the effectiveness or ineffectiveness of any individual's activity. The inexorable logic of the marketplace or other external arena has to be replaced by internal measures, mediated by managerial judgement. This is tricky.

Appraising performance is not a precise measurement but a subjective assessment. It has a long history of being damned for its ineffectiveness at the same time as being anxiously sought by people wanting to know how they are doing. It is difficult to do, it is frequently done badly with quite serious results, but on the rare occasions when it is done well it can be invaluable for the business, and literally life transforming for the appraisee. It is probably the most demanding and skilful activity for any manager to undertake and is dreaded by both appraisers and appraisees (Carroll and Schneier 1982; Grint 1993). Recent research about appraising the performance of British school teachers found that the appraisal itself was often accompanied by long periods of sickness absence due to stress. To a great extent this centred on the difficulty of appropriate criteria, particularly where

> headteachers link capability to personal qualities such as 'open-minded and prepared to adapt and take on new skills' or 'attitude' or where generalised descriptions such as 'unable to do the job properly' or 'not meeting standards' are offered. Measurement is also inevitably imprecise when it is subjective, making the judgement difficult to substantiate and prone to challenge. This leads to the risk that the yardsticks of acceptable performance chosen are those that can best be justified rather than those that are most important. (Torrington *et al.* 2003)

A selection of comments by those taking CIPD examinations underlines the point:

1. I cannot bring myself to tell people that they are less than brilliant because I would tie myself up in knots trying to justify it. However well-designed the scheme is it all boils down to people wanting to know if they are good or better than average. If you don't tell them that, they will interpret something you said to mean what they want to hear. Otherwise they will have you for infringing their human rights or discriminating against them. (from a large retail grocery company)
2. We have had approximately one new scheme per year over the last six years. These have ranged from a blank piece of paper to multi-form exercises, complete with tick boxes and a sentence of near death if they were not complete by a specified date. (from an international motor manufacturer)
3. Our scheme is not objective and has become a meaningless ritual. It is not a system of annual appraisal; it is an annual handicap. (from a public corporation)

With reactions like this, it makes the appraisal interview sound even more suspect than the selection interview, as we saw in the Part II Focus on skills. If it is so difficult to get right, why does it survive? Why persist with something that was described in 1993 as an idea whose time had gone (Fletcher 1993)?

One might just as well ask why marriage survives despite its extensive failure and the innumerable personal tragedies it produces. Why do teachers grade students' work? Why do we all seek advice? Why do audiences applaud? Why do wives and husbands seek the views of their spouses on the prospective purchase of a new suit/dress/shirt/hat? The reason is simple: we all seek approval and confirmation that we are doing the right thing, and most of us yearn to advise or direct what other people should do.

At work these basic human drives are classified into activities including objective setting, counselling, coaching or feedback on performance. They all have in common the feature of one person meeting face to face with another for a discussion focused on the performance of only one of them. It may initially seem strange that we use the performance appraisal interview as an example of the problem-solving approach to interaction, as so much individual performance is not problematic. The point is that the interactive approach involved is *joint* in a way that is distinct from enquiry or exposition, and it is a process of jointly finding out ways in which the performance might be enhanced.

There are appraisal schemes in all areas of employment. Once installed, schemes are frequently modified or abandoned, and there is widespread management frustration about their operation. Despite the problems, the potential advantages of appraisal are so great that organisations continue to introduce them and appraisal can produce stunning results. Here is an extract from another set of examination answers:

I have had [an] annual appraisal for three years. Each time it has been a searching discussion of my objectives and my results. Each interview has set me new challenges and opened up fresh opportunities. Appraisal has given me a sense of achievement and purpose that I had never previously experienced in my working life. (from an insurance company)

CONTRASTING APPROACHES TO APPRAISAL

There are two contrasting motivations that drive the appraisal interview: the motivation of management control and the motivation of self-development. These produce appraisal systems that show a mixture of both motivations, with the control approach still being the more common, especially when there is a link with performance-related pay, but the alternative development emphasis is gaining in popularity. Describing them as polar opposites helps to illustrate the key elements.

The management control approach starts with an expression of opinion by someone 'up there', representing the view of controlling, responsible authority, saying:

> We must stimulate effective performance and develop potential, set targets to be achieved, reward above-average achievement and ensure that promotion is based on sound criteria.

Despite the specious appeal of this most reasonable aspiration, that type of initiative is almost always resisted by people acting collectively, either by representation through union machinery or through passive resistance and grudging participation. This is because people whose performance will be appraised construe the message in a way that is not usually intended by the controlling authorities, like this:

> They will put pressure on poor performers so that they improve or leave. They will also make sure that people do what they're told and we will all be vulnerable to individual managerial whim and prejudice, losing a bit more control over our individual destinies.

It is the most natural human reaction to be apprehensive about judgements that will be made about you by other people, however good their intentions.

This approach is likely to engender:

- Conflictual behaviour and attitudes within the organisation, including resistance by managers to the amount of administrative work involved in the process.
- Negotiated modifications to schemes. These are 'concessions' made to ease the apprehension of people who feel vulnerable. These frequently make the schemes ineffective.
- Tight bureaucratic controls to ensure consistency and fairness of reported judgements.
- Bland, safe statements in the appraisal process.
- Little impact on actual performance, except on that of a minority of self-assured high achievers at one extreme and disenchanted idlers at the other.
- Reduced openness, trust and initiative.

This approach works best when there are clear and specific targets for people to reach, within an organisational culture that emphasises competition. There are considerable problems, such as who sets the standards and who makes the judgements. How are the judgements, by different appraisers of different appraisees, made consistent? Despite its drawbacks, this approach is still potentially useful as a system of keeping records and providing a framework for career development that is an improvement on references and panel interviews. It is most appropriate in bureaucratic organisations. The emphasis is on form filling.

The development approach starts with the question in the mind of the individual job holder:

> I am not sure whether I am doing a good job or not. I would like to find ways of doing the job better, if I can, and I would like to clarify and improve my career prospects.

This question is addressed by job holders *to themselves*. Not: 'Am I doing what you want?' but:

> Where can I find someone to talk through with me my progress, my hopes, my fears? Who can help me come to terms with my limitations and understand my mistakes? Where can I find someone with the experience and wisdom to discuss my performance with me so that I can shape it, building on my strengths to improve the fit between what I can contribute and what the organisation needs from me?

Those in positions of authority tend to put a slightly different construction on this approach, which is something like:

> This leads to people doing what they want to do rather than what they should be doing. There is no coordination, no comparison and no satisfactory management control.

This approach to appraisal:

- Develops cooperative behaviour between appraisers and appraisees and encourages people to exercise self-discipline, accepting autonomous responsibility.
- Confronts issues, seeking to resolve problems.
- Does not work well with bureaucratic control.
- Produces searching analysis directly affecting performance.
- Requires high trust, engenders loyalty and stimulates initiative.

This approach works best with people who are professionally self-assured, so that they can generate constructive criticism in discussion with a peer; or in protégé/mentor situations, where there is high mutual respect. The emphasis is on *interviewing*, rather than on form filling. Despite the benefits of this approach, there are two problems: the first is the lack of the *systematic* reporting that is needed for attempts at management control of, and information about, the process; the second is the problem of everyone finding a paragon whom they can trust.

Frances Storr describes an approach to performance appraisal that seeks to take out almost all the formality; it includes the appraisees choosing their own appraisers and usually the feedback is face to face, with virtually no form filling:

its purpose is stated clearly: to improve performance and enable people to learn and grow. We emphasise that appraisal is as much about celebrating people's achievements, as it is about helping them to identify areas in which they can improve. Within that framework it is up to individuals to decide how they will carry out their own 360 degree appraisal. In more than 90 per cent of cases, feedback is given face to face, with people talking to their appraisers as a group. Any written material . . . belongs to the appraisee, with the result that the appraisal has become a dialogue rather than a survey. (Storr 2000, p. 39)

ACTIVITY III.1

To what extent can the benefits of both approaches be created in a single scheme? Who should conduct the appraisal interview?

Appraisal is valueless unless the general experience of it is satisfactory. Appraisees have to find some value in the appraisal process itself and see tangible outcomes in follow-up. Appraisers have to find the appraisal process not too arduous and have to see constructive responses from appraisees. When general experience of appraisal is satisfactory, it becomes an integral part of managing the organisation and modifies the management process.

Who does the appraisal?

Individuals are appraised by a variety of people, including their immediate superior, their superior's superior, a member of the HR department, themselves, their peers or their subordinates. Sometimes, assessment centres are used to carry out the appraisal.

There are, however, many problems for those carrying out the appraisal. For example:

- *Prejudice* – the appraiser may actually be prejudiced against the appraisee, or be anxious not to be prejudiced; either could distort the appraiser's judgement.
- *Insufficient knowledge of the appraisee* – appraisers often carry out appraisals because of their position in the hierarchy rather than because they have a good understanding of what the appraisee is doing.
- *The 'halo effect'* – the general likeability (or the opposite) of an appraisee can influence the assessment of the work that the appraisee is doing.
- *The problem of context* – the difficulty of distinguishing the work of appraisees from the context in which they work, especially when there is an element of comparison with other appraisees.

Problems for both the appraiser and the appraisee include:

- *The paperwork* – documentation soon gets very cumbersome in the attempts made by scheme designers to ensure consistent reporting.

ACTIVITY III.2

Think of jobs where it is difficult to disentangle the performance of the individual from the context of the work. How would you focus on the individual's performance in these situations?

- *The formality* – although appraisers are likely to try to avoid stiff formality, both participants in the interview realise that the encounter is relatively formal, with much hanging on it.

WINDOW ON PRACTICE

In 1997 the Secretary of State for Education issued guidance to schools and local education authorities about capability procedures to deal with the problem of school teachers who did not perform satisfactorily. This degree of formality for dealing with performance is very rare outside schools and produced major problems. Teachers who were 'put on procedure' found that so humiliating that they rarely improved and usually spent long periods of absence from school suffering from stress. Throughout the education system there was a preference for informal arrangements to deal with this very difficult issue.

Among the other common problems, which often cause appraisal schemes to fail, are:

- *Outcomes are ignored* – follow-up action for management to take, although agreed in the interview, fails to take place.
- *Everyone is 'just above average'* – most appraisees are looking for reassurance that all is well, and the easiest way for appraisers to deal with this is by stating or inferring that the appraiser is doing at least as well as most others, and better than a good many. It is much harder to deal with the situation of presenting someone with the opinion that they are average; who wants to be average?
- *Appraising the wrong features* – sometimes behaviours other than real work are evaluated, such as time-keeping, looking busy and being pleasant, because they are easier to see.

The appraisal interview style

The different styles of appraisal interview were succinctly described over forty years ago by the American psychologist Norman Maier (1958). His threefold classification remains the most widely adopted means of identifying the way to tackle the interview. The *problem-solving* style has been summarised as:

> The appraiser starts the interview by encouraging the employee to identify and discuss problem areas and then consider solutions. The employee therefore plays an active part in analysing problems and suggesting solutions, and the evaluation of performance emerges from the discussion at the appraisal interview, instead of being imposed by the appraiser upon the employee. (Anderson 1993, p. 102)

This is certainly the most effective style, consistent with the development approach to appraisal set out at the opening of this Focus on skills, provided that both the appraiser and appraisee have the skill and ability to handle this mode. This Focus on skills is based on this style, but it is not the only style. Maier's alternatives included, first, *tell and sell*, where the appraiser acts as judge, using the interview to tell the appraisee the result of the appraisal and how to improve. This 'ski instructor' approach can be appropriate when the appraisees have little experience and have not developed enough self-confidence to analyse their own performance. *Tell and listen*, the second alternative, still casts the appraiser in the role of judge, passing on the outcome of an appraisal that has already been completed and listening to reactions. Both of these approaches could sometimes change the assessment, as well as enabling the two people to have a reasonably frank exchange.

Pryor (1985) offers a reappraisal of Maier's three styles, particularly the usefulness of tell and sell and tell and listen. He suggests that they can be effectively adapted to the needs of appraisees with little experience who require less participation in the appraisal interview.

It is tempting to identify the problem-solving approach as 'the best', because it appears to be the most civilised and searching, but not all appraisal situations call for this style, not all appraisees are ready for it and not all appraisers normally behave in this way.

The appraisal interview sequence

Certain aspects of the appraisal interview are the same as those of the selection interview discussed in the Part II Focus on skills. There is the inescapable fact that the appraiser determines the framework of the encounter, there is a need to open in a way that develops mutual confidence as far as possible and there is the use of closed and open-ended questions, reflection and summarising. It is also a difficult meeting for the two parties to handle:

> The appraisal interview is a major problem for both appraisers and appraisees. The appraiser has to have a degree of confidence and personal authority that few managers have in their relationship with all those who they have to appraise. The most contentious aspect of many appraisal schemes is the lack of choice that appraisees have in deciding who the appraiser should be. Interview respondents regularly cite the interview as something that they dread. (Torrington 1994, p. 149)

For the appraisee there are concerns about career progress, job security, the ongoing working relationship with the appraiser and the basic anxieties relating to self-esteem and dealing with criticism.

The fundamental difference between selection and appraisal that every appraiser has to remember is that the objective is to reach an understanding that will have some impact on the future performance of the appraisee: it is not simply to formulate a judgement by collecting information, as in selection. A medical metaphor may help. A surgeon carrying out hip replacements will select patients for surgery on the basis of enquiring about their symptoms and careful consideration of the evidence. The surgeon asks the questions, makes the decision and implements that decision. A physician examining a patient who is overweight and short of breath may rapidly make the decision that the patient needs to lose weight and take more exercise. It is, however, not the physician but the patient who has to implement that decision. The physician can help with diet sheets, regular check-ups and terrifying advice; the real challenge is how to get the patient to respond.

The easy part of appraisal is sorting out the facts. The difficult bit is actually bringing about a change in performance. The interview, like the discussion in the physician's consulting rooms, is crucial in bringing about a change of attitude, fresh understanding and commitment to action.

Preparation

The appraiser should brief the appraisee on the form of the interview, possibly asking for a self-appraisal form to be completed in advance. To some extent this is establishing rapport, with the same objectives, and makes the opening of the eventual interview easier.

Asking for the self-appraisal form to be completed will only be appropriate if the scheme requires this. As we have seen, self-appraisal gives the appraisee some initiative, ensures that the discussion will be about matters which the appraisee can handle and on 'real stuff'.

The appraiser has to review all the available evidence on the appraisee's performance, including reports, records or other material regarding the period under review. Most important will be the previous appraisal and its outcomes.

Most of the points made in the Part II Focus on skills about preparing for the selection interview apply to appraisal as well, especially the setting. Several research studies (e.g. Anderson and Barnett 1987) have shown the extremely positive response of appraisees who felt that the appraiser had taken time and trouble to ensure that the setting and supportive nature of the discussion was considerate of the appraisee's needs.

Interview structure

A recommended structure for a performance appraisal interview is shown in Figure III.1. Alternative frameworks can be found in Anderson (1993, pp. 112–13) and Dainow (1988).

Rapport is unusual because it attempts to smooth the interaction between two people who probably have an easy social relationship, but now find themselves ill at ease. This is not the sort of conversation they are used to having together, so they have to find new ground-rules. The pre-interview appraisee briefing is an important step towards this, but the opening of the interview itself still needs care. The mood needs to be light, but not trivial, as the appraisee has to be encouraged towards candour rather than gamesmanship.

1	**Purpose and rapport**	Agree purpose with appraisee Agree structure for meeting Check that pre-work is done
2	**Factual review**	Review of known facts about performance in previous period. Appraiser reinforcement.
3	**Appraisee views**	Appraisee asked to comment on performance over the last year. What has gone well and what has gone less well; what could be improved; what they liked; what they disliked; possible new objectives.
4	**Appraiser views**	Appraiser adds own perspective, asks questions and disagrees, as appropriate, with what appraisee has said.
5	**Problem solving**	Discussion of any differences and how they can be resolved.
6	**Objective setting**	Agreeing what action should be taken, and by whom.

Figure III.1 Structure for a performance appraisal interview

ACTIVITY III.3

What do you think of the following openings to appraisal interviews heard recently?

(a) 'Well, here we are again. I'm sure you don't like this business any more than I do, so let's get on with it.'

(b) 'Now, there's nothing to worry about. It's quite painless and could be useful. So just relax and let me put a few questions to you.'

(c) 'I wonder if I will end up conning you more than you will succeed in conning me.'

(d) 'Right. Let battle commence!'

Factual review is reviewing aspects of the previous year's work that are unproblematic. The appraiser should begin by reviewing the main facts about the performance, without expressing opinions about them but merely summarising them as a mutual reminder. This will include the outcome of the previous appraisal. This will help to key in any later discussion by confirming such matters as how long the appraisee has been in the job, any personnel changes in the period, turnover figures, training undertaken, and so forth.

The appraiser will still be doing most, but not all, of the talking, and can isolate those aspects of performance that have been disclosed which are clearly satisfactory, mention them and comment favourably. This will develop rapport and provide the basic reassurance that the appraisee needs in order to avoid being defensive. The favourable aspects of performance will to some extent be *discovered* by the factual review process. It is important that 'the facts speak for themselves' rather than appraiser judgement being offered. Not, for instance:

> Well, I think you are getting on very well. I'm very pleased with how things are going generally.

That sort of comment made at this stage would have the appraisee waiting for 'but . . .' as the defences have not yet been dismantled. A different approach might be:

> Those figures look very good. How do they compare with . . . ? That's X per cent up on the quarter and Y per cent on the year . . . That's one of the best results in the group. You must be pleased with that . . . How on earth did you do it?

This has the advantage of the evidence being there before the eyes of both parties, with the appraiser pointing out and emphasising, and it is specific rather than general, precise rather than vague. This type of approach invariably raises the question from appraisers about what to do in a situation of poor performance. Appraising stars is easy; what about the duds? The answer is that all appraisees have some aspects of their performance on which favourable comment can be made, and the appraisal process actually identifies strengths that might have been previously obscured by the general impression of someone who is not very good. The appraiser may discover something on which to build, having previously thought the case was hopeless. If there is not some feature of the performance that can be isolated in this way, then the appraiser probably has a management or disciplinary problem that should have been tackled earlier.

The appraiser then asks for the *appraisee's views* on things that are not as good as they might be in the performance, areas of possible improvement and how these might be addressed. These will only be offered by the appraisee if there has been effective positive reinforcement in the previous stages of the interview. People can only acknowledge shortcomings about performance when they are reasonably sure of their ground. Now the appraisee is examining areas of dissatisfaction by the process of discussing them with the appraiser, with whom it is worth having the discussion, because of the appraiser's expertise, information and 'helicopter view'. There are three likely results of debating these matters:

- some will be talked out as baseless;
- some will be shown to be less worrying than they seemed when viewed only from the single perspective of the appraisee, and ways of dealing with them become apparent;
- some will be confirmed as matters needing attention.

This stage in the interview is fraught with difficulties for the manager, and is one of the reasons why an alternative style is sometimes preferred:

> some employees prefer to be told rather than invited to participate . . . the manager receives extra pay and status for making decisions, so why should the manager expect them to do his or her job as well? (Wright and Taylor 1984, p. 110)

These, however, are problems to be recognised and overcome: they are not reasons for not bothering to try.

Appraiser views can now be used in adding to the list of areas for improvement. In many instances there will be no additions to make, but usually there are improvement needs that the appraisee cannot, or will not, see. If they are put at this point in the interview, there is the best chance that they will be understood, accepted and acted upon. It is not possible to guarantee success. Demoralised collapse or bitter resentment is always a possibility, but this is the time to try, as the appraisee has developed a basis of reassurance and has come to terms with some shortcomings that he or she had already recognised.

The appraiser has to judge whether any further issues can be raised and if so, how many. None of us can cope with confronting all our shortcomings, all at the same time, and the appraiser's underlying management responsibility is to ensure that the appraisee is not made less competent by the appraisal interview. There is also a fundamental moral responsibility not to use a position of organisational power to damage the self-esteem and adjustment of another human being.

Problem solving is the process of talking out the areas for improvement that have been identified, so that the appraisee can cope with them. Underlying causes are uncovered through further discussion. Gradually huge problems come into clearer and less forbidding perspective, perhaps through being analysed and broken up into different components. Possibilities for action, by both appraiser and appraisee, become clear.

These central stages of the interview, factual exchange, appraisee views, appraiser views and problem solving, need to move in that sequence. Some may be brief, but none should be omitted and the sequence should not alter.

The final stage of the encounter is to agree what is to be done: **objective setting.** Actions need to be agreed and nailed down, so that they actually take place. One of the biggest causes of appraisal failure is with action not being taken, so the objectives set must be not only mutually acceptable, but also deliverable. It is likely that some action will be needed from the appraiser as well as some from the appraisee.

Making appraisal work

There are many reports of businesses installing an appraisal system only to find that they have to change it or completely abandon it after only a short time. Others battle on with their systems, but recognise that they are ineffective or inadequate or disliked. What can be done to encourage the system to work as effectively as possible?

Effectiveness will be greater if all involved are clear about what the system is for. The personnel manager and senior managers need to work out what they want the appraisal system to achieve and how it fits in with the other HR activities that feed into it and are fed by it, such as career planning, training and HR planning. Those who have to operate the system also have to appreciate its objectives, otherwise they are just filling in forms to satisfy the irksome HR people, as we saw at the opening of this Focus on skills. Finally, those whose performance is to be appraised will answer questions and contribute ideas with much greater constructive candour if they understand and believe in the purposes of the scheme.

It is vital that the system is visibly owned by senior and line management in the business, and that it is not something that is done for the HR department. This may mean, for example, that appraisal forms are kept and used within the department and only selected types of data are fed through to the HR function or other departments. Ideally, the form itself should be a working document used by appraiser and appraisee throughout the year.

The more 'open' the appraisal system is, that is, the more feedback appraisees are given about their appraisal ratings, the more likely appraisees are to accept rather than reject the process. Similarly, the greater the extent to which appraisees participate in the system, the greater the chance of gaining their commitment, subject to the reservation already made: not all appraisees are ready and willing to participate, and not all organisational cultures support participative processes.

The involvement of both appraisers and appraisees in the identification of appraisal criteria has already been noted. Stewart and Stewart (1977) suggest that these criteria must be:

1 Genuinely related to success or failure in the job.
2 Amenable to objective, rather than subjective judgement, and helpful if they:
   (a) are easy for the appraiser to administer;
   (b) appear fair and relevant to the appraisee;
   (c) strike a fair balance between catering for the requirements of the present job while at the same time being applicable to the wider organisation.

Appraisers need training in how to appraise and how to conduct appraisal interviews. Appraisees will also need some training if they have any significant involvement in the process. An excellent performance appraisal system is of no use at all if managers do not know how to use the system to best effect.

The appraisal system needs to be administered so that it causes as few problems as possible for both parties. Form filling should be kept to a minimum, and the time allocated for this activity should be sufficient for it to be done properly, but not so much that the task is seen as unimportant and of low priority.

Appraisal systems need to be supported by follow-up action. Work plans agreed by appraiser and appraisee need to be monitored to ensure that they actually take place, or that they are modified in accordance with changed circumstances or priorities. Training needs should be identified and plans made to meet those needs. Other development plans may involve the HR department in arranging temporary transfers or moves to another department when a vacancy arises. In order to do this, it is vital that appraisal forms are not just filed and forgotten. Peter Goodge and Philip Watts are consultants working in the field of 360-degree appraisal and one of their suggestions demonstrates the importance of follow-up:

> We suggest that organizations should spend 20 per cent of the project's budget on the assessment and 80 per cent on the subsequent development support. (Goodge and Watts 2000, p. 51)

SUMMARY PROPOSITIONS

III.1 Performance appraisal has a poor track record, but it has considerable potential, when done well.

III.2 Among the problems of appraisal are prejudice, insufficient knowledge by the appraiser of the appraisee, the halo effect, the problem of context, the paperwork, the ignoring of outcomes, appraising the wrong features and the tendency for everyone to be just above average.

III.3 Three approaches to the appraisal interview are problem solving, tell and sell and tell and listen.

III.4 Features of the interview itself are the opening for preliminary mutual assessment; factual review; appraisee views on performance; appraiser views, to add perspective; problem solving; and objective setting.

III.5 Appraisers must follow up on interviews, making sure that all agreed action (especially that by the management) takes place.

III.6 Training in appraisal is essential for appraisers and for appraisees.

GENERAL DISCUSSION TOPICS

1 'What right does he have to ask me questions about my motivation and objectives? I come here to do a job of work and then go home. What I want to do with my life is my business.' How would you react to that comment by someone who had just emerged from an appraisal interview?

2 In what situations have you seen outstanding individuals depress the performance of a team where the other people were demoralised by the dominance of that individual? How do you cope with this?

FURTHER READING

Fletcher, C. (1999) *Appraisal: routes to improved performance*. London: CIPD

Lowry, D. (2002) 'Performance management', in J. Leopold (ed.) *Human Resources in Organisations*. London: Prentice Hall
The appraisal interview has not been the subject of much research in recent years, but the above reviews provide practical suggestions.

Redman, T. and McElwee, G. (1993) 'Upward appraisal of lecturers: lessons from industry', *Education and Training*, Vol. 35, No. 2, pp. 20–5

Redman, T., Snape, E., Thompson, D. and Kaching Yan, F. (2000) 'Performance appraisal in the National Health Service', *Human Resource Management Journal*, Vol. 10, No. 1, pp. 1–16

Torrington, D.P., Earnshaw, J.M., Marchington, L. and Ritchie, M.D. (2003) *Tackling Underperformance in Teachers*. London: Routledge Falmer
Recent studies of appraisal in specific professional contexts include the above, Redman and McElwee (1993) on further education, Torrington *et al.* (2003) on schoolteaching and Redman *et al.* (2000) on the National Health Service.

WEB LINKS

The book's website contains practical exercises in appraisal interviewing. General information about aspects of performance can be found at:

www.hrmguide.co.uk/hrm/chap10
www.som.cranfield.ac.uk (the Performance Management Association)

Trade unions, some employers and most public bodies provide information about the performance management arrangement on their websites. One example of general interest is at:

www.governyourschool.co.uk

Consultancy firms provide information about their particular approach. A selection of interesting sites (without any assessment of the value of their products) is:

www.hrwigwam.co.uk
www.targetimprovement.co.uk

www.openview.hp.com/solutions
www.hse.gov.uk (the Health and Safety Executive)
www.managingabsence.org.uk (a site supported by government and industry partners)
www.statistics.gov.uk (the National Statistics site)
www.cbi.org.uk (the Confederation of British Industry)
www.leadersdirect.com (an American site of the Self Renewal Group)
www.audit-commission.gov.uk (Best Value Performance Plan Toolkit from the Audit Commission)
www.apse.org.uk (Association for Public Service Excellence)
www.performance-appraisals.org (an American business site)
www.dti.gov.uk (Department of Trade and Industry)
www.employment-studies.co.uk (the Institute of Employment Studies site)
www.acas.org.uk (Advisory, Conciliation and Arbitration Service)

REFERENCES

Anderson, G.C. (1993) *Managing Performance Appraisal Systems*. Oxford: Blackwell.

Anderson, G.C. and Barnett, J.G. (1987) 'The characteristics of effective appraisal interviews', *Personnel Review*, Vol. 16, No. 4.

Carroll, S.J. and Schneier, C.E. (1982) *Performance Appraisal and Review Systems*. Glenview, Ill.: Scott Foresman.

Dainow, S. (1988) 'Goal-oriented appraisal', *Training Officer*, January, pp. 6–8.

Fletcher, C. (1993) 'Appraisal: an idea whose time has gone?' *Personnel Management*, September, Vol. 25, No. 9, pp. 34–8.

Goodge, P. and Watts, P. (2000) 'How to Manage 360 degree feedback', *People Management*, February, pp. 50–2.

Grint, K. (1993) 'What's wrong with performance appraisals? A critique and a suggestion', *Human Resource Managemnt*, Vol. R, No. 3, pp. 61–77.

Maier, N.R.F. (1958) *The Appraisal Interview: Objectives, methods and skills*. New York: John Wiley.

Pryor, R. (1985) 'A fresh approach to performance appraisal', *Personnel Management*, June.

Stewart, V. and Stewart, A. (1977) *Practical Performance Appraisal*. Aldershot: Gower.

Storr, F. (2000) 'This is not a Circular', *People Management*, May, pp. 38–40.

Torrington, D.P. (1994) 'Sweets to the sweet: performance-related pay in Britain', *International Journal of Employment Studies*, Vol. 1, No. 2, pp. 149–64.

Torrington, D.P., Earnshaw, J.M., Marchington, L. and Ritchie, M.D. (2003) *Tackling Underperformance in Teachers*. London: Routledge Falmer.

Wright, P.L. and Taylor, D.S. (1984) *Improving Leadership Performance*. Hemel Hempstead: Prentice Hall International.

REVIEW OF PART III

In the opening chapter of Part III we included this comment from an article in *People Management* in 2001:

> more than 30 studies in the US and UK leave no room for doubt; how organizations manage and develop people has a powerful – perhaps the most powerful – effect on overall performance, including the bottom line.

This is delivering performance and it lies at the core of human resource management. Reverting to the philosophy of human resource management set out at the beginning of the book:

> Human resource management is a series of activities which: first enables working people and the organisation which uses their skills to agree about the objectives and nature of their working relationship and, second, *ensures that the agreement is fulfilled* . . .

The words in italics describe the HR role in performance management. HR people do not personally lead groups outside the HR function, nor do they manage performance directly, but they do ensure that all these activities are carried out and they have a responsibility to ensure that the activities are understood, valued and carried out as effectively as possible. If they can deliver those three requirements – that the processes are understood, valued and carried out effectively – then they make a major contribution to the bottom-line performance referred to above.

A piece of contemporary history illustrates how significant the management of performance can be. When Britain and the United States invaded Iraq in 2003 there was a great deal of speculation about Iraq's possession of weapons of mass destruction. A BBC journalist, Andrew Gilligan, claimed that a British government document on this issue had been 'sexed up' to strengthen the case for war. This allegation was denied by government ministers.

Subsequently the BBC broadcast a television programme in which another journalist, John Ware, stated that Gilligan had previously been 'hauled over the coals' by his superiors for using loose language. Andrew Gilligan was outraged about this statement that had been broadcast by John Ware without any reference to him first. He also said that the interview referred to was with his manager:

> It was a meeting to say how well I had done in Iraq and I was criticized over one matter. It was 95 per cent praise. In no sense could it be described as a hauling over the coals. (*The Times*, 22 January 2004, p. 1)

He also said that he had checked with his manager, who agreed that he had not been hauled over the coals. This whole issue became one that caused intense interest and imperilled the government, but it illustrates how important running performance management in general, and the appraisal interview in particular, is; making adverse comments about someone's performance without them having the chance to explain or rebut can lead to serious difficulties. Although we have emphasised the importance of setting critical comments in the broader context of more favourable judgements, it is always important to ensure that the criticisms are understood and accepted.

We have said earlier that conducting an appraisal interview is one of the hardest things any manager has to do. For HR specialists managing the surrounding process, the task is not so daunting, but it has to be done very thoroughly indeed.

Part III CASE STUDY PROBLEM

BAKERSFIELD UNIVERSITY

Bakersfield (new) University is in a process of change in order to promote more effective service delivery to its customers within tight budget constraints. Teaching staff have increasingly taken on higher teaching hours as the staff to student ratio has increased from 1 : 18 to 1 : 28 over the past 12 years. The decrease in staff numbers has been managed through the non-replacement of leavers and a limited level of early retirement. In addition to taking on increased teaching loads staff have been exhorted to engage themselves in commercial work and in research to a much greater extent and to complete PhDs. The staff have increasingly felt under pressure, but have on the whole been dedicated workers. Those staff who were most seriously disillusioned by the changes taking place were generally those opting for early retirement, although this process also meant that much expertise was suddenly lost to many departments.

The pressure of work seems set to increase and the goodwill and relatively high performance of staff are increasingly at risk. In the current circumstances departments have found it difficult to recognise the good work of staff by promotion, which had been the traditional approach. Many department heads have tried to deal with this by holding out the hope of future promotion and by recognition of a good job done. Some department heads were more effective in this than others.

The university as a whole has decided to put two major schemes into place in relation to staff performance: first, a staff appraisal scheme and, second, an individual performance-related pay scheme. Standard forms were produced for all departments to use and guidelines were produced relating to the purpose and frequency of appraisal. All departments conformed in terms of carrying out the appraisals, but there were great differences in how this was handled in different departments. Those heads who had experience of successful systems elsewhere, or who were enthusiastic about this change, carried out the appraisals in a more thorough and committed way, and did try to integrate them into the running of the department and link them to departmental goals. Other heads failed to do this, and some were positively against the system as they saw it as impinging on academic freedom, and in any case had never seen themselves as true managers.

The reaction of staff was mixed, often depending on their past employment experiences and length of time employed by the university. In general staff were resistant and sceptical. The culture of the university had been easygoing with staff able to 'do their own thing', and relied on to focus on work that was important for the university and to organise themselves in a conscientious manner. Those who had come to the university from industry had been attracted by the opportunity to control the nature and content of their own work. The new system was perceived as wresting control away from the individual and as an indication that they were not trusted.

There were disparate reactions to the individual performance pay scheme. Department heads were each allocated a small pot of money to distribute as they saw fit between their staff. There were only two months between the announcement of the availability of this money and the date for distribution. Some department heads announced its availability and others never mentioned it. Some made allocations based on performance appraisal results and others made a separate judgement – perhaps allocating money only to someone who was highly valued and who had threatened to leave, but who was not necessarily the best performer. Others shared the money, in different amounts, between the top three high performers and one other shared the money out equally between all staff in the department. Most heads of department allocated the money without any consultation, indeed the heads never got together to talk about the new system and how to handle it. A small number of heads quickly formed a senior staff panel to judge the allocation and one head devised a peer assessment panel.

Staff reactions were mixed. Some were pleased that at last there was potential monetary recognition for the extra effort they had put in. But those who only found out about the system after the money had been allocated to others were angry. Some of the staff who had received the money were so embarrassed about it that they kept it secret. Union representatives complained about the 'shady' process in many departments. Only three heads announced the criteria which had been used to allocate the money. There were complaints about the timescale – but this was improved by the immediate announcement in the university's newsletter of a similar pot of money being made available for the following year. Many objected on principle, though, to the idea of individual performance pay and felt that it undermined the teamwork that was necessary for the department to run effectively. A number argued that if there was to be such pay next year, it should relate directly to the performance appraisal results, and hence became more concerned that these were carried out more thoughtfully.

Staff morale was damaged by these events and the university, which is aware that it mishandled these issues, is anxious to improve matters as quickly as possible.

Required

1. What were the main problems with the approach adopted by the university authorities?
2. What options does the university have for next year? What are the advantages and disadvantages of each?
3. Which option would you recommend, and how would you implement it?

Part III EXAMINATION QUESTIONS

1 'Equal opportunities legislation is an unnecessary interference for business.' Discuss.

2 Outline the major implications of the Disability Discrimination Act 1995. Why was the Act seen as necessary?

3 What is the business case for diversity management? How strong and persuasive do you regard this case to be?

4 Present arguments for and against linking pay to an assessment of individual performance. Having done this, explain whether or not you would like to be paid in this way, and why.

5 Discuss the reasons for the relative failure of women to move into the ranks of senior management in both private and public sector organisations.

6 Why is performance appraisal a process that frequently disappoints both appraisers and appraisees? How can these problems be overcome?

7 Given the models of best practice and the problems that have emerged in training for equal opportunities in the areas of both race and gender, suggest how these might influence equal opportunities training relating to the Disability Discrimination Act 1995.

8 As an HR consultant how would you evaluate client/customer satisfaction with your organisation's performance and why is it important to do so?

PART 4

DEVELOPMENT

Having set up appropriate methods of organisation and systems to ensure performance, we now have to consider in more detail the ways in which people acquire skill and knowledge in order to develop their capacity to perform effectively.

One feature of development is the national framework within which vocational skills can be acquired. Here the individual employer relies on the provision of the education system and the arrangements of professional and other bodies, which specify the appropriate standards for vocational competence. Individuals are developed further within the business, especially in management development, where the skills and knowledge needed tend to be much more organisation specific and the methods of development are geared to the ongoing processes of the business.

Individually we are all interested in our own careers. It is now unlikely that anyone will spend more than a few years with a single employer, especially at the start of their working life, so career development is something that we take on as our responsibility rather than as solely the responsibility of our employer.

Central to all development is the teaching interaction, whether it be the instructor developing the capacity of someone else to acquire a practical skill, such as driving a car or using a keyboard, or the mentor developing a protégé's self-confidence and effectiveness in social situations.

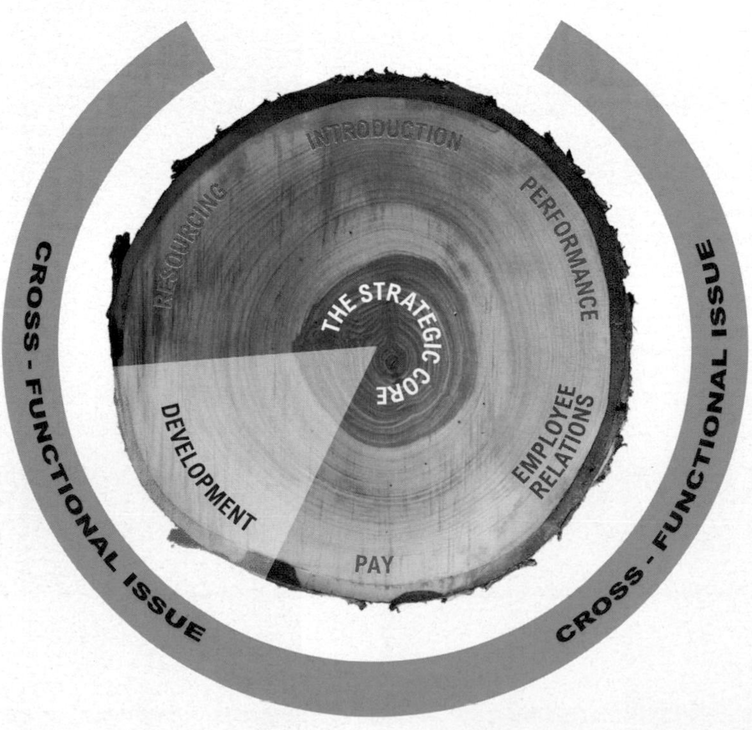

CHAPTER 16

STRATEGIC ASPECTS OF DEVELOPMENT

THE OBJECTIVES OF THIS CHAPTER ARE TO:

1. REVIEW THE ROLE OF TRAINING AND DEVELOPMENT IN THE UK
2. ANALYSE THE LINK BETWEEN BUSINESS STRATEGY AND HRD STRATEGY AND THE VARIOUS WAYS THAT THIS CAN BE PLAYED OUT
3. EXAMINE THE NEED TO ALIGN HRD STRATEGY WITH OTHER ASPECTS OF HR STRATEGY, AND THE INFLUENCE OF THE EXTERNAL LABOUR MARKET
4. EXPLORE THE RANGE OF HRD ROLES AND STAKEHOLDERS

WINDOW ON PRACTICE

First Monday of the month again – Board meeting. This was the opportunity I'd been waiting for – with some trepidation. My function had produced firm proposals on a new training and development strategy which I was to present to the Board. Development for all was the theme, with key competencies being identified at each level of the organisation and everyone being entitled to six days' off-job training per year, plus coaching on the job to meet individual development goals. A real step in the right direction at last. All I had to do was to get the Board's backing and we'd be off.

I began to present the scheme, complete with user-friendly overheads, information packs for employees and a manager guidance and support package. My colleagues listened intently, for about 5 minutes, then all hell broke loose.

'So what's going to happen to production when they're all off swanning around training – we're understaffed anyway?' – that was Gary, the Production Manager.

Brian from Marketing chipped in next: 'They'll be poached as soon as they're trained if word gets out about this – we'll be doing it for nothing'.

But worst of all was Karen, the MD: 'Why are you proposing this anyway? Granted we desperately need some skills training for those new machines and to encourage flexibility – but we didn't ask for all this. How will it improve business performance? What are we going to get out of all the money this is going to cost us?'

I had hoped more of Karen. She was usually very supportive when I came up with training proposals to solve business problems – well crises would be a better word – we did what I suggested and it usually worked.

This time my words fell on stony ground – no one was interested.

Where do we go from here??????

(Extract from the diary of Len Hodge, Human Resource Director)

ACTIVITY 16.1

Before you read on . . .

- What went wrong in the Board meeting?
- Why do you think that the Directors reacted as they did?
- What could Len have done differently to improve his chances of success?
- Where does Len go from here?

There seems to be general agreement that training and development is a good thing, and that it increases productivity, but the question is 'how much?' It is even difficult to show a causal link between HR development and organisational performance, partly because such terms are difficult to define precisely, and partly because the payoff from development may not be seen in the short term. It is also difficult to tie down performance improvements to the development itself and to understand the nature of the link. For example, is performance better because of increased or different HR development, because the reward package has improved or because we have a clearer set of organisational and individual objectives? If there is a link with HR development initiatives, is it that employees have better skills, or that they are better motivated, or that they have been selected from a more able group of candidates attracted to the organisation as it offers a high level of development?

In spite of these difficulties it is important to identify the contribution of HR development to business success, and wider measures for assessing business success, beyond the standard financial indicators, make this more feasible, as, for example, suggested by Kaplan and Norton (1992) and discussed in Chapter 10. While the search for 'evidence' goes on, the current climate encourages high levels of attention to HR development, which is increasingly seen not only as a route to achieving business strategy, but also as a means of building core competence over the longer term to promote organisational growth and sustained competitive advantage. Global competition and a fast pace of change have emphasised the importance of the human capital in the organisation, and the speed and ways in which they learn. A Green Paper produced by the Department for Education and Employment (1998) stated that 'investment in human capital will be the foundation of success in the 21st century'. Nationally the emphasis on qualifications is increasing and case 16.1 on the website focuses on the development of directors from this perspective.

In addition, levels and sophistication of training and development have received considerable attention in the context of the 'new psychological contract' and the need to promote employability, which we discuss in more detail in Chapter 19. There is some evidence that employee demand for training and development is increasing and that unions are beginning to engage in bargaining for development. Opportunities for training and development may be a vital tool in recruitment and retention, and considered to be a reward when promotion or monetary rewards are less available. However, Stewart and Tansley (2002) found significant structural and cultural barriers to formal and informal learning in organisations; in particular lack of time was identified as an issue.

THE NATIONAL PICTURE

Employee development has traditionally been seen as a cost rather than an investment in the UK, although this is certainly changing in some organisations. It has been argued that UK organisations give little support to training and development compared with our European partners (*see*, for example, Handy 1988; Constable and McCormick 1987). This lack of investment in training and development has been identified as a major factor in Britain's economic performance, and it has been argued that without such investment we will be trapped in a low wage, low skills economy (Rainbird 1994). Our national training framework is voluntarist, with the government's role limited to *encouraging* training rather than intervening, as in many other countries.

More recently it has been argued, however, that it is not a lack of investment in training that is the problem but the way such investment is distributed, that is, who it is spent on and the content of the training. It is generally agreed that training spend is unevenly distributed. For example Stevens (2001) argues that it is the people at the lower end of the hierarchy that miss out on training, and Westwood (2001) reports that:

> Access to workforce development is unequal with managers and professionals or those with a degree up to five times more likely to receive work based training than people with no qualification and/or unskilled jobs. (p. 19)

Thomson (2001) explains that broader development is concentrated on those at the beginning of their careers and those in more senior and specialist posts, rather than part-timers and those with fewer qualifications to begin with. In the aerospace and pharmaceuticals businesses, defined as high skills sectors, Lloyd (2002) found a conflict of interests between employees' desire for training and development and managerial short-term aims, lack of accreditation of skills, structured development focused on key employees, access to training being dependent on individual initiative, senior managers viewing training as a minor issue to be dealt with by lower-level managers and insufficient resources. She suggests that there was under-investment and lack of support for flexibility and employability. Westwood (2001) concludes that while we do not do as much training as in Europe, we do spend a lot of money on training that doesn't last very long and on the people who may not need it. In terms of training content there is evidence to suggest that much training is related to induction and particularly health and safety, and it has been argued that this does nothing to drive the development of a knowledge-based economy (*see*, for example, Westwood 2001).

Some view the solution to this problem as increasing state intervention, as many view voluntarism as having a limited effect (*see*, for example, Sloman 2001). It is argued that potential intervention would not mean a return to the levy system, but, for example, statutory rights for paid study leave and employer tax credits. Currently Employer Training Pilots (ETPs) are being experimented with. These reward employers with state funding for giving employees time off for training, and the scheme is being expanded.

However, there is another school of thought that suggests the problem lies with the demand side of the equation rather than the supply side. In other words the problem is not with government initiatives and measures to encourage training, development and learning but with the way that skills are used and jobs are constructed, and hence the employer demand for training, development and learning. In speaking of the Learning and Skills Councils (LSCs), Stevens (2002) says that he is less concerned with what the LSCs can do to encourage learning than with 'whether the UK can generate enough jobs for people who have learnt and can learn' (p. 44). The National Skills Strategy and Delivery Plan advocated a more demand-led system of learning and more help from employers. Lloyd (2002) suggests that the country cannot solve its problems just by developing skills, as it is critical to change the structure of jobs.

> All this suggests that we still have a situation in which the majority of organizations are using a reactive strategy: training only in response to the immediate short-term demands of the business, rather than being considered a strategic issue. (Ashton 2003, p. 23)

ORGANISATIONAL STRATEGY AND HR DEVELOPMENT STRATEGY

For training and development to be effective in terms of business success there is a well-rehearsed argument that it should be linked up front with business strategy. McClelland's research (1994) is one of many studies that show that organisations generally do not consider development issues to be part of their competitive strategy formulation, although he found that those that do so identified it to be of value in gaining as well as maintaining competitive advantage. Miller (1991), writing specifically of management development, points to a lack of fit between business strategy and development activity. Pettigrew and others (1988) did find, though, that development issues receive a higher priority when they are linked to organisational needs and take a more strategic approach. Miller makes the point that although at the organisational level it is difficult to identify quantitatively the direct impact of strategic investment in development, this impact is well supported by anecdotal evidence and easily demonstrated at the macro-level.

Those organisations that do consider HR development at a strategic level usually see it as a key to *implementing* business strategy in a reactive way. Luoma (2000) categorises this approach as a 'needs driven' approach, where the purpose of the HR development strategy is to identify and remedy skill deficiencies in relation to the organisational strategy. Luoma suggests that in many articles this is 'implicitly referred to as the only way of managing strategic HRD'. Miller, for example, has demonstrated how management development can be aligned with the strategic positioning of the firm, and this can be seen as coming within the broad remit of such approaches as a needs-driven approach. He has produced a matrix demonstrating how development content and processes can reflect stable growth, unstable growth, unstable decline and competitive positions, as shown in Table 16.1. He offers the model as suggestive, only, of the 'possibilities in designing strategically-oriented management development programmes'.

Luoma (2000), however, identifies a second approach to HR development strategy which is an 'opportunistic approach', where the impetus is external rather than internal. This would include applying leading ideas on development to the organisation in a more general way, rather than specifically in relation to meeting the current business objectives. Such ideas may be developed from benchmarking, case studies, networking and the academic and practitioner press. Such ideas could include content and method, for example the development of a corporate university, and the concept of developing non-employees who perhaps work for suppliers or who are contracted to the organisation. The abilities thus developed may indeed be relevant in achieving business objectives, but they may also be relevant in developing abilities and behaviours which may be the source of future competitiveness. Thus they may also be a means of achieving culture change and/or facilitating the strategy process itself by constructing it as a learning process. In this approach the learning potential of all employees will be emphasised, and the HR development strategy may meet reactive needs in implementation of business strategy, but may also be proactive in influencing the formation of future business strategy.

The third approach to the strategy link suggested by Luoma is based on the concept, which we discussed in Chapter 2, of organisational capability as the key to sustained competitive advantage, the resource-based view of the firm. This approach is proactive in that it focuses on the desired state of the organisation as defined in its

Table 16.1 Linking management development to strategic situations

	Environment condition			
	Stable	Unstable growth	Unstable decline	Competitive
Content	Environment scanning skills Understanding sources of stability (e.g. geographically isolated product market, state of technology) Defence strategies Industrial relations skills (but depends on source of stability)	Environment scanning skills Industry analysis skills Sales, marketing Financial control Creative thinking Team building Organisation structure skills Forecasting techniques	Stakeholder relations Executive retention skills Understanding competitor environment Negotiating skills Diversification skills (technology, human resources)	Competitive strategy development Competitor analysis Marketing/cost control (dependent on competitive strategy) Industry analysis (dependent on competitive strategy)
Process	Slow pace but 'eventful' Modest emphasis on individual development Non-competitive but 'aggressive' Reactive	Fast-moving High pressure Intense Team-oriented Proactive	Medium pace Co-operative environment Reactive	High pressure Competitive

Source: P. Miller (1991) 'A strategic look at management development', *Personnel Management*, August, p. 47. Reproduced with permission of the author.

future vision. Within this would come the interest in anticipatory learning, which has been attracting some interest, where future needs are predicated and development takes place in advance. The *Journal of Management Education and Development* (1994) devoted an entire issue to anticipatory learning, which included some ideas on how it might be identified and achieved.

ACTIVITY 16.2

How can future development needs, say five years out, be anticipated?

With a group of colleagues/students, brainstorm future needs for your own organisation, or the university/college which you attend.

Of paramount importance, therefore, is the ability to learn. Watkins (1987) suggests that development for strategic *capability*, rather than just targeting development on achieving business objectives, needs to reinforce an entrepreneurial and innovative culture in which learning is part of everyday work. He identifies the importance of acting successfully in novel and unpredictable circumstances and that employees acquire a 'habit of learning, the skills and learning and the desire to learn'. Within this same perspective Mayo (2000) suggests that intangible assets of the organisation are increasing in proportion to the value of tangible assets. He recognises that developing intellectual capital may be an 'act of faith', or one of budgetary allocation, and suggests that the most useful measures to track such investments are individual capability, individual motivation, the organisational climate and work-group effectiveness.

While he recognises the value of competency frameworks in respect of individual development he does point out that these neglect such features as experience and the networks and range of personal contacts, both of which are key to the development of core organisational competencies which are key to developing uniqueness.

In a slightly different but compatible approach McCracken and Wallace (2000) develop a redefinition of strategic HR development, based on an initial conception by Garavan (1991). They suggest nine characteristics of a strategic approach to HR development, which are that:

- HR development shapes the organisation's mission and goals, as well as having a role in strategy implementation.
- Top management are leaders rather than just supporters of HR development.
- Senior management, and not just HR development professionals, are involved in environmental scanning in relation to HR development.
- HR development strategies, policies and plans are developed, which relate to both the present and future direction of the organisation, and the top management team are involved in this.
- Line managers are not only committed and involved in HR development, but involved as strategic partners.
- There is strategic integration with other aspects of HRM.
- Trainers not only have an expanded role, including facilitation and acting as organisational change consultants, but also lead as well as facilitate change.
- HRD professionals have a role in influencing the organisational culture.
- There is an emphasis on future-oriented cost effectiveness and results, in terms of evaluation of HR development activity.

They suggest that each of these aspects needs to be interrelated in an open system. In the following sections we will address some of these characteristics in more detail.

THE EXTERNAL LABOUR MARKET AND HR STRATEGIC INTEGRATION

The external availability of individuals with the skills and competencies required by the organisation will also have an impact on employee development strategy. If skilled individuals are plentiful, the organisation has the choice of whether, and to what extent it wishes, to develop staff internally. If skilled individuals are in short supply, then internal development invariably becomes a priority. Predicting demographic and social changes is critical in identifying the extent of internal development required and also who will be available to be developed. In-depth analysis may challenge traditionally held assumptions about who will be developed, how and to what extent. For example, the predicted shortage of younger age groups in the labour market, coupled with a shortage of specific skills, may result in a strategy to develop older rather than younger recruits. This poses potential problems about the need to develop older workers some of whom may learn more slowly. What is the best form of development programme for employees with a very varied base of skills and experiences? Another critical issue is that of redeployment of potentially redundant staff and their development to provide skills that are in short supply.

Prediction of skills availability is critical, as for some jobs the training required will take years rather than months. Realising in January that the skills required in August by the organisation will not be available in the labour market is too late if the development needed takes three years!

The external labour market clearly has a big impact on employee development strategy, so it is important that there is effective integration between HR development strategy, other aspects of human resource strategy and overall organisational strategy.

Where there is a choice between recruiting required skills or developing them internally, given a strategic approach, the decision will reflect on the positioning of the organisation and its strategy. In Chapter 4 we looked at this balance in some depth and you may find it helpful to re-read this. A further issue is that of ensuring a consistency between the skills criteria used for recruitment and development.

From a slightly different perspective, the impact of the organisation's development strategy on recruitment and retention, either explicit or implicit, is often underestimated. There is increasing evidence to show that employees and potential employees are more interested in development opportunities, especially structured ones, than in improvements in financial rewards. Development activity can drive motivation and commitment, and can be used in a strategic way to contribute towards these. For these ends, publishing and marketing the strategy is key, as well as ensuring that the rhetoric is backed up by action. There is also the tricky question of access to and eligibility for development. If it is offered only very selectively, it can have the reverse of the intended impact.

However, not all employees see the need for, or the value of, development and this means that reward systems need to be supportive of the development strategy. If we want employees to learn new skills and become multiskilled, it is skills development we need to reward rather than the job that is currently done. If we wish employees to gain vocational qualifications, we need to reflect this in our recruitment criteria and reward systems. Harrison (1993) notes that these links are not very strong in most organisations.

Other forms of reward, for example promotions and career moves, also need to reflect the development strategy; for example, in providing appropriate, matrix, career pathways if the strategy is to encourage a multifunctional, creative perspective in the development of future general management. Not only do the pathways have to be available, they also have to be used, and this means encouraging current managers to use them for their staff. In Chapter 19 we explore such career issues more fully.

Finally, an organisation needs to reinforce the skills and competencies it wishes to develop by appraising *those* skills and competencies rather than something else. Developmentally based appraisal systems can clearly be of particular value here. Mabey and Iles (1993) note that a strategic approach to development differs from a tactical one in that a consistent approach to assessment and development is identified with a common skills language and skills criteria attached to overall business objectives. They also note the importance of a decreasing emphasis on subjective assessment. To this end many organisations have introduced a series of development centres, similar to the assessment centres discussed in Chapter 7, but with a clear outcome of individual development plans for each participant related to their current levels of competence and potential career moves, and key competencies required by the business.

TRAINING AND DEVELOPMENT ROLES

Salaman and Mabey (1995) identify a range of stakeholders in strategic training and development, each of which will have different interests in, influence over and ownership of training and development activities and outcomes. They identify senior managers as the *sponsors* of training and development, who will be influenced by professional, personal and political agendas; and business planners as the *clients* who are concerned about customers, competitors and shareholders. Third, they identify *line managers* who are responsible for performance, coaching and resources; and fourth, *participants* who are influenced by their career aspirations and other non-work parts of their lives. HRM staff are identified as *facilitators* who are concerned with best practice, budget credibility and other HR strategy. Lastly, training specialists are identified as *providers*, who are influenced by external networks, professional expertise and educational perspectives. The agendas of each of these groups will overlap on some issues and conflict on others. We have already noted how McCracken and Wallace (2000) have redefined the roles of top managers, line managers and HR professionals so that they are all more proactively involved in HRD strategy.

Most organisational examples suggest that the formation of training and development strategy is not something that should be 'owned' by the HR/HRD function. The strategy needs to be owned and worked on by the whole organisation, with the HR/HRD function acting in the roles of specialist/expert and co-ordinator. The function may also play a key role in translating that strategy into action steps. The actions themselves may be carried out by line management, the HR/HRD function or outside consultants. Stewart and Tansley (2002) suggest that the immediate and medium-term contribution of HRD professionals should focus on developing the competence and motivation of managers to manage learning and development. They confirm that such professionals need to act as facilitators and not instructors, and have a focus on the process and design of development rather than its content.

Involvement from line management in the delivery of the training and development strategy can have a range of advantages. Top management have a key role in introducing and promoting strategic developments to staff, for example, creating an organisation-wide competency identification programme; setting up a system of development centres or introducing a development-based organisational performance management system. Only if management carry out this role can employees see and believe that there is a commitment from the top. At other levels line managers can be trained as trainers, assessors and advisers in delivering the strategy. This is a mechanism not only for getting them involved, but also for tailoring the strategy to meet the real and different needs of different functions and departments.

External consultants may be used at any stage. They may add to the strategy development process, but there is always the worry that their contribution comes down to an offering of their ready-packaged solution, with a bit of tailoring here and there, rather than something which really meets the needs of the organisation. It is useful to have an outside perspective, but there is an art in defining the role of that outside contribution.

In delivery, external consultants may make a valuable contribution where a large number of courses have to be run over a short period. The disadvantages are that they can never really understand all the organisational issues, and that they may be seen as someone from outside imposing a new process on the organisation.

WINDOW ON PRACTICE

One large organisation had a well-established training function and on an annual basis they sat down to plan the year ahead. They would plan how many of what types of course would be needed, depending on the demand in the previous year and the availability of appropriate staff. New courses would be introduced where a need had been identified and were piloted. Course evaluation data (collected mainly from participants, but sometimes from their managers) were used to inform course demand and course structure and content.

Individuals were booked on training courses following discussion with their manager regarding their individual needs. There were often problems resulting from long waiting lists and individuals being nominated for courses for which they were not eligible (defined by the nature of their job) – it appeared that individuals sometimes nominated themselves and the manager rubber-stamped this.

Some years later, after efforts on the part of general management and training and development management to employ a more strategic approach to the business, the picture was very different. Performance management had been introduced as the cornerstone of people management, resulting from a multifunctional, high-level working party. A course was devised and delivered in chunks of one and two days and this was delivered to *all* staff, with slightly differing versions for managers and non-managers. The course was an integrating mechanism for all people management activities and most importantly it promoted a cohesive *style and philosophy* of people management that the organisation felt was critical in the achievement of its business objectives. Not only was senior general management involved in the initial stages of the course, but key line managers were involved in delivering the subsequent modules.

WINDOW ON PRACTICE

Holden and Livian (1992) compared some strategic aspects of training across 10 European countries.*

Training as a recruitment strategy

All 10 countries identified training as being used in recruitment strategy. In eight (not including Germany and Sweden) training for new recruits was seen as the most popular method (from a list of 11) of attracting recruits.

Knowledge of investment in training

Although all organisations had increased expenditure on training over the previous year, many were unclear about the actual money spent as a proportion of wages.

* The countries surveyed were Switzerland, Denmark, Germany, Spain, Finland, Italy, Norway, Netherlands, Sweden and the UK.

However, this varied by country. The three highest – Sweden (44 per cent of organisations did not know), Denmark (42 per cent of organisations did not know) and the UK (38 per cent of organisations did not know) – compare markedly with the lowest, France, where only 2 per cent of organisations did not know. This no doubt reflects the French taxation system, where a tax is levied if the organisation does *not* spend 1.2 per cent of the paybill on training.

Actual investment in training

In only Sweden and France do more than a quarter of the organisations surveyed spend above 4 per cent of the paybill on training. With the exception of France, the majority of organisations in each of the other countries spent less than 2 per cent of their paybill on training.

Time spent on training

Only some 10 per cent of organisations provided over 10 days' training per year – the exception to this being Spain, where 29 per cent of organisations provided this level of training. In all countries the amount of time for managerial training was greater than for other groups of employees.

Source: Summarised from L. Holden and Y. Livian (1992) 'Does strategic training policy exist? Some evidence from ten European countries', *Personnel Review*, Vol. 21, No. 1, pp. 12–23.

Website case 16.2 focuses on the changing roles of training and development specialists.

SUMMARY PROPOSITIONS

16.1 There is currently a voluntarist approach to training and development in the UK, which means that employers make their own choices about the extent to which they train. The government attempts to influence what organisations do by a range of supply-side initiatives.

16.2 HR development strategy needs to focus on the organisation's strategy and objectives and involves identifying the skills and competencies required to achieve this, now and in the future. HR development strategy may also be opportunistic and proactive and influence the development of organisational strategy.

16.3 It is important that HR development strategy is reinforced by, and reinforces, other HR strategy, and the context of the external labour market will be an influencing factor in how these strategies are framed.

16.4 The HR/HRD function does not own HR development strategy – it must be owned by the organisation as a whole.

GENERAL DISCUSSION TOPICS

1 Both the UK as a whole and organisations themselves would benefit if the government adopted an interventionist approach to training.
- Do you agree or disagree? Why?
- How might this intervention be shaped?

2 What opportunities are there for development strategy and reward strategy to be mutually supportive?
Think of examples (real or potential) where reward strategies undermine development strategies.

FURTHER READING

Grieves, J. (2003) *Strategic Human Resource Development*. London: Sage Publications
A thoughtful approach to strategic human resource development which considers its roots in organisational development and which rises above the level of training programmes. The book presents an ethical approach to change management and reviews the role of culture, the consultancy relationship and strategic HRD interventions.

Wright, P. and Geroy, G. (2001) 'Changing the mindset: the training myth and the need for world-class performance', *International Journal of Human Resource Management*, Vol. 12, No. 4, pp. 586–600
An interesting paper which challenges the link between training and productivity. The paper argues that training is used instead of addressing the problems of poor management, job design and physical aspects of the job. The authors argue that training is often not applied due to cultural barriers and too narrowly focused on current jobs. They suggest that training should be more broadly based on developing capability and that the training function needs to reinvent itself and have a broader-based approach rather than concentrating on skills development.

REFERENCES

Ashton, D. (2003) 'Training Trends: Past, Present and Future', in CIPD (ed.) *Reflections: New Developments in Training*. London: CIPD.

Constable, R. and McCormick, R.J. (1987) *The Making of British Managers*. London: BIM.

Department for Education and Employment (1998) *The LEARNING Age: A Renaissance for a New Britain*, Green Paper, Cm. 3790. London: HMSO.

Garavan, T. (1991) 'Strategic Human Resource Development', *Journal of European Industrial Training*, Vol. 11, No. 9, pp. 17–30.

Handy, C. (1988) *Making Managers*. London: Pitman.

Harrison, R. (1993) *Human Resource Management: Issues and Strategies*. Wokingham: Addison Wesley.

Holden, L. and Livian, Y. (1992) 'Does strategic training policy exist? Some evidence from ten European countries', *Personnel Review*, Vol. 21, No. 1, pp. 12–23.

Journal of Management Education and Development (1994) 'Anticipatory learning: learning for the twenty-first century', Vol. 12, No. 6.

Kaplan, R. and Norton, D. (1992) 'The balanced scorecard – measures that drive performance', *Harvard Business Review*, January–February, pp. 71–9.

Lloyd, C. (2002) 'Training and development deficiencies in "high skill" sectors', *Human Resource Management Journal*, Vol. 12, No. 2, pp. 64–81.

Luoma, M. (2000) 'Investigating the link between strategy and HRD', *Personnel Review*, Vol. 29, No. 6.

Mabey, C. and Iles, P. (1993) 'Development practices: succession planning and new manager development', *Human Resource Management Journal*, Vol. 3, No. 4.

McClelland, S. (1994) 'Gaining competitive advantage through strategic management development', *Journal of Management Development*, Vol. 13, No. 5, pp. 4–13.

McCracken, M. and Wallace, M. (2000) 'Towards a Redefinition of Strategic HRD', *Journal of European Industrial Training*, Vol. 24, No. 5, pp. 281–90.

Mayo, A. (2000) 'The role of development in the growth of intellectual capital', *Personnel Review*, Vol. 29, No. 4.

Miller, P. (1991) 'A strategic look at management development', *Personnel Management*, August, pp. 46–9.

Pettigrew, A.M., Sparrow, P. and Hendry, C. (1988) 'The forces that trigger training', *Personnel Management*, Vol. 20, No. 12, pp. 28–32.

Rainbird, H. (1994) 'Continuing training', in K. Sisson (ed.) *Personnel Management in Britain*. Oxford: Blackwell.

Salaman, G. and Mabey, C. (1995) *Strategic Human Resource Management*. Oxford: Blackwell Business.

Sloman, M. (2001) 'Sharing the power of learning', in CIPD (ed.) *The Future of Learning for Work*. London: CIPD.

Stevens, J. (2001) 'Training from the top down', *People Management*, Vol. 7, No. 11, 31 May, p. 53.

Stevens, J. (2002) 'Balancing Act', *People Management*, Vol. 8, No. 25, 26 December, p. 44.

Stewart, J. and Tansley, C. (2002) *Training in the Knowledge Economy*. London: CIPD.

Thomson, A. (2001) 'Too much apple pie', *People Management*, Vol. 7, No. 9, 3 May, p. 49.

Watkins, J. (1987) 'Management development policy in a fast-changing environment: the case of a public sector service organisation', *Management Education and Development*, Vol. 18, Pt 3, pp. 181–93.

Westwood, A. (2001) 'Drawing a line – who is going to train our workforce?' in CIPD (ed.) *The Future of Learning for Work*. London: CIPD.

An extensive range of additional materials, including multiple choice questions, answers to questions and links to useful websites can be found on the Human Resource Management Companion Website at **www.pearsoned.co.uk/torrington.**

CHAPTER 17

CONTEXT, COMPETENCE AND COMPETENCIES

THE OBJECTIVES OF THIS CHAPTER ARE TO:

1. INTRODUCE KEY ASPECTS OF THE NATIONAL TRAINING FRAMEWORK
2. REVIEW THE COMPETENCE MOVEMENT AND THE SHIFT FROM KNOWLEDGE TO SKILLS
3. IDENTIFY THE CHARACTERISTICS OF NVQS AND ANALYSE THEIR STRENGTHS AND WEAKNESSES
4. IDENTIFY THE CHARACTERISTICS OF BEHAVIOURAL COMPETENCIES AND ANALYSE THEIR STRENGTHS AND WEAKNESSES

The words competence, competency and competencies pervade much of the HRM literature, and it is argued that they provide a sound basis for the integration of HRM activities. The terms however are often used confusingly, so we will start with some definitions. The word 'competence' (plural 'competences') relates to the ability to carry out a specific task, and it is this interpretation of competence that forms the foundation for National Vocational Qualifications (NVQs), which could be described as job standards. The concept is therefore output, or performance based. In contrast the word 'competency' and its plural 'competencies' refer to behaviour (*see*, for example, Whiddett and Hollyforde 1999, p. 5) rather than task achievement, and there is general agreement that this concept is based on the work of Boyatzis (1982). There is a third definition, with which we are not concerned in this chapter, and that is the core competence of the organisation, which relates to the foundation for competitive advantage.

NATIONAL TRAINING FRAMEWORK

We referred in the last chapter to government initiatives intended to encourage the extent and nature of employer training and development in order to narrow the skills gap, and improve British industrial performance. NVQs are a key plank in this and there is therefore a political momentum behind the competency movement over and above considerations of education and training. It has been heavily promoted by the Training and Enterprise Directorate, latterly, and now by the Learning and Skills Council and the Department for Education and Employment. In this section we briefly review three government initiatives which have particular relevance for NVQs, before turning directly to competence and NVQs.

Investors in People (IiP)

As government initiatives go IiP has had a long-lasting impact since being introduced in 1991, but the more recent version is less prescriptive and has more emphasis on outcomes rather than the process by which the business achieves IiP recognition. There are four principles: commitment, planning, action and evaluation, and there are 12 criteria in total set against the four principles. Organisations go through a range of internal processes in order to meet the standard and provide evidence to be assessed by IiP UK, which may or may not result in accreditation. The intent of these processes is to ensure that the appropriate training and development policies and procedures exist to meet business goals, and more generally to promote a culture where this linkage is a key part of the way the organisation operates. The initial targets set for the number of employers seeking and achieving the IiP recognised status are proving to have been very ambitious, but Ruth Spellman, the Chief Executive of Investors in People UK, reports that by April 2002 25,000 organisations met the standard which represents a quarter of the UK workforce (Spellman 2002). She notes that if additional organisations that have already registered their commitment to IiP achieve the standard, this will rise to over one-third of the working population.

A commitment to IiP requires significant time and effort, particularly in relation to the processes involved in development. The benefits from gaining recognition of IiP status have been debated. Some studies have found an increase in commitment to HR development, a belief in the value of the process and perceived performance gains (*see*, for example, Alberga *et al.* 1997); other studies have found significant benefits, although organisations themselves found it difficult to identify these (Down and Smith 1998). There is a tendency in the IiP process to focus on formal qualifications, such as NVQs, and for the significance of informal development to be neglected (*see*, for example, Ram 2000). Some studies show that organisations struggle with the bureaucracy of the approach, and Ram also found considerable evidence that the standard is sought for its 'stamp of approval' rather than because of a genuine commitment to improving training and Down and Smith also argue convincingly that it is those organisations that have most to gain from pursuing the standard that are least likely to attempt to do this. In a study of a hospital trust Grugulis and Bevitt (2002) found that most of the soft HR initiatives employed had existed before accreditation. Hammond (2001) reports research carried out by Hoque, who found that a substantial minority of accredited workplaces did not adopt best practice. Although he also found that training is generally better in accredited organisations, they were still characterised by a lack of training opportunities and a deep cynicism.

Sector Skills Councils (SSCs)

SCCs have taken over from the old National Training Organisations (NTOs) and they are generally amalgamations of the olds NTOs covering a wider range of sectors and drawing in more employers. The SSCs have to apply to be licensed by the Sector Skills Development Agency (SSDA) before they can operate, and 15 had been licensed by the end of 2003, covering over half the UK workforce, and it is estimated that by the end of 2004 85 per cent of the workforce should be covered by SSCs (*see* Merrick 2003). Like the old NTOs, SSCs are empowered to set occupational standards (on which NVQs are based); promote training which will help to reduce skills shortages; and lobby on behalf of employers.

Learning and Skills Councils (LSCs)

As a result of the 1999 White Paper *Learning to Succeed* the LSCs have replaced the old Training and Education Councils (TECs). They are responsible for planning and funding all post-16 education and training, except for the university sector. The LSC has produced a national workforce development strategy in response to three key objectives (*see* Sanderson 2002): to stimulate demand from employers and individuals for education and training; to improve the responsiveness and flexibility of providers better to meet business needs; and to provide better labour market intelligence. However, evidence suggests that employers are not able clearly to differentiate LSCs from TECs (CIPD 2003). The same survey reports that most employers contact LSCs about qualifications, such as NVQs.

THE CONTEXT OF THE COMPETENCE MOVEMENT

There has always been a tension in education and training between what the trainee knows and what the trainee can do after the training is complete. Knowledge has an ancient history of being highly desirable and jealously guarded: look at the trouble the serpent got Eve into in the Garden of Eden. Our literature and our folklore are full of the value of knowledge, including the best-known aphorism in this area, that expressed by Francis Bacon four hundred years ago, that knowledge itself is power. This connection to power and influence is why access to knowledge is often surrounded by elaborate ritual requirements to ensure that possession of the knowledge remains valuable and rare.

In every country of the world education has been developed, with all its mystique and influence, to communicate knowledge and to develop understanding. In developing countries it is usually the first priority of economic growth. For all people the search for better understanding is a human quality that is self-perpetuating once the appetite has first been stimulated.

WINDOW ON PRACTICE

Many people love studying, but in some places it seems to have become a public nuisance. In a shopping mall on Orchard Road in Singapore a café proprietor concerned about the popularity of the establishment with students has a large notice: 'NO STUDYING IN THE CAFE.'

The search for knowledge also develops a prestige for certain types of knowledge and for the institutions that trade in that knowledge. In Britain and France the areas with the greatest prestige have been those that are closest to the arts and pondering the human condition: English, history, classical civilisation and language, philosophy and theology, followed by those allied to elite professions, such as medicine and the law. Science took longer to achieve a similar prestige and it is still physics and chemistry that are valued ahead of engineering. Knowledge rather than practical skills carries status, and the educational institutions with the highest prestige are those universities with the strongest representation in these areas.

This preference for knowledge has carried through into the labour market. We still pay more to people who manipulate words than to those who manipulate materials. Reading the news on television pays much more than making the world's most advanced aircraft or electronic equipment. Writing computer programs for arcade games pays much more than making the equipment on which the games run. It has become very difficult to recruit able students to study physics at university, and it is a bitter frustration for their teachers that many of them will move, on graduation, to merchant banking or accountancy.

Elsewhere it is different. The inevitable comparison is with Germany and Japan, countries where the practical skills of engineering, for instance, carry much greater prestige. This comparison has increasingly led policy makers and those in education to seek ways to shift the emphasis in education away from esoteric knowledge towards practical, vocational skills. This has proved remarkably difficult, as education is a large vested interest in any advanced society and change is resisted, however inevitable it may be. In the last sixty years there have been the moves to set up technical schools in the late 1940s, which failed almost completely. We have had technological universities, many of which became universities much like any other. We had degrees in technology that were designated as BSc, to show that they were not real degrees at all. We had the industrial training boards in the 1960s, rapidly followed by polytechnics in the 1970s, but the training boards were abolished and the polytechnics developed degrees in social sciences more rapidly than in vocational science and engineering.

By the early 1980s government policy achieved an unprecedented degree of centralised control of schooling through the national curriculum and of higher education through controlling student numbers and having differential fee regimes. Central to this control has been a heightened emphasis on practical vocational skills: what the student is able to do that is vocationally useful when the training is complete. The end result should be that the student is competent to do something that is useful. Furthermore, the education and training agenda has been placed under greater employer influence than previously. It is difficult to see that this has produced the desired results.

ACTIVITY 17.1

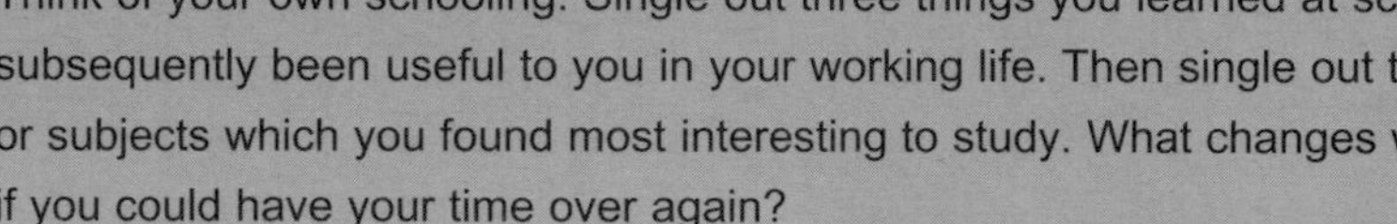

Think of your own schooling. Single out three things you learned at school that have subsequently been useful to you in your working life. Then single out the three topics or subjects which you found most interesting to study. What changes would you make if you could have your time over again?

COMPETENCES AND NVQS

Characteristics and benefits of NVQs

The vehicle for this attempted revolution has been an array of National Vocational Qualifications (NVQs), which have brought together a wide and unstructured range of previous vocational qualifications. Now vocational qualifications either are completed directly by the NVQ competence route itself, or, if they are of a different nature, will be identified as equivalent to a specific NVQ level. NVQs have been developed for all occupational areas, and within each occupation there are five levels of NVQ with level one relating to basic and routine work and level five relating to the most complex tasks. There are standards for the management occupation at levels three, four and five.

The basic idea of training for competence is that it should be criterion related, directed at developing the ability of trainees to perform specific tasks directly related to the job they are in or for which they are preparing, expressed in terms of performance outcomes and specific indicators. It is a reaction against the confetti-scattering approach to training as being a good thing in its own right, concerned with the general education of people dealing with general matters. The design of the standards themselves is somewhat complex. Each standard is first divided into job roles. For example in the updated (1997) level three management standards, seven job roles are identified, as shown in Table 17.1. This is a development on the four job roles which were in the original standard. The key roles are then subdivided into units of competence, which are then subdivided into elements of competence with attached performance criteria and range statements.

Table 17.1 Level three management standards

Key roles	
22	To manage activities
23	To manage resources
24	To manage people
25	To manage information
26	To manage energy
27	To manage quality
28	To manage projects

In the United Kingdom, competence standards have been developed in line with other aspects of change in education, such as experiential learning, problem-based learning, the national curriculum and GCSEs, as an attempt to develop the ability of learners to *do* rather than to *know*. This introduces greater flexibility into the learning process, so that career aspirants are not restrained by the elitist exclusiveness of either educational institutions or professional associations. The standards are designed so that the vast majority of work can be done 'on the job' with maybe small inputs from educational providers. Where this route is not possible the standards can be completed as part of a 'course'. Wherever they are done the individual's completed portfolio of work has to be assessed by a qualified and accredited assessor.

The principles of competencies leading to national vocational qualifications are:

1. **Open access.** There should be no artificial barriers to training, such as that it is available only to people who are members of a professional body, such as the Chartered Institute of Personnel and Development or the Law Society, or those in a particular age group. There are no previous qualifications required in order to embark on the NVQ process.
2. There is a focus on what people can **do**, rather than on the process of learning. Master's-degree students in a university typically cannot graduate in less than 12 months. With competence-based qualifications, you graduate when you can demonstrate competence, however long or short a period it takes you to achieve the standard.
3. **National** vocational qualifications, which are the same wherever the training takes place, so that the control is in the hands of the awarding body rather than the training body, and there is only one strand of qualification for each vocational area: no multiplication of rival qualifications. The overall control is with the National Council for Vocational Qualifications (NCVQ).
4. The feature of performance **standards** as the basis of assessment; not essays or written-up case studies, but practical demonstrations in working situations, or replicas, of an ability to do the job at a specified standard. Although training schemes are littered with euphoria about excellence, the competence basis has only one standard. The only degree of differentiation between trainees is the length of time taken to complete the qualification.

5 **Flexibility and modularisation.** People must be able to transfer their learning more or less at will between 'providers', so that they are not tied to a single institution or by needless regulations about attendance. Candidates can stop and start their work towards the standard as it suits their personal or work needs, and they can begin on any element of the standard and complete the elements in any order. This means that standards can be worked on in line with business demands.

6 **Accreditation of prior experience and learning.** You can accredit prior learning, no matter how you acquired it. If you have been able to acquire a competence by straightforward experience or practice at home, and if you can reach the performance standard, you can receive the credit for it. If prior experience enables you to demonstrate competence, you can receive credit for that as well.

7 The approach to training is the establishment of a **learning contract** between the provider and the trainee, whereby the initiative lies with the trainee to specify the assistance and facilities that are needed and the provider agrees to provide them. The idea of this is that the learner is active in committing to the learning process.

8 Flexibility in assessment is partly achieved by the **portfolio** principle, as you accumulate evidence of your competence from your regular, day-to-day working and submit it for assessment as appropriate. For further details of how technology can be used to enhance portfolio compilation, *see* case 17.1 on the website.

9 **Continuous development.** Initial qualification is not enough. Updating and competence extension will be needed and failure to do this will lead to loss of qualification.

10 The standards to be achieved are determined by designated **lead bodies**, which are large committees of practitioners, or professional bodies, so that vocational standards are decided by those in charge of the workplace instead of by those in charge of the classroom.

11 **Assessment.** Written examinations are not regarded as being always the most appropriate means of assessing competence. Assessment of whether or not the learner has attained the appropriate standard must be by a **qualified assessor**, who becomes qualified by demonstrating competence according to two units of the scheme produced by the Training and Development Lead Body. Assessment may be partly by portfolio (*see* 8 above), but has to be **work based.** Originally it was to be in the workplace, but that proved impracticable to implement in every case.

12 **General National Vocational Qualifications** (**GNVQs**) are school or college based and take the place of BTec and similar qualifications.

The general intention is that NVQs should run alongside traditional academic qualifications at undergraduate level.

The standards have strong support from some quarters as we have already stated, but there have been fewer reports of the benefits of pursuing the standards. Winterton and Winterton (1999) report that organisations adopting the management standards have been able to identify gaps in competence, identify competence development targets, develop a coherent structure for training and development and identify clearer criteria for human resource planning and career progression. In our own studies, again in relation to the management standards, it was found that participants developed self-confidence in their managerial role, became better organised and were motivated to focus on improvement (Hall and Holman 1996). Most critically, we found that following the standards was a rite of passage for those who were new to the managerial world (Holman and Hall 1996).

Problematic aspects of NVQs

NVQs have had a rough ride since the concept was first introduced, coming under some heavy criticism and not being extensively taken up. The most common reservations about NVQs are:

1. **Assessment.** The emphasis has been shifted away from learning towards assessment. The assessment process is itself somewhat laborious. Research by the Institute of Manpower Studies (1994) found that the most common problem about introducing NVQs was finding the time to organise the assessments. The study found that 5 per cent of employers were using NVQs and half of them reported this difficulty. In our own studies (Hall and Holman 1996) we found that candidates were heavily engaged in a 'paper chase' to gather evidence of their competence, and this seemed to take over from the importance of the learning process and what was being learned.
2. **Bureaucracy.** NVQs have developed an entire vocabulary to bring the concept into action, and this causes difficulties (*see*, for example, Priddley and Williams 2000). One of the key terms is 'range indicators' and at a meeting of 50 HR practitioners, no one could produce a definition that the rest of the group could accept. Also the assessment process specifies a number of different standards of performance that have to be demonstrated and assessed. Each of these has to be described succinctly and the performance measured.
3. **The generality of the standards.** Those employers who take up NVQs are likely to modify them for their own use. In a three-year research project at UMIST over twenty employer schemes for the management standards were examined, and each one was tailored to the needs of the particular business. This is for two reasons: (a) the national standards are seen as being too general, and (b) employers are concerned to train for their own needs rather than for national needs of skilled human resources. This begins to undermine the concept of a *national* qualification.
4. **The quality of the standards.** It is very difficult to ensure a satisfactory quality of assessment, where so much depends on a large number of individual assessors. The initial emphatic opposition to written examination has lessened, especially as NVQs are contemplated for some of the well-established professions, such as medicine and the law.
5. In relation to the management standards in particular there is a criticism that the standards are **reductionist**. In other words, because the standards try to spell out the detail of what management entails, the complexity of management gets lost as it is difficult to specify this in the structure and language of the standards.
6. A related criticism is that the **functional** approach (*see*, for example, Stewart and Hamblin 1992), used to identify what management is (that is, through specifying management activities), is a narrow and partial approach.

7 The early management standards were also criticised for being an **incomplete** representation of management, and yet in our research we found that those following the pre-1997 standard had not recognised any omissions, for example ethics and politics.

8 **Lack of attention to learning and cognitive processes** has also been identified (for example by Holman and Thorpe 1993), as the emphasis is on doing rather than thinking and understanding.

9 It has also been argued that following the standards rubber-stamps the level of competence already achieved, rather than stimulating further development.

10 **The training agenda.** Within a large vested interest such as British higher education, there is obviously some resistance to the idea that educators are not competent to set the training agenda.

> There seems to be a drift towards a training agenda in management education, such that students are technically equipped to take up a task but intellectually incapable of addressing the ideas that have shaped the creation of that task. (Berry 1990)

One quite damning piece of research has been produced by Peter Robinson of the London School of Economics. He demonstrates that the actual take-up of NVQs is very low and has not been associated with an increase in the training available to individuals:

> Between 1991 and 1995 the only net growth in the number of all vocational qualifications awarded was at level 1 and especially level 2. There was no growth at all in the number of awards at level 3, and a slight fall in the number of awards at levels 4 and 5. (Robinson 1996, p. 4)

Since they were introduced in 1987 there have been over 4 million NVQ/SVQ (Scottish Vocational Qualifications) awards made. However, in 2001/2 there was a 5 per cent drop in the number of all vocational qualifications awarded: 408,000 were awarded in this period compared with 428,000 in 200/1 (DfEE 2003). This drop is a continuing trend, with, for example 442,000 awards in 1998/9 (DfEE 2000). Awards of traditional vocational qualifications continue to outstrip NVQs, especially at higher levels. There were 474,000 vocational awards (or 499,000 if awards made outside the national framework are included) in 2001/2. However, these awards also appear to be falling at present.

NVQs are heavily concentrated in skilled trades occupations (23 per cent of awards in 2001/2), personal and protective services (20 per cent), and clerical and secretarial (18 per cent). The only other area where they have made an impact is in management and administration (DfEE 2000).

The initial failure of NVQs to take off stimulated a high-level review of the whole process; for example the management standards were redesigned in 1997 to make them more flexible, easy to understand and up to date (Whittaker 1998).

ACTIVITY 17.2

Interview at least three people who have followed the NVQ standards. They may be employees of your organisation, but this is not essential, so friends and family can be included. Ask your interviewees:

1 What were the most positive aspects of following the standards, and why?
2 What were the problematic aspects of following the standards, and why?
3 How might these negative aspects be overcome?

BEHAVIOURAL COMPETENCIES

Characteristics of behavioural competencies

The key piece of research on competencies is by Richard Boyatzis, who carried out a large-scale intensive study of 2,000 managers, holding 41 different jobs in 12 organisations. He defines a competency as: 'an underlying characteristic of a person which results in effective and/or superior performance in a job' (Boyatzis 1982, p. 21).

Competency may be a trait, which is a characteristic or quality that a person has, such as efficacy, which is the trait of believing you are in control of your future and fate. When you encounter a problem, you then take an initiative to resolve the problem, rather than wait for someone else to do it.

Competency may be a motive, which is a drive or thought related to a particular goal, such as achievement, which is a need to improve and compete against a standard of excellence.

Competency may be a skill, which is the ability to demonstrate a sequence of behaviour that is functionally related to attaining a performance goal. Being able to tune and diagnose faults in a car engine is a skill, because it requires the ability to identify a sequence of actions, which will accomplish a specific objective. It also involves being able to identify potential obstacles and sources of help in overcoming them. The skill can be applied to a range of different situations. The ability to change the sparking plugs is an ability only to perform that action.

Competency may be a person's self-image, which is the understanding we have of ourselves and an assessment of where we stand in the context of values held by others in our environment. For example: 'I am creative and innovative. I am expressive and I care about others.' In a job requiring routine work and self-discipline, that might modify to: 'I am creative and innovative. I am too expressive. I care about others and lack a degree of self-discipline.'

Competency may be a person's social role, which is a perception of the social norms and behaviours that are acceptable and the behaviours that the person then adopts in order to fit in. It may be a body of knowledge.

If these are the elements of competency, some of them can be developed, some can be modified and some can be measured, but not all.

Boyatzis makes a further distinction of the threshold competency, which is: 'A person's generic knowledge, motive, trait, self-image, social role, or skill which is essential to performing a job, but is not causally related to superior job performance', such

Table 17.2 The seven threshold competencies identified by Richard Boyatzis

Threshold competencies	
Use of unilateral power	Using forms of influence to obtain compliance.
Accurate self-assessment	Having a realistic or grounded view of oneself, seeing personal strengths and weaknesses and knowing one's limitations.
Positive regard	Having a basic belief in others; that people are good; being optimistic and causing others to feel valued.
Spontaneity	Being able to express oneself freely or easily, sometimes making quick or snap decisions.
Logical thought	Placing events in causal sequence; being orderly and systematic.
Specialised knowledge	Having usable facts, theories, frameworks or models.
Developing others	Helping others to do their jobs, adopting the role of coach and using feedback skills in facilitating self-development of others.

Source: R. Boyatzis (1982) *The Competent Manager*. New York: John Wiley.

as being able to speak the native tongue of one's subordinates. Table 17.2 summarises these elements.

Competencies are required for superior performance and are grouped in clusters, shown in Table 17.3. The goal and action management cluster relates to the requirement to make things happen towards a goal or consistent with a plan. The leadership cluster relates to activating people by communicating goals, plans and rationale and stimulating interest and involvement. The human resource management cluster relates to managing the coordination of groups of people working together towards the organisation's goals. The focus on others cluster relates to maturity and taking a balanced view of events and people. The directing subordinates cluster relates to providing subordinates with information on performance, interpreting what the information means to the subordinates, and placing positive or negative values on the interpretation.

The Boyatzis framework is set out at some length because of its influence. It is the basis of the work carried out by many consultants in the training field. It has, however, suffered criticism. Academics were sceptical about the methods of investigation, and practitioners found the framework too complex to translate into action. Boyatzis may be slipping into history, but his work remains an invaluable point of reference because of the way it demonstrates the scale and complexity of the management job. Subsequently tailor-made competency frameworks have come thick and fast from the training and development specialists (*see*, for example, Brewis 1996), and most large companies have produced such a framework. Most frameworks have clusters of competencies, like the Boyatzis model, and within each of the competencies within the cluster a list of behavioural indicators is usually attached. *See* Figure 17.1 for an example. Website case 17.2 concentrates on Goleman's emotional intelligence competencies which we discussed in Chapter 14 on leadership.

Advantages of behavioural competencies

Behavioural competencies are often seen as a way of expressing what is valued by the organisation as well as what characteristics have been seen to result in superior

Table 17.3 The five clusters of management competencies by Richard Boyatzis (1982)

Management competency clusters	
The goal and action management cluster	*Concern with impact*: Being concerned with symbols of power to have impact on others, concerned about status and reputation. *Diagnostic use of concepts*: Identifying and recognising patterns from an assortment of information, by bringing a concept to the situation and attempting to interpret events through that concept. *Efficiency orientation*: Being concerned to do something better. *Proactivity*: Having a disposition towards taking action to achieve something.
The leadership cluster	*Conceptualisation*: Developing a concept that describes a pattern or structure perceived in a set of facts: the concept emerges from the information. *Self-confidence*: Having decisiveness or presence; knowing what you are doing and feeling you are doing it well. *Use of oral presentations*: Making effective verbal presentations in situations ranging from one to one to several hundred people (plus threshold competency of logical thought).
The human resource management cluster	*Use of socialised power*: Using forms of influence to build alliances, networks, coalitions and teams. *Managing group process*: Stimulating others to work effectively in group settings (plus threshold competencies of accurate self-assessment and positive regard).
The focus on others cluster	*Perceptual objectivity*: Being able to be relatively objective, avoiding bias or prejudice. *Self-control*: Being able to inhibit personal needs or desires in service of organisational needs. *Stamina and adaptability*: Being able to sustain long hours of work and have the flexibility and orientation to adapt to changes in life and the organisational environment.
The directing subordinates cluster	*Threshold competencies* of developing others, spontaneity and use of unilateral power.

Source: R. Boyatzis (1982) *The Competent Manager*. New York: John Wiley.

performance. In addition they are seen to provide a critical mechanism for the integration of human resource practices which is considered essential to a strategic approach to HR. Thus, once a competency framework has been researched and designed it can be used in recruitment, selection, training, performance management and reward. In this way employees are given consistent messages about what is valued and what is expected of them. However, in practice this link is often weak; for example Abraham and his colleagues (2001) found organisations willing to identify a set of managerial competencies that described a successful manager, but did not place a corresponding emphasis on including these competencies in their performance appraisal. A further advantage of competency frameworks is that, as they can be expressed as behaviours, they are more easily measurable, and thus can be used explicitly in all HR processes. This means, for example, that in a development centre, assessors can be trained in how to observe a long list of behaviours. In the centre itself each assessor can then check the behaviours of the candidates under observation to record how many times that particular behaviour is displayed.

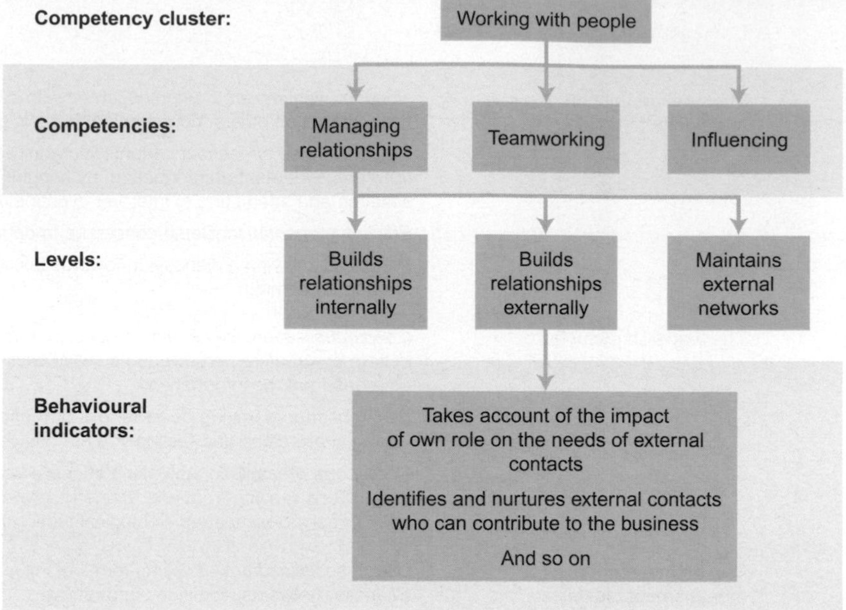

Figure 17.1 Typical content of a competency framework (Source: This material is adapted from *The Competencies Handbook* by S. Whiddett and S. Hollyforde (1999), p. 14, with the permission of the Chartered Institute of Personnel and Development, CIPD House, Camp Road, London, SW19 4UX.)

Problematic aspects of behavioural competencies

Criticisms of the approach have been focused around the complex process required to research the appropriate competencies for the organisation, and perhaps more importantly, the fact that such competencies, due to the research process itself, will be inevitably backward looking rather than future oriented. Antonacopoulou and FitzGerald (1996), for example, found that competency work focused on what managers do now rather than what is needed to perform effectively in the future. Hayes *et al.* (2000) also note that a competency framework may not include every aspect that is critical to superior performance, and also that while one set of competencies may result in high performance this does not necessarily mean that such performance may not be achieved via a different set of competencies. Whiddett and Kandola (2000) similarly argue that processes *solely* based on competencies are flawed and that a wider perspective needs to be taken. Without the wider perspective the scope for encouraging and using diversity may be diminished. In terms of performance management they also highlight that changes in behaviour may be due to factors other than competencies, and this, of course, has implications for development. A similar perspective is taken by Brittain and Ryder (1999) who suggest that organisations need to take into account the fact that a person's behaviour is not necessarily consistent, and may be affected by the environment and the situation. Salaman and Taylor (2002) suggest that there are five inherent weaknesses where organisations limit themselves to a behavioural competency approach for managers including: marginalisation of the cultural, social and organisational context, the fact that such frameworks emphasise a narrow set of behaviours and attitudes with a lack of emphasis on the long-term processes of management development, and that competencies are founded on the questionable assumption that managers behave rationally and are achievement driven.

SUMMARY PROPOSITIONS

17.1 Investors in People, Sector Skills Councils and Learning and Skills Councils are aspects of the national training framework which encourage the competence movement and NVQs.

17.2 Competence (plural: competences) is concerned with job standards and output, whereas competency (plural: competencies) refers to behaviour, that is, input.

17.3 The most recent attempt to strengthen vocational training has been the development of competence-based (or competency-based) qualifications, which are directed at developing the ability of trainees to perform specific tasks directly related to the work they are doing or which they are preparing to do. The main vehicle for learning to achieve competence is the array of National Vocational Qualifications (NVQs).

17.4 Ever since they were initially proposed, NVQs have been continually criticised, mainly because of queries about assessment, bureaucracy, generality and the quality of the standards.

17.5 Behavioural competencies are applauded as an integrative mechanism for HR processes. Problems with behavioural competencies are that they are backward, not forward looking, and are limiting and misleading if they are used alone.

GENERAL DISCUSSION TOPICS

1 The Boyatzis approach to competency-based management training has been criticised as being too complicated. To what extent do you agree and why?

2 In 1996 a review of NVQs included the following comment:

> A widely-held view was that NVQs/SVQs worked best when they were focused on the workplace and that they were less suitable for those preparing to enter employment . . . for unemployed people or those in employment seeking new job opportunities, there was difficulty in accessing workplace assessment.

How could that difficulty be overcome?

3 What are the differences between skill, competence and competency?

FURTHER READING

Harrison, R. (2002) *Learning and Development*. London: CIPD
Chapter 2, 'National Policy and framework', is an excellent overview of the government's vision for national vocational education and training, and its implementation. The chapter explains the development of the current approach and also addresses emerging concerns.

Smith, A., Boocock, G., Loan-Clarke, J. and Whittaker, J. (2001) 'IIP and SMEs: awareness, benefits and barriers', *Personnel Review*, Vol. 31, No. 1, pp. 62–85
The bureaucracy that has to be dealt with to achieve IiP status and the time that needs to be devoted to this has been viewed as a barrier for small and medium-sized enterprises (SMEs) and this article considers the significance of IiP to the SME sector. A quantitative and qualitative study was undertaken which addressed the levels of awareness, interest in and commitment to IiP; triggers for IiP commitment; inhibitors to IiP and the benefits of IiP.

REFERENCES

Abraham, S., Karns, L., Shaw, K. and Mena, M. (2001) 'Managerial competencies and the managerial performance appraisal process', *Journal of Management Development*, Vol. 20, No. 10, pp. 842–52.

Alberga, T., Tyson, S. and Parsons, D. (1997) 'An evaluation of the Investors in People Standard', *Human Resource Management Journal*, Vol. 7, No. 2, pp. 47–60.

Antonacopoulou, E. and FitzGerald, L. (1996) 'Reframing competency in management development', *Human Resource Management Journal*, Vol. 6, No. 1, pp. 27–48.

Berry, A.J. (1990) 'Masters or subjects?' *British Academy of Management Newsletter*, No. 5, February.

Boyatzis, R.E. (1982) *The Competent Manager*. New York: John Wiley.

Brewis, J. (1996) 'The "making" of the "competent" manager: Competency development, personal effectiveness and Foucault', *Management Learning*, Vol. 27, No. 1, pp. 65–86.

Brittain, S. and Ryder, P. (1999) 'Get complex', *People Management*, 25 November, pp. 48–51.

CIPD (2003) *Training and Development 2003*. London: CIPD.

DfEE (2000) *Vocational Qualifications in the UK 1998/9*, Statistical Bulletin No. 05/00. London: HMSO.

DfEE (2003) *Vocational Qualifications in the UK 2001/02*, Statistical Bulletin No. 02/03. London: HMSO.

Down, S. and Smith, D. (1998) 'It pays to be nice to people – Investors in People: the search for measurable benefits', *Personnel Review*, Vol. 27, No. 2.

Grugulis, I. and Bevitt, S. (2002) 'The impact of Investors in People: a case study of a hospital trust', *Human Resource Management Journal*, Vol. 12, No. 3, pp. 44–60.

Hall, L. and Holman, D. (1996) 'A competent experience?' *Organisations and People*, Vol. 3, No. 1, pp. 9–14.

Hammond, D. (2001) 'IIP companies "fail to implement best practice" ', *People Management*, Vol. 7, No. 8, 19 April, p. 6.

Hayes, J., Rose-Quirie, A. and Allinson, C. (2000) 'Senior managers' perceptions of the competencies they require for effective performance: implications for training and development', *Personnel Review*, Vol. 29, No. 1.

Holman, D. and Hall, L. (1996) 'The rites and wrongs of competence', *British Journal of Management*, Vol. 7, No. 2, pp. 191–202.

Holman, D. and Thorpe, R. (1993) 'MCI Management Competencies', paper presented at the Conference of the British Academy of Management, September 1993.

Institute of Manpower Studies (1994) *National and Scottish Vocational Qualifications: Early indications of employers' take-up and use*. Poole, Dorset: BEBC.

Merrick, N. (2003) 'Happy Returns?' *People Management*, Vol. 9, No. 5, 6 March, pp. 16–17.

Priddley, L. and Williams, S. (2000) 'Cognitive styles: enhancing the developmental component in National Vocational Qualifications', *Personnel Review*, Vol. 29, Issue 2.

Ram, M. (2000) 'Investors in People in small firms: Case study evidence from the businesses services sector', *Personnel Review*, Vol. 29, No. 1.

Robinson, P. (1996) *Rhetoric and Reality: Britain's new vocational qualifications*. London: London School of Economics, Centre for Economic Performance.

Salaman, G. and Taylor, S. (2002) 'Competency's consequences – changing the character of managerial work', paper presented at the ESRC *Critical Management Studies Seminar: Managerial Work*, The Judge Institute of Management, Cambridge.

Sanderson, B. (2002) 'The grand plan', *People Management*, Vol. 8, No. 22, 7 November, p. 51.

Spellman, R. (2002) 'Raising the standard', *People Management*, Vol. 8, No. 8, 18 April, p. 23.

Stewart, J. and Hamblin, B. (1992) 'Competence-based qualifications: the case for established methodologies', *Journal of European Industrial Training*, Vol. 16, No. 10, pp. 91–6.

Whiddett, S. and Hollyforde, S. (1999) *The Competencies Handbook*. London: IPD.

Whiddett, S. and Kandola, B. (2000) 'Fit for the job?' *People Management*, 25 May, pp. 30–4.

Whittaker, J. (1998) 'Pass notes', *People Management*, October, pp. 36–40.

Winterton, J. and Winterton, R. (1999) *Developing Managerial Competence*. London: Routledge.

An extensive range of additional materials, including multiple choice questions, answers to questions and links to useful websites can be found on the Human Resource Management Companion Website at **www.pearsoned.co.uk/torrington.**

CHAPTER 18

LEARNING AND DEVELOPMENT

THE OBJECTIVES OF THIS CHAPTER ARE TO:

1 EXPLORE FOUR PERSPECTIVES ON THE NATURE OF LEARNING AND CONSIDER THE IMPLICATIONS THAT EACH HAS FOR DEVELOPMENT PROVISION AND SUPPORT

2 REVIEW SOME OF THE PRACTICAL CHARACTERISTICS OF LEARNING AND DEVELOPMENT

3 EXPLAIN THE VARIOUS METHODS OF ADDRESSING LEARNING AND DEVELOPMENT NEEDS

4 INVESTIGATE THE NATURE OF EVALUATION IN THIS CONTEXT

There has been a considerable shift in the way that individual development is understood and characterised. We have moved from identifying training needs to identifying learning needs, the implication being that development is owned by the learner with the need rather than by the trainer seeking to satisfy that need. This also has implications for who identifies the needs and the way that those needs are met. Current thinking suggests that needs are best developed by a partnership between the individual and the organisation, and that the methods of meeting these needs are not limited only to formal courses, but to a wide range of on-the-job development methods and distance/e-learning approaches. There has also been a shift in the type of skills that are the focus of development activity. Hallier and Butts (1999) for example identify a change from an interest in technical skills to the development of personal skills, self-management and attitudes. Lastly, while the focus on development for the current job remains high, there is greater pressure for development which is also future oriented. These shifts reflect the changes that we have already discussed in terms of global competition, fast and continuous change and the need for individuals to develop their employability in an increasingly uncertain world.

THE NATURE OF LEARNING

For the purpose of this text we consider the result of learning to be changed or new behaviour resulting from new or reinterpreted knowledge that has been derived from an external or internal experience. There are broadly four theoretical approaches or perspectives to understanding the nature of learning, and the training and development that organisations carry out reflect the explicit or implicit acceptance of one or more perspectives. We will look at each perspective, in the evolutionary order in which they became important. There is no right or wrong theory – each has strengths and weaknesses.

The **behaviourist** perspective is the earliest which, reflecting the label, concentrates on changes in observable behaviour. Experiments with animals formed the foundation of this theory, for example the work of Skinner, Watson and Pavlov. Researchers sought to associate rewards with certain behaviours in order to increase the display of that behaviour. The relevance of this for organisations today may be seen for example in telesales training where employees are taught to follow a script and calls are listened to, to ensure that the script is followed. Reward or punishment follows depending on behaviour. Trainers are not interested in what is going on in the heads of employees, they merely want them to follow the routine to be learned. This approach has also been used for a range of interpersonal skills training. One American company, for example plays video sequences to trainees portraying the 'correct' way to carry out, say, a return to work interview. Trainees then practise copying what they have seen and are given cue cards to use when carrying out that particular interpersonal event. The problems with the perspective are that it is overtly manipulative, simplistic and limited. It may produce only temporary changes in behaviour and increase cynicism.

Cognitive approaches are based on an information-processing perspective and are more concerned with what goes on in the learner's head. This is a more technical perspective and maps out the stages of learning such as: expectancy to learn (motivation); attention and perception required; experience is coded (meaning is derived); meaning is stored in long-term memory; meaning is retrieved when needed; learning is applied; feedback is received (which may supply reinforcement). The strengths of this perspective are that it stresses the importance of learner motivation and individual needs, it recognises that the individual has some control over what is learned and it identifies feedback as an important aspect of learning. The weaknesses are that it assumes learning is neutral and unproblematic and it is a purely rational approach that ignores emotion. From this perspective useful development activities would be seen as formal courses offering models and ideas with lots of back-up paperwork. Activities to improve learning motivation are also important, for example helping employees to recognise their own development needs and providing rewards for skills development. Mechanisms for providing feedback to employees are also key.

The third perspective is based on **social learning theory**, in other words learning is a social activity and this is based on our needs as humans to fit in with others. In organisations this happens to some extent naturally as we learn to fit in with things such as dress codes, behaviour in meetings and so on. Fitting in means that we can be accepted as successful in the organisation, but it is not necessary that we internalise and believe in these codes. Organisations use often role models, mentors and peer support, and 'buddies', to intensify our natural will to fit in. The disadvantages of this perspective are that it ignores the role of choice for the individual and it is based, to some extent, on a masquerade.

The **constructivist** perspective is a development of the information-processing perspective, but does not regard learning as a neutral process: it is our perception of our experiences that count; there is no 'objective' view. This perspective accepts that in our dealings with the world we create 'meaning structures' in our heads and these are based on our past experiences and personality. New information and potential learning need to fit with these meaning structures in some way, which means that a similar new experience will be understood differently by different people. We tend to pay attention to things which fit with our meaning structures and ignore or avoid things that don't fit. As humans we are also capable of constructing and reconstructing our meaning structures without any new experiences. These meaning structures are mainly unconscious and therefore we are not aware of the structures which constrain our learning. We are generally unaware of how valid our meanings sets are, and they are deeply held and difficult to change. Making these structures explicit enables us to challenge them and to start to change them. This perspective recognises that learning is a very personal and potentially threatening process. We develop mechanisms to protect ourselves from this threat, and thus protect ourselves from learning. The implication of this is that learning support needs to encourage introspection and reflection, and providing the perspectives of others (for example as in 360-degree feedback, outdoor courses or relocations) may assist in this process.

PRACTICAL CHARACTERISTICS OF LEARNING AND DEVELOPMENT

Learning from experience

There has been a significant amount of work done which helps us understand how managers, and others, learn from their experiences. Kolb *et al.* (1984) argue that it is useful to combine the characteristics of learning, which is usually regarded as

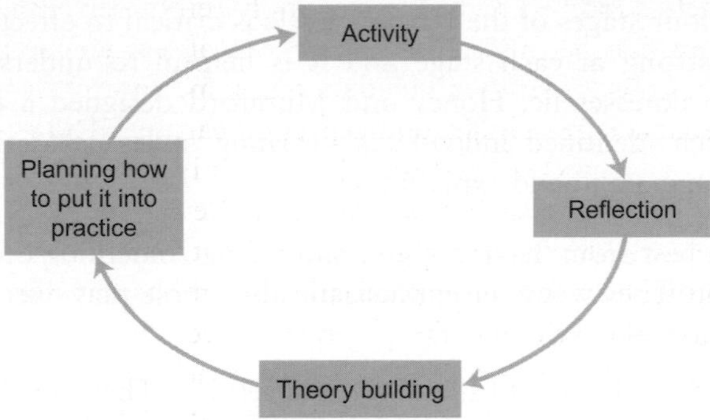

Figure 18.1 The learning cycle

passive, with those of problem solving, which is usually regarded as active. From this combination Kolb *et al.* developed a four-stage learning cycle, which was further developed by Honey and Mumford (1989).

The four stages, based on the work of both groups of researchers, are shown in Figure 18.1.

WINDOW ON PRACTICE

Gwen is a management trainer in a large organisation running a number of in-house management courses. She has just moved into this position from her role as section leader in the research department; the move was seen as a career development activity in order to strengthen her managerial skills.

Gwen is working with her manager to learn from her experiences. Here is an extract from her learning diary based on the learning cycle:

Activity – I've had a go at running three sessions on my own now, doing the input and handling the questions.

Reflection – I find the input much easier than handling questions. When I'm asked a question and answer it I have the feeling that they're not convinced by my reply and I feel awkward that we seem to finish the session hanging in mid-air. I would like to be able to encourage more open discussion.

Theory building – If I give an answer to a question it closes off debate by the fact that I have 'pronounced' what is 'right'. If I want them to discuss I have to avoid giving my views at first.

Planning practice – When I am asked a question rather than answering it I will say to the group: 'What does anyone think about that?' or 'What do you think?' (to the individual who asked) or 'What are the possibilities here?' I will keep encouraging them to respond to each other and reinforce where necessary, or help them change tack by asking another question.

Each of these four stages of the learning cycle is critical to effective learning, but few people are strong at each stage and it is helpful to understand where our strengths and weaknesses lie. Honey and Mumford designed a questionnaire to achieve this which identified individuals' learning styles as 'activist', 'reflector', 'theorist' and 'pragmatist', and explain that:

- **Activists** learn best from 'having a go', and trying something out without necessarily preparing. They would be enthusiastic about role-play exercises and keen to take risks in the real environment.
- **Reflectors** are much better at listening and observing. They are effective at reflecting on their own and others' experiences and good at analysing what happened and why.
- **Theorists'** strengths are in building a concept or a theory on the basis of their analysis. They are good at integrating different pieces of information, and building models of the way things operate. They may choose to start their learning by reading around a topic.
- **Pragmatists** are keen to *use* whatever they learn and will always work out how they can apply it in a real situation. They will plan how to put it into practice. They will value information/ideas they are given only if they can see how to relate them to practical tasks they need to do.

Understanding how individuals learn from experience underpins all learning, but is particularly relevant in encouraging self-development activities. Understanding our strengths and weaknesses enables us to choose learning activities which suit our style, and gives us the opportunity to decide to strengthen a particularly weak learning stage of our learning cycle. While Honey and Mumford adopt this dual approach, Kolb firmly maintains that learners *must* become deeply competent at all stages of the cycle. There has been considerable attention to the issue of matching and mismatching styles with development activities: *see*, for example, Hayes and Allinson (1996), who also consider the matching and mismatching of trainer learning style with learner learning style.

ACTIVITY 18.1

1. If you have not already done so obtain the Honey and Mumford questionnaire and work out your learning style(s).
2. Select your weakest style and try to identify two different learning activities which fit with this style, but that you would normally avoid.
3. Seek opportunities for trying out these learning activities. If you practise these activities on a regular basis this should help you strengthen the style you are working on.
4. Log your experiences and in particular what you have learned about these 'new' learning activities.

Table 18.1 Planned and emergent learning

Learner type	Planned learning score	Emergent learning score
Sage	High	High
Warrior	High	Low
Adventurer	Low	High
Sleeper	Low	Low

Source: Adapted from D. Megginson (1994) 'Planned and emergent learning: A framework and a method', *Executive Development*, Vol. 7, No. 6, pp. 29–32.

Planned and emergent learning

From a different, but compatible, perspective, David Megginson characterises learners by the extent to which they plan the direction of their learning and implement this (planned learning), and the extent to which they are able to learn from opportunistic learning experiences (emergent learning). Megginson (1994) suggests that strengths and weaknesses in these two areas will influence the way individuals react to self-development. These two characteristics are not mutually exclusive, and Megginson combines them to identify four learning types, as shown in Table 18.1.

Warriors are those who are strong at planning what they want to learn and how, but are less strong at learning from experiences they had not ancticipated. They have a clear focus on what they want to learn and pursue this persistently. On the other hand *Adventurers* respond to and learn from opportunities that come along unexpectedly, they are curious and flexible. However, they tend not to plan and create opportunities for themselves. *Sages* are strong on both characteristics, and *Sleepers* display little of either characteristic at present. To be most effective in self-development activities learners need to make maximum use of both planned and emergent learning. For a further explanation of this model also *see* Megginson and Whitaker (1996).

ACTIVITY 18.2

Consider your development over the past year: do you feel that your strengths are in planning your learning or in learning opportunistically?

Choose your weaker approach, and identify how you could strengthen this.

Learning curves

The idea of the learning curve has been promulgated for some time, and was developed in relation to technical skills development. The general idea was that we tend to learn a new task more rapidly at first, so that the learning curve is steep, and then gradually plateau after we have had significant experience. A slightly different shape of learning is more relevant to personal skills development: the curve is less likely to be smooth, or it may not even be curved. Ideally our learning would be incremental,

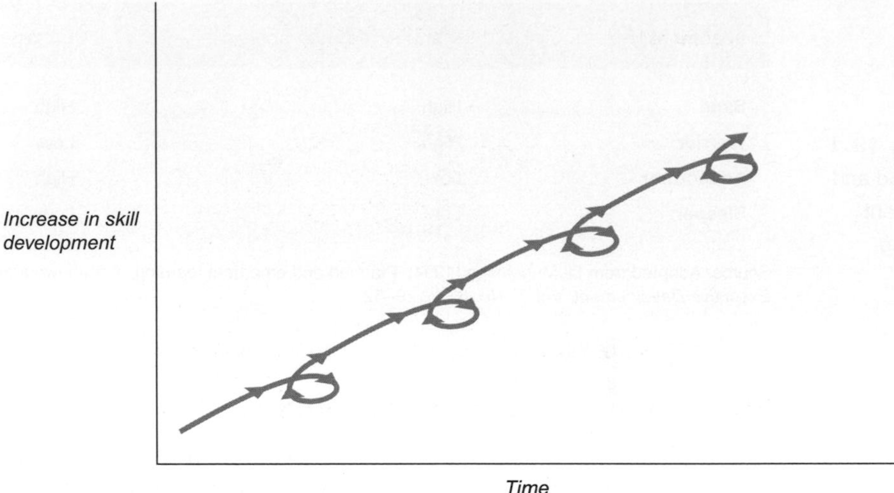

Figure 18.2 The reality of learning progress

improving bit by bit all the time; in reality, however, learning is usually characterised by a mix of improvements and setbacks. Although, with persistence, our skills gradually increase, in the short term we may experience dips. These dips are demotivating but they are a necessary part of learning. Developing personal skills usually requires us to try out a new way of doing things. This is risky because, although the skills we are developing may be quite personal to us, we usually have to experiment with new ways of doing things in public. Understanding that sometimes things get worse before they get better helps to carry us through the dips. Figure 18.2 shows the reality of learning progress.

Identifying learning and training needs

The 'systematic training cycle' was developed to help organisations move away from ad hoc non-evaluated training, and replace it with an orderly sequence of training activities, but this approach has been less prominent of late. Harrison (2002) contests that such a cycle is not necessarily the most appropriate to use as it falls far short of the messy world of practice, and does not focus adequately on learning. Sloman (2001) argues that it may have fitted the 1960s mood for rationality and efficiency, but it is somewhat mechanical and fits less well with our faster pace of continuous change. In spite of this the cycle does retain some value, and we describe an adaptation of such a model to make it more applicable to today's environment. The model is set within an external environment and within an organisation strategy and an HR development strategy. Even if some of these elements are not made explicit, they will exist implicitly. Note that the boundary lines are dotted, not continuous. This indicates that the boundaries are permeable and overlapping. The internal part of the model reflects a systematic approach to learning and to training. Learning needs may be identified by the individual, by the organisation or in partnership, and this applies to each of the following steps in the circle. This dual involvement is probably the biggest change from traditional models where the steps were owned by the

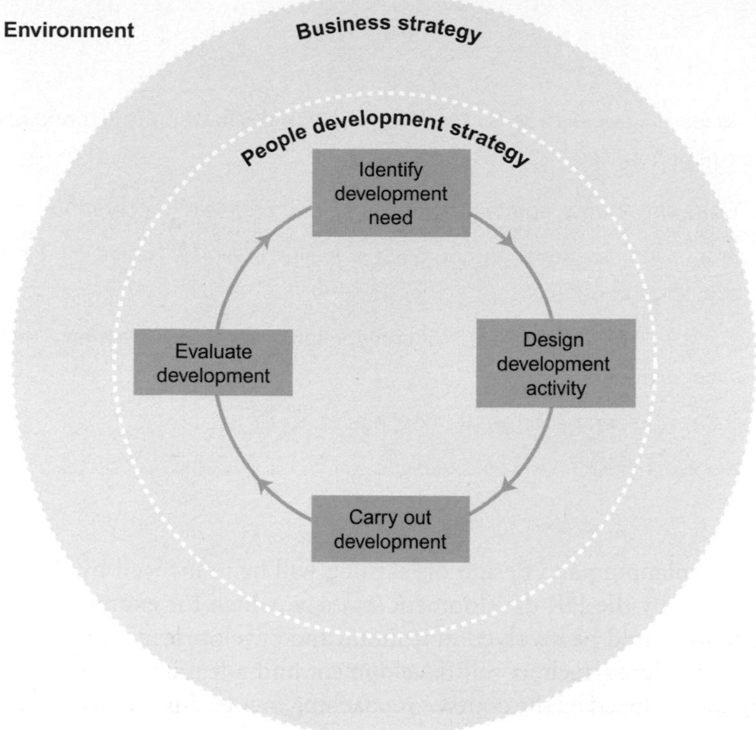

Figure 18.3 A systematic model of learning and training

organisation, usually the trainers, and the individual was considered to be the subject of the exercise rather than a participant in it, or the owner of it. The model that we offer does not exclude this approach where appropriate, but is intended to be viewed in a more flexible way. The model is shown in Figure 18.3.

There are various approaches to analysing needs, the two most traditional being a problem-centred approach or matching the individual's competency profile with that for the job that person is filling. The problem-centred approach focuses on any performance problems or difficulties, and explores whether these are due to a lack of skills and, if so, which. The profile comparison approach takes a much broader view and is perhaps most useful when an individual, or group of individuals, are new to a job. This latter approach is also useful because strategic priorities change and new skills are required of employees, as the nature of their job changes, even though they are still officially in the same role with the same job title. When a gap has been identified, by whatever method, the development required needs to be phrased in terms of a learning objective, before the next stage of the cycle, planning and designing the development, can be undertaken. For example, when a gap or need has been identified around team leadership, appropriate learning objectives may be that learners, by the end of the development, will be able 'to ask appropriate questions at the outset of a team activity to ascertain relevant skills and experience, and to check understanding of the task' or 'to review a team activity by involving all members in that review'.

ACTIVITY 18.3

Write learning objectives for the following individuals who are experiencing problems in their performance:

1 Tina, who always dominates meetings, and neglects the contribution of others.

2 Brian, who has never carried out a selection interview before, and is very unsure of how to go about this.

3 Mark, who feels he has lots of contributions to make at meetings, but never actually says anything.

4 Sara, who can never get to meetings on time.

The planning and design of learning will be influenced by the learning objectives and also by the HR development strategy, which for example may contain a vision of who should be involved in training and development activities, and the emphasis on approaches such as self-development and e-learning. Once planning and design have been specified the course, or coaching or e-learning activity, can commence, and should be evaluated at an appropriate time in the future to assess how behaviour and performance have changed.

METHODS OF LEARNING AND DEVELOPMENT

Off-job methods: education and training courses

Educational courses undertaken during a career are frequently done on a part-time basis leading to a diploma or master's degree with a management or business label, and/or qualification for a professional body. It is considered that such courses provide value for both the employer and the participant – and MBA study is a popular route. For advantages of such a course for the employee *see*, for example, Baruch and Leeming (2001). An alternative approach to qualification is the NVQ route which we discussed in the previous chapter, which is more closely tied to on-job experiences and not concerned with 'education'.

In addition there are consultancy courses. Varying from a half-day to several weeks in length, they are run by consultants or professional bodies for all comers. They have the advantage that they bring together people from varying occupational backgrounds and are not, therefore, as introspective as in-house courses and are popular for topical issues. They are, however, often relatively expensive and superficial, despite their value as sources of industrial folklore, by which we mean the swapping of experiences among course members.

The most valuable courses of this type are those that concentrate on specific skills or knowledge, such as developing time management, interviewing or disciplinary skills, or being introduced to a new national initiative. This short-course approach is probably the only way for individuals to come to terms with some new development, such as a change in legislation, because they need not only to find an interpretation of the development, but also to share views and reactions with fellow employees to ensure that their own feelings are not idiosyncratic or perverse.

In-house courses are often similar in nature to the consultancy courses, and are sometimes run with the benefit of some external expertise. In-house courses can be particularly useful if the training needs to relate to specific organisational procedures and structures, or if it is geared to encouraging employees to work more effectively together in the organisational environment. The drawbacks of in-house courses are that they suffer from a lack of breadth of content, and there is no possibility of learning from people in other organisations.

Alternatively, there are outdoor-type courses (sometimes known as Outward Bound, after the organisation that pioneered them). Outdoor courses attempt to develop skills involved in working with and through others, and aim to increase self-awareness and self-confidence through a variety of experiences, including outdoor physical challenges. Courses like these continue to be increasingly used, and their differential value is assumed to hinge on their separation from the political, organisational environment. A natural, challenging and different environment is assumed to encourage individuals to forsake political strategising, act as their raw selves and be more open to new ideas. Burleston and Grint (1996), based on ethnographic research into outdoor programmes, found that while most participants did gain from the experience, the idea of providing a de-politicised environment is a naive hope rather than a reality. Ibbetson and Newell (1999) did find, however, that non-competitive outdoor programmes were more effective in meeting teambuilding objectives than competitive programmes. More recently learning experiences based on drama are increasingly being used; in these participants are engaged in improvisation through role play and exercises. For a fascinating insight into the variety of forms this may take *see* Monks *et al.* (2001). There are other forms of simulation in addition to role play, such as games and computer simulations; for a good discussion of definitions and outcomes of such approaches *see* Feinstein *et al.* (2002).

One of the major concerns with these different types of off-job courses and activities is the difficulty of ensuring transfer of learning back to the workplace. As part of their research on the contribution of off-job courses to managers Longenecker and Ariss (2002) asked managers what helped them retain what they had learned and transfer it to the workplace. Developing goals/plans for implementing new skills was most frequently identified. In addition managers said that it helped to review materials immediately after the programme; be actively involved in the learning itself; make a report to peers/superiors on what they had learned; review material and development plans with their mentor/manager; and include development goals in performance reviews. It is generally agreed that a supportive climate helps transfer (for example line manager interest and involvement and development having a high priority in the organisation). Santos and Stewart (2003), for example, found that transfer was more likely if reward such as promotion or pay was attached to developmental behaviour change, and also where there was a helpful management climate in terms of pre- and post-course briefings and activities. In relation to MBAs Martin and Pate (2001) found, surprisingly, that a poor transfer climate did not affect transfer, but willingness to apply what was learned was related to the individual's positive feelings about the company and their intended continuance there.

While courses are no longer viewed as the key means of developing staff, they still have an important role to play, and in Interactive skill 4, in the Focus on skills at the end of Part IV, we therefore explore teaching and instructional skills.

Learning on the job

Manager coaching and teaching

The line manager's role in learning and development has increased with the devolution of HR tasks. Coaching is an informal approach to individual development based on a close relationship between the individual and one other person, usually their immediate manager, who is experienced in the task. The manager as coach helps trainees to develop by giving them the opportunity to perform an increasing range of tasks, and by helping them to learn from their experiences. They work to improve the trainee's performance by asking searching questions, actively listening, discussion, exhortation, encouragement, understanding, counselling and providing information and honest feedback. The coach is usually in a position to create development opportunities for the trainee when this is appropriate. For example, a line manager can delegate attendance at a meeting, or allow a trainee to deputise, where this is appropriate to the individual's development needs. Alternatively they can create the opportunity for a trainee to join a working party or can arrange a brief secondment to another department. Coaches can share 'inside' information with the individual they are coaching to help them understand the political context in which they are working. For example, they are able to explain who will have most influence on a decision that will be made, or future plans for restructuring within a department.

Skilled coaches can adapt their style to suit the individual they are coaching, from highly directive at one end of the scale to non-directive at the other. The needed style may change over time, as the trainee gains more confidence and experience. Useful texts on coaching include MacLennan (1995) who provides considerable detail on the nature of achievement, skills required for coaching, coaching issues, barriers to coaching and how to overcome them. Also, Mumford (1994) has written an excellent guide to the ways that managers can help other managers to learn.

In an exploratory study Carroll and Gillen (2001) found a variety of barriers to line manager acceptance of a teaching/coaching role, in particular lack of interpersonal competence, lack of time, performance pressures, and a feeling that the teaching role was not valued and was the role of the HR department. This same article also provides some excellent material on what makes an effective coach.

There has been an increasing trend to broaden the concept of coaching in terms of both content and who carries out the coaching. Peers and other managers may provide internal coaching, with external executive coaching being provided by consultancy organisations. Various forms of coaching may include career coaching, performance coaching, skills coaching, business coaching and life coaching.

Mentoring

Mentoring offers a wide range of advantages for the development of the protégé, coaching as described above being just one of the possible benefits of the relationship. The mentor would occasionally be the individual's immediate manager, but usually it is a more senior manager in the same or a different function. Kram (1983) identifies two broad functions of mentoring, the first of which is the career function, including those aspects of the relationship that primarily enhance career advancement, such as exposure and visibility and sponsorship. The second is the psychosocial function, which includes those aspects of the relationship that primarily enhance a sense of competence, clarity of identity and effectiveness in the managerial role.

Arnold (1997) found that the most common advantages of mentoring were perceived as role modelling and counselling. There is evidence that mentoring does benefit both parties (*see*, for example, Johnson *et al.* 1999), and Broadbridge (1999) suggests that mentors can gain through recognition from peers, increased job satisfaction, rejuvenation, admiration and self-satisfaction. The drawbacks to mentoring that were revealed in Broadbridge's research include the risk of over-reliance, the danger of picking up bad habits, the fact that the protégé may be alienated from other sources of expertise and the sense of loss experienced when a mentor leaves. In addition, the difficulty of dealing with conflicting views in such an unequal relationship was identified. Perceived benefits, however, considerably outweighed any drawbacks. Megginson (2000) identifies the issue of dysfunctional mentoring, and the danger of assuming that mentoring is unquestionably good.

Managers are also seen as responsible for developing talent, and while a mentor/protégé relationship might not naturally occur, mentorship may be encouraged or formalised. For example, there are systems where all new graduates are attached to a mentor as soon as they join the organisation. The difficulties of establishing a formal programme include the potential mismatch of individuals, unreal expectations on both sides and the time and effort involved. Conway (1998) provides useful advice on planning and implementing a mentoring scheme.

WINDOW ON PRACTICE

Tony Stott and Jenny Sweeney (1999) report on a structured mentoring scheme with a difference at Shell. While Shell runs a very flexible mentoring scheme appropriate for many different types of employee and purposes, it recognises the importance of the design of the scheme and good administration. The authors suggest that there are five critical elements in a good scheme:

- **A database.** Although the scheme is based on natural selection, that is, a mutual decision between a potential mentor and a new recruit, the database appears to be critical, in order to track the flow of mentees and the availability of mentors. Copies of mentor biographies are available for new recruits to read.
- **Mentor support.** Mentors are trained in their role and in recognising the limits of their abilities. There is also a support mechanism for mentors, and mentors meet to share their experiences.
- **Training.** Both mentors and mentees are trained, and this forms a key part of the induction programme for new recruits, with information on reasons for using mentoring, roles and expectations.
- **Resource materials.** These include websites for mentors. Guidance booklets for mentees are also produced.
- **Evaluation.** Shell found that a non-bureaucratic scheme, which gives ownership to the participants, was appreciated.

Source: Summarised from T. Stott and J. Sweeney (1999) 'More than a match', *People Management*, June, pp. 45–8.

Peer relationships

Although mentor–protégé relationships have been shown to be related to high levels of career success, not all developing individuals have access to such a relationship, and even formal schemes are often reserved for specific groups such as new graduate entrants. Supportive peer relationships at work are potentially more widely available to the individual and offer a number of benefits for the development of both parties. The benefits that are available depend on the nature of the peer relationship, and Kram and Isabella (1985) have identified three groups of peer relationships, which are differentiated by their primary development functions. These can be expressed on a continuum from 'information peer', based primarily on information sharing, through 'collegial peer', based on career strategising, giving job-related feedback and friendship, to 'special peer', based on emotional support, personal feedback, friendship and confirmation. Most of us benefit from one or a number of peer relationships at work but often we do not readily appreciate their contribution towards our development. Peer relationships most often develop on an informal basis and provide mutual support. Some organisations, however, formally appoint an existing employee to provide such support to a new member of staff through their first 12–18 months in the organisation. These relationships may, of course, continue beyond the initial period. The name for the appointed employee will vary from organisation to organisation, and sometimes the word 'buddy', 'coach' or 'mentor' is used – which can be confusing! Cromer (1989) discusses the advantages of peer relationships organised on a formal basis and the skills and qualities sought in peer providers, which include accessibility, empathy, organisational experience and proven task skills.

ACTIVITY 18.4

Consider each significant peer relationship that you have at work. Where does each fit on the continuum of relationships described above, and what contributions does it make towards your development?

If you are in full-time education consider the contribution that each of your relationships (whether at university, home or work) has to your development.

Action learning

Reg Revans was one of the first professors in the UK to specialise in management. Despairing of how management was being taught, Revans resigned his chair in Manchester and moved to Belgium to start his first action learning project based on his conviction that managers do not need education, but the ability to solve problems (Revans 1974). His method has been basically to organise exchanges, so that a manager experienced in one organisation is planted in another to solve a particular set of problems that is proving baffling. He or she brings a difference of experience and a freshness of approach, and is not dependent on new, temporary, organisational peers for career growth. They work on the problem for a period of months, having many sessions of discussion and debate with a group of other individuals similarly planted in unfamiliar organisations with a knotty problem to solve. The learning stems from the immediate problem that is presented, and from all the others that emerge, one by one, in the steps towards a solution. This presents a need that the student has to satisfy and all the learning is in terms of what they discover they need to know, rather than what someone else feels is necessary. It is an idea of startling simplicity, and has been adapted by both formal educational providers, often in master's courses and by organisations. Paauwe and Williams (2001) note that action learning is less effective when restricted to a single case within a single company, and when participants are all from the same company, and that the problems faced are too routine and familiar. It is therefore unfortunate that this is the way that action learning is often used.

Self-development

Natural learning is learning that takes place on the job and results from an individual's everyday experience of the tasks that they undertake. Natural learning is even more difficult to investigate than coaching, mentoring or peer relationships, and yet the way that we learn from everyday experiences, and our level of awareness of this, is very important for our development. To some extent self-development may be seen as a conscious effort to gain the most from natural learning in a job, and to use the learning cycle as a framework. Self-development can be focused in specific skills development, but often extends to attitude development and personal growth: for example Ireland's North Western Health Board is using an approach to action learning to promote a culture of continuous development (O'Hara *et al.* 2001).

ACTIVITY 18.5

The video *Groundhog Day* can be viewed as a journey of self-development. Watch the video and answer the following questions:

- How did Phil's attitudes change and how was this reflected in his behaviour?
- What do you think Phil learned?
- How did he learn it?
- Why is personal development so difficult?

The emphasis in self-development is that each individual is responsible for, and can plan, their own development, although they may need to seek help when working on some issues. Self-development involves individuals in analysing their strengths, weaknesses and the way that they learn, primarily by means of questionnaires and feedback from others. This analysis may initially begin on a self-development course, or with the help of a facilitator, but would then be continued by the individual back on the job. From this analysis individuals, perhaps with some help at first, plan their development goals and the way that they will achieve them, primarily through development opportunities within the job. When individuals consciously work on self-development they use the learning cycle in a more conscious way than in natural learning. They are also in a better position to seek appropriate opportunities and help, in their learning, from their manager.

Many of the activities included in self-development are based on observation, collecting further feedback about the way they operate, experimenting with different approaches and in particular reviewing what has happened, why and what they have learned. Self-development, however, is not a quick fix for, as Stansfield (1997) suggests, it requires time, patience, tenacity, adjustment and careful planning. Stansfield (1996) also recommends that more attention needs to be paid to the 'scaffolding' which supports the self-development process. To this end she suggests that extensive briefing and explanation of the theoretical underpinning of the self-development are both important. In addition she suggests direct skill development concerning the role, importance and nature of peer feedback, and further support in tracking personal learning needs to ensure a more rigorous learning journey. Woodall (2000) also notes difficulties around the support structure for self-development, and identifies confusion in terminology as unhelpful. Confusion in terminology is also raised by Antonacopoulou (2000) who highlights a much neglected influence on self-development – that the individuals themselves have to be capable of taking on this responsibility.

Self-development groups

Typically, a group of individuals is involved in a series of meetings where they would jointly discuss their personal development, organisational issues and/or individual work problems. Groups may begin operating with a leader who is a process expert, not a content expert, and who therefore acts as a facilitator rather than, but not to the complete exclusion of, a source of information. The group itself is the primary source of information and may operate without outside help as its members' process skills develop. The content and timings of the meetings can be very flexible, although they will require a significant level of energy and commitment if they are to operate well.

Self-development groups can be devised in a variety of contexts. They can be part of a formal educational course, for example a Diploma in Management Studies, where a group of managers from different organisations come together to support their development; they constitute the whole of a self-development 'course'; or they can be an informal support group within an organisation. However the group originates, it is important that the members understand what every member hopes to get out of the group, the role of the facilitator (if there is one), the processes and rules that the group will operate by and how they agree to interact.

Learning logs

Learning logs are a mechanism for learning retrospectively as they encourage a disciplined approach to learning from opportunistic events. The log may be focused around one particular activity and is usually designed to encourage the writer to explain what happened, how they have reflected on this, what conclusions they have made and what future learning actions they wish to make. Alternatively logs can be used in the form of a daily or weekly diary.

ACTIVITY 18.6

Identify a management skills area that you need to develop. (You may find it particularly helpful to choose an interpersonal area, for example, assertiveness, influencing others, presentation, being more sociable, contributing to meetings, helping others.)

Keep a learning diary over the next few weeks, logging anything that is relevant to your development area. Use the framework which Gwen used in a previous example (*see* Window on practice box at the beginning of this chapter).

At the end of the period review what you have learned in your development area and also what you have learned about the learning cycle.

Learning contracts

There is increasing use of learning contracts, sometimes used within more formalised self-development groups; on other management courses; as part of a mentoring or coaching relationship; or in working towards a competency-based qualification. These contracts are a formal commitment by the learner to work towards a specified learning goal, with an identification of how the goal might be achieved. They thus promote a proactive approach to learning. Boak (1991) has produced a very helpful guide to the use of such contracts and suggests that they should include:

- an overall development goal;
- specific objectives in terms of skills and knowledge;
- activities to be undertaken;
- resources required;
- method of assessment of learning.

The value that individuals gain from learning contracts is dependent on their choosing to participate, their identification of the relevant goal and the importance and value they ascribe to achieving it. Only with commitment will a learning contract be effective, because ultimately it is down to the individual learner manager to make it happen.

WINDOW ON PRACTICE

David wanted to improve his influencing skills and has sent the following draft learning contract to his manager for discussion:

Goal

To improve my influencing skills with both peers and more senior managers.

Specific objectives

- To prepare for influencing situations.
- To try to understand better the perspective of the other.
- To identify the interpersonal skills required – probably active listening, reflecting, summarising, stating my needs, collaboration (but maybe more).
- To be able to identify that I have had more influence in decisions made.

Activities

- Watch a recommended video on influencing skills.
- Re-read my notes from the interpersonal skills course I attended.
- Watch how others in my department go about influencing.
- Ask other people (supportive ones) how they go about it.
- Identify possible influencing situations in advance, and plan for what I want and what might happen.
- Reflect back on what happened, and work out how to do better next time.
- Ask for feedback.

Resources

- Video.
- Notes.
- The support of others.

Assessment

- I could ask for feedback from colleagues and my manager.
- My own assessment may be helpful.
- Make a log over time of decisions made and my originally preferred outcome.

Open, distance and e-learning

As technology enables interesting and interactive presentation of distance learning materials, there is evidence of considerable enthusiasm on the part of organisations to pursue this approach to development, and take advantage of the opportunities it presents. CIPD (2003) reports that one of the most significant changes in training over the last five years is the increased use of e-learning, although it is still most heavily used by IT staff. E-learning can be defined as 'learning that is delivered, enables or mediated by electronic technology' (Sloman and Rolph 2003, p. 1). While e-learning has been characterised as requiring high investment in terms of hardware, software and design time, it has also been characterised as cost-effective in the long run, with the ability to provide speedy and flexible training. Hammond (2001), for example, describes the case of Cisio which is constantly launching new IT-based products. The company has moved from 90 per cent classroom-based training for its sales representative to 80 per cent online training so that the large numbers of representatives can experience training immediately the product is launched. Channel Four (Cooper 2001) has a strategy to replace much of its classroom teaching activity with interactive learning, and the London Emergency Services are using virtual reality training to prepare employees for emergency events. For example Prickett (1997) reports how Hendon Police Training College uses virtual reality to prepare officers to deal with siege and hostage situations. Sloman and Rolph (2003) found that e-learning has been implemented in a variety of ways, from being introduced as a sweeping ambitious change to small incremental changes to the organisation's approach to training, and from a mandatory change to an offer to volunteers. They also report that key barriers are computer literacy of employees and access to the appropriate equipment.

However enthusiasm from the organisation is not sufficient. Sadler-Smith *et al.* (2000), for example, found that managers did not widely use such distance learning methods, and they were perceived as less effective than other methods. The support provided may well be critical, as may the way that such methods are introduced and used. E-learning covers a wide variety of approaches from using CD-roms to the company intranet and the internet. More sophisticated approaches do not confine e-learning to interactive learning at a distance. Increasingly, synchronous learning is used where all participants log on at the same time, with a tutor or facilitator being available. Individuals can progress through material alone or network with others to complete a task and use chat rooms and have a dialogue with the tutor. Video conferencing can also be used to bring participants together at the same time. For example, some MBAs have been delivered via video conferencing rather than classroom-based teaching, and further details of this are provided in cases 18.1 and 18.2 on the website. The concept of blended learning also has much appeal recently, but this term can be interpreted in different ways. Some use it to indicate the blending of e-learning with face-to-face learning experiences, while others use it more broadly to indicate 'a range of ways that e-learning can be delivered when combined with multiple additional routes that support and facilitate learning' (Sloman and Rolph 2003, p. 6).

WINDOW ON PRACTICE

Hills and Francis (1999), for example, suggest that computer-based learning is a solitary activity, and that social contact and interaction were a necessary ingredient in learning. They assessed the use of their local computer-based training centres in Lloyds TSB, and found that some were used much more than others. The extent of use was not related to geographical accessibility, but instead to the support provided by the centre administrator, before, during and after learning sessions, and also the support of local managers.

EVALUATION OF TRAINING AND DEVELOPMENT

One of the most nebulous and unsatisfactory aspects of the training job is evaluating its effectiveness, yet it is becoming more necessary to demonstrate value for money.

Phelps (2002) argues that training costs UK business £2 billion each year and yet there is no satisfactory return on investment calculation to prove its value, and that we remain unsure whether training breeds success or success breeds training. Evaluation is straightforward when the output of the training is clear to see, such as reducing the number of dispatch errors in a warehouse or increasing someone's typing speed. It is more difficult to evaluate the success of a management training course or a programme of social skills development, but the fact that it is difficult is not enough to prevent it being done.

A familiar method of evaluation is the post-course questionnaire, which course members complete on the final day by answering vague questions that require them to assess aspects of the course using only such general terms as 'good', 'very good' or 'outstanding'. The drawbacks with such questionnaires are, first, that there is a powerful halo effect, as the course will have been, at the very least, a welcome break from routine and there will probably have been some attractive fringe benefits such as staying in a comfortable hotel and enjoying rich food. Second, the questionnaire tends to evaluate the course and not the learning, so that the person attending the course is assessing the quality of the tutors and the visual aids, instead of being directed to examine what has been learned.

Hamblin (1974), in a much-quoted work, identified five levels of evaluation: (1) evaluating the training, as in the post-course questionnaire above; (2) evaluating the learning, in terms of how the trainee now behaves; (3) evaluating changes in job performance; (4) evaluating changes in organisation performance; and (5) evaluating changes in the wider contribution that the organisation now makes. Perhaps the most well-referenced approach to evaluation is Kilpatrick (1959) who suggested four levels of evaluation, somewhat similar to Hamblin: reaction level; learning level (have the learning objectives been met?); behaviour (how has the individual's behaviour changed back in the job?); and results (what is the impact of training on job performance?). Bramley (1996) suggests that performance effectiveness can be measured at individual, team and organisational levels, and that changes in behaviour, knowledge, skills and attitudes need to be considered. He makes the worthwhile point – as do others – that the criteria for evaluation need to be built into development activities from the very beginning, and not tagged on at the end. Bramley is a useful source of practical approaches to evaluation, as is Bee and Bee (1994). Sadler-Smith *et al.* (1999) provides a useful comparison of a wide range of evaluation frameworks.

In 1996 Canning noted that the body of knowledge on evaluation had not grown over the past ten years, and the difficulty of this task is no doubt an influence on lack of progress. Harrison (1997), for example, notes that due to high levels of change, and the gap between espoused and actual HR goals and strategy, it is 'therefore hard, if not impossible, to be certain about the specific outcomes of HR or HRD strategy' (p. 209). There is a need, however, to assess value for money, and this is generally worked out on a pay-back basis, which focuses attention on the short term. Lee (1996) suggests a 'pay-forward' approach to assessing value for money and this concept appears to be more consistent with the nature of training and development strategy and interventions then a pay-back approach, as the outcome may only be observed in the long term.

While organisations may desire a measure of the impact of training on the organisation, in practice this appears to be rarely achieved. Sadler-Smith *et al.*, for example, found in their study (1999) that the reasons for evaluating training were more often operational than strategic, and they state that evaluation information was used 'mostly for feedback to individuals, and to inform the training process, and less for return on investment decisions' (p. 369).

SUMMARY PROPOSITIONS

18.1 There are four perspectives on learning: behaviourist, cognitive, social and constructivist. Each has different implications for the approach taken to training and development.

18.2 The emphasis has moved from training to learning, with individuals taking ownership of their own learning needs. To be effective learners we need to understand the nature of learning and our own strengths and weaknesses.

18.3 The emphasis on formal development programmes is declining in favour of greater interest in approaches to on-the-job development, such as coaching, mentoring, peer relationships and self-development.

18.4 There has been an upsurge of interest in e-learning. However, the extent to which employees take advantage of such opportunities will be affected by the context and the support available.

18.5 Evaluation of development is critical but difficult. It is most effective when built into the design of the development activity rather than tagged on at the end.

GENERAL DISCUSSION TOPICS

1 If learning is an individual process, why is so much training done in groups? What are the implications of moving towards more individualised learning?

2 Discuss the view that the role of the trainer/facilitator is critically important in the effectiveness of a training programme.

FURTHER READING

Reynolds, J., Caley, L. and Mason, R. (2002) *How do People Learn? A Research report*. London: CIPD

This research report covers the background context to learning in today's organisations and considers the four theoretical perspectives on learning. The report also covers practical aspects of learning and e-learning. This report has been summarised by Jennifer Schramm (2002) in *The change agenda: How do people learn?* London: CIPD.

Thorne, K. (2003) *Blended Learning*. London: Kogan Page

A useful, broadly based handbook which explains how to get the best out of combining innovative and technological advances offered by e-learning with the best of traditional approaches to learning. Thorne considers the high-level support required for such approaches and the involvement of stakeholders as well as providing practical design solutions. A range of case studies shows, in particular, the various ways in which different approaches to learning can be combined.

REFERENCES

Antonacopoulou, E. (2000) 'Employee development through self-development in three retail banks', *Personnel Review*, Vol. 29, No. 4.

Arnold, J. (1997) 'Mentoring in early career', *Human Resource Management Journal*, Vol. 7, No. 4, pp. 61–70.

Baruch, Y. and Leeming, A. (2001) 'The added value of MBA studies – graduates' perceptions', *Personnel Review*, Vol. 30, No. 5, pp. 589–601.

Bee, F. and Bee, R. (1994) *Training Needs Analysis and Evaluation*. London: IPM.

Boak, G. (1991) *Developing Managerial Competencies. The management learning contract approach*. London: Pitman.

Bramley, P. (1996) *Evaluating Training*. London: IPD.

Broadbridge, A. (1999) 'Mentoring in retailing: a tool for success?' *Personnel Review*, Vol. 28, No. 4.

Burleston, L. and Grint, K. (1996) 'The deracination of politics: outdoor management development', *Management Learning*, Vol. 27, No. 2, pp. 187–202.

Carroll, S. and Gillen, D. (2001) 'Exploring the teaching function of the managerial role', *Journal of Management Development*, Vol. 21, No. 5, pp. 330–42.

Canning, R. (1996) 'Enhancing the quality of learning in human resource development', *Journal of European Industrial Training*, Vol. 20, No. 2, pp. 3–10.

CIPD (2003) *Training and Development 2003: Survey Report*. London: CIPD.

Conway, C. (1998) *Strategies for Mentoring*. Chichester: Wiley.

Cooper, C. (2001) 'Connect Four', *People Management*, February.

Cromer, D.R. (1989) 'Peers as providers', *Personnel Administrator*, Vol. 34, Pt 5, pp. 84–6.

Feinstein, A., Mann, S. and Corsum, D. (2002) 'Charting the experiential territory – Clarifying definitions and uses of computer simulations, games and role plays', *Personnel Review*, Vol. 21, No. 10, pp. 732–44.

Hallier, J. and Butts, S. (1999) 'Employers' discovery of training: self-development, employability and the rhetoric of partnership', *Employee Relations*, Vol. 21, No. 1.

Hamblin, A.C. (1974) *Evaluation and Control of Training*. Maidenhead: McGraw-Hill.

Hammond, D. (2001) 'Reality Bytes', *People Management*, January.

Harrison, R. (1997) *Employee Development*. London: IPD.

Harrison, R. (2002) *Learning and Development*. London: IPD.

Hayes, J. and Allinson, C.W. (1996) 'The implications of learning styles for training and development: a discussion of the matching hypothesis', *British Journal of Management*, Vol. 7, pp. 63–73.

Hills, H. and Francis, P. (1999) 'Interaction Learning', *People Management*, July.

Honey, P. and Mumford, A. (1989) *A Manual of Learning Opportunities*. Maidenhead: Peter Honey.

Ibbetson, A. and Newell, S. (1999) 'A comparison of a competitive and non-competitive outdoor management development programmes', *Personnel Review*, Vol. 28, No. 1/2.

Johnson, S., Geory, G. and Griego, O. (1999) 'The Mentoring Model theory: dimensions in mentoring protocols', *Career Development International*, Vol. 4, No. 7.

Kilpatrick, D. (1959) 'Techniques for evaluating training programmes', *Journal of the American Society of Training Directors*, Vol. 13.

Kolb, D.A., Rubin, I.M. and McIntyre, J.M. (1984) *Organization Psychology*, 4th edn. Englewood Cliffs, NJ: Prentice-Hall.

Kram, K.E. (1983) 'Phases of the mentor relationship', *Academy of Management Journal*, Vol. 26, No. 4.

Kram, K.E. and Isabella, L.A. (1985) 'Mentoring alternatives: the role of peer relationships in career development', *Academy of Management Journal*, Vol. 28, No. 1.

Lee, R. (1996) 'The pay-forward view of training', *People Management*, pp. 30–2.

Longenecker, C. and Ariss, S. (2002) 'Creating competitive advantage through effective management education', *Personnel Review*, Vol. 21, No. 9, pp. 640–54.

Martin, G. and Pate, J. (2001) 'Company-based education programmes: what's the pay off for employers?' *Human Resource Management Journal*, Vol. 11, No. 4, pp. 55–73.

MacLennan, N. (1995) *Coaching and Mentoring*. Aldershot: Gower.

Megginson, D. (1994) 'Planned and Emergent Learning: A framework and a method', *Executive Development*, Vol. 7, No. 6, pp. 29–32.

Megginson, D. (2000) 'Current issues in mentoring', *Career Development International*, Vol. 5, No. 4/5.

Megginson, D. and Whitaker, V. (1996) *Cultivating Self-development*. London: IPD.

Monks, K., Barker, P. and Mhanachain, A. (2001) 'Drama as an opportunity for learning and development', *Personnel Review*, Vol. 20, No. 5, pp. 414–23.

Mumford, A. (1994) *How Managers Develop Managers*. Aldershot: Gower.

O'Hara, S., Webber, T. and Murphy, W. (2001) 'The joy of sets', *People Management*, 8 Feb., pp. 30–4.

Paauwe, J. and Williams, R. (2001) 'Seven key issues for management development', *Journal of Management Development*, Vol. 20, No. 2, pp. 90–105.

Phelps, M. (2002) 'Blind faith', *People Management*, Vol. 8, No. 9, 2 May, p. 51.

Prickett, R. (1997) 'Screen savers', *People Management*, 26 June, pp. 36–8.

Revans, R.W. (1974) 'Action learning projects', in B. Taylor and G.L. Lippitt (eds) *Management Development and Training Handbook*. Maidenhead: McGraw-Hill.

Sadler-Smith, E., Down, S. and Field, J. (1999) 'Adding value to HRD: evaluation, Investors in People and small firm training', *Human Resource Development International*, Vol. 2, No. 4, pp. 369–90.

Sadler-Smith, E., Down, S. and Lean, J. (2000) '"Modern" learning methods: rhetoric and reality', *Personnel Review*, Vol. 29, No. 4.

Santos, A. and Stewart, M. (2003) 'Employee perceptions and their influence on training effectiveness', *Human Resource Management Journal*, Vol. 13, No. 1, pp. 27–45.

Sloman, M. (2001) 'Hardier laurels, please', *People Management*, Vol. 7, No. 25, 27 December, p. 39.

Sloman, M. and Rolph, J. (2003) *E-learning: The learning curve – The change agenda*. London: CIPD.

Stansfield, L. (1996) 'Is self-development the key to the future?' *Management Learning*, Vol. 27, No. 4, pp. 429–45.

Stansfield, L. (1997) '"Employee – develop yourself" Experiences of self-directed learners', *Career Development International*, Vol. 2, No. 6.

Stott, T. and Sweeney, J. (1999) 'More than a match', *People Management*, June, pp. 45–8.

Woodall, J. (2000) 'Corporate support for work-based management development', *Human Resource Management Journal*, Vol. 10, No. 1, pp. 18–32.

An extensive range of additional materials, including multiple choice questions, answers to questions and links to useful websites can be found on the Human Resource Management Companion Website at www.pearsoned.co.uk/torrington.

CHAPTER 19

CAREER DEVELOPMENT

THE OBJECTIVES OF THIS CHAPTER ARE TO:

1 EXPLAIN AND CRITIQUE HOW AND WHY CAREERS ARE CHANGING

2 INTRODUCE SOME DEFINITIONS OF CAREER AND CAREER DEVELOPMENT

3 REVIEW SOME OF THE MODELS AND THEORIES WHICH HELP US UNDERSTAND THE CONCEPT

4 EXPLORE PRACTICAL WAYS IN WHICH THE INDIVIDUAL CAN MANAGE THEIR CAREER, AND THE TYPES OF SUPPORT THE ORGANISATION CAN PROVIDE FOR CAREER DEVELOPMENT AND MANAGEMENT

WINDOW ON PRACTICE

Mallon (1998) reports on research with 24 ex-managers of one branch of the public sector who now had portfolio careers, and through in-depth biographical interviews set out to understand how they account for their career move. From the data she grouped the participants into three categories: 'refugees', 'missionaries' and 'reluctant missionaries'.

There were only two managers classified as 'refugees' and both were unexpectedly made compulsorily redundant, from senior positions. Since then they had not reconciled themselves to any alternative form of working other than full-time employment. One found a new job, after a year, in which she hopes to remain until retirement, the other still looks for jobs, but having been unsuccessful so far is developing his portfolio of work. Two others Mallon classified as 'ex-refugees'. Both experienced redundancy, both found other work, but both have since chosen the portfolio route. Their explanation for this centred around growing disillusionment with the 'employment' world stimulated by their bitter experiences of redundancy.

Mallon identified five of her respondents as 'missionaries'. All left voluntarily and two of these never felt that they fitted in the 'employed world'. Three made very well-planned decisions to move to a portfolio, reducing hours with their current employer in order to gradually build up work elsewhere, for example. These three felt that there were no further challenges in the organisation for them, they talked about 'new' careers, and about taking control for themselves. They clearly felt pulled by other opportunities.

The final, largest group, 'reluctant missionaries', were somewhere in between. Two were offered the choice between a different job or redundancy, and chose to leave, others felt a growing dissatisfaction with the organisation and being out of step with the organisation, and one felt that dismissal was looming. However, although these individuals were pushed into action they did report factors which pulled them towards a portfolio approach, such as integrity, time for childcare and doing the type of work that they wanted to do. Others fled the organisation because they felt their position was untenable but, at the time, they had no idea what they were going to do next, and their decision to go portfolio was a pragmatic response to the situation that they were in.

Source: Adapted from M. Mallon (1998) 'The portfolio career; pushed or pulled to it?' *Personnel Review*, Vol. 27, No. 5.

There is a considerable body of literature indicating that the foregoing examples are typical of a general and substantial move from long-term organisationally based careers to individually managed portfolio or boundaryless careers.

HOW AND WHY ARE CAREERS CHANGING?

Many writers over the past decade have provided a picture of dramatic change in the nature of careers that are possible in today's society. The traditional career within a single organisation, characterised by hierarchical progression, managed on a planned basis by the organisation, is gone, it is argued (*see*, for example, Arthur and Rousseau 1996a; Adamson *et al.* 1998). Organisations now have flatter structures and need to be flexible, fluid and cost-effective in the face of an uncertain and unpredictable future. Thus they can no longer offer long-term career progression in return for loyalty, commitment and adequate performance, which was an unwritten deal and part of the traditional psychological contract.

Kanter (1989), for example, suggests that managers can no longer rely on the organisation for their career future and must learn to manage themselves and their work independently as many professionals do. In particular, they must build portfolios of their achievements and skills, develop networks, make a 'name' for themselves and market themselves within the relevant industry sector rather than just within their current organisation. In a different sense Handy (1994) uses the words 'portfolio career' to mean 'exchanging full time employment for independence', which is expressed in the collection of different pieces of work done for different clients. Individuals starting off a portfolio career often continue to do some work for their previous organisation (on a fee-paying basis) and add to this a network of other clients. Arthur (1994) describes the 'boundaryless career' which includes moves between organisations and non-hierarchical moves within organisations where there are no norms of progress or success. This concept continues to capture interest and a whole part of the *International Journal of Human Resource Management* in 2003 was devoted to this and related issues.

However the evidence to support the reality that careers have fundamentally changed is 'shaky at best' (Mallon 1998). Guest and McKenzie-Davey (1996), for example, found the traditional organisation and the traditional career 'alive and well' (pp. 22–3), with the hierarchy still used for motivation and progression. Also, as we indicated in Chapter 8, where we looked at retention, statistics demonstrate that job tenure and the number of job changes has changed very little over the past thirty years. As yet there is insufficient research into the extent to which new career patterns are developing.

Some argue that the contradictions between the above views are a result of being in transition (*see*, for example, Burke 1998a), whereas King (2003) suggests that the 'new career' may be reflected in people's expectations rather than their labour market experiences. Another explanation may be that temporary and contract work are spread more evenly across different sectors (*see*, for example, Burke 1998b), and have therefore become more visible. Let us not forget that the traditional psychological contract was never available to everyone. Smithson and Lewis (2000) argue that public perceptions of increasing insecurity may have more to do with the characteristics of those whom the insecurity now affects, such as graduates and professional staff, rather than an increase in the phenomenon. Similarly, different groups have different sets of expectations and subjective feelings of job insecurity. Younger workers accept insecurity, almost as the norm (*see*, for example, Smithson and Lewis 2000), but older workers feel the psychological contract has been violated. Older workers may have the same expectations as before but realise that the employer is no longer going to fulfil their part of the bargain (*see*, for example, Herriot *et al.* 1997; Thomas and Dunkerley 1999).

A different explanation for these contradictory findings is that organisations project the image of a stable and predictable internal career structure, because it is in their interests to do so, whatever the reality. Adamson *et al.* (1998) suggest that it is

Table 19.1 The old psychological contract

Employee offers	Employer offers
Loyalty	Security
Commitment	Future career
Adequate performance	To look after the employee

Table 19.2 The new psychological contract

Employee offers	Employer offers
Continuous learning	Employability
Keep pace with change	Tools and environment to achieve this
Commitment to organisational success	Opportunities for assessment
Manage their own career	Opportunities for development
High productivity	Care

Source: Based on R.H. Waterman, J.A. Waterman and B.A. Collard (1994) 'Toward a career-resilient workforce', *Harvard Business Review*, July–August.

in the organisation's interests to maintain the illusion of such career structures so as to retain high-performance employees. It could also be argued that such structures are useful for the organisation in recruiting highly skilled employees, for whom career structures are likely to continue. Purcell *et al.* (2003) also showed that positive perceptions of career advancement opportunities are one of the most powerful determinants of employee commitment. However, if this is an illusion such a strategy may well backfire on the organisation.

If the psychological contract between employer and employee now needs to be renegotiated (*see*, for example, Herriot and Pemberton 1996), this does not mean abandoning the concept of career, rather, the idea of a new psychological contract is developing. Many articles identify a 'new psychological contract' in which the deal between the employer and their staff is different but still mutually beneficial. Employees offer high productivity and total commitment while with their employer, and the employer offers enhanced *employability* rather than long term employment. The offer of employability centres on enabling employees to develop skills that are in demand, and allows them opportunities to practise these and keep up to date. This equips the employee with the skills and experiences needed to obtain another appropriate job when he or she is no longer needed by their present employer (*see*, for example, Waterman *et al.* 1994). The difference between the old psychological contract and the new psychological contract, as they relate to careers, are shown in Tables 19.1 and 19.2. King (2003) found that graduates rated the offer of employability as of most importance in career terms, and they still expected the organisation to provide a career for them; she argues that the picture presented is one of lip service and a less than whole-hearted commitment to the concept of the 'new career'.

However, a further contradiction is apparent in the literature: the assumption that the 'new psychological contract' supplants the old when the original contract is violated, but the degree to which this happens is debatable (*see*, for example, Doherty *et al.* 1997). Herriot (1998) argues that the new psychological contract is just more rhetoric, and that in reality there are many different new deals, and Sparrow (1996) suggests that the solution to the fragmentation of the old psychological contract is a series of layered individualised career contracts. King also suggests that the organisation should not adopt an either/or career approach, but aim to offer both internal careers and employability support.

DEFINITIONS AND IMPORTANCE OF CAREER DEVELOPMENT

A career can be defined as the pattern or sequence of work roles of an individual. Traditionally, the word applied only to those occupying managerial and professional roles, but increasingly it is seen as appropriate for everyone in relation to their work roles. Also, the word career has been used to imply upward movement and advancement in work roles. As we have noted, many organisations no longer offer a traditional career, or only offer it to a selected few. Enforced redundancies, flatter structures, short-term contracts, availability of part-time rather than full-time work, all break the idealised image of career. We now recognise other moves as legitimate expressions of career development, including development and extension within the job itself, lateral moves and the development of portfolio work. Career can also be conceptualised more broadly in terms of 'the individual's development in learning and work throughout life' (Collin and Watts 1996), and thus includes voluntary work and other life experiences. Indeed Adamson *et al.* (1998) go so far as to say that a good curriculum vitae may:

> no longer be one with an impressive list of job titles of increasing seniority, but rather a rich cv (e.g. one which includes a variety of work and non-work activities). (p. 256)

Male careers are becoming increasingly similar to the traditional fragmented pattern of women's careers (Goffee and Nicholson 1994), and many men are generally keener to develop careers which take account of personal and family needs, including children's education, partner's career and quality of life. Career development is no longer a stand-alone issue and needs to be viewed in the context of the life and development of the whole person and not just the person as employee.

We view career development as something experienced by the individual (sometimes referred to as the *internal* career), and therefore not necessarily bounded by one organisation. This also means that the responsibility for managing a career is with the individual, although the organisation may play a key facilitating and supporting role.

The primary purpose of career development is to meet the current and future needs of the organisation and the individual at work, and this increasingly means developing employability. On this basis Walton (1999) argues that it is increasingly difficult to disentangle career development from general training and development. We could make a strong case for the value of self-development here. Career success is seen through the eyes of the individual, and can be defined as individual satisfaction with career through meeting personal career goals, while making a contribution to the organisation. Although in this chapter we prioritise the needs of the individual, in Chapter 3 we prioritise the needs of the organisation when we review replacement and succession planning.

We have given priority to the individual in career development, but it is worth noting the general benefits career development provides for the organisation:

- It makes the organisation attractive to potential recruits.
- It enhances the image of the organisation, by demonstrating a recognition of employee needs.
- It is likely to encourage employee commitment and reduce staff turnover.
- It is likely to encourage motivation and job performance as employees can see some possible movement and progress in their work.
- Perhaps most importantly it exploits the full potential of the workforce.

Before looking at how individuals can manage their career development with organisational support, we need to review some of the concepts underlying the notion of career.

UNDERSTANDING CAREERS

Career development stages

Many authors have attempted to map out the ideal stages of a successful career, matched against an age range for each stage. Schein (1978) offers nine stages of the career life cycle, while other authors, such as Super (1980) and Hall and Nougaim (1968), have suggested five. In this section we review the five stages outlined by Greenhaus and Callanan (1994). Few careers follow such an idealised pattern, and even historically such a pattern did not apply for all employees. However, the stage approach offers a useful framework for understanding career experiences, if we use it flexibly as a tool for understanding careers rather than as a normative model.

Stage 1: occupational choice: preparation for work

The first stage may last until around age 25, or may reappear for those who wish to change career later in life. It involves developing an occupational self-image. The key theme is a matching process between the strengths/weaknesses, values and desired lifestyle of the individual and the requirements and benefits of a range of occupations. One of the difficulties that can arise at this stage is a lack of individual self-awareness. There are countless tests available to help identify individual interests, but these can only complete part of the picture, and need to be complemented by structured exercises, which help people look at themselves from a range of perspectives. Other problems involve individuals limiting their choice due to social, cultural, gender or racial characteristics. Although we use role models to identify potential occupations, and these extend the range of options we consider, this process may also close them down. Another difficulty at this stage is gaining authentic information about careers which are different from the ones pursued by family and friends.

Stage 2: organisational entry

There is some overlap between Stage 1 and Stage 2 which occurs, typically, between the ages of 18 and 25, but is revisited by most of us a number of times. It involves the individual in both finding a job which corresponds with their occupational self-image, and starting to do that job. Problems here centre on the accuracy of information that the organisation provides, so that when the individual begins work expectations and reality may be very different. Recruiters understandably 'sell' their organisations and the job to potential recruits, emphasising the best parts and neglecting the downside. Applicants often fail to test their assumptions by asking for the specific information they really need. In addition, schools, colleges and universities have, until recently, only prepared students for the technical demands of work, ignoring other skills that they will need, such as communication skills, influencing skills and dealing with organisational politics. To aid organisational entry, Wanous (1992) has suggested the idea of realistic recruitment which we refer to in Chapter 8.

ACTIVITY 19.1

Think of three different jobs in your organisation (or any organisation with which you are familiar) which have been/may be recruited externally. If a 'realistic recruitment' approach were adopted:

- What information would you give to the candidates about each job and the organisation so that a balanced picture was presented?
- What methods would you use to communicate this information?

Stage 3: early career – establishment and achievement

The age band for early career is between 25 and 40 years.

The establishment stage involves fitting into the organisation and understanding 'how things are done around here'. Thorough induction programmes are important, but more especially it is important to provide the new recruit with a 'real' job and early challenges rather than a roving commission from department to department with no real purpose, as often found on trainee schemes. Feedback and support from the immediate manager are also key.

The achievement part of this stage is demonstrating competence and gaining greater responsibility and authority. It is at this stage that access to opportunities for career development becomes key. Development within the job and opportunities for promotion and broadening moves are all aided if the organisation has a structured approach to career development, involving career ladders, pathways or matrices, but not necessarily hierarchical progression. Feedback remains important, as do opportunities and support for further career exploration and planning. Organisations are likely to provide the most support for 'high fliers' who are seen as the senior management of the future and who may be on 'fast track' programmes.

Stage 4: mid-career

Greenhaus and Callanan (1994) suggest that the mid-career stage usually falls between the ages of 40 to 55, and may involve further growth and advancement or the maintenance of a steady state. In either case it is generally accompanied by some form of re-evaluation of career and life direction. A few will experience decline at this stage. For those who continue to advance, organisational support remains important. Some people whose career has reached a plateau will experience feelings of failure. Organisational support in these cases needs to involve the use of lateral career paths, job expansion, development as mentors of others, further training to keep up to date and the use of a flexible reward system.

Stage 5: late career

The organisation's task in the late career stage is to encourage people to continue performing well. This is particularly important as some sectors are experiencing skills shortages and there are moves by some companies to allow individuals to stay at work after the state retirement age. Despite the stereotypes that abound defining older workers as slower and less able to learn, Mayo (1991) argues that if organisations believe these employees will do well and treat them accordingly they will perform well. Greenhaus and Callanan point out that the availability of flexible work patterns, clear performance standards, continued training and the avoidance of discrimination are helpful at this stage, combined with preparation for retirement.

ACTIVITY 19.2

If you had a high degree of choice in terms of your career stages would you prefer to:

1 Remain with one organisation for life, or move around?
2 Stay with one occupation/profession for life or change your occupation/profession once or twice?
3 Prefer hierarchical job moves with more responsibility in the same area, or the opportunity to move into new areas without increasing your responsibility level?
4 Prefer to retire as soon as you can, or work for as long as you can?

Identify the reasons for your choice, and consider its advantages and disadvantages. How likely do you think it is that you will be able to fulfil your choice?

Career anchors

Based on a longitudinal study of 44 male graduates of Massachusetts Institute of Technology Sloan School of Management completed in 1973, 10–12 years after graduation, Schein (1978) identified a set of five 'career anchors' and proposed that these explained the pattern of career decisions that each individual had taken. Schein described career anchors as much broader than motivation, and including the following:

- self-perceived talents and abilities;
- self-perceived motives and needs;
- self-perceived attitudes and values.

Our perception of ourselves in these areas comes from direct experiences of work, from successes, from self-diagnosis and feedback. The conclusions that we draw both drive and constrain future career development. Schein sees career anchors as a holistic representation of the person, which takes into account the interaction between the factors identified above. Career anchors can identify a source of personal stability in the person which has determined past choices and will probably determine future choices.

The problematic aspect of career anchors is the accuracy of the individual's self-perceptions, and the question of what happens in mid-career to those who feel their attitudes and values are changing. Schein acknowledges that career anchors are learned rather than reflecting latent abilities and are the sorts of things that people are reluctant to abandon. Not only do we all need to identify and understand what our anchors are in order to make sure we are doing the right thing, we also need to appreciate that there are things that we shall continue to need even if we make a career change.

Schein originally identified five career anchors and later supplemented them with another four. The original five are:

Technical/functional competence

Those who have this as their career anchor are interested in the technical content of their work and their feelings of competence in doing this. They tend not to be interested in management itself, as they prefer to exercise their technical skills. They would, however, be prepared to accept managerial responsibilities in their own functional area.

Managerial competence

For those with this career anchor, the exercising of managerial responsibility is an end in itself, and technical/functional jobs just a way of getting there. These people are most likely to end up in general managerial jobs and possess three key competences: analytical competence to solve problems characterised by incomplete information in areas of uncertainty; interpersonal competence to influence and control; and emotional resilience, with the ability to be stimulated rather than paralysed by crises.

Security and stability

It is characteristic of those with this career anchor to be prepared to do what the organisation wants of them in order to maintain job security and the present and future benefits which go with this. Given the choice, most will therefore remain with one organisation for life, although there are alternative patterns such as remaining in the same geographical area but moving between different employers, and making separate financial provision for the future. Because they have not sought career success in terms of hierarchical promotion those with this career anchor often feel a sense of failure, and find it hard to accept their own criteria for career success. This group are more likely to integrate career with home life.

Creativity

Individuals with creativity as a career anchor feel the need to build something new. They are driven by wanting to extend themselves, get involved in new ventures and projects and could be described as entrepreneurial. Should their new venture turn into a thriving business they may become bored by the need to manage it and are more likely to hand this aspect over to others.

Autonomy and independence

The desire to be free of organisational constraints in the exercise of their technical/functional competence is what drives those with this career anchor. They tend to find organisational life restrictive and intrusive into their personal lives and prefer to set their own pace and work style. They will usually work alone or in a small firm. Consultants, writers and lecturers are typical of the roles that this group occupy.

The four additional anchors which Schein added later are:

Basic identity

Those with this career anchor are driven by the need to achieve and sustain an occupational identity. Typically they are in lower-level jobs where their role is represented visually perhaps with badges or uniforms. In this way their role is defined externally, and some may seek, for example, to be associated with a prestigious employer.

Service to others

The driving force here is the need to help others, often through the exercise of interpersonal competence or other skills. The need is not to exercise such competence as an end in itself, but for the purpose of helping others; typical examples here would be teachers and doctors.

Power, influence and control

This career anchor can be separate from the managerial anchor or may be a pronounced part of it. Those driven by this career anchor may pursue political careers, teaching, medicine or the church as these areas may give them the opportunity to exercise influence and control over others.

Variety

Those who seek variety may do so for different reasons. This career anchor may be relevant for those who have a wide range of talents, who value flexibility or who get bored very easily.

Career balance

Much of the original work done on describing career stages and career anchors was carried out by analysing the experiences of those who were both male and white, so the analyses are clearly inadequate for our contemporary world of work. Schein's development of his original set of career anchors shows understanding is being reshaped, but we still lack satisfactory explanations of career development that can embrace the full variety of ethnic backgrounds, gender and occupational variety.

There is considerable evidence that racial minorities and women limit their career choices, both consciously and unconsciously, for reasons not to do with their basic abilities and career motives. Social class identity may have the same impact. Employers need at least to be aware of such forces and ideally would explore such constraints with their employees to encourage individual potential to be exploited to the full.

The acceptance of such idealised career development stages as described above, particularly in an era of work intensification, leaves little room for family and other interference in career development, and until recently there has been no place in career development and even in the thinking about careers for those who do not conform to the stages outlined. There are hopeful signs of increasing recognition that career and life choices need to be explored in unison. There has also been little recognition of the commercial environment and the impact that this has on career development stages for many individuals. Considerable attention is being paid, currently, to the concept of work-life balance (*see* IDS 2000) where aspects of work are combined with other life choices and we devote Chapter 32 to this issue.

INDIVIDUAL CAREER MANAGEMENT

If we identify a career as the property of the individual, then clearly the responsibility for managing this rests on the individual, who should identify career goals, adopt strategies to support them and devise plans to achieve the goal.

In reality, however, many people fail to plan. Pringle and Gold (1989), for example, found a lack of career planning in their sample of 50 'achieving' men and women managers. Only around a quarter of people had plans for the future and many identified luck, opportunity or being in the right place at the right time as the reason they had achieved promotions. Harlan and Weiss (1982) found both men and women drifting into positions created through coincidences.

Of course, we do not know how well these people would have done had they planned – they might have done even better. We argue that planning is an essential ingredient of individual career management even if only to provide a framework for decisions about the opportunities that arise through identifying priorities. We also argue that the more an individual attempts to manage their career, the more likely it is that opportunities will arise and the more likely that they are to be able to do something constructive with them.

Mayo suggests that in defining a career goal it is too difficult for a person to try to specify the ultimate goal of their career. Career aiming points are more appropriate if based on a 10–15-year timespan, or maybe a shorter period.

A career goal will be specific to the individual, such as to become an internal senior organisational consultant by the age of 35. The range of strategies that a person may adopt in pursuit of their goal can be described in terms of more general groups. The list below describes the type of strategies, identified from a review of the literature by Gould and Penley (1984).

- **Creating opportunities.** This involves building the appropriate skills and experiences that are needed for a career in the organisation. Developing those skills that are seen as critical to the individual's supervisor and department are most useful, as is exercising leadership in an area where none exists at present.
- **Extended work involvement.** This necessitates working long hours, both at the workplace and at home, and may also involve a preoccupation with work issues at all times.
- **Self-nomination/self-presentation.** The individual who pursues this strategy will communicate the desire for increased responsibility to their managers. They will also make known their successes, and build an image of themselves as someone who achieves things.
- **Seeking career guidance.** This involves seeking out a more experienced person, either within the organisation or without, and looking for guidance or sponsorship. The use of mentor relationships would come into this category.
- **Networking.** Networking involves developing contacts both inside and outside the organisation to gain information and support.
- **Interpersonal attraction.** This strategy builds the relationship with one's immediate manager on the basis that they will have an impact on career progression. One form of this is 'opinion conformity'; that is, sharing the key opinions of the individual's manager, perhaps with minor deviations. Another is expressed as 'other enhancement', which may involve sharing personal information with one's manager and becoming interested in similar pursuits.

More recently Siebert and colleagues (2001) suggest that career success hinges on who you know as well as what you know, and often on the relationship between the two. In their research they found that it was better to have a large network of contacts and weaker ties, rather than a smaller network with stronger ties.

These strategies provide some difficulties for women:

> women in management often find it difficult to break into the male-dominated 'old boy network' and therefore are denied the contacts, opportunities and policy information it provides. (Davidson and Cooper 1992, p. 129)

The career strategies explored above are clearly most appropriate in the early and mid-career stages, and other strategies will best fit other stages.

There is evidence however, that individuals are generally not good at career self-management, as demonstrated by Sturges *et al.* (2002). Nevertheless, they did find that informal career support, perhaps in terms of mentoring, did reinforce self-management activities. This supports the partnership approach to career development. From a slightly different angle, Yarnall (1998) found that career education for employees helps them extract support from the business. In the 2003 career management survey by CIPD (2003) 95 per cent of respondents felt that individuals will be expected to take responsibility for their own careers in the future and 90 per cent felt that they must be offered organisational support to do this. Arguing that the public sector seems to depend more on the individual to drive their own career Hirsh (2003) suggests that this may be related to the lower effectiveness of the public sector.

ACTIVITY 19.3

What general types of career strategy would be appropriate for:

- organisational entry?
- late career?

Compare your views with those of people you know who are in each of these career stages.

While the strategies discussed above were derived from careers within an organisational context, similar strategies could be appropriate for employees forced to look more widely in developing their careers. Arthur and Rousseau (1996b) suggest that individuals need to develop career resilience, which they defined as bouncing back from disruptions to one's career, and Waterman *et al.* (1994), in an article on the career-resilient workforce, suggest that individuals need to:

- Make themselves knowledgeable about relevant market trends.
- Understand the skills and knowledge needed in their area and anticipate future needs.
- Be aware of their own strengths and weaknesses.
- Have a plan for increasing their performance and employability.
- Respond quickly to changing business needs.
- Move on from their current employer when a win/win relationship is no longer possible.

Ball (1997) identifies four career management competencies. Three of these are planning, engaging in personal development and balancing work and non-work. The fourth is optimising, which includes intelligence gathering, seeking a mentor, having a positive self-image and gaining the attention of others. However Hirsh (2003) argues that:

> If employees want to get on they should seek qualifications and training, greater responsibility and varied work experiences. They should not work reduced hours, take career breaks, work from home or get ill. (p. 7)

So far we have tended to focus on career moves within the organisation, but many people desire the next career move to be to another organisation or into a new type of career. The concept of a personal career agent has emerged for top-flight executives and for further details on this see case 19.1 on the website. However, most us of need to rely on our own skills and effort to make a career move. In particular, moving into a different type of career is very difficult for many of us and so we conclude this section by discussing why this is so difficult and what steps might be taken to improve one's chances of success. Drummond and Chell (2001) use two case studies

to illustrate some of the issues which embed us in our career. They explain, using Becker's theory of side bets, how other interests influence our choice of career in addition to the work itself, for example the likelihood of high earnings, status, travel and so on. If these desires are fulfilled but we are dissatisfied with our career we may find ourselves trapped. They also show how we use self-justification to defend the careers choices we have made and to stick with them, failure or problems being attributed to external causes. They suggest that decisions made early in life are hard to reverse and that the more we stick with what we have done and the more we rationalise this, the more likely we are to stick with it in the future. Ibarra (2002) also uses case studies to illustrate how individuals try to make the change but fail due to the way they go about it, in addition to the natural fear we have of change. There are cases where dramatic changes were attempted and failed, either because they turned out to be the same as before (moving to a new job in a new organisation, but finding the nature of the work just the same) or because they just did not work (as in a new start-up business that could not make sufficient profit). Not only is self-knowledge important, Ibarra argues, but much of this needs to be gained from real experiences. Planning to change and using advisers is insufficient. She suggests that:

> working identity, as a practice, is necessarily a process of experimenting, testing, and learning about our possible selves. (p. 43)

Her advice is to try out new activities on a small scale before making a major commitment to a new career path, for example, trying out additional work at the evenings or weekends, or on the basis of temporarily reduced hours, sabbatical or extended holidays, and maybe working on a voluntary basis. She also suggests developing new networks and reference groups in areas where we may be interested to work, as these people will not only provide information and possible opportunities but also a support network when different types of work are begun. Third, she suggests that we to seek out or create triggers and catalysts for change. For example, one may use redundancy as an opportunity to be free to try something different.

ORGANISATIONAL SUPPORT FOR CAREER DEVELOPMENT

Although career management is primarily the individual's responsibility, organisations can and should support this. This will be relevant whether careers are offered internally or whether employability is promoted, although the support may be different. Most organisations still see career management as optional rather than essential, its future orientation makes it slip down the business agenda, and there is always a tension between individual and organisational needs (Hirsh 2003). Successful career management is dependent on resolving these differences. CIPD (2003) argues that the factors contributing to effective career management are using career management activities valued by employees; training of line managers and HR staff in career management; line managers taking career management seriously; commitment of senior managers; a formal written career management strategy; integration with overall HR and business strategy. Based on the 2003 CIPD study Hirsh notes that the main barriers to career management are practical rather than philosophical and involve lack of time and resources, career management being seen as peripheral and lack of senior management commitment. Organisations can help individuals with:

- **Career exploration** – providing tools and help for self-diagnosis and supplying organisational information.
- **Career goal setting** – providing a clear view of the career opportunities available in the business, making a wider range of opportunities available to meet different career priorities.
- **Career strategies and action planning** – providing information and support; what works in this organisation; what's realistic; when considering working for other organisations may be appropriate.
- **Career feedback** – providing an honest appraisal of current performance and career potential.

Organisations can make this contribution through the following activities.

Career strategy

Although a career strategy is critical, less than a half of the organisations responding to the 2003 CIPD careers survey reported that a written career strategy existed, and only one-quarter of respondents had a career strategy that covered *all* employees. Most organisations concentrate on senior managers and key staff that the organisation wishes to retain. There appeared to be little support for traditionally disadvantaged groups such as part-time workers, those returning after long-term sick absence or a career break, women returning to work after bearing children and workers over age 50.

Career pathways and grids

A career path is a sequence of job roles or positions, related via work content or abilities required, through which an individual can move. Publicised pathways can help people to identify a realistic career goal within the organisation. Traditional pathways were normally presented as a vertical career ladder, emphasising upward promotion within a function, often formally or informally using age limits and formal qualifications for entry to certain points of the ladder. Joining the pathway other than at the normal entry point was very difficult. These pathways tended to limit career opportunities as much as they provided helpful information. The emphasis on upward movement meant that career progress for the majority was halted early on in their careers. The specifications of age and qualification meant that the pathways were restricted to those who had an 'ideal' career development profile but excluded those who had taken career breaks, or who had lots of relevant experience but no formal qualifications. This inflexibility tended to stifle cross-functional moves and emphasised progression via management rather than equally through development of technical expertise.

There is now increasing use of alternative approaches, often designed in the form of a grid, with options at each point, so that upwards, lateral, diagonal and even downwards moves can be made. These grids may also be linked into grids for other parts of the business, thereby facilitating cross-functional moves. Ideally, positions are described in behavioural terms, identifying the skills, knowledge and attitudes required for a position rather than the qualifications needed or age range anticipated. However, as organisations continue to change more and more rapidly even such a matrix may prove to be too rigid and career opportunities may need to be expressed in terms of groups of roles, and be fluid enough to integrate newly developed and unexpected types of roles.

Not only do career pathways and grids need to be carefully communicated to employees, they also need to reflect reality, and not just present an ideal picture of desirable career development. Managers who will be appointing staff need to be fully apprised of the philosophy of career development and the types of move that the organisation wishes to encourage. It is important that the organisation reinforces lateral moves by developing a payment system that rewards the development of skills and not just the organisation level.

Fast-track programmes

Fast-track programmes have been considered as a way of developing and retaining high performers. However, problems have been found with such accelerated progress. Hall (1999) reports that although individuals on such programmes perform well early on, they tend to experience derailment later in their career. He proposed four reasons for this. First, that moving through the organisation so quickly means that they have never been in one place long enough to develop a network of learning support. Second, that in their rapid progress they will have alienated a lot of people on the way. Third, that they have never been in one position long enough to experience failure and setbacks and learn how to deal with these, and, finally, this means that they have not received sufficient developmental feedback, which is critical to career success. Iles (1997) suggests that to make such careers more sustainable there needs to be greater emphasis on developing empowerment skills and more developmental feedback.

Career conversations

The lack of opportunity to discuss career options is frustrating for employees, and to discover the nature of helpful career conversations Hirsh and her colleagues (2001) asked individuals to explain positive career conversations in terms of where they took place, who was involved, how they were conducted and the impact that they had. They found that only around one-fifth of the discussions took place with the individual's line manager and many more had conversations with other managers in the organisation, and some with specialist advisers or HR. Around half the discussions took place informally, outside the remit of, say, an appraisal, development centre, mentoring, coaching, or any other formal system, and of these 40 per cent were unplanned. It was key that discussions were held with people who were trusted and open, prepared to be frank about the individual's skills and potential and who were genuinely interested in the individual. Around three-quarters of these conversations appeared to result in some form of career action. Hirsh and her colleagues note that these findings differ from current ideas of best practice which are to discuss career with one's line manager in an appraisal context.

Managerial support

In spite of the above findings managerial support remains critical, not only in terms of appointing staff, but also in terms of supporting the career development of their current staff. Direct feedback on current performance and potential is vital, especially in identifying strengths and weaknesses, and what improvement is required. The immediate manager is in a good position to refer the individual to other managers and introduce them into a network which will support their career moves. In addition the manager is in the ideal position to provide job challenges and experiences within the current job which will equip the incumbent with the skills needed for the desired career move.

Unfortunately, managers often do not see these responsibilites as part of their job and see them as belonging to the HR department, and Hirsh notes that managers often need to be cajoled by HR to play their part. Yarnall (1998) found low levels of support from managers, but also found that employees participating in self-development career initiatives did encourage management support. Managers often feel constrained by their lack of knowledge about other parts of the organisation, and often withdraw from giving accurate feedback about career potential, particularly when they know that what they have to say is not what the individual wishes to hear. CIPD (2003) notes that there appears to be a lack of training for line managers to support them in their career development role. It also found that the most common career goals explored by line managers were around short-term promotions and projects within the organisation at the expense of more complex issues such as lateral moves, secondments, work-life balance and career flexibility Managers are also sometimes tempted, in their own interests, to hold on to good employees rather than encouraging them to develop elsewhere.

ACTIVITY 19.4

As a member of the HR function pursuing an organisational philosophy of flexible career moves and continuous career development, how would you:

- encourage managers to adopt this philosophy?
- prepare them for the skills they will need to use?

What other career development support could immediate managers give in addition to the suggestions made above?

Career counselling

Occasionally immediate managers will be involved in career counselling, drawing out the strengths, weaknesses, values and interests of their staff. In many cases, however, those who seek such counselling would prefer to speak in confidence to someone independent of their work situation. In these circumstances a member of the HR department may act as counsellor. In more complex cases, or those involving senior members of staff, professionals external to the organisation may be sought. This is also more likely to be the case if the career counselling is offered as part of an outplacement programme resulting from a redundancy.

Career workshops

Career workshops are usually, but not always, conducted off-site, and offered as a confidential programme to help individuals assess their strengths and weaknesses, values and interests, identify career opportunities, set personal career goals and begin to develop a strategy and action plan. Career goals will not necessarily be restricted to the current employing organisation – and one objective of the workshop is often to broaden career perspectives. Workshops may last 2–3 days, and normally involve individual paper-and-pencil exercises, group discussions, one-to-one discussions and private conferences with tutors. For some people these can be quite traumatic events as they involve whole-life exploration, and often buried issues are confronted which have been avoided in the hurly-burly of day-to-day life. The most difficult part for many individuals is keeping the momentum going after the event by continuing the action planning and self-assessment of progress.

Self-help workbooks

As an alternative to a workshop there are various self-help guides and workbooks which can assist people to work through career issues by presenting a structure and framework. Organisations such as 'Lifeskills' provide a range of workbooks appropriate for different stages of career development.

Career centres

Career centres within organisations can be used as a focal point for the provision of organisational and external career information. The centre may include a library on career choices and exploration, information on organisational career ladders and grids, current opportunities to apply for, self-help workbooks and computer packages. Such centres appear to be relatively common in large organisations, yet CIPD (2003) reports that participants do not consider them to be very useful.

Assessment and development centres

Assessment centres for internal staff have traditionally taken the form of pass/fail assessment for a selected group of high-potential managers at a specific level. They were focused on organisational rather than individual needs. Recently changes to some of these centres have moved the focus to the individual, with less limitation on who is allowed to attend. These 'development centres' assess the individual's strengths and weaknesses and provide feedback and development plans so that each can make the most of his or her own potential. The outcome is not pass/fail but action plans for personal and career development.

Whatever career activities are in place in the organisation it is important to ensure that:

- There is a clear and agreed careers philosophy communicated to all in the organisation.
- Managers are supported in their career development responsibilities.

- Career opportunities are communicated to staff.
- There is an appropriate balance between open and closed internal recruitment.
- The reasons for the balance are explained.
- Knowledge, skills and attitude development are rewarded as well as achievement of a higher organisational level.
- Attention is given to career development within the current job.

Although all of these activities focus on careers within an organisation, most are still appropriate for employers providing development leading to employability rather than long-term employment. Waterman *et al.* (1994) stress that employers need to move to an adult/adult relationship with their employees from that of parent/child, be prepared to share critical organisational information and let go of the old notion of loyalty, thus accepting that good employees will leave. Hiltrop (1996) provides a good range of suggestions for managing the changing psychological contract.

ACTIVITY 19.5

- What are the advantages and disadvantages of open and closed internal recruitment?
- In which circumstances might it be appropriate to give a greater emphasis to closed recruitment?
- In which circumstances might it be appropriate to give a greater emphasis to open recruitment?

Perhaps the most outstanding challenge is to come to terms with the fact that careers have changed due to a changing organisation structure and competitive demands; individuals in our current labour market have a greater say in their career and how it relates to their whole life; and that alternative career profiles are equally legitimate. It is a sad reflection that in most research career development activities are not found to have a high profile (*see*, for example, Atkinson 2000).

SUMMARY PROPOSITIONS

19.1 The context of careers is changing from long-term careers in one organisation with upward movement to careers that are characterised by disruption, movement between employers and the development of portfolios of work. There is a school of thought that suggests this trend is overstated.

19.2 Careers are owned by individuals and the primary responsibility for managing them falls to the individual; organisations have a role in supporting and encouraging this.

19.3 Theories of career development include career stage theories and career anchors. Although these were developed in an era of more stable career structures they still have interpretive value if used in a flexible manner.

19.4 Individuals need to manage their careers and aim to become career resilient, so that they have developed the skills and knowledge to overcome career setbacks.

19.5 Organisations can support and encourage individual career management by providing flexible and realistic career grids, honest feedback, opportunities for individual career exploration and planning.

GENERAL DISCUSSION TOPICS

1 What is the career management challenge for the early twenty-first century? What appropriate strategies and actions might there be for employers and employees?

2 'No matter how much we encourage individuals to plan their careers, at the end of the day it comes down to opportunity and chance.'

Do you think that this comment is a fair reflection of the way that individuals manage their careers?

FURTHER READING

Daniels, I., Schramm, J. and Ryder, B. (2002) 'Evolution at work', *People Management*, Vol. 8, No. 11, 30 May, pp. 28–30

A thought-provoking article based on the views of six experts of what work and careers will look like in the future.

Hirsh, W. and Rolph, J. (2003) 'Snakes and Ladders', *People Management*, Vol. 9, No. 9, 1 May, pp. 36–7

An extremely useful summary of the CIPD 2003 survey report *Managing Employee Careers*, together with some brief material from CIPD's *Reflections: Trends and Issues in Career Management*. If you do not have time to read the full reports this is an accessible and informative alternative.

REFERENCES

Adamson, S., Doherty, N. and Viney, C. (1998) 'The meanings of career revisited: Implications for theory and practice', *British Journal of Management*, Vol. 9, pp. 251–9.

Arthur, M. (1994) 'The boundaryless career', *Journal of Organisational Behaviour*, Vol. 15, pp. 295–306.

Arthur, M. and Rousseau, D. (1996a) 'A career lexicon for the 21st century', *Academy of Management Executive*, Vol. 10, No. 4, pp. 28–39.

Arthur, M. and Rousseau, D. (1996b) *The Boundaryless Career: A New Employment Principle for a New Organisational Era*. Oxford: OUP.

Atkinson, C. (2000) 'Career management strategies in a major UK plc', paper presented to the British Academy of Management Conference, September, Edinburgh.

Ball, B. (1997) 'Career Management competencies – the individual perspective', *Career Development International*, Vol. 2, No. 2.

Burke, R. (1998a) 'Correlations of job insecurity amongst recent business school graduates', *Employee Relations*, Vol. 20/1, No. 2, pp. 92–100.

Burke, R. (1998b) 'Changing career rules: clinging to the past or accepting the new reality?' *Career Development International*, Vol. 3, No. 1.

CIPD (2003) *Managing Employee Careers – Issues, Trends and Prospects, Survey Report, June 2003*. London: CIPD.

Collin, A. and Watts, A. (1996) 'The death and transfiguration of career – and of career guidance?' *British Journal of Guidance and Counselling*, Vol. 24, No. 3, pp. 385–98.

Davidson, M.J. and Cooper, C. (1992) *Shattering the Glass Ceiling*. London: Paul Chapman.

Doherty, N., Viney, C. and Adamson, S. (1997) 'Rhetoric or reality – shifts in the philosophy and practice of graduate career management?' *Career Development International*, Vol. 2, No. 4.

Drummond, H. and Chell, E. (2001) 'Life's chances and choices: A study of entrapment in career dicisions with reference to Becker's side bet theory', *Personnel review*, Vol. 30, No. 2, pp. 186–202.

Goffee, R. and Nicholson, N. (1994) 'Career development in male and female managers – convergence or collapse?' in M.J. Davidson and R.J. Burke (eds) *Women in Management: Current Research Issues*. London: Paul Chapman.

Gould, S. and Penley, L. (1984) 'Career strategies and salary progression: a study of their relationships in a municipal bureaucracy', *Organisational Behaviour and Human Performance*, Vol. 34, pp. 244–65.

Greenhaus, J.H. and Callanan, G.A. (1994) *Career Management*. London: Dryden Press.

Guest, D. and McKenzie-Davey, K. (1996) 'Don't write off the traditional career', *People Management*, February.

Hall, D.T. (1999) 'Accelerate executive development at your peril', *Career Development International*, Vol. 4, No. 4, pp. 237–9.

Hall, D.T. and Nougaim, K. (1968) 'An examination of Maslow's need hierarchy in an organisational setting', *Organisational Behaviour and Human Performance*, Vol. 13, pp. 12–35.

Handy, C. (1994) *The Empty Raincoat: Making Sense of the Future*. London: Hutchinson.

Harlan, A. and Weiss, C.L. (1982) 'Sex differences in factors affecting managerial career advancement', in P.A. Wallace (ed.) *Women in the Workforce*. London: Auburn House, ch. 4.

Herriot, P. (1998) 'The role of the HRM function in building a new proposition for staff', in P. Sparrow and M. Machington (eds) *Human Resource Management: The New Agenda*. London: Financial Times/Pitman.

Herriot, P. and Pemberton, C. (1996) 'Contracting careers', *Human Relations*, Vol. 49, No. 6, pp. 757–90.

Herriot, P., Manning, W. and Kidd, J. (1997) 'The content of the psychological contract', *British Journal of Management*, Vol. 8, pp. 151–62.

Hiltrop, J.-M. (1996) 'Managing the changing psychological contract', *Employee Relations*, Vol. 18, No. 4, pp. 36–49.

Hirsh, W. (2003) 'Career management – meeting the challenge?' in CIPD (ed.) *Reflections: Trends and Issues in Career Management*. London: CIPD.

Hirsh, W., Jackson, C. and Kidd, J. (2001) 'A word with the wise', *People Management*, Vol. 7, No. 12, 4 June, pp. 42–6.

Ibarra, H. (2002) 'How to stay stuck in the wrong career', *Harvard Business Review*, December, pp. 40–7.

IDS (2000) *Work-life Balance*, IDS Study 698, November. London: IDS.

Iles, P. (1997) 'Sustainable high-potential career development: a resource-based view', *Career Development International*, Vol. 2, No. 7.

Kanter, R.M. (1989) *When Giants Learn to Dance*. New York: Simon and Schuster.

King, Z. (2003) 'New or traditional careers? A study of UK graduates' perceptions', *Human Resource Management Journal*, Vol. 13, No. 1, pp. 5–26.

Mallon, M. (1998) 'The portfolio career; pushed or pulled to it?' *Personnel Review*, Vol. 27, No. 5.

Mayo, A. (1991) *Managing Careers: strategies for organisations*. London: IPM.

Pringle, J.K. and Gold, U.O'C. (1989) 'How useful is career planning for today's managers?' *Journal of Management Development*, Vol. 8, No. 3, pp. 21–6.

Purcell, J., Kinnie, N., Hutchinson, S., Rayton, B. and Swart, J. (2003) *Understanding the people and performance link: Unlocking the black box*. London: CIPD.

Schein, E. (1978) *Career Dynamics: Matching individual and organisation needs*. Reading, Mass.: Addison-Wesley.

Siebert, S., Kraimer, M. and Liden, R. (2001) 'A social capital theory of career success', *Academy of Management Journal*, Vol. 44, No. 2, pp. 219–37.

Smithson, J. and Lewis, S. (2000) 'Is job insecurity changing the psychological contract?' *Personnel Review*, Vol. 29, No. 6.

Sparrow, P. (1996) 'Transitions in the psychological contract: some evidence from the banking sector', *Human Resource Management Journal*, Vol. 6, No. 4.

Sturges, J., Guest, D., Conway, N. and MacKenzie Davey, K. (2002) 'A longitudinal study of the relationship between career management and organisational commitment among graduates in the first ten years at work', *Journal of Organisational Behaviour*, Vol. 23, pp. 731–48.

Super, D.E. (1980) 'A life span, life space approach to career development', *Journal of Vocational Behaviour*, Vol. 16, pp. 282–98.

Thomas, R. and Dunkerley, D. (1999) 'Careering downwards? Middle managers' experiences in the downsized organisation', *British Journal of Management*, Vol. 10, pp. 157–69.

Walton, J. (1999) *Strategic Human Resource Development*. Harlow: Financial Times Prentice Hall.

Wanous, J.P. (1992) *Recruitment, Selection, Orientation and Socialisation of Newcomers*. Wokingham: Addison-Wesley.

Waterman, R.H., Waterman, J.A. and Collard, B.A. (1994) 'Toward a career resilient workforce', *Harvard Business Review*, July–August.

Yarnall, J. (1998) 'Line managers as career developers: rhetoric or reality?' *Personnel Review*, Vol. 27, No. 5.

An extensive range of additional materials, including multiple choice questions, answers to questions and links to useful websites can be found on the Human Resource Management Companion Website at www.pearsoned.co.uk/torrington.

Part IV FOCUS ON SKILLS

INTERACTIVE SKILL 4: TEACHING AND PRESENTATION

In February 2004, the British Learning and Skills Council published the results of a Survey of 72,000 public and private employers that showed 22 per cent of them reporting skill shortages as impeding the development of their businesses and impairing productivity. To some extent this seems to be an endemic British problem, with similar dire warnings being produced from time to time, for at least the last sixty years, as British output per worker continues to lag behind that of other Western economies. However, the need for training is universal and increasing, as few people can rely in their middle years on the skills they acquired in their youth. Indeed, few people can rely in the future on the skills they acquired last year.

A central function of HRM is to enable people to learn. There are all manner of ways in which this can be done, especially with the development of technical aids, but here we concentrate on the face-to-face learning situations of teaching and presentation. Many people visualise teaching as a process in which someone who knows instructs someone who does not; but enabling people to learn goes beyond simple instruction. Learners frequently have to discover for themselves, as this is the only way in which they will understand, and they frequently can only learn by their interaction with other people in a group, as it is the group process alone that can help them develop their social skills.

The objectives of this Focus on skills are to:

1 Review various approaches to learning
2 Describe different types of learner
3 Explain job instruction
4 Explain features of presentation

Teaching a person to do something is different from teaching someone to understand something, and understanding something intellectually is different from understanding and changing how you interact with other people.

Approaches to learning

Different types of learning require fundamentally different methods and approaches by the teacher. One popular classification is to distinguish between memorising, understanding and doing (MUD). This classification was the result of research by Downs and Perry (1987), who identified blockages to learning, especially by adults, and was widely promoted in the late 1980s by, among others, the Manpower Services Commission. A more detailed classification was shown in the CRAMP taxonomy (ITRU 1976), developed after a study of the work of the Belbins (Belbin and Belbin 1972) and following an earlier analysis by Bloom (1956). This system divides all learning into five basic types.

1 *Comprehension* is where the learning involves knowing how, why and when certain things happen, so that learning has only taken place when the learner understands: not simply when the learner has memorised. Examples include having enough understanding of how German grammar works to be able to get the words of a sentence in the right order, or knowing enough of the law of employment to decide whether or not someone has been dismissed unfairly.
2 *Reflex learning* is involved when skilled movements or perceptual capacities have to be acquired, involving practice as well as knowing what to do. Speed is usually important and the task needs constant repetition to develop the appropriate synchronisation and coordination. Many of the obvious examples lie outside the interests of most personnel managers, such as juggling, gymnastics or icing a cake, but there are many examples in most organisations, such as driving a fork-lift truck, spot welding, fault-finding and typing. One of the most widespread in management circles is the use of a keyboard.
3 *Attitude development* is enabling people to develop the capacity to alter their attitudes and improve their social skills. Much customer care training has this as its basis. The theory is that dealing with customers requires people to be confident of their own ability to deal with others, shedding some of their feelings of insecurity and discovering how they are able to elicit a positive response. This can partly be achieved by the process of 'scripting', whereby staff have a set formula to follow. We are all familiar with making a telephone call which brings a response along the lines of, 'Good morning. Bloggs, Blenkinsop, Huggins and Scratchit. Mandy speaking. How may I help you?' The woodenness of that method can be overcome by enabling people to develop positive attitudes about themselves and their relationships with others, so that they can cope effectively with other people in a variety of situations, including the telephone.

4 *Memory training* is a way of enabling trainees to remember how to handle a variety of given situations. Pharmacists learn by rote a series of maximum dosages, for example, and an office messenger will need to remember that all invoices go to Mr Brown and all cheques to Mrs Smith. Anyone who is good with figures has probably at some time learned their multiplication tables. When doing it, this is a terrible chore, yet it is fundamental to any facility with numbers. Police officers remember the registration numbers of cars better than most of us, and we all need to remember telephone numbers and PINs. Memory training is distinguished from comprehension because understanding is not necessary, only recall, and it is worth referring back to the example above of understanding German grammar. Learning grammatical rules by rote does not enable one to use that knowledge, because understanding is also required. Learning your PIN does not require any understanding at all.

5 *Procedural learning* is similar to memory except that the drill to be followed does not have to be memorised, but located and understood. An example is the procedure to be followed in shutting down a plant at Christmas, or dealing with a safety drill.

Most forms of training involve more than one type of learning, so that the apprentice vehicle mechanic will need to understand how the car works as well as practising the skill of tuning an engine, and the driver needs to practise the skill of coordinating hands, feet and eyes in driving as well as knowing the procedure to follow if the car breaks down. Broadly speaking, however, comprehension-type learning is best approached by a method that teaches the whole subject as an entity rather than splitting it up into pieces and taking one at a time. Here the lecture or training manual is typically used. Attitude change is now often handled by group discussion, but reflex learning is best handled by part methods, which break the task down into sections, each of which can be studied and practised separately before being put together as a complete performance, just as a tennis player will practise the serve, the smash, the forehand, the backhand and other individual strokes before playing a match in which all are used. Memory and procedural learning may take place either by whole or by part methods, although memorisation is usually best done by parts.

ACTIVITY IV.1

1 Think of things that you have learned in the recent past and identify whether the learning was comprehension, reflex, attitude development, memorisation or procedural.

2 How would you classify learning for the following?

Swimming	Selection interviewing
Calorie counting in a diet	Learning Russian
Parenting	Running a business
Safe lifting	Preparing for retirement

Types of learner

Learners differ according to their prior knowledge, the quality and nature of their previous education and their age. CRAMP (comprehension, reflex learning, attitude development, memory training, procedural learning) was based on research among adults and most of the teaching carried out under the aegis of HRM is with adults, so we need some understanding of how learners differ. An excellent analysis has been produced by Robert Quinn (1988) based on earlier work by Dreyfus *et al.* (1986). It also appears in Quinn's work on management skills (Quinn *et al.* 1990). He believes that mastery of an activity involves a learning process that takes place over an extended period of time and that the capacity to learn evolves at the same time. The inference of this is that our approach to organising facilities for others to learn will be influenced by how far their learning capacity has developed. There are five stages:

1. *The novice* learns facts and rules without criticism or discussion, accepting that there are ways of doing things that others have devised, and that's that.
2. *The advanced beginner* goes a little further by being able to incorporate the lessons of experience, so that understanding begins to expand and embellish the basic facts and rules. As you begin to experience working in an organisation, aspects of cultural norms become apparent that are just as important as the basic rules. You find out the subtleties of the dress code and working relationships and extend competence by trying out very slight departures from the rigidity of the rules.
3. *Competency* represents a further development of confidence and a reduced reliance on absolute rules by recognising a wider variety of cues from the working context. There is a greater degree of learning by trial and error, experimenting with new behaviours. It is not abandoning the rules, but being able to use them more imaginatively and with an interpretation that suits one's own personal strengths and inclinations.
4. *Proficiency* is where the learner transcends analysis and begins to use intuition:

> Calculation and rational analysis seem to disappear. The unconscious, fluid, and effortless performance begins to emerge, and no one plan is held sacred. You learn to unconsciously 'read' the evolving situation. You notice cues and respond to new cues as the importance of the old ones recedes. (Quinn *et al.* 1990, p. 315)

5. *Expert* is the term used to describe those rare people who produce a masterly performance simply by doing what comes naturally, because all the learning has fused together to develop a capacity based on having in their heads 'multidimensional maps of the territory' that are unknown to other people; they are thus able to meet effortlessly the contradictions of organisational life.

This is a neat and helpful model, although it could also be an excuse for sloppy thinking and an inability to see that there has been a sea change that undermines the expert's certainties. HR students have ground into them the risks of snap judgements in selection interviewing ('I can tell as soon as they come through the door') and there will always be a temptation for established managers to take short cuts on the basis of their assumed expertise without realising that the rules have been changed and they are now playing the wrong game.

WINDOW ON PRACTICE

David teaches a teacher-training course which has a mixture of students. Most are recent graduates with little working experience but well-developed study skills. A minority are a little older, usually mothers with growing children, who have experience, but whose study skills are rusty. He finds that the mature students tend to dominate discussion at the beginning of the course, as they constantly relate everything to their own experience and circumstances, while the recent graduates feel at a loss and put down. After a few weeks the younger students become more assertive in discussion as they gain confidence from their developing understanding, and the mature students are less dominant because they are beginning to question some of the taken-for-granted certainty of their earlier opinions. Mutual respect gradually develops and both groups learn from each other. David classifies the recent graduates as novices rapidly becoming advanced beginners and the mature students as competents who have to revert to being novices in order to move on to proficiency.

Job instruction

The first step in learning a skill is for the learner to understand the task and what needs to be done to produce a satisfactory performance. This provides the initial framework for, and explanation of, the actions that are to be developed later, although more information will be added to the framework as the training proceeds. The job of the teacher at this point is to decide how much understanding is needed to set up the training routine, especially if part methods are to be used for the later practice. Trainees are usually keen to get started with 'hands-on' experience, so long and detailed preliminaries are best avoided.

The second step is to practise the performance, so the instructor has to decide how to divide the task up into separate units or subroutines to aid learning. Typists begin their training by learning subroutines for each hand before combining them into routines for both hands together, but pianists spend very short periods of practice with one hand only. The reason for this seems to be that typists use their two hands in ways that are relatively independent of each other with the left always typing 'a' and the right always typing 'p', so that coordination of the hands is needed only to sequence the actions. In playing the piano there is a more complex integration of the actions performed by the two hands so that separate practice can impair rather than enhance later performance. A further aspect of learning to type is to practise short letter sequences that occur frequently, such as 'and', 'or', 'the', 'ing' and 'ion'. These can then be incorporated into the steadily increasing speed of the typist as the actions become automatic and reliable. The amateur typist will often transpose letters or hit the wrong key, writing 'trasnpose' instead of 'transpose' or 'hte' instead of 'the'. The skilled typist will rarely do this because the effect of the repeated drills during training will have made the subroutines not only automatic but also correct.

The third element is feedback, so that learners can compare their own performance with the required standard and see the progress they are making. The characteristics of good feedback are immediacy and accuracy. If the feedback comes immediately after the action, the trainee has the best chance of associating error with the part of the performance that caused it, whereas delayed feedback will demonstrate what was wrong, but the memory of what happened will have faded. If you are being taught to drive a car, one of the early lessons is changing gear. If you think you understand what the instructor tells you, you need to try it out straightaway, so that you have first the feedback of your own performance in seeing if you execute the manoeuvre effectively and then the feedback from the instructor, who confirms that you have done it right, but may add some ways to do it even better. If you are learning photography you do not have that element of immediate feedback, so that you have to recall everything that took place in taking the photograph when you eventually receive the prints.

The second characteristic of feedback is that it should be as accurate as possible in the information it provides on the result and the performance. The driving instructor may say, 'That's fine', or may say, 'That was better than last time because you found the gear you were looking for, but you are still snatching. Try again and remember to ease it in.' The second comment provides a general indication of making progress, it provides an assessment of the performance and specific comment that should improve the next attempt.

The job instruction sequence

Preparation

The instructor will have two sets of objectives: organisational and behavioural. Organisational objectives specify the contribution to the business that the learner will make at the end of training. It will be general but necessary. If a company trains its own word processor operators and secretaries, for instance, it might be that the organisational objectives will be to teach people to word process and to transcribe from handwritten copy or dictating machine, but not to take shorthand. These are different from educational objectives, which focus on the trainee or student rather than on organisational needs, so that tutors in secretarial colleges are more likely to arrange training round what will be useful in a number of occupational openings. The instructor will need to work out organisational objectives which may or may not include broader educational features.

Behavioural objectives are specifically what the learner should be able to do when the training, or training phase, is complete. Organisational objectives for trainee word processor operators may be simply to ensure a constant supply of people able to type accurately and at reasonable speed. In behavioural terms that would be made more specific by setting standards for numbers of words to be typed to a predetermined level of accuracy per minute.

ACTIVITY IV.2

Think of a training experience involving learning how to *do* something that you are contemplating for yourself or for someone else in your organisation. Note down organisational objectives and behavioural objectives for the training.

Next the instructor will decide what learning methods to use. We have already seen that the main elements of job instruction are understanding, practice and feedback, so the instructor decides how much initial explanation is needed, and how many other explanations will be needed at different stages of the training, together with the form that is appropriate. Words alone may be enough, but audio-visual illustration and demonstration will probably be needed as well. For some skills computer-based training and interactive video can provide frequent explanations and feedback on trainee performance.

Two questions about practice are to decide on the subroutines and any necessary simulation, such as the working of a flight simulator in pilot training. Most feedback is by the instructor talking to the learner, but it may be necessary to provide greater accuracy or speed to the feedback by methods such as television recording or photography. The most common method of job instruction is the *progressive part* method. This had its most comprehensive explanation by Douglas Seymour (1966). The task to be undertaken by the learner is broken down into a series of subroutines. The learner then practises routine 1, routine 2 and then 1 1 2.

The next step is to practise routine 3, then 2 1 3 and 1 1 2 1 3, so that competence is built up progressively by practising a subroutine and then attaching it to the full task, which is constantly being practised with an increasing number of the different components included. The components are only practised separately for short periods before being assimilated, so there is no risk of fragmentary performance.

This only works if the job can be subdivided into components. Where this is not possible, *simplification* offers an alternative. In this method the task to be performed is kept as a whole, but reduced to its simplest form. Skilled performance is then reached by gradually increasing the complexity of the exercises. In cookery the learner begins with simple recipes and gradually develops a wider repertoire.

There are some specialised methods of memory training which can be listed here, as well as ways of training for acquiring perceptual skills. Both types of ability appear to be increasing in importance in organisational life.

The most familiar way of memorising is the *mnemonic* or *jingle*, wherein a simple formula provides the clue to a more comprehensive set of data. 'Laser' is much easier to remember than 'light amplification by stimulated emission of radiation'. If the initial letters are not easily memorable, the mnemonic is replaced by the jingle. The denseness of 'ROYGBIV' has led generations of schoolchildren to remember 'Richard Of York Gave Battle In Vain' as a way of recalling the sequence of red, orange, yellow, green, blue, indigo and violet in the spectrum. 'Arthur Spits in Claude's Milk' is a rather less familiar way of remembering that there are five types of arthropod: Arthropods, Spiders, Insects, Crustaceans and Myriapods. One does have to be sure, however, both that the mnemonic or jingle will itself be remembered and that it will subsequently be possible to remember what is to be recalled.

ACTIVITY IV.3

What do the following sets of letters mean:

DERV, DfES, DSS, RADAR, TINA LEA, UNESCO, FCIPD?

Apart from the obvious, why should anyone remember the phrase, 'Most Engineers Prefer Blondes'?

For some tasks the use of *rules* reduces the volume of material to be memorised. There are many fault-finding rules, for instance, where the repairer is taught to use a systematic series of rules. The stranded motorist who telephones the vehicle rescue service for assistance will probably be asked a first question, 'Have you run out of petrol?' The answer 'Yes' identifies the fault, while 'No' leads to the second question, 'Is there any spark?' so that the engineer who comes to help already has some areas of fault eliminated.

Deduction is a method that puts information into categories so that if something does not fit into one category the learner then uses deduction to conclude that it must belong in another. At the beginning of this Focus on skills was the example of the office messenger remembering that invoices go to Mr Brown and cheques to Mrs Smith. If there was also a Ms Robinson, who received all sales enquiries, complaints, unsolicited sales promotion material, tax returns, questionnaires, applications for employment and so on, the messenger would not need to remember what did go to Ms Robinson, but what did not: invoices to Mr Brown, cheques to Mrs Smith and everything else to Ms Robinson. Some interesting examples of using deduction in training are to be found in Belbin and Downs (1966).

For memorisation of information the *cumulative part* method is slightly, but significantly, different from the progressive part method already described in that the learner constantly practises the whole task, with each practice session adding an extra component. This is distinct from the progressive part method in which components are practised separately before being built into the whole. This can be especially useful if the more difficult material is covered first, as it will then be rehearsed much more than that coming later.

A method for the development of perceptual skills is *discrimination*, which requires the learner to distinguish between items that appear similar to the untrained eye or ear. In a rough-and-ready way it is the procedure followed by the birdwatcher or the connoisseur of wine. First the trainee compares two items which are clearly dissimilar and identifies the points of difference. Then other pairs are produced to be compared, with the differences gradually becoming less obvious. Discrimination can be aided by *cueing*, which helps the learner to identify particular features in the early attempts at discrimination by providing arrows or coloured sections. Some people start learning to type with the keys coloured according to whether they should be struck with the left or right hand, or even according to the particular finger which is appropriate. Gradually the cues are phased out as the learner acquires the competence to identify without them.

Magnification is a way of developing the capacity to distinguish small faults in a process or even small components in machinery. Material for examination is magnified at the beginning of training and then reduced back to normal as competence is acquired. Inspectors of tufted carpet start their training by being shown samples of poor tufting that have been produced using much larger material than normal. Later they examine normal material under a magnifying glass and eventually they are able to examine the normal product. A helpful discussion of the magnification method can be found in Holding (1965).

The various training methods to be used are put together in a training programme. This sets out both what the instructor is going to do and the progress the trainee is expected to make. Of critical importance here is pacing; how much material has to be taken in before practice begins, how long the practice period is before the learner is able to proceed to a new part, and how frequently progress is checked by the teacher. Individual trainees will each have their own rate at which they can proceed and will need differing levels of initial explanation and demonstration before practice can start. Training programmes require sufficient flexibility to accommodate the varying capacities that learners bring to their training.

A useful feature of the training programme is providing scope for learners to be involved in determining their own rate of progress and some self-discovery, to avoid spoon-feeding. At the outset trainees are so conscious of their dependency that all measures that build up confidence, independence and autonomy are welcome.

The instruction

When instructor and trainee meet for the first time there is a mutual appraisal. The process is basically 'getting to know you', but the exchanges are important, as the two people have to work together and the learner will be uncertain in an unfamiliar situation, and absolutely dependent upon the instructor. It is essential that learners feel confident in the instructor as someone skilled in the task that is to be learned and enthusiastic about teaching it to others. They will also be looking for reassurance about their own chances of success by seeking information about previous trainees.

The explanation of procedure will follow as soon as the meeting phase has lasted long enough. Here is the first feature of pacing that was mentioned as part of preparation. There has to be enough time for meeting to do its work, but long, drawn-out introductions lead to impatience and wanting to get started.

The procedure is the programme, with the associated details of timing, rate of progress, training methods and the general overview of what is to happen. The most important point to the trainee is obviously the end. When does one 'graduate'? What happens then? Can it be quicker? Do many people fail? What happens to them? The instructor is, of course, more interested in the beginning of the programme rather than the end, but it is only with a clear grasp of the end that the trainee can concentrate on the beginning. Clarifying the goal reinforces the commitment to learning.

With long-running training programmes where an array of skills has to be mastered, the point of graduation may be too distant to provide an effective goal so that the tutor establishes intermediate goals: 'By Friday you will be able to . . .' This phase benefits from illustration: a timetable, a chart of the average learning curve, samples of work by previous trainees; all make more tangible the prospect of success and more complete the mental picture of the operating framework that the learner is putting together. It is also helpful to ensure that the explanation does not become mechanical, like the tourist guide at a stately home. If the instructor has explained the procedure so often that it has become automatic, it is no longer the vivid stimulus to learning that is so necessary. It is a time for as much interchange as possible, with questions, reiteration, further explanation, clarification and confirmation.

WINDOW ON PRACTICE

Repetition does not necessarily make material automatic. Acker Bilk played 'Stranger on the Shore' thousands of times, and many excellent teachers reuse exactly the same material repeatedly. The Scottish playwright James Barrie studied medicine in his youth and took with him to university a set of verbatim anatomy notes that had been compiled by his father thirty years earlier. His father said the lectures were so interesting that it would be better if he did not have to make notes. As Barrie attended the lectures, he was astonished to find that little had changed. At one point the lecturer took hold of a gas bracket and related an anecdote. On looking at his father's notes he saw, 'At this point Professor X took hold of a gas bracket and told this story . . .'

The task that the trainee has to perform is first demonstrated and explained. The purpose is not to display the teacher's advanced skills, but to provide a basis for the learner's first, tentative (and possibly incorrect) attempts. The demonstration is thus done without any flourishes, and as slowly as possible, because the teacher is not only demonstrating skill but also using skill to convince the trainees that they can do the job. Accompanying the demonstration, an explanation gives reasons for the different actions being used and describing what is being done so that the learners can watch analytically. Their attention is drawn to features they might overlook, the sequence of actions is recounted and key points are mentioned.

The task must be presented to the learner in its simplest possible form, with a straightforward, unfussy, accurate demonstration accompanied by an explanation which emphasises correct sequence, reasons why, features that might be overlooked in the demonstration and the key points that lead to success. Where possible, the tutor should not mention what not to do. Errors can be dealt with later; at this stage the direction should be on what to do.

The presentation is followed, and perhaps interrupted, by questions from the learners on what they did not follow or cannot remember. The success of this stage will depend on the skill of the instructor in going through the opening stages of the encounter. Many trainees are reluctant to question because they feel that the question reveals their ignorance, which will be judged as stupidity. The experienced instructor can stimulate the questioning and confirming by the trainees by putting questions to them. This is effective only when done well, as there is the obvious risk of inhibiting people by confronting them with their lack of understanding. The most unfortunate type of questions are those which cross-examine:

'Now, tell me the three main functions of this apparatus.'
'Can anyone remember which switch we press first?'

Little better are the vague requests for assent:

'Do you understand?'
'Am I making myself clear?'
'Is that all right, everybody?'

These are leading questions. They will be some use as there will be nods and grunts from the trainees to provide response, but it is most unlikely that people will do more than offer the easy, regular 'yes'. The job of the teacher is to help learners build the picture in their own minds without feeling that they are being tested. This will only come with good rapport. After the presentation the trainees have their first attempt at the task.

They expect to do badly and need confidence from the tutor, who has to steer a difficult path between too much or too little intervention. Too much and the trainees do not 'feel their feet' and acquire the confidence that comes from sensing the strength and purpose of their own first faltering steps. Too little intervention means that trainees learn about their lack of competence, which is reinforced by a performance that falls short of what the presentation had suggested as being possible. This shows the importance again of presentation, which has to be pitched at the level that will make initial performance feasible, without building up expectations that cannot be realised.

Among the considerations for teachers are the varying potential of individual trainees and the ritual elements of training. Some trainees will be able to make initial progress much more rapidly than others, so that pegging all to the same rate of advance will inhibit both. The ritual features depend on the trainee acknowledging the absolute, albeit temporary, superiority of the tutor. It has already been pointed out that there is a reluctance to question during presentation; there are also intermittent displays of deference to the teacher. This enables learners to perform badly during practice without losing face. However, deference to a superior figure is normally offered on the assumption that the novice is being helped towards the advanced level of skill that the superior possesses. If early practice of a taught skill produces abject performances by the learners, then they either lose confidence or resent the instructor for highlighting their inadequacy.

Learning theory tells us the importance of the law of effect, which practice makes possible, but it also tells us that there is likely to be a point at which the learner makes a sudden leap forward; the point at which the penny drops and there is a shared excitement. In the words of Professor Higgins about Eliza: 'I think she's got it. By Jove, she's got it.' Practice leads up to the point where the learning spurts forward and it then provides the reinforcement of that learning by continued rehearsal and confirmation.

The most effective reinforcement for learners is realising that they can perform, like the child who at last finds it possible to remain upright and mobile on a bicycle.

Learners cannot usually rely on their own interpretation of success: they will need constant assessment by the teacher. Many of the textbooks on teaching and learning emphasise the value of praise, a little of which apparently goes a long way, for example:

> When they are learning people need to know where they stand, they need to know how they are progressing. The knowledge of their progress spurs them on to greater achievements. In this respect praise is always far more helpful than criticism.
> (Winfield 1979)

Effective reinforcement enables trainees to understand both the result and the actions or behaviour that produced the result, so the tutor needs to identify the particular ways in which progress is being made and explain their merit, as well as explaining what caused the progress to happen. When trainees are approaching full competence, with the associated self-confidence, then they are able to cope with more direct criticism.

Presentation

The material above is directed mainly at instruction for the R and M of CRAMP: reflex skills and memorisation. Presentation is directed towards the C: comprehension. Much training takes this form, as people simply have to be told about things. Induction is partly experiential, in that a person is shown round and given a workspace and so forth, but much of it simply has to be known and understood. In the last ten years there has been a plethora of guides and self-help books on how to make an effective presentation. HR people constantly have to present on such matters as explaining a change of policy, clarifying details of a new trade union agreement or setting out the implications in a change of employment legislation. There may be presentations on career prospects in the organisation at careers conventions, pitching to a senior management group for an improvement in the budget, 'selling' the advantages of a new performance-related pay scheme, or explaining to a small group of job applicants the details of the post for which they have applied.

Objectives

As with almost every aspect of management, the starting point is the objective. What are you aiming to achieve? What do you want the listeners to do, to think or to feel? Note that the question is not 'What do you want to say?' The objective is in the response of the listeners. That starting point begins the whole process with a focus on results and payoff, turning attention away from ego. It also determines tone. If your objective is to inform, you will emphasise facts. If you aim to persuade, you will try to appeal to emotion as well as to reason.

The material

What is to be said or, more accurately, what should members of the audience go away having understood and remembered?

> Organise your material with an introduction that previews, a body that develops, and a conclusion that reviews. When you organize the body of your presentation, start by sorting out the theme. The theme is a planning device that holds together the various ideas you want to discuss. If the theme of your presentation is informative, then the body should provide facts. If the theme is persuasive, the body should develop persuasive arguments. (Fandt 1994, p. 159)

In the introduction the speaker establishes rapport with the audience. Apart from gaining their attention, the speaker will include here an answer to the unspoken question: is it going to be worth our while listening? Is this person worth listening to? The person who is worth listening to is someone who looks at the audience and looks friendly, knowledgeable and, above all, enthusiastic. A useful format for the introduction is to explain what the members of the audience will know or be able to do at the end. It is also helpful to sketch out the framework of what is to come, so that people can follow it more readily. But stick to what you promise. If you say there are going to be five points, the audience will listen for five to make sure that they have not missed one.

Having secured the attention of the listeners, you now have them waiting not just for what you say next, but with a framework in their heads of what they will hear, so they will be able to locate their understanding within that framework. The main body of the presentation is the message that is to be conveyed, the development of the argument and the build-up of what it is that the audience should go away having understood and remembered.

The main body will need to be effectively organised. This will not only help members of the audience to maintain attention, but also discipline the speaker to avoid rambling, distracting irrelevance or forgetting. The most common methods are:

- *Chronological sequence*, dealing with issues by taking the audience through a series of events. A presentation to an employment tribunal often follows this pattern.
- *Known to unknown, or simple to complex.* The speaker starts with a brief review of what the audience already knows or can easily understand and then develops to what they do not yet know or cannot yet understand. The logic of this method is to ground the audience in something they can handle so that they can make sense of the unfamiliar. This is the standard method of organising teaching sessions.
- *Problem to solution* is almost the exact opposite of simple to complex. A problem is presented and a solution follows. The understanding of the audience is again grounded, but this time grounded in anxiety that the speaker is about to relieve.
- *Comparison* is a method of organisation which compares one account with another. Selling usually follows this path, as the new is compared with the old.

Whatever the method of organisation for the material, the main body will always contain a number of key thoughts or ideas. This is what the speaker is trying to plant in the minds of the audience: not just facts, which are inert, but the ideas which facts may well illustrate and clarify. The idea that inflation is dangerously high is only illustrated by the fact that it is at a particular figure in a particular month.

The ideas in a presentation can be helpfully linked together by a device that will help audience members to remember them and to grasp their interdependence. One method is to enshrine the ideas in a story. If the story is recalled, the thoughts are recalled with it, as they are integral to the structure. The classic examples of this are the New Testament parables, but every play, novel or film uses the same method. Another method is to use key words to identify the points that are being made, especially if they have an alliterative or mnemonic feature, such as 'People Produce Prosperity'. In a lecture it is common to provide a framework for ideas by using a drawing or system model to show the interconnection of points.

Facts, by giving impact, keep together the framework of ideas that the speaker has assembled. They clarify and give dimension to what is being said. The danger is to use too many, so that the audience are overwhelmed by facts and figures which begin to bemuse them. If the presentation is to be accompanied by a hand-out, facts may be usefully contained in that, so that they can be referred to later, without the audience having to remember them.

Humour is the most dangerous of all aids to the speaker. If the audience laughs at a funny story, the speaker will be encouraged and may feel under less tension, but how tempting to try again and end up 'playing for laughs'. Laughter is a most seductive human reaction, but too many laughs are even more dangerous than too many facts. What will the audience remember, the joke, or what the joke was intended to illustrate? Attempted humour is also dangerous for the ineffective comedian. If you tell what you think is a funny story and no one laughs, you have made a fool of yourself (at least in your own eyes) and risk floundering.

Very few people speak effectively without notes. Although there is a tendency to marvel at those who can, relying solely on memory risks missing something out, getting a fact wrong or drying up completely. Notes follow the pattern of organisation you have established, providing discipline and limiting the tendency to ramble. It is both irritating and unhelpful for members of an audience to cope with a speaker who wanders off down a blind alley, yet this is very common. When an amusing anecdote pops up in your brain, it can be almost irresistible to share it.

There are two basic kinds of notes: headlines or a script. Headlines are probably the most common, with main points underlined and facts listed beneath. Sometimes there will also be a marginal note about an anecdote or other type of illustration. The alternative, the script, enables the speaker to try out the exact wording, phrases and pauses to achieve the greatest effect. The script will benefit from some marking or arrangement that will help you to find your place again as your eyes constantly flick from the page to the audience and back again. This can be underlining or using a highlighter. When using a script it is important not to make the reading too obvious. Head down, with no eye contact and little light and shade is a sure-fire way of turning off the attention of the audience. Public figures increasingly use electronic prompters which project the script progressively through the presentation on to a glass screen some way in front of the speaker. By this means the script can be spoken with little break in eye contact with the audience. This will be too ambitious for most HR people, but the important thing is that the words should be *spoken* rather than *read*.

There are many variations of these basic methods of organising the material, so that one approach is to use varying line length, while another is to use rows of dots to indicate pause or emphasis.

Some people like to have their notes on small cards, so that they are unobtrusive, but this is difficult if the notes are more than headlines. Standard A4 paper should present no problem, if the notes are not stapled, are well laid out and can be handled discreetly. Never forget to number the pages or cards, as the next time you speak they may slip off your lap moments before you are due to begin.

Most presentations benefit from using visual aids. You may use a model, a sample or even a person ('Here is our trainee of the month'), but mostly you will use visual images. Blackboards still exist and white boards are fairly common. Flip charts and overhead projector acetates are widely used. The most rapidly growing type of visual image in presentation is that from a computer, projected on a screen, usually using a PowerPoint package.

The rationale for visual aids is that we remember what we see for longer than we remember what we are told, and we can sometimes understand what we see better than we can understand what we hear. Overhead projectors and other devices are, however, aids to, and not substitutes for, the presentation. Too much displayed material can obscure rather than illuminate what is being said. Television news provides a good example of how much can be used. The dominant theme is always the talking head with frequently intercut pieces of film. Very seldom do words appear on the screen and then usually as extracts from a speech or report, where a short sentence or passage is regarded as being especially meaningful. The other way in which words and numbers appear is when facts are needed to illustrate an idea, so that ideas such as football scores or a change in the value of the pound sterling almost always have the figures shown on the screen to clarify and illustrate. Seldom, however, will more than two or three numbers be displayed at the same time. Speakers need to remember the size of what they are displaying as well as its complexity. Material has to be big enough for people to read and simple enough for them to follow. Material also has to be timed to coincide with what is being said.

A note of caution about PowerPoint is that it can be a most seductive toy for the presenter. The box of tricks is enormous and too many people give a show, with clever figures dancing across the screen and other distractions. We must always remember what the purpose of the presentation is; clever or spectacular forms of display can become what people remember rather than the message that is to be conveyed. Television news is again an illustration. Between programmes there may be all manner of clever visual entertainment in brief clips. Once the news report begins there are no such fancy tricks.

SUMMARY PROPOSITIONS

IV.1 A useful classification of types of learning is CRAMP: comprehension, reflex learning, attitude development, memory training, procedural learning.

IV.2 Selecting the right approach to learning is helped by identifying the learner as being at one of these stages: novice, advanced beginner, competent, proficient or expert.

IV.3 Alternative methods in job instruction are: progressive part, simplification, mnemonics or jingles, rules, deduction, cumulative part, discrimination and magnification.

GENERAL DISCUSSION TOPICS

1 There is an old saying, 'You can lead a horse to water, but you cannot make it drink'. How true is this of training and development and what are the HR implications?

2 Another saying is, 'What I hear I forget, what I see I can understand and what I do I know'. The relevance of that to job instruction is easy when considering manual skills, but what are the implications for aspects of training and development dealing with values and attitudes such as, for example, racist or sexist behaviour?

FURTHER READING

Belbin, E. and Belbin, R.M. (1972) *Problems in Adult Retraining*. London: Heinemann

Belbin, E. and Downs, S. (1966) 'Teaching and paired associates', *Journal of Occupational Psychology*, Vol. 40, pp. 67–74

Seymour, W.D. (1966) *Industrial Skills*. London: Pitman

Winfield, I. (1979) *Learning to Teach Practical Skills*. London: Kogan Page

Methods of teaching practical skills are so well established that most of the texts were published some time ago. Although 40 years 'old', Seymour (1966) (above) is the most thorough and practical. It can still be found in some libraries. The other works listed are slightly more recent and more widely available.

Fandt, P.M. (1994) *Management Skills: Practice and Experience*. St Paul, Minn.: West Publishing

Quinn, R.E. (1988) *Beyond Rational Management: Mastering the paradoxes and competing demands of high performance*. San Francisco: Jossey-Bass

Quinn, R.E., Faerman, S.R., Thompson, M.P. and McGrath, M.R. (1990) *Becoming a Master Manager*. New York: John Wiley

Material on management skills is everywhere, but in this context the above works are especially helpful.

Yate, M. and Sander, P. (2003) *The Ultimate Business Presentations Book*. London: Kogan Page

Presentation is also preached very widely. This excellent recent import from the United States covers the ground very thoroughly and readably.

WEB LINKS

On the book's website there is supplementary material on handling group discussion as a form of learning. This is the usual method for social skills training and attitude development. Other useful websites are:

www.lsc.gov.uk (Learning and Skills Council).
www.mmu.ac.uk/academic/studserv/learningsupport/studyskills/presentations (Manchester Metropolitan University).
www.spokenwordltd.com/coaching (Spoken Word Ltd, providing teaching and coaching in spoken word skills).
www.ft.com (this has a useful section 'Career Point', but you need to pay to subscribe).
www.ssda.org.uk (Sector Skills Development Agency).

REFERENCES

Belbin, E. and Belbin, R.M. (1972) *Problems in Adult Retraining*. London: Heinemann.

Belbin, E. and Downs, S. (1966) 'Teaching and paired associates', *Journal of Occupational Psychology*, Vol. 40, pp. 67–74.

Bloom, B.S. (1956) *Taxonomy of Educational Objectives: The cognitive domain*. London: Longman.

Downs, S. and Perry, P. (1987) *Helping Adults to Become Better Learners*. Sheffield: Manpower Services Commission.

Dreyfus, H.L., Dreyfus, S.E. and Athanasion, T. (1986) *Mind over Machine: The power of human intuition and expertise in the era of the computer*. New York: Free Press.

Fandt, P.M. (1994) *Management Skills: Practice and Experience*. St Paul, Minn.: West Publishing.

Holding, D.H. (1965) *Principles of Training: Research in Applied Learning*. Oxford: Pergamon.

ITRU (Industrial Training Research Unit) (1976) *Choose an Effective Style: A self-instructional approach to the teaching of skills*. Cambridge: ITRU Publications.

Quinn, R.E. (1988) *Beyond Rational Management: Mastering the paradoxes and competing demands of high performance*. San Francisco: Jossey-Bass.

Quinn, R.E., Faerman, S.R., Thompson, M.P. and McGrath, M.R. (1990) *Becoming a Master Manager*. New York: John Wiley.

Seymour, W.D. (1966) *Industrial Skills*. London: Pitman.

Winfield, I. (1979) *Learning to Teach Practical Skills*. London: Kogan Page.

REVIEW OF PART IV

It is a long time since Lord Weinstock, as Chairman of GEC, asked all his senior managers to tell him how they were going to save money, starting with management development. He can perhaps be forgiven for his shortsightedness as he was an accountant, and HR people tend to view the world differently from accountants. The thinking behind his request, however, lies in the difficulty that training and development so often face: does it work; is it worth the money? At the time of Lord Weinstock's comment a Director of Training in a different multinational business explained to one of the authors how his objective was to establish in the organisation 'a learning community within, but separate from, grim commercial pressures of the bottom line'. There is always the lurking suspicion that training is an escape from real life into a realm of chat and putting the world to rights. We all know that that is a total misrepresentation, but the suspicions remain. Another problem is the question of who should pay for it. Governments typically want employers to pay for training, while employers expect governments to pay for it, especially if those being trained at great expense are not going to remain for long with their current employer.

In Part IV we have considered the strategic questions in development and the ways in which we can understand how people learn and how they develop. The more specific chapters have dealt first with competence, a word that has taken on new potency in the last twenty years by concentrating on particular things that a person can do, and this is a far cry from chat and putting the world to rights at a training centre in a converted stately home somewhere. Second, we consider the development of careers and the way in which individuals take control of their own destiny within the constraints imposed, but using the benefits provided, by their employer.

Part IV CASE STUDY PROBLEM

Micropower is a rapidly growing computer software firm, specialising in tailor-made solutions for business. Increasingly, training for other businesses in their own and other software packages has occupied the time of the consultants. This it sees as a profitable route for the future and such training is now actively sold to clients. Consultants both sell and carry out the training. As an interim measure, to cope with increasing demand, the firm is now recruiting some specialist trainers, but the selling of the training is considered to be an integral part of the consultant's role.

Micropower has just issued a mission statement which accentuates 'the supply of and support for sophisticated computer solutions', based on a real understanding of business needs. The firm considers that it needs to be flexible in achieving this and has decided that multiskilling is the way forward.

All consultants need to sell solutions and training at all levels, and be excellent analysts, designers and trainers. Some 200 consultants are now employed; most have a degree in IT and most joined the firm initially because of their wish to specialise in the technical aspects of software development, and they spent some years almost entirely in an office-based position before moving into a customer contact role. A smaller proportion were keen to concentrate on systems analysis, and were involved in customer contact from the start.

In addition there are 300 software designers and programmers who are primarily office based and rarely have any customer contact. It is from this group that new consultants are appointed. Programmers are promoted to two levels of designer and those in the top level of designer may then, if their performance level is high enough, be promoted to consultant. There is some discontent among designers that promotion means having to move into a customer contact role, and there are a growing number who seek more challenge, higher pay and status, but who wish to avoid customer contact. Another repercussion of the promotion framework is that around a quarter of the current consultants are not happy in their role. They are consultants because they valued promotion more than doing work that they enjoyed. Some have found the intense customer contact very stressful, feel they lack the appropriate skills, are not particularly comfortable with their training role and are unhappy about the increasing need to 'sell'.

Required

1 What immediate steps could Micropower take to help the consultants, particularly those who feel very unhappy, perform well and feel more comfortable in their new roles?

2 In the longer term how can Micropower reconcile its declared aim of multiskilling with a career structure which meets both organisational and employee needs?

3 What other aspects of human resource strategy would support and integrate with the development strategy of multiskilling?

4 Micropower wishes to develop a competency profile for the consultant role. How would you recommend that the firm progress this, and how might the profile be used in the widest possible manner in the organisation?

Part IV EXAMINATION QUESTIONS

1. Outline the nature and purpose of National Vocational Qualifications. What has been their impact so far?
2. Discuss the advantages and disadvantages of on-the-job training and development compared with off-job training and development. In which circumstances might each be more appropriate?
3. Identify the factors which determine 'skill need' in an organisation. Discuss how managers ensure that workers develop the skills and knowledge necessary for their roles within organisations.
4. What practical steps would you take if you were the human resource manager in an organisation wanting to introduce training for people to enable them to manage their own careers more effectively?
5. What is a career, how is it changing and how should it be managed?
6. Choose one of the following: (a) career planning workshops; (b) mentoring; (c) succession planning. Define it and briefly describe the forms it can take in an organisation. Discuss the criteria on which its success can be evaluated and consider whether some criteria are (i) more appropriate, and (ii) more easily measured, than others.
7. Explain to a line manager the value of coaching as a way of developing a subordinate.
8. 'Employment development should be handed over to line managers.' Summarise your views on this statement.

PART 5

EMPLOYEE RELATIONS

All jobs have the potential to be alienating, making the job holder indifferent or hostile both to the job and to the management, who are seen as responsible for obliging the employee to continue doing the job.

Employee relations is largely concerned with preventing or alleviating that type of alienation. Because the issues are often collective, concerning a number of people in a similar situation, many procedures incorporate the recognition of trade unions and ways of making that recognition productive for both parties. Working safely in a healthy environment is included here as there is a legal obligation to involve employee representatives in monitoring management arrangements for safe working. Safe working is ultimately a matter of employees working safely because they understand and follow the practices that are provided for their personal safety.

Two parallel chapters, on diversity and equality, deal with the issue of people being treated fairly, not only because we all want to be fair in the way we do things, but also because there is a strong social justice theme to consider, as well as significant legal requirements. Furthermore, people who feel they are managed with due respect for their diversity and recognition of their equality are more likely to be resourceful humans than those who do not sense that respect and recognition.

Whether unions are recognised or not, there are always points of disagreement between managers and the managed and here we consider two rather 'heavy' areas: grievance and discipline. Few managers like to participate in grievance and discipline processes, but they are very interesting and provide the opportunity for major change and improvement for the manager who handles them well.

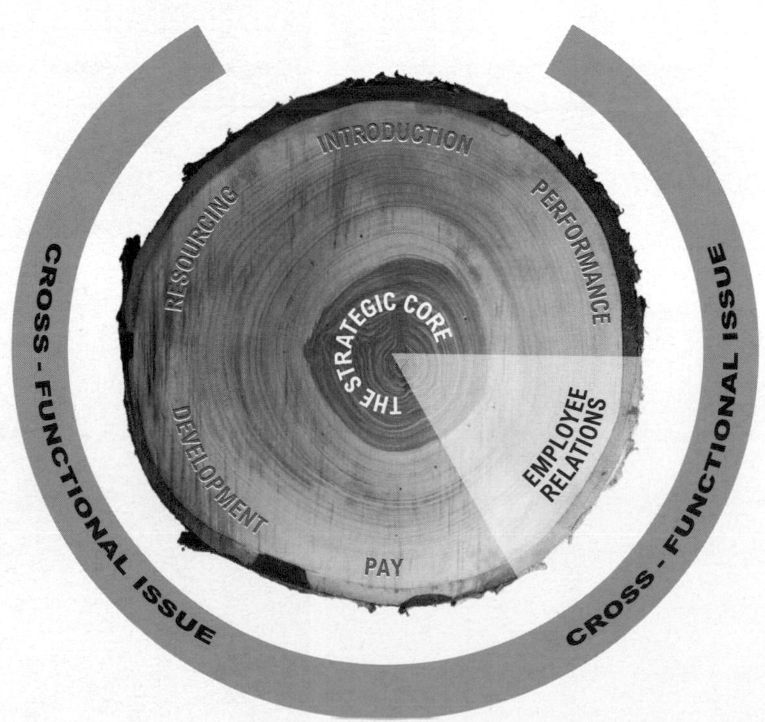

CHAPTER 20

STRATEGIC ASPECTS OF EMPLOYEE RELATIONS

THE OBJECTIVES OF THIS CHAPTER ARE TO:

1 EXPLAIN THE DECLINE OF TRADE UNIONS IN RECENT DECADES

2 REVIEW DEVELOPMENTS IN THE FIELDS OF COLLECTIVE BARGAINING AND INDUSTRIAL ACTION

3 ACCOUNT FOR THE SUBSTANTIAL AND ONGOING INCREASE IN THE EXTENT OF EMPLOYMENT REGULATION

4 EXPLORE THE IMPLICATIONS OF THESE TRENDS FOR THE STUDY OF EMPLOYMENT RELATIONS

5 SET OUT THE MAJOR CHOICES AVAILABLE TO MANAGERS IN THE AREA OF COLLECTIVE EMPLOYEE INVOLVEMENT

6 ASSESS THE VARIOUS APPROACHES USED AS A MEANS OF INVOLVING INDIVIDUAL EMPLOYEES IN THE MANAGEMENT OF ORGANISATIONS

had an adverse impact on the propensity of employees to join a union. There are far fewer large factories employing thousands on assembly lines than there used to be, and many more small-scale office and hi-tech manufacturing operations. Management styles in small workplaces, even when part of a much larger group, inevitably tend to be more ad hoc and personal. Grievances, disputes and requests for a pay rise are thus discussed and settled in face-to-face meetings or informally between people who know each other well, without the need to involve a trade union. Moreover, in the private services sector the proliferation of small workplaces means that alternative employment is readily available for suitably qualified people. When receptionists, shop workers, sales executives, call-centre staff or IT people are dissatisfied with their work, their workplace or their managers, they can simply look for another job and resign. They do not need to move house to find work and are unlikely, in the present economic climate, to suffer any decline in income. Their jobs thus matter less to them than was the case in the days of the steel town, the mining village or the city suburb in which one big employer provided the lion's share of all employment. In short, there is now less need to join a union because there are other ways of resolving problems at work and relieving discontent.

By 1998 47 per cent of UK workplaces employing over 25 people stated that they employed no union members at all (Cully *et al.* 1999, pp. 87 and 92), while in hundreds of thousands more unions have no influence of any significance. For most employees, therefore, the norm is now to work in a non-union workplace. As a result, employee relations has come to be characterised by a far greater variety of forms than had been the case throughout much of the past century, traditional approaches continuing to decline:

> What we find, therefore, is a marked split between the public sector, where traditional industrial relations appears to have survived, albeit with some adaptations, and a private sector which, with the exception of a declining set of large establishments, is predominantly non-union and without worker representation. . . . Management appears to be firmly in the driving seat, controlling the direction of employment relations.
> (Guest 2001, p. 99)

The question of whether continued trade union decline is inevitable has been considered by many and, as with most debates about the future, this one is characterised by diverse views. From a trade union perspective there are grounds for pessimism, despite years of new initiatives aimed at recruiting new members in the private sector. The proportion of younger people who choose to join unions has declined dramatically, suggesting that they do not see membership of a collective employee body as necessary or desirable. In 1991 as many as 37 per cent of people in the 25–34 age group were union members (Waddington 2003, p. 239). Ten years later, union density among the under 30s had fallen to just 16 per cent, compared with 34 per cent among those over the age of 30 (Freeman and Diamond 2003, p. 29). The second reason to anticipate further decline in the future relates to the continued growth of industries which have not traditionally been unionised. With the exception of some jobs in the public sector, the fastest-growing professions are all ones that have very low rates of union density (e.g. technicians, consultants, software engineers, nursery nurses, hairdressers and beauticians).

The alternative view rests first of all on the observation that trade unions have been through periods of steep decline before and have later recovered. Kelly (1998) shows how union membership declined steeply during the 1920s and early 1930s, density falling as low as 22 per cent in 1933, only to recover again afterwards. His theory of 'long waves' in industrial relations leads him to conclude that workers will only ever put up with so much 'exploitation and domination' by employers, before beginning to unite to fight back. Others take heart from research which shows that many employees in the non-union sectors (including young people) are neither strongly opposed to unions, nor unwilling to countenance joining a union in the future. Fifty per cent of those asked in a poll in 2001 said that they would be either 'very likely' or 'fairly likely' to join if one were available at their workplace (Charlwood 2003, p. 52). These figures suggest that unions could create a renaissance for themselves if they could find more effective ways of organising and marketing themselves in the private services sector.

WINDOW ON PRACTICE

Trade unions face a major problem in recruiting members in what are known as 'dispersed sectors' in which people are scattered across the country in small workplaces, working in small teams less than half a dozen strong or even alone. Traditional approaches involving communication from the union hierarchy through local shop stewards is clearly inappropriate for these groups. New methods such as the use of mobile phone text alerts thus have to be harnessed.

Despite the difficulties some of the larger unions have enjoyed some modest successes in recent years by setting up special sections for people working in these dispersed occupations. IRS (2003b) gives several interesting examples. The GMB union has recently started targeting professional boxers, London minicab drivers and workers in the sex industry, while the Transport and General Workers Union has signed up over 2,000 childcare workers in private nurseries. However, the biggest success story is probably Amicus's clergy and church workers' section which has over 2,500 members and recently succeeded in persuading the Church of England to recognise the right of clergymen not to be unfairly dismissed.

Collective bargaining and industrial action

A major consequence of the decline in trade union membership has been a simultaneous decline in the number of employees whose terms and conditions are determined through collective bargaining (i.e. negotiation with a union or unions). Here, too, dramatic changes have occurred over recent decades. We have moved from a position in which a large majority of people worked in establishments which recognised trade unions, to one in which a large majority do not. In 1970 over 80 per cent of the UK workforce was covered by collective agreements. Thirty-three years later, the figure was 35.6 per cent (Labour Market Trends, 2003a).

Table 20.1 Average number of working days lost due to strikes

1970–1974:	14.1 million
1975–1979:	11.6 million
1980–1984:	10.5 million
1985–1989:	3.9 million
1990–1994:	824,000
1995–2000:	594,000
2000–2002:	924,000

Source: Adapted from R. Taylor (1993) *The Trade Union Question in British Politics*. Oxford: Blackwell; and Labour Market Trends (2003c) 'Labour disputes in 2002', *Labour Market Trends*, June. London: HMSO.

Profound changes have also occurred within the sectors that remain covered by collective agreements, and continue to do so. Over several decades we have seen the breaking down of the system of national collective bargaining established in the middle years of the twentieth century. Agreements of this kind are now very rare outside the public sector whereas once they were the norm. They involve terms and conditions being agreed at industry level between representatives of the relevant unions and an employers association, resulting in an agreement to which all operating in the industry agree to adhere. One by one arrangements of this kind have collapsed as collective bargaining, where it continues at all, increasingly takes place at the level of the organisation or the individual workplace. In 1960, according to Brown *et al.* (2003), 60 per cent of UK employees were covered by industry-level collective agreements. By 1980 the proportion had fallen to 43 per cent and by 1998 to only 14 per cent. These remaining agreements are largely in the public sector and are themselves under robust attack from government ministers who see local bargaining as a more efficient and fairer way of distributing public money.

Another major change in employee relations has been the very marked decline in the incidence of industrial action in recent years. Contrary to commonly held perceptions, UK workers have never been more prone to take industrial action than their counterparts in other countries, but the 1970s and early 1980s did see the loss of millions of days' work as a result of strikes, not to mention the fall of at least two governments in the wake of major strikes. The position is now wholly transformed. The UK's strike rate has been below the average for both the European Union and the OECD countries in every year except one since 1992 (Labour Market Trends 2003b), while the subject has long ceased to be one which influences voting patterns. The number of stoppages varies from year to year. In 2002, for example, there was a marked increase due to a long-running dispute in the fire service, but the overall trend has been downwards for over a decade. The number of working days lost to strikes each year is now a fraction of what it was thirty years ago (*see* Table 20.1).

The rise of employment law

Until the 1960s there was no such thing as employment law in Britain. With the exception of basic protection for child workers and some health and safety regulations, the state 'kept its distance' from the relationship between employers and employees. This became known as the principle of voluntarism and it meant that the UK differed very markedly from most other industrialised countries. All workers and employers, it was argued, were free to enter into whatever contractual relationship they preferred and it was not for the state to determine people's terms and conditions or to set minimum standards. All the courts did was provide a mechanism for contracts of employment to be enforced when one side or the other breached them or sought to change them unilaterally without the consent of the other party. Protection from injustices perpetrated by managers and abuse of power was provided by trade unions and through collective agreements.

Over the past thirty years this position has wholly reversed. In 1965 the first major piece of modern employment legislation was introduced – a right for redundant workers to receive payments by way of compensation. In the years since a major new field of legal practice has been created as the law has intervened more and more in the regulation of the employment relationship. As trade unions have declined in terms of their size and influence, the law has stepped in to provide a minimum floor of rights and to deter employers from acting without proper employee relations procedures. In recent years many developments have originated at European level, but UK governments have pushed the agenda forward on their own account too.

Unfair dismissal law dates from 1971, sex discrimination law from 1975 and race discrimination law from 1976. Since 1974 we have had comprehensive health and safety law together with a government inspectorate to enforce it. Regulations relating to 'transfers of undertakings' were introduced in 1981, when it also became a formal requirement to consult collectively when making redundancies. The past ten years have seen an astonishing quickening of the pace. We now have disability discrimination law, a national minimum wage, restrictions on working time, compulsory union recognition, a host of new family-friendly measures, extensive data protection law and measures preventing discrimination against people employed on fixed-term and part-time contracts. 2003 saw the introduction of new regulations outlawing discrimination on grounds of sexual orientation and religion or belief, as well as significant improvements to the rights of people with family responsibilities. In 2004 new workplace dispute resolution measures were introduced, and 2005 will see major new obligations introduced in the field of information and consultation, while from 2006 we will have age discrimination legislation in placc.

Employment tribunals now oversee nearly 100 separate areas of jurisdiction (i.e. distinct types of claim that an aggrieved employee, ex-employee or job applicant can bring to court). In addition there are some thirty or forty separate types of claim rooted in the laws of contract, trust or tort that can be taken to the county courts. Over 100,000 claims are lodged with the Employment Tribunal Service each year, leading the government to reform procedures and adjust remedies so as to discourage parties from pursuing cases they are unlikely to win. Given the acceleration of developments in the field of employment law, it is not surprising that its implementation by organisations now comes so much higher up HR managers' agendas than more traditional employee relations concerns (IRS 2003a). In the vast majority of workplaces the nature of the relationship that is established between employers and employees, and the rules that govern it, owe far more to the requirements of employment law than to the demands of trade unions. This represents a total transformation from the position that prevailed a generation ago.

ACTIVITY 20.2

Why do you think employment practice in the UK moved from being unregulated to being so highly regulated in thirty years? Do you agree that we now have 'too much' employment law? If so, which statutes would you like to see kept and which repealed?

THE STUDY OF EMPLOYEE RELATIONS

The profound changes in the employee relations world outlined above have had, and continue to have, important implications for those whose job it is to study and conduct research into this area of organisational life. Until recently most of this work continued to be carried out within a frame of reference founded on the assumption that union membership and collective bargaining were the norm. The questions asked and the research undertaken focused for the most part on trade union organisation, forms of bargaining, industrial conflict and resolution, and the 'assaults' on established UK employment practices by employers and government. Since 1997 a great deal of attention has been given to the operation of the new institutions that have been set up to provide trade unions with a method of forcing employers to recognise them when they have sufficient support in the workforce, and to other measures introduced by the Blair government aimed at fostering partnership agreements between employers and employee representatives (*see* Chapter 21). The focus for many thus remains the formal, collective aspects of the employment relationship and the prospects of a revival in the fortunes of trade unions. The continued, widespread use of the term 'non-union firm', when such employers have constituted the large majority for many years, illustrates the lasting influence of this long-established frame of reference.

Increasingly academics specialising in this field are looking at employee relations from new perspectives and are asking different kinds of questions in their research. Some have firmly argued that the time has come for industrial relations specialists 'to move on' and focus on the lived reality of working in contemporary workplaces in which trade unions and collective bargaining are either peripheral or wholly irrelevant:

> the search for the familiar – committees, procedures and so on – could blind the discipline to the relative sociological marginality of many of these new forms. Whereas collective bargaining in 1968 was a central social institution comparable to supermarket shopping today in its impact on the economy and ordinary people's lives, these new institutions are of far lesser significance . . . The danger is that we cling to one small log that is being washed downstream by a mighty river of socio-economic change. The log is worth grasping, clearly, but Industrial Relations needs to address the encircling current too. Ackers and Wilkinson (2003, pp. 13–14)

We are thus now witnessing a very interesting period in the development of employee relations as an academic discipline. Prominent figures in the field are directing their minds to different types of issues and the development of new paradigms. Guest (2001), for example, has argued that developments in the state of the psychological contract between employers and employees (*see* Chapter 1) might provide a good focus for the study of employee relations in the future, while Rubery and Grimshaw (2003) make a good case for focusing on a wider range of employment institutions beyond those which derive from union recognition and collective bargaining. Their comparative studies look at regulatory practices in the areas of training, pay determination, working time, retirement, downsizing and employee involvement.

Because the last of these (employee involvement) has been studied in depth by UK researchers for some time, it provides a good reference point when thinking about strategic choices faced *today* by managers in the employee relations field, and it will provide our frame of reference for the remainder of this chapter. The key questions that need to be asked are the following:

- How far should employees be involved in decision making?
- Should their involvement be direct or through representatives such as trade unions?
- What form should the involvement take?
- At what organisational level should the involvement take place?
- Which issues should be the subject of involvement?

The answers vary from workplace to workplace. In some, particularly those in which trade unions are not well established, managers have a wide choice about how and to what extent they involve their employees in decision making. In others managers have limited room for manoeuvre if they are to avoid a deterioration in employee relations and/or their position in competitive labour markets. It is possible to run a successful business with minimal employee participation of any kind, but this is often not the best option. A strong case can be put for a substantial degree of worker involvement both directly and through the actions of legitimate representatives.

COLLECTIVE EMPLOYEE INVOLVEMENT

Management always needs the collective consent of its employees: it also needs a mandate to manage. This can partly be delivered by trade union recognition, but other approaches are also available. The recent changes in union membership, employment legislation and fluctuating unemployment levels have provided academic analysts with the challenge of describing how employee relations strategies have changed. We still lack a full explanation, but one of the best-known approaches has been the attempt of Purcell and Sisson (1983) to categorise management styles in industrial relations. These are summarised in Table 20.2 and the key distinguishing feature is a collective view of the workforce.

The categories in Table 20.2 are useful, although some organisations do not fit easily into any one of them. Most large, long-established companies will be in one of the last three; most public sector organisations will be in category 4; and many newer businesses will be in some version of category 2.

Table 20.2 Categories of management styles in employee relations

Style	Characteristics
Traditional	Fire-fighting approach. Employee relations not important until there is trouble. Low pay. Hostile to trade unions. Authoritarian. Typical in small, owner-managed businesses.
Paternalist	Unions regarded as unnecessary because of employer's enlightenment. High pay. Concentration on encouraging employee identification with business objectives.
Consultative	Union participation encouraged through recognition. Problem-solving, informal approach to employee relations. Emphasis on two-way communications.
Constitutional	Similar to consultative, but emphasis on formal agreements to regulate relationship between two powerful protagonists.
Opportunistic	Large company devolving responsibility for employee relations to subsidiaries, with no common approach but emphasis on unit profitability.

Source: J. Purcell and K. Sisson (1983) 'Strategies and practice in the management of industrial relations', in G.S. Bain (ed.) *Industrial Relations in Britain*. Oxford: Blackwell, pp. 112–18.

ACTIVITY 20.3

Which of the five categories in Table 20.2 most closely fits your establishment? Does the category vary for different groups of employees?

If we take a strictly managerial view of trade unions and their recognition, the interest is the degree to which recognition will deliver collective consent to a general framework of rules and guidelines within which management and employees operate. Collective consent implies the acceptance of a situation, while agreement has the more positive connotation of commitment following some degree of initiative in bringing the situation into existence. We are not, therefore, necessarily describing active employee participation in managerial decision making. The range is wider, and includes the variety of circumstances in which employees consent collectively to managerial authority, so long as they find it acceptable.

In order to couch the discussion in terms that can embrace a variety of styles, we set out seven categories of consent, in which there is a steadily increasing degree of collective employee involvement. We begin with a category in which there is straightforward and unquestioning acceptance of management authority, and then move through various stages of increasing participation in decision making and the necessary changes in management style as the power balance alters and the significance of bargaining develops and extends to more and more areas of organisational life.

1 **Normative.** We use this term in the sense of Etzioni (1961), who described 'normative' organisations as those in which the involvement of individuals was attributable to a strong sense of moral obligation. Any challenge to authority would imply a refutation of the shared norms and was therefore unthinkable. Many of the exercises in corporate culture are construed by some as strategies to develop this type of consent, with strong emphasis on commitment and the suppression of views opposed to managerial orthodoxy.

2 **Disorganised.** In organisations that are not normative there may be collective consent simply because there is no collective focus for a challenge; disorganised consent is where there may be discontent but consent is maintained through lack of employee organisation to articulate and endorse the dissatisfaction. A Victorian sweatshop would come into this category.

3 **Organised.** When employees organise it is nearly always in trade unions and the first collective activities are usually those dealing with general grievances. It is very unlikely that there will be any degree of involvement in the management decision-making processes. Employees simply consent to obey instructions as long as grievances are dealt with.

4 **Consultative.** Consultation is a stage of development beyond initial trade union recognition, even though some employers consult with employees before – often as a means of deferring – trade union recognition. This is the first incursion into the management process as employees are asked for an opinion about management proposals before decisions are made, even though the right to decide remains with the management.

5 **Negotiated.** Negotiation implies that both parties have the power to commit and the power to withhold agreement, so that a decision can only be reached by some form of mutual accommodation. No longer is the management retaining all decision making for itself; it is seeking some sort of bargain with employee representatives, recognising that only such reciprocity can produce what is needed.

6 **Participative.** When employee representatives reach the stage of participating in the general management of the business in which they are employed, there is a fundamental change in the control of that business, even though this may initially be theoretical rather than actual. Employee representatives take part in making the decisions on major strategic issues such as expenditure on research, the opening of new plants and the introduction of new products. In arrangements for participative consent there is a balance between the decision makers representing the interests of capital and those representing the interests of labour, though the balance is not necessarily even.

7 **Controlling.** If the employees acquire control of the organisation, as in a workers' cooperative, then the consent is a controlling type. This may sound bizarre, but there will still be a management apparatus within the organisation to which employee collective consent will be given or from which it will be withheld.

All of the above categories require some management initiative to sustain collective consent. In categories 1 and 2 it may be exhortation to ensure that commitment is kept up, or information supplied to defer organisation. In each subsequent category there is an increasing bargaining emphasis, which becomes progressively more complex.

The implication is that there is a hierarchy of consent categories, through which organisations steadily progress. Although this has frequently been true in the past, it is by no means necessary. Some may begin at 6 or 7: there is no inflexible law of evolution, and change can move in the opposite direction as well. Some instances of partial or complete de-recognition of trade unions could be characterised as examples of regression back down the hierarchy.

INDIVIDUAL EMPLOYEE INVOLVEMENT

Whether or not employees are involved and able to influence decision making collectively, there remains scope for direct individual involvement. Interest in this area of activity has increased in recent years, partly as a result of government interest and partly because employers have seen involvement as a means by which employee commitment and organisational communication can be improved. Involvement initiatives are particularly useful in an environment in which unions are absent or marginal – because they can provide an alternative means whereby managers gain an understanding of feelings and attitudes 'on the shop-floor'.

Direct forms of employee involvement are not incompatible with collective forms such as are associated with trade union recognition. However, they are generally initiated by employers and are often seen by critical writers as a method that is used to discourage trade union growth. The suggestion is that if employees' desire for involvement can be partially satisfied using individual initiatives, they will be less inclined to seek it through collective means. While it is clear from some surveys (for example IRS 1999) that some employers specifically design employee involvement initiatives to weaken trade unions, a good business case can be made on many other grounds. The major reasons are as follows:

- Employees like to be involved and appreciate involvement initiatives.
- Employee involvement initiatives improve organisational commitment.
- Involvement makes change easier for employees to accept.
- Involvement increases levels of job satisfaction.
- Involvement is associated with lower levels of staff turnover.

In theory, therefore, employee involvement can potentially be seen as making a significant contribution to improving organisational performance. While there is some evidence to support this contention (*see* Guest and Hoque 1994; Fernie and Metcalf 1996; IRS 1999b), it is very difficult to prove conclusively. The methodological limitations of research in this area are summarised by Marchington (2001, pp. 246–7). He states that all that can be said with certainty is that employees like the idea of involvement initiatives and prefer participative management styles to those which are autocratic in nature. The evidence is too tenuous to be a base for any firm claim that involvement leads to a change in employee attitudes or to improved organisational performance. The claim is nonetheless persuasive intuitively, and can explain the growth in direct involvement initiatives over recent years.

ACTIVITY 20.4

How far do you think that your own work performance is/would be affected by the presence of individual employee involvement initiatives at your workplace? What about your level of commitment to the organisation?

The major forms of direct involvement used in the UK are team briefing, the publication of company news sheets (often now web based), quality circles, suggestion schemes and attitude surveys. Teamworking is less common but has generated considerable interest among researchers because it involves individual workers, together with their colleagues, exercising substantial control over their own areas of work. It can therefore be characterised as the most far-reaching form of individual employee involvement.

Team briefing

Team briefing is an initiative that attempts to do a number of different things simultaneously. It provides authoritative information at regular intervals, so that people know what is going on, the information is geared to achievement of production targets and other features of organisational objectives, it is delivered face to face to provide scope for questions and clarification, and it emphasises the role of supervisors and line managers as the source of information:

> [Team briefings] are often used to cascade information or managerial messages throughout the organisation. The teams are usually based round a common production or service area, rather than an occupation, and usually comprise between four and fifteen people. The leader of the team is usually the manager or supervisor of the section and should be trained in the principles and skills of how to brief. The meetings last for no more than 30 minutes, and time should be left for questions from employees. Meetings should be held at least monthly or on a regular pre-arranged basis. (Holden 1997, p. 624)

With goodwill and managerial discipline, team briefing can be a valuable contributor to employee involvement, as it deals in that precious commodity, information. Traditionally, there has perhaps been a managerial view that people doing the work are not interested in anything other than the immediate and short term and that the manager's status partly rests on knowing what others do not know. For this reason all the managers and supervisors in the communications chain have to be committed to making it a success, as well as having the training that Holden refers to above. Team briefing gets easier once it is established as a regular event. The first briefing will probably go very well and the second will be even better. It is important that management enthusiasm and commitment do not flag just as the employees are getting used to the process.

During economic recessions there is a boost to the team briefing process because so many managements have so much bad news to convey. When you are losing money and profitability, there is a great incentive to explain to the workforce exactly how grim the situation is, so that they do not look for big pay rises. Whatever the economic climate, team briefing continues to be used widely and was found to operate in a majority of organisations featured in the 1998 WER Survey (Cully *et al.* 1999).

Quality circles

Originating in Japanese firms, quality circles comprise small groups of employees (10–15 maximum) who meet regularly to generate ideas aimed at improving the quality of products and services and of organisational productivity. They can also be used as problem-solving groups and as a means by which employee opinion is transmitted to senior management. Some quality circles consist of staff who work together within a team or organisational function, others are cross-functional and focus on interdepartmental issues. They can form part of total quality management approaches such as those we assessed in Chapter 11:

> These sorts of practice have several objectives, such as to increase the stock of ideas within an organisation, to encourage co-operative relations at work, and to legitimise change. These practices are predicated on the assumption that employees are recognised as *a* (if not *the*) major source of competitive advantage for organisations, a source whose ideas have been ignored in the past or who have been told that 'they are not paid to think'. (Marchington 2001, p. 235)

Not only, therefore, are quality circles a potential source of useful ideas for improving systems and saving costs. They also give people a welcome opportunity to contribute their thoughts and experience. A general positive impact on employee attitudes should thus result.

News sheets

Another common form of employee involvement occurs through the regular publication of in-house journals or news sheets either in paper or electronic form. On one level they simply provide a means by which information concerning finances, policy and proposed change can be transmitted by managers to employees. This is a limited form of employee involvement which does little more than improve the extent to which employees are informed about what is going on elsewhere in their organisations. This will engender a perception of greater involvement and belonging, but does not directly involve employees in any type of decision making. For that to occur the news sheet must be interactive in some way. It may, for example, be used as a means by which employees are consulted about new initiatives, or may provide a forum through which complaints and ideas are voiced.

Attitude surveys

Regular surveys of employee opinion are very useful from a management point of view, particularly where there are no unions present to convey to management an honest picture of morale and commitment in the organisation. In order to be effective (that is, honest), responses must be anonymous, individuals stating only which department they work in so that interdepartmental comparisons can be made. It also makes sense to ask the same questions in the same format each time a survey is carried out, so that changes in attitude and/or responses to initiatives can be tracked over time.

The major problems with attitude surveys are associated with situations in which they reveal serious problems which are then not properly addressed. This can easily lead to cynicism and even anger on the part of the workforce. The result is a poorer employee relations climate than would have been the case had no survey taken place. The same is true of suggestion schemes. It is counter-productive to involve employees if their contribution is subsequently ignored.

Teamworking

Teamworking is a direct descendant of the concept of autonomous working groups, which had their highest profile in the Volvo plant at Kalmar (now closed down), and a rather vague movement of the 1960s, called Quality of Working Life (QWL). At Volvo there were the twin aims of improving the quality of working life and enhancing productivity. The QWL was directed mainly at making life more tolerable, as the title implies, and it is difficult to see what impact it had. More recently teamworking has become more comprehensive in its approach and its objectives. It is very fully explained in the work of Buchanan (1993; Buchanan and McCalman 1989).

Teamworking aims to focus work activity among small groups of about a dozen members, who are mutually supportive and who operate with minimal supervision. Management sets performance targets (often after consultation) and allocates tasks, but it is for the team itself to decide exactly how these are to be achieved. The team organises its own activities, appoints its own leaders and works out for itself how to overcome problems. Teamworking can thus be characterised as a form of worker control, even though it operates within heavily prescribed limits. Managers refrain from giving day-to-day supervision, but are on hand to give advice or more direct assistance where necessary. Disciplining staff, for example, is a task carried out by managers and not by team members. Teamworking is often associated with situations in which several regionally based teams compete with each other to meet or exceed performance targets. Team-based remuneration then accounts for a proportion of the total pay received.

INTERNATIONAL PERSPECTIVES

Employee relations, more than other areas of HRM practice, varies considerably from country to country. Although some analysts believe that there has been a degree of convergence in recent years in response to increased global competition and new technologies, it is clear that substantial differences remain. In important respects different countries have witnessed different responses to the same environmental pressures (*see* Bamber and Lansbury 1998 for a summary of these debates).

Comparative studies undertaken in the industrialised countries reveal the continued effect of different industrial relations traditions on contemporary practice. They also identify the importance of historical experience and institutional differences in explaining the observed variations. The major dimensions across which national systems vary are as follows:

- high union membership v. low union membership;
- single-employer bargaining v. multi-employer bargaining;
- interventionist government role v. non-interventionist role;
- adversarial tradition v. consensual (or social partnership) tradition;
- autocratic management style v. involving management style.

ACTIVITY 20.5

Making reference to our description of employee relations trends above, consider in which ways the UK employee relations system has evolved along each of these dimensions in recent years.

Clearly, of course, there is a great deal of variation within as well as between national systems in all the above areas. It is also true that things do not remain static over time and that prevailing norms within any country evolve in new directions. However, it remains the case that certain approaches remain associated with particular countries. In Japan, for example, union membership is high and management practices relatively autocratic, but the unions themselves are enterprise based and there is a consensual tradition. In Germany and the Scandinavian countries the social partnership approach is well established, but here it is associated with industry-based unions, national-level bargaining, extensive employee involvement in decision making and heavy government intervention. Hence employers are obliged by law to consult and share decision making with their workforces through works councils. In France, by contrast, union membership is notoriously low, but the unions maintain a role in negotiating terms and conditions because they are empowered to do so in law. The government is further involved through the setting of minimum standards in areas such as training provision, holiday entitlements, wages, hours of work, health insurance and pensions. Government intervention is also extensive in the Eastern European countries, but here union membership remains high, while bargaining is often carried out at industry level.

The main practical implications associated with this variation in approach are for multinational organisations. They have an understandable impulse to strengthen their corporate culture by taking a standard approach to employee relations management across their operations, but also have to take account of local conditions. For them, success comes when they find ways of creating a company-wide, international strategy which is adaptable to the requirements of the various countries in which they operate. Employee relations considerations thus play a major role in determining which countries are chosen as the locations for their operations. They can also contribute to decisions about plant closures when retrenchment is deemed necessary.

SUMMARY PROPOSITIONS

20.1 Employee relations practice in the UK was dominated by trade unions and collective bargaining for most of the twentieth century.

20.2 Since 1979 trade union membership has declined along with the significance of collective bargaining.

20.3 As trade unions have become more marginal, managers have sought other forms of employee involvement over which they are able to exert more influence.

20.4 Increasingly it is the requirements of the law more than the demands of employees that shape the rules which govern employment relationships.

20.5 It is possible to identify seven categories of consent to illustrate variations in the level and type of collective employee involvement.

20.6 Individual employee involvement initiatives are direct; they do not operate through workforce representatives. The most common are team briefing, attitude surveys, quality circles, news sheets and teamworking initiatives.

20.7 Despite some evidence of convergence in recent years, national employee relations systems remain very different from one another in important respects.

GENERAL DISCUSSION TOPICS

1 Why should employees be involved and what should they be involved in?

2 To what extent do you agree with the proposition that the decline of trade unions in the form that they have traditionally taken is inevitable?

3 Which of the forms of direct employee involvement described in this chapter do you think is most attractive from an employee perspective and why?

FURTHER READING

Boeri, T., Brugiavani, A. and Calmfors, L. (eds) (2001) *The Role of Unions in the Twenty First Century*. Oxford: OUP

Gospel, H. and Wood, S. (eds) (2003) *Representing Workers: Union recognition and membership in Britain*. London: Routledge

There is no shortage of excellent scholarly writing on recent trends in employee relations, and in particular on the position of trade unions. An up-to-date summary of UK-based research is provided by the authors contributing to the book edited by Gospel and Wood (2003). For an international perspective Boeri, Brugiavani and Calmfors (2001) provide a good starting point.

Cully, M., Woodland, S., O'Reilly, A. and Dix, G. (1999) *Britain at Work: As depicted by the 1998 Workplace Employee Relations Survey*. London: Routledge

Milward, N., Bryson, A. and Forth, J. (2000) *All Change at Work*? London: Routledge

It is impossible seriously to study trends in employment relations in the UK without taking account of the findings of the vast Workplace Employee Relations Surveys which are undertaken periodically. The most recent survey was conducted in 1998 and the findings are extensively summarised in the above books.

Blyton, P. and Turnball, P. (2004) *The Dynamics of Employee Relations*, 3rd edn. London: Palgrave Macmillan

Geary, J. (2003) 'New forms of work organisation: still limited, still controlled, but still welcome?' in P. Edwards (ed.) *Industrial Relations: Theory and Practice*, 2nd edn. Oxford: Blackwell

Marchington, M. (2001) 'Employee Involvement at Work', in J. Storey (ed.) *Human Resource Management: A Critical Text*, 2nd edn. London: Thomson Learning

Developments in the field of employee involvement, both collective and individual, are discussed at length in the major texts on employee relations. Thought-provoking critical analyses which reach somewhat different conclusions are provided by the three works listed above.

REFERENCES

Ackers, P. and Wilkinson, A. (2003) 'Introduction: The British Industrial Relations Tradition – Formation, Breakdown, and Salvage', in P. Ackers and A. Wilkinson (eds) *Understanding Work and Employment: Industrial Relations in Transition*. Oxford: OUP.

Bamber, G. and Lansbury, R. (1998) 'An introduction to international and comparative employment relations', in G. Bamber and R. Lansbury (eds) *International and Comparative Employment Relations*, 3rd edn. London: Sage.

Brown, W., Marginson, P. and Walsh, J. (2003) 'The management of pay as the influence of collective bargaining diminishes', in P. Edwards (ed.) *Industrial Relations: Theory and Practice*, 2nd edn. Oxford: Blackwell.

Buchanan, D. (1993) 'Principles and practice of work design', in K. Sisson (ed.) *Personnel Management*, 2nd edn. Oxford: Blackwell.

Buchanan, D. and McCalman, J. (1989) *High Performance Work Systems*. London: Routledge.

Charlwood, A. (2003) 'Willingness to unionize amongst non-union workers', in H. Gospel and S. Wood (eds) *Representing Workers: union recognition and membership in Britain*. London: Routledge.

Cully, M., Woodland, S., O'Reilly, A. and Dix, G. (1999) *Britain at Work: As depicted by the 1998 Workplace Employee Relations Survey*. London: Routledge.

Dunn, S. and Gennard, J. (1984) *The Closed Shop in British Industry*. London, Macmillan.

Etzioni, A. (1961) *A Comparative Analysis of Complex Organisations*. New York: Free Press.

Fernie, S. and Metcalf, D. (1996) 'Participation, contingent pay, representation and workplace performance: Evidence from Great Britain', *Discussion Paper 232*. London: Centre for Economic Performance, London School of Economics.

Freeman, R. and Diamond, W. (2003) 'Young workers and trade unions', in H. Gospel and S. Wood (eds) *Representing Workers: union recognition and membership in Britain*. London, Routledge.

Geary, J. (2003) 'New forms of work organisation: still limited, still controlled, but still welcome?' in P. Edwards (ed.) *Industrial Relations: Theory and Practice*, 2nd edn. Oxford: Blackwell.

Guest, D. (2001) 'Industrial Relations and Human Resource Management', in J. Storey (ed.) *Human Resource Management: A Critical Text*, 2nd edn. London: Thomson Learning.

Guest, D. and Hoque, K. (1994) 'The good, the bad and the ugly: employment relations in new non-union workplaces', *Human Resource Management Journal*, Vol. 5, No. 1, pp. 1–14.

Holden, L. (1997) 'Employee Involvement', in I. Beardwell and L. Holden (eds) *Human Resource Management*, 2nd edn. London: Pitman.

IRS (1999) 'Trends in employee involvement', *IRS Employment Trends*, No. 683, July. London: Industrial Relations Services.

IRS (2000) 'Where next for HR?' *IRS Employment Trends*, No. 704, May. London: Industrial Relations Services.

IRS (2003a) 'HR Prospects 2003', *IRS Employment Review*, No. 775, May. London: Industrial Relations Services.

IRS (2003b) 'Part of the union', *IRS Employment Review*, No. 764, November. London: Industrial Relations Services.

Kelly, J. (1998) *Rethinking Industrial Relations: mobilization, collectivism and long waves*. London: Routledge.

Labour Market Trends (2003a) 'Trade Union Membership', *Labour Market Trends*, July. London: HMSO.

Labour Market Trends (2003b) 'International comparisons of labour disputes in 2001', *Labour Market Trends*, April. London: HMSO.

Labour Market Trends (2003c) 'Labour disputes in 2002', *Labour Market Trends*, June. London: HMSO.

Mackay, L.E. and Torrington, D.P. (1986) *The Changing Nature of the Personnel Function*. London: IPM.

Marchington, M. (2001) 'Employee Involvement at Work', in J. Storey (ed.) *Human Resource Management: A Critical Text*, 2nd edn. London: Thomson Learning.

Purcell, J. and Sisson, K. (1983) 'Strategies and practice in the management of industrial relations', in G.S. Bain (ed.) *Industrial Relations in Britain*. Oxford: Blackwell.

Rubery, J. and Grimshaw, D. (2003) *The Organization of Employment: An International Perspective*. Basingstoke: Palgrave Macmillan.

Taylor, R. (1993) *The Trade Union Question in British Politics*. Oxford: Blackwell.

Vissa, J. (2002) 'Why fewer workers join unions in Europe: a social custom explanation of membership trends', *British Journal of Industrial Relations*, Vol. 40, No. 3, pp. 403–30.

Waddington, J. (2003) 'Trade union organization', in P. Edwards (ed.) *Industrial Relations: Theory and Practice*. Oxford: Blackwell.

An extensive range of additional materials, including multiple choice questions, answers to questions and links to useful websites can be found on the Human Resource Management Companion Website at **www.pearsoned.co.uk/torrington.**

CHAPTER 21

RECOGNITION AND CONSULTATION

THE OBJECTIVES OF THIS CHAPTER ARE TO:

1. DEFINE THE TERM 'RECOGNITION' AS IT APPLIES TO THE RELATIONSHIP BETWEEN AN EMPLOYER AND A TRADE UNION
2. EVALUATE THE CASES FOR AND AGAINST RECOGNISING TRADE UNIONS FROM A MANAGEMENT PERSPECTIVE
3. DISCUSS THE SEVERAL FORMS THAT UNION RECOGNITION AGREEMENTS CAN TAKE
4. OUTLINE THE MAIN FEATURES OF THE LAW ON TRADE UNION RECOGNITION INTRODUCED IN 2000
5. SET OUT THE SITUATIONS AND SUBJECTS ABOUT WHICH UK EMPLOYERS ARE OBLIGED BY LAW TO CONSULT WITH THEIR EMPLOYEES COLLECTIVELY
6. EXPLAIN WHY CONSULTATION CONSTITUTES GOOD MANAGEMENT PRACTICE AND SHOW HOW THE HR FUNCTION CAN CONTRIBUTE IN A PRACTICAL WAY

According to the 1998 Workplace Employee Relations Survey (Cully *et al.* 1999, pp. 90–4), trade unions enjoy some presence in 53 per cent of all UK workplaces employing more than 25 people. In four-fifths of these (that is, in 45 per cent of all workplaces), managers negotiate with trade unions over the pay and employment conditions of some or all employees. The Labour Force Survey for 2002 (*see* www.statistics.gov.uk) showed that 8.7 million employees in the UK, accounting for 35.6 per cent of the total, worked for employers who recognised trade unions and determined pay and conditions through collective bargaining machinery. We can thus conclude that while the proportion of the workforce in unionised workplaces has fallen over the past twenty years, collective bargaining and trade union recognition remain important institutions in the UK. This is particularly true of the public sector and of industries which were previously nationalised, union membership being heavily concentrated in these sectors (Cully *et al.* 1999, p. 86). As a result of new legislation requiring recognition under certain circumstances, the number of workplaces in which managers negotiate with trade unions increased recently after many years of decline (Gall and Hammond 2000, p. 14).

We can therefore be sure that some HR managers are in establishments where unions are not recognised and where recognition is unlikely, some are in establishments where they are working towards recognition and many others are in a situation where unions are recognised to some degree for at least part of the workforce. A fourth group will have experienced, or may yet experience, situations in which unions have had recognition withdrawn. In most cases, therefore, the issue of the extent and type of union recognition remains an issue of some significance in the day-to-day management of the HR function.

When a trade union is recognised its officials and members, along with the union itself, gain important rights in law. Among the most important of these is the right to be consulted over issues such as redundancy, pensions and health and safety. Irrespective of the law, consultation with unions over a range of issues is an essential contributor to the development of a harmonious, high-trust relationship, as is consultation with employees more generally.

DEFINING RECOGNITION

Recognition, in the context of employee relations, is defined fairly narrowly in law. Section 178 of the 1992 Trade Union and Labour Relations (Consolidation) Act contains the established legal definition of recognition as being a situation in which, either via a formal written agreement or through custom and practice, employers engage in collective bargaining with union representatives about some or all of the following matters:

1. Terms and conditions of employment, or the physical conditions in which any workers are required to work.
2. Engagement or non-engagement, or termination or suspension of employment or the duties of employment of one or more workers.
3. Allocation of work or the duties of employment as between workers or groups of workers.
4. Matters of discipline.

5 The membership or non-membership of a trade union on the part of a worker.
6 Facilities for officials of trade unions.
7 The machinery for negotiation or consultation and other procedures, relating to any of the foregoing matters, including the recognition by employers or employers' associations of the right of a trade union to represent workers in any such negotiation or consultation or in the carrying out of such procedures.

The decision to recognise or to withdraw recognition from a trade union has implications far beyond the terms of the agreement itself. Once recognised, the union gains a raft of defined legal rights to exercise on behalf of its members. First, there is the right to be consulted before redundancies are made or before a business is transferred to new owners. Recognised unions also have consultation rights in the fields of health and safety and occupational pensions, and are empowered to conclude workplace agreements with employers concerning the working time and parental leave regulations. Second, officials of recognised unions and union-appointed learning representatives have a right to reasonable paid time off work in order to carry out their duties and for training purposes. Union health and safety representatives enjoy these rights as well as others giving them access to office facilities. Third, recognised unions have the right to receive information from managers to enable them to engage in meaningful collective bargaining. Finally, the Transfer of Undertakings Regulations 1981 require that union recognition continues and collective agreements remain in force after the transfer of an undertaking to new ownership, provided that the transferred undertaking retains 'an identity distinct from the remainder of the transferee's undertaking'.

A range of other rights such as protection from discrimination on trade union grounds, the right to accompany an employee at a serious disciplinary or grievance hearing, and the right to organise lawful industrial action apply to unions and their members irrespective of whether or not they are formally recognised. However, these rights are conditional on the union concerned being recognised as an independent entity by the Certification Officer who has the responsibility of maintaining the official list of trade unions.

ACTIVITY 21.1

What do you think should be the main criteria used to establish whether a body should or should not be granted the status of a trade union?

Traditionally the Certification Officer has placed a great deal of importance on independence from management, ensuring that staff associations that are limited to specific companies cannot qualify. Is this fair?

THE CASES FOR AND AGAINST UNION RECOGNITION

When a trade union has recruited a number of members in an organisation, it will seek recognition from the employer in order to represent those members. The step of recognition is seldom easy but is very important as it marks a highly significant movement away from unilateral decision making by the management.

If the employees want that type of representation, they will not readily cooperate with the employer who refuses. In extreme cases this can generate sufficient antagonism to cause industrial action in support of recognition. In such situations the employer may be forced to grant partial recognition or even concede the demand for full negotiating rights over a whole range of issues. Alternatively refusal may lead to a situation in which the employer is forced to recognise the union under the terms of the Employment Relations Act 1999 (*see* below).

However, there are also positive reasons for considering recognising trade unions, relating to the benefits that can flow as a result: there are employee representatives with whom to discuss, consult and negotiate so that communication and working relationships can be improved:

> There are a number of reasons why employers should choose to work with, rather than against, unions at the workplace. Firstly, management may regard trade union representatives as an essential part of the communication process in larger workplaces. Rather than being forced to establish a system for dealing with all employees, or setting up a non-union representative forum, trade unions are seen as a channel which allows for the effective resolution of issues concerned with pay bargaining or grievance handling. It is also the case that reaching agreement with union representatives, in contrast to imposing decisions, can provide decisions with a legitimacy which otherwise would be lacking. It can also lead to better decisions as well. (Marchington and Wilkinson 2002, p. 425)

There are also various arguments that can be put against choosing to recognise a trade union and resisting doing so. Employers are often apprehensive about the degree of rigidity in employment practice that union aims for security of employment appear to imply, and they therefore consider to what extent collective consent can be achieved by other means, provided that the management work hard at both securing and maintaining that consent.

A survey undertaken by IRS (1995, pp. 3–9) asked company representatives to outline the advantages and disadvantages of trade union recognition. The benefits suggested included the stable structure such a relationship gives to the management of employees, the promotion of smooth industrial relations and its role in providing a mechanism for upward communication from the staff. A further perceived advantage was its cost effectiveness as a communication tool when compared to more individualised approaches. The drawbacks principally related to a perception that unions tend to resist change and take a long time to get things done. The result is a reduction in the ability of managers to respond quickly and flexibly to market pressures and opportunities.

Data from the Workplace Employment Relations Survey shows that managers are split over the issue of trade union recognition. Cully *et al.* (1999, p. 87) report that in 29 per cent of workplaces managers are broadly in favour of union membership and that in 17 per cent they are opposed. The remaining 54 per cent stated either that they were ‘neutral’ or that it was simply not an issue in their workplaces.

WINDOW ON PRACTICE

An interesting footnote to British industrial relations is the elimination of trade unions at the Government Communications Headquarters (GCHQ) at Cheltenham. GCHQ produces signal intelligence to support the security, defence, foreign and economic policies of the British government. As in most public sector bodies, there has been a strong tradition of union representation among the several thousand staff who are employed there.

In the early 1980s the government became concerned about the possible risk to security of this type of representation in a body where such sensitive data were handled. There was a particular apprehension about the possibility of industrial action impeding urgent defence initiatives. In January 1984 union members were offered £1,000 each to 'buy out' their membership. All but a small number accepted the offer, but the action was regarded as a serious attack on union rights and there were a series of legal moves, including an appeal to the European Court of Human Rights, to have the ban declared invalid. In October 1988, 14 of the employees who had not resigned their union membership were dismissed.

The incoming 1997 government was pledged to restore negotiating rights, and fulfilled the pledge within two weeks of taking office, although maintaining a ban against industrial action. In July those who had been dismissed returned to work.

FORMS OF TRADE UNION RECOGNITION

Union recognition comes in various shapes and forms. It may be 'partial', in which case the range of topics subject to negotiation is limited, or it may be 'full', covering pay, conditions and all employer policies relating to the employment relationship. The irreducible minimum is assistance by a union representative for members with grievances, but the extent to which matters beyond that are recognised as being a subject of bargaining depends on the type of management regime that is in place. It also depends on the possible existence of other agreements that could take some matters out of the scope of local recognition. A feature of some collective agreements is an acceptance that certain matters are potentially subject to negotiation with the recognised union (e.g. pay and redundancy), while in other areas the union has the right only to be consulted or informed.

The second fundamental decision to be taken in respect of recognition concerns the number of unions to be recognised and the type of bargaining to be adopted. There are three basic alternatives:

1 **Multi-union bargaining** involves the recognition of several different unions, each of which negotiates separately on behalf of different groups of workers. Sometimes this leads to a situation in which the separate groups are employed on different sets of terms and conditions. Such an approach has traditionally been common in large public sector organisations such as the NHS, although union mergers in recent

years have tended to reduce the overall number that are recognised. As a rule different unions will represent different 'bargaining groups' such as unskilled manual workers, skilled manual grades and white-collar workers.

2 **Single-table bargaining** is a situation in which a number of unions are recognised, but where only one set of negotiations takes place over terms and conditions at a time. The full range of issues is thus determined for all groups of staff around a single table. It is usual for such arrangements to be associated with 'single-status' practices or harmonised terms and conditions, so that all workers enjoy the same basic entitlements as regards matters such as holiday, pensions, hours and sick pay.

3 **Single-union bargaining** is principally associated with situations in which only one union seeks recognition. However, it can also occur where an employer rejects multi-union bargaining and agrees instead only to recognise one union. These are popularly known as 'sweetheart' or 'new style' agreements and have been the subject of some controversy. They are typically found on greenfield sites and in businesses of technological sophistication, their essential novelty being the closeness and extent of the working relationship between management and union. Union officials find that they have less freedom of action on some matters than their members expect, but also find they are involved in the full range of human resource management questions, not simply the familiar terrain of collective bargaining. The agreements are also frequently accompanied by 'no strike' clauses, which supposedly remove the need for industrial action by providing for independent arbitration in situations where management and union fail to reach agreement. Single-status arrangements also often feature in single-union deals.

From a management perspective it is preferable, if possible, to conclude a **partnership agreement** with the union or unions which have been recognised. Such approaches have been actively encouraged by the government and by the TUC in recent years and may well become the dominant form in the future when European Works Councils become a statutory requirement in all larger organisations. Partnership deals represent an attempt to move away from the traditional, adversarial, low-trust form of union–management relationship towards one which is characterised by high trust and a willingness to engage in joint problem solving. Communication and consultation are watchwords, so that employees and their representatives are kept fully aware of the factors affecting management decision making and are themselves involved as far as is possible. Collective bargaining continues but is supplemented with other prominent institutions such as a company council:

> This is a representative body consisting of employer and union representatives, which has a number of functions. These normally include: acting as a negotiating forum; acting as a consultative forum; establishing sub-committees and working parties; facilitating the resolution of grievances and disputes; and promoting the agreed principles of employee relations between the employer and the union(s). (Farnham 2000, p. 248)

Another feature of many recent collective agreements is the inclusion of specific undertakings relating to flexibility and new technology. **Flexibility agreements** aim to reduce the significance of demarcation between different groups of workers so that greater numbers are willing and able to undertake tasks outside a tightly defined job role. They are typically introduced in response to intense competitive pressures and are concluded as a means of minimising job losses. In return for higher wages and appropriate training, the workforce agrees to become multiskilled and to abandon strict grade definitions that restrict which people can do which kinds of task. **Technology agreements** are concluded in order to facilitate the smooth introduction of new machinery and accompanying working practices. The result is a planned transfer to new systems in which employee representatives are fully involved. Issues that managers might otherwise consider unimportant (such as adjustments in the make-up of production teams) are thus included in discussions, while uncertainty and fears of job losses are kept to a minimum.

The third major way in which collective bargaining arrangements differ is in their level. Three approaches are commonly identified:

- multi-employer bargaining;
- single-employer bargaining;
- workplace bargaining.

All can operate within the same organisation at the same time with different matters being determined at different levels. However, in most organisations which recognise trade unions the most important decisions are taken in one forum.

Multi-employer bargaining used to be very common in the UK and remains so in many European countries. Negotiations over basic pay and conditions of employment take place at industry or national level through the auspices of employers associations. The result is the presence of industry norms, the same rates of pay and agreements on hours being honoured by all employers in a particular industry. The 1980s and 1990s saw a rapid decline in multi-employer bargaining in the UK, with the collapse of long-established agreements in industries such as engineering and textiles. According to Millward *et al.* (2000, pp. 184–99) only 6 per cent of UK workplaces engaged in manufacturing and 3 per cent of private services operations now determine pay through a multi-employer agreement. The figure for the public sector is a great deal higher (39 per cent), but here too there has been substantial decentralisation in recent years.

Most bargaining therefore takes place within organisations either at employer level, or in multi-site operations at the level of the workplace. The former is better where core terms and conditions are standardised across the organisation. It is also the more efficient approach as it ties up less managerial time than is the case where each workplace carries out its own negotiations.

ACTIVITY 21.2

What do you think are the main reasons for the breaking up of so many industry-level collective agreements in the UK over recent decades? Why have they survived in other countries such as Denmark and Italy?

DERECOGNITION

Derecognition of trade unions is often seen in published literature as being redolent of fundamentally undesirable 'macho' approaches to employee relations. While outright derecognition against the stated wishes of the workforce has been relatively rare, instances of employers withdrawing from collective bargaining arrangements increased somewhat during the 1990s (*see* Gall and McKay 1999). The comparative rarity of derecognition is also a finding of successive Workplace Employment Relations Surveys (*see* Millward *et al.* 2000, pp. 103–4), the majority of episodes relating to specific grades of employees rather than the entire workforce. In other cases partial derecognition has occurred where the scope of matters covered by collective bargaining is narrowed. Such situations often accompany moves by employers to establish personal employment contracts and/or to move towards pay rises based on individual performance or contribution. The result is the retention of collective bargaining machinery, but a tendency for it to be used more and more rarely in important decision making.

It could be argued that partial derecognition of this kind ultimately leads to full derecognition as fewer staff see any particular advantage in joining the union. Over time the union becomes so numerically weak that there is no longer a persuasive case for its continued recognition – even over the limited range of issues for which it retains bargaining rights.

In such circumstances there is a good case for accepting that the union is no longer performing a useful representative function and that employees' interests might thus be better served with the introduction of other forms of collective or individual involvement.

TRADE UNION RECOGNITION LAW

Since 2000 there has been in place a formal legal route which unions can use as a means of forcing employers to recognise them and to bargain with them in good faith about the pay and conditions of the workers they represent. The new law was introduced as part of the Employment Relations Act 1999 and is highly complex. A central role is played by the Central Arbitration Committee (CAC), a statutory body which is independent of government, to which union recognition claims are sent. The CAC is required to consider the claim and to seek voluntary agreement between the parties. Where this cannot be established it can either require management to recognise the union or organise a ballot of the workforce concerned. The law applies in all organisations employing more than 20 people where there is no existing collective bargaining arrangement in place.

The process is started by a union or a group of unions acting together making a formal recognition claim on behalf of a defined bargaining group. Management can then accept the claim, reject it outright or seek to negotiate a more favourable deal. If necessary the CAC panel dealing with the case will ask officials from the Advisory, Conciliation and Arbitration Service (ACAS) to help the parties reach a voluntary agreement. Only when such avenues fail are formal hearings held and decisions made. The CAC will consider the case if the bargaining group concerned is coherent, includes everyone who should be included and is generally 'compatible with effective management'.

Where it can be shown that over 50 per cent of the workers in the defined bargaining group are members of the union/unions bringing the claim, the CAC will order recognition unless there is evidence to suggest that sufficient members may not want their union to be recognised or where the panel is persuaded that it would not be in the interests of good industrial relations to require recognition without first organising a ballot. Where the union concerned shows that over 10 per cent of the bargaining group are members and produces evidence to suggest that a ballot for recognition stands a good chance of succeeding the CAC will order that a ballot should take place. In most cases the evidence required will be in the form of a petition of workers in the defined bargaining group.

Ballots ordered by CAC panels are funded jointly by employers and unions, and are supervised by independent scrutineers. Ballot papers are sent to employees' home addresses, to which campaigning literature can also be sent. In order to win the ballot, the union side must secure a majority of the votes cast and those of at least 40 per cent of the employees in the bargaining group. Strong support must therefore be shown for recognition among the workers concerned. A majority voting for recognition will not succeed if only a minority decide to vote. Once a ballot has been won and a recognition order served, the employer is obliged to bargain in good faith for at least three years. Only then is it possible to consider derecognition; in which case a further application has to be made to the CAC and another ballot held along similar lines.

In the UK, unlike in most other industrialised countries, collective agreements are not generally legally enforceable. They are binding on the parties 'in honour only', so if one side breaches the agreement no legal action can be taken to ensure that it is honoured. Elsewhere in the world, across Europe and in the United States, this is not the case. As a result collective agreements have the character of a contract and tend to be written in less unambiguous language than in the UK. An important exception to this rule has been made for collective agreements formed as a result of an order by the CAC. Where an employer is forced to recognise a trade union as a result of the legal procedure described above, the resulting agreement can be enforced in a court. Employers are thus prevented from formally recognising a trade union and then subsequently failing to engage with it in meaningful collective bargaining.

WINDOW ON PRACTICE

During the first three years of the compulsory recognition procedure the CAC received 255 applications from trade unions, of which 23 resulted in recognition without a ballot and a further 35 after a ballot had been held. These figures suggest that the law on recognition has had only a marginal impact, but this is not the case. Of the applications, 124 were withdrawn after an application to CAC had been made, most because a voluntary recognition agreement had been reached between the parties. In addition, over 700 further recognition agreements were signed between unions and employers in the four years following the announcement that this law was to be introduced and in its first years of operation (i.e. 1998–2002). This represents a very substantial increase in voluntary agreements that can only be explained by the presence of a compulsory recognition procedure. Because employers know that they may be forced to recognise a union or unions on terms decided by a third party, they prefer to do their own deal locally first (*see* Wood *et al.* 2003).

IDS (2000) provides several useful examples of recognition agreements signed in the aftermath of compulsory recognition. They show that some employers prefer to organise ballots themselves with the same rules as can be imposed by the CAC as a means of deterring trade unions from making formal applications.

COLLECTIVE CONSULTATION

Among the legal rights that are conferred on unions when they are recognised is a requirement to be consulted over particular issues. However, the duty on employers to consult with their workforces on a collective basis is not restricted only to those which recognise trade unions. The legal requirement to consult thus takes a variety of different forms. In this context the term 'consultation' means formally talking to employee representatives with a view to reaching agreement. There is no obligation on employers to negotiate or to conclude any formal deal, but an attempt must be made in good faith.

Redundancy

Where an employer proposes to make 20 or more people redundant there is an obligation to consult when formal proposals are drawn up. Where a union or unions are recognised, consultation must be with their representatives. In non-union organisations the obligation is to consult with representatives chosen by all relevant sections of the affected workforce. The aim of the consultation is to find ways of avoiding redundancies and/or to mitigate the consequences. Consultation should take place over issues such as the proposed selection procedure, the method used to determine the pool of affected employees and the basis on which redundancy payments are to be calculated.

Transfer of undertakings

The same regulations covering redundancies apply in transfer of undertakings cases (namely, situations in which one organisation is taken over by another, usually as a result of a sale). Consultation is a requirement placed on both the transferor and transferee companies. The duty to consult extends to representatives of employees whose work or conditions will be directly affected by the transfer. There is a more general duty to inform representatives of other workers about the reasons for the transfer and its longer-term implications.

Health and safety

Under the Health and Safety (Consultation with Employees) Regulations 1996 employers have a general duty to consult with worker representatives about all health and safety matters. Here too the obligation is to consult with trade union appointed safety representatives wherever a union is formally recognised. In other organisations employers can either consult with the workforce directly or set up a health and safety committee to which employee representatives are elected. There are specific duties to consult 'in good time' on the introduction of any measure (e.g. new technology or working arrangement) which substantially affects health and safety, and on procedural arrangements for managing health and safety issues.

Pensions

Recognised unions must be consulted where an employer proposes that its occupational pension should 'contract out' of the State Earnings Related Pension Scheme (*see* Chapter 29). They also have the right to receive on request information concerning a pension scheme's rules and membership numbers, as well as copies of its accounts and actuarial valuations.

European Works Councils

As of 2001, European Works Councils have to be set up in all 'community scale undertakings', defined as organisations which employ over 1,000 people in the European Union and including at least 150 in two EU states. They are not instruments of industrial democracy and there is no right to co-determination with management over areas of employment policy, as has long been the approach in Germany. The major requirements are as follows:

- Councils must have between 3 and 30 members.
- These individuals must be elected to the council by the workforce.
- Council meetings are to be held annually and at such meetings the management is obliged to give reports concerning progress, prospects, the financial situation and plans relating to sales, production, employment, investment and/or the corporate structure.
- Special meetings are to be held in 'exceptional' circumstances when, for example, large-scale redundancies or plant relocations are being contemplated.
- Councils have the right to be informed and consulted about 'any measure liable to have a considerable effect on employees' interests'.
- Only matters that are 'community scale' need be discussed. There is no legal requirement to cover affairs affecting employees in only one EU country.

Workplace agreements

Two recent pieces of legislation originating in Europe provide employers with the opportunity to determine their local application via workplace agreements. These are the Working Time Regulations 1998 and the Maternity and Parental Leave etc. Regulations 1999 (as they apply to parental leave). In both cases the basic rights are set out together with a 'default scheme' which contains more detailed rules on their application. However, employers are permitted to develop their own local rules to replace the government's default scheme, provided these are agreed through a formal workplace agreement. Where unions are recognised this can be achieved using established collective bargaining machinery. Otherwise the employer needs either to secure the explicit agreement of a majority of employees or to arrange for representatives to be elected to a consultative forum.

The Information and Consultation Directive

A major new EU directive extending information and consultation rights was agreed in March 2002. Its aim is to extend the European Works Council principle to all workplaces employing 50 or more people, but at the time of writing (early 2004) it is unclear how significant an impact it will have on UK employment relations in practice. Implementation will start in March 2005 for workplaces employing over 150 workers, later dates in 2007 and 2008 being earmarked for its introduction in smaller workplaces. The directive requires that workers in qualifying workplaces should regularly receive information from their employers and be consulted on all issues which affect their interests, these being defined as anything which affects employment prospects, changes in work organisation or substantial changes in terms and conditions of employment.

The UK government successfully opposed attempts by other EU countries with a tradition of works councils to impose a standard model on all organisations, negotiating a fair degree of flexibility. At the time of writing only draft regulations are available, and they may change, but most anticipate that the legislation implementing the directive in the UK will contain the following features:

1. The Central Arbitration Committee (CAC) will have the major enforcing role and not employment tribunals.
2. Quite substantial financial penalties for non-compliance (up to £75,000) will be payable.
3. New arrangements will only have to be put in place where 10 per cent of the workforce request their establishment.
4. Employers and employee representatives will be free to establish arrangements that suit local circumstances, a default system being designed for use where no agreement is reached.
5. Where there are existing consultation arrangements in place changes would only be introduced following a ballot of employees with the same rules as exist currently for union recognition (i.e. a majority vote including at least 40 per cent of the electorate).

The draft regulations set out the arrangements that will probably apply where management and workforce are unable to reach agreement about another system. This is likely to be the model that is adopted in most workplaces, as is currently the case with the working time and parental leave regulations, which also provide for local variation via workplace agreements (*see* above). The major features are as follows:

1. Appointment to an information and consultation committee will be via election, a secret ballot of all employees being held.
2. The maximum number of representatives will be 25, one person being elected for every 50 employees.
3. Management will be required to provide information to the committee in three areas:

a the recent and probable development of the undertaking's activities and economic situation;
b the situation, structure and probable development of employment – and about any threats to employment;
c decisions likely to lead to substantial changes in work organisation or contractual relations.

4 Management will be required to consult the committee on items **b** and **c** above, namely employment and work organisation.
5 Once established, the committee itself would determine how and in what way, if any, it wanted to move away from the default scheme – this could be achieved if management and a majority of members agreed.

ACTIVITY 21.3

The UK government is known to have opposed the extension of works councils beyond community-scale undertakings and sought, with other countries, to block the Information and Consultation Directive. Why do you think this might have been? What arguments could be put for and against requiring all substantial UK employers to operate works councils?

CONSULTATION IN PRACTICE

Irrespective of legal obligations, consultation is generally regarded as a hallmark of good management. An employer who fails to consult properly, particularly at times of significant change, is likely to be perceived as being unduly autocratic. The result will be dissatisfaction, low levels of motivation, higher staff turnover and poorer levels of customer service. Moreover, consultation has important advantages as a means by which good ideas are brought forward and weak ones challenged.

In workplaces where unions are recognised it is usual for consultation to take place over a range of issues and for permanent consultative institutions to be established. The joint consultative committee (JCC) is the most common form, being a forum in which managers and union representatives meet on a regular basis. Importantly, JCCs are kept distinct from negotiating forums – despite the fact that the membership is often the same:

> In Britain, voluntary collective bargaining and voluntary joint consultation have traditionally been seen as separate and complementary processes, with collective bargaining focusing on the divergent interests of employers and employees and consultation focusing on their common interests . . . This has meant in many cases that collective bargaining has been concerned with pay determination and conditions of employment and joint consultation with welfare, health and safety, training and efficiency. (Farnham 2000, pp. 81–2)

The partnership approach to recognition outlined above, in seeking to move away from adversarial approaches to employee relations, is associated with a process of strengthening or upgrading consultative forums (such as JCCs) at the expense of those used for bargaining.

JCCs are twice as common in union workplaces as in those where unions are not recognised (Millward *et al.* 2000, pp. 108–9), suggesting that they are mostly still used in parallel with collective bargaining machinery. However, research by Marchington (1989) found evidence that they were used in some workplaces as a substitute for collective bargaining or as a means of discouraging the development of a union presence. Managers in such workplaces believe that unions are less likely to gain support and request recognition if the employer keeps its staff informed of issues that affect them and consults with them before taking decisions. Consultative forums in non-union firms also provide a means whereby managers can put their case effectively without the presence of organised opposition.

In many workplaces, union or non-union, JCCs often play a very marginal role from the perspective of most employees. This typically is true where decision making is heavily decentralised to the level of the department or to individual teams of employees. If budgets are devolved too, people may also be uninterested in the outcomes of collective bargaining, because their pay and career prospects are effectively determined by their immediate managers. This poses a problem for management at times of significant change, because there is a need to engage everyone in proper consultation. Without it people will not understand the reasons for the proposed changes or the alternative strategies that are being considered, and will not have the opportunity to contribute their own ideas. From time to time, therefore, managers need to organise one-off consultation exercises as a means of making change management processes as smooth and effective as possible. Common examples are business reorganisations, major policy changes, the introduction of new product lines, organisational relocations and cultural change programmes.

From a management perspective, the great danger is that people come to believe that management is not genuinely interested in hearing their views or in taking them on board. Rose (2001, p. 391) refers to this approach as a 'pseudo-consultation' in which managers are really doing little more than informing employees about decisions that have already been taken. Cynicism results because there is perceived to be an attempt on the part of managers to use consultative forums merely as a means of legitimising their decisions. They can say that consultation has taken place, when in truth it has not. Pseudo-consultation typically involves assembling employees in large groups with senior managers present. The management message is then put across strongly and a short time is given for others to respond. In such situations employees have no time to give proper consideration to the proposals and are likely to feel too intimidated to articulate criticisms. The result is often worse in terms of employee morale and engagement with the changes than would have been the case had no consultation been attempted.

Even where managers genuinely intend to undertake meaningful consultation, they can very easily create an impression that it is no more than a 'pseudo' exercise. It is therefore important to avoid the approaches outlined in the above paragraph. Employees should be informed of a range of possible ways forward (not just the one favoured by management) and invited to consider them in small groups. The results of their deliberations can then be fed back to senior managers and given proper consideration. In this way the appearance of pseudo-consultation, as well as the reality, can be avoided.

WINDOW ON PRACTICE

An issue of significance for employers recognising trade unions for the first time is the need to reassure non-union members that their voices will still be heard. IDS (2000, p. 7) gives several examples of the way in which employers use consultative machinery to ensure that this is the case.

It is particularly important where a union is recognised even though it represents only a minority of the workforce. While union representatives necessarily dominate the staff side in collective bargaining institutions, this need not be the case with joint consultative committees, company councils or health and safety committees.

IDS describes the way that firms such as Yoplait Dairy Crest and Monarch Aircraft Engineering have reserved specific seats on key consultative committees for the representatives of both union members and employees who do not wish to join the recognised union.

HR ROLES IN RECOGNITION AND CONSULTATION

HR specialists play different roles in the recognition, bargaining and consultation processes, much depending on the status achieved by the HR function within the organisation. Broadly it is possible to identify three types of role: facilitating, advisory and executive.

The **facilitating** role is the most restricted. Here HR staff do little more than manage the administrative aspects of recognition and consultation. They organise the meetings, circulate agendas, take minutes and provide factual information, but do little more than support the line managers who take the leading role. The **advisory** role also involves the HR manager being present in a supporting capacity. Here, however, there is considerably more direct involvement with the substance of employee relations management. Specialist advice is provided on legal matters, procedure and precedent, as well as on the HR implications of different courses of action. Line managers chair meetings and take the lead in negotiations, but are directly assisted and supported by an HR specialist who participates in decision making. The third '**executive**' model is one in which employee relations management is largely devolved to the HR function. Here HR managers lead the negotiations, chair consultative meetings and are chiefly responsible for decision making concerning matters such as recognition and derecognition. The advisory role, in such situations, is played by line managers.

In order to carry out the advisory or executive roles effectively, HR managers need to be able to combine specialist knowledge with detailed knowledge of the organisation and its business strategy. Practical negotiation skills and experience of handling sensitive employee relations matters are also significant. HR managers' role has been enhanced in recent years by the great growth in the volume and complexity of legislation.

In the past HR advice used to be thoughtful and genuinely intended to be helpful, and was sometimes welcome, but its basis was simply general experience and good intentions. The recipient could use or ignore it at will, depending on the commonsense assessment of its value. Legislation has caused the need for advice of the type offered by a professional. This is thoughtful and intended to be helpful, but may not be welcome. It will be based on an informed examination of statute and precedent, and will include a full appreciation of the strategic implications of whatever is being considered. No HR manager can now regard the general company strategy as something of concern only to other members of the management team. Although this is such an obvious point, it needs reiteration as a number of those applying for courses in HRM retain a view that their role is to be much more even-handed, and some commentators castigate personnel managers for adopting a managerial approach. One commentary criticised HR managers for abandoning their social and religious principles, adopting a managerial rather than an independent professional stance, ignoring the **pluralistic** nature of work organisations and consolidating an exploitative relationship between people at work (Hart 1993). Today's HR manager is inescapably and necessarily a representative of management interests. In union recognition issues in particular, there is no point in having a personnel manager involved who does not adopt that perspective.

The HR manager therefore carries a specific type of authority. As well as receiving advice, the employer needs to see that all employment matters are administered in a way that is consistent with the legislative framework, and part of that requirement is that managerial actions should be consistent with each other. It may also be that people see the need not only for advice, but also for representation by someone who knows the esoteric rules of procedure and behaviour in a highly stylised form of discussion.

SUMMARY PROPOSITIONS

21.1 While trade union recognition is less common than it was 25 years ago, collective bargaining remains the main means by which pay and conditions are determined in a large minority of workplaces. It is still dominant in the public sector.

21.2 An employer is deemed in law to have recognised a trade union if it negotiates with it about pay, conditions or employment policy. Recognition gives trade unions and their representatives important rights in law.

21.3 There are compelling cases from a management perspective both in favour of and against trade union recognition. Their validity is determined by the circumstances of the organisation.

21.4 Collective bargaining varies in terms of its scope and its level and in the number of unions involved. Recent years have seen moves towards partnership agreements, as well as those designed to achieve flexibility and to facilitate the introduction of new technology.

21.5 Since 2000 there has been in place a legal route for trade unions to use as a means of securing recognition. The result has been an increase in the number of voluntary agreements reached.

21.6 Recognised unions have a right to be consulted about a range of issues. Collective consultation is also a legal obligation in non-union firms.

21.7 Consultation is a hallmark of a good employer. In order to be effective, consultation processes must be meaningful and genuine.

GENERAL DISCUSSION TOPICS

1 Why has trade union membership remained so high in the public sector when it has declined so markedly in the private sector?

2 How effective do you think the recognition provisions in the Employment Relations Act 1999 will turn out to be over the long term?

3 What are the arguments for and against extending the concept of the 'workplace agreement' to fields of employment law beyond working time and parental leave?

FURTHER READING

British Journal of Industrial Relations
There is no shortage of thoughtful, up-to-date and very well-researched literature on the subjects covered in this chapter because so many of our most prominent academics choose to focus their attention on industrial relations issues. The above journal is recommended as a place to read about the latest research on union recognition and collective consultation issues.

Barrow, C. (2002) *Industrial Relations Law*. London: Cavendish Publishing

Marchington, M., Wilkinson, A., Ackers, P. and Dundon, A. (2001) *Management Choice and Employee Voice*. London: CIPD

Morris, G. and Archer, T. (2000) *Collective Labour Law*. Oxford: Hart Publishing
Solid, detailed accounts of the various ways in which UK law requires employers to consult with their workforces are provided by Morris and Archer (2000) and by Barrow (2002). By contrast, Marchington *et al.* (2001) provide an effective assessment of the business case for meaningful consultation between employers and employees.

Wood, S., Moore, S. and Ewing, K. (2003) 'The impact of the trade union recognition procedure under the Employment Relations Act 2000–2002', in H. Gospel and S. Wood (eds) *Representing Workers*. London: Routledge
Several detailed evaluations of the compulsory recognition procedures contained in the Employment Relations Act 1999 have been published. The government's own assessment is carried on the Department of Trade and Industry website. This article provides a good, critical, up-to-date discussion of the procedure in action.

REFERENCES

Cully, M., Woodland, S., O'Reilly, A. and Dix, G. (1999) *Britain at Work: As depicted by the 1998 Workplace Employee Relations Survey*. London: Routledge.
Farnham, D. (2000) *Employee Relations in Context*, 2nd edn. London: CIPD.

Gall, G. and Hammond, D. (2000) 'Spectre of CAC prompts first waves of voluntary recognition', *People Management*, 7 December.

Gall, G. and McKay, S. (1999) 'Developments in union recognition and derecognition in Britain 1994–1998', *British Journal of Industrial Relations*, Vol. 37, No. 4, pp. 601–14.

Hart, T. (1993) 'Human resource management: time to exorcize the militant tendency', *Employee Relations*, Vol. 15, No. 3, pp. 29–36.

IDS (2000) *Union Recognition*, IDS Study 685. London: Incomes Data Services.

IRS (1995) 'Employee representation arrangements: the trade unions', *Employment Trends*, No. 586.

Marchington, M. (1989) 'Joint consultation in practice', in K. Sisson (ed.) *Personnel Management in Britain*. Oxford: Blackwell.

Marchington, M. and Wilkinson, A. (2002) *People Management & Development*. London: CIPD.

Millward, N., Bryson, A. and Forth, J. (2000) *All Change at Work?* London: Routledge.

Rose, E. (2001) *Employment Relations*. London: Financial Times Prentice Hall.

Wood, S., Moore, S. and Ewing, K. (2003) 'The impact of the trade union recognition procedure under the Employment Relations Act 2000–2002', in H. Gospel and S. Wood (eds) *Representing Workers*. London: Routledge.

An extensive range of additional materials, including multiple choice questions, answers to questions and links to useful websites can be found on the Human Resource Management Companion Website at **www.pearsoned.co.uk/torrington**.

CHAPTER 22

HEALTH, SAFETY AND WELFARE

THE OBJECTIVES OF THIS CHAPTER ARE TO:

1 DEFINE THE TERMS HEALTH, SAFETY AND WELFARE AND THE ROLE THEY PLAY IN HRM

2 EXPLAIN THE FRAMEWORK OF CRIMINAL LAW IN THE HEALTH AND SAFETY FIELD AND ITS ENFORCEMENT

3 ASSESS THE INCREASED ROLE PLAYED BY THE CIVIL LAW IN HEALTH AND SAFETY MANAGEMENT, PARTICULARLY IN RESPECT OF STRESS AT WORK

4 OUTLINE THE MAJOR METHODS AVAILABLE TO IMPROVE EMOTIONAL WELFARE AMONG STAFF

5 IDENTIFY THE MAJOR PROCESSES USED TO PREVENT PHYSICAL INJURIES FROM OCCURRING IN THE WORKPLACE

6 DESCRIBE THE ROLE THAT CAN BE PLAYED BY AN OCCUPATIONAL HEALTH FUNCTION

There is always a conflict between the needs of the employer to push for increased output and efficiency and the needs of the employee to be protected from the hazards of the workplace. In the mid-nineteenth century these tensions centred almost entirely on the long hours and heavy physical demands of the factory system. In the opening years of the twenty-first century the tensions are more varied and more subtle, but concern about them remains as great, being expressed by employers, employees, trade unions, government agencies and campaign groups.

Increasingly, aspects of protection are being provided by statute, much new legislation having a European origin. The most recent major addition is the body of measures contained in the Working Time Regulations 1998 which aim to reduce the number of hours we work each week, while also guaranteeing everyone a minimum period of paid holiday each year. In addition some aspects result from the initiatives of managements, employees and their representatives. No matter what the source of the initiative or the nature of the concern, the human resource manager is often the focus of whatever action has to be taken.

DEFINITIONS OF HEALTH, SAFETY AND WELFARE

The dictionary defines 'welfare' as 'well-being', so health and safety are strictly aspects of employee welfare, which have been separately identified as being significant areas of welfare provision for some time. There are two primary areas of benefit to the individual from the provision of welfare facilities, physical benefits and emotional/psychological benefits. Physical benefits stem primarily from measures to improve health and safety, as well as from the provision of paid holidays, reduced working hours and suchlike. Emotional welfare stems chiefly from any provisions made to improve mental health, for example, counselling, improved communications, or anything involving the 'human relations' needs of people at work. These benefits are, however, highly interrelated, and most welfare activities would potentially have both physical and emotional benefits. It can also be argued that employers provide for the material and intellectual welfare of their employees, in the material provisions of sick pay and pensions, and in the intellectual benefits that come from the provision of satisfying work and appropriate training and development. However, since these aspects are covered elsewhere in this book, we shall concentrate on physical and emotional welfare in this chapter.

HRM AND HEALTH, SAFETY AND WELFARE

The development of health, safety and welfare provision is to a large extent interrelated with the development of human resource management itself. As mentioned in Chapter 1, one of the early influences on the development of the profession was the growth of industrial welfare workers at the beginning of the twentieth century. Enlightened employers gradually began to improve working conditions for employees and the industrial welfare worker was often concerned in implementing these changes. Much of this work was carried out voluntarily by employers, although not necessarily from altruistic motives alone. Another influence was that of the 'human relations school', in particular the work of Elton Mayo at the Hawthorne plant of the Western Electric Company. Here there was an employee counselling programme, which operated from 1936 to 1955. It was found that such a programme was beneficial for both the mental health of the employees and their work. Other aspects of welfare provision, particularly in respect of safety, such as limitations on the hours of work of children, were enshrined in the law from as early as the 1840s and these again have become identified with the human resource function.

Our research shows that in 41 per cent of those firms with a safety officer, this person comes within the ambit of the human resource function. In those firms without a health and safety officer the human resource department has a primary responsibility for health and safety. As health and safety legislation has become more pervasive, in particular since the Health and Safety at Work etc. Act 1974, and the surge of regulations stemming from it (many resulting from the need to harmonise health and safety regulation throughout the EU), the human resource department has taken on the role of advising managers on the organisation's legal obligations.

The importance of health, safety and welfare from the employees' point of view is clear because their lives and futures are at risk. Health and safety has thus been given increasing emphasis by the trade unions in recent years and has been covered more extensively in the media. A convincing business case for addressing these issues has been articulated in the human resource management press, while the Health and Safety Executive campaigns vigorously to raise awareness of its validity among employers.

The business case is based on three propositions:

1 Illness and injury which is work related leads to avoidable absence.
2 Serious injury and illness can lead to litigation and substantial compensation being paid out by employing organisations.
3 A poor reputation for safety and welfare makes it harder for an organisation to recruit, retain and motivate its staff.

The number of serious injuries sustained at work by UK employees fluctuates substantially each year. The level has dropped since the 1970s with the fall in manufacturing employment, but the total number remains much higher than it should be. In the year to April 2003, for example, 226 people lost their lives in the UK as a result of accidents sustained at work, mostly as result of falls and motor vehicle accidents. It is further estimated that 6,000 people die each year from cancers caused by working conditions (HSE 2003). In addition, over a million people are reported by the Health and Safety Executive to suffer from some form of work-related illness each year. In 2001/02 40.1 million working days were lost in the UK due to injuries and illnesses sustained at work, a third of these being due to stress, depression or anxiety (IRS 2003). The total annual cost to employers runs to several billion pounds a year, including the costs associated with the early retirement of around 30,000 employees forced to give up work on grounds of ill health. If the number of incidents were reduced by only a small percentage, employers would thus save a considerable amount of money and trouble.

The reason that the numbers remain so high is the continual conflict between health, safety and welfare considerations and other business priorities. Leach (1995) reports a line manager who had previously been a safety officer as saying: 'I think in general managers don't see [health and safety issues] as important as . . . other issues that they would deal with disciplinary on. I mean you do take short cuts, I do myself. I mean I am not practising a lot of what I used to preach, there's no doubt about it. Managers know it is a part of their job, but I don't think they personally see [health and safety offences] as an offence as such.'

ACTIVITY 22.1

How convincing do you find the business case for the maintenance of a high level of health and safety? What additional arguments, other than those outlined here, could be deployed either for or against its validity in different workplaces?

HEALTH AND SAFETY LAW

In the area of health and safety legislative intervention has existed continuously for well over a century, longer than for any other matter we consider. Prior to 1974 the principal statutes were the Factories Act 1961, the Offices, Shops and Railway Premises Act 1963 and the Fire Precautions Act 1971. These three Acts, along with others relating to specific industries, were all brought up to date by the Health and Safety at Work etc. Act 1974 which remains the major statute governing the law in this area. In addition there are a host of health and safety regulations primarily extending the Health and Safety Act to expand specific areas of the legislation, the most significant of which are the Control of Substances Hazardous to Health (COSHH) Regulations 1988 and the series of 'daughter directives' issued by the EU concerning matters such as noise control, the manual handling of heavy loads, use of visual display units (VDUs) and use of carcinogens and biological agents. In addition there are specific sets of regulations covering matters such as violence at work, fire precautions, ventilation, the provision of sanitary facilities, safety signs and noise at work. In 1998 a major new piece of legislation came into UK law in the form of the Working Time Regulations which also have an EU origin. Many of the regulations are supplemented by Health and Safety Commission codes of practice which are not themselves legally enforceable, but which define the standard against which the authorities judge employers' actions.

The reason that EU directives have increased so rapidly in this area is that the Single European Act 1987 added another article to the Treaty of Rome. This allowed health and safety directives to be accepted by a qualified majority vote as a move towards harmonising EU health and safety legislation.

Health and safety law can be neatly divided into two halves, representing its criminal and civil spheres. The first is based in statute and is policed both by the Health and Safety Executive and by local authority inspectorates. The second relies on the common law and allows individuals who have suffered injury as a result of their work to seek damages against their employers. The former is intended to be preventative, while the latter aims to compensate individuals who become ill as a result of their work.

Criminal law

Health and safety inspectors potentially wield a great deal of power, but their approach is to give advice and to issue warnings except where they judge that there is a high risk of personal injury. They visit premises without giving notice beforehand in order to inspect equipment and make sure that the appropriate monitoring procedures are in place. They have a general right to enter premises, to collect whatever information they require and to remove samples or pieces of equipment for analysis.

Where they are unhappy with what they find, inspectors issue **improvement notices** setting out recommended improvements and requiring these to be put in place by a set date. In the case of more serious lapses, where substantial risk to health is identified, the inspectors issue **prohibition notices** which prevent employers from using particular pieces of equipment until better safety arrangements are established. Breach of one of these statutory notices is a criminal offence, as is giving false information to an inspector. Over a thousand prosecutions are brought each year for non-compliance with a Health and Safety Executive Order, leading to fines of up to £20,000. Prosecutions are also brought after injuries have been sustained where it can be shown that management knew of risks and had not acted to deal with them. Where fatalities result and an employer is found guilty of committing corporate manslaughter, fines of several hundred thousand pounds are levied. Moreover, in some cases custodial sentences have been given to controlling directors held to have been individually liable. A well-publicised case occurred in 1994 when the manager of an adventure company based at Lyme Bay was given a three-year prison sentence and fined £60,000 following the deaths of four teenagers. In recent years the government has come under pressure following rail accidents to create a new more clearly drawn offence of 'corporate killing'. This would extend criminal responsibility beyond directors to anyone acting in 'a management role' and could lead to their disqualification from such work.

The Health and Safety at Work etc. Act 1974 is the source of most health and safety law in the UK, under which more detailed sets of regulations are periodically issued. Its main purposes are as follows:

- to secure the health, safety and welfare of people at work;
- to protect the public from risks arising from workplace activities;
- to control the use and storage of dangerous substances;
- to control potentially dangerous environmental emissions.

The Act places all employers under a general duty 'to ensure, as far as is reasonably practicable, the health, safety and welfare at work' of all workers. In addition there are specific requirements to maintain plant and equipment, to provide safe systems of working, to provide a safe and healthy working environment, to consult with trade union safety representatives, to maintain an accident reporting book and to post on a noticeboard a copy of the main provisions contained in the 1974 Act. Where hazardous substances or equipment are in use, there is a further requirement to train people properly in their use and to have safe arrangements for their 'handling, transport and storage'. Where more than five workers are employed, employers are expected to have a written health and safety policy which must be kept up to date and made available to all staff.

In the case law, judges have interpreted the phrase 'as far as is reasonably practicable' relatively narrowly. Employers are expected to undertake formal risk assessments and to compare the level of risk against the costs involved in making a workplace safer. Wherever there is risk identified improvements must be made unless it would be unreasonable, for example on grounds of excessive cost, to expect an employer to do so.

The management of the organisation carries the prime responsibility for implementing the policy it has laid down; it also has a responsibility under the Act for operating the plant and equipment in the premises safely and meeting all the Act's requirements whether these are specified in the policy statement or not. A duty is also placed on employees while they are at work to take reasonable care for the safety of themselves and others, as well as their health, which appears a more difficult type of responsibility for the individual to exercise. The employee is, therefore, legally bound to comply with the safety rules and instructions that the employer promulgates and can be prosecuted for failing to do so. Employers are also fully empowered to dismiss on the grounds of misconduct employees who refuse to obey safety rules, especially if the possibility of such a dismissal is explicit in the disciplinary procedure.

WINDOW ON PRACTICE

An employee who refused to wear safety goggles for a particular process was warned of possible dismissal because the safety committee had decreed that goggles or similar protection were necessary. His refusal was based on the fact that he had done the job previously without such protection and did not see that it was now necessary. He was dismissed and the tribunal did not allow his claim of unfair dismissal (*Mortimer v. V.L. Churchill* (1979)).

Under the 1974 Act recognised trade unions have the right to appoint safety representatives who have specific duties and with whom managers are obliged to consult. Their role is to investigate complaints from staff about health and safety matters, to carry out their own inspections, to liaise with HSE inspectors and to attend meetings of health and safety committees. Managers are not permitted to prevent a representative from carrying out an inspection, but may be present during the process. Safety representatives are legally entitled to reasonable paid time off work to carry out their duties and to undertake necessary training, as well as to have facilities such as a noticeboard, telephone access, secure filing and photocopying. In 1993 new legislation gave safety representatives protection from victimisation, while case law has determined that managers cannot decide who is appointed to the role or for how long they remain in post.

The First Aid Regulations 1981 place employers under a general duty to provide adequate first aid equipment and facilities. The accompanying code of practice sets out what should be kept in a first aid box and what supplementary equipment is required in different types of workplace. In low-risk environments it is recommended that there should be one person with first aid training for every 50–100 employees, rather more being needed in high-risk workplaces such as construction sites and chemical plants.

The Control of Substances Hazardous to Health (COSHH) Regulations 1988 comprise 19 regulations and four approved codes of practice. The purpose of the legislation is to protect all employees who work with any substances hazardous to their health, by placing a requirement on their employer regarding the way in which and extent to which such substances are handled, used and controlled. The regulations apply to all workplaces, irrespective of size and nature of work. They therefore apply equally to a hotel as to a chemical plant, and in firms of a handful of employees as well as major PLCs. The regulations place a responsibility for good environmental hygiene not only on the employer, but on employees too. All substances are included, except for asbestos, lead, materials producing ionising radiations and substances underground, all of which have their own legislation (*see* Riddell 1989). The regulations require employers to focus on five major aspects of occupation in respect of hazardous substances. These are:

1 Assessing the risk of substances used, and identifying what precautions are needed. This initial assessment of substances already in use, and those that are intended for use is a major undertaking in terms of both the number of substances used and the competency of the assessor. Cherrie and Faulkner (1989) report that one employer in their survey used over 25,000 different substances!

2 Introducing appropriate measures to control or prevent the risk. These may include: removing the substance, by changing the processes used, substituting the substance or controlling the substance where this is practical. Examples include totally or partially enclosing the process, increasing ventilation and instituting safer systems of work and handling procedures.

3 Ensuring that control measures are used, that procedures are observed and that equipment involved is regularly maintained. Where necessary, exposure of employees to the substance should be monitored. This particularly applies where there could be serious health hazards were the measures to fail or be suboptimal. Records of monitoring should be made and retained.

4 Health surveillance. Where there is a known adverse effect of a particular substance, regular surveillance of the employees involved can identify problems at an early stage. When this is carried out, records should be kept and these should be accessible to employees.

5 Employees need to be informed and trained regarding the risks arising from their work and the precautions that they need to take.

The Management of Health and Safety at Work Regulations 1992 implemented the EU's Framework and Temporary Workers Directives. The Framework Directive is an umbrella directive, in a similar way that the Health and Safety at Work Act is an umbrella act. Additional rules known as 'daughter directives' covering specific areas have been issued within the framework of this directive. The following examples apply to workplaces generally. Others apply to specific industries such as construction, mining and chemicals.

- The Workplace (Health, Safety and Welfare) Regulations 1992 set out minimum design requirements, including provision of rest and no-smoking areas.
- The Provision and Use of Work Equipment Regulations 1992 set minimum standards for the safe use of machines and equipment.
- The Personal Protective Equipment at Work Regulations 1992 require employers to provide appropriate protective equipment, and workers to use this correctly.
- The Manual Handling Operations Regulations 1992 require employers to reduce the risk of injury by providing lifting equipment where appropriate and training in lifting.

- The Health and Safety (Display Screen Equipment) Regulations 1992 require employers to provide free eye tests, glasses where appropriate, regular breaks, appropriate training and organisation of equipment to reduce strain.
- The Protection of Pregnant Workers Directive 1994 was implemented in 1994 via a range of UK Acts and regulations. The major measures are now incorporated into the Employment Relations Act 1999. The most important element is that requiring employers to offer alternative work to a pregnant employee or to one who has recently given birth where there are identifiable health and safety risks.

The Health and Safety (Consultation with Employees) Regulations 1996 require employers to consult collectively with their employees about health and safety matters irrespective of whether a trade union is recognised. Consultation is defined as discussing issues with employee representatives, listening to their views and taking these into account when decisions are being made which have health and safety implications. Where trade unions are recognised the regulations require that their representatives are consulted. In situations where there are no recognised unions the employer must consult with employees as individuals directly or must make arrangements for employees to elect health and safety representatives. Elected representatives have the same rights to paid time off for training and to information disclosure as trade union appointed safety representatives.

The Working Time Regulations 1998 comprise the most significant recent addition to UK health and safety law. Like the other legislative instruments described above, they are enforced by officers of the Health and Safety Executive, but complaints can also be taken directly to employment tribunals by individuals whose employers deny them the various rights set out in the regulations.

The law on working time originates in the EU's Working Time Directive 1993. This was agreed by the Council of Ministers via qualified majority voting, with the UK government voting against. Moves were subsequently made to challenge the legality of its imposition in the UK on the grounds that it was essentially a social issue, and thus inapplicable in the UK, and not about health and safety at all. Predictably the government's case was turned down by the European Court of Justice, leading to the rather hurried introduction of the new regulations in October 1998.

As of 2004 the basic entitlements are as follows. They apply to all workers whether or not they work under a contract of employment:

- a working week limited to a maximum of 48 hours;
- four weeks' paid annual leave per year (in addition to bank holidays);
- a limitation on night working to eight hours in any one 24-hour period;
- eleven hours' rest in any one 24-hour period;
- an uninterrupted break of 24 hours in any one seven-day period;
- a 20-minute rest break in any shift of six hours or more;
- regular free health assessments to establish fitness for night working.

There are more restrictive, additional regulations relating to those aged between 16 and 18, while other groups such as transport workers, junior doctors and people who determine their own working time are excluded from the 48-hour week. Further complexity derives from the way the regulations permit more than 48 hours to be worked in some weeks and more than eight hours on some nights provided that the average number of hours worked over a 17-week period does not breach these limits. Individuals can agree with their employers in writing that they are excluded from the right to the 48-hour maximum working week, but all must be permitted to opt back into the scheme with reasonable notice if they so wish.

The regulations set out the basic rights, but they also allow for locally agreed variation on detailed matters through the mechanism of **workplace agreements**. Where trade unions are recognised, these can be drawn up and agreed through existing collective bargaining machinery. Where unions are not recognised a workplace agreement can be established in one of two ways:

1. The employer can draw up the text before asking employees to sign their approval. Once over half of the employees' signatures in a workplace are obtained, the agreement becomes valid.
2. The employer can arrange for representatives of employees to be elected to negotiate on behalf of everyone. An existing health and safety committee, provided it is properly elected, can fulfil this function.

It is likely that the EU will seek to tighten these regulations in future years. It is generally agreed that they have had no substantial impact on the UK's 'long hours culture' in their first years of operation because so many people either opt out or remain unaware of their rights under the regulations. Further restrictions will thus be necessary if the directive's health and safety objectives are to be met. At the time of writing (2004) the EU is reviewing the operation of its Working Time Directive and is considered likely to require the UK to give stronger effect to its principles. This could well lead to the end of opt-out arrangements and many of the other exemptions that mean some professions are not covered by parts of the regulations.

ACTIVITY 22.2

Devise a health and safety policy for your organisation. Include information about:

1. General policy on health and safety.
2. Specific hazards and how they are to be dealt with.
3. Management responsibility for safety.
4. How the policy is to be implemented.

Or:

Obtain the Health and Safety Policy from any organisation and assess the policy in the light of these four points.

Civil law

While distinct in origin and nature from the criminal sanctions, civil cases relating to health and safety are often brought alongside criminal proceedings in connection with the same incident. When someone is seriously injured or suffers ill health as a direct result of their work the health and safety authorities will bring a criminal prosecution, while the injured party will sue for damages in the civil courts. Most claims are brought under the law of contract (*see* Chapter 5), the injured party alleging that their employer breached its implied duty of care or its duty to provide safe systems of working. It is also possible in certain circumstances to sue for damages under the law of tort by claiming that an employer is guilty of negligence or of breaching its statutory duty.

Whatever the nature of the claim, the courts have to be satisfied that the employer failed to act reasonably and that the injury or illness was sustained 'during the course of employment'. Central here, as in the criminal law, are the notions of foreseeability and risk assessment. Cases often hinge on what the employer knew at the time the injury was sustained and whether or not reasonable precautions in the form of training or the provision of equipment had been taken. Employers can thus defend themselves effectively by satisfying the court that little else could have been done by any reasonable employer to prevent the accident from occurring. Importantly the principle of vicarious liability applies in this field, as in sexual harassment (*see* Chapter 23). This means that the employer is legally liable for the negligent actions of employees when they are at work. If one employee causes another to become injured, the claim is therefore brought against the employer and not the fellow employee who was responsible.

There are a number of defences open to employers which can result in no award being made or in reduced damages. These include situations in which an accident was not foreseeable (for example if someone was struck by a piece of masonry during exceptionally heavy winds), where the employee voluntarily assumed a risk despite being warned of possible danger, and where an injury which originated outside the workplace was worsened as a result of working. Most significant of all are situations where the employee is found to have contributed to their own injury in some way. This can happen where illnesses derive from lapses of concentration, professional misjudgement or simply stupid behaviour in the face of dangerous conditions. An example is the extraordinary case of *Jones* v. *Lionite Specialities (Cardiff) Ltd* (1961) where an employee fell into a tank of noxious liquid and died. The court held that he was wholly to blame as he had put himself at risk in order to take big whiffs of the liquid's vapour 'to which he had taken a liking'.

MANAGING STRESS AND EMOTIONAL WELFARE

Workplace stress is the welfare topic which has received the most coverage in recent years. It is also a source of litigation which has led to particularly high amounts of damages being paid to those who have sustained illnesses brought on directly as a result of work-related strain. An out-of-court settlement worth £175,000 was agreed following the High Court ruling in the landmark case of *Walker* v. *Northumberland County Council* (1995). Here a social work manager who had returned to work following a nervous breakdown was given inadequate support and an increased workload leading to a further breakdown. The court held that this amounted to a breach of the implied duty of care, because the second illness had been clearly foreseeable. In *Ingram* v. *Worcester County Council* (2000), a settlement of £203,000 was reached after a warden responsible for the regulation of travellers' sites suffered a single breakdown after having been subjected to physical and verbal abuse from site residents. The fact that he had been undermined in his efforts by senior council officials and had suffered 'prolonged and unremitting stress' led to the finding that the duty of care had been breached (*see* IRS 2000a, p. 4).

In recent years there have been fewer successful personal injury claims based on stress and lower amounts of damages awarded to victorious applicants. This trend follows guidance given by the Court of Appeal in four linked cases heard in February 2002. The Court overturned the judgments of lower courts in three of the cases and reduced the damages that had been awarded in the fourth. They made the following important points in their judgment:

- Employers are not obliged to make searching enquiries to establish whether an individual is at risk.
- Employees who stay in stressful jobs voluntarily are responsible for their own fate if they subsequently suffer stress-based illnesses.
- There must be indications of impending harm arising from workload in order for an employer to take action.
- The employer is only in breach where the risk is foreseeable 'bearing in mind the size of the risk, the gravity of the harm, the costs of preventing it and the justification of running the risk'.
- There are no occupations which should be regarded as intrinsically dangerous to mental health.
- Employers who offer confidential counselling services with access to treatment are unlikely to be found in breach.
- The illness must clearly be caused by breach of duty and not just by occupational stress.
- Damages must be reduced to take account of pre-existing disorders or the chance that the claimant would have fallen ill anyway.

Thanks to these rulings, employers were able to take a tougher line on stress-related absences and the management of these issues for much of 2002 and 2003. However, the respite was short-lived because in 2003 the Health and Safety Executive announced that its inspectors would soon be adding stress-related illnesses to their list of checks when visiting employer premises and that the first improvement notices concerning stressful working environments had been served. The Executive's guidance makes it clear that employers are now expected to treat stress like any other health hazard, and that there is consequently 'a legal duty to take reasonable care to ensure that health is not placed at risk through excessive and sustained levels of stress arising from the way people deal with each other at their work or from the day-to-day demands placed on their workforce' (Willey 2003, p. 414).

Stress at work is not a new idea, although it was originally viewed in terms of executive stress (*see* Levinson 1964), and seen only to apply to those in senior management positions. The literature on the subject of stress at work is large (for example, Cooper and Marshall 1980; Palmer 1989; Nykodym and George 1989; Roney and Cooper 1997; Jex 1998; Macdonald 1999). It is defined by Ganster and Murphy (2000) as a form of 'strain' provoked in response to situational demands labelled 'stressors' which occur 'when jobs are simultaneously high in demands and low in control':

> Stressors generally mean environmental factors that cause the individual to muster a coping response because they pose threat or harm. In the work domain examples of such stressors are high workloads, requirements for working fast and meeting strict deadlines, conflicting demands and interruption . . . Problems are seen to arise when exposure to such demands is chronic and elicits a strong enough pattern of responses to strain the individual's physical and mental resources. (Ganster and Murphy 2000, p. 36)

According to Willey (2003, p. 413) the incidence of chronic stress is often seen as a 'by-product' of management initiatives adopted in many countries, including the UK, in the past twenty years. These include delayering, downsizing, the intensification of work, increased monitoring of staff, moves towards greater flexibility at work and competitive tendering. Each has placed increased burdens on staff groups who have had to accept lower job security, greater levels of responsibility and longer hours of work. The inability to reconcile such demands with family life is a further cause of strain. The results are twofold:

- adverse health conditions (such as heart disease, high blood pressure, ulcers, depression and panic attacks);
- behavioural consequences (such as insomnia, anxiety, poor concentration and increased consumption of alcohol, tobacco and other substances).

Both can lead to increased rates of absence, high staff turnover, low levels of job satisfaction and the sustenance of a low-trust employee relations environment.

Stress and its consequences are often caused by a combination of strains originating in and outside work. A person who is normally able to cope well with the demands of a stressful job may cease to do so when home-based problems come to the fore, the major culprits being bereavement, debt and marital breakdown. There is thus a good business case for employers to provide formal mechanisms for emotional support, quite aside from the strong ethical case. The following are examples of available approaches.

Someone to talk to/someone to advise

A person to talk to could be the individual's manager, or the human resource manager, but it is often more usefully someone who is distinct from the work itself. Occupational health nurses, welfare officers or specialised counsellors are the sort of people well placed to deal with this area. There are two benefits that come from this, the first being advice and practical assistance. This would be relevant, for example, if the individual had financial problems, and the organisation was prepared to offer some temporary assistance. Alternatively, the individual could be advised of alternative sources of help, or referred, with agreement, to the appropriate agency for treatment. The second benefit to be gained is that of having someone just listen to the individual's problem without judging it, in other words, counselling. De Board (1983) suggests that the types of work-related problems that employees may need to be counselled on are: technical incompetence, underwork, overwork, uncertainty about the future and relationships at work. Counselling aims to provide a supportive atmosphere to help people to find their own solution to a problem.

Reorganisation of work

This is a preventive measure involving reorganisation of those aspects of work that are believed to be affecting the mental health of employees. This may include changes that could be grouped as 'organisational development', such as job rotation and autonomous work-groups. Eva and Oswald (1981) suggest greater control over the speed and intensity of work, an increase in the quality of work and a reduction in unsocial hours. Individually based training and development programmes would also be relevant here. Specifically for the executive, there is growing use of the 'managerial sabbatical'. Some American companies have begun to give a year off after a certain number of years' service in order to prevent 'executive burnout'. In the UK, the John Lewis Partnership has a programme allowing six months away from work.

Positive health programmes

Positive health programmes display a variety of different approaches aimed at relieving and preventing stress and associated problems, and promoting healthy lifestyles. There is increasing activity in terms of healthy eating and no-smoking campaigns and support, together with the provision of resources for physical activity. Corporate wellness programmes have been in place for a longer period in the USA, where the prime motivation was the reduction of medical costs (most employers covering these costs as a benefit for their employees). In the UK the programmes are more often seen as an employee benefit in themselves, with the hope that providing them will also encourage higher productivity and reduce absence levels. However, Mills (1996) argues that although there is a weak positive relationship between healthier lifestyles and the bottom line, there is little evidence that health promotion programmes are actually working. He argues that only a small number of employees are affected by such programmes and that these are likely to be those who already have healthier lifestyles. Mills suggests that blue-collar employees, who have the least control over their working lives, also tend to have less healthy lifestyles and are more resistant to health promotions. He suggests that all three factors are interrelated and connected in a complex manner with employee motivation. If Mills is right, this presents a challenge to organisations and suggests at the very least that they should evaluate positive health programmes as well as investigating the impact of the prevailing management style.

Some approaches to corporate wellness include the use of yoga and meditation. Others, such as 'autogenic training', are based on these principles, but are presented in a new guise. Autogenic training is developed through exercises in body awareness and physical relaxation which lead to passive concentration. It is argued that the ability to achieve this breaks through the vicious circle of excessive stress, and that as well as the many mental benefits, there are benefits to the body including relief of somatic symptoms of anxiety, and the reduction of cardiovascular risk factors (Carruthers 1982). Another approach is 'chemo feedback', which is geared towards the connection between stress and coronary heart disease, high blood pressure and strokes. Chemo feedback (Positive Health Centre 1985) is designed as an early warning system to pick up signs of unfavourable stress. The signs are picked up from the completion of a computerised questionnaire together with a blood test. This approach, like others such as the Occupational Stress Indicator (*see* IRS 2000b, pp. 13–16), is being offered as a 'stress-audit' tool for use on a company-wide basis.

MANAGING PHYSICAL WELFARE

There are a number of ways in which managerial responsibility can be discharged to implement the organisation's health and safety policy statement and to ensure compliance with legal requirements.

Making the work safe

Making the work safe is mainly in the realm of the designer and production engineer. It is also a more general management responsibility to ensure that any older equipment and machinery that is used is appropriately modified to make it safe, or removed. The provision of necessary safety wear is also a managerial responsibility – for example, making sure goggles and ear protectors are available.

Enabling employees to work safely

Whereas making the work safe is completely a management responsibility, the individual employee may contribute by his or her own negligence, working unsafely in a safe situation. The task of managers is twofold; first, the employee must know what to do; second, this knowledge must be translated into action: the employee must comply with the safe working procedures that are laid down. To meet the first part of the obligation management needs to be scrupulous in communication of drills and instructions and the analysis of working situations to decide what the drills should be. That is a much bigger and more difficult activity than can be implied in a single sentence, but the second part of getting compliance is more difficult and more important. Employee failure to comply with clear drills does not absolve the employer and the management. When an explosion leaves the factory in ruins it is of little value for the factory manager to shake his head and say: 'I told them not to do it.' We examine the way to obtain compliance shortly, in the course of our discussion about training and other methods of persuasion.

In larger organisations the initiative on safe working will be led by the professionals within the management team. They are the safety officer, the medical officer, the nursing staff and the safety representatives. Although there is no legal obligation to appoint a safety officer, more and more organisations are making such appointments. One reason is to provide emphasis and focus for safety matters. The appointment suggests that the management means business, but the appointment itself is not enough. It has to be fitted into the management structure with lines of reporting and accountability which will enable the safety officer to be effective and which will prevent other members of management becoming uncertain of their own responsibilities – perhaps to the point of thinking that they no longer exist. Ideally, the safety officers operate on two fronts: making the work safe and ensuring safe working, although this may require an ability to talk constructively on engineering issues with engineers as well as being able to handle training and some industrial-relations-type arguments.

The medical officer (if one is appointed) will almost certainly be the only medically qualified person and can therefore introduce to the thinking on health and safety discussions a perspective and a range of knowledge that is both unique and relevant. Second, the medical officer will probably carry more social status than the managers dealing with health and safety matters and he or she will be detached from the management in their eyes and his or her own. Doctors have their own ethical code, which is different from that of the managers. They are authoritative advisers to management on making the work safe and can be authoritative advisers to employees on working safely. They are invaluable members of the safety committee and potentially important features of training programmes. Occupational nurses also deal directly with working safely and often play a part in safety training, as well as symbolising care in the face of hazard.

Safety training and other methods of persuasion

Safety training has three major purposes: (1) employees should be told about and understand the nature of the hazards at the place of work; (2) employees need to be made aware of the safety rules and procedures; and (3) they need to be persuaded to comply with them. The first of these is the most important, because employees sometimes tend to modify the rules to suit their own convenience. Trainers cannot, of course, condone the short cut without implying a general flexibility in the rules, but they need to be aware of how employees will probably respond. In some areas the use of short cuts by skilled employees does not always mean they are working less safely, but there are many areas where compliance with the rules is critical, for example, the wearing of safety goggles.

Safety training needs to be carried out in three settings: at induction, on the job and in refresher courses. A variety of different training techniques can be employed, including lectures, discussions, films, role playing and slides. These methods are sometimes supplemented by poster or other safety awareness campaigns and communications, and disciplinary action for breaches of the safety rules. Management example in sticking to the safety rules no matter what the tempo of production can also set a good example.

Research by Pirani and Reynolds (1976) indicated that the response to a variety of methods of safety persuasion – poster campaigns, film shows, fear techniques, discussion groups, role playing and disciplinary action – was very good in the short term (over two weeks) but after four months the initial improvement had virtually disappeared for all methods except role playing. From this it can be concluded that: first, a management initiative on safety will produce gratifying results in the obeying of rules, but a fresh initiative will be needed at regular and frequent intervals to keep it effective; and, second, the technique of role playing appears to produce results that are longer lasting.

WINDOW ON PRACTICE

Health and safety and the use of contractors

As large firms increasingly contract out their operations the Health and Safety Commission is paying greater attention to this area, and Frank Davis, the Chair of the Commission warned: 'No firm – whatever the industrial sector – can afford to be complacent about the activities of contractors' (speaking at the Royal Society for Prevention of Accidents Congress, May 1996).

Lucas Industries (who subcontract a range of activities, some high risk), as part of a major reorganisation, reviewed their health, safety and environment systems in order to improve their performance. They concluded that current systems were reactive, not auditable or integrated with other systems, lacked clear ownership, were too dependent on internal specialists and did not address concerns about high-risk activities.

Their new approach seeks to rectify these problems. They developed a questionnaire for contractors to complete, relating to health and safety issues and they assessed this against what they could reasonably expect from a contractor of that size in that business. This enabled Lucas to take the initiative by assessing the risk and then discussing this assessment with the contractor. Where necessary, contractors were given encouragement and help to improve. Only those contractors who were already operating at the appropriate level, or who would improve to this level, would be on the Lucas Register of Contractors. Contractors were invited to attend a half-day awareness raising workshop based on the questionnaire topics and focused on risk assessment. A newly designed Contractors Registration Form was implemented to be completed jointly by the contractor and Lucas. This covers such issues as the task, materials, substances and equipment used, services needed, work environment and conditions and site hazards. Via this form the contractors and Lucas agree and record controls and precautions and safe systems of work. Where possible these forms are displayed where the work is carried out in order to make the risk assessment visible.

OCCUPATIONAL HEALTH DEPARTMENTS

Occupational health and welfare is a broad area which includes both physical and emotional well-being. The medical officer, occupational health nurse and welfare officer all have a contribution to make here. In a broader sense so do the dentist, chiropodist and other professionals when they are employed by the organisation. The provision of these broader welfare facilities is often found in large organisations located away from centres of population, especially in industrial plants, where the necessity of at least an occupational health nurse can be clearly seen.

In terms of physical care the sorts of facility that can be provided are:

1 Emergency treatment, beyond immediate first aid, of injuries sustained at work.
2 Medical, dental and other facilities, which employees can use and which can be more easily fitted into the working day than making appointments with outside professionals.
3 Immediate advice on medical and related matters, especially those connected with work.
4 Monitoring of accidents and illnesses to identify hazards and danger points, and formulating ideas to combat these in conjunction with the safety officer.
5 On-site medical examinations for those joining the organisation.

6 Regular medical examinations for employees.
7 Input into health and safety training courses.
8 Regular screening services (e.g. cervical cancer screening).

SUMMARY PROPOSITIONS

22.1 Occupational welfare is the 'well-being' of people at work, encompassing occupational health and safety.

22.2 The history of human resource management is interrelated with the development of welfare. Many HR managers find this association a disadvantage when trying to develop the authority and status of personnel management.

22.3 The legal framework for health and safety includes both the criminal and civil law. The former is policed by health and safety inspectors; the latter provides a vehicle for those who suffer illness or injury as a result of their work to claim damages.

22.4 The Health and Safety at Work etc. Act 1974 is a major piece of UK legislation in this field. The efforts of the EU to ensure harmonisation of health and safety resulted in a major surge of new legislation in the 1990s.

22.5 The period since the 1980s has seen increasing interest in occupational health and welfare, particularly related to stress, alcoholism and counselling.

GENERAL DISCUSSION TOPICS

1 'Good health is good business.' Discuss.

2 To what extent and by what processes can organisations reduce stress for employees who are members of dual-career families?

3 How can an organisation utilise training and development to foster a culture that is receptive to health and safety?

FURTHER READING

Boyd, C. (2003) *Human Resource Management and Occupational Health and Safety*. London: Routledge

This is a thorough critical study looking at the various ways that HR managers can and should contribute to health, safety and welfare. This book contains case studies focusing on the airline, call-centre and nuclear power industries.

Ganster, D.C. and Murphy, L. (2000) 'Workplace Interventions to Prevent Stress-Related Illness: Lessons from Research and Practice', in C. Cooper and E. Locke (eds) *Industrial and Organizational Psychology: Linking Theory with Practice*. Oxford: Blackwell

These authors provide an excellent summary of research and effective practice on the subject of stress-related illnesses. They conclude by suggesting a best practice approach to stress prevention.

Stranks, J. (2001a) *A Manager's Guide to Health and Safety at Work*, 6th edn. London: Kogan Page

Stranks, J. (2001b) *Health and Safety Law*, 4th edn. London: Prentice Hall
Jeremy Stranks is the most prolific writer on health and safety issues. He has written dozens of handbooks explaining the law and setting out the most recent guidance on reducing ill health and injuries in the workplace. Two of the most recent editions of his handbooks are listed above.

REFERENCES

Carruthers, M. (1982) 'Train the mind to calm itself', *General Practitioner*, 16 July.

Cherrie, I. and Faulkner, C. (1989) 'Will the COSHH regulations improve occupational health?' *Safety Practitioner*, February, pp. 6–7.

Cooper, C.L. and Marshall, I. (1980) *White Collar and Professional Stress*. Chichester: John Wiley.

De Board, R. (1983) *Counselling People at Work: an introduction for managers*. Aldershot: Gower.

Eva, D. and Oswald, R. (1981) *Health and Safety at Work*. London: Pan Books.

Ganster, D.C. and Murphy, L. (2000) 'Workplace Interventions to Prevent Stress-Related Illness: Lessons from Research and Practice', in C. Cooper and E. Locke (eds) *Industrial and Organizational Psychology: Linking Theory with Practice*. Oxford: Blackwell.

Health and Safety Executive (2003) HSC press release C038:03, 29 July 2003.

IRS (2000a) '£203,000 award for single breakdown', *Employee Health Bulletin 13*, February.

IRS (2000b) 'Stress auditing – the OSI', *Employee Health Bulletin 16*, August.

IRS (2003) 'Cold comfort in safety record', *IRS Employment Review* January, p. 41.

Jex, S.M. (1998) *Stress and Job Performance: Theory, Research and Implications for Managerial Practice*. Thousand Oaks, Calif.: Sage.

Leach, J. (1995) 'Devolution of personnel activities – the reality', MA dissertation, Manchester Metropolitan University.

Levinson, H. (1964) *Executive Stress*. New York: Harper & Row.

Macdonald, L. (1999) *Sensitive Issues in Employment*. Dublin: Blackhall.

Mills, M. (1996) 'Body and soul', *People Management*, 2 September, pp. 36–8.

Nykodym, N. and George, K. (1989) 'Stress busting on the job', *Personnel*, July, pp. 56–9.

Palmer, S. (1989) 'Occupational stress', *The Safety and Health Practitioner*, August, pp. 16–18.

Pirani, M. and Reynolds, J. (1976) 'Gearing up for safety', *Personnel Management*, February.

Positive Health Centre (1985) *Chemo Feedback*. London: Positive Health Centre.

Riddell, R. (1989) 'Why COSHH will hit hard on health and safety', *Personnel Management*, September, pp. 46–9.

Roney, A. and Cooper, C. (eds) (1997) *Professionals on Workplace Stress*. Chichester: Wiley.

Willey, B. (2003) *Employment Law in Context*, 2nd edn. London: Financial Times/Prentice Hall.

LEGAL CASES

Ingram v. *Worcester County Council* (2000) (in IRS 2000c).

Jones v. *Lionite Specialities (Cardiff) Ltd* (1961) 105SJ 1082.

Mortimer v. *V.L. Churchill* (1979).

Walker v. *Northumberland County Council* [1995] 1 All ER 737; [1995] IRLR 35.

An extensive range of additional materials, including multiple choice questions, answers to questions and links to useful websites can be found on the Human Resource Management Companion Website at www.pearsoned.co.uk/torrington.

CHAPTER 23

EQUALITY: THE LEGAL FRAMEWORK

THE OBJECTIVES OF THIS CHAPTER ARE TO:

1 REVIEW THE KEY LEGAL REQUIREMENTS IN THE AREAS OF DISCRIMINATION

2 EXPLAIN THE CORE PRINCIPLES OF DISCRIMINATION LAW

3 DISTINGUISH BETWEEN DIRECT AND INDIRECT DISCRIMINATION

4 EXPLAIN THE IMPORTANCE OF HARASSMENT IN DISCRIMINATION LAW

5 SET OUT THE MAJOR DEFENCES DEPLOYED BY EMPLOYERS IN DISCRIMINATION CASES

An important part of employment law in the UK is concerned with deterring employers from discriminating unfairly at any stage in their relationship with an individual worker. It is an area of law which is well established but which is also developing fast in new directions. As we write there are specific statutes making it unlawful to discriminate on the following grounds:

- sex;
- marital status;
- race;
- national origin;
- ethnicity;
- disability;
- sexual orientation;
- religion or belief;
- union membership or non-membership;
- that individuals are part-time workers;
- that individuals are fixed-term workers,
- that individuals are ex-offenders whose convictions are spent.

Discrimination law operates rather differently in the case of each of the above grounds, providing a greater degree of protection, for example, to those discriminated against on the grounds of sex or race than to union members or ex-offenders. In some cases the law allows employers to discriminate on certain grounds provided their action can be objectively justified, while in others the grounds for defence are very limited.

In recent years the UK has had to amend and extend its discrimination laws in order to comply with new European directives which establish a common framework across all member states in respect of discrimination on grounds of sex, race, sexual orientation, religion or belief, disability and age. By the end of 2006 this process will be complete, meaning that most of UK discrimination law will fall within the boundaries of European competence, the European Court of Justice being the final court of appeal.

In the following chapter we look more generally at employment policy on equality issues and at the practices associated with the effective management of diversity.

ACTIVITY 23.1

What other grounds, aside from those currently covered by the law, would you consider should be covered by discrimination law? Are there any that are currently covered that you think should not be?

DISCRIMINATION ON GROUNDS OF SEX OR MARITAL STATUS

The two major Acts of Parliament that govern sex discrimination matters in the UK are the Equal Pay Act 1970 and the Sex Discrimination Act 1975. Although both came into effect thirty years ago they have been subsequently amended in important ways. Sex discrimination is an area of law which has long been one of EU competence, so appeals can be made to the European Court of Justice. UK law can also be challenged in the European courts if it is considered that it fails to comply in some way with Article 141 of the Treaty of Amsterdam (formerly Article 119 of the Treaty of Rome) or with EU directives in the sex discrimination field.

Employer actions are policed to some extent by the Equal Opportunities Commission (EOC) which is required to keep the legislation under review, to conduct formal investigations into employer actions where it has reason to suspect there has been a contravention of the law, to issue codes of practice and to provide legal assistance to employees who consider themselves to be victims of unfair discrimination. On many occasions the EOC has itself represented employees before employment tribunals. It also brings its own test cases in a bid to push back the frontiers of sex discrimination law. In the future the EOC's current duties will be carried out by a new larger body with responsibilities extending across and beyond the major fields of discrimination law. At the time of writing the provisional title is the Commission for Equality and Human Rights.

The Equal Pay Act 1970

The Equal Pay Act 1970 was the first legislation promoting equality at work between men and women. Although passed in 1970, it only came into force in December 1975. It was subsequently amended, and its scope extended, by the Equal Pay (Amendment) Regulations 1983 and by the Sex Discrimination Act 1986. The Act is solely concerned with eliminating unjustifiable differences between the treatment of men and women in terms of their rates of pay and other conditions of employment. It is thus the vehicle that is used to bring a case to tribunal when there is inequality between a man's contract of employment and that of a woman. In practice the majority of cases are brought by women and concern discriminatory rates of payment, although there have been some important cases brought by men focusing on aspects of pension provision.

The Act, as amended in 1983, specifies three types of claim that can be brought. These effectively define the circumstances in which pay and other conditions between men and women should be equal:

1 Like work: where a woman and a man are doing work which is the same or broadly similar – for example where a woman assembly worker sits next to a male assembly worker, carrying out the same range of duties.

2 Work rated as equivalent: where a man and a woman are carrying out work which, while of a different nature, has been rated as equivalent under a job evaluation scheme. We cover this aspect of equal pay in greater detail in Chapter 27.

3 Work of equal value: where a man and a woman are performing different tasks but where it can be shown that the two jobs are equal in terms of their demands, for example in terms of skill, effort and type of decision making.

In order to bring a case the applicant must be able to point to a comparator of the opposite gender with whom he or she wishes to be compared. The comparator must be employed by the same employer and at an establishment covered by the same terms and conditions. When an equal value claim is brought which an employment tribunal considers to be well founded, an 'independent expert' is appointed to carry out a job evaluation exercise in order to establish whether or not the two jobs being compared are equal in terms of the demands they make.

Employers can employ two defences when faced with a claim under the Equal Pay Act. First, they can seek to show that a job evaluation exercise has been carried out which indicates that the two jobs are not like, rated as equivalent or of equal value. To succeed the job evaluation scheme in use must be both analytical and free of sex bias (*see* Chapter 27). Second, the employer can claim that the difference in pay is justified by 'a genuine material factor not of sex'. For this to succeed, the employer has to convince the court that there is a good business reason for the unequal treatment and that there has thus been no sex discrimination. Examples of genuine material factors that have proved acceptable to the courts are as follows:

- different qualifications (e.g. where a man has a degree and a woman does not);
- performance (e.g. where a man is paid a higher rate than a woman because he works faster or has received a higher appraisal rating);
- seniority (where the man is paid more because he has been employed for several years longer than the woman);
- regional allowances (where a man is paid a London weighting, taking his pay to a higher rate than that of a woman performing the same job in the Manchester branch).

The courts have ruled that differences in pay explained by the fact that the man and woman concerned are in separate bargaining groups, by the fact that they asked for different salaries on appointment or because of an administrative error are not acceptable genuine material factor defences. It is possible to argue that a difference in pay is explained by market forces, but evidence has to be produced to satisfy the court that going rates for the types of work concerned are genuinely different and that it is therefore genuinely necessary to pay the comparator at a higher rate.

In 2003 a questionnaire system was introduced to provide a vehicle for people who believe that they may have grounds for bringing a claim formally to ask their employers whether they are being paid less than a named comparator and, if this is the case, to give reasons. Legal action can then follow (or be threatened) if the reasons given are unsatisfactory. When someone wins an equal pay claim they are entitled to receive up to six years' back pay to make up the difference between their salary and that of their comparator.

WINDOW ON PRACTICE

Ms Smith was taken on to work for a company as a stockroom manager at a salary of £50 a week. After a few months she discovered that her predecessor (a man) had been paid £60 a week for doing the same job. As there was no suitable male comparator currently employed by the firm, she decided to bring an equal pay case using her predecessor as her male comparator. The European Court of Justice decided that this was acceptable under the terms of Article 119 of the Treaty of Rome. Ms Smith thus won her case.

In a more recent case, a woman who had been employed in a senior role resigned and was subsequently replaced by a man who was paid a considerably higher salary. She brought an equal pay claim against her former employer citing her successor as the male comparator. This too was ruled acceptable under the terms of the European Treaties.

Sources: *Macarthy's Ltd* v. *Smith* (1980), *Diocese of Hallam Trustees* v. *Connaughton* (1995).

The Sex Discrimination Act 1975

The Sex Discrimination Act also came into force in December 1975 and was designed to complement the Equal Pay Act 1970 by dealing primarily with non-contractual forms of sex discrimination such as employee selection, the provision of training opportunities, promotion, access to benefits and facilities and dismissal. It also applies outside the workplace, so case law that relates to events which have nothing at all to do with employment can be the source of important precedents. The Act covers all workers whether or not they serve under contracts of employment or are employed and all job applicants. The only groups excluded are ministers of religion, soldiers who may serve in front-line duties and people employed to work abroad. It thus remains permissible for firms recruiting employees to work in Saudi Arabia exclusively to select men. The Act applies equally to men and women, and also protects people from unfair discrimination on the grounds that they are married.

There are three headings under which claims are brought: direct discrimination, indirect discrimination and victimisation, the way the law works in each case being rather different.

Direct discrimination is straightforward. It occurs simply when an employer treats someone unfavourably and when sex or marital status is an important factor in this decision. In judging claims the courts use the 'but for' test, asking whether the woman would have received the same treatment as a man (or vice versa) but for her sex. Examples of direct sex discrimination include advertising for a man to do a job which could equally well be done by a woman, failing to promote a woman because she is pregnant or dismissing a married woman rather than her single colleague because she is known to have a working husband.

If an employer is found to have discriminated *directly* on grounds of sex or marital status, except in one type of situation, there is no defence. The courts cannot, therefore, take into account any mitigating circumstances or make a judgment based on the view that the employer acted reasonably. Once it has been established that direct discrimination has occurred, proceedings end with a victory for the applicant. The one exception operates in the area of recruitment, where it is possible to argue that certain jobs have to be reserved for either women or men. For this to be acceptable the employer must convince a court that it is a job for which there is a 'genuine occupational qualification'. The main headings under which such claims are made are as follows:

- **authenticity** (e.g. acting or modelling jobs);
- **decency** (e.g. lavatory or changing room attendants);
- **personal services** (e.g. a counsellor engaged to work in a rape crisis centre).

Direct discrimination on grounds of pregnancy or maternity is assumed automatically to constitute unlawful sex discrimination. This means that there is no defence of reasonableness whatever the individual circumstances. It is thus unlawful to turn down a job application from a well-qualified woman who is eight months pregnant, irrespective of her intentions as regards the taking of maternity leave.

Indirect discrimination is harder to grasp, not least because it can quite easily occur unintentionally. It occurs when a 'requirement or condition' is set which has the effect, in practice, of disadvantaging a significantly larger proportion of one sex than the other. In other words, if substantially fewer women than men can comply with the condition, even if it is applied in exactly the same way to both men and women, it is potentially unlawful. A straightforward example is a job advertisement which specifies that applicants should be taller than 5 feet 10 inches. This is indirectly discriminatory because a substantially smaller proportion of women are able to comply than men. The same rule applies in the case of discrimination on grounds of marital status, an example being that of an employer who offers promotion on the basis that the employee must be prepared to be away from home for considerable spells of time, when in reality such absence was never or rarely required.

Indirect discrimination differs from direct discrimination in that there are defences that an employer can deploy. For example, an employer can justify the condition or requirement they have set 'on grounds other than sex', in which case it may be lawful. An example might be a job for which a key requirement is the ability to lift heavy loads. It is reasonable in such circumstances for the employer to restrict recruitment to people who are physically able to comply, for example by including a test of strength in selection procedures. The fact that more men than women will be able to do so does not make the practice unlawful, provided the lifting requirement is wholly genuine.

In the USA the 'four-fifths rule' applies in judging cases of indirect discrimination, meaning that a practice is unlawful where the proportion of one sex that can comply with the condition is fewer than 80 per cent of the other. At present there is no such convention in the UK, meaning that it is for individual tribunals to decide what exactly constitutes 'a substantially smaller proportion' of men or women when judging these cases.

WINDOW ON PRACTICE

A leading case in indirect sex discrimination law is *Price* v. *Civil Service Commission* (1977). This concerned a requirement set by the Civil Service that applicants for posts of executive officer level should be between the ages of 17 and 28. Mrs Price, who was 36, claimed that an advertisement for an executive officer was indirectly discriminatory against women on the grounds that a substantially greater proportion of men could in practice comply with the age requirement. Her case was based on the contention that many women were outside the labour market during these ages bringing up children. The Employment Appeals Tribunal agreed with her and declared the age limitation to be unreasonable.

In the field of sex discrimination the term '**victimisation**' means the same as it does in other areas of employment law. An employer victimises workers if it disadvantages them in any way simply because they have sought to exercise their legal rights or have assisted others in doing so. An employee would thus bring a claim of victimisation to a tribunal if they had been overlooked for promotion having recently successfully settled an equal pay claim. Importantly victimisation covers situations in which someone threatens to bring an action or plans to do so even if no case is ultimately brought.

Positive discrimination

Positive sex discrimination involves directly or indirectly discriminating in favour of women in situations where they are underrepresented – usually at senior levels in an organisation or in occupational groups which are male dominated. Such practices are unlawful under UK law when they involve actively discriminating against men who are better qualified to fill the positions concerned. However, it is lawful to take positive action aimed at encouraging and supporting women provided it stops short of actually discriminating in their favour. It is thus acceptable to include an equal opportunities statement in a job advertisement as a means of indicating that the organisation welcomes applications from women. Similarly employers can design and offer training courses tailored specifically for women. As long as men are not prevented from participating, such action is lawful.

Dress codes

In relation to dress codes, a tribunal will only find valid a claim of sex discrimination if the applicant or applicants can be shown to have suffered a detriment as a result of the condition being imposed. Merely treating members of the two sexes differently is not in itself sufficient to constitute unlawful indirect discrimination. For this reason it is acceptable in principle for employers to impose different dress codes on male and female staff, provided the same broad 'standard of conventionality' is applied.

It is thus lawful, as far as sex discrimination law is concerned, to insist that male employees wear business suits at work while permitting women more choice about their attire. Over the years, however, tribunals have adapted their interpretation of the term 'standards of conventionality' to reflect changing social norms. As a result sex discrimination claims have been successfully won by men who wish to retain their long hair tied in a pony-tail and women who wish to wear trousers at work.

Transsexuals

Whereas homosexuals have had great difficulty over the years in persuading the courts that they have rights under sex discrimination law, transsexuals have been protected for some years. It is therefore unlawful to discriminate against someone on the grounds that he or she is a medically defined transsexual. The rights of people undergoing gender reassignment are now specifically protected by the Sex Discrimination (Gender Reassignment) Regulations 1999.

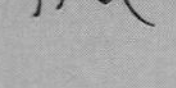

ACTIVITY 23.2

In making its judgment in *Rewcastle* v. *Safeway* (1989), a case that concerned the dismissal of a man who refused to cut his hair to a conventional male length, the tribunal made the following remark about the law on dress codes:

> Whilst we naturally accept the employer's right to determine standards of appearance and dress for its employees . . . we question whether a policy which is designed to mirror 'conventional' differences between the sexes can be reconciled with the underlying rationale of the sex discrimination legislation which is to challenge traditional assumptions about sexes.

To what extent do you agree with these sentiments?

Source: IRS (1993, p. 11).

Sexual harassment

While the area of sexual harassment is not specifically covered in the Sex Discrimination Act 1975, the courts have accepted for some years that allowing someone to be subjected to acts of harassment which have a sexual dimension amounts to unlawful sex discrimination. Although the law applies equally to men and women, the vast majority of cases are brought by women. The employer's liability in harassment cases arises from the application of the doctrine of **vicarious liability**, under which employers are held responsible for the commitment of civil wrongs by employees when they are at work. The doctrine also plays an important role in health and safety law, as we saw in Chapter 22.

Sexual harassment is defined in a European Union code of practice dating from 1991. It establishes the following:

(a) that it consists of unwanted conduct of a sexual nature or based on sex, which affects the dignity of men and women at work;

(b) that sexual harassment can be physical or verbal in nature;

(c) that the conduct *either* leads to material detriment (i.e. it affects promotion, pay, access to training, etc.) *or* creates an intimidating or humiliating work environment.

In judging cases the courts focus on the reaction of the victim and do not apply any general definitions of what types of conduct do and do not amount to unlawful harassment. Hence conduct which may not offend one person in the slightest can be found to constitute sexual harassment when directed at someone else who is deeply offended.

For an employer the only valid defences relate to the notion of vicarious liability. An employer can, for example, claim ignorance of the incident of which the victim is complaining or can claim that vicarious liability does not apply because it occurred away from the workplace and outside office hours. Finally the employer can defend itself by showing that all reasonable steps were taken to prevent the harassment from occurring or continuing. In order to succeed here, the employer needs to produce evidence to show that initial complaints were promptly acted upon and that appropriate action, such as disciplining the perpetrators or moving them to other work, was taken.

RACE DISCRIMINATION

UK race discrimination law is governed by the Race Relations Act 1976 and subsequent amendments. This area of law became one of European competence in 2003, but the principles established in the 1976 Act have not changed, and they remain very similar to those set out in the Sex Discrimination Act described above. The law applies to all workers except those recruited to work overseas or in private households. The 'direct' and 'indirect' forms of discrimination are defined in the same way as in sex discrimination law, as are the terms 'victimisation', 'positive discrimination' and 'harassment'. Moreover, the Commission for Racial Equality plays a similar facilitating role to that played by the Equal Opportunities Commission in the field of sex discrimination. Precedents from the sex discrimination arena can apply in that of race discrimination and vice versa. There is, however, no equivalent law to that contained in the Equal Pay Act operating in the field of race discrimination.

Importantly the Act extends beyond discrimination on grounds of race to embrace the notions of nationality and ethnic and national origin. It is thus as unlawful for an employer to discriminate against someone because they are French or American as it is to treat someone less favourably because of their racial origins. The term 'ethnicity' was defined by Lord Fraser in the case of *Mandla* v. *Lee* (1983) as applying to a distinct group within the population sharing the following essential characteristics:

- a long history of which the group is conscious as distinguishing it from other groups, and the memory of which keeps it alive;
- a cultural tradition of its own, often but not necessarily associated with religious observance;
- a common geographical origin, or descent from a small number of common ancestors;
- a common language, not necessarily peculiar to the group;
- a common literature peculiar to the group;
- a common religion different from that of neighbouring groups or from the general community surrounding it;
- being a minority or being an oppressed or a dominant group within a larger community.

According to this definition, merely practising a minority religion is an insufficient basis to constitute being of distinct ethnic origin. There also has to be a shared and long history of distinctiveness. As a result, until the introduction of law preventing discrimination based on religion in 2003, unless a religious group was ethnically distinct, its members could lawfully be treated less well because of their faith.

Genuine occupational qualifications (now known as genuine occupational requirements), as in sex discrimination law, permit discrimination on grounds of race at the recruitment stage for one or two kinds of job. The main grounds are authenticity and the provision of personal services to members of a particular racial community. In the case of race discrimination the defence of authenticity extends to employers of people to work in ethnic restaurants.

Most cases involving indirect discrimination under the Race Relations Act concern requirements being set for a high standard of English or for specific UK-based qualifications. As in sex discrimination law, it is necessary to be able to show objectively that these are necessary for the jobs in question. The courts will not allow employers to set conditions such as these unless it can be shown that there really is a *need* for such a condition. For example, in the case of *Hampson* v. *Department of Education and Science* (1990) a teacher was able to show that the requirement to have completed a three-year training course before being appointed to a teaching post in the UK unfairly discriminated against people of Chinese origin who had qualified in Hong Kong. She was successful because she was able to convince the Court of Appeal that her two-year qualification followed by eight years' classroom experience made her well qualified to teach in Britain.

A fine line has to be trodden when recruiting people from overseas countries because there is a need to stay on the right side of both the Race Relations Act 1976 and the more recent Asylum and Immigration Act 1996. The former makes it unlawful to treat an overseas application unfavourably in any way, while the latter makes it a criminal offence to employ someone who does not have the right of residence in the UK or a valid work permit. Great care is thus called for in handling such matters.

WINDOW ON PRACTICE

A race discrimination case with important implications was brought by two women in 1996.

This case concerned the appearance at a private function of Mr Bernard Manning in the guise of a comedian. The audience consisted of 400 men who were treated to a routine consisting in large part of racially and sexually offensive jokes. Two of the waitresses employed by the hotel at the function were black. Bernard Manning noticed them and made a number of remarks directed at them during his routine.

The two women sued the hotel group which employed them on the grounds that it was vicariously liable and that they had been allowed to suffer racial harassment. The employer contested this, saying that it could not be liable for offensive remarks made by someone who was not an employee – indeed was not even a guest in the hotel and thus had no contractual relationship with it at all.

The women won their claim, successfully arguing that the hotel's management had failed to take action to prevent the harassment from occurring by removing them from the function at the earliest possible time.

Source: *Burton* v. *De Vere Hotels Ltd* (1996).

DISABILITY DISCRIMINATION

The Disability Discrimination Act (1995) came into force in December 1996, since when several thousand cases have been lodged with employment tribunals. It replaced the Disabled Persons (Employment) Act 1944, which was widely criticised for being ineffective, only eight successful prosecutions having been brought during its fifty-year existence. From April 2000 the Disability Rights Commission has been in operation, with a remit in respect of discrimination against disabled people which is very similar to that of the Equal Opportunities Commission and the Commission for Racial Equality in their respective fields. Disability discrimination will come within the field of European competence in 2006. This has major consequences for countries which do not have established law in this area, but for the UK only relatively minor adjustments are necessary. The Disability Discrimination Act was thus amended in October 2004 so as to bring it into line with expected EU requirements.

While it shares some features in common with established legislation on sex and race discrimination, disability discrimination law is different in important respects The most significant is the restriction of protection to direct discrimination and victimisation. There are no provisions equivalent to those on indirect discrimination in the Sex Discrimination and Race Relations Acts. The key words are as follows:

> An employer discriminates against a disabled person if for a reason which relates to the disabled person's disability, he treats him less favourably than he treats or would treat others to whom that reason does not or would not apply. (Disability Discrimination Act 1995, s. 5(1))

The Act is thus concerned with preventing an employer from discriminating directly against an individual worker or job applicant who suffers from a disability. There is no specific prohibition on the setting of requirements for use in recruitment or promotion processes which might be held to discriminate against disabled people in general. It is thus lawful to list 'good record of health' as a desirable characteristic in a person specification – that alone cannot constitute discrimination under the terms of the Act. Employers only invite tribunal claims at the point that they actually discriminate against an individual.

However, this does not mean that employers can safely use language in job advertisements which could deter disabled people, because the advertisement can later be used by a rejected applicant as evidence in support of a disability discrimination claim. Newspapers and employment agencies which knowingly publish advertisements which are discriminatory may also face fines of up to £5,000 if successfully prosecuted.

The other important difference between direct discrimination on grounds of disability and that on grounds of sex or race is the existence of defences which an employer can employ. Essentially, 'less favourable treatment' is permitted if it is for a good reason. An example of this might be a typist who is required to type at a certain speed due to valid job demands. If a person with arthritis in their hands, who could only type at a much lower speed, applied for this job, they could lawfully be rejected on the grounds of their disability provided the potential employer had first explored whether any adjustment in the working environment could be made to overcome the mismatch. Discrimination is thus permitted if no 'reasonable adjustment' can be made to allow the person concerned to perform the job satisfactorily. Employers are nonetheless under a duty to consider reasonable adjustments in any situation in which 'a provision, criterion or practice puts the disabled individual at a substantial disadvantage'.

Since 2004 a distinction has been made between treating somebody less favourably 'because they are disabled' and treating somebody less favourably 'for a reason related to their disability'. There is now no defence that can be deployed in the former case, the established defence relating to reasonable adjustment remaining in the latter.

There are two key issues which the courts are required to rule on when determining cases brought under the Disability Discrimination Act:

1 What does and what does not constitute a disability for the purposes of the Act.
2 What is and what is not 'a reasonable adjustment' for an employer to make in order to accommodate the needs of a disabled person.

The first issue is decided with reference to the words used in the Act. These define someone as disabled if they have 'a physical or mental impairment which has a substantial and long term adverse affect on their ability to carry out normal day to day activities'. The term 'impairment' is taken by the courts to mean any kind of a loss of a key bodily function such as the ability to hear, see, walk or write. It also covers conditions involving loss of memory and incontinence. An impairment is 'substantial' if it is more than minor or trivial, while 'long term' is defined as a condition which has lasted or *might reasonably* be expected to last for 12 months or more.

The words 'normal day to day activities' have been the source of much confusion and litigation. This is because the courts have taken the phrase very much at face value. It is thus the case that someone is not disabled – and is thus not protected by the Act – if their condition stops them from climbing mountains or playing football, as these are not considered to be 'normal day to day activities'. It has to be an impairment which severely restricts someone's ability to carry out basic, commonplace tasks in the household or workplace.

However, provided the symptoms are serious in their impact, virtually all medical conditions can potentially be accepted as 'disabilities' for the purposes of the Disability Discrimination Act. This includes mental illnesses as well as those with physical symptoms. Hence the definition of disability in the Act has been found by the courts to encompass severe depression, bulimia and ME, as well as asthma, speech impairments and severe back pain. Severe facial disfigurement is also included as a relevant condition. The only exceptions are a few conditions with socially undesirable symptoms which have specifically been excluded. These include alcoholism, drug addiction, exhibitionism, kleptomania and pyromania. Hay fever is also excluded. Importantly it is irrelevant whether or not an individual has recovered from their disability. Discriminating against someone on the grounds that they have suffered from a condition in the past amounts to unlawful discrimination, provided the discrimination met the definition set out in the Act. The fact that someone can live and work normally because they are receiving treatment for their condition, for example in the form of drugs or psychiatric counselling, does not mean that they have ceased to be disabled under the terms of the Act. It is thus unlawful to discriminate against them on these grounds without an objectively justifiable reason.

WINDOW ON PRACTICE

In 1997 a Mr Quinlan was dismissed from his job as an assistant working at a garden centre after seven days because he refused to carry out the heavy lifting work that formed a part of the job. He would not do this because he had had open heart surgery some ten years previously and had been told that lifting heavy weights might injure his health. He brought a claim to a tribunal under the Disability Discrimination Act arguing that it would have been reasonable for the employer to omit from his work the requirement to lift heavy weights, and that his dismissal was thus unlawful.

He lost his case on the grounds that he was not disabled under the terms of the Act. This was because lifting heavy weights was not found to constitute 'a normal day to day activity'. He could only have succeeded had his illness not allowed him to lift everyday objects. There was no consideration given to questions of reasonable adjustment, because the Disability Discrimination Act was found not to apply to Mr Quinlan in the first place.

(*Quinlan* v. *B&Q plc* (1997) Employment Appeals Tribunal 1386/97).

Source: L. Macdonald (1998) 'Discrimination', *Personnel Manager's Factfinder*. London: Gee Publishing.

The burden of proof in disability discrimination cases passes to the employer to satisfy the tribunal that no reasonable adjustments could be made to accommodate the needs of a disabled person. The courts thus assume that adjustments are possible unless the employer can show that it would be unreasonable to expect them to be made. There are no general rules here, because the courts are obliged in reaching their judgments to take account of the size and resources of the employer concerned. The large PLC is thus expected to make bigger adjustments in response to the demands of the Act than the owner of a small corner shop.

It is expected that employers consider making adjustments to the physical working environment, working arrangements and working conditions. Minor building alterations are clearly covered; so unless the employer is very small and is unable to afford to make them, it would be expected that disabled toilets and/or wheelchair ramps would be installed to accommodate a disabled person. Other examples would include changing taps to make them easier to switch on, altering lighting for people with restricted vision and allocating specific parking spaces. However, the concept of 'reasonable adjustment' goes a great deal further, encompassing changes in all kinds of working practices. It is thus expected that employers reorganise duties, allocate ground-floor offices to wheelchair users, adjust working hours for a disabled person or allow someone to work from home if these changes would allow an individual disabled person to be employed. Of particular importance is the requirement to permit disabled people a greater amount of sick leave than other employees. Hence, as was shown in Chapter 9, it is no longer possible to dismiss a chronically ill employee on grounds of incapability, without first considering whether reasonable adjustments could be made to allow them to continue working. The courts expect to see evidence that the employer has given serious consideration to a request for adjustments and that no request is turned down without a proper investigation having first taken place.

When applicants win their cases at tribunal, there are three possible outcomes:

1 The tribunal issues a declaration affirming the complainant's rights (e.g. preventing an employer from making someone redundant).
2 The tribunal makes a recommendation (e.g. requiring a doorway to be widened to accommodate a wheelchair).
3 The tribunal makes a compensatory award.

In the case of the third outcome, there are no statutory limits on the compensation that can be paid, allowing the courts to fully recompense people for any past or estimated future losses they may have incurred.

DISCRIMINATION ON GROUNDS OF SEXUAL ORIENTATION

The Equality (Sexual Orientation) Regulations 2003 gave effect to EU law which seeks to protect people from discrimination on grounds of their sexual orientation. For many years test cases had been brought in a bid to establish rights of this kind using sex discrimination law. Occasionally applicants were successful, but almost all these rulings were subsequently overturned by the higher courts. The principle that such discrimination is unlawful has now been established in statute, but aspects of the 2003 regulations are controversial, and there are significant outstanding issues that will have to be addressed by the courts as cases come through the system. Research suggests that discrimination against people on grounds of their sexual orientation is common in the UK, so there are good reasons for anticipating substantial numbers of claims being brought to employment tribunals in the coming years.

All workers and job applicants are covered by the regulations. Former employees are also explicitly covered and could bring a claim, for example, were a discriminatory job reference to be written. Four types of claim can be brought, reflecting the standard approach to discrimination law which is now being developed in the statutes. The meanings of these terms are the same as for sex discrimination law (*see* above):

1 direct discrimination;
2 indirect discrimination;
3 harassment;
4 victimisation.

Harassment claims are likely to be common under the 2003 regulations, as evidence suggests that this is the major source of discrimination against gay and lesbian people. It is thus important for employers to put relevant policies in place and to take a very firm line with staff who perpetrate harassment of this kind if they wish to avoid a day in court defending their actions.

One of the most interesting issues the government had to wrestle with when drawing up the regulations was how to define the term 'sexual orientation'. After consulting extensively it was decided to define the term narrowly and specifically as meaning 'a sexual orientation towards persons of the same sex, persons of the opposite sex, or persons of the same sex and the opposite sex'. Importantly, the regulations make it unlawful to discriminate against someone 'on grounds of sexual orientation' and not simply because of their sexual orientation. This means that treating someone unfavourably because a relative is gay or because they have gay friends is as unlawful as discriminating against someone because they are themselves gay or perceived to be so. Discriminating against people because they are not gay is also equally unacceptable under the regulations. It remains to be seen how the courts will deal with situations in which someone claims to be in a gay relationship in order to gain access for a partner to a benefit of some kind (e.g. a staff discount scheme) but where the employer claims that they are not in fact in a gay relationship.

As is the case with existing law on sex and race discrimination, it is permissible to discriminate against people on grounds of sexual orientation where there is a 'genuine occupational requirement'. It is thus lawful in principle to refuse to employ someone, or to promote them, if the job concerned is only suitable for someone of a particular sexual orientation. However, the guidance notes issued by the government and ACAS suggest only two types of genuine occupational requirement that might apply:

1 Counselling/support services related to sexual matters.
2 Some roles in religious organisations.

A major source of complaint, and of litigation, over the years has been differential treatment given to heterosexual and homosexual people in the field of employee benefits. Pension scheme rules are the biggest issue, particularly widows' pensions and survivors' payments under life assurance terms, but some staff discount schemes have similarly been restricted to spouses and heterosexual partners. While the 2003 regulations make it unlawful for an employer to favour heterosexual partners over homosexual partners in the operation of any type of scheme, it remains possible to restrict benefits to married people. This aspect of the law has been the subject of much criticism and is likely to be the subject of legal challenges at an early opportunity.

DISCRIMINATION ON GROUNDS OF RELIGION OR BELIEF

The Employment Equality (Religion and Belief) Regulations also came into force in December 2003 and derive directly from the European Union's Equal Treatment Framework Directive. Their structure and content is the same as for sexual orientation, although the practical issues that they throw up are different. They had the effect of righting some anomalies in existing UK law, under which discrimination *purely* on grounds of religious belief was lawful except in Northern Ireland. Religious groups who do not share a common ethnicity are thus now protected from unfair discrimination.

The government stated from the outset that its intention was to define the term 'religion or belief' narrowly. However, the definition that appears in the draft regulations allows plenty of room for interpretation. The wording used is 'any religion, religious belief or similar philosophical belief'. Specifically excluded are 'philosophical or political beliefs unless those beliefs are similar to a religious belief'. The aim is to try to avoid a situation arising in which, for example, a member of a neo-nazi group could make use of the law to protect themselves from discrimination on grounds of their politics but, in the process, the regulations also ensure that people with pacifist or vegetarian convictions, or indeed those committed to any political creed, fall outside their protection. The explanatory notes issued alongside the new regulations state that courts should take a number of factors into account when deciding whether or not a 'belief' falls within the purview of these regulations. In particular, there should be evidence of collective worship, 'a clear belief system' and a 'profound belief affecting way of life or view of the world'. It will not be long before cases of discrimination on grounds of political belief start coming through European court systems and the European Court of Justice may well interpret the term 'religion and belief' more broadly than the UK government has chosen to.

As elsewhere in discrimination law the regulations on religion or belief permit direct discrimination to occur only where a post carries with it a genuine occupational requirement (GOR). This is likely to be one of the major areas in which the case law evolves as there are a number of obvious and common situations in which GORs will be an issue. The regulations permit GORs *both* where 'being of a particular religion is a genuine and determining occupational requirement for the job' *and* where 'the employer has an ethos based on religion or belief'. It is pretty clear therefore that a GOR would apply in the case of clerical roles, such as a hospital chaplain or a Christian outreach worker, but what about posts in denominational schools? More interesting is the case of organisations which do not have a religious purpose, but which claim to run themselves in accordance with a particular religious ethos. There are, for example, Christian medical practices, Islamic businesses and Jewish law firms which currently only employ members of a particular religious group, at least in senior roles.

For most employers, however, the most important practical consequence of the 2003 regulations has been a need to review policy on time off for religious holidays. Refusing to allow someone to take a day off to observe a Sabbath or religious festival constitutes indirect discrimination because the organisation has a rule in place which indirectly discriminates against members of certain religious groups. This means that it is only permissible to refuse time off if the rule can be objectively justified. In other words, there must be a credible business reason advanced for refusing requests. In its guidance ACAS states that where it would be possible to accommodate the request, and where sufficient notice has been given, it will normally be expected that employers should grant it. Examples of where it would be reasonable to refuse would be where a large proportion of the workforce wanted to take the same day off, making it impossible to continue operating or where the dates coincide with a very busy period.

TRADE UNION DISCRIMINATION

The freedom to join a trade union and take part in its lawful activities is generally regarded as a fundamental human right. It is included in both the European Convention on Human Rights and the founding conventions of the International Labour Organisation. Although this freedom is not couched in the language of positive rights, it is in practice difficult for a UK employer lawfully to discriminate against people simply because they have joined a union or have taken part in union activities. These rights are long established, but are now found in the Trade Union and Labour Relations (Consolidation) Act 1992. In 1990, equivalent rights were extended to people who do not wish to join a union or become involved in its activities. There are three basic rights:

1 the right not to be dismissed for a trade union reason;

2 the right not to suffer action short of dismissal for a trade union reason;

3 the right not to be refused a job on trade union grounds.

The first two of these protect people who take part (or refuse to take part) 'in the activities of an independent trade union at an appropriate time'. The protection, however, only extends to employees (i.e. people working under a contract of service) and does not apply in the police and armed services. In the case of dismissals, because trade union reasons are regarded as 'automatically unfair', there is no qualifying period of service. Full rights thus apply from the first day someone is employed at a particular establishment.

In order to gain the protection of the law in this area the organisation an individual joins or with which he or she becomes involved must be one which has been listed as an independent trade union by the Certification Officer. Moreover, the activities in which the individual engages must be authorised by the trade union concerned and must, if they take place during work time, be carried out with the consent of the employer. Industrial action is not included in the definition of 'the activities of an independent trade union at an appropriate time', but is the subject of other protective legislation.

Discrimination against prospective employees at the recruitment stage simply because they are or are not union members has been an unlawful practice since 1990. In the Employment Relations Act 1999 rights in this area were extended to cover any discrimination occurring as a result of an individual's past involvement in trade union activity. The aim was to prevent groups of employers from maintaining blacklists of individuals perceived to be union troublemakers.

PART-TIME WORKERS

Discriminating against a female part-time worker has long been taken by the courts to constitute indirect sex discrimination because the vast majority of part-time workers are female. Since 2000, however, it has not been necessary for part-time workers (of either gender) to use sex discrimination law to protect themselves. The Part-time Workers (Prevention of Less Favourable Treatment) Regulations 2000 were introduced to ensure that the UK complied with the EU's Part-Time Workers Directive. They now seek to ensure that part-time workers (not just employees) are treated equally with full-time workers in all aspects of work, the key features being as follows:

1 Part-time workers who believe that they are being treated less favourably than a comparable full-time colleague can write to their employer asking for an explanation. This must be given in writing within 14 days.

2 Where the explanation given by the employer is considered unsatisfactory, the part-time worker may ask an employment tribunal to require the employer to affirm the right to equal treatment.

3 Employers are required under the regulations to review their terms and conditions and to give part-timers pro rata rights with those of comparable full-timers.

4 There is a right not to be victimised on account of enforcing rights under the Part-time Workers Regulations.

Any term or condition of employment is covered by the regulations, as is any detriment caused as a result of failure to be promoted or given access to training. It is also now unlawful to select someone for redundancy simply because they work part-time.

There are a number of problems with the new regulations, including the absence of a statutory authority to enforce the third of the above points. One of the more complex issues involves how the term 'part-time worker' should be defined, because it is used differently in different workplaces. In some organisations someone working 35 hours a week is employed on a 'part-time contract' because full-time hours are 40 per week. Elsewhere, where everyone works 35 hours, such a worker would be regarded as a full-timer. The regulations simply state that a worker is part-time if they work fewer hours in a week than are worked by recognised full-timers. This obviously poses difficulties for organisations which do not employ people to work a set number of hours a week, or for whom patterns of hours vary considerably over the course of a year. There is also a need for part-time workers who consider themselves to have been less favourably treated to name a comparator employed in a broadly similar job who is employed on a full-time basis in the same employment. Where none exists it is effectively impossible to bring a claim.

FIXED-TERM WORKERS

The EU's Fixed-term Work Directive (brought into UK law via the Employment Act 2002) includes a range of important provisions designed to improve the position of the many employees who are employed on temporary contracts. The general requirement is that a fixed-term employee should not be treated less favourably than a comparable permanent employee unless less favourable treatment can be objectively justified. This has meant an end to the common practice of avoiding making redundancy payments when fixed-term contracts finish by including a waiver clause in the contract of employment. The statute extends to fixed-term employees the right to receive statutory sick pay (SSP) in the same way as permanent staff and also requires employers to inform fixed-term employees about permanent vacancies in the organisation.

However, the most significant change is the restriction on the employment of people on successive fixed-term contracts. In the past employers commonly used this device to give themselves numerical flexibility and, many would argue, to extract greater effort out of people who were in constant fear of the consequences of non-renewal. Employment of people on successive fixed-term contracts is now limited to four years unless further extentions can be objectively justified. It thus remains acceptable to extend a fixed-term contract beyond four years if the money to fund the post is limited or if a specific project is clearly coming to an end within a short period of time. However, in other situations, after four years the law treats all fixed-term contracts as if they were permanent.

The law gives fixed-term employees the right to ask for a written statement of reasons from their employer if they are being treated unfavourably as well as a statement that their contract has become permanent after four years. Where employers fail to honour these rights or to give satisfactory explanations, complaints can be taken to an employment tribunal.

EX-OFFENDERS

Another group who are given some measure of legal protection from discrimination at work are ex-offenders whose convictions have been 'spent'. The relevant legislation is contained in the Rehabilitation of Offenders Act 1974 which sets out after how many years different types of criminal conviction become spent and need not be acknowledged by the perpetrator. In the field of employment, protection from discrimination extends to dismissal, exclusion from a position and 'prejudicing' someone in any way in their employment. In other words, employers cannot dismiss someone, fail to recruit them or hold them back in their occupations simply because they are known or discovered to have a former conviction. Failing to disclose the conviction can also be no grounds for discrimination. Moreover, no one (the individual concerned or anyone else) is under any obligation to tell anyone else about the conviction once it has been spent. Effectively, the slate is wiped clean, allowing the ex-offender to live and work as if no conviction had been received.

The rehabilitation periods set out in the Act vary depending on the type of sentence that has been received. The tariff is as follows:

imprisonment over 30 months:	never spent
imprisonment 6 to 30 months:	ten years
less than 6 months' imprisonment:	seven years
fine or community service order:	five years
detention in a detention centre:	three years
conditional discharge:	one year
absolute discharge:	six months

The time runs from the date of the conviction, the times being cut in half for those who are under the age of 18 at this time. It is the sentence imposed that is relevant to the Act and not the sentence actually served.

Numerous jobs and occupations are excluded from the terms of the Act. Organisations which employ people to work in these positions are entitled to know about spent convictions and can lawfully discriminate against individuals on these grounds. The list includes all jobs which involve the provision of services to minors, employment in the social services, nursing homes and courts, as well as employment in the legal, medical and accountancy professions.

At the time of writing the government is proposing to make a series of relatively minor amendments to the law on the rehabilitation of offenders, but no date has been given for their introduction.

AGE DISCRIMINATION LAW

The final element of the EU's Equal Treatment Framework Directive that will be implemented in the UK is the outlawing of age discrimination from October 2006. This is a wholly new field of law which will require major changes to many existing statutes both within and outside the employment field. At the time of writing (early 2004) no detailed proposals have been published, but is clear from the government's consultation paper that a complex piece of legislation will be introduced requiring major changes to be made to common employment practices.

In terms of its basic structure and scope, age discrimination law will follow the same approach as has been established for the other types of discrimination law that fall within the area of European competence (i.e. sex, race, disability, sexual orientation and religion or belief). It will also extend beyond the world of employment to the activities of trade unions, professional bodies and institutions of further and higher education. However, it appears that in cases of direct age discrimination (i.e. treating an individual less favourably because of their age or for a reason related to their age), defences will be available. So it will remain possible for employers to discriminate on age grounds under certain types of circumstances. The consultation document labels these 'exceptional circumstances', but goes on to list situations which appear commonplace:

- health, safety and welfare reasons;
- facilitation of employment planning;
- encouraging or rewarding loyalty;
- the need for a reasonable period for employment prior to retirement.

The biggest issue of all in the field of age discrimination is mandatory retirement, and the government has yet to announce how it intends to legislate on this. It is currently acceptable for an employer to require all employees to retire, whether they want to or not, at a pre-determined age. This is 65 unless the employer has another 'normal' contractual retirement age. The government wants greater flexibility in this area, but also appears anxious to avoid a situation in which elderly people exercise a legal right to continue in jobs which they are no longer capable of carrying out. The likely outcome is a later compulsory retirement age, with lower ages being permitted for certain professions, but until the regulations are finalised employers are not able to plan ahead with confidence.

SUMMARY PROPOSITIONS

23.1 Discrimination law has grown rapidly in recent years, extending to new grounds such as age, sexual orientation and religion or belief.

23.2 Equal pay law requires men and women to be paid the same wage for doing work which is the same or which can be shown to be of equal value unless the employer can justify a difference on grounds other than sex.

23.3 In much discrimination legislation an important distinction is made between direct and indirect discrimination. The former relates to a situation in which someone is discriminated against because of a personal characteristic, the latter relates to the setting of a requirement by an employer with which fewer of one group can comply than another.

23.4 Harassment claims can be brought against any employer who allows a worker to be subjected to treatment which intimidates or humiliates the victim for reasons related to their sex, sexual orientation, race or disability.

23.5 The Disability Discrimination Act 1995 requires employers to consider making reasonable adjustments to working conditions to accommodate the needs of a disabled person before dismissing them or failing to offer them a job.

23.6 Limited protection from discrimination is given in law to trade union members, employees who do not engage in union activity, part-time workers, fixed term-workers and ex-offenders whose convictions are spent.

GENERAL DISCUSSION TOPICS

1 Which groups who are not currently protected would you like to see covered by anti-discrimination law? What arguments could be advanced for and against your proposition from an employer perspective?

2 How far do you think that UK discrimination law is effective in achieving its aims? What could be done to make it more effective?

FURTHER READING

Bowers, J. and Moran, E. (2002) 'Justification in sex discrimination law: breaking the taboo', *Industrial Law Journal*, Vol. 31, No. 4, pp. 307–20
Gill, T. and Monaghan, K. (2003) 'Justification in sex discrimination law: taboo upheld', *Industrial Law Journal*, Vol. 32, No. 2, pp. 115–22
An interesting debate was carried out in 2002 and 2003 in the pages of the *Industrial Law Journal* about whether or not there is a good case for allowing employers grounds for justifying direct sex discrimination in certain defined circumstances. This view was advanced by Bowers and Moran in 2002 and robustly rebutted a few months later by Gill and Monaghan.

Department of Trade and Industry (DTI)
IRS Employment Review (Industrial Relations Services)
The best way of keeping up to date with this fast evolving area of law is to visit the DTI website (**dti.gov.uk**). There is extensive coverage there of new discrimination law on the equality and employment pages. It is also possible to download research commissioned by the DTI looking at the background to new laws and their impact. Any significant new case law is reported fortnightly in *IRS Employment Review*.

Fredman, S. (2002) *Discrimination Law*. Oxford: OUP
This provides an excellent and thoughtful summary of the principles behind the law, the purposes it serves and the major critiques that are advanced. It also draws extensively on the experience of other countries.

REFERENCES

IRS (1993) 'Dress and Personal Appearance at Work', *IRS Law Bulletin*, No. 469, pp. 2–13.
Macdonald, L. (1998) 'Discrimination', *Personnel Manager's Factfinder*. London: Gee Publishing.

LEGAL CASES

Burton v. *De Vere Hotels Ltd* [1996] IRLR 596.
Diocese of Hallam Trustees v. *Connaughton* (1995) (EAT 1128/95).
Hampson v. *Department of Education and Science* [1990] IRLR 302.
Macarthy's Ltd v. *Smith* [1980] IRLR 209–10.
Mandla et al. v. *Lee et al.* [1983] IRLR 209.
Price v. *Civil Service Commission* [1977] IRLR 291.
Quinlan v. *B&Q plc* (1997) (EAT 1386/97).
Rewcastle v. *Safeway plc* (1989) (EAT 22482/89).

An extensive range of additional materials, including multiple choice questions, answers to questions and links to useful websites can be found on the Human Resource Management Companion Website at **www.pearsoned.co.uk/torrington.**

CHAPTER 24

EQUAL OPPORTUNITIES AND DIVERSITY

THE OBJECTIVES OF THIS CHAPTER ARE TO:

1. REVIEW THE CURRENT EMPLOYMENT EXPERIENCES OF THE MEMBERS OF SOME SOCIALLY DEFINED MINORITY GROUPS
2. ANALYSE THE DIFFERING APPROACHES TO ACHIEVING EQUALITY FOR THOSE GROUPS, IN PARTICULAR CONTRASTING THE MORE TRADITIONAL EQUAL OPPORTUNITIES APPROACH WITH THE MANAGEMENT OF DIVERSITY APPROACH
3. EXPLORE THE IMPLICATIONS WHICH MANAGING DIVERSITY HAS FOR ORGANISATIONS

Legislation, voluntary codes of practice and equality initiatives have resulted in some progress towards equality of treatment for minority groups, but there remains inescapable evidence of continuing discrimination. More recent approaches under the banner of management of diversity include the economic and business case for equality, the valuing and managing of diversity in organisations, culture change and the mainstreaming of equality initiatives. These approaches are partly a response to the insufficient progress made so far, yet there is only limited evidence that they have made a difference. They offer some useful perspectives and practices, although the underlying concepts also raise some issues and concerns.

CURRENT EMPLOYMENT EXPERIENCES OF SOCIALLY DEFINED MINORITY GROUPS

For the purposes of this section we will consider the experiences of five socially defined minority groups: women, racial/ethnic minorities, disabled people, older people and individuals who are lesbian, gay, bisexual or transsexual. In choosing these groups we have followed, broadly, Kirton and Greene (2003), although others, such as British Telecom, have identified as many as 12 aspects of difference between employees (Liff 1999). As identified in the previous chapter there are a larger number of other minority groups for whom legal protection against discrimination is available, and we have therefore been selective in the groups we have chosen to discuss in this chapter. At the time of writing there is no legal protection against age discrimination as this will not be in place until 2006.

It should also be noted that CIPD (2003) provides a much broader definition of diversity, going beyond social category diversity, as above, to include informational diversity (differences in terms of education, tenure and functional background) and value diversity (which includes differences in personality and attitudes).

Women

If **participation** in the labour force is an indication of decreasing discrimination then recent figures are encouraging. From 1971 to 2001 the female participation rate in employment increased from 56.8 per cent to 72 per cent, compared with the male participation rate which is slowly falling, and now at 84 per cent (Equal Opportunities Review (EOR) 2002). These trends are predicted to continue. Much of this increase has been due to the replacement of full-time jobs with part-time jobs. Indeed Hakim (1993) puts forward the strong argument, based on an alternative analysis of the census and employment data, that the increasing participation of women in employment between the 1950s and the late 1980s is a myth, although a real increase does appear to have taken place since the late 1980s. Her analysis shows that 'the much trumpeted rise in women's employment in Britain consisted entirely of the substitution of part-time for full-time jobs from 1951 to the late 1980s' (p. 102). Hakim concludes from the research that only an increase in full-time employment is likely to have a wider impact on women's opportunities at work and elsewhere.

Some of the more obvious signs of discrimination, such as in recruitment advertising, may have disappeared, and there is some evidence to suggest that women are beginning to enter some previously male-dominated occupations. For example, women have now been ordained as priests in the Church of England but not without deep and continuing debate. Similarly men are beginning to enter some previously female-only occupations, such as midwifery. However, there remains a high degree of subtle, for example in access to training and support for development and promotion, and not-so-subtle discrimination, as in the continued **gender segregation** in terms of both type and level of work undertaken. There are still few women in higher levels of management and not many male secretaries. People Management (2002) reports research undertaken by Cranfield which finds a 50 per cent increase over the previous year in women is executive directors in the FTSE 100 companies. However, even after the increase the percentage of executive directors who are women is still only 15 per cent. In the same year Higginbottom and Roberts (2002) report that the EOC found only 28 per cent of elected councillors, 12 per cent of elected council leaders, and 10 per cent of local authority chiefs were women. The majority of managers and administrators are men and most women remain in three occupational groups: clerical and secretarial, personal and protective services such as catering, caring, cleaning and selling occupations (Thair and Risden 1999). These occupations are often characterised by part-time work, and poor pay, and are in a mainly narrow range of industrial sectors. Part-time workers are often described as part of the secondary labour market with pay, conditions and employment rights being vastly inferior to those of full-time permanent workers, although legislation now provides for some equalisation.

WINDOW ON PRACTICE

Gender segregation at Deloitte Touche

McCracken (2000) reports how Deloitte Touche were good at recruiting women and felt they had achieved equal opportunities, but they were finding that women were leaving at a much higher rate than men and few women were made partners. On investigating the situation they found that women were leaving, not for domestic reasons as they had anticipated, but due to the male-dominated culture. Men were assigned high-visibility assignments in manufacturing, financial services, acquisitions and mergers, whereas women were offered non-profit organisations, healthcare and retail. They also found that women were genuinely assessed on their performance levels, but that men were also assessed on their potential, which women missed out on.

Deloitte Touche made efforts to change these practical features of working life and also tried to promote work-life balance. Having identified the real problems in achieving equality they found that more women partners were coming through and that money was being saved as they were losing fewer talented women.

Summarised from: D. McCracken (2000) 'Winning the talent war for women: sometimes it takes a revolution', *Harvard Business Review*, November–December, pp. 159–65.

Pay differentials between men and women have narrowed very little except for a hike of women's pay upwards when the Equal Pay Act 1970 came into force in 1975.

Table 24.1 Barriers to the achievement of gender-based equal pay

Starting pay is frequently individually negotiated	As men usually have higher previous earnings this means they can negotiate a higher starting rate
Length of service	Men generally have longer service and fewer career breaks, and while this may result in greater experience early in a career it is less of a performance-influencing factor as general length of service increases
Broadbanding	There is a lack of transparency in such systems and there is a lack of structured progression, managers are likely to have high levels of discretion and may be unaware of biases
Lack of equal access to bonus payments	There is evidence that appraisal ratings and assessments discriminate unfairly against minority groups
Market allowances not evenly distributed	Such allowances are more likely to be given to men
Different pay structures and negotiating bodies	As some jobs are done primarily by women and some primarily by men, direct comparisons are harder to make
Job evaluation	Such schemes often perpetuate old values and may be subject to managerial manipulation

Source: Based primarily on material in IDS (2004) 'Employers move on equal pay', *IDS Report No. 897*, January, pp. 10–18.

The 2003 New Earnings Survey reports that women's full-time average weekly pay without overtime was 18 per cent less than that for full-time men (IDS 2004), having increased from around 30 per cent lower prior to the Equal Pay Act. However, if overtime is included the current gap widens as men work a greater number of hours. The same survey shows that the hourly rate of part-time women is 40 per cent less than that for full-time men, with overtime excluded. While some progress has been made towards equal pay, these factors still remain as barriers to be overcome. The abolition of the Wages Councils has not helped in this respect, but the minimum wage has provided some limited support. IDS (2004) identify a range of unintentional consequences of pay systems which prove to be a barrier to achieving equal pay, and these are shown in Table 24.1.

Racial and ethnic groups

In spite of the legislation evidence of discrimination continues to exist. The EOR (2003) reports that the level of unemployment for black and Asian communities is 12 per cent compared with that for the white population of 5 per cent. This picture of **comparative level of unemployment** has barely changed over the last 18 years, and the gap appears to be widening rather than narrowing, although there are differences between the different ethnic groups. In addition, there is continued **segregation in the labour market**, with ethnic minority male employees being employed in the hotel, catering and repairs and distribution sectors, and manufacturing industry, to a much greater extent than their white counterparts. But for construction the reverse is true. Segregation also occurs vertically. Using Labour Force Survey data, the Trades Union Congress (TUC) (2000) reports that 30.4 per cent of white people were classified as managers compared with 24.7 per cent of black people. Again the gap appears to be widening rather than narrowing. Other evidence of vertical segregation has been found by the Runnymede Trust (2000) when surveying the FTSE 100 companies. They found that 5.4 per cent of employees were from ethnic minority groups, compared with the representation of ethnic minorities in the general population of 6.4 per cent, but that this proportion fell sharply at higher grades, with 3.2 per cent of junior managers from ethnic minorities and 1 per cent of senior managers. Yet all of these companies believed that they did not unfairly discriminate. Samir Sharma OBE, Chair of the Runnymede Trust, commented that 'there is still a sea of white faces in the boardrooms of Europe' (EOR 2000). Racial discrimination may also happen less blatantly. Rana (2003) reports on a project designed to understand why ethnic minority managers are underrepresented in senior levels of local government. The researchers found that in 360-degree feedback results the line managers' assessments of ethnic minority employees were less favourable for each individual than all other assessments, which were generally similar. This discrepancy did not occur when considering the ratings of white employees. In terms of **pay**, non-white workers are also comparatively disadvantaged.

WINDOW ON PRACTICE

The *Guardian* (4 November 2000) contained the following report:

The IT industry is often considered to be one which is more open to the employment of different racial groups. But while the workforce may look more diverse the top jobs are still mostly filled by white people. The article goes on to report the experiences of two non-white IT directors. The first, Rene Carayol, is Chief Executive of an e-business consultancy, and comments that he is shocked by the racial prejudice that he encounters. For example, when Rene and the team are visiting new offices, people who have not met them before look around the team for the white faces to work out who is the boss. He comments that it takes some time for people to get used to working with him, and feels that it took him longer to rise to his present position due to his race.

The second, Sarabjit Ubhey, Head of Operational Control at BUPA, identifies the glass ceiling above which there are few senior non-white IT people. She feels that the fundamental problem is awareness, pointing out, for example, that when social/networking events are held at a pub Muslims cannot be present. This, in addition to making them feel excluded, hinders their career progression.

Source: Adapted from R. Woolnough (2000) 'Racism reinforces the glass ceiling', *Guardian*, 4 November, p. 31.

Disabled people

Woodhams and Danieli (2000) point out that people who have a disability face common barriers to full integration into society and yet are a very varied group in that impairments can vary in severity, stability and type. There are 6.7 million people in the UK who have a current long-term health problem or disability which has a substantial adverse impact on their day-to-day activities and affects the work they can do (Bruyere 2000). People with a disability are more likely to be unemployed than their able-bodied counterparts, and once unemployed they are likely to remain so for a longer period (EOR 2003). The economic activity rate for disabled people is 53 per cent compared with 84 per cent for non-disabled people, and 49 per cent of disabled people are in employment compared with 81 per cent of non-disabled people (EOR 2003). Hammond (2002) notes that the media have a particularly poor reputation for employing disabled people. This is particularly unfortunate as this is a missed opportunity to create visible and influential role models.

Choice of job is often restricted for people with a disability, and where they do find work it is likely to be in low-paid, less attractive jobs. People with a disability are overrepresented in plant and machine operative jobs and in the personal and protective services, and are underrepresented in professional and managerial jobs (Skills and Enterprise Network 2000). Periods of high general unemployment exacerbate these problems.

Employers traditionally have had a wide range of concerns regarding the employment of disabled people, including worries about general standards of attendance and health, safety at work, eligibility for pension schemes and possible requirements for alterations to premises and equipment. The two ticks disability symbol is a government initiative and can be used by employers to demonstrate their commitment to employing disabled people. Employers who use the symbol make five commitments to action: a guaranteed job interview for disabled applicants, regular consultation with disabled employees, retaining employees if they become disabled during their employment, improving knowledge about disability for key employees, reviewing these commitments and planning ahead. However Dibben *et al.* (2001) note that the symbol appeared to have only a limited effect on support for disabled employees or potential employees.

WINDOW ON PRACTICE

The case of Val Milnes

Glover reports the experiences of Val Milnes in seeking employment after recovering from a skiing accident, which left her paralysed from the chest down. After being dismissed by her current employer six months after the accident, she began to look for work when she had been through a rehabilitation process. Her experiences of seeking employment are salutary. Little support was made in most organisations to enable her to compete on a 'level playing field', and she comments that HR professionals did not help. In terms of finding locations and carrying out interviews Val was constantly put at a disadvantage. She felt that on many occasions she was interviewed as a matter of procedure and as a way of complying with the two ticks symbol; and that there was no intention to consider her for employment. She suggests some very practical steps that employers could take to make people with a disability feel more welcome.

Source: Summarised from C. Glover (2003) 'Ticked off', *People Management*, Vol. 8, No. 2, 24 January, pp. 38–9.

Age

While advertisements are generally less obviously discriminatory in respect of age the EOR (1998) found that employers still used coded language to indicate that they were looking for a specific age group, and found phrases such as 'young', 'articulate youngsters', 'second jobber', and 'young dynamic environment'. There continue to be cultures that discriminate against older, and younger, people. There is frequently discrimination at both the shortlisting and interview stage, with line managers having negative perceptions of older workers, seeing them as less able to cope with change, training or technology and less interested in their careers. Higginbottom and Roberts (2002), reporting on a MORI poll of 2000 adults, found that they viewed age discrimination as the prime cause of discrimination at work. Philpott (2003) reports that in a survey of 600 retired people, two-fifths believe they had suffered discrimination in some way, age discrimination being the most frequent form. He goes on to argue that there are fewer older people in the workforce, not because they prefer to retire, but because they feel they have been discriminated against. Snape and Redman (2003) found partial support for this. Platman (2002) reports on National Opinion Poll (NOP) research funded by the Department for Work and Pensions which included people between the ages of 50 and 60, a quarter of whom believe that they were discriminated against when looking for a job. Nearly half the organisations in the survey had no staff aged 60 or over. Line managers said they were age friendly, although they appeared to be ignorant of the guidelines.

Given that by 2010 almost 40 per cent of the working population will be over 45 (Higginbottom 2002) and the current shortage of many skills, this presents a critical problem for organisations. Older workers are seen to be more loyal and conscientious, to have better interpersonal skills, to be more efficient in the job and their experience in the job counteracts any age-related factors lowering productivity; older workers are generally more satisfied with their jobs and have fewer accidents and a better absence record; and in any case there is considerable variation within individuals. Older workers also have lower turnover rates which saves the organisation money.

On the basis of their research Snape and Redman (2003) argue that discrimination for being too young is at least as common as that for being too old. Both forms of discrimination adversely affected commitment to the organisation, and hence, it could be argued, performance.

Sexuality

Lesbian, gay and bisexual discrimination is the most difficult to identify due to the fact that group membership is more easily concealed, usually due to the anticipation of discrimination. It is therefore difficult to quantify the extent to which these groups experience active discrimination. The protection now given to transsexuals means that they are not forced to offer historical information on their gender, but transsexuals in transition clearly cannot keep this confidential, and will need support and protection from harassment (Higginbottom 2002). Most employers have been slow to include sexual orientation in their diversity management initiatives (Ward 2003).

Wilson (2000) in an article reporting three case studies found that in two of the three organisations sexuality other than the heterosexual norm was not considered acceptable in the culture. In one engineering company, the researcher was told that you would have to be very discreet if you were gay, and that one gay person, who had not 'come out', had left the organisation. In the second, a professional partnership, the researcher was told that sexuality was 'under wraps'. Only in the third, a media organisation, were different sexual orientations considered acceptable.

In a TUC survey carried out at the end of 1998 (EOR 1999b), 44 per cent of the 440 gay, lesbian and bisexual respondents said they had experienced discrimination at work due to their sexuality. Forms of discrimination reported ranged from verbal abuse to dismissal. Even in jobs where employees feel sufficiently comfortable to disclose their sexuality, there is considerable discrimination in the terms and benefits they receive, although legislation is beginning to change this situation.

In summary

Although some of the more blatant aspects of discrimination have been significantly improved, there remain considerable discrimination and inequality in respect of minority groups in the workplace. To some extent we are only just beginning to understand the causes and nature of more subtle forms of discrimination which are the root of inequality. We now turn to the theoretical debate which underpins different organisational approaches to tackling discrimination.

DIFFERENT APPROACHES TO EQUALITY

There has been a continuing debate concerning the action that should be taken to alleviate the disadvantages that minority groups encounter. One school of thought supports legislative action, which we considered in detail in the previous chapter, and this approach is generally referred to as the equal opportunities, or liberal approach. The other argues that this will not be effective and that the only way to change fundamentally is to alter the attitudes and preconceptions that are held about these groups. This second perspective is embodied in the managing diversity approaches. The initial emphasis on legislative action was adopted in the hope that this would eventually affect attitudes. A third, more extreme, radical approach, which enjoys less support, comes from those who advocate legislation to promote positive or reverse discrimination to compensate for a history of discrimination against specified groups and to redress the balance more immediately. The arguments for and against such an approach are fully discussed by Singer (1993). In the UK legislation provides for positive action, such as special support and encouragement, for disadvantaged groups, but not positive or reverse discrimination (discriminating in their favour), although positive discrimination is legal in the USA. For a comparison of UK and US approaches to equality *see* Ford (1996).

The labels 'equal opportunities' and 'management of diversity' are used inconsistently, and to complicate this there are different perspectives on the meaning of managing diversity, so we shall draw out the key differences which typify each of these approaches, and offer some critique of their conceptual foundations and efficacy.

The equal opportunities approach

The equal opportunities approach seeks to influence behaviour through legislation so that discrimination is prevented. It has been characterised by a moral and ethical stance promoting the rights of *all* members of society. The approach, sometimes referred to as the liberal tradition (Jewson and Mason 1986), concentrates on the equality of opportunity rather than the equality of outcome found in more radical approaches. The approach is based on the understanding that some individuals are discriminated against, for example in the selection process, due to irrelevant criteria. These irrelevant criteria arise from assumptions based on the stereotypical characteristics attributed to them as members of a socially defined group, for example that women will not be prepared to work away from home due to family commitments; that a person with a disability will have more time off sick. As these assumptions are not supported by any evidence, in respect of any individual, they are regarded as irrelevant. The equal opportunities approach therefore seeks to formalise procedures so that relevant, job-based criteria are used (using job descriptions and person specifications), rather than irrelevant assumptions. The equal opportunities legislation provides a foundation for this formalisation of procedures, and hence procedural justice. As Liff (1999) points out, the use of systematic rules in employment matters which can be monitored for compliance is 'felt fair'. In line with the moral argument, and emphasis on systematic procedures, equal opportunities is often characterised as a responsibility of the HR department.

The rationale, therefore, is to provide a 'level playing field' on which all can compete on equal terms. Positive action, not positive discrimination, is allowable in order that some may reach the level at which they can compete equally. For example British Rail has given members of minority groups extra coaching and practice in a selection test for train drivers, as test taking was not part of their culture so that, when required to take a test, they were at a disadvantage.

Equal opportunities approaches stress disadvantaged groups, and the need, for example, to set targets for those groups to ensure that their representation in the workplace reflects their representation in wider society in occupations where they are underrepresented, such as the small numbers of ethnic minorities employed as firefighters and police officers, or the small numbers of women in senior management roles. These targets are not enforceable by legislation, as in the United States, but organisations have been encouraged to commit themselves voluntarily to improvement goals, and to support this by putting in place measures to support disadvantaged groups such as special training courses and flexible employment policies.

Differences between socially defined groups are glossed over, and the approach is generally regarded as one of 'sameness'. That is, members of disadvantaged groups should be treated in the same way as the traditional employee (white, male, young, able-bodied and heterosexual), and not treated differently due to their group membership, unless for the purpose of providing the 'level playing field'.

Problems with the equal opportunities approach

There is an assumption in the equal opportunities approach that equality of outcome will be achieved if fair procedures are used and monitored. In other words this will enable any minority groups to achieve a fair share of what employment has to offer. Once such minority groups become full participating members in employment, the old stereotypical attitudes on which discrimination against particular social groups is based will gradually change, as the stereotypes will be shown to be unhelpful.

The assumption that fair procedures or procedural justice will lead to fair outcomes has not been borne out in practice, as we have shown. In addition there has been criticism of the assumption that once members of minority groups have demonstrated their ability to perform in the organisation this will change attitudes and beliefs in the organisation. This is a naïve assumption, and the approach has been regarded as simplistic. Liff (1999) argues that attitudes and beliefs have been left untouched. Other criticisms point out that the legislation does not protect all minority groups (although it is gradually being extended); and there is a general lack of support within the organisation, partly because equality objectives are not linked to business objectives (Shapiro and Austin 1996). Shapiro and Austin, among others, argue that equal opportunities has often been the concern of the HR function, and Kirton and Greene (2003) argue that a weak HR function has not helped. The focus of equal opportunities is on formal processes and yet it is it not possible to formalise everything in the organisation. Recent research suggests that this approach alienated large sections of the workforce (those not identified as disadvantaged groups) who felt that there was no benefit for themselves, and indeed that their opportunities were damaged. Others felt that equal opportunities initiatives had resulted in the lowering of entry standards, as in the London Fire and Civil Defence Authority (EOR 1996). Shapiro and Austin argue that this creates divisions in the workforce. Lastly, it is the individual who is expected to adjust to the organisation, and 'traditional equal opportunities strategies encourage a view that women (and other groups) have a problem and need help' (Liff 1999, p. 70).

In summary the equal opportunities approach is considered simplistic and to be attempting to treat the symptoms rather than the causes of unfair discrimination.

The management of diversity approach

The management of diversity approach concentrates on individuals rather than groups, and includes the improvement of opportunities for *all* individuals and not just those in minority groups. Hence managing diversity involves everyone and benefits everyone, which is an attractive message to employers and employees alike. Thus separate groups are not singled out for specific treatment. Kandola and Fullerton (1994, p. 47), who are generally regarded as the main UK supporters of a managing diversity approach, express it this way:

> Managing diversity is about the realisation of the potential of all employees . . . certain group based equal opportunities policies need to be seriously questioned, in particular positive action and targets.

In the second edition of their book (1998, p. 11) they contest, in addition, that:

> if managing diversity is about an individual and their contribution . . . rather than about groups it is contradictory to provide training and other opportunities based solely on people's perceived group membership.

Further differences from an equal opportunities approach are highlighted in the following definition from the USA, where managing diversity is described as:

> the challenge of meeting the needs of a culturally diverse workforce and of sensitising workers and managers to differences associated with gender, race, age and nationality in an attempt to maximise the potential productivity of all employees.
>
> (Ellis and Sonnenfield 1994, p. 82)

Ignoring for a moment the fact that some groups are specifically excluded from this definition, we will focus, among other themes, on two key issues that this quotation raises: recognition of difference and culture. Recognition of difference is also demonstrated by the Institute of Personnel and Development (IPD, now CIPD) (1997) when they say that 'people have different abilities to contribute to organizational goals and performance' (pp. 1–2). Whereas the equal opportunities approach minimised difference, the managing diversity approach treats difference as a positive asset. Liff (1996), for example, notes that from this perspective organisations should recognise rather than dilute differences, as differences are positive rather than negative.

This brings us to a further difference between the equal opportunities approach and the managing diversity approach which is that the managing diversity approach is based on the economic and business case for recognising and valuing difference, rather than the moral case for treating people equally. Rather than being purely a cost, equal treatment offers benefits and advantages for the employer if it invests in ensuring that everyone in the organisation is valued and given the opportunities to develop their potential and make a maximum contribution. The practical arguments supporting the equalisation of employment opportunities are thus highlighted. Thompson and DiTomaso (reported by Ellis and Sonnenfield 1994) put it very well:

> [A] [m]ulticultural management perspective fosters more innovative and creative decision making, satisfying work environments, and better products because all people who have a contribution to make are encouraged to be involved in a meaningful way . . . More information, more points of view, more ideas and reservations are better than fewer.

A company that discriminates, directly or indirectly, against older or disabled people, women, ethnic minorities or people with different sexual orientations will be curtailing the potential of available talent, and employers are not well known for their complaints about the surplus of talent. The financial benefits of retaining staff who might otherwise leave due to lack of career development or due to the desire to combine a career with family are stressed, as is the image of the organisation as a 'good' employer and hence its attractiveness to all members of society as its customers. A relationship between a positive diversity climate and job satisfaction and commitment to the organisation has also been found (Hicks-Clarke and Iles 2000). Although the impact on performance is more difficult to assess, it is reasonable to assume that more satisfied and committed employees will lead to reduced absence and turnover levels. In addition, the value of different employee perspectives and different types of contribution is seen as providing added value to the organisation, particularly when organisational members increasingly reflect the diverse customer base of the organisation. This provides a way in which organisations can better understand, and therefore meet, their customer needs. The business case argument is likely to have more support from managers as it is less likely to threaten the bottom line. Policies that do pose such a threat can be unpopular with managers (Humphries and Rubery 1995).

Managing diversity highlights the importance of culture. The roots of discrimination go very deep, and in relation to women Simmons (1989) talks about challenging a system of institutional discrimination and anti-female conditioning in the prevailing culture, and the Macpherson Report (1999) identifies institutional racism as a root cause of discrimination in the police force. Culture is important in two ways in managing diversity: first, organisational culture is one determinant of the way that organisations manage diversity and treat individuals from different groups. Equal opportunity approaches tended to concentrate on behaviour and, to a small extent, attitudes, whereas management of diversity approaches recognise a need to go beneath this. So changing the culture to one which treats individuals as individuals and supports them in developing their potential is critical, although the difficulties of culture change make this a very difficult task.

Second, depending on the approach to the management of diversity, the culture of different groups within the organisation comes into play. Recognising that men and women present different cultures at work and that this diversity needs to be managed, is key to promoting a positive environment of equal opportunity, which goes beyond merely fulfilling the demands of the statutory codes. Masreliez-Steen (1989) explains how men and women have different perceptions, interpretations of reality, languages and ways of solving problems, which, if properly used, can be a benefit to the whole organisation, as they are complementary. She describes women as having a collectivist culture where they form groups, avoid the spotlight, see rank as unimportant and have few but close contacts. Alternatively, men are described as having an individualistic culture, where they form teams, 'develop a profile', enjoy competition and have many superficial contacts. The result is that men and women behave in different ways, often fail to understand each other and experience 'culture clash'. However, the difference is about how things are done and not about what is achieved. However, we must be aware that here we have another stereotypical view which simplifies reality.

The fact that women have a different culture, with different strengths and weaknesses, means that women need managing and developing in a different way, needing different forms of support and coaching. Women more often need help to understand the value of making wider contacts and how to make them. In order to manage such diversity, key management competencies for the future would be: concern with image, process awareness, interpersonal awareness/sensitivity, developing subordinates and gaining commitment. Attending to the organisation's culture suggests a move away from seeing the individual as the problem, and requiring that the individual needs to change because they do not fit the culture. Rather, it is the organisation that needs to change so that traditional assumptions of how jobs are constructed and how they should be carried out are questioned, and looked at afresh. As Liff (1999) comments, the sociology of work literature shows how structure, cultures and practices of organisations advantage those from the dominant group by adapting to their skills and lifestyles. This is the very heart of institutional discrimination, and so difficult to address as these are matters which are taken for granted and largely unconscious. The trick, as Thomas (1992) spells out, is to identify 'requirements as opposed to preferences, conveniences or traditions'. This view of organisational transformation rather than individual transformation is similar to Cockburn's

Aspect	Equal opportunities	Managing diversity
Purpose	Reduce discrimination	Utilise employee potential to maximum advantage
Case argued	Moral and ethical	Business case – improve profitability
Whose responsibility	HR/personnel department	All managers
Focuses on	Groups	Individuals
Perspective	Dealing with different needs of different groups	Integrated
Benefits for employees	Opportunities improved for disadvantaged groups, primarily through setting targets	Opportunities improved for all employees
Focus on management activity	Recruitment	Managing
Remedies	Changing systems and practices	Changing the culture

Table 24.2 Major differences between 'equal opportunities' approaches and 'management of diversity' approaches

(1989) 'long agenda' for equality, as she discusses changing cultures, systems and structures.

Finally, managing diversity is considered to be a more integrated approach to implementing equality. Whereas equal opportunities approaches were driven by the HR function, managing diversity is seen to be the responsibility of all managers. And, as there are business reasons for managing diversity it is argued that equality should not be dealt with as a separate issue, as with equal opportunities approaches, but integrated strategically into every aspect of what the organisation does; this is often called mainstreaming.

Table 24.2 summarises the key differences between equal opportunities and managing diversity.

Problems with the managing diversity approach

While the management of diversity approach was seen by many as revitalising the equal opportunities agenda, and as a strategy for making more progress on the equality front, this progress has been slow to materialise. In reality, there remains the question of the extent to which approaches have really changed in organisations. Redefining equal opportunities in the language of the enterprise culture (Miller 1996) may just be a way of making it more palatable in today's climate, and Liff (1996) suggests that retitling may be used to revitalise the equal opportunities agenda.

It has been pointed out by Kirton and Greene (2003) that only a small number of organisations are ever quoted as management of diversity exemplars, and EOR (1999b) notes that even organisations which claim to be managing diversity do not appear to have a more diverse workforce than others, and neither have they employed more minority groups over the past five years.

Apart from this there are some fundamental problems with the management of diversity approach. The first of these is its complexity, as there are differing interpretations, which we have so far ignored, and which focus on the prominence of groups or individuals. Miller (1996) highlights two different approaches to the management of diversity. The first is where individual differences are identified and celebrated, and where prejudices are exposed and challenged via training. The second, more orthodox, approach is where the organisation seeks to develop the capacity of all. This debate between group and individual identity is a fundamental issue:

> Can people's achievements be explained by their individual talents or are they better explained as an outcome of their gender, ethnicity, class and age? Can anything meaningful be said about the collective experience of all women or are any generalisations undermined by other cross-cutting ideas? (Liff 1997, p. 11)

The most common approach to the management of diversity is based on individual contribution, as we have explained above, rather than group identity, although Liff (1997) identifies different approaches with different emphases. The *individualism* approach is based on dissolving differences. In other words, differences are not seen as being distributed systematically according to membership of a social group, but rather as random differences. Groups are not highlighted, but all should be treated fairly and encouraged to develop their potential. The advantage of this approach is that it is inclusive and involves all members of the organisation. An alternative emphasis in the management of diversity is that of *valuing differences* based on the membership of different social groups. Following this approach would mean recognising and highlighting differences, and being prepared to give special training to groups who may be disadvantaged and lack self-confidence, so that all in the organisation feel comfortable. Two further emphases are *accommodating* and *utilising* differences, which she argues are most similar to equal opportunity approaches where specific initiatives are available to aid identified groups, but also where these are also genuinely open for all other members of the organisation. In these approaches talent is recognised and used in spite of social differences, and this is done, for example, by recognising different patterns of qualifications and different roles in and out of paid work. Liff's conclusion is that group differences cannot be ignored, because it is these very differences which hold people back.

There is a further argument that if concentration on the individual is the key feature, then this may reduce our awareness of social-group-based disadvantage (Liff 1999) and may also weaken the argument for affirmative action (Liff 1996). The attractive idea of business advantage and benefits for all may divert attention from disadvantaged groups and result in no change to the status quo (*see*, for example, Ouseley 1996). Young (1990) argues that if differences are not recognised, then the norms and standards of the dominant group are not questioned.

On the other hand, a management of diversity approach may reinforce group-based stereotypes, when group-based characteristics are identified and used as a source of advantage to the organisation. For example, it has been argued, in respect of women, that as these differences were treated previously as a form of disadvantage, women may be uncomfortable using them to argue the basis for equality. Others argue that a greater recognition of perceived differences will continue to provide a rationale for disadvantageous treatment.

In addition to this dilemma within managing diversity approaches, the literature provides a strong criticism of the business case argument, which has been identified as contingent and variable (Dickens 1999). Thus the business case is unreliable because it will only work in certain contexts. For example, where skills are easily available there is less pressure on the organisation to promote and encourage the employment of minority groups. Not every employee interacts with customers so if image and customer contact are part of the business case this will only apply to some jobs and not others. Also some groups may be excluded. For example, there is no systematic evidence to suggest that disabled customers are attracted by an organisation which employs disabled people. UK managers are also driven by short-term budgets and the economic benefits of equality may only be reaped in the longer term. Indeed as Kirton and Greene (2000) conclude, the business case is potentially detrimental to equality, when, for example, a cost–benefit analysis indicates that pursuing equality is not an economic benefit.

The CIPD (2003) argues that the jury is still out in respect of the business case for diversity; in other words, the evidence of performance improvements resulting from diversity is scanty. It also points to the importance of a conducive environment in gaining benefits. Furthermore it recites problems which can result from a more diverse workforce which include increased conflict, often resulting in difficulties in coming up with solutions, and poorer internal communication, with increased management costs due to these issues.

In addition there are concerns about whether diversity management, which originated in the USA, will travel effectively to the UK where the context is different, especially in terms of the demographics and the history of equality initiatives. Furthermore, there are concerns about whether diversity can be managed at all, as Lorbiecki and Jack (2000) note:

> the belief that diversity management is do-able rests on a fantasy that it is possible to imagine a clean slate on which memories of privilege and subordination leave no mark. (p. 528)

and they go on to say that the theories do not take account of existing power differentials.

Lastly, managing diversity can be seen as introspective as it deals with people already in the organisation, rather than with getting people into the organisation – managing rather than expanding diversity (Donaldson 1993). Because of this Thomas (1990) suggests that it is not possible to *manage* diversity until you actually have it.

Equal opportunities or managing diversity?

Are equal opportunities and managing diversity completely different things? If so, is one approach preferable to the other? For the sake of clarity, earlier in this chapter we characterised a distinct approach to managing diversity which suggests that it is different from equal opportunities. Miller (1996) identifies a parallel move from the collective to the individual in the changing emphasis in personnel management as opposed to HRM. However, as we have seen, managing diversity covers a range of approaches and emphases, some closer to equal opportunities, some very different.

Much of the management of diversity suggests that it is superior to and not compatible with the equal opportunities approach (see Kandola *et al.* 1996). There is, however, much support for equal opportunities and managing diversity to be viewed as mutually supportive and for this interaction to be seen as necessary for progress (*see* Ford 1996), although Newman and Williams (1995) argue that we are some way from a model which can incorporate difference and diversity in its individualised and collective sense. To see equal opportunities and management of diversity as *alternatives* threatens to sever the link between organisational strategy and the realities of internal and external labour market disadvantage.

IMPLICATIONS FOR ORGANISATIONS

Conceptual models of organisational responses to equal opportunities and managing diversity

A conceptual model of organisational responses to achieving equality, concentrating on perceived rationale and the differing contributions of equality of opportunity and managing diversity has been developed by LaFasto (1992). This is shown in Figure 24.1.

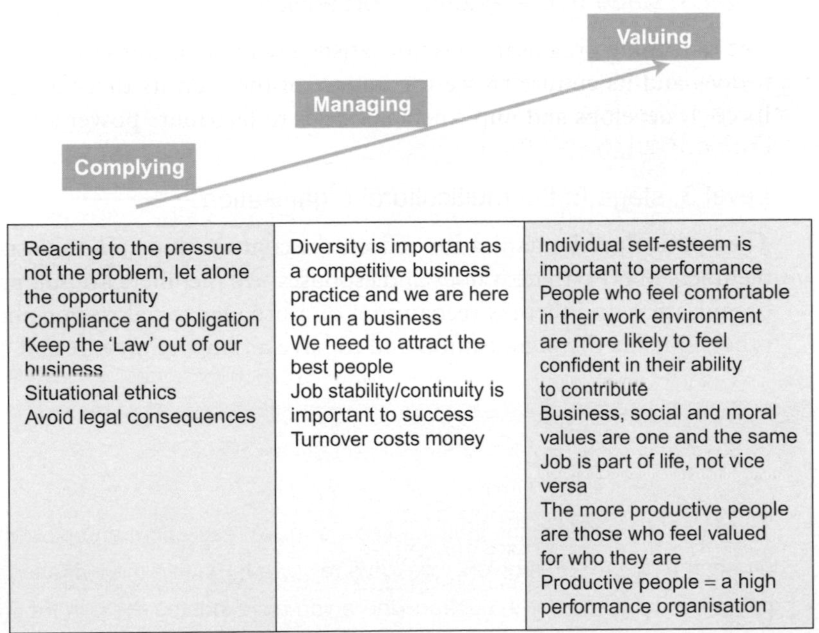

Figure 24.1 Conceptual model of diversity (Source: F. LaFasto (1992) 'Baxter Healthcare Organisation', in B.W. Jackson, F. LaFasto, H.G. Schultz and D. Kelly, 'Diversity', *Human Resource Management*, Vol. 31, Nos 1 and 2, Spring/Summer, p. 28. Reproduced with permission of John Wiley and Sons, Inc. Copyright © 1992 John Wiley and Sons, Inc.)

An alternative framework is proposed by Jackson *et al.* (1992) who, concentrating on culture, identify a series of stages and levels that organisations go through in becoming a multicultural organisation:

Level 1, stage 1: the exclusionary organisation

The exclusionary organisation maintains the power of dominant groups in the organisation, and excludes others.

Level 1, stage 2: the club

The club still excludes people but in a less explicit way. Some members of minority groups are allowed to join as long as they conform to predefined norms.

Level 2, stage 3: the compliance organisation

The compliance organisation recognises that there are other perspectives, but does not want to do anything to 'rock the boat'. It may actively recruit minority groups at the bottom of the organisation and make some token appointments.

Level 2, stage 4: the affirmative action organisation

The affirmative action organisation is committed to eliminating discrimination and encourages employees to examine their attitudes and think differently. There is strong support for the development of new employees from minority groups.

Level 3, stage 5: the redefining organisation

The redefining organisation is not satisfied with being anti-racist and so examines all it does and its culture to see the impact of these on its diverse multicultural workforce. It develops and implements policies to distribute power among all groups.

Level 3, stage 6: the multicultural organisation

The multicultural organisation reflects the contribution and interests of all its diverse members in everything it does and espouses. All members are full participants of the organisation and there is recognition of a broader social responsibility – to educate others outside the organisation and to have an impact on external oppression.

ACTIVITY 24.1

Think of five organisations that you know or have read about and plot where they are on each of the two frameworks we have reviewed. Explain the evidence and examples you have used in order to support where you have located them in the frameworks.

Equal opportunities and managing diversity: strategies, policies and plans

While the use of equal opportunities policies has grown very slowly such policies are now a feature of most organisations. Our research in 1984 indicated that such policies were only produced by 60 per cent of organisations, and that on the whole they were not seen as very useful. Indeed, a large number of organisations saw their policy as irrelevant. However, in 1994, using a similar sample, we found that 89 per cent of organisations had equal opportunities policies. Itzin and Phillipson (1993) also found that three-quarters of the 221 employers which responded to their questionnaire had an equal opportunities policy. A postal survey which was sent out in July–August

1999 (EOR 1999b) showed that 95 per cent of respondent organisations had an equal opportunities policy or statement, but Cully *et al.* (1999) found that 66 per cent of organisations in the Workplace Employee Relations (WER) Survey had policies or a statement. Clearly the existence of policy or statement depends on the nature of organisations surveyed. It would also be a mistake to assume that all policies cover all potentially disadvantaged groups (*see*, for example, EOR 1999b).

It is interesting that EOR reported that organisations tended to have equal opportunities policies rather than managing diversity policies, and equal opportunities and managing diversity appeared to be viewed as complementary means of achieving equality rather than different concepts. However, some organisations appear to move from one approach to the other. Maxwell *et al.* (2001), for example, express the difficulty of transition from an equal opportunities policy to a diversity policy. They explain the need to avoid the impression that the equal opportunities approach was inadequate or that those who promoted it were ill informed or mistaken.

However, despite the prevalence of policies there is always the concern that having a policy is more about projecting the right image than about reflecting how the organisation operates. For example, Hoque and Noon (1999) found that having an equal opportunities statement made no difference to the treatment of speculative applications from individuals who were either white or from an ethnic minority group and that 'companies with ethnic minority statements were more likely to discriminate *against* the ethnic minority applicant'. The Runnymede Trust (2000) in a survey on racial equality found that the way managers explained their equal opportunities policy was different from employee views about what happened in practice. Creegan *et al.* (2003) investigated the implementation of a race equality action plan and found a stark difference between paper and practice. Line managers who were responsible for implementing the plan were operating in a devolved HR environment and so had to pay for advice, training and support from HR. The consequence of this was that in order to protect their budgets they were reluctant to seek help. Employees felt that there was no ownership of the strategy or the plan within the organisation by senior or middle managers. In respect of women there is evidence that women in senior positions are not very supportive of equal opportunities policies which help other women get on in the organisation (Ng and Chiu, 2001).

ACTIVITY 24.2

Consider the equal opportunities policy in your own organisation, or another with which you are familiar.

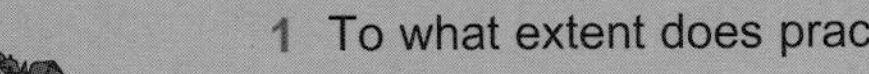

1 To what extent does practice match policy?

2 Explore the reasons for the achievement of a match or mismatch.

A process for managing diversity

Ross and Schneider (1992) advocate a strategic approach to managing diversity that is based on their conception of the difference between seeking equal opportunity and managing diversity. The difference, as they see it, is that diversity approaches are:

- internally driven, not externally imposed;
- focused on individuals rather than groups;
- focused on the total culture of the organisation rather than just the systems used;
- the responsibility of all in the organisation and not just the HR function.

Their process involves the following steps:

1 Diagnosis of the current situation in terms of statistics, policy and culture, and looking at both issues and causes.

2 Setting aims which involve the business case for equal opportunities, identifying the critical role of commitment from the top of the organisation, and a vision of what the organisation would look like if it successfully managed diversity.

3 Spreading the ownership. This is a critical stage in which awareness needs to be raised, via a process of encouraging people to question their attitudes and preconceptions. Awareness needs to be raised in all employees at all levels, especially managers, and it needs to be clear that diversity is not something owned by the personnel function.

4 Policy development comes after awareness raising as it enables a contribution to be made from all in the organisation – new systems need to be changed via involvement and not through imposition on the unwilling.

5 Managing the transition needs to involve a range of training initiatives. Positive action programmes, specifically designed for minority groups, may be used to help them understand the culture of the organisation and acquire essential skills; policy implementation programmes, particularly focusing on selection, appraisal, development and coaching; further awareness training and training to identify cultural diversity and manage different cultures and across different cultures.

6 Managing the programme to sustain momentum. This involves a champion, not necessarily from the HR function, but someone who continues in their previous organisation role in addition. Also the continued involvement of senior managers is important, together with trade unions. Harnessing initiatives that come up through departments and organising support networks for disadvantaged groups are key at this stage. Ross and Schneider also recommend measuring achievements in terms of business benefit – better relationships with customers, improvements in productivity and profitability, for example – which need to be communicated to all employees.

Ellis and Sonnenfield (1994) make the point that training for diversity needs to be far more than a one-day event. They recommend a series of workshops which allow time for individuals to think, check their assumptions and reassess between training sessions. Key issues that need tackling in arranging training are ensuring that the facilitator has the appropriate skills; carefully considering participant mix; deciding whether the training should be voluntary or mandatory; being prepared to cope with any backlash from previously advantaged groups who now feel threatened; and being prepared for the fact that the training may reinforce stereotypes. They argue that training has enormous potential benefits, but that there are risks involved.

While the ideal may be for organisations to work on all aspects of diversity in an integrated manner, the reality is often that organisations will target specific issues or groups at different times. Case 24.1 on the website is focused on improving diversity practice for people with disabilities.

WINDOW ON PRACTICE

Age equality at Derby City Council

Platman reports that in Derby City Council potential applicants would phone to find out if there was any point in applying for a particular job, expecting that their older age would rule them out. The Council felt that age discrimination restricted the pool of applicants and that they had to get rid of signals that age was not valued. They now have a code of practice which centres on dignity at work, and this applies to both councillors and employees. The aim of the code is to ensure that ageist behaviour, attitudes and language are avoided. The intention is to put across the message that the Council values the experience of older employees, and older employees are now specifically encouraged to apply for further training and promotions.

Source: Summarised from K. Platman (2002) 'Matured Assets', *People Management*, Vol. 8, No. 24, 5 December, pp. 40–2.

Changing culture is clearly a key part of any process for managing diversity. In 1995 Her Majesty's Inspectorate of Constabulory (HMIC) stressed the business case for diversity in the police force. The police force, over a number of years, has made considerable efforts to increase the recruitment and promotion of members of ethnic minorities (*see*, for example, EOR 1997). It began to tackle the issues of why individuals from different ethnic backgrounds would not even apply to the police for a career (for example, they may be seen, within some ethnic groups, as traitors for doing so). Some progress was made but the McPherson Report highlighted the issue of institutional racism, and further efforts were made to reduce discrimination. However, in 2004 there is still clear evidence of discriminatory cultures and attitudes, as evidenced by the television programme about the racist attitudes of new recruits into Manchester police. On Radio 4 on 20 January 2004 the Ali Desai case was discussed and it was argued that the metropolitan police service were racist in the way that they applied discipline to officers, picking up on smaller issues for racial minority groups than for white officers. The changes required to manage diversity effectively should not be underestimated.

Case 24.2 on the website considers the achievement of an ethnic mix on some MBA courses.

WINDOW ON PRACTICE

BT – Championing women in a man's world

BT is often used as an exemplar of an organisation which has taken significant steps to encouraging women in a male-dominated engineering environment and Equal Opportunities Review (1999a) reports on how BT has gone about this.

First, BT has top-level strategic support to increase the proportion of women at all levels in the organisation, and also has identified the need for line managers to be convinced of the economic value of such policies.

The initiatives introduced involve the appointment of a gender champion, assessing the HR director, partly on objectives relating to gender issues, and running a one-day workshop for all 5,000 managers to stress the business case and attempt to change attitudes.

In terms of access to employment BT has targeted universities with a higher proportion of women students, revised job titles and specifications and considered ways of developing eligibility criteria for jobs. BT has set improvement targets and encouraged 'take your daughters to work' days.

In respect of existing employees BT has: produced a women's development portfolio and a women's management development programme, developed strategic skills for senior women managers, a women's network and website and raised the issues of life-work balance and childcare.

Source: Summarised from EOR (1999a) 'BT: Championing women in a man's world', *Equal Opportunities Review*, No. 84, March–April, pp. 14–20.

ACTIVITY 24.3

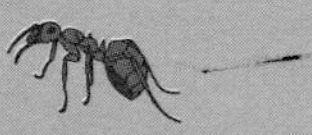

Prepare a strategy for managing diversity which would be appropriate for your organisation, or one with which you are familiar.

SUMMARY PROPOSITIONS

24.1 The essence of much HR work is to discriminate between individuals. The essence of equality is to avoid unfair discrimination. Unfair discrimination often results from people being treated on the basis of limited and prejudiced understanding of the groups to which they belong rather than on the basis of an assessment of them as individuals. People are not always aware when they are discriminating unfairly.

24.2 Legislation can have only a limited effect in achieving equality, and does not change attitudes, beliefs and cultures and structures. Organisations and their cultures, processes and structures are founded on the needs of the majority group and individuals from other groups are expected to adapt to this norm. This explains why progress towards equality of opportunity has been very slow.

24.3 Equal opportunities approaches highlight the moral argument for equal treatment, whereas managing diversity highlights the business case.

24.4 Actual changes in practice relating to equalising opportunity are taking place very slowly, and only long-term organisational transformation is likely to support equality.

24.5 Equal opportunities approaches and the management of diversity are best viewed, not as alternatives, but as complementary approaches which need to be interrelated.

GENERAL DISCUSSION TOPICS

1 Discuss Liff's (1997) question:

> 'Can people's achievements be explained by their individual talents or are they better explained as an outcome of their gender, ethnicity, class and age? Can anything meaningful be said about the collective experience of all women or are any generalisations undermined by other cross-cutting ideas.' (p. 11)

2 Which is preferable – the UK approach or the US approach to equal opportunities? What are the implications of each for all members of the organisation?

FURTHER READING

Benschop, Y. (2001) 'Pride, prejudice and performance: relations between HRM, diversity and performance', *International Journal of Human Resource Management*, Vol. 12, No. 7, pp. 1166–81
This a very illuminative article which presents the experience of the impact of workforce diversity in two case study organisations. The findings indicate that an organisation's strategy for diversity influences how employees perceive and understand diversity and the impact that it has on performance.

Mattis, M. (2001) 'Advancing women in business organisations', *Journal of Management Development*, Vol. 20, No. 4, pp. 371–88
This article examines the role of key players such as middle and first line managers in supporting gender diversity initiatives. A wide range of case examples are used and the article provides a range of practical activities to support gender diversity.

REFERENCES

Bruyere, S. (2000) 'Managing disability in the workplace', *Equal Opportunities Review*, No. 92, July–August.

CIPD (2003) *Diversity: Stacking up the evidence, Executive Briefing*. London: CIPD.

Cockburn, C. (1989) 'Equal Opportunities: the long and short agenda', *Industrial Relations Journal*, Vol. 20, No. 3, pp. 213–25.

Creegan, C., Colgan, F., Charlesworth, R. and Robinson, G. (2003) 'Race equality policies at work: employee perceptions of the "implementation gap" in a UK local authority', *Work, Employment and Society*, Vol. 17, No. 4, pp. 617–40.

Cully, M., Woodland, S., O'Reilly, A. and Dix, G. (1999) *Britain at Work: As depicted by the 1998 Workplace Employee Relations Survey*. London: Routledge.

Dibben, P., James, P. and Cunningham, I. (2001) 'Senior management commitment to disability', *Personnel Review*, Vol. 30, No. 4, pp. 454–67.

Dickens, L. (1999) 'Beyond the business case: a three pronged approach to equality action', *Human Resource Management Journal*, Vol. 9, No. 1, pp. 9–19.

Donaldson, L. (1993) 'The recession: a barrier to equal opportunities?' *Equal Opportunities Review*, No. 50, July–August.

Ellis, C. and Sonnenfield, J.A. (1994) 'Diverse approaches to managing diversity', *Human Resource Management*, Vol. 33, No. 1, Spring, pp. 79–109.

Equal Opportunities Review (1996) 'Ethnic minorities in the police service', *Equal Opportunities Review*, No. 68, July–August.

Equal Opportunities Review (1997) 'Ethnic minorities in the police service', *Equal Opportunities Review*, No. 73.

Equal Opportunities Review (1998) 'Tackling Age bias: code or law?' *Equal Opportunities Review*, No. 80, July–August.

Equal Opportunities Review (1999a) 'BT: Championing women in a man's world', *Equal Opportunities Review*, No. 84, March–April, pp. 14–20.

Equal Opportunities Review (1999b) 'Equal Opportunities Policies: An EOR survey of employers', *Equal Opportunities Review*, No. 87, September–October.

Equal Opportunities Review (2000) 'Businesses urged to shape up on race', *Equal Opportunities Review*, No. 90, March–April.

Equal Opportunities Review (2002) 'Trends in female employment', *Equal Opportunities Review*, No. 112, December, pp. 19–22.

Equal Opportunities Review (2003) 'Economic activity rates of disabled people and ethnic minorities', *Equal Opportunities Review*, No. 121, September, pp. 7–8.

Ford, V. (1996) 'Partnership is the secret of success', *People Management*, 8 February, pp. 34–6.

Glover, C. (2003) 'Ticked off', *People Management*, Vol. 8, No. 2, 24 January, pp. 38–9.

Hakim, C. (1993) 'The myth of rising female employment', *Work, Employment and Society*, Vol. 7, No. 1, March, pp. 121–33.

Hammond, D. (2002) 'TV industry tackles inequality', *People Management*, Vol. 8, No. 15, 25 July, p. 9.

Hicks-Clarke, D. and Iles, P. (2000) 'Climate for diversity and its effects on career and organizational attitudes and perceptions', *Personnel Review*, Vol. 29, No. 3.

Higginbottom, K. (2002) 'The wonder years', *People Management*, Vol. 8, No. 24, 5 December, pp. 14–15.

Higginbottom, K. and Roberts, Z. (2002) 'EOC urges local authorities to confront lack of senior women', *People Management*, Vol. 8, No. 12, 13 June, p. 7.

Hoque, K. and Noon, M. (1999) 'Racial discrimination in speculative applications: new optimism six years on?' *Human Resource Management Journal*, Vol. 9, No. 3, pp. 71–82.

Humphries, J. and Rubery, J. (1995) *Research Summary of the Economics of Equal Opportunity*. Manchester: EOC.

IDS (2004) *Employers move on equal pay*, IDS Report, No. 897, January, pp. 10–18.

Institute of Personnel and Development (1997) *Managing Diversity: A Position paper*. London: IPD.

Itzin, C. and Phillipson, C. (1993) *Age Barriers at Work: Maximising the potential of mature and older people*. London: Metropolitan Authorities Recruitment Agency.

Jackson, B.W., LaFasto, F., Schultz, H.G. and Kelly, D. (1993) 'Diversity', *Human Resource Management*, Vol. 31, Nos 1 and 2, Spring/Summer, pp. 21–34.

Jewson, N. and Mason, D. (1986) 'The theory and practice of equal opportunities policies: liberal and radical approaches', *Sociological Review*, Vol. 34, No. 2, pp. 307–34.

Kandola, P. and Fullerton, J. (1994, 2nd edn 1998) *Managing the Mosaic*. London: IPD.

Kandola, R., Fullerton, J. and Mulroney, C. (1996) *1996 Pearn Kandola Survey of Diversity Practice Summary Report*. Oxford: Pearn Kandola.

Kirton, G. and Greene, A. (2003) *The dynamics of managing diversity: a critical approach*. Oxford: Butterworth Heinemann.

LaFasto, F. (1992) 'Baxter Healthcare Organisation', in B.W. Jackson, F. LaFasto, H.G. Schultz and D. Kelly, *Human Resource Management*, Vol. 31, Nos 1–2, Spring/Summer.

Liff, S. (1996) 'Managing diversity: new opportunities for women?' *Warwick Papers in Industrial Relations* No. 57. Coventry: IRU, Warwick University.

Liff, S. (1997) 'Two routes to managing diversity: individual differences or social group characteristics?' *Employee Relations*, Vol. 19, No. 1, pp. 11–26.

Liff, S. (1999) 'Diversity and Equal Opportunities: room for a constructive compromise?' *Human Resource Management Journal*, Vol. 9, No. 1, pp. 65–75.

Lorbiecki, A. and Jack, G. (2000) 'Critical turns in the evolution of diversity management', *British Journal of Management*, Vol. 11, pp. S17–S31.

McCracken, D. (2000) 'Winning the talent war for women: sometimes it takes a revolution', *Harvard Business Review*, November–December, pp. 159–65.

Macpherson of Clung, Sir William (1999) *The Stephen Lawrence Inquiry. A Report by Sir William Macpherson of Clung*. London: HMSO.

Masreliez-Steen, G. (1989) *Male and Female Management*. Sweden: Kontura Group.

Maxwell, G., Blair, S. and McDougall, M. (2001) 'Edging towards managing diversity in practice', *Employee Relations*, Vol. 23, No. 5, pp. 458–82.

Miller, D. (1996) 'Equality management – towards a materialist approach', *Gender, Work and Organisation*, Vol. 3, No. 4, pp. 202–14.

Newman, J. and Williams, F. (1995) 'Diversity and change, gender, welfare and organisational relations', in C. Itzin and J. Newman, *Gender, Culture and Organisational Change*. London: Routledge.

Ng, C. and Chiu, W. (2001) 'Managing Equal Opportunities for women: sorting the friends from the foes', *Human Resource Management Journal*, Vol. 11, No. 1, pp. 75–88.

Ouseley, H. (1996) quoted in S. Overell, 'Ouseley in assault on diversity', *People Management*, 2 May, pp. 7–8.

People Management (2002) 'Call for women in senior roles', *People Management*, Vol. 8, No. 23, 21 November, p. 11.

Philpott, J. (2003) 'Time to tackle age-old problem', *People Management*, Vol. 9, No. 13, June, p. 22.

Platman, K. (2002) 'Matured Assets', *People Management*, Vol. 8, No. 24, 5 December, pp. 40–2.

Rana, E. (2003) 'Council appraisals discriminate', *People Management*, Vol. 9, No. 2, 23 January, p. 11.

Ross, R. and Schneider, R. (1992) *From Equality to Diversity – a business case for equal opportunities*. London: Pitman.

Runnymede Trust (2000) *Moving on up? Racial Equality and the Corporate Agenda, A Study of the FTSE 100 companies*. London: Central Books.

Shapiro, G. and Austin, S. (1996) 'Equality drives total quality', *Occasional Paper*. Brighton: Brighton Business School.

Simmons, M. (1989) 'Making equal opportunities training effective', *Journal of European Industrial Training*, Vol. 13, No. 8, pp. 19–24.

Singer, M. (1993) *Diversity-based Hiring*. Aldershot: Avebury.

Skills and Enterprise Network (2000) *Labour Market and Skills Trends*. Sheffield: DfEE.

Snape, E. and Redman, T. (2003) 'Too old or too young? The impact of perceived age discrimination', *Human Resource Management Journal*, Vol. 13, No. 1, pp. 78–89.

Thair, T. and Risden, A. (1999) 'Women in the labour market: results from the Spring 1998 Labour Force Survey', *Labour Market Trends*, March.

Thomas, R.R. (1990) 'From affirmative action to affirming diversity', *Harvard Business Review*, March–April.

Thomas, R.R. (1992) 'Managing diversity: a conceptual framework', in S. Jackson (ed.) *Diversity in the Workplace*. New York: Guildford Press.

Trades Union Congress (2000) *Qualifying for Racism*. London: TUC.

Ward, J. (2003) 'How to address sexual orientation', *People Management*, Vol. 9, No. 21, 23 October, pp. 62–3.

Wilson, E. (2000) 'Inclusion, exclusion and ambiguity – the role of organizational culture', *Personnel Review*, Vol. 29, No. 3.

Woodhams, C. and Danieli, A. (2000) 'Disability and diversity – a difference too far?' *Personnel Review*, Vol. 29, No. 3.

Woolnough, R. (2000) 'Racism reinforces the glass ceiling', *Guardian*, 4 November, p. 31.

Young, I.M. (1990) *Justice and the Politics of Difference*. Princeton, NJ: Princeton University Press.

An extensive range of additional materials, including multiple choice questions, answers to questions and links to useful websites can be found on the Human Resource Management Companion Website at www.pearsoned.co.uk/torrington.

CHAPTER 25

GRIEVANCE AND DISCIPLINE

THE OBJECTIVES OF THIS CHAPTER ARE TO:

1. EXAMINE THE NATURE AND EXPLAIN THE PLACE OF GRIEVANCE AND DISCIPLINE IN THE EMPLOYMENT CONTRACT

2. REVIEW THE MILGRAM EXPERIMENTS WITH OBEDIENCE AND USE THEM TO EXPLAIN OUR RESPONSE TO AUTHORITY

3. EXPLAIN THE FRAMEWORK OF ORGANISATIONAL JUSTICE IN THE BUSINESS

4. EXPLAIN GRIEVANCE AND DISCIPLINE PROCEDURES

Grievance and discipline are awkward words nowadays. They sound rather solemn and forbidding, more suitable for a nineteenth-century workhouse than a twenty-first-century business. They certainly have no place in the thinking of Britain's favourite entrepreneur, Sir Richard Branson:

> If you have the right people in place, treat them well and trust them, they will produce happy customers and the necessary profits to carry on and expand the work. (quoted in Handy 1999, p. 86)

We use the words as technical terms to describe the breakdown of mutual confidence between employer and employee, or between managers and managed. When someone starts work at an organisation there are mutual expectations that form the basis of the forthcoming working relationship. We explained in the opening chapter of this book how the maintenance of those mutual expectations is the central purpose of human resource management. Apart from what is written in the contract of employment, both parties will have expectations of what is to come. Employees are likely to expect, for instance, a congenial working situation with like-minded colleagues, opportunities to use existing skills and to acquire others, work that does not offend their personal value system, acceptable leadership and management from those more senior and opportunities to grow and mature. Employers will have expectations such as willing participation in the team, conscientious and imaginative use of existing skills and an ability to acquire others, compliance with reasonable instructions without quibbles, acceptance of the authority of those placed in authority and a willingness to be flexible and accept change.

That working relationship is sometimes going to go wrong. If the employee is dissatisfied, then there is potentially a grievance. If the employer is dissatisfied, there is the potential for a disciplinary situation. The two complementary processes are intended to find ways of avoiding the ultimate sanction of the employee quitting or being dismissed, but at the same time preparing the ground for those sanctions if all else fails.

Usually, the authority to be exercised in a business is impersonalised by the use of roles in order to make it more effective. If a colleague mentions to you that you have overspent your budget, your reaction might be proud bravado unless you knew that the colleague had a role such as company accountant, internal auditor or financial director. Everyone in a business has a role. Most people have several roles and each confers some authority. The canteen assistant who tells you that the steak and kidney pudding is off is more believable than the managing director conveying the same message. Normally in hospitals people wearing white coats and a stethoscope are seen as being more authoritative than people in white coats without a stethoscope.

Dependence on role is not always welcome to those in managerial positions, who are fond of using phrases like, 'I know how to get the best out of people'or 'I have a loyal staff'. This may partly be due to their perception of their role being to persuade the reluctant and command the respect of the unwilling by the use of personal leadership qualities, and it is indisputable that some managers are more effective with some groups of staff than with others, but there is more to it than personal skill: we are predisposed to obey those who outrank us in any hierarchy.

THE MILGRAM EXPERIMENTS WITH OBEDIENCE

Obedience is the reaction expected of people by those in authority positions, who prescribe actions which, but for that authority, might not necessarily have been carried out. Stanley Milgram (1974) conducted a series of experiments to investigate obedience to authority and highlighted the significance of obedience and the power of authority in our everyday lives.

Subjects were led to believe that a study of memory and learning was being carried out which involved giving progressively more severe electric shocks to a learner who gave incorrect answers to factual questions. If the learner gave the correct answer the reward was a further question; if the answer was incorrect there was the punishment of a mild electric shock. Each shock was more severe than the previous one. The 'learner' was not actually receiving shocks, but was a member of the experimental team simulating progressively greater distress, as the shocks were supposedly made stronger. Eighteen different experiments were conducted with over 1,000 subjects, with the circumstances between experiments varying. No matter how the variables were altered the subjects showed an astonishing compliance with authority even when delivering 'shocks' of 450 volts. Up to 65 per cent of subjects continued to obey throughout the experiment in the presence of a clear authority figure and as many as 20 per cent continued to obey when the authority figure was absent.

Milgram was dismayed by his results:

> With numbing regularity good people were seen to knuckle under to the demands of authority and perform actions that were callous and severe. Men who are in everyday life responsible and decent were seduced by the trappings of authority, by the control of their perceptions, and by the uncritical acceptance of the experimenter's definition of the situation into performing harsh acts. (1974, p. 123)

Our interest in Milgram's work is simply to demonstrate that we all have a predilection to obey instructions from authority figures, even if we do not want to. He points out that the act of entering a hierarchical system (such as any employing organisation) makes people see themselves acting as agents for carrying out the wishes of someone else, and this results in these people being in a different state, described as the agentic state. This is the opposite to the state of autonomy when individuals see themselves as acting on their own. Milgram then sets out the factors that lay the groundwork for obedience to authority.

1 Family. Parental regulation inculcates a respect for adult authority. Parental injunctions form the basis for moral imperatives, as commands to children have a dual function. 'Don't tell lies' is a moral injunction carrying a further implicit instruction: 'And obey me!' It is the implicit demand for obedience that remains the only consistent element across a range of explicit instructions.

2 Institutional setting. Children emerge from the family into an institutional system of authority: the school. Here they learn how to function in an organisation. They are regulated by teachers, but can see that the head teacher, the school governors and central government regulate the teachers themselves. Throughout this period they are in a subordinate position. When, as adults, they go to work it may be found that a certain level of dissent is allowable, but the overall situation is one in which they are to do a job prescribed by someone else.

3 **Rewards.** Compliance with authority is generally rewarded, while disobedience is frequently punished. Most significantly, promotion within the hierarchy not only rewards the individual but also ensures the continuity of the hierarchy.

4 **Perception of authority.** Authority is normatively supported: there is a shared expectation among people that certain institutions do, ordinarily, have a socially controlling figure. Also, the authority of the controlling figure is limited to the situation. The usher in a cinema wields authority, which vanishes on leaving the premises. As authority is expected it does not have to be asserted, merely presented.

5 **Entry into the authority system.** Having perceived an authority figure, an individual must then define that figure as relevant to the subject. The individual not only takes the voluntary step of deciding which authority system to join (at least in most of employment), but also defines which authority is relevant to which event. The firefighter may expect instant obedience when calling for everybody to evacuate the building, but not if asking employees to use a different accounting system.

6 **The overarching ideology.** The legitimacy of the social situation relates to a justifying ideology. Science and education formed the background to the experiments Milgram conducted and therefore provided a justification for actions carried out in their name. Most employment is in realms of activity regarded as legitimate, justified by the values and needs of society. This is vital if individuals are to provide willing obedience, as it enables them to see their behaviour as serving a desirable end.

Managers are positioned in an organisational hierarchy in such a way that others will be predisposed, as Milgram demonstrates, to follow their instructions. Managers put in place a series of frameworks to explain how they will exact obedience: they use *discipline*. Because individual employees feel their relative weakness, they seek complementary frameworks to challenge the otherwise unfettered use of managerial disciplinary power: they may join trade unions, but they will always need channels to present their *grievances*.

In later work Milgram (1992) made an important distinction between obedience and conformity, which had been studied by several experimental psychologists, most notably Asch (1951) and Abrams *et al.* (1990). Conformity and obedience both involve abandoning personal judgement as a result of external pressure. The external pressure to conform is the need to be accepted by one's peers and the resultant behaviour is to wear similar clothes, to adopt similar attitudes and adopt similar behaviour. The external pressure to obey comes from a hierarchy of which one is a member, but in which certain others have more status and power than oneself.

> There are at least three important differences . . . First, in conformity there is no *explicit* requirement to act in a certain way, whereas in obedience we are *ordered* or *instructed* to do something. Second, those who influence us when we conform are our *peers* (or equals) and people's behaviours become more alike because they are affected by *example*. In obedience, there is . . . somebody in *higher authority* influencing behaviour. Third, conformity has to do with the psychological need for acceptance by others. Obedience, by contrast, has to do with the social power and status of an authority figure in a hierarchical situation. (Gross and McIlveen 1998, p. 508)

In this chapter we are concerned only with discipline and grievance within business organisations, but it is worth pointing out that managers are the focal points for the grievances of people outside the business as well, but those grievances are called complaints. You may complain *about* poor service, shoddy workmanship or rudeness from an employee, but you complain *to* a manager.

HR managers make one of their most significant contributions to business effectiveness by the way they facilitate and administer grievance and disciplinary issues. First, they devise and negotiate the procedural framework of organisational justice on which both discipline and grievance depend. Second, they are much involved in the interviews and problem-solving discussions that eventually produce solutions to the difficulties that have been encountered. Third, they maintain the viability of the whole process which forms an integral part of their work: they monitor to make sure that grievances are not overlooked and so that any general trend can be perceived, and they oversee the disciplinary machinery to ensure that it is not being bypassed or unfairly manipulated.

Grievance and discipline handling is one of the roles in HRM that few other people want to take over. Ambitious line managers may want to select their own staff without HR intervention or by using the services of consultants. They may try to brush their HR colleagues aside and deal directly with trade union officials or organise their own management development, but grievance and discipline is too hot a potato.

The requirements of the law regarding explanation of grievance handling and the legal framework to avoid unfair dismissal combine to make this an area where HR people must be both knowledgeable and effective. That combination provides a valuable platform for influencing other aspects of management. The HR manager who is not skilled in grievance and discipline is seldom in a strong organisational position.

Everything we have said so far presupposes both hierarchy and the use of procedures. You may say that we have already demonstrated that hierarchy is in decline and that there is a preference for more flexible, personal ways of working than procedure offers. Why rely on Milgram's research, which is now thirty years old? Surely we have moved on since then? Our response is simply that hierarchical relationships continue, although *deference* is in decline. We still seek out the person 'in authority' when we have a grievance and managers readily refer problems they cannot resolve to someone else with a more appropriate role. Procedures may be rigid and mechanical, but they are reliable and we use them even if we do not like them.

WINDOW ON PRACTICE

At the end of the twentieth century schoolteaching in Britain saw the widespread introduction of procedures to deal with teacher capability. Research (Torrington *et al.* 2003) showed that these procedures were generally ineffective in restoring capability and effectiveness for teachers who had lost their way, because of the general reluctance by head teachers to use procedures rather than personal leadership in finding solutions. The result was that heads used an inordinate amount of time in dealing with situations and 'incapable' teachers were extremely distressed and frequently ill because matters were never properly dealt with.

WHAT DO WE MEAN BY DISCIPLINE?

Discipline is regulation of human activity to produce a controlled performance. It ranges from the guard's control of a rabble to the accomplishment of lone individuals producing spectacular performance through self-discipline in the control of their own talents and resources.

The Advisory, Conciliation and Arbitration Service (ACAS) has produced a code of practice relating to disciplinary procedures which makes precisely this point:

> Disciplinary procedures should not be viewed primarily as a means of imposing sanctions (but) . . . as a way of helping and encouraging improvement amongst employees whose conduct or standard of work is unsatisfactory. (ACAS 2000, p. 6)

First, there is managerial discipline in which everything depends on the leader from start to finish. There is a group of people who are answerable to someone who directs what they should all do. Only through individual direction can that group of people produce a worthwhile performance, like the person leading the community singing in the pantomime or the conductor of an orchestra. Everything depends on the leader.

Second, there is team discipline, where the perfection of the performance derives from the mutual dependence of all, and that mutual dependence derives from a commitment by each member to the total enterprise: the failure of one would be the downfall of all. This is usually found in relatively small working groups, like a dance troupe or an autonomous working group in a factory.

Third, there is self-discipline, like that of the juggler or the skilled artisan, where a solo performer is absolutely dependent on training, expertise and self-control. One of the few noted UK researchers working in the field of discipline concludes that self-discipline has recently become much more significant, as demonstrated in the title of his work, 'Discipline: towards trust and self-discipline' (Edwards 2000).

Discipline is, therefore, not only negative, producing punishment or prevention. It can also be a valuable quality for the individual who is subject to it, although the form of discipline depends not only on the individual employee but also on the task and the way it is organised. The development of self-discipline is easier in some jobs than others and many of the job redesign initiatives of recent years have been directed at providing scope for job holders to exercise self-discipline and find a degree of autonomy from managerial discipline. Figure 25.1 shows how the three forms are connected in a sequence or hierarchy, with employees finding one of three ways to achieve their contribution to organisational effectiveness. However, even the most accomplished solo performer has at some time been dependent on others for training and advice, and every team has its coach.

ACTIVITY 25.1

Note three examples of managerial discipline, team discipline and self-discipline from your own experience.

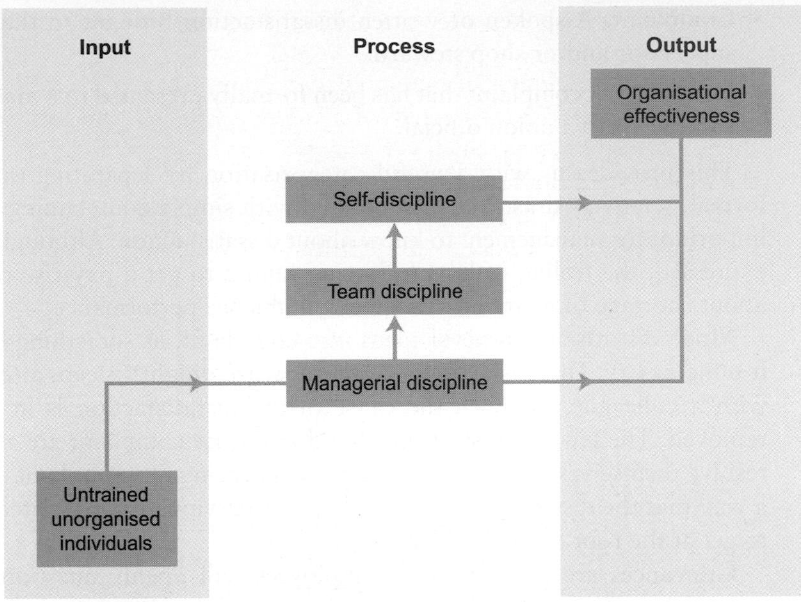

Figure 25.1 Three forms of discipline

Managers are not dealing with discipline only when they are rebuking latecomers or threatening to dismiss saboteurs. As well as dealing with the unruly and reluctant, they are developing the coordinated discipline of the working team, engendering that *esprit de corps* which makes the whole greater than the sum of the parts. They are training the new recruit who must not let down the rest of the team, puzzling over the reasons why A is fitting in well while B is still struggling. Managers are also providing people with the equipment to develop the self-discipline that will give them autonomy, responsibility and the capacity to maximise their powers. The independence and autonomy that self-discipline produces also brings the greatest degree of personal satisfaction, and often the largest pay packet. Furthermore the movement between the three forms represents a declining degree of managerial involvement. If you are a leader of community singing, nothing can happen without your being present and the quality of the singing depends on your performance each time. If you train jugglers, the time and effort you invest pays off a thousand times, while you sit back and watch the show.

WHAT DO WE MEAN BY GRIEVANCE?

Contemporary British texts virtually ignore grievance handling, but the Americans maintain sound coverage. Mathis and Jackson (1994) have a particularly helpful review. Some years ago Pigors and Myers (1977, p. 229) provided a helpful approach to the topic by drawing a distinction between the terms dissatisfaction, complaint and grievance as follows:

- **Dissatisfaction.** Anything that disturbs an employee, whether or not the unrest is expressed in words.

- **Complaint.** A spoken or written dissatisfaction brought to the attention of the supervisor and/or shop steward.
- **Grievance.** A complaint that has been formally presented to a management representative or to a union official.

This provides us with a useful categorisation by separating out grievance as a formal, relatively drastic step, compared with simply complaining. It is much more important for management to know about dissatisfaction. Although nothing is being expressed, the feeling of hurt following failure to get a pay rise or the frustration about shortage of materials can quickly influence performance.

Much dissatisfaction never turns into complaint, as something happens to make it unnecessary. Dissatisfaction evaporates with a night's sleep, after a cup of coffee with a colleague, or when the cause of the dissatisfaction is in some other way removed. The few dissatisfactions that do produce complaint are also most likely to resolve themselves at that stage. The person hearing the complaint explains things in a way that the dissatisfied employee had not previously appreciated, or takes action to get at the root of the problem.

Grievances are rare since few employees will openly question their superior's judgement whatever their private opinion may be and fewer still will risk being stigmatised as a troublemaker. Also, many people do not initiate grievances because they believe that nothing will be done as a result of their attempt.

HR managers have to encourage the proper use of procedures to discover sources of dissatisfaction. Managers in the middle may not reveal the complaints they are hearing, for fear of showing themselves in a poor light. Employees who feel insecure, for any reason, are not likely to risk going into procedure, yet the dissatisfaction lying beneath a repressed grievance can produce all manner of unsatisfactory work behaviours from apathy to arson. Individual dissatisfaction can lead to the loss of a potentially valuable employee; collective dissatisfaction can lead to industrial action.

There are three types of complaint that get progressively harder to handle. The first kind is factual and can be readily tested:

- 'The machine is out of order.'
- 'The stock we're getting now is not up to standard.'
- 'This adhesive won't stick.'

The second type is complaints that are based partly on subjective reactions:

- 'The work is messy.'
- 'It's too hot in here.'
- 'This job is too stressful.'

These statements include terms where the meaning is biologically or socially determined and can therefore not be understood unless the background of the complainant is known; seldom can their accuracy be objectively determined. A temperature of 18 degrees Celsius may be too hot for one person but equable for another.

The third, and most difficult, type of complaint is that involving the hopes and fears of employees:

- 'The supervisor has favourites, who get the best jobs.'
- 'The pay is not very good.'
- 'Seniority doesn't count as much as it should.'

These show the importance of determining not only what employees feel, but also why they feel as they do; not only verifying the facts, which are the *manifest* content of the complaint, but also determining the feelings behind the facts: the *latent* content. An employee who complains of the supervisor being a bully may actually be expressing something rather different, such as the employee's attitude to any authority figure, not simply the supervisor who was the subject of the complaint.

Each type of dissatisfaction is important to uncover and act upon, if action is possible. Action is usually prompt on complaints of the first type, as they are neutral: blame is placed on an inanimate object so individual culpability is not an issue. Action may be quick on complaints of the second type if the required action is straightforward, such as opening a window if it is too hot, but the problem of accuracy can produce a tendency to smooth over an issue or leave it 'to sort itself out' in time. The third type of complaint is the most difficult, and action is often avoided. Supervisors will often take complaints to be a personal criticism of their own competence, and employees will often translate the complaint into a grievance only by attaching it to a third party such as a shop steward, so that the relationship between employee and supervisor is not jeopardised.

ACTIVITY 25.2

Think of an example from your own experience of dissatisfaction causing inefficiency that was not remedied because there was no complaint. Why was there no complaint?

THE FRAMEWORK OF ORGANISATIONAL JUSTICE

The organisation requires a framework of justice to surround the employment relationship so that managers and supervisors, as well as other employees, know where they stand when dissatisfaction develops. An illustration of this is in Figure 25.2.

Organisation culture and management style

The culture of an organisation affects the behaviour of people within it and develops norms that are hard to alter and which provide a pattern of conformity. If, for instance, everyone is in the habit of arriving ten minutes late, a 'new broom' manager will have a struggle to change the habit. Equally, if everyone is in the habit of arriving punctually, then a new recruit who often arrives late will come under strong social pressure to conform, without need for recourse to management action. Culture also affects the freedom and candour with which people discuss dissatisfactions with their managers without allowing them to fester.

The style of managers in handling grievances and discipline reflects their beliefs. The manager who sees discipline as being punishment, and who regards grievances as examples of subordinates getting above themselves, will behave in a relatively autocratic way, being curt in disciplinary situations and dismissive of complaints. The manager who sees disciplinary problems as obstacles to achievement that do not necessarily imply incompetence or ill will by the employee will seek out the cause of

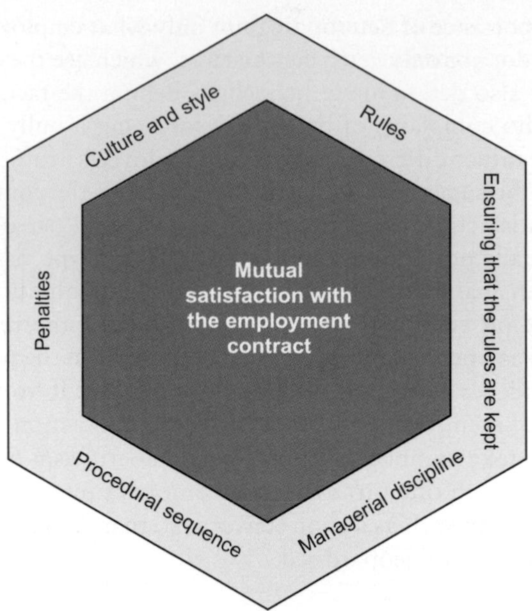

Figure 25.2 The framework of organisational justice

the problem. That problem may then be revealed as one requiring firm, punitive action by the manager, or it may be revealed as a matter requiring management remedy of a different kind. The manager who listens out for complaints and grievances, gets to the bottom of the problems and finds solutions will run little risk of rumbling discontent from people obsessed by trivial problems.

Rules

Every workplace has rules; the difficulty is to have rules that people will honour. Some rules come from legislation, such as the tachograph requirement for HGV drivers, but most are tailored to meet the particular requirements of the organisation in which they apply. For example, rules about personal cleanliness are essential in a food factory but less stringent in a garage.

Rules should be clear and readily understood; the number should be sufficient to cover all obvious and usual disciplinary matters. To ensure general compliance it is helpful if rules are jointly determined, but it is more common for management to formulate the rules and for employee representatives eventually to concur with them. Employees should have ready access to the rules through the employee handbook and noticeboard, and the HR manager will always try to ensure that the rules are known as well as published.

Rules can be roughly grouped into various types:

1 Negligence is failure to do the job properly and is different from incompetence because of the assumption that the employee can do the job properly, but has not.

2 Unreliability is failure to attend work as required, such as being late or absent.

3 Insubordination is refusal to obey an instruction, or deliberate disrespect to someone in a position of authority. It is not to be confused with the use of bad language. Some of the most entertaining cases in industrial tribunals have involved weighty consideration of whether or not colourful language was intended to be insubordinate.

4 Interfering with the rights of others covers a range of behaviours that are socially unacceptable. Fighting is clearly identifiable, but harassment or intimidation may be more difficult to establish.

5 Theft is another clear-cut aspect of behaviour that is unacceptable when it is from another employee. Theft from the organisation should be supported by very explicit rules, as stealing company property is regarded by many offenders as one of the perks of the job. How often have you taken home a box of paper clips or a felt tip pen without any thought that you were stealing from the employer?

6 Safety offences are those aspects of behaviour that can cause a hazard.

The value of rules is to provide guidelines on what people should do, as the majority will comply. It is extremely difficult to apply rules that do not command general acceptance.

WINDOW ON PRACTICE

In a recent discussion with a group of senior managers, employees identified the following as legitimately taken at will:

paper clips, pencils, disposable pens, spiral pads, local telephone calls, plain paper, computer disks, adhesive tape, overalls and simple uniform.

Among the more problematic were:

- Redundant or shop-soiled stock. One DIY store insisted that the store manager should personally supervise the scrapping of items that were slightly damaged, to ensure that other items were not slightly damaged on purpose.
- Surplus materials. One electricity supplier had some difficulty in eradicating the practice of surplus cable and pipe being regarded as a legitimate perquisite of fitters at the end of installation jobs, as they suspected their engineers were using the surplus for private work. Twelve months later the level of material requisition had declined by 14 per cent.

Ensuring that the rules are kept

It is not sufficient just to have rules; they are only effective if they are observed. How do we make sure that employees stick to the rules?

1 Information is needed so that everyone knows what the rules are and why they should be obeyed. Written particulars may suffice in an employment tribunal hearing, but most people conform to the behaviour of their colleagues, so informal methods of communication are just as important as formal statements.

2 **Induction** can make the rules coherent and reinforce their understanding. Rules can be explained, perhaps with examples, so that people not only know the rules but also understand why they should be obeyed.

3 **Placement or relocation** can avoid the risk of rules being broken, by placing a new recruit with a working team that has high standards of compliance. If there are the signs of disciplinary problems in the offing, then a quick relocation can put the problem employee in a new situation where offences are less likely.

4 **Training** increases awareness of the rules, improving self-confidence and self-discipline. There will be new working procedures or new equipment from time to time, and again training will reduce the risk of safety offences, negligence or unreliability.

5 **Reviewing the rules periodically** ensures that they are up to date, and also ensures that their observance is a live issue. If, for instance, there is a monthly staff council meeting, it could be appropriate to have a rules review every 12 months. The simple fact of the rules being discussed keeps up the general level of awareness of what they are.

6 **Penalties** make the framework of organisational justice firmer if there is an understanding of what penalties can be imposed, by whom and for what. It is not feasible to have a fixed scale, but neither is it wise for penalties to depend on individual managerial whim. This area has been partially codified by the legislation on dismissal, but the following are some typical forms of penalty:

a **Rebuke.** The simple 'Don't do that' or 'Smoking is not allowed in here' or 'If you're late again, you will be in trouble' is all that is needed in most situations, as someone has forgotten one of the rules, had not realised it was to be taken seriously, or was perhaps testing the resolution of the management. Too frequently, managers are reluctant to risk defiance and tend to wait until they have a good case for more serious action rather than deploy their own, there-and-then authority.

b **Caution.** Slightly more serious and formal is the caution, which is then recorded. This is not triggering the procedure for dismissal, it is just making a note of a rule being broken and an offence being pointed out.

c **Warnings.** When the management begins to issue warnings, great care is required. This is because the development of unfair dismissal legislation has made the system of warnings an integral part of disciplinary practice, and this has to be followed if the employer is to succeed in defending a possible claim of unfair dismissal at tribunal. For the employer to show procedural fairness there should normally be a formal oral warning, or a written warning, specifying the nature of the offence and the likely outcome if the offence is repeated. It should also be made clear that this is the first, formal stage in the procedure. Further misconduct could then warrant a final written warning containing a statement that further repetition would lead to a penalty such as suspension or dismissal. All written warnings should be dated, signed and kept on record for an agreed period. The means of appeal against the disciplinary action should also be pointed out.

d **Disciplinary transfer or demotion.** This is moving the employee to less attractive work, possibly carrying a lower salary. The seriousness of this is that it is public, as the employee's colleagues know the reason. A form of disciplinary transfer is found on assembly lines, where there are some jobs that are more attractive and carry higher status than others. Rule breakers may be 'pushed down the line' until their contempt is purged and they are able to move back up.

e **Suspension.** This is a tactic that has the benefit of being serious and avoids the disadvantage of being long lasting, as demotion is. The employer has a contractual obligation to provide pay, but not to provide work, so it is easy to suspend someone from duty with pay either as a punishment or while an alleged offence is being investigated. If the contract of employment permits, it may also be possible to suspend the employee for a short period without pay.

The important general comment about penalties is that they should be appropriate in the circumstances. Where someone is, for instance, persistently late or absent, suspension would be a strange penalty. Also penalties must be within the law. An employee cannot be demoted or transferred at managerial whim, and unpaid suspension can only be imposed if the contract of employment allows it.

Procedural sequence

This is the clear, unvarying logic of procedure, which should be well known and trusted. Procedure makes clear, for example, who does and who does not have the power to dismiss. The dissatisfied employee, who is wondering whether or not to turn a complaint into a formal grievance, knows who will hear the grievance and where an appeal could be lodged. This security of procedure, where step B always follows step A, is needed by managers as well as by employees, as it provides them with their authority as well as limiting the scope of their actions.

Managerial discipline

This preserves general respect for the justice framework by managers exercising self-discipline in how they work within it. With very good intentions some senior managers maintain an 'open door' policy with the message: 'My door is always open . . . call in any time you feel I can help you'. This has many advantages and is often necessary, but it has danger for matters of discipline and grievance if it encourages people to bypass middle managers. There is also the danger that employees come to see the settlement of their grievances as being dependent on the personal goodwill of an individual rather than on the business logic or their human and employment rights.

Managers must be consistent in handling discipline and grievance issues. Whatever the rules are, they will be generally supported only as long as they deserve support. If they are enforced inconsistently they will soon lose any moral authority, and will be obeyed only because of employees' fear of penalties. Equally, the manager who handles grievances quickly and consistently will enjoy the support of a committed group of employees.

The other need for managerial discipline is to test the validity of the discipline assumption. Is it a case for disciplinary action or for some other remedy? There is little purpose in suspending someone for negligence when the real problem is lack of training. Many disciplinary problems disappear under analysis, and it is sensible to carry out the analysis before making a possibly unjustified allegation of indiscipline.

GRIEVANCE PROCEDURE

Managers who believe that it introduces unnecessary rigidity into the working relationship often resent the formality of the grievance procedure: 'I see my people all the time. We work side by side and they can raise with me any issue they want, at any time they want . . .' The problem is that many people will not raise issues with the immediate superior that could be regarded as contentious, in just the same way that managers frequently shirk the rebuke as a form of disciplinary penalty. Formality in procedure provides a structure within which individuals can reasonably air their grievances and avoids the likelihood of managers dodging the issue when it is difficult. It avoids the risk of inconsistent ad hoc decisions, and the employee knows at the outset that the matter will be heard and where it will be heard. The key features of grievance procedure are fairness, facilities for representation, procedural steps and promptness.

1 Fairness is needed, to be just, but also to keep the procedure viable. If employees develop the belief that the procedure is only a sham, then its value will be lost and other means will be sought to deal with grievances. Fairness is best supported by the obvious even-handedness of the ways in which grievances are handled, but it will be greatly enhanced if the appeal stage is either to a joint body or to independent arbitration, as the management is relinquishing the chance to be judge of its own cause.

2 Representation can help the individual employee who lacks the confidence or experience to take on the management singlehandedly. A representative, such as a union official, has the advantage of having dealt with a range of employee problems and may be able to advise the aggrieved person whether the claim is worth pursuing. There is always the risk that the presence of the representative produces a defensive management attitude affected by a number of other issues on which the manager and union official may be at loggerheads, so the managers involved in hearing the grievance have to cast the representative in the correct role for the occasion.

3 Procedural steps should be limited to three. There is no value in having more just because there are more levels in the management hierarchy. This will only lengthen the time taken to deal with matters and will soon bring the procedure into disrepute. The reason for advocating three steps is that three types of management activity are involved in settling grievances. Nevertheless, it is quite common for there to be more than three steps where there is a steep hierarchy, within which there may be further, more senior, people to whom the matter could be referred. The reason for there being more steps has nothing to do with how to process grievances but is purely a function of the organisation structure.

The first step is the *preliminary*, when the grievance is lodged with the immediate superior of the person with the complaint. In the normal working week most managers will have a variety of queries from members of their departments, some of which could become grievances, depending on the manager's reaction. Mostly the manager will either satisfy the employee or the employee will decide not to pursue the matter. Sometimes, however, a person will want to take the issue further. This is the preliminary step in procedure, but it is a tangible step as the manager has the opportunity to review any decisions made that have caused the dissatisfaction, possibly enabling the dissatisfied employee to withdraw the grievance. In our experience it is rare for matters to be taken any further unless the subject of the grievance is something on which company policy is being tested.

The *hearing* gives the complainant the opportunity to state the grievance to a more senior manager, who is able to take a broader view of the matter than the immediate superior and who may be able both to see the issue more dispassionately and to perceive solutions that the more limited perspective of the immediate superior obscured. It is important for the management that the hearing should finalise the matter whenever possible, so that recourse to appeal is not automatic. The hearing should not be seen by the employees as no more than an irritating milestone on the way to the real decision makers. This is why procedural steps should be limited to three.

If there is an *appeal*, this will usually be to a designated more senior manager, and the outcome will be either a confirmation or a modification of the decision at the hearing.

4 Promptness avoids the bitterness and frustration that comes from delay. When an employee 'goes into procedure', it is like pulling the communication cord in a train. The action is not taken lightly and is in anticipation of a swift resolution. Furthermore, the manager whose decision is being questioned will have a difficult time until the matter is resolved. The most familiar device to speed things up is to incorporate time limits between the steps, specifying that the hearing should take place no later than, say, four working days after the preliminary notice and that the appeal should be no more than five working days after the hearing. This gives time for reflection and initiative by the manager or the complainant between the stages, but does not leave time for the matter to be forgotten.

Where the organisation has a collective disputes procedure as well as one for individual grievances, there needs to be an explicit link between the two so that individual matters can be pursued with collective support if there is not a satisfactory outcome. An outline grievance procedure is in Figure 25.3.

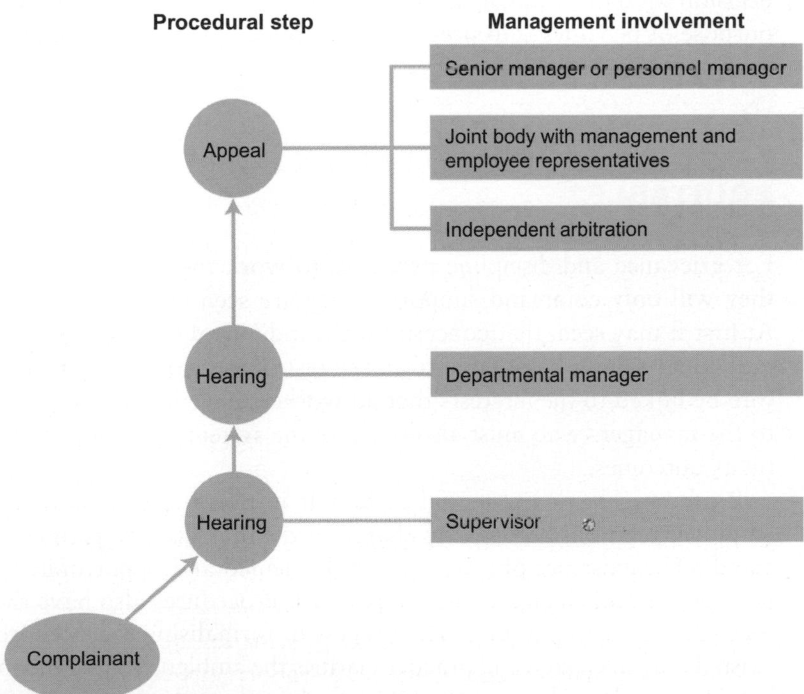

Figure 25.3 Outline grievance procedure

DISCIPLINARY PROCEDURE

Procedures for discipline are very similar to those for grievance and depend equally on fairness, promptness and representation. There are some additional features.

Authorisation of penalties

The law requires that managers should not normally have the power to dismiss their immediate subordinates without reference to more senior managers. Whatever penalties are to be imposed, they should only be imposed by people who have that specific authority delegated to them. Usually this means that the more serious penalties can only be imposed by more senior people, but there are many organisations where such decisions are delegated to the HR department.

Investigation

The procedure should also ensure that disciplinary action is not taken until it has been established that there is a problem that justifies the action. The possibility of suspension on full pay is one way of allowing time for the investigation of dubious allegations, but the stigma attached to such suspensions should not be forgotten.

Information and explanation

If disciplinary action is possible, the person to be disciplined should be told of the complaint, so that an explanation can be made, or the matter denied, before any penalties are decided. If an employee is to be penalised, then the reasons for the decision should be explained to make sure that cause and effect are appreciated. The purpose of penalties is to prevent a recurrence. An outline disciplinary procedure is in Figure 25.4.

ARE GRIEVANCE AND DISCIPLINE PROCESSES EQUITABLE?

For grievance and discipline processes to work they must command support, and they will only command support if they are seen as equitable, truly just and fair. At first it may seem that concern for the individual employee is paramount, but the individual cannot be isolated from the rest of the workforce. Fairness should therefore be linked to the interests that all workers have in common in the business, and to the managers who must also perceive the system as equitable if they are to abide by its outcomes.

Procedures have a potential to be fair in that they are certain. The conduct of employee relations becomes less haphazard and irrational: people 'know where they stand'. The existence of a rule cannot be denied and opportunities for one party to manipulate and change a rule are reduced. Procedures also have the advantage that they can be communicated. The process of formalising a procedure that previously existed only in custom and practice clarifies the ambiguities and inconsistencies within it and compels each party to recognise the role and responsibility of the other. By providing pre-established avenues for responses to various contingencies, procedures

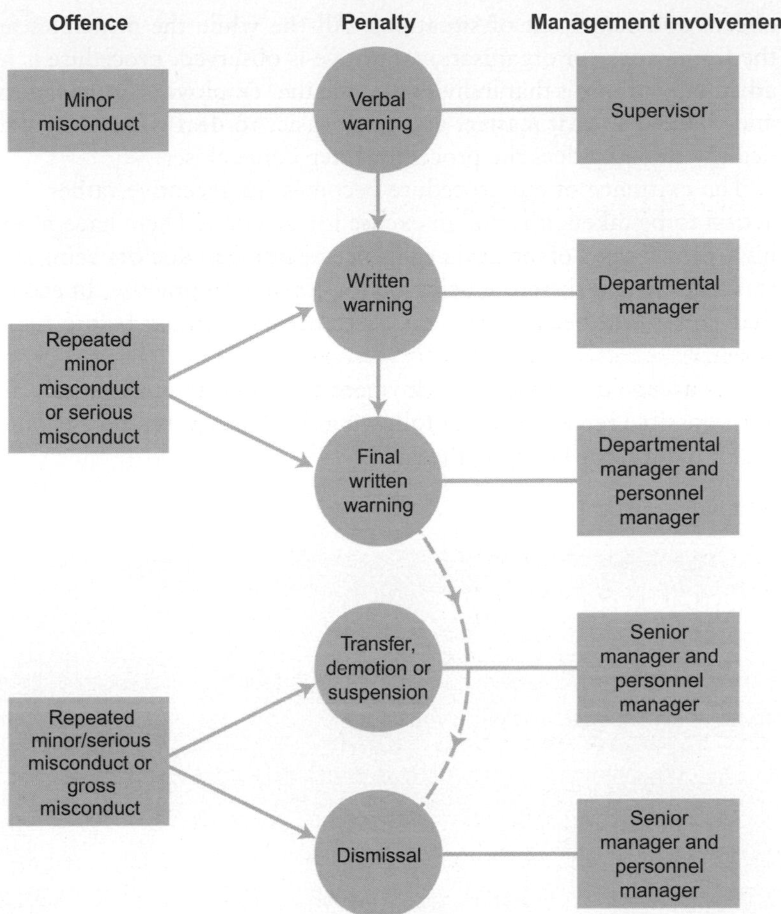

Figure 25.4 Outline disciplinary procedure

make it possible for the response to be less random and so more fair. The impersonal nature of procedures offers the possibility of removing hostility from the workplace, since an artificial social situation is created in which the ritual displays of aggression towards management are not seen as personal attacks on managers.

The achievement of equity may not match the potential. Procedures cannot, for instance, impart equity to situations that are basically unfair. Thus attempting to cope with an anomalous pay system through a grievance procedure may be alleviating symptoms rather than treating causes. It is also impossible through a grievance procedure to overcome accepted norms of inequity in a company, such as greater punctuality being required of manual employees than of white-collar employees.

A further feature of procedural equity is its degree of similarity to the judicial process. All procedures adopt certain legalistic mechanisms, such as the right of individuals to be represented and to hear the case against them, but some aspects of legalism, such as burdens of proof and strict adherence to precedent, may cause the application of standard remedies rather than the consideration of individual circumstances.

There is a nice irony in the fact that equity is best achieved when procedures are not used. Procedure is there in the background and expresses principles for fair and effective management of situations. All the while the **principles** are followed and the framework for organisational justice is observed, procedure is not invoked. The advantage of this is that individuals, whether employees or managers, are not named and shamed so that matters are much easier to deal with. Only when the matter is dealt with badly does the procedural step come closer.

The existence of the procedure becomes the incentive rather than the means for action to be taken: it is not an excuse for inaction. There have recently been several high-profile cases of medical negligence resulting in doctors being struck off the medical register and therefore being no longer able to practise. In each case it appeared that lapses had been allowed to continue for too long before remedial action was taken.

It is accepted that some employment situations require naming and shaming first, with possible remedial action following. In most sports there is on-the-spot penalising of players for breaking the rules.

WINDOW ON PRACTICE

The 'red-hot stove' rule of discipline offers the touching of a red hot stove as an analogy for effective disciplinary action:

1. The burn is immediate. There is no question of cause and effect.
2. You had warning. If the stove was red-hot, you knew what would happen if you touched it.
3. The discipline is consistent. Everyone who touches the stove is burned.
4. The discipline is impersonal. People are burned not because of who they are, but because they touch the stove.

ACTIVITY 25.3

Think of an attempt at disciplinary action that went wrong. Which of the features of the red-hot stove rule were missing?

Notions of fairness are not 'givens' of the situation; they are socially constructed and there will never be more than a degree of consensus on what constitutes fairness. Despite this, the procedural approach can exploit standards of certainty and consistency, which are widely accepted as elements of justice. The extent to which a procedure can do this will depend on the suitability of its structure to local circumstances, the commitment of those who operate it and the way that it reconciles legalistic and bargaining elements.

SUMMARY PROPOSITIONS

25.1 The authority of managers to exercise discipline in relation to others in the organisation is underpinned by a general predilection of people to obey commands from those holding higher rank in the hierarchy of which they are members.

25.2 The exercise of that discipline is limited by the procedural structures for grievance and discipline.

25.3 Grievance and discipline handling are two areas of human resource management that few other people want to take over, and provide HR managers with some of their most significant contributions to business effectiveness.

25.4 Discipline can be understood as being managerial, team or self-discipline, and the three types are connected hierarchically.

25.5 Dissatisfaction, complaint and grievance form another hierarchy. Unresolved employee dissatisfaction can lead to the loss of potentially valuable employees. In extreme cases it can lead to industrial action.

25.6 Grievance and disciplinary processes both require a framework of organisational justice.

25.7 The procedural framework of disciplinary and grievance processes is one of the keys to their being equitable.

25.8 Effective management of both discipline and grievance is achieved by following the principles of the procedures without invoking them in practice.

GENERAL DISCUSSION TOPICS

1 Do you think Milgram's experiments would have had a different outcome if the subjects had included women as well as men?

2 What examples can individual members of the group cite of self-discipline, team discipline and managerial discipline?

3 'The trouble with grievance procedures is that they encourage people to waste a lot of time with petty grumbles. Life at work is rarely straightforward and people should just accept the rough with the smooth.'

What do you think of that opinion?

FURTHER READING

Torrington, D.P., Earnshaw, J.M., Marchington, L. and Ritchie, M.D. (2003) *Tackling Underperformance in Teaching*. London: Routledge

This is a report on research regarding teachers' alleged lack of capability. The results, including a number of case studies, are really an object lesson in how *not* to deal with a problem. The reader will easily work out how the matters *should* have been dealt with. Whether they would actually have done any better is debatable. Handling misconduct is easy; handling lack of capability is much more difficult.

REFERENCES

Abrams, D., Wetherell, M., Cochrane, S., Hogg, M.A. and Turner, J.C. (1990) 'Knowing what to think by knowing who you are: Self categorization and norm formation', *British Journal of Social Psychology*, Vol. 29, pp. 97–119.

Advisory, Conciliation and Arbitration Service (2000) *Code of Practice on Disciplinary Practice and Grievance Procedures at Work*. London: HMSO.

Asch, S.E. (1951) 'Effect of group pressure upon the modification and distortion of judgements', in H. Guetzkow (ed.) *Groups, Leadership and Men*. Pittsburgh, Penn.: Carnegie Press.

Edwards, P. (2000) 'Discipline: towards trust and self-discipline', in S. Bach and K. Sisson (eds) *Personnel Management*, 3rd edn. Oxford: Blackwell.

Gross, R. and McIlveen, R. (1998) *Psychology: A New Introduction*. London: Hodder & Stoughton.

Handy, C.B. (1999) *The New Alchemists*. London: Hutchinson.

Mathis, R.L. and Jackson, J.H. (1994) *Human Resource Management*, 7th edn. Minneapolis/St Paul, Minn.: West Publishing.

Milgram, S. (1974) *Obedience to Authority*. London: Tavistock.

Milgram, S. (1992) *The Individual in a Social World*, 2nd edn. New York: Harper & Row.

Pigors, P. and Myers, C. (1977) *Personnel Administration*, 8th edn. Maidenhead: McGraw-Hill.

Torrington, D.P., Earnshaw, J.M., Marchington, L. and Ritchie, M.D. (2003) *Tackling Underperformance in Teachers*. London: Routledge.

An extensive range of additional materials, including multiple choice questions, answers to questions and links to useful websites can be found on the Human Resource Management Companion Website at **www.pearsoned.co.uk/torrington**.

Part V FOCUS ON SKILLS

INTERACTIVE SKILL 5: GRIEVANCE AND DISCIPLINARY INTERVIEWING

In concluding this Part we pick up on the theme of Chapter 25 by considering grievance and disciplinary interviewing. This type of interactive skill falls into the fourth category of face-to-face situations that we described in the first of our Focuses on skills, namely conflict resolution (*see* Figure I.1).

We said earlier that the appraisal interview was the hardest aspect of management for any manager to undertake. The subject now is the least popular of all management activities: talking to people when things have gone wrong. Reading most books on management you might think that things never go wrong. The writing has such an upbeat tone that it is *entirely* positive, enthusiastic, visionary, forward looking and all the other qualities that are so important. Sometimes, however, things really do go wrong and have to be sorted out. The sorting out involves at some point a meeting between a dissatisfied manager and an employee who is seen as the cause of that dissatisfaction, or between a dissatisfied employee and a manager representing the employing organisation that is seen as the cause of the employee's dissatisfaction. Procedures, as described in Chapter 25, can do no more than force meetings to take place: it is the meetings themselves that produce answers.

The objectives of this Focus on skills are:

1 To review concepts of discipline and grievance

2 To examine the nature of interviewing in grievance and discipline

3 To outline an approach to grievance and discipline interviewing by suggesting model sequences

Many present-day views of discipline are connected with the idea of punishment, as we saw in the last chapter; a disciplinarian is one seen as an enforcer of rules, a hard taskmaster or martinet. To discipline schoolchildren is usually to punish them by keeping them in after school or chastising them. Disciplinary procedures in employment are usually drawn up to provide a preliminary to dismissal, so that any eventual dismissal will not be viewed as unfair by a tribunal. This background makes a problem-solving approach to discipline difficult for a manager, as there is always the sanction in the background making it unlikely that the employee will see the manager's behaviour as being authentic. There will always be a feeling somewhere between outright conviction and lingering uncertainty that a manager in a disciplinary interview is looking for a justification to punish rather than looking for a more constructive solution. The approach of this Focus on skills is based on the more accurate notion of discipline implied in its derivation from the Latin *discere*, to learn and *discipulus*, learner. In disciplinary interviews the manager is attempting to modify the working behaviour of a subordinate, but the modification does not necessarily involve punishment.

The idea of grievance similarly has problems of definition and ethos. In the last chapter we used the convenient scale of dissatisfaction–complaint–grievance as an explanation, but that is a convenient technical classification. The general sense of the word is closer to the dictionary definitions which use phrases such as 'a real or imaginary wrong causing resentment' or 'a feeling of injustice, of having been unfairly treated'. Notions of resentment and injustice seem too heavy for situations where the basic problem is that the maintenance crew have fallen down on the job or the central heating is not working properly. Where we have unresolved problems about our jobs (even when we are deeply worried by them) we are often reluctant to construe our feelings as 'having a grievance'. We just want to get more information, or an opportunity for training, or a chance to talk to someone a bit more senior. Very few people indeed want to be seen to be grumbling. Customers are generally reluctant to grumble about the service they receive, because it is too much trouble, because no one would listen, or just because they do not want to make a fuss; yet they can simply walk away. Compared with customers, employees are much less inclined to complain, or even to point out problems, for fear of being categorised as a nuisance.

Despite the difficulties, our aim here is to formulate an approach to the interview that achieves an adjustment in attitude, with the changed attitude being confirmed by subsequent experience. Either the manager believes that the employee's subsequent working behaviour will be satisfactory, or the employee believes that his or her subsequent experience in employment will be satisfactory. The conflict of interest between the parties is resolved and the interview only succeeds when there is that confirmation.

In his profound and simple book of 1960, Douglas McGregor advocated an approach to management based on the strategy of *integration and self-control*. He regarded forms and procedures as having little value and emphasised the importance of social interaction as well as the difficulty of achieving any change in people's interactive behaviour:

> Every adult human being has an elaborate history of past experience in this field and additional learning is profoundly influenced by that history. From infancy on, his ability to achieve his goals and satisfy his needs – his 'social survival' – has been a function of his skills in influencing others. Deep emotional currents – unconscious needs such as those related to dependency and counterdependency – are involved. He has a large 'ego investment' and his knowledge and skill in this area, and the defences he has built to protect that investment are strong and psychologically complex. (McGregor 1960, p. 75)

Just as we set grievance and discipline alongside each other in the last chapter, similarly we examine here the grievance/disciplinary encounter in the same framework, as both are trying to tackle dissatisfaction where resolution of the problem is not straightforward. If Jim sets fire to the Plant Director's office and admits to the police that he did it for a lark because he was bored, then any disciplinary interview ought not be too difficult. If Joe is not working as well as he used to, but nobody quite knows why and he refuses to say anything about it to anyone, then there is the less straightforward situation with which the approach of this Focus on skills might help.

ACTIVITY V.1

What grievance or disciplinary incidents can you recall where the situation was not clear-cut and where an interview with a manager produced a resolution to the problem that was effective, although quite different from what had been anticipated by the manager at the beginning of the interview?

The nature of grievance and disciplinary interviewing

Many grievance or discipline interviews are simple: giving information, explaining work requirements and delivering rebukes, but from time to time every manager will need to use a problem-solving approach, involving sympathy, perception, empathy and the essential further feature that some managers provide only with reluctance: time. The method will be analytical and constructive; not only for the interviews built in to the grievance and discipline procedure, but also for interviews that avoid recourse to the rigid formality of procedure. We see such interviews as one of the means towards *self-discipline* and *autonomy* of employees, reducing the need for supervision. The sequence we advocate has discipline and grievance intertwined for much of the process but diverging in the interview itself (*see* Figure V.1).

As we have shown in the previous chapter, a grievance may be expressed only in manifest form, requiring interviewing to understand its latent content in order

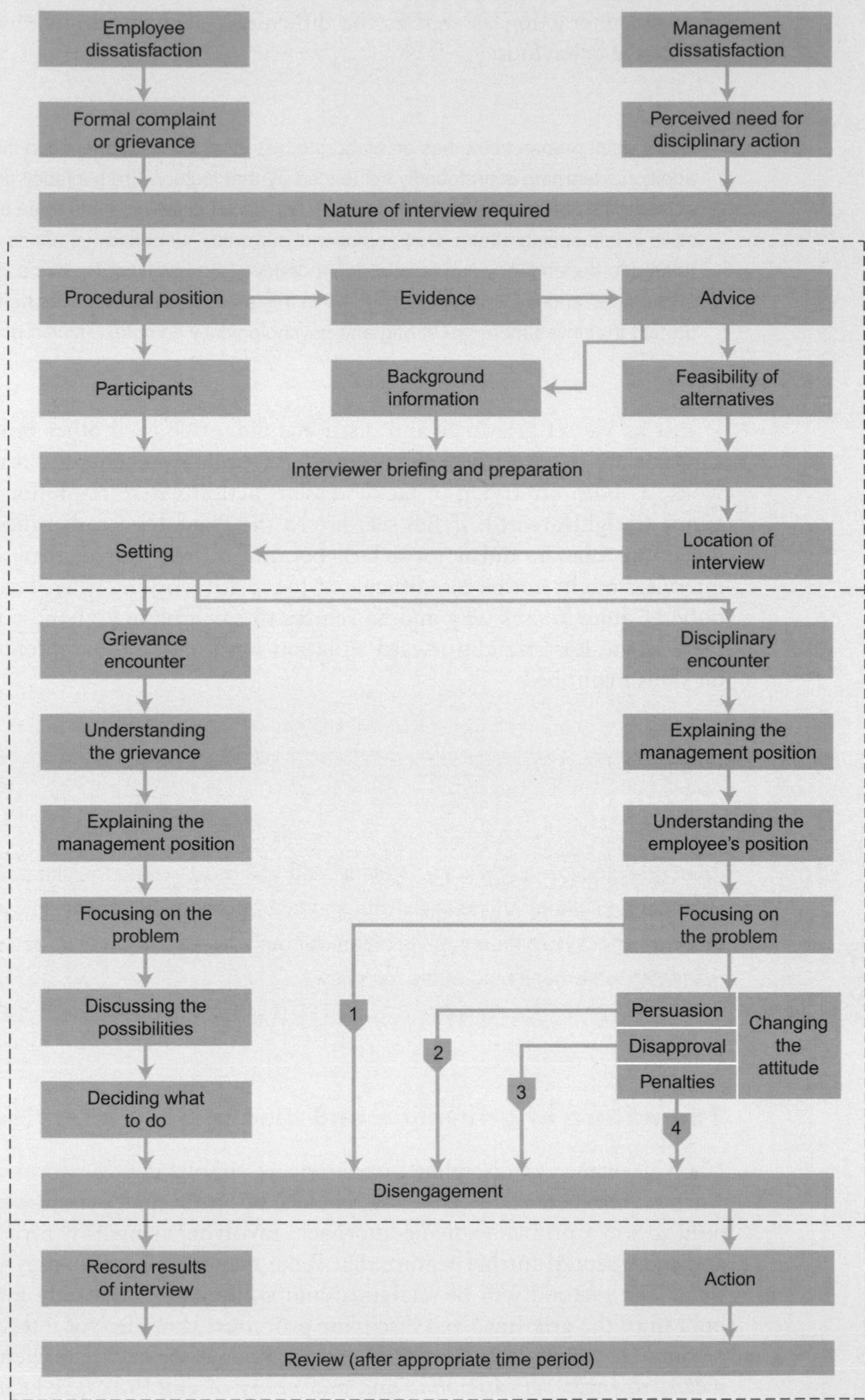

Figure V.1 The grievance and disciplinary interviews

that appropriate action is taken to remove the underlying dissatisfaction. Discipline problems will have underlying reasons for the unsatisfactory behaviour and these need to be discovered before solutions to the problems can be attempted.

The discipline and grievance sequence

Preparation

The first requirement is to check the procedural position and to ensure that the impending interview is appropriate. In a grievance situation, for instance, is the employee pre-empting the procedure by taking the matter to the wrong person or to the wrong point in the procedure? This is most common when the first-line supervisor is being bypassed, either because the employee or the representative feels that it would be a waste of time, or perhaps because the supervisor is unsure of the appropriate action and is conniving at the side-stepping of the procedure. It is also possible that the supervisor knows what to do but is shirking the responsibility or the potential unpopularity of what has to be done.

In disciplinary matters even more care is needed about the procedural step, as the likelihood of penalties may already have been set up by warnings, thus reducing the scope for doing anything else in the impending interview apart from imposing a further penalty. In the majority of cases we believe that interviews will precede procedure, in which case the parties to the interview are less constrained by procedural rules. In these situations the manager will be at pains to establish that the interview is informal and without procedural implications. Alternatively the interview may be in a situation where the likelihood of a move into procedure is so remote that the manager will be at pains to avoid any such reference, for fear of the complainant taking fright.

Who will be there? Here there are similar procedural considerations. In procedure there is the likelihood of employee representation; out of procedure there is less likelihood of that, even though the employee may feel anxious and threatened without it. If the manager is accompanied in the interview, the employee may feel even more insecure, and it is doubtful how much can be achieved informally unless the employee feels reasonably secure and able to speak frankly.

What are the facts that the interviewer needs to know? In grievance it will be necessary to know the subject of the grievance and how it has arisen. This type of information will have been filtered through the management hierarchy and may well have been modified in the process, so it needs to be considered carefully and any additional background information collected.

Disciplinary interviews always start at the behest of the management so the manager will again need to collect evidence and consider how it may have been interpreted by intermediaries. This evidence will include some basic details about the interviewee, but mainly it will be information about the aspects of the working performance that are unsatisfactory and why. Too often this information exists only in opinions that have been offered and prejudices that are held. This provides a poor basis for a constructive interview, so the manager needs to ferret out details, with as much factual corroboration as possible, and should try to make a shrewd guess about the interviewee's perspective on the situation.

It is almost inevitable that the interviewee will start the interview defensively, expecting to be blamed for something and therefore ready to refute any allegations, probably deflecting blame elsewhere. The manager needs to anticipate the respondent's initial reaction and be prepared to deal with the reaction as well as with facts that have been collected. Unless the interview is at an early, informal stage, the manager also needs to know about earlier warnings, cautions or penalties that have been invoked.

For both types of interview there will be more general information that is required. Not just the facts of the particular grievance or disciplinary situation, but knowledge to give a general understanding of the working arrangements and relationships, will be required. Other relevant data may concern the employee's length of service, type of training, previous experience, and so forth.

Most managers approaching a grievance or disciplinary interview will benefit from advice before starting. It is particularly important for anyone who is in procedure to check the position with someone such as a personnel officer before starting, as management ability to sustain any action will largely depend on maintaining consistency with what the management has done with other employees previously. The manager may also have certain ideas of what could be done in terms of retraining, transfer or assistance with a domestic problem. The manager needs to verify the feasibility of such actions before broaching them with an aggrieved employee or with an employee whose work is not satisfactory.

Where is the interview to take place? However trivial this question may seem it is included for two reasons. First, because we have seen a number of interviews go sadly awry because the parties arrived at different places; this mistake seems to happen more often with this type of encounter than with others. Second, because there may be an advantage in choosing an unusually informal situation, or an unusually formal location, according to the manager's assessment. A discussion over a pie and a pint in the local pub may be a more appropriate setting for some approaches to grievance and disciplinary problems, although they are seldom appropriate if the matter has reached procedure. Also employees frequently mistrust such settings, feeling that they are being manipulated or that the discussion 'does not count' because it is out of hours or off limits. If, however, one is trying to avoid procedural overtones, this can be a way of doing it.

Unusual formality can be appropriate in the later stages of procedure, especially in disciplinary matters, when proceedings take on a strongly judicial air. An employee is not likely to take seriously a final warning prior to probable dismissal if it is delivered over a pint in a pub. The large, impressive offices of senior managers can provide appropriate settings for the final stages of procedure.

ACTIVITY V.2

What incidents have you experienced or heard about where the location of the interview was clearly unsuitable for the nature of the encounter?

The grievance interview

The first step in the grievance interview is for the manager to be clear about what the grievance is; a simple way of doing this is to state the *subject* of the grievance and get confirmation from the employee that it is correct. The importance of this lies in the probability that the manager will have a different perspective on the affair from the employee, particularly if it has got beyond the preliminary stage. A supervisor may report to a superior that Mr X has a grievance and 'will not take instructions from me', but when the interview begins Mr X may state his grievance as being that he is unwilling to work on Saturday mornings. In other situations it might be the other way round, with the supervisor reporting that Mr X will not work Saturday mornings and Mr X saying in the interview that he finds the style of his supervisor objectionable. Even where there is no such confusion, an opening statement and confirmation of the subject demonstrate that the two parties are talking about the same thing.

Having clarified or confirmed the subject of the grievance, the manager will then invite the employee to state the case, explaining the nature and reasons for the dissatisfaction. This enables the employee to explain why he or she is aggrieved, citing examples, providing further information and saying not just 'what' but also 'why'. Seldom will this be done well. The presentation of a case is not a particularly easy task for the inexperienced, and few aggrieved employees are experienced at making a case of this type. Furthermore, there is the inhibition of questioning the wisdom of those in power and some apprehension about the outcome. Because of this the manager will need to ask questions after the declaration of the case in order to fill in the gaps that have been left by the employee and to clarify some points that were obscure in the first telling. As a general rule it seems better to have an episode of questioning after the case has been made, rather than to interrupt on each point that is difficult. Interruptions make a poorly argued case even more difficult to sustain. There may, however, be disguised pleas for assistance that provide good opportunities for questioning to clarify: 'I'm not very good with words, but do you see what I'm getting at?' 'Do you see what I mean?' or 'Am I making myself clear?' Among the communication ploys that the manager will need at this stage could be the method of *reflection* that was mentioned briefly in our first Focus on skills. Its application in this context is described more fully by Beveridge:

> a selective form of listening in which the listener picks out the emotional overtones of a statement and 'reflects' these back to the respondent without making any attempt to evaluate them. This means that the interviewer expresses neither approval nor disapproval, neither sympathy nor condemnation. Because the respondent may be in an emotional state, sympathy is liable to make him feel resentful and angry. Any attempt to get the respondent to look objectively and rationally at his problem at this stage is also likely to fail; he is still too confused and upset to be able to do this and will interpret the very attempt as criticism. (Beveridge 1968, p. 121)

After all the necessary clarification has been obtained the manager will restate the employee grievance, together with an outline of the case that has been presented, and will ask the employee to agree with the summary or to correct it. By this means the manager is confirming and demonstrating an understanding of what the grievance is about and why it has been brought. This is not agreeing with it or dismissing it; all that has happened is that the grievance is now understood.

This phase of the interview can be summarised in sequential terms:

Manager	Employee
1 States subject of grievance	
	2 Agrees with statement
	3 States case
4 Questions for clarification	
5 Re-states grievance	
	6 Agrees or corrects

The grievance is now understood

The next phase is to set out the management position on the grievance. This is not the action *to be taken* but the action that *has been taken*, with the reasons for the action; this phase may include an explanation of company policy, safety rules, previous grievances, supervisory problems, administrative methods and anything else which is needed to make clear why the management position has been what it has been. The manager will then invite the employee to question and comment on the management position to ensure that it is understood and the justifications for it are understood, even if they are not accepted. The objective is to ensure that the parties to the discussion see and understand each other's point of view.

The management position is now understood

Setting out the two opposed positions will have revealed a deal of common ground. The parties will agree on some things, though disagreeing on others. In the third phase of the interview the manager and employee sort through what they have discussed and identify the points of disagreement. At this stage the points on which they agree can be ignored, as the need now is to find the outer limits. This is very similar to the differentiation stage in negotiation, which is explained in the Part VI Focus on skills.

Points of disagreement are now in focus

As a preliminary to taking action in the matter under discussion, various possibilities can be put up for consideration. It is logical that the employee's suggestions are put first. Probably this has already been done either explicitly or implicitly in the development of the case. If, however, specific suggestions are invited at this stage they may be different ones, as the aggrieved employee now understands the management position and is seeing the whole matter clearly following the focusing that has just taken place. Then the manager can put forward alternatives or modifications, and such alternatives may include, or be limited to, the suggestion that the grievance is mischievous and unfounded so that no action should be taken. Nevertheless, in most cases there will be some scope for accommodation even if it is quite different from the employee's expectation. Once the alternative suggestions for action are set out, there is time for the advantages and disadvantages of both sets to be discussed.

Alternatives have now been considered

A grievance interview is one that falls short of the mutual dependence that is present in negotiation, so that the decision on action is to be taken by the manager alone; it is not a joint decision even though the manager will presumably be looking for a decision that all parties will find acceptable. In bringing a grievance the employee is challenging a management decision and that decision will now be confirmed or it will be modified, but it remains a management decision.

Before making the decision the manager may deploy a range of behaviours to ensure that the decision is correct. It may be useful to test the employee's reaction by thinking aloud, 'Well, I don't know, but it looks to me as if we shall have to disappoint you on this one . . .' There may be an adjournment for a while to seek further advice or to give the employee time to reflect further, but the manager has to decide and then explain the decision to the employee. In this way the manager is not simply deciding and announcing, but supporting the decision with explanation and justification in the same way that the employee developed the case for the grievance at the beginning. There may be employee questions, the employee may want time to think, but eventually the management decision will have to be accepted, unless there is some further procedural step available.

Management action is now clear and understood.

The disciplinary interview

Discipline arises from management dissatisfaction rather than employee dissatisfaction with the employment contract, so the opening move is for a statement of why such dissatisfaction exists, dealing with the *facts* of the situation rather than managerial feelings of outrage about the facts. This shows that the interview is being approached by the manager as a way of dealing with a problem of the working situation and not (at least not yet) as a way of dealing with a malicious or indolent employee. If an employee has been persistently late for a week, it would be unwise for a manager to open the disciplinary interview by saying, 'Your lateness this week has been deplorable' as the reason might turn out to be that the employee has a seriously ill child needing constant attendance through the night. Then the manager would be embarrassed and the potential for a constructive settlement of the matter would be jeopardised. An opening factual statement of the problem, 'You have been at least twenty minutes late each day this week . . .', does not prejudge the reasons and is reasonably precise about the scale of the problem. It also circumscribes management dissatisfaction by implying that there is no other cause for dissatisfaction: if there is, it should be mentioned.

WINDOW ON PRACTICE

In the booklet *I'd Like a Word With You*, Tietjen decribes types of difficult interviewee, one of which is 'the professional weeper':

> This is the person who can turn on tears like turning on a tap. Some people are quite unmoved by tears, but lots of bosses find tears and emotion very hard to cope with. They are either very embarrassed or very apologetic that their words could have had such an effect. (1987, p. 26)

Another difficult interviewee is the 'counter-attacker':

> who operates on the maxim that the best defence is attack. Once you have stated your reasons for the interview, he will leap straight into the discussion, relishing the opportunity to 'have it out'. The obvious danger is that you respond to his aggression, that a battle of words will ensue and that nothing else will happen. (p. 28)

Notice that Ms Tietjen leaves the gender open in the first instance and specific in the second!

Now the manager needs to know the explanation and asks the employee to say what the reasons for the problem are, perhaps also asking for comments on the seriousness of the problem itself, which the employee may regard as trivial, while the manager regards it as serious. If there is such dissonance it needs to be drawn out. Getting the employees reaction is usually straightforward, but the manager needs to be prepared for one of two other types of reaction. Either there may be a need to probe because the employee is reluctant to open up, or there may be angry defiance. Disciplinary situations are at least disconcerting for employees and frequently very worrying, surrounded by feelings of hostility and mistrust, so that it is to be expected that some ill feeling will be pent up and waiting for the opportunity to be vented.

First possible move to disengagement

If the employee sees something of the management view of the problem and if the manager understands the reasons for the problem, the next requirement is to seek a solution. We have to point out that a disciplinary problem is as likely to be solved by management action as by employee action. If the problem is lateness, one solution would be for the employee to catch an earlier bus, but another might be for the management to alter the working shift to which the employee is assigned. If the employee is disobeying orders, one solution would be for them to start obeying them, but another might be for the employee to be moved to a different job where orders are received from someone else. Some managers regard such thinking as unreasonable, on the grounds that the contract of employment places obligations on individual employees that they should meet despite personal inconvenience. However, the point is not how people *should* behave, but how they do. Can the contract of employment be enforced on an unwilling employee? Not if one is seeking such attitudes as enthusiasm and cooperation, or behaviour such as diligence and carefulness. The disenchanted employee can always meet the bare letter rather than the spirit of the contract.

The most realistic view of the matter is that many disciplinary problems require some action from both parties, some require action by the employee only and a small proportion require management action only. The problem-solving session may quickly produce the possibility for further action and open up the possibility of closing the interview.

This simple, logical approach outlined so far may not be enough, due to the unwillingness of employees to respond to disciplinary expectations. They may not want to be punctual or to do as they are instructed, or whatever the particular problem is. There is now a test of the power behind management authority. Three further steps can be taken, one after the other, although there will be occasions when it is necessary to move directly to the third.

Second possible move to disengagement: persuasion

A first strategy is to demonstrate to employees that they will not achieve what they want, if their behaviour does not change:

> 'You won't keep your earnings up if you don't meet targets.'
> 'It will be difficult to get your appointment confirmed when the probationary period is over if . . .'

By such means employees may see the advantages of changing their attitude and behaviour. If they are convinced, there is a strong incentive for them to alter, because they believe it to be in their own interests.

Third possible move to disengagement: disapproval

Another strategy is to suggest that continuing the behaviour will displease those whose goodwill the employee wishes to keep:

> 'The Management Development Panel are rather disappointed . . .'
> 'Some of the other people in the department feel that you are not pulling your weight.'

A manager using this method needs to be sure that what is said is both true and relevant. Also the manager may be seen by the employee as shirking the issue, so it may be appropriate to use a version of 'I think this is deplorable and expect you to do better'.

We asked for a restraint from judgement in the early stages of the interview, until the nature of the problem is clear. The time for judgement has now come, with the proper deployment of the rebuke or the caution.

Fourth possible move to disengagement: penalties

When all else fails or is clearly inappropriate, as with serious offences about which there is no doubt, penalties have to be invoked. In rare circumstances there may be the possibility of a fine, but usually the first penalty will be a formal warning as a preliminary to possible dismissal. In situations that are sufficiently grave summary dismissal is both appropriate and possible within the legal framework.

Disengagement

We have indicated possible moves to disengagement at four different points in the disciplinary interview. Now we come to a stage that is common to both grievance and disciplinary encounters from the point of view of describing the process, although the nature of disengagement will obviously differ. The manager now needs to think of the working situation that will follow. In a grievance situation can the employee now accept the decision that has been made? Are there faces to be saved or reputations to be restored? What administrative action is to be taken? In closing a disciplinary interview, the manager will aim for the flavour of disengagement to be as positive as possible so that all concerned put the disciplinary problem behind them. In cases where the outcome of the interview is to impose or confirm a dismissal, then the manager will be exclusively concerned with the fairness and accuracy with which it is done, so that the possibility of tribunal hearings is reduced, if not prevented. It can never be appropriate to close an interview of either type leaving the employee humbled and demoralised.

WINDOW ON PRACTICE

The American Eric Harvey has reduced what he calls 'positive discipline' to three simple steps:

1 Warn the employee orally.

2 Warn the employee in writing.

3 If steps 1 and 2 fail to resolve the problem, give the employee a day off, *with pay* (Harvey 1987).

A similar, very positive, approach was outlined in a seminal paper by Huberman in 1967.

SUMMARY PROPOSITIONS

V.1 Grievance and disciplinary interviews are central to the process of sorting things out when there is a management/employee problem, but most managers dislike such interviews intensely.

V.2 Grievance and disciplinary interviews are one of the means whereby people at work achieve self-discipline and autonomy, reducing the need for supervision and reducing the need for recourse to the formality of procedure.

V.3 The steps in conducting a grievance interview are first to understand the nature of the grievance, to explain the management position, to focus on the problem, to discuss possibilities and then to decide what to do.

V.4 The disciplinary interview starts the other way around, first explaining the management position, then understanding the employee's position and focusing on the problem. If that does not produce a satisfactory result, the manager may have to move through three more steps: persuasion, showing disapproval or invoking penalties.

GENERAL DISCUSSION TOPICS

1 Do individual grievance and disciplinary procedures weaken trade union organisation in a workplace by enabling the management to deal with employees individually rather than having to face the potential strength of collective action and representation?

2 In 1791 Edmund Burke, a British statesman, said, 'He that wrestles with us strengthens our nerves, and sharpens our skill. Our antagonist is our helper.' Do trade union officials help HR managers by strengthening their nerves and sharpening their skill?

FURTHER READING

Bouwen, R. and Salipante, P.F. (1990) 'Behavioural analysis of grievances', *Employee Relations*, Vol. 12, No. 4, pp. 27–32
Hook, C.M., Rollinson, D.J., Foot, M. and Handley, J. (1996) 'Supervisor and manager styles in handling discipline and grievance', *Personnel Review*, Vol. 25, No. 3, pp. 20–34
These recent studies cover behaviour in discipline and grievance interviewing.

Edwards, P.K. (2000) 'Discipline: towards trust and self-discipline?' in S. Bach and K. Sisson (eds) *Personnel Management: A comprehensive guide to theory and practice*. Oxford: Blackwell, pp. 317–37
Redman, T. and Wilkinson, A. (2001) *Contemporary Human Resource Management*. Harlow, Essex: Pearson Education, pp. 177–92
These studies provide further background and discussion of the place of interviewing in employment relations processes.

WEB LINKS

www.eoc.org.uk (the website of the Equal Opportunities Commission)
www.cre.gov.uk (the website of the Commission for Racial Equality)
www.ageconcern.org.uk (the website of the charity Age Concern)

REFERENCES

Beveridge, W.E. (1968) *Problem-Solving Interviews*. London: Allen and Unwin.
Harvey, E.L. (1987) 'Discipline versus punishment', *Management Review*, March, pp. 25–9.
Huberman, J.C. (1967) 'Discipline without punishment', *Harvard Business Review*, May, pp. 62–8.
McGregor, D. (1960) *The Human Side of Enterprise*. Maidenhead: McGraw-Hill.
Tietjen, T. (1987) *I'd Like a Word With You*. London: Video Arts Ltd.

REVIEW OF PART V

Part V has dealt with aspects of management that centre on a basic conflict of interest between those who employ and those who are employed. To a great extent that is a feature of all management, but here it is most apparent. The grievance or disciplinary interview both illustrates and symbolises that division, but also illustrates how the conflict can often be resolved and does not have to be destructive. Various forms of collective consent can be negotiated, employees can be involved, teams briefed and unions recognised. Health hazards can be modified and stressful working conditions alleviated. The extent to which people are disadvantaged or have their dignity affronted through discrimination can be lessened. When there is a real problem of dissatisfaction with the employment or psychological contract, that problem can be tackled through policy, procedure or face to face.

In 1776 Adam Smith, in his *Wealth of Nations*, made a sly comment about universities:

> The discipline of colleges and universities is in general contrived, not for the benefit of the students, but for the interest, or more properly speaking, for the ease of the masters.

All readers of this book, as well as its authors, will know that is certainly not true for all universities in the twenty-first century even if it may have been true in the eighteenth, but it remains a useful homily to underpin the management of employee relations, illustrated by part of a true story about an industrial dispute. In a small factory in Lancashire production was halted because of an unofficial strike. Attempts to solve the problem failed and the strike lingered on despite the fact that the strikers were not eligible for strike pay and were experiencing considerable hardship. One day the pickets heard that 'a man from London' was coming. Hopes rose for a breakthrough. Soon after 11.00 a.m. the General Manager drove to the station, returning with a passenger. Both went in to the offices to emerge after an hour with the Works Manager and the Production Manager. All four got into the car and drove out. The car and two passengers returned at 4.00 p.m: the man from London had obviously been returned to the station after a lengthy lunch. The following day it emerged that the meeting had not been about the strike at all, but to discuss replacement company cars for the Works and Production Managers. The strike continued for six more weeks and the plant closed completely seven months later.

Part V CASE STUDY PROBLEM

Industrial disputes at British Airways, 1997 and 2003

British Airways is an international company by any standards and, by 1990, was the world's most popular and most profitable airline, although this position was compromised after the events of September 2001, which had such a disastrous effect on air travel.

Because of its extensive network and the salient position of Heathrow as the world's busiest airport, it was relatively straightforward for BA to become the most popular airline, but achieving high profitability was more difficult. There was overstaffing and the need for radical measures:

> The organisation had a bureaucratic style of management, damaging industrial relations and a poor reputation for customer service . . . There was a drastic reduction in staff numbers from 60,000 to 38,000. This was achieved by a combination of voluntary severance and natural wastage. (Hopfl 1993, p. 117)

In order to maintain market leadership the airline embarked on a famous programme of staff training to develop commitment to customer service, and the quality of service to the customer improved markedly, so that British Airways was able to maintain its premier position despite ever-increasing competition.

There were, however, mounting problems with the staff as the pressure on margins continued. In 1996 a strike by pilots was narrowly averted, but 1997 brought one stoppage and the threat of another.

On 9 July a 72-hour strike by cabin staff began. It was an official stoppage called by the Transport and General Workers Union following protracted negotiations and a ballot among its members working for the airline. According to British Airways only 142 cabin crew formally joined the strike, but 1,500 (compared with a normal daily average of 120) reported sick – a novel strategy! The number that reported for work as usual was 834.

The management reaction was to announce that all strikers would forfeit travel perks and promotion prospects for three years. Film was also taken of strikers on picket lines. The threats were later withdrawn and the filming was stopped. The situation was complicated by the existence of a rival union, Cabin Crew '89, which had broken away from the TGWU in 1989. This union, known as CC89, supported the management position and all their members worked normally through the stoppage.

Another interesting feature of the dispute was reported by *The Times*:

> During the past few years, BA, like many companies in Britain, has appointed middle and senior managers who fear for their jobs. To get on, they believe, they must show they are tough. I have heard these 'performance managers' brusquely warning vacillating staff that if they follow their union and refuse to work, they will 'face the consequences.' This has irked the cabin crew far more than the dispute over pay and conditions. They no longer feel part of a team and believe they are being bullied. (Elliott 1997, p. 41)

As usual, the dispute moved on to talks to find a resolution, but BA had lost many flights and its reputation was as severely dented as its financial position. The share price dropped from 763p to 583p before recovering to 635p, and there were varying reports about how many millions of pounds the dispute was costing.

Four years later the terrorist attack on the World Trade Center in New York badly affected full-service airlines, especially those with transatlantic services like BA. Competition from low-cost airlines and anxiety about a war in Iraq added to the pressure, so cost-cutting had to slice even deeper. One method introduced was Automated Time Recording (ATR) that kept a tighter control on hours worked. Many check-in and engineering staff were alarmed at this innovation, fearing that it might lead to a reduction in flexibility about working hours, which was a major attraction for many who relied on this to fit in with their domestic arrangements. They were also angered by senior managers using terms such as 'feather-bedding' and making comments about high absenteeism in the summer. On 18 July 2003, on one of the busiest weekends of the year, BA's operations at Heathrow were paralysed by a wildcat strike by check-in and other groundstaff. It was expected to cost the airline £100 million.

Required

1 Do you think it is inevitable that the pressures of international competition drive companies into a situation where unilateral managerial decision making must prevail and there is simply no time for the consultation and compromise that is involved in union negotiation?

2 This case provides an excellent example of the problems that can arise from having two unions representing the same group of employees and competing with each other for membership. How would you have tried to deal with this situation in 1997 – not back in 1989?

3 How accurate do you regard Harvey Elliott's views to be as a general comment on current management practice?

4 'Informal arrangements for flexible manning, made by supervisors individually with employees, are better than electronic or similar controls.' Do you agree or disagree?

References

Elliott, H. (1997) 'BA is Plunging towards Disaster', *The Times*, 10 July.

Hopfl, H. (1993) 'Culture and Commitment: British Airways', in D. Gowler, K. Legge and C. Clegg (eds) *Case Studies in Organizational Behaviour and Human Resource Management*, 2nd edn. London: Paul Chapman Publishing, pp. 117–25.

Part V EXAMINATION QUESTIONS

1 Explain the difference between these four terms:
   (a) Industrial relations
   (b) Employee relations
   (c) Collective bargaining
   (d) Employee involvement

2 What are the aims and objectives of British trade unions?

3 What is meant by the term 'derecognition'? How extensive is derecognition in present-day Britain, and what employment practices, if any, have employers initiated to take the place of trade unions?

4 'Good health is good business.' Discuss.

5 How just can the framework of organisational justice ever be when managers have so much more power than employees?

6 Analyse critically the assertion that employers develop employee involvement schemes in order to empower their employees.

7 Explain the main components of a grievance procedure.

8 Explain the difference between bargaining and grievance handling.

PART 6

PAY

If we were all paid the same amount for working, life would be very straightforward, but not many of us would be satisfied with the arrangement! This part of the book deals with the ways in which what we are paid differs between us. There must always be a reason to justify the difference.

It may be that one person is paid more than another for having a higher level of skill, so the skilled artisan is paid more than the labourer, or it may be that the difference is justified by experience, so that the experienced schoolteacher will be paid more than the newly qualified teacher. Managers have always been interested in making arrangements for the better performer to be paid more than the average performer, and we can see many schemes currently that are working towards that objective. Aspects of payment do not only affect our working life; there is an effect also on our pension at the end of our working life and other effects on our attitudes to our work as a result of associated benefits that are provided.

Pay is a feature of management arrangements where fairness is always both important and problematic, so job evaluation is a means of introducing fairness into the calculations, and negotiation is a way in which the equity of changes to pay and working methods can be tested.

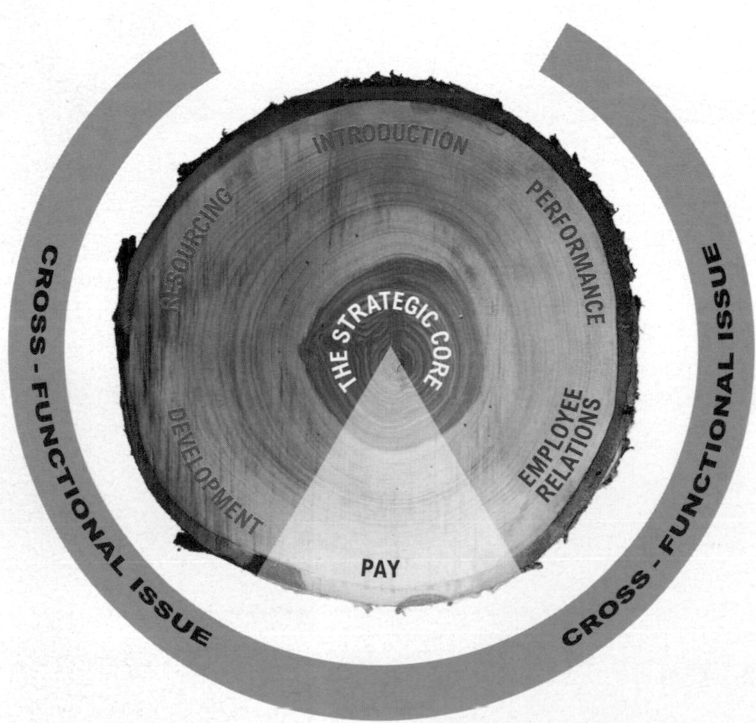

CHAPTER 26

STRATEGIC ASPECTS OF PAYMENT

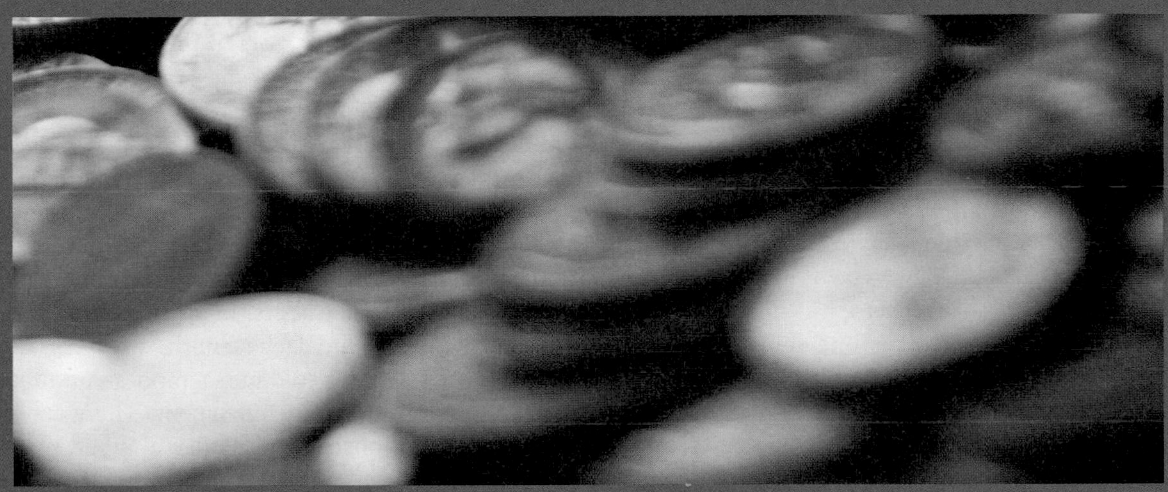

THE OBJECTIVES OF THIS CHAPTER ARE TO:

1 ASSESS THE MAJOR OBJECTIVES MANAGERS HAVE WHEN DETERMINING PAY RATES AND SYSTEMS

2 CONSIDER THE MAIN EMPLOYEE OBJECTIVES FROM A REWARD PACKAGE

3 EVALUATE THE MAJOR ALTERNATIVE METHODS OF SETTING BASE PAY RATES

4 INTRODUCE THE DIFFERENT ELEMENTS THAT MAKE UP A PAY PACKAGE

5 STATE THE SIGNIFICANCE OF EQUITY IN DESIGNING AND MAINTAINING EFFECTIVE REWARD SYSTEMS

6 DEBATE THE EXTENT TO WHICH REWARD MANAGEMENT HAS OR HAS NOT TAKEN ON A 'STRATEGIC' CHARACTER IN RECENT YEARS

Pay is all sorts of different things. It is basically a transaction, as an employer pays £X in exchange for generally specified time, skills, commitment and loyalty. But pay is also a label (the £3,000-a-day libel lawyer), a status symbol (professors are paid more than senior lecturers) and a determinant of standard of living. Pay is also likely to be a discriminator according to gender (average earnings are lower for women than for men) and social class (average earnings are lower for manual workers than for non-manual workers), and is one of the main influences on the degree to which people value their employment. It is not just the amount they are paid, but the nature of the contract. Salaried posts in the main are for what a person *is* as well as for what he or she does. The government minister in charge of the treasury is paid to *be* Chancellor of the Exchequer, not just to prepare and deliver an annual budget.

The reason why pay is a crucial issue for managers is that managers decide what employees should be paid, so they influence all of these factors in the lives of John Brown and Mary Smith. Managers mediate between the customer and the worker as a supplier of goods and services, and we are all highly sensitive to issues such as our social status. This is why trade unions were created and pay review bodies formed. This is why we have laws to control at least some aspects of the pay bargain. If you are an employee at any level someone decides what you are worth, and few things matter more to us than how we are valued.

This type of management mediation between customer and worker applies only to employees; it is different for the self-employed and sole traders. In writing this book we have one thing in common with J.K. Rowling and Delia Smith: we have all recently published books. Every copy of this book that is sold puts a modest amount of money in our pockets, that is predetermined by a royalty agreement. There is no employer intervention to vary the amount. If the publisher sells a huge number, then our royalty payments rise in strict proportion. If they sell few, then our royalty payments are disappointing, but there is no argument about worth or value, because there is no mediation.

In the following chapter we look in detail at the measurement and grading of jobs. In Chapters 28 and 29 the focus is on incentives and employee benefits. Here we introduce some of the fundamental choices that managers have to make in deciding how much and in what form to pay their employees.

TERMINOLOGY

A strange thing about payment is that managers seem to shy away from actually using the word. We hear about 'compensation', 'reward' or 'remuneration', yet the idea of compensation is that it involves making amends for something that has caused loss or injury. Do we want to suggest that work necessarily causes loss or injury? Reward suggests a special payment for a special act. Much current management thinking on pay issues concerns the need to induce more special effort by employees, but the bulk of the pay bargain for an individual is not affected by performance. Remuneration is a more straightforward word which means exactly the same as payment but has five more letters and is misspelled (as renumeration) more often than most words in the human resource manager's lexicon. We use the general term 'payment' as this part of the book includes material about pensions, sick pay and other benefits, but the current general term is certainly 'reward'. This term is used to identify the system of payment as a central, integrated feature of the approach to HRM. The traditional collective bargain was separated from the management of the people receiving the money: the concept of reward is to have some sort of multiple helix, where motivation, skill, career and performance are all intertwined to produce added value to the individual career and corporate aspects, with the pay reflecting, describing and moving with the other elements continuously. In recent years there has been increased interest in the concept of 'total reward' (*see* Armstrong and Brown 2001, pp. 3–5) which views pay as just one part of a far bigger package of rewards that employees derive from their work. Seen from this perspective, non-financial rewards such as recognition, career development opportunities and the ability to achieve an acceptable work-life balance play as much of a role as financial rewards in meeting organisational objectives.

ACTIVITY 26.1

How far do you agree with the proposition that managers should think in terms of 'total reward' as a means of recruiting, retaining and motivating their staff? Are praise and career development as important as pay? Would you trade some of your pay for greater recognition and development opportunities?

REWARD STRATEGY

A major current feature of the literature and rhetoric about payment systems has been a concern with defining and refining reward strategies. While different writers have different ideas about what exactly constitutes a strategic approach to the management of pay, most agree that it is primarily about aligning an organisation's payment arrangements with its business objectives. This means developing payment systems which enhance the chances that an organisation's employees will seek actively to contribute to the achievement of its goals. So if improved quality of service is the major business objective, this should be reflected in a payment system which rewards front-line staff who provide the best standards of service to customers. Alternatively, if increased productivity is sought, then a payment system which rewards efficiency would be more appropriate. But choices in this area are not always as straightforward as this because organisations are obliged to compete with one another for good staff as well as for customers. The extent to which organisations can impose payment arrangements which serve their business objectives is thus limited by the equally important need to recruit, retain and motivate staff to carry out the work. So a balance always has to be sought between the objectives of employers and employees when developing payment strategies.

Interestingly, and perhaps surprisingly, it is only in relatively recent years that managers have had the opportunity to think strategically about pay in this way. This is because until the 1970s (and much later in many industrialised countries) the majority of employees had their payment determined in large part through national or industry-level collective bargaining arrangements. Managers at the local level thus had little freedom of manoeuvre beyond determining who should be employed on which grade and how much overtime was worked. Multi-employer bargaining declined steeply during the 1980s and 1990s, so that by 2000 only 40 per cent of public sector employees and just 4 per cent of those employed in the private sector were covered by such arrangements (Brown *et al.* 2003, p. 202). As a result, unlike other areas of HRM, there have been relatively few years in which new approaches to the management of pay have been tried out, established and subsequently evaluated. To a great degree we are still at the experimentation stage with many newer approaches, and this means that fierce debates rage among commentators about the effectiveness, efficiency and fairness of systems which aim to enhance individual effort, encourage skills acquisition, reward specific employee behaviours and try to establish an identity of interest between employers and their staff.

EMPLOYEE OBJECTIVES FOR THE CONTRACT FOR PAYMENT

Those who are paid and those who administer payment schemes have objectives for the payment contract which differ according to whether one is the recipient or the administrator of the payments. The contract for payment will be satisfactory in so far as it meets the objectives of the parties. Therefore we consider the range of objectives, starting with employees.

First objective: purchasing power

The absolute level of weekly or monthly earnings determines the standard of living of the recipient, and will therefore be the most important consideration for most employees. How much can I buy? Employees are rarely satisfied about their purchasing power, and the annual pay adjustment will do little more than reduce dissatisfaction, even if it exceeds the current level of inflation. Enhanced satisfaction only occurs when a pay rise is given which surpasses expectations.

Second objective: felt to be fair

Elliott Jacques (1962) averred that every employee had a strong feeling about the level of payment that was fair for the job. In most cases this is a rough, personalised evaluation of what is appropriate. The employee who feels underpaid is likely to demonstrate the conventional symptoms of withdrawal from the job: looking for another, carelessness, disgruntlement, lateness, absence and the like. Perhaps the worst manifestation of this is among those who feel the unfairness but who cannot take a clean step of moving elsewhere. They then not only feel dissatisfied with their pay level, but also feel another unfairness too: being trapped in a situation they resent. Those who feel they are overpaid (as some do) may simply feel guilty, or may seek to justify their existence in some way by trying to look busy. That is not necessarily productive.

Third objective: rights

A different aspect of relative income is that concerned with the rights of the employee to a particular share of the company's profits or the nation's wealth. The employee is here thinking about whether the division of earnings is providing fair shares of the Gross National Product. The focus is often on the notion of need – the idea that someone has a right to a greater share because they or their families are suffering unjustly. These are features of many trade union arguments and part of the general preoccupation with the rights of the individual.

Fourth objective: relativities

'How much do I (or we) get relative to . . . group X?' This is a version of the 'felt to be fair' argument. It is not a question of whether the employee believes the remuneration to be reasonable in relation to the job done, but of whether they believe it reasonable in relation to the jobs other people do. There are many potential comparators, and the basis of comparison can alter. We may compare our own pay with that of the person sitting in the next desk, with an opposite number in a competitor company or we may be concerned more generally about comparisons with other professional or occupational groups.

Whichever comparator is chosen, it is often difficult to make a fair comparison. For example, basic pay may be very different from overall earnings, while jobs themselves can share a title or job description in common while carrying rather different levels of real responsibility.

Fifth objective: recognition

Most people have an objective for their payment arrangements, that their personal contribution is recognised. This is partly seeking reassurance, but also a way in which people can mould their behaviour and their career thinking to produce progress and satisfaction. It is doubtful if financial recognition has a significant and sustained impact on performance, but providing a range of other forms of recognition while the pay packet is transmitting a different message is certainly counter-productive.

Sixth objective: composition

How is the pay package made up? The growing complexity and sophistication of payment arrangements raises all sorts of questions about pay composition. Is £400 pay for 60 hours' work better than £280 for 40 hours' work? The arithmetical answer that the rate per hour for the 40-hour arrangement is marginally better than that for 60 hours is only part of the answer. The other aspects will relate to the individuals, their circumstances and the conventions of their working group and reference groups. Another question about composition might be: is £250 per week plus a pension better than £270 per week without? Such questions do not produce universally applicable answers because they can be quantified to such a limited extent, but some kernels of conventional wisdom can be suggested as generalisations:

1 Younger employees are more interested in high direct earnings at the expense of indirect benefits, such as pensions, which will be of more interest to older employees.

2 Incentive or performance-related payment arrangements are likely to interest employees who either see a reliable prospect of enhancing earnings through the ability to control their own activities, or see the incentive scheme as an opportunity to wrest control of their personal activities (which provide little intrinsic satisfaction) away from management by regulating their earnings.
3 Women with children are less interested in payment arrangements that depend on overtime than men often are.
4 Overtime is used by many employees to produce an acceptable level of purchasing power particularly among the lower-paid.

ACTIVITY 26.2

Which of the above objectives do you consider to be most important to you? How far do you think priorities in this area change with age?

EMPLOYER OBJECTIVES FOR THE CONTRACT FOR PAYMENT

In looking at the other side of the picture, we consider the range of objectives in the thinking of employers, or those representing an employer interest *vis-à-vis* the employee.

First objective: prestige

There is a comfortable and understandable conviction among managers that it is 'a good thing' to be a good payer. This seems partly to be simple pride at doing better than others, but also there is sometimes a feeling that such a policy eliminates a variable from the contractual relationship. In conversation with one of the authors a chief executive expressed it this way:

> 'I want to find out the highest rates of pay, job-for-job, within a fifty-mile radius of my office. Then I will make sure that all my people are paid 20 per cent over that. Then I know where I am with them as I have taken money out of the equation. If they want to quit they can't hide the real reason by saying they're going elsewhere for more cash: they can't get it. Furthermore, if I do have to fill a job I know that we won't lose a good guy because of the money not being right.'

Whether high pay rates succeed in bestowing on an organisation the reputation of being a good employer is difficult to see. What seems much more likely is that the low-paying employer will have the reputation of being a poor employer.

Second objective: competition

More rational is the objective of paying rates that are sufficiently competitive to sustain the employment of the right numbers of appropriately qualified and experienced employees to staff the organisation. A distinction is drawn here between competition thinking and prestige thinking, as the former is designed more to get a good fit on one of the employment contract dimensions than simply to overwhelm it. It permits consideration of questions such as: how selective do we need to be for this range of jobs? and: how can we avoid overpaying people and inhibiting them from moving on? Every employer has this sort of objective, even if only in relation to a few key posts in the organisation.

Third objective: control

There may be ways of organising the pay packet that will facilitate control of operations and potentially save money. The conventional approach to this for many years was the use of piecework or similar incentives, but this became difficult due to the unwillingness of most employees to see their payment fluctuate wildly at the employer's behest. Theoretically, overtime is a method of employer control of output through making available or withholding additional payment prospects. In practice, however, employees use overtime for control more extensively than employers. Other ways in which employers could control their payroll costs have been eliminated or made more difficult by legislation. Redundancy, short-term layoff and unfair dismissal are all now more expensive, and it is unlawful to regard women as a reservoir of inexpensive, temporary labour as once was common.

Fourth objective: motivation and performance

Employers also seek to use the payment contract to motivate employees and thus to improve their work performance. The subject of incentive payment systems is discussed in detail in Chapter 28, but some features of payment and its influence on performance are worth mentioning here.

Until recently incentive payment systems were primarily used as part of the payment package for manual workers and sales staff. The design of such schemes is simple, with a built-in bias towards rewarding the volume of products manufactured or sold. Wherever the quality of output is a matter of significance such approaches are, therefore, inappropriate. Two extreme examples indicate the weakness of this approach. Someone engaged in the manufacture of diamond-tipped drilling bits would serve the employer poorly if payment were linked to output. If it were possible to devise a payment system that contained an incentive element based on high quality of workmanship or on low scrap value that might be more effective. If schoolteachers were paid a 'quantity bonus' it would presumably be based either on the number of children in the class or on some indicator like the number of examination passes. The first would encourage teachers to take classes as large as possible, with probably adverse results in the quality of teaching. The second might increase the proportion of children succeeding in examinations, but would isolate those who could not produce impressive examination performance.

WINDOW ON PRACTICE

The case of the AIDS counsellor

The difficulty of determining a fair and satisfactory rate of pay for particular individuals is illustrated in the following example of a nurse employed by a large NHS hospital as a counsellor for haemophilia patients who have contracted AIDS through blood transfusion.

The nurse concerned was employed on a senior sister's grade but was required to work in the community, undertaking counselling duties with patients and their families. The nature of the job, however, meant that she was required to work very irregular and unpredictable hours and could not delegate duties to anyone else or share the burden of cases with others. She requested a regrading with the full support of her managers who perceived her to be a uniquely good performer. No performance-related scheme had, however, been developed and regrading the nurse was not straightforward. The first stumbling block came when her duties were assessed according to grading criteria negotiated by the relevant NHS Whitley Council. Although several attempts were made to try to make the job fit the criteria for the higher grade, the task proved impossible. Authorising a regrading on these grounds would have set a precedent leading to large numbers of regrading claims.

The next approach taken was to analyse the nurse's job using the hospital's computerised job evaluation system. This route also failed because the results of the analysis suggested that the job was already graded too highly. To regrade in spite of this would render the decision indefensible were an equal value claim to be brought by a male nurse employed at the same grade.

Finally an attempt was made to justify the proposed regrading by discovering at what level other hospitals paid nurses undertaking similar roles. It was found, however, that other AIDS counsellers were paid on the same or lower grades.

It thus proved impossible to pay the nurse concerned a rate which she and her managers regarded as 'fair' because no decision to regrade could be objectively justified.

In recent years a great deal of attention has been paid to the development of incentive payment systems which go beyond rewarding the quantity of output to take account of job performance as a whole. In particular there has been a marked increase in the use of performance-related pay (PRP) for management and professional staff, especially for senior managers; organisations have sought either to re-establish or to introduce for the first time schemes which reinforce the messages required to produce improved performance and increased productivity. Private sector employers in particular now increasingly believe that they are not providing an appropriate or competitive package for their directors and senior executives unless there is some element of risk money to add on to the basic salary and reward the achievement of company growth, profitability and success. At the same time, companies have been re-examining the use of bonus schemes for more junior employees in order to increase motivation and to reward them for their contribution. The use of PRP is also growing in the public sector following active promotion of its benefits by government ministers.

Fifth objective: cost

Just as employees are interested in purchasing power, the absolute value of their earnings, so employers are interested in the absolute cost of payment, and its bearing on the profitability or cost effectiveness of their organisation. The importance of this varies with the type of organisation and the cost of employees relative to other costs, so that in the refining of petroleum employment costs are modest, in teaching or nursing they are substantial. The employer's interest in this objective is long term as well as short term. Not only do employees expect their incomes to be maintained and to carry on rising, rather than fluctuating with company profitability, but the indirect costs of employing people can also be substantial.

Sixth objective: change management

Pay can be used specifically as one of a range of tools underpinning change-management processes. The approach used is to tie higher base pay, bonuses or promotion to the development of new behaviours, attitudes or skills gained by employees. Pay works far more effectively than simple exhortation because it provides a material incentive to those whose natural inclination is to resist change. It also sends out a powerful message to employees indicating the seriousness of the employer's intentions as regards proposed or ongoing changes.

APPROACHES TO SETTING BASE PAY RATES

One of the most important decisions in the design of payment systems concerns the mechanism or mechanisms that will be used to determine the basic rate of pay for different jobs in the organisation. There are, of course, restrictions on management action in this area provided by the law. Since 1999 the UK has had a National Minimum Wage (£4.50 an hour in 2004) to which workers over the age of 22 are entitled; a lower minimum rate is set for those aged 18–22. Equal pay law is a further way in which the state intervenes, providing a mechanism for employees to complain when they consider their pay to be unjustifiably lower than that paid to a colleague of the opposite sex. Moreover, in many countries incomes policies are operated as tools of inflation control. These restrict the amount of additional pay that people can receive in any one year while remaining in the same job. While formal incomes policies were abandoned in the UK after the 1970s, similar thinking continues to underpin government decision making in the area of public sector pay (Thorpe 2000, pp. 34–5).

A further restriction on management action is the nature of the product markets in which their organisations operate. The extent of this influence varies according to how important labour costs are in deciding product cost, and how important product cost is to the customer. In a labour-intensive and low-technology industry such as catering, there will usually be such pressure on labour costs that the pay administrator has little freedom to manipulate pay relationships. In an area such as magazine printing, the need of the publisher to get the product out on time is so great that labour costs, however high, may be of relatively little concern. In this situation the pay negotiators have much more freedom of manoeuvre.

It is possible, notwithstanding the above restrictions, to identify four principal mechanisms for the determination of base pay. They are not entirely incompatible, although one tends to be used as the main approach in most organisations.

External market comparisons

In making external market comparisons the focus is on the need to recruit and retain staff, a rate being set which is broadly equivalent to 'the going rate' for the job in question. The focus is thus on **external relativities**. Research suggests that this is always a major contributing factor when organisations set pay rates, but that it increases in significance higher up the income scale. Over 75 per cent of employers look to the external market when determining pay for senior managers, but only 55 per cent say they do so when setting rates for manual staff (CIPD 2004, p. 21). Some employers consciously pay over the market rate in order to secure the services of the most talented employees. Others 'follow the market', by paying below the going rate while using other mechanisms such as flexibility, job security or longer-term incentives to ensure effective recruitment and retention. In either case the decision is based on an assessment of what rate needs to be paid to compete for staff in different types of labour market. Going rates are more significant for some than for others. Accountants and craftworkers, for instance, tend to identify with an external employee grouping. Their assessment of pay levels is thus greatly influenced by the going rate in the trade or the district. A similar situation exists with jobs that are clearly understood and where skills are readily transferable, particularly if the employee is to work with a standard piece of equipment. Driving heavy goods vehicles is an obvious example, as the vehicles are common from one employer to another, the roads are the same, and only the loads vary. Other examples are secretaries, switchboard operators and computer operators. Jobs that are less sensitive to the labour market are those that are organisationally specific, such as most semi-skilled work in manufacturing, general clerical work and nearly all middle-management positions.

There are several possible sources of intelligence about market rates for different job types at any one time. A great deal of information can be found in published journals such as the pay bulletins issued by Incomes Data Services (IDS) and Industrial Relations Services (IRS), focusing on the hard-to-recruit groups such as computer staff. More detailed information can be gained by joining one of the major salary survey projects operated by firms of consultants or by paying for access to their datasets. Information on specific types of job, including international packages for expatriate workers, is collected by specialised consultants and can be obtained on payment of the appropriate fee. White (2000, pp. 44–5) identifies a range of other sources of UK pay data including the Confederation of British Industry's Pay Databank and the Office of Manpower Economics. In addition there are more informal approaches such as looking at pay rates included in recruitment advertisements in papers and at job centres. New staff, notably HR people, often bring with them a knowledge of pay rates for types of job in competitor organisations and can be a useful source of information. Finally, it is possible to join or set up salary clubs.

These consist of groups of employers, often based in the same locality, who agree to share salary information for mutual benefit.

Internal labour market mechanisms

Just as there is a labour market of which the company is a part, so there is a labour market within the organisation which also needs to be managed so as to ensure effective performance. According to Doeringer and Piore (1970) there are two kinds of internal labour market: the enterprise and the craft. The enterprise market is so called because the individual enterprise defines the boundaries of the market itself. Such will be the market encompassing manual workers engaged in production processes, for whom the predominant pattern of employment is one in which jobs are formally or informally ranked, with the jobs accorded the highest pay or prestige usually being filled by promotion from within and those at the bottom of the hierarchy usually being filled only from outside the enterprise. It is, therefore, those at the bottom that are most sensitive to the external labour market. Doeringer and Piore point out that there is a close parallel with managerial jobs, the main ports of entry being from management trainees or supervisors, and the number of appointments from outside gradually reducing as jobs become more senior. This modus operandi is one of the main causes of the problems that redundant executives face.

Recent American research has stressed the importance of this kind of internal labour market in determining pay rates. Here the focus is on **internal differentials** rather than external relativities. An interesting metaphor used is that of the sports tournament in which an organisation's pay structure is likened to the prize distribution in a knock-out competition such as is found, for example, at the Wimbledon Tennis Championships. Here the prize money is highest for the winner, somewhat lower for the runner-up, lower again for the semi-final losers and so on down the rounds. The aim, from the point of view of the tournament organisers, is to attract the best players to compete in the first round, then subsequently to give players in later rounds an incentive to play at their peak. According to Lazear (1995, pp. 26–33), the level of base pay for each level in an organisation's hierarchy should be set according to similar principles. The level of pay for any particular job is thus set at a level which maximises performance lower down the hierarchy among employees competing for promotion. The actual performance of the individual receiving the pay is less important.

The second type of internal labour market identified by Doeringer and Piore is the craft market, where barriers to entry are relatively high – typically involving the attainment of a formal qualification. However, once workers are established in the market, seniority and hierarchy become unimportant as jobs and duties are shared among the individuals concerned. Such arrangements are usually determined by custom and practice, but are difficult to break down because of the vested interests of those who have successfully completed their period of apprenticeship. Certain pay rates are expected by those who have achieved the required qualification and it is accepted by everyone that this is a fair basis for rewarding people.

Job evaluation

We assess job evaluation in some detail in the next chapter. Here it is necessary only to define the term and identify it as one of the four principal mechanisms of pay determination. Job evaluation involves the establishment of a system which is used to measure the size and significance of all jobs in an organisation. It is defined by Bloom (1998, p. 185) as follows:

> Job evaluation is a systematic process designed to aid an establishment in establishing differentials across jobs within a single employer . . . The culmination of this appraisal process is a hierarchy of jobs denoting their relative complexity and value to the organisation.

The focus is thus on the relative worth of jobs within an organisation and on comparisons between these rather than on external relativities and comparisons with rates being paid by other employers. Fairness and objectivity are the core principles, an organisation's wage budget being divided among employees on the basis of an assessment of the nature and size of the job each is employed to carry out. Usage of job evaluation has increased in recent years. It is currently used by just over half UK organisations in some shape or form (CIPD 2004, p. 21).

Collective bargaining

The fourth approach involves determining pay rates through collective negotiations with trade unions or other employee representatives. Thirty years ago this was the dominant method used for determining pay in the UK, negotiations commonly occurring at industry level. The going rates for each job group were thus set nationally and were adhered to by all companies operating in the sector concerned. Recent decades have seen a steady erosion of these arrangements, collective bargaining being decentralised to company or plant level in the manufacturing sector, where it survives at all. Meanwhile the rise of service sector organisations with lower union membership levels has ensured that collective bargaining arrangements now cover only a minority of UK workers. According to Cully *et al.* (1999, pp. 241–2) only 41 per cent now have any of their terms and conditions determined in this way. The experience of many other countries is similar, but there remain regions such as Eastern Europe and Scandinavia where collective bargaining remains the major determinant of pay rates. Where separate clusters of employees within the same organisation are placed in different bargaining groups and represented by different unions, **internal relativities** become an issue for resolution during bargaining.

In carrying out negotiations the staff and management sides make reference to external labour market rates, established internal pay determination mechanisms and the size of jobs. However, a host of other factors come into the equation too as each side deploys its best arguments. Union representatives, for example, make reference to employee need when house prices are rising and affordable accommodation is hard to find. Both sides refer to the balance sheet, employers arguing that profit margins are too tight to afford substantial rises, while union counterparts seek to gain a share of any increased profits for employees. However good the case made, at the end of the day what makes collective bargaining different from the other approaches is the presence of industrial muscle. Strong unions which have the support of the majority of employees, as is the case in many public sector organisations, are able to ensure that their case is heard and taken into account. They can thus 'secure' a better pay deal for their members than market rates would allow.

ACTIVITY 26.3

Which of the four mechanisms outlined above do you think is usually most efficient for setting the following?

1 Base pay
2 Annual cost of living increases
3 Executive remuneration packages
4 Bonus schemes

THE ELEMENTS OF PAYMENT

Once the mechanisms for determining rates of pay for jobs in an organisation have been settled, the second key strategic decision relates to the make-up of the pay package. Here there is a great deal of potential choice available. What is included and to what extent are matters which should be decided with a view to supporting the organisation's objectives and encouraging the necessary attitudes and actions on the part of employees. The payment of an individual will be made up of one or more elements from those shown in Figure 26.1. Fixed elements are those that make up the

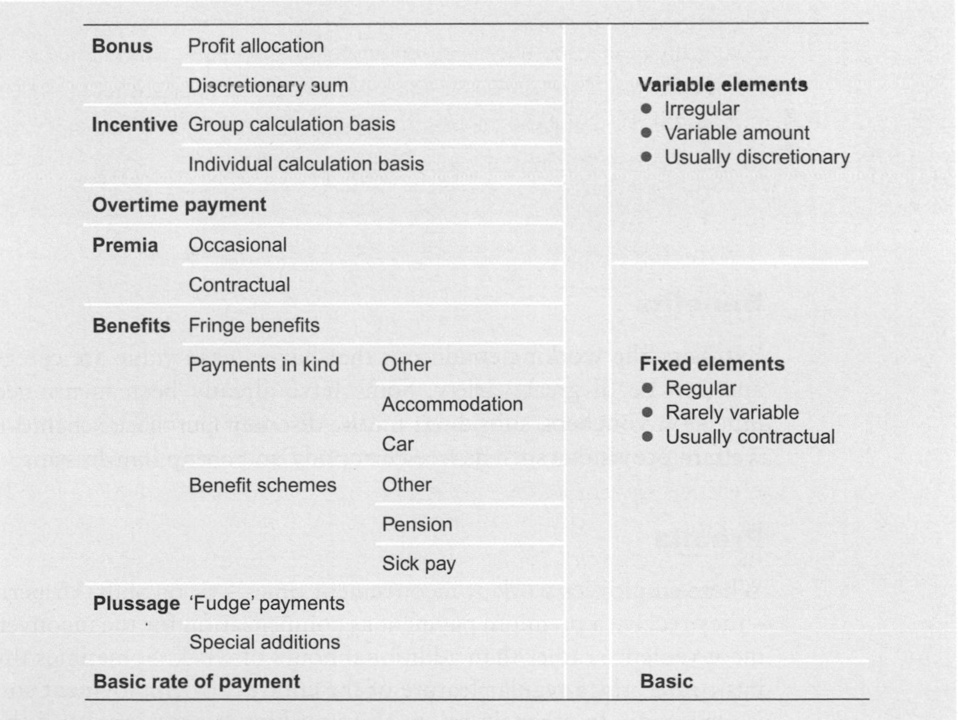

Bonus	Profit allocation		**Variable elements** • Irregular • Variable amount • Usually discretionary
	Discretionary sum		
Incentive	Group calculation basis		
	Individual calculation basis		
Overtime payment			
Premia	Occasional		
	Contractual		**Fixed elements** • Regular • Rarely variable • Usually contractual
Benefits	Fringe benefits		
	Payments in kind	Other	
		Accommodation	
		Car	
	Benefit schemes	Other	
		Pension	
		Sick pay	
Plussage	'Fudge' payments		
	Special additions		
Basic rate of payment			**Basic**

Figure 26.1 The potential elements of payment

regular weekly or monthly payment to the individual, and which do not vary other than in exceptional circumstances. Variable elements can be varied by either the employee or the employer.

Basic rate

The irreducible minimum rate of pay is the basic. In most cases this is the standard rate also, not having any additions made to it. In other cases it is a basis on which earnings are built by the addition of one or more of the other elements in payment. Some groups of employees, such as operatives in the footwear industry, have little more than half of their earnings in basic, while primary and secondary schoolteachers have virtually all their pay in this form. Indeed, according to the New Earnings Survey as many as 60 per cent of employees receive no additional payments at all beyond their basic pay (Grabham 2003, p. 398).

Plussage

Sometimes the basic has an addition to recognise an aspect of working conditions or employee capability. Payments for educational qualifications and for supervisory responsibilities are quite common. There is also an infinite range of what are sometimes called 'fudge' payments, whereby there is an addition to the basic as a start-up allowance, mask money, dirt money, and so forth.

ACTIVITY 26.4

If your employer offered you a 'remuneration package', which could be made up from any of the items in Figure 26.1 provided that the total cost was no more than £X, what proportion of each item would you choose and why? Does your answer suggest ideas for further development of salary policies?

Benefits

Extras to the working conditions that have a cash value are categorised as benefits and can be of great variety. Some have already been mentioned; others include luncheon vouchers, subsidised meals, discount purchase schemes and the range of welfare provisions such as free chiropody and cheap hairdressing.

Premia

Where employees work at inconvenient times – or on shifts or permanently at night – they receive a premium payment as compensation for the inconvenience. This is for inconvenience rather than additional hours of work. Sometimes this is built into the basic rate or is a regular feature of the contract of employment so that the payment is unvarying. In other situations shift working is occasional and short-lived, making the premium a variable element of payment. The New Earnings Survey records that shift premia are now received by just 11 per cent of UK workers, but that it accounts on average for as much as 12 per cent of their total pay (Grabham 2003, p. 399).

Overtime

It is customary for employees working more hours than are normal for the working week to be paid for those hours at an enhanced rate, usually between 10 and 50 per cent more that the normal rate according to how many hours are involved. Seldom can this element be regarded as fixed. No matter how regularly overtime is worked, there is always the opportunity for the employer to withhold the provision of overtime or for the employee to decline the extra hours. Overtime is earned by over a quarter of the UK workforce, more than two-thirds of the recipients being men (Grabham 2003, p. 398). It is particularly associated with less well paid manual work. Where overtime is paid it tends to account for a major portion of an individual's gross pay (18.2 per cent on average in 2002).

Incentive

Incentive is here described as an element of payment linked to the working performance of an individual or working group, as a result of prior arrangement. This includes most of the payment-by-results schemes that have been produced by work study, as well as commission payments to salespeople, skills-based pay schemes and performance-related pay schemes based on the achievement of agreed objectives. The distinguishing feature is that the employee knows what has to be done to earn the payment, though he or she may feel very dependent on other people, or on external circumstances, to receive it. One in seven workers receives a portion of their pay via incentives of one kind or another, more men being rewarded in this way than women. On average incentive pay contributes 22 per cent towards their overall salaries (Grabham 2003, p. 398).

Bonus

A different type of variable payment is the gratuitous payment by the employer that is not directly earned by the employee: a bonus. The essential difference between this and an incentive is that the employee has no entitlement to the payment as a result of a contract of employment and cannot be assured of receiving it in return for a specific performance. The most common example of this is the Christmas bonus.

We include profit sharing under this general heading although the ownership of shares confers a clear entitlement. The point is that the level of the benefit cannot be directly linked to the performance of the individual. Rather, it is linked to the performance of the business. In some cases the two may be synonymous, with one dominant individual determining the success of the business, but there are very few instances like this, even in the most feverish imaginings of tycoons. Share ownership or profit sharing on an agreed basis can greatly increase the interest of the employees in how the business is run and can increase their commitment to its success, but the performance of the individual is not directly rewarded in the same way as in incentive schemes.

THE IMPORTANCE OF EQUITY

Whatever methods are used to determine pay levels and to decide what elements make up the individual pay package, employers must ensure that they are perceived by employees to operate equitably. It has long been established that perceived inequity in payment matters can be highly damaging to an organisation. Classic studies undertaken by J.S. Adams (1963) found that a key determinant of satisfaction at work is the extent to which employees judge pay levels and pay increases to be distributed fairly. These led to the development by Adams and others of **equity theory** which holds that we are very concerned that rewards or 'outputs' equate to our 'inputs' (defined as skill, effort, experience, qualifications, etc.) and that these are fair when compared with the rewards being given to others. Where we believe that we are not being fairly rewarded we show signs of 'dissonance' or dissatisfaction which leads to absence, voluntary turnover, on-job shirking and low-trust employee relations. It is therefore important that an employer not only treats employees equitably in payment matters but is *seen* to do so too.

While it is difficult to gain general agreement about who should be paid what level of salary in an organisation, it is possible to employ certain clear principles when making decisions in the pay field. Those that are most important are the following:

- a standard approach for the determination of pay (basic rates and incentives) across the organisation;
- as little subjective or arbitrary decision making as is feasible;
- maximum communication and employee involvement in establishing pay determination mechanisms;
- clarity in pay determination matters so that everyone knows what the rules are and how they will be applied.

These are the foundations of procedural fairness or 'fair dealing'. In establishing pay rates it is not always possible to distribute rewards fairly to everyone's satisfaction, but it should always be possible to do so using procedures which operate equitably.

ARE WE BECOMING MORE STRATEGIC?

At the start of this chapter we explained how the decline in collective bargaining as the principal mechanism of pay determination in the UK had provided managers with new opportunities to develop their own pay strategies aimed at underpinning the achievement of organisational objectives. The extent to which such opportunities have in practice been taken up is a hotly debated question. More 'reward managers' are nowadays employed in organisations than 'salary administrators', but how big a change in practice does the change in job titles actually represent?

Many consultants working in the reward field believe that there has been a major shift in a strategic direction. Armstrong and Murlis (1998, pp. 12–14), for example, go so far as to argue that present-day practice is characterised by an acceptance of a 'new pay philosophy' in which decisions about payment levels and packages 'flow from the overall strategy' of the organisation. According to their view pay policy now increasingly underpins employer objectives and promotes change by rewarding 'results and behaviour consistent with the key goals of the organisation'. Similar claims are made by specialist managers working in the field of pay. Brown (2001, pp. 2–3), for example, draws on survey evidence from Towers Perrin which reveals that '80 per cent of organisations now have an explicit reward strategy' and that 'these strategic plans have driven the 94 per cent of them who introduced significant reward changes in the past three years'.

Academic researchers have tended to take issue with this assessment, often quite stridently. While they agree that major developments have occurred in pay determination over recent decades, they dispute the claims made about the extent of change and question how far organisations are taking a long-term strategic approach to the management of pay. Smith (1993) and Thompson (1998), in particular, have argued that managers are just as short-termist and reactive when making decisions about pay as they always were. Changes are introduced for damage limitation reasons, to respond to immediate recruitment difficulties or in response to government initiatives rather than as a means of aligning practices with organisational goals.

Kessler (2001) and Poole and Jenkins (1998) also report considerable gaps in many organisations between the rhetoric and reality of strategic activity in pay management. They did, however, also find evidence of the development of genuinely original approaches in some larger private sector organisations. For most, however, the story is one of incremental changes being made in order to improve features of existing systems rather than step-shifts involving the adoption of new strategic approaches (Cox and Purcell 1998; Brown 2001; Thompson and Milsome 2001).

WINDOW ON PRACTICE

Attitudes towards payment arrangements vary radically between different countries. In a survey in Singapore 1,500 respondents were asked to pick three of the following five factors which they believed would have a significant impact on wage determination: wages in the same industry, wages in a different industry, union representation, government influence and productivity. The proportion of respondents identifying the five factors as significant were:

Productivity	33.5%
Government	29.1%
Wages in the same industry	27.1%
Unions	18.3%
Wages in a different industry	14.8%

The same survey demonstrated that the main cause of differences between individual perspectives was the quality and quantity of information that they had received from their employers about their businesses.

Source: D.P. Torrington and Tan Chwee Huat (1994) *Human Resource Management for South East Asia*. Singapore: Simon & Schuster.

SUMMARY PROPOSITIONS

26.1 In payment matters employees are principally concerned with purchasing power, fairness and recognition of effort and skills. Employers are concerned with recruitment, retention, motivation and minimising the wage budget.

26.2 Employers are restricted in pay matters by the law and the realities of their product markets.

26.3 There are four main alternative methods of setting base pay rates: external labour market comparisons, internal labour market mechanisms, job evaluation and collective bargaining.

26.4 The main elements of payment are basic rate, plussage, benefits, premia, overtime, incentives and bonus.

26.5 Procedural equity is essential to the design of successful payment systems.

26.6 Analysts disagree about how far UK managers have embraced more strategic approaches to reward management in recent years.

GENERAL DISCUSSION TOPICS

1 Can payment ever be truly fair?

2 The chapter lists employer and employee objectives in relation to payment. What changes would you make to these lists?

3 Do you think it is possible to identify 'best practice' in payment policy? What elements would you consider should make up any such package?

FURTHER READING

Chartered Institute of Personnel and Development
The Chartered Institute of Personnel and Development carries out a big annual survey of reward management policy and practice which is published in February each year. It can be downloaded from the institute's website. They also published two useful broad surveys of the reward field in 2001; a research report entitled 'Reward Determination in the UK' and an executive briefing exploring *The future of reward*.

Kessler, I. (2001) 'Reward System Choices', in J. Storey (ed.) *Human Resource Management: A Critical Text*, 2nd edn. London: Thomson Learning
This excellent chapter assesses different conceptions of reward strategy and reviews the evidence on the extent to which any have been adopted in the UK. The author is particularly good at explaining links between pay policy and the broader debates about HRM strategy we discussed in Chapter 2.

Thorpe, R. and Homan, G. (2000) *Strategic Reward Systems*. London: Financial Times/Prentice Hall
Several of the chapters in this volume take forward the main points made in the present chapter. Many contain case study examples which illustrate the problems organisations face putting pay strategy into action in practice.

REFERENCES

Adams, J.S. (1963) 'Towards an understanding of inequity', *Journal of Abnormal and Social Psychology*, Vol. 67, pp. 422–36.

Armstrong, M. and Brown, D. (2001) *New Dimensions in Pay Management*. London: CIPD.

Armstrong, M. and Murlis, H. (1998) *Reward Management: A handbook of remuneration strategy and practice*. London: Kogan Page.

Bloom, M.C. (1998) 'Job evaluation methods', in L.H. Peters, C.R. Greer and S.A. Youngblood (eds) *Blackwell Encyclopedic Dictionary of Human Resource Management*. Oxford: Blackwell.

Brown, D. (2001) 'Reward futures, visions and strategies . . . who needs them?' in *The Future of Reward*, CIPD Executive Briefing. London: CIPD.

Brown, W., Marginson, P. and Walsh, J. (2003) 'The management of pay as the influence of collective bargaining diminishes', in P. Edwards (ed.) *Industrial Relations: Theory and Practice*, 2nd edn. Oxford: Blackwell.

CIPD (2004) *Reward Management 2004: A survey of policy and practice*. London: CIPD.

Cox, A. and Purcell, J. (1998) 'Searching for leverage in payment systems: trust, motivation and commitment in SMEs', in S.J. Perkins and S.J. Sandringham (eds) *Trust, Motivation and Commitment*. Farringdon: Remuneration Research Centre.

Cully, M., Woodland, S., O'Reilly, A. and Dix, G. (1999) *Britain at Work: As depicted by the 1998 Workplace Employee Relations Survey*. London: Routledge.

Doeringer, P.B. and Piore, M.J. (1970) *Internal Labour Markets and Manpower Analysis*. Washington, DC: Office of Manpower Research, US Department of Labor.

Grabham, A. (2003) 'Composition of Pay', *Labour Market Trends*, August.

Jacques, E. (1962) 'Objective measures for pay differentials', *Harvard Business Review*, January–February, pp. 133–7.

Kessler, I. (2001) 'Reward System Choices', in J. Storey (ed.) *Human Resource Management: A Critical Text*, 2nd edn. London: Thomson Learning.

Lazear, E.P. (1995) *Personnel Economics*. Boston: Massachusetts Institute of Technology.

Poole, M. and Jenkins, G. (1998) 'Human Resource Management and the Theory of Rewards: Evidence from a national survey', *British Journal of Industrial Relations*, Vol. 36, No. 2, pp. 227–47.

Thompson, M. (1998) 'Trust and Reward', in S.J. Perkins and S.J. Sandringham (eds) *Trust, Motivation and Commitment*. Farringdon: Remuneration Research Centre.

Thompson, P. and Milsome, S. (2001) *Reward Determination in the UK*. London: CIPD.

Thorpe, R. (2000) 'Reward Strategy', in R. Thorpe and G. Homan (eds) *Strategic Reward Systems*. London: Financial Times/Prentice Hall.

Smith, I. (1993) 'Reward management: A retrospective assessment', *Employee Relations*, Vol. 15.

Torrington, D.P. and Tan Chwee Huat (1994) *Human Resource Management for South East Asia*. Singapore: Simon & Schuster.

White, G. (2000) 'Determining pay', in G. White and J. Druker (eds) *Reward Management: A Critical Text*. London: Routledge.

An extensive range of additional materials, including multiple choice questions, answers to questions and links to useful websites can be found on the Human Resource Management Companion Website at **www.pearsoned.co.uk/torrington.**

CHAPTER 27

JOB EVALUATION

THE OBJECTIVES OF THIS CHAPTER ARE TO:

1. INTRODUCE AND ASSESS THE OPERATION OF TRADITIONAL GRADING STRUCTURES AND PAY SPINES
2. EXPLAIN THE CONCEPT OF 'BROADBANDING'
3. APPRAISE DIFFERENT APPROACHES TO JOB EVALUATION
4. DEMONSTRATE THE IMPORTANCE OF EMPLOYEE INVOLVEMENT IN DESIGNING JOB EVALUATION SCHEMES
5. EXAMINE THE INTEGRATION BETWEEN JOB EVALUATION AND EQUAL PAY LAW

One of the main tasks of payment administration is setting the differential gaps. It is necessary always to juggle the three factors of performance, market rate and equity. It is rarely possible or wise to pay people only according to their performance or contribution, and linking payment only to developments in the labour market can make working relationships very difficult. There is always the vexed question of how much more than Y and how much less than Z should X receive? The relative contribution of each individual of the three is difficult to measure, so some acceptable assessment of each job is made. The difficult problem of assessing performance is overlaid with the even more difficult problem of making comparisons.

The standard way of tackling this problem is to use a form of job evaluation, a long-established technique which appears to be used by more and more UK employers each year. Steady growth was reported during the 1990s despite the approach being criticised by advocates of greater flexibility in pay determination (IRS 1998a). Large-scale surveys (*see* Thompson and Milsome 2001; IDS 2003a; and CIPD 2004) confirm the continuation of this trend in more recent years, also providing evidence of further likely take-up in the future. Much of the recent growth has been in the public sector, local authorities and the NHS being examples of major employers establishing new schemes in recent years, but the surveys suggest that job evaluation is very widely used in the private sector as well. Moreover, few organisations abandon it, once introduced. The maxim that 'job evaluation is the one management tool that refuses to go out of fashion' thus continues to hold true.

The chief reason for the introduction of job evaluation is to achieve fairness in pay policy and to increase employees' sense of fairness. It is also commonly used as a tool in organisation restructuring and in harmonising the terms and conditions enjoyed by different groups of employees, for example following a merger or acquisition, or the signing of a single-status agreement with a trade union. Another important reason for the increased use of job evaluation is the need to comply with the Equal Pay Act 1970, as modified in 1984, which places as central in assessing equal pay claims the question of whether or not a job evaluation scheme is in use.

SALARY STRUCTURES

Most organisations of any size have in place a form of grading structure which is used as the basis for determining the basic rate of pay for each job. Moves towards person-based and performance-related reward in recent years have tended to be used to determine the level of bonus or progression within a grading structure. They have thus been used in addition to and not instead of established job-based systems.

The traditional approach involves developing a salary structure of groups, ladders and steps, whereby different groups or 'families' of jobs in an organisation are identified, each having a separate pay scale. This principle is illustrated in Figure 27.1.

Job families

The first element of the structure is the broad groupings of salaries, each group being administered according to the same set of rules. The questions in making decisions about this are to do with the logical grouping of job holders, according to their common interests, performance criteria, qualifications and, perhaps, bargaining arrangements and trade union membership. Massey (2000, p. 144) suggests the following as a typical seven-way division of jobs into distinct families:

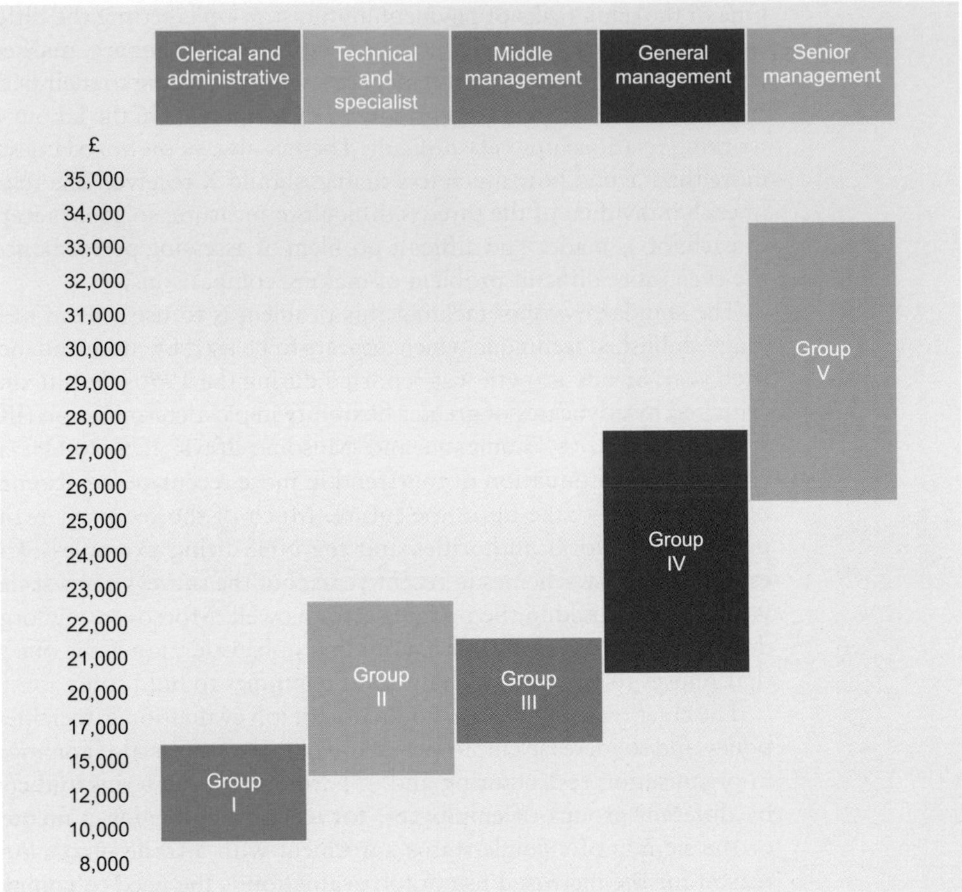

Figure 27.1 Typical salary groups

1 Executives
2 Management
3 Professional
4 Technical
5 Administrative
6 Skilled manual
7 Manual

The broad salary ranges are then set against each group, to encompass either the maximum and minimum of the various people who will then be in the group or – in the rare circumstance of starting from scratch – the ideal maximum and minimum levels.

As the grouping has been done on the basis of job similarity, the attaching of maximum and minimum salaries can show up peculiarities, with one or two jobs far below a logical minimum and others above a logical maximum. This requires the limits for the group to be put at the 'proper' level, with the exceptions either being identified as exceptions and the incumbents being paid a protected rate or being moved into a more appropriate group.

Salary groups will not stack neatly one on top of another in a salary hierarchy. There will be considerable overlap, recognising that there is an element of salary growth as a result of experience as well as status and responsibility. No overlap at all (a rare arrangement) emphasises the hierarchy, encouraging employees to put their feet on the salary ladder and climb, but the clarity of internal relativities may increase the dissatisfaction of those on the lower rungs and put pressure on the pay system to accommodate the occasional anomaly, especially if climbing is not well supported. Overlapping grades blur the edges of relativities and can reduce dissatisfaction at the bottom, but introduce dissatisfaction higher up.

Another reason why pay scales for different job families usually overlap is to accommodate scales of different length. A family with a flat hierarchy will tend to have a small number of scales with many steps, while the steep hierarchy will tend to have more scales, but each with fewer steps. One of the main drawbacks of overlapping scales is the problem of migration, where an employee regards the job as technical at one time and makes a case for it to be reclassified as administrative at another time, because there is no further scope for progress in the first classification. Another aspect of migration is the more substantive case of employees seeking transfer to other jobs as a result of changes in the relative pay scales, which reduce rigidity in the internal labour market.

Ladders and steps

Because employees are assumed to be career oriented, salary arrangements are based on that assumption, so each salary group has several ladders within it and each ladder has a number of steps (often referred to as 'scales' and 'points'). In the traditional model increments are awarded annually, reflecting individual seniority. Hence the new starter normally enters employment with the organisation at the lowest rung of the ladder in the grade for the job. At the end of each completed year of service they are then awarded an increment until after six or seven years they reach the top of the ladder – the ceiling for the relevant grade. At this point pay progression stops, except for any annual cost of living rise. The only way a higher income can be gained within the organisation is to secure promotion to a more highly graded job. This involves moving up on to a new ladder, at which point annual incremental pay awards commence again. Such approaches are still common in the public sector, although, as in many private sector organisations, incremental progress is increasingly linked to satisfactory performance or to the achievement of agreed objectives.

As with groups there is considerable overlap, the top rung of one ladder being rather higher than the bottom rung of the next. Taking a typical general management group as an example, we could envisage four ladders, as shown in Figure 27.2. The size of the differential between steps varies from £200 to £600 according to the level of the salary, and the overlapping could be used in a number of ways according to the differing requirements. Steps 6 and 7 on each ladder would probably be only for those who had reached their particular ceiling and were unlikely to be promoted further, while steps 4 and 5 could be for those who are on their way up and have made sufficient progress up one ladder to contemplate seeking a position with a salary taken from the next higher ladder.

The figures attached to the ladders in this example are round, in the belief that salaries are most meaningful to recipients when they are in round figures. However,

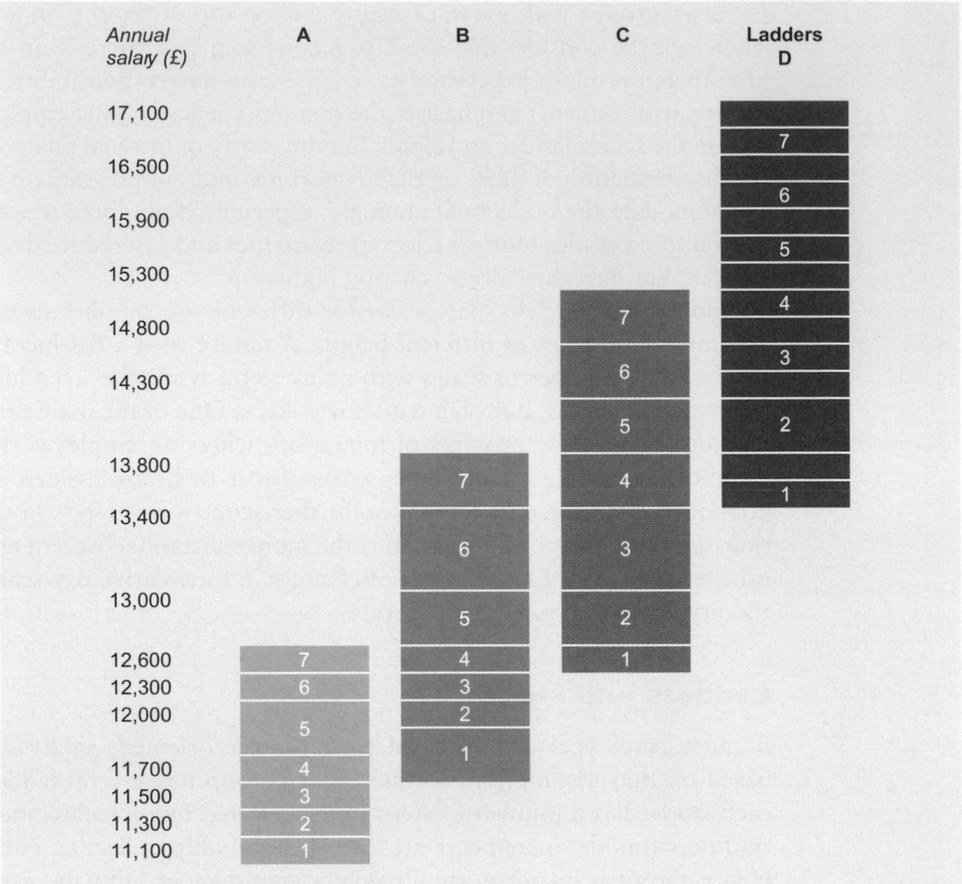

Figure 27.2 Ladders and steps in a salary group

ladders are sometimes developed with steps having a more precise arithmetical relationship to their relative position, so that each step represents the same percentage increase. Equally, some ladders have the same cash amount attached to each step. Some commentators place importance on the relationship of the maximum to the minimum of a ladder, described as the span, and the relationship between the bottom rung of adjacent ladders, referred to as the differential. According to Armstrong and Murlis (1998, pp. 174–5), a span of 50 per cent above the minimum or 20 per cent on either side of the midpoint 'is fairly common and was orthodox practice a decade or more ago'. Differentials of 20 per cent are also seen as typical, but there is no inscrutable logic behind these precise figures. There is a neatness and symmetry about the method, which can commend itself to salary recipients.

The self-financing increment principle

It is generally believed that fixed incremental payment schemes are self-regulating, so that introducing incremental payment schemes does not mean that within a few years everyone is at the maximum. The assumption is that just as some move up, others retire or resign and are replaced by new recruits at the bottom of the ladder. This will clearly not be the case when staff turnover is low.

ACTIVITY 27.1

If incremental scales cease to be self-financing through lack of labour market movement, what advantage is there to the employer in keeping them?

Why not one big (happy) family?

An important question is whether there should be subgroupings within the organisation at all, or whether all employees should be paid in accordance with one overall salary structure. Internal relativities disappear; there is only a differential structure.

This arrangement has many attractions, as it emphasises the integration of all employees and may encourage them to identify with the organisation as a whole, it is administratively simple and can stimulate competition for personal advancement. It also allows more flexibility in the pay that is arranged for any individual. Interest in the development of single pay structures has increased in recent years for a number of reasons. It has accompanied a more general preference among employers for taking a company-wide approach to a whole range of HR initiatives. New technologies often demand a more flexible workforce, leading to a blurring of the organisational distinction between groups of workers. Harmonisation of the terms and conditions of employment follows, so that all employees work the same number of hours, are given the same training opportunities and enjoy the same entitlement to occupational pensions, sick pay and annual leave. Such practices have also been conspicuously imported into British subsidiaries of Japanese and American companies, which typically have longer experience of single-status employment practices.

Interest has also arisen following recent judgments in which courts have awarded equal pay to employees who have sought to compare their jobs with those of other individuals in wholly different job families. As a result, employers who continue to operate different mechanisms for determining the pay of different groups of employees have had difficulty in defending their practices when faced with equal value claims.

The argument against such a system is that it applies a common set of assumptions that may be inappropriate for certain groups. In general management, for instance, it will probably be an assumption that all members of the group will be interested in promotion and job change; this will be encouraged by the salary arrangements, which will encourage job holders to look for opportunities to move around. In contrast, the research chemist will be expected to stick at one type of job for a longer period, and movement into other fields of the company's affairs, such as personnel or marketing, will often be discouraged. For this reason it will be more appropriate for the research chemist to be in a salary group with a relatively small number of ladders, each having a large number of steps; while a general management colleague will be more logically set in a context of more ladders, each with fewer steps.

Moreover, in practice it is very difficult to develop a single pay structure which is acceptable to all parties in an organisation. The more diverse the skills, values and union affiliation of the employees, the more difficult is such a single job family. The factors used to compare job with job always tend to favour one grouping at the expense of another; one job at the expense of another. The wider the diversity of jobs that are brought within the purview of a single scheme, the wider will be the potential dissatisfaction, with the result that the payment arrangement is one that at best is tolerated because it is the least offensive rather than being accepted as satisfactory.

ACTIVITY 27.2

In what type of situations do you think a single, integrated pay structure would be appropriate? Where would such a pay structure be inappropriate? What are the most likely management problems in each case?

WINDOW ON PRACTICE

In 2003 the National Health Service started the process of moving towards a single streamlined pay structure for all its staff except doctors and dentists by securing agreement with its many trade unions to pilot a scheme in 12 NHS Trusts. The new pay scales form part of a wider package of measures being introduced by the government under the heading 'agenda for change'. The intention is for national implementation to begin in 2004 and 2005.

The new pay structure radically simplifies established NHS pay practices. Instead of each professional group negotiating its own grading structure, the agenda for change approach creates a standard pay scale which covers everyone. Six hundred and fifty different pay grades are being replaced with just 16 pay bands (two spines each with eight grades) along with harmonised terms and conditions which will apply across the whole NHS.

All existing jobs are being allocated to one of the eight new bands using a job evaluation scheme which takes account of five factors:

- the level of responsibility held by the job holder
- the extent of knowledge, training and experience needed to do the job
- the extent to which the job holder has freedom to act independently
- the level and type of skills deployed by the job holder
- the nature of the working environment and amount of effort required to carry out the job.

The number of incremental steps varies from band to band. Band 1 (mainly for lower-skilled ancillary and clerical roles) contains four steps, while Band 7 (specialist nurses and section managers) contains nine. Progression is mainly based on seniority, so after each completed year of service, the employee is awarded one increment and climbs a step. But two steps in each band (the second from the bottom and one higher up the scale) can only be attained if the job holder satisfies a competency-based assessment.

Sources: IDS (2003b) 'Pay modernisation in the NHS', *IDS Report 884*, July. London: IDS; and Department of Health website (www.doh.gov.uk/agendaforchange).

BROADBANDING

Attention has recently been given to the introduction of 'broadbanding' as a way of retaining the positive features of traditional pay scales while reducing some of the less desirable effects (*see* Armstrong and Brown 2001, CIPD 2004). One of these less desirable effects is the built-in incentive to focus on being promoted rather than on performing well in the current job. This can lead to individuals playing damaging political games in a bid to weaken the position of colleagues or even undermine their own supervisors. Inflexibility can also occur when individuals refuse to undertake duties or types of work associated with higher grades. Moreover, in making internal equity the main determinant of pay rates within an organisation, rigid salary structures prevent managers from offering higher salaries to new employees. This tends to hinder effective competition in some labour markets.

Broadbanding essentially involves retaining some form of grading system while greatly reducing the numbers of grades or salary bands. The process typically results in the replacement of a structure consisting of ten or a dozen distinct grades with one consisting of only three or four. Pay variation within grades is then based on individual performance, skill or external market value rather than on the nature and size of the job. The great advantage of such approaches is their ability to reduce hierarchical thinking. Differences in pay levels still exist between colleagues but they are no longer seen as being due solely to the fact that one employee is graded more highly than another. This can reduce feelings of inequity provided the new criteria are reasonably open and objective. As a result, teamwork is encouraged as is a focus on improving individual performance in order to secure higher pay.

In theory, therefore, broadbanded structures increase the extent to which managers have discretion over the setting of internal differentials, introduce more flexibility and permit organisations to reward performance or skills acquisition as well as job size. Their attraction is that they achieve this while retaining a skeleton grading system which gives order to the structure and helps justify differentials. Time will tell how acceptable such approaches are to the courts when it comes to judging equal value claims.

JOB EVALUATION METHODS

Job evaluation is the most common method used to compare the relative values of different jobs in order to provide the basis for a rational pay structure. Among the many definitions is this one from ACAS:

> Job evaluation is concerned with assessing the relative demands of different jobs within an organization. Its usual purpose is to provide a basis for relating differences in rates of pay to different in-job requirements. It is therefore a tool which can be used to help in the determination of a pay structure. (ACAS 1984)

It is a well-established technique, having been developed in all its most common forms by the 1920s. In recent years it has received a series of boosts. First, various types of incomes policy between 1965 and 1974 either encouraged the introduction of job evaluation or specifically permitted expenditure above the prevailing norm by companies wishing to introduce it. In the 1980s the use of job evaluation became the hinge of most equal pay cases. More recently organisations have found it useful as part of moves towards single-status contractual arrangements and resolving pay issues following organisational mergers (IDS 2000, p. 2).

Despite its popularity it is often misunderstood, so the following points have to be made:

1 Job evaluation is concerned with the job and not the performance of the individual job holder. Individual merit is not assessed.
2 The technique is systematic rather than scientific. It depends on the judgement of people with experience, requiring them to decide in a planned and systematic way, but it does not produce results that are infallible.
3 Job evaluation does not eliminate collective bargaining. It determines the differential gaps between incomes; it does not determine pay levels or annual pay rises.
4 Only a structure of pay rates is produced. Other elements of earnings, such as premia and incentives, are not determined by the method.

There are many methods of job evaluation in use and they are summarised by Armstrong and Murlis (1998, pp. 81–102), Smith and Nethersall (2000) and IDS (2003a). Where a non-analytical or 'whole job' scheme is used a panel of assessors examines each job as a whole, in terms of its difficulty or value to the business, to determine which should be ranked more highly than others. No attempt is made to break each job down into its constituent parts. By contrast, an analytical scheme requires each element or factor of the job to be assessed. Since 1988 it has been the practice of courts only to accept the results of analytical schemes in equal pay cases.

The most widely used analytical schemes are based on points-rating systems, under which each job is examined in terms of factors such as skill, effort and responsibility. Each factor is given a weighting indicating its value relative to the others and for each factor there are varying degrees. A score is then given depending on how demanding the job is in terms of each factor, with the overall points value determining the relative worth of each job – and hence its grade in the organisation's pay structure. Traditionally the analysis was carried out by a panel of managers and workforce representatives examining each job description in turn and comparing it, factor by factor, against grading definitions. In recent years there has been increased interest in computer-assisted job evaluation systems which award scores to each job on the basis of information gathered from job analysis questionnaires.

A well-known set of factors, weightings and degrees was devised for the National Electrical Manufacturers Association of the United States, but the International Labour Organisation has produced a list of the factors used most frequently (*see* table below). It would be unusual for more than a dozen of these to be used in any one scheme, most taking account of six to ten different factors.

The points values eventually derived for each job can be plotted on a graph or simply listed from the highest to the lowest to indicate the ranking. Then – and only then – are points ratings matched with cash amounts, as decisions are made on which points ranges equate with various pay grades. This process is illustrated in Figure 27.3, each cross representing a job. The most common approach involves using a graph on which one axis represents the *current* salary for each job evaluated and

- Accountability
- Accuracy
- Analysis and judgement
- Complexity
- Contact and diplomacy
- Creativity
- Decision making
- Dexterity
- Education
- Effect of errors
- Effort
- Initiative
- Judgement
- Know-how
- Knowledge and skills
- Mental effort
- Mental fatigue
- Physical demands
- Physical skills
- Planning and coordination
- Problem solving
- Resources control
- Responsibility for cash/materials, etc.
- Social skills
- Supervision given/received
- Task completion
- Training and experience
- Work conditions
- Work pressure

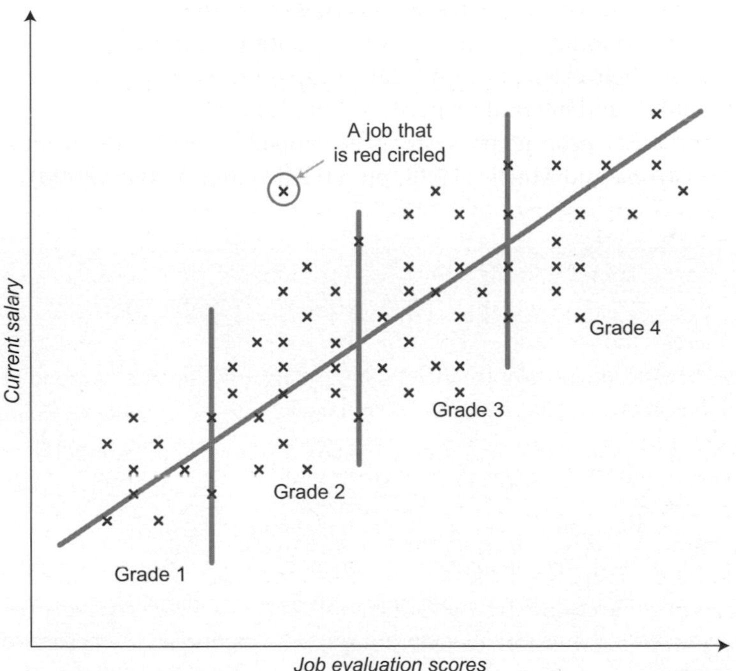

Figure 27.3 Job evaluation analysis

the other the number of *job evaluation points* awarded. A line of best fit is then drawn and each job assigned to a grade. Salary-modelling software is widely available to help with this process.

It is virtually inevitable that some jobs will be found to be paid incorrectly after job evaluation has been completed. If the evaluation says that the pay rate should be higher then the rate duly rises, either immediately or step by step, to the new level. The only problem is finding the money, and introducing job evaluation always costs money. More difficult is the situation where evaluation shows the employee to be overpaid. It is not feasible to reduce the pay of the job holder without breaching the contract of employment. There have been two approaches. The first, which was never widespread and appears almost to have disappeared, is buying out. The overpaid employee is offered a large lump sum in consideration of the fact of henceforth being paid at the new, lower rate. The second and more general device used is that of the personal rate or **red-circling**. An example could be where the rate for the job would be circled in red on the salary administrator's records to show that the employee should continue at the present level while remaining in that post, but a successor would be paid at the lower job-evaluated rate.

A very widely used proprietary scheme is the Hay Guide Chart-Profile Method (E-reward 2003), which is particularly appropriate for the evaluation of management jobs. The method is based on an assessment of four factors; know-how, problem solving, accountability and working conditions. Jobs are assessed by using each of three guide charts, one for each factor. A profile is then developed for the job showing the relationship between the factors, a ranking is eventually produced and the rates of pay of the jobs considered in order to produce a new pay structure. At this stage comes one of the greatest advantages of this system. The proprietors have available a vast amount of comparative pay data on different undertakings using their system, so their clients not only can compare rates of pay within their organisation (differentials and internal relativities) but also can examine their external relativities. This and other proprietary systems developed by firms of consultants are described by Armstrong and Murlis (1998, pp. 602–15) and by IDS (2000).

WINDOW ON PRACTICE

In 1997 the National Joint Council for Local Authority Services agreed in principle to abolish the long-standing division in UK local government between manual workers and white-collar officers. This harmonisation deal included the introduction of a single national pay spine covering all workers. In order to assist local authorities to implement the new payment arrangements, the negotiating parties at national level developed a single-status job evaluation scheme which can be used to assess the size of jobs across the various employee groupings. No authority is obliged to evaluate jobs using this particular scheme, but many are doing so. Potentially, 1.5 million workers could ultimately be covered. The main motivation for moving towards a single pay spine was the threat of equal value claims.

The local government scheme contains four principal factors: knowledge and skills, effort demands, responsibilities and environmental demands. Each is broken down into a number of subfactors which are weighted differently. Under 'effort demands' four headings are listed: initiative and independence, physical effort, mental effort and emotional effort, the first being weighted as having double the significance of the others. The aim is to ensure that different types of 'effort' are rewarded properly, those typically associated with male jobs being given equal standing to those that are characteristic of female-dominated jobs.

Sources: IRS (1998b) 'From status quo to single status: job evaluation in local government', *IRS Employment Trends 663*, September, and S. Hastings (2000) 'Grading systems and estimating value', in G. White and J. Druker (eds) *Reward Management: A Critical Text*. London: Routledge.

EMPLOYEE PARTICIPATION IN JOB EVALUATION

The degree of participation by non-managerial employees in job evaluation varies from one business to another. In some cases the entire operation is conducted from start to finish without any employee participation at all. Some degree of participation is more common and is sensible if acceptance of a new scheme is to be gained. Apart from negotiating on pay levels and bargaining units, the main opportunities for employee contribution are discussed below.

Job families

Employees collectively need to consent to the family structure and they can probably add to the deliberations of managers about what that structure should be, as they will be well aware of the sensitive points of comparison.

Job descriptions

Traditionally job descriptions have been crucial to the evaluation and it is common for job holders to prepare their own, using a pro-forma outline, or for supervisors to prepare them for jobs for which they are responsible. Superficially, this is an attractive method, as there is direct involvement of the employee, who cannot claim to have been misrepresented. Also, it delegates the task of writing job descriptions, enabling it to be completed more quickly. The drawback is similar to that of character references in selection. Some employees write good descriptions and some write bad ones: some overstate while others understate. Inconsistency in job descriptions makes consistency in evaluation difficult.

An alternative is for job descriptions to be compiled by job analysts after questioning employees and their supervisors, who subsequently initial the job description which the analyst produces, attesting to its accuracy.

Panel evaluation

The awarding of points is usually done by a panel of people who represent between them the interests and expertise of management and employee. This is not only being 'democratic', it is acknowledging the need for the experience and perspective of job holders as well as managers in arriving at shrewd judgements of relative worth. Naturally, panel memberships alter so that employees are not asked to evaluate their own jobs. Although there is an understandable general tendency for employee representatives to push ratings up, and for management representatives to try to push them down, this usually smooths out because both parties are deriving differential rankings and not pay levels. The only potential conflict of interest will be if employee representatives and managers have divergent objectives on the shape of the eventual pay structure, with big or small differential gaps.

Job analysis questionnaires

Proprietary, computer-assisted job evaluation methods involve trained analysts putting a series of detailed questions to job holders from a multiple-choice questionnaire. The results are then fed into a computer which generates a score for each job. There is therefore no need for a panel to reach decisions based on written job descriptions. While there is clearly direct employee involvement in providing answers to the job analysis questionnaire, the absence of a panel including workforce representatives can reduce the level of employee influence on the outcome of the exercise. This is particularly the case with those proprietary schemes which are customised to meet the needs of the purchasing organisation.

EQUAL VALUE

One of the major reasons for the growth in job evaluation in recent years has been the development of equal pay law. When assessing the validity of equal pay claims, tribunals employ the principles of job evaluation as a starting point, appointing a job analyst to undertake a comparison of the content of different jobs if necessary. Importantly, from the employer perspective, this means that the use by an organisation of an analytical job evaluation scheme can be a very effective defence when an equal pay claim is brought. The employer can simply claim that the jobs in question have both been evaluated and have been found to be of different value for specific reasons. Provided the scheme itself is free of sex bias, this should serve to deter aggrieved employees from bringing cases in the first place.

The Equal Pay Act 1970 established that a woman could bring a case to an employment tribunal claiming entitlement to equal pay with a man working at the same establishment if the claimant and her chosen comparator were engaged in 'like work' or work rated as equivalent under an employer's job evaluation study. A man can equally bring a case comparing his pay to that of a female colleague but this has rarely occurred in practice outside the field of pension entitlements. An amendment to the Act, which came into effect in 1984, broadened the definition of 'equal value' so that it became possible for a case to be brought if the claimant believes that her work is equal to that of her comparator in terms of the demands made upon them. This amendment followed a European Court ruling which judged the existing Equal Pay Act to fall short of the standard established by the EEC Equal Pay Directive. Since then other European Court rulings have further extended the scope of equal value law.

Like work

When presented with a claim for equal pay an employment tribunal will first seek to establish whether the claimant is engaged in 'like work' with the more highly paid man she has named as her comparator. The work does not have to be identical to justify equal pay under this heading, but must be either the same or of a broadly similar nature. In practice this means that the difference in pay can only be justified if there is 'a difference of practical importance' in the work done or if there is 'a genuine material factor' which justifies the higher rate of pay enjoyed by the male comparator.

An example of a difference of practical importance might be the level of responsibility of the man's job when compared to that of the claimant. An employer might, for example, be justified in paying a man more than his female colleague working on a comparable production line if the articles being manufactured by the man were of substantially greater value. Similarly a discriminatory payment could be justified if a man worked under less supervision than a woman engaged in otherwise like work. A common example would be a man working without supervision on night shifts.

Where there is no practical difference of this kind a discriminatory payment can only be justified where there is a 'genuine material factor other than sex' which can explain the difference in pay levels.

Work rated as equivalent

Cases brought under this section of the Act relate to jobs which are different in nature but have been rated as equivalent under the employer's job evaluation study. The existence of such a study can also provide the basis of an employer's defence in equal value claims. A definition of a job evaluation scheme is included in the Act:

> A woman is to be regarded as employed on work rated as equivalent with that of any man if her job and his have been given an equal value, in terms of the demand made on a worker under various headings (for instance, effort, skill, decision), on a study undertaken with a view to evaluating in these terms the jobs done by all or any of the employees in an undertaking. (Equal Pay Act 1970, s. 1.5)

Case law has further narrowed the definition of acceptable job evaluation schemes. In the case of *Bromley* v. *H. & J. Quick* (1988) the Court of Appeal ruled that the identification of benchmark jobs and paired comparisons was 'insufficiently analytical' as this did not involve evaluation under headings as required by the Act. The widely used method of job evaluation whereby only a sample of benchmark jobs are analysed cannot, therefore, be relied upon as a basis for an employer's defence. The jobs of the applicants and their chosen comparators must each have been evaluated analytically. In addition, a tribunal will look at the means by which scores derived from a job evaluation scheme are used to determine the rate of pay and will take account of a job evaluation study which has been completed but not implemented.

To be acceptable to a tribunal the job evaluation scheme in use must also be free of sex bias. Employers should ensure, therefore, that the factor weightings do not indirectly discriminate by overemphasising job requirements associated with typical male jobs, such as physical effort, at the expense of those associated with jobs predominantly undertaken by women, such as manual dexterity or attention to detail.

Work of equal value

A woman who is not engaged in like work, work of a broadly similar nature or work rated as equivalent is still entitled to bring an equal pay claim if she believes her work to be of equal value. In these cases the claimant names as her chosen comparator a man employed by the same undertaking who may be engaged in work of a wholly different nature. If the tribunal decides that there are grounds to believe that the work is of equal value, it will then appoint an independent expert, nominated by ACAS, to carry out a job evaluation study. The report of the expert will then be used by the tribunal as a basis of the decision on whether or not to make an award of equal pay to the claimant. A woman may bring an equal value claim in this way even if she has male colleagues engaged in like work and paid at the same rate as she.

A number of significant equal value cases have been brought to tribunals over the years. In *Hayward* v. *Cammell Laird* (1984) a cook was awarded pay equal to that of men employed as joiners and laggers, but only after an appeal to the House of Lords three years after making the initial complaint. In 1990 the shopworkers' union USDAW dropped an equal value case against Sainsbury's when the employer agreed to carry out a job evaluation exercise. The union had claimed that predominantly female check-out operators were engaged in work of equal value to that of predominantly male warehousemen. This led to an 11 per cent rise in Sainsbury's retail wage bill and to a series of similar USDAW settlements with other major retailers during 1990 and 1991. The impact of these cases has been very substantial, leading to the restructuring of pay arrangements across industry and the public services.

Genuine material factor defences

If it is established, to the satisfaction of an employment tribunal, that the claimant is engaged in like work, work rated as equivalent or work of equal value, the employer must show that the difference in the respective rates of pay is not due to sex discrimination but to a 'genuine material factor not of sex'. There are many defences which potentially fall into this category, some of which are described in Chapter 23. Among the most significant, as far as job evaluation is concerned, is the practice of red-circling whereby an individual's rate of pay is protected for a period following redeployment or a new job evaluation exercise. In most cases, provided it can be clearly shown that the red circle was awarded for reasons other than the individual's sex, this will be an acceptable material factor defence.

WINDOW ON PRACTICE

The Ontario Pay Equity Act

A major purpose of equal pay law is the reduction of inequality between payment for jobs which are principally performed by men and those which are mostly carried out by women. Although improvements have occurred since the 1970s when the legislation was first brought in, women's gross average hourly earnings remain around 80 per cent of men's (Shaw and Clark 2000). Equal pay law is thus failing to achieve one of its principal aims, or is doing so too slowly. This has led many to argue that the current law is inadequate and that more radical approaches are needed.

A model often cited by supporters of change is the approach used in the Canadian province of Ontario, where an inspectorate has a policing role. This means that there is less need for individual women or their representatives to prepare court actions. The following are the key features of the Ontario pay equity regime:

- Employers of more than 100 people are required to have written policies which identify 'female' job classes – defined as being over 60 per cent female.
- They then have to carry out job evaluation to establish whether or not there is a discrepancy between male and female classes.

- Where there is, they have to draw up a 'pay equity plan' setting out what they intend to do to narrow the gap – that is, make pay equity adjustments – over a number of years if necessary.
- There are derogations similar in nature to the UK's genuine material factors which employers can deploy to defend unequal pay.

Aileen McColgan (1993, p. 251) makes the following observation about the system:

> The potential of Ontario's legislation lies in its effective reversal of the burden of proof. Rather than encouraging employers to ignore issues of equal pay save in the unlikely event of an individual's complaint, the Pay Equity Act obliges them, in co-operation with any bargaining agent, to scrutinise their own pay practices for evidence of discrimination and eliminate it.

SUMMARY PROPOSITIONS

27.1 Traditional salary structures assign each job to a grade in which there are a number of incremental steps.

27.2 Recent years have seen moves towards single pay spines covering all jobs in an organisation. Separate scales for different 'job families' remain common.

27.3 Another recent development is a move towards broadbanded structures which reduce the number of grades in each salary scale to allow managers greater flexibility in setting pay levels for individual employees.

27.4 Job evaluation involves using a standard system to measure the size or importance of jobs in an organisation. Systems can be analytical or non-analytical. Modern computerised systems are highly analytical in nature.

27.5 Key decisions in designing job evaluation schemes are which factors to include and what weighting to give to each.

27.6 A major reason for the growth in the use of job evaluation in recent years has been the development of equal value law which uses the principles of job evaluation as the basis for deciding cases.

GENERAL DISCUSSION TOPICS

1. 'Job evaluation does not produce equitable payment: it merely produces a ramshackle method of justifying the status quo.' Do you agree with this statement?
2. What would be the main arguments for and against introducing legislation that is similar to the Ontario Pay Equity Act in the UK?
3. What do you think would be the major organisational problems associated with a move from a narrow to a broadbanded payment stucture?

FURTHER READING

Armstrong, M. and Baron, A. (1995) *The Job Evaluation Handbook*. London: IPD

Hastings, S. (2000) 'Grading systems and estimating value' in G. White and J. Druker (eds) *Reward Management: A Critical Text*. London: Routledge

IDS (2003a) 'Job evaluation is alive and well despite market-driven pay', *IDS Report 875*, February. London: Incomes Data Services

Lawler, E. (1990) *Strategic Pay*. San Francisco: Jossey Bass

IDS (2003a) and Armstrong and Baron (1995) provide the best practical guides to job evaluation processes, including case studies from different sectors. The most widely quoted critique of job evaluation is found in Lawler (1990), in which the author sets out the case for the adoption of new approaches in many organisational scenarios. Hastings (2000) provides a good summary of various other critical perspectives.

Armstrong, M. and Brown, D. (2001) *New Dimensions in Pay Management*. London: CIPD

IPD (1997) *The IPD Guide on Broadbanding*. London: IPD

A great deal has been written about broadbanding in recent years and the likelihood that it will be adopted to a greater extent in the future. The best general introduction to the topic is IPD (1997), a more detailed account being provided by Armstrong and Brown (2001).

Leslie, S., Hastings, S. and Morris, J. (2003) *Equal Pay: A practical guide to the law*. London: The Law Society

Rubery, J. (ed.) (1998) *Equal Pay in Europe? Closing the Gender Wage Gap*. London: Macmillan

Shaw, S. and Clark, M. (2000) 'Women, pay and equal opportunities', in R. Thorpe and G. Homan (eds) *Strategic Reward Systems*. London: Financial Times/Prentice Hall

Equal pay issues are debated and discussed in many books and articles. Good starting points are Shaw and Clark (2000) and Leslie *et al.* (2003). The book of articles edited by Jill Rubery (1998) contains detailed analysis of pay equity issues in different industries in Germany, Italy and the UK.

REFERENCES

ACAS (1984) *Job Evaluation*. London: Advisory, Conciliation and Arbitration Services.

Armstrong, M. and Brown, D. (2001) *New Dimensions in Pay Management*. London: CIPD.

Armstrong, M. and Murlis, H. (1998) *Reward Management*. London: Kogan Page.

Chartered Institute of Personnel and Development (2004) *Reward Management 2004: A survey of policy and practice*. London: CIPD.

E-reward (2003) 'What is happening to job evaluation today: a large-scale survey', www.e-reward.co.uk.

Hastings, S. (2000) 'Grading systems and estimating value', in G. White and J. Druker (eds) *Reward Management: A Critical Text*. London: Routledge.

IDS (2000) *Job Evaluation*, IDS Studies Plus, Autumn. London: Incomes Data Services.

IDS (2003a) 'Job evaluation is alive and well despite market-driven pay', *IDS Report*, No. 875, February. London, Incomes Data Services.

IDS (2003b) 'Pay modernisation in the NHS', *IDS Report*, No. 884, July. London: IDS.

IPD (1997) *The IPD Guide on Broadbanding*. London: IPD.

IRS (1998a) 'There is value in job evaluation', *IRS Employment Trends*, No. 665, October.

IRS (1998b) 'From status quo to single status: job evaluation in local government', *IRS Employment Trends*, No. 663, September.

McColgan, A. (1993) 'Equal Pay: A New Approach', in A. McColgan (ed.), *The Future of Labour Law*. London: Cassell.

Massey, C. (2000) 'Strategic reward systems – pay systems and structures', in R. Thorpe and G. Homan (eds) *Strategic Reward Systems*. London: Financial Times/Prentice Hall.

Shaw, S. and Clark, M. (2000) 'Women, pay and equal opportunities', in R. Thorpe and G. Homan (eds) *Strategic Reward Systems*. London: Financial Times/Prentice Hall.

Smith, P. and Nethersall, G. (2000) 'Job Evaluation', in R. Thorpe and G. Homan (eds) *Strategic Reward Systems*. London: Financial Times/Prentice Hall.

Thompson, P. and Milsome, S. (2001) *Reward Determination in the UK*. London: CIPD.

LEGAL CASES

Bromley v. *H. & J. Quick* [1988] ICR 623.

Hayward v. *Cammell Laird Shipbuilders Ltd* [1984] TLR 52.

An extensive range of additional materials, including multiple choice questions, answers to questions and links to useful websites can be found on the Human Resource Management Companion Website at **www.pearsoned.co.uk/torrington.**

CHAPTER 28

INCENTIVES

THE OBJECTIVES OF THIS CHAPTER ARE TO:

1 SET OUT THE MAJOR CHOICES FACED BY EMPLOYERS CONTEMPLATING SETTING UP OR REVIEWING INCENTIVE PAYMENT SCHEMES

2 EXPLORE THE QUESTION OF HOW MANY PEOPLE ARE PAID DIFFERENT TYPES OF INCENTIVE IN THE UK

3 OUTLINE THE MAIN FORMS OF PAYMENT BY RESULTS (PBR) SCHEMES AND DISCUSS THEIR ADVANTAGES AND DISADVANTAGES

4 DEBATE THE MERITS OF INDIVIDUAL PERFORMANCE-RELATED PAY (PRP)

5 INTRODUCE SKILLS-BASED PAY AND DISCUSS ITS MAJOR ADVANTAGES AND DISADVANTAGES

6 OUTLINE THE MAJOR FORMS OF PROFIT-SHARING SCHEMES THAT OPERATE, INCLUDING THOSE SPONSORED BY THE GOVERNMENT

Incentive payments remain one of the ideas that fascinate managers as they search for the magic formula. Somewhere there is a method of linking payment to performance so effectively that their movements will coincide, enabling the manager to leave the workers on automatic pilot, as it were, while attending to more important matters such as strategic planning or going to lunch. This conviction has sustained a continuing search for this elusive formula, which has been hunted with all the fervour of those trying to find the Holy Grail or the crock of gold at the end of the rainbow.

In recent years incentives of all kinds have been the source of much debate among HR professionals, consultants, trade unionists and academic writers. While particular attention has been given to the pros and cons of individual performance-related reward systems, much has also been written in support of and against the use of team-based incentives and those which reward the acquisition of defined skills. Profit sharing and employee share ownership have been the subject of significant government initiatives and have thus also become topics about which a great deal is written.

BASIC CHOICES

While incentive payment systems are common in the UK, there are millions of employees who do not receive this kind of reward and many employers who use them only in a limited way (often in the remuneration of senior managers). It is thus perfectly possible, and some would argue desirable, to recruit, retain and motivate a workforce by paying a simple, fixed rate of pay for each job in the organisation. There is other equipment in the HR manager's toolkit which can be used to reward effort and maintain good levels of job satisfaction. The most fundamental question is therefore whether or not to use an incentive payment system at all. In the opinion of Sisson and Storey (2000, pp. 123–4) many organisations in the UK have introduced schemes in recent years for 'ideological reasons' as a means of impressing stockmarket analysts, reinforcing management control or undermining established collective bargaining machinery. These, they suggest, are poor reasons which have generally met with little long-term success. Incentive schemes should only be used where they are appropriate to the needs of the business and where they can clearly contribute to the achievement of organisational objectives.

There is a long tradition in the academic literature of hostility to incentive schemes in general and those which focus on the individual in particular. In 1966, Frederick Herzberg argued that pay was a 'hygiene factor' rather than a 'motivator'. He claimed that its capacity to motivate positively was limited, while it can very easily demotivate when managed poorly. It follows that there is little to be gained and a great deal to lose from the introduction of incentive schemes. Others (for example, Thompson 2000) have focused on the way that incentives are perceived by employees as tools of management control which reduce their autonomy and discretion. This, it is argued, causes resentment and leads to dissatisfaction and industrial conflict.

A different school of thought argues in favour of incentives on the grounds that they reward effort and behaviours which the organisation wishes to encourage. As a result they not only are a fair basis for rewarding people, but also can enhance organisational effectiveness and productivity. Advocates of **expectancy theory** hold this position with their belief that individual employees will alter their behaviour (e.g. by working harder or prioritising their actions differently) if they believe that in so doing they will be rewarded with something they value. Hence, where additional pay is a valued reward, employees will seek it and will work to secure it. A positive outcome for both employer and employee is achievable provided the incentive is paid in return for a form of employee behaviour which genuinely contributes to the achievement of organisational objectives.

The research evidence points both ways on the question of how far incentives actually lead to performance improvements at the organisational level. Some studies suggest a correlation between superior performance and some types of incentive scheme (e.g. Huselid 1995), while others (e.g. Thompson 1992) have found no evidence of any link. Much seems to depend on the circumstances. Incentives are not universally applicable, but can play a role in enhancing individual effort or performance where the conditions and scheme design are right. Problems occur when the wrong system is imposed, on the wrong people, in the wrong circumstances or for the wrong reasons.

Where an incentive scheme is used, the next choice relates to the way the scheme is to operate. There are two basic approaches that can be used: bonus payments and incremental progression. In the case of the former, the employee is rewarded with a single payment (possibly made in stages) at the end of a payment period. In the case of profit sharing it will often be an annual payment, while sales commission is usually paid monthly. Whatever the timing, the key principle is that the pay is variable. Good performance in one period is rewarded, but the same individual could earn rather less in the next if their performance deteriorates. Some writers refer to such systems as putting 'pay at risk', because earnings vary from period to period depending on how much incentive is earned. The alternative approach involves making incremental progression dependent on the individual's contribution. The reward takes the form of a general pay rise over and above any cost of living increment being paid in a particular year. The incentive payment thus becomes consolidated into overall earnings and is not variable or 'at risk' after it has been earned.

ACTIVITY 28.1

What in your view are the main advantages and disadvantages of these alternative approaches from a management perspective? Would you be more motivated by the prospect of a pay rise or a one-off bonus payment?

Another basic choice concerns the extent of the incentive. In practice this is a decision of rather greater importance than the type of incentive scheme to be used, although it is given rather less coverage in the literature. There is the world of difference, in terms of cost and employee perception, between a scheme which rewards people with 3 per cent or 4 per cent of salary and one which pays a sum equivalent to 25 per cent. Studies undertaken in the USA, reported by Bartol and Durham (2000, p. 14), suggest that the minimum level of bonus or pay rise 'necessary to elicit positive perceptual and attitudinal responses' is between 5 per cent and 7 per cent of salary. Lesser payments are thus unlikely to provide meaningful incentives and will have only a peripheral impact. According to Hendry *et al.* (2000, p. 54) this has been a major problem for schemes introduced in the public sector where incentives have tended to be worth a maximum of only 2 per cent or 3 per cent of salary. Armstrong and Murlis (1998) offer the following advice:

> As a rule of thumb, those whose performance is outstanding may deserve and expect rewards of 10% and more in their earlier period in a job. People whose level of performance and rate of development is well above the average may merit increases of between 7 and 9%, while those who are progressing well at the expected rate towards the fully competent level may warrant an increase of between 4% and 6%. Increases of between 0% and 3% may be justified for those who are not making such good progress but who are still developing steadily. Performance-related increases of less than 2–3% are hardly worth giving. Much also depends on current market movement and this affects expectations. (Armstrong and Murlis 1998, pp. 286–9)

The final choice concerns the level at which the incentive will be paid. Some schemes reward individuals for individual performance, others reward a group of employees or team for their collective performance. Finally there are schemes which share incentive payments out among all employees in the organisation or within individual business units. These are not mutually exclusive. It is possible, for example, to reward a salesperson with three types of incentive, one from each level. The basic pay would thus be enhanced with commission calculated individually, with a performance-based payment made to all in his/her sales team to reflect excellent customer feedback, and finally with a profit-related bonus paid to all employees in the organisation. Team-based incentives have tended to get a better press in recent years than individual incentives, a major problem with the latter being their tendency to undermine teamworking in situations where it is an important contributor to competitive advantage (*see* Pfeffer 1998, pp. 218–20).

WINDOW ON PRACTICE

Peter and Patrick are sales consultants for a financial services company and both had business targets for a six-month period. Peter met his target comfortably and received the predetermined bonus of £6,000 for reaching on-target earnings. Patrick failed to reach his target because his sales manager boss left the company and poached two of Patrick's prime customers just before they signed agreements with Patrick, whose bonus was therefore £2,000 instead of £6,250.

Joanne was a sales consultant for the same company as Peter and Patrick. Before the sales manager left, he made over to her several promising clients with whom he had done considerable preparatory work and who were not willing to be 'poached' by his new employer. All of these signed agreements and one of them decided to increase the value of the deal tenfold without any reference to Joanne until after that decision was made, and without knowing that she was now the appropriate contact. Her bonus for the period was £23,400.

Henry is a production manager in a light engineering company with performance pay related to a formula combining output with value added. Bonus payments were made monthly in anticipation of what they should be. One of Henry's initiatives was to increase the gearing of the payment by results scheme in the factory. Through peculiarities of company accounting his bonus payments were 'justified' according to the formula, but later it was calculated that the production costs had risen by an amount that cancelled out the value-added benefits. Also 30 per cent of the year's output had to be recalled due to a design fault.

Patrick had his bonus made up to £6,250. Joanne had her bonus reduced to £8,000, but took legal advice and had the amount cut restored, whereupon Peter and Patrick both threatened to resign until mollified by *ex gratia* payments of £2,000 each. Peter resigned three months later. Henry was dismissed.

THE EXTENT TO WHICH INCENTIVES ARE PAID

There is conflicting evidence about how widespread incentive payments are in the UK and about whether or not they are becoming more or less common. Each year the government's New Earnings Survey selects a sample of over 100,000 employees from across the country and asks their employers to fill in a form outlining their earnings in the previous tax year. One of the questions asks about incentive payments 'such as piecework, commission, profit sharing, productivity and other incentives/bonuses'. In 2003 (ONS 2003) the survey results revealed that only 14 per cent of employees were receiving such payments, but no occupational breakdown was provided. However, previous editions of the survey have shown that the proportion of manual workers being paid through incentive schemes (around 25 per cent) is considerably higher than is the case for non-manual workers (10 per cent), suggesting that the most common use of incentives involves the use of traditional piecework or payment by results schemes in the manufacturing and agricultural sectors. Other approaches, such as individual performance-related pay, appear restricted to relatively small numbers of employees.

However, other surveys paint a rather different picture. The authors analysing the 1998 Workplace Employment Relations Survey (Millward *et al.* 2000, pp. 212–13) concluded that around 60 per cent of the 2,191 workplaces in their sample operated either a payment by results or a merit pay incentive scheme. They concluded that, on balance, the proportion was similar to that reported in the 1990 survey, indicating no overall change in the extent of incentive schemes. In 1998 an IPD survey of 1,158 organisations found that 40 per cent of the respondents operated a merit pay system and that the median percentage of employees covered by the schemes was between 70 and 80 per cent. This survey (IPD 1998) also produced evidence of growth, a majority of the schemes in operation having been started within the previous five years. More recent published data (*see* Thompson and Milsome 2001 and CIPD 2004) tells the same story, a majority of respondents stating that they operate a variable payment scheme of some kind. Other smaller surveys such as those described by Brown and Armstrong (2000, pp. 19–23) lead to a similar conclusion – namely that incentive schemes of one kind or another are common and are steadily becoming more widespread.

It is not easy to reconcile the diverse results produced by these surveys. One possibility is that the different results may reflect the different samples used. The New Earnings Survey covers workplaces of all sizes, including the very smallest, while the others tend to focus on larger employers. It could therefore be the case that incentive schemes are largely used in bigger firms with more sophisticated management practices. Another possibility is that a high proportion of the schemes in operation reward employees with performance-based incremental payments (that is, a pay rise) rather than a one-off annual bonus. These might well not be picked up by the New Earnings Survey, which asks specifically about the amount of incentive payment received in the previous tax year. A further possibility is that many of the schemes in operation only apply to senior managers and not to the generality of staff.

ACTIVITY 28.2

What other factors might account for the different results picked up by these surveys? How could a survey be designed which would give definitive information about the extent of incentive payments in the UK?

It is thus difficult to reach a firm conclusion. It would appear that a majority of larger employers operate some form of incentive scheme, but that the majority of the UK workforce are not covered. There has been some growth in recent years (*see* IRS 2003, pp. 31–3), but this is patchy and cannot conceal the fact that many schemes are withdrawn as well as established each year. Team-based incentive schemes and skills-based approaches, such as those based on individual performance, are also growing in number but are operated only by a small proportion of employers.

PAYMENT BY RESULTS SCHEMES

Historically, the most widely used incentive schemes have been those which reward employees according to the number of items or units of work they produce or the time they take to produce them. This approach is associated with F.W. Taylor and the phase in the development of personnel management described in Chapter 1 under the heading 'Humane bureaucracy'. Little attention has been paid to the operation of piecework schemes in recent years and there is clear evidence to show that they are in decline, both in terms of the proportion of total pay which is determined according to PBR principles and in terms of the number of employees paid in this way. The results of the annual New Earnings Surveys, however, show that PBR is still widely used, in some shape or form, by employers of manual workers.

Individual time saving

It is rare for a scheme to be based on the purest form of piecework, a payment of *X* pence per piece produced, as this provides no security against external influences which depress output such as machine failure or delays in the delivery of raw materials. The most common type of scheme in use, therefore, is one where the incentive is paid for time saved in performing a specified operation. A standard time is derived for a work sequence and the employee receives an additional payment for the time saved in completing a number of such operations. If it is not possible to work due to shortage of materials or some other reason, the time involved is not counted when the sums are done at the end of the day.

Standard times are derived by the twin techniques of method study and work measurement, which are the skills of the work study engineer. By study of the operation, the work study engineer decides what is the most efficient way to carry it out and then times an operator actually doing the job over a period, so as to measure the 'standard time'. Work-measured schemes of this kind have, however, been subject to a great deal of criticism and are only effective where people are employed on short-cycle manual operations with the volume of output varying between individuals depending on their skill or application.

The main difficulty, from the employee's point of view, is the fluctuation in earnings that occurs as a consequence of a varying level of demand for the product. If the fluctuations are considerable then the employees will be encouraged to try to stabilise them, either by pressing for the guaranteed element to be increased, or by storing output in the good times to prevent the worst effects of the bad, or by social control of high-performing individuals to share out the benefits of the scheme as equally as possible.

Measured daywork

To some people the idea of measured daywork provides the answer to the shortcomings of individual incentive schemes. Instead of employees receiving a variable payment in accordance with the output achieved, they are paid a fixed sum as long as they maintain a predetermined and agreed level of working. Employees thus have far less discretion over the amount of effort they expend. Theoretically, this deals with the key problem of other schemes by providing for both stable earnings and stable output instead of 'as much as you can, if you can'.

The advantage of measured daywork over time-saving schemes, from the management point of view, is the greater level of management control that is exercised. The principal disadvantage is the tendency for the agreed level of working to become a readily achievable norm which can only be increased after negotiation with workforce representatives.

Group and plant-wide incentives

Sometimes the principles of individual time saving are applied to group rather than individual output to improve group performance and to promote the development of teamworking. Where jobs are interdependent, group incentives can be appropriate, but it may also put great pressure on the group members, aggravating any interpersonal animosity that exists and increasing the likelihood of stoppages for industrial action. Group schemes can also severely reduce the level of management control by allowing the production group to determine output according to the financial needs of individual group members.

A variant on the group incentive is the plant-wide bonus scheme, under which all employees in a plant or other organisation share in a pool bonus that is linked to the level of output, the value added by the employees collectively or some similar formula. The attraction of these methods lies in the fact that the benefit to the management of the organisation is 'real' because the measurement is made at the end of the system, compared with the measurements most usually made at different points within the system, whereby wages and labour costs can go up while output and profitability both come down. Theoretically, employees are also more likely to identify with the organisation as a whole, they will cooperate more readily with the management and each other, and there is even an element of workers' control. The difficulties lie in the fact that there is no tangible link between individual effort and individual reward, so that those who are working effectively can have their efforts nullified by others working less effectively or by misfortunes elsewhere.

Commission

The payment of commission on sales is a widespread practice about which surprisingly little is known as these schemes have not come under the same close scrutiny as incentive schemes for manual employees. They suffer from most of the same drawbacks as manual incentives, except that they are linked to business won rather than to output achieved.

ACTIVITY 28.3

A problem with sales commission is its tendency to reward the quantity of goods sold without having regard to the quality of service provided by sales staff. In which circumstances might this have negative consequences? How could a commission-based incentive scheme be adapted to incorporate measures of quality as well as quantity?

DISADVANTAGES OF PBR SCHEMES

The whole concept of payment by results was set up to cope with a stable and predictable situation, within the boundaries of the workplace. External demands from customers were irritations for others – such as sales representatives – to worry about. The factory was the arena, the juxtaposed parties were the management on the one hand and the people doing the work on the other, and the deal was output in exchange for cash. The dramatic changes of the past twenty years, which have swept away stability, dismantled the organisational boundary and enthroned the customer as arbiter of almost everything have also made PBR almost obsolete.

According to the New Earnings Survey the proportion of manual workers receiving PBR payments has been in steady decline since 1983. This trend can be explained, in part, by changing technologies and changes in working practices. A payment system that puts the greatest emphasis on the number of items produced or on the time taken to produce them is inappropriate in industries where product quality is of greater significance than product quantity. Similarly a manufacturing company operating a just-in-time system will rely too heavily on overall plant performance to benefit from a payment scheme that primarily rewards individual effort.

In addition to the problem of fluctuating earnings, described above, there are a number of further inherent disadvantages which explain the decline of PBR-based remuneration arrangements.

Operational inefficiencies

For incentives to work to the mutual satisfaction of both parties, there has to be a smooth operational flow, with materials, job cards, equipment and storage space all readily available exactly when they are needed, and an insatiable demand for the output. Seldom can these conditions be guaranteed and when they do exist they seldom last without snags. Raw materials run out, job cards are not available, tools are faulty, the stores are full, customer demand is fluctuating or there is trouble with the computer. As soon as this sort of thing happens the incentive-paid worker has an incentive either to fiddle the scheme or to negotiate its alteration for protection against operational vagaries.

Quality of work

The stimulus to increase volume of output can adversely affect the quality of output, as there is an incentive to do things as quickly as possible. If the payment scheme is organised so that only output meeting quality standards is paid for, there may still be the tendency to produce expensive scrap. Operatives filling jars with marmalade may break the jars if they work too hurriedly. This means that the jar is lost and the marmalade as well, for fear of glass splinters.

Renewed emphasis on quality and customer satisfaction mean that employers increasingly need to reward individuals with the most highly developed skills or those who are most readily adaptable to the operation of new methods and technologies. PBR, with its emphasis on the quantity of items produced or sold, may be judged inappropriate for organisations competing in markets in which the quality of production is of greater significance than previously.

The quality of working life

There is also a danger that PBR schemes may demotivate the workforce and so impair the quality of working life for individual employees. In our industrial consciousness PBR is associated with the worst aspects of rationalised work: routine, tight control, hyper-specialisation and mechanistic practices. The worker is characterised as an adjunct to the machine, or as an alternative to a machine. Although this may not necessarily be the case, it is usually so, and generally expected. Payment by results in this way reinforces the mechanical element in the control of working relationships by failing to reward employee initiative, skills acquisition or flexibility. There is also evidence to suggest that achieving high levels of productivity by requiring individuals to undertake the same repetitive tasks again and again during the working day increases stress levels and can make some employees susceptible to repetitive strain injuries.

The selective nature of the incentive

Seldom do incentive arrangements cover all employees. Typically, groups of employees are working on a payment basis which permits their earnings to be geared to their output, while their performance depends on the before or after processes of employees not so rewarded, such as craftsmen making tools and fixtures, labourers bringing materials in and out, fork-lift truck drivers, storekeepers and so forth.

The conventional way round the problem is to pay the 'others' a bonus linked to the incentive earned by those receiving it. The reasoning for this is that those who expect to earn more (such as the craftspeople) have a favourable differential guaranteed as well as an interest in high levels of output, while that same interest in sustaining output is generated in the other employees (such as the labourers and the storekeepers) without whom the incentive earners cannot maintain their output levels. The drawbacks are obvious. The labour costs are increased by making additional payments to employees on a non-discriminating basis, so that the storekeeper who is a hindrance to output will still derive benefit from the efforts of others, and the employees whose efforts are directly rewarded by incentives feel that the fruits of their labour are being shared by those whose labours are not so directly controlled.

Obscurity of payment arrangements

Because of these difficulties, incentive schemes are constantly modified or refined in an attempt to circumvent fiddling or to get a fresh stimulus to output, or in response to employee demands for some other type of change. This leads to a situation in which the employees find it hard to understand what behaviour by them leads to particular results in payment terms. This same obscurity is often found in the latest fashion in PRP. In a recent unpublished study comparing performance management in two blue-chip companies, less than half the people in management posts claimed to understand how the payments were calculated. Many of those actually misunderstood their schemes!

PERFORMANCE-RELATED PAY

Arguments about the advantages and disadvantages of individual PRP have been some of the most hotly contested in recent decades. The topic has formed the basis of numerous research studies and remains one which attracts much controversy, as was shown in recent debates about the introduction of PRP for teachers working in state schools. The main reason is the apparent contrast between the theoretical attractiveness of such systems – at least from a management perspective – and their supposed tendency to disappoint when operated in practice. While there are many different types of scheme available, all involve the award of a pay rise or bonus payment to individual employees following a formal assessment of their performance over a defined period (normally the previous year). Two distinct varieties of scheme can be identified.

Merit-based systems simply involve the immediate supervisor undertaking an appraisal of each subordinate's work performance during the previous year. This will typically be done following a formal appraisal interview and often requires the completion of standard documentation drawn up by an HR department. A proportion of future remuneration is then linked to a score derived from the supervisor's assessment. Some systems require supervisors to award a percentage mark against different criteria, while others oblige them to assess individual performance as 'excellent', 'good', 'satisfactory' or 'inadequate'. Merit-based systems are generally regarded as unsatisfactory because they allow considerable scope for assessors to make subjective judgements or to allow personal prejudice to colour their assessments. There is also a tendency to give undue weight to recent events at the expense of achievements taking place early in the appraisal period.

Goal-based systems are more objective, but are not appropriate for all kinds of job. They are, however, particularly well suited for the assessment of managerial work. Here the supervisor and subordinate meet at the start of the appraisal period and agree between them a list of objectives which the appraisee will seek to meet during the coming months. Examples would be the completion of particular projects, the establishment of new initiatives, undertaking a course of training or making substantial progress towards the solving of a problem. Many employers nowadays seek to link individual objectives directly to defined organisational goals for the year as a means of reinforcing their significance and ensuring that all are pulling in the same direction. At the end of the year the employee is assessed on the basis of which objectives have or have not been met. A score is then derived and a bonus payment or pay rise awarded. Where performance in a job can meaningfully be assessed in this way, such systems are recommended because they are reasonably objective and straightforward to score. Where the nature of the job involves the consistent achievement of a defined level of performance, and cannot usefully be assessed in terms of the achievement of specific objectives, the goal-based approach has less to offer. It may still be possible to assess part of the job in this way, but there will also have to be a merit-based element if the appraisal is to reflect all of a person's activity during the appraisal period.

ACTIVITY 28.4

Make a list of five jobs that you consider would be best rewarded by a merit-based system and five more that are best rewarded via the goal-based approach.

The attractions of PRP

It is not difficult to see why PRP has attracted the interest of managers, consultants and government ministers. Its theoretical attractions are considerable and include the following:

- attracting and retaining good performers;
- improving individual and corporate performance;
- clarifying job roles and duties;
- improving communication;
- improving motivation;
- reinforcing management control;
- identifying developmental objectives;

- reinforcing the individual employment relationship at the expense of the collective;
- rewarding individuals without needing to promote them.

In short PRP aims to provide a flexible and cost-effective means of distributing rewards fairly between the good and poorer performers while also contributing towards improved organisation performance. Moreover, it is based on principles to which most people, employees as well as managers, seem to adhere (Brown and Armstrong 2000, pp. 11–13). Most of us are very happy to see individuals rewarded for superior performance and/or effort and would like payment decisions to be based on such criteria. The problems arise when attempts are made to put the principles into practice. A system which is fair and objective in theory can easily fail to achieve these objectives when implemented.

Critiques of PRP

Performance-related pay attracted a great amount of criticism from academic researchers in the 1980s and 1990s during a period when its virtues were frequently asserted by HR managers and consultants. The attacks came from several quarters. Occupational psychologists tended to question the ability of PRP to motivate positively (e.g. Kohn 1993), while sociologists saw it as a means of reinforcing management control at the expense of worker autonomy (e.g. Hendry *et al.* 2000). A further source of criticism has come from those who suspect that PRP is used as a means of perpetuating gender inequality in payment matters (e.g. Rubery 1985). However, the most colourful and damning criticisms have come from management thinkers such as W. Edwards Deming who advocate Total Quality Management approaches (*see* Chapter 11) and for whom PRP represents exactly the wrong kind of initiative to introduce. The whole basis of their philosophy is the substitution of 'leadership' for 'supervision', removing organisational hierarchies and managing people with as little direction and control as possible. They see PRP as having the opposite effect. It reinforces the hierarchy, enhances the power of supervisors and strengthens management control.

For many critics, including those cited above, PRP has fundamental flaws which cannot be overcome. Kohn, for example, argues that incentives can only succeed in securing temporary compliance. Their use cannot change underlying attitudes, while the attempt to do so ultimately damages the long-term health of an organisation by undermining relationships and encouraging employees to focus on short-term aims:

> Managers who insist that the job won't get done right without rewards have failed to offer a convincing argument for behavioural manipulation. Promising a reward to someone who appears unmotivated is a bit like offering salt water to someone who is thirsty. Bribes in the workplace simply can't work. (Kohn 1993, p. 60)

A second stream of criticism is more moderate, arguing that PRP can have a role to play in organisations, but that its positive effects are limited. Moreover, while not fundamentally flawed, PRP is very difficult to implement effectively in practice. As a result, systems fail as often as they succeed. The arguments are summarised well by Gomez-Mejia and Balkin (1992, pp. 249–55), Cannell and Wood (1992, pp. 66–101), Pfeffer (1998, pp. 203–4) and Purcell (2000). The major points made by these authors are as follows:

1 Employees paid by PRP, especially where the incentive is substantial, tend to develop a narrow focus to their work. They concentrate on those aspects which they believe will initiate payments, while neglecting other parts of their jobs.

2 PRP, because of its individual nature, tends to undermine teamworking. People focus on their own objectives at the expense of cooperation with colleagues.

3 PRP, because it involves managers rating employees, can lead to a situation in which a majority of staff are demotivated when they receive their rating. This occurs where people perceive their own performance to be rather better than it is considered to be by their supervisors – a common situation. The result is a negative effect on the motivation of the staff who are unexceptional, but loyal and valued. These are often the very people on whom organisations depend most.

4 Employees are rarely in a position wholly to determine the outcomes of their own performance. Factors outside their control play an important role, leading to a situation in which the achievement or non-achievement of objectives is partially a matter of chance.

5 Even the most experienced managers find it difficult to undertake fair and objective appraisals of their employees' performance. Subjective judgements are often taken into account leading to perceptions of bias. Some managers deliberately manipulate ratings for political reasons, allowing their judgement to be coloured by the effect they perceive the outcome will have on particular employees. Low ratings are thus avoided, as are very high ratings, where it is perceived this will lead to disharmony or deterioration of personal relationships.

6 In organisations subject to swift and profound change, objectives set for the coming year may become obsolete after a few months. Employees then find themselves with an incentive to meet goals which are no longer priorities for the organisation.

7 PRP systems tend to discourage creative thinking, the challenging of established ways of doing things and a questioning attitude among employees.

8 Budgetary constraints often lead managers to reduce ratings, creating a situation in which excellent individual performance is not properly rewarded.

9 It is difficult to ensure that each line manager takes a uniform approach to the rating of their subordinates. Some tend to be more generously disposed in general than others, leading to inconsistency and perceptions of unfairness.

10 When the results of performance appraisal meetings have an impact on pay levels, employees tend to downplay their weaknesses. As a result development needs are not discussed or addressed.

11 PRP systems invariably increase the paybill. This occurs because managers fear demotivating their staff by awarding low or zero rises in the first years of a system's operation. Poorer performers are thus rewarded as well as better performers.

Using PRP effectively

Despite the problems described above it is possible to implement PRP successfully, as is shown by the experience of case study companies quoted by Brown and

Armstrong (2000), IRS (2000) and IDS (2003). It will only work, however, if it is used in appropriate circumstances and if it is implemented properly. Part of the problem with PRP has been a tendency in the HR press to portray it as universally applicable and as a panacea capable of improving performance dramatically. In fact it is neither, but is one of a range of tools that have a useful if limited role to play in some situations. Gomez-Mejia and Balkin (1992) specify the following favourable conditions:

1 Where individual performance can be objectively and meaningfully measured.
2 Where individuals are in a position to control the outcomes of their work.
3 Where close team working or cooperation with others is not central to successful job performance.
4 Where there is an individualistic organisational culture.

In addition, Brown and Armstrong (2000) rightly point to the importance of careful implementation and lengthy preparation prior to the installation of a scheme. Moreover, they argue that PRP should not be looked at or judged in isolation from other forms of reward, both extrinsic and intrinsic. Success or failure can hinge on what else is being done to maximise motivation, to develop people and to improve their job security.

Ultimately PRP has one great advantage which no amount of criticism can remove: it helps ensure that organisational priorities become individual priorities. Managers can signal the importance of a particular objective by including it in a subordinate's goals for the coming year. If the possibility of additional payment is then tied to its achievement, the chances that the objective concerned will be met increases significantly. Organisational performance is improved as a result. Where the achievement of such specific objectives forms a relatively minor part of someone's job, PRP can form a relatively minor part of their pay packet. Other rewards can then be used to recognise other kinds of achievement.

WINDOW ON PRACTICE

Many job descriptions for supervisory positions include reference to responsibility for ensuring that the appropriate health and safety at work regulations are adhered to. Few supervisors, however, left to themselves would see this aspect of their work as a priority. In one organisation known to the authors it was decided to try to raise the profile of health and safety issues by including objectives in this field into managers' annual performance targets. It therefore became clear that the level of PRP in the following year would, in part, be determined by the extent to which the health and safety objectives had been met.

The result was the swift establishment of departmental health and safety committees and schemes whereby staff could bring safety hazards to the attention of supervisors.

SKILLS-BASED PAY

A further kind of incentive payment scheme is one which seeks to reward employees for the skills or competencies which they acquire. It is well established in the United States and, according to IRS (2003), is becoming a good deal more common among British employers. It is particularly prevalent as a means of rewarding technical staff, but there is no reason why the principle should not be extended to any group of employees for whom the acquisition of additional skills might benefit the organisation.

There are several potential benefits for an employer introducing a skills-based pay scheme. Its most obvious effect is to encourage multiskilling and flexibility enabling the organisation to respond more effectively and speedily to the needs of customers. A multiskilled workforce may also be slimmer and less expensive. In addition it is argued that, in rewarding skills acquisition, a company will attract and retain staff more effectively than its competitors in the labour market. The operation of a skills-based reward system is proof that the sponsoring employer is genuinely committed to employee development.

Most skills-based payment systems reward employees with additional increments to their base pay once they have completed defined skill modules. A number of such schemes are described in detail in a study published by Incomes Data Services (1992). Typical is the scheme operated by Venture Pressings Ltd where staff are employed on four basic grades, each divided into 10 increments. Employees progress up the scale by acquiring specific skills and demonstrating proficiency in them to the satisfaction of internal assessors. New starters are also assessed and begin their employment on the incremental point most appropriate to the level of skills they can demonstrate. In many industries it is now possible to link payment for skills acquisition directly to the attainment of National Vocational Qualifications (NVQs) for which both the setting of standards and the assessment of individual competence are carried out externally.

A skills-based pay system will only be cost effective if it results in productivity increases which are sufficient to cover the considerable costs associated with its introduction and maintenance. A business can invest a great deal of resources both in training its workforce to attain new skills, and in rewarding them once those skills have been acquired, only to find that the cost of the scheme outweighs the benefit gained in terms of increased flexibility and efficiency. Furthermore, in assisting employees to become more highly qualified and in many cases to gain NVQs, an employer may actually find it harder to retain its staff in relatively competitive labour markets.

The other major potential disadvantage is associated with skills obsolescence. Where a business operates in a fast-moving environment and needs to adapt its technology regularly, a skills-based payment system can leave the organisation paying enhanced salaries for skills which are no longer significant or are not required at all. Employers seeking to introduce skills-based systems of payment therefore need to consider the implications very carefully and must ensure that they only reward the acquisition of those skills which will clearly contribute to increased productivity over the long term.

ACTIVITY 28.5

A number of commentators praise skills-based pay as a system which avoids some of the pitfalls associated with PRP schemes. Look back at the list of practical problems with PRP schemes above and consider which do and which do not apply to skills-based incentive systems.

PROFIT SHARING

There are a number of different ways in which companies are able to link remuneration to profit levels. In recent years the government has sought to encourage such schemes and has actively promoted their establishment with advantageous tax arrangements. Underlying government support is the belief that linking pay to profits increases the employee's commitment to his or her company by deepening the level of mutual interest. As a result, it is argued that such schemes act as an incentive encouraging employees to work harder and with greater flexibility in pursuit of higher levels of take-home pay. Other potential advantages for employers described by Pendleton (2000, pp. 346–51) are better cost flexibility, changed attitudes on the part of employees and the discouragement of union membership.

Cash-based schemes

The traditional and most common profit-sharing arrangement is simply to pay employees a cash bonus, calculated as a proportion of annual profits, on which the employee incurs both a PAYE and a national insurance liability. Some organisations pay discretionary profit bonuses on this basis, while others allocate a fixed proportion of profits to employees as a matter of policy. **Gainsharing** is a variation on cash-based profit sharing which is widely used in the USA and which can be used in non-profit-making organisations as well as those operating in the commercial sector. Here the bonus relates to costs saved rather than profit generated in a defined period. So if a workforce successfully achieves the same level of output at lower overall cost, the gain is shared between employer and employees.

Between 1987 and 2000 the government operated an approved profit-related pay scheme which became increasingly popular. By 1996 there were over 14,000 schemes in operation, covering 3.7 million employees. The attraction was the ability profit-related pay schemes gave employers to give pay rises to all employees, while recouping the cost through tax concessions. The scheme was phased out and has now been replaced by the Share Incentive Plan (*see* below).

Share-based schemes

There are several methods of profit sharing which involve employees being awarded shares rather than cash. Here too there are government-sponsored schemes in operation which involve favourable tax treatment.

The Savings-Related Share Option scheme permits organisations to grant share options to directors and employees in a tax-effective manner. This means that they are given the opportunity to buy shares in their own companies at a future date, but at the current price. The hope is that the value will have increased in the meantime, allowing the purchaser to cash in a tidy profit. This particular government-sponsored scheme requires participants to put between £5 and £250 of their monthly pay aside and then to use the proceeds of the accumulated fund, after three, five or seven years, to buy shares at a discount of 20 per cent of the price they were when the plan started.

From 2001 it has also been possible for employers to set up Inland Revenue approved Share Incentive Plans (previously called All-Employee Share Schemes) that allow employees to obtain shares in their own companies while avoiding tax and national insurance contributions. Employers can give such shares to employees to a maximum value of £3,000 per year. Some can be given in recognition of individual or team performance, making it possible to award some employees more shares than others. Where employees subsequently hold these shares for three years or more, there is no tax liability when they are sold. In addition, under the scheme, employees can buy up to a further £1,500 worth of shares out of pre-tax income and subsequently avoid a proportion of the tax owed when they are sold. Companies are also allowed to give 'free' matching shares for each share purchased by an employee under the scheme. Employers as well as employees gain tax advantages from operating these schemes. Deductions in corporation tax can be made equivalent to the amount of salary used by employees to purchase shares, as well as monies used in establishing and operating the scheme.

Disadvantages of profit-related schemes

The obvious disadvantage of the schemes described above from the employee's point of view is the risk that pay levels may decline if the company fails to meet its expected profit levels. If no profit is made it cannot be shared. Share values can go down as well as up. Companies are not permitted to make guarantees about meeting payments and will have their schemes revoked by the Inland Revenue if they do so. In any event it is likely that profit-based incentives will vary in magnitude from year to year.

For these reasons it is questionable to assert that profit-sharing schemes do in fact act as incentives. Unlike PRP awards they do not relate specifically to the actions of the individual employee. Annual profit levels are clearly influenced by a whole range of factors which are both internal and external to the company. An employee may well develop a community of interest with the company management, shareholders and other employees but it is unlikely seriously to affect the nature of his or her work. Furthermore, both poor and good performers are rewarded equally in profit-related schemes. The incentive effect will therefore be very slight in most cases and will be restricted to a general increase in employee commitment.

SUMMARY PROPOSITIONS

28.1 Incentive schemes should be used where they are appropriate to the needs of the business and where they can clearly contribute to the achievement of organisational objectives.

28.2 Incentive payment schemes either involve the payment of a bonus or form the basis of incremental progression systems. In either case, the reward should represent at least 7 per cent of salary if there is to be a meaningful incentive effect.

28.3 The extent to which different types of incentive arrangement are used in the UK is unclear. There is evidence of growth in recent years, but the majority of employees are not covered by such schemes.

28.4 Methods of payment by results include individual time saving, group incentives, measured daywork, plant-wide schemes, productivity schemes and commission.

28.5 Performance-related pay systems are either merit based or goal based. They have been the subject of notable debate in recent years, many researchers finding a mismatch between their theoretical attractions and practical outcomes.

28.6 Skills-based pay involves linking incentives to the achievement of defined competencies or qualifications. It rewards what people bring to the job rather than the results of their efforts.

28.7 Profit sharing has been promoted by governments for many years. The Share Incentive Plan is the latest attempt to encourage employees to hold shares in their own companies.

GENERAL DISCUSSION TOPICS

1 What are the relative advantages of: (a) a system of straight salary that is the same each month, and (b) a system of salary with an individual performance-related addition so that the total payment each month varies?

2 In what circumstances might it be appropriate to base individual payment on team performance?

3 What do you think about Peter, Patrick, Joanne and Henry in the Window on practice box early in this chapter?

FURTHER READING

Brown, D. and Armstrong, M. (2000) *Paying or Contribution: real performance-related pay strategies*. London: Kogan Page

Kohn, A. (1993) 'Why Incentive Plans Cannot Work', *Harvard Business Review*, September–October, pp. 54–63

The debate about the merits of individual performance-related pay is so polarised that it is rare to find a balanced account that sets out the views of those who are for and those who are against. It is best to read the partisan accounts. Kohn's (1993) article contains an eloquent and damning critique of such schemes, while Brown and Armstrong (2000) paint a more positive picture.

Incomes Data Services

Industrial Relations Services
Information about trends in the design of incentive payment schemes is regularly provided in the IDS and IRS publications. They also commonly feature case studies which show exactly how the various schemes operate in practice as well as regular surveys of current practice that can be used for benchmarking processes.

Thorpe, R. and Homan, G. (eds) *Strategic Reward Systems*. London: Financial Times/Prentice Hall
Several chapters in this book concern incentive payment systems of one kind or another. The book includes extensive material on PRP, skills-based pay, gainsharing, profit-sharing and team-based incentives.

REFERENCES

Armstrong, M. and Murlis, H. (1998) *Reward Management*, 4th edn. London: Kogan Page.
Bartol, K.M. and Durham, C.C. (2000) 'Incentives: Theory and Practice', in C. Cooper and E. Locke (eds) *Industrial and Organizational Psychology*. Oxford: Blackwell.
Brown, D. and Armstrong, M. (2000) *Paying for Contribution: real performance-related pay strategies*. London: Kogan Page.
Cannell, M. and Wood, S. (1992) *Incentive Pay: Impact and Evolution*. London: IPM.
CIPD (2004) *Reward Management 2004: A survey of policy and practice*. London: CIPD.
Gomez-Mejia, L. and Balkin, D. (1992) *Compensation, Organizational Strategy and Firm Performance*. Cincinnati, Ohio: South Western Publishing.
Hendry, C., Woodward, S., Bradley, P. and Perkins, S. (2000) 'Performance and rewards: cleaning out the stables', *Human Resource Management Journal*, Vol. 10, No. 3, pp. 46–62.
Herzberg, F. (1966) *Work and the Nature of Man*. Cleveland, Ohio: World Publishing.
Huselid, M. (1995) 'The impact of HRM practices on turnover, productivity and corporate performance', *Academy of Management Journal*, June.
IDS (1992) *Skills-based pay*, IDS Study No. 500. London: IDS.
IDS (2003) *Bonus Schemes*, IDS Study 742. London: IDS.
IPD (1998) *Reward Management Survey*. London: IPD.
IRS (2000) 'The truth about merit pay', *IRS Pay and Benefits Bulletin 501*, August.
IRS (2003) 'Looking Ahead: the 2004 pay round', *IRS Employment Review*, No. 787, November.
Kohn, A. (1993) 'Why Incentive Plans Cannot Work', *Harvard Business Review*, September–October, pp. 54–63.
Millward, N., Bryson, A. and Forth, J. (2000) *All Change at Work?* London: Routledge.
Office for National Statistics (2000) *New Earnings Survey*. London: The Stationery Office.
Pendleton, A. (2000) 'Profit-sharing and employee share ownership', in R. Thorpe and G. Homan (eds) *Strategic Reward Systems*. London: FT/Prentice Hall.
Pfeffer, J. (1998) *The Human Equation: Building profits by putting people first*. Boston: Harvard Business School Press.
Purcell, J. (2000) 'Pay per view', *People Management*, 3 February, pp. 41–3.
Rubery, J. (1995) 'Performance-related pay and the prospects for gender pay equity', *Journal of Management Studies*, Vol. 32, No. 5, pp. 637–54.
Sisson, K. and Storey, J. (2000) *The Realities of Human Resource Management*. Buckingham: Open University Press.

Thompson, M. (1992) *Pay and Performance: The Employer Experience*. Institute of Manpower Studies Report 218. London: IMS.

Thompson, M. (2000) 'Salary progression systems', in G. White and J. Druker (eds) *Reward Management: A Critical Text*. London: Routledge.

Thompson, P. and Milsome, S. (2001) *Reward Determination in the UK*. London: CIPD.

An extensive range of additional materials, including multiple choice questions, answers to questions and links to useful websites can be found on the Human Resource Management Companion Website at **www.pearsoned.co.uk/torrington**.

CHAPTER 29

PENSIONS AND BENEFITS

THE OBJECTIVES OF THIS CHAPTER ARE TO:

1. INTRODUCE THE DIFFERENT TYPES OF PENSION SCHEME PROVIDED BY THE STATE, BY EMPLOYERS AND BY FINANCIAL SERVICES ORGANISATIONS
2. EXPLAIN THE CAUSES AND SIGNIFICANCE OF CURRENT TRENDS IN THE PROVISION OF OCCUPATIONAL PENSIONS
3. OUTLINE THE ROLES PLAYED BY HR PROFESSIONALS IN THE FIELD OF OCCUPATIONAL PENSIONS
4. DISTINGUISH BETWEEN STATUTORY SICK PAY (SSP) AND OCCUPATIONAL SICK PAY (OSP)
5. ASSESS RECENT DEVELOPMENTS IN THE PROVISION OF COMPANY CARS BY UK EMPLOYERS
6. EXPLORE THE POTENTIAL OF FLEXIBLE BENEFITS SYSTEMS IN THE UK CONTEXT

Employee benefits commonly used to be known as 'fringe benefits', suggesting a peripheral role in the typical pay packet. The substantial growth in the value of most benefits packages over the past ten or twenty years means that the title 'fringe' is no longer appropriate. An increasing proportion of individual remuneration is made up of additional perks, allowances and entitlements which are mostly paid in kind rather than cash. The total value of benefits 'paid' by employers to employees commonly represents between 20 per cent and 50 per cent of an organisation's salary budget, depending on what is included (IDS 1999). Pensions alone can easily account for 20 per cent, to which must be added the costs of providing some or all of the following: company cars, sick pay, meals, live-in accommodation, parking facilities, private health insurance, crèche facilities, mobile phones, Christmas parties, staff discounts, relocation expenses and any holiday or maternity allowances paid in excess of the required statutory minima. Smith (2000a, p. 153) shows that these extra elements of pay are distributed unevenly between members of staff. Those earning at the top of the scale (especially directors and senior managers) tend to gain rather more than average employees, 30 per cent or 40 per cent of their take-home pay being accounted for by benefits of various kinds.

Despite these developments, there remains a big question-mark over how far employees value the benefits provided to them by their employers or appreciate the extent of the costs involved in their provision. A survey of 13,000 employees carried out by Towers Perrin (IRS 2000a, pp. 5–9, Thompson and Milsome 2001, pp. 55–62) found that a majority were dissatisfied with the level of benefits provided and that only 21 per cent were interested in improving the package by reducing their take-home pay. They concluded that 'traditional benefits are not a significant factor in the recruitment, retention and motivation of most employees' because there was 'a misalignment between their needs and the extent to which their employers are meeting those needs'. This does not mean, of course, that employers can easily stop offering benefits. While the full cost may not be appreciated by employees, they are generally in favour of the benefits and would resent their removal. Poor publicity would also inevitably follow the withdrawal of rewards such as pensions which are generally seen as being the hallmark of a good employer. The alternative courses of action involve communicating the true value of benefits to employees more effectively and providing them with a degree of choice as to which benefits they wish to receive. The latter approach, involving the provision of 'flexible' or 'cafeteria' benefits, has become very common in the USA and has received a great deal of attention in the UK too.

PENSIONS

Occupational pensions are increasingly seen as a form of 'deferred pay' rather than a reward for a lifetime of employment, and as such are attracting more attention from employees, trade unions, government and the media. Once a peripheral concern of most HR departments, and many reward management specialists, they have now, as a result of recent developments, moved to the centre of the stage. The trade union AMICUS recently stated that pensions are the top priority issue for its members, while the CIPD's annual survey on reward management practices now places the section on pensions at the beginning, ahead of all other pay topics (CIPD 2004).

The role of employers in providing pensions has moved up the agenda for several reasons, but underlying all of them are the long-term demographic trends which have called into question the ability of the established UK pension system to provide an adequate income to older people after they retire. On the one hand people are living increasingly longer and thus require a bigger pension to provide them with an income across their years of retirement. On the other, fewer children are being born, leading to an increase in the **dependency ratio**, by which is meant the proportion of retired people *vis-à-vis* working people in the economy. At present in the UK there are around 3.3 people working for every pensioner, but this figure will reduce quite rapidly after 2010. By 2030 it is expected to fall to 2.7 and to continue declining for two further decades (Hopegood 1994). This has major implications for the government, which will have to raise taxation very considerably in order to fund decent state pensions for so many retired people, in addition to providing for their health, welfare and other care needs. The government is seeking to tackle this issue in different ways. Overseas immigration is being allowed to rise considerably for the first time in decades, while the state pension age is likely to rise to 70 in the near future. However, an important part of the strategy is to shift the burden of providing pension income from the state to the private and occupational sectors. For this strategy to succeed ways must be found to encourage today's working population to save a great deal more for their own retirement than is currently the case. Employers will also have to be persuaded both to make contributions themselves and to provide pension schemes which encourage workers themselves to contribute. Unfortunately, in recent years the opposite trend has occurred. Far from growing, the occupational sector is declining in terms of both the number of people covered and the size of pension that is being provided to retirees. In fact, since 2000 we have witnessed the dismantling of large parts of the established occupational pensions structure. A majority of larger employers have downgraded their pension commitments, reducing the amount of money they contribute to funds and shifting investment risks on to employees. This ongoing situation is regularly seen in the press and by pensions experts as constituting a 'pensions crisis' (IRS 2003a).

ACTIVITY 29.1

Robert Noble-Warren (1986) talks about 'lifetime planning' as a series of 'rest and recuperation' periods throughout life as well as the planning of financial provision. Lifetime planning has to start with a statement of your life's objectives. What are your life's objectives and what work, rest and financial plans can you make to achieve these?

State schemes

The state runs two schemes: a basic scheme and the State Second Pension (S2P) scheme. The latter replaced SERPS (the State Earnings Related Pension Scheme) in 2002, but people who contributed to SERPS have all their accrued entitlements under that scheme protected. Every employee is obliged to contribute a standard amount to the basic scheme, which currently provides an old age pension at the age of 65 for men and 60 for women. By 2020 the pensionable age for both men and women will be 65 and in the 10 years prior to this date there will be a gradual phasing in of the new pensionable age for women. Anyone earning above a 'low earnings threshold' determined by the government (£10,800 in 2003) makes payments towards S2P through their national insurance contributions, it being intended that the scheme will pay out an additional flat-rate state pension to those who retire after April 2006 or 2007 (IDS 2002a, pp. 22–3). SERPS operated along similar lines, but produced a second state pension that varied in size depending on how much had been contributed by the individual retiree.

The state pension scheme is organised on a pay-as-you-go basis. This means that there is no state pension fund as such, and the money that is paid to today's pensioners comes from today's taxes and national insurance contributions. The money that will be paid to today's contributors, when they become pensioners, will come not from the investment of their and their employers' contributions, but from the contributions of the workforce and their employers in the future. This is why there is growing concern about the ability of future governments to be able to fund state pensions for many more retired people beyond a basic subsistence level.

Occupational schemes

The UK has had, for many years, one of the most extensive and effective systems of occupational pension provision in the world. There are over 150,000 separate schemes in operation with combined assets worth approximately £600 billion. Just over 10 million people are members of occupational pension schemes, while around eight million pensioners draw an income from their funds (Government Actuary's Department 2003). Although there has been some reduction recently in the proportion of the workforce covered by occupational pensions, they remain by far the most significant employee benefit in terms of their cost to employers.

In general, occupational schemes provide an additional retirement pension on top of the state pension, providing better and wider-ranging benefits than the state schemes and a great deal more flexibility. They are most often found in large organisations and the public sector, but some smaller organisations also run such schemes. Men and women have equal access to occupational schemes and, since 1990, have had to be treated equally in respect of all scheme rules. Yet, in spite of this, men and women continue to fare differently in terms of pensions benefits due to the typical pattern of women's employment being different from male patterns and women's longer average life expectancy. A higher proportion of managerial and professional workers have occupational pensions than other groups, blue-collar workers being the least likely to be in schemes. It is no longer lawful for an employer to exclude part-time or temporary workers.

With the exception of one or two in the public sector, occupational schemes do not pay their pensioners in the pay-as-you-go manner operated by the state, but create a pension fund, which is managed separately from the business. The advantage of this is that should the organisation become bankrupt, the pension fund cannot be seized to pay debtors because it is not part of the company. The money in the pension fund is invested and held in trust for the employees of the company at the time of their retirement.

Larger organisations administer their own pension funds through an investment or fund manager. The manager will plan how to invest the money in the fund to get the best return and to ensure that the money that is needed to pay pensions and other benefits will be available when required. An actuary can provide mortality tables and other statistical information in order to assist planning and must be hired regularly to carry out a formal actuarial assessment of the scheme's assets and liabilities. Smaller organisations tend to appoint an insurance company or a bank to administer their pension funds, and so use their expertise. Pension funds can be invested in a variety of different ways, and are often worth more than the market value of their sponsoring companies. As a result they have come to dominate investment on the stockmarket.

During the 1990s as the worth of stocks and shares increased, the typical pension fund found itself in surplus. It thus had more assets than it needed to pay its liabilities. As a result benefit levels were increased and many employers were able to enjoy lengthy 'contribution holidays', meaning that they did not have to put any money into their funds. In recent years this position has changed radically as stockmarkets have fallen, life expectancy has risen, the amount of taxation levied on the funds has been increased and costly new regulations have been imposed. By the end of 2002 all but nine of the FTSE 100 companies (i.e. the largest in the country) had pension funds in deficit, the combined shortfall amounting to £77 billion. This was equivalent to 93 per cent of their annual operating profits. The figures for smaller companies were even worse, their fund deficits representing over 130 per cent of operating profits (IRS 2003). New accounting regulations, known as FRS17 standards, threaten to make the situation worse after 2005 as they will require companies to include details of pension fund assets (and hence the substantial deficits) in their annual accounts. The current picture, from an employer's point of view, is thus one of very substantial escalating costs and far less predictability about how much by way of a contribution the organisation will have to make each year. This has resulted in profound changes being made by many private sector funds, which have substantially reduced the likely level of pension that many employees will receive when they retire. At the time of writing (early 2004) an improved stockmarket position has led some commentators to contend that the worst is over and that we will begin to see a reversal of recent trends, but there is little sign of this happening in practice (IRS 2004, p. 31). Occupational pensions take one of three basic forms.

Defined benefit schemes dominated for the past thirty or forty years, but the number of people with access to them has declined hugely in the last two or three years. Virtually all the public sector schemes take this form, but they now account for just 42 per cent of the schemes offered by private sector employers. Even among larger employers, only 66 per cent now operate defined benefit schemes (National Association of Pension Funds, 2003). Here contributions are made into a single organisation-wide fund which is invested on behalf of members by a fund manager. Retired employees then draw a pension from the fund calculated according to a defined formula. Most defined benefit schemes take the final salary form, in which the value of the pension is determined by the level of salary being received by each individual at the time of retirement. In the private sector it is common for this to be calculated on a 'sixtieths' basis, whereby the retiree is paid an annual pension equivalent to 1/60th (1.67 per cent) of their final salary multiplied by the number of years' pensionable service they have completed. In the public sector it is usual for the figure to be based on 'eightieths', with a tax-free lump sum being paid in addition at the time of retirement. In either case the size of pension is heavily related to the length of scheme membership, the maximum pension payable equalling two-thirds of final salary. Examples of final salary calculations are given in Figure 29.1.

Figure 29.1 Final salary schemes – examples of various contribution periods with a 1/60th and a 1/80th scheme

Sixtieths scheme	
Final salary	= £24,000
Contributions for 5 years	= 1/60 × 24,000 × 5
Pension	= £2,000 per year
Final salary	= £24,000
Contributions for 25 years	= 1/60 × 24,000 × 25
Pension	= £10,000 per year
Final salary	= £24,000
Contributions for 40 years	= 1/60 × 24,000 × 40
Pension	= £16,000 per year
Eightieths scheme	
Final salary	= £24,000
Contributions for 25 years	= 1/80 × 24,000 × 25
Pension	= £7,500 per year
Lump sum	= 3/80 × 24,000 × 25 = £22,500

Another form of defined benefit scheme bases the pension calculation on the average salary earned over a period of 5, 10 or 20 years prior to retirement rather than on pay in the final year. Unless most of someone's pensionable service has been spent earning close to the final salary level, such schemes are less generous than the final salary variety in terms of the amount of pension paid. High levels of inflation also reduce the value of pensions calculated on an average salary basis.

Most defined benefit schemes are contributory. This means that monies are paid into the fund on a regular basis by both the employer and the employee. In the case of employees the contribution is fixed as a percentage of salary (typically 5 per cent), a sum which is subject to tax relief. Employers, by contrast, are obliged only to pay in sufficient funds to ensure that the scheme remains solvent. When the pension fund is in surplus, as many were in the 1980s and 1990s, employers can take 'contribution holidays'. By contrast, when the fund is in deficit, the employer has to contribute whatever is necessary to ensure that assets are sufficient to meet possible liabilities. This means that the amount of employer contribution can vary considerably, year on year, in an unpredictable fashion. In 2003 contribution rates for employers were averaging 15–16 per cent of salary (NAPF 2003). Employers, like employees, gain from tax relief on contributions paid.

In some industries, as well as parts of the public sector, it has been traditional for occupational pensions to be non-contributory. In such schemes the employee makes no contribution at all, but nonetheless draws a pension calculated according to the final salary. Civil servants benefit from this kind of arrangement, as do many employees in the banking and finance sectors. Defined benefit schemes typically offer extra benefits such as ill-health pensions for those forced to retire early and death-in-service benefits for widows and widowers.

Defined contribution schemes (also known as money purchase schemes) are organised in a totally different way from defined benefit arrangements, and there are no promises about what the final level of pension will be. Employees and employers both contribute a fixed percentage of current salary to these schemes, usually 5 per cent or 6 per cent on a monthly basis. The pension benefits received are then entirely dependent on the money that has been contributed and the way that it has been invested. Where investments perform well, a good level of pension can be gained.

Where investments are disappointing, the result is a low level of pension. Further uncertainty derives from the way that money purchase schemes result in the payment of a single lump sum to the employee when he/she retires. This is then used to buy an annuity from an insurance company from which a weekly or monthly income is paid for life. Annuity rates vary considerably from year to year, and there is also considerable variation between the deals offered by different providers. In essence this means that the risk associated with pension investments is carried by the employee in a defined contribution arrangement, rather than by the employer as in a final salary scheme. For this reason defined contribution schemes are generally less satisfactory than defined benefit schemes when seen from an employee's perspective. Investments have to perform unusually well while inflation remains low for a money purchase scheme to give an equivalent level of benefit. However, despite these drawbacks, money purchase schemes are more flexible and more easily transferable than defined benefit arrangements. For people changing jobs frequently or working on a self-employed basis for periods of time, particularly during the early years of a career, they can thus be a more attractive option.

In recent years there has been a strong trend away from defined benefit schemes and towards defined contribution provision. At the time of writing 62 per cent of all UK schemes are of the money purchase variety, compared with only 5 per cent in 1990 (National Association of Pension Funds 1992 and 2003). The majority of newly established schemes take the defined contribution form, while many organisations now offer only a money purchase scheme to new employees. By 2003 all but 19 per cent of final salary schemes in the private sector had been closed to new members.

The trend has coincided with a period in which long contribution holidays have come to an end and in which the amount of regulation to which defined benefit schemes are subject has increased substantially. Employers have thus taken the opportunity to reduce their own liabilities and to move to a form of provision which is more predictable financially from their point of view. Many employees are less well served as a result, but the lack of appreciation and understanding of pensions issues referred to above has allowed employers to make the change without becoming any less attractive in the labour market.

Hybrid schemes too are becoming more common, although as yet they represent a small minority of UK pension funds. These, in various different ways, combine elements of the defined benefit and defined contribution forms of provision. The most common form is the 'money purchase underpin' which is basically a final salary arrangement, but one which calculates pensions and transfer values on a money purchase basis where these are higher. Such schemes seek to combine the best aspects of both main types of scheme. They offer a generous, secure and predictable pension, but also incorporate the flexibility associated with defined contribution schemes.

ACTIVITY 29.2

Which of these three types of occupational pension scheme would you find most attractive at the current stage in your career? Under what circumstances might you change your preference?

Group personal pensions

Since the 1980s there has been substantial growth in the market for personal pensions. Self-employed people have always needed to be concerned with making their own provisions for retirement, as they have been excluded from joining S2P, and before that SERPS. More general attention has been focused on this area due to increasing job mobility and the perceived greater portability of personal pensions. A personal pension is arranged, usually through an insurance company, and the individual pays regular amounts into their own 'pension fund' in the same way that they would with a company fund. The employer may also make a contribution to the fund, but at present there are very few employers who have chosen to do so.

An alternative arrangement is a Group Personal Pension plan (GPP) set up by an employer instead of an occupational pension scheme. From a legal and taxation perspective a GPP is no different from any individual personal pension arrangement, but charges are lower because the employer is able to arrange a bulk discount. The scheme is administered by an insurance company, the employer making contributions as well as the employee. Pensions are calculated on the same basis as an occupational money purchase scheme, but tend to be less extensive because employees are responsible for paying some of the administrative charges. From an employee perspective a GPP is inferior to an occupational pension scheme, but is better than a situation in which no employer provision is made at all. Such arrangements are mainly entered into by small firms, but one or two big companies have also set them up in place of conventional occupational pensions.

WINDOW ON PRACTICE

Pension scandals

Following the introduction of personal pensions in 1988 many thousands of employees who were members of occupational schemes were persuaded by salespeople working for insurance companies to leave their employers' schemes and take out inferior personal pension products instead. This became known as the 'pensions mis-selling scandal' because so many people lost out as a result. The government has required the companies concerned to compensate the individuals who were mis-sold pensions, but by 2001 there were still thousands of cases outstanding and waiting to be settled. This scandal, combined with the discovery in 1992 of the defrauding of the Mirror Group pension funds by Robert Maxwell, served to harm the reputation of the UK pensions industry. Mr Maxwell had used the funds to prop up ailing businesses owned by his group. Their combined worth was greater than the value of the companies themselves. When the group collapsed, the funds intended to pay past and present pensioners were found to have disappeared. Robert Maxwell committed suicide.

The government responded to public concern by setting up a committee under the chairmanship of Professor Roy Goode to examine the whole field of pension fund regulation. The result was the Pensions Act 1995, which substantially altered UK law on pension funds. In more recent years many have argued that the measures introduced in 1995 went too far in imposing new regulation. Government now talks about reducing the regulatory burden, but in terms of action the trend continues in the opposite direction.

Stakeholder pensions

A new form of government-sponsored pension arrangement, the stakeholder pension, was established in 2001. These are aimed primarily at the five million or so middle income earners (that is, those earning in the £10,000 to £20,000 a year range) who do not have access to an occupational scheme. The aim is to reduce the number of people in future decades who are reliant on state pensions for their retirement income.

A stakeholder pension scheme can be operated by an employer, a financial services company or a trade union. They operate along money purchase lines and are regulated by established authorities. Charges are kept low because providers are obliged to follow minimum standards set by the government. Employers are not obliged to make contributions to a stakeholder pension, but must provide access to one through their payroll. If employees join a scheme, for example one provided by their trade union, the employer is therefore obliged to make deductions via the payroll out of pre-tax income.

Views vary on whether or not the stakeholder scheme can be hailed as a success. Supporters point to the fact that over 600,000 plans have now been been set up, while critics stress that 80 per cent of these are 'designation only' which means that no money has actually been invested in them. Moreover, because many of the schemes which are being used are set up by employers to replace existing money purchase plans, it would seem that relatively few of the 5 million target group are actually benefiting in practice.

OCCUPATIONAL PENSIONS AND HRM

While occupational pension schemes are governed by a board of trustees which includes member representatives, in most organisations the pensions manager and pensions department are part of the HR function. It is thus important that HR professionals are familiar with the types of scheme offered and the main operating rules so that they can give accurate and timely advice to staff and to potential recruits. They also need to be familiar with the regulatory environment for occupational pensions, which has changed considerably in recent years. Aside from new legislation outlawing discrimination on grounds of sex or against part-time and temporary staff, several other important regulatory changes have been made and new regulatory bodies established. The Pensions Act 1995 now sets out in detail what information must be disclosed to scheme members on request and what must be sent to them automatically each year. The Act also requires all occupational funds to meet a defined minimum funding level so that they are always able to meet their liabilities in the event of the employing company being wound up. Moreover, strict restrictions are now placed on 'self-investment', making sure that fund assets cannot be invested in property or other business ventures controlled by the sponsoring organisation. However, the most important single piece of legislation was the Social Security Act 1985 which put in place a series of measures to protect 'early leavers', ensuring that people who switch employers during their careers do not suffer substantial loss in the value of their pensions.

Early leavers now have one of three options in making their pension arrangements when they begin work for a new employer. One option is to claim back the contributions that the individual has made into the former employer's pension scheme. Deductions are made in accordance with tax laws, and of course, the employer's contribution is lost, but a substantial sum can be reinvested in the new employer's scheme or in a personal pension. Another alternative involves opting for a preserved pension. With a final salary scheme, if there were no inflation, and if the individual progressed very little up the career ladder, a preserved pension from an old employer plus a pension from the recent employer would equate well with the pension they would have received had they been with the new employer for the whole period. However, if these conditions are not met, which in recent times they have not been, individuals who have had more than one employer lose out in the pension stakes. Past employers are required to revalue preserved pensions in line with inflation (to a maximum of 5 per cent), but the value of such a pension remains linked to the level of salary at the date of leaving.

The third option is usually preferable, but is only open (in 2004) to people who have completed two years' membership of a scheme. This involves the transfer of the pension from the old employer's fund into that of the new employer. The process is straightforward in the case of a money purchase scheme, because the worth of each person's pension is readily calculated. It is simply the value of the employee's contributions, plus those of the employer, together with funds accrued as a result of their investment. The process is more complicated in the case of a final salary scheme, the transfer value being calculated according to standard actuarial conventions which take account of the employee's age, their length of pensionable service, the level of salary at the time of leaving and the current interest rate. All things being equal, 'early leavers' still fare worse than 'stayers' in terms of final pensions, but the difference is a great deal less than used to be the case.

Aside from giving advice and taking overall responsibility for pensions issues, HR managers are concerned with determining their organisations' pension policy. Is an occupational pension to be offered? If so, what form should it take? What level of contribution is the employer going to make? It is quite possible to make a judgement in favour of generous occupational provision simply on paternalistic grounds. Many organisations have thus decided that they will offer pensions because it is in the interests of their staff that they should. Occupational schemes represent a convenient and tax-advantageous method of providing an income in old age; it therefore makes sense to include a pension in the total pay and benefits package. The problems with such a commitment, particularly in the case of defined benefit schemes, are the cost and the fact that the long-term financial consequences are unpredictable. This, combined with the fact that many employees do not seem to appreciate the value of an occupational pension, means that many employers are now questioning their commitment to final salary schemes and to pension provision in general.

Research suggests that interest in and understanding of occupational pensions varies considerably from person to person (Goode 1993; Taylor 2000). Older people, professional workers and those working in the financial services sector usually have a clearer perception of their value than other groups of staff. For these groups pensions are important, and their labour market behaviour will be affected as a result. A firm which does not offer a good pension will thus find it harder to recruit and retain them than one which does. By contrast, a firm which largely employs younger people, and/or workers in lower-skilled occupations, may find that it makes more sense to offer additional pay in place of an occupational scheme.

ACTIVITY 29.3

It has been argued that by making occupational pensions readily transferable, by increasing the complexity of the regulatory regime and by increasing taxation levied on pension funds, successive governments have provided a major disincentive to employers considering the establishment of a scheme. To what extent do you agree with this point of view?

SICK PAY

As with pension schemes, the provision of sick pay is seen as the mark of a good employer. Sick pay is an important issue due to the need for control and administration of absence. Research suggests that sickness absence represents around 4 per cent of working time (CBI 2000), although there are large differences between sector and job type. The HR manager and the HR department have a variety of roles to play in relation to sick pay, particularly since the introduction of statutory sick pay in 1983 when state sick pay in addition to occupational sick pay became managed by the employer.

Statutory sick pay (SSP)

Statutory sick pay is a state benefit that has been in existence for several decades. It provides a basic income (£64.35 per week in 2004) to employees who are incapable of going to their normal place of work as a result of illness. SSP, however, is not claimed from a benefit office; it is administered by employers and paid through the payroll according to regulations set out in statute.

Since 1994 employers have been required to take full financial responsibility for SSP for the first four weeks of absence, after which they can claim back a portion of the costs from the state through reduced employer national insurance contributions. However, the method of calculation used now ensures that smaller employers are able to claim back a very considerably higher proportion of the costs than larger employers who usually have to fund it all themselves. Most employees are entitled to state sickness benefit; however, there are some exceptions: employees who fall sick outside the EU, employees who are sick during an industrial dispute, employees over pensionable age and part-timers whose earnings are below the lower earnings limit (£77 per week in 2004). These groups, as well as self-employed people, are obliged to claim state incapacity benefit instead from the Benefits Agency. SSP is built around the concepts of qualifying days, waiting days, certification, linked periods, transfer to the Department for Work and Pensions (DWP) and record periods.

Qualifying days are those days on which the employee would normally have worked, except for the fact that he or she was sick. For many Monday-to-Friday employees this is very straightforward. However, it is more complex to administer for those on some form of rotating week or shift system. Sick pay is only payable for qualifying days.

Waiting days have to pass before the employee is entitled to receive sick pay – at present the number of days is three. These three days must be qualifying days, and on the fourth qualifying day the employee is entitled to sickness benefit, should he or she still be away from work due to sickness.

Certification from a doctor is required after seven days of sickness absence. Prior to this the employee provides self-certification. This involves notifying the employer of absence due to sickness by the first day on which benefit is due – that is, immediately following the three waiting days.

Linked periods of illness mean that the three waiting days do not apply. If the employee has had a period of incapacity from work (PIW) within the previous eight weeks, then the two periods are linked and treated as just one period for SSP purposes, and so the three waiting days do not have to pass again.

The employer does not have to administer SSP for every employee indefinitely. Where the employee has been absent due to sickness for a continuous or linked period of 28 weeks the responsibility for payment passes from the employer to the state. A continuous period of 28 weeks' sickness is clearly identifiable. It is not so clear when linked periods are involved. An employee who was sick for five days, back at work for four weeks, sick for one day, at work for seven weeks and then sick for two days would have a linked period of incapacity of eight days. Alternatively, an employee who was sick for four days, back at work for ten weeks and then sick for five days would have a period of incapacity this time of five days. The DWP requires employers to keep SSP records for three years so that these can be inspected.

Occupational sick pay

There is no obligation on employers to pay employees for days of absence due to sickness beyond what is required under the state's SSP scheme. However, most employers choose to do so via a benefit known as occupational sick pay (OSP). The most common approach is to continue paying the full salary for a set period of time, but other schemes involve reducing the pay rate for days taken off as a result of illness. In either case a sum in excess of the statutory minimum is paid, the portion accounted for by SSP being reclaimed from the state where possible. Paying the full salary is straightforward for those staff who receive a basic salary with no additions. It is more difficult to define for those whose pay is supplemented by shift allowances or productivity bonuses.

Occupational sick pay arrangements tend to be most generous in unionised environments and in the public sector, although professional and managerial employees are usually well covered in most organisations. The common public sector approach involves paying full pay for the first six months of an illness, once three years' service have been completed, before moving the employee on to half-pay for a further six months. Thereafter OSP ceases. At the other end of the scale are employers who pay no OSP at all. They take the view that occupational sick pay will be abused and so pay only what is due under the state scheme. Another approach involves paying a predetermined flat rate in addition to money provided via SSP.

Occupational sick pay schemes also vary according to the period of service required. Some employers provide sick pay for sickness absence from the first day of employment. Others require a qualifying period to be served. For some this is a nominal period of four weeks, but the period may be three or six months, or a year or more. There is a major difference here between OSP and SSP. With SSP pay is available immediately after employment has begun.

We covered the methods used in order to support the section on managing absence effectively in Chapter 15.

COMPANY CARS

A form of employee benefit which is a great deal more common in the UK than in other countries is the company car, nearly 2 million employees enjoying this benefit in 2000 (IRS 2000b, p. 2). Managers from overseas often take some persuading that cars are necessary to attract and retain high-calibre managers, but the received wisdom is that they are. Their importance to employees is demonstrated by the comparative lack of take-up of cash alternatives where these are offered (Smith 2000a, p. 161). After pensions, they are the second most significant employee benefit in cost terms, and are provided for some employees by over 90 per cent of large and medium-sized companies.

There are a number of sound reasons underlying the provision of company cars. First, for some there is a need as part of their jobs to travel very widely and regularly. Not everyone can be assumed to own a reliable car, so it is sometimes necessary to provide one simply to enable an employee to carry out his/her day-to-day job duties. In the case of sales representatives and senior managers the impression created when travelling on company business can be important. It is therefore often considered necessary to provide them with upmarket and up-to-date models to ensure that clients and potential clients are suitably impressed. A case can also be made on cost efficiency grounds for people who clock up a great number of business miles each year. The cost of paying them a reasonable mileage allowance to drive their own cars is often greater than the cost of providing them with a company vehicle; it costs £9,000 a year to reimburse someone who has travelled 30,000 miles at 30p per mile.

However, most possessors of company cars do not fit either of the above categories. Their car entitlements simply come as an expected part of the pay package for middle and senior managers. As such, they signify the achievement of a certain level of status. Indeed, in many companies the cars offered become steadily more imposing as people climb up the corporate hierarchy. Being upgraded to a more impressive car thus signifies in a very manifest way the company's approval. Downgrading, of course, has the opposite effect.

One of the reasons that company cars are so significant in the UK is historical, because before April 1994 they were a highly tax-efficient benefit. It was a good deal cheaper to drive a company car than to purchase one's own out of taxed income, so it made sense for people to be 'paid' in part with a car. This is now far from being the case.

The current tax regime introduced in April 2002 encourages employers to lease or purchase cars which are environmentally friendly. Until then company cars were simply taxed according to the number of miles driven on company business, the annual tax paid by the driver being equivalent to a percentage of the car's list price. The more business miles clocked up, the less tax was paid. In addition there were substantial discounts for people who drove older cars. Now the tax paid depends on carbon emissions or engine size and there are no reductions for people who drive a great number of miles or use an older vehicle. So there is a substantial incentive for people who drive a great deal as part of their jobs to use smaller cars or larger ones with low carbon emissions. Most employers offer cash alternatives equal to the tax payable on the car (IDS 2002b, p. 1), but many of those eligible choose not to take these up despite the fact that there are no longer any obvious tax advantages associated with driving a company car. This is partly because company cars tend to be more expensive than individuals could justify spending from their own income, but mainly because of the substantial savings that still accrue in terms of insurance, maintenance and repair costs. The tax changes have, however, led to a preference for 'trading down'. This means where a choice is given, employees are increasingly opting for a smaller car and more cash in their pay packets.

A major policy choice faced by employers in the provision of cars is whether to buy or lease their fleet. There are advantages and disadvantages associated with both approaches, much depending on the nature of the deal that is struck with a leasing company. Where the company is reputable and where the agreement provides for insurance, maintenance and repair of vehicles, the financial case for leasing is strong.

ACTIVITY 29.4

Assume that you have been offered a new job which comes with either the use of a new company car or a cash allowance. The salary is £35,000 per year. The car is worth £15,000, giving you an annual tax bill of £5,250. This is also the amount being offered by way of an annual cash allowance. Which option would you choose and why?

LONDON ALLOWANCES

Most larger employers pay a standard, organisation-wide allowance or salary weighting to employees working in central London. In some cases such allowances are also paid to employees working in the region around London. The purpose is to attract and retain staff who are obliged to live and commute in the capital where the cost of property, transport and parking is so much higher than it is elsewhere in the country. The typical level of allowance is between £3,000 and £4,000 a year, the highest sums being paid by the finance houses of the City and the lowest by the retailers and public sector employers. According to IDS (2002c), the level of allowances has tended to rise more slowly than wage inflation generally and have often been frozen for a number of years. This has occurred because employers are increasingly moving towards the development of wholly separate London-based salary scales. The flat-rate allowance has thus become a less significant part of the total pay packet, allowing employers to target resources on the groups who are hardest to recruit. In tight labour markets, therefore, there is now a greater differential between pay rates in and out of London than was the case ten years ago.

FLEXIBLE BENEFITS

Flexible benefits or 'cafeteria plans' have proliferated in the United States over recent years where they are specifically recognised in the tax regime. By contrast, take-up of the idea in the UK has been slow (Smith 2000b, p. 379). However, several high-profile organisations have moved towards greater flexibility, and the case for others doing so is strong. Such flexibility involves giving individual employees a choice as to how exactly their pay packet is made up. The overall value of the package is set by the employer, but it is for employees to choose for themselves what balance they wish to strike between cash and the different kinds of benefit. Those who have children, for example, can opt for benefits that are of value to them such as childcare vouchers, access to a company crèche or additional holidays. A young person in their first job might well prefer to forgo most benefits in return for higher take-home pay, while an older person may wish to purchase additional years of pensionable service in exchange for cash or perhaps a car.

There are a number of good reasons for considering such an approach. First, it helps ensure that employees are only provided with benefits which they are aware of and appreciate. Resources that would otherwise be wasted by providing unwanted benefits are thus saved. The employer gets maximum value per pound spent, while at the same time allowing employees to tailor their own 'perfect' benefits mix. The result should be improved staff retention and a better motivated workforce.

WINDOW ON PRACTICE

In 1998 a large-scale merger took place between two of the world's largest professional services firms – Price Waterhouse and Coopers & Lybrand. The merged firm, called PricewaterhouseCoopers, employs 150,000 people in 150 different countries. While the two organisations were culturally similar, they had rather different traditions in the provision of benefits. Rather than continue with different people employed on different sets of terms and conditions, partners decided to harmonise everyone as soon as was possible. This process was made a great deal easier and less contentious by the decision to develop a new flexible benefits scheme called 'Choices'. It allows employees to trade cash for additional holiday, a choice of car, childcare vouchers, retail vouchers, insurance of various kinds and a pension. No one was required to alter their existing benefits package as a result of the merger unless they wished to.

Source: O. Franks and D. Thompson (2000) 'Rights and rites of passage', *People Management*, 17 February.

Flexible benefits plans take many different forms, the main distinction being between those that are 'fully flexible' and those that allow a degree of flexibility within prescribed limits. The former allow employees a free hand to make up their own package and to change it at regular intervals. Under such a regime an employee could theoretically swap all benefits for cash, or could double their holiday entitlement in exchange for a pay cut. A degree of restriction is more common, a compulsory core of benefits being compulsory, with flexibility beyond that. Under such a scheme everyone might be required to take four weeks' holiday and invest in a minimal pension, but be allowed freedom to determine whether or not they wished to benefit from private health insurance, gym membership, discounts on company products, etc. Typical plans also permit some choice of the make and model of car.

A third approach is administratively simpler but is more restrictive in terms of employee choice. This involves 'prepackaging' a number of separate benefits menus designed to suit different groups of employees (rather like a pre-set banquet menu in a Chinese restaurant). Employees must then opt for one package from a choice of five or six, each having the same overall cash value. One is typically tailored to meet the needs of older staff, another is for those with young families, a third for new graduates and so on.

A number of disadvantages with flexible benefits systems can be identified which may well explain their slow development in the UK. These are summarised by Smith (2000b) as follows:

> Objections include difficult administration; problems connected with handling individual employee choices; the requirement for complex costing and records; difficulty in getting employees to make effective choices; employees making mistakes (for example leaving themselves with inadequate pension cover); employees' circumstances changing over time leaving his or her package inappropriate and giving the employer the costly headache of re-designing the package; and finally the possible hiring of expensive specialist or consultant skills and financial counselling to support the move to flexibility.

Uncertainty about the future tax position may also be a deterrent, especially where changes have the potential to throw a whole system out of kilter (as happened in 1997 when the Chancellor of the Exchequer substantially extended taxation on pension fund investments). Good advice about how to overcome these obstacles, together with examples of UK-based schemes in operation, is provided in IDS (1998). A case study outlining the approach taken by Lloyds TSB, which operates one of the largest UK schemes, is provided in IRS (2003b).

SUMMARY PROPOSITIONS

29.1 Between 20 per cent and 50 per cent of the typical employer's pay bill is spent on the provision of supplementary benefits. Evidence suggests that most employees do not appreciate the true financial value of such benefits.

29.2 Occupational pensions are a tax-efficient means of providing funds for retirement in excess of what is provided by state and personal pension schemes.

29.3 Occupational pensions take one of three forms: defined benefit, defined contribution and hybrid. Employers can choose as an alternative to set up a group personal pension or to provide a stakeholder pension under the government's scheme.

29.4 Employers are required to facilitate the payment of statutory sick pay to employees who are away from work as a result of an illness. Most pay occupational sick pay in addition either as a result of moral obligation or in order to attract, retain and motivate their workforces.

29.5 Company cars are commonly provided by UK employers for senior staff. The tax regime introduced in 2002 aimed to discourage demand for larger cars which are not environmentally friendly.

29.6 In theory, flexible benefits plans have a great deal to offer employees. It is likely that their use will grow more widespread in the next few years.

GENERAL DISCUSSION TOPICS

1 Why do you think so few people seem to have an appreciation of the value of their occupational pensions and other benefits? What could be done to raise awareness of the costs involved in their provision?

2 Draw up three flexible benefits packages; one aimed at new graduates, one at employees in their thirties, and one for those aged over 50.

FURTHER READING

Chartered Institute of Personnel and Development
CIPD provides up-to-date information about organisational policy on pensions and benefits, as well as about priorities for benefits managers, in this annual survey (published in February each year).

CIPD (2002) *Pensions and HR's role: a guide*. London: CIPD
This useful guide reviews all the current pressures facing organisations seeking to offer decent occupational pensions for their employees and puts forward suggestions about possible ways forward from an HR perspective.

Employee Relations
A special edition of *Employee Relations* also focused on occupational pensions from an HR point of view.

Incomes Data Services

Industrial Relations Services
Extensive coverage to these issues is given in the IDS and IRS publications listed in the References below.

Smith, I. (2002a) 'Benefits', in G. White and J. Druker (eds) *Reward Management: A Critical Text*. London: Routledge

Smith, I. (2002b) 'Flexible plans for pay and benefits', in R. Thorpe and G. Homan (eds) *Strategic Reward Systems*. London: Financial Times/Prentice Hall
These two chapters provide the best introductions to flexible benefits in the UK context.

REFERENCES

CBI (2000) *Focus on Absence*. London: CBI.
CIPD (2002) *Pensions and HR's role: a guide*. London: CIPD.
CIPD (2004) *Reward Management 2004: A Survey of policy and practice*. London: CIPD.
Franks, O. and Thompson, D. (2000) 'Rights and rites of passage', *People Management*, 17 February.

Goode, R. (1993) *Pension Law Reform: The Report of the Pension Law Review Committee*, Volume 2: Research. London: HMSO.

Government Actuary's Department (2003) *Occupational Pension Schemes: Eleventh Survey*. London: HMSO.

Hopegood, J. (1994) 'Money-go-round: solving the age-old SERPS puzzle', *Daily Telegraph*, 19 March.

IDS (1998) *Flexible benefits*, IDS StudyPlus, July. London: IDS.

IDS (1999) *Benefits: costs and values*, IDS Focus 89, March. London: IDS.

IDS (2002a) *Pensions in Practice 2002/2003: From primary legislation to practical implementation*. London: IDS.

IDS (2002b) *Company Cars and Business Travel*, IDS Study 733, August. London: IDS.

IDS (2002c) *London Allowances*, IDS Study 738, November. London: IDS.

IRS (2000a) 'Managing benefit provision', *IRS Pay and Benefits Bulletin*, No. 487, January. London: IRS.

IRS (2000b) 'Cash or car?' *IRS Pay and Benefits Bulletin*, No. 498, June. London: IRS.

IRS (2003a) 'Occupational pensions in crisis', *IRS Employment Review*, No. 773, April.

IRS (2003b) 'Banking on flexible benefits at Lloyds TSB', *IRS Employment Review*, No. 768, January.

IRS (2004) 'Innovation in occupational pensions', *IRS Employment Review*, No. 794, February.

NAPF (1992) *Seventeenth Annual Survey of Occupational Pension Funds*. London: National Association of Pension Funds.

NAPF (2003) *Pension Scheme Changes – a snapshot*. London: National Association of Pension Funds.

Noble-Warren, R. (1986) 'Lifetime planning', in Institute of Directors, *The Director's Guide to Pensions*. London: The Director Publications Ltd.

Smith, I. (2000a) 'Benefits', in G. White and J. Druker (eds) *Reward Management: A Critical Text*. London: Routledge.

Smith, I. (2000b) 'Flexible plans for pay and benefits', in R. Thorpe and G. Homan (eds) *Strategic Reward Systems*. London: Financial Times/Prentice Hall.

Taylor, S. (2000) 'Occupational pensions and employee retention: debate and evidence', *Employee Relations*, Vol. 22, No. 3, pp. 246–59.

Thompson, P. and Milsome, S. (2001) *Reward Determination in the UK*. London: CIPD.

An extensive range of additional materials, including multiple choice questions, answers to questions and links to useful websites can be found on the Human Resource Management Companion Website at www.pearsoned.co.uk/torrington.

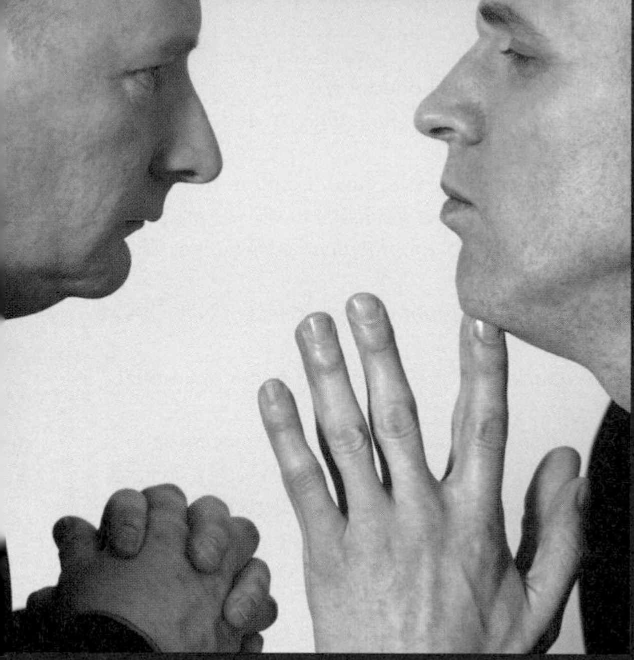

INTERACTIVE SKILL 6: NEGOTIATION

Negotiation is a long-standing art which has developed into a major mode of decision making in all aspects of social, political and business life, even though there is always a feeling that it is no more than a substitute for direct, decisive action. In employment we have developed the institutions of collective bargaining as a means of regulating some parts of the employment relationship between employer and organised employees. The essence of the process is to find not just common ground between two parties but a new relationship with greater constructive potential than the one that preceded it. To some this is the cornerstone of industrial democracy and the effective running of a business, but to others it is seen as impairing efficiency, inhibiting change and producing the lowest, rather than the highest, common factor of cooperation between management and employees. There is growing concern among union leaders as well as in parts of management that there is a lack of both experience and expertise in bargaining.

> . . . for over a decade it has been possible to shape an HR career without coming into contact with unions. Industrial relations expertise has been lost as those who forged their skills in the 1970s have moved on, many into retirement . . . Some employers are looking outside their organizations to bring in industrial relations expertise. But this can not be a permanent solution. (Roberts 2002, p. 37)

This Focus on skills deals directly with that field of expertise. Because negotiation has been out of fashion, most of the academic work on negotiation is of relatively long standing, although there is a recent thorough review in Hiltrop and Udall (1995) and a particular angle described in Grint (1997). There have also been a number of more practical books recently, including Kennedy (1998).

The objectives of this Focus on skills are to:

1 Examine the place of conflict in the employment relationship, its sources, benefits and drawbacks

2 Explain bargaining strategies and tactics

3 Explain the negotiating sequence

4 Consider some aspects of bargaining with individuals

Since the summer of 2000 trade unions have had restored to them a statutory right to recognition by an employer that had been removed from them twenty years before. Recognition means the right to require an employer to negotiate on matters such as hours, pay and holidays: not to consult, but to negotiate. A useful summary is in Younson (2000).

Is negotiation rightly viewed as an activity that is only second best to unilateral decision making? If the outcome is no more than compromise, the choice seems to be between negotiation and capitulation. Some would argue that capitulation by one side would be a better outcome for both than a compromise that ignores the difficulties and dissatisfies both. There is, however, an alternative to splitting the difference in negotiation and that is where the differences in view and objective of the parties are accommodated to such an extent that the outcome for both is better than could have been achieved by the unilateral executive action of either.

Any negotiation takes place because there are some goals that are common to both parties and some goals that conflict. Between employer and employees the desire to keep the business in operation is a goal they usually have in common, but some of their other goals may conflict. Consequently the two parties negotiate a settlement because the attempt by one to force a solution on the other either would fail because of the other's strength or would not be as satisfactory a settlement without the approval of the other party.

Traditionally, negotiation on employment matters has been assumed to deal with the collective aspects of the relationship, the management or the employers being pitched against the unions or the workers. Now, however, we include material on the negotiation of the bargain between the management and an individual person or consultancy selling services. Another recent change has been the growing interest of language specialists in the various processes of negotiation (for instance, Mulholland 1991).

The nature of conflict in the employment relationship

The approach to collective negotiations depends on the view that conflict of interests is inevitable between employer and employee because there is an authority relationship in which the aims of the two parties will at least sometimes conflict. A further assumption is that such conflict does not necessarily damage that relationship.

This has led some commentators to discuss negotiation in terms of equally matched protagonists. The power of the two parties may not actually be equal, but they are both willing to behave as if it were. Negotiation thus has the appearance of power equalisation in the search for a solution to a problem. When both sides set out to reach an agreement that is satisfactory to themselves and acceptable to the other, then their power is equalised by that desire. Where the concern for acceptance by the other is lacking, there comes the use of power play of the forcing type described later in this Interactive skill:

> negotiators seek to increase common interest and expand cooperation in order to broaden the area of agreement to cover the item under dispute. On the other hand, each seeks to maximize his own interest and prevail in conflict, in order to make the agreement more valuable to himself. No matter what angle analysis takes, it cannot eliminate the basic tension between cooperation and conflict that provides the dynamic of negotiation. (Zartman 1976, p. 41)

The relative power of the parties is likely to fluctuate from one situation to the next; this is recognised by the ritual and face-saving elements of negotiation, where a power imbalance is not fully exploited, both to make agreement possible and in the knowledge that the power imbalance may be reversed on the next issue to be resolved.

The classic work of Ann Douglas (1962) produced a formulation of the negotiating encounter that has been little modified by those coming after her. However, this needs further thought when applied to negotiations between representatives of management and representatives of employees about terms and conditions of employment because of the clear inequality of power and access to resources between them.

Sources of conflict in the collective employment relationship

Most texts on organisational behaviour include sections on reducing conflict, and management talk is full of the need for teamworking, corporate culture and collaboration, so why do we find one area of working life where conflict is readily accepted, even emphasised?

Although the processes of civilisation tend to constrain it there is a natural human impulse to behave aggressively to some degree at some time. It has a number of outlets, for example, watching football, wrestling or boxing. Another outlet for aggression is in negotiations within the employing organisation, which is a splendid arena for the expression of aggressiveness and bravura without actually incurring the physical risks that would be involved in violent combat. Dr Johnson summed up the attractions of vigorous disagreement when he said, 'I dogmatise and am contradicted, and in this conflict of opinions I find delight'. Probably the main source of industrial relations conflict is divergence of interests between those who are classified as managers and those who are seen as non-managers. One group is seeking principally such things as efficiency, productivity and the obedience of others to their own authority. The members of the other group are interested in these things, but are more interested in features such as high pay, freedom of action, independence from supervision, scope for the individual and leisure. To some extent these invariably conflict.

Potential benefits of such conflict

Although it is widely believed that conflict of the type described here is counter-productive, there are some advantages.

Introducing new rules

Employment is governed by a number of rules, formal rules that define unfair dismissal and the rate of pay for various jobs, as well as informal rules such as dress codes and modes of address. Management/union conflict is usually a disagreement over the rules and the bargain that is struck produces a new rule: a new rate of pay, a new employment practice or whatever. It may be the only way of achieving that particular change, and it is a very authoritative source of rule making because of the joint participation in its creation.

Modifying the goals

The goals that management sets can be modified as a result of conflict with others. Ways in which management's goals will be unpopular or difficult to implement may be seen for the first time and modifications made early instead of too late. A greater range and diversity of views is brought to bear on a particular matter so that the capacity for innovation is enhanced, but modification of goals can be difficult for managers to accept.

Clash of values

More fundamental is the possible clash of values, usually about how people should behave. Frequently the clash is about managerial prerogative. Managers like to believe and proclaim that management is their inalienable right, so that those who question the way their work is done are ignorant or impertinent. Non-managers may regard management as a job that should be done properly by people who are responsive to questioning and criticism.

Competitiveness

One of the most likely sources of conflict is the urge to compete for a share of limited resources. Much of the drive behind differential pay claims comes from competing with other groups at a similar level, but there may also be competition for finance, materials, security, survival, power, recognition or status.

Organisational tradition

If the tradition of an organisation is to be conflict prone, then it may retain that mode obdurately, while other organisations in which conflict has not been a prominent feature may continue without it. It is axiomatic that certain industries in the United Kingdom are much more likely to display the manifestations of extreme conflict in industrial relations than others. Indicators such as the number of working days lost through strikes show a pattern of distribution which varies little between different industries year by year. The nature of the conflict can range between the extremes of pettiness, secrecy, fear and insecurity on the one hand, to vigorous, open and productive debate on the other, with many organisations exhibiting neither.

Understanding of respective positions

Combatants will come to a better understanding of their position on the issue being debated because of their need to set it forth, develop supporting arguments and then defend those arguments against criticism. This enables them to see more clearly what they want, why they want it and how justifiable it is. In challenging the position of the other party, they will come to a clearer understanding of where they stand, and why.

Potential drawbacks of such conflict

The above advantages may not be sufficient to balance the potential drawbacks.

Waste of time and energy

Conflict and the ensuing negotiations take a great deal of time and energy. Conflict can be stressful when over-personalised, and individuals become obsessed with the conflict itself rather than what it is about. Negotiation takes much longer than simple management decree.

Emotional stress for participants

People vary in the type of organisational stress to which they are prone. To be involved in negotiation is stressful for some people, while others find it stimulating.

Accommodating conflict often causes some inefficiency through the paraphernalia that can accompany it: striking, working to rule, working without enthusiasm, withdrawing cooperation or the simple delay caused by protracted negotiation.

Risks

Negotiation may be the only way to cope with a conflictual situation, but there is the risk of stirring up a hornets' nest. When conflict is brought to the surface it may be resolved or accommodated, or it may get worse if the situation is handled badly.

The quality and amount of communication is impaired. Those involved are concerned more to confirm their own viewpoint than to convey understanding, and there are perceptual distortions such as stereotyping and cognitive dissonance. The attitudes behind the communications may also become inappropriate as there are greater feelings of hostility and attempts to score off others.

Bargaining strategies

Managers and managements adopt various strategies to cope with conflict. We need to recognise these and appreciate some of the likely effects.

Avoidance

To some extent conflict can be 'handled' by ignoring it. For a time this will prevent it surfacing so that it remains latent rather than manifest: the danger being that it is harder to deal with when it eventually does erupt. Opposing views cannot be heard unless there is apparatus for their expression. The management of an organisation can fail to provide such apparatus by, for instance, not having personnel specialists, not recognising trade unions and not recognising employee representatives. If the management organises the establishment as if conflict of opinion did not exist, any such difference will be less apparent and its expression stifled. This strategy is becoming harder to sustain because of the developing legal support for employee representation, but it has obvious short-term advantages.

Smoothing

A familiar strategy is to try to resolve conflict by honeyed words in exhortation or discussion where the emphasis is on the value of teamwork, the assurance that 'we all agree really' and an overt, honest attempt to get past the divergence of opinion, which is regarded as a temporary and unfortunate aberration. This is often an accurate diagnosis and represents an approach that would have broad employee support in a particular employment context, but there is always the risk that smoothing ignores the real problem, like giving a massage to someone who has suffered a heart attack.

Forcing

The opposite to smoothing is to attack expressions of dissent and deal with conflict by stamping it out. This is not easy and has innumerable, unfortunate precedents in both the political and industrial arenas.

Compromise

Where divergence of views is acknowledged and confronted, one possibility is to split the difference. If employees claim a pay increase of £10 and the management says it can afford nothing, a settlement of £5 saves the face of both parties but satisfies neither. However common this strategy may be, and sometimes there is no alternative, it has one major drawback: both parties fail to win.

Confrontation

The fifth strategy is to confront the issue on which the parties differ. This involves accepting that there is a conflict of opinions or interests, exploring the scale and nature of the conflict and then working towards an accommodation of the differences which will provide a greater degree of satisfaction of the objectives of both parties than can be achieved by simple compromise. This sounds ambitious, but we suggest that this is the most productive strategy in many cases and offers the opportunity of both parties winning. It is this strategy that we consider in the remainder of this Interactive skill.

ACTIVITY VI. 1

Consider an industrial dispute or disagreement which you have recently witnessed or read about.

1 Was the management strategy one of avoidance, smoothing, forcing, compromise or confrontation?

2 Was this an inappropriate strategy?

3 If the answer to the last question was 'yes' why was an inappropriate strategy used?

Bargaining tactics

In preparing for negotiation there are a number of matters that the parties must review before they begin.

Resolution or accommodation

Conflict can be *resolved* so that the original feelings of antagonism or opposition vanish, at least over the issues that have brought the conflict to a head. The schoolboy story of how two boys 'put on the gloves in the gym' after a long feud and thereafter shook hands and became firm friends is a theoretical example of a conflict resolved. This type of outcome has a romantic appeal and will frequently be sought in industrial relations issues because so many people feel acutely uncomfortable when involved in relationships of overt antagonism.

Alternatively, the conflict may be *accommodated*, so that the differences of view persist, but a modus vivendi, some form of living with the situation, is discovered. In view of the inevitability of the conflict that is endemic in the employment relationship, accommodation may be a more common prospect than resolution, but an interesting question for a negotiator to ponder when approaching the bargaining table is: which is it – resolution or accommodation?

Tension level

Most negotiators feel they have no chance to determine the timing of encounters. This is partly due to reluctance; managers in particular tend to resort to negotiation only when necessary, and the necessity is usually a crisis. A more proactive approach is to initiate encounters, at least trying to push them towards favourable timings.

A feature of timing is the tension level. Too much, and the negotiators get the jitters, unable to see things straight and indulging in excessive interpersonal vituperation:

too little tension, and there is no real will to reach a settlement. Ideal timing is to get a point when both sides have a balanced desire to reach a settlement.

Power balance

Effective negotiation is rarely limited to the sheer exploitation of power advantage. The best settlement is one in which both sides can recognise their own and mutual advantages (Fowler 1990, pp. 11–16). The background to any negotiation includes the relative power of the disputants. Power parity is the most conducive to success:

> Perceptions of power inequality undermine trust, inhibit dialogue, and decrease the likelihood of a constructive outcome from an attempted confrontation. Inequality tends to undermine trust on both ends of the imbalanced relationship, directly affecting both the person with the perceived power inferiority and the one with perceived superiority.
> (Walton 1969, p. 98)

The greater the power differential, the more negative the attitudes.

Synchronising

The approaches and reactions of the two parties need a degree of synchronising to ensure that an approach is made at a time when the other party is ready to deal with it. Management interpretation of managerial prerogative often causes managers to move quickly in search of a solution, virtually pre-empting negotiation. When what they see as a positive overture is not reciprocated, they are likely to feel frustrated, discouraged and cross; making themselves in turn unready for overtures from the other side.

Openness

Conflict is handled more effectively if the participants are open with each other about the facts of the situation and their feelings about it. The Americans place great emphasis on this, as openness is more culturally acceptable in the United States than in the United Kingdom, but we note their concern that negotiators should own up to feelings of resentment and anger, rather than mask their feelings behind role assumptions of self-importance.

WINDOW ON PRACTICE

John Dunlop is known as one of the great theorists of industrial relations and the processes in collective bargaining (*see* Dunlop 1984). David Farnham summarises the ten points of his framework for analysing the negotiating process:

1. It takes agreement within each negotiating group to reach a settlement between them.
2. Initial proposals are typically large, compared with eventual settlements.

3 Both sides need to make concessions in order to move towards an agreement.

4 A deadline is an essential feature of most negotiating.

5 The end-stages of negotiating are particularly delicate, with private discussions often being used to close the gap between the parties.

6 Negotiating is influenced by whether it involves the final, intermediate or first stages of the conflict resolution process.

7 Negotiating and overt conflict may take place simultaneously, with the conflict serving as a tool for getting agreement.

8 Getting agreement does not flourish in public.

9 Negotiated settlements need procedures to administer or interpret the final agreement.

10 Personalities and their interactions can affect negotiating outcomes.

Source: D. Farnham (1993) *Employee Relations*. London: IPM, p. 337.

The negotiation sequence

In the various stages of the negotiating encounter aspects of ritual are especially important. They can make for formality and awkwardness rather than relaxed informality, but these ritual steps are not time-wasting prevarication: they are an inescapable feature of the process, which is summarised in Figure VI.1.

Agenda

The meeting needs an agenda or at least some form of agreement about what is to be discussed. Some people nurture a naive conviction that there is benefit in concealing the topic from the other party until the encounter begins, believing there is something to be gained from surprise. In fact, this only achieves a deferment of discussion until members of the other party have had a chance to consider their position. The nature of the agenda can have an effect on both the conduct and outcome of the negotiations. It affects the conduct of the encounter by revealing and defining the matters that each side wants to deal with. It is unlikely that other matters will be added to the agenda, particularly if negotiations take place regularly between the parties, so that the negotiators can begin to see, before the meeting, what areas the discussions will cover.

The sequence of items on the agenda will influence the outcome as the possibilities of accommodation between the two positions emerge in the discussion. If, for instance, all the items of the employees' claim come first and all the management's points come later, the possibilities do not turn into probabilities until the discussions are well advanced. An agenda that juxtaposes management and employee 'points' in a logical fashion can enable the shape of a settlement to develop in the minds of the negotiators earlier, even though there would be no commitment until all the pieces of the jigsaw were available. Many negotiations take place without an agenda at all, sometimes because there is a crisis, sometimes because neither party is sufficiently well organised to prepare one. Morley and Stephenson (1977, pp. 74–8) review a

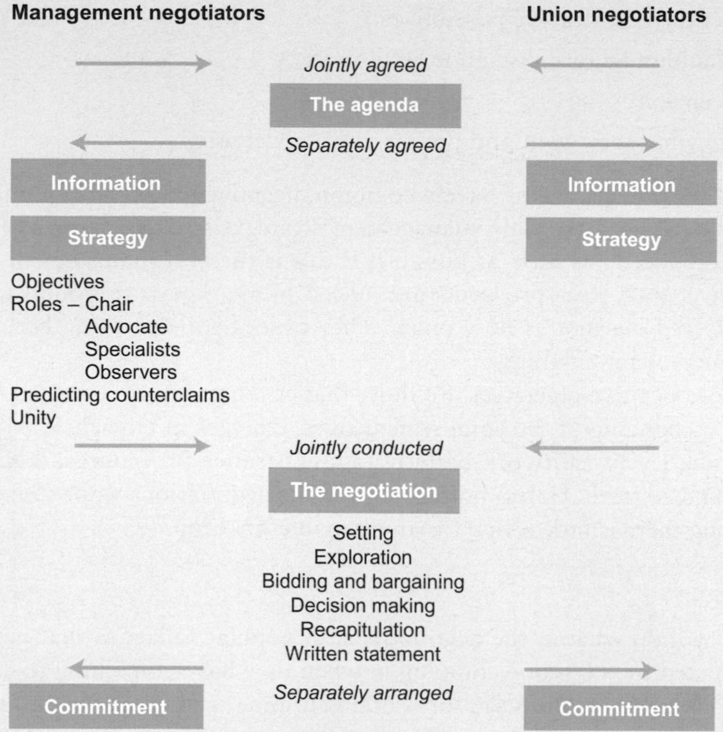

Figure VI.1 The negotiating process

number of studies to draw the conclusion that agreement between negotiators is facilitated when there is the opportunity for them to experience 'orientation', considering on what to stand firm and on what to contemplate yielding, or where there is an understanding of the issues involved. An agenda is a prerequisite of orientation.

Information

Both parties need facts to support their argument in negotiation. Some information will be provided to employee representatives for the purposes of collective bargaining and both sets of negotiators have to collect what they need, analyse it so that they understand it, and confirm that the interpretation is shared by each member of their team.

Strategy

The main feature of preparation is for each set of negotiators to decide their strategy. Probably the most helpful work on negotiation strategy has been done by Fowler (1990), with his careful analysis of bargaining conventions and possibilities. Here we limit our considerations to four aspects of strategy.

Objectives

What do the negotiators seek to achieve? They need clear and helpful objectives. When the question has been put to management negotiators entering either real or contrived negotiations in recent years the following have been some of the statements of objectives:

- 'Get the best deal we possibly can.'
- 'Maintain factory discipline at all costs.'
- 'Keep cool.'
- 'See what they want and put up a strong defence.'

All these declarations have a common, negative quality. The initiative is with the other party and the only management strategy is to resist for as long as possible and to concede as little as possible. If this is the best management negotiators can contrive, then their prospects are indeed bleak. They are bound to lose; the only unresolved question is how much. They cannot gain anything because they do not appear to want anything.

More positive objectives are those that envisage improvements which could flow from a changing of the employment rules, changes in efficiency, working practices, manning levels, shiftwork patterns, administrative procedures, flexibility, cost control, and so forth. Unless both parties to the negotiations want something out of the meeting there is little scope for anything but attrition.

Roles

Who will do what in the negotiations? A popular fallacy is that negotiation is best conducted by 'everyone chipping in when they have something to say' and 'playing it by ear'. This is the style for a brainstorming, problem-solving group discussion; negotiation is quite different. Problem solving implies common interests; negotiation implies conflicting interests between groups who are opposed in debate. Negotiators need a specific role, in which they remain. The roles are:

1 Chair. In the majority of cases the management provides this function, and one of the management team will chair the discussion and control the meeting.

2 Advocate. Each party requires one person who will be the principal advocate to articulate the case and to examine the opposing case. This provides focus to the discussion and control of the argument. Although it is common for the roles of chair and advocate to be combined in one person for status reasons, this can put a great strain on the individual, who is bowling and keeping wicket at the same time.

3 Specialists. The third role is that of specialist. There is one person who fully understands the details of the management proposal or arrangement that is being questioned, another to provide expert comment on any legal points, and so forth. The important emphasis is on what the specialist does *not* do. One would not expect this particular negotiator to become involved in the general debate, as this is confusing and moves control from the advocate. The specialist's role is to provide advice when required, rather like the civil servants who regularly pass notes to ministers appearing before House of Commons Committees. Negotiating does not benefit from free-for-all, unstructured discussion.

4 Observers. There is no need for all those attending to speak in order to justify their presence. There is an important role for those who do no more than observe the discussions. They get less emotionally involved in the interplay and point scoring, and are able to evaluate the situation as it develops. When there are adjournments the observers often initiate the discussions within their team as strategy is redefined and further tactics considered.

Predicting counterclaims

No strategy survives intact the first encounter with the opposition, but its chances are improved if the negotiators have tried to predict what they will hear from the opposition. In this way they will be prepared not only to advance their own arguments, but also to respond to arguments put to them.

Unity

Because negotiations are the confrontation of different sets of interests, each team works out a united position before negotiations begin and expresses that unity in negotiation. If the position is to be modified, then they will agree the modification. This is another aspect of the vital difference between this activity and problem solving. It is the differences between the parties that have to be handled; differences within the parties are simply a nuisance.

The negotiation

Setting

The number of people representing each side will influence the conduct of negotiations. The larger the number, the greater the degree of formality that is needed to manage the meeting; this is an argument in favour of negotiations between very small teams. On the other hand, meetings between two or three people in 'smoke-filled rooms' give rise to allegations of manipulation and are difficult for members of trade unions to countenance in view of their dependence on democratic support. Another problem is that different phases of negotiation call for different arrangements. Relatively large numbers can be an advantage at the beginning, but are often a hindrance in the later stages:

> it is not uncommon for the trade union side to field a sizeable team – a union official, perhaps, supported by a shop stewards' committee. It is unwise for a single manager to attempt to negotiate alone with such a team. Negotiation demands a high level of concentration and quick thinking and it is difficult for one person to maintain full attention to everything that is said, and to detect every nuance in the discussion. This does not mean that the management team must equal the trade union team in size. Indeed, to go beyond a fairly small number runs the risk of poor coordination between team members and the possibility that differing views will emerge within the team as negotiations proceed. (Fowler 1990, p. 35)

When asked to suggest an appropriate number, most experienced negotiators opt for three or four on each side.

The nature of the seating arrangements needs to reflect the nature of the meeting, and that means that the sides face each other, with the boundaries between the two being clear. The importance of the physical arrangements were demonstrated by the Paris Peace Talks, which were intended to bring an end to the Vietnam War. The start of talks was delayed for some weeks due to the delegations not being able to agree about the shape of the table.

Negotiating

The opening stage of the negotiations is one of *exploration*. Negotiators begin by making it clear that they are representing the interests of people who are much more important than the negotiators themselves: 'the membership', 'the board' and 'the shareholders' are just a sample of the powerful decision makers behind the negotiators. They also emphasise the strength and righteousness of their case as well as the impossibility of any movement from the position they are declaring. Both sides know but do not acknowledge that there will be movement from the positions that they are busy declaring to be immovable. The displays of strength are necessary for the negotiators to convince themselves that they are right and to impress the opposition, who have previously only been able to see the rightness of their own position.

The substantive element of this phase is to clarify what the differences are and how important or intransigent each feature of the opposing case is. By the time it draws to a close the negotiators should be quite clear on the matters that divide them, where and how. This, of course, is an important part of the process: differentiation precedes integration.

An important part of the ritual at this point is for the participants to keep down the level of interpersonal animosity. This is a part of the emphasis on their representative role that has already been mentioned. Different behaviours are needed later that depend on an open, trusting relationship between the negotiators, so this must not be impaired by personal acrimony at the opening. Ann Douglas (1962) described this stage as 'inter-party antagonism'.

After the differences have been explored, there is an almost instinctive move to a second, integrative stage of the encounter. Here negotiators are looking for possibilities of movement and mutual accommodation:

> Douglas distinguishes between the public role-playing activities of the first stage and the 'psychological' (individual) activities of the second stage as being concerned, respectively, with inter-party and interpersonal exchange. Behaviourally the inter-party exchange is characterized by official statements of position, ostensibly committing the party or parties to some future action congruent with that position. The interpersonal exchange, on the other hand, is characterized by unofficial behaviours which do not so commit the parties in question. (Morley and Stephenson 1970, p. 19)

This second stage is *bidding and bargaining*. The statements made by negotiators are much more tentative than earlier, as they sound out possibilities, float ideas, ask questions, make suggestions and generally change style towards a problem-solving mode. This has to be done without any commitment of the party that is being represented, so the thrusts are couched in very non-committal terms, specifically exonerating the party being represented from any explicit authorisation of what is being said. Gradually, the opportunities for mutual accommodation can be perceived in the background of the discussion. We can now incorporate the idea of target points and resistance points advanced by Walton and McKersie (1965).

The target point of a negotiating team is the declared objective, what they would really like to achieve. It will be spelled out in the exploration phase. The resistance point is where they would rather break off negotiations than settle. This point is never declared and is usually not known either. Although negotiators frequently begin negotiations with a feeling of 'not a penny more than . . .', the point at which they would actually resist is seldom the same as that at which they think they would resist. Normally the resistance points for both parties slide constantly back and forth during negotiations.

Decision making

Through the stage of bidding and bargaining all the variations of integration will have been considered and explored, even though negotiators will have veered away from making firm commitments. The third phase of their encounter is when they reach an agreement, and it is interesting to pause here with the comment that agreement is inevitable in all but a small minority of situations, because the bargainers need each other and they have no one else with whom to negotiate. The employees want to continue working for the organisation. Even if they take strike action, they will eventually return to work. The management needs the employees to work for it. Employees collectively cannot choose a different management with whom to negotiate and managers can seldom choose a replacement workforce with whom to bargain. They have to reach agreement, no matter how long it takes.

After an adjournment the management will make an offer. The decision about what to offer is the most difficult and important task in the whole process, because the offer can affect the resistance point of the other party. The way in which the other's resistance point will be affected cannot be predetermined. A very low offer could move the other's resistance point further away or bring it nearer; we cannot be sure until the negotiations actually take place.

The offer may be revised, but eventually an offer will be accepted and the face-to-face negotiations are over, but the full process is not yet complete.

Negotiations on the contract for collective consent are thus significantly different from those other types of bargaining in which people engage. The negotiations to purchase a secondhand car or a house may seem at first sight to be similar, but in both of those situations either party can opt out at any stage and cease to deal any further. The possibility of losing the other is always present, just as is the possibility of negotiating with a different 'opponent'. For this reason the political analogies are more helpful. A peace treaty has to be agreed between the nations that have been at war, and no one else.

Recapitulation

Once a bargain has been struck the tension of negotiation is released and the natural inclination of the negotiators is to break up and spread the news of the agreement that has been reached. It is suggested that they should resist this temptation and first recapitulate all the points on which they have agreed and, if necessary, make arrangements on any minor matters still outstanding that everyone had forgotten.

In the wake of a settlement there are usually a number of such minor matters. If they are dealt with there and then they should be dealt with speedily because of the overriding relief at reaching agreement that is felt. If discussion of them is deferred because they are difficult, then agreement may be hard to reach later as the issues stand on their own, instead of in the context of a larger settlement.

Written statement

If it is possible to produce a brief written statement before the meeting is ended, both parties to the negotiations will be greatly helped. The emphasis here is on producing a brief written statement *before* the meeting ends, not as soon as possible afterwards. This will help all the negotiators to take away the same interpretation of what they have done and make them less dependent on recollection. In most circumstances it can also be used to advise non-participants: retyped as a memorandum to supervisors, put up on noticeboards, read out at union meetings, and so on. This will reduce the distortion that can stem from rumour. Until the agreement is in writing it rests on an understanding, and understanding can easily change.

Commitment of the parties

So far agreement has been reached between negotiators only, and it is of no value unless the parties represented by those negotiators accept it and make it work. This requires acceptance at two levels: first in words and then in deeds.

Employee representatives have to report back to their membership and persuade them to accept the agreement. To some extent management representatives may have to do the same thing, but they customarily carry more personal authority to make decisions than do employee representatives.

Although this is a difficult and uncertain process, it is no more important than the final level of acceptance, which is where people make the agreement work. Benefits to the employees are likely to be of the type that are simple to administer, such as an increase in the rates of pay, but benefits to the business, such as changes in working practices and the variation of demarcation boundaries, are much more difficult. They may quickly be glossed over and forgotten unless the changes are painstakingly secured after the terms have been agreed.

WINDOW ON PRACTICE

Lemuel Boulware, Vice-President for Employee Relations in the General Electric Company of the United States, tried to side-step the ritual dance described above by developing a strategy which he called 'truth in bargaining'. The essence was that his first offer was also his last. He claimed that in conventional bargaining everyone knew that the first offer would be improved, so it was artificially low. He intended to be direct and truthful, making one offer that would not be varied so as to save time and speculation about the final outcome.

This policy had short-run success, but trade unions objected to Boulwarism on the grounds that it eliminated the constructive interchange of normal bargaining and diminished the importance of union representatives in negotiation. Eventually they challenged the policy successfully in the US courts on the grounds that it was not bargaining in good faith.

ACTIVITY VI. 2

1 What was Lemuel Boulware's mistake?

2 Why is the process (as well as the result) of negotiating important to both management representatives and employee representatives?

3 Is the process of negotiation important to the members of management and the employees who are represented, but not participating in the negotiations; or are they only interested in the result?

4 In view of the assertive, take-it-or-leave-it approach of some managements at the end of the twentieth and the beginning of the twenty-first centuries, is Boulware just a historical footnote, or is there still a lesson to be learned from his experience?

Negotiating with individuals

The majority of people at work are employed at the rate for the job, even though there may be some marginal variations in individual circumstances. There are, however, a small number of people who genuinely negotiate an individual arrangement. Sometimes they are employees, more often they are freelance providers of specialist services.

Although there are not the same elaborate rituals that surround the collective bargain, there is still a fundamental conflict of interest in that the two parties are not 'on the same side', but there is also the key difference in that the parties can walk away from each other. They are not (yet) bound to each other by a contract of employment; the employer can readily decide to contract with a different supplier and the supplier of services will not be wholly dependent on a single employer. Also the employer is keen that the supplier should produce a *performance*, not simply honouring the agreement with poor grace, but performing at a high level.

Some individuals get great satisfaction from the idea of negotiating their own deal. It gives them a clear sense of their own value and a feeling of autonomy, being in control of their own destiny. It was earlier suggested that collective negotiations are at least partly a way of people dealing with their aggressive tendencies. In individual situations it is slightly different in that the gaming element is stronger and everyone becomes their own entrepreneur.

The negotiating process is broadly the same in that the first stage is to muster all the information that is needed. Exactly what is the task to be done? What is the standard to which it has to be completed? What are the timescales? What latitude is there? When the parties sit down to negotiate, there is again the general searching stage of defining the negotiating range, clarifying what is wanted and hearing what the supplier wants and needs. The employer has the useful advantage that the prospective supplier has to tender, knowing that there are, or may be, others tendering for the same work, so the supplier has to pitch the tender at a level attractive enough to interest the employer not only in the price but also in the quality of service being offered.

Those employing services have to know what they can and cannot do. William Oncken (1984) has coined the term 'freedom scale' to describe the degree of discretion you want to enjoy. His scale is:

- Level 5 – Act on your own, routine reporting only.
- Level 4 – Act, but advise at once.
- Level 3 – Recommend, then take resulting action.
- Level 2 – Ask what to do.
- Level 1 – Wait until told.

Although Level 5 sounds very status-full and macho, employers may prefer in some negotiations to have less freedom, so that they cannot be expected to commit themselves without time for thought. Remember the representation element that was so central to collective negotiation.

WINDOW ON PRACTICE

Roger Fisher and William Ury (1986) suggest four basic rules to govern any negotiation:

1. Separate the people from the problem. Don't focus on the clash of personalities or bruised egos, but on the problem that needs resolution.
2. Focus on interests, not positions. If you get locked into a particular position, you may not achieve the real objective of your negotiation. Always be looking for alternative possibilities.
3. Make the pie bigger. Generate other possibilities beyond what your 'opponent' is asking for by thinking of options that are low cost to you and high benefit to them.
4. Insist on using objective criteria. Prevent the negotiation becoming a contest of wills by looking for objective standards or criteria that can be used by both parties to test the reasonableness of any position that is adopted.

SUMMARY PROPOSITIONS

VI.1 The practice of negotiation is based on a need to resolve or accommodate matters on which there is a conflict of interest about the appropriate rate for the job between those who employ and those who are employed.

VI.2 In collective issues negotiation can clear the air, introduce new rules, modify an unworkable management position or produce better understanding of respective positions.

VI.3 Among the problems of negotiation are the waste of time, the stress and the risks.

VI.4 The most common bargaining strategies are avoidance, smoothing, forcing, compromise or confrontation.

VI.5 Aspects of preparation are setting the agenda, collecting information, deciding a strategy, agreeing objectives and roles.

VI.6 The stages in collective negotiation are exploration, bidding and bargaining, decision making, recapitulation, agreeing a written statement and ensuring the commitment of the parties.

VI.7 In individual negotiations a negotiator will want to get agreement to an appropriate position of the 'freedom scale'.

GENERAL DISCUSSION TOPICS

1 In 1735 Benjamin Franklin said that 'necessity never made a good bargain'. Do you agree with this when applied to collective negotiations?

2 Is negotiation necessary in payment matters or is it just a form of game playing that appeals to people who like doing deals?

FURTHER READING

Fisher, R. and Ury, W. (1986) *Getting to Yes: Negotiating agreement without giving in*. New York: Penguin
This is very sound on the basics and probably the most thorough recent treatment.

Hiltrop, J.M. and Udall, B. (1995) *The Essence of Negotiation*. Hemel Hempstead: Prentice Hall International
A relatively recent thorough treatment of the process, it has an especially useful review of the literature.

Kennedy, G. (1998) *The New Negotiating Edge*. London: Nicholas Brealey
Written by a professor in a business school, who combines academia with running an international consultancy, this book combines some of the merits of both spheres of work. It proposes an approach to negotiating that is a modification of what is set out here. It is described as trading behaviour with four stages: prepare, debate, propose and bargain.

Mulholland, J. (1991) *The Language of Negotiation*. London: Routledge
This book is quite different from most texts which take an industrial relations perspective of negotiation, as it uses the distinctive approach of analysing the linguistic subtleties of the process.

Scott, W.P. (1981) *The Skills of Negotiating*. New York: Wiley
This book has probably the best explanation of the interactive skills involved in negotiating.

WEB LINKS

Most websites deal with negotiating sales but two that could be useful are:

www.core-solutions.com (a consultancy, Core Solutions); and
www.unison.org.uk/bargining (the trade union, UNISON).

REFERENCES

Douglas, A. (1962) *Industrial Peacemaking*. New York: Columbia University Press.
Dunlop, J.T. (1984) *Dispute Resolution*. London: Auburn.
Farnham, D. (1993) *Employee Relations*. London: IPM.
Fisher, R. and Ury, W. (1986) *Getting to Yes: Negotiating agreement without giving in*. New York: Penguin.

Fowler, A. (1990) *Negotiation Skills and Strategies*. London: IPM.

Grint, K. (1997) *Fuzzy Management*. London: Sage.

Hiltrop, J.M. and Udall, B. (1995) *The Essence of Negotiation*. Hemel Hempstead: Prentice Hall International.

Kennedy, G. (1998) *The New Negotiating Edge*. London: Nicholas Brealey.

Morley, I. and Stephenson, G.M. (1970) 'Strength of case, communication systems and the outcomes of simulated negotiations', *Industrial Relations Journal*, Summer.

Mulholland, J. (1991) *The Language of Negotiation*. London: Routledge.

Oncken, W. (1984) *Managing Management Time: who's got the monkey?* Englewood Cliffs, NJ: Prentice-Hall.

Roberts, Z. (2002) 'A Square Deal', *People Management*, September, Vol. 8, No. 18, pp. 37–40.

Walton, R.E. (1969) *Interpersonal Peacemaking: Confrontations and third party consultation*. Reading, Mass.: Addison-Wesley.

Walton, R.E. and McKersie, R.B. (1965) *Towards a Behavioural Theory of Labour Negotiations*. London: McGraw-Hill.

Younson, F. (2000) 'How to handle a union recognition claim', *People Management*, Vol. 6, No. 15.

Zartman, I.W. (1976) *The 50% Solution*. New York: Anchor Press/Doubleday.

REVIEW OF PART VI

When Friedrich Engels came to Manchester from Germany in the 1840s he acted as agent for his family firm at what is now known as Jackson's Mill, for many years housing the Chemical Engineering Department of the University of Manchester. Looking out of his small first floor office he saw the squalid hovels of his workers in nearby Ancoats, with overcrowding, lack of sanitation and a level of poverty such that the average life expectancy was less than 30. This was a life-transforming experience for the young man who had left behind the elegant buildings and broad thoroughfares of Dresden. He wrote *The Condition of the Working Classes in England in 1844* and four years later collaborated with Karl Marx to write *The Communist Manifesto*. Here was the economic analysis that was to provide the intellectual underpinnings of the labour movement and of trade unionism for a hundred years. Fundamentally antagonistic, the interests of capitalists and workers were bound to cause class conflict and struggle as those who controlled the means of production wrestled to extract a surplus from the producers.

The management of employee relations is not now quite so stark, but the processes rest on the same fundamental premise of conflict between two different sets of interests, and much of that is about money. How will it be distributed? Who will decide on fair shares? How will the inevitable disagreements be dealt with? Pay is the mechanism of exchange at the centre of the employment contract. It not only rewards contribution and determines standard of living, it also reflects social status and financial security. Every aspect of human resource management has an important impact on the lives of all those involved, whether they be managing or managed, although the distinction between those who manage and those who are managed is hardly clear. Pay has a more significant impact on people's lives than some of the matters we have considered in this book.

Part VI CASE STUDY PROBLEM

Offshoring to India

Since 2000 dozens of large corporations based in the UK, USA and Canada have transferred parts of their operations to cities such as Bangalore and Mumbai in India. In the main the activities that are 'offshored' are those carried out in call centres, such as customer enquiries, telemarketing and back-office administration. Some 50,000 such jobs are estimated to have been switched from the UK to India between 2000 and 2004. Most of the larger finance companies either have made such a move or are actively considering doing so. The same is true of many e-businesses, mail-order retailers and other service sector companies. Rail and airline enquiries may well soon be answered down the phone from India, while some larger legal firms rely on secretarial services based in India to type up dictated letters. Offshoring has clearly become a major business trend.

The potential advantages are very evident. The salary that has to be paid to a call-centre worker in India is around 20 per cent of the figure required to secure the services of someone in the UK. This means that call centres in India operate at around 40 per cent of their cost in the UK once international telephone charges have been taken into account. Setting up a 850-seat centre in India costs about £20 million, but can easily yield annual savings of £15 million once it is established. Savings of that kind are just too significant to pass up in highly competitive industries that must cut costs wherever possible if they are to survive and grow.

Moreover, by Indian standards, these are well-paid jobs which attract highly educated people, including graduates, who perform more effectively and more quickly than the typical UK call-centre worker. Employers report that as well as having lower salary expectations, Indian employees are more adaptable to change and more responsive to management demands than their UK counterparts. Their level of spoken English is generally very high too. It is thus argued that costs are saved and quality is increased when an organisation offshores its operations to India.

Offshoring has been criticised vigorously by trade unions representing the British workers whose jobs are put at risk by the offshoring trend. They argue that it is no more than a 'corporate fashion' which cannot be justified over the longer term. They point to the very high levels of staff turnover that are found in many Indian call-centre operations and to persistent power maintenance problems. Over the long term, the critics argue, shortages of appropriately qualified staff will emerge as the Indian economy develops its own high-tech industrial sector. Cost savings will thus reduce substantially within 10 years. Critics also point to well-publicised instances of poor quality services being provided by some Indian operations.

It appears that in order to be successful, a great deal of effort must be put into training Indian staff to adopt Western personas, particularly in the telesales operations. They have to make 200 calls to the UK or the USA on each shift that they work, and these yield more sales if the operator poses as someone called Jack or Cathy and is able to chat about the weather in the UK or the latest television programmes.

Questions

1 Companies transferring their call-centre operations to India can either outsource to one of the established India-based providers (which typically operate 10,000-seat centres), or set up their own bespoke operation via a subsidiary company. What are the major advantages and disadvantages of each of these options from the perspective of the corporation?

2 Critics of offshoring often claim that the practice is unethical, when seen from the perspective of both UK and Indian employees. To what extent do you agree with this view and why? What steps might be taken by a company that aims to be a champion of corporate social responsibility to ensure that it acted ethically when offshoring?

3 A great deal of customer demand for call-centre services is concentrated in the evenings and at weekends, and this is also the prime time for selling goods and services to UK and US-based consumers via cold calling. What implications does this have for the achievement of a work-life balance for Indian call-centre workers?

4 Some companies have already outsourced parts of their HR function to India – mainly basic back-office tasks such as payroll administration, the maintenance of databases and intranet systems, generation of standard letters and sets of documentation and benefits administration. How much further do you think this process could be taken? To what extent would it be feasible to offshore some of the advisory functions carried out by HR specialists as well as the basic administrative tasks?

Sources

Crabb, S. (2003) 'East India companies', *People Management*, 20 February, pp. 28–32.
Articles downloaded from the BBC News website (www.bbc.co.uk).

Part VI EXAMINATION QUESTIONS

1 Explain the difference in the objectives of employer and employee when considering the payment arrangements of the employee.

2 What are the differences between wages and salaries?

3 'Job evaluation is redundant: it is only the Equal Pay Act that keeps it going.' Discuss.

4 How effective are payment systems in improving effort levels and performance?

5 If you are managing a system of payment with the objective that those being paid should regard the system as being fair, would you relate the payment to the demands of the job or to the relative performance of individuals doing the job?

6 'Individual performance pay is only one ingredient of a performance management system and a relatively insignificant one at that.' Do you agree or disagree with this statement? Explain your reasons.

7 What are the advantages and disadvantages of broadbanded pay structures?

8 What should be the main benefits of an employee benefits policy?

PART 7

CROSS-FUNCTIONAL ISSUES

As we come to the close of the book, we have a different sort of Part. We are not considering activities in a specific functional grouping, but issues that tend to influence all functional areas. The international dimension to HR work may have very little influence in some businesses, but in others it may be considerable. Education authorities have recruited schoolteachers in foreign countries and health authorities have many different nationalities in their ranks. Some organisations have many overseas activities, which have to be staffed and with which there may be some difficult comparisons when terms and conditions of employment are being discussed.

Some aspects of working internationally have a strong ethical dimension, as do many features of employment within a single country and again inter-country comparisons can be very difficult. In many Western countries, particularly the UK, the matter of the balance between hours spent working and hours spent at home has recently received a great deal of attention.

The effectiveness of the HR function is frequently questioned so all HR people need to consider how valuable their contribution is and how it can be effectively measured. Finally we conclude our series of Interactive skills by considering the activity of chairing meetings.

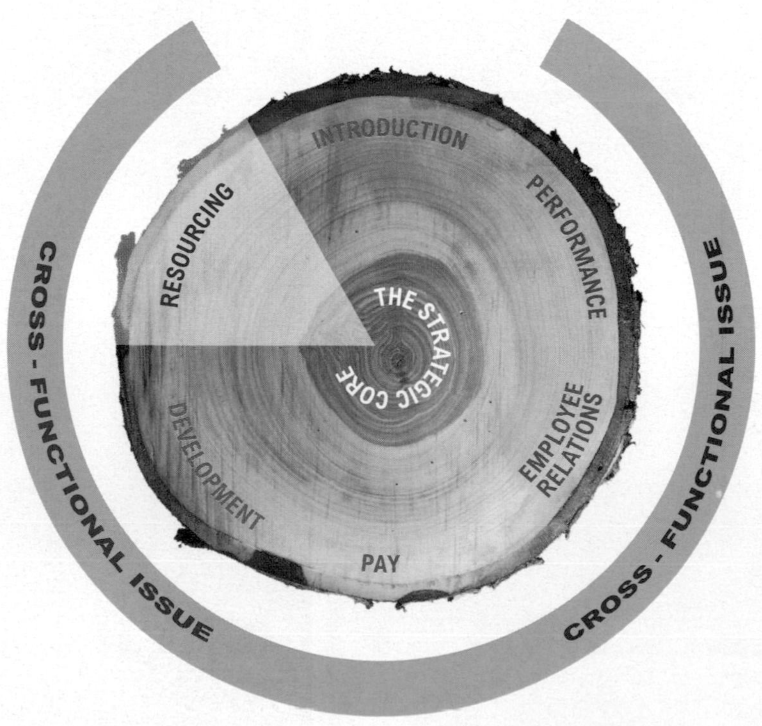

CHAPTER 30

THE INTERNATIONAL DIMENSION

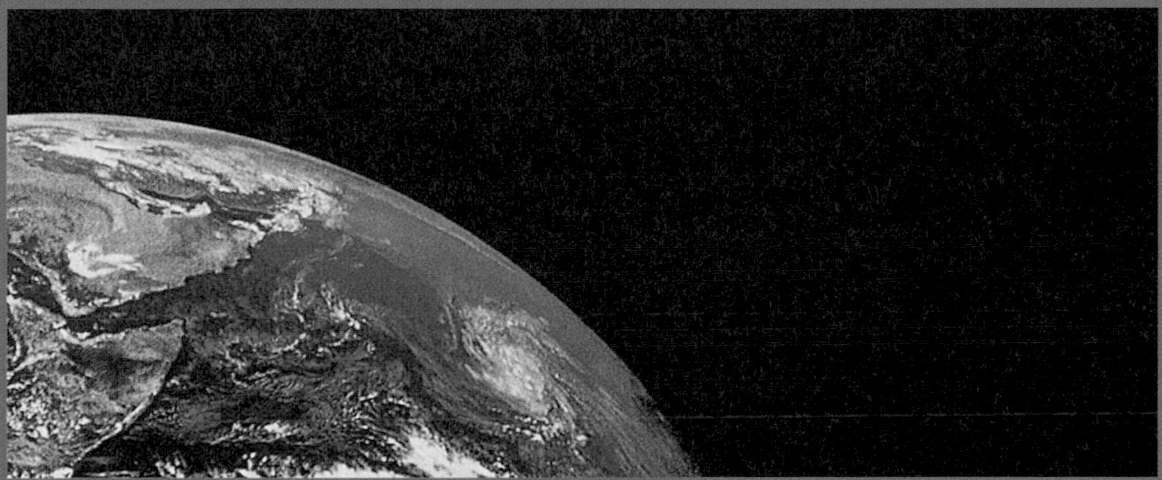

THE OBJECTIVES OF THIS CHAPTER ARE TO:

1. DEFINE INTERNATIONAL HRM
2. PRESENT AN ANALYSIS OF CULTURAL DIFFERENCES IN MANAGEMENT
3. REVIEW ASPECTS OF INTERNATIONAL COMMUNICATION AND COORDINATION

A frequent axiom about any form of international management is 'global thinking; local action'. This is not just a neat form of words, it sums up precisely the spread of understanding that international management activity requires. It is particularly apposite for human resource management and derives from a sentence in one of the seminal works on international management:

> Successful international managers, whether mobile or non-mobile, must be prepared to act locally, but to plan and think strategically and globally. (Barham and Rassam 1989, p. 149)

Global thinking in an international business is concerned with all the things that are different in doing business in more than one country at the strategic level, and how (on earth) the activities can be coordinated effectively. For HR managers these are issues such as how the cultural differences between countries can be accommodated and how effective communication can be maintained across long distances, different time zones, different managerial assumptions, varying national norms and different languages. There are also the differences in legislation, training methods, education systems, social security arrangements and pension provision. This is HRM at its most intellectually demanding because of the deep understanding that is needed of so many complex issues.

Local action is informed by global thinking, but carried out quite separately as all action is local and has to be decided by reference to aspects of employment in one locality only. Human resource management deals with people who are employed within only one set of legal, cultural, demographic and physical conditions. A debug technician may be employed in Italy to do exactly the same job on exactly the same range of products as another employee of the same company in Iowa or Indonesia, but the terms and conditions of employment, social conventions and accepted management practices will be totally different.

The range of this topic is therefore vast, as dealing adequately with local action would require a library full of books. In other chapters there have already been references to certain aspects of local action in different contexts. Here we shall introduce the general topic and then deal with just two aspects of global thinking that are particularly important to international HRM.

INTERNATIONAL HUMAN RESOURCE MANAGEMENT

> Systems which in most countries have evolved incrementally over the course of many decades – even centuries – have each acquired a distinctive coloration, adapted to the idiosyncrasies of national socio-economic structure, national political regimes, and perhaps also national temperaments. (Ferner and Hyman 1992, p. xvii)

The above comment was written specifically about Europe, but it applies even more when the comparison is extended beyond a single continent. Europeans share a common heritage, no matter how bloodstained it may be, through fighting against each other in various combinations for a thousand years, throughout which time the

Christian religion has been shared by all nationalities. North Americans stopped fighting each other on any big scale 150 years ago and share a common religious tradition with the Europeans, as well as sharing one of the European languages. Europe and North America also share the concept and practices of 'Westernisation', but there is still ample scope for misunderstanding between the two continents. Contrasts become even starker when one moves to Arab countries, to India, to China or to South East Asia. This is just an illustration of the diversity that international HRM has to encompass.

Towards the end of the twentieth century there grew a concern about the ever-increasing significance of the multinational company as the means whereby individual economies are integrated into a global economy, with a small number of very large companies accounting for a disproportionately large number of the people in employment.

> There are 53,000 MNCs that control 450,000 subsidiaries, and these MNCs account for approximately one quarter of output in the developed economies . . . As companies and organisations expand their cross-border activities there has been a concomitant increase in business activity together with an increase in the cross-border integration of their production and services. This in turn has created an increasing in the processes by which management co-ordination and control can be exercised. (Beardwell *et al.* 2004, p. 585)

Globalisation has become a dirty word, sparking demonstrations and being blamed for many of the ills in the developing world, yet HRM in any business has to contend with the human resource implications of globalisation. There is always an HRM dimension to any strategic initiative, and international moves perhaps present the strongest case for the HRM specialist to be involved at the beginning in formulating the overall approach, simply because the HRM implications and opportunities are not immediately obvious.

International HRM is a particular type of decentralisation and expansion of the HR role. As an organisation increases its international activities, it inevitably steps up the degree of decentralisation, but internationalisation is not simply a form of decentralisation. It is the most complex form of decentralising operations and involves types of difference – language, culture, economic and political systems, legislative frameworks, management styles and conventions – that are not found in organisational growth and diversification that stay within national boundaries.

In these circumstances HRM logically follows, as well as helping to shape, the strategic direction set by the financial, marketing and operational decisions. In practice there may be a different pattern, as HR often remains one of the last centralising forces because of the importance of such features of management as equity, order, consistency and control. Although the personnel function will relinquish these aspects of HRM reluctantly, they are likely to have other contributions to make in operating the corporate internal labour market:

> The loss of some central tasks through decentralisation – especially the orchestration of central bargaining, and the management of pay structures and job evaluation – and gaining new ones . . . represent a significant shift in the corporate personnel role. (Hendry 1990, p. 102)

Decentralisation is needed to empower the subsidiaries, so that they become autonomous units within a corporate family instead of being overseas subsidiaries of a parent company. Some features, such as recruitment and industrial relations negotiations, are almost entirely decentralised, so that there is little need for a coordinated, centrally driven policy.

ACTIVITY 30.1

Review the HR activities within your own organisation or one with which you are familiar and decide which you feel should be coordinated on an international basis and which should be decentralised.

Integration is expansion of the HR role to achieve the necessary coordination so that the business remains whole. New features are added, such as advanced schemes of remuneration for expatriate employees, new forms of communication to ensure the necessary 'corporate glue'. Although nearly all recruitment and selection is decentralised, a new activity will develop in the recruitment, selection and training for an elite corps of international managers.

CULTURAL DIFFERENCES IN MANAGEMENT

The history of the European Union in attempting to establish a supranational institution is one of constant, but reluctant recognition of the stubbornness of national differences and the accentuation of regional differences among, for instance, the Basques, the Flemish and the Scots. The cultural diversity and intensity of feeling on national issues in a close-knit and economically developed region like Western Europe indicates the significance of cultural difference on a global scale. Nationality is important in HRM because of its effect on human behaviour and the consequent constraints on management action.

Some things that initially appear specific to a particular national culture turn out to be understood and welcomed in almost all cultures. Italian pizza has been adopted in most countries of the world, and the expansion has been largely brought about by Pizza Hut, which is owned by Pepsi-Cola, an American company known for a drink that has also gone to every corner of the globe. Who would have expected that Muscovites would daily queue up outside the largest McDonald's in the world until it was overtaken by the branch in Beijing? Few brands are more obviously global than Microsoft.

Newspapers and magazines in social democracies and socialist republics frequently devote more space in 12 months to the British Royal Family than to any other topic, despite the fact that the institution is utterly British and theoretically alien to their political system. Countless millions every day follow the fortunes of some very ordinary people in the fictional Australian setting of Ramsey Street, Erinsborough, and even more watch association football. The wide international acceptability of these things could suggest that we are all members of the global village with converging tastes and values. Yet certain facets of national culture remain deeply rooted and have a way of undermining that argument.

> It is difficult to prove that any given language determines management behaviour in specific ways. Nevertheless, it seems incontestable that the French have developed their language as a precision tool for analysis and conceptualisation; that the Japanese use their language as an emollient for creating an atmosphere conducive to harmonious interaction; and that the Americans use their version of English as a store of snappy neologisms to excite, distract and motivate. (Holden 1992)

Managers in organisations with an international dimension, and HR professionals in particular, have a job that is forcing them to be more internationally minded almost daily, yet seldom are they aware of the impacts of different national cultures on management practices.

Cultural diversity in management practice is so extensive that anyone's brain hurts when trying to comprehend it and then trying to remember the details. For example, to the European, Israel is in the Middle East and has a government. To the Malaysian, Israel is in West Asia and has a regime. The cultural range is so great that there is a danger of international managers operating simply at the level of caricature, folklore and trivia, such as learning how to present one's business card to a Japanese, or what it means when a German takes his jacket off. Is there any framework for fitting together the maze of cultural diversity? One classic study by Geert Hofstede was published in 1980 and then re-visited in 1984, 1988 and 1991. As with any original piece of work it has been criticised, but it remains the most convincing analysis. One of his critics acknowledges:

> The importance and value of Hofstede's work cannot be overstated . . . the criticisms levelled against him are dwarfed by the strengths of [his] work in comparing cultures and applying cultural analysis to practical management problems . . . The four dimensions tap into deep cultural values and allow significant comparisons to be made across national cultures. To ignore his findings would be inexcusable. (Tayeb 2003, p. 71)

Differences in national cultures

Hofstede (1980) analysed 116,000 questionnaires administered to employees of IBM in seventy different countries and concluded that national cultures could be explained by four key factors:

1 **Individualism.** This is the extent to which people expect to look after themselves and their family only. The opposite is collectivism which has a tight social framework and in which people expect to have a wider social responsibility to discharge because others in the group will support them. Those of a collectivist persuasion believe they owe absolute loyalty to their group.

2 **Power distance.** This factor measures the extent to which the less powerful members of the society accept the unequal distribution of power. In organisations

Table 30.1 Cultural differences between nations

Criterion	High	Low
Power distance	Mexico Philippines Venezuela Yugoslavia	Austria Denmark Israel New Zealand
Uncertainty avoidance	Belgium Greece Japan Portugal	Denmark Hong Kong Singapore Sweden
Individualism	Australia Canada Great Britain United States	Colombia Pakistan Peru Venezuela
Masculinity	Austria Italy Japan Venezuela	Denmark Norway Sweden Yugoslavia

Source: Based on material in G. Hofstede (1991) *Cultures and Organizations: Software of the Mind*. London: McGraw Hill.

this is the degree of centralisation of authority and the exercise of autocratic leadership.

3 Uncertainty avoidance. The future is always unknown, but some societies socialise their members to accept this and take risks, while members of other societies have been socialised to be made anxious about this and seek to compensate through the security of law, religion or technology.

4 Masculinity. The division of roles between the sexes varies from one society to another. Where men are assertive and have dominant roles these values permeate the whole of society and the organisations that make them up, so there is an emphasis on showing off, performing, making money and achieving something visible. Where there is a larger role for women, who are more service oriented with caring roles, the values move towards concern for the environment and the quality of life, putting the quality of relationships before the making of money.

Hofstede found some clear cultural differences between nationalities. A sample of scores on the four criteria are in Table 30.1.

Clusters of national cultures and organisational principles

Hofstede's findings were then compared with the large-scale British study of organisations carried out in the 1970s (Pugh and Hickson 1976) and some unpublished analysis of MBA students' work at INSEAD, which suggested that there were clusters of national cultures that coincided with different organisational principles, when Hofstede's results were plotted against two of his dimensions: uncertainty avoidance and power distance. Hofstede argues (1991, pp. 140–6) that countries emphasising large power distance and strong uncertainty avoidance were likely to produce forms of organisation that relied heavily on hierarchy and clear orders from superiors: **a pyramid of people.**

Pyramid of people	Well-oiled machine	Village market	Family
Arab-speaking	Austria	Australia	East Africa
Argentina	Costa Rica	Britain	Hong Kong
Belgium	Finland	Canada	Indonesia
Brazil	Germany	Denmark	India
Chile	Israel	Ireland	Jamaica
Colombia	Switzerland	Netherlands	Malaysia
Ecuador		New Zealand	Philippines
El Salvador		Norway	Singapore
France		South Africa	West Africa
Greece		Sweden	
Guatemala		United States	
Iran			
Italy			
Japan			
Korea			
Mexico			
Pakistan			
Panama			
Peru			
Portugal			
Spain			
Taiwan			
Thailand			
Turkey			
Uruguay			
Venezuela			
Yugoslavia			

Table 30.2 Clusters of national cultures

Source: Based on material in G. Hofstede (1991) *Cultures and Organizations: Software of the Mind*. London: McGraw Hill.

In countries where there is small power distance and strong uncertainty avoidance there would be an implicit form of organisation that relied on rules, procedures and clear structure: **a well-oiled machine.**

The implicit model of organisation in countries with small power distance and weak uncertainty avoidance was a reliance on ad hoc solutions to problems as they arose, as many of the problems could be boiled down to human relations difficulties: **a village market.**

The picture is completed by the fourth group of countries where there is large power distance and weak uncertainty avoidance, where problems are resolved by constantly referring to the boss who is like a father to an extended family, so there is concentration of authority without structuring of activities. The implicit model of organisation here is: **the family**. Table 30.2 shows which countries fit the different organisation models.

So now we have a classification of cultural diversity that helps us. Table 30.2 tells us that the implicit form of organisation for Britain is a village market, for France it is a pyramid of people, for Germany it is a well-oiled machine and for Hong Kong it is a family. If we can get to grips with the organisational realities and detail in those four countries, then this can provide clues about how to cope in Denmark, Ecuador, Austria or Indonesia because they each share the implicit organisational form and implicit organisational culture of one of the original four.

It is not quite as easy as that, because the clusters show only relative similarities and, inevitably, other studies do not entirely agree with Hofstede (for example,

Ronen and Shenkar 1985), but there is sufficient agreement for us to regard the four-way classification as useful, if not completely reliable, although all the research material was gathered in the 1970s: there may have been radical changes since then.

Time orientation

Hofstede's second book (1991) produces a refinement of the uncertainty avoidance dimension: 'Confucian dynamism', or long-term versus short-term orientation. Later he used the term 'time orientation' instead. Management researchers are typically from Western Europe or the United States, with all the cultural bias that such an orientation involves. Working with the Canadian Michael Bond, Hofstede used a Chinese value survey technique in a fresh study and uncovered a cultural variable that none of the original, Western, questions had reached. This was long-term orientation, and the highest scores on this dimension were from China, Hong Kong, Taiwan, Japan and South Korea. Singapore was placed ninth. Leaving out the special case of China, we see that the other five are those known as the 'Five Dragons' because of their dramatic rate of economic growth in the 1980s.

Hofstede argues that countries in the West have derived their culture largely from the three religions of Judaism, Christianity or Islam, all of which are centred on assertion of truth that is accessible to true believers, whereas none of the religions of the East are based on the assertion that there is a truth that a human community can embrace:

> They offer various ways in which a person can improve him/herself, however these do not consist in believing but in ritual, meditation, or ways of living . . . What one does is important. (ibid., p. 171)

The 'Confucian' values found attached to this long-term orientation included perseverance, clearly maintained status differentials, thrift and having a sense of shame. In many ways these values are valuable for business growth, as they put social value on entrepreneurial initiative, support the entrepreneur by the willing compliance of others seeking a place in the system, encourage saving and investment, and put pressure on those who do not meet obligations.

This suggests that international companies should consider the location of some of their strategic activities in the East. This idea was reflected in a comment from an expert on international human resource issues:

> Philips is establishing centres of competence . . . their centre for long-range technology development was recently moved from the United States to the Far East, where the time orientation was seen as more conducive to innovation than the 'quick fix' mentality of North America. (Evans *et al.* 1989, p. 116)

Considering the fact that Eastern cultures might have features that Western investigators could not initially see is a relatively recent development for management researchers, if not for anthropologists. It indicates the persistence of the Western assumption, well justified until very recently, that Europe and the United States dominated the world's commerce: therefore they also were the centre for understanding universal aspects of management and business.

Hofstede's work ignores Russia and most of the countries of Eastern Europe, as well as the People's Republic of China. The globalisation of management is now more real than at any time previously, but our understanding of how different cultures alter the HRM process is still slight.

Strategic implications of cultural diversity

From a strategic perspective cultural diversity has many implications for HRM. Hodgetts and Luthans (1991, p. 36) have selected some of these where the culture of a society can directly affect management approaches.

1 **The centralisation of decision making.** In some societies (especially the pyramid of people type) all important decisions are taken by a small number of managers in senior positions. In other societies (like the village markets) decision making is more decentralised. In a joint venture between two dissimilar societies, not only will these differences of approach need to be recognised, but management systems will have to devised to enable members of the two cultures to understand each other and work together.

2 **Rewards and competition.** The level of financial rewards between countries can be a problem, when those in country A appear to receive much more money than those in country B for doing the same job, but a more subtle difference is the way in which rewards are disbursed. In some instances there is a culture favouring individual recognition, while elsewhere there is a convention of group rewards. Similarly some societies encourage competition rather than cooperation, and in others the reverse applies.

3 **Risk.** As Hofstede demonstrated in his first study, attitudes towards taking risks are a clear discriminator between cultures, with marked variations of uncertainty avoidance.

4 **Formality.** The well-oiled machine cultures place great emphasis on clear procedures and strict rules, while pyramid of people cultures emphasise clear hierarchies and observance of rank. This contrasts strongly with the village market type societies where relationships are more informal and ad hoc action more likely.

5 **Organisational loyalty.** In Japan there tends to be a strong sense of loyalty to one's employer, while in Britain and the United States there is a growing sense of identification with one's occupational group, rather than with a particular employer. The long-standing importance of professional bodies and the declining long-term reliability of corporations as wagons to which to hitch one's career star have increased this sense of loyalty to one's occupation rather than to one's employer.

6 **Short or long-term orientation.** Hofstede's identification of an Eastern predilection for the long term is beginning to influence strategic decisions on where to locate those organisational activities for which long-term thinking is particularly appropriate.

Table 30.2 gives us a rough guide to similarities between national cultures and the classification gives us some route markings through the cultural maze. We also have the long-term orientation of Confucian dynamism, which can guide thinking on a number of strategic issues in international management.

INTERNATIONAL COMMUNICATION AND COORDINATION

Communicating across geographical, ethnic and national boundaries is a major challenge for HR people. Not only 'What did he say?' but also 'What did he mean?' Remembering Hofstede's analysis of cultural variations, we realise, for instance, that people from cultures with a wide power distance are not likely to provide feedback which is other than straightforward assent. They are inhibited by the feeling that their questions will indicate criticism.

WINDOW ON PRACTICE

Mead (1990, p. 47) gives the example of hotel managers in South East Asia, who will say 'Yes' to a question such as 'Can the refrigerator in my room be repaired today?' even if it cannot:

> His cultural priorities tell him to give a pleasing answer and to satisfy immediate needs; the long-term problem can be resolved at a later date or may disappear. The guest may decide that he doesn't need to use the refrigerator; or will change his travel plans and move out that day; or can be accommodated in another room.

Brandt and Hulbert (1976) studied organisational feedback in a number of multinational companies that had their headquarters in Europe, Japan and the United States. They found that the American organisations had many more feedback reports and meetings between headquarters and subsidiaries than their European or Japanese counterparts. In contrast, Pascale (1978) found that Japanese managers in Japan used face-to-face contacts more than American managers as well as more upwards and lateral communication. Japanese managers in America used communication in the same way as Americans.

ACTIVITY 30.2

In your place of work or in your college, what differences in behaviour do you notice among people with a different cultural background from your own? How do these differences affect your working relationship with them?

SOME BARRIERS TO EFFECTIVE INTERNATIONAL COMMUNICATION

There are various ways in which expectation determines communication content and all can impair the accuracy of message transmission. Several of these – the frame of reference, stereotyping and cognitive dissonance – were explained in the Part I Focus on skills. Such problems are compounded by geographical distance, cultural differences and subtleties of language.

Frame of reference

Few of us change our opinions alone. We are influenced by the opinions developed within the group with which we identify: our reference group, which provides our *frame of reference*, was referred to in our opening chapter. The clearest example of contrasted frames of reference is when international expansion is by the route of acquisition. Employees in the acquired company will feel a greater sense of community with each other than with those who have acquired them. They will see corporate affairs from their own standpoint and will tend to be cautious in their behaviour and suspicious in their interpretation of what they hear from their new owners. Every acquisition has this problem, but international acquisition is beset by particular problems.

Despite all attempts to forge a common identity, companies in different countries will take pride in their own accomplishments and informally disparage the accomplishments of other nationality groups. As long as this stimulates healthy competition, rivalry can benefit the business, but it can quickly become destructive, like the situation of the car assembly plant in Britain which constantly rejected and returned gear boxes made by the same company in Germany. National boundaries produce distorted ideas about the 'other' people, whose achievements are underestimated and undervalued in comparison with the achievements of your own group, which may be overestimated.

Stereotypes

It is quite common for the British and some Americans to hold a stereotypical expectation of certain types of behaviour and intention from the Irish ('Never stop talking and always ready for a fight'). Other crude stereotypes are that Germans are thorough and unimaginative, the French are romantic and obsessed with status, the Chinese all look the same, Americans are loud and brash, the English are reserved and aloof, Arabs are fatalists, Spaniards are haughty, and so on.

Our review of culture was partly an account of national stereotypes and exemplifies the problem: we need to understand general differences in behaviour and attitude that are rooted in cultural diversity, otherwise we will be misunderstood in what we say and will misinterpret what we hear, but we must avoid the trap of assuming that all nationals conform precisely to a single model. Not all the Irish are loquacious and not all the Scots are mean.

In dealing with foreigners, some well-informed stereotyping can avoid initial offence and misunderstanding, but it must give way to more sensitive behaviour as the other person is evaluated and better understood.

Cognitive dissonance

Cognitive dissonance does more than lead to misunderstanding; it can also distort or inhibit action. Not only do recipients of information find it difficult to understand, remember and take action, they will also grapple with the dissonance that the problematical new information presents. One of the ways in which they do this is to distort the message so that what they actually hear is what they expect to hear and can easily understand rather than the difficult, challenging information that is being put to them.

WINDOW ON PRACTICE

A Portuguese manager of a small company in Bombay received an instruction from his head office about closing one of his plants, so he called in the manager of the plant and showed him the letter. He was baffled when the plant manager begged him to destroy the letter. The Portuguese saw this as a pointless symbolic act; the Indian saw it as a way of making the instruction void.

A young Swiss woman in London was equally baffled when, paying for an item in a store by using a cheque, she was told to cross the cheque. Having tried folding it in half, she required great persuasion to draw two straight lines across the face of it. Not only did this seem strange to her, but it was also directly counter to her previous experience and beliefs.

Language

There are frequent problems with language. In Shell International there is a term to describe the purpose of certain types of meeting as 'flocking', which is a wonderfully precise term to express the nature and purpose of those particular gatherings that take place, yet French and German people have great difficulty in understanding the nuances of the term, because neither language has an equivalent that distinguishes between, for example, flocking and herding.

We can also fall into the trap of misunderstanding a word which is not what it sounds as if it should be. An example which causes problems for English speakers in Italian hotels is the word 'caldo', which means 'hot', on bathroom taps.

Even the most scrupulous translation can be tricky. The following English translation of a government edict in Prague seems to have lost something in translation:

> Because Christmas Eve falls on a Thursday, the day has been designated a Saturday for work purposes. Factories will close all day, with stores open a half day only. Friday, December 25 has been designated a Sunday, with both factories and stores open all day. Monday, December 28, will be a Wednesday for work purposes. Wednesday, December 30, will be a business Friday. Saturday, January 2, will be a Sunday, and Sunday, January 3, will be a Monday.

Jargon

The problem of jargon is where a word or a phrase has a specialised meaning that is immediately understandable by the cognoscenti, but meaningless or misleading to those who do not share the specialised knowledge. The Maslovian hierarchy of human needs is by now quite well known in management circles. On one occasion a lecturer was describing the ideas that were implicit in this notion and was surprised some months later in an examination script to see that one of the students had heard not 'hierarchy' but 'high Iraqui'. The unfamiliarity of the word 'hierarchy' had been completely misinterpreted by that particular receiver, who had imposed her own meaning on what she heard because of the need to make sense of what it was that she received. Professor Eugene McKinna relates how he was lecturing on the same subject of motivation, describing job enlargement and job enrichment. After the lecture a puzzled student asked him, 'what exactly was the job in Richmond?'

The value of jargon in international management is that the jargon quickly becomes universally understood by the experts, no matter what their nationality. Botany, Medicine and Chemistry are fields where a specialist can probably understand a technical paper no matter what the language may be. Sheet music is covered in Italian words that have no neat translation and no need for translation as they are universally understood by musicians. Management is moving in that direction, with JIT, QWL, TQM and the rest.

Corporate culture

A quite different aspect of communication for the HR people in the international company is disseminating information and other messages within the organisation to help develop corporate culture, a sense of collaboration across national boundaries in order to integrate the business, with members of the different units in the business understanding, for instance, why a company has been acquired in South America, even though it seems to threaten the livelihood of some parts of the parent organisation. Comprehensive communication can raise awareness of the wider market and the opportunities that are waiting to be grasped. Foulds and Mallet (1989, p. 78) suggest the following as purposes of international communication:

- to reinforce group culture so as to improve the speed and effectiveness of decision taking;
- to encourage information exchange in internationally related activities and prevent the 'reinvention of the wheel';
- to form the background to the succession planning activity – certain cultures demand certain types of people;
- to establish in peoples' minds what is expected of them by the parent company;
- to facilitate change in a way acceptable to the parent company;
- to undermine the 'not invented here' attitudes and thereby encourage changes;
- to improve the attractiveness of the company in the recruitment field – particularly where the subsidiary is small and far from base;
- to encourage small activities, which may be tomorrow's 'cream', and give such activities a perspective within the international activities.

There is a need for constant communication throughout the business to disseminate information and to sustain changing values. The organisation must operate holistically. It is not the sum of its parts: the whole exists in every part, like the human body. If you are ill a doctor can obtain information about your illness from any part of you. A sample of your blood or the taking of your temperature is just as good wherever it comes from. If you are to be protected against cholera, which attacks the intestines, you have an injection in your arm. If you are about to be shot in the chest, your entire body will shiver in fear.

When a company is operating internationally the work-flow pattern may be very clear and provide the logical main channel for communication. If a washing machine is produced by manufacturing electronic components in California, subassemblies and wiring harnesses in Korea and final assembly in Scotland, there is an easy sequence to follow. Job instructions, guidance notes, queries, telephone calls, specifications, requisitions, authorisations, order forms are some of the many ways in which groups of people communicate with those before and after in the work flow, or critically adjacent to the process, such as the HR people. Among the most effective international communicators are airlines, as their entire business is moving not only customers but also staff constantly across national boundaries to different organisational outposts of the business: the business activity creates the communications. All international businesses require centralised, coordinated communications to create common purpose and to share ideas and benefits, but those that do not have a natural work-flow link across national boundaries will have this need more highly developed.

Individual behaviour

As in any organisation, the communications management challenge for international human resource management is at two extremes. At one extreme is the personal behaviour and skill of individual organisation members in making themselves understood, persuading others to do things, negotiating agreements with people from different cultural backgrounds, overcoming language barriers, appreciating different frames of reference and developing heightened sensitivity to varying behavioural norms and conventions. Communication is an individual activity, reflecting personal style, and the HRM requirement is for cultural awareness and perhaps language training. In this type of communication the manager is a skilled solo performer.

Communication channels

The other extreme is impersonal and systemic, more concerned with channels of communication than with individual behaviour, and more concerned with systematic distribution of carefully chosen information and the organisation of communications opportunities. In this type of communication the manager both writes the score and conducts the orchestra.

Although the forms of communication are so different, they are also linked. Organisational communication is only as good as the quality of interpersonal communication that is taking place.

> consistent patterns of interaction begin to develop when a group of individuals, in response to certain characteristics and needs of the environment, create a system of patterned activities for the accomplishment of a specific task. The process by which these relationships are formed and maintained is interpersonal communication. (Baskin and Aronoff 1980, p. 7)

It is not practicable for employees to develop confidence in a communications system; they can only acquire confidence in what the system produces and in those other members of the organisation with whom they interact. That confidence is built by the substance of what people say and do, but also by a climate in which people feel encouraged to express ideas, make suggestions and question the validity of decisions they cannot understand. Communications and behaviour are so closely interlinked that everything which influences behaviour also influences communication.

COORDINATION

Managers working internationally give themselves major problems of coordination by adopting measures that they see as necessary for business success. On the one hand they have to encourage diversity of local action, so that what is done fits local circumstances. On the other hand their global thinking requires careful coordination as the way to synergy, so that the global business does more and better together than it could possibly achieve as a number of independent units.

Bartlett and Goshal (1989) described three conventional approaches to coordination that were used, stemming from the nationality of the parent company, the Japanese, the American and the European.

Japanese centralisation

The typical Japanese approach is where a strong headquarters group retain for themselves all major decisions and frequently intervene in the affairs of overseas subsidiaries. This appears to stem from their difficulty in dealing with foreigners:

> a major strategic challenge for Japanese firms is to accept that non-Japanese must somehow be given more direct responsibility and opportunity for promotion within the company at local level . . . there has to be letting-go from the centre. But this is no easy thing. For companies must overcome severe impediments associated with wariness, distrust and lack of knowledge about the world beyond Japan. (Holden 1994 p. 127)

American formalisation

The American approach is described as formalisation. Power is vested not in headquarters or in the managers of local companies, but in formal systems, policies and standards, so that it is the systems that drive the business. Many American businesses went international at the time that the use of control systems was being rapidly developed to cope with the large size of the businesses. The idea of delegation and holding others accountable by means of extensive computerised information systems seemed eminently suitable for operating the increasing number of overseas units, especially when one remembers the apparent unpopularity of overseas postings among American managers (*see* e.g., Tung and Miller 1990).

European socialisation

In European companies the approach to coordination is described as socialisation. There has been a reliance on key, highly skilled and trusted individuals. These people were carefully selected and developed a detailed understanding of the company's objectives and methods. Their personal development included the establishment of close working relationships and mutual understanding with colleagues. Once groomed these key decision makers were despatched to manage the subsidiaries, so that the headquarters and the subsidiaries were both strengthened.

> . . . because it relies on shared values and objectives, it represents a more robust and flexible means of co-ordination. Decisions reached by negotiations between knowledgeable groups with common objectives should be much better than those made by superior authority or by standard policy. (Bartlett and Ghoshal 1989, p. 163)

These three different approaches or emphases worked best for companies which had their headquarters in those three regions of the globe. As the world becomes smaller and companies become more diverse with subsidiaries that are fully mature, more sophisticated methods are needed: companies are not international, but global.

INCREASING THE RANGE OF COORDINATION METHODS

The strength of the three approaches described above should not be underestimated, but any management will benefit from considering additional methods of coordination. Some will fit well with their current practice, adding to their strength; others will not seem suitable yet, others will not seem suitable at all.

Evangelisation

The first suggestion is summed up, with some hesitation, by using the word *evangelisation*, to describe the process of winning the acceptance throughout the business of a common mission and a shared purpose. The idea of needing to win hearts and minds has been a common thread in management thinking for many years, but it takes on particular significance in the international or global business because of the number of barriers to be surmounted in coordination, especially the barriers of language, culture, national boundaries and parochial self-interest. It is indeed a remarkable management team who will be able to commit themselves with enthusiasm to closing down their local operation on the grounds that the business as a whole will benefit if an operation in another country is developed instead.

Evangelisation is used hesitantly to describe this process because it is the language of religion. Using it in relation to business will be heretical to some and irrelevant to others, but the processes of evangelisation contain many of the methods that are needed in coordination and evangelists confront the same barriers as those dealing in the world of global business. One of the most successful of all the great international companies has been Matsushita, the founder of which established in 1932 a development plan that was set out to cover a 250-year period. All employees undertake a programme of cultural and spiritual training and all worldwide units of the company have a daily assembly ritual. The very thought of a 250-year plan is inconceivable to most managers, but the fact of over sixty years of business success makes their mouths water. The American electronics giant IBM has moved on from its previous practices, but throughout its early years of market leadership, the company had some evangelistic features, including the IBM hymn, which caused one team of French analysts to describe it as 'la nouvelle eglise' (Pages *et al.* 1979).

ACTIVITY 30.3

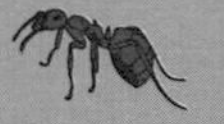

Within any organisation with which you are familiar, what examples can you think of where the methods of evangelisation described here have been effective in communication and coordination?

Shared belief

Coordination through evangelisation works through **shared belief.** The beliefs may be interpreted in different ways and may produce varied behaviours, but there is the attempt to promulgate relatively simple doctrines to which members of the organisation subscribe and through which they are energised. Some readers of this book will have learned their catechism as children, or will know the Gettysburg Address by heart. Although this may seem inappropriate to the business world, the Matsushita case provides at least one example of its current application in commercial circles. In the 1970s a British company, Vitafoam, was established by a man who required his senior executives to copy out his annual policy statement by hand, three times, before handing it back to him. It is now commonplace for companies to have mission statements, which come close to being unifying articles of faith.

> At the top is the mission statement, a broad goal based on the organization's planning premises, basic assumptions about the organization's purpose, its values, its distinctive competencies, and its place in the world. A mission statement is a relatively permanent part of an organization's identity and can do much to unify and motivate its members. (Stoner and Freeman 1992, p. 188)

Parables

Evangelisation also works through **parables.** We all love a good story, and religion flourishes as tales of the founder and of current heroes are recounted and we learn from the message that the parable conveys. Ed Schein (1985, pp. 237–42) identified 'stories and legends' as one of the key mechanisms for articulating and reinforcing the organisation's culture. In pursuing the religious analogy, it is interesting that almost every Western-based multinational company will have one or more voluminous documents, colloquially known as 'the Company Bible', yet it is invariably a set of rules and procedures, rather than stories, legends or articles of faith.

The company house magazine partially serves the purpose of circulating the good news about heroic deeds in all parts of the company network. Better are the word of mouth exchanges and accounts of personal experience. Those who visit another country have to be fully exploited when they return. Returning expatriates have stories to tell to all members of the company to which they are coming back, not just to the senior managers conducting the debriefing. There are many problems in repatriation, but one of the best ways of getting re-established is to share one's overseas experience widely, with as many people as possible, and fully, covering the entire gamut of their experiences. Occasional visitors to other branches of the business also need to be encouraged to tell their stories. They return with important technical understandings that need to be shared, but they also return with all sorts of other awareness of the visited company which can contribute to the bonding between units. On a tedious flight between Istanbul and Singapore, an Australian businesswoman spent over an hour sorting through a large number of holiday snaps, explaining that she regarded them as the most important present she could bring back. Her male colleagues brought back photographs of machine parts, warehouse layout, operational equipment and production processes. These were used at important debriefing sessions with fellow managers. She took back pictures of people and places, of food and mealtimes, of cluttered offices and what was put up on the office walls. These were handed round and explained in casual encounters over coffee, on the way to and from meetings and at dinner parties.

Apostles

Evangelisation can use **apostles**, ambassadors sent out to preach the faith. These are those management role holders who are constantly on the move. Because of their frequent movement they know the worldwide organisation well and can describe one component to another, explaining company policy, justifying particular decisions and countering parochial thinking. They can also move ideas around ('In Seoul they are wondering about . . . what do think?') and help in the development of individual networks ('Try getting in touch with Oscar Jennings in Pittsburgh . . . he had similar problems a few weeks ago').

At times of crisis, apostles are likely to be especially busy, countering rumour and strengthening resolve. In mature companies apostles will have home bases in different regions, just as expatriates will move in various directions and not simply from the centre out, but before the business reaches maturity it will probably be important that most of the apostles come from headquarters and have personally met, and can tell stories about, the founder.

Standards and norms

Coordination can be improved by the development and promulgation of *standards and norms*. Many British companies have sought the accreditation of BS 5750, the

British Standard for quality; others claim to be equal opportunity employers. Global companies will wish to set standards for many aspects of their operation. Cynthia Haddock (1994) describes how Shell develops and maintains standards relating to alcohol and drug abuse. If standards are adopted throughout a global company, they become a form of coordination. Furthermore, it is not necessary for all of them to be developed at the centre. Decentralised standard formulation can enable different parts of the global business to take a lead as a preliminary to universal adoption of the standard they have formulated: an excellent method of integration.

Few businesses will be able to develop universally applicable standards in all aspects of human resource management. Many manufacturing developments in Asia have taken place explicitly to enjoy the benefits of low labour costs. It is most unlikely that the American, European or Japanese parent company would develop a company-wide standard on the level of pay rates in manufacturing. In contrast a company-wide standard set of terms and conditions for expatriate assignment would be much more feasible. The CIPD library in London has just such a document from IBM in the form of a sample letter of 24 pages!

Systems

There is obvious scope for coordination through *systems*. Many global businesses are dominated by a single system, which reaches every part of the business. Any international airline has a ticketing and booking system which links thousands of computer terminals in order to operate the airline. The system is only useful if it provides the global link, and provided the systems link constantly reinforces with all personnel the interrelationship of the activities in all countries where the airline operates. Although that is a specialised example, all businesses have systems and they can be developed to avoid duplication and overlap, so that in one country a team develops a spare part retrieval system that is quickly adopted for use throughout the business, while in another country they concentrate on an aspect of accounting procedures or systematic advice on training opportunities.

Concentration of capability

A similar approach is to consider the concentration of *capability* by seeking to encourage the development of particular expertise in different locations, but for group-wide application and exploitation. Bartlett and Ghoshal (1989, p. 106) offer the intriguing example of how Teletext was developed by Philips. Because of an interest from the BBC, the British Philips subsidiary began work on the possibility of transmitting text and simple diagrams through a domestic television set. Within Philips generally it was regarded as 'a typical British toy – quite fancy but not very useful'. Despite little encouragement and sales that were initially disappointing, the British persisted. Ten years after starting work, there were 3 million Teletext receivers in use in Britain and Philips had established a world lead in a product for which there was initially only a British market.

SUMMARY PROPOSITIONS

30.1 International HRM is a subject that still lacks an accepted definition and content.

30.2 Much international management activity is through multinational companies and their policies of globalisation.

30.3 Understanding cultural diversity is crucial. Work by Hofstede has identified four distinguishing factors of national culture: individualism, power distance, uncertainty avoidance and masculinity. He later added a fifth, Confucian dynamism or time orientation.

30.4 Hofstede also concluded that organisations within certain cultures had one of four dominant value systems, so that they would resemble a pyramid of people, a well-oiled machine, a village market or a family.

30.5 Hodgetts and Luthans then suggested that these findings influenced the following aspects of management: centrality of decision making, rewards and competition, risk, formality, organisational loyalty, short- or long-term orientation.

30.6 Problems of communication in any international business are exacerbated by different frames of reference, stereotyping, cognitive dissonance and language.

30.7 Traditional forms of coordination can be roughly stereotyped as Japanese centralisation, American formalisation or European socialisation.

30.8 More particular forms of coordination include evangelisation, standards and norms, systems and locating capability.

GENERAL DISCUSSION TOPICS

1 Multinational companies tend to be unpopular with activists, who mount demonstrations against their apparent greed and serious impact on some of the societies in which they operate. What are the arguments for and against this point of view?

2 Can an HRM manager from one culture carry out a line management role working in a different culture?

3 Have you come across examples of American formalisation, Japanese centralisation and European socialisation? How do they conflict? What is the practical implication of these variations?

FURTHER READING

Dowling, P.J., Welch, D.E. and Schuler, R.S. (1999) *International Dimensions of Human Resource Management*. Cincinnati, Ohio: South Western College Publishing
Texts on international HRM are very varied and usually eclectic in concentrating on one or two aspects at the expense of others (like this chapter). Dowling *et al.* is one exception. There is a very well-informed chapter in Tayeb (*see* below) by P.S. Budhwar.

Mead, R. (1990) *Cross-Cultural Management Communication*. Chichester: Wiley
This book is useful on communication.

Tayeb, M. (2003) *International Management: Theories and Practices*. Harlow: Prentice Hall
This book provides a recent general treatment of international management. It has five chapters on culture, two on communication and three on managing employees in different cultures.

Trompenaars, F. and Hampden-Turner, C. (1998) *Riding the Waves of Culture: Understanding Cultural Diversity in Business*, 2nd edn. New York: McGraw-Hill
This book is a major work on culture that complements those referred to in the chapter. It sets out the authors' extensive research findings, but also includes much practical advice.

REFERENCES

Barham, K. and Rassam, C. (1989) *Shaping the Corporate Future*. London: Unwin & Hyman.

Bartlett, C.A. and Ghoshal, S. (1989) *Managing Across Borders*. London: Random House.

Baskin, O.W. and Aronoff, C.E. (1980) *Interpersonal Communication in Organizations*. Santa Monica, Cal.: Goodyear Publishing.

Beardwell, I., Holden, L. and Claydon, T. (2004) *Human Resource Management: A Contemporary Approach*, 4th edn. Harlow, England: Prentice Hall.

Brandt, W.K. and Hulbert, J.M. (1976) 'Patterns of Communication in the Multinational Company', *Journal of International Business Studies*, Spring, pp. 57–64.

Evans, P., Doz, Y. and Laurent, A. (1989) *Human Resource Management in International Firms*. London: Macmillan.

Ferner, A. and Hyman, R. (1992) *Industrial Relations and the New Europe*. Oxford: Blackwell.

Foulds, J. and Mallet, L. (1989) 'The European and International Dimension', in T. Wilkinson (ed.) *The Communications Challenge*. London: IPM.

Haddock, C. (1992) 'How Shell's Organisation and HR Practices Help it to be Both Global and Local', in D.P. Torrington (ed.) *International Human Resource Management*, London: Prentice Hall International.

Hendry, C. (1990) 'Corporate Management of Human Resources under Conditions of Decentralisation', *British Journal of Management*, Vol. 1, pp. 91–103.

Hodgetts, R.M. and Luthans, F. (1991) *International Management*. New York: McGraw-Hill.

Hofstede, G. (1980) *Culture's Consequences: International Differences in Work-Related Values*. Beverly Hills, Cal.: Sage Publications.

Hofstede, G. (1991) *Cultures and Organizations: Software of the Mind*. London: McGraw-Hill.

Holden, N.J. (1992) 'Management Language and Euro-Communications: 1992 and Beyond', in M. Berry (ed.) *Cross-Cultural Communication in Europe*. Proceedings of Conference on Cross-Cultural Communication, Helsinki. Turku: Institute for European Studies.

Holden, N.J. (1994) 'NEC: International HRM with Vision', in D.P. Torrington (ed.) *International Human Resource Management*. London: Prentice Hall International.

Mead, R. (1990) *Cross-Cultural Management Communication*. Chichester: Wiley.

Pages, M., Bonnetti, M., de Gaulejac, V. and Descendre, D. (1979) *L'Emprise de l'Organisation*. Paris: Presses Universitaires de France.

Pascale, R.T. (1978) 'Communication and Decision Making Across Cultures: Japanese and American Comparisons', *Administrative Science Quarterly*, March, pp. 91–110.

Pugh, D.S. and Hickson, D.J. (1976) *Organisational Structure in its Context*. Farnborough: Saxon House.

Ronen, S. and Shenkar, O. (1985) 'Clustering Countries on Attitudinal Dimensions: A Review and Synthesis', *Academy of Management Review*, Vol. 10, No. 3, pp. 435–54.

Schein, E.H. (1985) *Organizational Culture and Leadership*. San Francisco, Cal.: Jossey-Bass.

Stoner, J.A.F. and Freeman, R.E. (1992) *Management*, 5th edn. Englewood Cliffs, NJ: Prentice-Hall Inc.

Tayeb, M. (2003) *International Management: Theories and Practices*. Harlow Prentice Hall.

Tung, R.L. and Miller, E.L. (1990) 'Managing in the Twenty-first Century: The Need for Global Orientation', *Management International Review*, Vol. 30, pp. 5–18.

An extensive range of additional materials, including multiple choice questions, answers to questions and links to useful websites can be found on the Human Resource Management Companion Website at **www.pearsoned.co.uk/torrington.**

CHAPTER 31

ETHICS AND CORPORATE SOCIAL RESPONSIBILITY

THE OBJECTIVES OF THIS CHAPTER ARE TO:

1 INTRODUCE THE TOPIC OF ETHICS AND CORPORATE SOCIAL RESPONSIBILITY

2 CONSIDER THE PARTICULAR ASPECTS OF ETHICS THAT AFFECT HRM

3 REVIEW THE VARIATIONS OF ETHICAL PRACTICE ACROSS NATIONAL BOUNDARIES

4 SUGGEST PARTICULAR ETHICAL QUESTIONS FACING HRM PEOPLE IN THE FUTURE

WINDOW ON PRACTICE

In January 2004 the Treasury Select Committee of the British Parliament criticised chief executives of large insurance companies for taking big pay rises at a time when the profitability of their companies and the value of endowment policies was falling, both after a period during which endowment policies had been mis-sold. Between 1999 and 2002 the value of payouts from endowment policies had declined by an average of 25 per cent, the companies' share prices had declined by 50 per cent and the chief executives' remuneration had risen by amounts between 45 per cent and 70 per cent to sums ranging up to £1.3 million. The chairman of the committee said, 'The industry is going downhill like a slalom skier . . . Why do you think you're worth so much?'

Source: Based on A. Senior (2004) 'MPs attack insurers over chiefs' pay', *The Times*, 28 January, p. 26.

This could be a starting point for the fourth general discussion topic at the end of this chapter.

THE ETHICAL DIMENSION

Human resource management has always had an ethical dimension. In Chapter 1 we defined the first phase of its evolution as a preoccupation with social justice, and when the second phase of preoccupation with developing bureaucracy began it was the development of *humane* bureaucracy. The odd thing is that practitioners have for so long been trying to bury this aspect, while academic commentators have grumbled that personnel practitioners fail to deliver on it. Thirty-five years ago it was possible to write a chapter in a book on personnel management with the title 'The Social Role of Personnel' (Torrington 1968, pp. 147–60) and generate a series of reviews that all vehemently disagreed with the implicit proposition that there actually *was* a social role for the personnel manager in the business. In 1977 Peter Anthony reminded his readers of an earlier statement by Michael Fogarty at an IPM conference, 'the business of business is business' before adding his own comment, 'it is the business of the industrial relations specialist to make sure that the business can get done'.

Since then there has been some increase of interest in ethics, but now it is not a vain attempt of the nice personnel people to act as the conscience of the company. Instead, it is a much more general management interest. Kenneth Blanchard is an American academic and consultant of considerable reputation, including being the author of the best-selling *The One-Minute Manager*. He teamed up with Norman Vincent Peale, who had written in 1952 *The Power of Positive Thinking*, which had sold no fewer than 20 million copies. Together they produced a slim, popular book about ethics in management which they described as follows:

> ethical behaviour is related to self-esteem. We both believe that people who feel good about themselves have what it takes to withstand outside pressure and to do what is right rather than do what is merely expedient, popular or lucrative. We believe that a strong code of morality in any business is the first step toward its success. We believe that ethical managers are winning managers. (Blanchard and Peale 1988, p. 7)

It is interesting that the idea is 'sold' as a means to an end rather than as an end in itself, and it sounds almost as 'expedient, popular or lucrative' as the alternative that they are disparaging. We will return to the general management interest in business ethics later in the chapter, but we can get Blanchard and Peale in clearer perspective if we consider some definitions.

Any dictionary will indicate that ethics can be both singular and plural. In the singular it relates to:

> the moral value of human conduct and the principles that ought to govern that conduct.

The plural form describes:

> a social, religious or civil code of behaviour considered to be correct, especially that of a particular group or profession.

In the business context we can therefore understand ethics as a part of the culture of the individual business corporation that sets norms of behaviour by which people in the business will abide because the norms have some moral authority as well being convenient. It is also a set of guidelines followed by people in a particular group or profession because it makes practical sense in enabling them to do their jobs. Barristers will not represent two different clients if there is likely to be a conflict of interest between the clients. Doctors will generally refrain from sexual relationships with their patients. In both cases there are sound practical reasons, quite apart from any moral dimension.

Early management concern with ethics

The early management concern with ethics was discussed in Chapter 1, where comments were made about some of the Victorian philanthropists, such as Lord Leverhulme. An American contemporary was Andrew Carnegie, who was born in Scotland but made a considerable fortune after emigrating to the United States and devoted the last years of his life to giving most of it away. In 1900 he wrote a book called *The Gospel of Wealth*, which set out a statement of corporate social responsibility that was quite as paternalist as that of his British counterparts. He believed that corporate social responsibility had two principles, charity and stewardship. The more fortunate in society had an obligation to aid the less fortunate (charity) and those with wealth should see themselves as owning that wealth in trust for the rest of society by using it for purposes which were socially legitimate (stewardship).

Carnegie was very influential, largely because he dispensed charity on such a massive scale, but the paternalism gradually drew more and more criticism and the involvement in social responsibility waned. It was more or less destroyed altogether by Milton Friedman, who argued that those in business were not qualified to decide on the relative urgency of social needs. He contended that managers who devoted corporate resources to pursue personal interpretations of social need might be misguided in their selection and would unfairly 'tax' their shareholders, employees and customers:

> There is one and only one social responsibility of business: to use its resources and energy in activities designed to increase its profits as long as it stays within the rules of the game, engaging in open and free competition, without deception and fraud. (Friedman 1963, p. 163)

Renewed interest in business ethics

The 1980s saw the return of interest in business ethics, although to many people it remains an incongruous concept:

> Many persons educated in the humanities (with their aristocratic traditions) and the social sciences (with their quantifying, collectivist traditions) are uncritically anti-capitalist. They think of business as vulgar, philistine, and morally suspect . . . Three accusations come up.
>
> (a) In pursuit of profits, won't businesses act immorally whenever necessary?
>
> (b) Aren't executive salaries out of line? Isn't dramatic inequality wrong?
>
> (c) Isn't it wrong to subject workers and middle managers in their mature years to so much insecurity? Isn't it wrong to let people go abruptly and without a parachute? (Novak 1996, pp. 7–8)

That was an American perspective, but would be echoed by many people in Europe. There is also the more general feeling that any commercially driven activity has dominant motivations that are inevitably opposed to social considerations. Another version of the same view, echoing Friedman, is that those in management positions should *not* make moral judgements as they have no authority to do so. Instead they should respond to public opinion as expressed by customers' purchasing decisions, demonstrations by pressure groups or trade unions or by government legislation.

WINDOW ON PRACTICE

One relatively recent form of control on management decision making is *whistle blowing*, which describes the practice of an employee metaphorically blowing a whistle to attract attention from the outside to some ethical malpractice within the business. Originally this was done by lone individuals taking great risks with their employment, but the method has now altered through the establishment of a charity, *Public Concern at Work*, which gives free legal advice to potential whistle blowers. Its director claims that most issues are now settled within the business:

> 90 per cent of clients who follow our advice report a successful outcome. This has much to do with our policy that, if raised responsibly within the organisation, concerns about malpractice will be addressed properly by those in charge. (Dehn 1997)

An alternative point of view sees business practice as a product of its past:

> Wealth or values creation is in essence a moral act. The individual entrepreneurs who first organised production systematically were steeped in largely Nonconformist religious convictions that blocked most customary routes to advancement in British society of the eighteenth and early nineteenth centuries [who] . . . shared a belief that their works on this earth would justify them, that the Kingdom of Heaven was to be built by them, here and now. (Hampden-Turner and Trompenaars 1993, p. 3)

These authors then argue that the moral values that drive wealth creation are rooted in the national and organisational cultures of the wealth-creating corporations, although that is frequently forgotten because of the prominence given to the 'value-empty' discipline of economics, of which Milton Friedman was the supreme example:

> The qualities of work performed by these corporations depend as much on the durable values of their work cultures as they once depended on the values of their founders. In our survey of 15,000 executives we found that culture of origin is the most important determinant of values. In any culture, a deep structure of beliefs is the invisible hand that regulates economic activity. (Friedman 1963, p. 4)

The need for ethical guidelines

The further simple logic supporting the need for ethical guidelines is that actions in business are the result of decisions by human beings, and human beings tend to seek justification for their actions beyond the rule of value for money. Frequently this takes the form of grotesque rationalisation. The various Mafia families apparently have a very robust code of conduct, based on strong family cohesion and a convenient interpretation of the Roman Catholic faith. This 'justification' enables them to peddle drugs, launder money, run large-scale prostitution and extortion, to say nothing of killing people, without a sense of guilt. Osama bin Laden apparently is motivated by a personal interpretation of Islam that legitimises terrorism.

Fortunately most people do not resort to such extreme behaviour, but will still seek to justify to themselves actions they take that can have unpleasant consequences for other people. The person who is totally rational in decision making is a rare creature in business life. In Chapter 25 there was an account of Milgram's work, which showed people acting in a most extreme way when they were put in an 'agentic state', whereby the responsibility lay somewhere else, absolving the individual of any guilt or responsibility associated with their actions. Recent concern about responsibility for fatal accidents has created great interest in the concept of corporate manslaughter. Who is responsible for a train crash, the train driver or those in overall charge of the business who did not arrange for suitable training, supervision or other facilities?

Moral justification

Sometimes the moral justification comes from a value system that is independent of the business itself and where individual opinions can be sharply divided. Some doctors and nurses are happy to work in abortion clinics, while others refuse, as some people are passionately committed to the woman's right to choose and others are equally passionately pro-life. Some people are enraged about the destruction of green land to build motorways, while others are enthusiastic. Other actions and decisions are more generally supported by the external value system. Few would disagree that people at work should be honest and that claims about a product or service should be accurate. Most would also agree with the general proposition of equal opportunity for all, although there may be sharp disagreement about what exactly that means in practice.

Ethical principles

Some standards of ethics derive from voluntary agreement by members of a particular industry, such as editors of national newspapers, or statutory 'watchdogs' such as those monitoring the activities of privatised public utilities. The problem of pensions and similar financial services being mis-sold has produced the Personal Investment Authority, which has quite swingeing powers intended to prevent a repetition of that sort of problem. Then there are the ethical standards that are generated within a particular business. The Royal Dutch/Shell Group of Companies relies largely for its international effectiveness on the values shared by all its companies and employees. No new joint venture will be developed unless the partner company accepts them.

> The business principles are a set of beliefs which say what the Shell group stands for and covers in general terms its responsibilities to its principal stakeholders, its shareholders, employees, customers and society. They are concerned with economic principles, business integrity, political activities, the environment, the community and availability of information. (Haddock and South 1994, p. 226)

These principles were first set out in 1976 and were not imposed from the top, but were a codification of already accepted behaviour. The principles are revised from time to time and one of the challenging tasks for the central HR function was to introduce a code of practice relating to drugs and alcohol, which took considerable discussion and consultation before agreement could be reached.

Individuals encounter moral dilemmas frequently in their working lives and are likely to find them very difficult. In carrying out research a few years ago about performance appraisal practice in a large building society, it was possible to see the rise in sickness absence at the time of the annual appraisal discussion, and this was most marked among appraisers: those who had to pass on bad news. We saw in Chapter 25 that few managers wish to take over responsibility for grievance and discipline from HR people, and making the decision to dismiss someone for almost any reason other than gross misconduct is a most unpopular management task because it seems that the interests of the business are being considered at the expense of the interests of individual employees. At times like this managers are very anxious to find some justifying framework for their actions.

ACTIVITY 31.1

Eric was deaf, mute and suffered from cerebral palsy. He had been unemployable all his adult life, but in his late twenties he started to follow round the local authority refuse collectors emptying dustbins. As the lorry reached the end of a street, Eric would go ahead of it and drag dustbins out from behind the houses to the front. His handicap made it a very slow and painful process, but it was something he could do and he worked until he dropped with exhaustion. This completely unofficial arrangement was accepted by the refuse collectors as they were able to complete their rounds quicker and they were on an incentive payment arrangement and Eric's participation enabled them to complete their rounds in slightly less time. At the end of the week they had a collection and gave Eric a few pounds. This transformed his life, as he had a purpose and had some mates.

1 Do you feel that Eric was being exploited by the refuse collectors?
  Local authority officials heard about what Eric was doing and said it had to stop.
2 Why do you think they made this decision? Do you agree with it?
  A personnel manager in the neighbourhood heard about Eric and arranged for him to be taught to operate a sewing machine. He was then employed in the personnel manager's factory to maintain and repair all the overalls: a straightforward job carried out skilfully and conscientiously.
3 Do you feel that Eric was being exploited by the personnel manager?
4 As Eric was able to draw invalidity benefit, do you feel that the job should have been offered first to someone who was able-bodied? In the following three years investigations twice demonstrated that the overalls could be repaired cheaper by subcontracting the work to another company, but that decision was not taken. Eric carried on as an employee.
5 Why do you think they did not make that decision? Do you agree with it?

Codes of ethics

By the early 1990s one-third of leading British companies had a written code of ethics, which was nearly double the number in 1987. The key issue with ethical codes is the extent to which they are supported by the people to whom they apply. They are not rules that can be enforced by penalties for non-compliance. It is necessary that they are understood, appreciated and willingly honoured by the great majority of those who are affected. There will then be considerable social pressure on the few who do not wish to comply. Imposing ethics is very tricky. While examining equal opportunities some years ago, researchers found an interesting situation in an American computer company with a rapidly growing British subsidiary. The company had a high-profile commitment to 'positive action to seek out and employ members of disadvantaged groups'. This was reinforced in the annual appraisal system for managers, who had to indicate what they had done in the last 12 months to implement a 'programme of employment and development for minorities'. The company annual report made a claim that this initiative was advancing at all international locations. In Britain, however, it was found in practice that:

> Without exception, all managers to whom we spoke ignored that part of their appraisal . . . They put a line through the offending clause and wrote 'not applicable in the UK' . . . despite the corporate objective of 'citizenship', applicable in the UK, requiring recruitment officers to seek out the disadvantaged in the community . . . Suggestions by the researchers that such an active recruitment policy was an obligation on the part of management . . . invoked the reaction, 'we're not a welfare organisation'. (Torrington, Hitner and Knights 1982, p. 23)

ETHICS AND HUMAN RESOURCE MANAGEMENT

Criticisms of the HRM approach to ethics

Some academics have criticised HR managers for management failures in the employment field and derided them as powerless because of their inability to carry out 'simple' tasks such as introducing genuine equality of opportunity and humanising the workplace. Forty years ago Flanders criticised them, and their managerial colleagues, for getting the balance wrong between who did what in management:

> Confusion over the role of personnel management can produce a compromise that gets the worst of all worlds. In major areas of industrial relations policy – such as employment, negotiations, communications and training – line management may shed all the details of administration, while retaining ultimate authority and an illusion of responsibility. (Flanders 1964, p. 254)

WINDOW ON PRACTICE

One of the most telling caricatures of the HR manager comes from a Tyneside shop floor:

> Joe, an old labourer, is trudging through the shipyard carrying a heavy load on his shoulders. It is a filthy, wet day and the sole of his shoe is flapping open. The personnel manager, passing at the time, stops him, saying 'Hey Joe, you can't go round with your shoe in that state on a wet day like this' and reaching into his back pocket takes out a bundle of bank notes. Joe beams in anticipation. 'Here' says the personnel manager, slipping the elastic band off the bundle of notes, 'put this round your shoe, it will help keep the wet out'. (Murray 1972, p. 279)

The most vigorous denunciation of personnel people for not putting the world to rights has been from Tim Hart (1993) with his onslaught on HRM, which had three points of criticism:

1 HRM is amoral and anti-social because it has moved away from the principles of the famous social philanthropists who realised that the standard economic paradigm of labour utility needed to be tempered with social and religious values. HRM ignores the pluralistic nature of work organisations and personnel managers have abandoned their welfare origins.

2 Personnel managers, aided and abetted by the Institute of Personnel Management, have lost their claim to independent professional standing, as HRM is a managerial rather than professional approach, producing a purely reactive response to situations.

3 HRM is ecologically destructive because it consolidates an exploitative relationship between people at work which is then reproduced in our approach to relationships in the wider society and with our environment.

Other management specialists do not receive these criticisms, either because their activities are more limited in their social implications or because their academic commentators are more interested in the technical than the social aspects of what they are doing.

HR interest in ethics

The 'welfare' concept

HR people have long held a strong interest in ethics, although it was usually caricatured as welfare. Some of the academic critics argue that personnel managers should remain aloof from the management hurly-burly so that 'professional values will be paramount and prevail over other interests' (Hart 1993, p. 30). The problem with that simplistic argument is that HR people do not have a separate professional existence from the management of which they are a part. HRM is a management activity or it is nothing. The company doctor and the company legal adviser are bound by codes of professional ethics different from those of managers, but they are employed for their specialist, technical expertise and they are members of long-established, powerful professional groupings with their own normal places of work. When they leave their surgeries or their courtrooms to align themselves with managers in companies, they are in a specialised role. They can maintain a non-managerial, professional detachment, giving advice that is highly regarded, even when it is highly unpopular. Furthermore they advise; they do not decide. For instance, any dismissal on the grounds of ill health is a management decision and not a medical decision, no matter how explicit and uncompromising the medical advice may be.

HR specialists do not have separate places and conventions of work which they leave in order to advise managements. They are employed in no other capacity than to participate closely in the *management* process of the business. They do not even have the limited degree of independence that company accountants have, as their activities are not subject to external audit, and it is ludicrous to expect of them a fully-fledged independent, professional stance, although there is a move in that direction since the professional body became chartered. The chartered personnel practitioner can only retain that particular cachet after regular reassessment of professional competence.

The change in general management orientation during the 1980s and 1990s towards the idea of leaner and fitter, flexible organisations, downsizing, delayering, outplacement and all the other ideas that eventually lead to fewer people in jobs and fewer still with any sort of employment security have usually been implemented by personnel people. HR and personnel managers cannot behave like Banquo's ghost and be silently disapproving of their colleagues' actions. What they can do is to argue vigorously in favour of what they see as the best combination of efficiency and justice, but they can only argue vigorously if they are present when decisions are made. If they are not generally 'on side', they do not participate in the decision making and they probably do not keep their jobs. Either they are a part of management, valued by their colleagues, despite their funny ideas, or they are powerless. There are no ivory towers for them to occupy, and no more employment security for them than for any other member of the business.

The 'deviant innovator'

In the different era of the 1970s Legge (1978) propounded her formulation of the conformist and deviant innovator as alternative strategies for the personnel manager to pursue. The conventions of employment security then, especially those of managers, were such that personnel specialists could perhaps pursue a deviant path with impunity. Now it is more difficult:

> The 'deviant innovator' bolt hole based on a plea to consider the merits of social values and to ponder the value of an independent 'professional stance' appeared to be offering a less secure refuge. (Storey 1992, p. 275)

They can still take such an approach, if they are valued by their managerial colleagues for the wholeness of their contribution, and if they accept the fact that they will often lose the argument: they cannot do it by masquerading as an unrepresentative shop steward. They have no monopoly of either wisdom or righteousness, and other members of the management team are just as likely as they are to be concerned about social values.

Lob enrichment and humanising the workplace

HR managers have not abandoned their interest in welfare; they have moved away from an approach to welfare that was trivial, anachronistic and paternalist. In the HR vocabulary the term 'welfare' is code for middle-class do-gooders placing flowers in the works canteen. Personnel managers increasingly shun the traditional approach to welfare not for its softness, but because it is ineffectual. It steers clear of the work that people are doing and concentrates on the surroundings in which the work is carried out. It does not satisfy the HR obsession with getting progress in the employment of people, and it certainly does not do enough to satisfy the people who are employed. In many undertakings HR specialists are taking their management colleagues along with them in an enthusiastic and convinced attempt to give jobs more meaning and to humanise the workplace. Their reasoning is that the business can only maintain its competitive edge if the people who work there are committed to its success, and that commitment is volitional: you need hearts and minds as well as hands and muscle. Investment in training and the dismantling of elaborate, alienating organisation structures do more for employee well-being than paternalistic welfare programmes ever did.

WINDOW ON PRACTICE

The CIPD Code

The CIPD Code of Professional Conduct (IPD 1996) identifies seven areas in which its members must respect standards of conduct:

Accuracy. They must maintain high standards of accuracy in the information and advice they provide to employers and employees.

Confidentiality. They must respect the employer's legitimate needs for confidentiality and ensure that all personnel information (including information about current, past and prospective employees) remains private.

Counselling. With the relevant skills, they must be prepared to act as counsellors to individual employees, pensioners and dependants or to refer them, where appropriate, to other professionals or helping agencies.

Developing others. They must encourage self-development and seek to achieve the fullest possible development of employees in the service of present or future organisation needs.

Equal opportunities. They must promote fair, non-discriminatory employment practices.

Fair dealing. They must maintain fair and reasonable standards in their treatment of individuals.

Self-development. They must seek continuously to improve their performance and update their skills and knowledge.

ETHICS ACROSS NATIONAL BOUNDARIES

The international dimension of the social responsibility question has still to be developed. Logging operations in South America are ravaging the rainforests, which are essential to life continuing on the planet. Error, or neglect, in the management of manufacturing processes can produce a tragedy like that of Bhopal in India, Chernobyl in Ukraine or the various discharges of crude oil that have occurred all over the world. We have already referred to the concern about values in Shell, yet this business suffered serious difficulties about its plans for the disposal of the Brent Spar oil rig. Since the first formal warning by the American Surgeon General about the risks of smoking, tobacco consumption has been falling in Western countries, so the tobacco companies have increased their marketing in less developed countries.

Ethical standards vary. The Recruit affair was a major Japanese scandal involving allegations of corruption among the country's most senior politicians. In the aftermath there was much American criticism of Japanese business practices and a flurry of righteous indignation in Western newspapers about the need to use 'slush funds' in various countries to obtain business. Becker and Fritzsche (1987) carried out a study of different ethical perceptions between American, French and German executives. Thirty-nine per cent of the Americans said that paying money for business favours was unethical. Only 12 per cent of the French and none of the Germans agreed. In the United States Japanese companies have been accused of avoiding the employment of ethnic minority groups by the careful location of their factories (Cole and Deskins 1988, pp. 17–19). On the other hand, Japanese standards on employee health and safety are as high as anywhere in the world (Wokutch 1990). In Southeast Asia the contrast in prosperity between countries such as Malaysia and Singapore on the one hand and Indonesia and the Philippines on the other means that there are ethical questions about the employment of illegal immigrants that are superficially similar to those applying to Cubans and Mexicans in the United States, but which do not occur in other parts of the world. There are very low wages and long working hours in China, and in Europe, Britain initially refused to accept the social chapter of the Maastricht Treaty harmonising employment conditions across the European Union.

The disparate nature of ethical standards between countries will be one of the key HR issues to be addressed in the future. There will gradually be a growing together of national practice on working hours, but it will take much longer for rates of pay to harmonise. One can visualise common standards on health and safety developing much quicker than equality of opportunity between the sexes and across ethnic divisions.

It seems that games are played between governments and multinational companies:

> Corporations in the international arena . . . have no real desire to seek international rules and regulations . . . that would erode the differential competitive advantage which accrues as a consequence of astute locational decisions. Indeed the strategies are centred on endless negotiations, or the ability to play off the offer from one nation against that of another . . . Examples of this strategy can be found in the recent negotiations over CFC restrictions, ozone depletion and the preservation of the Amazon rain forest. (McGowan and Mahon 1992, p. 172)

SOME CURRENT AND DEVELOPING ETHICAL DILEMMAS

We conclude this chapter by suggesting some of the less obvious ethical dilemmas for those in management positions. Issues such as the environment and equalising opportunity are extensively discussed, but there are others that receive less attention.

Life in the business

What sort of quality does working life have and what sort of quality will it have in the future? Twenty years ago there was a team of experts employed at government expense in a Quality of Working Life Unit. Their task was to suggest ways in which that quality could be improved, mainly through job redesign initiatives. Since then the general belief is that quality of working life has declined, partly through overwork and partly through fear of losing employment. At the beginning of the twenty-first century workplace stress is one of the most common causes of absence and the place of work is an arena where newspapers would have us believe that harassment, poor supervision and bullying are rife, to say nothing of problems with passive smoking.

> Few people go off to work these days with a song in their hearts . . . many people dread each day because they have to work in places where they feel abused and powerless. What is happening to us? Why are talented, productive people being thwarted and sabotaged? Why do we treat each other so badly? Why are tyrannical bosses tolerated? Does the bottom line really justify the hurt and frustration we experience? (Wright and Smye 1996, p. 3)

As we saw at the beginning of this book, we now lack the comfortable feelings of security that the employing organisation used to provide. Whether people really are more or less secure in their jobs is debatable, but there is no doubt that they *feel* less secure. Furthermore, delayering and downsizing to become leaner and fitter has mainly affected people in middle-range posts, who used to be the most secure and who valued their security most highly.

As the gradual shift in organisation from entity to process continues we shall have to find ways that make work less stressful and more satisfying, despite the absence of certain of its traditionally most attractive features: security and community.

Information technology and the workplace

We have plenty of predictions of what the computer, the internet and the microprocessor can do and what will then logically happen: manufacturing will progressively be taken over by robots, rapid transfer and manipulation of data, the paperless office, people working from home instead of coming into a centre, and so forth: the golden age of the post-industrial society and the information superhighway. The ethical dilemma is to wonder what will be done to make up for what the computer will take from us: the conviviality and communal feeling of organisational life.

Managers have long had the opportunity to spend more of their time, and make more of their decisions, by rational planning and operational research methods than in fact they do. The strange thing is that there continues to be a preference among managers in general and HR managers in particular to spend their time talking with people and to make their decisions as a result of discussion and shrewd judgement. Will managers now begin to eschew face-to-face discussion in favour of face-to-terminal decision making, or will they continue to confer and keep busy while others feed to them an ever-increasing flow of processed information requiring interpretation, evaluation and further discussion? Research findings suggest that managers work the way they do at least partly because they like it that way.

> The manager actually seems to prefer brevity and interruption in his work. Superficiality is an occupational hazard of the manager's job. Very current information (gossip, hearsay, speculation) is favoured; routine reports are not. The manager clearly favours the . . . verbal media, spending most of his time in verbal contact. (Mintzberg 1973, pp. 51–2)

The date and male gender of that quotation may be significant. Most of the studies of managerial work have been of men and of men and women working in a male-dominated culture. It may be that the increasing proportion of managerial jobs done by women will alter the stereotype. The women authors of *Corporate Abuse* are quite clear about the need to care for souls:

> Studies of work flow suggest there is five times more opportunity to experience joy in the workplace on a daily basis than in the home environment if it is a workplace that is in tune with the needs of the soul . . . Once we have a community of fully nurtured souls, the possibility of creativity is limitless. Everyone in the workforce will be tapped into his or her own power source as well as being part of a larger community of effort and partnership. (Wright and Smye 1996, pp. 248–9)

This rings strangely in management ears, but maybe this is the way to rediscover the sense of community that employing organisations used to provide.

How great will the influence of the computer on HRM work actually become? How will we make up for what the computer takes away? If there is a general tendency for people to work at home, taking their terminal with them, how popular will that turn out to be? It is over a century since the household ceased to be the central productive unit and the men, and later the women, began to spend a large part of their waking hours at a different social centre: the factory, shop or office – the organisational entity. To be housebound has become a blight. We can see how it used to be:

> In 1810 the common productive unit in New England was still the rural household. Processing and preserving of food, candlemaking, soap-making, spinning, weaving, shoemaking, quilting, rug-making, the keeping of small animals and gardens, all took place on domestic premises.
>
> Although money income might be obtained by the household through the sale of produce, and additional money be earned through occasional wages to its members, the United States household was overwhelmingly self-sufficient . . . Women were as active in the creation of domestic self-sufficiency as were men. (Illich 1981, pp. 111–12)

Since that time we have dismantled, or allowed to wither, all the social mechanisms that supported that self-sufficiency, and developed instead the social institution of the workplace as the arena for many of our human needs, such as affiliation, interaction, teamworking and competition. It really seems most unlikely that the move away from working in the household will be reversed. In every country of the world roads and railways are jammed with people at the beginning and end of the day going to work or returning, despite the tendency for the organisational entity to decline.

The World Wide Web may not turn everyone into a homeworker, but it is still having a significant impact. There is the slightly isolating nature of the work that computerisation produces. The individual employee is not one of many in a crowded workshop, but one of a few scattered around a mass of busy machines. The clerical employee spends more time gazing at a computer terminal and less talking to colleagues. What employee behaviour will this engender and what attitudes will be associated with that behaviour?

WINDOW ON PRACTICE

Susan is not a high-flier, but an extremely competent and conscientious PA/secretary who is happy to work part-time so as to maintain an active family role. She explains what she has progressively 'lost':

> When I started I worked for one boss. He was a bit of a pain at times, but I got very involved, partly because he was so disorganised. He relied on me and I could follow all the ups and downs of his office politics. There was good camaraderie with other secretaries, who really ran the place. Not at all PC, but interesting and worthwhile. Nowadays there is more concentration on just doing the basic job of setting out letters and endless hours staring at that bloody screen. I feel more and more isolated.

As more people become able to use the computer there is a net loss of jobs. This has been seen in its most dramatic form in the publishing of newspapers, where typesetting has been eliminated through journalists typing their copy directly at a computer terminal.

The central ethical dilemma seems to be that we are allowing information technology gradually to take away the social institution of the organisation on which we have become so dependent. How will this scenario unfold?

ACTIVITY 31.2

What difference has the computer made to your working life so far? What further effect do you expect it to have in the next five years? How readily would you be (or are you) a homeworker?

Employment

If employing organisations are not to provide the security of a job for life, how will people find employment, both as a way of earning their livelihood and as a means of finding their place in society? There has been much brave talk of people managing their own careers and concentrating on ensuring their continuing employability. Charles Handy enunciated his concept of portfolio living, whereby people put together a portfolio of different activities so that they could control their own lives without becoming dependent on a single employer. This is fine for the able, well educated and independently minded, but human society has not evolved to the point where that description fits everyone; it probably fits only a minority.

There have always been large proportions of any society who were dependent. The golden age of Ancient Greece was based on slavery, as was the earlier Pharoanic period in Egypt. The lord of the manor had his tenants, mass production required masses of people and the world has always required large numbers for their armies. Not only were there dependent people, but society depended on them. We are now moving into this strange new world where there seems to be no place for that large proportion of the population.

It is unrealistic to expect every middle-aged redundant unskilled operative or every school-leaver without GCSEs to develop their own flexible employability. They need someone or something to provide them with the opportunity to work. Current economic wisdom is that jobs can only come through the activity of the market. This is one of the common political debating points: where are the jobs going to come from? Surely, however, it is one of the salient questions for human resource management. If personnel managers have social responsibility, how will *they* improve job prospects in the economy?

Self-improvement

For a long time we have lived with inflation that was, in many ways, the engine of growth. Not only did we spend in order to avoid higher prices next month, but we always felt we were making progress when our take-home pay kept going up. Rationally we know that we were not necessarily doing better at all, but it vaguely *felt* as if we were. Recently the level of inflation has been so firmly controlled that we no longer have that spurious feeling of making progress, as cost-of-living adjustments either do not exist or seem so small.

Without the mirage of progress provided by inflation, people need to have a more genuine sense of being able to do better. We have already considered the advantages and drawbacks of relating pay to performance, which is the main way in which it has been possible recently to see an improvement in one's material circumstances, but this really pays off only for a minority.

Delayering has taken out another yardstick of progress, as the scope for promotion is much reduced. This may reduce costs and may replace the phoney improvement of promotion by the possibility of real improvement through finding new opportunities, but we should remember that the business that is 'lean and mean' feels very mean indeed to the people who are inside it.

A nice HR challenge is to develop novel aspects of corporate culture that will recognise achievement and give a sense of progress for all those who seek it, without generating envy:

> Conspicuous privilege, ostentation, and other forms of behaviour, even when not necessarily wrong, typically provoke envy. Unusually large salaries or bonuses, even if justified by competition in a free and open market, may offer demagogues fertile ground on which to scatter the seeds of envy. It is wise to take precautions against these eventualities. (Novak 1996, p. 144)

Personal (note: not personnel) management

One ethical challenge in HRM is to ensure that the processes of management are seen to be carried out by people who can be seen, talked to, argued with and persuaded.

While it is clearly important for managers to avoid an overpreoccupation with procedural trivia, which reinforces the status quo and inhibits change, management is not all about strategy, and HRM has only a modest strategic element. It is the operational or technical aspects that require the skill and confer the status. Is there anything harder for a manager to do well than carry out a successful appraisal interview? Are there many more important jobs to be done than *explaining* strategy, or making the absolutely right appointment of someone to a key role? This is operational management for HR specialists, yet so often we find that they have retreated to the strategy bunker to think great thoughts and discuss the shape of the world with like-minded people consuming endless cups of coffee, while the appraisal and the selection and the communication is left to 'the line'.

There used to be a management approach knows as MBWA, or management by walking about. This exhorted managers to get out of their offices and walk about to see what was going on and to be available. We have already referred in this chapter to the apparent preference among managers to spend their time in face-to-face discussion rather than in solitary activities. The trouble is that more and more of their contacts are with other managers rather than with people in the front line.

We suggest that it is important to maintain the work of HR as largely 'a contact sport', dealing face to face with people in all sorts of jobs in all parts of the business, so that, although the business employs the HR manager, there is an agent of that employing business with whom that manager can reason and debate.

Future HR managers will need a shrewd strategic sense and a set of operational managerial skills. They will also need an ethical sense, able to set management action in its context, understanding the implications for the enterprise, for each person and for the community at large. Many aspects of management work can be developed into a science: successful HRM is an art.

WINDOW ON PRACTICE

There has recently developed an interest in corporate social responsibility or CSR. Reviewing this development Stefan Stern (2004) made the following comment:

> CSR is bound to fail in companies where it is adopted simply for reasons of public relations . . . It may be successful in changing attitudes to your company in the short term, but if your activities are morally dubious they will eventually be exposed. CSR, if it is to mean anything, it cannot be a bolted-on attitude or a departmental annexe . . . It is not about 'putting something back' – it is about how you make your money in the first place. (. . . In any case, if you really feel the need to 'put something back', doesn't that suggest you have taken too much already?) (Stern, 2004, p. 35)

SUMMARY PROPOSITIONS

31.1 In the business context, ethics are part of the corporate culture that sets norms of behaviour by which people in the business will abide because they have some moral authority as well as being convenient.

31.2 Ethical standards vary been different national cultures, making international standards difficult.

31.3 Ethical codes are only valid if they are appreciated and willingly implemented by the great majority of those to whom they apply.

31.4 Personnel management has always had a strong ethical dimension, although personnel managers and the practice of HRM are regularly criticised for failure in social responsibility.

31.5 The CIPD has a code for its members, setting standards of conduct in accuracy, confidentiality, counselling, developing others, equal opportunities, fair dealing and self-development.

31.6 Among current and developing ethical dilemmas are the quality of life in the business, information technology in the workplace, employment, self-improvement and personal management.

GENERAL DISCUSSION TOPICS

1 The chapter opens by explaining that personnel managers for years played down their ethical/welfare role. Why do you think this was?

2 To what extent do you regard Tim Hart's criticisms as valid?

3 What examples can members of the group produce that would put you in the position of feeling that the demands of your job were in conflict with what you regarded as being right?

How would you deal with this and how do the Milgram experiments on obedience explain, or fail to explain, your actions?

4 Most people agree that differences in rates of pay according to value or effort are justified, but that some differences are 'obscene'. What criteria would you suggest for setting pay differentials within a business that both are seen as fair and are effective in being able to attract and retain appropriate people from the labour market?

FURTHER READING

Fisher, C. and Lovell, A. (2003) *Business Ethics and Values*. Harlow: Prentice Hall

McEwan, T. (2001) *Managing Values and Beliefs in Organisations*. Harlow: Prentice Hall
Both of these books provide useful reviews of ethical issues for managers in general. Both are up to date and have sections of particular interest to HRM people.

People Management (2003), 10 July
This issue of the journal is dedicated to examining corporate social responsibility.

Redman, T. and Wilkinson, A. (2001) *Contemporary Human Resource Management*. Harlow: Prentice Hall
There is an excellent chapter on employment ethics by Peter Ackers in this volume.

REFERENCES

Anthony, P.D. (1977) *The Conduct of Industrial Relations*. London: Institute of Personnel Management.

Becker, H. and Fritzsche, D.J. (1987) 'A comparison of the ethical behavior of American, French and German managers', *Columbia Journal of World Business*, Winter, pp. 87–95.

Blanchard, K. and Peale, N.V. (1988) *The Power of Ethical Management*. London: Heinemann.

Cole, R.E. and Deskins, D.R. (1988) 'Racial factors in site location and employment patterns of Japanese auto firms in America', *California Management Review*, Fall, p. 11.

Dehn, G. (1997) 'Blow the whistle, save a life', *The Times*, 8 April.

Flanders, A. (1964) *The Fawley Productivity Agreements*. London: Faber & Faber.

Friedman, M. (1963) *Capitalism and Freedom*. Chicago: University of Chicago Press.

Haddock, C. and South, B. (1994) 'How Shell's organisation and HR practices help it to be both global and local', in D.P. Torrington (ed.) *International Human Resource Management*. Hemel Hempstead: Prentice Hall International.

Hampden-Turner, C. and Trompenaars, F. (1993) *The Seven Cultures of Capitalism*. New York: Doubleday.

Hart, T.J. (1993) 'Human resource management; time to exorcize the militant tendency', *Employee Relations*, Vol. 15, No. 3, pp. 29–36.

Illich, I. (1981) *Shadow Work*. London: Marion Boyars.

Institute of Personnel and Development (1996) *Code of Professional Conduct*. London: IPD.

Legge, K. (1978) *Power, Innovation and Problem-solving in Personnel Management*. Maidenhead: McGraw-Hill.

McGowan, R.A. and Mahon, J.F. (1992) 'Multiple games, multiple levels: gamesmanship and strategic corporate responses to environmental issues', *Business and the Contemporary World*, Vol. 14, No. 4, pp. 162–77.

Mintzberg, H. (1973) *The Nature of Managerial Work*. London: Harper & Row.

Murray, J. (1972) 'The role of the shop steward in industry', in D.P. Torrington (ed.) *Handbook of Industrial Relations*. Epping: Gower.

Novak, M. (1996) *Business as a Calling: work and the examined life*. New York: Free Press.

Senior, A. (2004) 'MPs Attack Insurers over Chiefs' Pay', *The Times*, 28 January, p. 26.

Stern, S. (2004) 'The Perils of CSR', *Royal Society of Arts Journal*, January.

Storey, J. (1992) *Developments in the Management of Human Resources*. Oxford: Blackwell.

Torrington, D.P. (1968) *Successful Personnel Management*. London: Staples Press.

Torrington, D.P., Hitner, T.J. and Knights, D. (1982) *Management and the Multi-Racial Workforce*. Aldershot: Gower.

Wokutch, R.E. (1990) 'Corporate social responsibility, Japanese style', *Academy of Management Executive*, May, pp. 56–72.

Wright, L. and Smye, M. (1996) *Corporate Abuse*. New York: Macmillan.

An extensive range of additional materials, including multiple choice questions, answers to questions and links to useful websites can be found on the Human Resource Management Companion Website at **www.pearsoned.co.uk/torrington.**

CHAPTER 32

WORK-LIFE BALANCE

THE OBJECTIVES OF THIS CHAPTER ARE TO:

1 ANALYSE THE DRIVERS FOR WORK-LIFE BALANCE

2 OUTLINE THE LEGISLATIVE CONTEXT

3 EXPLORE A RANGE OF WORK-LIFE BALANCE PRACTICES

4 ASSESS THE BENEFITS OF WORK-LIFE BALANCE

5 ASSESS THE BARRIERS TO, AND PROBLEMS WITH, WORK-LIFE BALANCE

this position will change in the future as a result of decisions in the courts. For this to happen a woman whose request for flexible working had been turned down would have to bring a test case using the new regulations in tandem with the established law of indirect sex discrimination. If she could successfully show that a requirement to work full time constituted a rule with which considerably more men could comply than women, it would follow that a refusal to grant her request amounted to an act of indirect sex discrimination (*see* Chapter 23). The employer might still be able to defend itself, but to do so it would have to show that its decision was objectively justifiable. In other words, it would have to justify its decision in some detail rather than simply to state that one of the eight grounds for refusing a request applied.

Debates about family-friendly legislation

Views are divided about how, and indeed whether, further extensions of the family-friendly rights outlined above would be justified. Some mooted changes are uncontroversial, such as allowing a couple to choose whether it is the mother or the father who exercises the right to take additional maternity leave (AML), but others are strongly resisted by employers' associations. These include paying women at the higher rate of SMP throughout ordinary maternity leave (OML), giving employees returning from maternity leave a legal right to work part time and requiring larger employers to provide access to crèche facilities. Many employers argue that such measures would unacceptably add to their costs and make them less competitive internationally. There is also evidence of growing discontent about such measures from employees who do not have families, and a fear that too much regulation of this kind actually serves to hinder rather than help women's employment prospects by acting as a 'disincentive to hiring women of prime child-bearing age' (Lea 2001, p. 57).

However, strong public policy arguments can also be put in favour of family-friendly legislation and these hold sway in current government circles. In short, it is believed that such measures are needed to provide gateways which allow parents (particularly mothers) to combine working with their family responsibilities and hence to put much needed skills and experience at the disposal of the economy. They also serve to encourage single mothers and those with unemployed partners to come off welfare benefits and to take up paid employment instead. Helping fathers to take a greater share of domestic responsibilities contributes to this aim as much as removing the barriers which discourage mothers from returning to work following a pregnancy. In a tight labour market, where skills shortages are common, a compelling case can thus be made for family-friendly regulation on purely economic grounds (*see* Collins 2002, pp. 454–5).

ACTIVITY 32.2

Where do you stand in this debate about family-friendly legislation? Does it serve to underpin economic prosperity or reduce international competitiveness? What further measures would you welcome and which would you oppose?

WORK-LIFE BALANCE PRACTICES

Work-life balance options focus on three different types of work flexibility. First, there is flexibility in terms of the number of hours worked; second, the exact timing of those hours; and, third, the location at which the work is carried out. Clearly some options may reflect all three types of flexibility. While the legislation only addresses the need of parents, there is a strong lobby for flexible work options to be potentially available for all employees. There are potentially many possible work-life balance options, and clearly not all of these options are appropriate for all jobs or employees, and employers will need to be convinced of the business benefits of any work-life balance option. In addition work-life balance will mean different things to different people, depending on their age, life circumstances, values, interests, personality and so on. At present flexible options are predominantly taken by women (IRS 2002). Table 32.1 lists the main options.

Table 32.1 Options for achieving work-life balance

Part-time	Term-time working	Unpaid leave
Flexitime	Job share	Unpaid sabbaticals
Compressed week	Self-rostering	Work from home
Annual hours	Shift swapping	

Some items on this list are self-evident, but others require an explanation. While flexitime has been used for some time the systems tended to be formal, with limits, and there is currently an emphasis on less formal approaches and a more ad hoc approach to flexible hours, with, for example, days off for urgent domestic issues and time made up later. Compressed hours allow an employee to work perhaps a nine-day fortnight by working a little extra each day to allow for one whole day off. Self-rostering has been used particularly in the health service and allows nursing teams to design shift patters and staffing around the demands of work (for example getting the right mix of skills on each shift and taking account of patient care needs) and their own needs. IDS (2000) has produced a useful volume containing case studies of six organisations explaining how each has implemented work-life balance.

WINDOW ON PRACTICE

Work-life balance at Lloyds TSB

Lloyds TSB has won praise for its work-life balance policies, and Rana (2002) highlights the key role of the line manager is being open to new ideas and coming up with a work-life solution to meet both individual and business needs. Lloyds TSB introduced Work Options in March 1999 and in 2002 just under 3,600 employees were working flexibly as a result of this. An important foundation of policy at Lloyds TSB is that applications to work flexibly are now 'reason neutral', as it was felt that taking a reason into account forced managers into making value judgements. Now all that matters is making a viable business case.

Originally work-life balance policies were not embraced as fully as the bank would have liked; in particular men did not feel that it was legitimate to work flexibly and felt that doing so would damage their careers. This position is gradually improving and 16 per cent of those using work options are men and 18 per cent are managers.

However, there is still some way to go. A union representative explained that flexible options did not sit easily with the old culture of long hours and unclaimed overtime pay, and that employees were still inhibited in requesting flexibility. The representative was also concerned that staff shortages may limit the viability of many work options.

Source: Summarised from E. Rana (2002a) 'How does it really work in practice?' *The Guide to Work-life Balance*. London: CIPD.

Glynn *et al.* (2002) suggest that in fixed hours cultures, such as a supermarket, work-life balance policies which detail specific options for flexibility will help. In a long hours culture, like consultancy work, they argue that it is harder to achieve work-life balance, and a more viable option is to allow individuals more informal discretion to work their hours at the times and in the location that best suit business and personal needs.

There is some evidence that the public sector makes much better provision for work-life balance and Walton and Gaskell (2001) give some excellent examples of senior public sector employees working in a variety of flexible ways. Case 32.1 on the website focuses on the public sector.

WINDOW ON PRACTICE

Gap years for grown-ups

Saga Magazine (2003) reports on the increasing trend for those in their 50s and 60s to take off into the unknown for a gap year. While some of these may be retired, many are still in employment and are taking a year out, returning to work refreshed and with a new perspective on life with rediscovered drive and enthusiasm. Examples given in the article are individuals who feel they have had little freedom in the past due to work and family commitments, and want to do something while they are still fit and active.

There can be powerful advantages in the work environment from employers making such long periods of leave available, not only in retaining people who might otherwise give up their job, but as one of their interviewees explained, 'I don't bother with the trivia now. And I came back to my job far more resilient, resourceful and tolerant.'

BENEFITS OF WORK-LIFE BALANCE

Work-life balance practices have been shown in some instances to reduce absence (especially unplanned absence), raise morale and in increase levels of job satisfaction. Increased levels of performance have also been found as employees are less tired and so work more effectively when they are working. Kodz *et al.* (2002) in their research found that productivity and quality of work had both improved, as had staff retention and the ability to recruit staff. Perry-Smith and Blum (2000) found that bundles of work-life balance policies were related to higher organisational performance in a US survey of 527 firms. In the early 1970s the UK experienced some intensive industrial action which caused the government to introduce a three-day week throughout the economy, accompanied by regular power cuts to conserve energy. For that short period industrial production dipped by less than the 40 per cent that working hours were reduced. Control and choice are important characteristics of working life and Kodz *et al.* found that

> there is increasing acceptance that choice, control and flexibility are important *in work*, that personal fulfilment is important *outside work*, and, further, that satisfaction *outside work may enhance employees' contribution to work.* (Kodz *et al.* 2002, p. 1, italics in original)

Sabbaticals in particular can give individuals space and time to develop in other ways. Davidson (2002) reports on Elan, an IT company, that funds sabbaticals for employees to develop in new ways if there is a possibility this can transfer back into the workplace. They have supported such interests as horse whispering, surfing, performance music and neuro-linguistic programming and argue that 'sabbaticals give people the security of knowing they have a job to return to, and they bring fresh ideas back into the workplace' (p. 37).

In a baseline study covering employers and employees, conducted by the Institute for Employment Research at the University of Warwick and IFF Research Ltd (Hogarth *et al.* 2001), 91 per cent of employers and 96 per cent of employees felt that people work better when they can balance their work with other aspects of their lives. Employers can also find that such policies can meet business needs for flexibility and can be a way of addressing diversity issues.

Some employers have argued that staff on shorter working hours are still producing the same amount of work that they did on full-time hours; however, this was found to be, at least in part, due to the fact they were working longer than part-time paid hours, as the Window on practice in the following section demonstrates.

Case 32.2 on the website presents two different perspectives on the value and importance of work-life balance.

BARRIERS TO, AND PROBLEMS WITH, WORK-LIFE BALANCE

The take-up gap

There is considerable evidence that the demand for flexible work options is much greater than the take-up so far, and this has been referred to as the take-up gap.

Hogarth (2001) reports that 47 per cent of employees not currently using flexitime would like to do so, and 35 per cent would like a compressed week. Some work-life balance strategies cost the organisation money and financial limits are set for such practices to be viable. The AA experienced difficulties in setting up teleworking at home. Productivity was greater than that of site-based staff, but in order to offset the cost of technology and infrastructure such workers had to be more than 1.5 times as productive as site staff. To gain such productivity tight management and measurement of home-based teleworkers is necessary (Bibby 2002).

Policies and some line managers may limit access to work-life balance to certain groups. There is evidence that some employers fail to have a strategic approach to work-life balance, but use such practices in a fire-fighting manner, to deal with situations when they reach breaking point (for example in a case study of a Further Education college, *see* Glynn *et al.* 2002).

WINDOW ON PRACTICE

Who is entitled to work-life balance? A cautionary tale

In a government office there is a work-life balance policy with a range of options available. The options, however, are seen as being available only for women with children and this is causing much resentment among other staff. One manager, however, arranged, informally, in a specific year to have Friday afternoons off so that she could take her disabled husband up to the Lake District, avoiding the stressful Friday evening rush hour. To do this she worked extra time every other day of the week to make up her full-time hours. There were no problems resulting from this arrangement. She requested that the arrangement should continue the following year, but was told that she now had to make a formal application. She did this and was turned down on the basis that it was not compatible with work demands, and that she was needed in the office on a Friday afternoon. Stunned by this the manager wrote back explaining that she had two children, and it was on this basis that she needed the Friday afternoon off. Her application was granted.

There is evidence in the literature that work-life balance requests for childcare reasons would be dealt with more favourably that requests or any other basis. The association that work-life balance practices have with women bringing up children creates two problems. The first is that work-life balance is 'ghettoised' (*see*, for example, Rana 2002b), as something done for women with children who are not interested in real careers. The second is that this causes alienation from the rest of the workforce who are not allowed these special privileges. In particular, working part time has been a popular option in combining work and other commitments, and yet there is considerable evidence that this limits career development (*see*, for example, MacDermid *et al.* 2001).

ACTIVITY 32.3

Discuss the following statement. To what extent do you agree or disagree with it, and why?

'Employees should be equally entitled to work-life balance options, as long as business needs are met. It doesn't matter whether the reason is childcare, the desire to engage in sports activities, do extra gardening, or just loll around on the sofa watching television.'

The take-up of work-life balance options is often equated with lack of commitment to one's career or to the organisation. In the baseline study Hogarth *et al.* (2001) found that two-thirds of male employees felt that their career prospects would be damaged if they worked part time, and CIPD (Rana 2002b) found strikingly similar results in their survey of work-life balance.

In addition there are many employees who are committed to full-time hours because financial commitments mean that they require full-time pay. This severely limits the type of flexibility that they feel is appropriate for themselves. Heavy workloads may prevent requests for flexible working, and where departments are inadequately staffed flexible options are severely curtailed. High levels of work, combined with pressure from the organisational culture may also have unexpected consequences for those employees opting to reduce their hours to part time from full time, as is shown in the Window on practice.

WINDOW ON PRACTICE

Unpaid work

Glynn *et al.* (2002) in their research for the Institute for Employment Studies found examples of individuals reducing their hours to part time, but actually continuing to work more like their original hours as the workload had not reduced. As one interviewee who had done this explained:

> 'I end up working almost full time, just not visibly in the office. I do it at home once the kids are in bed.'

Managers appeared to be aware of these situations, and one manager explained:

> 'she produces almost exactly the same amount, of the same quality, as when she was working full time . . . she feels she has to prove she's still committed . . . she's not actually working less, she's working the same but in a different location . . . at a different time . . . she's not being paid for it and her access to other benefits [is] reduced . . . I worry that it is not sustainable for her.'

Source: Summarised from: C. Glynn, I. Steinberg and C. McCartney (2002) *Work-life balance: The role of the manager.* Horsham: Roffey Park Institute.

Furthermore in many organisations individuals have to be proactive and come up with flexible solutions which meet business needs and this is difficult when there are few precedents and a lack of understanding of what is available or possible. In addition the majority of organisations in an IRS survey had no procedure for employees to use to request flexible working (IRS 2002).

The CIPD survey (Rana 2002b) reports that 74 per cent of respondents believed that working hours is not an indication of commitment, 84 per cent felt that individuals working part time were not less committed and 77 per cent believed that organisations should allow employees to attend to personal commitments in working time, and then make the time up. However, while these figures demonstrate that there have been some shifts in attitudes, culture remains a major barrier to take-up. Long hours cultures with early and late meetings are hard to shift. It is argued that more middle and senior manager role models are needed of flexible working and that there need to be work-life balance champions.

Managers' role in implementing work-life balance

Whether or not there is a work-life balance policy in existence, it is often line managers who will be the 'main arbiters of whether work-life balance policies become a reality . . . both by their attitudes and management practices' (Glynn *et al.* 2002, p. 5). The Work Foundation found that managers were the main barrier to introducing and implementing work-life balance policies (CIPD 2003). Managers have to manage performance targets of the team and often feel that flexible working damages this, and flexible working for some may mean higher workloads for others. There is a pressure on line managers to be fair and their decisions about who can work flexibly and in what way are under scrutiny and may result in a backlash. On top of this managers may receive a bonus for meeting team performance targets, which may be jeopardised by flexible working. MacDermid *et al.* (2001) found that managers had three concerns relating to employees working reduced hours. The first concerned helping employees develop professionally while not working full time, the second, what to do if more employees wanted to work reduced hours as it could be a nightmare to manage a host of different alternative work arrangements, and third, that some jobs were just not do-able on anything less than a full-time basis. Managing workers who are not visible (working at home for example) is a particular concern for line managers. Felstead *et al.* (2003) report the fear that working at home is a 'slacker's charter', but they also found that homeworkers themselves had fears about not being able easily to demonstrate their honesty, reliability and productivity. Some managed this by working more hours than they should in order to demonstrate greater output. To counteract this fear, managers in Felstead's study introduced new surveillance devices, set output targets and brought management into the home via home visits. Managers also felt that home working represented a potential threat to the integration of teams and the acceptance of corporate culture, and that it impeded the transmission of tacit knowledge. There is also a concern that only some employees have the characteristics to be successful homeworkers, and Felstead *et al.* (2003) develop this idea in some detail.

It is becoming apparent that a range of key management skills is needed in managing flexibility. For example Janman (2002) suggests that key skills are communication, empowerment, performance management and coaching. Glynn *et al.* (2002) are more specific in their recommendations. They suggest that line managers need to be able to 'push back' work demands from other parts of the organisation which they feel are unrealistic; plan and schedule; delegate in a fair and equitable way and understand the capacity and skills of those who report directly to them. They suggest that it is important for managers to be able to crack down hard on individual breaches of trust without cracking down across the board.

The Work Foundation (CIPD 2003) suggests that implementing work-life balance requires managers to shift the way that they measure staff, requiring more effort in judging performance and output rather than time spent doing the job. Managers clearly have to learn how to manage at a distance. But all this needs to be supported by the organisational culture:

> To thrive, work-life balance needs a supportive organizational culture that has sympathetic values and practices at its core. Arguably, training practitioners have one of the most important and strategic roles in creating and supporting that culture through imaginative and appropriate training programmes. (McCartney 2003, p. 39)

Unfortunately Kodtz *et al.* (2002) found that line managers felt abandoned and did not get the support that they needed.

McCartney goes on to give the example of Ford Europe which provides seminars related to work-life balance topics such as stress management, how individuals should manage their own working arrangements, maternity and returning to work and new fathers' workshops. Also reported is BT, which offers e-learning packages on skills to enable balance, optimising the performance of flexible teams and judging which roles are suitable for home working.

Limits on access to work-life balance

So far we have treated work-life balance as an option potentially available for a majority of employees, but this is not the case in reality. Felstead *et al.* (2003) reveal that the option to work at home is usually the privilege of the highly educated and/or people at the top of the organisational hierarchy. People in these jobs, they suggest, have considerably more influence over the work processes they are engaged in. They also report that although more women work at home than men, there are more men who have the choice to work at home. Nolan and Wood (2003) also note that work-life balance is not for the lower paid. They report that 5 per cent of such employees hold more than one job, and usually work in low-paid, low-status jobs in catering and personal services. A similar scene is painted by Polly Toynbee (2003). She also reports that many of these low-paid workers work for agencies and as such are distanced from the ultimate 'employer'. In these circumstances work-life balance policies are unlikely to be available in any case. Even working only for one employer Toynbee reports a hospital porter saying, 'you can't survive, not with a family, unless you do the long, long hours, unless you both work all the hours there are' (p. 59). Felstead *et al.* (2002) highlight an assumption in the work-life balance literature, which portrays working at home as always a 'good thing'. They argue that what is important is the *option* to work at home, as some people work at home doing low-paid unsatisfying jobs with no choice of work location, such conditions not necessarily being conducive to work-life balance.

White *et al.* (2003) argue that organisations are using flexibility to attempt to offset the damage being caused by high-performance work practices, but they argue that they are only enjoyed by a small proportion of the workforce at the moment, and in any case only have a small effect on the problem. They argue for more fundamental changes in working practices with safeguards to protect work-life balance, such as giving teams themselves the responsibility for addressing work-life balance issues when setting output targets for themselves.

> Successful implementation of flexible working is a culture-change programme, one that has relatively distinct goals in terms of values and beliefs, processes and behaviours. Viewing flexible working as culture changes places the topic firmly on the strategic agenda. (Jarman 2002, p. 17)

Few organisations monitor and evaluate the take-up of work-life balance options or measure their costs and benefits (IRS 2002). However, McCartney (2003) found that in BT the company used an annual survey, web chats, career life planning discussions, and employee networks to do this.

SUMMARY PROPOSITIONS

32.1 Demographic factors, the changing composition of the workforce, recruitment and retention problems, work intensification and the 24-hour society are all drivers for work-life balance initiatives.

32.2 There is increasing legislation encouraging employers to support work-life balance, but the emphasis is on family-friendly measures, and not on work-life balance for all.

32.3 Work-life balance policies generally provide options around how many hours are worked, exactly when these hours are worked and where they are worked.

32.4 When employees are given some control over their work-life balance they are likely to be more satisfied with work, have greater commitment to work, be more productive and stay longer in the organisation.

32.5 Barriers to work-life balance include understaffing, line manager fears, worries about career damage and organisational culture.

GENERAL DISCUSSION TOPICS

1. It is important to measure the costs and benefits of work-life balance. In what ways could this be done?
2. Discuss a range of measures that could be taken in an organisation to help line managers manage work-life balance successfully.

FURTHER READING

Duggan, M. (2003) *Family-Friendly Policies: A handbood for employer and employee*. Welwyn Garden City: Emis Publishing
This book on family-friendly employment legislation is comprehensive and up to date.

Holder, R. and Bradshaw, B. (2002) *Balancing Work and Life*. London: Dorling Kindersley Ltd
This is a useful, practical handbook which focuses on the steps readers can take in order to balance their work life with other aspects of their life. The book guides the reader through exercises which help them to recognise what success means for them as a person, understand themselves better, make changes in their work life and sustain these. The emphasis is on issues that are within the individual's control whether or not the organisation has any work-life balance policy or flexible options available.

McColgan, A. (2000) 'Family Friendly Frolics: The Maternity and Parental Leave etc Regulations 1999', *Industrial Law Journal*, Vol. 29, No. 2
This provides a sharply critical and thought-provoking appraisal of the measures taken by the government. The author shows how the UK has a great deal further to go in terms of legal provision if parents here are to enjoy the kind of rights that are common in many other EU countries.

REFERENCES

Bibby, A. (2002) 'Home start', *People Management*, Vol. 8, No. 1, 10 January, pp. 36–7.

CIPD (2003) 'Managers obstruct flexibility', *People Management*, Vol. 9, No. 18, p. 9.

Collins, H. (2002) 'Is There a Third Way in Labour Law?' in J. Conaghan, R.M. Fischl and K. Klare (eds) *Labour Law in an Era of Globalization: Transformative Practices and Possibilities*. Oxford: Oxford University Press.

Davidson, E. (2002) 'What lies beneath', *People Management*, Vol. 8, No. 25, pp. 36–7.

Felstead, A., Jewson, N., Phizacklea, A. and Walters, S. (2002) 'The option of working at home: another privilege for the favoured few', *New Technology, Work and Employment*, Vol. 17, No. 3, pp. 204–23.

Felstead, A., Jewson, N. and Walters, S. (2003) 'Managerial control of employees working at home', *British Journal of Industrial Relations*, Vol. 41, No. 2, June, pp. 241–64.

Glynn, C., Steinberg, I. and McCartney, C. (2002) *Work-life balance: The role of the manager*. Horsham: Roffey Park Institute.

Hogarth, T., Hasluck, C., Pierre, G. with Winterbotham, M. and Vivian, D. (2001) *Work-life Balance 2000: Results from the baseline study*. Research Report 249. London: DfEE.

Holbeche, L. and McCartney, C. (2002) *The Roffey Park Management Agenda*. Horsham: Roffey Park Institute.

IDS (2000) *Work-life balance*, IDS Study, No. 698, November. London: IDS.

Institute of Management (2001) *The Quality of Working Life Report*. London: Institute of Management.

IRS (2002) 'Hanging in the balance', *IRS Employment Review*, No. 766, 30 December, pp. 6–11.

Janman, K. (2002) 'How to . . . improve work-life balance in your organisation', *The Guide to Work-life Balance*. London: CIPD.

Kodz, J., Harper, H. and Dench, S. (2002) *Work-life Balance: Beyond the Rhetoric*, Institute for Employment Studies Report No. 384. Brighton: Institute for Employment Studies.

Lea, R. (2001) 'The Work-Life Balance and all that: The re-regulation of the labour market' IoD policy paper. London: Institute of Directors.

McCartney, C. (2003) 'Addressing the balance', *People Management*, Vol. 9, No. 17, 28 August, p. 39.

MacDermid, S., Lee, M., Buck, M. and Williams, M. (2001) 'Alternative work arrangements among professionals and managers', *Journal of Management Development*, Vol. 20, No. 4, pp. 305–17.

Mahoney, C. (2002) 'Only intensive care can save NHS staff', *in The Guide to Work-life Balance*. London: CIPD.

Nolan, P. and Wood, S. (2003) 'Mapping the future of work', *British Journal of Industrial Relations*, Vol. 41, No. 2, pp. 165–74.

Noon, M. and Blyton, P. (1997) *The Realities of Work*. London: Macmillan Business.

Perry-Smith, J. and Blum, T. (2000) 'Work-family human resource bundles and perceived organizational performance', *Academy of Management Journal*, Vol. 43, pp. 1107–17.

Rana, E. (2002a) 'How does it really work in practice?' *in The Guide to Work-life Balance*. London: CIPD.

Rana, E. (2002b) 'Balancing Act Earns UK respect', *in The Guide to Work-life Balance*. London: CIPD.

Saga Magazine (2003) 'See the world and change your life', *Saga Magazine*, April, pp. 47–50.

Toynbee, P. (2003) *Hard Work: Life in low-pay Britain*. London: Bloomsbury.

Walton, P. and Gaskell, L. (2001) 'Pliable Alternatives', *People Management*, Vol. 7, No. 6, 22 March, pp. 26–31.

White, M., Hill, S., McGovern, P., Mills, C. and Smeaton, D. (2003) '"High performance" management practices, working hours and work-life balance', *British Journal of Industrial Relations*, Vol. 41, No. 2, June, pp. 175–95.

An extensive range of additional materials, including multiple choice questions, answers to questions and links to useful websites can be found on the Human Resource Management Companion Website at **www.pearsoned.co.uk/torrington.**

CHAPTER 33

MEASURING HR: EFFECTIVENESS AND EFFICIENCY

THE OBJECTIVES OF THIS CHAPTER ARE TO:

1 CLARIFY THE MEANING OF THE TERM 'MEASURING HR'

2 EXPLAIN A RANGE OF MEASURES WHICH ARE FREQUENTLY USED

3 EXPLORE THE USE OF SCORECARDS AND OTHER STRATEGIC FRAMEWORKS IN MEASURING HR

4 EXPLORE CURRENT METHODS TO MAKE THE PROVISION OF HR MORE EFFECTIVE AND EFFICIENT

We have explored in some detail some of the research which indicates that differing HR activities will impact on the bottom-line performance of the firm, and that intangible assets are critical to a firm's value. This focus is growing in importance. In addition there is a recognition that traditional accountancy measures are inadequate, as they are unable to reflect the value of people to the organisation. Measures are needed which can demonstrate how people are an asset which adds value to the business rather than just a cost. This, together with the anticipation of the need to report people measures in a company's annual report, have provided a context where the measurement of HR has become increasingly important. However, there remains resistance by the HR function to measurement and IRS (2003) reports that less than half of respondents to its survey calculate measures of HR value.

WHAT DOES 'MEASURING HR' MEAN?

The research referred to in previous chapters has a very clear focus on measuring or assessing a range of best practices in terms of workforce organisation and management (such as self-managing teams, high training spend, reduced status differentials) and relating these to impact on productivity and profitability. This is a very specific approach to 'proving' that HR practices affect bottom-line performance. In this chapter we include this type of measurement, but we are taking a much wider perspective and will review a broader range of measures which are used to demonstrate how the HR function and HR capital contribute to the organisation.

HR measures are sometimes talked about in the context of measuring the contribution of the HR function. An example of such measures might be the staffing costs of the HR function, recruitment speed, training delivery, management satisfaction with HR advice and services, and so on. Such factors are clearly down to the people in the HR function and are under their control. There are many more measures, however, which may be only partly within the control of members of the HR function, and partly within the control of others in the organisation, and indeed there are some measures over which the HR function may have no control, particularly in an organisation where HR is devolved to line managers. For example absence and employee turnover are typical measures in many organisations. But to what extent are absence levels, for example, the result of the absence policy (and HR may or may not have designed this alone), the way the policy is implemented by line managers, the influence of other policies (such as work-life balance), the influence of the way that work is structured and commitment to peers (as for example in self-managing teams)? The list could go on. It could be argued that the HR function has an ultimate responsibility for all of this, but in reality this is not a tenable view, and there is also a much greater emphasis on partnership in HR requiring many activities to be business

ACTIVITY 33.1

Employee turnover is frequently measured in organisations. Identify which aspects of the organisation have an influence on this and who in the organisation would be seen as having a responsibility for these aspects.

driven and owned rather than HR driven and owned. Thus many HR measures represent aspects of human capital in the organisation on which the HR function has some influence. IRS (2002a) in its survey found that respondents commented on the inherent difficulty in identifying the contribution of the HR function in many measures.

FREQUENTLY USED MEASURES

IRS (2002a) divides measures into hard and soft measures, with training days, for example, being a hard (objective) measure and employee satisfaction, for example, being a soft measure. In its survey IRS found that employers most frequently calculated absence rates (96 per cent), employee turnover (98 per cent) and expenditure on training (88 per cent). However, these figures are based on a small sample, so actual percentages should be treated with caution. Other popular measures were employee relations indicators (such as number of grievances and tribunal cases), training days, cost to fill vacancies, time to fill vacancies, HR costs as a proportion of profit or total costs and time spent communicating with staff. Only 9 per cent of the organisatons surveyed measured productivity.

In terms of soft measures, IRS found that 85 per cent of the sample measured employee satisfaction, 72 per cent measured line manager satisfaction, 68 per cent measured senior manager satisfaction and 60 per cent measured customer satisfaction. Employee satisfaction was considered to be the most effective soft measure.

Such measures are frequently collected in an ad hoc manner, are not integrated or tied in with business strategy and may not result in action being taken. Below we look at some of the more popular measures in more detail.

Absence analysis and costing

For aggregate analysis the **absence rate** is the number of days of absence, that is, when attendance would have been expected, of all employees. The **absence percentage rate** is this figure divided by the total number of actual working days for all employees over the year, multiplied by 100. This simple percentage figure is the one most often used and enables the organisation's absence level to be compared with national figures, or those of other organisations in the same sector.

The **absence frequency rate** is the number of spells of absence over the period, usually a year. Comparing this and the absence percentage rate gives critical information about the type of absence problem that the organisation is experiencing.

Absence data, as well as enabling external comparisons, can be analysed by department, work-group, occupation, grade and so on. In this way the analysis will throw up problem areas, and additional analysis can be used to try to identify the causes of differing levels of absence in different parts of the organisation. The data may be supplemented by information from questionnaires or interviews with employees or line managers.

The purpose of producing this information is to understand the causes and extent of absence in order to manage it effectively. So, for example, such analysis may result in a new absence policy, employee communications about the impact of absence, appropriate training for line managers, changes to specific groups of jobs and the introduction of a new type of attendance system such as flexitime. The information provides a base for future monitoring. Absence data can be analysed further to provide benchmarks of 'high', 'medium' and 'low' absence levels in the organisation, and can be used to set improvement targets. This analysis can also be used to trigger specific management actions when an employee reaches different benchmark levels. For example, a trigger may be the number of days or number of spells per year or, as in the Bradford factor (*see* Figure 15.2 on p. 324 for the formula), a combination of both.

The costing of absence needs to have a wider focus than just the pay of the absent individual. Other costs include:

- line manager costs in finding a temporary replacement or rescheduling work;
- the actual costs of the temporary employee;
- costs of showing a temporary employee what to do;
- costs associated with a slower work rate or more errors from a temporary employee;
- costs of contracts not completed on time.

These costs can be calculated and provide the potential for productivity improvement.

Equal opportunities analysis

Equal opportunities analysis aims to provide an organisational profile of, most frequently, ethnic origin, gender, age and disability. The resulting percentages from this can be compared with national and local community figures to give an initial idea of how representative the organisation is. Further analyses break these figures down to compare them by department, job category and grade. It is in this type of analysis that startling differences are likely to be found, for example as shown in Figure 33.1.

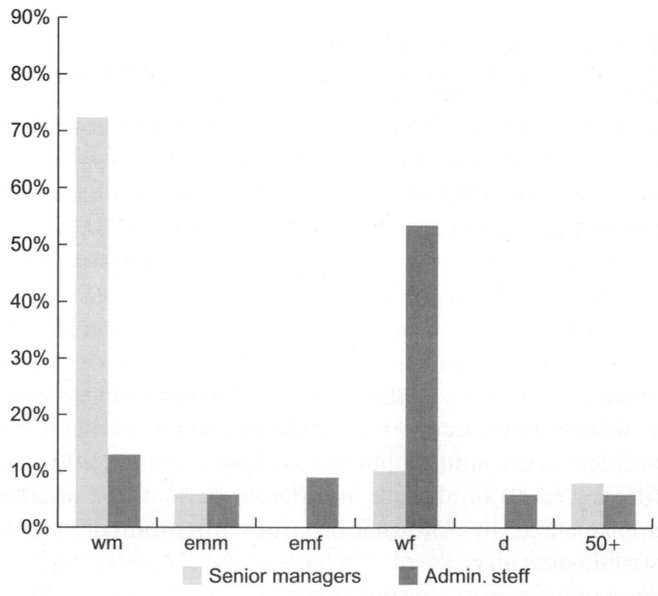

Figure 33.1 Breakdown of senior manager staff group and administrative staff group

The information gleaned can be used to:

- question the extent and spread of disadvantaged groups in the organisation;
- identify specific barriers to a more representative spread;
- formulate appropriate policy and action plans;
- set targets to be achieved and to monitor year on year compared with these base figures.

Other analyses can be carried out to show promotion, internal moves and secondment figures for disadvantaged groups compared with advantaged groups, for example, white males. Further mention is made of these and the recruitment system in the following section.

ACTIVITY 33.2

What metrics does your HR function calculate?
What is the purpose of each one?
How are the results translated into action?
To what extent are these measures related to business strategy?
To what extent are these measures integrated?

Turnover analysis and costing

We cover this aspect in Chapter 8 on Retention.

The workforce and organisational performance

There is a range of analyses which can relate the contribution of the workforce to organisational performance. These relationships can be used to control headcount, measure organisational effectiveness and compare this with that of similar organisations. The information can also be used to communicate to employees what their contribution is to the business. Turnover per employee and profit per employee can be calculated in order to monitor performance and to demonstrate to each employee the importance of cost consciousness. If an employee of an organisation employing 3,000 employees realises that profit per employee is only £900 this means far more to that individual than expressing profit as £2.7 million. Cost consciousness suddenly becomes important as the fragile and marginal nature of profits is demonstrated. A further calculation expresses the cost of employees in relation to the total costs of production. To work this out, turnover less profit (that is, the cost of production) is compared with employee costs (salary plus on-costs). The percentage of production costs accounted for by employees will vary markedly according to the nature of the business. For example, in some pharmaceutical businesses people costs will account for 70 per cent of all production costs (due to a heavy emphasis on research and development) whereas in a less people-intensive business, as found in other parts of the manufacturing sector, people costs may only account for around 15 per cent. Changes in the percentage of people costs over time would need to be investigated.

People costs are a good way of communicating to employees just how important they are to the success of the business.

WINDOW ON PRACTICE

HR survey: What do managers need from the function?

Cathy Cooper (2001) reports on how Fidelity International redesigned its annual manager survey so that it became a meaningful tool in helping the company to improve people management. The original survey which had been used for five years tended to be a 'popularity contest for HR'. The first stage in redesign was to investigate what the survey should focus on. To this end an external consultant was employed to carry out focus groups with HR staff to establish the strengths and weaknesses of the department. The survey manager then held one-to-one interviews with managers to establish their concerns. The interview data were then used to frame topics for the survey. The focus taken in the survey was on how well we (all managers, including HR) manage our people, and not on how well or badly HR is doing. The survey was designed to take 10 minutes to complete and asked respondents to identify the extent to which they agreed or disagreed with a number of statements. Respondents were invited to make any additional comments they wished. Some questions were retained, however, to get specific information on HR's performance. The survey was delivered by the company intranet to make responding easy. Of the 500 managers they invited to participate they received completed questionnaires from over half.

The results of the survey were used to develop 12 broad goals for the HR function with which individual objectives will be aligned. Senior managers have been involved in how the goals could best be met, and then HR directors and their teams in different locations will develop a project action plan.

Source: Summarised from C. Cooper (2001) 'Win by a canvass', *People Management*, Vol. 7, No. 2, 25 January, pp. 42–4.

Measures can be benchmarked externally against other similar organisations which would allow a meaningful comparison, such as competitors. They can also be benchmarked internally by comparing departments, different locations and so on. IRS (2002a) found that around one-third of the organisations it surveys regularly carried out external benchmarking and the same percentage regularly carried out internal benchmarking.

USING SCORECARDS AND OTHER FRAMEWORKS FOR MEASUREMENT

Considerable attention has been given to the use of scorecards, such as the balanced scorecard (Kaplan and Norton 1992) and, later, the HR scorecard (Becker *et al.*

2001), in linking people, strategy and performance. These are perhaps the best-known scorecards, but many different scorecards have been developed over the last decade or so. Such scorecards utilise a range of measures of HR which are viewed as critical to the success of the business strategy, and which move the process of measurement on from an ad hoc to a strategic and integrated approach. Kaplan and Norton widened the perspective on the measurement of business performance by measuring more than financial performance. Their premise is that other factors which lead to financial performance need to be measured to give a more rounded view of how well the organisation is performing. This means that measures of business performance are based on measures of strategy implementation in a range of areas. Kaplan and Norton identify three other areas for measurement in addition to financial measures: customer measures, internal business process measures and learning and growth measures. In each of these areas critical elements need to be identified and then measures devised to identify current levels and measure progress. Some organisations implementing this scorecard have developed the learning and growth area to include a wider range of HR measures.

Becker *et al.* (2001) argue that it is important to have a 'measurement system [that] convincingly showcases HR's impact on business performance' (p. 4), otherwise, they argue, the HR function cannot show how it adds value and risks being outsourced. The system they suggest focuses on 'HR architecture', and by this they mean the 'sum of the HR function, the broader HR system, and the resulting employee behaviours' (p. 1). This is therefore a broad view of HR measurement, as we discussed in the first section of this chapter. Becker and his colleagues have designed a seven-step process to clarify and measure HR's strategic influence:

Step 1. Clearly define business strategy in a way that involves discussing how the strategy can be implemented and communicated.

Step 2. Develop a business case for HR as a strategic asset explaining how and why HR can facilitate business strategy – Becker and his colleagues suggest how current research relating HR to firm performance can be useful here.

Step 3. Create a strategy map – which should involve managers across the organisation, and needs to address the critical strategic goals, identify the performance drivers for each goal, identify how progress towards goals can be measured, identify barriers to goal achievement, identify required employee behaviour for goal achievement, question whether the HR function is developing employee competencies and behaviours needed to meet the goals, and if this is not happening, what needs to change.

Step 4. Identify HR deliverables from the strategy map – which may include performance drivers and enablers; for example low turnover, high levels of specific competencies and so on may be needed to reduce product development time.

Step 5. Align HR architecture with the deliverables in step 4. Policies can be developed to result in these deliverables – for example policies encouraging low turnover may be supported by family-friendly and work-life balance policies, diversity policies, career development opportunities and so on.

Step 6. Design a strategic HR measurement system. This requires that valid measures of HR deliverables are developed. For example in specifying low turnover it would be important to identify which particular staff groups this applies to, whether voluntary turnover only is to be calculated, whether internal job moves are included and so on.

Step 7. Implement management by measurement – Becker and his colleagues suggest that once the measurement system has been developed this can then become a powerful management tool.

In designing measures Becker and his colleagues suggest that HR efficiency as well as deliverables need to be measured. Efficiency measures tend to be cost measures, for example cost per new hire, or HR cost per employee. They suggest that these are both lagging indicators. Leading indicators can also be measured. These are defined as measures of 'high performance work system' and HR system alignment. The high-performance work system appears to be defined in terms of best-practice-type measures, for example hours training received each year by each employee, or percentage of the workforce regularly undergoing annual appraisal. HR system alignment indicates the extent to which the high-performance work system is tailored to business strategy via supporting each HR deliverable. Useful lists of HR deliverables and efficiency measures can be found in Ulrich (1997).

An alternative framework for monitoring, measuring and managing human capital is the 'human capital monitor' and this has been developed in the UK by Andrew Mayo (2001). The human capital monitor is designed to connect the intrinsic value of the human capital in the organisation with the working environment. It includes processes and systems which impact on employees' behaviour together with the value that is created by people. As with the previous models discussed this is not specifically designed for the HR function to monitor itself. The model adds together the value of people as assets (box 1) and the motivation and commitment (box 2) to produce the people contribution to added value (box 3). The model is shown in Figure 33.2.

The first box in the model, people as assets, provides a method of balancing people costs with a measure of the value that they contribute. Mayo argues that calculating the value of people is important for four reasons. First, resourcing decisions should be about more than just cost; second, it important to understand relative values of individuals and teams; third, it helps make informed investment decisions showing the relative benefits of investing in people as opposed to other assets; and finally, it enables the company to monitor whether its talent is increasing or decreasing. To demonstrate the types of measures that Mayo suggests, we use the example of capability, where the following measures are provided: personal behaviour; business and professional know-how; network of contacts; qualifications and experience; attitudes and values. In terms of maximising human capital we will look at potential. Here Mayo suggests that success in acquisition could be measured by total human asset worth, average IAM (individual asset multiplier) of new recruits and the increase in strategically important core capabilities. The drivers for acquisition of potential include employer brand and acceptance rates, among others.

We turn now to the second box concerning motivation and commitment. Here Mayo suggests such measures as absence levels, satisfaction surveys, attrition rates and reasons for leaving, among others. He suggests five influencing factors as listed in the model, and for the work-group, for example, he proposes two measures: team assessments of working practices and a team stability index.

THE HUMAN CAPITAL MONITOR

People as assets		People motivation and commitment		People contribution to added value
Human asset worth = Employment costs × Individual asset multiplier (IAM)/1000		Measures – How successful are we?		The value added to each stakeholder
IAM = a function of • capability • potential • contribution • values alignment	+	**The work environment that drives success**	=	• Financial • Non-financial
Maximising human capital • Acquisition – How successful are we? • Retention • Growth – What drives success?		• Leadership • Practical support • The work-group • Learning and development • Rewards and recognition		• Current • Future

Figure 33.2 Mayo's human capital monitor (Source: Adapted from A. Mayo (2001) *The human value of the enterprise: Valuing people as assets – monitoring, measuring and managing*. London: Nicholas Brealey, p. 65.)

In the final box, people contribution to added value, Mayo suggest that the focus should be on wealth creation, which is a much broader concept than profit, as some of the wealth created can be reinvested in the business. To this end he compares a conventional income statement with a value-added financial statement, which goes beyond seeing people as just costs. In assessing current value Mayo suggests that work needs to be analysed into work which creates value and non-value added work (such as redoing work, duplication, computer downtime, cross-charging and so on), and that the percentage of each type of work needs to be a focus. He argues that building future value is dependent on innovation and that measures of this need to be derived.

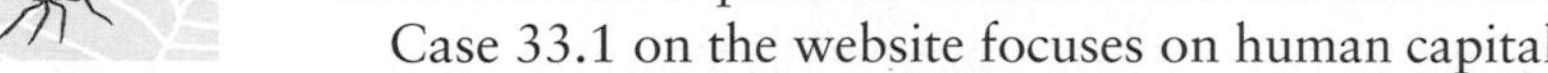

Case 33.1 on the website focuses on human capital.

EFFECTIVE AND EFFICIENT HR PROVISION

The literature has for some time been replete with articles about the decentralisation and devolution of HR management as methods of integrating HR activities with day-to-day line management. The thrust has been for the line to take ownership of HR activities, with HR specialists acting as a consultant, coach, facilitator and strategic partner. The advantages of this approach to restructuring HR activities and the issues in implementation have been dealt with in detail and we do not intend to rehearse these issues here. For further details *see*, for example, Hall and Torrington (1998). Emerging approaches to improve the efficiency and effectiveness of the HR function are outsourcing, HR service centres and e-HR.

Outsourcing

HR administration has typically been outsourced, for example pensions, payroll and recruitment. But more specialist aspects have been subject to outsourcing too, such as training and legal work. IDS (2003) argues that the delivery channels for outsourcing HR administration involve e-HR and HR service centres. We will deal with these separately, while recognising that there may be some overlap in approach.

The drivers for outsourcing HR are frequently quoted as reducing costs and improving service delivery. Outsourcing appears to encourage the measurement of the value of HR, and IDS (2003) suggests that this comes about through the need for service-level agreements and key performance indicators with a greater focus on customer satisfaction. Outsourcing has also been introduced as a vehicle for effecting changes that would be hard to implement internally. For example in large organisations outsourcing has been used to bring different parts of the organisation together to reduce costs, apply common standards and share best practice (*see*, for example, Pickard 2002), and provide access to innovative IT solutions. A further advantage that is claimed is that the internal HR function can now concentrate on driving the direction of HR rather than carry out more mundane tasks.

WINDOW ON PRACTICE

Prudential outsources HR in USA

Higginbottom (2002) reports on Prudential's move to outsource HR to Exault in the USA. Core administrative services, including payroll and benefits administration, have been transferred to Exault. Exault also manages an HR call centre, provides HR information services, and looks after employee data and records. In addition Exault will take responsibility for training. Exault argues that this will improve Prudential's HR processes, enhance services to employees and reduce costs. Michele Darling, executive vice-president for HR, suggests that as the deal provides efficiencies and a better costs structure this will enable the internal HR function to intensify its focus on strategic issues. The group has not said whether the same approach will be taken in the UK.

Source: Summarised from K. Higginbottom (2002) 'Prudential outsources HR in US', *People Management*, Vol. 8, No. 2, 24 January, p. 10.

However, time is needed to select and develop a relationship and trust with a service provider. Also Rippin and Dawson (2001) identify the importance of fit with the service provider and warn that organisations choosing to outsource in order to save costs should not expect immediate returns. Outsourcing the whole of HR is also a very different proposition from outsourcing differentiated activities, which has been happening in an ad hoc manner for a much longer time. Blackburn and Darwen Borough Council, for example, has outsourced all its HR to Capita, including strategic HR (IDS 2003), which is the one part that most organisations retain in-house.

ACTIVITY 33.3

We noted that outsourcing the whole of the HR function is a different proposition from outsourcing some specific aspects. In the context of your own organisation, or one that you are familiar with:

1 If you were to outsource some specific aspects of HR, what would they be and why have you chosen those aspects?

Or

What aspects of HR are already outsourced and how effective has this proved to be and why?

2 If you were to outsource the whole function what reactions would you anticipate from employees and line managers, why do you think they would react like this and what could be done to support them through this change?

Or

If your organisation has already outsourced the totality of HR how effective has this proved to be and why?

Some organisations have clearly experienced advantages from outsourcing, although many of these are based in the USA and there is a question as to the extent to which such an approach should be applied in the same way in the UK. Hammond (2002), on the basis of a recent survey, reports that firms in the UK are resisting outsourcing. He argues that BP experienced only limited success when it outsourced to Exault, and that outsourcing for such big companies is a different proposition from what it is for smaller organisations. This same survey found that managers have a number of fears concerned with outsourcing HR such as loss of control, loss of the personal touch and doubts about the quality and commitment of external staff. However, the research reported was commissioned by Northgate Information Solutions and this fact needs to be taken into account when interpreting the results, as this company has a product to sell. John Hofmeister, director of HR at the Royal Dutch/Shell group, attacks outsourcing as leading to the corrosion of HR departments, and he argues that only high levels of internal HR staffing can lead to and maintain high levels of HR practices (People Management 2002). In a slightly different vein Gratton (2003) argues that outsourcing combined with other trends such as devolution fragments the HR function, and she identifies a growing alienation between different providers (ousourcing agencies, line managers and remaining specialists in the HR function). She argues that HR would provide greater added value as a totality rather than the sum of the different fragments. Gratton proposed four mechanisms through which the function can be integrated to provide greater added value. IRS (2003) also suggests that such outsourcing has been dogged with many problems, to the extent that some organisations have brought HR back in-house.

In spite of any concerns, outsourcing is predicted to continue to increase, and in particular outsourcing overseas – sometimes referred to as ‘offshoring’, although in some cases the outsourcing may be to wholly owned subsidiaries or may be the movement of an internal service centre (Crabb 2003). India is a favoured destination but Eastern Europe is also popular. However, cultural and legal differences will inevitably restrict the range of activities that can be successfully outsourced in this way. The popularity of the outsourcing idea is underlined by the fact that the CIPD now runs a course entitled 'Outsourcing HR' to help specialists understand the procurement process.

Key issues of implementation involve a careful choice of partner so that there is sufficient fit, clear performance specifications, IT system compatibility, reassurance regarding the impact on HR staff, line managers and employees, promotion of new arrangements, good contract management and monitoring of performance.

Case 33.2 on the website focuses on HR outsourcing.

HR service centres

Some organisations argue that a better alternative to outsourcing is to use an HR service centre or shared service centre (*see*, for example, Pickard 2002). Shared service centres are sometimes referred to as partnership service centres or insourcing, depending on the circumstances. For example the Window on practice shows how Rotherham Borough Council has entered into a strategic partnership with BT.

WINDOW ON PRACTICE

Rotherham Brought Together (RBT)

IDS (2003) reports how Rotherham Borough Council and BT created RBT. RBT is responsible for HR administration and payroll, the management of IT functions, procurement, customer contact and revenues and budgets.

Five hundred council staff have been seconded to RBT on their existing terms and conditions, and new appointees will be on the same conditions. For their part BT has invested heavily in RBT, and will take the profit from the operation. However, after a certain level of profit has been achieved the profit will be shared with Rotherham BC.

RBT includes an integrated HR/payroll system, self-service HR through an intranet, and an HR service centre to deal with transactional and operational HR issues. The first port of call is intended to be the intranet and then the service centre, but for some issues such as discipline and grievance a specialist adviser will be made available.

Alongside the creation of RBT line managers have been given more responsibility for HR, and HR staff have been centralised, although some senior HR staff remain in Rotherham BC with a remit which includes strategy, policy, OD, and culture change, among other issues.

There is a plan to take on work from other clients in the future.

Source: Summarised from IDS (2003) *Outsourcing HR administration*, IDS Study Plus, Spring.

IDS (2003) suggests that developing an HR service centre is often the linchpin in a company's drive to achieve a more efficient form of HR delivery. IDS suggests that this is primarily achieved by streamlining and centralising routine HR processes and transactions. In addition such a service centre is usually the primary point of reference for line managers with HR queries. The benefits they identify are savings from lower transaction costs, the removal of unneeded duplication, a more consistent HR approach across the whole of a company and an HR service which is more customer focused and more responsive to business needs.

Service centres may be HR centres or may be a shared centre with other functions, such as IT or finance. Other terms used are HR call centre or client centre. In terms of operation many centres will have staff based in the 'back office' dealing with administration and transactions, and different staffing for the 'front office' where enquiries from line managers are handled. Alternatively staff may be organised in terms by specialist function or client group (IDS 2003). Staff at the service centre would have electronic access to personal employee details and HR policies and so on.

One of the advantages of such centres is the metrics that can be derived to assess their performance. Examples are call waiting time, call count, call length, time taken to resolve queries, accuracy and satisfaction measures from users. There is usually a system of escalation where queries can be fed up to the next level if the original call centre operator cannot resolve them.

WINDOW ON PRACTICE

HR service centres: task limits

Recruitment administration is a task that a service centre would be likely to take on, and IDS (2001b) provides an example of how this would work in practice. IDS suggests that:

Service centre staff would:

- Place advertisements
- Issue application forms
- Receive application forms
- Deal with candidate management
- Provide information for shortlisting and interviewing
- Arrange interviews and assessment dates
- Prepare and send offer and reject letters
- Draw up and send out contracts
- Request references
- Send out starter packs
- Enter new starters on records system
- Monitor equal opportunities

Line managers, perhaps supported by a local HR adviser, would:

- Determine the need for the vacancy
- Confirm/draw up job and person specifications
- Define selection and assessment processes
- Shortlist
- Carry out interviews
- Make the final selection decision
- Co-determine salary package

Source: Summarised from IDS (2001b) *HR Service Centres*, IDS Study, No. 707, April.

The problems with the service centre structure are that local knowledge and business solutions may be lost in the changeover, many low-level administrative roles are created with little potential for career development and there may be an obsession with measurement at the expense of service delivery.

e-HR

One of the difficulties with e-HR is that it can be defined in a wide range of ways. It can incorporate HR and corporate intranets with static information, interactive HR and corporate intranets, email-based initiatives and the internet. The emphasis here is on intranets.

As with other initiatives, much of the drive for such systems has come from the need to liberate the personnel function from its administrative tasks to allow it to focus on more strategic matters (Trapp 2001). Such systems are often introduced alongside the introduction of HR service centres, with the intention that the system should be the first port of call, before the service centre. In this way the pressure on service centres should be reduced in the long run. Different surveys have produced very different results concerning the extent of use (*see*, for example, Trapp 2001 compared with IRS 2002b), and we will not dwell on the figures. However, it is generally agreed that more sophisticated applications are still not very common and are most likely to be found in IT or related companies. IRS (2003) found that improvement in communications (73 per cent) was most frequently cited as the specific reason for introducing e-HR, followed by reduction of routine administration (60 per cent), compared with only 37 per cent looking specifically for cost savings. Tyler (2001) also suggests empowering employees as another reason for introduction.

In terms of static information intranets are likely to contain HR policies, rules and regulations, details of training courses, standard forms, staff handbooks, induction information and information on benefits.

ACTIVITY 33.4

We have referred to the 'loss of the personal touch' in the introduction to this discussion of these alternative means of providing HR services.

How important is 'the personal touch' to employees of today, and why do you think this is so?

More sophisticated systems include such features as the ability to update one's personal details (password access), reviewing and changing the flexible benefits that one has chosen, checking one's remaining leave entitlement and requesting leave, submitting expense claim forms, asking questions (such as pension projection figures), performance management and salary review tools. IRS (2002b) identifies three user groups of such systems: HR service centres or HR function, line managers and employees. In terms of employees such systems are often referred to as self-service or self-management systems.

Some of these applications will clearly require changes in the organisational culture. In addition there are concerns about the loss of the personal touch and security of information (Trapp 2001). There are also issues about the access to computers and the computer literacy of some staff. Some companies have introduced kiosks where computers can be used by a range of staff, but there are issues about the extent to which staff will prefer to use their coffee breaks booking holidays on the computer.

SUMMARY PROPOSITIONS

33.1 Measuring HR may involve direct measurements of the HR function's contribution, but there may also be wider measures of aspects of HR capital in the organisation which are influenced by all managers.

33.2 Ad hoc measures are likely to include absence and turnover analysis and equal opportunities monitoring, but these measures are frequently not strategically integrated and do not necessarily lead to action.

33.3 The balanced scorecard (Kaplan and Norton 1992), the HR scorecard (Becker *et al.* 2002) and the human capital monitor (Mayo 2001) have all been used as a framework for measuring the effectiveness and efficiency of HR. Such frameworks integrate measures and relate them to organisational strategy.

33.4 Outsourcing, service centres and e-HR are all present-day approaches to improving the added value of HR.

GENERAL DISCUSSION TOPICS

1 'Quantitative measures mean nothing. The way that questions are asked, the subjective understanding of what the question means, biased response patterns, and the way that data is analysed and presented, all mean that statistics can be made to say whatever the author of them wishes.' To what extent do you agree or disagree with this statement, and why?

2 To what extent do you agree with Linda Gratton's view that a fragmented HR function contributes less value than a fully integrated function? What evidence have you used to support this view?

FURTHER READING

Crabb, S. (2003) 'East India Companies', *People Management*, Vol. 9, No. 4, 20 February, pp. 28–32

Crabb describes the increasing number of organisations moving operations to the Indian subcontinent, and in this context reviews the extent to which HR will be swept along with this tide. Crabb also reviews the *compound growth rate* in all offshoring for HR activities, which appears to be greater than for other functional areas. Crabb notes that organisations report this issue as being politically sensitive.

IDS (2001a) *HR Intranets*, IDS Study, No. 713

This is a very useful guide to a wide range of HR intranet usage. The study explores the challenges of intranets, design, promotion required, content and application, and includes seven case studies: Shell, Argos, Cisco systems, Prudential, Ford, ICL and Cable and Wireless.

REFERENCES

Becker, B., Huselid, M. and Ulrich, D. (2001) *The HR Scorecard: Linking People, Strategy and Performance*. Boston: Harvard Business School Press.

Crabb, S. (2003) 'HR faces offshore boom', *People Management*, Vol. 9, No. 4, 20 February, p. 7.

Cooper, C. (2001) 'Win by a canvass', *People Management*, Vol. 7, No. 2, 25 January, pp. 42–4.

Gratton, L. (2003) 'The Humpty Dumpty Effect', *People Management*, Vol. 9, No. 9, 1 May, p. 18.

Hall, L. and Torrington, D.P. (1998) *The Human Resource Function: The dynamics of change and development*. London: Financial Times Pitman Publishing.

Hammond, D. (2002) 'Firms resist outsourcing', *People Management*, Vol. 8, No. 12, 13 June, p. 8.

Higginbottom, K. (2002) 'Prudential outsources HR in US', *People Management*, Vol. 8, No. 2, 24 January, p. 10.

IDS (2001a) *HR Intranets*, IDS Study, No. 713, August.

IDS (2001b) *HR Service Centres*, IDS Study, No. 707, April.

IDS (2003) *Outsourcing HR administration*, IDS Study Plus, Spring.

IRS (2002a) 'Measure for measure', *IRS Employment Review*, No. 754, June, pp. 8–13.

IRS (2002b) 'e-HR: evolution or revolution?' *IRS Employment Review*, No. 764, 25 November, pp. 8–14.

IRS (2003) 'HR goes strategic', *IRS Employment Review*, No. 733, 4 April, pp. 9–14.

Kaplan, R. and Norton, D. (1992) 'The balanced scorecard – measures that drive performance', *Harvard Business Review*, January–February, pp. 71–9.

Mayo, A. (2001) *The human value of the enterprise: Valuing people as assets – monitoring, measuring and managing*. London: Nicholas Brealey.

Pickard, J. (2002) 'A source of inspiration?' *People Management*, Vol. 8, No. 14, 11 July, pp. 36–42.

People Management (2002) 'HR departments are corroded by the extent of outsourcing', *People Management*, Vol. 8, No. 20, 10 October, p. 10.

Rippin, S. and Dawson, G. (2001) 'How to outsource the HR function', *People Management*, Vol. 7, No. 19, 27 September, pp. 42–3.

Trapp, R. (2001) 'Of mice and men', *People Management*, Vol. 7, No. 13, 28 June, pp. 24–32.

Tyler, E. (2001) 'The click step', *People Management*, Vol. 7, No. 8, 19 April, pp. 50–2.

Ulrich, D. (1997) 'Measuring human resources: an overview of practice and a prescription for results', *Human Resource Management*, Vol. 36, Fall, pp. 303–20.

An extensive range of additional materials, including multiple choice questions, answers to questions and links to useful websites can be found on the Human Resource Management Companion Website at **www.pearsoned.co.uk/torrington**.

INTERACTIVE SKILL 7: CHAIRING MEETINGS

Part VII has been a mixture of topics having in common the single feature that they potentially affect all of the functional areas dealt with in the earlier parts of the book. For that reason our examination of an interactive skill now considers an activity that is dealing with coordination in a rather different way: making meetings work. Meetings do not constitute the whole of management but they are an inescapable part of the management process and they are frequently less successful than they should be. Leading, or chairing, meetings is a challenging skill but a rewarding aspect of human resource management. Chairing meetings is also a position that is associated with authority. Company boards, benches of magistrates, Cabinet committees, employment tribunals, political parties, debating societies are among the many activities that are led by the person in the chair. Professors in universities are appointed to chairs, not because they are too weary or lazy to stand up, but because the occupation of a chair represents authority.

WINDOW ON PRACTICE

In courts of law there is a standard opening to proceedings whereby everyone present stands for the entry of the judge or the magistrates. If there is more than one person on the bench, the chair for the central person usually has a higher back than the others to emphasise the authority of the office that this person holds.

The objectives of this Focus on skills are to:

1 Review some of the different types of meeting HR people have to chair

2 Explain the stages of running a meeting: preparation, conduct of the meeting itself, follow-up and implementation of proposals

Types of meeting

HR specialists have many meetings to chair, including selection panels, meetings with union officials, health and safety committees, job evaluation groups and many more. It is not sufficient just to know why a meeting is being held for it to be a success: the processes by which a meeting works have to be understood as well. In one of our research projects 433 meetings were observed, and many showed the chair to have such limited understanding of the basic mechanics of meetings that there was inadequate discussion, understanding and action about important matters. Poor meetings not only fail to achieve objectives, but also do harm, as members become frustrated about lack of progress or about not being able to get their point of view across. It is not just the fault of the person in charge: all participants have to learn meeting mechanics. The analogy of the orchestra is apt. The conductor is responsible for the final quality of the coordinated act, but every instrumentalist has to make a distinctive, but not individualistic, contribution that blends with all the others.

We have to pay careful attention to the details of running the meeting. Good intentions and the importance of the matter to be considered are not enough on their own. The person in charge takes the blame for things not being right. Those who feel overlooked or outmanoeuvred are merciless with those who have overlooked them, however unintentional this was by the person in the chair. The person in charge may feel very uncomfortable and may lose respect in the eyes of colleagues, but something is still usually achieved: catharsis for group members and some information exchange.

The basic necessities are a clear format, purpose and preparation, with the leader being in control. Those attending the meeting can then concentrate on content rather than fretting about the way the meeting is being conducted. People will only attend and make a success of meetings they see as useful.

WINDOW ON PRACTICE

An ICI Plant Manager has on the wall of his office a framed citation confirming that he is a full member of 'The Institution of Meetings Engineers'. This is obviously a spoof, non-existent body dreamt up by a few engineers who felt that most meetings were a waste of time. The inscription included phrases such as, 'Members shall attend all meetings called, regardless of their value . . . Any member falling asleep shall have membership suspended until he wakes up . . . A member finding a meeting useful should send a full report to the General Secretary of the Institution before seeking medical attention.'

Many readers will empathise with those comments, having attended meetings which seem pointless, or boring, or too long or all three. People who can chair meetings effectively are a rare breed, highly regarded by their colleagues.

Preparation

Making effective arrangements for a meeting help it to be an effective meeting. It is useful to run through a series of check questions.

Who should attend the meeting?

A large group will ensure that a wide range of interests is represented, so that there should be few problems of people complaining that they were excluded. Large numbers are usually appropriate when pressing matters of major importance are to be discussed and a lot of people have to be informed quickly. The problems are that the more people who attend, the more likely it is that the business will grind to a halt. Also the more people who attend, the less likely it is that there will be any useful discussion.

A small group makes discussion easier and more productive as there are fewer people competing to have their say and it is easier for the person in the chair to blend together a range of contributions in finding a consensus.

Ideally you want people either who have expertise in the matter being discussed or who have a stake in it. This ensures focus for the discussion and should help outcomes, as there is an old axiom that people will support that which they have helped to create. Observers or 'freeloaders' can be a nuisance as they do not have the discipline of having to deliver on whatever is agreed and may therefore become more concerned to make an impression as someone with bright ideas rather than thinking of practical solutions.

You may want a variety of personalities and styles to ensure a lively discussion. There is discussion of this in Chapter 13.

What is the brief or terms of reference of the meeting?

Does this meeting have the power to take a decision, or to make a recommendation, or simply to exchange information? All of these are equally valid objectives for a meeting, but it helps to be clear on this basic question of what sort of meeting it is.

Sometimes there is a limit to how wide the discussion can usefully range. Some aspects will be outside the competence of the meeting and such discussion could distract those present from dealing with the matter they should be discussing. An example is where a decision has already been made elsewhere that cannot be changed. If it has been decided elsewhere that a plant should close, there will then be a number of other meetings to decide how that decision should be implemented. It is rarely appropriate for a management meeting to try to get that decision changed. If members spend time deploring the decision that has been made, it might be worth while if they then are able to move on, having expressed their feelings.

As well as explicit terms of reference that define the range of discussion, there may well be some conclusions that would be unacceptable. The chair needs to have sufficient common sense to be aware of what these are and to whom they would not be acceptable, so that they can either be ruled out in discussion or questioned if suggested.

What should the agenda be?

There are two questions about the agenda, one more obvious than the other: what do we need to consider, and in what order?

The content of the agenda is usually drafted and proposed by the Chair or, in more formal meetings, the Chair in consultation with the Secretary. The topics for consideration need to be clearly described, so that members of the group can come to the meeting with a clear understanding of them and with a focus on the key issues. There is a risk in putting too many items on the agenda so that some are rushed, or put off to another occasion.

The sequence of items can be affected by the consideration of which chicken needs to come before which egg. Getting the right things early on the agenda can make it easier to resolve later matters provided they are in the right order; otherwise decisions are half-made and then deferred 'until we have dealt with item x'.

With meetings where there are minutes to review, matters arising and any other business, this can take up a lot of time unless there is careful planning.

ACTIVITY VII.1

Reflect on a meeting you attended recently that you felt was not well organised and run. Were the terms of reference for the meeting clear to all attending? Was the sequence of items on the agenda conducive to a successful meeting? Would the meeting have been more effective if the sequence had been different?

What about the physical location and arrangements?

How often have you attended a meeting where one or more of the following occur:

- Two people do not come because they were not told about it (or so they say).
- Three people arrive late because they could not find the room.

- Two of the late arrivals immediately leave to try to borrow chairs from another room because there are not enough.
- Coffee arrives ten minutes after the meeting has started and is served (or distributed) by catering assistants who swap comments with each other in loud voices such as, 'One more down here, Flo'.
- Several people mutter that they had specifically asked for tea, whereupon Flo produces a docket and reads out what it says so as to clear Flo and her colleague of any responsibility for the fact that tea has not been provided.
- After half an hour a succession of people arrive for a completely different meeting, because the room has been double-booked (or so they say. Probably they forgot to book it. You're sure that *you did* book it, aren't you?).
- The room is noisy, too hot or too cold, the wrong shape or in the wrong place, and the toilets are miles away.

Incidents like these can wreck a meeting, or at least send the Chair into convulsions, yet most of them can be avoided with good organisation, so that you merely have to contend with the people who have brought the wrong papers or do not know what is going on as they have not opened their email since last month.

What is the meeting for?

The person leading the meeting needs a clear view of what type of meeting it is going to be. This will affect the way it is run and the way in which those attending are asked to participate.

The meeting may be *to convey information*. Then the sole focus is on the Chair, who is passing on information, or analysis or news to a gathering of those who need to know. The only role for others attending the meeting is to listen, perhaps ask questions and probably mutter explanations and reiterations to each other to check their understanding. The reason for holding a meeting for this purpose rather than distributing a memorandum is to give the opportunity for further clarification through questions; there is also the symbolic impact of information being passed on personally rather than impersonally. Meetings are therefore usually held to convey information of weight and significance.

If a meeting is *to share information* the Chair is the coordinator rather than the fount of all wisdom. A case conference is a typical example and the Chair needs skill to elicit constructive participation, encourage a free flow of information at the same time as preventing such a free flow that the meeting becomes chaotic and loses any sense of direction.

A meeting *to make a decision* will have a different style again. The expertise needed to make the right decision is distributed among the members of the group, so that much of the time is spent sharing information, but there has to be joint ownership of, or support for, the decision that is eventually made. A board meeting is the obvious example and the actual dynamics of the encounter itself will vary according to the relative status and authority of those present. The Chair may be so dominant that the meeting is to win the support of members to a decision that is already made. In other situations it is necessary for a consensus to be identified as the discussion develops so that it can be articulated for everyone to accept or modify until it wins general acceptance and commitment. Some decisions are reached by voting.

Although these are not common in management meetings, it is still essential that the Chair moves to a vote only when a consensus is apparent. A majority of one is scarcely a majority at all and talking should continue until the weight of opinion is more substantial.

Conduct of the meeting itself

How can contributions be stimulated and controlled?

For each item on the agenda, the Chair needs to consider:

- Who has something to say?
- How can I get them to say it?
- How can I keep the long-winded brief?
- When should I nudge the meeting towards a decision/the next item?

Few people are accustomed to expressing a point of view in a meeting, and most are likely to find it inhibiting. They speak best when asked to do so, and when speaking on something about which they are knowledgeable. Leaders of meetings get contributions by asking people to speak, picking up non-verbal cues of a desire to speak or reaction to what someone else has said. Statements of fact rather than expressions of opinion are the easiest way for people to make their first contribution. Experienced members of groups can help the less experienced by 'shaping' the clumsy or over-emotional comments of their colleagues and agreeing with them (for example: 'I would like to agree with what Hilary was saying and make the further point . . .' NOT, 'I think Hilary was trying to say . . .').

Inexperienced leaders of meetings sometimes show their worry about losing control by constantly emphasising the limited time available, but this makes it harder for people to make coherent contributions. People speak more effectively and come to the point more quickly when not under time pressure.

Curbing the excesses of the verbose is a true test of chairing skill. Making a succinct and focused contribution is a competence not found often among people attending meetings, so the Chair has to be skilled not only in eliciting contributions, but also in closing people down when they are running out of control. Here are some suggestions:

- Use eye contact with the speaker to indicate encouragement or discouragement. When you begin to lose interest, or become mildly irritated, the speaker will receive that silent message and respond to it.
- For those who will not respond, use more direct signals, such as looking away or looking anxiously at your watch.
- Use focus questions. The speaker will be rambling on and on, so you focus what is being said by interrupting with a question to focus the speaker and to elicit an answer that is likely to be brief. Examples are:

> 'How long will it take for X's performance to improve?'
> 'What will it cost?'
> 'Have you got it cleared?'

Bringing people in

An aspect of control is finding ways to bring people into the discussion at the time when their contribution is most appropriate. Ways to do it are like this:

- Pick out someone who you think should have a relevant or constructive comment to make and invite them: 'What is your view, Henry?' or 'I wonder if Sheila could help us with the exact figures' or, 'Well I know that Harry has direct experience of this sort of problem'.
- Pick out someone whose body language indicates a potential willingness to speak. This might be a raised hand, or an obviously angry reaction to a comment from someone else, a worried expression, a vigorous nod of agreement or a sudden change in someone's demeanour showing that they have just had a brainwave. The tricky thing is to decide who to bring into the discussion when, bearing in mind that people raising their hands or looking angry will have to have their say eventually.

Keeping it going

A meeting is best chaired when the Chair takes part constantly in the discussion, not necessarily expressing an opinion, nor declining to do so, but watching the pattern develop and helping everyone to see the pattern and concentrate on it.

- Summarise sparingly, but summarise well. It is pointless to summarise every individual contribution, as the contributors will not see that their own, crystal-clear, succinct comments need any summarising from anyone else. Summarising is needed when there are a number of contributions that have to be pulled together and a pattern found.
- An exception to the last sentence is where someone has not expressed themselves at all well, and is prepared to acknowledge it: 'I have not put that very clearly, but do you see what I am driving at?' Because you have been listening closely, you are able to move things forward by saying something like, 'Well what I got from that was . . . Have I got it right?' The person will then confirm that you got it right or will modify it. Either way they will be grateful to you. Do not say, 'I think what you were trying to say was . . .' That shows you to be patronising and the other person to be inadequate.
- Be ready to summarise where the discussion has reached, but do not summarise in search of a conclusion until you are confident that there is at least a partial consensus among all those present. Picking the right time is risky but unavoidable. If you go for a conclusion too quickly, you may not carry the meeting with you and you seriously undermine your necessary authority. Leaving it too late makes everyone fed up because things are dragging on. People grumble about meetings, but they rarely grumble about the (very few) meetings that are well run.
- Where things are really difficult, try getting a series of partial solutions. This is trying to split up an issue into parts and identifying a part where there appears to be general agreement and confirming that with the rest of the group, even if it is conditional on some other problem being resolved later. This helps the group by giving everyone a sense of some agreement and progress. Once there are two or three small matters on which there is agreement, it is surprising how much more progress can be made.

And what about your own input?

The person chairing the meeting is not simply enabling everyone else to have their say, like the Speaker of the House of Commons. There is usually a strong personal contribution to be made, often a leading contribution. People will want to hear what you have to say, maybe looking to you for a lead, but you still need to carry them with you.

There are basically two alternative approaches: playing the waiting game or leading from the front. Playing the waiting game is setting up the discussion of different points by a brief, summary introduction of the issue and eventually shaping the discussion with your own views and reaction. Leading from the front is setting out your position and then inviting suggestions. Neither is better than the other; they are simply different approaches that suit different situations and people.

Winding it up

Finally the Chair sums things up by reiterating the points upon which agreement has been reached and the nature of that agreement. There may well be further points of clarification and even argument, but the Chair has to nail down what people will accept and commit to. Equally important is to sum up the remaining points of disagreement, again with as much succinct clarity as possible. This is when you might just get your lucky break, because your summary might make someone realise that they really have been a bit petty and it is time for a magnanimous gesture. Also someone may have been doggedly hanging on to a position in the hope of movement elsewhere and is now prepared to shift because they are simply not going to win their argument. No one likes to be the reason for a group failing to agree.

ACTIVITY VII.2

On the basis of the suggestions in the last few pages formulate some forms of words that would be effective for your own personal style in various aspects of chairing a meeting, such as:

Stimulating and controlling contributions.
Curbing the verbose.
Bringing people in.
Keeping it going.
Making your own input.

Members of the group need to disperse feeling that their time has been well spent and that they had their day, knowing what has been agreed and what is outstanding, and knowing what happens next.

Follow-up

When the meeting has finished, the leader of the meeting still has work to do.

Minutes or report of the meeting

Formal meetings have minutes. Less formal meetings have notes. Informal meetings may not have any agreed record at all, but people will still have made jottings in their diary, on a clipboard or in the margin of the agenda. You have no control over what notes people at the meeting make for their own use, but the way you run the meeting will, of course, affect what they write.

The more formal minutes or notes will be written by the Secretary, if there is one, or by the Chair. The purpose is to produce a stimulus to appropriate action, not to write historical analysis. Sometimes it is important to describe the discussion and issues, so that those not in attendance can understand not simply what was agreed but at least some of the reasoning. In other cases it is sufficient simply to list the action points and who is responsible for following them through.

Activity VII.3 has the framework of an administrative drill for a committee secretary to follow. To make this illustration concrete we are assuming a meeting once a month on Day 28.

ACTIVITY VII.3

Day	**Phase One: MINUTES AND PRELIMINARIES**
1, 2	Write draft of minutes for yesterday's meeting, including notes of action items.
5	Clear minutes with Chair and confirm date and time of next meeting.
6, 7	Type, copy and distribute minutes.
10	Book room for next meeting.
	Phase Two: AGENDA
18	Ask committee members for items to be included on next agenda.
21	Discuss order of agenda and inclusion/deferment of items with Chair. Suggested sequence:
(a)	Announcements (apologies, introduction of new members, Chair's points).
(b)	Minutes of previous meeting and matters arising, where matter involves brief report. Matters arising for further discussion to be separate agenda items.
(c)	Items requiring decision but involving little controversy.
(d)	Most difficult item. (possible break)
(e)	Next most difficult item.
(f)	Items requiring discussion but not decision.
(g)	Easy items.
(h)	Any other business.
(i)	Provisional date of next meeting.
	Phase Three: RUN-UP
22	Circulate agenda and other papers to members, with note of date, time and venue.
26	Check seating, catering, visual aids. Collate all papers, past minutes, apologies.
28	Attend meeting and take notes for minutes.

Implementation of proposals

The meeting will have ended with general understanding that various actions would follow. Some of these will follow at once, as people scurry away to make their phone calls or look up information. Other actions will be forgotten unless there is a reminder. This is where the circulation of the minutes can be useful. Other actions will probably need the Chair to push them along and pull together actions by different people as the situation changes in the days after the meeting.

SUMMARY PROPOSITIONS

VII.1 Chairing meetings is an aspect of management that is crucial to making and implementing management decisions.

VII.2 Key aspects of preparing for a meeting are: who should attend, what is the brief, what is the agenda, what about physical location and arrangements, what is the meeting for: to convey information, to share information or to make a decision?

VII.3 Key features of conducting the meeting itself are: how contributions can be stimulated and controlled, bringing people in, keeping it going, making your own input and winding it up.

VII.4 An administrative drill for a meeting secretary deals with minutes and preliminaries, agenda and run-up.

GENERAL DISCUSSION TOPICS

1 What advantages and drawbacks do you see in an arrangement where everyone takes it in turn to chair a meeting of a particular group?

2 Why do so many people complain about the amount of time they spend in meetings?

3 To what extent could video conferencing or a web-based chat room be an alternative to a conventional meeting?

FURTHER READING

Hutton, W. and Giddens, A. (2000) *On the Edge: Living with Global Capitalism*. London: Jonathan Cape
Combines journalistic incisiveness with distinguished scholarship. An interesting European contrast to the American Stiglitz (*see* below).

Nugent, H. (2004) 'Pensioners forced back to work', *The Times*, 5 February

Stiglitz, J.E. (2002) *Globalisation and its Discontents*. New York: Norton
Provides a clear analysis of the problems facing current patterns of globalisation in business.

Taylor, R. (2003) 'Generation Next', *People Management*, Vol. 9, No. 18
A quick summary of the Future of Work programme is a helpful starter to looking on the website below.

WEB LINKS

The Future of Work programme of research has a great and varied output. Details are at www.leeds.ac.uk/esrcfutureofwork
The International Labour Organisation is at www.ilo.org

Another international body is the World Federation of Personnel Management Associations at www.wfpma.com

A selection of national bodies is:
Australian Human Resources Institute at www.ahri.com.au
British Chartered Institute of Personnel and Development at www.cipd.co.uk
Hong Kong Institute of Human Resource Management at www.hkihrm.org
Japanese Society for Human Resource Management at www.jshrm.org
United States Society for Human Resource Management at www.shrm.org

REFERENCES

ILO (1944) *Income Security Regulations*. Geneva: International Labour Office.

Economic and Social Research Council, *The Future of Work*. Details are at: www.leeds.ac.uk/esrcfutureofwork.

REVIEW OF PART VII

This final part of the book has covered some diverse topics, having in common the fact that they cannot be pigeon-holed in a specific area of HR practice like those of Parts II–VI. They are also issues that have come to the fore of consideration more recently than the main areas of HR work, where practice is long established, no matter how often it has to be modified and brought up to date. Another common feature is that they cannot be parcelled up and 'passed to Personnel'. They are aspects of management that have an HR dimension and indicate the fact that HRM is increasingly a part of all management that cannot be just dumped somewhere, although the need for specialised, expert input will grow and some administrative aspects should sensibly be collected together.

As with everything else we have looked at, there are important social and political aspects to the first three chapters on the international dimension, ethics and work-life balance, while the measurement of HR effectiveness almost implies questioning the value of everything that has gone before in this book, and chairing meetings is a skill that all managers need.

Where do we go to from here? Futurology is a flawed science, but there are some questions with which to close.

How will international HRM develop?

We have made several references to globalisation, but the extent to which this will be the future framework for international HRM is not clear. The social and political implications of globalisation are such that there is a strong, worldwide resistance to it. If finance ministers of major economies meet, they will have to endure excessive security and massive public demonstrations from people seeking to prevent the destabilising effect of the way in which financial markets work and the inequalities of income between the richer countries and developing countries. This is often accompanied by objections to capitalism and to the proliferation of Western values.

Within the European Union there is an attempt to control the more destructive effects of international financial markets, so this could lead to some stability within the Eurozone and beyond, but it depends on political aspirations of member states being curbed in the interest of the greater good. This may be too much to ask. As the EU enlarges, there are matters with a direct bearing on HR in the freer movement of labour around the zone, but the stronger economies face a paradox in needing immigration, but not all immigrants. The relatively low birth rate in Western Europe, with a corresponding increase in the number of older citizens, produces a demand for immigrants with useful practical skills. At the same time there is a reluctance bordering on paranoia to avoid immigration by people 'who will be a burden on the state'. So there is the paradox: those needing asylum become increasingly unwelcome, while those with useful skills should probably be encouraged to remain in their home countries to develop those struggling economies.

How will the ethical questions for HRM evolve?

Many ethical questions in HRM for the future are closely associated with the international dimension. What are the implications for Western capitalism of the rise of confidence and assertiveness in Islam? This is not simply a question for politicians; it is a challenge to HR managers in how they respond to issues such as the provision of prayer facilities and time off for religious festivals. It is a matter of how well prepared employees are to go and work in countries where the Western ethic is not dominant, and how well incipient racism is handled at home as well as abroad. The ESRC research programme on the Future of Work, referred to earlier in this book, raises a number of such issues. Satisfaction with work decreased during the 1990s, despite generally higher living standards and average job tenure being longer that it was in the previous decade. This is popularly attributed to longer hours and increased stress, although that seems an overly simplistic explanation. HR people always want to make the most of the input from the resourceful humans they employ and an important prerequisite is that those employed should be satisfied with their part of the bargain in the employment contract. The law may be able to deliver on specific human rights that are a compensation for having to work, such as pay, hours, holidays and union representation, but the law does not work well in delivering job satisfaction. In the opening chapter we offered a philosophy for human resource management that included:

> Only by satisfying the needs of the individual contributor will the business obtain the commitment to organisational objectives that is needed for organisational success, and only by contributing to organisational success will individuals be able to satisfy their personal employment needs. It is when employer and employee – or business and supplier of skills – accept this mutuality and reciprocal dependence that human resource management is exciting, centre stage and productive of business success.

That is tough to ask of any HR person, yet nothing less will do. The Future of Work programme also concluded that most workplaces do not pursue HR management techniques. By now readers will appreciate that HRM is much, much more than *techniques*. The continuing ethical question is, as it has been for over a century, how to achieve efficiency with justice and how to combine performance with satisfaction.

How will the work-life balance change?

Work-life balance is an ethical question as well as an efficiency issue. This, of course, is a combination that extends to most HR work, but the Future of Work programme tells us that family-friendly policies are few and rarely amount to more than the legal minimum, despite the clear advantages found in businesses that adopt them with enthusiasm and commitment to their success.

A slightly different aspect of work-life balance is in the length of working life. Although there was a general tendency through the last half of the twentieth century for people to retire earlier, this has eased in the last decade as the associated costs have become so substantial. The gradual raising of the official retirement age for women in the UK symbolised this change. The point at which people end their working life is obviously closely linked with the level of pensions and the standard of living they will then enjoy, as the expectations of retirement have risen sharply. In 1944 the International Labour Office defined the age of retirement simply as:

> The prescribed age should be that at which persons commonly become incapable of efficient work, the incidence of sickness and invalidity becomes heavy, and unemployment, if present, is likely to be permanent. (ILO 1944)

Sixty years later none of us is satisfied with that picture of retirement being a time of living in the shadows, incapable, unwell and probably not wanted. Our expectations have risen, with ideas of early retirement from choice, 'while you're still young enough to enjoy it', and an expectation that retirement should not necessarily be a time for penny-pinching, but a time to reap the rewards from one's work and to do things that there was never time for before. It is now seen more as a beginning than an end, and consequently the pensions that support this new beginning are seen as more important at an earlier age than before. Helen Nugent (2004), reporting on research carried out for a major bank, claims that nearly 3 million pensioners in the UK are returning to work because they cannot afford to live on their retirement pension, although very few work more than a modest number of hours a week. Other commentators argue that it is unfair that people should be obliged to relinquish full-time work simply because they have reached an arbitrary age. For whatever reason, the balance between years spent working and later years spent not working is likely to be an interesting HR issue in the future.

These are just three of the daunting challenges and exciting prospects ahead of HRM and, as we saw in the last chapter, HR will have to deliver and the effectiveness of its delivery will have to be measurable. It is a twin challenge: to meet reasonable 'bottom line' expectations of contribution to the financial viability of the business, whether public, private or voluntary, and to meet the human expectations of those who work in the business and those outside the business who expect it to provide employment, social responsibility and economic growth. In the twenty-first century membership of CIPD, the British professional body, stands at a record 120,000 and growing. If HR does not deliver, that number will stop growing.

Part VII CASE STUDY PROBLEM

Morris and Young

Morris and Young Associates is a training and development consultancy that started trading in 2004. It is based in a town in Shropshire and works with organisations across the West Midlands of the UK. With thirty years' experience between them of both training and the care field, Felix Morris and Bill Young undertake assignments for all manner of organisations, but their special strengths are, first, a detailed knowledge and experience of social care and, second, an expertise in electronic assessment for NVQs.

NVQs were introduced in Chapter 17, where the comment was made that they have not been universally popular in the early years since their introduction. Care is an area where the take-up has been appreciably higher than the national average, partly because of the large number of people working in the field who have not previously had the opportunity to gain qualification.

Morris and Young provide training in a number of areas that will be familiar to all readers of this book, such as leadership and motivation, interviewing, recruitment and selection, performance management and supervisory skills. They are also very busy with internal verification, which is an integral part of NVQ training and uses some of the methods of measuring HR effectiveness that were set out in Chapter 33. Some aspects of their technical expertise in the care field, such as life story work and handling aggressive behaviour, might have applications elsewhere. Samples of their material on personal development are included on the website for this book. It is based on the method of transactional analysis (*see* Stewart and Jaines 1987) developed by Eric Berne (1966), which has been used rather differently in management development programmes for many years.

Required

1. In what circumstances might you use a new consultancy like this rather than approach a well-established national or international business?
2. How would you relate their expertise to the needs of your business and what further information would you need before approaching them?
3. In what areas (if any) do you think Morris and Young should develop their offerings to be of value outside the caring professions?
4. What is the place of consultants in the future of HRM?

References

Berne, E. (1966) *Games People Play*. Harmondsworth, Middlesex: Penguin.

Stewart, I. and Jaines, V. (1987) *TA Today: A New Introduction to Transactional Analysis*. New York: Life Space Publishing.

www.morrisyoung.net (website of Morris and Young).

Part VII EXAMINATION QUESTIONS

1. In what ways does the expansion of the European Union in 2004 affect human resource management in a member state? Identify a particular member state in which to base your answer.
2. What are the practical implications of 'think globally: act locally'?
3. To what extent can HR managers act ethically within the culture of an organisation that does not always encourage the ethical standards that the HR manager holds?
4. A notice on the staff noticeboard in a British company reads as follows:

   'Service engineers always put customer needs first. If this sometimes involves parking in a restricted area, the company will reimburse the engineer the full cost of any fine that is imposed.'

   What is your view of this explicit invitation to break the law?
5. Family-friendly policies to ensure work-life balance could be seen as unfair as they provide more benefits for those with children than for those without. Do you agree?
6. To what extent can the effectiveness of the HR function be measured by quantitative methods?
7. 'Human resource management is an integral part of the work of everyone in a managerial post, so having a separate HR function meddles and dilutes responsibility.' How would you counter that point of view?
8. 'Human resource management is the essential lubricant of the organisational machine and can therefore only be judged on its long-term effectiveness.' To what extent do you agree with this view?

Glossary

The terms in this glossary have been taken selectively from the text. Rather than repeating definitions that are already in the text, we have selected those terms which are neologisms that may not appear in a dictionary, or are invented words, such as outsourcing, which do not yet appear in a dictionary. We also include terms, such as bureaucracy, which require more interpretation than we have provided in the text.

Emboldened words have their own entry in the glossary.

Aims. *See* **Mission.**

Benchmarking. Originally a benchmark was a mark on a work bench that could be used to measure off a standard size. This idea of comparative measurement is used in HRM to describe the process of checking some aspect of work in one's own business against an external standard, such as the average number of days lost through absence across the working population as a whole, or in a particular industry, by age, occupation, gender and so forth. It is slightly different from 'yardstick', which is literally a measuring stick a yard long (i.e. just under one metre). This is sometimes used as a rough and ready measure for some aspect of management effectiveness, but it lacks the dimension of external comparison.

Best fit/Fit. In many fields of human endeavour there is an aim to find and implement the one best way, or the right way of doing things. An alternative is to work out the best way of doing things in this or that situation. There is no single approach or method that is always right.

Bottom line. A term derived from accountancy, where it is the final total in a profit and loss statement or other financial document. In management generally it is used as the ultimate criterion or most important factor: financial viability.

Brand. A term taken from marketing to describe a company or product name that is very distinctive and powerful. Examples are Coca-Cola, Microsoft, Rolls Royce or Virgin. It was illustrated by the retail director of a fashion chain who said, 'If I buy a ready meal from X and I don't like it, I take it back. If I buy it from Marks & Spencer, either I haven't followed the instructions or there is something wrong with my cooker.' To HR people the company brand can be very important in matters of **commitment** and **recruitment.**

Bureaucracy has become almost a term of abuse, describing rigidity, lack of responsiveness by staff, lack of willingness to take responsibility and too much emphasis on the rules. It is, however, a time-honoured method of making any large organisation work. In current business usage it describes a type of centralised social order that makes things happen by having guidelines of policy, procedure and precedent to empower role holders to do their jobs, conferring appropriate authority for action as well as limiting the scope for individual whim or prejudice. It is therefore both more acceptable and more practical as a method of organisation for any large undertaking than relying on the autocratic alternative of everything being decided by a small number of people at the centre, while everyone else waits and grumbles. Human resource managers are occasionally derided by some of their colleagues in other functions for their apparent preoccupation with the 'rules' of procedure and employment law. These colleagues are, of course, wrong, but bureaucracy has a serious inherent flaw in that it always grows, requiring frequent pruning and review.

Career. The whole issue of careers is explored in Chapter 19, but the idea of a career involving moving from job to job is relatively recent. For most people a career was an occupation, such as nursing or teaching or carpentry or bricklaying. It was only in **bureaucracies** that people looked for a promotional ladder. In most of the long-standing professions a career was a lifetime of doing the same job, although perhaps introducing a change of emphasis. A clergyman was a clergyman, even though a few might become deans or bishops. A writer was a writer, although there might be a move from writing poetry to writing novels. An architect is an architect, a dentist is a dentist, a driver is a driver. In some areas the idea of moving 'up' has been created artificially by inventing new pay grades and titles. Until the 1970s British nursing had three levels of nurse, sister and matron. In order to provide a career structure, new jobs were introduced, nursing officer, senior nursing officer and principal nursing officer. The flattening of hierarchies is changing the emphasis.

Casual work is where someone is employed on a temporary and probably irregular basis without any obligation of either party to further employment when a spell is complete.

Change/Initiatives. These are often regarded as invariably desirable, particularly by consultants trying to sell you something. Although constantly advocated in HRM, change has to be balanced against other issues such as stability and security. Furthermore, few changes in HR practice can be made quickly and easily. The ideas are usually easy or obvious. Getting them accepted and making them work requires a great deal of hard work, which means that changes have to be worth the trouble and not just some transitory idea that will have been overtaken by something else in six months' time. 'Initiative fatigue' is a term used to describe the experience of some people who have scarcely got used to one new initiative before another is imposed that contradicts the first.

Clocking on (or in) is a term still in common usage, although the practice is not now widespread. In the heyday of large-scale production businesses, manual employees registered their arrival for work by operating an automatic time recording machine, usually by punching a hole in a personal card. Sometimes they clocked out as well as on. This gave a reliable record of hours worked and enabled pay calculations to be made. Although initially seen as a way to be fair, it eventually became a symbol of close, overbearing control – 'The tyranny of clocking on'. It has become less common although variants are used by, for example, security staff who clock their arrival at various parts of the premises at regular times during the night, or by managers of motorway service stations to demonstrate that they have recently checked the cleanliness of the toilets. A refinement and extension of clocking is the tachograph in road haulage vehicles.

Coach/Mentor/Protégé. A coach is someone who gives specialised training and guidance as well as general support and encouragement. This may be to an individual, for example a tennis player, or to a team, as in cricket. A mentor gives the same sort of service to an individual in what is often a very close personal relationship, requiring from the protégé a high degree of trust in the integrity and goodwill of the mentor. A protégé is someone who is guided by a mentor, acknowledging a need for that person's greater standing and expertise. Tiger Woods is the world's most successful golfer, but still needs a coach: he is not the coach's protégé. One of the most ghastly and needless bits of management jargon is the word 'mentee', presumably invented by someone who could not cope with three syllables, as an alternative to protégé.

Commitment is widely used in current HR practice to describe the quality of being dedicated to the cause, and various methods are used (*see* Chapter 10, for example) to develop this quality among the members of the workforce in their dedication to the cause of company success. Some may be committed to a career or to employment security that is associated with the success of the business, while others are committed to the success of their **career**, perhaps at the expense of the business, and others have no commitment at all. In these circumstances the value of the **brand** may be important.

Competitive advantage. Any business has to be competitive, no matter how much many of its members may not like the idea. A school has to be seen by parents to be at least as good as other schools, otherwise parents will remove their children and the pupils will not have self-respect. Commercial organisations seek competitive advantage for more immediate reasons of survival, but schools, hospitals, charities and churches will all decline and may close if they do not meet the current needs and expectations of their 'clients', although they will quite rightly cavil at the terms 'customers' or 'clients'.

Consideration. *See* **Contract.**

Contingency is a word much used in sociology and organisation theory. Apart from its normal usage to describe a possible future event that cannot be predicted with certainty, in management it is used to differentiate from the absolute. Solutions to problems are seldom invariably right: it depends on the particular circumstances of the event.

Contract/Consideration. In this book the material about contracts is mainly about legal agreements, although there is also reference to psychological contracts. The fundamental principle of a legal contract is that there must be consideration. A contract is a spoken or written agreement that is intended to be enforceable at law, but the offer of agreement by one party only becomes legally enforceable when there is consideration from the other party, that is, an undertaking of some sort, to do something or to stop doing something or to abandon a claim. An offer of employment, for instance, is not legally binding on the employer making the offer until and unless the prospective employee accepts the offer and agrees to provide the work (consideration) that the employer is offering. This same sense of reciprocity is equally fundamental to the psychological contract: there must be an agreed exchange. Contracting out (from a pension scheme, for instance) involves withdrawing from an agreement and thereby relinquishing the benefits that would otherwise have been received.

Culture/Organisational culture. In management circles interest in culture is an attempt to grasp the realities of collective life in a department or organisation that cannot be easily seen and described by means of such identifiers as job titles, departments and organisation charts. It is an aspect of the **hard/soft** distinction. Recently culture has been especially important in explaining the differences in management practice in various countries, but organisational culture refers to the beliefs, conventions and general patterns of behaviour that characterise a particular organisation.

Delayering is a method of **downsizing** that reduces the number of people in a **hierarchy** by removing a tier in the organisational structure.

Demographics describes statistical data relating to the age and gender structure of the population. This is an important element of the labour market.

Diversity is subtly different from equality and refers principally to the value to management of making the most of employees from two distinct groups, women and those from ethnic minorities, rather than assuming that core employees are white and male. Theoretically diversity could also apply to people who are older than average, but thus far that aspect of diversity has received little attention.

Downsizing describes an approach to increasing organisational efficiency by reducing the number of people employed in the business and therefore reducing the costs associated with their employment. The main methods are **delayering** and **outplacement/outsourcing.**

Employee relations/Industrial relations are not simply different terms for the same activities; they denote a significant change of emphasis. Concern with industrial relations developed when the emphasis was on collective relationships within an industry, such as engineering, agriculture or teaching. Each business within the ambit of that industry observed the terms and conditions agreed between employers' representatives and unions, which bound every employer. Employee relations have little regard for industry criteria and focus on collective arrangements within an individual business.

Environment. We typically think nowadays of elements of the physical environment in which we live: pollution, greenhouse gases, GM crops, vulnerable species and so forth. In HRM it is more likely to refer to the social, political and legal environment of the business.

Fit. *See* **Best fit.**

Flexibility is something managers try hard to achieve and trade unions and the legal system try to limit. The flexible workforce makes managerial life easier by giving more scope to managers to manipulate the labour supply, as do flexible hours arrangements. Flexibility agreements with unions reduce rigidity in work practices. All these practices reduce the problems of **bureaucracy** but the advantages for employees may be more mixed. Flexible hours are probably the most attractive, but there are always disadvantages for employees with flexibility initiatives that at least slightly erode their personal security.

Gender. *See* **Sex**.

Hard/Soft. Hard data are precise and can be accurately measured by numbers and statistical calculation. Soft data are less precise but may be more important in planning. They include judgement, assessment and informed guesswork.

Hierarchy is the system of organisation which ranks all the people according to their status or authority. This is used for all manner of purposes, ranging from the trivial, such as who has the biggest office and who is allowed to travel first class, to the identification of who is empowered to do what, as the hierarchical system includes titles or labels to make sense of the jobs that people do. In Britain the growth of hierarchy received a boost when an early management theorist, E.F.L. Brech, advanced his theory of the span of control, saying that no manager should supervise directly the work of four or five subordinates, *whose work interlocks*. Many people accepted the theory but conveniently forgot the last three words.

Human capital. Economists, rather reluctantly, conceded that any economic analysis of an organisation or an economy needed to include the concept of a value or cost assigned to skills, knowledge or experience of the population. It has proved a more acceptable and useful concept than the sterile accountancy technique of human asset accounting. Its main value to HR practitioners is the idea that human capital requires investment.

Human Relations School, The. A school of thought that developed in the 1930s as a reaction against the perceived mechanical thinking of **Scientific Management**. It aimed to develop high productivity by concentrating on the well-being of the individual worker and the surrounding social relationships in the workplace, with an emphasis on adapting the task to the worker rather than adapting the worker to the task.

Industrial relations. *See* **Employee relations**.

Initiatives. *See* **Change**.

Labour market. *See* **Marketplace**.

Marketplace/Labour market. The importance of both these concepts (taken from economics) in HRM is to emphasise that people management can never be entirely inward in focus. The business has to operate in a context in which there is a market for its products or service, and the business has to survive in that market no matter how inconvenient it may be for the people inside the business. Equally there is an external market for labour and skills, which cannot be ignored. Even employees totally loyal to the business will be aware of prevailing conditions elsewhere, not only how much people are paid but also conditions of work, hours and fringe benefits.

Matrix is a term that has recently come into popular currency because of film and television programmes using it in a very specialised way. In management it has long been used to describe a particular form of organisation in which levels of specialisation, accountability and responsibility are set out in vertical columns crossed by horizontal lines, with points of intersection identifying individual people who have a line of communication in one direction (line management) as well as a distinct accountability to someone else. An office manager, for instance, might be responsible for most things to the immediate superior, but accountable to the HR manager for health and safety issues. 'The line' is often mentioned in this book and refers to the vertical line of accountability.

Mentor. *See* **Coach**.

Meta-analysis. Meta is a scientific term indicating a change in condition, such as metamorphosis. In social sciences it denotes something beyond, of a higher order kind.

Mission/Aims/Objectives/Targets. These are all terms used quite loosely in management jargon and are in a rough hierarchy from the broad to the specific. Mission comes from religion and is used in a business to describe what the organisation is for, what its purpose is. It is fashionably set in a mission statement and is typically vague and general, but can be useful in developing **commitment**. Aims and objectives describe the more specific purposes of individual functions, departments, teams or individuals within the mission framework. Targets are very specific and usually short term as stages on the way for teams and individuals to achieve longer-term objectives.

Objectives. *See* **Mission.**

Occupational health. Many businesses describe their medical departments as 'Occupational Health', regardless of the skills possessed by the people who work in them, but it is worth bearing in mind that occupational medicine is a defined specialism, not general practice in an occupational setting. Both doctors and nurses can acquire qualifications in occupational medicine, but they are most likely to be needed in a business with specific hazards, such as radiation or toxic materials.

Organisational culture. *See* **Culture.**

Outplacement/Outsourcing. There is a small difference between these two terms. Outplacement describes taking a complete activity and shifting it to a supplier, while outsourcing describes looking outside the business for human resources.

Peers is an equivocal term in Britain because it has two meanings. One is to describe members of the aristocracy: earls, baronets, dukes, marquesses and viscounts. In this book, and in more general usage, it describes people of the same age, status, ability or qualification as oneself. A peer group is therefore a group of one's equals, not one's superiors.

Performance. Everyone wants effective performance. The individual wants the satisfaction of achievement and results, managers want individuals to be effectively coordinated and productive, customers want a good product and good service at the right price, governments want efficient businesses in a growing economy. Achieving performance is complicated. It is not simply paying people lots of money, although not paying people enough money may well inhibit performance. It is not simply being nice to people and releasing them from supervision, as they may then do the wrong things. Achieving effective performance also varies according to the work done. A symphony orchestra requires members with great expertise playing different instruments, yet all must work to an identical score under the strict leadership of the conductor, with very little scope for individual flair. The jazz quartet is more loosely coordinated with many individual riffs. Those working for a courier firm or in the operating theatre of a hospital can only perform well by following a tight schedule arranged by someone else. Those working in an advertising agency have a much looser rein in order to encourage their creativity.

Portfolio is a collection of items that represent a person's work. Very familiar for people whose work can best be demonstrated by examples, such as painters or cartoonists, it is also now much used by all classes of worker to demonstrate their skills and accomplishments, thereby justifying a qualification to practise.

Pluralist. *See* **Unitarist.**

Proactive. *See* **Reactive.**

Protégé. *See* **Coach.**

Reactive/Proactive. This distinction is important in HRM because there is a natural emphasis in people matters to await developments and deal with them (reactive). Many HR people report that they spend much of their time putting right problems created by the impetuosity or thoughtlessness of their colleagues in other functions. There is also a need, however, to create opportunities for growth and change and to think ahead of issues so that problems can be averted. A well-rounded HR/personnel function is able to maintain a balance between both types of approach, vigorously and calmly sorting out problems or disasters but also taking matters forward in a creative way when the problems are all under control.

Recruitment/Selection. Recruitment is the process whereby a business seeks applicants either generally or for particular vacancies. Potential applicants are interested but there is no mutual obligation. Selection is the process whereby not only does the employer choose between two or more interested applicants, but applicants also select, deciding how much further they wish to pursue their original enquiry. The end of the process is a legally binding agreement.

Resourcing. This term has only recently come into common usage and means simply providing the needed resources. For HR people this is providing the human resources that are needed, although some pedantic academics (such as at least one of your authors) dislike the term 'employee resourcing' as it is the employing organisation that is being provided with resources; not the employees. Also employees are not the only source of human resources for the business. Consultants or subcontractors are alternative sources.

Ritual is a series of actions or a type of behaviour invariably followed in accordance with a convention. Developed originally to help people feel secure in the mysteries of religious practices, they are widespread in present-day society (the ritual of going to the pub on Friday after work, the ritual of the pre-match huddle, the ritual of Prime Minister's Question Time). All provide the benefit of enabling people to feel comfortable and accepted in a social situation, and are therefore important in many employment situations where there is a felt need to conform to existing conventions. The selection interview is the most obvious. Others examples are the 'leaving do', collections before a marriage, negotiations, and the office party.

Scenario. A method of envisaging the future is to bring together various bits of evidence, both hard and soft, and fit them together in a way that describes a reliable version of the future in *X* years' time.

Scientific Management. The first modern theory of management, formulated by F.W. Taylor and using the principles of industrial engineering to raise productivity by adapting the worker to the machine or the process. It relied heavily on adjusting the worker's earnings to the level of individual output. The basic ideas remain in place and are at the root of many payment systems, but most management academics and commentators throughout the last three-quarters of the twentieth century disparaged and deplored the 'mechanistic and inhuman' practices spawned by scientific management. (*See also* **Human Relations School** for a reaction to this.)

Selection. *See* **Recruitment.**

Sex/Gender. The word sex is pretty clear in its meaning as describing either a range of interesting activities, or to describe the biological distinction between male and female. Until recently gender was a grammatical term to distinguish between classes of noun or pronoun in some languages, loosely based on natural distinctions of sex: masculine, feminine or neuter. It is now also used to refer to social and cultural differences between the sexes.

Statutory rights. Rights of the individual citizen or citizens that derive explicitly from a statute or Act of Parliament.

Stress presents managers with two problems. An employee may be absent from work suffering from stress, but this is a condition that is easy to fake and not easy to diagnose. How does a manager detect malingering and take appropriate action? More significantly a manager may exacerbate or cause stress in someone. How can this be avoided and what remedies are available to employees? A further complication is that stress is not necessarily undesirable. Any football fan will suffer periods of intense stress when the wrong team is winning a match, but this only makes sweeter the euphoria when the right team wins. Stress can be stimulating as well as harmful and some jobs are best done and most enjoyed where there is frequent stress followed by achievement (two examples being journalists, who have to meet tight deadlines, and surgeons, who have to deal with crises).

Targets. *See* **Mission.**

Tells. 'I love you' is a statement by one person to another that is normally accompanied by certain actions and behaviours that demonstrate to the recipient how sincere the feeling is. Sometimes, however, we say things that we do not believe, or of which we are unsure. Then the listener may try to guess what we really mean, not just what the words say. We give clues to our uncertainty or our truthfulness by what we do, especially what we cannot help doing. These are tells. Blushing shows we are embarrassed, many people put their hands to their mouths when they feel guilty. HR managers need to learn what tells to look for in situations such as selection, where not all candidates are strictly accurate in what they say, or in appraisal, where people may be very guarded in what they say.

Tribunal here refers almost only to the three-person panel that makes up the Employment Tribunal deciding matters of employment law, although it can be any sort of body used to settle disputes. Not always made up of three people, it is normal to have an odd number to avoid deadlock.

Unitarist/Pluralist. For HRM these terms come from industrial relations analysis. A unitarist thinker believes that all authority and all responsibility is centred in one place or person, so that senior management can, and must, decide on all key issues, while other people involved simply have to accept the consequences. The pluralist says that is both unacceptable and impractical. Employees have a legitimate interest in the business that cannot be disregarded and the local community is another important stakeholder.

Index

Note: text within windows on practice and activities has not been indexed.

D

E

F

G

N

O

P

Q

R

S

Y

Z